L

Th
va
cc
Le
siv
Ol
of
of-
ha
by
vic
Tr
an
bei
tiv

RIC
and
An
for
Re
He
Otl
wel

CAMBRIDGE STUDIES IN LAW AND SOCIETY

Founded in 1997, Cambridge Studies in Law and Society is a hub for leading scholarship in socio-legal studies. Located at the intersection of law, the humanities, and the social sciences, it publishes empirically innovative and theoretically sophisticated work on law's manifestations in everyday life: from discourses to practices, and from institutions to cultures. The series editors have longstanding expertise in the interdisciplinary study of law, and welcome contributions that place legal phenomena in national, comparative, or international perspective. Series authors come from a range of disciplines, including anthropology, history, law, literature, political science, and sociology.

Series Editors

Mark Fathi Massoud, *University of California, Santa Cruz*
Jens Meierhenrich, *London School of Economics and Political Science*
Rachel E. Stern, *University of California, Berkeley*

A list of books in the series can be found at the back of this book.

LAW'S TRIALS

The Performance of Legal Institutions
in the US "War on Terror"

Richard L. Abel
UCLA

CAMBRIDGE
UNIVERSITY PRESS

CAMBRIDGE
UNIVERSITY PRESS

University Printing House, Cambridge CB2 8BS, United Kingdom

One Liberty Plaza, 20th Floor, New York, NY 10006, USA

477 Williamstown Road, Port Melbourne, VIC 3207, Australia

314–321, 3rd Floor, Plot 3, Splendor Forum, Jasola District Centre, New Delhi – 110025, India

79 Anson Road, #06-04/06, Singapore 079906

Cambridge University Press is part of the University of Cambridge.

It furthers the University's mission by disseminating knowledge in the pursuit of education, learning, and research at the highest international levels of excellence.

www.cambridge.org
Information on this title: www.cambridge.org/9781108429757
DOI: 10.1017/9781108555227

© Richard L. Abel 2018

First published 2018

Printed in the United States of America by Sheridan Books, Inc.

A catalogue record for this publication is available from the British Library.

Library of Congress Cataloging-in-Publication Data
Names: Abel, Richard L., author.
Title: Law's trials : the performance of legal institutions in the US "War on Terror" / Richard L. Abel.
Description: Cambridge [UK]; New York, NY: Cambridge University Press, 2018. | Series: Cambridge studies in law and society | Includes bibliographical references and index.
Identifiers: LCCN 2018007064 | ISBN 9781108429757 (hardback)
Subjects: LCSH: Terrorism – Prevention – Law and legislation – United States. | Rule of law – United States. | Civil rights – United States. | Prisoners of war – Civil rights – Cuba – Guantánamo Bay Naval Base. | Detention of persons – United States. | Habeas corpus – United States. | War on Terrorism, 2001–2009. | BISAC: LAW / General.
Classification: LCC KF9430.A925 2018 | DDC 344.7305/325–dc23
LC record available at https://lccn.loc.gov/2018007064

ISBN 978-1-108-42975-7 Hardback

CONTENTS

TABLES

FOREWORD

Do courts in fact preserve the rule of law? We all assume they do, but we rarely study precisely how they do it, and when and why they fail. The real test comes not in ordinary times, but when judges are under the most intense stress and political pressure to trade off the rights of those brought before them for unquantifiable, yet not easily dismissed, claims of national security. Nearly two decades after September 11, 2001, a broad and confusing landscape of legal actions has unfolded – courts-martial, criminal prosecutions, military commissions, habeas corpus petitions, and civil actions for grave civil liberties and human rights violations – that finally give us the kind of ecosystem-shocking episode that is ripe for serious scholarly examination. But how do we know which legal institutions in fact best protected the rule of law, and which have abjectly failed?

Understanding how and why trials mattered during this bracing historical era is one of the central challenges facing those who want to understand better the interaction between law and society. For while this is ground overtilled by many, it has been notably underexamined by serious scholars who conscientiously research where, when, and how challenges to the rule of law arise; how legal institutions weather those challenges; and how those responses compare with other responses by parallel institutions in other societies or during other historical eras. Over his long and most distinguished academic career, Richard L. Abel has consistently proven himself to be one of our most discerning law and society scholars. In the 1990s he instructed us on how law and lawyers mattered in winning another searing social justice challenge: the decades-long struggle against apartheid. In this prodigious volume, and its equally ambitious companion *Law's Wars*, Abel offers a nuanced, deeply thoughtful, and overarching vision of how law can preserve its essential core under intense political pressure, and what long-term overall impact the so-called "war on terror" has had on our nation's bedrock values.

These volumes should be read and remembered by historians, political scientists, sociologists, anthropologists, as well as lawyers willing to draw the fundamental lessons of this era. Those of us who have lived through these decades as observers and participants have often anguished when we have sought deeper understanding, only to find transient commentary. We both need and should learn from Abel's essential and painstaking research, which provides the kind of detailed quantitative and qualitative analysis that has been too sadly missing from the daily blogosphere's spontaneous reactions. Abel's moving final chapter – which after surveying more than one hundred other social justice campaigns, suggests that most remedial rule-of-law projects take a generation or more to reach fruition – offers comfort and insight at the same time as it demands patience. Abel's greatest achievement may be in reminding us that the vigilance that preserves liberty is sadly unceasing, and demands the kind of dogged persistence and perseverance we wish we could be spared from, but will always be both destined and obliged to provide.

Harold Hongju Koh[+]

[+] Sterling Professor of International Law and former Dean (2004–09), Yale Law School, Legal Adviser (2009–13), and Assistant Secretary of State for Democracy, Human Rights and Labor (1998–2001), US Department of State.

FOREWORD

Professor Rick Abel's stunning new book tells the story of how the US Constitution has failed since September 11, 2001, and during crises throughout American history. As Professor Abel describes, so often since the earliest days of the nation, when there has been a crisis – especially a foreign-based crisis – the response has been repression. In hindsight, we realize that the country was not made any safer by taking away rights. The goal of ensuring safety and security is a noble one, but its pursuit too easily has led to the compromise of our basic values.

Professor Abel's focus is on what has occurred since September 11, 2001. He paints a bleak picture of how our institutions have failed to uphold the rule of law and to live up to even basic notions of human rights. He shows how this continues to this day, more than sixteen years after 9/11, a period far longer than any war in American history and that shows no prospect of ending.

This, of course, is not the first book to be written about the loss of rights since 9/11. But it is different from any others. In part, this is because of its scope, especially combined with its companion volume, *Law's Wars*. This is the most comprehensive book yet on what has occurred over the last decade and half as part of the "war on terror." It focuses not just on the Supreme Court, or even the courts, but on all of the actors in the legal system, telling the story of each of the criminal prosecutions, of the military tribunals, of the habeas proceedings, of the civil suits. Although this is not its primary purpose, it is going to be a vital reference book for what has occurred in the legal system since 9/11.

But what most distinguishes the book is its sociolegal perspective. It focuses on the people involved: the parties, law enforcement officers, prosecutors, defense lawyers, and judges. Ultimately, it is a story of how well-intentioned people – and there is no doubt that the vast majority of those involved were acting to protect the country – came to undermining the Constitution and basic norms of human rights. It is a powerful story of how US courts largely have failed in their willingness to convict on inadequate evidence, their refusal to grant habeas corpus, and their dismissal of civil suits. It forces the reader to think about how the institutions of American government so easily can be used for repression and how the checks and balances that should protect everyone can fail.

Professor Abel recognizes that there is much more to know and consider. He suggests questions for further research, knowing that this era of American history will be studied for generations to come.

The sheer comprehensiveness of Professor Abel's effort is what makes it so powerful – and frankly, so distressing. The only conclusion from all of this is that the US legal system has profoundly failed. It requires us to think about whether it realistically could have done better. I believe so. But we must think about what it would take for government institutions to adhere to the rule of law even in a time of crisis, such as in fighting the war on terror.

Professor Abel concludes on an optimistic note. He details the many instances in which other countries have come to recognize their human rights abuses and act to reconcile with them. But it is an open question whether the United States will do so. Even the Obama administration steadfastly refused to prosecute the war crimes committed in the earlier years, such as in torture and inhumane treatment of detainees. Surely, the Trump administration – which wants to expand the use of Guantánamo – is not going to do so.

Professor Abel reminds us that future generations may learn from our mistakes and will be less likely to repeat them. The repression of free speech during World War I – which Professor Abel describes early in the book – did not happen again. The internment of Japanese Americans during World War II is almost universally condemned, and that has prevented a subsequent similar experience.

The most hopeful conclusion from this book is that by telling this history, and realizing the tragic mistakes since 9/11, we are less likely to repeat them. I hope Professor Abel is right, though there is no way to know how the future will look at what has occurred and what lessons will be drawn from it.

Ultimately, Professor Abel tells us of how a society that prides itself on observing the rule of law has compromised it in pursuing security above all else. Underlying his story is how government officials charged with combating terrorism pursued that even when it meant violating the Constitution and basic norms of human rights. Can we ever change this so that they see their role as much as upholding the Constitution as protecting society? That is the question that every reader must ask after finishing this magnificent book.

Erwin Chemerinsky
Dean and Jesse H. Choper Distinguished Professor
of Law, University of California, Berkeley School of Law

PREFACE

The "war on terror," which the USA launched after the 9/11 attacks, profoundly challenged the rule of law during the 16 years of the Bush and Obama administrations. In the companion volume, *Law's Wars*, I define the rule of law, explain its importance, and chart its fate across five contested terrains: Abu Ghraib, Guantánamo Bay, interrogation and torture, electronic surveillance, and battlefield law of war crimes. I focus on the roles of two state institutions (executive and legislature) and civil society (media, lawyers, and NGOs) in defending the rule of law. Because the judiciary claims to be independent and apolitical, it is seen as the ultimate bulwark of the rule of law. The present volume, therefore, deals exclusively with judicial proceedings. Chapter 1 draws on history, primarily US and especially in moments of crisis, to derive research questions about when and how courts successfully defend the rule of law. The book then discusses six legal processes: criminal prosecutions of accused terrorists; courts-martial of military service members for law of war violations; military commissions for Guantánamo prisoners, especially the so-called high-value detainees; habeas corpus petitions by Guantánamo detainees (and a few others); civil damages actions by (and compensation schemes for) victims of both the "war on terror" and terrorism; and civil liberties violations and responses to Islamophobia. The concluding chapter compares the fate of the rule of law across these six domains, as well as with the contested terrains examined in *Law's Wars*. Although the two volumes address some of the same issues, they contain almost no overlap and can be read separately.

Many other books have done an excellent job of explicating and criticizing the legal doctrine spawned by the "war on terror." My goal is different: to understand when and why courts preserved the rule of law in the face of (sometimes overwhelming) pressure to sacrifice liberty for (an often illusory) security. My method, therefore, is sociolegal: investigating the actions of all those who sought to defend the rule of law (parties, law enforcement officers, prosecutors, defense lawyers, and judges), how they did so, the rhetoric they deployed, and the outcomes. For this reason, I do not restrict myself to the most recent majority decision by the highest court (the only authoritative source of doctrine); I am equally interested in lower court decisions and concurrences and dissents, process as well as outcome. That broader vision allows me to engage not only in qualitative analysis of the reasons for actions but also in quantitative analysis of the actions themselves, asking whether judges' votes are correlated with their political orientations (as measured by the party of the appointing president) and how this differs across domains.

By examining more than a hundred other campaigns to redress major social wrongs, the concluding chapter offers a historical context for understanding the efforts described in this book to correct the deplorable errors of the "war on terror." I advance the tentative hypothesis that such remedial projects often take a generation or more to bear fruit, offering hope to those discouraged by the performance of US legal institutions during the "war on terror." This reminds us of what several early nineteenth-century commentators observed: eternal vigilance is the price of liberty. I hope the narratives and analyses of these hundreds of cases from the first 16 years of the "war on terror" will offer insight and inspiration to those who must persevere in unending defense of the rule of law.

ACRONYMS AND ABBREVIATIONS

1st Lt.	First Lieutenant
2nd Lt.	Second Lieutenant
ABA	American Bar Association
ACLU	American Civil Liberties Union
ADL	Anti-Defamation League
ADMAX SHU	Administrative Maximum Special Housing Unit
AFB	Air Force Base
AFDI	American Freedom Defense Initiative
AG	Attorney General
AI	Amnesty International
AK-47	Kalashnikov assault rifle
AP	Associated Press
AQAP	Al-Qaeda in the Arabian Peninsula
AR 15–6	Army Regulation 15–6 (governing criminal investigations)
ARB	Administrative Review Board
Art. 32	Military equivalent of civilian court arraignment or grand jury indictment
ATA	Anti-Terrorism Act
ATS	Alien Tort Statute, 28 U.S.C. §1350
AUEC	alien unlawful enemy combatant
AUMF	Authorization for the Use of Military Force
AUSA	Assistant US Attorney
AWOL	Absent Without Official Leave
BDO	Behavioral Detection Officer
BDS	DoS Bureau of Diplomatic Security
BGen.	Brigadier General
BoI	Bureau of Investigation
BoP	US Bureau of Prisons
CA	Military Commissions Convening Authority (also called Appointing Authority)

CAIR	Council on American–Islamic Relations
Capt.	Captain
CAT	Convention Against Torture
CBC	Canadian Broadcasting Corporation
CBS	Columbia Broadcasting System
CBP	Customs and Border Patrol (DHS)
CCR	Center for Constitutional Rights
CD Cal	US District Court for the Central District of California
CD Ill	US District Court for the Central District of Illinois
CENTCOM	US Central Command
CIA	Central Intelligence Agency
CID	Criminal Investigation Command (Army)
CLEAR	Creating Law Enforcement Accountability and Responsibility (CUNY Law School project)
CMCR	Court of Military Commission Review
CMDR	Commander
CNN	Cable News Network
Col.	Colonel
CPA	Coalition Provisional Authority
Cpl.	Corporal
CS	confidential source
CSO	Court Security Officer
CSRT	Combatant Status Review Tribunal
CUNY	City University of New York
D Az	US District Court for the District of Arizona
D Colo	US District Court for the District of Colorado
D Hi	US District Court for the District of Hawaii
D Id	US District Court for the District of Idaho
D Mass	US District Court for the District of Massachusetts
D Md	US District Court for the District of Maryland
D Minn	US District Court for the District of Minnesota
D Mont	US District Court for the District of Montana
D NJ	US District Court for the District of New Jersey
D Ore	US District Court for the District of Oregon
D RI	US District Court for the District of Rhode Island
D SC	US District Court for the District of South Carolina
D Utah	US District Court for the District of Utah
DCI	Director of the CIA

DDC	US District Court for the District of Columbia
DHS	Department of Homeland Security
DIA	Defense Intelligence Agency
DNI	Director of National Intelligence
DoD	US Department of Defense
DoE	Department of Energy
DoJ	US Department of Justice
DoS	Department of State
DSC	US District Court for the District of South Carolina
DTA	Detainee Treatment Act of 2005
EC	enemy combatant
ECHR	European Court of Human Rights
ED Cal	US District Court for the Eastern District of California
ED Mich	US District Court for the Eastern District of Michigan
ED Va	US District Court for the Eastern District of Virginia
ED Wash	US District Court for the Eastern District of Washington
EDNY	US District Court for the Eastern District of New York
EEOC	Equal Employment Opportunities Commission
EIT	enhanced interrogation technique
EO	Executive Order
EPIC	Electronic Privacy Information Center
FBI	Federal Bureau of Investigation
FDR	Franklin D. Roosevelt
FISC	Foreign Intelligence Surveillance Court
FOIA	Freedom of Information Act 2000
FSIA	Foreign Sovereign Immunities Act
FTCA	Federal Tort Claims Act
GAO	Government Accountability Office
Gen.	General
Gitmo	Guantánamo Bay Naval Base
GTMO	Guantánamo Bay Naval Base
HASC	House Armed Services Committee
HIG	Hezb-I-Islam Gulbuddin
HJC	House Judiciary Committee

HLF	Holy Land Foundation
HPSCI	House Permanent Select Committee on Intelligence
HRF	Human Rights First
HRW	Human Rights Watch
HUAC	House Committee on Un-American Activities
Humvee	High Mobility Multipurpose Wheeled Vehicle (HMMWV)
HVD	high-value detainee
IATA	International Air Transport Association
ICC	International Criminal Court
ICE	Immigration and Customs Enforcement (DHS)
ICRC	International Committee of the Red Cross
ICTR	International Criminal Tribunal for Rwanda
ICTY	International Criminal Tribunal for the former Yugoslavia
IED	improvised explosive device
IG	Inspector General
IMU	Islamic Movement of Uzbekistan
INA	Immigration and Naturalization Act
IRA	Irish Republican Army
IS	Islamic State
ISIS	Islamic State of Iraq and Syria
ITRSHRA	Iran Threat Reduction and Syria Human Rights Act
IWW	International Workers of the World
JAG	Judge Advocate General
JCS	Joint Chiefs of Staff
JFK	John F. Kennedy Airport
JTF	Joint Task Force
KKK	Ku Klux Klan
KMT	Kuomintang (Taiwan)
KSM	Khalid Sheikh Mohammed
LAPD	Los Angeles Police Department
LAX	Los Angeles Airport
LCpl.	Lance Corporal
LGen.	Lieutenant General
LOAC	Law of Armed Conflict
Lt.	Lieutenant
LtCol.	Lieutenant Colonel

LtCdr.	Lieutenant Commander
Maj.	Major
MAM	military-aged male
MC	military commission
MCA	Military Commissions Act of 2006, 2009, or 2015
MD Tn	US District Court for the Middle District of Tennessee
MDC	Metropolitan Detention Center (federal prison in Brooklyn)
MEJA	Military Extraterritorial Jurisdiction Act
MEK	Mujaheddin-e-Khalq (People's Mujaheddin Organization of Iran)
MGen.	Major General
MNF-I	Multi-National Force–Iraq
MP	Military Police
MPAC	Muslim Public Affairs Council
MTA	Metropolitan Transportation Authority
NBC	National Broadcasting Company
NCIC	National Crime Information Center (FBI)
NCIS	Naval Criminal Investigative Service
NDAA	National Defense Authorization Act
ND Cal	US District Court for the Northern District of California
ND Fla	US District Court for the Northern District of Florida
ND Ill	US District Court for the Northern District of Illinois
ND Ok	US District Court for the Northern District of Oklahoma
NGO	nongovernmental organization
NPR	National Public Radio
NSA	National Security Agency
NYC	New York City
NYCB	New York City Bar
NYCLU	New York Civil Liberties Union
NYPD	New York Police Department
NYPD OIG	New York Police Department Office of the Inspector General
NYU	New York University

OLC	Department of Justice Office of Legal Counsel
OMC	Office of Military Commissions
PA	Palestine Authority
PFC	Private First Class
PIVF	Passenger Identity Verification Form
PLO	Palestine Liberation Organization
PO3	Petty Officer 3rd Class (Navy)
POM	Presiding Officer Manual (MCs)
POW	prisoner of war
PRT	Privilege Review Team
PTSD	post-traumatic stress disorder
Pvt.	Private
RAdm.	Rear Admiral (Navy)
Ret.	retired
RFRA	Religious Freedom Restoration Act
RNC	Republican National Committee
ROE	Rules of Engagement
SASC	Senate Armed Services Committee
SD Fla	US District Court for the Southern District of Florida
SD Tex	US District Court for the Southern District of Texas
SDNY	US District Court for the Southern District of New York
SEPTA	Southeastern Pennsylvania Transportation Authority
SNP	Spanish National Police
SSCI	Senate Select Committee on Intelligence
Sgt.	Sergeant
SJA	Staff Judge Advocate
SJC	Senate Judiciary Committee
SOP	Standard Operation Procedure
SOUTHCOM	Southern Command
SPC	Specialist
SPOT	Screening Passengers by Observation Techniques (TSA)
SSgt.	Staff Sergeant
SUV	sport utility vehicle
TEI	Terrorism Enterprise Investigation (NYPD)
TIDE	Terrorist Identities Datamart Environment

TRIP	Traveler Redress Inquiry Program (DHS)
TRO	Temporary Restraining Order
TSA	Transportation Security Administration
TVPA	Torture Victims Protection Act
UA	undercover agent
UCLA	University of California, Los Angeles
UCMJ	Uniform Code of Military Justice
UEC	unlawful enemy combatant
UECRB	Unlawful Enemy Combatant Review Board
USSC	US Supreme Court
VAdm.	Vice Admiral
WD Ky	US District Court for the Western District of Kentucky
WD Ok	US District Court for the Western District of Oklahoma
WD Pa	US District Court for the Western District of Pennsylvania
WD Wash	US District Court for the Western District of Washington

CHAPTER ONE

JUDGING THE JUDGES

Courts are the ultimate arbiters of the rule of law, both when handling routine cases and when reviewing the actions of the executive and legislature.[1] This volume deals with six categories of cases: criminal prosecutions, courts-martial, military commissions, habeas corpus petitions, civil damages actions, and civil liberties. The present chapter draws on two strands of historical scholarship – first focusing on courts and then on wartime distortions of law – to contextualize and frame the questions I will address in the later chapters.

COURTS

Analyzing the predicament of antebellum judges asked to enforce the fugitive slave laws, Robert Cover identified four alternatives – prioritizing law over conscience or conscience over law, manipulating the law, or resigning – and explained judges' choices in terms of their personalities, beliefs about natural law, preferences for liberty and the constraints of the judicial function.[2] South African legal scholars fiercely debated whether judges should resign rather than administer apartheid laws.[3] Methods of selection and retention shape judicial action (as shown by the intense politicization of federal court nominations and the increasing influence of campaign contributions on state judicial elections). Courts of general jurisdiction tend to be more independent than specialized tribunals (which can be captured by the domain they adjudicate, just like regulatory agencies).[4] Although routine prosecutions generally convict by negotiating a guilty plea (which may tacitly condone procedural irregularities), show trials conspicuously respect the rule of law, sometimes acquitting.[5] It is generally easier to resist government action defensively, using law as a shield, than to challenge it actively, wielding law as a sword, which allows the government to raise questions of standing and invoke state secrets, political question, and act of state doctrines. But a proactive government can forum-shop for the most favorable venue in which to prosecute.

Like the executive and the legislature, the judiciary may subordinate liberty to security in times of apparent crisis.[6] During the Civil War, courts denied habeas corpus to Clement Vallandingham, even though the writ had not been suspended in the jurisdiction where he was held.[7] Sentencing International Workers of the World members who opposed World War I, ND Ill Judge Kenesaw M. Landis pronounced: "You have a legal right to oppose, by free speech, preparations for war. But once war is declared, that right ceases."[8] In a 1919 opinion Justice Holmes wrote for a unanimous Supreme Court upholding the convictions of Charles Schenck and Elizabeth Baer for denouncing conscription. "[I]n many places and in ordinary times the defendants would have been within their constitutional rights." But "the character of every act depends upon the circumstances in which it is done." Announcing his famous test, Holmes said their words created a "clear and present danger." Justice John H. Clarke wrote the *only* dissent to World War I convictions for speech, denouncing the "flagrant mistrial" of the *Philadelphia Tageblatt*, which was "likely to result in disgrace and great injustice ... because this Court hesitates to exercise the power, which it undoubtedly possesses, to correct, in this calmer time, errors of law which would not have been committed but for the stress and strain of feeling prevailing in the early months of the late, deplorable war."[9]

One of the Supreme Court's most shameful moments was its approval of internment of Japanese Americans during World War II.[10] Unanimously affirming Gordon Hirabayashi's conviction, Chief Justice Stone revealed his discomfort in a triple negative:[11] "[W]e cannot say that the war-making branches of the Government did not have ground for believing that in a critical hour such persons could not readily be isolated and separately dealt with, and constituted a menace to the national defense and safety."

Advancing an analogy that would embarrass even a first-year law student, Stone saw no difference between uprooting more than 100,000 Americans, nearly two-thirds of them citizens, and interning them indefinitely in harsh conditions hundreds or thousands of miles from home, and "the police establishment of fire lines during a fire." The great civil libertarian, Justice Douglas, concurred because "we must credit the military with as much good faith in that belief" about necessity "as we would any other public official acting pursuant to his duties." Affirming the conviction of Fred Korematsu a year later, Justice Black echoed Douglas's credulous deference in his own double negative: "we cannot reject as unfounded the judgment of the military authorities."[12] He protested (unconvincingly) that "to cast this case into the outlines of racial prejudice ... confuses the issue." And he offered government a flimsy veil of false necessity – "it was impossible to bring about an immediate segregation of the loyal from the disloyal" – declaring that "hardships are part of war," as though they were borne equally by Japanese Americans and all others.

This time, however, there were dissents. Justice Murphy (Roosevelt's former Attorney General) explicitly rebuked Black: relocation goes "over 'the brink of constitutional power' and falls into the ugly abyss of racism" (prompting Black's disavowal, perhaps motivated by unresolved rumors of his earlier KKK membership). And Justice Jackson presciently warned that:

> a judicial construction of the due process clause that will sustain this order is a far more subtle blow to liberty than the promulgation of the order itself ... the Court for all time has validated the principle of racial discrimination in criminal procedure and of transplanting American citizens. The principle then lies about like a loaded weapon ready for the hand of any authority that can bring forward a plausible claim of an urgent need.

Justice Rutledge, who joined the majority in both cases, later wrote in extenuation that he had suffered "more anguish" over *Hirabayashi* than any other case. And Douglas claimed he had "always regretted that I bowed to my elders," conceding that the Court "is not isolated from life ... the state of public opinion will often make the Court cautious when it should be bold."

During the post-World War II anti-communist hysteria, courts convicted all 11 defendants in the first Smith Act prosecution and 93 of 113 in the second, both of them show trials staged to help Truman win the 1948 election, cheered on by both the *New York Times* and the *Washington Post*.[13] Dissenting from the affirmation in the first case, Justice Black wrote:

> Public opinion being what it is now, few will protest the conviction of these Communist petitioners. There is hope, however, that in calmer

times, when present pressures, passions and fears subside, this or some later Court will restore the First Amendment liberties to the high preferred place where they belong in a free society.

National security prosecutions require courts to decide whether to relax the procedural protections they extend to other accused: admitting illegally obtained or secret evidence, withholding exculpatory evidence, and closing hearings to the public. During the McCarthy era, appellate courts twice reversed Judith Coplon's conviction for espionage and conspiracy because of unlawful FBI surveillance; Learned Hand even publicly rebuked J. Edgar Hoover.[14] In 1972 the government dropped weapons charges against Bill Ayers rather than reveal unlawful wiretaps; but in other Weather Underground prosecutions the Supreme Court invoked national security to uphold the government's refusal to disclose surveillance.[15] CD Cal Judge Byrne dismissed the case against Daniel Ellsberg for leaking the Pentagon Papers because the White House "plumbers" had burgled his psychiatrist's office.

Even during the Civil War, when the US faced a mortal threat, some judges resisted executive pressure to subordinate liberty to security. Chief Justice Taney granted John Merryman's habeas petition, declaring that only Congress could suspend the writ.[16] The Supreme Court reversed Lambdin Milligan's military commission conviction because civilian courts had exclusive jurisdiction whenever they were open. Justice Davis wrote:

> [T]he Constitution … is a law for rules and people, equally in war and in peace, and covers with the shield of its protection all classes of men, at all times, and under all circumstances. No doctrine, involving more pernicious consequences, was ever invented by the wit of man than that any of its provisions can be suspended during any of the great exigencies of government.

During World War I, D Mont Judge George Bourquin directed the acquittal of a man charged under the Espionage Act because his alleged statements were matters of opinion rather than fact.[17] Bourquin granted habeas to a man facing deportation as a communist, declaring that "he and his kind are less of a danger to America than those who indorse or use the methods that brought him to deportation." (Critics unsuccessfully tried to remove Bourquin from office.) Declaring that the Sedition Act contained "every evil of the old definition of treason," Eighth Circuit Judge Charles Fremont Amidon dismissed more than half the cases brought under the Act against socialists and agrarian reformers but sustained convictions of German Americans opposed to the war. In Boston, D Mass Judge George W. Anderson secretly arranged to hear the habeas petitions of 20 alleged communists threatened with deportation, asked Harvard law professors Zechariah Chafee and Felix Frankfurter to argue on their behalf, challenged the use of informants, personally questioned government officials, and freed the prisoners, declaring: "this case seems to have been conducted under the modern theory of states-manship: Hang first and try later." "The government's spy system ... destroys trust and confidence and propagates hate. A mob is a mob, whether made up of government officials acting under instructions from the Department of Justice, or criminals, loafers and the vicious classes." [18]

SDNY Judge Learned Hand consciously jeopardized his chance of promotion to the Second Circuit by enjoining enforcement of the Espionage Act against *The Masses*.[19] After being reversed, he instructed the jury that "every man has the right to have such economic, philo-sophic or religious opinions as seem to him best whether they be socialist, anarchistic or atheistic." (He was passed over for a vacant position on the Court of Appeals that year but appointed to it seven years later.)

Five months after upholding Schenck's conviction, Justice Holmes qualified that opinion (and his "clear and present danger" test) in lan-guage that became even more influential when he dissented from the Court's affirmation of the Espionage Act convictions of Jacob Abrams and others.[20] (Holmes probably was influenced by meeting Zechariah Chafee, who had written a critical article about the *Schenk* opinion, and by corresponding with Learned Hand and Harold Laski.[21])

> [N]obody can suppose that the surreptitious publishing of a silly leaflet by an unknown man, without more, would present any immediate danger that its operations would hinder the success of the government's arms ... [W]hen men have realized that time has upset many fighting faiths, they may come to believe even more than they believe the very foundations of their own conduct that the ultimate good they desire is better reached by free trade in ideas – that the best test of truth is the power of the thought to get itself accepted in the competition of the market, and that truth is the only ground upon which their wishes safely can be carried out ... That at any rate is the theory of our Constitution. It is an experiment, as all life is an experiment ... we should be eternally vigilant against attempts to check the expression of opinions that we loathe and believe

to be fraught with death, unless they so imminently threaten immediate interference with the lawful and pressing purposes of the law that an immediate check is required to save the country.[22]

Holmes's insistence three times in the final sentence that the danger must be "imminent" or "immediate" was telling, given his earlier requirement that it only had to be "present."

Six years later Holmes dissented from the affirmation of Benjamin Gitlow's conviction for violating New York's Criminal Anarchy Law by publishing a "Left Wing Manifesto." "It is said that this manifesto was more than a theory, that it was an incitement. Every idea is an incitement. It offers itself for belief and if believed it is acted on unless some other belief outweighs it or some failure of energy stifles the movement of its birth." [23]

A few years after that, Brandeis (joined by Holmes) wrote in a concurrence upholding Charlotte Whitney's conviction under California's Criminal Syndicalism Act for belonging to the Communist Labor Party:

> Those who won our independence ... believed liberty to be the secret of happiness and courage to be the secret of liberty. They believed that freedom to think as you will and to speak as you think are means indispensable to the discovery and spread of political truth ... [that] discussion affords ordinarily adequate protection against the dissemination of noxious doctrine; that the greatest menace to freedom is an inert people ... [that] it is hazardous to discourage thought, hope and imagination; that fear breeds repression; that repression breeds hate; that hate menaces stable government ... Fear of serious injury alone cannot justify suppression of free speech and assembly. Men feared witches and burnt women.[24]

The Governor of California quoted their opinion when pardoning Whitney a month later.

In a dissent two years later, Holmes offered another memorable formulation: "if there is any principle of the Constitution that more imperatively calls for attachment than any other it is the principle of free thought – not free thought for those who agree with us but freedom for the thought that we hate."[25] Invalidating a California law prohibiting display of a red flag, Chief Justice Hughes wrote in 1931 that "the maintenance of the opportunity for free political discussion to the end that government may be responsible to the will of the people and that changes may be obtained by lawful means is a fundamental principle of our constitutional system."[26]

Soon after the USA entered World War II, the Supreme Court upheld a Pennsylvania school district's expulsion of Jehovah's Witnesses for refusing to salute the flag. "[W]e live by symbols," Frankfurter explained, and the flag "is the symbol of our national unity, transcending all internal differences." But the Court, in a rare action, reversed itself just three years later (symbolically on July 4). "[I]f there is any fixed star in our constitutional constellation," Justice Jackson wrote, "it is that no official, high or petty, can prescribe what shall be orthodox in politics, nationalism or other matter of opinion or force citizens to confess by word or act their faith therein." The "freedom to differ is not limited to things that do not matter much. That would be a mere shadow of freedom. The test of its substance is the right to differ as to things that touch the heart of the existing order." [27]

That year the Court overturned the denaturalization of Communist Party president William Schneiderman, declaring: "There is a material difference between agitation and exhortation calling for present violent action which creates a clear and present danger of public disorder ... and mere doctrinal justification or prediction of the use of force under hypothetical conditions at some indefinite future time." [28]

After upholding the early Smith Act convictions, the Supreme Court gradually changed course in the wake of Stalin's death, the end of combat in Korea, Senate condemnation of Joseph McCarthy, and the replacement of four Justices. [29] The Court declared that "mere doctrinal justification of forcible overthrow" of the government, even "if engaged in with the intent to accomplish overthrow," was not punishable because it was "too remote from concrete actions." In another case the Court held that government could not punish membership in an organization unless the individual knew of its illegal advocacy, was an "active" member, and had a "specific intent" to further its illegal ends. Elsewhere the Court limited the use of paid informants and let the defense see FBI surveillance evidence. It ruled that the Loyalty Review Board lacked authority to conduct post-audit hearings after two other boards had exonerated an individual; [30] only civil servants with access to sensitive information could be summarily dismissed; [31] federal sedition law preempted state laws; [32] and New York could not treat invocation of the Fifth Amendment as resignation from employment. [33] But though the government lost all 12 prosecutions involving communists during the 1956 term, the Court upheld the convictions of witnesses who refused to testify before the House Committee on Un-American

Activities (HUAC), perhaps to deflect efforts to strip courts of jurisdiction in national security matters.[34]

Although Lyndon Johnson's Attorney General, Ramsey Clark, refused to prosecute organizers of the anti-war demonstrations at the 1968 Democratic National Convention in Chicago, Nixon's Attorney General, John Mitchell, secured indictments of eight, leading to a notorious travesty of justice.[35] ND Ill Judge Julius Hoffman displayed blatant hostility to the defendants during the four-and-a-half-month trial, binding and gagging Bobby Seale before declaring a mistrial and sentencing him to four years for contempt of court. The jury acquitted the others of conspiracy but convicted five of crossing state lines with intent to incite a riot.

Judge Hoffman sentenced them to the maximum of five years and both them and their lawyers to another 2.5–4 years for contempt. After the Seventh Circuit reversed all the convictions, the government retried the contempt charges. The new judge convicted three defendants and one lawyer on just 13 of the original 175 contempt charges, but declined to sentence them because they had been goaded by Judge Hoffman's improper, provocative, and "condemnatious" conduct.

When the Department of Justice (DoJ) prosecuted White Panther Party members for bombing the CIA office in Ann Arbor, Attorney General Mitchell declared the FBI could wiretap without a warrant in whatever it "deems a 'national security' case."[36] ED Mich Judge Damon Keith ordered the government to disclose its surveillance or drop the case, and the Supreme Court unanimously affirmed. Justice Powell (a Nixon appointee) wrote that the Fourth Amendment "cannot properly be guaranteed if domestic surveillance may be conducted solely within the discretion of the executive branch."

Other courts also overturned convictions of government critics. After Benjamin Spock, William Sloane Coffin Jr., Mitchell Goodman, and Michael Ferber were convicted of conspiracy to aid draft violators and sentenced to two years for what D Mass Judge Francis Ford called an act "in the nature of treason," the First Circuit reversed on technical grounds, and the government did not retry them.[37] Prosecutions of those protesting the Vietnam War or the draft in Catonsville, Maryland, Kansas City, Missouri, Evanston, Illinois, and Gainesville, Florida collapsed or were dismissed or reversed on appeal because of unlawful surveillance. Mass arrests of demonstrators required courts to deal with evidentiary flaws and due process violations.[38]

After police arrested 13,400 protesters camped on the Washington Mall in May 1971, courts convicted only 745 for demonstrating without a permit.[39] Three years later a federal jury awarded $12 million to those wrongly arrested on the Capitol grounds. Six months after that a federal judge found massive civil liberties violations during every major Washington demonstration between 1969 and 1975 and ordered all arrest records expunged.

The Supreme Court granted constitutional protections to a variety of 1960s protesters. It extended conscientious objector status to those who did not believe in a Supreme Being[40] and struck down the Selective Service reclassification and induction of anti-war demonstrators.[41] Affirming the right of a high school student to wear a black arm band to oppose the war, Justice Fortas wrote that students do not "shed their constitutional rights to freedom of speech or expression at the schoolhouse gate."[42] Justice Harlan reversed a flag-burning conviction, declaring that the First Amendment protected "excited public advocacy of the idea that the United States should abandon, at least temporarily, one of its national symbols."[43] Overturning a conviction for wearing a shirt declaring "Fuck the Draft" in a government building, Justice Harlan echoed Holmes:

> The constitutional right of free expression is a powerful medicine in a society as diverse and populous as ours. It is designed and intended to remove governmental restraints from the arena of public discussion, putting the decision as to what views shall be voiced largely in the hands of each of us, in the hope that use of such freedom will ultimately produce a more capable citizenry and more perfect polity and in the belief that no other approach would comport with the premise of individual dignity and choice upon which our political system rests. [44]

Explicitly limiting Holmes's "clear and present danger" test, the Court reversed a KKK member's conviction because the actions he advocated were not imminent.[45] When lawyers began asking courts to enforce human rights treaties in the 1980s, judges appointed by Democratic presidents were more likely to do so than those appointed by Republicans.[46]

Juries may resist government pressure to convict. A jury acquitted the publisher Andrew Zenger, charged with defaming the royal governor of New York, even though truth was no defense to seditious libel.[47] John Merryman was accused of treason for allegedly burning bridges during the Civil War but never tried because no Maryland jury would convict him.[48] Juries hung in both prosecutions of *The Masses* under the Espionage Act of 1917. The government indicted 27 Communist Party members for the 1920 bombing of J.P. Morgan and Co. (which killed 38 and injured hundreds, making it one of the worst terrorist attacks in the USA until 9/11), even though it was almost certainly perpetrated by anarchists.[49] But the jury convicted only the Party's president and could not agree about another defendant after being told it had to find he had "advocated crime, sabotage, violence and terrorism." The government never tried the rest. Juries refused to convict some who protested the draft and the Vietnam War.[50]

Latin American countries have been less protective of the rule of law in times of crisis.[51] Chilean courts rejected almost all the thousands of habeas petitions filed on behalf of those missing or detained by the Pinochet regime.[52] On the rare occasions when courts granted a petition, the junta ignored them. Even after the restoration of democracy, the Chilean Supreme Court held that international treaties could not retroactively abrogate the amnesty Pinochet had granted his subordinates, and civilian courts could not hear cases against the military. By 1994, however, the Appeals Court circumvented the amnesty by finding that kidnapping was a continuing offense. In 2006 the Supreme Court invoked the Convention against Torture (CAT) to hold there could be no amnesty for crimes against humanity and no statute of limitations for grave human rights violations like torture. The following year the Appeals Court found there had been a systematic pattern of state violence abrogating fundamental human rights and the government had a duty to prosecute. El Salvador courts failed to punish the military for murdering five priests, their housekeeper, and her daughter.[53] When Spain tried to prosecute those responsible (because some victims were Spanish), El Salvador rebuffed the extradition request. Guatemalan courts were unable to convict and punish numerous human rights violators.[54] The Constitutional Court reversed the conviction of Efraín Ríos Montt (a former general, president, and president of Congress) for genocide and crimes against humanity. When Peruvian courts blocked accountability for a military massacre, victims obtained a default judgment in a US court but could not execute it.[55]

Soon after the first intifada began in Israel in 1987 the Landau Commission endorsed "moderate physical" and "non-violent psychological" pressure during interrogations.[56] Starting in 1994 human rights lawyers brought every case of suspected torture to the Supreme

Court, but it evaded the issue for eight years, dismissing 17 cases as not involving torture. Even Chief Justice Barak thought the Knesset should decide the question. But in 1996 he wrote for a unanimous Supreme Court:

> It is our duty to safeguard the legality of the regime even with difficult decisions. Even when the cannons roar and the muses are silent the law exists in practice and determines what is permissible and what forbidden, what is legal and what is illegal. And where the law exists, there is also a court which determines what is permissible and what forbidden, what is legal and what is illegal. Some of the public will be pleased with our decision; another part will oppose it. Conceivably, neither will peruse our reasoning. But we shall perform our task, this is our work and this is our duty as judges ... we are one of the branches of government, and it is our function to oversee that the other branches act within the framework of the law in order to ensure the rule of law in government. The branches of government hold a high place, but the law is higher than all of us. [57]

Several years later (echoing Justice Jackson's warning) Barak reflected:

> It is a myth to think that it is possible to maintain a sharp distinction between the status of human rights during a period of war and the status of human rights during a period of peace. It is self-deception to believe that we can limit our judicial rulings so that they will be valid only during wartime, and that we can decide that things will change in peace time ... A wrong decision in a time of war and terrorism plots a point that will cause the judicial graph to deviate after the crisis passes. [58]

Lord Denning took the opposite approach during the Irish Republican Army (IRA) bombing campaign in Britain.[59] Dismissing civil actions against the West Midlands police by the Birmingham Six, who had challenged their convictions on grounds of misconduct, he wrote that if the accused won,

> it would mean that the police were guilty of perjury; that they were guilty of violence and threats; that the confessions were involuntary and improperly admitted in evidence; and that the confessions were erroneous. That would mean that the Home Secretary would have either to recommend that the accused be pardoned or to remit the case to the Court of Appeal. That was such an appalling vista that every sensible person would say, "It cannot be right that these actions should go any further."

Fortunately, "sensible" judges disagreed, and the action ultimately succeeded.

THE PATH OF THE LAW IN WARTIME

Wartime heightens the tensions between liberty and security.[60] As early as 1798, Federalists played on fears of a French invasion and fifth-column traitors to enact laws authorizing the removal of aliens from countries that had declared war on the USA, empowering the president to deport those "he shall judge dangerous," and criminalizing anyone who uttered "false, scandalous and malicious" words about Congress or the president. Robert Goodloe Harper (a Federalist) asked if the country had to wait "until a judicial process can be entered up? To stay until the dagger is plunged into our bosoms …?" Robert Livingston (a Republican) replied: "we must legislate upon facts, not on surmises." Denouncing the Sedition Act as "a weapon used by a party now in power, in order to perpetuate their authority and preserve their present places," Albert Gallatin demanded that Federalists "prove that the necessity now exists which heretofore did not exist." The government used the Act to prosecute four of the five leading Republican newspapers (and many others), convicting Thomas Cooper for accusing President Adams of incurring "the expense of a permanent navy" and impairing the country's credit. Matthew Lyon was imprisoned for four months for declaring that under President Adams "every consideration of the public welfare was swallowed up in a continual grasp for power, in an unfounded thirst for ridiculous pomp, foolish adulation, and selfish avarice."

When the debate over slavery intensified a half century later, the federal government condoned Southern repression of abolitionist advocacy.[61] President Andrew Jackson and his Postmaster General supported Southern postmasters who refused to deliver abolitionist newspapers and tracts. Jackson urged Congress to prohibit anyone mailing "incendiary publications intended to instigate the slaves to insurrection" (an implausible strategy, given how few could read). The Postmaster General took the bizarre position that "the States are still independent, and may fence round and protect their interest in slaves" by any laws, including those limiting "the carrying on [of] discussions" or "distribution of printed papers." But Congress refused to interdict mail to the South, and an 1836 law made it a crime not to deliver mail (although no postmaster was prosecuted for disobedience). Congress refused to debate slavery but declined to block petitions against it. Lincoln began raising an army, empowering his top army general to suspend habeas corpus three months before Congress declared war. A month after doing so, Congress ratified his actions. Soon thereafter Lincoln authorized military tribunals to try "all Rebels and Insurgents, their aiders and abettors ... and all persons discouraging volunteer enlistments, resisting militia drafts, or guilty of any disloyal practice."

Foreshadowing President Trump a century earlier, President Wilson announced to the Daughters of the American Revolution two years before the USA entered World War I: "I am in a hurry for an opportunity to have a line-up and let the men who are thinking first of other countries stand on one side and all those that are for America first, last, and all the time on the other."[62] At the end of that year he warned Congress:

> [T]he gravest threats against our national peace and safety have been uttered within our own borders. There are citizens of the United States ... born under other flags but welcomed by our generous naturalization laws to the full freedom and opportunity of America, who have poured the poison of disloyalty into the very arteries of our national life.

He proclaimed "once and for all that loyalty to this flag is the first test of tolerance." In 1916 he helped draft the Democratic Party platform plank on loyalty, which condemned "every group or organization, political or otherwise, that has for its object the advancement of the interest of a foreign power ..." Sen. Albert Fall (R-NM) declared that due process did "not apply" in wartime. Sen. William Borah (R-Id) contended that if soldiers risked their lives to protect "our form of government, our Constitution and our flag" it was not "too much to ask complete devotion upon the part of those who remain at home." Sen. James Lewis (D-Oh) said any disloyal citizen should forfeit his citizenship. Former President Theodore Roosevelt, who still enjoyed enormous respect, was even more inflammatory: "every disloyal native-born American should be disenfranchised and interned" (anticipating his fifth cousin's actions a quarter century later).

Urging Congress to pass the Sedition Act of 1918, Wilson asserted that the "authority to exercise censorship is absolutely necessary to the public safety." But the American Newspaper Publishers Association protested, and the *New York Times* editorialized: "while we are warring to make democracy safe in the world, let us keep it safe in the United States." Sen. Henry Cabot Lodge (D-Mass) warned that government was "going very dangerously too far" in attempting "to deny to the press all legitimate criticism of either Congress or the Executive. And Theodore Roosevelt now attacked "foolish or traitorous persons who endeavor to make it a crime to tell the truth," declaring that if Congress passed the bill he would "give the government the opportunity to test its constitutionality" by defying it. Sen. Joseph France (R-Md) proposed an amendment that "nothing in this act shall be construed as limiting the liberty … of any individual to publish or speak what is true, with good motives and for justifiable ends." Although the Senate passed it unanimously, the conference committee recommended against it after being warned by Assistant Attorney General O'Brian that "the most dangerous type of propaganda" was "religious pacifism" and claims that "this war is one between capitalists and the proletariat." The amendment was defeated, and the Act passed overwhelmingly. Wilson thundered on Flag Day: "Woe be to the man or group of men who seeks to stand in our way in this day of high resolution when every principle we hold dearest is to be vindicated and made secure for the salvation of the nation." But O'Brian refused to defend the law's constitutionality, and Attorney General Gregory directed all US Attorneys to obtain his approval before prosecuting violations. The law "should not be permitted to become the medium whereby efforts are made to suppress honest, legitimate criticism of the administration or discussion of Government Policies." When the US Attorney for SDNY proposed to indict the National Civil Liberties Board for defending those accused of sedition, O'Brian replied that "as the avowed purpose at least of this Bureau is the protection of civil liberties … it is of the first [importance] that no action be taken by arrest, suppression or otherwise unless it be based upon facts showing a violation of the express provisions of the law." He added later that "the organization of defense of persons accused of a crime" is not "in and of itself a crime."

Asking Congress to declare war, Wilson asserted that "Germany has filled our unsuspecting communities and even our offices of government with spies and set criminal intrigues everywhere afoot against our national unity of counsel, our peace within and without, our industries and our commerce."

He immediately signed an executive order restricting the movement of aliens and empowering DoJ to arrest and imprison without trial any foreigner deemed disloyal. The next day a secret executive order (EO) authorized department heads to remove any employee deemed a loyalty risk; other EOs empowered the War Department to censor messages sent abroad and Postmaster General Burleson to censor all foreign language newspapers. A week later Wilson used his emergency powers to create the Committee on Public Information to disseminate propaganda.

Within a month, Burleson had banned 15 left-wing publications, including *The Masses*. When Max Eastman (its editor and Wilson's friend) objected, the president supported Burleson. Postmasters refused to deliver International Workers of the World (IWW) mail. The Supreme Court upheld Burleson's ban on the *Milwaukee Leader*. More than a thousand were convicted under the Espionage Act of 1917 for speaking against the war. Rose Pastor Stokes was sentenced to ten years for saying "no government which is for profiteers can also be for the people." When Eugene Victor Debs denounced her sentence, he also was convicted and sentenced to ten years. But Wilson opposed a bill allowing war offenses to be tried in military courts, which "would make an impression with regard to the weakness of our ordinary tribunals which would not be justified."

Less than a month before the Armistice, Congress passed the Alien Act, which the Secretary of Labor used to deport nearly 12,000 aliens after a secret administrative process found they belonged to an anarchist organization. A jury took only 39 minutes to convict Emma Goldman and Alexander Berkman of violating the Draft Act 1917 after SDNY Judge Julius Mayer instructed them that "no issue of free speech was involved"; Mayer sentenced them to the two-year maximum. Wilson backed Attorney General Gregory's effort to exploit the war frenzy to attack the IWW; a jury deliberated less than an hour before convicting 96 of 113 leaders of violating the Espionage Act. The *New York Times* cheered: the government should "make short work of these treasonable conspirators," who were "in effect, and perhaps in fact, agents of Germany." Hundreds of others were arrested and 165 convicted, some imprisoned for 20 years. Gregory told the American Bar Association (ABA): "we are going to urge capital punishment in any case where the facts justify it." He also waged a campaign against "slackers" who had not registered for the draft, declaring that the greatest threat to national security was the "respectable" pacifist – a "physical or moral degenerate." The Council of National Defense encouraged action against those who failed to buy Liberty Bonds. The Bureau of Investigation (BoI, precursor of the FBI) and 400 police and military, backed by 2,000 volunteers from the 250,000-member American Protective League, arrested between 50,000 and 65,000 (although only 5 percent were shown to be draft dodgers). Gregory boasted that, assisted by the Knights of Liberty, Boy Spies of America, Sedition Slammers, and Terrible Threateners, DoJ had been able "to investigate hundreds of thousands of complaints and to keep scores of thousands of people under observation. We have

15

representatives at all meetings of any importance." But even the pro-Wilson *New York World* condemned this "Amateur Prussianism in New York," this "rape of the law – this ravishing of the very spirit of American institutions."

The backlash forced Gregory and the BoI chief to resign. In 1922 the Ninth Circuit found American Protective League arrests unconstitutional and awarded damages.

A. Mitchell Palmer, Gregory's successor, arrested an estimated 6,000 to 10,000 in his eponymous raids in response to anarchist bombings (one of which targeted him).[63] J. Edgar Hoover (the new BoI chief) declared with stunning hyperbole that "civilization faces its most terrible menace of danger since the barbarian hordes overran west Europe and opened the dark ages." Wilson warned that the Russian Revolution could bring "the poison of disorder, the poison of revolt, the poison of chaos" to the USA.

> You have got to watch [revolutionaries] with secret agencies planted everywhere. And you can't do that under free debate. You can't do that under public counsel. Plans must be kept secret. Knowledge must be accumulated under a system which we have condemned, because we have called it a spying system. The more polite call it a system of intelligence.

He authorized black bag jobs, in which the BoI's Radical Division and the Office of Naval Intelligence broke into embassies and consulates. The *Washington Post* applauded: "there is no time to waste on hairsplitting over infringement of liberty." Only after Coolidge became president in 1923 did his Attorney General, Harlan Fiske Stone, begin to correct some of these abuses.

Roger Baldwin created the Civil Liberties Bureau (the precursor of the American Civil Liberties Union (ACLU)), within the American Union Against Militarism, to defend conscientious objectors and oppose conscription.[64] After passage of the Espionage Act, it became the National Civil Liberties Bureau and shifted strategies from negotiating with the White House to defending the IWW, whose objectives it shared. Baldwin defiantly refused conscription, attracting national attention and widespread sympathy. When vigilantes in Kentucky attacked Rev. Herbert S. Bigelow, pastor of a predominantly German American Cincinnati church, DoJ refused to act because it viewed him as disloyal. Baldwin organized a meeting to support Bigelow, which was widely publicized and sold out even though boycotted by liberal organizations and leaders. When the government responded by blocking all National Civil Liberties Bureau mail and raiding its New York office, the Bureau won an order from SDNY Judge Augustus Hand that the Post Office deliver its mail (but not its pamphlet "The Truth About the I.W.W.").

As World War II approached, the USA seemed to have learned from experience.[65] At the ACLU's 1939 Conference on Civil Liberties in the Present Emergency, Attorney General Murphy (a member) assured the audience that "an emergency does not abrogate the Constitution or dissolve the Bill of Rights." Three days after Pearl Harbor, Attorney General Biddle exhorted Americans: "it is essential at such a time as this that we keep our heads, keep our tempers, – above all, that we keep clearly in mind what we are defending." Roosevelt designated December 15, 1941 as Bill of Rights Day, declaring: "We will not, under any threat, or in the face of any danger, surrender the guarantees of liberty our forefathers framed for us in the Bill of Rights." But just hours after Pearl Harbor (with Roosevelt's approval), Hawaii's governor proclaimed martial law, suspended habeas corpus, closed local courts, and transferred the government to the military (which retained power until October 1944). On December 14 Roosevelt warned that "some degree of censorship is essential in war time, and we are at war." And a month later he suggested to FBI Director Hoover that it might be time to "clean up a number of these vile publications."

In May 1940 Roosevelt wrote Attorney General Jackson that, even though the Supreme Court had excluded wiretapping evidence, he was convinced:

> it never intended any dictum in the particular case which it decided to apply to grave matters involving the defense of the nation ... It is too late to do anything about it after sabotage, assassination and "fifth column" activities are completed. You are, therefore, authorized and directed in such cases as you may approve, after investigation of the need in each case, to authorize the necessary investigation agents that they are at liberty to secure information by listening devices direct [sic] to the conversations or other communications of persons suspected of subversive activities against the Government of the United States ... [but] limit them insofar as possible to aliens.[66]

Biddle (Jackson's successor) dismissed the first three Espionage Act indictments immediately after Pearl Harbor and instructed all US Attorneys to get his approval before filing others.[67] But after a March

1942 Cabinet meeting unanimously supported Roosevelt's demand for "vigorous action" against seditious speech and publications, DoJ indicted 28 fascist supporters. The left was no more tolerant: *The Nation* exhorted the government to "curb the Fascist press"; the Communist Party urged Biddle to "lock them up"; and the National Lawyers Guild advocated suppression of Father Coughlin's *Social Justice*. Biddle signed orders to detain 3,846 German, Italian, and Japanese aliens, but rejected Hoover's demand to prosecute black leaders who "exhibited sentiments in a manner inimical to the Nation's war effort."

When eight German agents were captured after landing by submarine in New York and Florida, legislators and the media demanded their death.[68] Biddle and Secretary of War Stimson expressed concern that the plot had not matured sufficiently to convict the men of serious offenses. But two days later Roosevelt urged Biddle to try them in a military commission (MC) because "the death penalty is called for by usage and by the extreme gravity of the war aim and the very existence of our American government ... Surely they are just as guilty as it is possible to be ... and it seems to me that the death penalty is almost obligatory." Biddle now agreed that MCs had decisive advantages: secrecy, speed, ease of proving war violations, the death penalty, and no habeas corpus. "All the prisoners can thus be denied access to our courts." On his advice, Roosevelt issued two EOs asserting the jurisdiction of MCs and empowering them to make their own rules. They could hear any evidence that would, "in the opinion of the President of the Commission, have probative value to a reasonable man" and convict by a two-thirds vote (rather than the unanimity required of civilian juries). After they confessed at their secret trial, Roosevelt sentenced them to death, but Biddle persuaded him to commute the two American citizens' sentences to imprisonment. The Supreme Court confirmed the MCs' legality before the verdict but did not issue its opinion until after the six were executed. Justice Byrne refused to recuse himself even though he served as adviser to the administration.

Two months after Pearl Harbor the *New York Times* reported that the FBI claimed (falsely) to have found ammunition and contraband among Japanese residents in Monterey Bay.[69] The next day Walter Lippmann fulminated in the *Washington Post* about "The Fifth Column on the Coast," declaring that the absence of any attack "is a sign that the blow is well-organized and that it is held back until it can be struck with maximum effect." California Governor Earl Warren assured Congress that "it would seem ... beyond doubt that the presence" of Japanese on the coast "is not coincidence" (although many had lived there for decades). He boasted he could determine the loyalties of Germans and Italians by observation, but justified internment of all the inscrutable Japanese because "we are in an entirely different field and we cannot form any opinion that we believe to be sound." "[T]here is more potential danger among the group of Japanese who are born in this country than from the alien Japanese who were born in Japan." Gen. John L. DeWitt, who directed the relocation, pronounced that "the very fact that no sabotage has taken place to date is a disturbing and confirming indication" that Japanese Americans had hidden it.

Although a few religious organizations and fair play committees opposed internment, most civil liberties groups remained silent. The ACLU initially denounced the relocation but soon split over the issue.[70] Alexander Meiklejohn compared EO 9066 to a measles quarantine, asserting that "Japanese citizens, as a group, are dangerous both to themselves and to their fellow-citizens." Morris Ernst (ACLU co-founder and general counsel) denied there was "any possible constitutional question if there is military necessity." The ACLU board voted 52 to 26 that government had the right to remove people. Roger Baldwin (ACLU Director) congratulated Gen. DeWitt on conducting the evacuation "with a minimum of hardship." Although the ACLU participated in *Hirabayashi*, it did not attack the EO's constitutionality, and the national organization ordered the Northern California branch to remove its name from the *Korematsu* brief challenging the EO. By the end of 1943 Biddle and Interior Secretary Ickes urged the immediate release of all Japanese Americans; Stimson joined them six months later; but Roosevelt delayed for fear of alienating voters in the 1944 election.

Initial opposition to the Vietnam War focused on its legality (*jus ad bellum*) rather than specific acts of misconduct (*jus in bello*).[71] Elite lawyers lobbied Congress through the Lawyers Committee concerning American Policy in Vietnam, published a book-length critique of the administration's belated justification for the war, and tried to raise the issue during the Supreme Court confirmation hearing for William Rehnquist, who had drafted the legal justification for the Cambodian invasion. But in 1968 the International League for the Rights of Man published a report signed by prominent intellectuals and international lawyers decrying "the departure on a massive scale from observance of the Geneva and Hague Conventions relative to the conduct of the war." Seymour Hersh's exposé of the My Lai massacre, followed by Ron

Haeberle's *Life* magazine photos, intensified criticism. But two-thirds of Americans felt My Lai was just the kind of incident that was "bound to happen in a war." Sen. Thomas Dodd (D-Ct) denounced anti-war demonstrations as "tantamount to open insurrection"; Sen. Richard Russell (D-Ga) warned that "every protest will cause the Communists to believe they can win if they hold on a little longer." A Senate Internal Security Subcommittee report concluded that the anti-war movement was controlled by "communist and extremist elements who are openly sympathetic to the Vietcong and openly hostile to the United States." HUAC agreed.

In addition to suppressing perceived security threats, wartime governments prosecute military crimes. In 1879 Gen. Sherman told Congress that military and civilian judicial systems were and should be as "wide apart as the poles."[72] "The object of civil law is to secure to every human being in a community all the liberty, security, and happiness possible, consistent with the safety of all. The object of military law is to govern armies composed of strong men, so as to be capable of exercising the largest measure of force at the will of the nation."

Consequently, military justice tended to be far more favorable to those accused of crimes than civilian courts. Although 88 percent of army trials during World War I resulted in convictions, nearly 70 percent of the sentences were reduced by Convening Authorities (CAs) (a form of executive interference anathema to civilian courts, except in the rare instances of clemency or pardon). After the war an effort to conform military trials to civilian justice was defeated, but a second attempt following World War II produced the 1950 Uniform Code of Military Justice, which required an Art. 32 proceeding prior to a general court-martial and granted the accused a wide panoply of rights: to counsel, to cross-examine witnesses and submit evidence, against self-incrimination, to a jury of military peers, and to review by the Court of Military Appeals. The Military Justice Act 1968 sought to insulate courts-martial from command influence. For every general court-martial during the Vietnam War there were more than 25 special and summary courts-martial (limited to 12 months' imprisonment and noncustodial sentences, respectively) and more than 170 nonjudicial punishments. Although general court-martial conviction rates for crimes against civilians were comparable to or perhaps higher than those in civilian courts, those penalties also were reduced, often drastically. The 15 Marines who were convicted of murder for actions committed during the Vietnam War and sentenced to life actually served an average of only 12 years. A soldier who killed a Vietnamese while trying to knock off his hat (for a trophy) served only 11 months; by contrast, a black soldier who killed a white buddy who had attacked him served ten years.

In the notorious My Lai massacre, two platoons raped and sodomized villagers, killing 200–500.[73] After the cover-up was exposed, Lt. William Calley was charged just before leaving the service. The Army Criminal Investigation Command (CID) recommended charges against 30 soldiers, but only 14 were prosecuted. Although an Art. 32 proceeding found that MGen. Samuel W. Koster knew of the cover-up, the charges were dismissed because he was at the end of a distinguished career (which included being Superintendent of West Point). His deputy received an administrative punishment. Although eyewitnesses testified before Congress that Sgt. David Mitchell had killed My Lai villagers, exclusion of that evidence in his court-martial led to an acquittal. Sgt. Charles Hutto was acquitted even though he admitted killing under orders. Capt. Medina, who ordered the platoons into the village, was charged with command responsibility but was acquitted by a jury that deliberated less than an hour. The CA dismissed charges against seven others, including one accused of multiple rapes and sodomy. Although Calley was convicted of killing at least 22 people, the CA reduced his life sentence to 20 years, the Secretary of the Army then cut that in half, and Nixon released him after he had served just 3.5 years under house arrest.

RESEARCH QUESTIONS

This brief history of the judicial response to tensions between liberty and security offers many examples of both principled assertions of fundamental liberties and craven capitulation to executive and legislative invocations of security (often later exposed as factitious). That experience suggests a broad range of research questions.

How do judges react when law offends their moral intuitions about how to resolve tensions between liberty and state power? How is their reaction related to the nature and magnitude of the alleged threat to national security? When do judges defer to the executive or the military? What reasons do they give? What deontological or consequentialist counterarguments are offered by judges who decline to defer?

How do judges' political orientations (measured by the proxy of the appointing president's party affiliation) shape their responses? How do prospects of promotion or threats of recall influence judicial actions?

21

Do general jurisdiction Art. III courts respond differently from specialized courts (e.g., Foreign Intelligence Surveillance Court (FISC), military commissions)? Are there differences among District Courts, Courts of Appeal, and the Supreme Court?

Which criminal cases become show trials? Are they handled differently from ordinary crimes? How do judges deal with defendants who defy their authority?

Are private litigants more successful when they use law as a shield against the government than when they invoke law as a sword to compel the government to act? How does the government exploit its control over forum choice to maximize its chances of getting a conviction? When is habeas corpus effective as a means of challenging detention?

Which fundamental liberties are limited in the name of security? Are there differences in the treatment of the freedoms of speech and the press? How do courts decide what security requires? When do courts restrict procedural protections against illegally obtained or secret evidence, the accused's right to see exculpatory evidence, and public hearings? When do courts accept government claims that state secrets preclude adjudication? When does the executive assert plenary, incontestable power? How do courts respond? Do courts treat citizens and noncitizens differently? Immigrants and native-born? Racial and religious minorities?

When are liberty rights vindicated despite the state's security claims? When do judges overturn convictions because of procedural error? What challenges do mass arrests pose for the criminal process? When do courts limit the government's power to criminalize speech or membership in political organizations? How does all this change over time? How do earlier judicial actions influence later ones (both when judges follow precedent and when they repudiate bad decisions)? When do juries refuse to convict in national security cases?

How do NGOs and the media respond to wartime measures and other restrictions on civil liberties?

Do the executive, legislature, or judiciary differentiate between what the government can do in the name of criminal prosecutions and intelligence gathering?

When does the executive invoke war to justify limiting liberty? What evidence does it offer for the dangers it seeks to avert? When does it try to use war and national security threats for political gain? Does the executive ever encounter internal dissent? At what levels? How does it respond? How does the legislature respond in wartime? Does either branch resist limitations on liberty? Does the judiciary?

When does the government prosecute crimes in military commissions rather than Art. III courts? How do those commissions differ from conventional criminal trials? In terms of constitutional protections? Separation of powers?

How do the executive, military, and judiciary respond to law-of-war violations, especially atrocities? How do courts-martial differ from Art. III courts and military commissions, in structure, composition, process, outcome, and sentence? Do courts-martial respond differently to charges against enlisted personnel and officers and among officers by rank?

The following chapters seek to answer those questions (and others that history did not anticipate) by documenting and analyzing how US courts have dealt with threats to liberty in the name of security during the years since 9/11.

CHAPTER TWO

CRIMINAL PROSECUTIONS

Conservatives have accused those defending the rule of law of committing "lawfare": abusing law to obstruct the government's essential and legitimate conduct of the "war on terror." But "lawfare" better characterizes how the government itself has deployed law in waging that "war."[1] Criminal prosecutions have been an essential strategy. On October 25 Attorney General John Ashcroft declared: "We will seek every prosecutorial advantage."[2] Within weeks, DoJ filed more than a hundred terrorism-related indictments.[3] A 2003 guide for US Attorneys encouraged "strategic overinclusiveness." Although the material support law had rarely been used before 9/11 (18 U.S.C. §2339A twice, 18 U.S.C. §2339B four times), it was charged against 140 defendants in 2001–07 and accounted for 18 percent of all convictions after 9/11. Those statutes have a lower *mens rea* threshold (knowledge rather than purpose), apply to a wide variety of conduct, do not require an agreement (as in conspiracy) or much by way of action, and do not require that any harm resulted.[4]

The FBI shifted so many resources to fighting terrorism that prosecutions of white-collar crime fell by half from 2001 to 2008.[5] But DoJ may have exaggerated its emphasis on terrorism by including immigration, credit card and marriage fraud, and money-laundering cases.[6] And prosecutors rejected a high and increasing proportion of terrorism referrals: 77% in 2003, 65% in 2004, 84% in 2005, and 91% in the first half of 2006. Indeed, after spiking in 2002, the number of national security prosecutions fell just as sharply, returning to the level they had reached during the last few months of 2001.[7]

Attorney General Mukasey said in 2008 that the government would use "any available charge."

> This may well mean that certain plots are charged at early stages, before the evidence is fully developed. I would rather explain to the American people why we acted when we did, even if it is at a very early stage, than try to explain why we failed to act. [8]

Terrorism *is* different from other crimes. Because of the magnitude of the harm feared (especially after 9/11), government is under enormous pressure to prevent it rather than punish after the fact in order to deter others – the response to ordinary crimes – especially since committed terrorists cannot be deterred (witness the 9/11 suicide attackers). Indeed, only five of the hundreds convicted actually attempted terrorist acts – Richard Reid (shoe bomber), Umar Farouk Abdulmutallab (underwear bomber), Faisal Shahzad (Times Square bomber), Ahmed Ghailani (East African embassy bombings), and Dzhokhar Tsarnaev (Boston Marathon bomber) – and the first three attempts failed. But by intervening early – choosing to risk false positives rather than false negatives – the government punished defendants who might never have committed the crimes they were accused of planning, assisting, or attempting.

One case can introduce many of the issues raised by terrorism prosecutions.[9] Ehsanul Islam Sadequee, 19, born in the USA of Bangladeshi parents, and Syed Haris Ahmed, 21, a naturalized citizen born in Pakistan, both studying engineering at Georgia Tech, traveled to Canada in March 2005 to discuss with others possible attacks on oil refineries and military bases.[10] (Canada convicted one of those men, Chiheb Esseghaier, of planning to bomb a New York–Montreal train.[11]) Interviewed at JFK Airport on his return, Sadequee claimed he had made the trip alone to stay with an aunt and was charged with lying to federal authorities (a common place-holder). The indictment alleged Sadequee and Ahmed had engaged in military training in the mountains (by firing guns – hardly unusual in rural Georgia). They also had visited Washington DC to videotape potential targets, including the Capitol, Pentagon, and World Bank headquarters. A voice-over said: "this is where our brothers attacked the Pentagon." They videotaped the Masonic Temple because "we had been told they worship the devil or whatever." They included oil storage tanks because oil was "Muslim property, and it's being stolen." An attack would "raise the prices so that people over there will get more money." Ahmed told the FBI: "There is nothing to be worried about. We are just stupid, childish." They had shaved their beards before visiting Washington, which was their chance "to be spies for the people over there." "It's like, uh, thrilling to be undercover and stuff like that." The video "means nothing"; they took it to impress people associated with radical websites who, Ahmed hoped, could get them admitted to a militant training camp in Pakistan. But when he visited Pakistan, his cousins and Islamic teachers dissuaded him from going to a Lashkar-e-Taiba camp. The US Attorney explained that though the two had "not proceeded to the point that they posed an imminent threat to the United States," "we no longer wait until a bomb is built and ready to explode."

Ahmed was convicted of material support. Sadequee fired his lawyers against his family's wishes and the judge's strong advice. His opening statement was brief: "There was a lot of talk about doing a lot of things. But no one in fact did anything." He had gone to Bangladesh to get married. "If everything is a question mark, can there be a plan?" During the trial, he questioned prosecution witnesses about Superman and the Antichrist. "We were immature young guys who had imaginations running wild. But I was not then, and am not now, a terrorist." In closing he described himself as one of those young men who "type faster than they think." The jury took just five hours to convict. Ahmed got 13 years, Sadequee 17.

This case exhibits elements found in many other terrorism prosecutions: immature, suggestible defendants with delusions of grandeur, inchoate offenses, preemptive prosecution, pretextual charges, words rather than actions, and bravado combined with pleas for mercy.[12] This chapter analyzes five cases in detail before examining their commonalities with a wide range of other "war-on-terror" cases. This analysis allows us to ask how terrorism prosecutions differed from others across a wide variety of variables: the identities of the accused, their actions (both before and during trial), the behavior of the FBI (especially the use of informants and undercover agents), the actions of prosecutors, defense counsel, judges and juries, and verdicts and sentences.

HAMID AND UMER HAYAT (LODI)[13]

Naseem Khan, born in Peshawar in 1973, came to the USA at 16, speaking little English. After attending high school in three states and picking up a conviction for passing a bad check, he moved to Lodi in California's Central Valley in 1999 but left after a couple of years for Bend, Oregon, where he had a minimum wage job at a convenience store. A month after 9/11 the FBI questioned him about bin Laden and Muslim fundraising organizations (having confused him with a suspect bearing the same name). Nine days later they showed him photos of alleged terrorists and inquired about Lodi. He claimed to have seen three leading figures in the Lodi mosque: Ayman al-Zawahiri (al-Qaeda's number two), Ahmed Mohammed Hamed (a suspect in the East African embassy bombings), and Abdelkarim Hussein Mohamed al-Nasser (a suspect in the 1996 al Khobar Towers bombing in Saudi Arabia). "Every time I would go to the mosque" Zawahiri (to whom Naseem claimed to have spoken) "would be coming or going." Naseem told the FBI he "could still picture the priest-like al-Zawahiri standing up in front of the audience, speaking Urdu, and lecturing about Allah." (Al-Zawahiri, an Egyptian doctor, spoke Arabic, not Urdu.) FBI agent Rachel Pifer "thought the probability that [Naseem] saw Zawahiri during this period of time was probably pretty slim." (Indeed, it was impossible; Naseem based his identification of Zawahiri on videos he had seen on television.) But Pifer made Naseem an undercover agent (UA) and became his handler, paying him $230,000 in salary and expenses and helping him obtain citizenship. A former girlfriend said Naseem "really liked the work. It fit his dream of someday going into law enforcement." He had taken criminology courses at the local community college and sometimes shot with police friends at the local pistol range.

In summer 2002 Naseem returned to Lodi at the FBI's direction, renting an apartment overlooking the mosque and befriending Shabbir Ahmed, imam at the Farooqia Islamic Center, and Muhammad Adil Khan, imam at the Lodi Muslim Mosque. He took Khan's younger children to amusement parks and gave Ahmed a cell phone. After they grew suspicious and severed contact, he focused on Hamid Hayat, sometimes sleeping in his home. The US-born Hamid, a high school dropout ten years younger than Naseem, worked sporadically in a food packing plant and was flattered by the attention and impressed by Naseem's money, new cars, and fashionable clothes. In March 2003 he called Naseem his best friend. Naseem advised Hamid's father Umer (a naturalized Pakistani American), who drove an ice cream truck, that the best way to send money to Islamic causes in Pakistan was through Naseem's company. In one conversation, Umer agreed to give Naseem $4,000 for an unnamed political party and promised another $4,000; but he never delivered on either. Naseem often steered the conversations (which he secretly taped) to militant training camps, complaining that Muslims in America were "cowards to take action" and "should not sit idle." But Umer wanted Hamid to finish his religious education in Pakistan in order to become an imam in Sacramento. In April 2003 Hamid went to

Pakistan with his mother and sister (later joined by Umer) and married a Pakistani woman. In phone calls initiated and recorded by Naseem, Hamid sought to display his Islamic fervor, declaring that the US "is mine in name only, understand? My heart is in Pakistan" and that killing Daniel Pearl was "a good job." He lied about joining a Taliban attack and doing time in a Pakistan prison, talked about a fictitious Pakistani political party and terrorists using nonexistent pay phones, and bragged that one relative led a radical opposition group and another was close to Mullah Mohammed Omar (the Taliban leader). He also claimed his father frequently sent money to Pakistani political groups with secret branches in every US state. But his admission that he had not yet attended a training camp angered Naseem.

NASEEM: You're just sitting around doing nothing.
HAMID: I do one thing. I pray. That's it.
NASEEM: You fucking sleep for half a day. You wake up. You light a fucking cigarette. You eat. You sleep again. That's all you do. A loafer guy.
HAMID: What else am I going to do?
NASEEM: You sound like a fucking broken bitch. Come on. Be a man. Do something.
HAMID: Whatever I can do, I'll do that, man.
NASEEM: When I come to Pakistan and I see you, I'm going to fucking force you, get you, from your throat and fucking throw you in the madrassa.
HAMID: Yes, God willing. After Ramadan. God willing. I'll study and become a religious scholar.

Hamid returned to the USA on May 30, 2005. Four days later he was interrogated at home and then voluntarily at the FBI office in Sacramento from 11 a.m. until early the next morning. He was Mirandized after several hours and waived legal representation. He claimed to have attended a training camp consisting of calisthenics, jogging, and shooting, but was unclear whether the targets were bull's-eyes or photos of American leaders. He fired a pistol three times, but found it heavy and never learned to reload, and fired a shotgun just once because the recoil was too powerful. He spent most of his time washing vegetables. He contradicted himself repeatedly about whether he was housed in a mud hut or a multi-story building, whether there were 35 trainers or 200, and whether they spoke Urdu, Pashto, or English. He gave six different locations for the camp, all in remote forest: two in Afghanistan and the others in Kashmir, near the family home, and close to Islamabad. But he could not find any on a map of Pakistan and concluded "the final thing I'll say was in Afghanistan." Before Hamid mentioned any of this the FBI agent suggested the province where the camp was located, described the type of training, named Pakistani terrorist organizations, and spoke of "killing of American soldiers."

AGENT: So jihad means that you fight and you assault something?
HAMID: Uh-huh.
AGENT: Give me an example of a target. A building?
HAMID: I'll say no buildings. I'll say people.
AGENT: OK, people. Yeah. Fair enough. People in buildings … I'm trying to get details about plans over here.
HAMID: They didn't give us no plans.
AGENT: Did they give you money?'
HAMID: No money…
AGENT: Guns?
HAMID: No.
AGENT: Targets in the U.S.?… buildings. Sacramento or San Francisco?
HAMID: I'll say Los Angeles and San Francisco.
AGENT: Financial, commercial?
HAMID: I'll say finance and things like that.
AGENT: Hospitals?
HAMID: Maybe…
AGENT: Who ran the camp?
HAMID: Maybe my grandfather.
AGENT: Al-Qaeda? Al-Qaeda runs?
HAMID: I'll say they run the camp.

The FBI affidavit declared that Hayat "specifically requested to come to the United States to carry out his Jihadi mission" but was vague about the targets until the agent suggested they included unnamed "hospitals and large food stores" and "big buildings, like finance buildings." Later, at the agent's suggestion, Hamid mentioned "Justice," the "FBI building," the Pentagon, and the White House. He agreed he was just awaiting orders. A search of his home found a scrapbook of articles collected during his trips to Pakistan. Although one depicted a Taliban machine gun, many featured his grandfather, a well-known religious leader and politician. When Hamid was detained he had a handwritten Arabic prayer, which a government expert translated as: "Oh Allah, we place you at their throats, and we seek refuge in you from their evil."

The FBI also conducted a ten-hour interrogation of Hamid's father Umer, who admitted paying his son's air fare and giving him $100 a month, knowing he would attend a camp. Umer claimed to have visited three or four camps but placed the one in which Hamid trained in a huge basement near Rawalpindi, where Umer (implausibly) remembered seeing nearly a thousand terrorist trainees, masked like Ninja turtles, slashing curved swords at dummies of Bush, Rumsfeld, and Colin Powell, and pole-vaulting "like 50 feet" to cross rivers. Umer's wife, Salma, punctured this boast, saying her husband was with her in their village when he allegedly visited the training camp.

The FBI persuaded Umer to wear a wire and talk to Shabbir Ahmed and Muhammad Adil Khan (the two Lodi imams), whom the Bureau later detained for immigration violations together with Khan's son. The lead FBI agent said he had found "information that the [proposed Lodi] madrassah is part of a long-term plan, similar to madrassahs in Pakistan, during which students would be spotted and assessed and maybe eventually be ready to commit acts of violence in the U.S." "[T]he word [to attack] would come from Shabbir and or Muhammad Adil Khan." But instead of prosecuting them, the government deported both to Pakistan.

President Bush praised the FBI's "use of intelligence and the follow-up." "[W]hat the American people need to know" is "that when we find any hint about any possible wrongdoing or a possible cell … we'll follow up." The US Attorney in Sacramento said: "we have detected, we have disrupted and we have deterred, and whatever was taking shape in Lodi isn't going to happen now." An FBI official said "this investigation is going to lead to other people. It will just take awhile to unravel [sic]." Director of National Intelligence (DNI) Negroponte called the five suspects a "home-grown jihadist cell."

The government charged Hamid and Umer with lying to the FBI and Hamid with providing material support to terrorists. A magistrate judge denied bail, declaring this "one of the most serious flight-risk cases that have been before me in my eight years on the bench." Another magistrate judge recommended bail for Umer, but ED Cal Judge Burrell found the collateral offered insufficient. (Burrell, a former Marine, had conducted the Unabomber trial.) Just 13 days before the trial, prosecutors gave the defense 253 compact discs and 45 audiotapes of the defendants' nearly 1,000 hours of conversation with Naseem. In her opening statement, the prosecutor said Hamid "talked about training camps. He talked about acts of violence. He talked about jihad, jihad, jihad." Hamid's lawyer, Wazhma Mojaddidi (trying her first criminal case just three years out of McGeorge Law School) said her client's statement had been made under duress. Seeking a purpose in life, he had exaggerated his activities in Pakistan. Umer's lawyer, Johnny L. Griffin III (a former state and federal prosecutor), said his client had been "psychologically bullied and emotionally pressured into doing whatever the FBI agents wanted him to say or do." A prosecution expert in Islamic studies testified that anyone carrying the prayer found on Hamid would be "a person who was engaged in jihad," "who perceives him or herself as being engaged in war for God against an enemy" and was "completely ready" to commit "an act of warfare against a perceived enemy." The defense sought to present former FBI agent James J. Wedick (who had been decorated for his work in the Sacramento office) to impeach the agents who interrogated Hamid in that office. But Judge Burrell ruled that his testimony had "the potential for confusing the jury, wasting time and presenting needless cumulative evidence." During the eight weeks of trial, 15 witnesses testified for the prosecution and seven for the defense.

A woman released from the jury four weeks into the trial (after disclosing she had dated a Sacramento police officer) expressed concern that FBI agents had "badger[ed]" Hamid during a late-night interrogation. "He was giving the information because they refused to believe that he didn't know anything." They seemed to be coaching him. "I didn't see him volunteering anything." He "could have been just a young guy trying to impress an older guy." In the sixth week of this lengthy trial, Naseem disclosed that he had failed to give the defense a 20-minute tape of a conversation, claiming to have found it while rearranging his CD collection. In closing, the prosecutor said Hamid had "a jihadi heart and a jihadi mind," had celebrated the killing of Daniel Pearl, and had referred to the president as "Bush, the worm." His lawyer replied that "reading about jihad doesn't make you a jihadi."

During deliberations the jury asked to rehear five hours of FBI interrogation. But the separate jury for each defendant could not hear the other defendant's confession and see the inconsistencies noted above. In response to a question, Judge Burrell told jurors they could not consider a proposed cash transfer as evidence of material support. Umer's jury made a third request to rehear testimony about his interrogation. But they could not agree, even after the judge told them to keep trying, and hung after deliberating for eight days. Arguing against retrying Umer, Griffin said the jury was "evenly split." A juror who favored conviction said those voting to acquit "couldn't accept that Umer understood" the FBI's questions, asking "Why didn't they have an interpreter? Why didn't they tape the first interview when they talked to [Umer] at his home?" Although the US Attorney planned to retry the case, Umer pleaded to a different count of lying to customs agents at Dulles Airport about the $28,000 he and his family were carrying to Pakistan, which he had said was for Hamid's wedding. He was sentenced to the 11 months he had served.

After deliberating nine days, the other jury convicted Hamid. The US Attorney exulted: "today's verdict makes clear that we can prevent acts of terrorism by winning convictions against those who would plot to commit violence against our citizenry in the name of an extremist cause." "Much of the satisfaction we're deriving from this case was in the successful pursuit of heading off a potential terrorist act." Attorney General Gonzales called the country "a safer place" because of the conviction. "[J]ustice has been served against a man who supported and trained with our terrorist enemies in pursuit of his goal of violent jihad."

Joe Cote, foreman of Hamid's jury, said the evidence "was overwhelmingly in favor of guilt." "He admits he attended a camp … the man had his heart and mind committed to terrorism." Cote emphasized Naseem's recordings, Hamid's confession to the FBI, and the prayer in his wallet, "which carried a lot of weight. A supplication is only carried in the country of the enemy. He would never carry it in Pakistan. Even though he's an American citizen, his love and his home are in Pakistan."

Lori Macias, another juror, did not believe the confession was coerced. "What person in their right mind does all that and doesn't ask for a lawyer?" Star Scaccia, a third juror, said Hamid's scrapbook of clippings about militant political parties "showed where his alliances were. It showed where his heart was." "I hope it gets the message out: Don't mess with the United States. It's not worth it." Jurors were influenced by rehearing Hamid's FBI interrogation and the judge's instruction that "the government may utilize a broad range of schemes and ploys to ferret out criminal activity." On the seventh day of deliberations, a Friday, with one juror holding out for acquittal on the material support charge, foreman Cote sent Judge Burrell a note: "There is an impasse with a juror who does not seem to fully comprehend the deliberation process. I'm available to discuss this with you and counsel at any time." Burrell conferred with counsel, sealed the note, and instructed the jury to continue. After the trial Cote conceded "I may have chosen the wrong language. That was the end of the day, end of the week." The holdout changed her mind on Monday. Cote insisted she reached her conclusion by "thinking about it over the weekend," without any pressure.

Mojaddidi complained that "outside influences" had affected the jury's decision. "It is suspect that after only two days of deliberation [i.e., the weekend] that this juror suddenly decided to convict." She moved for a new trial based on an affidavit by the holdout, Arcelia Lopez (a school nurse), that she "never once throughout the deliberation process and the reading of the verdict believed Hamid Hayat to be guilty." "I was emotional during the reading of the verdict, and when the jury was polled I responded to the court that I agreed with the verdict. In fact, I did not. I never believed Hamid Hayat was guilty." She had been bullied.

> Cote told the jury that we had to reach a verdict and he refused to accept my position. He personally attacked me repeatedly as someone who couldn't process the information and who just couldn't see that [Hamid] was guilty because he thought I didn't have the mental capacity to understand.

Another juror told Lopez: "if I didn't change my vote, she would consider getting off the jury herself due to the stress." "I deeply regret my decision." Disregarding Burrell's instructions, jurors read newspaper accounts of the case, discussed statements to the press by the excused juror, and brought written materials into the deliberation room. Cote repeatedly made a gesture of putting a noose around his neck, declaring, "Hang him," and insisted Muslims "all look alike." Two jurors, an African American woman and a white man, called those comments "insulting and inappropriate." Cote also told the jury something he had heard about the case on television. When Lopez learned Cote had sent a note to Burrell, she challenged his right to do so without her knowledge. He retorted: "I'm the foreman. I'm in charge. I can do what I want." That weekend she felt so stressed she went to a medical clinic with "extreme headaches." "I was under so much stress and pressure that I decided to change my vote." Burrell revealed that the foreman contacted an alternate juror about Lopez the same day he wrote the judge about her.

After the verdict, Cote told an *Atlantic Monthly* journalist that the prosecution's expert witness was "probably the most learned man I have ever encountered." The prayer was "like, 'Put the knife at the throat of my enemies.'" After 9/11 there were "new rules of engagement, and I don't want to see the government lose its case." "Can we … put this kid on the street … on the basis of what we know of how people of his background have acted in the past?"[14] Star Scaccia, another juror, said: "The Muslims are everywhere. Or, I don't know if they're Muslims or exactly who they are – but they all pretty much look alike. They all have beards, they all have the longer hair … it's hard to distinguish within the race who is who."

Judge Burrell denied the new trial motion.[15] He disbelieved Lopez's allegations and believed Cote's denials. "Even assuming Cote made all of the statements in the *Atlantic Monthly* article … [it] reveals that the jurors, and Cote himself, thoroughly and thoughtfully deliberated regarding Hayat's guilt or innocence." "The only concrete example that Hayat provides to support his contention that Cote made racist remarks during trial (that all Egyptians wearing the same garb look alike) is not racist, in light of the context in which it was made, since Cote was trying to explain how Khan could have misidentified certain individuals." (This is a striking conclusion, given that Burrell is African American.) "[T]here is no indication that Cote's telephone call to Watanabe [the alternate juror] constituted *prejudicial* misconduct." There was "no reasonable possibility" that any discussion of media coverage of the trial "affected the verdict."

Before sentencing, the US Attorney credited "prosecutions like this" for the absence of attacks since 9/11. Burrell sentenced Hamid to 24 years (he faced up to 39), including the 15-year maximum for material support. Evidence "suggested a likelihood of recidivism and an unlikelihood of rehabilitation." Hamid appealed on grounds of jury misconduct, exclusion of evidence, and a conflict of interest by his trial attorney.

The Ninth Circuit affirmed.[16] Judge Berzon (writing for Judge Schroeder) agreed with Judge Burrell that Cote's statement "did not indicate an actual racial, ethnic, or religious bias." It found plausible the nonbiased explanations for Cote's alleged post-verdict statements. By referring to "people of [Hamid's] background," the foreman might have meant "people who have expressed anti-American views and attended terrorist training camps" rather than "young Muslims or Pakistani males in general." His embrace of "new rules of engagement" under which it was "absolutely better to run the risk of convicting an innocent man than to let a guilty one go" free did not refer to "this particular case." Because Cote contacted the excused juror and referred to media coverage of the trial only after deliberations began, these actions did not show he had prejudged the case. The court upheld Judge Burrell's rulings on the admissibility of evidence but suggested they might be attributable to failures by Hamid's lawyer, possibly amounting to ineffective assistance of counsel. For procedural reasons, the court declined to review Hamid's post-sentencing motion alleging that his lawyer "had a conflict of interest because she relied heavily for legal and strategic advice on the more experienced lawyer representing Hayat's father."

Judge Tashima began his dissent by calling the case "a stark demonstration of the unsettling and untoward consequences of the government's use of anticipatory prosecution as a weapon in the 'war on terrorism.'" Even though Hamid's lawyer did not raise this issue,

Tashima addressed it because of "the primary constitutional duty of the Judicial branch to do justice in criminal prosecutions." He would reverse "because the district court plainly erred in preventing Hayat from introducing exculpatory evidence" by "preventing [Naseem] Khan from answering the question whether Hayat said he never intended to go to a camp." It also erred "in allowing inflammatory expert testimony" about Hamid's alleged "jihadi intent," thereby "usurp[ing] the jury's role as finder of fact." Tashima analogized Hamid carrying a prayer (in Arabic, a language he neither read nor spoke) to a Christian with a piece of paper containing "Onward Christian soldiers, marching as to war." Expert testimony about that defendant's intent in having such a paper would be "laughable."

LIBERTY CITY[17]

Narseal Batiste was a Haitian immigrant and sometime construction worker who walked around Liberty City, Florida, in flowing robes and a head wrap, carrying a shepherd's staff, calling himself sheikh, and preaching against drugs and domestic violence in a park on Sundays. His chapter of the Moorish Science Temple claimed to be autonomous from the government, like Native Americans. In September 2005 Abbas al-Saidi, a Yemeni-born Miami resident with arrests for assault and marijuana possession, told the FBI (for which he had been an informant) about Batiste and his group. A month later al-Saidi notified the FBI that the group was "training for hand-to-hand combat" and had asked him to use a forthcoming trip to Yemen to "get them contacts with al-Qaeda." Spending a night at Batiste's "embassy," al-Saidi saw the men with guns, practicing karate and fighting with machetes. The FBI paid him nearly $20,000 in income and expenses. A month later the FBI used him to introduce Batiste to Elie Assad, aka "Brother Mohammed," a more experienced Syrian-born informant impersonating a financier. The FBI paid Assad $117,000 and supported his political asylum application. Batiste asked Assad for uniforms, automatic handguns, Nextel cell phones, and a black SUV; two days later he added a mini .223 Bushmaster rifle. On December 22 Batiste told Assad he planned to destroy the Sears Tower in Chicago (where he had once made deliveries for FedEx), using secret tunnels that could be flooded from "Lake Toronto." Claiming expertise as a building contractor, Batiste (who did drywalling) boasted: "If I can put a building up, I can take it down." He would exploit the ensuing chaos to liberate Muslims from the nearby jail, who would force the government to recognize the "Sovereign Moors" – an offshoot of the Moorish Science Temple. He also wanted to blow up the Empire State Building. "With those two buildings down, all radio communications is out." A week later he asked for more firearms, radios, binoculars, boots (specifying shoe sizes), bulletproof vests, SUVs and $50,000 cash, inviting Assad to accompany him to Chicago to case the tower and meet "two top generals." The trip never occurred, and he got only the boots. In mid-January 2006 Assad offered Batiste, rent-free, a warehouse large enough for training (because the FBI could not easily surveil his "embassy," which was located in a high-crime area where agents would be spotted).

Growing mistrustful of al-Saidi, Batiste suspended contact. Al-Saidi responded by telling Batiste's closest associate that AQAP (Al-Qaeda in the Arabian Peninsula) had approved his plan: when bin Laden next threatened to strike the USA, he would be referring to Batiste's mission. Assad told Batiste a European explosives expert (actually a Scotland Yard agent) was ready to help. In Assad's apartment on February 19 Batiste outlined his plan to conduct a "full ground war" and "kill all the devils we can," starting by "taking down the Sears Tower." When Batiste grew impatient about the money promised, Assad stalled by swearing him into al-Qaeda with an English translation of the loyalty oath (in a ceremony recorded by the FBI). After the FBI wired the warehouse for sound and video, Assad administered the oath to the other six members of Batiste's group, four calling themselves "princes" and two "brothers." Rotschild Augustine misstated the oath, pledging allegiance to *himself* rather than al-Qaeda. Both informants made it clear that the oath was a prerequisite for the money. When Batiste complained it was taking too long to get the money, Assad replied that al-Qaeda planned to attack the FBI in Washington, Chicago, Los Angeles, New York, and Miami, giving Batiste a camera to make a videotape of the Miami office, "which would be sent back to al-Qaeda overseas." In late March, driving a van provided by Assad, Batiste and two others videotaped and photographed the FBI building, federal courthouse and detention center, and Miami police headquarters. After Assad asked to meet the Chicago associates, offering to pay their air fare, Batiste phoned Charles James Stewart (aka Sultan Khan Bey), leader of the Moorish Science Temple in Chicago (whose long rap sheet included rape and other serious crimes), giving him and his wife $3,500 to travel to Miami.

On April 11 Stewart and Batiste discussed opening a shop to sell marijuana and drug pipes (even though Batiste preached against drugs). Stewart wanted to build a Moorish Nation of 10,000, making his wife, Queen Zakiyaah, ambassador so she would enjoy diplomatic immunity. Moorish soldiers would wear green uniforms, learn to use bows and arrows, and receive night training, including jumping into water from 20 feet above. But Batiste and Stewart disagreed about the mission and who would be in charge. When the conflict climaxed on April 17, Stewart tried Batiste under Moorish law for treason and insubordination, questioning "his relationship and association with the Arabian or Nigerian mafia," i.e., Assad. Two days later Stewart, now running what was left of the group, was arrested after shooting at Master G.J.G. Atheea, Batiste's religious mentor. Wearing a wire, Atheea told Batiste: "I'm talking about dealing with a spiritual war. It seems like you're talking about a physical war." Batiste replied: "I was offered weapons ... anything I needed[,] to do whatever I needed to do for the mission." Rejecting Atheea's objection that he was contemplating "doing subversive working against this nation in a diabolical way," Batiste said, "I don't consider this, this place here to be a legitimate nation." Batiste curtailed his contact with Assad, whom he correctly suspected of working for the FBI. On May 5, after being charged with federal weapons offenses, Stewart told the FBI that Batiste's mission was "starting to get serious" and agreed to testify against the group. At the group's final meeting on May 24, Batiste told Assad "he was experiencing delays because of various problems within his organization."

In dual news conferences in Miami and Washington on June 22, the FBI announced the arrests of Batiste and his associates – Lyglenson Lemorin, Rotschild Augustine and Burson Augustin (brothers), Patrick Abraham, Stanley Grant Phanor, and Naudimar Herrera (all African American) – at least five of whom had arrest records for assault, drugs, or weapons. All pleaded not guilty and were denied bail. The next day the FBI Deputy Director said the group was "more aspirational than operational." But while conceding they had neither weapons nor explosives and posed "no immediate threat," Attorney General Gonzales insisted "they did take sufficient steps" to justify prosecution. "Our philosophy is that we try to identify plots in the earliest stages possible, because we don't know what we don't know about a terrorism plot" (parroting Donald Rumsfeld's *bon mot* about "unknown unknowns"). It would be too risky to decide in advance whether "this is a really dangerous group" or "this is not a dangerous group." Homegrown terrorists "may prove to be as dangerous as groups like al-Qaeda." Like the 2004 Madrid bombing and 2005 London underground attack, this plot represented "a new brand of terrorism" by "smaller, more loosely defined cells that are not affiliated with al-Qaeda, but who are inspired by a violent jihadist message." Deputy Attorney General Paul. J. McNulty said that though the group was unsophisticated – more talk than action – the government was committed to "prevention through prosecution." "We really don't have the option of waiting for the plotters and conspirators to take the next step." The US Attorney said "this case clearly demonstrates our commitment to preventing terrorism through energetic law enforcement efforts aimed at detecting and thwarting terrorist acts." Nathan Clark, representing Rotschild, retorted that it was "clearly a case of entrapment." The oath was "induced by the government."

Assistant US Attorney (AUSA) Richard Gregorie opened the trial by asserting that the defendants "came together with the sole purpose of creating a holy war against the United States." "They say the war has to be fought here. And it can't be just a bombing. It's got to be chaos." The plot involved "things as small as poisoning salt shakers in restaurants and as big as blowing up the Sears Tower in Chicago and killing any survivors." Batiste called bin Laden "an angel" and "cheered" the 9/11 attack. Batiste's lawyer, Ana Jhones, mocked her client as a "wannabe religious leader" who suffered delusions of grandeur and told the informants what they wanted to hear just to get the $50,000. "There was a dual con going on in this case." Defense lawyers said their clients were victims of two "mercenaries," who approached the FBI with stories about of having infiltrated a terrorist cell. The defendants were homeless, living in the "embassy": a windowless cinderblock storage room without running water. Other than the nunchakus, machetes, and swords with which they played at martial arts "training," their only weapon was a handgun legally registered to Lemorin, who left it behind when he moved to Atlanta two months before the arrests. Batiste spent eight days on the stand insisting he had only played along with the informants to extract money to start a construction business. Phanor's lawyer denied that Batiste spoke for the others; the schemes were "jive talking." In her summation, AUSA Jacqueline M. Arango replayed the video of the seven swearing an oath administered by Assad, who called himself "a representative of Sheik Osama bin Laden." "It doesn't matter whether the defendants did so for philosophical reasons or for money." "The government need not wait until buildings come down or people get shot to prove people are terrorists." The planned attacks were "just as good [as] or greater than 9/11." "They weren't going to be able to accomplish these grandiose plans alone ... That's why Batiste sought an unholy alliance with a foreign terrorist organization. They were a ready-made terrorist cell here for al-Qaeda." Prosecutors pointed to the fact that several defendants had security guard licenses and planned to infiltrate government buildings; but Burson's lawyer noted his client had gotten his *before* meeting Batiste. Jhones said "manipulation" by the government "cannot be tolerated because of the war on terror."

Raymond Tanter (an advocate for regime change in Iran) testified as a prosecution expert that all the defendants were in the fourth and final stage of what the New York Police Department (NYPD) called the "radicalization process." "The defendants have organized themselves as if they are a military organization with a definite hierarchy and leadership." "I strongly believe [Batiste] was talking about violent jihad, not introspection." Batiste declared: "I wanted the money for support. That was the only reason" [he met Assad]. "I'm exhausted financially; that's why I'm here." "I was behind a couple of months on the rent, the children had no clothes. There was no food for a couple of days." "Just from watching the movies" he "made up" the story of blowing up the Sears Tower so that, like dominos, it would topple over and destroy other buildings, which would fall into Lake Michigan to create a tsunami.

Three weeks into the trial a Miami police counterterrorism pamphlet was found in the jury room. Rejecting a defense motion for a mistrial, SD Fla Judge Lenard dismissed the two jurors and an alternate who admitted having read it. She instructed jurors that the government did not have to prove an act or even that the plot was feasible. After deliberating four days, the foreman said the jury had reached an impasse on all defendants. Lenard told them to keep trying, although both sides agreed it was too early for an Allen charge (urging a deadlocked jury to continue deliberating and seek to agree on a verdict). When jurors reiterated three days later that they were still deadlocked, Lenard gave the Allen charge: "the trial has been expensive in time, effort, money and emotional strain to both the defense and the prosecution. If you should fail to agree upon a verdict, the case will be left open and may have to be tried again." Four days later the jury acquitted Lemorin but hung on all the others. The foreman, an educator at a local synagogue, said "it was evenly split on a lot of counts." Other jurors said they deadlocked because the FBI found no explosives, weapons, or blueprints for terrorist activity and relied on informants of dubious credibility. The prosecution immediately vowed to retry the case, and Judge Lenard scheduled the new trial in a month, barring lawyers on both sides from talking. Immigration authorities began deportation proceedings against

Lemorin the day after he was acquitted, based on the same charges. Issuing the deportation order, the immigration judge said: "a finding by a jury is not binding on this court in removal proceedings."

In the retrial the prosecution said Batiste thought he was appointed by God "to destroy the devil" and his followers were "soldiers – dedicated to overthrowing the United States." Jhones dismissed the loyalty oath as a "drive-by pledge" led by Assad, whom she called "the muscle" to distinguish him from al-Saidi, "the little thug." Assad was so desperate to implicate the defendants that he cried during the oath, saying in effect "don't do it for al-Qaeda – do it for me." "They were framed from day one." Early in their deliberations the jurors asked Judge Lenard: "Is it against the law to swear an oath to al-Qaeda, agreeing to abide by the directives of al-Qaeda?" The lawyers disagreed, and Lenard simply reiterated that jurors should follow her instructions. On the tenth day they said they could not agree on any defendant. Lenard denied Jhones's motion for a mistrial and told the jury to keep deliberating. After the third jury note on the twelfth day Lenard declared a second mistrial.

The government tried them a third time, an action the *Washington Post* called "exceedingly rare and … usually reserved for murder cases," raising "serious questions about whether prosecutors are more concerned with saving face than seeking justice." The disclosure that there had been just one holdout "gives some legitimacy to a retrial" of Batiste, but the government should reduce or drop charges against the others in exchange for cooperation. "The more prosecutors appear to insist on repeat trials when they don't like the outcomes, the more the legitimacy of the system is eroded." The two trials had been hugely expensive – $1 million just for security. The jury foreman in the second trial expressed "disbelief" in the government's decision, fearing "the jurors will hang or they will have the same issues we did." The vast majority had wanted to convict Batiste and Abraham but acquit Herrera and Rotschild; they split equally on the other two. Some jurors thought the defendants really intended to ally with al-Qaeda, but others believed they were just interested in money. Many were troubled by the informants and skeptical that the defendants were committed to executing the plot. The jury foreman in the first trial agreed "there was really nothing that indicated that this was a real threat." Most jurors had felt that al-Saidi "had no credibility" and Assad "was trying to lead these guys on."

During selection of the third jury prosecutors moved to strike a prospective juror overheard declaring "they're never going to convict." At the prosecution's request Judge Lenard excluded a young Haitian

American man. After prosecutors objected to blacks and the defense to Hispanics, 56 jurors were questioned to seat 11: three blacks, four Hispanic whites, and four non-Hispanic whites. The defense then moved (unsuccessfully) to strike the entire panel on the ground it was not racially representative.

In her opening, Arango called Batiste a "power-hungry vicious man who wanted to make his mark on the world." She tried to show he admired Jeff Fort, a Chicago gang leader convicted in 1987 of conspiring with Libya to attack the USA. Batiste's group "agreed to sell out their country for money." Jhones retorted that the case was "a 100 percent set-up ... a manufactured crime." The government had tried to "buy [its] way to a conviction." The prosecution objected to Jhones's assertion that "taking an oath to al-Qaeda is not a crime."

On the third day of deliberations (after a three-month trial) Lenard dismissed a black male juror for illness. Although the prosecution wanted to proceed with 11, the defense asked Lenard to suspend deliberations for a week until the ill juror recovered, but she refused because of the length of the trial: "It's really not an issue of race, it's an issue of illness." After determining that the five remaining alternates had followed her instructions not to watch media accounts after the trial ended, she added a Hispanic woman, instructing the jury "to wipe your minds clean. Each of you said you could do so."

The next day Lenard learned that juror No. 4, a black woman, was turning her back on the others. The foreman, a Hispanic man, said "she doesn't open the book and follow what we're doing. She refuses to answer our questions. Her mind is made up." "She feels deliberating is a waste of time." She "mumbles words that should not be said," which "offend others." A white non-Hispanic woman added: "she's made a statement that we could sit there for years and we weren't going to change her mind." Juror No. 4 wrote Lenard that no one "respects my answers, and I feel I'm being attacked every time I open my mouth." One juror had "threatened to come over the table and stood up as if to" do so. "I may have said something recently about the law, which was misinterpreted," but I "would love to continue" serving "and see th[e] trial to the end." The following Monday she phoned the court to say that she was too ill to appear, but Judge Lenard later said juror No. 4 "did not have plans to go to the doctor and was vague as to the extent of her illness." The foreman wrote Lenard that juror No. 4 had said the previous Friday: "I don't believe in the law. I don't trust the law." Lenard then asked each juror whether anyone was refusing to deliberate, follow the court's instructions on the law, or apply the law to the evidence. All agreed juror No. 4 had refused to deliberate and all but one that she had refused to follow the court's instructions on the law and apply the law to the evidence.

When juror No. 4 arrived at court, Lenard found that she "responded evasively" to the same questions "and never indicated she was being physically threatened." She said "I'm willing to follow the law. But I'm still entitled to my own – you know, what I feel." When she began to cry, Lenard called a recess. Asked again if she was willing to deliberate, juror No. 4 said "I'm really unwilling because I think I'm making myself very ill." "I'm not agreeing with what some of the other jurors are saying and they're holding that against me ... all the negativity is directed at me." Lenard removed her for having "violated her oath and duty as a juror," substituting a black man and telling the jury to "disregard all initial deliberations and votes as if they had never occurred." After two weeks of deliberation, the jury convicted Batiste on all counts, Abraham on two, Rotschild, Burson, and Phanor on one, and acquitted Herrera. The special agent in charge of the FBI's South Florida office said the nation was a "much safer place" because of the prosecution. Although prosecutors had sought 30 years, Lenard sentenced Batiste to 13.5 years, Rotschild to 7, Burson to 6, and the others between 5 and 8 years.

The Eleventh Circuit affirmed.[18] The evidence that the defendants participated "in the photographing of the FBI building – under the direction and control of Al-Qaeda" (which they believed but which was not actually the case) was sufficient to support a conviction for material support for al-Qaeda. That their motivation may have been financial was irrelevant. The use of informants was not so "shocking to the universal sense of justice" that denying the motion to dismiss constituted plain error. "[T]he government only provided means to those who were 'willing and predisposed.'" Judge Lenard had acted properly in replacing juror No. 4.

THE NEWBURGH FOUR[19]

Shahed Hussain entered the USA illegally through Texas with his wife and two children in 1994, using a forged passport, and obtained asylum in 2003, claiming political persecution in Pakistan. While working as a translator for the Department of Motor Vehicles, he illegally helped people in the Albany area get driver's licenses. He pleaded guilty to fraud and got probation and time served in exchange for becoming an FBI informant, working on more than twenty cases (including two men convicted for the alleged sale of a missile launcher).[20] In 2007 the Bureau sent him to mosques in upstate New York to "listen, to hear, to talk with the attendees." He sported designer clothes and drove a Hummer, BMW, or Mercedes, because "at the mosque, nobody wants to talk to a poor guy." After failing to find suggestive targets at Masjid al-Noor mosque in Wappingers Falls, he began visiting Masjid al-Ikhlas mosque in Newburgh. Calling himself "Maqsood," Hussain would sit in the parking lot and approach men leaving Friday prayers, focusing on younger African Americans and visitors. He invited them to lunch, offering one a job in his construction firm and giving another a cell phone and computer. On three occasions he asked the mosque's former treasurer for a complete list of members, saying he wanted to approach potential customers. He sought meetings with the assistant imam and overpaid for a sandwich at a mosque fundraiser. But many were suspicious. After one reported that Hussain spoke of violence and offered a lot of money to join his "team," the imam warned members to stay away.

In June 2008 – after 12 fruitless visits over 9 months – Hussain finally recruited James Cromitie (and then stopped attending the mosque). While claiming to be Muslim, Cromitie had 27 arrests (a dozen for drug offenses) and still drank alcohol. He worked part-time at Walmart. At their first encounter in the mosque parking lot Cromitie waited by Hussain's car, introduced himself in an Arabic accent as Abdul Rahman, and admired Hussain's sandals, which he claimed were "my country's sandals" because his father was from Afghanistan – a country he had visited three times and to which he wanted to return (all complete fabrications). He talked about becoming a martyr and "do[ing] something to America." In unrecorded conversations he railed against Jews and the government, threatening to kill the "Antichrist" Bush 700 times. During hours of recordings he cursed loudly, boasted he wanted to make "a big noise," threatened violence, complained of discrimination, and denounced Jews. When Jewish people looked at him wearing Muslim clothing "like they would like to kill me," it "makes me want to jump up and killing one of them." "Don't be surprised if one day you might see me in handcuffs again. I have zero tolerance for people who disrespect Muslims." Watching the funeral of a man killed in the Mumbai terrorist attack, Cromitie told Hussain:

> Look at the Jewish guy. You're not smiling no more, you fucker. I hate those bastards ... I hate those motherfuckers. Those fucking Jewish

43

bastards ... I'd like to get one of those. I'd like to get a synagogue. Me, yeah, personally ... the one in New York City and Brooklyn. That one is like the mother of the synagogues ... You think the World Trade Center was something? That was nothing ... When you hit those spots like synagogues ... that bothers them ... I don't care if it's a whole synagogue of men.

He bragged about committing fictitious crimes: sending "ashcan" bombs to a Bronx police station, stealing three guns from the Walmart where he worked (which did not sell them), killing a drug dealer's son, and using a gun obtained from his brother, a NYPD officer, for which he claimed to have served 15 years. He contemplated attacking a Brooklyn synagogue and power plant, but also said "I know Allah didn't bring me here to fight a war." Hussain told Cromitie about terrorist attacks in Pakistan and India and said Obama's advisers were Jewish, declaring: "I think that evil is reach too high at a point where you, me, all these brothers have to come up with a solution to take the evil down." But when Hussain said Jews should be "eliminated" because they "are responsible for all the evils in the world," Cromitie responded "I don't wanna go that far." "With your intelligence," he told Hussain, "I know you can manipulate someone. But not me, because I'm intelligent. I'm Muslim. I know how far to go."

In July, when Hussain claimed to be a member of Jaish-e-Muhammad (a Pakistani militant group with ties to al-Qaeda), Cromitie said he wanted to "do jihad" because the USA was killing Muslims in Afghanistan and Pakistan, and he proposed attacking a synagogue because he hated Jews. On December 5, when he asked for "rockets" and "devices" for attacks, Hussain offered C-4 plastic explosive. Five days later, when Cromitie dragged his feet, Hussain berated him for not having picked a target, chosen equipment, devised code words, or recruited others. "You've not started on the first step, brother. Come on." When Hussain promised rewards in paradise, Cromitie temporized: "maybe it's not my mission, then. Maybe my mission hasn't come yet."

On December 17 Cromitie wanted to case the Stewart Airport (a public military facility in Newburgh) in preparation for attacking military planes. But the next day Hussain left for Pakistan, returning on February 22. During those two months the FBI stopped following Cromitie, acknowledging he was unlikely to do anything without Hussain. Indeed, Cromitie admitted on Hussain's return "I ain't do nothing ... since you been gone, I been, like okay I guess everything's down the drain now ... I just dropped everything." To revive Cromitie's interest, Hussain offered a BMW and as much as $250,000. Cromitie said: "OK, fuck it. I don't care. Ah, man, Maqsood, you got me." But he still did little for another two months, repeatedly refusing to accept Hussain's phone calls and rebuffing his pressure: "I'll do something when I decide to do something." "Allah will tell me when it's time." This changed in April, when Cromitie called Hussain after being fired by Walmart: "I have to try to make some money, brother." Hussain retorted: "I told you, I can make you 250,000 dollars, but you don't want it brother." Cromitie capitulated: "Okay, come see me brother." Hussain also promised a two-week Puerto Rico vacation, a BMW, and $70,000 to buy a barbershop.

Cromitie then recruited three others. Onta Williams (aka Hamza) had been addicted to crack and cocaine since he was 15. He spent 12 years in prison, where he converted to Islam but still drank. He worked unloading trucks. His uncle, with whom he had lived, said Onta was "a follower, not a leader. He's easy to push around." David Williams (aka Daoud) (not a relative) also converted to Islam in prison and had "Allah" and "Akbar" tattooed on his hands. Laguerre Payen (aka Amin), a Haitian immigrant, raised suspicion in the mosque with his disheveled appearance and odd behavior. His latest arrest (2003) was for shooting two teenagers with a BB gun while driving around and snatching two purses.

When approached by Cromitie, David said he needed money for his brother's liver transplant and agreed to participate but only if there was no violence. Cromitie "was like 'this guy is offering me $250,000, and I'll give you half for your little brother's operation.'" "Just be a lookout. You don't have to worry about anything. Nothing is going to happen." On April 10 Cromitie went to Walmart with David and Hussain to buy a camera and then to the Bronx to photograph a synagogue and the Riverdale Jewish Center. Several days later the group discussed getting a Stinger heat-seeking missile in Connecticut (reprising Hussain's earlier successful sting) and synchronizing an attack on the Stewart Airport. Onta said the military was "killing Muslim brothers and sisters in Muslim countries, so if we kill them here with I.E.D.'s [improvised explosive devices] and Stingers, it is equal." He joked about also using Stinger missiles to attack the Newburgh courthouse (where he had been convicted). In Hussain's presence, David bought a pistol for $700 from a Brooklyn Bloods gang leader, later bragging that had he been alone he would have shot the seller and kept the $700. On May 6 all five picked up the explosives and (nonfunctional) Stinger from a Stamford warehouse the FBI had wired, and tested bomb detonators to be set off with a cell phone, stashing everything in a Newburgh storage container and shouting "Allahu Akbar." Preoccupied with evading capture, the men discussed how the police might respond to the attack and how to dispose of their cell phones. On May 20 they drove to the Bronx with the bombs. Reminded by Hussain to lead the others in prayer, Cromitie anxiously asked: "should I do that real quick?" Knowing they were being recorded, Hussain urged him to "lead it loud, so everybody can understand." The four were arrested trying to detonate the disabled bombs.

Acting US Attorney Lev L. Dassin said the men "wanted to engage in terrorist attacks. They selected targets and sought the weapons necessary to carry out their plans ... While the weapons provided to the defendants by the cooperating witness were fake, the defendants thought they were absolutely real."

AUSA Eric Snyder said "it's hard to envision a more chilling plot." The defendants were "eager to bring death to Jews." Rep. Peter T. King (R-NY) said "it shows how real the threat is from homegrown terrorists." New York City (NYC) Mayor Bloomberg and NYPD Chief Kelly visited the Riverdale Jewish Center to praise the FBI and police, whom Bloomberg said had prevented "what could have been a terrible event." Joseph M. Demarest, head of the FBI's New York office, said: "It was their plot and their plan that they pushed forward. We merely facilitated ... They did leave the packages of what they believed to be real explosives, the bags, in front of two temples in the Bronx."

SDNY Judge McMahon directed the government to disclose what it spent on Hussain, but denied a defense motion seeking information about his efforts to recruit for other plots. When the prosecution delayed in complying, she threatened to grant a motion to dismiss. Claiming it was not exculpatory, prosecutors belatedly turned over a memo by FBI lead agent Robert Fuller reassuring officials that Cromitie would case Stewart Airport but posed no danger without Hussain. When the prosecution said some information might be classified, requiring defense counsel to obtain security clearances, McMahon angrily replied it should have warned the defense much earlier. But while agreeing that the evidence against the defendants was weak, she denied bail. The prosecution showed the jury videos of the defendants inspecting bombs and Stinger missile launchers, and casing Stewart Airport, and it displayed fake bombs packed with 500 ball bearings.

The defense played tapes of Cromitie's conversations with Hussain to show entrapment. Although Cromitie said "I don't want anyone to get hurt" and agreed with Hussain that women and children should be spared, he also boasted "I don't care if it's a whole synagogue of men, I will take them down. I'm not worried about nothing. What I'm worried about is my safety." Fearing Cromitie had lost interest after weeks of silence, Fuller instructed Hussain to encourage Cromitie to buy an illegal gun because he wanted to have at least one criminal charge "in our back pocket if things went south." (McMahon excluded this evidence.) An April 2009 email from Fuller's colleague expressed concern that Cromitie had become preoccupied with selling marijuana and no longer needed Hussain's money, or was having second thoughts. When Cromitie explained he had been out of state trying to make money and seemed reluctant to proceed with the plan, Hussain offered the $250,000. In another conversation Cromitie reminded Hussain of his offer to pay $25,000 for a look-out: "If you can assure them that they gonna see that much money, they gonna go for it." When Hussain emphasized ideology, Cromitie retorted "they will do it for the money. They're not even thinking about the cause." Hussain had to keep reminding the men of their extremist sponsors, downplaying the role of what he called the "jihad money" from Jaish-e-Mohammed. When Hussain told the men "I'm not running the show, [Cromitie is] running the show," a suspicious Cromitie retorted "ain't nobody running the show. Why do you keep saying that?" Cromitie told Hussain privately that the other men had families who depended on them and needed "bread money." He complained "we have nothing to show for why we did what we did," adding sarcastically: "You know, like I just did that for free." But he also told the others "it's not about money. It's about Jaish-e-Mohammed." Onta agreed: "the money helps. But I'm doing it for the sake of Allah."

The trial was suspended for two days when Payen became completely unresponsive and had to be brought to court in a wheelchair. He closed his eyes, let his head loll from side to side, and talked to himself. His lawyer said he was "intellectually challenged" and took medication for schizophrenia. But AUSA David Raskin called him "a faker." After being disciplined for sharing his phone card code with another inmate, he refused to leave his cell. Dr. Elissa Miller, chief psychiatrist for the Metropolitan Correctional Center, said her staff suspected he was malingering to avoid trial. He had complained of hallucinations, including the Virgin Mary, lights, dead people, bugs crawling on him, and people demanding he play chess. But the last was "not a common visual hallucination" and "improbable." Citing Payen's history of exaggeration and deceit dating back to 2003, McMahon concluded he was "just faking it" and denied a defense request for a mental health examination. Another defense lawyer moved to sever because his client was being "held hostage to Mr. Payen's behavior." Denying the motion, McMahon upbraided Payen for making a spectacle of himself. "At 9:30 tomorrow morning, the marshals will have you in that seat." "I hope you walk into court on your own steam." Payen just kept talking to himself, "sleeping" when the prosecution questioned Hussain but waking for cross-examination.

Defense lawyers tried to discredit Hussain, who had lied in applying for asylum and on job applications, bounced checks, and hidden assets when filing for bankruptcy. They accused him of perjury in this trial, asking the prosecution to investigate. They exposed his mistakes about dates and more important facts in documents or testimony. (The cross-examination grew so tedious that one juror fell asleep.) Cromitie's lawyer, Vincent L. Bricetti, tried to show that Hussain dominated the defendants, leading them in Arabic prayers and teaching them about the November 2008 terrorist attack in Mumbai. When Hussain asked if Cromitie would say "Allahu Akbar" if God asked you to "go to the jihad," Bricetti claimed his client "doesn't exactly say yes, but he doesn't exactly say no. In fact, that was your problem." In one conversation Cromitie voiced strong doubts about the plot before agreeing to it. "I'm trying to survive, that's all. I really don't have to do nothing crazy as of yet." Hussain expressed the fear that his life would be in danger if Cromitie backed out: "If my brother tells me cut your head off, I cut my head off, you know." When Hussain claimed he was just creating the "impression" of offering money – his boast that the defendants could make $250,000 was a "code" and not a genuine offer – Bricetti retorted "if this was not about money, there would be no reason to tell them it's not about money 50 or 100 times." When Hussain said in early May he was going to Florida to get their money, Cromitie shouted "oh my God" and quickly promised Payen that "the cash rolls in."

Judge McMahon often reprimanded Hussain for not giving simple yes or no answers. Pointing to "inconsistencies" in his testimony, she told the lawyers "I am skeptical of some of the things he has said. But I am not the trier of facts." At one point she shouted "I'm tired of your playing games with the questions," prompting Hussain to shrink into his seat. Prosecutors protested she had effectively told jurors he was "being slippery." Outside their hearing a prosecutor complained "the government is entitled to a fair trial." McMahon retorted: "Oh, boy, are you getting a fair trial from me … I'm tired of reminding him." But she later apologized to Hussain. Defense lawyers claimed that Hussain intentionally failed to record some conversations, including one discussing payments. When Bricetti asked about omissions in the sworn financial disclosure form Hussain provided the US Probation Office in 2003 before being sentenced for identity fraud, he meandered. McMahon yelled: "Yes, or no?" She later sought to mollify the lawyers. "Nerves are frayed. My nerves are frayed, and it showed this morning. I don't want you calling each other names. I want all of us – especially the judge – to take the temperature down a little." When she dismissed the jury at the end of the day she added: "I was a little testy this morning. I apologize for my outburst. I apologize to you, Mr. Hussain." At the end of his 13 days on the stand, Hussain admitted lying on a 2001 immigration form and applying for the earned income tax credit even though he had a family trust worth $10–15 million, from which he had withdrawn nearly $700,000 over 14 years.

The lawyers predictably clashed over the entrapment instruction. The defense objected to the statement that their clients could be predisposed to commit a crime "even though they lacked the capability to commit the crime before the government came along."

> The charge is really suggesting that the government could go up to a guy sleeping in Grand Central Station, and say, "Do you want to be involved in a conspiracy to build a nuclear bomb?" "And even though the guy is, like, lying there in his seven-day-old clothes and stuff, that if he says yes, it doesn't matter."

The prosecution responded:

> The government is allowed to walk up to a complete stranger and say, "Do you want to do this horrible thing?" – without any information of who that person is or what they are like. And if they say, "Yes, I do," and that's it, and they do it, they were not entrapped.

In closing, the prosecution said the defendants knew "there is a terrorist behind the wheel and there are three bombs in the car." "There aren't a lot of people like the defendants. Not a lot of people are going to get in that car, no matter how much money you offer them." An innocent person needed convincing, but "the criminal person doesn't." Bricetti retorted that selling for just $50 the surveillance camera Hussain had given him was "compelling evidence that James Cromitie was not ready and willing." After disappearing for several weeks in spring 2009, his client contacted Hussain only because he needed money. "If he was predisposed, why does it take so long to get him interested in this?" "This case is Hussain's meal ticket. He needs you to punch it."

The defense moved for a mistrial on the ground that transcripts of two defendants' prison phone calls – not admitted at trial – were improperly included in the jurors' evidence binders. In one, David told his father: "the lawyers are going with, like, two different types of entrapment." "The case is based on the, um, the first dude," i.e., Cromitie. David's lawyer objected that the transcript "fairly can be read as a defendant characterizing the entrapment defense, which has been the focus of this trial, as a ploy by 'the lawyers.'" In the other conversation, Onta bragged about how much he was paid to participate: "he was like 10,000 [dollars], just walk 'em down the street, that's it." Onta's lawyers argued that "a juror would have to be a mental Olympic gymnast to put out of his or her mind the extra-record information." Bricetti joined the application reluctantly "in light of the several jury notes suggesting that the jury is seriously considering the entrapment defense." Judge McMahon interrupted deliberations to determine how much the jurors had read. Apologizing for the "inadvertent error," prosecutors said the jurors who had read part of David's conversation had not seen "the most prejudicial information," and Onta's conversation was actually "helpful to the defense." McMahon denied the motion.

After deliberating for eight days, the jury convicted all four defendants of conspiracy to use weapons of mass destruction and Cromitie and David of an attempt to kill US officers and employees. Bricetti moved to set aside the verdicts on the ground of outrageous government misconduct. If Cromitie "was predisposed, they would not have had to offer him rewards." The prosecution said "this was an elaborate sting operation, but it was a lawful one. Nothing about the government's conduct shocks the conscience." If the defendants were motivated by jihad, then "money didn't matter to these guys." McMahon interjected: "Really? It was painfully obvious that the reason they did it was for the money." The fact that they had committed a crime did not show they had been predisposed to do so. But she denied the motion.[21]

> The Government indisputably "manufactured" the crimes of which defendants stand convicted. The Government invented all of the details of the scheme – many of them, such as the trip to Connecticut and the inclusion of Stewart AFB as a target, for specific legal purposes of which the defendants could not possibly have been aware … The Government

selected the targets. The Government designed and built the phony ordnance that the defendants planted ... at Government-selected targets. The Government provided every item used in the plot ... The Government did all the driving (as none of the defendants had a car or a driver's license). The Government funded the entire project. And the Government ... offered the defendants large sums of money, contingent on their participation in the heinous scheme ... no one thought it necessary to check before offering a jihadist opportunity to a man who had no contact with any extremist groups and no history of anything other than drug crimes ... the Government saw fit to create roles for persons other than Cromitie – who at least had uttered malicious and threatening statements about Jews and the United States – who had no history of terrorist leanings.

Still, she found it "relatively easy to conclude that the government committed no outrageous misconduct" with respect to Cromitie, who "expressed interest, even enthusiasm, for the idea of jihad from the early days of his dealings with Hussain" and "justified the Government's persistence when he proved to be ready and willing to commit terrorist acts." There was "no coercion of any sort, no suggestion of duress and no physical deprivation."

Nevertheless, there was "something decidedly troubling about the Government's behavior." McMahon was "left with the firm conviction that if the Government had simply kept an eye on Cromitie ... nothing like the events of May 9, 2009 would ever have occurred." "Hussain was the prime mover and instigator of all the criminal activity that occurred, right up until the last moments of the conspiracy, when he had to stop the car he was driving and 'arm' the 'explosive device' because the utterly inept Cromitie could not figure out how to do it." It took "fully nine months" for "Cromitie to take the bait that was offered." In the end, however, Cromitie "affirmatively re-injected himself into what he knew to be a criminal situation." The entrapment claim on behalf of the others was even weaker: "they were offered money to participate in criminal activity, and they said yes. It is of no moment that they were poor and needed money." It was "troubling" that "for many months, the Government dangled what had to be almost irresistible temptation in front of an impoverished man from what I have come (after literally dozens of cases) to view as the saddest and most dysfunctional community in the Southern District of New York." "In the end, however, it is not the province of the courts to tell the executive how to investigate potentially criminal situations."

51

Before sentencing, Cromitie apologized for "letting myself be caught up in a sting like this one. I've never been a terrorist and I never will be a terrorist." Onta was "sorry I ruined my life." Citing evidence that the defendants believed the bombs contained ball bearings, the prosecution sought life. But McMahon sentenced each to the 25-year minimum. Cromitie was "utterly inept." "Only the government could have made a 'terrorist' out of Mr. Cromitie, whose buffoonery is positively Shakespearean in scope." Nevertheless, their crimes were "as serious a set of offenses as is imaginable." They had been "prepared to do real violence." "What you attempted to do was beyond despicable." "You were not religious or political martyrs; you were thugs for hire, pure and simple." Cromitie became an "enthusiastic jihadist," who "showed no compunction" about the bombs. The nature of their crimes and the length of their sentences "virtually guarantee" they would be imprisoned under the harshest possible conditions. "I imagine you will be far from here, and quite isolated. I doubt that you will receive any training or rehabilitation treatment of any sort. Your crimes were terrible. Your punishment will indeed be severe." "25 years in the sort of conditions I anticipate you are facing is easily equivalent to life in other conditions."

A new team of defense lawyers appealed on grounds of entrapment. "When Cromitie said 'I love you' to Hussain, it was no mere pleasantry." "Without the love that Hussain pretended to have for Cromitie, and that Hussain fully exploited, this supposed crime would never have occurred." (Indeed, while the appeal was pending, an FBI target near Pittsburgh identified Hussain as the informant who sought to entrap him into terrorism.) During oral argument, Chief Judge Jacobs asked: "is there any other case that you can talk about where the government's level of involvement in creating and animating and realizing the offense was so all encompassing?" The prosecution replied that what distinguished the case "is not so much the involvement of the government, but the gravity of the criminal conduct." The government's role was primarily to remove "logistical hurdles." Judge Raggi said: "I don't think that's all the government did. It would be one thing if the defendant had conceived the crime and then, as obstacles arose, the government removed them. But I think you have to deal with the problem of the full circumstances here. The government comes up with the idea, picks the target, provides all the means, removes the obstacles."

The prosecution replied that Cromitie's declaration that he wanted to die a martyr and do "something to America" was "reason enough for the FBI to move forward with the investigation." Considering Cromitie's remarks and enthusiasm "about wanting to commit a crime like this," the government had "no choice but to follow up and reach the point where either the defendant walks away or we have some clarity about his character." A defense lawyer argued that the case was "not so much about terrorism as about the power of the government, through a corrupt informer, to entrap its citizens in crimes they never would have committed if they had been left alone." But Judge Newman quoted Cromitie "as saying at the first meeting that he wanted to do something to America. Granted, it's open-ended, but it's cause for concern."

The panel affirmed.[22] Judge Newman rejected the defense claim of entrapment as a matter of law because the defendants exhibited the necessary predisposition. "We doubt that the potential terrorists who are available to be recruited by Al-Qaeda or similar groups have already 'formed' a 'design' to bomb specific targets." He seconded McMahon's statement at sentencing: "I believe beyond a shadow of doubt that there would have been no crime here except the government instigated it, planned it, and brought it to fruition." But Cromitie's statements to Hussain at their first meeting "revealed a pre-existing design to commit terrorist acts." Newman also rejected the defense claim of outrageous government misconduct: "government creation of the opportunity to commit an offense, even to the point of supplying defendants with materials essential to commit crimes, does not exceed due process limits."

Jacobs dissented in part, finding that Cromitie was entrapped as a matter of law. "The design here was entirely formed by the government, and fed to Cromitie. He liked it, but he didn't form it." "All of Cromitie's statements regarding the specifics of the attack – such as targets – were made in direct response to Hussain's badgering."

> It is clear that Cromitie in his unmolested state of grievance would … have continued to stew in his rage and ignorance indefinitely, and had no formed design about what to do. The government agent supplied a design and gave it form, so that the agent rather than the defendant inspired the crime, provoked it, planned it, financed it, equipped it, and furnished the time and targets. He had to, because Cromitie was comically incompetent, possibly the last candidate one would pick as the agent of a conspiracy.

TAREK MEHANNA[23]

Tarek Mehanna, a pharmacy college graduate, was arrested in November 2008 as he was about to board a flight to Saudi Arabia, and was initially charged with having lied to the FBI in 2006 that Daniel Maldonado, a friend, was in Egypt, when Mehanna knew Maldonado had undergone terrorist training and was fighting in Somalia. Mehanna had gone to Yemen in February 2004, allegedly in an unsuccessful attempt to get terrorist training. He was subsequently charged with Ahmad Abousamra (who had fled the country) and others with conspiring to kill two prominent US government officials overseas, attack US troops in Iraq, and shoot at shoppers in US malls and the emergency personnel who would come to their rescue.

Mehanna's parents, brother, and dozens of supporters attended the first day of trial. Supporters organized a large march from Occupy Boston headquarters to the courthouse. Americans for Peace and Tolerance also planned a rally. Laila Murad, leader of the Tarek Mehanna Support Committee, said he was guilty of nothing more than "having a political and religious discussion, just like every American has on everything from marriage to U.S. foreign policy." The ACLU filed a motion to dismiss, citing the First Amendment. D Mass Judge O'Toole refused a defense request to introduce photos of the Constitution and the offensive Westboro Baptist Church demonstrations at military funerals (which had been protected by the Supreme Court).

AUSA Aloke Chakravarty said in his opening: "this is a material support case; this is about killing people." Mehanna translated "jihad material ... that would encourage others to participate in jihad, which was itself a service to al-Qaeda." The texts included Mullah Muhammed Omar's "39 Ways to Serve and Participate in Jihad" – which was "essentially training material to get ready to serve and participate in that fight" – as well as "Make Martyrdom What You Seek" and "Guiding the Confused on the Permissibility of Killing the Prisoners." In summer 2005 al-Qaeda "personally solicited" Mehanna to translate the group's second in command, al-Zawahiri. Mehanna "viewed himself as part of the media department of the terror group. It meant killing, it meant bullets, it meant martyrdom." A photo showed him striking a happy pose at Ground Zero. "He was going to celebrate what happened on that day." But "this case is not about what the defendant believed, whether he was against the war, whether he didn't like America."

Defense lawyer J.W. Carney Jr. called Mehanna "a young man his mom could be very proud of." He showed photos of the boy sitting on a shopping mall Santa's lap and playing baseball. "I'm not here to convince you to believe that his view and the view of millions of others was correct ... I am asking you to find that you can hold that view in the United States of America even if the government does not want you to hold that view." Mehanna translated documents because "he wanted others to understand the point of view." He went to Yemen to study fifteenth-century Arabic law, not to join terrorists.

Prosecutors introduced documents promoting jihad and videos seized from Mehanna's home depicting "jihadist scenes, combat scenes, in areas of conflict around the globe." Ali Aboubakr, a younger friend granted immunity, testified for four hours about Mehanna's praise of al-Qaeda leaders and the "blood donations" of suicide bombers and denunciations of Bush, as well as their dream to join jihad. Mehanna had sent him videos promoting suicide bombings, which Mehanna had subtitled in English; others featured al Zarqawi (leader of al-Qaeda in Iraq). Mehanna felt the World Trade Center had been a legitimate target because it symbolized the "infrastructure of the United States." Mehanna had asked: "if I tried to go again [on jihad], would you come?" Aboubakr replied: "Yes, dude, I am serious. Let's go donate blood." In 2006 Mehanna wrote: "I looked at [bin Laden] as my truth [sic] father in a sense." After Mehanna delivered a provocative sermon at the Islamic Center of New England, the Board of Directors confronted his father.

On cross-examination by Janice Bassil, Aboubakr agreed they were not a terrorist cell and Mehanna never said he had gone to Yemen to kill American soldiers in Iraq. Aboubakr admitted he initiated conversations about books or songs promoting jihad, but often was just joking, because jihad referred generally to Muslims' struggle to defend and spread their faith. He agreed that the proposed trip to the Middle East was not about seeking death as a martyr. "I can't recall a time where watching the videos [of wars in Chechnya and Bosnia] actually led to [Mehanna] saying, 'well, we have to actually get up and do something.'"

Prosecutors showed violent videos (some produced by al-Qaeda) depicting suicide bombings and glorifying the 9/11 attack, as well as internet chats in which Mehanna encouraged friends to watch videos and discussed bombings and beheadings. FBI Special Agent Andre Khoury described but did not screen a video that "shows a brutal beheading by ... al-Qaeda members in Iraq." He acknowledged that another showed hospitalized children suffering because of international sanctions against Iraq and some portrayed mujahideen shooting at Soviet troops. When Khoury mentioned bin Laden, Carney asked: "Do you want to say that name any more times?", repeating it several more himself and adding sarcastically: "I'm just trying to help the government out." He moved for a mistrial twice, complaining that "one of the goals of the prosecution is to mention Osama bin Laden as much as possible and to mention the twin towers as much as possible."

Hassan Masood, a former friend, testified that he brought Mehanna, Abousamra, and Kareem Abuzahra to Logan Airport to fly to Yemen for terrorist training. Prosecutors argued that though they failed to find a terrorist camp, Mehanna returned home with a new interest in jihad. Masood said Mehanna believed "there was an obligation for Muslims to stand up and fight against the invasion in Iraq and U.S. forces in Iraq." The three had "found someone who was going to help them in Yemen. They wanted to go to Yemen to look for training camps there." Mehanna often spoke of violent jihad, watched violent videos with friends, and supported attacks on US military targets, though he opposed suicide bombings. But Masood acknowledged he heard most of this from Abousamra and just assumed Mehanna shared that perspective. Actually, Mehanna had far less extreme views on Islam, seemed more interested in studying Islamic law, and often cited the Koran: "for Tarek, it was always about what Islam required or Islam permitted or Islam forbids." Seeking to impeach Masood, Carney got him to admit that Mehanna's prosecutors had convicted his father of visa fraud; he also was facing deportation, but denied expecting favorable treatment in exchange for testifying.

Jason Pippin, a Muslim convert, said Abousamra visited him in California in 2003 to discuss contacts in Yemen who would help him get terrorist training to fight in Iraq. Asked to join him, Pippin demurred; as a Westerner "I'd stick out as a sore thumb." Abousamra described "a circle of friends" including Mehanna, who were "like-minded that were set to be jihadi." But after returning from Yemen, Abousamra said online that he had failed to find training camps. Pippin, who had gone to Yemen because Yemenis spoke pure Arabic and accommodation was cheap, never talked to Mehanna about the latter's Yemen trip. Pippin acknowledged that Mehanna often took moderate stands on political issues and said Americans were not accountable for their country's war in Iraq.

FBI Agent Brad Davis testified that in December 2006 Mehanna claimed he had gone to Yemen two years earlier "for the purpose of finding an Arabic language school and an Islamic religious school," and "he and Abousamra went for the same purpose." Questioned four days before that, Abousamra also said they had gone to Yemen to study, but then immediately called Mehanna, warning him to get a lawyer and not talk to the FBI. "They asked me about my trip … and then they showed me a picture of you and Kareem" Abuzahra. In a second conversation that evening Abousamra said he had told the FBI he had visited schools, but had left because Yemen was "disgusting."

Daniel Maldonado testified that, after converting to Islam in 1999, he sought guidance from Mehanna, who became his best friend. They debated Islamic law and watched videos promoting jihad, which incited him. Facing a life sentence for military training in Egypt and Somalia, he cooperated with the government in exchange for a ten-year sentence. Mehanna had called the 9/11 attacks legitimate "because the same thing has happened to Muslims throughout the world." When Maldonado talked about fighting in Somalia, Mehanna said: "if we ever have the chance, we should make way to go." But when Maldonado was in Egypt in 2006, Mehanna discouraged him from fighting in Somalia, urging him to think of his wife (who later died of malaria in Somalia). Mehanna had declined Maldonado's plea to join him fighting in Somalia; he was only interested in whether he could find bookstores and a wife there. Maldonado agreed that Mehanna was "growing up and away from Ahmad [Abousamra] and his ideas."

Daniel Spaulding (another friend testifying under immunity, who had renounced Islam) said Mehanna reported in 2006 that his father had prohibited him from giving any more sermons after his controversial speech. A mosque board member had told his father: "if we didn't know he was your son, we would say he was a member of al-Qaeda." Mehanna's father also told him not to visit a questionable Islamic website or read certain books because they "fuel" his ideas.

Mehanna would discuss jihad with people only after ascertaining their views about 9/11. But he used jihad to mean protecting Muslims from invaders and resented being identified with al-Qaeda. He embraced the principle that anyone living in a country that let him practice Islam had a duty to obey that country's laws and dismissed as "silly" and "stupid and impractical" the proposal by Abousamra and Abuzahra to shoot up a shopping mall.

Kareem Abuzahra (also testifying under immunity) said Mehanna and he grew more attached to Islam in 2002. Abousamra, Mehanna, and he supported the 9/11 attack because "Americans had been pushing around everyone for so long, this was a way to get back at them." The three began to speak of jihad after the 2003 invasion of Iraq. "We saw it as an invasion on Islam, and we saw the Americans as valid targets." They considered going to Iraq, but concluded it was too difficult. They also contemplated shooting at Hanscom AFB or a shopping mall, or assassinating Condoleezza Rice and John Ashcroft. "We had to do something ... participate in jihad against the U.S. It was our duty. Defending Muslims and defending jihad." In 2003 they discussed getting weapons for a local attack from Maldonado (a former gang member), but scrapped the plan. "The goal was to get into Iraq." The three conspired to travel to Yemen in 2004 in search of terrorism training. Abuzahra paid for their plane tickets and made a video for his family in case he did not return. "The purpose of the trip was to go to war." Mehanna was exultant: "We're actually doing it. We're finally doing it." But after Abuzahra abandoned the others on learning during a stopover in the UAE that his father was ill, his relationship with Mehanna deteriorated. Questioned by the FBI in summer 2006, Abuzahra initially gave their cover story of seeking language training in Yemen, but agreed to cooperate when he "realized the interest in me by the government was more than I originally expected."

At a December 2006 meeting in Abousamra's home (secretly recorded by Abuzahra) the men discussed the FBI's interest in them and how to get their stories straight. Abousamra said "there's no testimony about us going for such and such false reasons, because we went there for one reason, to study." "[A]nything else is speculation." Mehanna, more cautious, said "I'm going to leave it at things that are documented, that I can't deny." But he was determined to return to Yemen. "The way we did it was very hasty and immature, but not the idea itself. I don't regret it for a second. Those were the best two weeks of my life, for once not sitting on my butt, telling people to do something I wasn't going to do."

Only when Maldonado was arrested a month later did Mehanna start to worry what his friend was telling the government. "Overall, they know generally I didn't go there to graze goats." "Dan knows everything." Abuzahra also sought to differentiate his two friends. He discussed domestic terrorist attacks with Abousamra, sometimes without Mehanna, who was always carrying books and Islamic texts and sought to calm down Abousamra. "Tarek was all about trying to figure out what the rules were, and following those rules," and he had debated extremists on web fora.

The prosecution's final witness was Evan F. Kohlmann, whom it offered as an expert on al-Qaeda and jihad. Mehanna translated materials and posted them on the Tibyan Publications site. Kohlmann said the web performed "a crucial function, because it allowed al-Qaeda to reach an audience ... a captive audience." But he admitted he did not speak Arabic, had never taught at an academic institution, lacked security clearance, and based much of his professional work on what he had learned in college. He had helped the Nine Eleven Finding Answers Foundation post on its website 37 videos glorifying jihad and 103 statements by bin Laden, Zawahiri and others, similar to those Mehanna had translated.

When the prosecution rested after five weeks, the defense offered its own experts. Andrew F. March, associate professor of political science and religious studies at Yale, showed that Mehanna debated and rejected radical views on Islamic websites, contending that military facilities and personnel were the only acceptable targets and civilians could not be attacked just because their taxes funded the war. In one post he repudiated the views of al-Awlaki and noted that the USA had produced some of the biggest anti-war demonstrations. Gregory Johnsen, a Princeton doctoral student specializing in Yemen, said the country was respected worldwide for teaching Islamic jurisprudence and speaking a pure form of Arabic. Mohammed Fadel, associate professor of law at University of Toronto, said Mehanna "wrote about the most mundane topics of Islam, such as whether you should sleep on your left side, your right side, or on your stomach." Marc Sageman, a former CIA agent and psychiatrist, contrasted his own "scientific method" with that of Kohlmann, who just "tells stories." Al-Qaeda had recruited most of its members before 9/11 in countries with little access to the Internet. Resting after little more than a week, the defense unsuccessfully sought a special verdict form in which the jury would record whether it thought Mehanna had violated federal laws by translating documents.

In closing, Chakravarty said the case was about Mehanna "besmirching Islam, so that he could do what it is he wanted to do." "If he had been successful in completing what he set out to do ... then on this day, when people are coming back from Iraq, there might be a bit fewer of them." Bassil replied for the defense that the prosecution showed pictures of bin Laden and the Twin Towers "to scare you," never giving "the whole story of whom [sic] Tarek Mehanna is." AUSA Jeffrey Auerhahn said Mehanna "revealed the true intentions of his trip to Yemen by refusing to discuss it with people outside his circle," and introduced others to al-Qaeda's ideology as "part of their one-on-one recruitment." Bassil retorted that "the only idea Tarek Mehanna shared with al-Qaeda was that Muslims had the right to defend themselves when they were attacked in their own land." Mehanna held that belief "because that's what the Koran teaches." "I'm not asking you to respect Tarek's beliefs, but I am asking you to respect his rights to independent advocacy."

The jury convicted Mehanna on all seven counts. Bassil called it "an incredibly sad day ... for civil rights." But the *Boston Herald* said Mehanna's First Amendment claims "essentially fell apart" when he sought terrorist training and translated jihadist documents. The director of the Massachusetts ACLU replied that translating had "never been a crime" and making it one "raises serious First Amendment concerns."

Before sentencing, Mehanna said that, when arrested at Logan Airport, he had been en route to a Saudi Arabian hospital where he had been asked to create a new diabetes treatment clinic. After being released on bail, he had taught math, science, and religion at a local Islamic private school, "the most fulfilling experience of his life." Asking for 5 to 6.5 years, his lawyers said he went to Yemen looking for religious schools when he was just 21 and "entirely unsophisticated," and never received terrorist training or "actually threatened United States security interests." Prosecutors asked for 25 years (not the maximum of life). Mehanna lived a "double life," posing as "dutiful and scholarly" when he actually was an "angry, callous, calculating man who obsessed about violence against Americans for most of his adult life." He "has never disavowed his extremist views or expressed any remorse."

After receiving more than a hundred pages of letters seeking lenience, Judge O'Toole sentenced Mehanna to 17.5 years, expressing concern about his "apparent absence of remorse." Mehanna's statement after sentencing confirmed this. The government charged him with these "crimes" only because he refused to become an informant. When he was just six years old he began reading comic books that "introduced me to a paradigm" in which "there are oppressors, there are the oppressed, and there are those who step up to defend the oppressed." Examples included Native Americans, the American Revolution, the fight against slavery, socialists, Anne Frank and the Holocaust, Nelson Mandela and the struggle against apartheid, and civil rights. His hero was Malcolm X, whose "life taught me that Islam is not something inherited ... it's a way of life." "I stand before you ... as a very proud Muslim." "[E]verywhere I looked, I saw the powers that be trying to destroy what I loved": Soviets

in Afghanistan, Serbs in Bosnia, Russians in Chechnya, Israel in
Lebanon and Palestine, and the USA in Iraq during the first Gulf War,
the subsequent sanctions, and the 2003 invasion. He listed American
atrocities: Haditha, the gang-rape of a 14-year-old girl, and the mass
murder of 17 civilians. (I describe these in Chapter 3.) "[E]ach Muslim
woman is my sister, each man is my brother." Jihad is just what the
Minutemen did at Concord. "Muslims should defend their lands from
foreign invaders." He had not been tried by a jury of his peers "because
with the mentality gripping America today, I have no peers."

The US had come to regret slavery, Jim Crow, and internment of
Japanese Americans. "[E]verything is subjective – even this whole
business of 'terrorism'." "[O]ne day, Americans will change and people
will recognize this day for what it is."

The First Circuit affirmed.[24] Judge Selya (joined by Howard and
Thompson) began by characterizing terrorism as an "existential
threat," "the modern-day equivalent of the bubonic plague." The
government's "predictably" "fierce" response compelled the court
"to patrol the fine line between vital national security concerns and
forbidden encroachments on constitutionally protected freedoms
of speech and association." There was ample evidence from which a
jury could find that Mehanna "traveled to Yemen with the specific
intent of providing material support to al-Qa'ida." With respect to his
translation activities, Judge Selya praised Judge O'Toole for having
"explained to the jury in no fewer than three different ways that independent advocacy" for a foreign terrorist organization or its goals "does
not amount to coordination," which had been criminalized as material
support. Selya rejected the government's argument – "breathtaking
in its scope" – that it could introduce anything Mehanna saw or read
on the ground that it shaped his worldview. "An objective observer
might well regard the sprawling taxonomy suggested by the government as a thinly disguised effort to saddle defendants indiscriminately
with the criminal and cultural baggage of internationally notorious
terrorists." But Selya deferred to O'Toole's judgment on "the point at
which relevant and admissible evidence lapses into relevant but cumulative (and therefore inadmissible) evidence." "It should not surprise
a defendant that proof of his participation in conspiracies to provide
material support to terrorist organizations and to kill Americans here
and abroad will engender the presentation of evidence offensive to
the sensibilities of civilized people … Terrorism trials are not to be
confused with high tea at Buckingham Palace."

AHMED KHALFAN GHAILANI[25]

Ghailani was indicted in 1998 for the bombings that year of the US embassies in Nairobi and Dar es Salaam, which killed 224 people and wounded hundreds more. He and others were alleged to have bought seven large gas tanks and a truck, which he had modified to hold two large batteries in a lockable compartment, and to have hid blasting caps in his residence. A day before the attack he used a false passport to fly with al-Qaeda leaders to Pakistan. After capturing him in July 2004, Pakistan handed him over to the CIA, which subjected him to enhanced interrogation techniques (EITs) in a secret prison until President Bush transferred him (with other high-value detainees (HVDs)) to Guantánamo in September 2006. He was interrogated further there and, in March 2008, charged before a military commission (which ruled out the death penalty). President Obama suspended the military commissions in January 2009, transferring Ghailani for trial in SDNY four months later. Sen. Mitch McConnell (R-Ky) said the transfer ignored the "clear desire of Congress and the American people that these terrorists not be brought to the United States." But Sen. Russell Feingold (D-Wisc) replied: "any system that permits the government to indefinitely detain individuals without charge or without a meaningful opportunity to have accusations against them adjudicated by an impartial arbiter violates basic American values and is likely unconstitutional."

Ghailani pleaded not guilty. His defense team of six lawyers included a specialist in the death penalty (although the government later decided not to seek it). Three lawyers traveled to Tanzania to meet his family, interview potential government witnesses, and visit the Kariakoo market where Ghailani allegedly bought the bomb ingredients. Their strategy was to portray him as one of hundreds of enterprising young men who frequented the market, running errands, hustling deals, and hoping for commissions and tips. Prosecutors declared they would not use any statements made "while [Ghailani] was in custody of other government agencies" (a euphemism for the CIA), and they acceded to the defense request to preserve evidence from the secret prison where he had been held.

Ghailani made a number of pretrial challenges. Invoking the Sixth Amendment right to counsel, he asked the court to enjoin the reassignment of the two military lawyers who had represented him before the MC. Judge Kaplan rejected the government's argument that this was

nonjusticiable, but found that Ghailani "is not entitled to choose particular government-paid counsel ... and he does not have a right to
the continued services of previously appointed counsel."[26] His civilian
counsel deplored this "tremendous loss to the defense."

Judge Kaplan granted some but not all defense discovery motions.[27]
Although a DoJ memorandum was exempt from disclosure, and
the government had not waived its privilege with respect to other
documents, Kaplan authorized discovery of materials in the
possession of Main Justice. Because Ghailani was charged with a
crime that "commanded the attention of the highest levels of our
government," "responsible officials within the Department of Justice
who were involved in making the series of decisions ... were sufficiently involved with the prosecution properly to be considered 'the
government.'" But Kaplan denied Ghailani's motion to dismiss on
the ground that he had been tortured by the CIA.[28] Because the government had refrained from using anything he said in CIA custody,
or the fruits of those statements, any due process violations would not
taint the subsequent criminal process.

Ghailani sought an order that the Bureau of Prisons (BoP) stop
conducting rectal examinations when he entered or left the prison for
court appearances.[29] Choosing not to find that Ghailani had failed to
exhaust administrative remedies, Kaplan heard testimony by a clinical
psychologist appointed to assist the defense (to whom prosecutors did
not object) that because Ghailani suffered post-traumatic stress disorder
(PTSD) as a result of his treatment by the CIA, such examinations
would render him incapable of assisting his defense. Nevertheless,
Kaplan found the examination "justified by the legitimate governmental interest in protecting the safety of prison and court personnel
and other inmates."

Ghailani moved to dismiss on the ground that the five-year delay
since his apprehension violated his constitutional right to a speedy
trial.[30] The defense said "this case presents possibly the most unique
and egregious example of a speedy trial violation in American jurisprudence to date." Prosecutors replied that because Ghailani "was believed
to have, and in fact did have, actionable intelligence about al-Qaeda,"
his detention and interrogation "was done, simply put, to save lives."
Declaring that "our nation decided over 200 years ago that the Speedy
Trial Clause ... applies to all, regardless of their citizenship or the crimes
of which they are accused," Judge Kaplan ordered prosecutors to review
DoJ files and give the defense any materials showing that decisions to

detain him "were for a purpose other than national security." But Kaplan ultimately denied the motion to dismiss. "[T]he decisions that caused the delay were not made for the purpose of gaining any advantage." Two years "served compelling interests of national security." None of the delay "subjected Ghailani to a single day of incarceration that he would not otherwise have suffered" as an enemy combatant, and there was "no persuasive evidence that the delay in this prosecution has impaired Ghailani's ability to defend himself." The *Los Angeles Times* praised the ruling in an editorial expressing concern that Attorney General Holder might abort the civilian prosecution of the five HVDs (as he did).

The most momentous pretrial issue turned on Ghailani's motion to suppress the crucial testimony of Hussein Abebe, who allegedly sold him explosives in Arusha to transport to Dar es Salaam. Tanzania arrested Abebe in Arusha in August 2006 and flew him to Zanzibar, where it questioned him with the FBI for about a week. But Ghailani argued that his own custodial statements (made under coercion) had led to Abebe, whose testimony thereby became "fruit of the poisonous tree." Although the government claimed it would have found Abebe without Ghailani's evidence, Kaplan said "that would have been roughly comparable to finding a particular individual named John or Bill in a state with a population around the size of Maine or New Hampshire ... while knowing little more about him than that he was regarded as prominent in a significant industry in the state.

The government called Abebe a willing witness. But it offered no affidavit from him, and "the circumstances of Abebe's initial questioning ... suggest that he is not simply a public spirited citizen who 'has come forward [to] offer evidence entirely of [his] own volition.'" Kaplan ruled that a hearing was necessary to determine whether Abebe truly would be the volunteer that the government claimed, that unlawfully obtained evidence did not play a role in securing Abebe's cooperation, or that the interval between the alleged misconduct in obtaining from Ghailani the information that led to Abebe and Abebe's agreement to cooperate was as long as the government doubtless would have it.

During the three-day hearing Abebe claimed he sold TNT to Ghailani believing it would be used for mining, learning otherwise only after seeing a television report on the bombing. Although an FBI agent said Abebe claimed to live in constant fear of being found out, Abebe told defense lawyers he had no such anxiety. He testified that Tanzanian officials encouraged him to cooperate with the

FBI so he could return home. He agreed to do so out of anger at having been deceived and discovering that his explosives had been used to kill. Cooperation "was not a must." But Kaplan noted that Abebe had been released only after he "promised to appear as a witness." "There is at least some evidence that there was an ongoing interactive process between the efforts to smoke out Hussein [Abebe], identify him and find him, and the interrogation of Ghailani by the C.I.A." "Somebody in Tanzania" came up with "a great theory" of where Abebe might be," leading to "further interaction with Ghailani." Kaplan found that the government "failed to prove that Abebe's testimony is sufficiently attenuated from Ghailani's coerced statements to permit its receipt in evidence."[31]

> The Court has not reached this conclusion lightly. It is acutely aware of the perilous nature of the world in which we live. But the Constitution is the rock upon which our nation rests. We must follow it not only when it is convenient, but when fear and danger beckon in a different direction. To do less would diminish us and undermine the foundation upon which we stand.

In a subsequent elaboration, Kaplan said Abebe feared being arrested if he did not cooperate. "He was no volunteer. Quite the contrary. He was induced to testify only out of fear of the consequences of not doing so, including possible prosecution, and conceivably worse." "[T]he link between the C.I.A.'s coercion of Ghailani and Abebe's testimony is direct and close." Although the CIA's "predominant motives" were "intelligence oriented … if the government is going to coerce a detainee to provide information to our intelligence agencies, it may not use that evidence" or its fruits "to prosecute the detainee for a criminal offense." Prosecutors did not appeal so as not to delay the trial.

To empanel a jury, Kaplan had more than a thousand prospective jurors complete an 11-page questionnaire requested by the defense, even though prosecutors had objected to its length and Kaplan was no "fan" of questionnaires. A pretrial hearing established that Ghailani was fit to stand trial. An FBI clean team had re-interrogated him after his transfer from the secret CIA prison to Guantánamo, but the prosecution decided not to use his new statements, even though they contained admissions he had trained with al-Qaeda in Afghanistan, been a bodyguard for bin Laden, and realized that the Dar es Salaam embassy would be attacked after "putting the pieces of the puzzle together." He believed military bases and soldiers were legitimate targets, but not embassies, and was "really bothered" by the number of Africans killed but was not bothered by American deaths.

In his opening, AUSA Nicholas Lewin said Ghailani participated "because he and his accomplices were committed to al-Qaeda's overriding goal, killing Americans." With co-conspirators, he escaped to Pakistan the day before the embassy bombings using a false name and fake passport. Prosecutors would exhibit chunks of charred metal from the truck used in the explosion, with a vehicle ID number that helped investigators trace it to Ghailani; shrapnel from some of the twenty 150-pound cylinders used to make the bomb; plane tickets for his flight; and recollections of blast survivors. Ghailani's lawyers said he was innocent, immature, trusting, and naive – a "creature of his surroundings," who liked to watch cartoons and had been duped by real terrorists. He was "neither a member of al-Qaeda nor does he share their goals." He did not know what his friends or al-Qaeda were planning, but had fallen in with older men who "at some point in their lives trained and became part of al-Qaeda."

The jury heard many accounts of the blast. The chargé d'affaires saw a blackened, charred body "in his last gasps of life." A marine heard "metal striking metal" and witnessed chaos. One woman heard a sound so loud "it went through my chest. It was physical." A Nairobi embassy employee was hurled through the air. "All I could see were bodies." Videos showed gray smoke, blaring car alarms and medics with stretchers in Dar es Salaam, and mounds of rubble, hoses spraying burning cars, pools of water tinged with blood, charred corpses, and a bus blown apart in Nairobi.

In his closing, a prosecutor called the defendant "a mass murderer" who "sat here calmly, day in and day out" knowing he "has the blood of hundreds on his hands." Ghailani helped buy the truck and gas tanks and stored detonators for explosives; his cell phone was the "operational phone." Although "he still looks pretty young for his age," he had been 24 at the time of the attack. The defense called Ghailani an al-Qaeda "dupe." He assumed the purchases of the truck and gas cylinders were routine commercial deals in the Kariakoo market. "It's not like you're buying a gun." The prosecution replied that Ghailani was "not one of the people being lied to. He's one of the liars." He told family and friends he was going to Yemen or Germany when he fled to Pakistan just before the bombing. "He knows what's coming the next day is mass murder – he's been preparing for it."

On the second day of deliberations the jury asked for the results of the FBI search of Ghailani's home, including testimony that it had found a blasting cap. Defense lawyers had called the search flawed and the cap planted. Just before lunch on the third day a juror wrote the judge, asking to be dismissed. She felt alone and attacked "for my conclusion." "I have come to my conclusion but it doesn't agreed [sic] with the rest of the juror [sic]." "My conclusion, it [sic] not going to change." The 53-year-old Bronx resident had been a crime victim and had a close friend or relative who had been charged with a crime. After Kaplan read her note to the lawyers, a defense lawyer was "beyond despondent." "I couldn't believe with those facts, I'd lost 11 that quickly." The defense opposed replacing her. After Kaplan talked to the jurors, the defense moved for a mistrial: "to do anything else would force a verdict on the jury." The prosecution responded that the jury had deliberated only two full days. "There is no plausible ground for arguing they're hopelessly deadlocked." Kaplan denied the defense motion and refused to replace the juror. Nothing in her note supported "the view that there is any kind of personal disharmony" among jurors rather than a "strenuous disagreement." With the concurrence of both sides, Kaplan re-read the jury his instructions:

> Each of you must decide the case for yourself, but you should do so only after consideration of the case with your fellow jurors, and you should not hesitate to change an opinion when convinced that it is erroneous … You are not bound to surrender your honest convictions.

After four days the jury asked Kaplan about the defense argument of "conscious avoidance" or willful blindness. If Ghailani suspected something illegal was happening but buried his head in the sand, could he still be convicted? If so, did he need to know the plot's specific objectives as charged in the indictment? Prosecutors argued that Ghailani only needed to know "some illegal purpose." The defense countered that he had to know the conspiracy's ultimate aims. Kaplan proposed language closer to the defense: Ghailani had to know the specific objectives, not just that "some crime" would be committed. The prosecution countered with a proposal allowing conviction with less knowledge. At 5:30 the next morning the defense drafted a three-page letter rejecting the government proposal as a "nonstarter." Kaplan's new instruction included most of the defense language.

That afternoon the jury acquitted Ghailani of 284 counts but convicted him of conspiracy to destroy government property. A defense lawyer called the verdict "a reaffirmation that this nation's judicial system is the greatest ever devised ... truly a system of laws and not men." Human Rights Watch (HRW) and Human Rights First (HRF) praised the process. Former MC chief prosecutor Morris Davis said the trial "delivered justice ... safely and securely, while upholding the values that have defined America." But there was criticism from both ends of the political spectrum. The Center for Constitutional Rights (CCR) questioned "the ability of anyone who is Muslim to receive a truly fair trial in any American judicial forum post-9/11." Republicans sought to exploit the verdict for political advantage. Calling it "all the proof we need that the administration's approach to prosecuting terrorists has been deeply misguided and indeed potentially harmful as a matter of national security," Sen. McConnell demanded President Obama offer assurances that "terrorists will be tried from now on in the military commission system that was established for this very purpose at the secure facility in Guantánamo Bay, or detained indefinitely, if they cannot be tried without jeopardizing national security." Sen. Jon Kyl (R-Az) declared "this trial came dangerously close to failure" and hoped "that the administration heard this wake-up call and will return to the policy of trying these kinds of terrorists in military commissions." Rep. Tom Price (R-Ga) called the verdict "a gross miscarriage of justice." Former Attorney General Michael Mukasey denounced the "cruel travesty" of convicting Ghailani of the single count when he "murdered" more than 200 people. Liz Cheney, Debra Burlingame (for a group of 9/11 victims' families), and Bill Kristol called the verdict not "just embarrassing" but "dangerous" because "it signals weakness in a time of war." Rep. King was "disgusted at the total miscarriage of justice," which "demonstrates the absolute insanity of the Obama administration's decision to try al-Qaeda terrorists in civilian courts." Kaplan's rulings "doomed" the case.

The *New York Times* denounced King's "shocking disdain for the 12 jurors" and praised Kaplan for "respecting the Constitution and the law." The *Los Angeles Times* agreed "the outcome demonstrates the deliberateness and fairness of civilian" trials, which "show the world that even those accused of the most heinous crimes will receive the full protections of American law." The *Washington Post* called the "stunning" verdict "an embarrassment for the Obama administration," but still favored criminal prosecutions over MCs. "The fact that a jury sitting in a terrorism case just blocks from ground zero declined to rubber-stamp the government's assertions shows not the weakness of the federal court system but one of its principal strengths: independence." Marc Thiessen denounced the "debacle" in his *Washington Post* column. The *New York Post* said the "tortured" process resulted in an "obscene" verdict.

The defense moved to set aside the verdict on the ground that the evidence was insufficient to sustain it in light of Ghailani's acquittal on more than 280 counts. Kaplan denied the motion: "a verdict of 'not guilty' means only this – the jury said no. It doesn't mean they found any facts." "It may be that what you had here was 11 for conviction, one absolutely adamant that there would be no conviction and a bargain at the end, so everybody could go home." The defense also asked him to dismiss the separate jury finding that Ghailani's conduct had "directly or proximately caused death to a person," thereby reducing the maximum to 20 years. Kaplan declined, commenting: "kind of hard to argue with that, don't you think?"

The defense sought leniency because of Ghailani's mistreatment in custody. The government sought life, introducing statements he subsequently said were voluntary but had been inadmissible in the guilt phase because he had not been Mirandized. He had obtained fertilizer and more than 100 detonators and helped load TNT and other components onto the truck. A plotter told him of the plans "about a week before [the embassy] was bombed." A senior al-Qaeda operative gave him $500 so that "as he fled from Africa using his false passport, he could bribe local immigration officials as necessary." Prosecutors introduced 33 letters from victims, almost all calling for a life sentence.

Ghailani chose not to address the court before sentencing. The prosecution said he "took away hundreds, hundreds of lives. In response to that, Your Honor, you should take away his freedom, and you should take it away forever." Agreeing, Kaplan sentenced Ghailani to life.

> It was a cold-blooded killing and maiming of innocent people on an enormous scale. The very purpose of the crime was to create terror by causing death and destruction ... This trial has been as divorced from any questionable practice that may have been engaged in by anybody other than the defendant as this human being is capable of having made it. I simply put all of that out of my mind ... Mr. Ghailani knew and intended that people would be killed as a result of his own actions and of the conspiracy that he joined.
>
> Ghailani might have other remedies for any illegal or improper actions by our government. But that is a matter for another time and another place. Today is about justice, not only for Mr. Ghailani, but for the victims of his crime.

Holder said the sentence "shows yet again the strength of the American justice system in holding terrorists accountable for their actions." The ACLU, Amnesty International (AI), and HRW agreed the case demonstrated the value of civilian justice. But Rep. Lamar Smith (R-Tex) called the trial "a close call," "a near disaster."

The Second Circuit (Cabranes, with Laval and Parker) affirmed.[32] It rejected Ghailani's speedy trial claim: nothing in the clause "requires the government to choose between national security and an orderly and fair justice system." Ghailani had not shown he was prejudiced at trial by the delay. The court upheld Judge Kaplan's instruction on "conscious avoidance" and his sentence.

COMMONALITIES WITH OTHER PROSECUTIONS

These five cases illustrate some of the most significant issues "war on terror" prosecutions pose for criminal justice. The remainder of this chapter locates those and related issues in the context of a wide variety of other criminal cases.

Informants
Informants played a central – arguably essential – role in many of these cases, initiating contact with the accused, suggesting the terrorist actions, and providing indispensable technical support and materiel.[33] We will never know whether Hamid Hayat would have attended a terrorist training camp without the constant badgering of Naseem Khan, whether Narseal Batiste and his followers would have cased Miami federal buildings and "sworn an oath to al-Qaeda" without the guidance of Elie Assad, or whether James Cromitie and his cronies would have attempted to bomb the Riverdale Jewish Community Center without Shahed Hassan's leadership. All these accused displayed reluctance and often seemed to lose interest in the plot. The latter two groups were motivated by money at least as much as, if not more than, ideology. Like Khan, Assad, and Hassan, many informants were unsavory characters, vulnerable to government pressure because of their criminal records, motivated by greed and the desire to become citizens. They lied to the government as well as the accused and failed (deliberately?) to record essential conversations. Yet none of this constituted the very restrictive legal definition of entrapment or otherwise helped the defense.[34]

Many other cases displayed similar patterns. Shahawar Siraj and James Elshafay might not have planned to bomb New York's Herald

Square subway station without the urging of Osama Eldawoody, a much older Egyptian American informant who boasted of expertise in nuclear weapons.[35] Yassin Aref and Mohammed Hossain might never have become involved in a bizarre scheme to sell a missile launcher to imaginary terrorists in order to raise $50,000 to improve a pizzeria without the contrivance of Shahed Hussain (the informant in the Newburgh 4 case).[36] Tarik Shah (a jazz musician) and Rafiq Sabir (an ER doctor) might never have devised a plan to teach martial arts to potential jihadis without the intervention of an informant (an ex-con and former Black Panther).[37] Craig Monteilh blew the whistle after the FBI paid him to induce members of the Islamic Center of Irvine, California, to engage in jihadist activity (echoing the FBI's use of Shahed Hussain in upstate New York).[38] Hosam Smadi might never have attempted to attack a 60-story Dallas office building had undercover FBI agents not given him a fake bomb and car.[39] Shaker Masri might never have tried to go to Somalia for jihad had the confidential source not furnished money for the trip and a cover story about traveling to trade in gold.[40] Sami Hassoun might never have attempted an attack near Chicago's Wrigley Field had an undercover agent not paid him $2,700 and given him the fake bomb and a camcorder to videotape the site.[41] Jose Pimentel would not have had the money, technical ability, or mental capacity to make pipe bombs without an informant's help (part of the reason why only state, not federal, prosecutors brought charges).[42] A US Attorney also declined to prosecute Ahmed Ferhani and Mohamed Mamdouh, apparently believing that police informants had crossed the line into entrapment.[43] Walli Mujahidh and Abu Khalid Abdul-Latif might not have proceeded with their plan to attack a Seattle military recruitment center had an informer not given them firearms.[44] Matthew Llaneza might never have attacked an Oakland Bank of America building had an undercover agent not helped him build and try to detonate the "bomb."[45] Hafiz Khan might never have sent money to the Taliban but for the encouragement of David Mahmood Siddiqui, an FBI informant.[46] Harouna Touré and Idriss Abdelrahman might have stuck to drug trafficking had an informant not suggested involving al-Qaeda.[47]

The Accused[48]
Like Hamid Hayat, James Cromitie, and Narseal Batiste, many other accused indulged in hate speech, empty boasts, and grandiose schemes. The government emphasized these exaggerated threats in order to claim it was defending Americans from an existential threat. Hayat

repudiated the USA and praised Daniel Pearl's killers; Cromitie spouted anti-Semitism; Batiste praised the 9/11 attack, ludicrously asserting immunity from US law as a religious leader; Mehanna posed triumphantly at Ground Zero. Some were fantasists: Umer Hayat claimed to have seen a thousand terrorist trainees dressed as ninjas pole-vaulting across rivers in an underground training camp; Batiste planned a Moorish Nation of green-suited soldiers, wielding bows and arrows and jumping 20 feet into rivers. Batiste bragged he could destroy the Sears Tower and Empire State Building (because he had delivered packages to the former and worked installing drywall), and this would paralyze American communications. Like Batiste's and Cromitie's followers, many defendants were weak, dependent, with drug habits and criminal records, and nursing grievances about poverty and racism.

Seeking a sense of meaning through identification with a larger group and cause, many were easily manipulated. Three related cases are illustrative. Colleen LaRose was sexually abused by her father from the age of eight, married twice (the first time at 16), worked as a prostitute and abused drugs, and then lived for five years with Keith Gorman, caring for his father but, according to a neighbor, "mainly notorious for getting drunk and getting into fights."[49] She converted to Islam and surfed the Internet, "desperate to do something somehow to help" suffering Muslims. After corresponding for a year with an Egyptian living in Sweden, she agreed to marry him, stole Gorman's passport for her new fiancé, and flew to Sweden the day after Gorman's father died, declaring it would be "an honor & great pleasure to die or kill" for her new husband. "[O]nly death will stop me now that I am so close to the target" (Lars Vilks, the Swedish cartoonist who had caricatured Mohammed). (In 2017 Ali Charaf Damache, LaRose's husband, was extradited from Spain for trial in the US.[50]) Jamie Paulin-Ramirez had been married at least three times. After converting to Islam, she flew to Ireland with her 6-year-old son and, the next day, married an Algerian she had never met before, soon becoming pregnant by him. LaRose stayed with the couple for two weeks. Mohammad Hassan Khalid, born in Pakistan but raised in Maryland, began corresponding with LaRose when he was just 15 and soliciting funds for her.

Some defendants, like Batiste and Cromitie, were attracted by money, even just dress-up clothes, betraying their professed fervor for Islam (about which they knew virtually nothing) by drinking or smoking dope. Others, like Laguerre Payen (in Newburgh), exhibited signs of mental illness or disability. Mohamed Alessa, 20, had had anger management problems from childhood but refused medication, leading to his expulsion from ten schools. He told his informant: "My soul cannot rest until I shed blood." "I wanna, like, be the world's known terrorist [sic]."[51] He and a 24-year-old friend were arrested at JFK Airport trying to fly to Somalia. Ahmed Ferhani had been hospitalized with mental illness 20–30 times in 15 years (once involuntarily by the police), had abused drugs, and had a criminal record. He pleaded guilty to a plan to attack New York synagogues, concocted with an undercover NYPD officer.[52] Mansoor Arbabsiar, a naturalized US citizen from Iran, suffered from bipolar disorder.[53] Depression confined him to bed for days; during one manic episode on an airplane he treated the pilot, flight attendants, and nearby passengers to expensive bottles of perfume. He admitted accepting $100,000 from the Iranian Quds Force to pay the Mexican Los Zetas gang $1.5 million to traffic drugs, murder the Saudi Ambassador to the USA, and bomb the Israeli embassy in the USA and the Israeli and Saudi embassies in Argentina. Jose Pimentel was unemployed, smoked dope, and freeloaded on an uncle after his mother threw him out; he once tried to circumcise himself. Rezwan Ferdaus told undercover agents he was anxious, depressed, and troubled by "intrusive thoughts."[54] A Massachusetts police officer once found him standing immobile in the road, having wet his pants. With two undercover agents, he planned to use drones to fly explosives into the Pentagon and the Capitol. He declaimed to the court before sentencing: "I the other, the uniquely dressed, the lone man in these shoes, I speak of humanity. No dehumanization can serve as justification for inhumanity in other places." "I hope for better and, God willing, I will aspire for more." (He got 17 years under a plea agreement.)

Just as Batiste could not have toppled the Sears Tower, other accused lacked the resources and technical knowledge to execute equally harebrained schemes. Ralph Deleon, a 23-year-old Philippine American convert to Islam, wanted to drive a truck loaded with C-4 explosives "into, like, the baddest military base." "I'm gonna take out a whole base. Might as well make it, like, big, ya know." He was arrested on his way to fight in Afghanistan, via Mexico City and Istanbul.[55] Shahawar Siraj, 22, bragged he would blow up Staten Island's four bridges, three police stations, and prison to "teach these bastards a lesson" (unconsciously parodying the famous London Times headline: "Heavy Fog in Channel. Continent Cut Off"). Pointing to the New York skyline, Siraj gloated "See, two twin towers are already gone, you cannot see no more" and laughed. Driving past a policeman, he taunted sotto voce: "Hello, pig. Hi, pig. By [sic], pig … You, pig, will learn the lesson someday." He wanted nuclear weapons to make "a big explosion that can take over the, like, army, army of America … with one punch." Russell Defreitas, a 63-year-old retired JFK Airport cargo worker who lived by selling used books on New York City street corners and shipping broken home appliances to Guyana, boasted he could detonate an explosion in the airport's fuel storage containers and pipes, which "will take out the whole entire area. The whole of Kennedy will go up in smoke."[56] The plan included distracting security guards by releasing a horde of rats inside the main terminal. But all he ever did was drive around the airport perimeter with the informant and parrot President Bush's embarrassing claim: "mission accomplished." The pipeline had safety mechanisms to prevent cascading explosions, and the fuel may not have been explosive.

Frederick Thomas, 73, a self-styled Georgia militia member, proclaimed at a secretly recorded meeting that he had a "bucket list" of government employees, politicians, business leaders, and media figures who had to be "taken out" to "make the country right again."[57] "There is no way for us, as militiamen, to save this country, to save Georgia, without doing something that's highly, highly illegal: murder." He surveilled Internal Revenue Service and Bureau of Alcholol, Tobacco, Firearms and Explosives buildings in Atlanta, and described the explosives and weapons the group would need to blow up buildings and kill employees, modeling his plot on an online novel, *Absolved*, by Mike Vanderboegh, a former Alabama militia leader. (Vanderboegh denounced this "Alzheimer's gang." "I don't understand what was going on in the minds of these Georgia idiots.") An undercover agent sold Dan Roberts, 67, a silencer and parts to make a rifle fully automatic. Samuel Crump, 68, described how to make ricin, and Ray Adams, 65, provided the ingredients. One had worked for the Centers for Disease Control and Prevention, the other for the Department of Agriculture. But a government expert said manufacturing and weaponizing ricin was "beyond the capabilities of anyone except professional weapons scientists." And before sentencing, Adams protested: "I would not have hurt anyone. I get angry at the government sometimes, but no more than anyone else." Crump maintained: "there were only words, no actions." "There's no way I could make that stuff."

But notwithstanding their character defects, technical incompetence, and informants' seductions, some accused, like the Newburgh 4, clearly intended to commit the serious crimes with which they were charged. And they shared the government's exaggerated claims about the harm they would inflict. Assem Hammoud wanted to bomb a Port Authority Trans Hudson (PATH) train to destroy New York's Holland Tunnel, even though he never even began surveillance and could not have flooded lower Manhattan, as the sensationalist *New York Daily News* warned.[58] (New York City is still above sea level, notwithstanding the real threat of climate change.) The three Duka brothers and their four associates really did want to attack Fort Dix, even though they had been cheered on by two informants and were still waiting for a fatwa and were attempting to buy automatic weapons.[59] One pronounced that "when someone is trying to attack your religion, your way of life, then you go jihad." Another hoped to "hit four, five, six Humvees and light the whole place up and retreat completely without any losses." Although a confidential source (CS) gave Sami Osmakac money to buy weapons from a UA, the accused was recorded planning to detonate a bomb and then "get in somewhere where there's a lot of people" and take hostages to exchange for the release of Muslim prisoners.[60] He also wanted to blow up bridges linking Tampa to the Florida mainland, which "will crush the whole economy." Mohamed Osman Mohamud, 19, wanted to detonate a van full of explosives at a crowded Christmas tree lighting ceremony in downtown Portland, Oregon (although the bomb was a dud supplied by UAs).[61] He persevered in his plan, even after being stopped at the airport because he was on the FBI watch list, telling agents he had wanted to go to Yemen. Rebuffing the UAs' suggestion that he perform jihad by prayer, he insisted on being "operational." He did not care that women and children would be killed: Americans should "be attacked in their own element with their families, celebrating the holidays." He hoped for 10,000 victims: "I want whoever is attending that event … to leave either dead or injured." "It's gonna be a fireworks show … a spectacular show." He was arrested as he dialed a cell phone to set off the fake bomb and yelled "Allahu Akbar!"

Some brazenly defied the law. Abdel Hameed Shehadeh repeatedly tried to fight abroad.[62] In June 2008 he flew to Pakistan on a one-way ticket, but was denied entry and was interviewed by the FBI on his return. Four months later he was rejected by an Army recruiter for concealing the Pakistan trip. The same month he was turned back from Jordan. On his return to the USA, he told the FBI he had tried to contact al-Awlaki. The next year he bought a ticket to Dubai; he also told the FBI he wanted to go to Somalia but was on the no-fly list. He boasted to boyhood friends (who were FBI confidential informants) he wanted to die a martyr. In 2010 he told the FBI he wanted to join the Taliban. He was finally arrested trying to fly to Hawaii.

Farooque Ahmed practiced using firearms and was videotaped telling a confidential informant he wanted to kill Americans in Afghanistan and "of course" was willing to die as a martyr.[63] But first he surveilled Washington DC Metrorail stations, targeted one, and diagramed where he would place the bombs to kill the most people. Antonio Martinez, a Muslim convert, also wanted to fight American soldiers abroad.[64] But first, working with a CS, he planned to bomb a military recruiting station outside Baltimore. Although the CS repeatedly offered him opportunities to withdraw, Martinez insisted: "I came to you about this, brother." He was arrested as he tried to detonate the fake bomb. Khalid Aldawsari confided to his diary:

> I excelled in my studies in high school [in Saudi Arabia] in order to take advantage of an opportunity for a scholarship to America. And now, after mastering the English language, learning how to build explosives, and continuous planning to target the infidel Americans, it is time for jihad.[65]

Studying in Lubbock, he researched the Dallas homes of George Bush and three Americans who had served in Abu Ghraib, declaring in an email: "one operation in the land of the infidels is equal to ten operations against occupying forces in the land of Muslims." His other targets included reservoirs and dams in Colorado and California. He made extensive, partly successful attempts to buy bomb-making materials. Ulugbek Kodirov emigrated from Uzbekistan after being accepted by Columbia Medical School only to end up in a minimum wage job in Alabama when poor English kept him from matriculating.[66] Claiming to have acted at the direction of the Islamic Movement of Uzbekistan, he made repeated threats to a CS to kill President Obama and bought an automatic rifle and four hand grenades from a UA. Amine el Khalifi first told a UA he wanted to bomb a Washington DC restaurant frequented by military officials, shooting those who fled the blast.[67] But the day he and the UA detonated a bomb in a West Virginia quarry, el Khalifi decided on a suicide attack on the Capitol. Frustrated by repeated questions about his commitment to the plot, he angrily told the agent to "stop asking him if he wanted to do this." The next month he donned a vest containing what he believed to be a bomb and was arrested walking toward the Capitol. Quazi Nafis, the son of a Bangladeshi banker, came to the USA to study in Missouri but ended up working in a New York hotel.[68] Claiming close connections to al-Qaeda, he told a UA he wanted to "destroy America" through its economy. "I don't want something that's like small. I just want something big. Something very big. Very, very, very, very big, that will shake the whole country." "You know what, this election might even stop." He assembled what he thought were explosives, parked them in a car next to the Federal Reserve on Wall Street, walked to a nearby hotel to record a video, and was arrested trying to detonate the fake bombs.

Interrogation and Other Procedural Issues

If reliance on informants was the most distinctive and pervasive feature of terrorism prosecutions, some cases also exhibited troubling interrogations.[69] Hamid Hayat was Mirandized only after being questioned for hours – and then continued answering questions during a night-long interview after "waiving" his right to a lawyer. Ahmed Ghailani was subjected to EITs more than a hundred times in a secret CIA prison. After being photographed naked, Sulaiman abu Ghaith was interrogated during the 14-hour flight from Amman to New York while wearing a hood and blackout goggles.[70] He claimed he was given only a small bottle of water and a single orange, soiled himself trying to urinate with his hands shackled to his waist, and was forced to clean the small airplane toilet wearing those restraints. Abdallah Higazy was accused of having an aviation radio in his Millennium Hilton hotel room near the World Trade Center on 9/11 after an FBI agent extracted a false confession by threatening that Egyptian security officers would abuse his family in Cairo.[71] Ahmed Omar Abu Ali, accused of plotting to assassinate President Bush, claimed he had been tortured by Saudi security officials asking questions posed by FBI agents.[72] After a six-day hearing, ED Va Judge Lee admitted the confession. A juror later reported being convinced by a 13-minute videotape made after the interrogation that Abu Ali had not been tortured: "He was laughing; he was joking. It was chilling. He was leaning back, rocking in his chair, asking for water, laughing, smiling. He wasn't moving as though he was in pain." Mohamed al-'Owhali claimed he had been insulted and threatened with violence against himself and his family during interrogation by American and Kenyan officials in Nairobi, but the Second Circuit upheld his conviction.[73] Mansoor Arbabsiar's lawyers questioned whether his consent to 12 days of interrogation without counsel had been knowing and voluntary, given a defense expert's finding that he "was likely cycling in and out of manic episodes during the period."[74] But he pleaded in exchange for a reduced sentence.

Nevertheless, prosecutors and judges ameliorated or corrected some of these abuses. After harsh interrogations, the FBI Mirandized Ahmed Abdulkadir Warsame,[75] Mohamed Ibrahim Ahmed,[76] and Nazih Abdul-Hamed al-Ruqai,[77] and had "clean teams" question them. SDNY Judge Castel scrupulously investigated the prosecution claim that Ahmed's "clean" interrogation was untainted by its "dirty" predecessor. The prosecution refrained from using even Ghailani's "clean team" interrogation, and Judge Kaplan excluded Abebe's testimony as poisoned by Ghailani's mistreatment. Higazy's "confession" was thrown out, and he was compensated for his mistreatment (see Chapter 6).

Defendants raised other objections. Hamid Hayat offered experts who challenged the prosecution expert's interpretation of the Arabic prayer in his wallet. A prosecution "expert," who testified that the Liberty City 7 were in the fourth and final stage of an invariant "radicalization process," was exposed as an advocate of regime change in Iran. Tarek Mehanna's lawyers undermined the qualifications of Evan Kohlmann, the prosecution's expert witness.

After the Second Circuit overturned Sheik Mohammed Ali Hassan al-Moayad's conviction for conspiracy to support al Qaeda and Hamas because the trial judge had improperly admitted prejudicial evidence – thereby nullifying the accused's 75-year sentence – prosecutors accepted a plea to material support, and a new trial judge sentenced him to time served.[78] A District Court dismissed some of the terrorism charges and ordered a new trial for Karim Koubriti and two others because prosecutors failed to disclose exculpatory evidence; and the DoJ took the unprecedented step of prosecuting US Attorney Richard Convertino for this misconduct (though it failed to convict him).[79] After Edward Snowden's exposure of National Security Agency (NSA) spying, Solicitor General Donald B. Verrilli Jr. assured the Supreme Court the government would disclose electronic surveillance to accused. When Verrilli discovered this was *not* DoJ policy, he directed US Attorneys to inform defendants if evidence had been obtained by this means, and several defendants subsequently raised the issue.[80]

Political Pressure for Military Commissions

The greatest threat to criminal prosecutions was external rather than internal: demands by Congressional Republicans and conservative media that the government hold terrorism suspects as enemy combatants (ECs) and try them in military commissions (if at all). Although Attorney General Holder bowed to political pressure by withdrawing criminal charges against five high-value detainees (discussed in Chapter 4), he refused to do so in the successful prosecutions of Ghailani and several others, despite harsh criticism. Sen. DeMint (R-SC) declared that Umar Farouk Abdulmutallab (the "underwear bomber") should have "immediately been interrogated military-style rather than given the rights of an American and lawyers. We probably lost valuable information."[81] (He offered no evidence for this supposition.) Sen. Lieberman (D-Ct) called that prosecution a "very serious mistake." Sen. Bond (R-Mo) said "trying terrorists in federal court comes at a high price." The *Wall Street Journal* asserted that interrogating Abdulmutallab as an EC should have been "a far higher priority."

Even though Abdulmutallab pleaded guilty, the debate revived after Faisal Shahzad attempted to bomb Times Square.[82] Sen. McCain (R-Az) said "our top priority should be finding out what intelligence [suspects] have that could prevent future attacks and save American lives ... [not] telling them they have a right to remain silent." Sen. Bond agreed that "we've got to be far less interested in protecting the privacy rights of these terrorists." Rep. Lamar Smith (R-Tex), a ranking member of the House Judiciary Committee (HJC), warned that "treating terrorists like common criminals makes Americans less safe." But Rep. Adam Smith (D-Wa) (no relative!) retorted that "we have proven in this country for a long, long time that you can get very valuable information out of people after you Mirandize them." And the conservative political commentator Glenn Beck (surprisingly) reminded listeners that Shahzad was "a citizen of the United States, so I say we uphold the laws and the Constitution on citizens ... We don't shred the Constitution when it's popular." Sen. Lieberman responded with legislation to strip American citizenship from those charged with terrorism.

A third iteration of this debate occurred when the government tried Ahmed Abdulkadir Warsame in SDNY, after interrogating him aboard a Navy ship for nearly 10 weeks.[83] The MC chief prosecutor met DoJ officials in New York to urge them to let him prosecute Warsame. Rep. McKeon (R-Ca) said "the transfer of this terrorist detainee directly contradicts Congressional intent and the will of the American people." Senate Minority Leader McConnell (R-Ky) warned that "the administration has purposefully imported a terrorist into the U.S. and is providing him all the rights of a U.S. citizen in court ... harming the national security ... Why is a man who is a known terrorist and enemy of the United States, being afforded these protections?" Sen. Durban (D-Ill) retorted that "second guess[ing]" President Obama was "totally unfair." And the *Washington Post*, *Los Angeles Times*, and *New York Times* endorsed the decision to prosecute in a civilian court. Warsame later pleaded guilty and cooperated with many other investigations.[84]

Even after Waad Raadan Alwan, an Iraqi arrested in the USA, pleaded guilty to material support and got a 40-year sentence for helping to secure life sentences for his co-conspirators, Sen. McConnell argued that "the military should have had custody ... to begin with for purpose of intelligence, detention and punishment."[85] At Guantánamo he could have been "fulsomely [*sic*] and continuously interrogated without having to overcome the objections of his civilian lawyers." Rep. Rogers (R-Mich), chair of the House Permanent Select Committee on Intelligence (HPSCI), said "the U.S. court system is not the appropriate venue" for Sulaiman abu Ghaith.[86] Sens. Graham (R-SC) and Ayotte (R-NH) agreed. But several who had successfully opposed trying the HVDs in SDNY now supported prosecuting abu Ghaith there. Julie Menin, former chair of NYC's Community Board 1, called this a "very different situation," as did Mayor Bloomberg (the mentor she was seeking to succeed). And Rep. King (R-NY) hoped abu Ghaith would "face swift and certain justice." (He was convicted and sentenced to life.) Sens. Graham and Ayotte also opposed the prosecution of Nazih Abdul-Hamed al-Ruqai.[87] Sen. Chambliss (R-Ga) warned: "he is going to get lawyered up ... he's going to be silent and we're not going to be able to gather any information from this individual." But Rep. Ruppersberger (D-Md), HPSCI ranking member, was "sure with the evidence we have right now, we would win the case." And Rep. Schiff (D-Ca) said "nothing must be done to compromise ... the ability of the Justice Department prosecutors to seek justice." (Al-Ruqai died before he could be tried.)

After Ahmed abu Khattala, principal suspect in the 2012 siege of the US consulate in Benghazi, was seized by the USA in Libya, interrogated on board ship for 13 days, and indicted in Washington DC, Sen. Graham said: "the last thing we want is for this terrorist suspect to hear the statement 'you have the right to remain silent.'"[88] He and Sens. McCain, Rubio (R-Fla) and Cruz (R-Tex) wanted abu Khattala held in Guantánamo. Rep. McCaul (R-Tex), House Homeland Security Committee chair, complained that "rather than prosecuting a war, we're prosecuting criminal cases." "We have brought a foreign terrorist and given him due process rights under our Constitution here in the United States, right down the street from where you and I are in the nation's capital." Rep. Rogers said: "We want intelligence that is useful – 10 days is not enough … To me these are enemy combatants and if we start saying they're criminals, I don't know how you fight back." But the Benghazi attack victims' relatives applauded the prosecution and were seconded by former MC chief prosecutor Morris Davis and the *Washington Post*. In his *Washington Post* column, Dana Milbank praised the fact that at the bail hearing abu Khattala "was treated with dignity: He sat unshackled, and, through his lawyer, he entered a request for a halal diet and an Arabic-language Koran." His lawyers sought to exclude his statements to the FBI "clean team" on the ground that he had been beaten badly during his apprehension, interviewed by the CIA for four days, and made an ambiguous statement waiving his right to counsel, and the 13-day presentment delay was unreasonable. On August 16, 2017, DDC Judge Cooper denied those motions. The following month he allowed the prosecution to introduce some but not all evidence of "other acts" related to the charges.

The debate replayed after the arrest of Dzhokhar Tsarnaev for the Boston Marathon bombing.[89] Rep. Rogers urged the FBI not to Mirandize him. Rep. King declared him an EC because "there are so many questions unanswered. There are so many potential links to terrorism here. Also, the battlefield is not the United States." Sen. Graham said: "the least of our worries is a criminal trial which will likely be held years from now." (It was held in less than two.) "Under the law of war, we can hold this suspect as a potential enemy combatant not entitled to Miranda warnings or the appointment of counsel." Sens. Ayotte, McCain, and Angus King (I-Me) agreed. But Sen. Levin (D-Mich), chair of the Senate Armed Services Committee (SASC), said the laws of war did not apply because Tsarnaev was not "part of any organized group." Sen. Feinstein (D-Ca) agreed it would be unconstitutional to try him in an MC. Graham replied that Tsarnaev still could be held because of "his radical Islamist ties and the fact that Chechens are all over the world fighting with al-Qaeda." The *New York Times* ridiculed Graham's "thermal imaging device for detecting" Tsarnaev's motivation and criticized the senator and his colleagues for opposing "access to a lawyer or the fundamental rights that distinguish this country from authoritarian regimes." Andrew Rosenthal wrote in his *New York Times* column that "the argument that we should treat Mr. Tsarnaev as an enemy combatant boils down to his religious and ethnic origin." Charles Lane wrote in his *Washington Post* column that "insisting on reading [Tsarnaev] his rights immediately ... seems formalistic." But the *Post* called much of the criticism not "very intelligent." The statement by Graham and his colleagues was "breathtakingly shortsighted." It "matter[ed] greatly whether Mr. Tsarnaev ... is held accountable for his alleged crimes – and that the United States is seen by the world as capable of responding to a serious terrorist attack under the rule of law." The *Wall Street Journal* cavalierly dismissed "due process": "the greatest danger to liberty would be to allow more such attacks that would inspire an even greater public backlash against Muslims or free speech or worse." Sen. Graham ultimately conceded that "military commission trials are not available in cases like this." But Rep. Rogers remained adamant:

> We can't have, in a case like this, the judiciary deciding, because it's on television and it might look bad for them ... that they were going to somehow intercede in this. It's confusing, it is horrible God-awful policy, and dangerous to the greater community.

The *St. Louis Post-Dispatch* responded: "the tough thing about the United States Constitution is that it contains no asterisks ... when there's confusion about how something should be applied, the Supreme Court gets to decide ... this is called the rule of law ... [and] is the glory of the nations that follow it."

After Tsarnaev's lawyers effectively conceded his guilt, the jury quickly convicted. He was sentenced to death.

When Spain extradited Ali Charaf Damache to stand trial in New York for attempting to murder Lars Vilks (the Swede who caricatured Mohammed), the *New York Times* praised this as the "right move."[90] "[F]ederal prosecutors have won about 200 'jihadist related' terrorism and national security cases since Sept. 11," while "not a single Sept. 11 defendant has been convicted under the Guantánamo military commissions." And HRF lawyer Raha Wala wrote the *Times* that sending suspects to Guantánamo for detention and MC trial "is not only ineffective policy, but also a travesty of justice."

Defiant Defendants

If conservative politicians and pundits sought to abort criminal trials, defiant defendants tried to politicize them. Some invoked their right to free speech. Tarek Mehanna claimed he had just translated others' words, maintaining his innocence through to sentencing. Ali al-Timimi was convicted of conspiracy, attempting to aid the Taliban, soliciting treason, and encouraging others to wage war against the USA through his North Virginia mosque sermons and internet writings. At sentencing, he declared himself a "prisoner of conscience": "I will not admit guilt nor seek the court's mercy … because I am innocent." He got life imprisonment.[91] Although Sami al-Arian claimed to have been prosecuted for his pro-Palestinian views, he pleaded to one count of conspiring to support the Palestinian Islamic Jihad (designated as a terrorist organization) in exchange for a sentence close to time served.[92] Abu Hamza al-Masri's lawyer admitted that his client, the imam of London's Finsbury Park mosque, had said "a lot of harsh things" about the U.S.," but "these are views, not acts."[93] Al-Masri "needed to be outrageous" to "reach the entire spectrum of his community," where he sought to be a moderating influence, criticizing al-Qaeda and holding "a lot of independent views." But he was convicted for his role in kidnapping tourists in Yemen, including two American citizens. Although he claimed to have been just "a mouthpiece" for the kidnappers, he later told a victim that "Islamically," kidnapping "is a good thing to do." He was sentenced to life.

Sulaiman abu Ghaith insisted he had given religious speeches only at the request of Osama bin Laden (his father-in-law), who wanted him to make al-Qaeda fighters merciful because they had had a "hard life."[94] He had sent his pregnant wife and six children to Kuwait two days before the 9/11 attacks because "I had heard something would happen but I didn't know what," and he stayed in Afghanistan two weeks more because travel was difficult. He knew bin Laden was suspected in the attacks, but still "wanted to get to know that person." The day after the attack he appeared in a video holding an AK-47 and seated next to bin Laden, speaking from the latter's "quotes and points" and warning that "the storm of airplanes" would not abate. If "oppression befalls … any category of people, that category must revolt at some point." "Muslims must bear some responsibility to defend themselves." At the trial he said he hoped his speech would convince the USA to say, "let's go and sit down and talk and solve this problem." At sentencing, he refused to "ask for mercy from anyone except God."

> Islam is the religion that does not die when its followers die or get killed, and it does not come to a stop when they get captured or imprisoned. At the same moment where you are shackling my hands and intend to bury me alive, you are the same time unleashing the hands of hundreds of

Muslim youth, and you are removing the dust of their minds ... soon, and very soon, the whole world will see the end of these theater plays that are also known as trials.

He got life.

Lynne Stewart was convicted of violating her Special Administrative Measures affirmation by helping her client, Sheikh Omar Abdel-Rahman (imprisoned for conspiring to commit terrorist attacks after the first World Trade Center bombing) authorize followers in Egypt to discuss resuming terrorist activities there.[95] While admitting her actions at sentencing, Stewart insisted "my only motive was to serve my client as his lawyer. What might have been legitimately tolerated in 2000–2001, was after 9/11 interpreted differently and considered criminal." She had been "naive" and "careless," "blind" to the fact that the government "could misunderstand and misinterpret my true purpose." Outside the courthouse she defiantly pronounced her 28-month sentence "a great victory against an overreaching government." "I hope the government realizes their error, because I am back out. And I am staying out until after an appeal that I hope will vindicate me." Two years in jail was not "anything to look forward to. But – as some of my clients once put it – I can do that standing on my head." The Second Circuit upheld her conviction but remanded for resentencing in three opinions totaling almost 100 pages, with Judge Walker denouncing the "breathtakingly low sentence." The day after losing her appeal Stewart told a television interviewer: "I would do it again. I might handle it differently, but I would do it again."

Reporting to jail, Stewart denounced the Second Circuit opinion and its timing "on the eve of the arrival of the tortured men from offshore prison in Guantánamo." Her sentence was a warning to lawyers to "toe very close to the line that the government has set out." "[T]his is a case that is bigger than just me personally." She comforted supporters: "This is the day they executed Joe Hill, and his words were, 'Don't mourn me, Organize.' I hope that will be the message that I send, too ... They can put me in jail, but my love, my ideas, my forcefulness I hope will remain with all of you. And I will return."

On remand, SDNY Judge Koeltl increased her sentence to ten years. Although supporters had written 400 letters, her comments showed "the original sentence was not sufficient" because of her "lack of remorse." She retracted those comments before he pronounced the heavier sentence, because prison was far worse than she had imagined. On appeal, the Second Circuit upheld the new sentence:

From the moment she committed the first act for which she was convicted, through her trial, sentencing and appeals, Stewart has persisted in exhibiting what seems to be a stark inability to understand the seriousness of her crimes ... the breadth and depth of the danger in which ... [they had] placed the lives and safety of unknown innocents, and the extent to which they constituted an abuse of her trust and privilege as a member of the bar.

Judge Koeltl released her at the end of 2013 on the BoP's recommendation and finding that she was suffering from terminal cancer.

Other defendants tried to use their trials as political platforms. Aafia Siddiqui, accused of shooting at American soldiers after being captured in Afghanistan, asked prison guards to send her food to her son in Afghanistan, fearing he was being starved.[96] At her competency hearing, the prosecution's psychiatrist concluded she "most likely fabricated reported psychiatric symptoms." She repeatedly interrupted the hearing: "I didn't fire any bullets." "I'm really not against America." "I'm not psychotic." SDNY Judge Berman found her competent. After prosecutors noted the lack of outbursts, she "became much more loquacious, outspoken and difficult in the courtroom." During voir dire she declared: "I'm boycotting the trial ... there's too many injustices." She refused to cooperate with her lawyers, maintaining she would defend herself "whenever God wills but not in this courtroom. There's too much lies and hypocrisy here." She was ejected numerous times during the 14-day trial. Over her lawyers' objections she testified that she had never held a weapon and had been trying to escape Afghan custody because she feared torture. "I don't know how to make a dirty bomb." "[I] couldn't kill a rat myself." After being convicted she shouted: "this is a verdict coming from Israel and not from America." During discussion of the sentencing date, she again repudiated her lawyers. At sentencing, she rolled her eyes and made dismissive gestures when a lawyer argued for her. In a long, rambling statement she denied being mentally ill and forgave the judge and the soldier who had shot her. "I am a Muslim, but I do love America, too. I do not want any bloodshed." She was sentenced to 86 years. After the Second Circuit affirmed, she wrote Judge Berman seeking to terminate another appeal: "I refuse to participate in this system of total injustice that has punished and tortured me repeatedly, and continues to do so, without my having committed a crime."

Barry Walter Bujol Jr. was arrested after boarding a ship in Texas with a GPS, telephone, calling cards and military compass, all obtained from an informant, which he planned to give to al-Qaeda in Yemen.[97] He wrote al-Awlaki: "I've been searching adamantly for information about jihad and my responsibility as a Muslim in America. I have been convinced beyond a doubt that I need to step up to the plate and contribute in some form or fashion." After three failed attempts to reach Yemen, he used a false identity card obtained from the informant to gain access to the ship, leaving his wife a video saying he had met someone from AQAP and was going for jihad. After SD Tex Judge Hittner banned Bujol from communicating with the court, he wrote the *Houston Chronicle*:

> In all the time and money squandered on this terrorist extravaganza sponsored by your tax dollars, all the government could finally do was coax me to take a knapsack of items to the informant's friends ... I just want to be left alone, to be a father, a husband and to mind my own business ... I tried to leave the United States as an expression of not only a desire to determine my own destiny but also as an expression of disdain for American foreign policy.

He opted to be tried by Judge Hittner, fired his court-appointed lawyer, and told the court:

> I did have radical Islamic views, and I was interested in leaving the United States of America ... not to harm the U.S. or U.S. nationals ... but simply to express my discontent and displeasure with my tax dollars and what I was doing as a citizen with foreign policy objectives I didn't agree with.

He was convicted after a four-day trial in which he did not testify or present witnesses, and was sentenced to the 20-year maximum.

Naser Jason Abdo obtained conscientious objector status on the eve of his deployment to Afghanistan, after concluding that Islam prohibited his service in any war.[98] But before he could be discharged from the Army, he was referred to a court-martial for possessing child pornography and responded by going AWOL from Fort Campbell, Kentucky. When he was arrested near Fort Hood, Texas, police found a pistol, shotgun shells, an article on "How to Make a Bomb in your Kitchen," timers, a pressure cooker, a shopping list of explosives, and a military uniform with Fort Hood patches in his possession. Abdo admitted planning to attack the base "because I don't appreciate what my unit did in Afghanistan," and he shouted support for Nidal Hassan (who had committed the Fort Hood massacre). He was also accused of spitting blood on a jailer and other officers. After being sentenced to life, he declared: "I will continue until the day the dead are called to account for their deeds."

Several who defied the criminal justice system at the outset ended up pleading guilty. Najibullah Zazi bought bomb ingredients in Colorado and drove to New York to plant bombs in subways but aborted the plot when he realized he was under surveillance.[99] Declaring "I have nothing to do with this" and calling the allegations "more shocking every hour," he submitted to lengthy questioning by the FBI, insisting he had nothing to hide, and pleaded not guilty. But four months later he changed his plea, agreeing to cooperate in the prosecution of his alleged co-conspirators. One of them, Zarein Ahmedzay, also pleaded guilty but pronounced that the Zionist conspiracy "destroying this country from within" was a greater threat than al-Qaeda. The other, Adis Medunjanin, maintained his innocence. He had sought to evade arrest in a car chase that reached 100 mph, during which he phoned 911 and shouted: "There is no God but Allah and Muhammed is his messenger. This is Adis. We love death more than you love life." After the arrest he called himself a prisoner of war (POW) and asked to be exchanged for an American soldier held by the Taliban. He lectured interrogators on religion, trying to convert them to Islam. At the end of the trial, his lawyer said the three young men wanted to go to Afghanistan "to fulfill some romantic version of jihad" in retaliation for the oppression of Muslims in the USA. After a jury convicted Medunjanin on all counts, EDNY Judge Gleeson explained that a life sentence was mandatory on the explosives charge, but the defendant could seek leniency on the others. Instead, Medunjanin recited the Koran, denounced Abu Ghraib, waterboarding, and the killing of innocent civilians in Iraq, and concluded: "I had nothing to do with any subway plot or bombing plot whatsoever. I ask Allah to release me from prison." Judge Gleeson added 95 years to his life sentence.

Several accused tried to subvert the legal process. Daniel Boyd and his sons Dylan (22) and Zakariya (20), together with Hysen Sherifi, Ziyad Yaghi, Omar Aly Hassan, and Anes Subasic, were charged with conspiracy to provide material support and to murder, kidnap, and maim.[100] Several of them had made unsuccessful attempts to do jihad in the Middle East. After the three Boyds pleaded guilty and testified for the prosecution (receiving sentences of 18, 8 and 9 years), Sherifi, Yaghi, and Hassan were convicted. Dozens from the Raleigh, North

Carolina Muslim community made a five-hour round-trip to attend the sentencing hearing. Sherifi declared he was innocent and the prosecutors were tyrants. After getting 45 years, he was accused of plotting from jail with his brother Shkumbin and a female friend to pay an informant $5,000 to kill prosecution witnesses. They pleaded and agreed to testify against him, resulting in a second conviction and four life terms. Refusing the court-appointed lawyer, he said before sentencing: "the Koran is the truth that invalidates all other religions. If you do not submit [God] will severely judge you and on the day of judgment you will enter hellfire."

Before his trial for planning to bomb a bar in Chicago, Adel Daoud allegedly asked another inmate to arrange the killing of the UA who had supplied what Daoud thought was an explosive device.[101] In 2015 Yahya Farooq Mohammad was indicted for conspiring to travel to Yemen to give money to Anwar al-Awlaki.[102] Awaiting trial in prison, a year later he told an inmate he wanted to kill the judge. The inmate introduced him to an undercover FBI agent, to whom Mohammad's wife gave $1,000, promising that the rest of the money was coming from Dubai.

Three of the most notorious terrorists mixed defiance with guilty pleas. Zacarias Moussaoui (alleged to have been the twentieth 9/11 hijacker) pleaded guilty to six counts of conspiring with al-Qaeda, but vigorously fought the death penalty.[103] During jury selection for the penalty phase, he repudiated his lawyers as "enemies" because they were American, declaring "This trial is a circus … For four years I have waited. I will tell them the truth I know." Before one lunch break he shouted: "God curse you and America." Against his lawyers' advice, he testified that he and Richard Reid intended to fly a fifth plane into either the White House or the Sears Tower, though planning "was only in the most preliminary stages." He "consider[ed] every American to be my enemy" and was "grateful to be a member of al-Qaeda." "[E]very American is going to want my death because I want their death." After the jury found the facts rendering him eligible for the death penalty, Moussaoui shouted: "you will never get my blood. God curse your souls." Taking the stand again before the second part of the penalty phase, Moussaoui declared "no regret, no remorse." Witnesses expressing grief for 9/11 victims were "disgusting." Moussaoui was "regretful" that one man in the Pentagon had not died; the death of another "ma[d]e my day"; Timothy McVeigh was "the greatest American." Moussaoui had tried "to the best of my ability" to destroy the United States and would kill Americans "anytime, anywhere." He was ejected from the court-room shouting "death to the Jew" (referring to his own lawyer).

When the jury voted for a life sentence, Moussaoui exulted: "America, you lost! ... I won!" After victims' relatives testified at the sentencing, Moussaoui said Americans had "an amount of hypocrisy which is beyond any belief."

> You have branded me a terrorist or whatever, a criminal ... a thug. You should look at yourself first. I fight for my belief, and I'm a mujahid, and you think that you own the world, and I would prove it that you are wrong ... We will come back another day ... God save Osama bin Laden – you will never get him.

Early in his prosecution, Umar Farouk Abdulmutallab, the "underwear bomber," fired his lawyers and refused help from the standby lawyers ED Mich Judge Edmunds appointed.[104] At various times he yelled out that "Osama's alive," "Anwar" (al-Awlaki) was alive, and "the mujahedin will wipe out the U.S. cancer." He filed unusual motions, including one declaring he could "only be judged and ruled by the law of the Koran." After the judge remonstrated with him for wearing a T-shirt, he asked for a Yemeni robe with a traditional belt and dagger. But on the second day of trial he pleaded guilty to all counts, ensuring a sentence of life without parole. He maintained he had used:

> a blessed weapon to save the lives of innocent Muslims, for U.S. use of weapons of mass destruction on Muslim populations in Afghanistan, Iraq, Yemen and beyond. The United States should be warned that if they continue to persist and promote the blasphemy of Muhammad and the prophets, the United States should await a great calamity that will befall them through the hands of the mujahedin soon ... if you laugh at us now, we will laugh at you later on the last day of judgment.

At the sentencing hearing, he shouted "Allahu Akbar" five times, declaring Muslims were "proud to kill in the name of God, and that is what God told us to do in the Koran." Bin Laden and other dead al-Qaeda leaders were "alive and shall be victorious by God's grace." Attacks would continue "until the Jews are driven out of Palestine." "Today is a day of victory."

Although Faisal Shahzad almost managed to flee the country after failing to detonate a bomb in Times Square, he admitted his actions, waived his rights, cooperated with interrogators, and pleaded guilty.[105]

> I'm going to plead guilty 100 times over because until the hour the U.S. pulls its forces from Iraq and Afghanistan and stops the drone strikes in Somalia and Yemen and in Pakistan, and stops the occupation of Muslim lands, and stops killing Muslims, and stops reporting the Muslims to its government, we will be attacking U.S., and I plead guilty to that.

He chose Times Square on a Saturday evening, hoping to kill at least forty people. He planned to detonate a second bomb in New York two weeks later and keep doing so until he was captured or killed. He "would not consider it a crime" because he was "a Muslim soldier" and "the people select the government; we consider them all the same." "[T]he drone hits in Afghanistan and Iraq … they kill women, children. They kill everybody. It's a war. And in war, they kill people." After receiving the mandatory life sentence, he delivered a rambling denunciation, claiming for the first time that he had sought and been denied his Miranda rights.

> If I am given a thousand lives, I will sacrifice them all for the sake of Allah … [The U.S. military had] occupied the Muslim lands … we are proud terrorists, and we will keep on terrorizing you until you leave our land and people at peace … The Koran gives us the right to defend, and that's all what I'm doing … The defeat of the U.S. is imminent … Brace yourselves, because the war with Muslims has just begun … Blessed be [bin Laden] who will be known as no less than Saladin of the 21st century crusade, and blessed be those who give him asylum … Allahu Akbar.

Routinizing Terrorism Cases

Unlike these high-profile trials, most terrorism prosecutions resembled routine criminal cases. The material support statute facilitated conviction by eliminating the requirement of specific intent and encompassing a wide variety of behaviors, such as buying software for secure internet communications[106] or attempting to smuggle a fictitious member of Tehrik-e-Pakistan from Latin America into the USA.[107] The government had little difficulty convicting Somali Americans of supporting or trying to join al-Shabab by planning to travel to Somalia.[108] And like other criminal accused, most of those charged with terrorism offenses pleaded guilty in order to obtain a lower sentence. After being hyped as the "American Taliban," John Walker Lindh pleaded to one count of material support and one of carrying an explosive during commission of a felony, dropping his (clearly substantiated) claim of abuse in custody and accepting the 20-year maximum sentence in order to avoid the death penalty.[109] David Coleman Headley also escaped the death penalty for his alleged participation in a plot to murder Kurt Westergaard (who published a cartoon of Mohammed in the Danish newspaper *Morgenavisen Jyllands-Posten*), together with his involvement in the November 2008 attack in Mumbai (which killed 170, including six Americans), by pleading guilty and assisting the prosecution of his co-conspirator Tahawwur Husain Rana (who received a 35-year sentence).[110] By pleading guilty to the plot to kill Lars Vilks (who also caricatured Mohammed), Colleen LaRose got 10 years (with credit for 51 months in custody) instead of life. For helping convict LaRose, Jamie Paulin-Ramirez got eight years instead of ten, and Mohammad Hassan Khalid got five (and credit for three years served).[111]

Zachary A. Chesser and Jesse Morton threatened the writers of an episode of the television show *South Park* for ridiculing Mohammed by portraying him in a bear suit. Chesser also planted suspicious but innocent packages in public places to desensitize law enforcement in anticipation of leaving real bombs, and he twice tried to fly to Somalia (once with his infant son) to fight with al-Shabaab. After pleading guilty, Chesser got 25 years and Morton (facing more than 15) got 11.5.[112] Bryant Neal Vinas, a convert to Islam, pleaded to conspiring to murder US nationals abroad, material support, and military training, and cooperated in the prosecution of Zazi, Medunjanin, and Ahmedzay in exchange for lenience.[113] At his sentencing hearing more than eight years after being apprehended, the government praised him as "the single most valuable cooperating witness." Facing life, he got time served plus 90 days. Two of Dzhokhar Tsarnaev's friends – Dias Kadyrbayev and Khairullozhon Matanov – pleaded guilty to attempting to conceal evidence of Tsarnaev's guilt.[114]

Not all accused terrorists had the most effective representation: Hamid Hayat's lawyer was trying her first criminal case. But many received zealous expert advocacy. Ghailani's six lawyers (including a death penalty specialist, even though Ghailani did not face execution) helped him win acquittal from 284 of the 285 charges against him. Although Zacarias Moussaoui pleaded guilty, repeatedly disrupted the penalty phase, was his own worst enemy, and maligned his lawyers, they aggressively – and successfully – saved him from the death penalty.[115] Elizabeth Fink vigorously represented both Aafia Siddiqui and Ahmed Ferhani. Federal Public Defender Steven Wax, who exculpated Brandon Mayfield, energetically represented Mohamed Osman Mohamud.[116] Stanley Cohen constantly tested the boundaries in his representation of Mohamed Alessa and Carlos Almonte,[117] and especially abu Ghaith.[118] And the lawyers representing Dzhokhar Tsarnaev repeatedly (if unsuccessfully) sought a change of venue from Boston and strategically conceded their client's guilt in the hope of avoiding the death penalty.

If Judge Garland seemed hostile to Hamid and Umer Hayat, other judges displayed impartiality – criticizing prosecutors as well as defense counsel – and forbearance in handling difficult defendants. In his dissent from the Ninth Circuit's affirmance, Judge Tashima addressed issues not raised by Hamid because courts had a duty to "do justice." In the Newburgh 4 trial, Judge McMahon carefully dealt with material the jury should not have seen, repeatedly reprimanded the informant for evasive answers, and criticized the government for how it had used him, though she did not find entrapment. Judge Selya thoroughly explained to the jury how to distinguish Tarek Mehanna's constitutionally protected free speech from potentially criminal conduct. Judge Kaplan took the correct but politically unpopular step of excluding Abebe's testimony as fruit of the poisoned tree of Ghailani's coercive interrogation. D Colo Judge Kane ordered Jamshid Muhtorov released from custody the day after he petitioned for habeas because he had been held for more than five years without trial (only to have the order stayed by the Tenth Circuit).[119]

Other judges confronted even greater challenges. Zacarias Moussaoui oscillated between defiance and compliance, boastfully admitting and then denying guilt.[120] His erratic behavior repeatedly raised questions about his competence to stand trial. ED Va Judge Brinkema suspended Moussaoui's self-representation after he compared her to the Nazi SS. She had to eject him from court several times and then address the possibility that his disruptions had prejudiced the jury. She granted motions to let the defense interview some HVDs in Guantánamo and to preclude the death penalty (only to be reversed on appeal). She reprimanded the prosecution for suggesting that Moussaoui's "failure to act is sufficient for the death penalty." Threats to due process climaxed when a government lawyer violated Brinkema's explicit orders by giving trial transcripts to seven officials and coaching their testimony. The exasperated judge said that during more than two decades on the bench she had "never seen a more egregious violation of the rule about witnesses." Declaring that it affected both "the constitutional rights of this defendant" and "the integrity of the criminal justice system," she invited a defense motion to terminate the penalty phase and sentence

Moussaoui to life. After interviewing six of the seven witnesses who had been tampered with and uncovering further "egregious errors" – including efforts to prevent a defense witness from testifying – she said: "I don't think in the annals of criminal law there has ever been a case with this many significant problems." Overruling heated prosecution objections, she excluded the six tainted witnesses. After the jury made the factual findings necessary to let them vote on the death penalty, Brinkema persuaded Moussaoui to reverse his embrace of martyrdom. During the final phase, she warned the prosecution to moderate its emotional appeals to jurors and focus on *who* died on 9/11, not *how* they did so. Denying prosecution objections, she let nearly a dozen relatives of 9/11 victims testify for the defense. When the jury voted for life, Brinkema praised defense lawyers but also sought to comfort prosecutors: "the government wins when justice is done. Justice is not necessarily what the outcome is but how it was achieved." But passing sentence, she cut off Moussaoui's rambling tirade:

> Mr. Moussaoui, when this proceeding is over, everyone else in this room will leave. They are free to go anyplace they want … You will spend the rest of your life in a Supermax prison … you came here to be a martyr, in a great big bang of glory, but to paraphrase the poet T.S. Eliot, instead you will die with a whimper. [She silenced his interruption.] You will never get a chance to speak again and that's an appropriate and fair ending.

The Fourth Circuit denied his request to withdraw his guilty plea.

After Abdulmutallab fired his lawyers and insisted on representing himself, against the advice of ED Mich Judge Edmunds, she appointed standby lawyers to assist him during discovery.[121] When he disregarded their suggestions, Judge Edmunds directed the lawyers to continue receiving documents from the prosecution. Even after Abdulmutallab pleaded guilty, his lawyers persisted in opposing the mandatory life sentence.

Judge Kaplan (who had tried Ghailani) strived for balance in responding to a wide range of problems in the trial of abu Ghaith.[122] When the defendant sought to replace his Federal Public Defender with the flamboyant Stanley L. Cohen, Kaplan warned that Cohen was under federal indictment in Syracuse and federal investigation in Manhattan, creating a potential conflict of interest. (Cohen later pleaded guilty, accepting an 18-month sentence and disbarment.) Kaplan said several of Cohen's claims bordered on the frivolous: that prosecutors had gained access to privileged communications and the government had confused the accused with a Guantánamo detainee (despite the differences in name, age, national origin, and appearance). Kaplan admitted statements abu Ghaith made during his long plane trip, finding he had been advised of his rights before the "vast bulk of the questioning began." But over prosecutors' objections, Kaplan allowed the defense to submit questions to Khalid Sheikh Mohammed (KSM) and admitted the answers (while denying the request to have KSM testify). Kaplan also refused to allow anonymous testimony by a prosecution witness who had openly discussed his involvement in the alleged crimes. When a woman lost her job for serving on the jury, Kaplan appointed a lawyer at government expense to get her rehired. (The Second Circuit affirmed abu Ghaith's conviction.)

WD Wash Judge Coughenour struggled publicly over sentencing Ahmed Ressam, who had pleaded to conspiring to bomb Los Angeles Airport (LAX) in the Millennium plot.[123] Ressam initially fulfilled his plea agreement by cooperating in other investigations, but stopped after four years. Calling the decision the most agonizing of his career, Coughenour gave Ressam 22 years. He praised the government for choosing "the sunlight of a public trial" over a "secret military tribunal." "The tragedy of Sept. 11 shook our sense of security. Unfortunately some believe this renders our Constitution obsolete. If that view is allowed to prevail, the terrorists will have won." After the Ninth Circuit reversed and remanded, prosecutors asked for life, noting that Ressam had recanted his testimony in at least three cases. But Coughenour imposed the same sentence, finding that solitary confinement and repeated inter-rogation had provoked Ressam to cease cooperating. The Ninth Circuit reversed again, and the en banc Circuit agreed. (Dissenting, Judge Schroeder said: "our courts are well equipped to treat each offense and offender individually, and we should not create special sentencing rules and procedures for terrorists.") Coughenour capitulated, sentencing Ressam to 37 years, but criticized the government for shifting its pos-ition and demanding a more stringent sentence while acknowledging Ressam's cooperation. "The threat of terrorism is twofold. It threatens our security, and it challenges our values. Paramount among our values is justice for all persons, no matter how dangerous or reviled." If nearly a decade of solitary confinement had made Ressam defiant, the court had an "ethical responsibility" not to use that defiance as a justification for more punishment. "I will not sentence a man to 50 lashes with a whip and then 50 more for getting blood on the whip."

After Judge Lee sentenced Abu Ali to 30 years, the Fourth Circuit reversed (over a strong dissent by Judge Motz), finding the downward departure from the sentencing guidelines impermissible; ED Va Judge Lee then sentenced Abu Ali to life, which was affirmed.[124]

Like judges, jurors generally performed their difficult duties responsibly. Judges invested substantial resources in jury selection, as both sides sought to seat a sympathetic panel. During the Moussaoui penalty phase, Judge Brinkema spent five days choosing 67 potential jurors from a panel of 500. Judge Kaplan had 1,000 prospective jurors complete an 11-page questionnaire in the Ghailani trial, even though he disliked such surveys. Kaplan reviewed a panel of 540 to select jurors for abu Ghaith, seating a lawyer over prosecution objections that he had represented Guantánamo detainees. The venire for the Fort Dix 7 contained 1,500 people.[125] In the Boston Marathon bombing trial, Judge O'Toole denied three change of venue motions, but got both sides to accept a jury pool of 2,000.[126]

In Hamid Hayat's trial, Judge Garland dismissed defense criticism of jury deliberations, rejecting a juror's claim that her vote to convict had been coerced after nine days of deliberation and allegations of misconduct by the foreman and other jurors. But in other cases, jurors exercised the freedom to vote according to their consciences. A jury deliberated eight days before convicting the Newburgh 4. Rather than giving an Allen charge to jurors having difficulty reaching a verdict on Ghailani, Judge Kaplan affirmed their right to dissent. After deliberating for 13 days, a jury acquitted Sami al-Arian on eight counts and deadlocked on the rest.[127] When Youssef Megahed and Ahmed Mohamed were arrested for speeding near a military base, a search of their car trunk revealed bomb-making materials and a laptop with a video about bomb construction.[128] Mohamed pleaded guilty and got 15 years. But Megahed claimed ignorance of the trunk's contents and was acquitted. Although he had immigrated to the USA at 11, was just three credits short of his BA, and had applied for citizenship, Immigration and Customs Enforcement (ICE) sought to deport him because of the charge for which he had just been acquitted (as it had already done to an acquitted Liberty City defendant). Four jurors wrote to denounce this "blatant disregard" of their verdict. "This sure looks and feels like some sort of 'double jeopardy.'" After deliberating six days and convicting five of the Fort Dix 7 of some charges but acquitting them of attempted murder, the jury asked the judge to read a statement in court:[129]

This has been one of the most difficult things that we have ever had to do. During these last six days, we have held the fate of these five defendants in our hands, and we have not reached our conclusion lightly. The burden imposed on us has been heavy, but we are confident that our verdict has been reached fairly and impartially.

Dissenting jurors powerfully influenced many cases (if not Hamid Hayat's). After a six-month trial, a jury deliberated for another month before convicting Lynne Stewart on all charges.[130] One of the two holdouts wrote Judge Koeltl after the verdict that she had voted to convict "as a result of the fear and intimidation I was made to feel for my of life." Another juror, convinced of Stewart's guilt by a "smoking gun," also feared retaliation for his vote. Juries in the first two Liberty City trials deadlocked after deliberating 11 and 12 days. The foreman in the first trial attributed the fact that the jury "was evenly split on a lot of counts" to "just different takes by different people." After deliberating eight days, a jury acquitted Ghailani of 284 of the 285 counts. Speculating that this bizarre compromise verdict might have been necessary to convince the sole dissenter to vote for the single conviction, Judge Kaplan praised the jury for demonstrating "that American justice can be delivered calmly, deliberately and fairly, by ordinary people – people who are not beholden to any government, including this one."[131] DoJ also expressed its "respect" for the verdict.

In the prosecution of Holy Land Foundation for Relief and Development officials for material support of Hamas, the jury balked on the ninth day of deliberations when one member refused to vote; after ten more days, the jury acquitted on some counts and deadlocked on others.[132] When polled, two members maintained that the verdict did not accurately reflect their votes. Both had dozed during the trial; and one who fell asleep during deliberations voted guilty from the beginning, was confused by the evidence, and often declined to deliberate. The judge declared a mistrial. One juror, who had worked in military intelligence, said the panel was evenly split on most of the disputed charges. He regarded the entire prosecution as "a waste of time" because the government's case had "so many gaps" and "was strung together with macaroni noodles."

Osama Awadallah was arrested as a material witness ten days after 9/11, when FBI agents found a scrap of paper with his old phone number in the car left at Dulles Airport by Nawaz Alhazmi, a hijacker who had steered a plane into the Pentagon.[133] After appearing before a grand jury, Awadallah was charged with perjury for claiming not to remember another hijacker's name. Jury deliberations were so inflamed that shouting could be heard through the walls. The jury sent SDNY Judge Scheindlin many questions, such as "How do we do justice in this case? Please define reasonable doubt." She dismissed an ill juror, leaving a panel of 11, the least that could decide without the defense's consent. That afternoon the jury deadlocked, but Scheindlin urged them to continue. Two days later the jury asked her to replace a juror who admitted making up his mind before deliberations began. Questioned by Scheindlin, the dissenter – a former subway conductor turned nurse – insisted he was deliberating in good faith. "For the last six days, I felt like the eye of the storm." One juror had called him a terrorist sympathizer. "Everyone was completely convinced of [Awadallah's] guilt. I wasn't completely convinced of his innocence but I had reasonable doubts ... I'm not the brightest bulb on earth and I'm not the dimmest. I'm just an average guy, but I'm trying to do the right thing."

Scheindlin declared a mistrial, observing that "the dissenter just disagreed with [the other jurors] virtually throughout the deliberations, and he wasn't able to convince them and they weren't able to convince him. If we go around calling that a refusal to deliberate, we're essentially not accepting dissent."

CONCLUSION

Terrorism prosecutions since 9/11 both differed from and resembled other criminal cases. The considerable differences reflected the fact that, whereas criminal law is reactive – seeking to reduce crime by incapacitating perpetrators after the fact and deterring them and others from committing future crimes – the "war on terror" sought to anticipate and prevent terrorist acts.[134] It did so in part because it was responding to the worst attack on the mainland in US history, which was committed by suicidal terrorists who could not be deterred, generating fears of another similar or even worse atrocity. But in its effort to prevent terrorism, the criminal justice system had to charge inchoate crimes. Indeed, only a few suspects were prosecuted for committing terrorist acts, and only some of those succeeded in inflicting harm. (In addition to Ghailani and Tsarnaev, discussed above, the latter included Iranian cybercriminals,[135] Paul Anthony Ciancia's 2013 attack at LAX,[136] the San Bernardino shootings by Rizwan Farook and Tashfeen Malik,[137] Omar Mateen's massacre at the Pulse nightclub in Orlando,[138] Ahmad Khan Rahimi's New York City bombing,[139] Dahir

Adan's shooting in a Minnesota mall,[140] Esteban Santiago's shooting at the Fort Lauderdale Airport,[141] and Sayfullo Saipov's truck attack in lower Manhattan.[142] Counterterrorism officials failed to anticipate *any* of these. And criminal prosecutions were impossible in some: the Iranians were charged in absentia; and Farook, Malik, Mateen and Adan died in the attacks.)

The focus on inchoate crimes had two consequences. First, the government greatly increased its use of the material support statute (passed shortly before 9/11 but rarely used until afterwards), obviating the need to prove an actual agreement to act (as in conspiracy) or a significant step (as in attempt) or specific intent to do harm.[143] This allowed the USA (unlike European countries) to convict anyone who sought to support or join designated terrorist organizations operating abroad. The Liberty City convictions rested on theatrical "oaths" administered by an informant pretending to represent a terrorist organization. Because prosecutors could not point to terrorist acts, they used other tactics to sway (even inflame) juries: quoting hateful speech by the accused (which was protected by the First Amendment) and invoking arch villains (Osama bin Laden), terrorist organizations (al-Qaeda), and the "war on terror's" defining event – the 9/11 attacks. (José Padilla, initially accused by Attorney General Ashcroft of intending to detonate a "dirty bomb," was convicted only of having sworn *bayat* (an oath of allegiance) to bin Laden, whom prosecutors repeatedly named during the trial.[144])

The government relied far more heavily on informants in "war-on-terror" prosecutions than it did in most other criminal cases: to excite the target's initial interest in terrorist activity and sustain that commitment when it flagged; and to provide the plan and means to execute the crime, which the target otherwise lacked, even furnishing (inoperable) weapons and (dummy) explosives.[145] (By contrast, when determined terrorists independently sought to commit atrocities, and sometimes succeeded, informants played no role in obtaining advance intelligence, according to an investigation by three prominent conservative lawyers.[146]) Informants influenced targets – often strongly – by force of personality, relative age, pretensions to Islamic piety and militancy, alleged connections to foreign terrorist groups, flashy clothes and cars, and, of course, promises of money, often far more than the targets had ever seen. Many informants were disreputable characters – convicted criminals, pathological liars – motivated by money or the prospect of citizenship. But since their only function was secretly to record suspects' words, not to testify, their lack of credibility was irrelevant. And their behavior, however repugnant, failed to meet the high threshold for an entrapment defense.[147]

The focus on inchoate crimes let the government reassure the public it had never been in danger. But that strategy also raised doubts about whether the defendants would have engaged in the acts for which they were convicted – or indeed *any* terrorist activity – without the informant's intervention. (Retiring after two decades on the SDNY bench, Judge Sheindlin said of the Newburgh 4: "you sort of feel if they were never approached and urged on, they didn't have the brains or the wherewithal to pull this off."[148]) Many of the accused were life's losers: poor, uneducated, minority or immigrant, un- or under-employed, substance abusers or addicts, mentally ill, often with long criminal records and years in prison.[149] Unsurprisingly, they sought to vent generalized rage at the world. At other historical moments, some might have become anarchists, communists, black nationalists, white supremacists, or militia members. They were politically naive, possessing only a dim, often badly distorted understanding of the nature, ideology, and strategy of the terrorist groups they purported to embrace. Some were motivated by money rather than religion. Others – Muslim immigrants or converts (the latter often knowing little about Islam and rarely complying with its strictures) – sought an identity that would give their lives meaning and confer a sense of membership in a community (even though hardly any had connections to terrorist groups). Although a few emulated the 9/11 criminals by attempting to be suicide bombers, their ill-conceived plans often seemed to invite apprehension. Like the government (if for different reasons), they exaggerated the crimes they sought to commit and their ability to execute them.

These distinctive features raise serious questions about whether terrorism prosecutions constituted the best use of government resources and whether the enhanced security (if any) was worth the corrosive enmity informants provoked in Muslim American communities (not to mention the decades during which these hapless, misguided defendants languished in prison and the cost of keeping them there).[150] More than 400 people convicted of terrorism have been released without any reports of "recidivism."[151] But, as Judge McMahon suggested, those questions involve policy choices more than threats to the rule of law. And in most other respects, terrorism prosecutions resembled ordinary criminal cases, exhibiting their virtues and vices.[152] Quantitative statements are problematic because of controversies about how the government defined and categorized terrorism prosecutions.[153] But the limited evidence suggests that plea bargaining, conviction rates and sentence lengths were similar to those for ordinary crimes.[154] By contrast, civilian judges, like the courts-martial discussed in Chapter 3, could be exceptionally lenient when US military contractors killed Afghans. Don M. Ayala shot to death Abdul Salam, a handcuffed Afghan civilian, shortly after he threw burning gasoline on an American member of a Human Terrain Team, who died from her burns two months later. Ayala was charged with second-degree murder, pleaded to manslaughter, for which he faced 15 years, but received only probation and a small fine.[155] Justin Cannon and Christopher Drotleff were charged with second-degree murder for the deaths of two Afghan men; but though they were convicted for killing one and faced up to eight years, Cannon got 30 months and Drotleff 37.[156]

A few of the accused were horribly abused by the CIA. But the FBI, prosecutors, and judges took care to ensure that improperly obtained evidence did not contaminate the trial, which is all the exclusionary rule can do; other mechanisms must correct abuses committed during investigations. The administration successfully resisted strident, sometimes hysterical, pressure to abort civilian prosecutions in favor of indefinite detention or MC trials (most recently those concerning Ahmad Khan Rahimi and Ali Charaf Damache),[157] winning every one of these politically contested cases. Some accused sought to make their trials political platforms to propound their perverted versions of Islam and denounce America's alleged crimes. But their brief courtroom tirades were soon forgotten, and only a few defendants (Mehanna, Sherifi, al-Arian) attracted political support. Judges displayed great forbearance and admirable impartiality in the face of defiant, disruptive defendants, some of whom insisted on representing themselves or disregarding their lawyers' advice. Judges corrected prosecutorial misconduct in the courtroom and used their power to reduce sentences to acknowledge abuses outside the criminal justice system. (D Minn Judge Michael Davis courageously experimented with noncustodial dispositions to discourage Somali American youth from succumbing to the allure of al-Shabaab.[158]) Whereas judges' political orientations (indicated by the appointing president's party) were strongly correlated with responses to civil claims by both "war on terror" and terrorism victims (see Chapter 6), they were *not* significantly related to judges' decisions in criminal prosecutions. (Indeed, Democrats were slightly more likely than Republicans to favor the prosecution.)[159]

Table 2.1 Judges' Criminal Prosecution Rulings, by Appointing President's Party

Appointing President	# Ruled for Prosecution	% Ruled for Prosecution	# Ruled for Defendant	% Ruled for Defendant	Total number of judges
Democrat	30	70	13	30	43
Republican	16	59	11	41	27
Total	46	66	24	34	70

Chi-Square = 09.1, p = .37

Defense counsel were zealous and effective, challenging prosecutors and plea bargaining for better sentences for their clients (if rarely winning acquittals). Both sides fought hard to empanel favorable jurors, whose lengthy deliberations suggested they took their responsibilities seriously; and the hung juries showed that some members felt free to vote according to their consciences. As I completed this book, two trials demonstrated the federal judiciary's ability to accord due process to accused terrorists. Following two weeks of hearings (in which the defense offered no witnesses) and just four hours of deliberation, a jury convicted Ahmad Khan Rahimi of all eight counts for bombings in New York and New Jersey, finding that a second bomb failed to explode for technical reasons and not because the repentant defendant had disarmed it; the verdict carried a mandatory life sentence.[160] Ahmed Abu Khattala was on trial in DDC for the Benghazi embassy attack.[161] And despite President Trump's misguided enthusiasm for military commissions, his administration continued to choose civilian trials for alleged terrorists captured abroad, including Mustafa al-Imam, another Libyan charged with participation in the Benghazi attack.[162] After the November 2017 terrorist attack in which Sayfullo Saipov killed eight people and injured many others in lower Manhattan, Trump threatened to transfer him to Guantánamo, declaring: [163]

> We … have to come up with punishment that's far quicker and far greater than the punishment these animals are getting right now. They'll go through court for years, at the end … who knows what happens. We need quick justice, and we need strong justice, much quicker and much stronger than we have right now. Because what we have right now is a joke and it's a laughingstock.

He followed this with a tweet: "SHOULD GET DEATH PENALTY!" In an uncharacteristic criticism of Trump, Sen. Lindsey Graham accused the administration of making "a huge mistake" by reading Saipov his Miranda rights instead of interrogating him as an enemy combatant. (Saipov waived his rights and boasted about his actions.) Then in a rare nod to facts, Trump conceded that "statistically" the military commission "process takes much longer than going through the Federal system." (Even Attorney General Sessions, who as senator had attacked President Obama for prosecuting alleged terrorists in civilian courts, now claimed his DoJ had "gotten results" from such prosecutions.) But Trump again anticipated both verdict and sentence by tweeting "DEATH PENALTY!" (The *Washington Post* warned that Trump's tweets "undermine not only the government's case against [Saipov] but also the strength and independence of the U.S. justice system.") And venting his anger at the absence of investigations and prosecutions of Hillary Clinton and other Democrats, Trump complained that "the saddest thing is that because I'm the President of the United States, I am not supposed to be involved with the Justice Department … [or] the FBI."

Because the American criminal justice system is imperfect, its recurrent problems and failings inevitably affected terrorism prosecutions. But it successfully resisted political pressure from both vigilantes baying for blood and zealots seeking martyrdom, performing at least as well as it does when dealing with ordinary crime, and perhaps even better in the glare of unwonted publicity.

CHAPTER THREE

COURTS-MARTIAL

The US Department of Defense (DoD) takes great pride in its system of courts-martial for trying violations of the Uniform Code of Military Justice, created in the aftermath of World War II.[1] This chapter presents courts-martial for seven egregious Law of Armed Conflict (LOAC) violations in Afghanistan and Iraq, civilian prosecutions of an accused who had left service and a group of military contractors, and courts-martial for other offenses.[2] How do they compare with each other and with civilian criminal prosecutions and military commissions? What is the response to allegations of violations of LOAC by the US military and Congress, by victims and their political leaders? How do investigators determine what happened? How does the accused's rank influence charge, verdict, and sentence? How do accused justify their behavior, and how does that influence verdict and sentence? Are cases resolved by pleas or trials? What influence do superior officers exercise? How does procedure differ in courts-martial and civilian courts; how do those differences affect outcomes? Are there differences in attrition from initial allegations to final outcomes? What explains the exceptions to these patterns?

HADITHA

On November 19, 2005, an improvised explosive device (IED) struck a Humvee near Haditha, Iraq, killing LCpl. Miguel (T.J.) Terrazas (one of the most popular members of his platoon) and wounding two others.[3] The next day a military communique reported that "a U.S. Marine and 15 civilians were killed yesterday from the blast of a roadside bomb in

Haditha. Immediately following the bombing, gunmen attacked the convoy with small arms fire. Iraqi Army soldiers and Marines returned fire, killing eight insurgents and wounding another." But three months later *Time* magazine published Tim McGirk's very different account. Eyewitness evidence and a video showed that *Marines* had killed 15 unarmed civilians, including seven women and three children in their homes. (McGirk told *Frontline* that photos showed the dead "women and children … in their pajamas. And Iraq, it's a very traditional society. People don't go wandering around on the streets in their pajamas to get hit by an IED.") The military now said Marines in a house corridor, hearing what they believed was an AK-47 being racked (i.e., prepared to fire), broke down two doors and fired into the rooms, killing seven, including two women and a child, and shot a man running away. Believing they had taken fire from a second house, they broke down its door and threw in a grenade, igniting a kitchen propane tank and killing seven: a blind 76-year-old man in a wheelchair, his wife, her sister, and the couple's three young daughters and two-year-old son. Marines also raided a third house, finding only women and children, and then a fourth, where they killed a man holding an AK-47 and another reaching into a wardrobe for a weapon. They now admitted killing 24: 15 noncombatants and 9 alleged enemy fighters (including four youths found near the IED). Dr. Wahid al-Obeidi, Haditha Hospital director, said Marines delivered 24 bodies that night, claiming they had been killed by IED shrapnel. "But it was obvious to us that there were no organs slashed by shrapnel. The bullet wounds were very apparent. Most of the victims were shot in the chest and the head – from close range."

The next day a Haditha journalism student videotaped the morgue and the homes where the killings took place, giving the tape to a local human rights group that cooperated with HRW, which shared it with *Time*. It showed many victims still in nightclothes. Although the insides of the houses were sprayed with shrapnel (from grenades), bullet holes, and blood, there were no bullet holes outside. Soon after the killings Haditha's mayor led an angry delegation of elders to the Marines, where a "captain admitted that his men had made a mistake." But the military maintained the original story until *Time* gave the video and witness statements to the US military spokesman in Baghdad, who passed it up the command. After spending a week in Haditha in February 2006 interviewing Marines, survivors, and doctors, Army Col. Gregory Watt concluded that Marines had killed the civilians and the first two houses had contained no insurgents. But he called the deaths "collateral damage." The US paid $2,500 to relatives of each of the 15 dead civilians, less for those injured.

On April 7 MGen. Richard Natonski (1st Marine Division commander) stripped LtCol. Jeffrey R. Chessani (3rd Battalion commander, on his third tour in Iraq, having fought in Fallouja in 2004), Capt. James S. Kimber (Company I commander) and Capt. Lucas M. McConnell (Company K commander) of their commands for "lack of confidence in their leadership abilities," but he filed no charges. In May the military still insisted Marines had come under fire, though not from the houses where civilians were killed. But Rep. Murtha (D-Pa), an ex-Marine and House Armed Services Committee (HASC) senior minority member, demanded an investigation, claiming:

> they actually went into the houses and killed women and children. And there was about twice as many as originally reported by *Time*. ... Our troops overreacted because of the pressure on them, and they killed innocent civilians in cold blood. And that's what the report is going to tell. ... Now, you can imagine the impact this is going to have on ... our effort in trying to win the hearts and minds. We can't sustain this operation.

HASC chair Hunter (R-Ca) said the Committee would hold an inquiry and expected SASC to do so. But he "totally reject[ed]" Murtha's statement and "did not want the actions of one squad in one city on one morning to be used to symbolize or characterize or tar the actions of our great troops ... There has been no war in our history in which you didn't have people doing the wrong thing at one time or another."

Army MGen. Eldon Bargewell was investigating how the military had handled the incident. He had risen from Special Forces Staff Sergeant in Vietnam (where he was awarded four Purple Hearts and the Distinguished Service Cross) to Delta Force commander.

On May 25 Gen. Michael W. Hagee (Marine Corps commandant) flew to Iraq to exhort troops about the importance of complying with the Geneva Conventions. "There is a risk of becoming indifferent to the loss of human life, as well as bringing dishonor on ourselves." Rep. Murtha now said the incident was "much worse than reported": five Iraqis had been pulled out of a taxi and shot. Rep. Kline (R-MN), another ex-Marine, said "This was direct fire by Marines at civilians. This was not an immediate response to an attack. This would be an atrocity," a "horrific aberration." A senior Marine Corps officer briefed Congress several times. BGen. David M. Brahms (a retired Marine

Judge Advocate General (JAG)) said: "when these investigations come out, there's going to be a firestorm. It will be worse than Abu Ghraib." After a briefing by Hagee and the Marine Corps legislative liaison, Sen. Warner (R-Va), a former Marine and Navy Secretary, said the allegations about "significant loss of life" were "very, very serious." The Marine Corps said it took the allegations "very seriously" and was conducting an "on-going" investigation.

The *Los Angeles Times* reported that Marines had believed the IED was detonated from nearby. The newspaper had seen photos showing that the civilians had been killed execution-style, with bullet wounds in the head and back. Rep. Kline accused the Marines of "lying about it and covering it up – there is no question about it." But he had no "reason now to think there was any foot dragging" by the Marine investigation. The *Washington Post* quoted an eyewitness who had seen Marines kill a man pleading for his life and then kill his wife and four children. In the house closest to the IED Marines shot a 76-year-old man in a wheelchair nine times in his chest and abdomen, killing him as well as three middle-aged men, a woman, and a four-year-old boy. In another house Marines threw grenades into the kitchen and bathroom and shot a mother and five young girls; a sixth survived because their blood made her appear dead. In a third house Marines killed four brothers.

The Marine Corps reported that official military photos showed no bodies; but investigators had found a second set of photos, which a Kilo Company member took right after the shootings and sent to a friend in the USA. Rep. Kline said "there's no doubt that the Marines allegedly involved in doing this – they lied about it. They certainly tried to cover it up." Rep. Murtha reiterated: "there was no firefight. There was no IED that killed those innocent people." "Our troops ... killed innocent civilians in cold blood." "One Marine was killed and the Marines just said, 'We're going to take care of it.'" "It's as bad as Abu Ghraib, if not worse." *Time* now reported that a taxi with four students from the local technical institute had arrived at the scene just before the IED. Marines ordered the driver and passengers to lie on the ground and killed them when they ran off. When McGirk first approached the military, Capt. Jeff Pool replied: "I cannot believe you're buying any of this. This falls into the same category of AQI [al-Qaeda in Iraq] propaganda." Although the Iraqi government had not visited or sent condolences, Islamic Resistance distributed pamphlets in Haditha about "the dirty deeds of the Americans." But Army LtCol. Barry Johnson, a more senior officer in Baghdad, notified LGen. Peter Chiarelli (number two commander in Iraq), who instructed Pool to tell McGirk about the military investigation. When Johnson said there had been none, Chiarelli directed Col. Watt to conduct it.

The *New York Times* reported Hiba Abdullah's eyewitness account of the Marines shooting her wheelchair-bound father-in-law in the chest, his 66-year-old wife in the back, and their four-year-old son in the chest. (Confusion about the identities and relationships of the dead is indicative of the difficulty of ascertaining the facts.) An elderly woman, mother, and child were killed "in what appeared to be a prayer position." Some victims had a single bullet wound to the head. One home where people had been killed had no bullet marks on the walls. On ABC's *This Week* Sen. Warner said there were serious questions about "what was the immediate reaction of the senior officers in the Marine Corps." Rep. Murtha said on the same program that Marine Corps officials told him troops shot one woman "in cold blood" as she was begging for mercy. "Who said 'We're not going to publicize this thing. We're not even going to investigate it?'" The immediate investigation "was stifled," and "there was no serious investigation" until March. But the "decision to make payments to the families" "happens at the highest level," showing that officers up the chain of command knew about the events.

Joint Chiefs of Staff (JCS) Chairman Gen. Peter Pace told CNN:

> We want to find out what happened and we'll make it public. If the allegations, as they are being portrayed in the newspaper, turn out to be valid, then of course there will be charges ... We should, in fact, as leaders take on the responsibility to get out and talk to our troops and make sure that they understand that what 99.9 percent of them are doing, which is fighting with honor and courage, is exactly what we expect of them.

He assured CBS: "We'll get to the bottom of the investigation and take appropriate action." His predecessor, Gen. Richard B. Myers, told ABC he had "no idea" what happened, but there "has been and there is an ongoing, thorough investigation."

At the end of May it emerged that Col. Watt had seen death certificates showing wounds to victims' heads and chests from gunshots, not IED shrapnel. SSgt. Frank Wuterich (the senior noncommissioned officer on the patrol, his first combat operation) and LtCol. Chessani said the Marines took gunfire from the houses. With approval from higher levels, Chessani authorized the payment of $38,000 to the victims' families. The soldier who delivered the money told a city council member it was because the dead "were deemed not to be involved in combat," not because there had been a "mistake." Chiarelli referred Watt's March 9 report to the senior Marine commander in Iraq, who ordered a criminal investigation, which began on March 12.

Chiarelli also directed Bargewell to conduct a parallel investigation into a possible cover-up. Defense Secretary Rumsfeld and Pace were informed on March 10; Rumsfeld said it was "really, really bad – as bad or worse than Abu Ghraib." President Bush learned the next day. The Naval Criminal Investigative Service (NCIS) began a criminal investigation on March 12. The Marines started briefing Congress on March 13. *Time* appeared on March 19.

The *Los Angeles Times* said that:

> If Marines "avenged" the killing of a comrade by terrorizing and killing innocent Iraqis, they disgraced their uniform and must be punished. The same is true of anyone higher in the chain of command who helped conceal what happened … If the allegations of a massacre are corroborated – and a full disclosure is overdue – the debate about the wisdom of the U.S. mission in Iraq inevitably will become even more inflamed.
>
> Although Rep. Murtha had blamed "the fog of war and the confusion of battle," no amount of fog, no level of confusion, can obscure the fact that this is a nation of laws, and when the U.S. condones the deliberate murder of civilians it becomes, as Murtha said, no better than its enemy.

Iraqi Prime Minister Nouri al-Maliki said: "it is not justifiable that a family is killed because someone is fighting terrorists." Iraq "will ask for answers not only about Haditha" but whenever something "happened by 'mistake,' and we will hold those who did it responsible." (The Iraqi Human Rights Minister said to *Frontline* he had presented a "complete file" to the USA but been told: "we could not be part of the investigation.") Gen. George W. Casey, US commander in Iraq, supported an inquiry and rejected the earlier military investigation. Hours after presenting his credentials, the new Iraqi ambassador to the USA called for an inquiry. He had gotten no response to his formal request two months earlier for copies of the military reports. The previous year US troops in Haditha had "intentionally" and "unnecessarily" killed his 21-year-old cousin, who had let troops search his house. The military claimed self-defense, but had found only one unloaded weapon.

Although Bush learned about Haditha from the March *Time* article, he did not comment until June: "I am troubled by the initial stories. I am mindful that there is a thorough investigation going on. If, in fact, the laws were broken, there will be punishment ... I've talked to General Pete Pace about the subject, who is a proud Marine, and nobody is more concerned about these allegations than the Marine Corps."

NCIS said they were conducting the largest investigation since the war began, involving 50 people. The nation has "a willingness to deal with issues like this in an upfront way and an open way and correct problems." Bargewell's initial investigation found that Marines killed without provocation, sometimes execution style, and then lied to cover up.

Salam al-Zubaie, Iraqi Deputy Prime Minister, Acting Defense Minister, and one of the most powerful Sunnis, said: "We in the Ministers' Cabinet condemned this crime and demanded that coalition forces show the reasons behind this massacre. As you know, this is not the only massacre, and there are a lot. The Coalition forces must change their behavior. Human blood should be sacred regardless of religion, party and nationality." A committee of five ministers, including interior and finance and defense, would investigate.

A week after Hagee's visit to Iraq, Maliki said: "we cannot tolerate violations against the dignity and security of the Iraqi people." Some troops had "no respect for citizens ... killing on suspicion or a hunch." Sen. Warner urged Secretary of Defense Rumsfeld to complete the investigation because "public opinion on this matter is being influenced by misinformation, leaks and undocumented and uncorroborated facts." Rumsfeld assured a security conference in Singapore that "we'll soon know the answers, and my impression is that the Marine Corps is handling it well." Sen. McCain warned that, if there had been a cover-up, "obviously more senior people would have to be the subject of hearings." MGen. William Caldwell said at least three or four allegations of wrongdoing were being investigated. This "tragic incident" was "in no way representative of how coalition forces treat Iraqi civilians." Hagee went to Camp Lejeune to address the 2nd Marine Expeditionary Force on compliance with international law and military rules of engagement.

The *New York Times* said the:

> "apparent cold-blooded killing" will be hard to dispose of with another Washington damage control operation ... this affair cannot simply be dismissed as the spontaneous cruelty of a few bad men ... it will not do to ... ignore the administration officials, from President Bush on down, who made the chances of this sort of disaster so much greater by deliberately blurring the rules governing the conduct of American soldiers

in the field. The inquiry also needs to critically examine the behavior of top commanders ... and of midlevel officers who apparently covered up ... These damage control operations have done a great job of shielding the reputations of top military commanders and high-ranking Pentagon officials. But it has been at the expense of things that are far more precious: America's international reputation and the honor of the United States military.

Warning that "delays in getting out the official findings of fact due to a protracted review process will mean a mixture of information, disinformation and unconfirmed facts will continue to spiral in the public domain," SASC planned to hold hearings "at the earliest possible date" and asked Rumsfeld to make Bargewell available. Sen. Levin (D-MI) complained that the military "were very slow in notifying the committee, just like they were very slow in doing everything else." They "knew something was amiss" but did not start investigating until March 9. Bargewell submitted his 3,300-page report to the US Central Command (CENTCOM) Marine Corps commanding general in June.

Lawyers for those under investigation offered their justifications. Wuterich denied anyone had been rattled by Terraza's death. At the scene of the IED a group of "military-aged men" ignored orders to stop and ran away; Standard Operation Procedure (SOP) was to shoot to kill. After a report of shots from a house, platoon leaders decided to clear it. When his four-man team heard people behind a closed door, Wuterich kicked it open and tossed in a fragmentation grenade. The other Marines, who had had experience in Falloujah, fired a series of "clearing rounds." At the second house they again used a fragmentation grenade and clearing fire in a room full of people. Wuterich reported collateral damage of 12–15 civilians; he never said any had been killed by the IED. Wuterich's fitness evaluation praised his leadership in this operation, resulting in a promotion. Capt. McConnell, Kilo Company commander, said he had reported Wuterich's account to the 3rd Battalion executive officer that afternoon. Within a few days the battalion intelligence chief gave a PowerPoint presentation to senior Marine commanders.

Expecting to be court-martialed, Wuterich accused DoD of having "deliberately provided [Murtha] with inaccurate and false information." Wuterich sued Murtha for defamation to force Murtha to disclose what the Department had told him. Wuterich's lawyers said: "this case is not about money. It's about clearing Frank Wuterich's name." Murtha replied that he had spoken about Haditha "to draw attention to the horrendous pressure put on our troops in Iraq and to the cover-up of the incident." "Our troops are caught in the middle of a tragic dilemma, the military trains them to fight a conventional war and use overwhelming force to protect U.S. lives. I agree with that policy, but when we use force, we often kill civilians."

Calling Haditha "an ugly, ugly scene," Murtha said Pentagon officials believed Marines had "deliberately shot" civilians. Wuterich's lawyers accused DoD of "an effort to vilify and isolate these men before they ever have a chance to demonstrate their lack of guilt." They also demanded an apology from Rep. Kline, who responded within an hour: "As a retired colonel in the U.S. Marines, I am especially proud of the sacrifices our men and women make day in and day out, especially in combat situations ... I would never want to publicly insinuate, implicitly or explicitly, that I have prejudged what took place that day on the battlefield or afterwards."

Bargewell, who planned to retire in 2006 after nearly forty years of service, harshly criticized the aftermath of the killings. "Virtually no inquiry at any level of command was conducted into the circumstances surrounding the deaths" despite "a number of red flags and opportunities to do so." "Initial reports of Kilo company and its subordinate units were untimely, inaccurate and incomplete ... conflicted, poorly vetted and forgotten once transmitted." Although the 2nd Marine Division comptroller responsible for compensation payments told the Staff Judge Advocate (SJA) that the incident "might require further reporting," that office "did not forward any reports of the incidents to higher headquarters." Bargewell's documentation was four feet long.

In July Gen. Chiarelli criticized the senior staff of the 2nd Marine Division and the 2nd Regimental combat team for failing to investigate the killings. Although his report was not released, some of it leaked a month later. The official company logbook was missing all the pages for the day of the killing; later that day Wuterich had been on duty at the operations center where it was kept. A drone video of the IED site showed the bodies of five men stacked on top of one another close to their car; Marine officers initially told investigators the video was unavailable, producing it only after Chiarelli intervened. The Marine Corps reiterated that it was "committed to a full and thorough investigation."

Chessani had told investigators on March 20 he "did not suspect any wrongdoing from my Marines" and had no "reason to believe that this was anything other than combat action." "I just saw this as a large combat action that had been staged by the enemy ... [the] enemy has picked the place, he has picked the time, and the location for a reason ... he wanted to make us look bad." At the time he had not seen the Marine Corps statement that the Iraqis had been killed by the IED. Shown it three months later, he said "I knew this was inaccurate."

On December 6 (more than a year after the killings) LGen. Natonski briefed HASC on the Marine Corps investigation in a closed-door session. Later that month Capt. McConnell was relieved of his command. A few days after that four Marines were charged: Wuterich with unpremeditated murder, lying to authorities, and urging another Marine to make a false report; and Sgt. Sanick Dela Cruz and LCpls. Sharratt and Tatum with unpremeditated murder. Charges of dereliction of duty for failure to ensure a thorough investigation were filed against Chessani and McConnell, Capt. Randy W. Stone (3rd Battalion military lawyer) and Lt. Andrew Grayson (the Marine intelligence officer on the team that photographed the aftermath).

The NCIS report of thousands of pages, completed in January 2007, found that Marines who went to rescue those injured by the IED took enemy rifle fire from several locations. (Defense lawyers asked LGen. James Mattis, CENTCOM commander, to order an investigation into the leak of the report, which troubled NCIS.) Although Wuterich claimed he felt threatened by the five men who got out of the taxi, other Marines said the men were unarmed and clearly had surrendered. Dela Cruz said Wuterich kept shooting them with his M-16 rifle as they lay on the ground and then urinated on them. Wuterich asked Dela Cruz to back up claims that the men had been trying to flee. Believing they were receiving fire, 2nd Lt. William T. Kallop (heading the quick reaction force in his first combat operation) told Wuterich, Salinas, Tatum, and LCpl. Humberto Mendoza to "take the house." Wuterich said he "told them to treat it as a hostile environment. I told them to shoot first, ask questions later." True, the Rules of Engagement (ROE) were "ALWAYS minimize collateral damage" – targets had to be positively identified as threats before Marines could open fire; but "nothing ... prevents you from using all force necessary to defend yourself." After Tatum reported hearing an AK-47 being racked, they tossed grenades into rooms and sprayed rifle fire. At the second house Mendoza shot a man through the glass kitchen door "because I had been told the house was hostile and I was following my training that all individuals in a hostile house are to be shot." They "cleared" that house in the same way. Tatum said: "Knowing what I know now, I feel badly about killing Iraqi civilians who may have been innocent, but I stand fast in my decision that day, as I reacted to the threats that I perceived at the time. I did not shoot randomly with the intent to harm innocent Iraqi civilians." Hours later Sharratt, Wuterich, and Salinas went to two other houses after seeing men peering at them suspiciously. Iraqi witnesses said the Marines took all the men into the fourth house and shot them.

Marines initially classified eight dead civilians as "insurgents" and then reported at least fifteen civilians killed in "crossfire" with the enemy. McConnell told his Marines they had done a good job, but he reported the civilian deaths to superiors. That day Chessani also reported the civilian casualties to his regimental commander, Col. Stephen W. Davis, who said no investigation was needed. Davis later told investigators "there was nothing out of the ordinary about any of this, including the number of civilian dead, that would have triggered anything in my mind that was out of the norm." MGen. Huck, the division commander, learned about the civilian casualties that day but thought they were caused by the IED and ensuing gun battle. Three days later, when told about Marines "clearing houses," he said "nothing in the brief caused any concern to me." In February 2006 Chessani said he had authorized $38,000 in compensation payments in December, even though "the enemy chose the time and place of his ambush," fighting "from the bedrooms and living rooms of civilian-occupied houses" in "callous disregard for the lives of innocent bystanders." When *Time* magazine sent a list of questions based on the video, suggesting that Marines had massacred civilians inside houses and executed the men in the taxi, Huck, Davis, and others dismissed the allegations as insurgent propaganda. When Maj. Samuel H. Carrasco (battalion operations officer) and the battalion executive officer suggested Chessani investigate, he shouted angrily: "my men are not murderers." Col. Watt agreed the Marines had reason to be suspicious of the men in the taxi and it might have been "unrealistic to expect" the Marines to positively identify those in the house before shooting. There was no indication they had "intentionally targeted, engaged and killed noncombatants." But he suggested NCIS investigate.

On April 2 the military dropped the murder charge against Dela Cruz; two weeks later it dismissed all other charges against him in exchange for his testimony. He told NCIS he had shot into the bodies of the men from the taxi in revenge for Terrazas's death and only because he believed they had already been killed by Wuterich. Wuterich now told CBS News' *60 Minutes* he did not fire a single shot inside the houses.

Granted immunity on April 3, Kallop told NCIS that after he ordered the team to "take the house," they had done so "the way they had been trained to clear it, which is frags [fragmentation grenades] first." "I'm convinced that we did nothing wrong." He had reported civilian cas- ualties up the chain of command. But in his just-released 130-page declassified summary, Bargewell found that the chain of command had ignored "obvious signs" of "serious misconduct."

> All levels of command tended to view civilian casualties, even in signifi- cant numbers, as routine and as the natural and intended result of insur- gent tactics ... Statements made by the chain of command ... suggest that Iraqi civilian lives are not as important as U.S. lives, their deaths are just the cost of doing business, and that the Marines need to get "the job done" no matter what it takes.

Although trained correctly, some Marines "did not follow proper house and room techniques." Kilo company officers and the 3rd Battalion com- mander passed insufficient information to the regimental commander, and he and 2nd Marine Division officers ignored signs of problems.

Although Capt. Pool received battalion commanders' reports accur- ately describing Marines killing civilians, his news release blamed insurgents because the killings were a response to the IED. "The way I saw it was this. A bomb blast went off, or was initiated, that is what started, that is the reason they're getting this, is a bomb blew up, killed people. We killed people back, and that's the story." He had since been promoted and was a public affairs officer in Anbar province. Neither the photos showing women and children killed in their beds nor the more than $40,000 distributed as condolence payments prompted further investigation. Bargewell said "the most remarkable aspect of the follow- on ... was the absence of virtually any kind of inquiry at any level of command into the circumstances surrounding the deaths." Chessani's refusal to investigate even after the *Time* inquiry showed "an unwilling- ness, bordering on denial."

> There was evidence of an attitude that portrayed noncombatants as not necessarily innocents, which may have fostered a willingness to accept reported circumstances that might otherwise appear dubious. A duty to inquire further was so obvious in this case that a reasonable person with knowledge of these events would certainly have made further inquiries.

Chessani's lawyers replied that he had reported the deaths up the chain of command the same day, but Col. Davis, the regimental commander, "expressed only mild concern over the potential negative ramifications of indiscriminate killing based on his stated view that the Iraqis and insurgents respect strength and power over righteousness." Davis told Bargewell: "Frankly, what I am looking at is the advantage [McGirk is] giving the enemy." Col. R. Gary Sokoloski, Huck's lawyer and chief of staff, had approved the news release blaming insurgents for the deaths in order "to get that out for the press" before the insurgents issued their own statement. They all saw McGirk as a naive conduit for Haditha's mayor, whom they viewed as an insurgent. Capt. Stone said the regimental SJA had told him: "we don't do investigations for 'troops in contact' situations." Stone expressed "disappointment that the Marine Corps decided that, in the entire chain of command, that I am the one who should be held accountable."

Newly declassified documents included an email from the battalion operations officer within three hours of the attack informing the regiment that 15 civilians had been killed, "seven of which were women and kids." Although senior commanders maintained that those reports were passed to Huck's staff, he could not recall seeing them. "I didn't know at the time whether [the dead] were bad guys, noncombatants, or whatever." "They may have been guys pulling the trigger, for all I knew." He did not recall the commander's critical information requirement that he alert superiors and investigate whenever the number of dead civilians was three times the number of US military deaths. Three days after the episode, in the midst of two other combat operations, Huck saw Chessani's PowerPoint presentation on the attack, which did not mention civilian deaths. "[N]o bells and whistles went off." Ten weeks later Huck sent Chessani the PowerPoint presentation, saying "I support our account and do not see a necessity for further investigation." But less than five hours later Chiarelli forwarded it to BGen. Campbell, asking for a meeting "at the first possible moment tomorrow morning. We're going to have to do an investigation."

In Capt. Stone's Art. 32 proceeding (the first ever brought against a legal officer in wartime and extensively covered by leading US and foreign media), Kallop said he had been "shocked" to find only unarmed women and children dead in one house, but still felt his men acted appropriately because Wuterich and Salinas had expected to "walk into a machine gun." His platoon had been told Haditha was "an insurgent-controlled-and-occupied city." "I essentially told them to try and bust them out – find the [bomb] triggerman, find the insurgents." A week after the attack Sgt. Albert Espinosa told Stone: "I thought we need to do an investigation," but was assured it was being conducted at the battalion level. Huck explained why he had not ordered an investigation: "In my mind's eye I saw insurgent fire. I saw Kilo fire, and I saw Iraqi security forces fire. I could see how 15 neutrals in those circumstances could have been killed." "I had no suspicion that a Law of Armed Conflict violation had been committed." "While the number [of deaths] is big, it is the circumstances of how this was reported" that reassured him. Capt. Timothy Strabbing said an investigation was discussed only after *Time* emailed Kilo Company's executive officer on January 5. Chessani responded: "there is no reason to do an investigation. This was a bona fide combat action." 1st Lt. Adam Mathis said that the killings demonstrated "the extent that the enemy's willing to go to … how cheap they considered human lives, that they would conduct attacks from a populated area." He and the battalion's commander and executive officer had dismissed McGirk's questions as "sensational," "questionable." "It sounded like bad, negative spin. We tried to weed out the grievances that Mr. McGirk had against the Bush administration." "This guy is looking for blood because blood leads headlines."

Huck said Sokoloski and Davis had kept him in the dark. When he learned more details from Chiarelli on February 12, 2006 Huck was "highly irritated," asking Sokoloski: "Am I the last guy in this outfit to find out about this?" His superiors – Chiarelli and his predecessor, MGen. Stephen T. Johnson (the top Marine commander in Iraq) – had ignored earlier reports. Huck wrote Chiarelli: "I support our account and do not see a necessity for a further investigation." Johnson told investigators he had been more concerned about IEDs than civilian deaths: "15 people killed as a result of an attack, in a built-up area that involved I.E.D.'s and a coordinated attack, I still think that probably my reaction was, 'that's too bad, but they got caught somehow' … Hey, if the enemy hadn't done it, those people wouldn't have got killed." Col. John Ewers, who participated in Bargewell's inquiry, initially saw the killings as a "reckless application of the rules of engagement" and was "astonished" that Chessani had not ordered an investigation. But he testified that though Stone "didn't cover himself with glory," his behavior did not rise "to the level of criminal dereliction." Maj. Kevin Gonzalez, the battalion executive officer, said Stone "was not expected to take affirmative action." LtCol. Kent Keith, divisional SJA, said "it appeared the noncombatants were killed because of the IED and a subsequent ambush, and I saw no reason to investigate that. It's not a [law of war] violation if there is incidental loss of life." Maj. Carrasco said

McGirk's email "hit me in the chest like a baseball bat." Even though he felt the questions were not "based in reality," he told Chessani: "the allegations are pretty serious, probably something we want to look at" because "where there's smoke, there's a little bit of fire." But at their January 6, 2006 meeting Chessani twice declared to Gonzalez and him: "my men are not murderers."

Maj. Thomas McCann, presiding over the Art. 32 hearing, asked rhetorically: "at what point do we have to scratch our heads that we killed a lot more civilians than enemy?" He asked Capt. Jeffrey Dinsmore, who had inspected the scene: "if there had been 150 bodies n.k.i.a. [noncombatants killed in action] that day, where would we be?" The 21-year veteran replied: "You let loose Marines in a t.i.c. [troops in contact] against a hostile situation, taking small-arms fire, they don't have the training nor do they have the presence of mind to differentiate between civilians and insurgents."

Maj. Carroll Connolly, representing Davis (who had been granted immunity), argued that there was no need to investigate civilians killed during combat but could offer no legal authority for that assertion. Noting that officers had to report significant civilian deaths up the chain of command, the former head of the Army JAG Law School's international law division asked: "how can you report it if you don't see an obligation to investigate it in the first place?"

In the week after the killings, the Haditha mayor, town council, and 14 other local leaders spent a "heated and emotional" 45 minutes meeting with officers, describing the deaths, and submitting a written demand in English to investigate this "crime of war." Chessani, Sgt. Edward Sax (the senior enlisted man) and McConnell, who met with them, did not report up the command. A day after the incident, when two Iraqi civilians claimed the killings were murders, Capt. James Haynie, the battalion information officer, replied that their informants had lied: "Marines do not execute innocent civilians." Huck said he had trusted Chessani, who had visited the scene. "In a counterinsurgency, things are decentralized. You have to rely on trust tactics." All his superiors, including Gen. Casey, knew within hours that civilians had been killed in their homes. Huck sent a report to Johnson, who forwarded it to LGen. John Vines (Marine Corps commander), who "forwarded it to force." No further inquiry was needed because of the Marine dictum "trust tactics," requiring commanders to rely on subordinates to report events accurately and completely. Early reports blamed the 15 civilian deaths on the IED and insurgent gunfire, with

Marine fire just "further adding" to those casualties. Chessani had not told Huck that Marines had killed the five unarmed men ordered out of their taxi. The Haditha leaders' written demand – which Chessani had not seen – made it sound like "a law-of-armed-conflict violation," which "should have been reported." But on June 9, 2006 Maj. McCann had recommended no charges against Stone, urging that the matter be handled administratively.

In his Art. 32, hearing Chessani was represented by two military attorneys and lawyers from the Thomas More Law Center acting pro bono, one of whom had served with Chessani in the battle of Falloujah. (One wonders what the "heavenly" saint would think.) The Center raised more than $300,000 for Chessani's legal defense and issued press releases accusing anti-war agitators led by Rep. Murtha and *Time* magazine of making their client a "political scapegoat." It also complained to the Secretary of the Navy that NCIS had abused witnesses, interrogating them for up to eighteen hours, yelling and throwing things at them, and preventing them from eating, drinking, or using the bathroom. The Secretary declined to investigate. Chessani's father led a group of motorcyclists on a support ride from Seattle to Camp Pendleton (the Marines' base), helping to raise $80,000 for his defense.

Maj. Carrasco vouched for Chessani, whose "truthfulness is beyond reproach," but he added: "there's not a day that goes by that I don't wish we had done a better job." Col. Christopher Conlin, the hearing officer (who had led an infantry battalion during the 2003 assault on Baghdad), said other commanders would have visited the scene rather than relying on a grainy drone video. Instead, Chessani authorized a report to superiors with few details, misrepresenting that he had inspected the scene, rendering further investigation unnecessary.

Mathis said Chessani later dismissed *Time*'s questions as a trap: "If we follow up with an investigation, it will be an admission of guilt." Kallop testified that none of his troops had positively identified insurgents in the houses before he ordered them cleared "to get the bad guys, and to protect our guys." When he later found no AK-47s, shells, or other evidence, he exclaimed to Cpl. Salinas: "What the crap? Where are the bad guys?" Wuterich had not disclosed that Marines threw grenades and fired M-16s inside the houses, instead falsely reporting that insurgents had fled into the second house. Kallop asked few questions at the scene. He denied his troops had gone on a rampage. "They did not have grief in their eyes" about Terrazas. Wuterich "was personally the least aggressive leader," a "professional" who "knows his job." Capt. Oliver Dreger testified that officers rejected without discussion the town council's demand for an investigation because the mayor was suspected of insurgent ties and the petition was seen as "posturing, political maneuvering." (Dinsmore told *Frontline* that "the city council demonstrated ... that their allegiances largely lied [sic] ... with the insurgency." He also dismissed the Iraqi journalist who made the videotape as an "insurgent propagandist.")

1st Lt. Max Frank testified (under immunity) that the six children and two women, whose bodies he collected from a bed and photographed, had multiple bullet wounds, but "my assumption was my Marines were doing the right thing ... as they were taking fire." When the Iraqis did not obey an order to come out, the Marines "cleared the room with a fragmentation grenade, whose smoke would have obscured the Iraqis' identities." But he found no signs that insurgents had been using the houses or any shell casings from Iraqi guns. When he arrived at the morgue with the remains in 4–5 body bags and the rest in trash bags, some Iraqi workers vomited. Superiors told him to tell hospital officials: "the Marines were sorry about this, but this is what happens when you allow terrorists to use homes to attack Marines." Capt. Haynie said that two days after the killings an Iraqi man complained that his relatives had been pulled from their homes and shot, and another insisted that the taxi passengers were students going to Ramadi. Capt. McConnell later told him there were AK-47s in the taxi and some of the men wore suicide vests, but there was no evidence of either of these things. Sgt. Sax said Chessani was "by far the strongest moral leader I have ever served with in my life." He was sure Chessani would have investigated the deaths "without batting an eye" if he believed the Marines had done something wrong. But he later heard that Wuterich had told the Marines to "shoot first and ask questions later," which Sax called "a bad and damning comment."

Witnesses described two men shot through the head; a young woman shot in the back of the neck in a "cowering position"; two women trying to protect three girls and a young boy, all shot lying on a bed, some in the head; and five young men killed near the taxi, standing still, some with their hands in the air. A senior DoD lawyer, who wrote the first manual on investigating LOAC violations, said "the substantial number of head shots does not suggest a resisting force." Rules adopted after My Lai required commanders to investigate any "possible, alleged or suspected" crimes. But Mathis and

Kallop testified they did not believe the slayings violated LOAC. Huck said he had "some questions" about whether Chessani reported "everything he knew." Chessani never told him about the complaint by local leaders that three whole families had been killed. "If that document was presented, this needs to be reported and that commander should be thinking 'Perhaps I should get an investigation started.'" Chessani also should have reported that the taxi passengers were students. Maj. Connelly said the initial report was that civilians had been killed by the IED and cross fire. "My understanding ... was that they were out in the open" and "moving past the vehicles." He did not learn until later that women and children had been killed inside a house. "It was something different than what I had always pictured." He also did not hear about the town council's formal demand for an investigation.

Capt. Dinsmore, who had served 20 years as an intelligence officer, said no investigation was needed. "Politically, the Marine Corps made a decision to hang Col. Chessani out to dry." Intelligence had warned of a complex attack, including Syrian fighters waiting to ambush them. A drone spotted an insurgent involved in a firefight running into a nearby house and re-emerging in different clothes, carrying a baby. But SSgt. Justin Laughner testified (under immunity) that when Lt. Grayson and he were preparing a statement for higher officers and McGirk, attributing the deaths to cross fire, Grayson ordered him to destroy photos of the bodies and lie about whether they had been taken. (They remained on the camera.) Laughner now admitted: "it's not right, but I didn't say anything." Wuterich had told him that the men in the taxi had "engaged" the Marines with weapons, Marines had received insurgent fire from the house and they had found AK-47s there – all of which were lies. Wuterich never told him Marines had killed women and children. Searching the house, Laughner found no evidence of insurgents but rather a girl screaming that "the Marines came into her house and killed her family."

1st Lt. Mark Towers, Chessani's adjutant, called his superior "a godly man" who read the Bible for half an hour every morning. But he agreed that Chessani's report that he had examined the scene falsely "implied that he went there." Col. Brennan Bryne called Chessani a "Christian, an upright man," with "impeccable integrity," whom "[I] would trust ... with my life." LtCol. Eric Smith, an expert witness on the duties of battalion commanders, did not believe "for a nanosecond" that Chessani had had reason to believe war crimes had been committed. Mathis said the lesson of Haditha was that troops looking for insurgents had two choices: let them escape or fight back and risk "being part of an investigation for the next year and a half."

Chessani told NCIS that the enemy "had set this up so that there would be collateral damage" to "make us look bad." He testified that "I do not believe my decisions and actions were criminal." The day of the shootings was "non-stop action," with bombings and firefights in and around Haditha. He left the command center only once, to visit the site of the most significant battle, where 11 Marines had been injured. (But because he was not under oath he could not be cross-examined.)

Chessani, Gonzalez, McConnell, and Mathis responded to McGirk's email by preparing a five-page internal critique on January 29, 2006:

MCGIRK: How many Marines were killed and wounded in the I.E.D. attack that morning?

MEMO: If it bleeds, it leads. This question is McGirk's attempt to get good bloody gouge [sic] on the situation. He will most likely use the information he gains from this answer as an attention gainer.

MCGIRK: Were there any officers?

MEMO: By asking if there was an officer on the scene the reporter may be trying to identify a point of blame for lack of judgment. If there was an officer involved, then he may be able to have his My Lai massacre pinned on that officer's shoulders ... the reporter would most likely seek to discredit the U.S. government (one of our officers) and expose victimization of the American people by the hand of the government (the enlisted marines under the haphazard command of our "rogue officer.") Unfortunately for McGirk, this is not the case. ... McGirk's story will sell if it can be spun as "Iraq's My Lai massacre." Since there was not an officer involved, this attempt will not go very far. We must be on guard, though, of the reporter's attempt to spin the story like incidents from well-known war movies, like "Platoon" ... [which had] a classic "runaway sergeant" storyline where in [sic] the audience is supposed to be sickened by the sergeant's brutality and equally sickened by the traumatic effects war has on soldiers. This scheme is especially fruitful for McGirk because if he tries to adapt our situation to this model it simultaneously exposes a "war crime cover-up" and shows the deteriorative (albeit exaggerated) effects of war on U.S. marines (the best of the best), which could be expanded by the general press as a testament for why the U.S. should pull out of Iraq. [Chessani substituted a blunt "no" for their answer to this question.]

MCGIRK: How many marines were involved in the killings?

MEMO: First off, we don't know what you're talking about when you say "killings." One of our squads reinforced by a squad of Iraqi Army soldiers were engaged by an enemy initiated ambush on the 19th that killed one American marine and seriously injured two others. We will not justify

121

that question with a response. Theme; Legitimate engagement: we will not acknowledge this reporter's attempt to stain the engagement with the misnomer "killings."

MCGIRK: Were there any weapons found during these house raids – or terrorists – where the killings occurred?

MEMO: Again, you are showing yourself to be uneducated in the world of contemporary insurgent combat. The subject about which we are speaking was a legitimate engagement initiated by the enemy.

MCGIRK: Is there any investigation ongoing into these civilian deaths, and if so have any marines been formally charged?

MEMO: No, the engagement was a bona fide combat action ... By asking this question, McGirk is assuming the engagement was a LOAC violation and that by asking about investigations, he may spurn [sic] a reaction from the command that will initiate an investigation.

MCGIRK: Are the marines in this unit still serving in Haditha?

MEMO: Yes, we are still fighting terrorists of Al-Qaida in Iraq in Haditha. ("Fighting terrorists associated with Al-Qaida" is stronger language than "serving." The American people will side more with someone actively fighting a terrorist organization that is tied to 9/11 than with someone who is idly "serving," like in a way one "serves" a casserole. It's semantics, but in reporting and journalism, words spin the story.)

LtCol. Sean Sullivan, the prosecutor, argued that court-martialing Chessani would show he was being held to the same high standards obeyed by "99.99% of Marine officers and enlisted." A defense attorney replied that the hearing officer knew "that civilian deaths are a regrettable consequence of this war," and a court-martial would hurt morale. Col. Conlin recommended a court-martial because Chessani "did not take personal action to fully investigate the actions leading to civilian deaths," "failed to thoroughly and accurately report and investigate a combat engagement that clearly needed scrutiny," and "suffered from a fatal misunderstanding that loyalty to his marines meant vigorously defending their actions to the detriment of determining what those actions actually were."

In LCpl. Sharratt's Art. 32 hearing an Air Force pathologist said none of the victims with head wounds had been shot from less than two feet (i.e., they had been executed). But an NCIS forensic consultant concluded that two Iraqi men were shot "while crouched or sitting," one against a wall, the other inside a closed closet. He conceded, however, that one man might have been moving when shot. Sharratt (who had fought in Falloujah) said in a sworn statement to NCIS that he could "use any means necessary and my training to eliminate the hostile threat." He claimed to have heard the sound of an AK-47 being prepared to fire. "I knew if there were insurgents inside that room with weapons ... I had to move fast to establish fire superiority." In one room he found a man holding an AK-47 and shot him in the face. In another he shot a man holding an AK-47 two feet away. He then shot a third man who seemed to be moving and a fourth as well. Wuterich, behind him, shot 5–7 rounds into "bodies on the ground to make sure that none were capable of grabbing a weapon and firing back at us." Sharratt said: "We did not execute any Iraqi males ... I did exactly as I was trained to do." He claimed he gave the two captured AK-47s to a Marine that day, but there was no clear record of weapons being recovered at the house. Sgt. Frank Wolf testified that Haditha was "a hostile environment. I would put that day up there with Fallujah." Sgt. Travis Fields, who instructed the battalion in ROEs, said he told the Marines: "don't hesitate." They could shoot if someone was pointing a weapon at them or if they felt in imminent danger. But "they were not trained to anticipate meeting someone inside a home with a weapon." LCpl. James Prentice, Sharratt's friend, told NCIS that a few hours after the shooting Sharratt told him that Wuterich and he were going to use "a story" that the men inside the room were killed after one pointed a rifle at Sharratt.

In unsworn testimony, Sharratt said two of the three men he killed had pointed AK-47s at him. The third died as he emptied his pistol into the room.

> I could not tell while I was shooting if they were armed or not ... but I felt threatened because the first two individuals had rifles and I assumed [the others] had some sort of weapon ... I kept firing until my magazine was empty because I didn't know if they had body armor or suicide vests. As I fired at the other insurgents in the room, I felt as though they were coming toward me ... they all had a round in their chambers and were ready to fire what appear to be full magazines.

At the end of the hearing LtCol. Paul Ware (the hearing officer) told prosecutors "your theories don't match the reason you say we should go to trial." "The most important issue is whether the Marines perceived a hostile threat." "What the evidence points to is that the version of the Iraqis isn't really supported." The same day that Sullivan recommended a court-martial for Chessani, Ware recommended against one for Sharratt, who "responded instinctively, assaulting into the room and emptying his pistol. Whether this was a brave act of combat against the enemy or tragedy of misperception born out of conducting combat with an enemy that hides among innocents, Cpl. Sharratt's actions were in accord with the roe."

Physical evidence showing the shots had been fired from a distance was "inconsistent with an execution."

> To believe the government version of facts is to disregard clear and convincing evidence to the contrary and sets a dangerous precedent that ... may encourage others to bear false witness against marines as a tactic to erode public support of the Marine Corps and mission in Iraq. Even more dangerous is the potential that a Marine may hesitate at the critical moment when facing the enemy.

Expressing satisfaction, Sharratt's civilian lawyers said: "prejudgment within some elements of the media and by certain members of Congress was particularly offensive to us."

At his Art. 32 hearing LCpl. Tatum, charged with the murder of two Iraqi girls, negligent homicide of two men, a woman, and a child, and assault on a boy and girl, said he had been responding to a legitimate threat. NCIS agent Matthew Marshall testified that Tatum had told him: "knowing it was a kid, I shot him anyway." Tatum twice said he had identified those in the room as women and children. "He stated that women and children can hurt you, too, as a justification for shooting them." But Tatum said at least once that he had "unknowingly" shot women and children. In unsworn testimony Tatum told the hearing: "I didn't know there was women and children in that house until later. Otherwise, I would have physically stopped everybody in that room from shooting." In the first house "visibility was horrible." "Dust was in the air. Smoke was in the air. I really couldn't make out more than targets." In the second "it was dark. Couldn't make out a whole lot. Just targets." However, LCpl. Humberto Mendoza said that after he told Tatum frightened women and children were cowering in a bedroom, Tatum ordered him to kill them. When he refused, Tatum pushed past him into the room, after which Mendoza heard either a grenade or gunfire. But under cross-examination he admitted shooting two unarmed men during the raid, initially lying to investigators, not reporting the above conversation for more than a year, and hoping NCIS would release his citizenship application.

Ware, again the hearing officer, asked if the ROEs were "more" (he meant less) "restrictive than the common law, where [a civilian] can kill someone who points a gun at you?" The lawyer who briefed

Marines in Iraq before combat testified they could kill people fleeing IEDs, even if they were unarmed and there was no proof of their involvement. But the DoD LOAC expert had testified in Chessani's Art. 32 hearing that "the fact that [insurgents] use human shields doesn't give us authority to start firing and say, 'the fault is yours, not ours.'" And the prosecutor said: "Marines are required to positively identify a target, even a house that is considered hostile. Is it challenging? Yes. Unfortunately that's the reality we have." Tatum's lawyer said his client had been following the most important rule: coming to the aid of other Marines firing at targets inside a house. "You cannot sit back in this air-conditioned room at Camp Pendleton and second-guess these young men."

Ware recommended dropping all charges against Tatum.

> What occurred in house 1 and house 2 are tragedies. The photographs of the victims are heart wrenching, and the desire to explain this tragedy as a criminal act and not the result of training and fighting an enemy that hides among innocents is great. However, in the end, my opinion is that there is insufficient evidence for trial. Cpl. Tatum shot and killed people in houses 1 and 2, but the reason he did so was because of his training and the circumstances he was placed in, not to exact revenge and commit murder ... On 19 November 2005, in the mere seconds Cpl. Tatum had to make a decision, he acted in accord with training, to engage targets that a fellow marine was firing at, without time to fully assess the situation and reflect on what Sgt. Wuterich was doing. It is only in hindsight that we can start to question why Sgt. Wuterich was firing his weapon at children and conclude that Cpl. Tatum should have deemed such actions were unwarranted.

Gen. Mattis dismissed all the charges against Sharratt, calling him "innocent."

> Operational, moral and legal imperatives demand that we Marines stay true to our own standards and maintain compliance with the law of war in this morally bruising environment. With the dismissal of these charges, you may fairly conclude that you did your best to live up to the standards, followed by U.S. fighting men throughout our many wars, in the face of life or death decisions made by you in a matter of seconds in combat ...
>
> The intense examination into this incident, and into your conduct, has been necessary to maintain discipline standards and, in the words of the marine hymn, "To keep our honor clean" ... You have served as a marine infantryman in Iraq where our nation is fighting a shadowy

enemy who hides among the innocent people, and routinely targets and intentionally draws fire toward civilians.

Mattis also dismissed the charges against Stone, whose "mistakes" were not a crime.

> Capt. Stone and his fellow marines served in the most ethically challenging combat environment in the world. Nonetheless, marines are expected to withstand the extreme and fatiguing pressures inherent in counterinsurgency operations, protecting the innocent, while tirelessly fighting the enemy with relentless vigor. I have no doubt that he now understands the absolute necessity for objective inquiry into the combat actions of our marines in such an environment, especially when innocent lives are lost.

And Mattis exonerated MGen. Johnson, but issued letters of censure for Huck, Sokoloski, and Davis for their "lack of due diligence." Huck failed to ensure that his field commanders determined how and why so many civilians had been killed. Sokoloski waited two weeks to tell Huck about the *Time* inquiry. Davis failed to seek detailed explanations from battalion commanders about the civilian deaths. Huck was said to be the highest ranking active duty officer to be formally punished during the Iraq war. Marine Commandant Gen. James T. Conway endorsed the decision. The Marine Corps also exonerated Capt. McConnell.

In Wuterich's Art. 32 hearing, Dela Cruz testified under immunity that he saw the accused shoot five unarmed Iraqi men moments after the IED exploded. After a comrade had been wounded by an IED a week earlier, Wuterich said: "if we ever get hit again, we should kill everybody in that vicinity ... so to teach them a lesson." After Haditha, Wuterich told him: "if anyone asks, say they were running away." But cross-examination exposed inconsistencies in Dela Cruz's testimony. Although he had said earlier that Iraqi army soldiers with his unit had killed the five men, he acknowledged: "I did lie about that." But he maintained that after giving at least two false statements and contesting portions of others, now he was telling the truth. He admitted urinating on the head of a dead Iraqi but disputed another Marine's allegation that he had kicked a dead man's head while boasting "I killed that [expletive]." He also admitted abusing prisoners, kicking detainees so as not to leave bruises, and firing eight rounds into the men Wuterich had killed. He had agreed to tell Wuterich's cover story out of fear that his own shots into a dead body could lead to murder charges. SSgt. Laughner said Wuterich falsely told him the men had been running from the taxi when they were shot.

Wuterich testified (not under oath) that the five men he shot had been running away, perhaps to detonate a bomb in their car. "Engaging was the only choice. The threat had to be neutralized." "We were taking fire from that house. It was a hostile structure we were going into." "[O]n approach, I advised the team something like 'shoot first and ask questions later' or 'don't hesitate to shoot.'"

Ware recommended that Wuterich be court-martialed for negligent homicide in the deaths of the seven women and children but not for the other ten deaths. He found Dela Cruz "wholly incredible." "The evidence is contradictory, the forensic analysis is limited, and almost all the witnesses have an obvious bias or prejudice." "Although I believe the government will fail to prove beyond a reasonable doubt that [Wuterich] committed any offenses other than dereliction of duty, due to the serious nature of the charges I recommend referral to a general court-martial."

Gen. Mattis ordered that Chessani be court-martialed for dereliction of duty and failing to obey a direct order to conduct a full-scale investigation. Although Ware had recommended dismissal of all charges against Tatum, Mattis ordered that he be court-martialed for involuntary manslaughter, reckless endangerment, and aggravated assault, but dismissed the murder charges. After replacing Mattis at Camp Pendleton, MGen. Samuel T. Helland ordered that Wuterich be court-martialed for voluntary manslaughter, aggravated assault, reckless endangerment, dereliction of duty, and obstruction of justice.

Chessani's lawyers responded by alleging that Mattis's decision to charge had been subject to unlawful command influence. Col. John Ewers had assisted Bargewell's investigation and had taken Chessani's statement before becoming Mattis's legal adviser. Mattis testified: "I make my own decisions." Although Ewers might have been at meetings about Haditha, "he had no input, he was not asked for his opinion, nor did he offer it. Nor would I have accepted it." It was LtCol. William Riggs who had responsibility for advising Mattis about Haditha. Mattis had had no improper congressional contact, and "nobody in the Pentagon ever talked to me" about the case. Marine Corps commandants never mentioned the case. The media "had no influence whatsoever"; indeed, Mattis did not own a television. He had read more than 9,000 pages of evidence so he could "bluntly challenge" prosecutors and because he did not want information "filtered" through others.

Nevertheless, Col. Steven Folsom, hearing Chessani's court-martial, dismissed the charges because the prosecution had failed to prove beyond a reasonable doubt that there had been no such influence, which was "the mortal enemy of military justice … as devastating as actual manipulation of a trial." Ewers had participated in dozens of meetings about Haditha, thereby "tainting" the charges. Folsom denied a motion to reconsider, heatedly telling the prosecutor he had 72 hours to appeal. But the appeals court affirmed the dismissal. Although there was no evidence that Mattis had been influenced by Ewers, "an objective disinterested observer fully informed of all the facts and circumstances would harbor significant doubt about the fairness of the proceeding." Although the prosecution sought en banc review, the military decided not to pursue the appeal but instead convene a board of inquiry about whether Chessani should be demoted before retirement.

Lt. Grayson was the first to be tried, for ordering Laughner (during the early stages of the military investigation three months after the killings) to delete photos of the dead. Col. Watt testified that Grayson told him at that time there were no photographs. SSgt. Lee Sentino testified that he told Laughner to delete the photos because Grayson had said it was Marine policy to do so when dead Iraqis were found not to be insurgents. Laughner said he had lied to five investigators, telling the truth for the first time in August 2006. The judge dismissed the obstruction of justice charge because the prosecution had not alleged that Grayson knew of the criminal investigation when he ordered the photos destroyed. (The Bargewell inquiry was administrative, not criminal.) The prosecution said Grayson had engaged in "a pattern of lies … in order to avoid accountability." His civilian lawyer argued that Grayson had been charged because Watt, who was leading the Bargewell inquiry, "had an ax to grind." After deliberating six hours, the jury acquitted Grayson of all counts. He had refused an offer to plead to reduced charges and get no jail time.

Hearing Wuterich's court-martial, LtCol. David Jones rejected an allegation of unlawful command influence. Prosecutors had "overwhelmingly" met the burden of proving beyond a reasonable doubt that "there was no chilling effect. The court must deal with facts, not conjecture." The trial began in January 2012, more than six years after the killings. All but one of the prospective jurors had heard an order to "clear" a house of insurgents during combat in Iraq. One said he would have to be confident he was under fire before throwing grenades and firing his M-16. Nearly all said they had first separated military-age males (MAMs) from women and children; none had killed anyone in the process, but many acknowledged that the deaths of women and children were often a tragic result of war. Most had lost a fellow Marine. Jones instructed them they could decline to impose a prison sentence even if they convicted because "the conviction itself is the punishment." The prosecution showed a 60 Minutes interview in which Wuterich said no Marine violated his orders. "All the actions ... were taken as they should have been done." Col. Watt testified that Wuterich had told him several times he instructed the squad "to shoot first, ask questions later." LtCol. David Mendelson said Wuterich acknowledged he had not positively identified his targets. LCpl. Tatum (testifying under immunity) said that after Wuterich had labeled the house "hostile," there was no need to distinguish between combatants and noncombatants before killing them. Having heard shots, "I did not feel I had to [positively identify] individuals" as threats. Wuterich led the assault inside the house: "he was muzzle up and ready to engage any individuals coming out of those two doors." "The only thing that gave me the idea that there was hostile intent was Staff Sgt. Wuterich firing." Smoke and dust from guns and grenades made it impossible to tell targets' ages or gender. "They were just silhouettes." Based on his own experience in Falloujah, he did not feel Wuterich had done anything wrong. "I'm trained to shoot two to the head and two to the chest and I followed my training."

Dela Cruz testified that the five men from the taxi who were shot by Wuterich "were just standing around." He had shot the bodies lying on the ground "because I wanted to make sure they were dead." He admitted urinating on one – "my emotions got the best of me" – but denied kicking another. Despite their anger at Terrazas's death, Dela Cruz and others searched several occupied houses without killing anyone. Kallop testified that once a house had been declared "hostile," any use of force was justified without the need to distinguish between combatants and noncombatants. The prosecution offered a Marine lawyer to rebut this. A defense witness testified that the motto of the battle of Falloujah was "every room with a boom." But there, most civilians had already fled. (In a January 2006 report recommending Wuterich for a medal, Kallop had said Wuterich led a counter-attack on a building from which Marines were receiving fire, which "turned the tide of the ambush and killed a number of insurgents still attempting to fight or attempting to flee the area." The report praised his "tactical proficiency, aggressive leadership, and attention to detail.")

After the defense conducted devastating cross-examinations of three prosecution witnesses who had changed their stories when granted immunity, Col. Jones abruptly recessed the trial and told both sides to "look for options." Five days later Wuterich pleaded guilty to dereliction of duty, saying:

> When my marines and I cleared those houses that day, I responded to what I perceived as a threat. And my intention was to eliminate that threat in order to keep the rest of my marines alive. So when I told my team to "shoot first and ask questions later," the intent wasn't that they would shoot civilians, it was that they would not hesitate in the face of the enemy.

He originally faced 152 years, and Col. Jones had planned to recommend the 90-year maximum sought by the prosecution, declaring: "it's difficult for the court to fathom negligent dereliction of duty worse than the facts of this case." But the deal provided no jail time, only a reduction in rank to private and a general discharge under honorable conditions.

Wuterich said to the relatives of those killed: "words cannot express my sorrow for the loss of your loved ones." But the cousin of one victim said the outcome was "not new for the American citizens that already did little about Abu Ghraib and other crimes in Iraq." "We will resume the cases through all international courts." Another relative said the sentence "shows the lies of the Americans." A man whose four brothers were killed called the deal "another crime committed against the victims and their families." A teacher who saw the attack asked: "was the marine charged with dereliction of duty because he didn't kill more? Is Iraqi blood so cheap?" The Provincial Council member for Haditha said the punishment was "suitable for a traffic violation." An Iraq government spokesman said: "we will follow up [with] all legal procedures and judiciary measures."

HAMDANIA

On April 26, 2006, a month after *Time* exposed the Haditha killings, soldiers from Kilo Company, 3rd Battalion in the same Marine regiment killed a civilian in Hamdania.[4] The military quickly returned the suspects to Camp Pendleton, putting some in the brig and restricting the others to the base. Rep. Murtha again rushed to judgment, asserting on ABC television: "Some Marines pulled somebody out of a house, put them next to an IED, fired some [AK-47s] so they'd have cartridges there, and then tried to cover that up." MGen. Richard Zilmer, the top Marine in Iraq, announced that "sufficient information existed to recommend a criminal investigation." John Jodka complained that the military put his son (PFC John Jodka II) in the brig "to show 'we're in charge, we're cleaning up our act'" after Haditha. One general had concluded: "if a few privates and corporals have to take it, that's the price of keeping my stars."

Two months later Sgt. Lawrence Hutchins III, Cpl. Trent Thomas, LCpl. Tyler Jackson, PFC John Jodka II, LCpl. Jerry Shumate Jr., LCpl. Robert Pennington, Cpl. Marshall Magincalda, and Navy PO3 Melson Bacos were charged with conspiracy, murder, assault, lying to investigators, and obstruction of justice for pulling Hashim Ibrahim Awad al-Zobaie – an unarmed disabled 52-year-old former police officer and father of 11 – from his house and shooting him to death. This was the largest number of Marines ever charged in a wartime killing.

J. Richardson Brannon, representing Hutchins, maligned the victim as "a relative of the terrorist." Hutchins had reported to superiors that his unit "spotted a man digging on the side of the road from our ambush site. I made the call and engaged." The deceased had a shovel and an AK-47. Maj. Haytham Faraj, representing Thomas, accused NCIS of threatening some defendants with the death penalty unless they talked. Ret. BGen. David M. Brahms represented Pennington, "an all-American boy" he would be "proud" to have as his son. "It's hard to imagine him conspiring with others to commit the dastardly deed." Brahms accused DoD of leaking details before announcing the charges. "The bastards ... should be hung in a public square." "My Marines are being thrown under the goddamn bus." Jeremiah J. Sullivan III said his client, Bacos, who had earned a Purple Heart in earlier combat tours in Iraq, was being subjected to "cruel and unusual punishment" by being threatened with the death penalty and held in the brig under more restrictions than "known terrorists": in solitary except for a brief period walking in the recreational yard with his hands, legs, and waist shackled. (Shackling ended a week later.) Sullivan also complained that "the reports of Haditha are having an impact on everything." Joseph Casas, representing Jodka, called the incident a "legitimate, command-sanctioned ambush" in a locale where insurgents were known to plant IEDs. "I will adamantly say that what the government believes happened did not happen on that night." NCIS forced Jodka to sign a false statement by interrogating him in Iraq for more than seven hours without food, water, or bathroom breaks and threatening him with the death penalty. NCIS responded that all the statements were voluntary and each suspect had had "the opportunity to review the statement and make any changes to it before signing." Defense attorneys suggested that the victim's family had concocted the story to get money. The body was exhumed and brought to the USA for autopsy. Angered by the accused's confinement in the brig, 200 demonstrated outside the base with flags and signs saying "God Bless Our Heroes" and "Liberate the Pendleton 8." Smaller rallies continued weekly. The legal defense fund raised $60,000.

In August, Hutchins, Thomas, and Shumate, with LCpl. Saul H. Lopezromo, PFC Derek I. Lewis, and LCpl. Henry D. Lever, were charged in separate incidents uncovered during the investigation into Awad's killing. They were accused of beating Khalid Hamad Daham on April 10; and Hutchins was charged with choking Hassam Manza Fayall and placing a loaded pistol in the mouth of Ali Haaz Rbashby. Victor Kelley, representing Thomas, denounced this "false" allegation as an attempt to extract information about Awad's killing. In September, 2nd Lt. Nathan Phan was also charged in those assaults.

More than ninety journalists attended the Art. 32 proceeding against Magincalda and Jodka on August 30. Prosecutors (who had ruled out the death penalty) said Hutchins and Thomas admitted killing Awad. They stormed into his home after failing to find a suspected insurgent believed to live next door, slammed him to the ground in front of his family, and bound his hands and feet. Hutchins, Thomas, and Shumate shot him with their M-16 rifles, and Jackson and Jodka with their M-249 rifles. Magincalda collected the shell casings. To frame Awad, Bacos fired an AK-47 taken from another house and Pennington wiped off squad members' fingerprints, placing the AK-47 and a stolen shovel next to the body. Hutchins, the squad leader, reported by radio that after the unit had been fired on by a man they spotted digging, they killed him in a firefight. Pennington had given a statement about the cover-up. Jane Siegel (once the Marine Corps chief defense counsel), representing Jodka, sought to prevent prosecutors from reading defendants' statements in court. "To openly discuss the contents will completely pollute the local and national jury pool. Some of it is very inflammatory." Casas said: "all we have are unreliable, uncorroborated statements and no physical evidence." Iraqi witnesses were inherently incredible. "Their culture is so different from our own that when they narrate a story, they tell it in the first person" even if they only heard it from others. Magincalda's lawyer denied the defendants' statements were admissions of guilt. Jodka's lawyer said the defendants had been coerced. In order to avoid a public airing, defense lawyers agreed to let the hearing officer base his recommendation on reading them. Siegel accused the government of "doing its damned best to try and provoke one of these Marines to testify against the others in accordance with its theory of the case. None of these men are going to do that." Jodka sought to waive his Art. 32 hearing, which Casas called "a meaningless exercise because military prosecutors have refused to grant his attorneys access to important evidence that supports his claim of innocence." Shumate, Thomas, and Magincalda followed suit. The Marine Corps refused to agree, but allowed the hearing officer to rely exclusively on exhibits not disclosed to the public.

Shumate's lawyer initially insisted on hearing the prosecution's witnesses in open court, but two weeks later also agreed to let the hearing officer rely on exhibits. In September, Shumate was referred to court-martial. NCIS Special Agent Kelly Garbo had interviewed the accused on May 11, obtaining handwritten maps, diagrams, and statements that the prosecution called confessions. She denied claims that the defendants had been coerced, insisting Shumate had cooperated after being told that NCIS already knew "the real story." The Art. 32 hearing officers recommended a court-martial for Jodka but made no recommendation for Magincalda. Gen. Mattis referred Jodka, Magincalda, and Shumate for court-martial but ruled out the death penalty and dismissed charges against Lever.

A few days later Sullivan posted on the web a video of his client, Bacos, talking about his combat experience (but not the charges). "Unless you sit down and listen to this young man, you can't get a feel for the combat he has experienced." But the day after that, Bacos pleaded guilty to lesser charges and agreed to testify.

The squad had been on a late-night mission to catch insurgents. Hutchins wanted to kill an Iraqi suspected of planting IEDs. When they could not find him, Hutchins decided to capture and kill Awad, whom he believed had insurgent connections. Bacos watched the Marines line up and shoot Awad. Hutchins then did a "dead check," firing three more rounds into Awad's head, and Thomas fired 7–10 rounds. Bacos had stolen an AK-47 from the Iraqi's home; he fired it in the air so Marines would have shell casings to leave at the body. He had asked the squad to release Awad, but Magincalda refused, calling Bacos a "weakling."

Although "shocked and sick to my stomach," Bacos felt unable to intervene. "They were going to do what they were going to do." "Why didn't I do more to stop it? Why didn't I just walk away? The answer is I wanted to be part of the team." Later that night he told other Marines: "I want you to remember something – we're different. We're not like these men." He asked the dead man's family to forgive him and apologized "to our country, to the Navy and the Marine Corps for not living up to the values of honor, courage and commitment. I've learned from this mistake, and to tell the truth is the only honorable thing I can do." The judge, Col. Steven Folsom, watched a 19-minute tape of Awad's relatives describing him and the killing. Prosecutors had sought 10–15 years and a dishonorable discharge. The defense wanted just a few months. Folsom would have given Bacos ten years and a dishonorable discharge but was bound by the plea agreement to give him just a year and let him remain in the Navy. (He was released after ten months with credit for good conduct.) Folsom had denied a motion by other defense lawyers to close the hearing. Hutchins's lawyer questioned Bacos's credibility: "if the chances of spending the rest of your life in prison are on the line, you will say whatever it takes to be able to go home."

Several weeks later Jodka pleaded guilty to aggravated assault and conspiracy to obstruct justice. At his sentencing hearing he said the squad planned to kidnap Saleh Gowad and shoot him in a setting contrived to look like he had been surprised digging a hole for an IED. "If anyone asked, we would say that we had seen this man approach with a shovel and begin digging and that he engaged us and that we had lawfully engaged him." Gowad had been identified as a "high-value individual" by military intelligence and arrested three times by the squad, only to be released days later. Jodka claimed to have been unaware they had kidnapped and killed the wrong man. But he admitted knowing the plan was illegal: "civilians and noncombatants are not lawful targets." He had "agonized" over the decision to plead guilty.

> In the end, it was the right thing to do. The most difficult part for me is that I had to weigh my own integrity and need for the truth with the loyalty to the Marines that I had bonded with in Iraq ... In combat there is nothing but your squad ... If you can't depend on those men, you'll never survive combat.

Sgt. Jacob Fernandez, called as a character witness, said the infantry motto is "if we die, we're going to die together." "When the shit hits the fan, I know that Marine on my left and on my right has my back. If he dies, I die."

At sentencing, Jodka said this tragedy had taught him that "anything that gets reported becomes ammunition" for "an argument against the war." He apologized "to the Awad family for the suffering my actions in Iraq caused." Urging a five-year sentence, prosecutors showed a video the squad made two days after the killing in which Jodka and others used profanity and joked about killing more people. Casas blamed the whole plot on Hutchins, "an unscrupulous squad leader." The original charges carried a life sentence, and the judge would have given Jodka 5 years and a dishonorable discharge; but the plea bargain called for 18 months (with credit for 6 while awaiting trial) and a general discharge.

Jackson and Shumate pleaded guilty to aggravated assault and conspiracy to obstruct justice; they faced 15 years, prosecutors sought 10, the judge would have given them 8, but under the plea bargain they got just 21 months. Jackson said he deliberately shot above Awad's head.

After his wife raised $14,000 for his legal defense, Thomas pleaded to kidnapping, murder, conspiracy, making a false official statement, larceny, assault, and housebreaking. Asked by the judge why the squad killed an innocent man, Thomas said they had devised "Operation Vigilante" to "get someone else to make a statement that Marines, we were sick and tired of getting bombed." He admitted they had no evidence that Awad had ties to insurgents. As they marched him a thousand yards from his house, he repeatedly pleaded "Why, mister, why?" When he struggled to break free, Thomas and others bound his hands and feet and Pennington tried to choke him unconscious. Hutchins reported over the radio that the squad had spotted a man digging a hole. After someone fired the first shot, Thomas and others followed suit, and Bacos shot an AK-47 to make it look like a gunfight. Once several had shot Awad, Hutchins fired three more rounds into his head. Thomas also pleaded guilty to beating another Iraqi so badly he could not stand and had to be hospitalized on April 10. In his unsworn pre-sentencing statement he said: "every marine I ever served with knows [I have] his back." But on the third day of the sentencing hearing Thomas withdrew his guilty plea, claiming he now believed he had been "acting under the color of lawful authority." The refiled charges included premeditated murder (withdrawn as part of the earlier agreement).

In a hearing on the admissibility of his statement to NCIS, Pennington claimed he had been threatened with the death penalty. "I mulled that over for about 5 seconds and then said, 'if that's what you're going to charge me with, I want a lawyer,'" which he was denied. But after two NCIS agents disputed this, Pennington acknowledged signing a declaration confirming he had read and corrected his statement and then pleaded guilty to kidnapping and conspiracy. Although he regretted his actions, he and other Marines were frustrated by the ill-defined mission and their inability to tell friend from foe. "As callous as it sounds," every Iraqi was "guilty until proven otherwise." When the squad could not find Gowad, they planned to grab one of his brothers to "affect the insurgency and send a message. We felt that just catching them would be an exercise in futility – they would just be released a few days later."

At the sentencing hearing, Bacos said Pennington had stuffed a bandage into Awad's mouth as a gag, exclaiming at one point: "this [expletive] is trying to bite me." After the killing, Pennington "took [Awad's] hand and kind of played with it and made Mr. Awad hit himself. He said, 'Quit hitting yourself.'" Helping to put the body in a bag, Pennington joked about Awad's splattered brain matter and whether he had rigor mortis. Other witnesses testified that, after the killing, the platoon distributed a flier in Arabic warning that anyone digging a hole like Awad would be killed. Prosecutors asked for 20 years; the judge would have given him 14 and a dishonorable discharge; but the plea agreement stipulated 8 (and he received credit for nearly a year served).

2nd Lt. Nathan Phan, who commanded the unit that killed Awad but had not been present at the killing, had an Art. 32 hearing on charges of assaulting three Iraqis on April 10 and falsely reporting that one had been released. He had acknowledged to NCIS that he had placed an unloaded pistol near the lips of one detainee. Hutchins told NCIS that Phan had participated in or knew of all three assaults; he "was the brains and I was the brawn." The defense denounced Hutchins as a "murderer and inveterate liar." Shumate and Lopezromo both testified that Phan was not present at one assault. Phan's lawyer, David Sheldon, warned that "you will see some serious questions about outrageous tactics used by NCIS to obtain statements." The military announced it would bring a victim and three witnesses from Iraq. LCpl. Christopher Faulkner's statement to NCIS said Phan had placed a loaded pistol in a detainee's mouth. Faulkner now denied this, and the defense introduced a new statement that Phan had merely been present during the interrogation. The defense also wanted Shumate and Lopezromo to testify, presenting affidavits claiming that NCIS had changed their statements.

During a break, Sheldon told LtCol. William Pigott, the hearing officer, that NCIS agents had committed criminal misconduct. Pigott said he wanted testimony by those agents, some of whom were out of state. When the hearing resumed, NCIS Special Agent Michael Austin acknowledged that though Faulkner's statement (prepared by the agent conducting the interrogation) said Phan watched a sergeant choke the detainee, Austin's own interrogation notes said Faulkner was uncertain who had choked the detainee. Jodka testified he never saw Phan assault any Iraqi. LCpl. Andrew Kraus had given NCIS a sworn statement implicating Phan in the assault, but had since given the defense a sworn affidavit denying he had said that to NCIS. Threatened with a perjury charge, Kraus asked for a lawyer before testifying. Pigott said he would ask Mattis to order two investigations: one into perjury by the three defense witnesses and how NCIS obtained their statements; the other into whether any attorneys engaged in improper contact with witnesses. The defense also called a former police detective, who criticized NCIS for failing to videotape statements. At the end of the hearing Sheldon asked Pigott to reconsider admitting evidence the Marine Corps called classified. Pigott replied that the hearing was officially closed. When Sheldon objected, Pigott screamed this, ordering Sheldon to sit down and shut up. Sheldon muttered that Pigott's ruling was "bullshit." Pigott retorted: "Did you just threaten me? Don't swear at me." Sheldon also accused Pigott of improperly declaring that he believed government officials like NCIS agents were truthful.

When the hearing resumed, Pigott cleared the courtroom and made embedded reporters sign a nondisclosure agreement before letting the prosecutor read the secret ROE requiring Marines to follow a four-step process before firing an M-16: show, shout, shove, shoot. Marines had to positively identify the target as a threat demonstrating hostile action, not just intent; but the definitions were subjective. Phan testified that a few days before Awad's killing, his Marines had watched the 1999 film *The Boondock Saints*, in which young men in Boston killed gangsters. On other occasions Phan had ordered unauthorized tactics, including choking suspects and putting a gun in a suspect's mouth. "It was a gray area, and I thought I was doing the right thing to get information to save marines' lives."

Gen. Mattis ordered that Phan be court-martialed for two assaults but dismissed charges for the third, as well as for making a false statement. Six weeks later Mattis withdrew all the assault charges, ruling that Phan would face only administrative punishment. As part of the deal,

Phan admitted exceeding "the permissible limits of the official rules of engagement regarding interrogation of insurgents" and acknowledged ordering Hutchins to use a "blood choke" hold, rendering one detainee unconscious, and to point an unloaded pistol at another. Phan was reprimanded, restricted to base for a month and docked a half month's pay.

LtCol. David Jones, the judge, ordered a board of mental health professionals to determine whether Thomas could evaluate the legality of an alleged order to commit the killing. Defense lawyers sought to suppress his alleged admission to NCIS. LtCol. David Furness (the company commander) testified that he sought "to impress upon the Marines … discretion in the use of force." Although he initially believed Awad's killing fell within the ROE, Bacos's NCIS statement raised doubts. Furness ordered a formal investigation because "Haditha had just blown up and I believed it was prudent to protect the command, the Marines and the Marine Corps." Jones denied the suppression motion and ruled that an Art. 32 hearing was unnecessary because Thomas had earlier waived it for similar charges. Jones also ruled that jurors would not be told Thomas faced a mandatory minimum sentence of life if convicted of premeditated murder but would hear details of the other plea agreements. Jones excluded an interview Thomas gave to CNN the day before he withdrew his guilty plea, in which he said the squad killed Awad to "set an example for any future terrorists that are going to put an IED on this road." Thomas had compared the Marines to an abused wife. "They're getting shot at. They're getting blown up every day. And they get mad, and they go out and do something. Is it justified?"

Prosecutors called the case "an old-fashioned premeditated conspiracy to kill." Faraj, one of six defense lawyers, said that after Hutchins "issued the command … Cpl. Thomas had no other alternative other than to do what he did." Victor Kelley, the lead defense attorney, said evidence would show Thomas suffered from traumatic brain injury and PTSD. Jackson testified that Hutchins had formulated the plot to kidnap and kill Gowad. "Killing the number one HVI [high-value insurgent] in the area did not sound like a bad idea to me." Bacos said Gowad's release "really made us mad. We did all this work to find terrorists and then they let them go."

The jury of three officers and six enlisted men convicted Thomas of conspiracy to commit murder and kidnapping but acquitted him of premeditated murder, larceny, housebreaking, and making a false official statement. Before sentencing, Thomas testified about growing up in poverty in St. Louis. "I came from nothing. Here, I am at home. It is my all." "I've never been really good at anything until I came into the Marine Corps." He faced a life sentence; prosecutors sought 15 years; the defense asked for the 14 months he had already served, which he got, with a bad-conduct discharge. He said he still felt that killing Awad had deterred insurgent attacks on Marines.

Magincalda also demanded a jury trial and sought to ask prospective panel members more than twenty questions, including their favorite books and television shows and their politics and club memberships. The judge ruled that jurors could not hear the plea deals other defendants negotiated or the fact that the minimum sentence for premeditated murder was life. Prosecutors said Magincalda "helped kill this man and then he lied about it." The defense claimed that Magincalda refused to participate in the actual killing. "He said, 'I ain't gonna do it.'" Phan testified that he had been "frustrated, agitated and irritated" that "I send my boys out to risk their necks to capture these individuals and they are subsequently released."

The six-person jury of a captain and five sergeants found Magincalda guilty of housebreaking, larceny, and conspiracy to commit murder, but not premeditated murder. In his unsworn pre-sentencing statement he said: "I am very sorry for the offenses that I've done ... I would like to think I will go on to do good things in my life." Dr. Jennifer Morse, the psychiatrist who had been treating him in the brig, testified that "he was simply a broken man." He faced up to life; prosecutors sought 10 years; but he was sentenced to time served (448 days) and demoted to private.

Although Brannon claimed that Hutchins, his client, had asked for and been denied a lawyer, the judge admitted the seven-page single-spaced statement Hutchins typed and signed for NCIS, as well as his verbal statement that he had fired three bullets into Awad's head as he was dying. The judge held a closed hearing on whether to admit unidentified classified information (presumably the ROE). In a pretrial hearing Brannon said he planned to argue "partial mental responsibility." "It was 'cowboy country' and they are living in it. It was terrific stress. Can you imagine laying [sic] down every night knowing that people who want to kill you are only a hundred yards away?" The prosecution called Hutchins "the mastermind behind the plan," which "was an execution." Brannon said Hutchins and his squad were pressured by commanders to "get things done." "Their task was trying to stop the IEDs and the snipers and anybody who was hurting the American troops." Bacos testified that Hutchins shot as a "dead check," turning Awad's head into bloody pulp to prevent identification. Afterwards, Hutchins pronounced: "Congratulations gents, we've just gotten away with murder." Pennington testified: "we were sick of their rules and decided to write our own rules to protect ourselves." Brannon argued that his client's actions were the result of poor leadership and tacit approval of violence. The jury convicted Hutchins of unpremeditated murder, larceny, and false statement, but acquitted him of kidnapping, assault, housebreaking, and obstruction of justice. In his unsworn pre-sentence statement he said he had acted "out of a sense that it was part of our mission." He had joined the Marines right out of high school, following his father, uncle, and grandfather. His wife begged jurors to let him come home to her and their two-year-old daughter, who sat on her grandfather's lap in the courtroom. His mother said: "I gave him to the marines, now I want you to give him back to me." Arguing that Hutchins had destroyed his squad by persuading seven soldiers to commit crimes, the prosecutor sought 30 years. The jury recommended 15 and a dishonorable discharge. Mattis reduced this to 11.

After visiting Jackson and Shumate in prison, Mattis ordered their release after nine months, having "balanced many factors," including "their military experience, relative rank and position of authority, and their specific involvement in the death." Jodka and Bacos were already free, following sentence reductions for good behavior. A few days later Mattis freed Pennington after 15 months. On April 22, 2010 the Military Court of Appeal overturned Hutchins's conviction because of procedural errors. Having served about half his sentence, he was back at Camp Pendleton and restored to sergeant. He wanted to be reunited with his seven squad members. The prosecution appealed the reversal, but the Court of Appeals for the Armed Forces agreed that Hutchins's constitutional rights had been violated when he was held in solitary without access to a lawyer for seven days during his interrogation in Iraq. In a second trial more than five years later a jury again convicted him of murder after deliberating just three hours, but sentenced him to time served (about seven years) and a bad-conduct discharge. In 2017 Ray Mabus, who had been Navy Secretary at the time, said he had not been "as harsh" with lower ranks. "You have to have a degree of humanity when you're given the authority to lock your own troops up in jail for the rest of their life because they have the guts to volunteer to go into that situation."

MAHMUDIYAH

On March 12, 2006 in this rural town in the Sunni triangle, members of B Company, 1st Battalion, 502nd Regiment of the Army's 4th Infantry Division allegedly raped and killed Abeer Qasim Hamza (variously estimated as 14 or 20 years old), killed her father Qasim Hamza Raheem, mother Fakhriyah Taha Musin, and 7-year-old sister Hadeel Hasim Hamza, burned their home to conceal the crime, and blamed insurgents.[5] The soldiers manned a traffic checkpoint 650 feet from the Hamza house, which they had visited. A neighbor ran to Abu Firas Janabi (a neighbor and Fakhriyah's cousin) to say the house was on fire with bodies inside. Janabi said "Never in my mind could I have imagined such a gruesome sight. Kasim's corpse was in a corner of the room, and his head was smashed to pieces." Hadeel was beside him. Fakhriyah's arm had been broken. Abeer was in another room, naked, burned, her head smashed. Three days earlier Abeer had told her mother in Janabi's presence that American soldiers constantly searched her house, sexually harassing her. Villagers told Janabi that the killers wore black shirts and military pants. Even though he suspected the Americans manning the checkpoint, who would have heard shots, Janabi reported the atrocity to another American checkpoint. Army investigators (including two of the perpetrators!) took 15 photos of the bodies, attributing the deaths to "insurgent activity, which is common in the area." LtCol. Thomas Kunk (battalion commander) told Mahmudiyah's mayor that "a homicide was committed here." Kunk wanted to exhume the bodies but respected the family's religious scruples. A sheikh of the family's tribe reported the killings to a senior Iraqi police official.

On June 20 PFC Justin Watt (a medic in the unit) reported the incident to a combat stress counselor, accusing Sgts. Paul E. Cortez and Anthony W. Yribe, SPC James B. Barker, and PFCs Jesse V. Spielman, Bryan L. Howard, and Steven D. Green. (Previously in November 2005, Watt had treated a boy badly wounded by Yribe's ricochet shot; six days later Watt failed to save a woman hit by another Yribe ricochet shot; Yribe and Cortez, who had dated sisters as civilians and so knew each other before they joined the Army, covered up the second shooting.) When Watt's story was reported up the command, a sergeant said: "it makes Haditha look like child's play." After interviewing four suspects, who denied all knowledge, Kunk notified Army CID, which obtained statements from these four, as well as a fifth soldier to whom Green had boasted of the crimes. An Associated Press (AP) reporter wrote detailed accounts of the accusations. The White House said: "the President has full confidence in the military to investigate alleged crimes and to punish anyone convicted of abhorrent behavior that dishonors the proud traditions of our military." JCS Chairman Gen. Pace said rape or murder was "totally unacceptable." Gen. Casey (commander of US forces in Iraq) and Ambassador Zalmay Khalilzad apologized, promising the investigation would be a "vigorous and open process." "The alleged events of that day are absolutely inexcusable and unacceptable behavior."

Janabi told an American investigator the family did not want compensation but rather "punishment in the same level of the crime … committed." Iraqis initiated their own investigation by the local mayor, judge, town councilor, hospital director, and police chief, and an Iraqi Army representative. But this was suspended, partly because the rape was too shameful to discuss. The Iraqi Islamic Party human rights officer said: "the American soldiers violated everything. All the trials conducted by the Americans have so far been theater. We demand they impose punishments that will prevent such crimes." Prime Minister Maliki complained that immunity from Iraqi prosecution encouraged such atrocities and should be revoked: "Our people cannot tolerate that every day there is an ugly crime such as that in Mahmudiya." Kurdish and Sunni leaders concurred. The Minister of Justice said on television that the UN should ensure the soldiers were punished. The Minister of Human Rights agreed that "Maliki will present it to the Security Council."

A week later the military charged Cortez, Barker, Spielman, and Howard with rape and murder and Yribe with dereliction of duty for failing to report the crime. (Green had been discharged.) David Sheldon objected that an alleged confession by his client, Barker, was coerced. "At the end of the eight hours [of interrogation], the agents made SPC Barker type out his 'confession' line by line, telling him what to write nearly word for word. It is incredible that in a case of this magnitude army investigators did not tape the interrogation."

Between September 2005 (when the unit deployed) and June 2006 at least 17 battalion members had been killed, 2 after being captured and mutilated; 8 of the dead were from the 110-member Bravo Company; dozens more were seriously wounded. In February 2006, a fire in the abandoned factory used as a barracks destroyed most of their personal items. Three months before the killings an Iraqi in civilian clothes walked up to the checkpoint, shook hands with the soldiers, and then shot two sergeants in the head, fatally wounding both. Spielman shot the attacker, while Green threw one of the wounded onto a Humvee hood and tried to keep him alive on the ride to the base. Six of Barker's friends had been killed. The unit had a reputation as a "hard luck platoon." The previous month it had been ordered to spend 30 days continuously at the checkpoint, instead of the previous 3–5 day rotation. The respected squad leader and platoon commander were both on leave. On the verge of a nervous collapse, the company commander had been sent to Baghdad in February for "environmental recuperation." In December 2005 the battalion commander had begun sending soldiers home on several weeks' leave.

The military sought to close the Art. 32 hearing at Fort Campbell, Kentucky, but Barker's lawyers objected. An NCIS Special Agent testified that Barker said the men at the checkpoint had been playing gin rummy, drinking Iraqi whiskey mixed with an energy drink, and hitting golf balls when Green insisted he wanted to kill some Iraqis. He asked Barker if Cortez would go along and then approached Cortez (the acting squad leader), who asked what Barker thought.

Barker replied: "It's up to you." Cortez gave Howard the radio to be a look-out at the checkpoint. Green, Barker, Cortez, and Spielman donned black thermal underwear and ski masks and entered the house. Cortez held Abeer while Barker raped her. She was crying and speaking Arabic, but Barker told her to "shut up." Then Barker held her while Cortez raped her. After they heard gunshots from the bedroom where Green had taken her parents and sister, he returned, agitated, and said something like "They're all dead – I just killed them." Then Cortez held Abeer while Green raped her and shot her in the face with an AK-47. Barker doused her with kerosene from a lamp, and someone set her on fire. Green opened the propane tank and shouted "we need to get out of here" because the house was going to blow up. Green threw the AK-47 into the canal. They returned to the checkpoint, where Barker grilled chicken wings.

Watt said Yribe (who had remained at the checkpoint) told him Green had confessed in confidence, adding that a shotgun shell had been found in the house, from which the soldiers had taken rifles and a shotgun. Although many Iraqis had AK-47s, shotguns were rare. Seeking to "confirm my suspicions" that "there were American forces involved," Watt asked Howard, who said Green, Barker, and Cortez planned to rape a girl while he was the look-out. They returned from the house "covered in blood." Watt sought guidance from his father, who had served in the military in the 1970s. He counseled: "If it is as heinous as you say, you can't let your loyalty to your men get in the way of doing what is right." Watt spoke up because it "had to be done."

> If you have the power to make something right, you should do it ... if something went down – something terrible like that – then it's my obligation to come forward ... We'd come through hell with each other and there were a lot of good men who died. And this happened, for what? We're just trying to do a little good over there.

After he reported to the combat stress counselors he feared for his life: "everyone has a weapon and grenades." His superiors had been "extremely skeptical" about his allegations. (Indeed, the only officer who wrote Watt's father to compliment his son's "moral courage" received a letter of reprimand for doing so "without any consideration for the professional courtesy and loyalty due your fellow commander and this brigade.")

Kunk testified that the company had a particularly dangerous assignment: 800 IEDs were found or detonated during the 11-month deployment. Barker, when questioned, was "very flippant, very confident, and more than willing to answer the questions I had. He said, 'No sir, no coalition soldier was responsible for the ... murder of that family and the rape and murder of that little girl.'" Howard denied knowing who was responsible. Hearing that Green had said "all Iraqis are bad people," Kunk told him "that wasn't true and that 90% to 95% of the Iraqi people are good people and they want the same thing that we have in the United States." But he had asked if Green intended to kill Iraqis. An NCIS agent said Spielman passed the lie detector test when he said he did not kill or have sex with anyone.

An Iraqi Army medic said he found the naked, burned body of a girl with a bullet hole in her left eye and her legs splayed. In the next room a five-year-old girl had the back of her head smashed by a bullet. Her father was shot in the head: "the brain was on the floor and parts of the head were all over the place." Her mother had been shot repeatedly in the abdomen and chest. The scene left him "sick for almost two weeks."

Other soldiers in the company testified that fear and violence had driven some to mix painkillers, cough syrup, and Iraqi whiskey. They spent weeks without hot food, showers, or contact with home, on constant foot patrols for IEDs. PFC Justin Cross testified: "You feel like every step you might get blown up ... You're just walking a death walk."

A defense lawyer said: "these soldiers are not robots. They are humans with emotions, and the command structure hung them out to dry." But the prosecutor replied that this was "murder, not war. Rape, not war." "Cold food, checkpoints, personnel assignments … didn't kill that family … didn't rape and murder that 14-year-old little girl." Barker's lawyer blamed Green for the deaths: "He's the one who should be facing capital murder." Soldiers said Green had set a puppy on fire and thrown it off the roof.

A month later the hearing officer recommended that Barker, Spielman, Howard, and Cortez be court-martialed for rape, premeditated murder, and arson, and Yribe for dereliction of duty for failing to report their confessions. The prosecution sought the death penalty for Cortez, Barker, and Spielman, but Spielman's attorney said his client was only the "look-out." The Pentagon said "today's events clearly show … the United States military is committed to investigating any allegations of this nature thoroughly."

Three weeks later Barker, who faced death or life without parole, pleaded guilty, admitting he had agreed to kill the family and had raped Abeer. Sheldon said: "He who gets to the courthouse fastest often is the smartest." The accused were sleep-deprived and had been drinking whiskey; Barker had "acute stress syndrome." Asked why he did it, Barker said: "I hated Iraqis, your honor. They can smile at you, then shoot you in your face without even thinking about it." He got 90 years and could be paroled in 20. Yribe negotiated an "other than honorable" discharge. Howard pleaded to obstruction of justice and being an accessory after the fact, receiving 27 months' imprisonment (of which he served 17) and a dishonorable discharge.

Cortez pleaded guilty to rape, murder, arson, breaking into the house, and obstruction of justice. He said Barker and Green had talked about having sex with Abeer. Having visited the house, they knew it would be "an easy target" because there was only one man. They dressed in black so as not to be recognized as American soldiers. While Barker and Cortez raped Abeer, "she kept squirming and trying to keep her legs closed and saying stuff in Arabic." After Barker was done, Green came out of the bedroom and said "he had killed them all." The judge sentenced Cortez to life, but the plea agreement entitled him to 100 years (making him eligible for parole in 10) and a dishonorable discharge. A defense psychologist testified that Cortez and the others had stress from fatigue and trauma. Cortez said: "I don't know why [I did it]." "I want to apologize for all of the pain and suffering I have caused the al Janabi family."

145

Spielman pleaded guilty to arson, conspiracy to obstruct justice, wrongfully touching a corpse, and drinking, but was tried on more serious charges. Barker and Howard had told investigators that Spielman knew in advance of the plan to rape Abeer (although Spielman now denied it).

Cortez testified that Spielman stood guard. He was convicted of conspiracy to commit rape, rape, housebreaking with intent to commit rape, and four counts of felony murder. Before sentencing, he said: "I don't really blame anybody. I could have stopped it. I take responsibility for my actions." The jury recommended life, but because Spielman had pleaded to the lesser charges, his sentence was limited to 100 years, and he could be paroled in 10.

Green had been honorably discharged for "personality disorder" on May 16, a month before the crime was uncovered. A week after committing it, he had referred himself to the Army combat stress team in order to get out of the Army, reporting that he had thrown a puppy off the roof. He had been found to have "homicidal ideations" when he first sought help from the combat stress team on December 21, 2005, but was just given small doses of Seroquel, told to get some sleep, and returned to duty the next day. He had enlisted on February 16, 2005 under a "moral waiver" a few days after being released from jail for possession of alcohol as a minor, his third misdemeanor conviction. (The Army increased the number of "moral waivers" by nearly half after 9/11 to have sufficient troops to fight the wars in Afghanistan and Iraq.) A school classmate said Green "was always, like, in trouble." "He did not mix well with other people. He was basically mad." Another classmate thought Green "did drugs and drink in junior high school." When his mother was jailed for drunk driving, Green returned to his divorced father but dropped out of school in tenth grade. The only contact he listed for the Army was a former step-father, not his father or mother.

He was charged in the District Court for the Western District of Kentucky (WD Ky) (his Division's home) under the Military Extraterritorial Jurisdiction Act (MEJA). An affidavit by an FBI special agent said Green had drunk alcohol before committing the crime. He and four others had gone to the house (which they previously visited) armed with three M-4 rifles and a shotgun. One guarded the door. Green covered his face with a brown T-shirt, killed Abeer's parents and sister, and told the others he had done so. Then he and another raped Abeer, and Green killed her. They returned to the checkpoint with blood on their clothes, which they burned. They stole an AK-47 from the house, later throwing it into a canal. Hoping to subject himself to military rather than civilian justice, Green (unsuccessfully) sought to re-enlist in the Army and challenged the court's MEJA jurisdiction. Prosecutors rejected his offer to plead guilty and avoid the death penalty.

The Iraqi Human Rights Minister attended the trial's first day, at which the Janabi family's paternal grandmother and two surviving sons testified, as did the five soldiers who had pleaded guilty. Green was convicted on all 17 counts, including rape and four premeditated murders. A member of the Iraq Parliament's Human Rights Committee and the head of the victims' tribe demanded the death penalty. The defense argued that officers knew the platoon was grieving over members' deaths and a stress counselor had urged it be removed from the front lines. When the jury hung (6–6) on the death penalty after deliberating for just a day, the judge sentenced Green to five consecutive life terms without parole. A tribal leader said "according to our tribal traditions, this soldier should have been killed and crucified." At the sentencing hearing, Green said to the Janabi family members who were present: "I am truly sorry for what I did in Iraq … I helped to destroy a family and end the lives of four fellow human beings … I know you wish I was dead … If I was in your place, I am convinced beyond any doubt that I would feel the same way."

The Sixth Circuit rejected a challenge to the District Court's MEJA jurisdiction. In a December 2010 interview Green blamed his behavior on the deaths of fellow soldiers. "There's not a word that would describe how much I hated" Iraqis. "I wasn't thinking these people were human." Five years after his conviction Green committed suicide. He had been placed in protective segregation after a dispute with other inmates, but showed no signs of depression and was anticipating a visit from a documentary filmmaker.

THARTHAR LAKE (SALAHUDDIN)[6]

On May 9, 2006 SSgt. Raymond L. Girouard (the squad leader), SPC William B. Hunsaker, PFC Corey R. Clagett and SPC Justin R. Graber of the 3rd Brigade of the Army's 187th Infantry allegedly killed three Iraqi men and covered up the murders by claiming they had tried to flee. About twenty US and six Iraqi soldiers had been conducting an operation on an island in Tharthar Lake, Salahuddin Province, where Special Forces previously had come under fire. It was believed to contain a training camp with at least twenty al-Qaeda members. On their way to being questioned about the operation by CID on May 29, all but Graber allegedly threatened to kill PFC Bradley Mason if he talked. Girouard told investigators: "the ROE was to kill all military age males on Operation Murray." The AR 15–6 report found that "the Soldiers clearly acted in self-defense fearing for their safety as they were physically assaulted by the detainees." But charges were filed when witnesses changed their testimony after repeated interviews.

Girouard said he and the others shot and killed a man in a window and then rushed the house, where they found three men hiding behind two women and another holding a two-year-old girl in front of him. After removing the women and child, the soldiers took the three men into custody but claimed that they attacked the soldiers and ran. Hunsacker was stabbed; Clagett was "struck on the face with a fist or something." The soldiers said they had found an AK-47, ammunition, and gun parts. Sgt. Leonel Lemus saw the Iraqis killed but thought it was justified. Clagett's lawyer, Paul Bergrin (who also represented an accused at Abu Ghraib and later was himself convicted of homicide and disbarred), said if the defendants "did want to kill these men, they could have [done so] and been within the rules of engagement." Defense lawyers said two of the unit's officers, Col. Michael Steele (who had led the 1993 Somalia rescue mission depicted in *Black Hawk Down*) and Capt. Daniel Hart, admitted giving orders to kill all MAMs. After the capture, SFC Eric J. Geressy asked over the radio: "why did you take them prisoner? Why didn't you kill them?"

At the Art. 32 hearing Lemus changed his story, describing a deliberate plot to kill the three detainees. Ten minutes after they were handcuffed and blindfolded, Girouard took him and the three other soldiers to a nearby house, telling them to "bring it in close" so he could talk quietly. Speaking in a "low-toned voice" and talking "with his hands," he made it clear he was going to kill the detainees. Lemus said he "didn't like the idea, so I walked toward the door." Girouard "looked around at everyone and asked if anyone else had an issue or a problem." No one spoke. Soon thereafter Lemus heard shouts and gunfire and saw the detainees running and falling. Asked what had happened, Girouard "couldn't answer. He just looked at the bodies and had this frozen look on his face." Girouard cut Hunsacker as part of the cover-up. Lemus said "they both have ranger school backgrounds and they are pretty close friends. They would always talk about the French Foreign Legion and renegade mercenaries running around from country to country." Girouard threatened to kill anyone who squealed. Three days later

Clagett told Lemus "he couldn't stop thinking about it" and "dreamed about it over and over." Lemus "told him it was all right that he felt like that." Lemus had been afraid to intervene at the time and remained silent because "I have to be loyal to the squad." Girouard gathered the four men and warned them "not to go bragging or spreading rumors," threatening that "if he found out who told anything about it he would find that person after he got out of jail and kill him or her." Geressy said that when he talked to Girouard by radio during the operation, "I was wondering why they did not kill the enemy during contact." But "at no point did I ever try to put any idea into those soldiers' heads to execute or do any harm to the detainees." Col. Steele took the rare step of refusing to testify.

Mason (who admitted lying to investigators) said to the prosecutor in late May 2006 that Clagett "told me they cut the detainees loose and shot them. Him and SPC Hunsaker." Girouard had punched Clagett and cut Hunsaker as part of the cover-up. Mason testified under immunity that even before the unit arrived in Iraq, Girouard had declared: "every man, woman and child in Iraq deserves to die." American soldiers viewed the ten Iraqi soldiers and interpreters attached to their company as "terrorists." The night before the raid Steele had told the soldiers to "kill all of them." Although they encountered no Iraqi gunfire on the island, Mason unleashed a burst of 6–9 rounds as they approached the first house, killing an "old man" at the window. "We were told to kill all the males on the island. We don't fire warning shots." Whenever soldiers killed anyone, Girouard gloated: "that's another terrorist down. Good job." Clagett and Hunsaker had smiled when Girouard said they were going to kill disarmed, handcuffed detainees. But Mason had said: "I'm not down with it. It's murder." Officers failed to investigate the shooting after his report.

1st Lt. Justice Werheim confirmed that Steele had said: "We're going in tomorrow. We're going to hit the ground shooting and kill all the al-Qaeda in Iraq insurgents." Werheim said that Hart (who also refused to testify without immunity) had unambiguously described the ROE several times: "We were to positively identify and kill any military-age male on the island." PFC Jason R. Joseph confirmed that they expected heavy fire and were to "kill all military-age males that were not actively surrendering … any males who didn't have their hands in the air." Capt. Jason A. Sienko said: "we were to kill or engage any males on the island that were military-age" unless they were "actively surrendering." Steele had said: "we're not just going to the island and shoot everyone … make sure you have well-aimed shots. Make sure you're killing people that need to be killed." But Steele had also introduced "kill boards" recording how many Iraqis each soldier had killed and had given knives to those with kills. At the bottom of Company C's kill board he wrote: "Let the bodies hit the floor." Clagett and Hunsaker had not earned any kills before this raid. Geressy had said he wanted "three hundred kills."

The unit initially encountered barefoot men and women, sheep, and bags of raw wool; the only weapons were a pistol and a few Kalashnikovs. This "surprised" SPC Micah Bivens, who had no instructions to kill unarmed MAMs. As a medic, he checked Hunsaker's wound, which was "big enough that it could have used stitches." Cpl. Brandon Helton saw the accused shoot at three men hurrying toward "a tractor, cow, couple of sheep." He then saw the men "running at full sprint," having pulled down their blindfolds, and fall after being shot. Sgt. Armando Acevedo, the Company C team leader, heard three radio transmissions. The first said the unit had killed one Iraqi in action and captured three. In the second, a sergeant (Geressy) complained that "we're bringing these detainees back when they should be dead," but told the unit to put them on a helicopter and fly them to the base. In the third, Girouard said three more had been killed in action.

Girouard said the mission was "hit the first house, kill all military-age males, hit any secondary houses." As they approached the first house, Lemus, Hunsaker, Graber, Mason, and he fired at a man in the window. Inside they found three Iraqi men hiding behind two women, a known al-Qaeda tactic. The unit separated the men, and Mason searched them thoroughly: "If there was a dollar bill on them, I would have found it." Graber guarded the men, who were lying face down with their hands bound behind. In a second house they found a fourth man, Shelish, using a baby as a shield. Girouard radioed Geressy that they had killed one man. Acevedo paraphrased Geressy, asking why "we're bringing back these detainees when they should be dead." Although Geressy denied saying this, Lemus insisted Girouard "mentioned that SFC Geressy transmitted over the radio that the detainees should have been killed." Lemus said Girouard told Mason and him that Hunsaker and Clagett would kill the detainees after cutting off their wrist ties and ordering them to run away. Lemus and Mason left, wanting no part of this.

Girouard sent Helton, Lemus, and four other soldiers to hold Shelish at a pickup zone for the incoming helicopter. Mason (guarding the women inside the house) heard Hunsaker shout an expletive. Mason and those at the pickup zone heard fire from Clagett's machine gun and

Hunsaker's M-4. Ryan and Helton saw the three prisoners sprinting away. Ryan heard "gunshots as the men fell." Clagett and Hunsaker told investigators they had cut off the flimsy wrist ties in order to replace them with thicker plastic cuffs. Girouard radioed headquarters that he now had three "k.i.a's."

Sgt. Hamed Muhammad of the Iraqi Army testified that the soldiers had killed the 70–75-year-old man in the window. Girouard left Hunsaker and Clagett to guard the three detainees, thus violating tactical procedures. Muhammad wondered "where were these three barefooted detainees running? There was nowhere of concealment to go." "Once we detain these people, it became our duty to protect them." Gunfire killed two and left one dying. Graber and SPC Thomas Kemp ran back from the pickup site. When a medic declared the dying man beyond help, Girouard said "put him out of his misery." Kemp did not believe in "mercy killings" and quickly left. Graber fired, missed, and fired again, bringing the muzzle within four feet of the man's cheek. "I felt it was the human thing to do."

The Art. 32 hearing officer recommended charging Girouard, Hunsaker, and Clagett with conspiring to commit premeditated murder and threatening a soldier not to talk, and Graber with murder; all should be eligible for the death penalty. Bergrin said that "using reasonable and necessary force," the accused "shot and killed three detainees who were known terrorists." Hunsaker's lawyer argued that when the detainees "resisted and started to run, they dropped into hostile status again." Graber pleaded guilty to aggravated assault, getting nine months. Hunsaker's lawyer called this a betrayal "when we've been disclosing our strategy" to Graber's lawyers for months.

Steele was formally but secretly reprimanded in summer 2006, blocking any chance for promotion. Several soldiers gave sworn statements that he told them to kill all MAMs. Steele denied using "specific language" to order the killings but agreed he had told them: "Guys, you are going to get shot coming off the helicopter. If you don't get shot, you ought to be surprised." The classified report said: "a person cannot be targeted on status simply by being present on an objective deemed hostile by an on-scene commander." But it recommended only an admonition in light of Steele's "honest belief in the correctness of the mission r.o.e." In November 2006 he was reassigned to an administrative job at Fort McPherson, Georgia, whose duties included teaching soldiers how to handle enemy detainees. A separate report by the 101st Airborne Division lawyers found that "confusion regarding the r.o.e.

was the proximate cause of the death of at least four unarmed individuals, none of whom committed a hostile act or displayed hostile intent." The 70-year-old Iraqi was unarmed and not a legitimate target. After the raid, soldiers saw blindfolds and plastic handcuffs on three bodies. Steele had ordered a junior officer to investigate the deaths but report back only to him, not the divisional commander.

Hunsaker pleaded guilty to killing two unarmed Iraqis and trying to kill a third, conspiracy, and obstruction of justice. Clagett also pleaded guilty, admitting he had lied to "make it look like the detainees tried to escape and give us justification to shoot them." He told the judge: "we were gonna kill 'em for no reason." "My actions made the Army look bad. It was wrong." Both faced life without parole but got 18 years and could be freed in 5.

A legal defense fund in Girouard's hometown (population 6,000) raised $19,000. Its director warned the military: "when you mess with our boys you have to deal with us." The First Assembly of God Church, to which Girouard belonged, raised $6,600. The vice commander of the American Legion post complained that Girouard was being "railroaded." Clagett's family supported Girouard, even though Clagett testified for the prosecution as part of his plea bargain.

In the court-martial, the prosecutor said Girouard "orchestrated, planned and had his subordinates carry out the murders of three Iraqi detainees." His lawyer retorted that "the trigger-pullers" had falsely implicated Girouard in return for reduced sentences. Hunsaker testified "I got tired of lying about it." But he expressed no remorse: "I didn't want to spend the rest of my life in prison for the deaths of what, in my eyes, were three terrorists." Hunsaker and Clagett testified that Girouard punched Clagett and sliced Hunsaker to make it seem they had been attacked by the detainees. Two other squad members testified that Girouard threatened to kill anyone who talked. Hunsaker said Steele and Hart ordered them to kill all MAMs, and Steele offered knives and coins for kills. Hunsaker reported the radio transmission and Girouard's comment to the squad: "the first sergeant, he's pretty pissed these guys aren't dead. He wants them dead. Make it look good." Hunsaker understood "that's what [Geressy] wanted. That's why I proceeded." But Geressy testified he had made the statement believing the Iraqis had been shooting at the squad. Graber testified that Girouard stood beside him over the dying detainee and said "go ahead and put him out of his misery." Pvt. Zack Hicks said Hunsaker told him in the brig that he planned to implicate Girouard falsely "to get a lesser sentence."

But under cross-examination he admitted that Hunsaker never said he planned to lie under oath. Kemp said he stood near Graber before the mercy killing and did not hear Girouard order it. But under cross-examination he admitted hearing an unidentified voice mention putting the detainee out of his misery.

"Positive" he had not ordered the killings, Girouard claimed to have been "shocked" when Hunsaker and Clagett shot the three detainees. Just before the deaths Hunsaker told him: "we should kill [them], they're terrorists." Instead, Girouard told Hunsaker and Clagett to replace the zip ties with stronger plastic flex cuffs. He was escorting Shelish to the landing zone when he heard shots and was pretty "smoked up" when he learned of the killings. Hunsaker had said he fired in self-defense after a detainee broke free and cut him. But because the small cut "didn't look believable," Girouard engaged in "split-decision thinking" and cut Hunsaker again. "I wanted to help him be believable. He screwed up real bad." On cross-examination, however, he admitted "I had no right to cut" him and offered no answer when asked if "loyalty to your men trumps the law." He claimed to have punched Clagett in the face "out of sheer anger," shouting "you deserved it, you idiot!" But he acknowledged agreeing with Hunsaker and Clagett to make the killings look like self-defense.

The jury found Girouard not guilty of premeditated murder but guilty of negligent homicide and obstruction of justice. Facing 21 years, he got 10 (and credit for a year served), reduction in rank, and a dishonorable discharge. Clagett and Girouard were released after 3.5 years and Hunsaker after 6. In 2011 the Court of Appeals for the Armed Forces overturned Girouard's negligent homicide conviction based on a recent decision that this was not a lesser-included offense. He was reinstated at his former rank (with benefits and four years' back pay) and given a "general discharge under honorable conditions."

5TH STRYKER COMBAT BRIGADE[7]

The 5th Stryker Combat Brigade, 1st Infantry Division deployed in Maywand District, Kandahar Province, Afghanistan, in July 2009 and experienced heavy fighting, suffering 33 combat deaths (and three others). When they returned to Joint Base Lewis–McChord, PFC Andrew Holmes, SPC Michael Wagnon II, SPC Adam Winfield, SSgt. Calvin Gibbs, and SPC Jeremy Morlock were charged with killing 15-year-old Gul Mudin (Gulbaddin) on January 15, 2010, Marach Agha on February 22, and Mullah Adahdad on May 2. The accused allegedly began talking about a "kill team" in December 2009, soon after the arrival of Gibbs, who bragged it had been easy to get away with "stuff" when he served in Iraq in 2004. On January 15 the 3rd Platoon was providing perimeter security for a meeting between Army officers and tribal elders when Gul Mudin walked toward them. Morlock threw a fragmentation grenade, Holmes fired at the victim, and others joined in firing when the grenade exploded. Morlock told investigators that Gibbs gave him the grenade and others knew of the plot. But Holmes denied knowing, claiming he fired only after Morlock ordered him to do so.

On February 14 Adam Winfield told his father, Christopher (a former Marine), via Facebook that the platoon had gotten away with murder and was bragging about finding another victim. Because Adam was frightened, Christopher left messages on the Army Inspector General (IG)'s hotline and at the office of his senator, Bill Nelson (D-Fl). He talked to the sergeant on duty at Fort Lewis, who said that unless Adam was willing to tell his superiors, the Army could do little. Eight days later Gibbs, Morlock, and Wagnon allegedly murdered Agha. Wagnon, who had served in Iraq, also possessed an Afghan skull. In March, Gibbs, Wagnon, SSgt. Robert G. Stevens, Sgt. Darren N. Jones and PFC Ashton A. Moore allegedly shot at three Afghan men. On May 2 Gibbs, Morlock, and Winfield allegedly threw a grenade at Mullah Adahdad and then shot him to death. Winfield claimed that he shot only because he had been ordered to do so and deliberately missed. When tribal leaders complained to the Army that the cleric had been unarmed, 1st Lt. Stefan Moye returned to the village three days after the killing to declare: "this guy was shot because he took an aggressive action against coalition forces. We didn't just [expletive] come over here and just shoot him randomly." "I don't know why a mullah would just be carrying around a [expletive] Russian hand grenade." (An embedded reporter videotaped this exchange.)

A few days later the Military Police (MP) investigated hashish use by the platoon. Members severely beat PFC Justin A. Stoner, whom they suspected of admitting this. Gibbs threatened him with finger bones he had collected from Afghan corpses. But when Stoner reacted by telling MPs about the killings, the suspects were quickly arrested. The brigade commander barred disclosure of photos of the dead or wounded because of "the risk of potential prejudice to the substantial rights of the accused as well as the negative impact on the reputation of the Armed Forces."

During Morlock's Art. 32 proceeding his lawyer moved to suppress his earlier statements, arguing his client had been heavily medicated for sleep deprivation, pain, and muscle distress. Investigators replied that Morlock was tired but coherent, and his detailed recollection had been corroborated by other unit members. In the videotaped interrogation he said Gibbs expressed "pure hatred" for Afghans. He "just really doesn't have any problems with [expletive] killing these people. And so we identify a guy. Gibbs makes a comment, like, you know, 'you guys gonna wax this guy or what?'" Gibbs threw a grenade and told Morlock and Winfield: "wax this guy. Kill this guy." Morlock admitted the victim posed no threat. After Gibbs shot the second victim, he planted an AK-47 next to the corpse and ordered Morlock and another to fire it to simulate a shootout. Morlock said Gibbs had talked about killing Winfield, for fear he might squeal, by dropping a weight on his neck in the gym or dropping a tow bar on him in the motor pool. Stoner also feared being killed like the three Afghans: "it wouldn't be hard for them to take me out and do the same to me and blame it on the Taliban." Members "would blatantly smoke" marijuana before deployment. Morlock had gone AWOL for a week to avoid the final drug test. PFC Ashton Moore had told investigators that Gibbs said he was looking for a soldier who "could kill anybody without any kind of regret ... shoot the dude just because he could shoot the dude." PFC Adam W. Kelley, accused of assaulting Stoner and possessing hashish, said he and others admired Gibbs. "I believe that because of his experience that more people came back alive and uninjured than would have without him having been part of the platoon." Morlock was referred for a court-martial.

The Brigade's motto was "Strike and Destroy." Col. Harry D. Tunnell IV, its commander, prohibited officers from mentioning counterinsurgency strategy, declaring he was interested only in killing as many Taliban as possible, not in winning the trust of Afghan people. At the request of US, Dutch, and Canadian officials, the regional commander remonstrated with Tunnell, but to no effect. When platoon members killed a second unarmed Afghan within a two-week period in January 2009, Capt. Matthew Quiggle "furious[ly]" told soldiers "they needed to search until they found something" to justify the second shooting. Gibbs and others planted the magazine from a contraband AK-47 next to the corpse "to give the appearance the Afghan was an insurgent." Morlock said 1st Lt. Roman Ligsay permitted this. Ligsay was removed because the platoon had regularly been killing dogs and discharging weapons without reasons. Digital photos of soldiers posing with the corpses circulated widely within the unit. CNN broadcast the video of Morlock's interrogation and another in which a platoon member said they used drugs on "bad days, stressful days, days that we just needed to escape."

Because Gibbs barely attended high school, earning just one of the 20 credits needed to graduate, his parents sent him to an alternative school that steered boys into the military. He gained his General Equivalency Diploma (for high school) after enlisting. He refused to speak to investigators but explained his tattoo of skulls and crossed pistols, three for his Iraq kills and three for those in Afghanistan. Other soldiers said Gibbs had photos of bodies from his Iraq deployment.

At Gibbs's Art. 32 hearing his lawyer said the case rested largely on statements by soldiers who refused to testify (14 of the 18 military witnesses). Because the army did not want to offend Afghan religious objections to autopsies, there was almost no forensic evidence. The CID Special Agent said he had not interviewed Afghan villagers nor done more crime scene work because he needed permission from Gen. Petraeus for this. "If you go and interview Afghan civilians, basically saying U.S. soldiers had wrongfully killed your family member, when there's a battalion element still out there, it puts them at risk." Investigators visited only one crime scene, identifying neither grenade shrapnel nor blood, and later deleting all their photos. They heard that Gibbs had illegally confiscated AK-47 rifles, C-4 explosive, mortar rounds, rocket-propelled grenades (RPGs), and a Claymore mine to use as props, and had stolen severed fingers and leg bones from Afghan graves. Morlock told investigators that Gibbs "just really doesn't have any problems with ... killing these people." He "pulled out one of his grenades ... throws it, tells me where to go to whack this guy, kill this guy." "[W]e present [other soldiers] with a scenario, and nobody ever questioned it." Moye said: "I had no reason not to believe" that "what was described to me" on May 2 was "how it played out."

Winfield told investigators that on May 2 the platoon kept watch while Moye questioned villagers inside a compound. Adahdad, standing nearby, "seemed friendly. He didn't seem to have any sort of animosity towards us." Gibbs told Winfield and Morlock to walk Adahdad to a nearby ditch and make him kneel. Sgt. Gibbs said, "this is how it's going to go down. You're going to shoot your weapons, yell grenade. And then I'm going to throw this grenade. And after it goes off, I'm going to drop this grenade next to him."

Gibbs threw the grenade and told Morlock and Winfield: "All right, dude, you know, wax this guy. Kill this guy. Kill this guy." After they shot and the grenade exploded Gibbs walked up to the body and shot "probably about two more times in the head." Rushing to the scene, other platoon members found the dead man lying next to an unexploded Russian-made grenade. Gibbs led a team of three soldiers assigned to collect the body and record fingerprints. Seeing him cut off the left pinky finger with a medical scissors, Cpl. Emmitt R. Quintal called Gibbs "a savage." Quintal also saw Gibbs remove a tooth with his bare hands.

The military referred Winfield and Gibbs to court-martial. Morlock pleaded guilty. The prosecution sought life without parole, but he got 24 years (and could be paroled in seven). Of the seven men charged with lesser misconduct, two pleaded guilty; the longest sentence was six months.

Der Spiegel published some of the hundreds of photos the Army had sought to suppress. Two showed Morlock and Holmes grinning while holding a severed head next to the rest of the partly naked bloody corpse. Another displayed two dead bodies propped against a post.

Holmes's lawyer said his client had been "ordered to be in the picture by superiors" and criticized the Army for trying to conceal it. *Rolling Stone* posted 17 photos and two videos, accusing the Army of hiding them from even defense attorneys, fearing a scandal like Abu Ghraib. President Karzai said they should prompt international indignation "if there is conscience left in the west."

> They killed a young boy for entertainment, they killed an old man for entertainment, and even planned to kill children – to throw candy and then fire on them. It's very sad. It's a tragic story ... the people of the United States are undoubtedly good and compassionate people ... They are not cruel.

Winfield faced 17 years; the prosecution asked for 10; he pleaded guilty under an agreement that set a maximum of 8, got 3, and was released in a year. He accused Gibbs of pulling an Afghan man in his fifties away from his wife and children and insisting that Winfield and another shoot him while Gibbs lobbed a grenade. "I was afraid, and I wish I was braver." Gibbs had threatened to kill him if he talked: "he said several times he'd make it seem like I'd stepped on an IED."

Holmes pleaded guilty to unpremeditated murder, possession of a finger bone, and marijuana use. The judge would have given him 15 years; prosecutors asked for 13.5, and the defense sought 3; he got 7 and was released after 5. He called Morlock "psychopathic … the kind of leader who made me eat dirt, just to eat dirt."

In Gibbs's court-martial, Morlock said the photograph of him smiling with a corpse "was just more of a keepsake, a trophy photograph." He participated in the killings because he was frustrated with "meet and greets" to improve relations with Afghans. "The whole idea of the infantry mindset is to get into firefights and engage the enemy." After a nine-day trial, the jury deliberated just four hours before convicting Gibbs of three counts of murder, conspiring to murder, assaulting a fellow soldier, taking fingers and teeth from the dead, and other counts. He said he did not view the body parts as human but rather "like keeping the antlers from a deer you'd shot." He had been "trying to be hard, a hard individual" and still maintained the victims posed a threat. Prosecutors asked for life without parole. The jury gave him life, but he could be paroled in less than ten years. Wagnon had been referred to court-martial against the recommendation of the hearing officer, but the army dropped the charges "in the interest of justice."

NISOUR SQUARE[8]

On September 16, 2007 a car bomb exploded near a State Department motorcade in Baghdad. Soon thereafter a convoy of four SUVs belonging to military contractor Blackwater drove into Nisour Square, a mile away, and shot wildly, killing 17 Iraqi civilians and wounding 24. Blackwater claimed its convoy had taken fire "from close to 360 degrees." Because one vehicle had been disabled, guards were authorized to use "aimed fire" at anyone with weapons. Blackwater said "this convoy was violently attacked by armed insurgents, not civilians, and our people did their job to defend human life." Secretary of State Condoleezza Rice phoned Prime Minister Maliki to apologize and promised to investigate. An embassy spokesperson said it was "launching a full investigation in cooperation with the Iraq authorities." The Assistant Secretary of State for Public Affairs said: "there was a firefight. We believe some innocent life was lost. Nobody wants to see that. But I can't tell you who was responsible for that." The Iraqi Interior Minister called it "a big crime that we can't stay silent in front of." The Iraqi National Security Adviser sought review of Coalition Provisional Authority (CPA) Order 17 immunizing contractors from liability under Iraqi law. The Department of State (DoS) later offered the bereaved and injured $10,000–12,500, which many refused.

The Iraqi Interior Ministry report concluded that Blackwater had shot without provocation. When a white Kia failed to stop quickly enough, Blackwater killed the driver and a woman passenger. The report said no Iraqis fired, although witnesses claimed an Iraqi soldier in a watchtower had done so. Making no mention of civilian casualties, a two-page report by the US Embassy said Blackwater's Tactical Support Team 22 was encircled by "Iraqi Army and Iraqi Police units" pointing "large caliber machine guns" at it. (It was later revealed that a Blackwater contractor wrote the report.) The convoy had come under small-arms fire from 8–10 people at "multiple nearby locations with some aggressors dressed in civilian apparel and others in Iraqi police uniforms." But a traffic policeman said Iraqi police did not fire "a single bullet." Blackwater guards "were the only ones shooting." A senior Iraqi police official said they "were shooting in every direction," using "a rocket launcher or grenade launcher" and "supported by two helicopters who were shooting from the air." Five Iraqi eyewitnesses insisted Iraqis did not fire on Blackwater guards. ABC News quoted sworn statements by Blackwater guards, four of whom had fired on the white car.

Journalists offered a detailed account. After the initial burst of bullets killing the driver of the white Kia, Blackwater guards fired wildly. The driver's father later counted 40 bullet holes in the car. At least one car had bullet holes in its roof, suggesting it had been shot from a helicopter. One guard shouted to the others "No! No! No!" Not a single Iraqi witness heard or saw Iraqi gunfire. At a point 150 yards after leaving the square, the convoy again fired into a crush of cars, killing one Iraqi and injuring two.

Blackwater CEO Erik Prince gave a diametrically opposed account:

> When the second team arrived in Nisour Square, they came under small-arms fire and notified the first team to proceed along a different route. The vehicle team still in the intersection continued to receive fire, and some team members returned fire at threatening targets. Among the threats identified were men with AK-47s firing on the convoy, as well as approaching vehicles that appeared to be suicide bombers ... Some of those firing on this Blackwater team appeared to be wearing Iraqi National Police uniforms, or portions of such uniforms. As the withdrawal occurred, the Blackwater vehicles remained under fire from such personnel.

Maliki's spokesman said the commission investigating the shootings concluded the convoy had not been fired on "directly or indirectly, and was not even hit by a stone." "This is a deliberate crime against civilians. It should be tried in court and the victims should be compensated." Guards had shot people 200 feet away. Neither Iraqi nor US military investigators were given access to the guards. DoS explained it was just "a matter of bureaucratic arrangement that [we] have the lead."

The US military unit that reached the square 20–25 minutes after the shooting found shell casings from guns commonly fired by US contractors and military but none from those used by insurgents or Iraqi forces. LtCol. Mike Tarsa, the commander, said the incident "had every indication of an excessive shooting." "I did not see anything that indicated they were fired upon." Based on observation, eyewitness accounts, and discussions with Iraqi police, the unit found "no enemy activity involved" and called the shootings a "criminal event."

When FBI investigators returned from Baghdad six weeks after the shootings, senior officials said the DoS Bureau of Diplomatic Security (BDS) had given all the Blackwater guards use immunity in exchange for answering questions. Under federal court decisions, that made their answers involuntary and hence inadmissible. The FBI had been barred from reading the BDS interrogations, and guards refused to talk to them. Blackwater had repaired vehicles allegedly damaged by gunfire, making it impossible to evaluate the claims. DoJ responded by reassigning the investigation from the Criminal Division (whose lawyers had read the statements) to the National Security Division. The Departments of State and Justice both said the immunity offer would not derail the investigation. But the *Los Angeles Times* said the "scandalous" "rogue grant of immunity" had "badly compromised" the "appearance of fairness." Sen. Leahy (D-Vt) called this another example of the Bush administration's refusal to hold "their team" accountable.

Rep. David E. Price (D-NC) expressed the hope that Michael Mukasey, the new Attorney General, would prosecute the contractors under the War Crimes Act. Price said investigators had found no support for Blackwater's claim that employees had taken fire from Iraqis. The FBI did not arrive for more than two weeks, did not know the number of fatalities, could not recover some bodies, and was unable to reconstruct the crime scene. Some of the shells found could not be tied to the shootings because "the city is littered with brass." Four of the five contractors believed to have shot would not speak to the FBI without counsel. Nevertheless, the FBI found 14 of the 17 killings unjustified. The *New York Times* called this "hardly surprising" considering "the 'spray and pray' tactics favored by many of these contractors."

The US Attorney for the District of Columbia subpoenaed the 14 contractors who had been in Nisour Square but did not fire weapons, and sought Blackwater records, employee work histories, and military service files. Eight prosecutors and FBI agents spent two weeks in Baghdad hoping to interview about 25 witnesses. An ED Va grand jury issued subpoenas to Blackwater and other private security firms. Deputy Secretary of Defense Gordon England wrote Rep. Price that the guards "were not engaged in employment in support of the Department of Defense mission" and therefore could not be prosecuted in the federal court. But DoJ reiterated that the obstacles to prosecution were not insurmountable. By August 2008 federal prosecutors had sent target letters to six guards. In December prosecutors indicted Paul A. Slough, Dustin I. Heard, Evan S. Liberty, Nicholas A. Slatten, and Donald W. Ball in DDC on 14 counts of voluntary manslaughter and 20 of attempted manslaughter. (The charges against Ball were later dropped.) The *Washington Post* and *Los Angeles Times* applauded. The accused pleaded not guilty. Four Iraqi witnesses had been interviewed extensively by the FBI and would testify.

AUSA Kenneth Kohl met with victims' families in Baghdad. The FBI, prosecutors, and forensic experts made at least four trips to Baghdad. The assistant director of the FBI's Washington field office called the shootings "shocking and a violation of basic human rights."

James P. Ridgeway pleaded guilty to one count of voluntary manslaughter and one of attempted manslaughter (carrying a sentence of up to 17 years) and agreed to cooperate. He and other guards pumped hundreds of rounds of machine gun fire into the white Kia, killing Ahmed Haithem Ahmed al Rubia'y and his mother. Judge Urbina denied a motion to dismiss for lack of jurisdiction because the 2004 amendment to MEJA added those working "in support" of the DoD mission. Prosecutors alleged that at least one guard fired an automatic weapon "without aiming" and another fired in order to "instigate gun battles." Liberty had fired his automatic weapon without aiming on other occasions in May and September 2007. Slatten had said "he wanted to kill as many Iraqis as he could as payback for 9/11 and he repeatedly boasted about the number of Iraqis he had shot." Liberty, Slatten, and Slough routinely threw frozen water bottles, frozen oranges, and other objects at unarmed civilians and vehicles "to break automobile windows, injure and harass people, and for sport."

Judge Urbina held three weeks of closed hearings about whether evidence had been tainted by statements taken from the accused after

DoS had granted them immunity and threatened them with firing. The *Washington Post* and *Los Angeles Times* criticized the closure. Prosecutors dropped the charges against Slatten. At the end of 2009 Urbina dismissed the entire case, finding the statements had been coerced.[9]

Gen. Ray Odierno, commander of Multi-National Force–Iraq (MNF-I), called the ruling "a lesson in the rule of law." Rep. Jan Schakowsky (D-Ill) disagreed: it showed that "private military contractors [can] get away with murder." A Maliki spokesman said "the investigation conducted by specialized Iraqi officials confirmed without a doubt the Blackwater guards had committed murder." The *Washington Post* called the ruling "infuriating" but "correct." The *New York Times* agreed Urbina had "correctly" found that the government had violated the defendants' right against self-incrimination. The *Los Angeles Times* said the case was dismissed because of a "shocking violation of [the guards'] Fifth Amendment right against forced self-incrimination."

But Judge Urbina wrote an additional opinion declaring that the dismissal was without prejudice.[10] After meeting Iraqi leaders, Vice President Biden said the government was "disappointed" and would appeal. In April 2011 the DC Circuit reversed, instructing Judge Urbina to determine which prosecution evidence had been tainted.[11] The *Los Angeles Times* applauded the decision. "But regardless of what happens next, the legal process will have shown Iraqis how much this country values constitutional rights, including the right against self-incrimination."

New charges were filed against Heard, Liberty, Slatten, and Slough. On March 26, 2014, after a closed six-day hearing, Judge Lamberth (who inherited the case after Urbina retired) denied the motion to dismiss.[12] But the DC Circuit now held that its revival of the case did not apply to Slatten (whose charges had been dismissed by prosecutors); and the five-year statute of limitations for voluntary manslaughter had expired with respect to him. Judge Lamberth angrily called for an investigation.

> If the Department of State and the Diplomatic Security Service had tried deliberately to sabotage this prosecution, they could hardly have done a better job. It is incredible the way these defendants were coerced into making statements … Even more egregious, though, was the leaking to the news media of all the statements given … It is unclear … whether the Diplomatic Security Service or the State Department even had the authority to grant immunity to the defendants in exchange for their testimony absent approval from the Attorney General. Nor is the court aware

if the State Department sought any legal advice regarding the decision to grant immunity – a decision that was questionable at best.

Two weeks after the DC Circuit decision, the government charged Slatten with first-degree murder (which was not barred by the statute of limitations). Judge Lamberth held this was not vindictive.[13]

Prosecutors brought more than four dozen Iraqis to testify in Washington, the largest number of foreign witnesses ever appearing in a federal criminal trial. After the first one broke down describing his 9-year-old son shot in the head in the back seat of a car, Judge Lamberth called a recess. The next day he excused a juror who had been unable to sleep. A man shot in the abdomen saw his companion shot to death as he tried to run away. Matthew Murphy, a turret gunner, described waving his arms to get Iraqis to lie down: "my teammate's been firing wildly, and I don't want these kids to get shot." He heard AK-47 gunfire but never saw anyone shooting. It was "the most horrible, botched thing I've ever seen in my life." When the team discussed the operation the next day, the leader warned: "if we had problems with what happened out there, maybe we were the ones with the problem. And maybe we needed to find new lines of work." Adam Frost, another guard, said "we've been in firefights before. This one just felt different." "I saw people huddled down in their cars trying to shield their children with their bodies." But at the time he had been certain the convoy was under fire, and his teammates had responded appropriately to the white Kia.

Prosecutors called 71 witnesses, including 30 Iraqis; the defense called just 4. But there was evidence on both sides. It was unclear whether a Blackwater truck's radiator had been ruptured by bullets or by shrapnel from Blackwater grenades. Through "a series of innocent oversights," prosecutors failed to give the defense photos of eight spent shell casings that would fit an AK-47. The defense accused the government of suppressing for seven years "plainly exculpatory [evidence] on the central disputed issue" and wanted the jury informed. Blackwater guards had been told before the shooting that several cars loaded with explosives – including a white Kia – were roaming Baghdad looking for targets. But though the defense claimed the Kia had been speeding toward the guards, prosecutors said it only started creeping toward them at idling speed after the guards killed the driver, whose foot remained on the gas pedal. Prosecutors introduced evidence that Slatten and Liberty hated Iraqis and Slough sometimes shot at them without provocation. Prosecutors could not identify which defendant shot which victim, but argued: "why shoot all of these people who are running away? Why shoot women and children who are unarmed?"

After deliberating for an unprecedented 28 days, the jury found Slatten guilty of first-degree murder and the other three of multiple counts of voluntary manslaughter, attempted manslaughter, and gun violations. The *New York Times* praised the verdict for bringing "a measure of justice for the innocent victims and their families." A man whose mother was shot said: "I had faith in [America] to realize justice." But some survivors said only the death penalty would satisfy them. And Erik Prince blamed "politics" for the fact that the government spent "tens of millions of dollars on this, now trying it even years after the event, and 7,000 miles from where it happened." Finding that the defendants had committed wild, unprovoked actions that "just cannot ever be condoned by a court," Judge Lamberth sentenced Slatten to life and the other three to 30 years. But in August 2017 the DC Circuit reversed. It ordered a new trial for Slatten because Judge Lamberth had erroneously excluded a co-defendant's statement made soon after the attack that he had fired the shots for which Slatten was charged.[14] And the court directed Lamberth to resentence the others to lesser terms. Because the machine gun law under which the latter three were convicted was intended to punish those who intentionally used dangerous weapons to execute violent crimes, the 30-year sentences were "grossly disproportionate" to the culpability of those using government-issued weapons in a war zone.

ROBERT BALES[15]

On the night of March 11, 2012, SSgt. Robert Bales, in his fourth deployment, left a checkpoint in Panjwai District, Kandahar Province, Afghanistan, and killed 16 civilians, including 9 children and 3 women, and then tried to burn the corpses. Furious villagers took the bodies to the nearby military base. President Karzai condemned the "inhuman and intentional" act. President Obama and Defense Secretary Panetta called Karzai to offer condolences and promise an investigation. Obama said: "the United States takes this as seriously as if this was our own citizens and our own children who were murdered." Declaring that "once again Afghans have run out of patience," its parliament urged the USA "to punish the culprits and put them on trial in an open court." An Afghan government delegation visited the scene and distributed about $2,000 for each death and $1,000 for each person wounded. In Jalalabad a thousand people burned Obama in effigy and blocked the highway, demanding an immediate public trial. Religious leaders in Qalat City said Bales should be prosecuted in Afghanistan, and their statements were echoed by the Kandahar MP participating in the parliamentary investigation. Another Kandahar MP said Karzai should refuse to sign the strategic partnership agreement then being negotiated. After meeting the victims' relatives, Karzai insisted that more than one person had been involved and declared: "clearly the Americans should leave our villages." The USA refused to cooperate with the parliamentary investigation. The *New York Times* called for a "fast, transparent and conclusive" investigation and "swift" punishment.

Bales refused to speak to investigators, invoking his right to counsel. Because the USA had no long-term detention center for service members in Afghanistan, he was flown to Kuwait to allow "proper pre-trial confinement" and "access to legal services." The military disclosed that he had been injured twice in combat. His lawyer, John Henry Browne, said that a day before the killings Bales had seen a fellow soldier lose a leg to an IED. Bales's wife had previously blogged that he was disappointed at not being promoted to SFC. Now she acknowledged that he did not seem to suffer from PTSD, but added that he "shielded me from a lot of what he went through." A 2002 criminal assault charge was dismissed after Bales completed an anger management assessment; in 2003 he and some colleagues were convicted of financial fraud and fined more than $1.2 million (which they never paid); in 2008 he received a 12-month deferred sentence after fleeing a single-car rollover. Panetta denounced the massacre as a "criminal act" and "suspect[ed]" there had been a confession.

Bales was charged with 16 counts of murder, illegal steroid use, and alcohol consumption. Declaring that "there's no crime scene. There's no DNA. There's no confession, although they're leaking something," Browne complained of being denied access to witnesses, investigative files, medical records, and a surveillance video. The USA paid $50,000 for each of the 17 deaths and $11,000 for each of the 6 wounded, but the District Council deputy chair said that "didn't mean that [the families and victims] forgave the killer." Because Browne could not be present, he instructed Bales not to cooperate with the Sanity Board Hearing.

At the Art. 32 hearing at Joint Base Lewis–McChord, the prosecutor said Bales had been "lucid, coherent and responsive" when he returned from killing. Having visited one of the compounds, he knew it housed women and children. Cpl. David Godwin testified (under immunity) that he had drunk alcohol with Bales and Sgt. Jason McLaughlin that night and watched *Man on Fire*, a movie about a former intelligence operative who sought violent revenge after a girl's kidnapping. When taken into custody, Bales said: "I thought I was doing the right thing."

Fellow soldiers testified he was angry his unit had not done more to find who had set the IED in the week before the killings. Before leaving the base at midnight, Bales had a "hugely important" conversation with Special Forces team members, expressing his admiration and desire to join. He talked about domestic problems and his frustration with the ROE, which he blamed for the IED explosion: "they should have done something the very next day to find the people that planted the IED." SFC Clayton Blackshear said the day before the killing Bales had "expressed quite a bit of concern over our actions after the incident." McLaughlin testified that Bales was anxious about being promoted. That night an agitated Bales had barged into his room, flicked on the light, and boasted he had been to Alkozai and shot up some people. When McLaughlin expressed disbelief, Bales asked McLaughlin to smell his weapon. He declared: "I'm going to Najban, I'll be back at 5," and asked McLaughlin to "take care of my kids." After hearing reports of shots being fired and an Afghan guard's statement that an American soldier had left the base, McLaughlin and Godwin were sent to the main entrance. Seeing Bales return dressed in a dark cape, they leveled their guns and demanded he drop his weapon. He responded: "Mac, did you rat me out?" As Bales was being readied to move to a larger base, he bragged to McLaughlin about how many he had killed: "My count is 22."

When SFC James Stillwell asked why Bales was covered with blood, he replied "You guys are going to thank me." Between the two massacres he asked Godwin for help bleaching his blood-stained clothing and grabbed his laptop from another soldier, breaking the screen (but not damaging the hard drive). PFC Damian Blodgett, who was on guard duty, heard 30–40 minutes of gunfire from Alkozai. PFC Derek Guinn called Bales bipolar: "sometimes he was in a really good mood, and he seemed really angry sometimes, or easily annoyed." After being taken into custody, Bales mentioned an earlier incident in which troops had been pinned down for half an hour by an insurgent's machine gun, asserting "that's not going to happen again."

When Army CID Special Agent Matthew Hoffman finally was able to visit the village – three weeks later because of residents' anger – he found bloodstains on walls and floors, shell casings consistent with Bales's weapons, and a piece of fabric resembling the cape Bales wore after the killings. An Army doctor who treated wounded villagers testified that a young girl had a large bullet wound in the top of her head and a woman had wounds to her chest and genitals. An Army DNA expert testified that Bales's clothes contained the blood of at least four victims. Testifying by video, Mullah Khamal Adin said 11 members of his cousin's family were killed. "Their brains were still on the pillows." He found boot prints on some bodies, including the head of a child who had been shot and stomped or kicked. Another child had been "grabbed from her bed and thrown on the fire." A 14-year-old boy saw a "grandmother," whose clothes had been "ripped off," die of her wounds. A 7-year-old girl saw her father die, cursing in pain and anger. Browne tried to elicit testimony that there had been more than one shooter, but eyewitnesses denied that. Another defense lawyer sought to show that the soldiers who testified had been drinking that night. The prosecution sought the death penalty. Bales was referred for court-martial with the possibility of the death penalty. There had been 16 death sentences passed since the Uniform Code of Military Justice (UCMJ) was amended in 1984, but 9 had been set aside on appeal and 2 commuted to life. No one had been executed since 1961.

The military flew six male relatives of victims to Seattle to familiarize them with the US judicial system in preparation for testifying. One, who had lost his wife and three other family members, said: "I thought we were going to America to see [Bales] hanged. Instead they showed us a courtroom and kept us in rooms asking us more and more questions." He did not want to return for the trial; another man agreed: "we will only go if he is hanged." A victim's widow twice changed her story about whether there had been one gunman or two.

Five months after floating the possibility of a "mental health" defense and asking that Bales be examined in their presence by a neuropsychologist with expertise in traumatic brain injuries, Bales pleaded guilty to avoid the death penalty. He admitted every charge, declaring he had acted on his own, without compunction or mercy or under orders by a superior. He had taken steroids to get "huge and jacked," which "definitely increased my irritability and anger." In Afghanistan, survivors and relatives of the dead expressed their fury that Bales had escaped execution. The military flew seven men and boys to Seattle for the sentencing hearing. The defense described Bales helping his father garden, caring for a mentally disabled neighbor, and making his children chocolate chip pancakes. The prosecution described him as unhappy with his family, deeply in debt, and bitter at being denied promotion. Bales testified:

> What I did is an act of cowardice. I'm truly, truly sorry for those people whose family members I've taken away … if I could bring their family members back I would in a heartbeat. I can't comprehend their loss. I think about it every time I look at my kids. I know I murdered their family. I took that away from them.

He apologized for shaming the Army and staining the reputation of "really good guys, some heroes." After deliberating just 90 minutes, the jury sentenced him to life without parole. Outside of court one Afghan called Bales's apology a "fraud" and another objected that "we came all the way to the U.S. to get justice. We didn't get that."

CONCLUSION

Returning from the first wave of killing, Robert Bales told a buddy he had shot some villagers (offering the smell of gunpowder on his weapon as proof) and said he was going to shoot some more; after the second massacre he boasted of killing 22 people, declaring: "You guys are going to thank me." But he was the exception; all the other perpetrators sought to cover up their crimes. Nevertheless, only one case (Mahmudiyah) resembled a traditional "whodunit." Because there was no conceivable justification for the rape, the perpetrators blamed Iraqis, even pretending to "investigate" the crime scene. In all other cases the accused responded like white-collar criminals, claiming their actions had been legal, even necessary. Often they did so by disseminating a fabricated account, protected by the code of silence common in small homogeneous groups: the Mafia's *omertà*, the police blue wall, the reluctance of doctors, lawyers, and politicians to expose peer malpractice. When one soldier swore to another "I've got your back," that oath applied not just to combat but also to its aftermath. Officers had a stake in believing subordinates: misconduct reflected badly on superiors and could fuel enemy propaganda. Even more than other government officials, the military are suspicious of journalists, believing them congenitally opposed to warfare. There were numerous instances of the military seeking to control or limit publicity: issuing a false official story about Haditha; closing or dispensing with Art. 32 hearings; and suppressing sensational evidence, especially photographs. Many cover-ups succeed. But it is hard to keep a secret. Some perpetrators could not resist boasting about their exploits, or at least confiding in others. Some of their auditors felt obligated to blow the whistle (perhaps after seeking outside advice, e.g., from their ex-military fathers), even though they encountered skepticism from superiors, ostracism from peers, and threats or violence from perpetrators handy with weapons. Officers were legally obligated to investigate, especially when subordinates had fulfilled their duty to report up the chain of command (as evidenced by the payment of compensation, which could only be authorized at higher levels). And others were highly motivated to expose misconduct: journalists, NGOs, legislators, even the military itself when suspects were Blackwater contractors who threatened the military mission.

Because these killings (and the one rape) were so egregious, publicity compelled an official response. Grandstanding by members of Congress (some furious at the stain on the honor of a military they had proudly served) increased the pressure. The military quickly promised thorough investigation, which sometimes – like Bargewell's report on Haditha – pilloried the military's own handling of the matter (as had MGen. Taguba's report on Abu Ghraib). (It may be significant that Bargewell was about to retire.) The military's goal was to characterize the allegations as either unfounded (because the conduct was justified) and thus not deserving significant punishment, or as heinous (and therefore aberrational) but appropriately punished. Either choice obviated the need for fundamental change. The USA also had to respond to outrage in Iraq and Afghanistan. But though Presidents Maliki and Karzai fulminated for the benefit of domestic audiences, everyone knew they were impotent. The USA sought to pacify the immediate victims – the wounded and relatives of those killed – by offering compensation (cheap, given the local standard of living, even when the USA paid 25 times the usual rate, as in the massacre committed by Bales) and bringing them to testify in or observe American military and civilian trials (Nisour Square involved the largest number of foreign witnesses ever brought to federal court). But neither blood money nor Western justice could satisfy the call for a traditional *lex talionis*, which demanded a life for a life.

Military and civilian courts heard various explanations for the crimes, none entirely satisfying. Combat-related justifications – PTSD or Combat and Operational Stress Reaction, grief for comrades killed or maimed, fury when suspects evaded culpability – were advanced as mitigating circumstances (although they were not always accepted). Extrinsic motivations – anger at being denied promotion, a disintegrating marriage, mounting debt – offered no excuse and might actually be aggravating. The military sought to portray some accused as bad apples (Green, Gibbs, and Bales – like Graner in Abu Ghraib), even though this raised troubling questions about its lax recruitment standards (lowered to enable it to fight the wars in Iraq and Afghanistan by admitting those with minimal education and records of crime and substance abuse), its inadequate training, and its perfunctory response to emotional trauma (quickly returning soldiers to the battlefield with a few pills). Other accused seemed willing, even eager, to follow these ringleaders in order to display the toughness that confers status in the military.

Motive was relevant more to penalty than guilt. The accused offered other justifications in the guilt phase. As at Abu Ghraib, they complained about deplorable living conditions; but chronic poverty (and the attendant hardship) never excuses ordinary crime. They claimed to have been threatened by armed insurgents hiding behind women and children or running away; and the standard for self-defense was greatly relaxed by the fog of war. Nevertheless, actions must be proportionate to the military threat and minimize civilian casualties. Grief about casualties suffered by buddies or other soldiers was understandable, even admirable, but could easily engender blood lust for revenge. This combustible mix of uncertainty and anger aroused in many an indiscriminate hatred of all Iraqis and Afghans, casually anathematized as hajjis (as US military in earlier wars had used similar slurs to dehumanize enemies as slants, commies, Japs, and krauts). Soldiers and Marines competed for kills, sometimes incited by superiors pitting units against each other and offering rewards. Accused invoked the ROE, whose ambiguity (inevitable? deliberate?) justified their own actions while failing to implicate the officers who had issued them. Such a "bureaucratic excuse" let everyone off the hook, as Phil Klay (a combat veteran) powerfully depicted in his short story "Prayer in the Furnace."[16]

Courts-martial closely resembled civilian criminal prosecutions in one central respect: prosecutors worked their way up the ladder of culpability, offering those on lower rungs plea bargains and lesser penalties in exchange for testifying (under immunity) against superiors. Although this risked impugning the credibility of witnesses who jettisoned earlier protestations of innocence to implicate others, it did produce convictions. But courts-martial compared unfavorably to civilian criminal procedure in several other ways. The hierarchical

nature of the military blurred civilian courts' strict separation of executive and judicial powers. Commanding officers exercised plenary
authority over charges and sentences. Unlawful command influence
during the guilt phase could lead to dismissal of the prosecution with
prejudice. (After SSgt. Joseph Chamblin pleaded guilty to posing for
photos and videos while urinating on three dead Taliban, the Navy
Marine Corps Court of Criminal Appeals overturned the conviction
because Gen. James F. Amos, the Corps' commandant, had fired the
investigator who recommended against a general court-martial, saying
he wanted all the Marines involved "crushed."[17]) NCIS and CID agents
(mostly recent recruits) seemed much less professional than career FBI
agents: missing or losing essential evidence, detaining suspects under
harsh conditions, inadequately advising them of their rights, and failing
to tape their statements. In other cases, loss of the victim's remains
compromised the prosecution.[18] BDS was even worse, threatening
Blackwater contractors with losing their jobs while making (probably
unlawful) offers of immunity, all of which led Judge Urbina to take the
unprecedented step of dismissing the entire prosecution. But even the
most competent investigators faced extraordinary challenges: inability
to reach (much less secure) the crime scene for hours, days, sometimes
weeks (because of ongoing combat, logistical problems, and senior
officers' reluctance to give victims any opportunity to complain);
local witnesses who were intensely (and understandably) suspicious of
Americans (who had just killed their relatives or neighbors); cultural
and linguistic differences impeding both investigation and testimony;
and an Islamic proscription of autopsies. Procedural defenses rarely
successful in civilian prosecutions were surprisingly effective in courts-
martial: evidence excluded because of the failure to give a Miranda-like
warning; a conviction overturned because negligent homicide was not a
lesser included offense; an expired statute of limitations. Only in courts-
martial could accused testify not under oath, thereby avoiding cross-
examination. Jurors were chosen for their combat experience (whereas
civilian jurors are *excluded* if they or their relatives have any experience
with crime).

All legal systems selectively engage social action. Sociologists depict
civil litigation as a pyramid: its base is populated by eligible events (torts,
contract breaches), the vast majority of which never lead to claims; most
claims are settled out of court; a small fraction are tried; and a miniscule
number at the pinnacle are appealed.[19] Similarly, criminologists track
attrition from the "dark figure" of criminal acts through arrests, charges,

prosecutions, convictions (usually via plea bargains) to sentences. We know that this pyramid tapers even more rapidly when institutions address their own members' misconduct, as in lawyer discipline.[20] We should not be surprised to find the same pattern in courts-martial. The dark figure is even more opaque than usual because the military keep no public records of misconduct or even the statistics on arrests and convictions routinely maintained by police departments and the FBI. Nevertheless, there are some fragmentary data. The Clemency Board created by the War Department after World War II commuted 85 percent of the sentences in serious cases. Most life sentences imposed during the Vietnam War were reduced to a few years after it ended. Most notoriously, Lt. William Calley Jr., convicted of the My Lai massacre of 347–504 unarmed civilians, was given a life sentence but ended up serving only a few weeks in prison.[21] Through the end of 2011 only 18 of the 74 members of the military charged with homicide received any jail time.[22]

Table 3.1 charts the trajectories of the courts-martial narrated above, and reveals the striking lenience of courts-martial compared to the likely outcomes had comparable crimes been committed and tried outside the military.[23] In Haditha, soldiers killed 24 innocent civilians, including seven women and three children in their own homes. Yet the accused successfully claimed to have behaved appropriately in a combat setting. Charges were dismissed against two; one was acquitted; and one pled to a lesser offense, serving no jail time. Charges were dismissed against three of the officers accused of failing to investigate or covering up, two were exonerated or acquitted, and one was censured. In the Tharthar Lake combat operation, soldiers killed an unarmed elderly man (resulting in no charges) and murdered three detainees. One accused got 9 months; two got 18 years but were freed in 6 and 3.5 respectively. Although the ringleader was sentenced to 10 years, this was overturned on procedural grounds and he was awarded back pay. The officer who allegedly ordered the other accused to kill all "MAMs" received only a secret reprimand. In Hamdania, soldiers committed a premeditated murder and several other assaults. Charges were dismissed against one; seven spent about a year in jail (some after substantial sentence reductions by the commanding officer); and the ringleader had his 15-year sentence cut to 11 years and was re-sentenced to time served (about 7 years) after his second trial. The sole officer received an administrative punishment. Numerous other cases[24] confirm this pattern of lenience for abusing or assaulting[25] or killing[26] Iraqi or Afghan civilians

Table 3.1 Courts-Martial for Violations of the Law of Armed Combat in Iraq and Afghanistan

Case	Accused	Trial or Plea	Highest Initial Charge	Highest Conviction	Max. Sent. Yrs.	Pros. Request Yrs.	Sentence Yrs.	Time Served Yrs.
Haditha	LtCol. Chessani		Dereliction of duty	None				
	SSgt. Wuterich	Plea	Unpremed. murder	Dereliction of duty	152	90	0	
	Sgt. Dela Cruz		Unpremed. murder	None				
	LCpl. Sharratt		Unpremed. murder	None				
	LCpl. Tatum		Unpremed. murder	None				
	Capt. McConnell		Dereliction of duty	None				
	Capt. Stone		Dereliction of duty	None				
	Lt. Grayson	Trial	Dereliction of duty	None				
Hamdania	PFC Jodka	Plea	Murder	Aggravated assault	Life		18 months	

(continued)

Table 5.1 (continued)

174

Case	Accused	Trial or Plea	Highest Initial Charge	Highest Conviction	Max. Sent. Yrs.	Pros. Request Yrs.	Sentence Yrs.	Time Served Yrs.
	Sgt. Hutchins	Trial	Murder	Unpremed. murder		30	11	7
	Cpl. Thomas	Trial	Premed murder	Conspiracy to murder	Life	15	14 months	
	LCpl. Jackson	Plea	Murder	Aggravated assault		10	21 months	9 months
	LCpl. Shumate	Plea	Murder	Aggravated assault		10	21 months	9 months
	LCpl. Pennington	Plea	Murder	Murder	Life	20	8	15 months
	Cpl. Magincalda	Trial	Murder	Conspiracy to murder	Life	10	14 months	
	PO3 Bacos	Plea	Murder			10–15	1	10 months
	LCpl. Lopezromo		Assault					
	PFC Lewis		Assault					
	LCpl. Lever	Plea	Assault	None				
	2nd Lt. Phan	Plea	Assault	None				
Mahmudiyah	Sgt. Cortez	Plea	Rape, murder	Rape, murder	Death		100[1]	

	Plea					
Sgt. Yribe	Plea	Dereliction of duty	Dereliction of duty		0	
SPC Barker	Plea	Rape, murder	Rape, murder	Death	90[2]	
PFC Spielman	Trial	Rape, murder	Rape, murder	Death	100[3]	
PFC Howard	Plea	Rape, murder	Accessory after fact		27 months	17 months
PFC Green[4]	Trial	Rape, murder	Rape, murder	Death	Life without parole	
Tharthar Lake SSgt. Girouard	Trial	Premed. murder	Negl. Homicide[5]	21	10	3.5
SPC Hunsaker	Plea	Premed. murder	Premed. murder	Life	18	6
PFC Clagett	Plea	Premed. murder	Premed. murder	Life	18	3.5
SPC Graber	Plea	Murder	Aggravated assault		9 months	
5th Stryker PFC Holmes	Plea	Premed. murder	Unpremed. murder	13.5	7	5
SPC Wagnon		Premed. murder	None			
SPC Winfield	Plea	Premed. murder	Premed. murder	17	3	1
SSgt. Gibbs	Trial	Premed. murder	Murder		Life[6]	
SPC Morlock	Plea	Premed. murder	Premed. murder	Life without parole	24[7]	

(continued)

Table 3.1 (*continued*)

Case	Accused	Trial or Plea	Highest Initial Charge	Highest Conviction	Max. Sent. Yrs.	Pros. Request Yrs.	Sentence Yrs.	Time Served Yrs.
Nisour Square[8]	Ridgeway	Plea	Manslaughter	Manslaughter	17			
	Slough	Trial	Manslaughter	Manslaughter			30	
	Heard	Trial	Manslaughter	Manslaughter			30	
	Liberty	Tria	Manslaughter	Manslaughter			30	
	Slatten	Trial	Murder	Murder			Life	
	Ball		Manslaughter	None				
Panjwai	SSgt. Bales	Plea	Murder	Murder	Death		Life without parole	

1 Eligible for parole in 10 years.
2 Eligible for parole in 20 years.
3 Eligible for parole in 10 years.
4 Civilian trial.
5 Reversed on appeal.
6 Eligible for parole in less than 10 years.
7 Eligible for parole in 7 years.
8 Civilian trial; the DC Circuit found the sentences of Slough, Heard, and Liberty excessive, remanding the case for resentencing, and it ordered a new trial for Slatten.

during combat, desecration of corpses,[27] burning Korans,[28] mock executions,[29] "mercy" killings,[30] drowning a civilian in a river,[31] and even premeditated murder,[32] sometimes aggravated by a cover-up.[33]

Some of the most egregious miscarriages of justice involved detainees tortured to death during interrogation. Dilawar and Habibullah were hung by their arms from the ceiling and beaten to death during interrogation at Bagram (Dilawar's legs were "pulpified").[34] CID initially said it could not determine responsibility and quit interviewing three weeks after the deaths, questioning superiors only 15 months later. Computer records and written logs of the interrogation vanished. Blood taken from Habibullah (essential for the autopsy) was stored in a butter dish in the CID office refrigerator and lost when the office moved. Although CID recommended criminal charges against 27, only 15 were prosecuted. Charges against three were dismissed before trial, and four were acquitted; some accused who were not prosecuted received administrative punishments. Of those who pleaded guilty or were convicted at trial, four got brief jail sentences (5, 3, 2, and 1.5 months) and the others no jail time. None of the four soldiers charged in connection with the death of MGen. Abed Hamed Mowhoush during interrogation received any jail time.[35] Although Lt. Andrew K. Ledford admitted beating Manadel al-Jamadi during the eight-hour interrogation in which he died, a court-martial acquitted him in just three hours.[36]

My four other cases offer illuminating comparisons. The three premeditated murders committed by the 5th Stryker Combat Brigade were exposed as gratuitous thrill-seeking when some accused were revealed to have cut off body parts as trophies and photographed themselves gloating over the corpses.[37] (Photos also played a crucial role in exposing Abu Ghraib; and the CIA destroyed videotapes of torture.) Charges were dropped against one man, and another was released in a year. However, one man got 7 years, another 24 (but could be paroled in 7), and the ringleader received life (but could be paroled in less than 10). Although the Nisour Square massacre resulted in fewer deaths than Haditha (17 compared with 24) and there was (strongly disputed) evidence of incoming fire, three of the contractors prosecuted in civilian court were sentenced to 30 years and the fourth got life. (After successful appeals, the first three will receive lower sentences and the fourth will be retried.) A court-martial, by contrast, treated an analogous event much more leniently. After being attacked by a suicide bomber near Jalalabad, Afghanistan, a Marine Special Operations convoy raced 7 miles back to its base shooting wildly, killing 10–19 innocent civilians (including a 12-year-old boy, a 16-year-old girl and a 75-year-old man) and wounding many more.[38] A military investigation the next day found no evidence of hostile gunfire after the bombing but later discarded the 125 US bullet casings it recovered. No one was court-martialed.

The responses to the Mahmudiyah rape and murders (of the rape victim and her father, mother, and younger sister) also illustrate the distinctive reaction to behavior devoid of any conceivable combat justification and the difference between courts-martial and civilian courts. The two accomplices got either no jail time or 17 months, and the three soldiers court-martialed got 90–100 years but could be paroled in 10–20. By contrast, the one ex-soldier tried in civilian court got life without possibility of parole. In another case, however, neither the courts-martial nor the civilian prosecution held anyone accountable for the murder of four detainees.[39] Bales's sentence to life without parole for 16 murders (including 3 women and 9 children) showed that even a court-martial could mete out appropriate punishment for such a highly publicized gratuitous mass killing (although he would have gotten the death penalty in many civilian courts). And the few other gratuitous killings also led to significant penalties.[40]

The lenient treatment of heinous crimes against civilians in combat zones appears even more striking when compared to courts-martial for other offenses.[41] Gen. William Ward, who initiated the new Africa Command, retired after being demoted and ordered to repay $82,000 he spent on luxury travel for himself and his family.[42] After the Malaysian defense contractor "Fat Leonard" Francis pleaded in federal court to bribing military officers, the Navy reviewed the conduct of 440 active duty and retired personnel, including 60 admirals.[43] In two separate incidents, the Navy discharged 92 sailors for using a synthetic drug that mimicked marijuana.[44] Soldiers who kill *Americans* are punished as harshly by courts-martial as they would be in civilian courts, receiving sentences of life imprisonment or death.[45] Yet injuries and deaths inflicted in training are dealt with much more leniently.[46] Pvt. Danny Chen committed suicide after suffering a long campaign of racist hazing. Under pressure from Congress, the community, and the media, the military conducted a very public investigation and prosecution.[47] But though charges were brought against eight of his tormentors, they were dropped against two, two were acquitted, one got just a month, and three others received only administrative penalties. After a Muslim Marine recruit fell to his death in an apparent suicide following a campaign of racist physical abuse by a Parris Island senior drill instructor, the Marines investigated 20 commanders, senior advisers, and drill instructors for hazing and assault, partly in response to pressure from the dead man's Representative, and disciplined 13 of them.[48] Gunnery Sgt. Joseph A. Felix was found guilty on almost all counts and sentenced to ten years (three more than prosecutors requested); two other trials were pending at the time of writing.

The mixed responses to two other categories of crime raise additional questions about courts-martial. Sexual offenses by men against other men are treated harshly: Capt. Devery L. Taylor got 50 years for raping four men and attempting to rape others he had drugged and kidnapped;[49] a Catholic priest got 12 years (10 suspended) for forcible sodomy.[50] The military even condones vigilantism. After pressure from Congress, the Army reversed its discipline and reinstated SFC Charles Martland, a Green Beret discharged for beating an Afghan Local Police commander who kidnapped an Afghan boy to keep as a sex slave (a custom in Afghanistan, if not actually legal).[51] Channeling Nathaniel Hawthorne three centuries later, the military demoted a four-star general for adultery (the only instance in modern times), passing sentence the day his divorce was finalized, nearly a year after he and his wife had separated.[52] The Air Force retroactively demoted retired Gen. Arthur Lichte two ranks for "inappropriate" (but apparently consensual) sexual acts with a subordinate.[53] Heterosexual behavior was also punished when it compromised security (because it involved an Iraqi woman whose father was detained as a former Baath party official)[54] or threatened discipline (a career-ending censure for an aircraft carrier commander who starred in homophobic, pornographic, and coprophagic videos used to entertain the crew).[55] The civilian criminal justice systems of host countries like Japan, South Korea, and the Philippines severely punished rapes of their citizens by members of the US military.[56] Otherwise the military has tended to wink at male heterosexual misconduct (change is slow and erratic).[57] After a marital rape conviction was overturned, the accused was given back pay and allowances of more than $250,000.[58] The nine members of the military protecting President Obama during his trip to Colombia received nonjudicial punishment for using prostitutes.[59] BGen. Jeffrey A. Sinclair, who pleaded guilty to maltreating a much younger female captain on his staff with whom he had an affair, suffered only a reprimand and a fine.[60] The exposé of massive sexual harassment at Lackland Air Force Base in 2011 revived painful memories of similar misconduct at the Tailhook event in Las Vegas in 1991, Aberdeen Proving Ground in 1996, and the Air Force Academy in 2002.[61] But though SSgt. Luis Walker was sentenced to 20 years, Sgt. Bobby D. Bass got only 6 months, and others were punished administratively.[62] Since then the military has successfully blocked Congressional efforts to abolish the commanding officer's power over charge and sentence.[63] Nevertheless, the number of officers disciplined for sexual offenses in FY2013, 2014, and 2015 was about twice the number disciplined in FY2012.[64] Publication of photos of nude female Marines by their male colleagues prompted harsh criticism; and the Army quickly suspended Fort Benning drill sergeants following accusations of sexual assault.[65] By contrast, political pressure forced the military to respond quickly and effectively to charges of medical negligence at the former Walter Reed Army Medical Center and the mishandling of human remains at Arlington National Cemetery and the Dover Air Force Base mortuary.[66]

The military has also exhibited ambivalence about insubordination. Senior officers often received significant punishment. The Navy removed a ship's commander and his top aide because of sailors' misbehavior in port.[67] Gen. Stanley McChrystal resigned after *Rolling Stone* published his alleged slurs against President Obama and other high administration officials.[68] The Army discharged MGen. Peter Fuller for calling President Karzai "erratic" and ungrateful, and Afghans "isolated from reality."[69] But when enlisted men and women refused to deploy or continue serving, the military tended to impose mild penalties and discharge them (perhaps fearing contamination).[70] Even 1st Lt. Ehren K. Watada, who sought to publicize "the deception used to wage" the Iraq war and "the lawlessness that has prefaced every aspect of our civilian leadership," was allowed to resign after his court-martial ended in a mistrial and a federal judge enjoined a retrial as double jeopardy.[71]

Two notorious cases demonstrate the military's ability to punish misconduct severely when it wishes, despite significant obstacles. Maj. Nidal Malik Hasan murdered 13 soldiers and civilians and wounded 32 others at Fort Hood, Texas, on November 5, 2009.[72] Determined not to compromise the court-martial, DoD refused to provide Congress with access to potential witnesses or investigative reports. John P. Galligan, a retired Army colonel retained by the accused's family, mounted a vigorous defense until Hasan fired him. At the Art. 32 hearing, prosecutors called 24 witnesses, including 17 of the wounded. The trial was repeatedly postponed while Hasan resisted the judge's order that he be forcibly shaved, eventually prevailing in the US Court of Appeals for the Armed

Forces. When Hasan also fired his military lawyers, the judge ordered them to remain as standby counsel. The trial was further delayed while Hasan (unsuccessfully) advanced a "defense of others" justification for the massacre. The Army spent $5 million on pretrial proceedings and another $4 million during the trial. In his opening statement Hasan acknowledged committing the acts charged. Prosecutors called 44 witnesses; Hasan offered no defense. The jury convicted him on all 45 counts. After listening to 20 victims and relatives and deliberating for just two hours, the jury sentenced him to death, ending the trial just under four years after the murders (although appeals were mandatory).

In June 2010 Bradley (now Chelsea) Manning, an intelligence analyst, was arrested for allegedly giving WikiLeaks 260,000 classified US diplomatic cables and videos of US airstrikes that killed civilians.[73] She had told Adrian Lamo (a convicted hacker who reported Manning to the government) that the documents contained "incredible things, awful things ... that belonged in the public domain." She wanted "people to see the truth" in order to stimulate "worldwide discussion, debates and reforms." After being held in Kuwait for two months, Manning was categorized as a "maximum custody detainee" in the Quantico brig under a "protection of injury order": confined to her cell 23 hours a day without a pillow or sheets and forbidden ever to exercise or to sleep between 5 a.m. and 10 p.m. She was allowed her eyeglasses just an hour a day and dressed only in underwear. In a deliberate act of sexual humiliation, she was required to strip naked every morning and wait outside her cell until the other prisoners were awakened, before her underwear was returned. Guards checked on her every five minutes, night and day. The Assistant Secretary of State for Public Affairs called this treatment "ridiculous, counterproductive and stupid," resigning the next day. The British Foreign Office expressed concern about Manning (whose mother was British). After the UN Special Rapporteur on Torture and major US newspapers condemned her treatment, Manning was transferred to Fort Leavenworth and housed with other pretrial prisoners. She was charged with theft of public records, transmitting defense information, computer fraud, wrongfully causing intelligence to be published, violating regulations on information security, and "aiding the enemy" (the last carrying the death penalty). Although prosecutors presented overwhelming evidence of her actions, her lawyer argued that negligence by the military had facilitated the alleged crimes and sought to show her actions had caused no harm. After prosecutors rejected Manning's offer to plead to eight charges, she read a statement in open court admitting that, after failing to interest the *Washington Post* or *New York Times*, she provided secret files to WikiLeaks in order to inform the public about "what happens and why it happens" and "spark a debate about foreign policy." She was convicted of six counts of violating the Espionage Act and most of the other charges (though not aiding the enemy). Prosecutors contended the maximum sentence was 136 years, but the judge cut this to 90 because some offenses were closely related. Manning apologized for the "unintended consequences of my actions," which she had believed were "going to help people." "At the time of my decisions … I was dealing with a lot of issues" (namely, gender identity disorder). Prosecutors sought 60 years. Little more than three years after her arrest, Manning was sentenced to 35 years; with credit for time in custody and abusive treatment she would be eligible for parole in about seven. She attempted suicide twice in 2016. More than 100,000 signed an online petition supporting her request for commutation. Days before leaving office (despite DoD opposition), President Obama commuted her sentence to six years, allowing her to be released in May 2017.[74] A month later DoD acknowledged that a 2011 report by its Information Review Task Force concluded that her leaks had no strategic impact on the US military.

As this chapter has shown, courts-martial are far more politicized than civilian prosecutions. They impose harsh punishment when the accused kills Americans (Hasan) or endangers national security (Manning). (Another politicized example was the court-martial of Bowe Bergdahl on charges exposing him to life imprisonment, a decision made against the recommendation of the preliminary hearing officer, following pressure by Congress.[75] As a presidential candidate, Donald Trump called Bergdahl "a dirty rotten traitor" and pantomimed a firing squad. On the day of Trump's inauguration, Bergdahl's lawyer moved to dismiss the case on the ground of unlawful command influence. Although the military judge regretted the "disturbing and disappointing" remarks, he found them to be mere "campaign rhetoric" and was upheld by the Army Court of Criminal Appeals. But after Bergdahl pleaded guilty, his lawyers renewed the motion when Trump invoked his earlier remarks. Col. Nance, the judge, characterized Trump as saying: "I shouldn't comment on that, but I think everyone knows what I think on Bowe Bergdahl." Nance denied the motion but said Trump's comments would constitute mitigation evidence. And though prosecutors sought 14 years, Nance sentenced Bergdahl to a dishonorable discharge, forfeiture of his $1,000/month salary for ten months, and reduction in rank to private. Trump promptly called this "a complete disgrace to our Country and to our Military.") Even when victims were foreign, courts-martial imposed appropriately severe penalties if the crime was unrelated to combat and highly publicized (Hamandiya, Bales). Yet comparisons among courts-martial and between them and civilian prosecutions reveal many disturbing differences. Civilian courts imposed harsher penalties than courts-martial in the same incident. They also punished contractors more severely than courts-martial did military personnel, in incidents that were otherwise similar (compare Nisour Square with Jalalabad). Courts-martial punished some forms of sexual behavior and insubordination more severely than others. The military confronted its systemic problems in the mishandling of remains and medical malpractice in the treatment of veterans but not the much more pervasive problem of sexual harassment. Most disturbing was the response to offenses related to combat (or even training). Offenders counted on comrades to keep mum and superiors to look the other way. Crimes surfaced only as a result of a few courageous whistle-blowers or persistent journalists. Ambiguous ROEs, competition for kills (often stoked by superior officers), an expansive concept of self-defense, and the fog of war justified or excused offenses against foreign civilians. Inadequate investigations and procedural errors undermined prosecutions. Enlisted ranks were far more likely than officers to be prosecuted, convicted, and significantly punished. Plea bargains let off most accused with little or no punishment. A pervasive belief that troops had to be supported at all costs led to acquittals and lenient punishment of those found guilty. The experience of the Afghan and Iraq wars raised the question, once again, whether military justice in combat settings is as oxymoronic as military music.[76]

CHAPTER FOUR

MILITARY COMMISSIONS

> I would certainly favor using every appropriate method of interrogation
> and put off for quite a while whether or not to seek a conviction because
> a conviction is pretty easy to get, I would think, in most of these cases.
>
> Senate Majority Leader Mitch McConnell[1]

A month after the 9/11 attacks President Bush issued an Executive
Order (drafted by David Addington, Vice President Cheney's counsel,
bypassing a JAG team) establishing military commissions.[2] They could
admit any evidence that had "probative value to a reasonable person"
and convict and sentence by a two-thirds vote, with review limited to
the Secretary of Defense.[3]

Attorney General Ashcroft explained:

> Foreign terrorists who commit war crimes against the United States, in
> my judgment, are not entitled to and do not deserve the protection of the
> American Constitution, particularly when there could be very serious
> and important reasons related to not bringing them back to the United
> States for justice.[4]

At a hearing of the Senate Judiciary Committee (SJC) he excoriated
critics:

> [T]o those who scare peace-loving people with phantoms of lost lib-
> erty, my message is this: Your tactics only aid terrorists, for they erode
> our national unity and diminish our resolve. They give ammunition to
> America's enemies, and pause to America's friends …
>
> When we come to those responsible for this, say, who are in
> Afghanistan, are we supposed to read them the *Miranda* rights, hire a
> flamboyant defense lawyer, bring them back to the United States to

create a new cable network of Osama TV or what have you, provide a worldwide platform from which propaganda can be developed? [5]

Two weeks later Alberto Gonzales, White House counsel, wrote in a *New York Times* op ed that the commissions:

> spare American jurors, judges and courts the grave risks associated with terrorist trials. They allow the government to use classified information as evidence without compromising intelligence or military efforts. They can dispense justice swiftly, close to where our forces may be fighting, without years of pretrial proceedings or post-trial appeals. And they can consider the broadest range of relevant evidence to reach their verdicts. For example, circumstances in a war zone often make it impossible to meet the authentication requirements for documents in a civilian court, yet documents from al-Qaeda safe houses in Kabul might be essential to accurately determine the guilt of Qaeda cell members hiding in the west. [6]

He dismissed criticisms "based on misconceptions." Defendants would only be charged with "offenses against the international laws of war." "Enemy war criminals are not entitled to the same procedural protections as people who violated our domestic laws." Proceedings "will be as open as possible consistent with the urgent needs of national security." They would be "full and fair." "The American military justice system is the finest in the world." "[A]nyone arrested, detained or tried in the United States by a military commission will be able to challenge the lawfulness of the commission's jurisdiction through a habeas corpus proceeding in a federal court." "Military commissions do not undermine the constitutional values of civil liberties or separation of powers."

But there was considerable criticism.[7] Hundreds of law professors and lawyers wrote SJC chair Leahy that President Bush's EO "undermines the tradition of the Separation of Powers" because "Congress, not the President, has the power to define and punish ... Offenses against the Law of Nations." The *New York Times* wrote that "John Ashcroft Misses the Point." Its conservative columnist William Safire wrote that Bush, "misadvised by frustrated and panic-stricken Attorney General" Ashcroft, had seized "what amounts to dictatorial power to jail or execute aliens." An ABA Task Force on Terrorism and the Law questioned the Order.

Although defense lawyers and other critics repeatedly denounced the confusion and chaos of a legal process created (and recreated) from scratch, the Office of Presiding Officers issued Military Commission

Presiding Officer Manual (POM) #16 on February 16, 2006, for the purpose of "maintaining the decorum and dignity of Commission proceedings." It specified the clothing to be worn by members of the military and civilians. Accused would not appear in prison attire; they would not be restrained unless the Presiding Officer approved, and then with "reasonable measures … so that the wearing of restraints is not obvious to the Commission members." "Counsel will drink from a plain paper, soft plastic, or Styrofoam cup, without logos or labels." All communications would be "in civil, non-sarcastic language."

On the day after the Supreme Court decided *Rasul* (see Chapter 5), DoD announced MC trials of Ali al-Bahlul, David Hicks, and Ibrahim al Qosi; two weeks later it added Salim Hamdan. This chapter analyzes the five completed prosecutions, 14 stalled or aborted prosecutions, and ongoing prosecutions of six HVDs. It raises the following questions. Who resisted the MCs or sought to conform them to civilian trials? How were MCs perceived by Art. III judges, bar leaders, the media, and US allies? How did MCs differ from courts-martial and civilian trials? How did they cope with being *tabulae rasae*? How much independence did MC judges display? How did military juries perform? What distinctive challenges did defense lawyers confront in fulfilling their responsibilities as zealous advocates? How did prosecutors deal with pressures to convict from superiors and the Convening Authority? How did MCs cope with defiant defendants, especially those who insisted on representing themselves? How effective were MCs in convicting and punishing terrorists, publicizing their crimes, and demonstrating procedural fairness?

COMPLETED PROSECUTIONS[8]

Salim Ahmed Hamdan[9]

On July 3, 2003 President Bush designated Hamdan for MC trial. LtCdr. Charles Swift, appointed as Hamdan's military counsel on December 18, sought a statement of charges and a speedy trial under the UCMJ. (On February 23, 2004 the legal adviser to the Convening Authority ruled that the UCMJ did not apply because Hamdan was being held as an enemy combatant.) On July 13, 2004 Hamdan was charged with one count of conspiracy "to commit … offenses triable by military commission" for serving as Osama bin Laden's bodyguard and driver. In early 2004 Swift had told Hamdan that the government was offering a 20-year sentence in exchange for a guilty plea and full cooperation. Hamdan replied: "How can I plead guilty if I don't know what I've done?" A few days later he agreed to let Swift petition for habeas on his behalf. WD Wash transferred Hamdan's habeas petition to DDC following the Supreme Court's *Rasul* decision and the Ninth Circuit's *Gherebi* decision (see Chapter 5). In Guantánamo, Hamdan despaired, going on hunger strike for a week and making a sufficiently convincing suicide threat to be seen by psychiatrists.[10] In August, Swift conducted an extensive voir dire, first of Army Col. Peter Brownback, the judge, and then of the five jurors.[11] When Brownback denied having said Hamdan had no right to a speedy trial, Swift replied he had a tape on which Brownback said just that. Brownback put his head in his hands for 90 seconds and finally said the tape had been made without his permission but that Swift could give it to John Altenberg, the CA. (Altenberg later disqualified three of the five jurors, making it easier to convict, but did not disqualify Brownback.)

On November 8, DDC Judge Robertson (a former naval officer) granted Hamdan's habeas petition, staying his MC hearing 30 minutes after it began.[12] The Combatant Status Review Tribunal (CSRT) (established in response to the Supreme Court's *Hamdi* decision – see Chapter 5), which had found Hamdan to be an EC, was not adequate to adjudicate "detainees' status under the Geneva Conventions."[13] Although the president had determined that al-Qaeda members were not POWs under the terms of the Geneva Conventions, "the President is not a 'tribunal.'" There was no authority for the government's assertion that the president, as commander-in-chief, had "untrammeled power to establish military tribunals." The third Geneva Convention "requires trial by court-martial as long as Hamdan's POW status is in doubt."

> The government has asserted a position starkly different from the positions and behavior of the United States in previous conflicts, one that can only weaken the United States' own ability to demand application of the Geneva Conventions to Americans captured during armed conflicts abroad … Because the Geneva Conventions were written to protect individuals, because the Executive branch of our government has implemented the Geneva Conventions for fifty years without questioning the absence of implementing legislation, because Congress clearly understood that the Conventions did not require implementing legislation except in a few specific areas … the Third Geneva Convention is a self-executing treaty.

Unlike a court-martial, an MC could exclude accused from hearings and forbid their lawyers from describing them.

> It is obvious beyond the need for citation that such a dramatic devi-
> ation from the confrontation clause could not be countenanced in any
> American court … It is also apparent that the right to trial "in one's
> presence" is established as a matter of international humanitarian and
> human rights law.

In March 2005 DoD produced a draft MC manual, giving defendants
more power to challenge evidence and excluding any "confession or
admission that was procured from the accused by torture," defined as
any act "specifically intended to inflict severe physical or mental pain
and suffering."[14] But Addington was strongly opposed. And when the
rules were approved at the end of August, they allowed defendants to be
present only "to the extent consistent with the need to protect classified
information" and admitted all probative evidence, even if extracted by
torture.

In June 2005 Swift told a Senate hearing he had been directed to
negotiate a guilty plea.[15] Col. Fred Borch, the chief prosecutor, had
written Swift that he would have access to Hamdan only "so long as we
are engaged in pretrial negotiations." At the end of the hearing Swift
said: "When we go to hold accountability, sirs, it says as much about the
society that holds the trial, as it does about the individual before it. Our
trials in the United States reflect who we are."

A month later the DC Circuit reversed Judge Robertson's grant
of habeas.[16] Judge Randolph (joined by Roberts) found that the
Authorization for the Use of Military Force (AUMF) had authorized
the president to establish MCs. Relying on the Supreme Court's
Eisentrager decision (see Chapter 6), the Court of Appeals found that
the Geneva Conventions were not judicially enforceable. Even if they
were, Hamdan was not a POW, and the Geneva Conventions did not
apply to al-Qaeda. Even if they did, Hamdan would have to exhaust his
military remedies before challenging MC procedures in federal court.
Furthermore, the UCMJ "imposes only minimal restrictions upon the
form and function of military commissions … and Hamdan does not
allege that the regulations establishing the present commission violate
any of the pertinent provisions." An MC was a "competent tribunal"
under Army Regulation 190–8 to determine whether he was a POW.
Attorney General Gonzales was pleased the court had reaffirmed the
president's "critical authority." In August it emerged that, as White
House Counsel, Gonzales had interviewed Roberts for nomination
to the Supreme Court six days before oral argument; Vice President
Cheney, White House Chief of Staff Card and Deputy Chief of Staff

Rove interviewed Roberts a month later; and President Bush did so on the day the Circuit Court issued its decision.[17] Several legal ethicists (Stephen Gillers, David Luban, and Steven Lubet) said Roberts should have recused himself, but others disagreed (Deborah Rhode, Thomas Morgan, and Ronald Rotunda). Sens. Feingold and Schumer questioned Roberts's participation.[18]

The Supreme Court granted certiorari on November 7 (after conferencing the case weekly beginning September 26).[19] Declaring *Hamdan* "perhaps the most important case of the term," the *Washington Post* preferred the "proven method" of courts-martial.[20] MCs were "a disaster" that "undermined the prestige of American justice."

On March 8, 2006 Justice Scalia told an audience in Switzerland:[21]

> War is war, and it has never been the case that when you captured a combatant you have to give them a jury trial in your civil courts. It's a crazy idea … I mean, give me a break … If [Hamdan] was captured by my army on a battlefield, [an MC] is where he belongs. I had a son on that battlefield and they were shooting at my son, and I'm not about to give this man who was captured in a war a full jury trial. I mean it's crazy.

Before the case was argued three weeks later, a group of retired generals and admirals asked Scalia to recuse himself.[22] He refused. The *New York Times* later said Scalia "keeps ignoring" the "duty to avoid off-the-bench behavior hurtful to the Court's reputation and mission."[23] In February Scalia had said that those who did not share "his originalist philosophy of judging are 'idiots.'" The *Times* urged Scalia's colleagues to "help persuade him that [reconsidering his recusal] is the right thing to do."

After the Detainee Treatment Act (DTA) was passed by Congress on December 21, 2005 Republican Senators inserted 21 pages in the *Congressional Record*, seeking to construct a fictitious legislative history declaring that it retroactively stripped federal courts of jurisdiction in pending habeas petitions.[24] Sens. Kyl and Graham (the Act's sponsors) invented a nonexistent dialogue in which Kyl allegedly had said the DTA "expels lawsuits brought by enemy combatants from U.S. Courts." "The system of litigation that Rasul has wrought is unacceptable." Graham had supposedly added: "I agree entirely." (Sen. Levin recalled that the Bush administration had wanted the Act to be retroactive, but "we successfully opposed" that.) In their amicus brief, Kyl and Graham declared that the fact that their colloquy "appears in the *Congressional*

Record prior to the Senate's adoption" of the bill made it "unmistakably clear" that the law was retroactive. The exchange was "a genuine expression of the senators' understanding of, and intention regarding, the jurisdictional provisions." The Supreme Court took the highly unusual step of rejecting that amicus brief (while accepting five others). But arguing (unsuccessfully) for dismissal of the appeal, DoJ still claimed the "legislative history supports the conclusion that Congress was aware that the Act's jurisdiction-ousting rule would extend to pending cases, including this case."

The *New York Times* said the case, which had "become a focus of Mr. Bush's imperial vision of the presidency," was "a critical test of judicial independence," since "the Republican majority has decided to allow President Bush to usurp Congress's role in matters of national security."[25] Bush had "invented" the term "unlawful enemy combatant" to "deny the protections of the Geneva Conventions, international statutes, or United States law to certain prisoners." The *Times* agreed with Hamdan that "the commissions are not legitimate because prisoners are routinely barred from seeing evidence, much less confronting their accusers or having access to real legal representation." But the "larger battle" in this "first attempt to suspend habeas corpus on American territory since the Civil War" concerned Bush's claim that he had "the power to put prisoners beyond the reach of the law at his choosing." "At a minimum, we hope the Court will rule that Congress and the president may not deny the Justices the power to review pending cases. But it should also reject the defective military commissions, as well as the idea denying access to the courts for future valid claims."

Four days before the case was argued on March 28, 2006 DoD issued an MC rule barring "any statement determined by the prosecution to have been made as a result of torture," defined as an "act specifically intended to inflict severe physical or mental pain or suffering."[26] After argument, the *Los Angeles Times* said that since 9/11 "the nation's judicial branch seemed to be as much in the government's cross hairs as any alleged terrorist."[27] "Both the White House and Congress have tried to curtail judicial review of proceedings against detainees picked up on the battlefield (a somewhat amorphous concept in this war)." "This makeshift judicial system" did "not provide the same procedural safeguards accorded defendants in a court-martial or as required under the Geneva Convention."

On June 29, the Supreme Court (5–3) nullified the MCs in six opinions extending over a hundred pages.[28] Justice Stevens (joined by Breyer, Kennedy, Souter and Ginsburg) rejected the government's argument that the jurisdiction-stripping provision applied to pending cases, accepting Sen. Levin's statements on the floor that the Act was not retroactive and rejecting contrary statements by Sen. Kyl, which "appear to have been inserted into the Congressional Record *after* the Senate debate." Neither the AUMF nor the DTA authorized the president to create the MCs. "[T]he government has failed even to offer a 'merely colorable' case for inclusion of conspiracy among those offenses cognizable by law-of-war military commission."

> Hamdan's tribunal was appointed not by a military commander in the field of battle, but by a retired major general stationed away from any active hostilities … Hamdan is charged not with an overt act for which he was caught redhanded in a theater of war and which military efficiency demands be tried expeditiously, but with an *agreement* the inception of which long predated the attacks of September 11, 2001, and the AUMF [original emphasis].

The Court rejected the government's claim that Hamdan should be content to challenge procedures after conviction. He "*already has been* excluded from his own trial" [original emphasis] and would have no automatic right of appeal to a court were he sentenced to less than ten years. MC procedures violated UCMJ Art. 36, requiring that they follow those of courts-martial "as far as practicable." "The 'practicability' determination the President has made is insufficient to justify variances"; the fact that this flouted "one of the most fundamental protections" – the "right to be present" – was "particularly disturbing." MCs also violated the Geneva Conventions, an integral part of the law of war, compliance with which "is the condition upon which [UCMJ authority] is granted." Rejecting the Circuit Court's opinion, the Supreme Court held that "even if the relevant conflict is not between signatories" to the Geneva Conventions, Common Article 3 "requires that Hamdan be tried by a regularly constituted court affording all the judicial guarantees which are cognized as indispensable by civilized peoples." A "regularly constituted court" is defined as an "ordinary military court … established and organized in accordance with the laws and procedures already in force in a country." "The right to be tried in [one's] presence" was surely one of the "safeguards to which all persons in the hands of an enemy are entitled." "[I]n undertaking to try Hamdan and subject him to criminal punishment, the Executive is bound to comply with the rule of law that prevails in this jurisdiction."

Justice Breyer (with Kennedy, Souter, and Ginsburg) concurred separately to emphasize that "Congress has not issued the Executive a 'blank check'" (invoking O'Connor's language in *Hamdi*). Judicial insistence on consultation with Congress "strengthens the Nation's ability to determine – through democratic means – how best" to deal with terrorism. "The Constitution places its faith in those democratic means. Our Court today simply does the same." Justice Kennedy (with Souter, Ginsburg, and Breyer) agreed that Congress "has considered the subject of military tribunals and set limits on the President's authority," which Bush exceeded in creating the MCs. "The Constitution is best preserved by reliance on standards tested over time and insulated from the pressures of the moment." That the Appointing Authority could resolve "dispositive issues in the middle of the trial" raised "concerns that the commission's decisionmaking may not be neutral." Furthermore, "the review process here lacks structural protections designed to help ensure impartiality." Kennedy would not decide the applicability of the Geneva Conventions.

Justice Scalia (with Thomas and Alito) dissented in characteristically extreme language. The DTA "unambiguously" stripped the courts of jurisdiction. The majority had reached its "patently erroneous" conclusion despite this "plain directive." "Worst of all is the Court's reliance on the legislative history." That some of the "floor statements" were inserted into the *Congressional Record* after the Senate debate "makes no difference unless one indulges in the fantasy that Senate floor speeches are attended (like the Philippics of Demosthenes) by throngs of eager listeners." Scalia accused the majority of "opportunism" in choosing which statements to credit. "[T]he Court has made a mess of this statute." As a result, habeas petitions from "a purported 600" Guantánamo detainees will "keep the courts busy for years to come." Hamdan's claim that applying the DTA to his case would violate the Suspension Clause "is easily dispatched" because "it is clear that Guantánamo Bay, Cuba, is outside the sovereign 'territorial jurisdiction' of the United States." (Scalia's only authority for this was his *dissent* in *Rasul*.) Scalia condemned the majority's "audacity" in contradicting the "political branch's" finding that "military necessity" required MC trials. The District Court's enjoining of Hamdan's MC "brings the Judicial Branch into direct conflict with the Executive in an area where the Executive's competence is maximal and ours is virtually nonexistent." Justice Thomas (joined by Scalia and Alito) dissented because the majority "openly flouts our well-established duty to respect the Executive's judgment in matters of military operations and foreign affairs." Justice Alito (joined by Scalia and Thomas) dissented because the MC was "a regularly constituted court."

Administration officials promptly responded that they were considering amending the UCMJ to remove any reference to the Geneva Conventions.[29] Sens. Graham and Kyl were "disappointed" but believed that "Congress and the administration can draft a fair, suitable and constitutionally permissible tribunal statute." Graham said "the Geneva Convention aspects of this decision are breathtaking." He did not believe that "al-Qaeda members who do not sign up to the Geneva Convention, who show disdain for it, who butcher our troops" should "be given the protections of a treaty they're not part of." "Congress has the ability to restrict the application of Common Article III to terrorists." John Yoo wrote in *USA Today* that the Supreme Court was now "part of the problem" in the war on terrorism, having "tossed aside centuries of American history, judicial decisions of long standing," and the DTA. He accused the Court of "attempting to suppress creative thinking." Its "effort to inject the Geneva Convention into the war on terrorism … smacks of judicial mismanagement." Sen. McConnell said Congress had to address the Court's "very disturbing" finding that international law applied. House Majority Leader Boehner said there was "a clear choice between Capitol Hill Democrats who celebrate offering special privileges to violent terrorists, and Republicans who want the president to have the necessary tools to prosecute and achieve victory in the global war on terror."[30] When House Minority Leader Pelosi said the decision "reaffirms the American ideal that all are entitled [to] the basic guarantees of our justice system," Rush Limbaugh called her "deranged." A senior administration official said "members of both parties will have to decide whether terrorists who cherish the killing of innocents deserve the same protections as our men and women who wear the uniform." Rep. Peter King warned: "we can't be turning over evidence and discovery and giving the benefit of the doubt to terrorists in these cases. This is different from other wars."

The *Washington Post* welcomed "a victory for law" and "fundamental human values."[31] The Bush administration had chosen "to set aside the standing legal procedures and treaties for fighting this country's enemies and make up rules of its own – at the expense of violating human rights, tarnishing U.S. prestige around the world, and undermining the checks and balances of American democracy." Warning that "some in Congress now want to rush through legislation that would rubber-stamp the regime that the Court rejected," the *Post* said "there's nothing practical to be gained by gratuitously repudiating Geneva or U.S. laws that mandate compliance with it – and much that would be lost." But the newspaper also favored amending the law to make conspiracy a crime (ignoring the fact that this could not be retroactive). The *Los Angeles Times* noted that "for the second time in two years, the U.S. Supreme Court has rebuked President Bush for overreaching in the war on terror."[32] "Instead of passing a measure that rubber-stamps the inadequate procedures laid down by the administration, the House and Senate should expeditiously authorize tribunals that satisfy the requirements of the Uniform Code of Military Justice and the Geneva Convention." The *New York Times* said: "Justice Stevens's impassioned opinion found fault not only with the tribunals but the Bush administration's broader claims that the president has inherent power to execute the war on terror as he sees fit."[33]

> The challenge for Congress is simply to create a vehicle for giving the prisoners their day in court that contains the protections that Americans believe any human being deserves before he can be locked away in an isolated prison forever …The division … is between an executive branch that seems bent on proving that the president has unlimited war powers and those who believe that the Constitution and the rule of law did not crumble along with the World Trade Center.

About two weeks after the decision LtCdr. Swift, was denied promotion to commander, forcing him to retire in 2007 after 20 years of service.[34] He planned to continue representing Hamdan as a civilian. The *New York Times* said this "deeply troubling" decision drowned out the "lot of noise" the administration had made about "its respect for the uniformed lawyers of the armed forces."[35]

On July 7 Assistant Secretary of Defense Gordon England issued a memo affirming that "the Supreme Court has determined that Common Article 3 to the Geneva Conventions of 1949 applies as a matter of law to the conflict with al-Qaeda." But DoD insisted the memo "doesn't indicate a shift in policy."[36] The *Los Angeles Times* said the administration "grudgingly and gracelessly" had acknowledged that *Hamdan* required compliance with the Geneva Conventions.[37] But in his *New York Times* column, Bob Herbert was skeptical the administration would "actually make an attempt to emerge from the middle ages."[38]

Sens. Graham and Cornyn wanted to ensure that the Geneva Conventions did not apply.[39] HASC chair Hunter said the USA needed a system "that doesn't tie us into knots trying to prosecute the people who have killed Americans in large numbers." "In time of war it may not be practical to apply to [sic] rules of evidence that we do in civilian trials or court-martials for our troops." "We have to give the executive the tools to fight this war." SASC chair Warner (a former Secretary of the Navy) disagreed: "we've got to structure this law in such a way that if it ever comes back up through the Supreme Court, it will not be struck down." Sen. Specter said: "we're not going to give the DoD a blank check." Sen. Leahy said MCs "should be consistent with a high standard of American justice." ABA President Michael S. Greco wrote Specter and Leahy (chair and ranking minority member of the SJC) urging that MCs "provide the rights afforded in courts-martial, and … fully comply with our treaty obligations." The *Los Angeles Times* said the new rules should not be "a rubber-stamping of the flawed procedures unilaterally adopted by the Bush administration."[40] "The burden of proof … should be on those who would depart from the protections accorded by courts-martial."

At the SJC hearings, Specter said "the Constitution is explicit that the Congress has the authority, responsibility to establish the rules of trials on capture on land or sea." But denouncing the Court's "surprising and disappointing" decision, Steven Bradbury, head of the DoJ Office of Legal Counsel (OLC) declared that "only the president has the decision to introduce legislation" and insisted the administration's position had been "completely reasonable." "The court-martial procedures are wholly inappropriate … and would be infeasible." How much evidence MC defendants could see "should be left up to the DoD." He favored a substantial evidence standard for conviction. DoD's principal deputy general counsel Daniel Dell'Orto said approving "the system as currently configured … would be a very expeditious way to move these trials forward." "It would be ludicrous" to give detainees all the protections of courts-martial. Graham replied that administration lawyers would be "well served to forget about" the commissions. Outside the hearing, White House Counselor Dan Bartlett continued to insist that ECs "do not qualify for protections under Geneva," but said the administration would comply with the Court's decision. The *New York Times* was "pleased to see the Defense Department finally recognize the power of the Supreme Court over prisoners of the military," but expressed concern that it had "argued for what would be the worst possible outcome: that Congress just approve what Mr. Bush did and enact exceptions to the Geneva Conventions."[41]

At the HASC hearings Rep. Candice S. Miller, who boasted of having neither a college nor a law degree, denounced the *Hamdan* decision as "incredibly counterintuitive."[42] "This could be easy. We could just ratify what the executive branch and the [DoD] have done and move on." Dell'Orto agreed that "would be a very desirable way to proceed."

> I don't want a soldier when he kicks down a door in a hut in Afghanistan searching for Osama bin Laden to have to worry about … whether he's got to advise them of some rights before he takes a statement. I don't want him to have to worry about filling out some form that is going to support the chain of custody when he picks up a laptop computer that has the contact information for all manner of cells in the world.

For national security reasons, 73 military rules of evidence and 145–150 UCMJ articles would have to be amended, "gutting" the UCMJ, because otherwise the MCs would have to exclude hearsay, call soldiers from the front, and allow defendants to seek testimony from al-Qaeda leaders. Bradbury said: "there's obviously a spectrum" of "coercive questioning"; "I don't think you can make an absolute rule." HASC chair Hunter said: "it may not be practical on the battlefield to read the enemy their Miranda warnings. We have to give the executive the tools to fight this war. This is not a separation of powers issue. It is an issue of how to defeat the enemy."

He "instinctively" saw a problem with the UCMJ – "a body of law meant to extend privileges to the men and women who wear the uniform of the United States." But MGen. Scott Black, the Army JAG, said: "I believe the accused should see that evidence." Pressed by Hunter, Black said a case should be dropped if it could not be prosecuted without secret evidence. Attorney General Gonzales said "there are a series of procedures and processes and rights," such as Miranda warnings and the exclusion of hearsay, "that I think it is appropriate to ask, is this what we want to provide to terrorists?"[43] He continued to quarrel with the Supreme Court: "As a lawyer, I think words should mean something, so when I read a treaty that says it applies to conflicts 'not of an international character,' I take those words to mean what they say." And Bradbury warned that "the application of Common Article 3 will create a degree of uncertainty for those who fight to defend us from terrorist attack." The *Washington Post* said the "real question" was would the administration work "with the legislature to create fair trials, authorized by law" or seek "to muscle Congress into rubber-stamping the flawed system it created on its own?"[44] "The past five years have shown the grave difficulty of trying to build a legal system from scratch." It favored "the court-martial system the military uses every day, tailoring it as need be." Lawyers for the four branches of the military told SASC they favored the UCMJ.[45] The *New York Times* "wanted to weep" that their advice had not been heeded earlier. Sens. Inhofe and Cornyn cautioned about the "ambiguity" of the Geneva Conventions. But Sen. Graham was "very optimistic" that the UCMJ would be "the model but with substantial differences."

The *New York Times* warned it had become clear that the Bush administration's war on terror "had far less to do with fighting Osama bin Laden than with expanding presidential power."[46] "This effort to undermine the constitutional separation of powers ... grew out of Vice President Dick Cheney's long and deeply held conviction that ... the president needed more power and that Congress and the courts should get out of the way." "For one brief, shining moment, it appeared that the administration realized it had met a check that it could not simply ignore." "But by the week's end it was clear that the president's idea of cooperation was purely cosmetic." "Administration officials and obedient Republican lawmakers offered a lot of silly talk about not coddling the masterminds of terror." "Undoing the Geneva Conventions would further endanger the life of every member of the American military." The *Times* mocked the administration claim that the Geneva Conventions were "too vague." "Which part of 'civilized peoples,' 'judicial guarantees' or 'humiliating and degrading treatment' do they find confusing?" In his *New York Times* column, Bob Herbert condemned the "kangaroo courts" and "slapstick justice" of a "Marx Brothers republic."[47] Three days later he repeated that these "kangaroo courts" were "an unmitigated outrage," "patently illegal."[48] "They stomped all over the rights of the defendant. The inquisitors of the Middle Ages would have smiled knowingly at Guantánamo." "The rumbling you hear is the sound of the Founding Fathers spinning in their graves."

Attorney General Gonzales told the SJC that:

> [MC's] current procedures carefully address in a balanced fashion specific concerns. For example, no one can expect members of our military to read Miranda warnings to terrorists captured on the battlefield ... or provide terrorists on the battlefield immediate access to counsel ... or maintain a strict chain of custody for evidence. Nor should terrorist trials compromise sources and methods for gathering intelligence, or prohibit the admission of probative hearsay evidence ... Second, we must

eliminate the hundreds of lawsuits from Guantánamo detainees that are clogging our court system.

He wanted the DTA's jurisdiction-stripping "to apply to all of the existing Guantánamo detainee lawsuits." Sen. Graham warned Gonzales: "I'm going to be on the other side of you on classified information. If the only way we can try this terrorist is disclose classified information, and we can't share it with the accused, I would argue don't do the trial. Just keep him [as a detainee]. Because it could come back to haunt us."[49] Bradbury told the committee that "courts have always had a very difficult time defining what [coercion] is," but the military judge would be the "gatekeeper." Although the National Security Council had earlier assured senators the White House could accept the UCMJ as a starting point, a week later the Council made clear that the administration wanted to begin with the MCs and just make a few changes.[50] Sen. Sessions was supportive: "the UCMJ was designed to try American servicemen ... it was never designed to try unlawful combatants."

At the end of July, the administration circulated its bill, drafted by Bradbury.[51] But though Gonzales claimed it followed the hearsay rules of the International Criminal Tribunals of the former Yugoslavia (ICTY) and Rwanda (ICTR), international lawyers disagreed. Under the bill, a military judge would preside over a military jury of at least five people. MCs would exclude statements obtained by torture, but would admit coerced statements and hearsay unless a judge found them unreliable or lacking in probative value. The judge could close the trial to everyone but a single military defense counsel. Prosecutors had to disclose exculpatory evidence and prove guilt beyond a reasonable doubt. The jury had to convict by a two-thirds vote, three-fourths if it sentenced the accused to ten years or more, and unanimously to impose the death penalty. Those convicted could appeal to the Court of Military Commission Review, then to the DC Circuit, and finally seek certiorari in the Supreme Court. The DTA's jurisdiction-stripping was explicitly made retroactive. Gonzales said on August 2 that "our deliberations have included detailed discussion" with military attorneys, whose "multiple rounds of comments ... will be reflected in the legislative package." Actually, the bill was drafted by OLC, which had just one meeting with a working group of military lawyers on July 28, at the start of which OLC announced there was no point in debating the issue of secret evidence.[52] The *Washington Post* said the draft had "some significant positive elements and some terrible elements,"[53] but its "fundamental problem" was the decision "to create a wholly new trial mechanism rather than adapting the one America uses every day."

At a SASC hearing, McCain asked Gonzales whether statements gathered "through illegal, inhumane treatment" would be admissible.[54] After nearly a minute's silence, Gonzales said:

> The concern that I would have about such a prohibition is, what does it mean? How do you define it? I think if we could all reach agreement about the definition of cruel and inhumane and degrading treatment, then perhaps I could give you an answer … I can foresee a situation where, depending on the definition, I would say no. But depending on your definition of something as degrading, such as insults or something like that, I would say that information should still come in.

McCain replied: "I think that if you practice illegal, inhumane treatment and allow that to be admissible in court, that would be a radical departure from any practice that this nation" has seen. Graham said disregarding the UCMJ rules against hearsay would "not serve us well."

The *New York Times* said "the chief lawyers of the armed services provided a withering condemnation" of "the thinly disguised kangaroo courts known as military commissions."[55] They "unanimously rejected the administration's notion that prisoners could be excluded from their trials, or that judge and jury could see evidence kept secret from the accused," and they opposed coerced testimony, hearsay, and empowering the Defense Secretary to "invent crimes." The *Times* said "the tribunals should be constructed within the UCMJ, with specific and detailed changes only when absolutely necessary." Talk about rewriting "America's understanding of the [Geneva] Conventions" was "extremely dangerous." The *Los Angeles Times* said the "good news" was that the legislation "borrows heavily from the UCMJ."[56] But the "bad news" was that "the administration still clings to the notion that the end justifies the means" on issues like "the use of hearsay and evidence obtained by coercive or inhumane interrogation." It warned that "the administration persists in playing word games." "Defendants should be able to attend their trials and see the evidence against them." Jack Goldsmith and Eric Posner (law professors at Harvard and Chicago) wrote a *Washington Post* op ed arguing that "terrorist trials are both unnecessary and unwise" and detainees should just be held until the war ended.[57]

On September 6, Bush announced to an audience of relatives of 9/11 victims that he had transferred 14 HVDs from secret CIA prisons to Guantánamo, and he simultaneously submitted the Military Commissions Act to Congress.[58] "As soon as Congress acts to authorize the military commissions I have proposed, the men our intelligence officials believe orchestrated the deaths of nearly 3,000 Americans on Sept. 11, 2001, can face justice." The bill allowed the admission of hearsay and evidence obtained by coercion and denied suspects and their civilian lawyers the right to see classified evidence. Sen. Levin said: "if the defense cannot see what the jury sees and argue against it in some way, then it's inconsistent with our current federal rules." Sen. Graham agreed: "I do not think we can afford to again cut legal corners that will result in federal court rejection of our work." "I do not believe it is necessary to have a trial where the accused cannot see the evidence against them." But he was confident the differences with the administration "can be overcome." Sen. Cornyn supported Bush: "as a matter of principle that you don't unnecessarily share classified information with terrorists in the course of a military tribunal."

The *Washington Post* called Bush's actions "major steps ... toward cleaning up the mess his administration has made of the detention, interrogation and prosecution of those captured in the war on terrorism."[59] But the Military Commissions Act (MCA) 2006 would allow trials "modeled principally on the ad hoc ones the military set up unilaterally." The *Post* warned that "a grossly abbreviated legislative process in the midst of an election season in which one party is trying to label the other as soft on terrorism is not a propitious moment for sober action." The *Los Angeles Times* called the proposal "overdue" but "still flawed" in allowing the admission of coerced evidence.[60]

Military lawyers remained critical.[61] BGen. James Walker, the Marine JAG, said "no civilized country denied an accused the right to see the evidence, and the U.S. should not be the first." MGen. Black, the Army JAG, agreed. RAdm. Bruce MacDonald, the Navy JAG, said military law let a judge receive classified evidence and prepare an unclassified version for the accused. Sen. Graham said "it would be unacceptable, legally ... to give someone the death penalty in a trial where they never heard the evidence against them." Such a rule would be struck down by courts "in 30 seconds." But Sens. Cornyn and Sessions were prepared to endorse the administration bill. Sen. Warner said 90 percent of the administration's proposals resembled his own bill. "I feel this bill has got to pass what I call the federal court muster, so this thing doesn't get tangled up in the courts again and go all the way to the Supreme Court, and then goes down again." The *Washington Post* wrote that Sens.

Warner, McCain, and Graham had drafted "a remarkably good alternative bill … in almost all respects superior to the president's proposal."[62] The accused would see the evidence, and coerced evidence would be excluded. There would be "flexibility on the use of hearsay evidence." But the appeals process was too "constrained." And the *Post* opposed jurisdiction-stripping.

A week after the president introduced the MCA 2006, senators were still resisting his proposal to deny the accused access to evidence.[63] Graham said the clause prohibiting defense lawyers from sharing classified information with clients was "the killer. I fell over when I read it." "It will result in putting the commissions in legal jeopardy and eroding our standing in the world community." "How many more times do we need to create legislation that's defective … that's got not a snowball's chance in hell of passing Supreme Court muster?" "It would be a tragedy to take one of the masterminds of 9/11, hold them accountable, only to have the case rejected by the Supreme Court for no good reason." McCain and Warner agreed, proposing a compromise in which the judge would review classified evidence and summarize it to the accused. Their bill excluded evidence obtained through cruel, inhuman, or degrading treatment and stripped federal courts of habeas jurisdiction retroactively. HASC passed Rep. Hunter's version of the administration bill 52–8 after rejecting (on party lines, 26–32–1) Rep. Skelton's alternative, which resembled Warner's.[64]

The *Washington Post* said Warner's draft had changed "in some respects for the better, in one big respect for the worse."[65] Jurisdiction-stripping "would reduce badly needed oversight and judicial review of detentions and trials." The *Post* invoked "rules that preserve rights democracies have recognized for centuries – such as the ability of defendants to be present at trial and to know and confront the evidence against them."

> To authorize trials that needlessly depart from international norms will only invite skepticism about the convictions they deliver, further degrade the United States in the eyes of the world, and make martyrs of those condemned to prison or death.

Nine retired federal judges wrote Congress to "applaud" Warner's bill for ensuring that MCs "prohibit the use of secret evidence and evidence gained by coercion."[66] But they opposed jurisdiction-stripping. Deciding habeas petitions was "an easy matter" and "the most hallowed judicial role in our constitutional democracy." Eliminating them "would raise serious concerns under the Suspension Clause."

McCain and Graham informed Warner on September 13 that negotiating with the administration was futile. After an impromptu news
conference, Warner told Majority Leader Frist. The next day SASC
approved the Warner bill 15–9 (McCain, Warner, Graham, and
Collins joining the Democrats).[67] The day after the vote, wearing a tie
given him by Reagan declaring "Democracy is not a spectator sport,"
Warner said the issue was bigger than the fate of the "20-odd individuals" likely to be tried. "It's how America's going to be perceived in the
world, how we're going to continue the war against terrorism." Graham
wrote Condoleezza Rice: "where in American jurisprudence do you find
support for the concept that a person accused can be tried and convicted
on evidence which that person has no opportunity to see, confront or
rebut?" Noting that Bush made an "unaccustomed trip" to Congress to
lobby against Warner's bill, the *Washington Post* warned that the administration "wants the right to try ... detainees, and perhaps sentence
them to death, on the basis of evidence that the defendants cannot
see and that may have been extracted during ... abusive interrogation
sessions." Rep. Hunter warned that the SASC bill would lead to "the
lawyer brigade" being attached to combat troops to counsel detainees.

The *New York Times* devoted almost its entire editorial page to
denouncing the "Stampeding Congress."[68] The administration bill
"could cause profound damage to justice and the American way." Bush
wanted Congress to endorse MCs "the Supreme Court has already
ruled unconstitutional" and "permit the use of coerced evidence, secret
hearings, and other horrific violations of American justice." Sens.
Warner, McCain, and Graham "deserve enormous credit for standing
up to Mr. Bush's fearmongering – something many Democrats seem
too frightened to do ... [but] their bill still has serious shortcomings,
and should not be rushed through Congress in the current atmosphere,
which has very little to do with stopping terrorists and everything to do
with winning seats in November."

Bob Herbert wrote in his *Times* column that "in civilized countries, evidence obtained by torture is inadmissible in a court of law."[69]
Preventing the accused from seeing the evidence against him "is a concept that is so far beyond the pale it makes most legal scholars gasp."
The *Los Angeles Times* was cheered that it had been "a disappointing
week for the president – and a heartening one for anyone outside the
White House."[70]

New York City Bar President Barry M. Kamins wrote the majority
and minority leaders of both Armed Services Committees that the

MCA 2006 "runs afoul of *Hamdan* ... reflects a pointed disregard of the opinions of the senior JAGs and other military leaders, and ... undercuts this nation's well-earned role as the chief proponent of human rights and the rule of law around the world." The proposal for MCs "reflects a stunning disregard for *Hamdan's* citation to the Common Article 3's requirement of a 'regularly constituted court affording all the judicial guarantees which are recognized as indispensable by civilized peoples.'" "The administration has made no serious effort to show why accused terrorists require a wholly different judicial system" from the UCMJ. "This system is sure to be regarded by observers around the world as a mockery of justice. Convictions secured by it would thereby be discredited."

Sen. Graham remained firmly committed to jurisdiction-stripping.[71] "There are 400 and something lawsuits filed against our guys complaining about the food, the tv access, all kinds of crap. Prisoners of war don't sue their captors." Sen. Specter objected to the White House proposal to deny classified information to detainees.[72] He also criticized Warner's bill for eliminating habeas corpus retroactively. But Sen. Frist insisted on "protect[ing] classified information from terrorists who could exploit this information in planning attacks against the American people."

He threatened to filibuster both Specter's SJC bill and Warner's SASC bill. After five former JCS chairs opposed the administration's redefinition of US obligations under the Geneva Conventions, the White House dropped that element. Objecting to the administration draft, ABA President Karen J. Mathis wrote representatives urging that MCs be guided by the UCMJ. The HJC first voted 20–17 against the MCA 2006 and then just barely (20–19) passed a compromise excluding evidence obtained by techniques that violated the DTA.

The *New York Times* condemned the "bad bargain."[73] Marine Maj. Michael Mori (who represented David Hicks) called the bill "worse than the system that was in place before," because it would prevent defense lawyers from learning whether evidence against their clients had been obtained by coercion. Marine Col. Dwight Sullivan, chief defense counsel, said "it replaces the old broken" system with "a new broken commission system." The *Washington Post* deplored that "after barely three weeks of debate ... rather than carefully weigh the issues, Congress has allowed itself to be stampeded into a vote on hastily written but far-reaching legal provisions in a pre-election climate in which dissenters risk being labeled as soft on terrorism."[74] The bill did not meet Sen. Warner's test: "the United States can be proud of it ...

the world will see it as fair and humane, and … the Supreme Court can uphold it."

But the House approved it overwhelmingly (253–168, 34 Democrats voting for, 7 Republicans against).[75] Rep. Hunter said that once MCs began:

> [Americans could] watch all those rights being accorded to people who designed the attack against the United States and decide whether or not they agree with the Democrats that there weren't enough rights given to the defendants. My instincts are that they will probably … come to the conclusion that … we gave them too many rights … We are dealing with the enemy in war, not defendants in our criminal justice system. In time of war it is not practical to apply the same rules of evidence that we apply in civil trials or courts-martial for our troops.

Rep. Hastert denounced "Democrat Minority Leader Nancy Pelosi and 159 of her Democrat colleagues" for voting "in favor of MORE rights for terrorists." Sen. Levin criticized a provision that excluded coerced testimony only if it was obtained after December 20, 2005 (the effective date of the DTA). Sens. Robert Byrd and Barack Obama proposed an amendment that would sunset MCs in five years.

President of the New York City Bar (NYCB) Kamins wrote Frist that his association "shares the view presented by the service JAGs that the existing court-martial system … provides an appropriate process for trial of battlefield detainees." Shifting the burden to the accused to show that hearsay was not probative or reliable "is inconsistent with historical practice and would probably taint the proceedings themselves," and might "constitute a grave breach of Common Article 3." The American Jewish Committee wrote senators that its 150,000 members opposed the MCA, 2006, which "permits the prosecution to introduce evidence that has not been provided to a defendant in a form sufficient to allow him or her to participate in the preparation of his or her defense," and "unduly restricts defendants' access to exculpatory evidence available to the government." The *New York Times* said an "irresponsible Congress" had "railroad[ed] a profoundly important bill to serve the mindless politics of a midterm election."[76] "Reliable" coerced evidence (which would be admissible) was "a contradiction in terms." "American standards of justice prohibit evidence and testimony that is kept secret from the defendant."

The Senate defeated Warner's bill 43–54, with only one Republican (Lincoln Chafee, who quit the party the next year) joining the Democrats.[77] After more than ten hours of debate, the Senate approved the administration bill 65–34 (12 Democrats – 5 facing re-election – joined the 52 Republicans voting for; only 1 Republican and 1 Independent joined the 32 Democrats opposed). Leahy reported that the Democrats cited the 2002 defeat of Max Cleland (a Vietnam veteran and triple amputee), saying "we have to go along with [the MCA 2006] because we'll never be able to explain it back home." The House then approved the Senate bill 250–170. Bush declared that "the party of FDR and the party of Harry Truman has become the party of cut and run." Voters faced a choice between parties "with two different attitudes on this war on terror." Democrats "offer nothing but criticism and obstruction and endless second-guessing." Sen. Frist asked whether Americans "want to be voting for a party that does unabashedly say, 'we're going to have victory in this war on terror,' or a party that says, 'we've got to surrender'?" Rep. Hastert said that Democrats "are so bent on protecting criminals … they're not allowing us to prosecute these people."

The *Washington Post* deplored that "the artificial emergency Mr. Bush created has served his political purpose … to press opponents to cave to his will" and let him "create an issue allowing his party to tar the opposition as soft on terrorism."[78] Sen. Dodd wrote in a *Los Angeles Times* op ed that he had learned from his father, Thomas, who had helped Robert Jackson prosecute Nazis, that America fought World War II for:

> the idea that laws should rule the land, not men; that the principles of justice embodied in our Declaration of Independence and Constitution – of due process, of innocence until proven guilty, of the right to a fair trial – do not get suspended for vengeance. At Nuremberg, we rejected the certainty of execution for the uncertainty of a trial … Just as the word "Nuremberg" once defined the United States' moral authority and commitment to justice, what we risk today is that, one day, the loss of that moral authority and a commitment to injustice may also be defined by a single word: "Guantánamo."[79]

Signing the MCA 2006 before an audience of 9/11 victims, President Bush said it would "allow us to prosecute captured terrorists for war crimes through a full and fair trial."[80] "[N]o matter how long it takes, justice will be done." "Military commissions will provide a fair trial, in which the accused are presumed innocent, have access to an attorney, and can hear all the evidence against them." House Speaker Hastert said: "the Democrat's plan would gingerly pamper the terrorists who plan to destroy innocent American lives." They "put their liberal agenda ahead of the security of America." House Minority Leader Pelosi retorted: "Democrats want terrorists who kill Americans tried, convicted and punished through a constitutionally sound process that will be upheld on appeal. That goal will not be achieved by the bill President Bush signed into law today."

At the end of November 2006 John D. Altenburg Jr. resigned as CA and was replaced in February 20007 by Susan J. Crawford, who had been DoD IG, Army General Counsel, Special Counsel to Dick Cheney as Secretary of Defense under President George H.W. Bush, and then a judge on the US Court of Appeals for the Armed Forces from 1991 to 2006.[81]

On December 13, Judge Robertson granted the government motion to dismiss Hamdan's habeas corpus petition because the MCA 2006 had stripped him of jurisdiction.[82] Although this was not a constitutionally valid suspension, since "neither rebellion nor invasion was occurring at the time the MCA was enacted," Hamdan had no constitutional entitlement to the writ since he was a noncitizen detained outside US sovereignty.

In April 2007 Hamdan was again charged with conspiracy as well as a new crime: material support for terrorism.[83] In June, Navy Capt. Keith J. Allred, the judge, dismissed the charges because Hamdan's CSRT had not determined he was an "unlawful" enemy combatant, as the MCA 2006 required.[84] (Judge Brownback made a similar decision in Khadr's MC the same day, see below. After the Court of Military Commission Review (CMCR) reversed in Khadr's case, the prosecution asked Allred to find that Hamdan was an unlawful enemy combatant (UEC).) In September the Supreme Court refused to hear Hamdan's new challenge to the MCs.[85] Allred denied his motion to call three HVDs recently transferred to Guantánamo and three witnesses from Yemen.[86] Robert McFadden, a DoD counterintelligence official, testified that Hamdan had confessed to collecting and delivering weapons for bin Laden and had pledged allegiance to him on condition that al-Qaeda remained focused on fighting for the liberation of the Arabian peninsula and against "Jews and Crusaders." Another interrogator said Hamdan admitted driving bin Laden and his son around Afghanistan after 9/11 to avoid detection. Maj. Henry Smith testified he had seen two SA-7 missiles in a silver hatchback allegedly driven by Hamdan; but the prosecution's photo showed the missiles on the tailgate of a blue pickup truck. On December 19 Capt. Allred found that the prosecution had proved Hamdan was a UEC.

In June 2007 chief prosecutor Morris Davis fiercely defended the MCs.[87]

Some imply that if a defendant does not get a trial that looks like Martha Stewart's and ends like O.J. Simpson's, then military commissions are flawed. They are mistaken. The Constitution does not extend to alien unlawful enemy combatants … the rights afforded Americans are not the benchmark for assessing rights afforded enemy combatants in military tribunals … any statement by a person whose freedom is restrained by someone in a position of authority can be viewed as the product of some degree of coercion. Deciding how far is too far is the challenge. I make the final decision on the evidence the prosecution will introduce.

But four months later Davis abruptly quit.[88] He had clashed repeatedly with BGen. Thomas W. Hartmann, whom Crawford had made her legal adviser in the summer. In August, Hartmann had challenged Davis's authority and pressed his subordinates to quickly charge more detainees with terrorism accusations that would attract public attention. Davis filed a formal complaint against Hartmann for exceeding his authority and creating a conflict of interest, since Hartmann had to assess the adequacy of prosecution filings. "For the greater good, BG Hartmann and I should both resign and walk away or higher authority should relieve us of our duties." When DoD sided with Hartmann, Davis resigned.

Despite "direct orders not to comment with the media about the reasons for my resignation or military commissions," Davis did just that two weeks later. In September 2006 senior DoD officials had discussed the trials' "strategic political value," pressuring him to pursue "sexy" cases rather than those that were strong and ready to try. "There was a big concern that the election of 2008 is coming up. People wanted to get the cases going. There was a rush to get high-interest cases into court at the expense of openness." Soon after being appointed, Hartmann engaged in "nano-management," requesting detailed information on pending cases, defining the order in which they would be brought, and taking over pretrial negotiations with defense attorneys. Hartmann had decided to use classified evidence in closed sessions, whereas Davis wanted to focus on cases with enough declassified evidence that the public could see the entire trial. "No matter how perfect the trial is, if it's behind closed doors, it's going to be viewed as a sham." Hartmann had told Davis that "the way we were going to validate the system was by getting convictions and good sentences. I felt I was being pressured to do something less than full, fair and open." Although DoD's investigation of Davis's charges concluded that Hartmann did not try to coerce prosecutors, it urged him to "diligently avoid aligning himself with the

207

prosecutorial function so that he can objectively and independently provide cogent legal advice" to the CA.

In December, just before Davis was to testify before the SJC sub-committee on terrorism, technology, and homeland security that MCs were vulnerable to improper political influence, including pressure to use coerced evidence, DoD ordered him not to appear, declaring that "Hartmann is the best informed and most capable witness for this hearing."[89] A month earlier DoD had blocked Marine LtCol. Stuart Couch (another prosecutor) from testifying before an HJC subcommittee about his refusal to prosecute Mohamedou Ould Slahi because Slahi's "admissions" had been produced by torture (see below). Although Couch's superiors had no objections, DoD General Counsel William Haynes said his testimony would be "improper." HJC chair Conyers was "outraged."

A day after being silenced, Davis wrote in a *Los Angeles Times* op ed that the CA "was not living up to [its] obligation" to conduct trials "in an atmosphere of honesty and impartiality."[90] "Altenburg's staff had kept its distance from the prosecution to preserve its impartiality. Crawford, on the other hand, had her staff assessing evidence before the filing of charges, directing the prosecution's pretrial preparation of cases ... drafting charges against those who were accused and assigning prosecutors to cases."

Crawford "thought it unnecessary to wait" for the "time-consuming" classification review process "because the rules permit closed proceedings." Furthermore, two memos by Deputy Secretary of Defense England put Davis under the command of DoD General Counsel William Haynes, who had played a "role in authorizing the use of aggressive interrogation techniques some called torture" and who, Davis feared, might order him to use evidence obtained by waterboarding. "The first step, if these truly are military commissions and not merely a political smoke screen, is to take control out of the hands of political appointees like Haynes and Crawford and give it back to the military."

Hartmann replied in his own *Los Angeles Times* op ed.[91] "Crawford has not directed or influenced the way any military commission case will be tried." Hartmann, "without any political interference, directed [Davis] to evaluate more carefully the evidence, the cases, the charging process, the materiality of the cases, the speed of charging, the training program and the overall case preparation in the prosecutors office." Davis "knows that the [MC] process offers unprecedented rights to alleged war criminals." "Military commissions are now moving forward fairly and transparently."

In February 2008 a defense brief alleged that Hamdan was being held in "a regime of isolation with no access to natural light or air, for 22–23 hours a day."[92] A psychiatrist who had interviewed Hamdan for 70 hours said he had nightmares, amnesia, anxiety, irritability, insomnia, and a sense of "hopelessness and helplessness." Two months later his lawyers moved to recess the trial until he was transferred to a less restrictive setting. Davis testified for the defense that he had felt pressure to expedite cases to help Republicans in the 2006 election. Top DoD officials, including England, had made it clear that charging HVDs before the election could have "strategic political value." "Once you got the victim families energized and the cases rolling, whoever won the White House would have difficulty stopping the proceeding." When Davis said *acquittals* would give the commissions greater legitimacy, Haynes expostulated: "We can't have acquittals. We've been holding these guys for years. How can we explain acquittals? We have to have convictions." When Davis objected that "to allow or direct a prosecutor to come into the courtroom and offer evidence they felt was [the product of] torture ... puts a prosecutor in an ethical bind," Hartmann was dismissive, saying "everything was fair game – let the judge sort it out." Col. Lawrence Morris, who had replaced Davis, attributed his complaints to "bitterness" toward Hartmann, an aggressive tactless general. But LtCol. William Britt, another prosecutor, confirmed that Hartmann wanted to prioritize some cases because they would "seize the imagination of the American public" and make a splash in the media.

During the subsequent pretrial hearing Hamdan sometimes seemed in a daze but still engaged in a 40-minute colloquy with Allred about being denied human rights. "I would like the law, I would like justice. Nothing else. Just try me with the law and justice." "There is no such thing as justice here." Hamdan asked: "why did they change the law after his Supreme Court victory 'just for my case'?" Allred acknowledged Hamdan's "eloquent" statement and sympathized with his frustration at long confinement, but added:

> This trial will give you an opportunity to see the evidence against you, after all these years. It will give you the opportunity to call your witnesses, and a group of people who we hope will be fair and impartial will make a decision about your guilt or your innocence ... You should have great faith in American law. You have already been to the Supreme Court. The Supreme Court of the United States said to the president, "You can't do

that to Mr. Hamdan." You were the winner. Your name is printed in our law books.

Hamdan said he was addressing the government, not Allred. "You want us to confess to things we did not do. Right now I personally will admit to anything you want me to, but give me a just court." He left the room, declaring "I refuse participating in this, and I refuse all the lawyers operating on my behalf," but returned in the afternoon. After he threatened a boycott, Hartmann said "the trials are not going to be held up because an accused exercises his right not to be present." The commissions offered "astounding" rights, greater than those under the UCMJ.

Four days later Allred criticized Hartmann's "nanomanagement of the prosecutor's office" and ordered him to have no further involvement in Hamdan's case.[93]

> Telling the chief prosecutor (and other prosecutors) that certain types of cases would be tried and that others would not be tried, because of political factors such as whether they would capture the imagination of the American people, be sexy, or involve blood on the hands of the accused, suggests that factors other than those pertaining to the merits of the case were at play. ... [Use of] evidence that the chief prosecutor considered tainted and unreliable, or perhaps obtained as a result of torture or coercion, was clearly an effort to influence the professional judgment of the chief prosecutor ... National attention focused on this dispute has seriously called into question the legal adviser's ability to continue to perform his duties in a neutral and objective manner.

Allred asked DoD to replace Hartmann in this case because he had compromised the independence of the CA, whom he had called "an independent, quasi-judicial figure."

In mid-May Allred postponed the start of Hamdan's trial from June 2 to July 21 – after the Supreme Court's anticipated ruling in *Boumediene* (see Chapter 5) – to avoid "the potential embarrassment, waste of resources, and prejudice to the accused that would accompany an adverse decision mid-trial, or need to retry the case."[94] He also ordered an evaluation of Hamdan's fitness to stand trial. When pretrial hearings resumed, Hamdan again declared a boycott and slept through the next day's proceedings.[95] Allred agreed to hear testimony from eight defense witnesses, including KSM and four other HVDs, possibly through time-delays or videotaped depositions to protect national security. DoJ had objected strongly: "the prosecution is charged with protecting the national security of the United States. The detainees that [the defense] wants access to hold in their heads some of the most serious national security and intelligence sources and methods that the United States has." But Allred replied: "I want the government to know that I see this as relevant, necessary and exculpatory. I just believe the defendant cannot have a fair trial without this evidence."

The next day Hamdan testified that a female interrogator "came close to me, she came very close, with her whole body towards me. I couldn't do anything." She touched his thigh. "I said to her, 'what do you want?' She said, 'I want you to answer all of my questions.'" He did so. Just days earlier the prosecution had finally complied with a discovery order, producing 600 pages of detention records, which disclosed for the first time that Hamdan had been subjected to 50 days of sleep deprivation in "Operation Sandman." A defense lawyer called that torture. Hamdan testified that tight fetters during the long plane trip to Guantánamo had inflamed a back injury, causing "such severe pains, I cannot really explain." Although he had been held briefly in Camp 4, where "you share a room with other people and have almost a normal life," he spent most of his time in solitary confinement in Camps 5 and 6, with only a toothbrush, blanket, and towel (and sometimes not even those). Camp Echo, where he was held at the time of the trial, "is like a graveyard where you place a dead person in a tomb."

On July 3 (after *Boumediene*), Judge Robertson ordered an accelerated schedule to respond to Hamdan's motion to enjoin the trial. Although several hundred current and former European officials submitted an amicus brief asking Robertson to block the trial, he ruled on July 17 that it could proceed because the MCA 2006 had made "significant improvements" in procedures and allowed Hamdan to raise constitutional challenges on appeal to the CMCR and DC Circuit.[96] "The eyes of the world are on Guantánamo Bay. Justice must be done there, and must be seen to be done there, fairly and impartially." The same day Allred ruled that *Boumediene* allowed defendants to raise constitutional questions in their MCs, but rejected two of Hamdan's challenges: that the charges violated the *Ex Post Facto* clause because they were based on a law passed after he had been detained; and that MCs violated the Equal Protection clause because they could try only noncitizens. Noting that MCs offered a "substantial array of privileges and protections," including legal representation, a public trial, and proof of guilt beyond a reasonable doubt, Allred ruled that the Equal Protection clause did not apply at Guantánamo. Morris confidently predicted that the unfamiliarity of the procedure would quickly diminish, comparing MCs to the now routine space shuttle flights (conveniently ignoring the Challenger disaster). Over prosecution objections, Allred allowed defense lawyers to interview prospective detainee witnesses, including KSM.

On July 21 Allred seated a jury of six senior military officers.[97] He barred Hamdan's statements made at Bagram as coerced, but ruled that statements at made Guantánamo were admissible, finding no evidence that access to medical care had been conditioned on cooperation with interrogators. In its opening, the prosecution said Hamdan's intimate connection to bin Laden was shown by the fact that he was one of very few who knew details of the 9/11 attack (after it occurred), including the fact that the fourth plane had targeted the Capitol. The defense portrayed Hamdan as a poor man who had worked as a mechanic for bin Laden in order to support his family. Prosecution witnesses offered conflicting evidence about the circumstances of Hamdan's arrest and which vehicle contained two SA-7 missiles. At a news conference later that day, the defense complained that prosecutors had delayed for months complying with discovery orders, delivering 500 pages just 12 hours before the trial began. Telling the government "you're on the hot seat because of unsatisfactory performance of discovery," Allred presumptively excluded Hamdan's 2003 interrogation unless prosecutors could show by clear and convincing evidence it was reliable and should be admitted in the interests of justice. Morris continued to maintain that the commission was "the most just war crimes trial that anybody has ever seen."

The court saw a videotaped interrogation after Hamdan's capture on November 24, 2001, when he was driving his family to safety in Pakistan. He told an interrogator he had borrowed the car from a friend, who owned the two missiles, weapons license, and related documents. Three cards found in the car contained numbers corresponding to words al-Qaeda members used in radio communications to identify leaders and military actions. Ali Soufan, an FBI interrogator, testified that videos of Hamdan driving bin Laden to news conferences and speeches at terror training camps showed the leader's trust in the accused. Under cross-examination, FBI Special Agent Craig Connachie conceded that Hamdan performed only low-level functions for al-Qaeda. He had been trained in weapons at an al-Qaeda camp, but had never used them. He had cooperated during 40 interrogations in Guantánamo, identifying 30 other bin Laden bodyguards. He told Ammar Barghouty (another detainee) that Abd

Rahim al-Nashiri had bragged about the *USS Cole* bombing and offered to testify against him. The defense noted that Abu Assaum Maghrebi, head of bin Laden's bodyguard staff (and thus Hamdan's boss), was released in 2003; and Said Boujaadia, arrested at the same roadblock minutes after Hamdan, was released in 2007.

Prosecutors screened part of a 90-minute film, *The Al-Qaeda Plan*, produced by Evan Kohlmannn (a self-styled terrorism expert), showing mangled corpses from the US East Africa embassy bombings. Allred then reversed an earlier decision excluding the last seven segments graphically depicting the 9/11 attacks (in which Hamdan had not been involved) because "it's not any more prejudicial" than what jurors had already seen. Morris agreed that the film was "prejudicial," which "is why we show it." After prosecutors convinced Allred that Hamdan's 2003 interrogation was uncoerced, McFadden testified that the defendant had sworn *bayat* to bin Laden. The defense raised questions about McFadden's competence in Arabic, noting that he claimed to read from a statement that was upside down. Hamdan testified that he never admitted swearing *bayat* and had spoken only to Soufan, not McFadden.

The defense offered an expert who testified that al-Qaeda members were "the Harvard of the terrorist movement … multilingual, adept at infiltration, very talented operatives" with advanced degrees. "I don't see Salim Hamdan by any stretch of the imagination fitting this profile." The defense submitted a secret government document (produced to them the day before trial) in which a female interrogator described sexually humiliating Hamdan. A law-of-war expert testified that the USA had not been at war in Afghanistan during the period before 9/11 when Hamdan committed most of the alleged acts. Col. Morgan Banks, an army psychologist and survival, evasion, resistance, and escape (SERE) expert, testified in secret. In response to defense questions, KSM submitted a 16-page statement declaring that Hamdan's "nature was more primitive (Bedouin) person and far from civilization." "He was not with the ideology of Osama bin Laden, and people like him, he was only searching for pleasure and money in this life." Anyone believing a mere driver would be involved in attacks "is a fool." Hamdan

> did not play any role. He was not a soldier, he was a driver and auto mechanic. He was not fit to plan or execute. But he is fit to change trucks' tires, change oil filters, wash and clean cars and fasten cargo in pickup trucks. I personally was the executive director of 9/11, and Hamdan had no previous knowledge of the operation, or any other one.

Walid bin 'Attash (another HVD) agreed in a written statement that Hamdan "did not play any role in any planning."

In closing, the defense urged the jury to "look at the information Mr. Hamdan provided to the United States when it mattered most" and "how we squandered the opportunity" to capture bin Laden. The prosecution replied that bin Laden "hosted a wedding feast for the accused. This shows just how close he was to the very top of this terrorist conspiracy."

After the defense rested, Deputy Chief Defense Counsel Mike Berrigan called the trial "an obscenity," "a day America should be ashamed of." It was so limited by secrecy that the public did not see "big chunks" of evidence. Morris said: "it has been an open and fair and thorough process. I think it has gone extremely well." While the jury was deliberating, prosecutors objected that Allred had wrongly instructed the jury that though Hamdan was charged with transporting missiles to be used against US forces, jurors had to find that the missiles were to be used against civilians not involved in hostilities. Allred conceded the error but said the prosecution had waived its challenge by not raising it earlier.

After deliberating eight hours over three days, the jury convicted Hamdan of material support but acquitted him of conspiracy.[98] The White House called the MC "a fair and appropriate legal process for prosecuting detainees." Morris said Hamdan was "a career al-Qaeda warrior, pledged to ensuring the personal security of Osama bin Laden." Allred barred the only witness that prosecutors offered at sentencing – an FBI agent injured in the 9/11 attack – because his testimony would "prejudice" Hamdan by "appearing to hold him responsible for 9/11" when he "was such a small player." Hamdan pleaded for a light sentence, apologizing for 9/11: "it was a sorry or sad thing to see innocent people killed. I personally present my apologies to them if anything I did has caused them pain." When he learned of the attacks, "it was a big shock for me when someone [like bin Laden] who had treated you … with respect and regard and cordially, and then you realize what they were up to." But "I had no choice." Calling Hamdan "a hardened al-Qaeda member," the prosecution said: "once you see your boss killing people, you leave." The defense showed jurors photos of Hamdan's daughters, 7 and 9 (he had never seen the younger daughter), and a video of his wife talking about the hardships of raising the children without a husband or income. Although the prosecution asked for 30 years (after originally seeking life), the jury (after deliberating only an hour) sentenced

Hamdan to 5.5, and Allred (over prosecution objections) gave him credit for time served, making him eligible for release in just five months. Allred said to Hamdan: "I wish you Godspeed, Mr. Hamdan. I hope the day comes when you are able to return to your wife and daughters and your country." Hamdan replied: "Inshallah." After sentencing, a juror said the case "was kind of like using the hand grenade on the horsefly." "In none of the evidence presented did you ever see him brandishing a weapon at all." The juror was unmoved by the prosecution warning that Hamdan would be a threat to the USA.

> Do you really think [a-Qaeda] are going to take him back with open arms, even if he felt any inclination to go back, which we don't think he did? ... there are plenty of guys down there that are really bad guys that need to have the book thrown at them, but if you do a 30 [year] min [sentence], which was the prosecution's request, and they would have preferred life, where do you step up from that?

DoD maintained that Hamdan would still be an EC after serving his sentence. But the juror warned that would greatly annoy him and the other jurors: "after all, what did we come down here for?"

The *Washington Post* called the "stunning verdict and sentence" "remarkable" because "it appeared to be measured, thoughtful and fair – or as fair as a hopelessly flawed system could hope to produce."[99]

> The result was reached under a system that allows introduction of hearsay evidence and statements gleaned using coercive tactics. It is a system that restricts the ability of the defense lawyers to rebut government allegations – and the rights of defendants even to be aware of certain evidence. It is a system, in short, that should be shuttered.

The *Los Angeles Times* said the MC "wasn't a kangaroo court, but it also wasn't what American justice should be." MCs needed "to be fairer and more transparent, and an acquittal must mean more than a return trip to a prison cell." Releasing Hamdan after he served his sentence would be "the right thing. It's also smart policy." The *New York Times* called the verdict "a hollow victory in the war on terror, a blow to America's standards of justice and image in the world." A *Denver Post* cartoon showed Bush saying "seven years after 9/11, we've nailed that S.O.B.'s chauffeur" and Cheney rubbing his hands and adding "next, we go after his hair stylist." Ridiculing the trial as "the most historic session of traffic court ever," Stephen Colbert said it would not be long "before we track down Ayman al-Zawahiri's dermatologist."

A month later prosecutors asked Allred to order a new sentencing hearing, arguing that Hamdan should not have received credit for time served because he had been held as an EC, not on the charges for which he was tried.[100] LtCdr. Mizer, one of his military defense lawyers, said: "if the government doesn't honor the verdict of the jury, it clearly demonstrates these really are show trials." Allred denied the motion. DoD transferred Hamdan to Yemen on November 25 to serve the last month of his sentence, and Yemen released him on January 10, 2009.

A three-judge CMCR panel heard the appeal on January 10, 2009. Nine months later, without deciding, the Court announced en banc review.[101] On June 24, 2011 the seven-judge CMCR affirmed in an 89-page opinion extensively discussing international law and the history of the law of war.[102] It found that "international conventions and treaties provided an additional basis in international law that [Hamdan's] conduct in support of terrorism was internationally condemned and criminal." "International law recognizes joint criminal enterprise (JCE) as a theory of criminal liability." It rejected Hamdan's claim that he was being punished by an *ex post facto* law. "It strains credibility [*sic*] to contend that the accused would not recognize the criminal nature of the acts alleged in the indictment." "Creation of a new court to assume the jurisdiction of an old court does not implicate *ex post facto* prohibitions so long as the 'substantial protections' of 'the existing law' are not changed to the prejudice of the accused."

> [T]he evidence supporting the 2006 M.C.A. offense of providing material support for terrorism as a pre-existing law of war offense far exceeds even the "substantial showing" standard advanced in *Hamdan* that "the Government must make a substantial showing that the crime for which it seeks to try a defendant by military commission is acknowledged to be an offense against the law of war" … the M.C.A.'s restriction to prosecution of AUECs [alien unlawful enemy combatants] does not constitute a prohibited invidious discrimination against aliens, and appellant does not have a fundamental constitutional right to criminal procedures identical to those of U.S. citizens.

In October 2012 the DC Circuit reversed.[103] Judge Kavanaugh began: "The United States is at war against al-Qaeda, an international terrorist organization" whose "stated goals are, among other things, to drive the United States from posts in the Middle East, to devastate the State of Israel, and to help establish radical Islamic control over the Greater Middle East."

"To avoid the prospect of an Ex Post Facto Clause violation here, we interpret the Military Commissions Act of 2006 so that it does not authorize *retroactive* prosecution for conduct committed before enactment of that Act unless the conduct was already prohibited under existing U.S. law as a war crime triable by military commission."

But "material support for terrorism was not a war crime under the law of war ... at the time of Hamdan's conduct." Although "it is often difficult to determine what constitutes customary international law ... here, the content of customary international law is quite evident." Even the government conceded that "material support for terrorism was not a recognized violation of the international law of war as of 2001 (or even today, for that matter)." Therefore, the court vacated the conviction.

David Hicks

Hicks, a young Australian who entered Afghanistan in January 2001, was seized by a Northern Alliance soldier after 9/11, handed over to the USA for a reward soon thereafter, and flown to Cuba in 2002. In May 2003 three civilian interrogators spent half a day eating, drinking, and smoking with him before promising he could go home within three months – if he just signed a confession.[104] After negotiating its content, he signed and a month later was moved to a less punitive cell. In December 2003 he was contacted by Maj. Michael Mori, who had been assigned to defend him.[105] David's father Terry had organized demonstrations in Australia to free his son and retained Steven Kenny, an Australian lawyer acting pro bono. Hicks was also a plaintiff in *Rasul* (having petitioned for habeas on February 19, 2002, see Chapter 5). On June 10, 2004 he was charged with conspiracy, attempted murder by an unprivileged belligerent, and aiding the enemy, and was arraigned in August. Learning that the charges were based in large part on the "diary" of Feroz Abbasi, another detainee, Hicks met with Feroz, who repudiated the statements.[106] Pretrial hearings continued in November 2004, but the CA stayed them on December 10 in response to Judge Robertson's ruling invalidating Hamdan's MC. In April 2005 the Australian ambassador visited the White House and the Pentagon to express his government's frustration with the slow pace of the proceedings.[107] DoD replied that Australian officials had publicly acknowledged that MCs "can provide full and fair trials and have consented to the United States bringing David Hicks to trial in military commission proceedings." Indeed, in July Prime Minister Howard said that after the "changes that were made to the process, Australia is satisfied that the military commission process in relation to David Hicks ... will provide a proper measure of justice."[108]

But Air Force Capt. John Carr and Maj. Robert Preston quit the prosecution team in 2005 to protest the failure to disclose exculpatory evidence.[109] Preston wrote Borch, the chief prosecutor:

> I sincerely believe that this process is wrongly managed, wrongly focused and a blight on the reputation of the armed forces ... Frankly, I became disgusted with the lack of vision and in my view the lack of integrity long ago and I no longer want to be part of the process ... professionally, ethically, or morally ... writing a motion saying that the process will be full and fair when you don't really believe it will be is kind of hard.

Carr also wrote Borch:

> An environment of secrecy, deceit and dishonesty exists within our office ... emails are being sent out admitting that we don't have the evidence to prove the general conspiracy, let alone the specific accused's culpability ... In our meeting with OGA [Other Government Agency – a euphemism for the CIA) they told us that the exculpatory information, if it existed, would be in the 10% that we will not get with our agreed upon searches ... you told me the rules were written in such a way as to not require that we conduct such thorough searches and that we weren't going to worry about it ... You have repeatedly said to the office that the military panel will be handpicked and will not acquit these detainees.

Capt. Carrie Wolf quit the prosecution team about the same time (without publicizing her reasons).

There also were protests in Australia.[110] GetUp! collected 7,000 signatures on a petition to free Hicks. Jim Spigelman, New South Wales Chief Justice, said: "military justice bears the same relationship to justice as military music does to music." Bill Hayden, the former Governor-General of Australia, called Prime Minister Howard a "servile accomplice" to injustice. The New South Wales Director of Public Prosecutions said it was "patently obvious" that MCs were "wrong," "un-objective," and "fundamentally flawed." Sir Gerard Brennan, the former federal Chief Justice, condemned his country's passivity in the face of the injustice as "morally impoverished." DoD announced in September that MC trials would resume, possibly starting with Hicks in November.[111] But that month DDC Judge Kollar-Kotelly stayed his trial pending the Supreme Court's decision in *Hamdan*.[112] Hicks applied for UK citizenship (his mother was British) in the hope that Britain, which did not accept the MCs' legitimacy, would advocate for him more vigorously than Australia had.[113] In April 2006 the UK Court of Appeal rejected the Home Secretary's challenge to his application, and he was granted citizenship.

Hicks went on hunger strike following the three suicides in Guantánamo in July 2006 (see the companion volume *Law's Wars*), but ended it when he learned of the Supreme Court's decision in *Hamdan*.[114] After Bush signed the MCA 2006 in October, Hicks despaired of being released and privately drafted a possible guilty plea. (He had previously been offered 20 years and then, just before *Hamdan*, only 2.) When he realized the government had secretly photographed his papers, he drafted a private repudiation and ensured it was copied as well.[115] In January 2007 Prime Minister Howard said that if Hicks were not charged by February, Australia would demand his release.[116] On January 9, DoD General Counsel Haynes asked chief military prosecutor Davis how quickly he could charge Hicks. Davis said he could not do so until the MC Manual was completed. But on February 2 (five days before the appointment of a CA), under pressure from Haynes, Davis charged Hicks with attempted murder and material support (and also charged Hamdan and Khadr). Mori told Hicks he had heard from Howard's staffer that the Prime Minister would not let him return unless he pleaded guilty. On February 18 the Australian Foreign Minister corroborated this, saying that if Hicks were convicted, "we've made an arrangement with the Americans, which was confirmed to me 10 days ago by the Secretary of Defense, Robert Gates, that David Hicks will be able to serve his sentence or the remainder of his sentence in Australia." Behind in the polls and facing an election (which he lost in November), Howard was under pressure to get Hicks home. On February 23, Howard told visiting Vice President Cheney that he wanted the case "brought on as soon as humanly possible." On March 2 the new CA confirmed only the material support charge (which Hicks's lawyers complained had not been made a crime until 2006). Sen. Graham was "pleased to see this trial is going forward." Hicks's lawyers asked the Federal Court of Australia to order the government to demand that he be brought home for trial. GetUp! had raised more than Aus$200,000 for his defense. Both Labor and Conservative Party leaders were calling for his return. Mori made seven trips to Australia, where he had become a local folk hero. But Davis threatened to present charges under the UCMJ for using contemptuous language against American officials if Mori engaged in further "politicking." "Certainly in the U.S. it would not be tolerated having a U.S. Marine in uniform actively inserting himself into the political process." On March 13 Davis wrote the CA that Mori had violated the UCMJ. Mori retorted defiantly: "Are they trying to intimidate me?" The *Washington Post* accused Davis of engaging in "the attack-the-defense-lawyers act." His "unsubtle effort to quiet Maj. Mori may be even more disturbing" than Charles "Cully" Stimson's attacks on the pro bono habeas lawyers (see the companion volume *Law's Wars*). "It's the prosecution that really needs reining in." Prime Minister Howard repeated that the case "has taken too long."

On March 12 Hicks's lawyers moved to enjoin his MC trial pending Supreme Court review of *Boumediene* (which was certain to be appealed from the recent DC Circuit decision); but DDC Judge Kollar-Kotelly denied the motion on March 23 because of the MCA 2006's jurisdiction-stripping provisions.[117] Before the trial began on March 25, Joshua Dratel, one of Hicks's civilian lawyers, said his client would plead not guilty.[118] At the arraignment, Mori complained it was "groundhog's day." "When you don't have established rules and procedures, you risk convicting innocent people or allowing someone who is truly guilty to escape justice." He planned to seek Davis's removal. Davis retorted that "the idea that we've created this Frankenstein, cobbled-together system is not accurate." He confirmed that in January the prosecution had discussed a guilty plea in exchange for prison in Australia. The next day Marine Col. Ralph H. Kohlmannn, the judge, expelled Hicks's two civilian lawyers: Rebecca Snyder on the ground that she was a DoD employee, and MC rules allowed civilian lawyers only if there was no expense to the government (she was on leave and not being paid by the government); and Dratel for not agreeing to comply with rules the Secretary of Defense had not yet created. Dratel objected that "I can't sign a document that provides a blank check on my ethical obligations." Kohlmannn said: "I find no merit in the claim that this is beyond my authority. That's sometimes what courts do, they find a way to move forward." Hicks was "shocked because I just lost another lawyer." When Kohlmannn asked if he wanted Dratel to remain in the room, Hicks asked: "what's the sense of him sitting here if he's not my lawyer and can't represent me?" After Mori argued for four hours that he needed more time to prepare, Hicks pleaded guilty late that night to the single charge of material support. Davis (who had been excluded from the plea negotiations) said: "I don't look at it as a victory." DoD declared that the outcome showed that MCs were "transparent, legitimate and moving forward."

At the March 30 sentencing hearing, the prosecution and defense each used a peremptory challenge to eliminate a juror, leaving a panel of eight senior military officers.[119] The prosecution portrayed Hicks as especially dangerous because of his ability to blend into Western society, and claimed he had been determined to kill Americans. Invoking the attacks on the USS Cole and the US embassies in East Africa (which had nothing to do with the case), the prosecutor said: "Today in this courtroom we are on the front line of the war on terrorism, face to face with the enemy." Mori portrayed his client as a ninth-grade dropout who got scared in Afghanistan and abandoned his post. He said Hicks (who was too nervous to speak) "wants to apologize to Australia and to the United States" and thank the US armed services, who treated him professionally. The jury sentenced Hicks to the maximum term of seven years (he had faced life under the original charges). But all this was an elaborate charade. The panel had not been told that the plea agreement assured him a maximum of nine months, which he would serve in Australia after being returned within 60 days. Hicks was required to acknowledge that the government had the evidence to prove he had trained with al-Qaeda, carried an AK-47, and was prepared to fight Americans in Afghanistan. He had to declare he "has never been illegally treated" in captivity and promise not to sue over his treatment or "communicate in any way with the media" for a year. (The Australian Attorney General said the gag order might not be enforceable.) DoD said Hicks's allegations of mistreatment "have proven to be unsubstantiated." (His book, published in 2010, detailed that mistreatment at length.)

Davis complained afterwards that the plea deal had been negotiated between Mori and the CA without his input: "I wasn't considering" any sentence "that didn't have two digits" (which was impossible, given the single charge). Hicks was "very fortunate. He's getting a second chance." An Office of Military Commissions (OMC) spokeswoman appeared to acknowledge the role of politics: "like it or not, the detainees at Guantánamo are from different countries, and that sometimes is a factor." Cheney had actually negotiated the deal with Howard a month earlier in Australia. A year later Crawford, who signed off on it, denied feeling any political pressure. "I'm sick of the Vice President getting credit for my work." (She had been DoD IG when Cheney was Defense Secretary.) Howard was equally defensive: "the sentence was imposed by the military commission and the plea bargain was worked out between the military prosecution and Mr. Hicks's lawyers." "That it has something to do with the Australian elections is absurd." But a

Law Council of Australia observer called it an "amazing" coincidence that Hicks was barred from speaking in public until after the November election. An Australian lawyer wrote in *The Age* that "the charade that took place at Guantánamo Bay would have done Stalin's show trials proud." The Australian Bar Association awarded Mori an honorary life membership.

The *Washington Post* said the outcome "vividly demonstrates the folly of the legal scheme for detainees that Congress hastily approved last year."[120] It "demonstrated that the commissions can be politically twisted in a way that would be inconceivable in a credible court of law." The plea agreement was approved by a "Bush political appointee." Ben Wizner, who had observed the trial for the ACLU, wrote in a *Los Angeles Times* op ed that it would be a "colossal understatement" to say that the trial "lacked the dignity and gravitas of Nuremberg."[121]

Hicks was returned to Australia on May 19, 2007 and left prison on December 28, but was still subject to a control order under Australian anti-terror laws.[122] He finally told his story in his 2010 book (which sold 30,000 copies) and a February 2011 interview.[123] Australia threatened to seize the book profits, but abandoned the effort after Hicks repudiated the plea agreement as the product of torture. In November 2013 he appealed the conviction, claiming his plea bargain had been coerced.[124] In August 2014 he also appealed on the ground that material support was not a war crime.[125] On February 18, 2015 the CMCR set aside his conviction.[126] It found that his waiver of the right to appeal was ineffective because he had not filed it within 10 days of the CA's action, as required. Both parties agreed that, under *al-Bahlul* (see below), the conviction could not stand.

Omar Ahmed Khadr

Hours after the Supreme Court granted certiorari in *Hamdan*, DoD charged Khadr, a 19-year-old Canadian citizen, with murder, conspiracy to commit murder, attempted murder, and aiding the enemy.[127] The government alleged that when he was 15 he threw a grenade in Afghanistan, killing SFC Christopher Speer and blinding SFC Layne Morris. Khadr sought to replace his designated military counsel, Army Capt. John Merriam, who had never represented a criminal defendant. Muneer Ahmad, one of Khadr's civilian lawyers, objected to chief prosecutor Davis, calling it "nauseating" that a journalist had described Khadr as a "fresh face in the full bloom of adolescence," pronouncing him "guilty" and a "terrorist," and declaring: "when these guys went to camp, they weren't making s'mores and learning how to tie knots." Marine Col. Robert S. Chester, the military judge, admonished both sides against trying the case in the press.

MC proceedings often resembled theater of the absurd; the April 5, 2006 pretrial hearing offered just one of many examples of their Alice-in-Wonderland quality. Marine LtCol. Colby Vokey, Khadr's military defense lawyer, said his client wanted the defense to be assisted by two Canadian lawyers. Chester admitted that "I don't know, quite frankly, what the procedure would be" for deciding whether he could allow that. Acknowledging he had not prepared a motion or brief and the Canadians were not in Guantánamo, Vokey added that "it seems kind of useless to file a brief" if the judge did not know whether he had authority to order the relief.

> VOKEY: There is [sic] no procedures for this … We don't know who to request it from, the Presiding Officer, the Appointing Authority. There are no rules here.
> CHESTER: Colonel Vokey there is—
> VOKEY: The rules keep changing.
> CHESTER: —a very simple rule…
> VOKEY: Sir, is there anything beside [sic] POM 4-3 that we need to look at in order to brief this issue?
> CHESTER: I am not going to tell you how to do your research, Colonel Vokey…
> VOKEY: I don't know of any authority that even speaks to this … Now we can come up with some kind of brief, but it seems kind of crazy if the Presiding Officer does not have the power to act on it…
> CHESTER: [O]ne way to learn whether or not I have that authority would be to brief it, argue it here in the courtroom, and have me decide it.
> VOKEY: Sure, sir. Another way would be to have clear rules that told us exactly—
> CHESTER: Colonel Vokey—
> VOKEY: —[what] to do before we start.

Khadr boycotted the pretrial hearings to protest his transfer to the extremely restrictive maximum security Camp 5. Chester refused to address the conditions of confinement issue because it had not been briefed. Vokey replied that he had only learned of it two days earlier.

> VOKEY: Perhaps if, when I get here, we get quick access to the client, this would have come up a little bit sooner … Every time we come down here, this incredible burden, just to do our normal job…
> CHESTER: [Y]ou have not even given me the courtesy of telling me, "Hey, there is a problem that might need your assistance with" … If you want relief from me on that issue then it is incumbent upon

you to, number one, give me a head's up, which you [could] have done, so—

VOKEY: No, sir, I could not have done that.

CHESTER: You couldn't have approached me—

VOKEY: [slams hand on podium] Sir, yesterday afternoon that is what we discussed [slams hand on podium] all afternoon was that very same issue.

CHESTER: We are in recess.

After the recess Vokey said: "Sir, maybe I haven't made myself clear as to why this is such a serious issue." Chester replied: "it is not important to me, quite frankly, why it is important to you." "I don't know the significance" of Khadr's transfer to Camp 5. "I have never been down to the camps." When Chester asked "can we go forward?", Vokey replied: "We don't believe so."

> We want to avoid a conflict between an instruction from you, to defense counsel, to move forward, and an instruction from our client saying that that would exceed the bounds of the representation as he has defined it … Appointing Authority Regulation 3 says that … if there is a conflict between a rule of the Commission and what we understand to be our ethical obligations, we can't move forward until the legal adviser to the Appointing Authority coordinates with … the appropriate officials of other jurisdictions.

Chester asked if Vokey had legal authority and whether he would provide it to the court (disregarding what Vokey had just cited). Vokey replied: "If we think that something that we are being asked to do is a violation of our ethical obligations, our obligation, respectfully, is not to prove that to you … because, sir, you don't enforce the ethical rules." When Chester asked if Vokey had "sought or received any clear guidance from your bar," Vokey replied there had been no time between the end of his meeting with Khadr at 4:30 p.m. the previous day and the beginning of this day's hearing. Maj. Groharing, the prosecutor, said Vokey should withdraw. "We cannot stop these proceedings every time the accused places limitations on their counsel" or "doesn't like what he had for breakfast." When Chester asked if Khadr could "put off" the conditions of confinement complaint so the judge could "take up those issues that we need to take up that protect your rights here in this courtroom," the defendant replied: "I am sorry, sir, I can't." Chester warned: "You understand that if you don't" agree to proceed "and I tell your counsel to press forward and they don't do anything, you will have waived those rights?" After consulting Khadr, Vokey told Chester: "I think you came very close to the line, if not [a]cross the line, of interfering with our relationship in telling him that you want him to change his mind."

When Ahmad and Richard Wilson (another civilian defense lawyer) joined the boycott, Chester ordered Vokey and Merriam to continue the voir dire or he would view it as waived.

Proceeding "under protest," Vokey asked what law governed. Chester replied: "I will follow the law as I determine what the law is." When he referred to "Commission Law," Vokey objected: "the term, 'Commission Law,' is not really law, is it?" Chester replied: "I don't agree it is not law." Reprising their earlier squabble, Vokey asked who had the power to respond to a motion about conditions of confinement or to suppress evidence. Chester said "one way to find out; file a motion."

> VOKEY: Would you agree, sir, it would be a lot easier if there were already rules out there telling how to practice law?
> CHESTER: No, I won't ... The purpose of the voir dire, Colonel Vokey, is to find out if there is a basis to challenge the Presiding Officer ... if you are going to continue to ask what law applies about filing motions, how you go about getting things decided, I am not going to allow you to ask any more of those questions.
> VOKEY: All right, sir, but these questions do go to the heart of the matter.

Chester refused to say whether a DDC case between the same parties would control in the MC. But then he volunteered: "I think that we will look to international law, I think that we will look through military law, I think that we will look through federal criminal law, I think that we will look at a lot of sources to – to flesh out the procedural rules that govern this proceeding." At the end of the voir dire, the defense challenged Chester on two grounds: his "extensive research and search for media articles, gathering up, looking at other information and evidence of the case" and his "application for jobs with both the Department of Justice and the Department of Defense ... especially the application for the immigration law judge." Immigration judges were appointed by the Attorney General, who had an interest in Khadr's habeas petition pending in the DC Circuit (raising many of the same issues as those in his MC) and who had attended the Supreme Court argument in *Hamdan* the previous week. If Khadr were convicted and appealed to the DC Circuit, DoJ would represent the government. Chester rejected both challenges.

At the end of 2006 Groharing, the prosecutor, acknowledged the case had proceeded in "fits and starts" because intelligence agencies refused to give him information, fearing he would disclose it to the defense.[128]

Groharing said that when Khadr was informed of the charges, he looked "a bit arrogant, cocky," "somewhat hardened, far from a typical teenager." Davis bragged he expected to file 70 MC cases and was confident of convicting Khadr: "we have a crime scene, we have facts, we have witnesses." Vokey was initially barred by his commander from talking to reporters after he filed an affidavit accusing Guantánamo guards of abusing detainees. Ahmad said Khadr had been subjected to years of abuse: shackled until he soiled himself and then used as a "human mop" to clean up his urine, and threatened with deportation to Egypt where he would be raped.

In February 2007 the military drafted new charges.[129] Confirming them in April, Crawford removed several references to Khadr's deceased father (an alleged jihadist) to prevent potential jurors from learning about Omar's early exposure to radical Islam. At the end of May Khadr sought to fire all his American lawyers. Defense lawyers argued that international law prohibited war crime prosecutions of anyone under 18. In April DoD deputy general counsel Dell'Orto told a Senate hearing:

> [T]ransferring trials before military commissions from the security facility at Guantánamo Bay to the continental United States would hamstring the nation's ability to prosecute terrorist war crimes. The existing civilian court system is ill equipped to handle the dispensation of justice in the chaotic and irregular circumstances of armed conflict.[130]

But in June Col. Peter E. Brownback III, the trial judge, dismissed the case because Khadr's CSRT had not found he was an "*unlawful* enemy combatant" as required by the MCA 2006.[131] Marine Col. Dwight Sullivan, now heading the defense team, said "the military commissions are a model that has repeatedly shown itself incapable of rendering justice." The prosecution sought a 72-hour delay to consider appealing to the CMCR. The OMC belittled the problem as just "a technical matter." The CA legal adviser maintained: "this process has to go on because there is no alternative." DoD said it would ask Brownback to reconsider. Davis promised: "you'll see the evidence when we get into the courtroom of the smiling face of Omar Khadr as he builds bombs to kill Americans."

Sen. Leahy said: "these court decisions underscore that, far from being beyond reproach, the system set up by this administration in the weeks before the last election is not adequate and cannot be trusted with the liberties of millions of people." Sen. Kennedy said that "yet again the administration has botched their cases against detainees at Guantánamo. It is time to abandon military tribunals and use the well-established American justice system to try detainees." Sen. Specter had "an uncomfortable sense about the whole Guantánamo milieu. There's just a sense of too many shortcuts in the whole process." It was "dead wrong" to claim that Congress intended to permit prosecution of detainees who had not been declared UECs. Sen. Dodd said Congress had to fix the law's "egregious flaws." "The current system of prosecuting enemy combatants is not only inefficient and ineffective, it is also hurting America's moral standing in the world." The White House replied that "in no way does this decision affect the appropriateness of the military commission system." And Sen. Warner complained that "Congress can't suddenly begin to rewrite laws every time a federal district court judge or somebody change their view of the law." The *Washington Post* said "the Bush administration's chronically failing attempt to invent a new legal system for holding and trying terrorism suspects has suffered yet another setback." AI Canada, two former Foreign Affairs Ministers, 25 current and former MPs, and many others signed a letter urging Canada to seek Khadr's return. But the Canadian Foreign Affairs Minister said his government would wait until the appeals process ended.

In August, Col. Francis Gilligan (ret.) argued for the prosecution in the CMCR that the MC could either read the CSRT as declaring Khadr a UEC because al-Qaeda does not follow the rules of war, or make that finding itself.[132] In September the CMCR accepted the latter argument and remanded. Brownback had "abused his discretion in deciding this critical jurisdictional matter without first fully considering" the government's evidence.

Just before arraignment on November 7, the DC Circuit denied an emergency stay.[133] Dennis Edney, Khadr's Canadian lawyer, filed a written objection to LtCdr. Kuebler as lead defense counsel, claiming he was a tax lawyer with no criminal or trial experience and, rather than preparing for trial, had been waging an unsuccessful campaign to persuade Canada to demand Khadr's repatriation. Rejecting Edney's objection, Army Col. Steve David, the chief defense lawyer, accused him of disrupting the defense team and barred him from the hearing. Kuebler complained that only on November 6 had prosecutors told the defense they had an eyewitness to the alleged July 2002 attack, whose identity had been known for more than five years. Prosecutors also belatedly produced 700 pages of documents. (MC rules did not require the prosecution to make timely disclosure of its witnesses or make them available to the defense before trial.) An FBI agent scheduled to testify for the prosecution refused to meet with the defense. An ABA observer said such practices "would be virtually inconceivable in federal criminal courts" and constituted prosecutorial misconduct. The arraignment was suspended until at least late January to resolve disputes about defense access to prosecution witnesses and evidence. Col. David complained that the prosecution had 30 lawyers while the defense had just 6, 2 of whom planned to leave. Brownback barred the defense from challenging the constitutionality of the MCs at this stage. Kuebler resisted, disclosing that Brownback had said at a closed-door meeting that he had "taken a lot of heat" from DoD and the White House after ruling that the MCs lacked jurisdiction. Expressing irritation that Kuebler had repeated that conversation, Brownback insisted: "I never said anyone who had any influence over me said anything." At the end of November it emerged that Brownback had ruled on October 15 that Khadr's lawyers could not tell him or anyone else the names of prosecution witnesses, some of whom would testify behind a screen or in disguise. Maj. Groharing had argued that "it is conceivable, if not likely, that al-Qaeda members or sympathizers could attempt to target witnesses" (most of whom were in Guantánamo). "Potential witnesses have previously expressed reservations with [sic] participation in the military commission process because of fear of retaliation from al-Qaeda." Kuebler responded to Groharing and Brownback: "The manner in which this is being dealt with (i.e., off the record, via e-mail), creates an added level of difficulty by making it appear that the government is trying to keep the secrecy of the proceedings a secret itself."

In January 2008 the defense moved to dismiss on the ground that Khadr had been a child at the time of the alleged acts.[134] Brownback denied that at the end of April. Groharing urged Brownback to accelerate the proceedings, echoing Edney's complaint that Kuebler had spent his time trying to pressure Canada to seek Khadr's repatriation instead of preparing for trial.[135]

The judge should set a trial date "so we can try this case before a military commission, not before the media and not before a foreign government." Kuebler claimed that some witnesses to the firefight said Speer might have been killed by friendly fire. Although the government initially maintained that Khadr was the only enemy fighter still living when Speer's unit stormed the compound and there had been only one grenade blast, a US officer's diary just made available to the defense reported that at least one other person was still alive then, and other grenades had been thrown in the final confrontation. Having learned from a Canadian diplomat visiting Guantánamo that his government received a US agency report on the firefight soon after it occurred, Kuebler asked the court to obtain it. The prosecution had claimed the document had "gone missing" in the USA. At the end of the month Kuebler warned the Canadian House of Commons subcommittee on international human rights that Khadr would not receive a fair trial from the MC and probably would be convicted.

In March Brownback ordered prosecutors to give the defense classified records of Khadr's mistreatment in Afghanistan, threatening on May 8 that "we stop" if they were not provided by May 22.[136] At the end of the month the CA replaced Brownback with Col. Patrick Parrish. Although the OMC called this a "mutual decision" by Brownback and the Army, Brownback said he had been "badgered and beaten and bruised" by Groharing to move the case quickly. Just before being replaced, Brownback was told by Groharing that the defense was not entitled to the records and was urged to set a trial date. Kuebler called it "very odd" that "the judge who was frustrating the government's forward progress in the Khadr case is suddenly gone."

In June Kuebler claimed DoD had advised Guantánamo interrogators to destroy their notes in case they had to testify about harsh interrogation, preventing him from challenging Khadr's alleged confessions.[137] The January 2003 SOP manual said that because "the mission has legal and political issues that may lead to interrogators being called to testify, keeping the number of documents with interrogation information to a minimum can minimize certain legal issues." Although the manual was mentioned in the 2005 Schmidt–Furlow investigation of detainee abuse, that section had not previously been made public.

A secret report by the Canadian Director of Foreign Intelligence, disclosed to Khadr's Canadian lawyers under a Canadian court order, reported that before a 2004 visit to Guantánamo by a Canadian official, Khadr had been subjected to the "frequent flyer program" in order to render him "more amenable and willing to talk" by moving him to a new cell every three hours for three weeks.[138] Documents described him in tears during interrogation, repeatedly crying "kill me," claiming not to recognize a photo of his family, then urinating on it, and later looking at it affectionately. Khadr's Canadian lawyers released ten minutes from more than seven hours of videotapes. The judge who had ordered their release warned that Canada "became implicated in the violation" of international law. Prime Minister Harper was unmoved:

> This videotape is several years old, and the Canadian government is not changing course in terms of the process that will determine Mr. Khadr's fate. He's obviously facing very serious charges. We believe his fate should be decided through a judicial process rather than a political process.

DoD said: "Guantánamo provides an environment for detainees that is stable, secure, safe and humane. This environment sets the conditions to successfully gain valuable information from detainees built on a relationship of trust, not fear."

In August Kuebler asked the court to let two psychologists interview Khadr so they could testify about the reliability of his "confessions."[139] Groharing objected, claiming that government experts were adequate and defense experts would cost $60,000. He also said the prosecution had erred in letting the defense see reports on detainee abuse. Parrish reprimanded the prosecution for the delays in deciding whether a report could be given to the defense and set a deadline two weeks later.

At the beginning of September Parrish became the third judge to disqualify Hartmann, whose "active approach to his supervisory responsibilities of the prosecutors in this case has created the appearance that he will be unable to remain neutral and impartial during the post-trial process in the accused's case."[140] Kuebler complained that Parrish had waited until after Hartmann had denied the defense request for two mental health experts; Parrish then postponed the trial to November to decide whether to order the government to fund them. "The evidence suggests that the accused was involved in an incident in 2002, was severely injured, has been held in custody since then and was 15 years old at the time of the alleged offenses. I think those circumstances alone merit some consideration about assistance." In October Kuebler sought further delay because the defense had recently learned that medical records disclosed by the prosecution in June omitted Khadr's psychiatric examinations. Parrish demanded an explanation, warning the prosecution that when parties violate court orders, "those decisions have consequences." He rescheduled the trial for January 26, 2009. On November 24, 2008 DDC Judge Bates stayed Khadr's habeas petition until the end of his MC.[141]

In January 2009 it emerged that when the OMC reconstituted the panels after the September 2008 resignation of Darrel Vandeveld, who had prosecuted eight cases (see the section on the Jawad MC below), it withdrew all the charges (originally referred on April 24, 2007) and re-referred them on December 17, 2008.[142] This required rearraignment, and some defendants challenged the way the substitutions were made. But on his first full day in office, President Obama issued an executive order suspending all MCs (discussed in the section on HVD cases below).

On April 3 Air Force Col. Peter Masciola, chief defense counsel, fired Kuebler for unspecified ethical violations after Kuebler accused Masciola of a conflict of interest for trying to ensure that his office would represent detainees in civilian courts if Obama permanently closed the MCs.[143] A few days later Kuebler was reinstated after Parrish ruled *he* had to approve any such firing, which could only occur for cause. Masciola accused Parrish of misreading the rules. In June Khadr told Parrish he wanted to fire all his military lawyers. Kuebler and Snyder were replaced by civilians Barry Coburn and Kobie Flowers (former federal prosecutors, Khadr's tenth and eleventh lawyers), who said they would have to visit "the alleged crime scene" and might need six months to prepare for trial. When Coburn objected to guards "perusing" the notes Khadr took while talking to his lawyers, Capt. John Murphy, the chief prosecutor, said this was necessary for "force protection." Coburn replied that it violated the attorney–client privilege. When Parrish asked what happened in federal maximum security prisons, Coburn explained that "notes like that are usually kept in the cell with an inmate and are protected by the privilege." In October Murphy told Parrish that DoJ was reviewing the case and expected to make a "forum decision" by November 16. In December Army Maj. Jon Jackson, a new military defense attorney, said prosecutors had told him the MC would still hear the case, starting in July 2010. DoD said "the forum [decision] in the Khadr case was made after a careful assessment of all the factors identified." Responding to objections that Khadr had been 15 at the time of the alleged offense, Murphy said "even in our traditional court system we try 15-year-olds, and we try them as adults." In February 2010 CBC television screened a program documenting Khadr's torture and accusing the USA of disseminating "a demonstrably false version of what took place" during the alleged crime. "Some evidence that supported Omar's claims of innocence was systematically withheld from defense lawyers, while other exculpatory evidence was altered to make him look guilty."

Just before pretrial hearings were to begin at the end of April, DoD finally issued its 281-page MC manual. During those hearings,

Groharing maintained the "confessions" were not "wrestled from Omar Khadr. He talked openly, confidently, and comfortably about his knowledge of al-Qaeda."[144] FBI agent Robert Fuller said his partner and he never used duress when interrogating Khadr in Bagram. Four other interrogators testified that Khadr cooperated with them. Prosecutors played a 25-minute video showing Khadr building roadside bombs with alleged al-Qaeda operatives, wiring Russian anti-vehicle mines, and sitting next to an AK-47.

The defense sought to exclude the tape, claiming the government had learned about it through abusive interrogation. The defense said it would call "Interrogator #1," who would testify to having threatened Khadr in 2002 with being sent to Egypt to be raped. The *Toronto Star* reported that prosecutors had offered Khadr a deal of five more years in prison. Coburn said there had been negotiations but no "firm offer," and Khadr refused the government demand that he admit throwing the grenade.

The *New York Times* warned that "if the Obama administration wants to demonstrate that it is practical and just to try some terrorism suspects in military tribunals instead of federal courts, it is off to a very poor start."[145] Khadr would be "the first person in decades to be tried by a western nation for war crimes allegedly committed as a child." His conditions of confinement "have been in clear violation of the Geneva Conventions and international accords on the treatment of children." The pretrial hearing revealed that "his initial questioning at Afghanistan's Bagram prison occurred while he was sedated for pain and shackled to a stretcher following his hospitalization for severe wounds suffered in the fighting." His first interrogator was Army Sgt. Joshua Claus, "later convicted of detainee abuse" (in the deaths of Dilawar and Habibullah, discussed in the companion volume *Law's Wars*), who "used threats of rape and death to frighten the teenaged Omar Khadr into talking." "There's already a bad lingering taste from the hearing, which began just hours after Defense Secretary Robert Gates formally approved a new set of rules for the tribunals and before Mr. Khadr's lawyers or the judge had a chance to review them." "After Mr. Khadr's eight-year ordeal, it would be no disrespect to Sgt. Speer to return Mr. Khadr to his home country under terms designed to protect public safety and strive for his rehabilitation." On July 20, DDC Judge Bates again stayed Khadr's habeas petition pending the outcome of his MC.[146]

When the trial began in July, Khadr sought to fire his lawyers and boycott the hearing because of "the unfairness and injustice of it."[147]

"Not one of the lawyers I've had, or human rights organizations …
ever say that this commission is fair or looking for justice … it has been
constructed to convict detainees not to find the truth." He had been
offered a plea bargain of 30 years (25 suspended) "to make the U.S. government look good in the public eyes." It took two hearings to convince
Parrish he wanted no defense. When Parrish ruled that Khadr still had
to be represented by Jackson, the latter asked for time to consult with
professional responsibility experts in Arkansas (where he was licensed)
and the Army JAG. When the hearing resumed, Jackson objected to
the admission of Khadr's "confessions."

During jury selection in August, Groharing used his single peremptory challenge to exclude a serving Army lieutenant colonel who agreed
with Obama that Guantánamo should be closed.[148] But the hearing
was immediately suspended for at least 30 days when Jackson collapsed
and had to be medevaced from Guantánamo. A week later Parrish
denied the motion to suppress Khadr's "confessions," finding "no credible evidence" of torture. At 15, "he was not immature for his age" and
"had sufficient training, education and experience to understand the
circumstances in which he found himself." There was "no evidence" that
Sgt. Claus telling Khadr a fictional story about an Afghan captive sent
to a US prison and raped by "four big black guys" "caused the accused
to make any incriminating statements then or in the future." Parrish
admitted the videotape of Khadr learning to make and plant IEDs.

DoD lifted the ban on journalists reporting information from
Guantánamo that the military considered privileged, if it had been
publicly revealed or independently verified.[149] But the *New York Times*
said: "the changes are not remotely good enough. They only serve to
remind us of the Obama administration's original error, which was to
try Mr. Khadr for war crimes allegedly committed when he was a child,
based on evidence tainted by torture and abuse."

The *Times* criticized the "intolerable limitations" on journalists
"trying to cover" the trial. "Four of the most experienced and knowledge-
able reporters" had been expelled for a "laughable" reason: publishing
an interrogator's name that "had long been in the public realm."

In mid-October Parrish delayed resuming the trial to let the parties
negotiate a plea agreement.[150] On October 25 Khadr pleaded guilty
to murder in violation of the law of war, attempted murder, material
support, conspiracy, and spying. He admitted constructing and planting
IEDs and throwing the grenade that killed SFC Speer. Murphy declared
that the agreement "puts a lie to the long-standing lie by some that Omar

Khadr is a victim. He's not. He's a murderer, and he's convicted by the strength of his own words." At the sentencing hearing Speer's widow, Tabitha, spoke so movingly about the effect of her husband's death on her children that many in the courtroom wept. Dr. Michael Welner, a forensic psychiatrist, testified that Khadr "is devout. He is angry." He had been "marinating in a radical Islamic community" in Guantánamo. Khadr apologized to Tabitha Speer. Parrish refused to admit a statement by Sgt. Claus that he had threatened Khadr and rejected Khadr's own affidavit as "unbelievable." Parrish also rejected a defense plea that he take Khadr's conditions of confinement into account in sentencing. The jury of 7 officers sentenced him to 40 years, even though the prosecution asked for only 25.

However, under the terms of the plea agreement (which the jury did not know), he was sentenced to a symbolic 30 years but would not have to serve more than 8 and, if repatriated to Canada, would be eligible for parole after serving a third of that sentence (i.e., 32 months). Canada refused to seek his immediate repatriation but said it would be inclined to accept his request after another year.

The *New York Times* said "the Obama administration achieved its political goal of avoiding having this disturbing case be the first to go to trial under its revamped military commissions. But this is not a legal victory anyone can feel proud about."[151] Parrish's admission of Khadr's confessions was "appalling." The eight years he had already spent in Guantánamo "should have been enough."

In April 2011 the defense asked VAdm. Bruce McDonald, the CA, to reduce the sentence to four years.[152] Although it claimed prosecutors had threatened to revoke the plea deal if they challenged Welner's expert credentials, defense counsel showed that he had been influenced by a notorious Danish psychologist, Nicolai Sennels, who had called the Koran a "criminal book that forces people to do criminal things" and urged Western countries to halt all Muslim immigration. Parrish had said at the time: "Dr. Welner would have been as likely to be accurate if he used a Ouija board." McDonald refused the defense request.

On the anniversary of Khadr's plea, Vic Toews, the Canadian Public Safety Minister, said: "I put the safety of Canadians first. A decision will be made on this file, as in all applications, in due course."[153] When BGen. Mark Martins had become chief military prosecutor earlier that fall, he aggressively sought to negotiate pleas with other detainees; but they were reluctant to agree until Khadr was repatriated. Sufyian Barhoumi's lawyer said: "the fact that Khadr remains at Guantánamo beyond when he was supposed to be transferred is a significant hindrance in my client's willingness to participate in negotiations with the government." In March 2012, Canada said the USA had not approved Khadr's transfer application. Defense Secretary Panetta said in Ottawa: "I don't have a specific timetable for signing" the application. But he did so in April. In July Khadr's Canadian lawyers asked a court to order Toews to act. Former chief military prosecutor Davis and Canadian Liberal Senator Romeo Dallaire appealed on Khadr's behalf. Toews first claimed he was waiting for a report from Canada's prison agency and then said he needed Khadr's interrogation videotapes and complete reports from Guantánamo psychiatrists in order "to assess the mental state of Mr. Khadr" (even though one of those psychiatrists, Welner, had been discredited). More than half of Canadians considered Khadr a security threat. The USA provided the material in August, and Khadr was transferred in September. Toews then opposed Khadr's application for parole. When Edney moved to have him transferred from a maximum security prison to a provincial jail in September 2013, Prime Minister Harper objected that Khadr had "pleaded guilty to very serious crimes including murder and it is very important that we continue to vigorously defend against any attempts, in court, to lessen his punishment for these heinous acts." But in April 2015 Judge June Ross approved his release, and Edney offered him a place to live.[154] Although the government argued his release would damage relations with the USA, DoS denied this. He was freed on May 7 after the Alberta Court of Appeals said the government had failed to show his release would cause "irreparable harm" to Canada's international obligations. In a rare unanimous decision from the bench, the Canadian Supreme Court rejected the federal government's argument that Khadr was an adult offender.

After the DC Circuit overturned al-Bahlul's conviction (see below), Edney wrote Bryan Broyles, deputy chief defense counsel, on January 29, 2013 that Khadr wanted to appeal his convictions to the CMCR (even though he had waived his right to do so as part of his plea deal). In November 2013, days after Hicks appealed his conviction, Khadr did the same on the grounds of abuse in custody and that throwing a grenade in combat was not a war crime. The CMCR stayed its consideration while the DC Circuit considered al-Bahlul's challenge to its composition (see below).[155] Meanwhile, the DC Circuit denied Khadr's petition for mandamus seeking the disqualification of a CMCR judge who maintained a part-time private law practice. In July 2017 Canada settled Khadr's civil claim for its complicity by apologizing and paying him Can$10.5 million.[156] Announcing the settlement, Public Safety Minister Ralph Goodale said to critics: "you may want to dismiss the rule of law and the constitution. But if you do that, you are fundamentally undermining the integrity of the country." Justice Minister Jody Wilson-Raybould said the payment signified that "our rights are not subject to the whims of the government of the day. And there are serious costs when the government violates the rights of its citizens." Speer and Layne Morris asked a Canadian court to apply the money to the $134 million default judgment they had won in D Utah two years earlier.

Ali Hamza Ahmad Suliman al-Bahlul

Al-Bahlul, a Yemeni, was accused of being bin Laden's bodyguard and making al-Qaeda videos. During a pretrial hearing in August 2004, he asked to represent himself.[157] Col. Brownback, the judge, refused. A translator had rendered Al-Bahlul's next statement as: "I have some idea about practicing law in Yemen." But other interpreters corrected this to: "I know some people that do practice or are familiar with law in the country of Yemen." Al-Bahlul asked that one of them assist an American lawyer, if he could not be the principal lawyer, adding: "If I do have that choice, I'd rather not be here" to observe future hearings. Asked if he understood that he might not be allowed to see some prosecution evidence, al-Bahlul objected: "I don't think it is fair. The accused cannot defend himself without seeing such evidence for himself." The translation of his next statement was incomprehensible:

> It's well known in all those – the civilian, or the local – the decision is the evidence, especially as the decision is under no pressure, and based on the person without any – without being placed under any pressure, and based on personal decision or preference.

Again, other translators corrected this: "It's well known in both secular and religious law that a confession is evidence, particularly a confession given free of coercion and as a result of the person's own decision." Al-Bahlul continued: "*I am from al Qaeda and the relationship between me and 9/11*" until Brownback interrupted, telling jurors al-Bahlul had not been under oath and "none of this is evidence in any way."

Al-Bahlul spoke for ten minutes at his January 2006 arraignment, praising Allah and denouncing "your allies, the Jews."[158] "I am telling the judge do what you have to do. Rule what you have to rule. This life will go on and end at some point. God will rule based on justice, and those who call on other than God are not calling on anything." He then held up a paper with the word *Muqataa* (boycott in Arabic) and said it three times in English, refusing to enter a plea.

Complaining he had been denied a Yemeni lawyer, al-Bahlul again asked to represent himself. Brownback ruled that an accused who boycotted the hearing could not proceed pro se. His military lawyer, Army Maj. Thomas Fleener, objected that "for four years they wouldn't let detainees have lawyers; now they're shoving one down his throat." Requiring him to represent an unwilling client was an effort "to add some air of legitimacy to an otherwise wholly illegitimate process" and could violate the ethical rules of Iowa and Wyoming, where he was licensed. When he sat behind the defense table, Brownback told him to move to the counsel table. Fleener asked: "is that an order?" Brownback replied: "Do you need an order?" Fleener answered "yes" and then moved to withdraw. Brownback denied the motion. Fleener then sought to abate the proceedings by challenging Brownback's authority to preside alone, saying the president's order required all commission members to be present. Brownback refused but ordered that Fleener receive assistance because there were four prosecutors.

At the end of February chief prosecutor Davis compared the MC defendants to vampires.[159] "Remember if you dragged Dracula out into the sunlight he melted. Well that's kind of the way it is trying to drag a detainee into the courtroom. The facts are like sunlight to Dracula. The last thing they want is to face the facts in the courtroom. But their day is coming."

In April Fleener argued that al-Bahlul should be able to represent himself, noting his client's intelligence and decorum and citing Zacarias Moussaoui's civilian trial (a peculiar precedent, since Moussaoui had repeatedly interrupted his trial, see Chapter 2).[160] The National Institute of Military Justice, a group of Wyoming lawyers, and Kuebler sought to file amicus briefs. The prosecution raised no objection. But the CA had already denied al-Bahlul's request the previous June.

Al-Bahlul was charged in February 2008. The government alleged that in February 1999 he had gone to Afghanistan to get training and join al-Qaeda. As bin Laden's secretary, he had created a propaganda video, *The Destruction of the American Destroyer U.S.S. Cole*, drafted martyrs' wills for hijackers Mohammed Atta and Ziad al Jarrah, researched the economic effects of the 9/11 attacks, and operated the media commission equipment.

At the beginning of an August 15 hearing al-Bahlul demanded the *Muqataa* sign he had created in 2006, citing nine "political and legal reasons."[161] When prosecutors could not find it, he asked derisively: "if such a document is lost, what kind of court is this?" He insisted he wanted to return to his cell until the sign was found. When Air Force Col. Ronald Gregory, the judge, warned him of the consequences of being absent, al-Bahlul vowed to appear in court only to hear his sentence. "I don't really care how you will exercise this legal circus." He asked Gregory to withdraw his habeas petition. Gregory sent al-Bahlul back to his cell and canceled his pro se representation. Because al-Bahlul fired every military lawyer, the judge appointed Army Maj. David J.R. Frakt as "standby counsel." Frakt said he would follow al-Bahlul's instructions, although his client had refused to meet him again. "I think my obligation is to do what he wants – nothing ... Ali al Bahlul is my boss." Waiving all pretrial motions, Frakt declared he was ready for trial.

Al-Bahlul appeared at an October 2008 hearing but again refused to participate.[162] Frakt said: "I will be joining Mr. Al Bahlul's boycott of the proceedings, standing mute at the table." When Frakt asked to leave, Gregory ordered him to remain but said he could honor al-Bahlul's wishes. In an earlier hearing al-Bahlul had expressed loyalty to bin Laden and called the judge his enemy and the proceedings a "legal farce." But Gregory ruled that these statements could not be used against him because they occurred during his explanation for the boycott. Al-Bahlul was silent as a jury of nine officers was chosen. Of the 13 voir-dired, 6 had served on the Hicks MC. Gregory questioned them about this and their attitudes toward Islam.

Army Maj. Dan Cowhig, the prosecutor, described the accused as bin Laden's "media man," who sought "to grow the organization" and overcome Muslim resistance to suicide bombing. He sometimes was confused with bin Laden's bodyguard because he carried a rifle and grenades. He failed to connect a satellite receiver to watch the 9/11 attack, but listened to radio reports with bin Laden. In Guantánamo, al-Bahlul tried to send a note to KSM and bin al-Shibh: "The Americans have killed some of us and we have killed some of them. They have harmed us and we have harmed them, and they have captured some of us. I swear by Allah the Almighty – I am not just saying this, we will act upon it – with Allah's will, we will capture some of them and will treat them the same way they treated us."

Al-Bahlul smiled and nodded while the jury watched his two-hour video recruiting viewers to jihad. Former FBI agent Ali Soufan testified that during a 2002 interrogation al-Bahlul had boasted of producing the video, whose message was: "go to Afghanistan. Join al-Qaeda. Join martyrdom operations. Hate life. Love Death." Soufan said al-Bahlul "does not consider anyone protected persons ... as long as you are American, as long as you pay taxes, you are a target." Three men convicted in the Lackawanna Six terrorism trial testified that al-Bahlul had recruited them. After calling 14 witnesses over four days, Cowhig said in his closing that al-Bahlul was part of "a band of lawless wretches in armed conflict with the United States," who incited suicide bombers to kill Americans. His work inspired the 9/11 hijackers "to shred themselves and hundreds of others through the towers of the WTC [World Trade Center] and the walls of the Pentagon and a field in Pennsylvania." Gregory twice reminded the jury that al-Bahlul "is under no obligation to say or do anything to establish his innocence." When Cowhig sought to provoke al-Bahlul by declaring that "the evidence has shown in the past few days that you are a terrorist and a war criminal," Gregory directed Cowhig to address the jurors, not the accused.

The jury convicted al-Bahlul on all counts after deliberating for just four hours. At the sentencing hearing, Cowhig asked rhetorically: "When will it be safe for this man to leave confinement? Never!" Al-Bahlul spoke for 45 minutes, submitting a 60-line poem celebrating the attack on the "infidels' trade towers." "We will fight any government that governs America. We are the only ones on earth who stand against you." He called the proceedings a farce and regretted they did not receive more coverage. After deliberating less than an hour, the jury sentenced him to life. Davis (now a critic) said that after three trials in seven years the government had convicted "a dupe" (Hicks) and "a driver" (Hamdan) and won "a default" (al-Bahlul).

On September 9, 2011, the CMCR affirmed the conviction in an opinion of almost 150 pages.[163] It found that al-Bahlul was an AUEC and that material support, joint criminal exercise, complicity, and aiding the enemy were war crimes when he committed them. The court also found that conspiracy and solicitation were offenses under the law of armed conflict. The court rejected al-Bahlul's First Amendment, Bill of Attainder, and Equal Protection challenges.

On January 25, 2013 the DC Circuit vacated the conviction after the government agreed this was required by the Circuit's decision in

Hamdan.[164] Although the Guantánamo Bay Review Task Force had said in 2010 that 36 detainees could be prosecuted, chief prosecutor Martins now said that, given the DC Circuit ruling, no more than 20 could be tried.[165] Six were currently on trial (five HVDs and al-Nashiri), and seven more would be tried, including Ahmad al-Darbi and Abdul Hadi al-Iraqi.

On July 14, 2014 the en banc DC Circuit issued five opinions extending to over 150 pages, vacating the convictions for material support and solicitation for violating the *Ex Post Facto* clause.[166] Judge Henderson wrote that by refusing to participate in his hearing, al-Bahlul had forfeited any appellate challenges, which would be considered only for "plain error." The finding that material support or solicitation were law of war crimes at the time they had been committed was plain error, but not the finding that conspiracy was a law of war crime. The en banc court remanded the other challenges to the panel. Writing separately, Henderson would not have found that al-Bahlul could invoke the *Ex Post Facto* clause. Judge Rogers would have vacated the conspiracy conviction as well. Judge Brown would not have found that al-Bahlul had waived his objections, but would have upheld his conspiracy conviction against an *Ex Post Facto* challenge. "In the case of the terrorist attacks of September 11, involving the murder of thousands of civilians, the attackers knew the civilized world would condemn their actions." Judge Kavanaugh would have vacated the same two counts and only remanded for sentencing on conspiracy.

On June 25, 2015 the original panel vacated al-Bahlul's remaining conviction for conspiracy in three opinions extending over 80 pages.[167] Judge Rogers (joined by Tatel) wrote that the government conceded that conspiracy was not an international law of war crime. The Supreme Court had rejected the view that the Define and Punish clause gave Congress open-ended authority to create new war crimes. Because al-Bahlul's MC fell outside the historical Article III exception for law of war MCs, "there is no question that this usurps 'the essential attributes of judicial power.'" Judge Henderson wrote an angry dissent. With biting sarcasm she accused her colleagues of finding that Justice Jackson apparently failed to factor in an additional constraint on the political branches' combined war powers: international law.

> My colleagues contend – as a matter of *constitutional* law, not simple comity – that the Congress cannot authorize military-commission trials unless the international community agrees, jot and tittle, that the offense

in question violates the law of war. And the content of international law is to be determined by – who else? – the Judiciary, with little or no deference to the political branches ... And the beneficiary of today's decision could not be less deserving.

She quoted her concurrence in the en banc review declaring that al-Bahlul, "like Hitler's Goebbels – led Osama bin Laden's propaganda operation."

The *New York Times* called the decision "a major rebuke to the government's persistent and misguided reliance on the tribunals, which operate in a legal no man's land, unconstrained by standard constitutional guarantees and rules of evidence that define the functioning of the nation's civilian courts."[168]

But on September 25 the Circuit granted another en banc rehearing, and on October 20, 2016 it reinstated the conspiracy conviction in five opinions extending over 69 pages.[169] Four judges (Henderson, Brown, Griffith, and Kavanaugh) found that Congress could make conspiracy an offense triable by MC. "We are aware of no credible support for the notion that Congress has believed itself bound by international law in this context." Millett found that the conspiracy conviction was not plain error. Wilkins found that al-Bahlul's conviction was consistent with international law. Rogers, Tate, and Pillard dissented because conspiracy was not a crime under the international law of war and Congress's attempt to make it one violated "the judiciary's power to preside over the trial of all crimes" under Article III. In September 2017 the Supreme Court declined to review.[170]

Mohammed Jawad

In October 2007 the military charged Jawad, an Afghan, with trying to cause serious bodily harm to two US soldiers by lobbing a grenade into their car on February 17, 2002, when he had been 17.[171] Jawad told his CSRT he had falsely confessed after being tortured by Afghan police. At his arraignment the prosecution, referring to evidence Jawad could not see, said he had told a "senior Afghani police officer that he was proud of what he had done and, if he were let go, he would do it again." Jawad denied having said that. Although Jawad subsequently refused to attend hearings or allow Maj. Frakt to represent him, he later let Frakt challenge the MC and improve his conditions of confinement. In June 2008 Frakt moved to dismiss the charges because of the abuse suffered by Jawad. Although DoD claimed to have banned sleep deprivation in March 2004, prison records showed that in May Jawad had been subjected to the "frequent flyer program," having been moved from cell to cell 112 times in 14 days, usually at night, for no apparent reason. Army Maj. Jason Orlich testified it was standard operating procedure, approved by senior officers, to follow a "Discipline Synch Matrix" to keep detainees "off balance." Col. Morris, the prosecutor, admitted this but said Jawad had confessed without duress after being captured. The defense motion was "just a broad argument that says you ought to give him this colossal relief because the government may have stumbled some in how he was treated." Jawad interrupted testimony by a defense sleep disorder expert, almost rushing the witness stand when his shackles were removed. "Day and night they were shifting me from one place to another. Nobody answered why they were giving me this punishment." The defense called former chief prosecutor Davis, who testified that Hartmann, the CA legal adviser, had fast-tracked Jawad's trial before the case was ready because he believed that bloodshed in the alleged crime "captured the imagination of the American people." The audio malfunctioned for 22 minutes while prosecutors were answering defense questions about alleged DoD misconduct, and portions of the hearing were drowned out by a hearing in an adjacent courtroom. Frakt said in closing:

> The Feb. 7, 2002, order of President Bush invited the rule of law to be circumvented ... America lost a little of its greatness that day ... Today, Your Honor, you have an opportunity to restore a bit of America's lost luster ... to set us on a path that leads to an America which once again stands at the forefront of the community of nations in the arena of human rights.

In August the judge, Army Col. Stephen Henley, banned Hartmann from further participation in the trial and ordered the CA to review the charges.[172] He found that Hartmann's behavior "compromised the objectivity necessary to dispassionately and fairly evaluate the evidence and prepare the post-trial evaluation." Hartmann had failed to give the CA the defense counsel's analysis of "mitigating and extenuating circumstances," namely the abuse of Jawad in Bagram and Guantánamo. On September 24 Henley denied motions to dismiss for lack of subject matter jurisdiction and lack of personal jurisdiction based on the fact that Jawad had been a child soldier, but found that he had been tortured.

In September LtCol. Darrel Vandeveld resigned as prosecutor.[173] He said in a four-page declaration that "evidence we have an obligation [to disclose] as prosecutors and officers of the court has not been made available to the defense." "I now accept that Jawad was under the age of eighteen when apprehended. I suspect that he was duped by Hezb-e Islami Gulbuddin into joining the organization, and it seems plausible to me that Jawad may have been drugged before the alleged attack." The Afghan Interior Minister had said two other men had confessed to the crime. Troubled by Jawad's treatment in US custody, Vandeveld declared that the withholding of evidence had transformed him from "a true believer to someone who felt truly deceived." "As a juvenile at the time of his capture, Jawad should have been segregated from the adult detainees, and some serious attempt made to rehabilitate him."

Learning in the previous May that Jawad had attempted suicide over Christmas 2003 (after being held in solitary for six months), Vandeveld had tried to negotiate a plea agreement with Frakt. "I am a father, and it's not an exercise in self-pity to ask oneself how you would feel if your own son was treated in this fashion." But discovering that Vandeveld had admitted the abuse of Jawad in response to Frakt's motion to dismiss, supervisors reprimanded him and made him resubmit his response without the admission. In summer 2008 he saw photos and reports documenting Jawad's abusive interrogation in Afghanistan. "I am a resolute Catholic and take as an article of faith that justice is defined as reparative and restorative and that Christ's most radical pronouncement – command, if you will – is to love one's enemies." Higher authorities had rebuffed his concerns. "I am highly concerned, to the point that I believe I can no longer serve as a prosecutor at the Commissions, about the slipshod, uncertain 'procedure' for affording defense counsel discovery."

Frakt moved to call Vandeveld to testify about his ethical concerns and how he had wanted to offer Jawad a plea leading to a quick release. Because Vandeveld's superiors blocked his testimony, Frakt wanted to ask Henley to compel it. Morris dismissed Vandeveld's moral qualms, claiming the prosecutor said he was quitting for personal reasons and because he was "disappointed that his superiors did not agree with his recommendations." Morris refused to say whether his office had rejected a plea deal while insisting "we are the most scrupulous organization you can imagine in terms of disclosure to the defense." "When in doubt we disclose every scrap of paper and piece of evidence." He was angered by Vandeveld's "broad blast at some very ethical and hardworking people whose performances are being smudged groundlessly." Michael J. Berrigan, deputy chief defense counsel, said his lawyers and human rights organizations had raised similar concerns, "but we never had anyone on the inside who could validate those claims." When the defense called Vandeveld, the prosecution prevented him from traveling to Guantánamo, but Henley let him appear by video. Vandeveld initially asked for immunity and a lawyer, but then agreed to testify without them. Before being removed, he had been ordered by Hartmann to submit to a psychiatric examination; but Frakt said Walter Reed Hospital had cleared Vandeveld to remain on active duty. Henley ordered the prosecution to hand over three documents by October 3.

On October 28 Henley granted the defense motion to suppress Jawad's December 17, 2002 "confession" to Afghan police.[174] He found that Jawad was under 18 at the time of the alleged attack and appeared to be drugged. A high-level Afghan official had threatened: "you will be killed if you do not confess to the grenade attack" and "we will arrest your family and kill them if you do not confess." Henley said: "while the torture threshold" for excluding evidence "is admittedly high, it is met in this case." A month later Henley excluded statements made on December 17–18 after Jawad had been transferred to US custody because the USA had used techniques to maintain Jawad's "shock and fearful state" at arrest by blindfolding and hooding him. "The effect of the death threats which produced the … first confession to the Afghan police had not dissipated by the second confession to the U.S. government interrogator." The government appealed to the CMCR, which heard argument in January 2009. But though it ordinarily ruled on interlocutory motions within 30 days, in this case it postponed doing so until May (over defense objections) and finally dismissed the appeal as moot after the government withdrew the charges following the DDC action (see below).

In January 2009 Vandeveld filed a declaration in Jawad's habeas petition: "it is my opinion, based on my extensive knowledge of the case, that there is no credible evidence or legal basis to justify Mr Jawad's detention."[175] Morris reiterated that Vandeveld resigned only because he was "disappointed when I did not choose him to become a team leader." Opposing the petition, the government continued to rely on the confessions Henley had excluded. In July DDC Judge Huvelle suppressed every statement Jawad had made, calling the case "unbelievable," an "outrage," "riddled with holes. She granted habeas, and Jawad was returned to Afghanistan in August (see Chapter 5). Marine Corps Maj. Eric Montalvo, one of Jawad's defense lawyers, said he had spoken to all "the government's star witnesses," who had "received some sort of U.S. government compensation, from shoes and a trip to the United States to $400 for cooperation, which is a princely sum in Afghanistan." Frakt confirmed that "they acknowledged it on tape. It was in the context of 'well, they gave me $00, what can you do for me?'"

In May 2008 Frakt wrote Col. David, the chief military defense counsel: "I am reporting a suspected loac violation that I have uncovered in the course of my duties as a defense counsel assigned to the Office of Military Commissions Defense."[176] He believed Jawad had been tortured in violation of the Geneva Conventions, domestic and international law, and DoD regulations. When he got no response he wrote the commander in charge of SOUTHCOM-JTF-GTMO on October 7, copying four lawyers in the DoD Office of General Counsel, noting that David had forwarded Frakt's memo to their office on June 1. He added that Col. Henley had found that Jawad had been subjected to "abusive conduct and cruel and inhuman treatment" and had recommended disciplinary action for this "flagrant misbehavior." Frakt asked for "an update on the status of the mandatory loac violation investigation." He got no response. In January 2009 he again wrote the commander and lawyers, commenting that "it has now been over seven months since this report was filed." "On receipt of a loac violation report, a formal investigation is mandatory and should be done by the most expeditious means available." He never got an answer.

INCOMPLETE OR ABORTED PROSECUTIONS

Mohamedou Ould Slahi

LtCol. Stuart Couch served in the Marines for more than a decade before leaving for private practice in the 1990s.[177] After patriotically volunteering to return to active duty following 9/11, he was assigned to the OMC in August 2003 and given several prosecution files, including Slahi. On his first visit to Guantánamo in October he saw a detainee shackled to the floor and subjected to strobe lights and heavy metal music. When Slahi suddenly began offering evidence against other detainees in December, Couch, assisted by an NCIS investigator, tried to find out what had made him break. What he learned convinced him Slahi was being tortured: Slahi had been threatened with death and with having his mother brought to Guantánamo where, as the only woman detainee, she would be in danger of being raped. Couch consulted two brothers-in-law (a retired Marine and a theologian), as well as other Marine lawyers. At a baptism in May the priest reminded parishioners of the duty to "respect the dignity of every human being." Couch said: "when I heard that, I knew I got to get off the fence." That month he told the chief prosecutor, Army Col. Bob Swann, that Slahi's treatment violated the CAT, and he "refused to participate in [the Slahi] prosecution in any manner." He was taken off the case. (Slahi was never charged and was released on October 17, 2016.)

Couch then flew to Afghanistan to investigate other cases, after being warned by Swann "not to ask questions about detainee treatment." On his return he sent Swann a memo on "Prosecution Standards." He had found "incomplete information provided by agencies ... regarding the circumstances of detainee capture, interrogation and internment," had been denied such information, and had been stonewalled by the CIA. "*Ethically*, we have a duty to disclose to the defense all known statements by the accused, both unclassified and classified." "*Morally*, some of the interrogation techniques that have been used with some detainees resulting in statements they have provided are deplorable." He urged that these policies be changed and expressed his willingness to request reassignment. He then refused to use coerced confessions against al-Qahtani. When he uncovered evidence of the torture of KSM and Juma al-Dossari, those prosecutions also halted. Couch was assigned the prosecution of Mamdouh Habib, an Egyptian-born Australian citizen. After pushing to see the entire file, Couch learned that the damning evidence had been obtained by torture. When he reported that to BGen. Hemingway, the CA legal adviser, he was told to charge Habib anyhow. Couch took the matter to Altenburg, the CA, who ordered him to file the charges but promised not to approve them. (All these prosecutions are discussed below.) At the end of his three-year term of duty Couch left the prosecutor's office to become a military judge on the Navy-Marine Corps Court of Criminal Appeals.

Ghassan Abdullah al-Sharbi

In November 2005 al-Sharbi, a Saudi, was charged (at the same time as Khadr) with conspiracy to attack civilians and civilian objects and to commit murder, destruction of property, and terrorism.[178] He had a BA in electrical engineering from Embry-Riddle Aeronautics University (where he was studying on 9/11) and spoke fluent English. He was arrested on March 28, 2002 at an alleged al-Qaeda safe house in Faisalabad, Pakistan. At his CSRT he asked: "how can I defend myself" without the right to confront witnesses. He denounced the USA as "the infidel against God" and assailed capitalism and homosexuality. "May God help me fight the infidels or the unfaithful ones." At his April 2006 MC he refused to be represented by military or civilian lawyers and denounced the tribunal and his detention. He insisted on wearing prison clothing even though Navy Capt. Daniel O'Toole, the judge, warned it might prejudice commission members. "I'm going to make this short and easy for you guys. I'm proud of what I did and there isn't any reason of hiding." He would testify that "I fought against the United States. I took up arms … I did not come here to defend myself. I came in to tell you I did what I did and am willing to pay the price, no matter what it is. Even if I spend hundreds of years in jail that would be an honor to me … I'm not going to be violent or cause trouble. I'm not going to make commotions."

Asked if he was familiar with the process, he retorted: "Same circus, different clown." When O'Toole persisted in asking about representation, al-Sharbi reiterated: "I understand and I advise you not to waste time with me on that point. It's my decision and I'm not going to change it." But finding that al-Sharbi was not competent to represent himself and Military Commission Order 1 required military defense counsel, O'Toole assigned LtCdr. Kuebler. When Kuebler said the California Bar had ruled it was unethical to represent a competent individual against his wishes, O'Toole took that under consideration. On May 12, 2006 DDC Judge Sullivan enjoined the commission until the Supreme Court decided *Hamdan*.[179] In May 2008 charges were refiled against al-Sharbi.[180] But they were dismissed without prejudice five months later because the prosecution needed more time to prepare for trial following Vandeveld's resignation. Chief prosecutor Morris said: "we have plenty of evidence to convict all of them." The charges were dismissed without prejudice again on January 31, 2013.

Jabran Said bin al-Qahtani

Jabran al-Qahtani, a Saudi, was charged on November 7, 2005, the same day as al-Sharbi and with the same charges.[181] At his arraignment in April 2006 he said: "I don't want this court. I don't want an attorney. You judge me and you sentence me the way you want, if this is God's will." Army LtCol. Bryan T. Broyles phoned his bar (Kentucky) during the hearing and was told to respect al-Qahtani's wishes. But O'Toole ordered Broyles to represent al-Qahtani over his client's objections. He voir dired O'Toole, raising two challenges: prior rulings showed partiality to the prosecution, and the fact that his wife worked at NCIS.

O'Toole rejected both. The charges were dismissed without prejudice on January 28, 2013.

Mohammed al-Qahtani

In February 2008 Mohammed al-Qahtani – who allegedly was to have been the "20th hijacker" on 9/11 but had been denied entry to the USA several months earlier – was designated for prosecution along with the five HVDs (see below).[182] Three months later, however, the charges against him were dropped. Defense lawyers saw a memo from legal adviser Hartmann to CA Crawford advising that the death penalty would be inappropriate – presumably because al-Qahtani had been tortured in Guantánamo (see the companion volume *Law's Wars*). In his 2006 Administrative Review Board (ARB), al-Qahtani said he had been fed information by interrogators and never made a statement except under torture, which he described.

The *Washington Post* wrote that "the ghosts of interrogations past have come back to haunt the Bush administration."[183] The MC decision was "a palpable reminder of the inhumane acts committed by U.S. personnel and sanctioned by top officials in the name of protecting Americans from extremists." "[P]erhaps … the proceedings against Mr. Qahtani had to be halted to keep a litany of abuses from being recounted within earshot of the rest of the world." "Mr. Qahtani's experience shows that the horrors portrayed in the photographs from Iraq's Abu Ghraib prison, which have so deeply damaged U.S. prestige and influence around the world, were not invented by the night shift there, as Mr. Rumsfeld claimed, but were approved by him."

In November, after President Obama's election, chief prosecutor Morris said the prosecution would refile the charges because there was "independent and reliable evidence" against al-Qahtani, aside from his confessions.[184] "His conduct is significant enough that he falls into the category of people who ought to be held accountable by being brought to trial." Several defense lawyers said Hartmann had recently prepared a briefing urging the incoming Obama administration to continue the MCs. But in January 2009 Crawford, in her first interview since being appointed CA in February 2007, said she would not approve al-Qahtani's prosecution even though "there's no doubt in my mind he would've been on one of those planes had he gained access to the country in August 2001." "We tortured Qahtani. His treatment met the legal definition of torture. And that's why I did not refer the case" for prosecution. "This was not any one particular act; this was just a combination of things that … hurt his health. It was abusive and uncalled for. And coercive. Clearly coercive. It was that medical impact that pushed me over the edge" to call it torture. "For 160 days his only contact was with the interrogators … 48 of 54 consecutive days of 18- to 20-hour interrogations. Standing naked in front of a female agent. Subject to strip searches. And insults to his mother and sister."

Coerced testimony should not be allowed in the MCs: "you don't allow it in a regular court." When Crawford became CA in 2007 "the prosecution was unprepared" to go to trial. Two years later prosecutors still "were lacking in experience and judgment and leadership. A prosecutor has an ethical obligation to review all the evidence before making a charging decision and they didn't have access to all the evidence, including medical records, interrogation logs, and they were making charging decisions without looking at everything." "Certainly in the public's mind, or politically speaking, and certainly in the international community it may be too late" to rehabilitate the MCs.

She was the first senior Bush administration official to acknowledge torture. DoD said its own investigation concluded that the interrogation techniques "were lawful." A few days later (just before Obama's inauguration) chief defense counsel Masciola urged Crawford to drop the charges against all the detainees in light of her admission that some of the 22 facing trial had been tortured.[185] Crawford retired in January 2010.

Sufyian Barhoumi

Barhoumi, an Algerian, was charged with those people already discussed in this section. In April 2006 his lawyer, Capt. Wade Faulkner, moved to have him returned from Camp 5 to the communal Camp 4.[186] Judge O'Toole rejected the motion. Barhoumi planned to boycott the hearings and refuse Faulkner's representation. The government failed to grant Barhoumi's civilian attorney security clearance. Charges were refiled against Barhoumi in May 2008 but dropped in October (to avoid using the evidence of abu Zubaydah, which was tainted by his torture). The charges were refiled in 2009 (just before Obama's inauguration) but dropped again in January 2013.

Binyam Mohamed

Mohamed – an Ethiopian citizen, Muslim convert, and electrical engineer who had lived in the UK since he was a teenager – was charged with those people already discussed in this section. His indictment alleged that he had gone to Afghanistan in May 2001, received weapons training in al-Qaeda's al Farouq camp, and heard bin Laden say "something big is going to happen in the future." He attended a city warfare course in Kabul in August 2001 and fought with the Taliban against the Northern Alliance in September. He got explosives training in Kabul with Richard Reid (the "shoe bomber"). Abdul Hadi al-Iraqi (discussed below) told him al-Qaeda had a mission for him. He traveled with abu Zubaydah from Khowst to Pakistan, where he met José Padilla, Ghassan al-Sharbi, and Jabran Said al-Qahtani. At a guesthouse in Lahore he and Padilla got instructions on how to make a dirty bomb, which al-Sharbi translated into Arabic. In Lahore he and Padilla discussed with abu Zubaydah plans for an attack on the USA, including a dirty bomb, blowing up gas tankers, and spraying people with cyanide in nightclubs. He and Padilla went to Karachi to meet Saif al-Adel (head of al-Qaeda security) and KSM. Both of them told Mohamed to target high-rise apartment buildings by igniting the natural gas used for heating, as well as gas stations. In April 2002 he was given $6,000 and met KSM for the last time. On April 4 he and Padilla were detained at passport control in Karachi but released the next day. KSM got him a different forged passport. On April 10 he was arrested at Karachi airport trying to fly to London on a forged passport and handed over to the USA.

At his April arraignment, Mohamed held up a small sign reading "Con mission" and declared "this is not a commission. This is a con mission. It is out to con the world."[187] "What happens in America goes around the world." He denied meeting Padilla and said he did not speak Arabic. He wore a Pakistani tunic, which his lawyer had dyed prison orange, and had unsuccessfully sought to be brought in fully shackled because any lesser constraint would be "dishonest." He claimed the CIA had rendered him to Morocco, where he was held for 18 months and tortured before being taken to a prison in Afghanistan. He now objected that he had been misidentified as Binyam Muhammad (a different spelling). "I don't understand what kind of system – after four years of renditions and torture – gets the wrong man. I don't know if Congress gave you the right to change names; they gave you the right to change laws." "I'm innocent. I'm not supposed to be here." Col. Ralph Kohlmannn, the judge, said he had to call the defendant something. Mohamed suggested Count Dracula. Informed of his right to counsel, he said sarcastically: "I have been four years without rights and now all of a sudden I have rights? What are these rights ... where did these rights come from?"

Mohamed wanted to represent himself and did not trust Maj. Yvonne Bradley, who was "under orders to be my enemy." "If you were arrested in Saudi Arabia and Osama bin Laden said, 'I'm going to force you to have a military lawyer,' and gave you some bearded turbaned person, I don't think you would agree with that." He had trouble trusting an American lawyer because of the horrible things that had happened to him in custody. He wanted to use Clive Stafford Smith and Joseph Margulies, both civilian lawyers, as advisers. Bradley said she had a conflict of interest because other military defense lawyers represented clients who had made statements against each other. Dismissing those concerns, Kohlmannn ordered her to represent Mohamed vigorously. She invoked the Fifth Amendment three times on the ground that she would be breaching legal ethics by representing Mohamed without a lawyer–client privilege; and she declined to answer Kohlmannn's questions about pretrial motions. He admonished her "unprofessional attitude," "inappropriate grinning," and failure to address him as sir. He refused to let her consult with a private lawyer when threatened with contempt and indefinite detention in the brig. He called a recess and then asked Bradley, Stafford Smith, and Margulies to submit briefs. Unless the conflict of interest issues were resolved, the lawyers would have to withdraw. "We're not just going to be stuck in never-never land." Kohlmannn tried to enter a not guilty plea for Mohamed. When the lawyers declined to voir dire him, Kohlmann pronounced himself competent, provoking Mohamed to retort: "I don't think so." His lawyers called it a "rush to charge as many people as possible at Guantánamo Bay prior to President Bush leaving office."

The charges were withdrawn in October after DDC Judge Sullivan ordered the government to turn over all exculpatory evidence, including 42 classified British intelligence documents recording communications with the USA. The British High Court ordered their release to Mohamed's lawyers. In February 2009 he was transferred to Britain and released unconditionally. A month later it was reported that he had rejected a deal to serve another three years in prison in Britain, abandon his efforts to obtain documents about his torture, and agree not to speak or sue the USA or its officials.

Abdul Zahir

In January 2006 Zahir was charged with translating for the Taliban in 1997 and conducting financial transactions for al-Qaeda.[188] In early 2002 he allegedly joined Abdul Hadi al-Iraqi in planning bomb attacks on foreign civilians in Afghanistan. He was captured in July, three months after a grenade was thrown through a car window, seriously injuring a Canadian reporter. In his September 2004 CSRT Zahir said he worked at a guesthouse run by the Taliban, translating and running errands for Hadi. When in April 2006 Army LtCol. Thomas Bogar, his military counsel, asked the judge, Col. Robert S. Chester, what law would govern, Chester replied: "it's above my pay grade. The Supreme Court is going to tell us what to do." "I suppose we will look at military criminal law and federal criminal laws and procedures." Asked to be more specific, Chester refused "to speculate as to what is or what is not controlling."

Although Zahir had been given the charges in English, Arabic, and Pashto, Chester ordered that he be provided with them in Farsi, as well as a Farsi interpreter. The CA stayed the trial in June.

Ahmed Mohammed Ahmed Haza al-Darbi

Al-Darbi, a Saudi and brother-in-law of 9/11 hijacker Khalid al-Mihdhar, was charged in December 2007 with planning unconsummated attacks on vessels in the Strait of Hormuz.[189] (Several years earlier Stuart Couch had found evidence that al-Darbi had been tortured, resulting in the case being put on hold.)

Al-Darbi had allegedly traveled to Jalalabad, met bin Laden, trained at an al-Qaeda camp, served as a weapons instructor at another, and from 2001–02 transferred money for the attacks, traveled to several countries to buy equipment, and registered the attack boat in his name. In May 2009 Army Col. James L. Pohl, the judge, scheduled a hearing on defense motions to introduce two documentaries – *Torturing Democracy* and *Taxi to the Dark Side* – in support of claims that al-Darbi's "confessions" at Bagram were produced by torture. But Pohl then postponed it to September. Charges were withdrawn in November but refiled in August 2012 and again in February 2014. Al-Darbi pleaded guilty and agreed to cooperate with prosecutors and testify against al-Nashiri (see below). He would spend at least 3.5 years in Guantánamo before being sentenced and then 9–15 years in Saudi Arabia (on top of the 12 he had already served). He had faced life if convicted at trial. He admitted planning an al-Qaeda operation to sink a civilian petroleum tanker near the Strait of Hormuz, which resulted in the attack on the MV *Limburg*, killing a Bulgarian crew member and wounding 12 sailors. In October 2017 he was sentenced to 13 years, a term that began when he pleaded in February 2014 and which he would serve in Saudi Arabia from February 2018.[190]

Majid Shoukat Khan

In his April 2007 CSRT Khan denied all of the charges and the evidence to support them.

> I am not al-Qaida. To be al-Qaida, a person needs to be trained in Afghanistan and needs to take an oath in front of USAMA BIN LADEN. I have never been to Afghanistan and I have never met UBL. I cannot possibly be a member of al-Qaida. I admit I can't prove that I am not al-Qaida. It is very difficult to prove that someone is not al-Qaida.

In February 2012 Khan was charged with conspiracy, murder, attempted murder, material support, and spying by joining al-Qaeda in Pakistan to plan attacks in the USA, Indonesia, and elsewhere.[191] A week later he agreed to plead and testify against others (including KSM, Hambali, and al-Baluchi); sentencing would be postponed for four years, after which he would be eligible for transfer to Pakistan. He would serve no more than 19 years (in addition to the 9 he had already spent in detention); if convicted at trial, he faced life. His military defense counsel said "this is his best shot at going home." CCR, his civilian counsel, said: "we have a fundamental obligation to act in his best interest and to try and help him achieve the best outcome for him – regardless of how that might be viewed politically." As part of the deal he described meeting KSM in Karachi in 2002 and talking about plots, including blowing up gasoline tanks in the USA and a suicide bombing of President Pervez Musharraf. He delivered $50,000 to finance the bombing of the Marriott Hotel in Jakarta in 2003. Andrew Rosenthal wrote in his *New York Times* column that the case showed MCs were "an enormous and easily avoidable mistake." The *Washington Post* praised the "fair but appropriately tough plea deal that should smooth the way for a military trial of the alleged 9/11 perpetrators." "By vastly improving military commissions," the 2009 law gave them "legitimacy," which "rightly helped to ward off legal challenges to the system and paved the way for last week's progress." Khan's February 2016 sentencing hearing was postponed for three more years because the MCs in which he was to testify (especially al-Nashiri's) had not proceeded.[192]

In September 2016 Khan withdrew his guilty plea in light of the DC Circuit's 2014 decision in *al-Bahlul* that material support was not a war crime (even though this would not change his sentence).[193] He wanted "to show some kind of compunction to the families that my ... grotesque and pernicious actions, may have caused some understandably nonvenal pain."

Ibrahim Ahmed Mahmoud al Qosi

After al Qosi was charged in February 2008, he refused to participate in the MC.[194] "The only war crime I committed and for which I'm being tried today before you and which I admit having committed is, in truth, my nationality. My crime is that I'm a Sudanese citizen." Declaring he would represent himself, he quoted an Al Jazeera report that the 9/11 attacks had dealt a harsh blow to the US "militarily, economically, in security and spiritwise."

> After the collapse of the towers, after the collapse of the Pentagon, all these false masks fell away and your wrongs were exposed. The whole world has had a headache from your hypocrisy that you are the land of justice.

He said that MCs were sham courts that "move at the pace of a turtle in order to gain some time and keep us in these boxes without any human or legal rights." Cmdr. Susan Lachelier, his military defense counsel, quickly interrupted her client, urging Air Force LtCol. Nancy J. Paul, the judge, to order a psychiatric examination and noting that al Qosi had twice refused to meet with her. But he resisted: "I am not in any disturbed state." He had been waiting years to have his say. Paul let him read his prepared statement but ordered Lachelier to represent him against his wishes. Lachelier asked for time to consult the ethical rules in California and Virginia. She also said al Qosi's decisions might have been influenced by the fact that he had been shackled, hooded, and made to wear noise-canceling headphones on his way to court. But Paul denied Lachelier's request to meet al Qosi in his cell.

In December 2009 Paul denied a prosecution motion to amend the charges. In July 2010 al Qosi pleaded guilty to material support and conspiracy. He acknowledged following bin Laden from Sudan to Afghanistan in 1998 and serving as quartermaster, cook, bodyguard, and driver. A month later he was sentenced to 14 years. But the military jury was not told that a secret plea bargain limited this to only two more years in detention in addition to the eight he had already served. Paul ordered that the true sentence be kept secret until he was released. The CA approved the sentence in February 2011, suspending everything in excess of two years. On July 10, 2012, when al Qosi had completed the two extra years, he was transferred to Sudan. His appellate counsel, Navy Capt. Mary McCormick, moved to extend the two-year period within which he could petition for a new trial, but this was denied by the CMCR in February 2013 and CA in December 2013. The reason was that McCormick could not prove al Qosi wanted to petition; but in a typical military Catch-22 both bodies denied her funds to travel to Sudan to ask him. The CMCR affirmed the conviction on the same ground in April 2014, and the DC Circuit denied review in May 2015. However, in June 2016 the CMCR found that Lachelier had demonstrated an attorney–client relationship, and remanded to the CA to order an MC hearing on whether al Qosi had authorized the appeal and was an unprivileged enemy belligerent currently engaged in hostilities against the USA or coalition partners. In April 2017 chief defense counsel BGen. John Baker asserted the MCA 2009 gave every convict an automatic appeal unless he explicitly waived it, and a guilty plea was not a waiver. "The whole system is insane."

Mohammed Kamin

At his first pretrial hearing on May 20, 2008, Kamin, an Afghani, had visible injuries on his face.[195] Air Force Col. W. Thomas Cumbie, the judge, had had him forcibly extracted from his cell (because attendance at arraignment is compulsory) and said Kamin had bit and spit on a guard. Kamin declared: "I don't want any trial. The trials are yours, the courts are yours. How can I trust you? I don't expect anything good from you. I am helpless. You have the force." Asked if he understood his rights, he said he trusted only Allah. "Whatever is God's will, I will face. My judge is the God who created the sky and the land. He will be my lawyer and represent me. I wait for his decision. That is enough." "I don't want [Navy Lt. Richard Federico, his assigned military lawyer]. I don't want another one. I didn't want to come to court." He was the sixth detainee to boycott his trial; seven of the eight arraigned had either fired their lawyers or refused to attend after arraignment. Federico said his ethical obligation would be "to essentially not represent him." Cumbie ruled that unless Federico produced an ethical ruling from the Indiana bar, he would have to represent Kamin. Federico replied: "it is a legitimate defense to boycott. This is what he has clearly indicated he wants to do. So then what authority do I have in defining the scope of representation?" Federico had met Kamin twice. "He's unequivocally stated, 'I don't want your help.' I don't feel that he understands his options. I don't feel that he has good exposure, experience or understanding, at all ... of his fundamental rights and due process in the American legal system."

The prosecutor had told Federico that Kamin's medical records exhibited signs of mental illness. Cumbie told the prison camp to give them to the prosecutor, who should read them and give relevant portions to the defense. In July the prosecution requested a three-month delay.

After Holder announced in November 2009 that the five HVDs would be tried in civilian court, Federico said to Cumbie: "the fact that we are standing here in this courtroom today suggests that we are going to proceed to military commissions." Cumbie replied: "that would be my assumption too." But DoD had not yet released the new MC rules required by the MCA of 2009. After 18 months of pretrial motions the prosecution finally gave the defense the interrogation log showing that Kamin had been questioned 17 times, but summaries or transcripts of only four interrogations were included. Capt. Clay West, the other military defense counsel, said two Afghan men initially interrogated Kamin; but they could not be found by the USA, and Cumbie suggested "they might be dead." Federico said the charge of material support could not be tried in an MC; Cumbie took that under consideration. Federico moved to dismiss because MCs were empowered to try "enemy combatants," but the new administration called them "unprivileged belligerents." Cumbie warned he might forcibly extract Kamin to compel his attendance. But the charges were dismissed without prejudice in December 2009, a Periodic Review Board cleared Kamin for transfer in October 2015, and he was sent to UAE in August 2016.

Noor Uthman Muhammed

In October 2008 the government dismissed the charges against Muhammed, a Sudanese accused of training al-Qaeda recruits in Afghanistan.[196] This followed Vandeveld's resignation, although Morris insisted the actions were unrelated. Charges were refiled in April 2010 before Navy Capt. Moira Modzelewski. In February 2011 Muhammed pleaded guilty to material support and conspiracy, admitting he had left Sudan for Afghanistan in 1994 to get military training at Khalden Camp. But he denied this was an al-Qaeda facility and maintained he was not a member.

He fled Afghanistan after the US invasion, ending up in a safe house in Pakistan, where he made IED detonators. At his sentencing hearing his lawyers described how he had been shackled in Bagram, subjected to heat, cold, and deafening music, and stripped naked in front of female soldiers. Although the jury sentenced him to 14 years, a secret plea agreement capped this at 34 months. He was sent back to Sudan in December 2013. His conviction was overturned in January 2015 because the CA found that material support was not a war crime.

Abdul Hadi al-Iraqi

Hadi was charged in June 2013, and a conspiracy charge was added in February 2014.[197] Although the DC Circuit had rejected such a charge in *al-Bahlul,* that case dealt with conduct predating the MCA of 2006, whereas Hadi was captured in late 2006 or early 2007. He was arraigned in June 2014 on charges of overseeing plots to attack US forces in Afghanistan and assassinate former Pakistani President Pervez Musharraf. In November, Navy Capt. J.K. Waits, the judge, ordered an end to the use of female guards to move Hadi to meetings with his lawyers. Prosecutors had barred prison staff from talking to defense lawyers about this (claiming they had misunderstood the SJA's advice). And prosecutors also drafted a document advising potential defense witnesses that they had the right not to testify. RAdm. Kyle Cozad, the prison commander, was "opposed to discrimination" in his guard force and claimed to be unaware that women guards had not touched HVDs for years. Prosecutors said the order "ignores established precedent requiring deference to prison administrators." Women are "enmeshed and essential ... to the safe and effective function of the HVD camp." Female guards filed a sex discrimination complaint challenging the ban. A defense lawyer responded by asking the judge to expand the ban. Waits preemptively rejected any claim that he might be influenced by the sex discrimination complaint but rescinded his order on February 24; defense lawyers considered an appeal. They also moved to dismiss for lack of personal jurisdiction because the MCA 2015 violated the Equal Protection and Due Process Clauses and to dismiss co-conspirator liability, but Waits postponed that until trial.

In July 2015 Hadi said he wanted to fire his military lawyers, with whom he had a "very disturbed relationship." Waits declared an indefinite recess, observing: "we're in a little bit of a limbo." Marine LtCol. Sean Gleason, who had been reassigned from Hadi to al-Hawsawi in 2013, had documents recording conversations (between the two defendants) that could harm Hadi. Hadi was satisfied with his other military lawyer, LtCol. Tom Jasper, who said his client had never consented to Gleason's transfer. Hadi told Waits: "Gleason has lots of information concerning me, and I don't know in the future whether he'll use it for me or against me." The defense objected to receiving at the last minute a 10-page document the prosecution had had for years, which forced them to review it in only two days. Jasper himself had joined the defense team only in September 2014 (when another military lawyer, Col. Chris Callen, returned to civilian life). Air Force Maj. Ben Stirk was the only defense lawyer who had attended all five hearings. In September 2015 Hadi fired Jasper and Stirk. The new chief defense counsel, Marine BGen. John Baker, appointed Army Maj. Robert Kinkaid to try to develop a relationship with Hadi, but Kinkaid did not have the necessary security clearance for this. In November Baker detailed three new military defense counsel, accepted two pro bono civilian defense counsel and was hiring a DoD civilian defense counsel. As a result, Waits canceled hearings scheduled for November 2015 and January and April 2016. In July the defense sought a delay while its four new pro bono civilian lawyers obtained security clearance. Accusing the defense of stalling, the chief prosecutor replied that because the death penalty did not apply, Hadi was entitled to only one civilian lawyer. Waits advised the prosecution: "this is not a court in the United States. Why aren't you talking about" whether the Constitution applies at all. When the prosecutor attributed his failure to do so to "constitutional avoidance," the defense retorted that he could not invoke that doctrine unless the Constitution applied. In November Waits (who had been commuting from Italy) was replaced by Marine Col. Peter S. Rubin, who allowed himself to be voir dired. In January 2017 Hadi appeared in court with bruises he claimed were the result of resisting being touched by a female guard. In April Hadi's civilian lawyer Brent Rushforth asked whether Hadi would be released if found innocent, moving to abate the proceedings until the question was answered. The prosecution called that "an impossible request." The judge said: "it depends, asterisk, on a number of factors unknown at this time." Later that year, hearings were repeatedly postponed to treat injuries inflicted during detention.[198]

Faiz al Kandari

In June 2012 prosecutors dropped four-year-old charges that Faiz al Kandari trained with al-Qaeda, was a driver for bin Laden, and produced recruitment videos.[199] The same day the Kuwaiti ambassador disclosed that he was talking to the USA about releasing al Kandari and the only other Kuwaiti detainee. Al Kandari was transferred to Kuwait on January 8, 2016.

HIGH-VALUE DETAINEES: 9/11 CONSPIRATORS AND AL-NASHIRI (*USS COLE*)[200]

The 19 cases discussed above were just a prelude to the central drama. The real test of the MCs was how they compared to the Nuremberg Trials in prosecuting the ringleaders of the "war on terror": the five HVDs, accused of the 9/11 attacks, and Abd al-Rahim al-Nashiri, accused of attacking the *USS Cole*.

Ramzi bin al-Shibh refused to appear at his March 9, 2007 CSRT. His personal representative reported that the detainee had been "uncooperative and unresponsive" during four meetings over the previous month. At his CSRT the next day, by contrast, Khalid Sheikh Mohammed (KSM) declared on oath (through his personal representative) that he had sworn *bayat* to bin Laden and was a member of the al-Qaeda Council, media operations director under al-Zawahiri, and operational director for the 9/11 attack. He boasted he had been responsible for the 1993 World Trade Center and shoe bomber operations and the Bali nightclub attack, had "decapitated with my blessed right hand the head of the American Jew, Daniel Pearl," and had planned the second wave of attacks in the USA, and others there and elsewhere (all of which he specified). In his CSRT on March 12, Walid Muhammad Salih Mubarek bin 'Attash's personal representative said the "detainee stated the facts on the operations" against the US embassies in East Africa and the *USS Cole* "were mixed up, but the facts are the facts. Facts of the operation are correct and his involvements are correct, but the details are not correct. Detainee did not wish to correct the details." In his CSRT on March 14, al-Nashiri declared that his "confession" had been produced by torture and denied most of the specific and general allegations, including that he was a member of al-Qaeda. In his CSRT on March 21, Mustafa Ahmed Adam al-Hawsawi admitted most of the factual allegations. He denied having been a member of al-Qaeda but admitted knowing al-Zawahiri and KSM and training at al-Qaeda camps. He had met bin Laden had but not sworn allegiance to him. In his CSRT on March 30, Ali Abdul Aziz Ali (aka Ammar al-Baluchi) admitted he was KSM's nephew but denied all the specific and general allegations. "I do not belong to al-Qaida, the Taliban or associated organizations. I do not have any I.D. card showing that I am a member. I have never received any military training in Afghanistan. I refuse to be called or classified as an enemy combatant."

In February 2008, the military charged the five HVDs and Mohamed al Kahtani (Qahtani) with conspiracy, murder, attacking civilians and civilian objects, destruction of property, terrorism, and material support, and also charged the first four with hijacking (all accused were subject to the death penalty).[201] The *Los Angeles Times* declared that "in the eyes of many in this country and the world, the jury-rigged system of justice for detainees at Guantánamo Bay will be on trial along with the defendants." "Military prosecutors could spare the country further embarrassment by announcing that they would not need to present any testimony coerced by waterboarding," but Hartmann had left that to the judges. "[T]he possibility that a suspect could be put to death in the United States based on statements coerced from him by torture is an abomination." Unless the trial excluded coerced evidence, it "will fail at its most important task: to show the world that the 9/11 terrorists were not noble freedom fighters but common criminals, who committed mass murder." The *Washington Post* reminded readers that when the 1946 convictions of 73 Nazi officers and soldiers for killing a hundred US POWs were shown to have been obtained "through coercive methods, including torture," the "indignation at the treatment of the defendants at the hands of the U.S. government" was so great that "none of the defendants was executed, and eventually all were released." Those "lessons should be heeded." The goal of a "fair trial worthy of the world's leading democracy" was "in doubt because of the flaws inherent in military commissions," including coerced evidence, hearsay, and the inability of lawyers to discuss classified evidence with their clients. The *New York Times* predicted that "instead of being what they could and should be – a model of justice dispensed impartially, surely and dispassionately – the trials will proceed under deeply flawed procedures that violate this country's basic fairness." It cited the same defects as the *Post*, adding that "hanging over it all is the Kafkaesque fact that even if the defendants were somehow to beat the charges, they would not be set free." Former chief prosecutor Davis wrote in a *New York Times* op ed that "an obvious step" in recovering "the moral high ground" would be "to prohibit the use of evidence derived by waterboarding in criminal proceedings."[202] He had been "overruled on the question, and I resigned my position to call attention to the issue." He expected to be called as a witness for Hamdan and was "more than happy to testify." When DoD general counsel Haynes had boasted to him in August 2005 that "these trials will be the Nuremberg of our time," Davis had replied: "if we come up short and there are some acquittals in our cases it will at least validate the process." Haynes's eyes widened, and he said: "wait a minute, we can't have acquittals. If we've been holding these guys for so long, how can we explain letting them get off? ... we've got to have convictions."

In April, Morris (who had succeeded Davis as prosecutor but also resigned) said he had been told to focus on a detainee with "blood on his hands" to excite the public.[203] Pressure increased after the HVDs were sent to Guantánamo. "There was that consistent theme that if we didn't get this thing rolling before the election, it was going to implode. Once you got the victim families energized and the cases rolling, whoever won the White House would have difficulty stopping the proceeding." Davis said he was denied a medal for two years of work on the MCs because he had resigned and spoken out.

Prosecutors dropped the charges against al-Qahtani in May.[204] Crawford later explained: "We tortured Qahtani," which "tainted everything going forward." Hartmann claimed this showed "the strength of the system and the careful, deliberative and fair legal process in place at Guantánamo." The five HVDs moved before Kohlmann, the judge, to dismiss the charges because Judge Allred had found in the *Hamdan* MC that Hartmann had engaged in "unlawful influence."[205] In a June interview Hartmann said "the protections provided to" MC defendants "are very, very similar to the protections that would be provided to me in connection with a military court-martial."[206] Even in Nuremberg – "the gold standard" – there were no rules of evidence, guilt did not have to be proved beyond a reasonable doubt, and death sentences were carried out in a week "because there were no appellate rights." The five HVDs and al-Nashiri had ten military and eight civilian lawyers. Prosecutors had told Hartmann "that the amount of classified information that will be used in the cases will be relatively minor." "We've been required to make sure" MCs are "fair, open, just, honest, and we're going to do that."

The five HVDs were arraigned on June 5.[207] Before the hearing began they were allowed to interact for 15–20 minutes for the first time in years. Speaking first, KSM railed against Bush and "crusades" and disavowed the MC, refusing representation from any American citizen. "I consider all American laws under the Constitution to be evil and not of God." When Kohlmann interrupted, KSM said "go ahead," giving him permission to speak, but then expostulated: "all of this has been taken under torturing. Then after torturing, they transfer us to inquisition land here at Guantánamo, and you tell everyone to sit down, sit down." The others followed his lead. Al-Baluchi said:

everything that has happened here is unfair and unjust ... The government is talking about lawyers free of charge. The government also tortured me free of charge all these years. Lawyers are decorative. They cannot talk on our behalf ... But the court already made decision that is behind the desk. This is a staged play. I don't want anyone to bother with my case.

Army Maj. John Jackson (representing al-Hawsawi) objected to letting the defendants converse. He had spent 20 hours building rapport, only to see his client's demeanor change in the courtroom. "It was clear Mr. Mohammed was trying to intimidate Mr. al-Hawsawi into not having us as counsel. He was shaking." Calling this "the most prejudicial use of joinder" he had ever seen, Jackson said he would move to sever. LCdr. Brian Mizer said al-Baluchi had agreed to accept legal representation but changed his mind in court. Bin al-Shibh's lawyers said they had only learned at 9 p.m. the previous night that their client was taking psychotropic drugs, which could affect his ability to make decisions.

Kohlmann denied KSM's request that the five be allowed to plan their joint defense. He allowed military counsel to serve as standby advisers to KSM, bin 'Attash and al-Baluchi. The role of civilian counsel remained unclear, as did the question of how classified information would be shared with pro se defendants. The sound was cut off a half-dozen times, twice when KSM discussed torture. After al-Baluchi said "if I was given a lawyer the first day when they arrested me," the audio cut out for 90 seconds. When bin al-Shibh started explaining why he was taking psychotropic drugs, it shut off for four minutes. Navy Capt. Prescott Prince, KSM's chief military defense counsel, said it was "impossible to ethically and properly represent our clients." "In a capital murder case involving thousands of victims, it is just unbelievable that many members of the defense team have barely been able to meet with their clients, and some not at all." David Nevin, a civilian lawyer, had met KSM for just five hours two days earlier. He objected to Kohlmann's questions about choice of counsel and the defendants' competence. But Kohlmann had denied requests for a postponement by Nevin and Tom Durkin (bin al-Shibh's civilian counsel). Al-Baluchi asked: "if my case is a capital case, shouldn't I have a capital defense team before my arraignment?" But Kohlmann said "this is not a MCA rule." Only some of the accused had read the charges. Asked if he had examined the evidence, bin 'Attash replied that some papers were "secret," but he did not know what that meant. Al-Baluchi said he had seen the evidence if

Kohlmann meant "the information that was forced out of me." Asked if they understood the death penalty, KSM declared: "I have [been] looking to be a martyr from long time." The others followed suit. Bin al-Shibh said: "I have been seeking martyrdom for five years. I tried for 9/11 to get a visa, and I could not. If this martyrdom happens today, I welcome it. God is great." Bin 'Attash said they all wanted to be martyrs. Al-Hawsawi was confused: "you expect me to face death? You expect me to accept punishment when I have not looked at the charges?" Some 9/11 victims' relatives objected that the DoD's invitation to just one observer – Debra Burlingame, who "has made clear her support for the Bush Administration" – was "but the latest example of a covert, politicized military commission system that has little hope of bringing any legitimate outcome."

The *Washington Post* compared the "far less fair" MCs to Zacarias Moussaoui's civilian trial (see Chapter 2).[208] The government "has made a mockery of the proceedings by refusing detainees some basic elements of due process." Although KSM had been waterboarded, he could not "raise questions about his treatment." "The detainees are prohibited from seeing or responding to certain evidence that may prove crucial to their defense." If the Supreme Court were to hold in *Boumediene* (a decision expected within weeks) that Guantánamo detainees possessed constitutional rights, "Congress and the administration should remake the system to provide detainees with as many as possible of the protections that are available in federal court. This would not only bolster the legitimacy of the proceedings, it would also help to restore the image of the United States in the eyes of the world."

In response to questions, OMC said: "it is possible that an accused representing himself will not be able to directly review some evidence; in such circumstances, his standby defense counsel might be involved." Hartmann had declared in February: "there will be no secret trials. Every piece of evidence, every stitch of evidence, every whiff of evidence that goes to the finder of fact ... will be reviewed by the accused, subject to confrontation." Now the OMC reaffirmed that "if the military judge agrees that the classified information is relevant and material to the defense and that there is no reasonable alternative, then the military judge may order the prosecution to disclose the classified information or dismiss the charge and specification to which the classified information pertains."

Al-Nashiri was charged at the end of June 2008.[209] He was alleged to have been the primary planner of the 2000 attack on the *USS Cole*, to have attempted to bomb the USS *The Sullivans* in 2000, and to have been involved in the attack on the French supertanker MV *Limburg* in 2002. He had been waterboarded. The CA confirmed the charges in December 2009. After President Obama was inaugurated, the prosecution requested a 120-day delay, but Col. Pohl, the judge, found its reasoning "unpersuasive" and refused (although all the other judges granted those requests). A week later Crawford dropped the charges.

In separate hearings in July 2008, KSM and bin 'Attash (acting pro se with military backup attorneys) complained they had not received recent court filings or got them in only English.[210] Three letters KSM had written to backup counsel more than a month earlier had not been delivered. When bin 'Attash asked why he could not read classified reports since he expected to be executed, Kohlmann replied that he did not have the necessary security clearance. Al-Baluchi said he had written two letters and a legal motion that never reached the judge.

KSM complained that guards refused to give him paper to prepare motions. Kohlmann seemed shocked and – in a typical Catch-22 – promised to investigate if defendants filed a motion. He told al-Hawsawi and al-Baluchi: "it would be best for you to accept the assistance of counsel. If it sounds as if I am trying to talk you out of representing yourself, that would be accurate." They could not communicate with potential witnesses and would have to draft opening and closing statements and legal motions. "All of these things are usually done in a trial better by a lawyer with special knowledge and experience with the laws and procedures. In addition, you will not be given access to classified materials before trial." Prosecutors had asked him to give this advice. Kohlmann ordered individual hearings to determine whether the other defendants had been unduly influenced by KSM. But al-Hawsawi and al-Baluchi insisted they had not been coerced. Al-Baluchi declared: "nobody is in a position to give such an order. I'm a free human being. I'm not a slave." "There are a lot of reasons" why he wanted to represent himself: "some religious issues, ethical issues and, third, I am not satisfied with the proceedings." KSM's lawyers complained that the government had decreed that anything he said or wrote was classified. After bin al-Shibh refused to attend his hearing, Kohlmann ordered that a "Sanity Board" of military medical staff report on him, but refused a defense request for an examination by independent psychiatrists.

In July WD Wash Judge Coughenour, who had tried Ahmed Ressam (the Millennium bomber, see Chapter 2), wrote in a *Washington Post* op ed that federal courts "are not only an adequate venue for trying terrorism suspects but are also a tremendous asset in combating terrorism."[211] "Do we want our courts to be viewed as another tool in the 'war on terrorism,' or do we want them to stand as a bulwark against the corrupt ideology upon which terrorism feeds?" "Courts guarantee an independent process, not an outcome. Any tribunal purporting to do otherwise is not a court." "If politically vulnerable actors start redesigning courts, it is conceivable that popular pressure would soon demand the admission of statements obtained by harsh interrogation techniques, or dictate that defense counsel cannot access information needed to mount a defense." The *Washington Post* replied in an editorial the same day that "modern realities strongly argue against using federal courts as the exclusive arena to hold or try all terrorism suspects."[212] "The openness of federal court proceedings risks handing unclassified but valuable information to those who would harm this country." The *Post* advocated a national security court with "slightly more relaxed evidentiary standards."

In September KSM (on behalf of the other HVDs) voir dired Kohlmann for several hours.[213] "The government considers all of us fanatical extremists. How can you, as an officer of the U.S. Marine Corps stand over me in judgment?" He asked about Kohlmann's religious affiliation and views about torture, offering sarcastic political commentary: "I believe that we are part of an inquisition." "We are your enemy." Kohlmann threatened to terminate KSM's self-representation: "I will not allow you to act in a manner that is disrespectful to this court." Bin al-Shibh initially refused to attend, but changed his mind after the other defendants (at Kohlmann's request) asked him to do so. Saying he also wanted to represent himself, he joined the voir dire: "As far as I know, your last name is Kohlmann, which is a Jewish name." The judge replied he was Protestant but not particularly religious. The defendants and their lawyers submitted another list of obstacles to a fair trial: lawyer–client conversations were not confidential; translators were incompetent; and defense lawyers could not talk to friends and family of the accused without prosecutors knowing. In October Kohlmann allowed bin al-Shibh's lawyers to inspect his conditions of confinement as part of the inquiry into his mental health.[214]

Defense lawyers objected to interpreter incompetence.[215] One rendered al-Hawsawi's statement as: "in the beginning of the timing of the laws, I said there is no difficulties base." Al-Baluchi, a fluent English speaker, corrected another interpreter, who admitted his error. A defense linguist estimated that half of what al-Hawsawi said was incorrectly translated, and al-Hawsawi did not understand at least 25 percent of what was said in English. Translators' identities were classified, and defense lawyers could not examine their resumes. But the defense learned that one was a former schoolteacher with no prior experience in simultaneous translation; and another, after arriving in Guantánamo, announced he was unqualified. Kohlmann removed an interpreter who rendered the words "Osama bin Laden's driver" as "Osama bin Laden's lawyer." Al-Baluchi complained that when he said "top secret" in Arabic, it was translated as "very, very private." Kohlmann responded by telling defense lawyers to raise their hands when interpreters made an error (how would the lawyers know?) and asking everyone to speak more slowly.

In September Hartmann was removed as legal adviser to the CA but remained as director of operations, planning, and development.[216] DoD acting general counsel Dell'Orto said: "in no small part because of [Hartmann's] efforts and his dedication, the commissions are an active, operational legal system." A month later DoD revealed that Internal Affairs was investigating Hartmann after a preliminary inquiry found evidence that he: bullied prosecutors, logistics officials, and others at Guantánamo into taking cases to trial before they were ready and prosecuting at least one individual on unwarranted charges; advocated using coerced evidence over prosecutors' objections; and made intentionally misleading statements in public and during proceedings to downplay his direct role in overseeing all prosecutions. Separately, the DoD OIG was investigating complaints by at least two military officials about Hartmann's abusive and retaliatory behavior. One complainant was a defense lawyer, Maj. Frakt, who believed Hartmann "has acted in a manner that raises substantial questions as to his honesty, professionalism and fitness as a lawyer, and ... his conduct has been prejudicial to the fair administration of justice." In November Hartmann submitted his retirement papers.

The military planned to fly some relatives of 9/11 victims to Guantánamo for the HVD hearings and enable hundreds of others to watch them through video links on military bases.[217] Deputy Defense Secretary England said they "will have the opportunity to see firsthand the fair, open and just trials."

In November 2008 Kohlmann announced his retirement (which had been scheduled for April 2008).[218] He was replaced in the HVD MC by Army Col. Stephen Henley, who would have to hold a new voir dire. In December Col. Pohl replaced Kohlmann as chief judge. On

December 8 Henley began the proceedings by reading a statement the five HVDs had prepared during 27 hours of joint meetings.[219] (Although the defendants had submitted it a month earlier, Henley read it only the day before the proceedings because he could read communications from HVDs only in a secure facility, to which he had lacked access. KSM expressed amazement: "are the military commissions using carrier pigeons or what?") The defendants wanted to "withdraw all motions … and wished to enter pleas in what was termed as confessions in this case … We all five have reached an agreement to request from the commission an immediate hearing session in order to announce our confessions … without being under any kind of pressure, threat, intimidations or promise from any party."

Four had expressed their desire to die as martyrs during their June arraignment; al-Hawsawi now joined them. KSM said: "we don't want to waste our time with motions. All of you are paid by the U.S. government. I'm not trusting any American." Al-Baluchi said: "all of these decisions are undertaken by us without any pressure or influence by Khalid Sheik." Bin al-Shibh said: "We the brothers, all of us, would like to submit our confession." But given the opportunity to enter pleas later that day, KSM, bin 'Attash and al-Baluchi (who were representing themselves) declined out of concern that pleading without the jury present might render them ineligible for execution.

Morris, the prosecutor, said the UCMJ prohibited pleas in capital cases. Col. Henley asked both sides for briefs on whether he could accept a plea. He refused to let bin al-Shibh and al-Hawsawi represent themselves until he reviewed their psychological evaluations. Learning they could not plead together, the five decided to wait. At the end of the day bin al-Shibh said: "I want to send my greetings to bin Laden and I want to reaffirm my allegiance. I hope the jihad continues and strikes the heart of America with all kinds of weapons of mass destruction."

Nine relatives of 9/11 victims watched the hearing in Guantánamo. Hamilton Peterson said the defendants' "demeanor showed a complete absence of contrition." "They seemed to view these proceedings as a joke." Alice Hoagland opposed the death penalty. "There are worse things than death, and one would be to spend their lives under the total control of people they hate. They do not deserve to be dealt with as martyrs. They do not deserve the glory of execution." A letter from other relatives, coordinated by the ACLU, said: "many of us do not believe these military commissions to be fair, in accordance with

American values, or capable of achieving the justice that 9/11 family members and all Americans deserve."

The *Washington Post* said the MCs:

> have again become a forum for the absurd. Henley should reject the defendants' pleas, which seem clearly aimed at undermining the legal process and scoring a propaganda coup for their warped cause. This is made all the more possible because of the deeply flawed nature of the Guantánamo proceedings, which deny the detainees basic due-process rights that are available in civilian courts ... Mr. Obama should either work with Congress to revamp the military commissions to include far more transparency and robust rights for defendants, or he should suspend them in favor of federal court trials ... [which] would immediately infuse a level of legitimacy that has been sorely lacking in the Guantánamo proceedings.

After Obama's election, his legal advisers met with OMC and DoD officials.[220] Hartmann vigorously defended the MCs. But Navy Capt. Patrick McCarthy, a senior lawyer who worked closely with Hartmann, gave a sworn deposition stating that Hartmann had demanded prosecution access to all sorts of sensitive records, including International Committee of the Red Cross (ICRC) reports and "videotapes of foreign delegations meeting with their nationals." The previous spring Hartmann had argued that medical and intelligence records should be available to prosecutors and rejected claims of doctor–patient privilege.

Henley signed a protective order presumptively classifying any reference to the CIA, FBI, or DoS, allowing the court to classify information already in the public domain, and presumptively classifying "any statements made by the accused."[221] Waving a copy of a *Washington Post* interview in which Crawford said al-Qaeda members had been tortured, KSM declared: "Everybody knows this order was written by the CIA. Their true reason is to protect themselves against their own wrongdoing." Chief prosecutor Morris said the order contained "standard language used in numerous other counterterrorism, counterespionage or habeas detainee cases in federal court." Defense lawyers were under a secret order not to discuss any document in the case until it was released by the judge.

On his first full day in office, Obama suspended the MCs.[222] The *New York Times* praised this "obvious and vital step." They were "a mockery of American standards of justice and due process." "There is no good reason to restart these trials." The *Washington Post* said

Obama "has moved one step closer to ending the discredited practices for handling detainees that have blemished the United States' reputation worldwide." "Relying on a deeply flawed and unjust legal process such as the one in place at Guantánamo is untenable." At the beginning of February 2009 Obama assured 40 relatives of 9/11 victims that those responsible for the attack would be brought "to a swift and certain justice."[223] He had only hit the "pause button" by suspending the 21 prosecutions.

In March the five HVDs, calling themselves the "9/11 Shura Council," filed a 9-page document with the judge entitled "The Islamic Response to the Government's Nine Accusations."[224] "To us, they are not accusations. To us they are a badge of honor, which we carry with honor." "Your intelligence apparatus, with all its abilities, human and logistical, had failed to discover our military attack plans before the blessed 11 September operation. We are terrorists to the bone."

At the beginning of May, administration officials said some HVDs would be prosecuted in federal courts but MCs would remain an option.[225] A week later the administration said MCs would resume under new rules excluding evidence obtained by coercion, tightening the admissibility of hearsay, and giving detainees more freedom in choosing lawyers. Obama said: "this is the best way to protect our country, while upholding our deeply held values." "Military commissions have a long tradition in the United States. They are appropriate for trying enemies who violate the laws of war, provided that they are properly structured and administered." But Maj. Frakt dismissed the new rules as "minor cosmetic changes." He said that detainees had not complained about the particular lawyers assigned. "The problem is they don't want military counsel at all." Sen. McConnell called it "an encouraging development." Sen. Levin said MCs could play "a legitimate role in prosecuting."

The *New York Times* condemned the president's "lack of resolve" about "Bush's kangaroo courts," which presidential candidate Obama had "denounced passionately and frequently during the 2008 campaign," declaring on August 7: "I have faith in America's courts ... As president, I'll ... reject the MCA ... Our Constitution and our UCMJ provide a framework for dealing with terrorists." The *Times* said the rule changes were "not enough. The entire edifice must be scrapped and the laws that long governed military and civilian criminal trials put back in force." The HVDs "should be tried in civilian criminal courts ... treating them as warriors not only demeans civilian and military justice, but it gives terrorists the martyrdom they crave." The *Washington Post* called the changes "welcome" but said "more robust protections" were necessary, including ways to share classified information and a clear path for appeal. The *Wall Street Journal* ridiculed the changes. "Enemy combatants already have better access to attorneys – white shoe and pro bono, no less, than nearly every criminal defendant in America." The existing rules about hearsay "are nearly indistinguishable from those of the ICC [International Criminal Court]." Obama had "decided to pre-serve a tribunal process that will be identical in every material way to the one favored by Dick Cheney" and offer "the fairest and most open war-crimes trial in U.S. history."

In June the administration circulated a secret proposal to let those charged with death penalty offenses plead guilty (which the UCMJ prohibited).[226] Addressing the SJC a week later, Attorney General Holder estimated that about a quarter of the Guantánamo detainees (57) might be tried. In testimony before SASC, DoD General Counsel Jeh Johnson said: "where feasible, we would seek to prosecute detainees in [federal] courts." Those acquitted or given short sentences might be detained after release. David Kris, Assistant Attorney General for National Security, said defendants before the MCs were protected by some due process guarantees; but Johnson added they "do not enjoy the full panoply of constitutional rights." Darrel Vandeveld, the former prosecutor, said MCs were "broken and beyond repair."

The *New York Times* said the MCA 2009 introduced by Sen. Levin and unanimously approved by SASC was "a good first draft."[227] It gave defendants access to more evidence and barred coerced evidence (but was too vague in defining cruel, inhuman, or degrading treatment). Prosecutors had to justify the introduction of hearsay. The *Times* agreed with Johnson and Kris that MCs should not hear charges of material support. And it agreed with defense lawyers that their resources should equal those of the prosecution. In October the *Washington Post* said the bill "does a good job of ensuring fairness for detainees while giving the government a solid framework to prosecute alleged war criminals," but the *Post* reiterated that "the federal courts should be the preferred venue." Congress passed the Act on October 22.

In August the Guantánamo Detainee Task Force referred a "signifi-cant number of cases" to US Attorneys in SDNY, EDNY and ED Va for possible prosecution.[228] Sens. Graham, Lieberman, McCain, and Webb protested to Obama. "Such trials would treat the war on terrorism as a law enforcement operation, rather than a war, and would treat its alleged perpetrators as common criminals, instead of violators of the law of war."

A month later the *New York Times* endorsed civilian trials, denouncing Bush's "military tribunals where guilty verdicts were guaranteed." "[R]esistance to criminal trials for the worst terrorism suspects does not come only from a desire to safeguard what the intelligence agencies know. It also springs from a desire to cover up what the agencies did."

At a September hearing, KSM, bin 'Attash, and al-Baluchi read aloud a letter to Henley saying they had no objections to the government's proposed 60-day delay.[229]

> We send our greeting to [bin Laden, al-Zawahiri and Mullah Omar] on the occasion of the anniversary of eight years past on the most noble victory known to history over the forces of oppression and tyranny in the Washington and Manhattan attack ... I put my trust in Allah, so devise your plot ... then pass your sentence on me and give me no respite.

That month bin al-Shibh's lawyers filed an emergency mandamus petition in the DC Circuit, seeking to enjoin his MC.[230] During a July hearing, Henley had cut off discussion after consulting with the court security officer and instructed counsel to discuss only what happened to bin al-Shibh after he left CIA custody. The two court-appointed military psychiatrists found bin al-Shibh had a "delusional disorder" and was taking psychotropic medicines. The defense still wanted its own experts to examine him. Defense lawyers also complained that an FBI investigation of allegations that military defense counsel gave some clients classified information had "destroyed the attorney–client relationship." The Circuit Court dismissed the mandamus petition in July 2010.

In October the House version of the National Defense Authorization Act (NDAA) allowed detainees to be transferred to the USA to stand trial.[231] Attorney General Holder and Defense Secretary Gates opposed a bill sponsored by Sens. Graham, McCain, and Lieberman to block DoJ from prosecuting detainees in civilian court. After an impassioned debate, the Senate rejected the senators' proposal 45–54. On November 13, DoD and DoJ announced that the five HVDs would be tried in SDNY, while MCs would resume against al-Nashiri, al-Darbi, Khadr, al Qosi, and Noor Uthman Muhammed.[232]

> Justice has been delayed too long. Prosecutors in both departments are committed to moving forward with all these cases as quickly as possible and to working together to see that justice is served, consistent with our nation's values.

Holder explained that al-Nashiri would be tried in an MC because he was alleged to have attacked "a United States warship."[233] But another reason was that much of the evidence would be hearsay inadmissible in federal court. LtCdr. Stephen Reyes objected that his client "could be convicted and put to death without ever seeing any one of his accusers take the stand." DoD agreed: "the fact that many of the potential witnesses are citizens of other nations who cannot be compelled to attend trial in the United States is one of several evidentiary concerns that make trial by military commissions the proper legal venue." In his CSRT, al-Nashiri had denied responsibility. "I had nothing to do with this bombing. We were planning to be involved in a fishing project. I left the thing; I left the project and left." Salim Hamdan, who had been at the same al-Qaeda guesthouse, claimed to have heard al-Nashiri boast about the plot. Ali Soufan, an FBI special agent, might testify about what two alleged co-conspirators told him.

In August 2010 in a DC Circuit case, DoJ said "no charges are either pending or contemplated with respect to al-Nashiri in the near future." But he was charged again in an MC in April 2011. Reyes complained that two others had been indicted in New York for the USS Cole bombing. "But here, the only difference is that Nashiri was tortured. And the government wants to make the evidence of this disappear by sentencing him to death in a makeshift system." "Anyone who approved or participated in the torture of my client should be prepared to take the witness stand." Defense lawyers made a number of arguments against the referral of capital charges: lack of meaningful discovery; the judge consulting the prosecution about what resources to give the defense; the torture of al-Nashiri; and the ten-year delay since he was seized.[234] They noted that eight of the ten capital sentences ever rendered in courts-martial had been reversed, and one was still on appeal 23 years later. In this case, the destruction of al-Nashiri's interrogation videotapes made reversal even more likely. Furthermore, all three of the alleged attacks or attempts occurred when the USA was not engaged in hostilities.

Holder called the HVD referral "the toughest decision I've had to make as Attorney General." The prosecutions would be "truly the trial of the century." The pivotal factor was a confidential security study by the US Marshals Service finding SDNY the safest option.

Prominent New York politicians applauded. Mayor Bloomberg said it was "fitting that 9/11 suspects face justice near the WTC [World Trade Center] site where so many New Yorkers were murdered." NYPD

Commissioner Kelly and Sen. Schumer (D-NY) supported the decision. Rep. Nadler, whose district included the courthouse, said "New York is not afraid of terrorists. Any suggestion that our prosecutors and our law enforcement personnel are not up to the task of holding and success-fully prosecuting terrorists on American soil is insulting and untrue." Although Holder had claimed that New York Governor Paterson also approved, a day later Paterson said: "this is not a decision that I would have made," but he still promised his "fullest cooperation."[235] SJC chair Leahy said: "by trying them in our federal courts, we demonstrate to the world that the most powerful nation on earth also trusts its judicial system."

But Republicans assailed the decision. Warning that prosecutions could end with acquittals, mistrials, or short sentences, Rep. Smith (HJC senior minority member) said Republicans would increase efforts to block them. Sen. Cornyn called the action "unconscionable." Sen. Sessions warned the trials "will turn lawyers, juries, and judges into targets, and will needlessly endanger Americans living nearby," and would give KSM "an international stage to mock America and advance his own celebrity and jihad." House Minority Leader Boehner said the "irresponsible" decision "puts the interests of liberal special interest groups before the safety and security of the American people." Rep. King (NY) said "we should not be increasing the danger of another terrorist strike against Americans at home and abroad." John Yoo said the trial would be "an intelligence bonanza for al-Qaeda" and "cripple American efforts to fight terrorism." Former NYC Mayor Giuliani called it "an unnecessary advantage to give to the terrorists." And some Democrats joined the attack. Sen. Lieberman declared the defendants were not "entitled to all the constitutional rights American citizens have in our federal courts." Sen. Webb warned the trials "will be disrup-tive, costly and potentially counterproductive." Relatives of the 9/11 victims were split. A poll found that 54 percent of Americans (60 per-cent of Republicans) favored MCs.[236]

The Los Angeles Times praised the decision as "an eloquent statement about the Obama administration's determination to avenge the victims of terrorism within the rule of law."[237] "What matters is that [the accused] will be afforded the panoply of rights enjoyed by defendants in U.S. courts, including a prohibition on the use of illegally obtained evidence." The New York Times applauded the "bold and principled step … toward repairing the damage wrought by former President George W. Bush with his decision to discard the nation's well-established systems of civilian and military justice." This was "an enormous victory for the rule of law." But the *Times* regretted the revival of the MCs. The recent revisions did not "cure the problem of relying on a new system outside the regular military justice system. Nor does it erase the appearance that the government is forum-shopping to win convictions." The *Washington Post* called the decision "an important step for the victims, their families and the country." The federal courts were "unquestionably legitimate in the eyes of most of the world."

A few days later Obama assured those offended by KSM being given constitutional protections that they would not find it "offensive at all when he's convicted and when the death penalty is applied to him."[238] Holder told the SJC he had instructed prosecutors that "failure is not an option." Sen. Grassley called that "ludicrous," since a single juror could block conviction. Sen. Sessions praised the "clear advantages" of MCs and warned of the "spectacle of a trial, with high-paid defense lawyers." Sen. Graham feared that future interrogators would worry about jeopardizing possible criminal prosecutions. All the Democrats on the SJC supported Holder.

Sen. Feingold said the trial "shows the world that this country stands firmly behind its legal system and the Constitution." But some of those attending the hearing said they had brought a petition against the trial with the signatures of 100,000 New Yorkers. (On Christmas Day, Umar Farouk Abdulmutallab tried to bomb a plane landing in Detroit. Chapter 2 discusses opposition to his criminal prosecution, which led to a guilty plea and life sentence.)

In January 2010 the Bloomberg administration asked the Office of Management and Budget to reimburse the prosecution's costs, estimated at $200 million a year.[239] Julie Menin, chair of Community Board 1, which included the courthouse, warned about the expense and "disrupting the lives of people who have homes and jobs in lower Manhattan." She recommended moving the trial to Governor's Island, which the Board's Executive Committee approved but NYPD Commissioner Kelley said was impractical. Rep. King introduced a bill to prohibit the use of DoJ funds for such a trial, calling it "one of the worst decisions ever made by any president." In late January Bloomberg changed his mind, objecting to the cost (which he claimed would be $1 billion) and the disturbance. The president of the Real Estate Board of New York said a trial "would destroy the economy in lower Manhattan." Six senators (two Democrats, three Republicans, and Lieberman, an "Independent") wrote Holder that a trial would give the defendants "one of the most visible platforms in the world to exalt their past acts."

Days later the Obama administration abandoned a trial in SDNY, although White House Press Secretary Gibbs promised that "KSM is going to meet justice, and he's going to meet his maker."[240] Sen. Graham said this showed "what a dumb idea it was in the first place." The *New York Times* criticized "caving in to political pressure" as "the wrong move." It was "baffled" by Sen. Feinstein's warning against "media and public attention." "[I]sn't the idea of a public trial a bedrock principle of American justice?" The *Washington Post* said failing to consult Bloomberg in advance was a "breach of common sense." But it still felt a civilian trial "is a better choice that offers greater legitimacy." The *Los Angeles Times* had never thought it "crucial" that the trial be in New York City, but hoped Obama would still "show the world that even accused terrorists will receive due process in this country." The Mayor of Newburgh proposed his city: "a poor place," which "could really use the economic stimulus that a federal program like this could bring."

Eight senators (five Republicans, two Democrats, and Lieberman) tabled a bill to block all civilian trials of the HVDs.[241] Obama denounced opposition to civilian trials as "pretty rank politics." Sen. Webb retorted that "it's not about 'rank politics.'" Civilian trials "benefit the international terrorist movement." Sen. Lieberman called the trials "justice according to 'Alice in Wonderland.'" Michael Mukasey (Bush's last Attorney General) said: "I can't understand the choice to bring it to New York in the first place other than showboating." Holder's "vacillation" "makes it look like amateur night" at DoJ and "makes us look weak." "It is a mockery of the rule of law to take people who are charged with violating all the rules of war and put them in a situation that's better than the one they would have been in if they had followed the rules of war." But Ali Soufan, an FBI agent who had testified in two MCs, said in a *New York Times* op ed that "civilian courts are often the more effective venue."[242] "It's very disappointing to see politicians and pundits smear the law enforcement community, to imply that the United States Attorneys and the F.B.I. cannot do their job properly under the law."

Sens. Leahy and Feinstein wrote Obama that "our system of justice is strong enough to prosecute the people who have attacked us."[243] The president said he would participate in the ultimate decision, adding "I have not ruled ... out" New York City. The White House explained it would "take into account security and logistical concerns" and "the cost of the trial." Holder said:

> I think I make the final call, but if the president is not happy with that final call, he has the ability to reverse it … Trying the case in an Article III court is best for the case and best for our overall fight against al-Qaeda. The decision will be driven by: how can we maximize our chances for success and bring justice to the people responsible for 9/11, and also to survivors … I'm not sure the location or even the forum is as important as what the world sees in that proceeding … What we have to ensure is that it's done as transparently as possible and with adherence to all the rules.

Sen. Graham warned Holder and White House Chief of Staff Emanuel that "of all the issues they have dealt with, this is the one that could bring the presidency down. Most Americans don't look at these folks as common criminals who were trying to rob a liquor store." Emanuel himself favored MCs: "you can't close Guantánamo without Senator Graham, and K.S.M. was a link in that deal." The latest public opinion poll showed that 55 percent preferred MCs and only 39 percent civilian courts; two months earlier there had been an even split.

MC chief prosecutor Murphy complained to the *New York Times*[244] that its article suggested that military prosecutors do not have the legal experience to handle these cases. "Nothing could be further from the truth. I'm honored to be part of a distinguished team of prosecutors who work on complex legal cases involving potential law-of-war violations. The DoD and Justice Department lawyers assigned to the Office of Military Commissions have decades of courtroom experience and have successfully prosecuted or judged hundreds of cases."

In early March Graham made clear that his support for closing Guantánamo was contingent on trying the HVDs in MCs.[245] The media reported that the White House was prepared to do that. Marine Col. Jeffrey Colwell, acting chief defense counsel, said this would be a "sad day for the rule of law." "I thought the decision where to put people on trial … was based on what was right, not what is politically advantageous." The *New York Times* observed: "Congressional Republicans often say that the United States should use every legal means to combat terrorism – and they are right, which makes it deeply puzzling that they want to deprive the government of the single most effective way of bringing terrorists to justice." It accused Graham of an "affront to justice – a damaging meddling in another branch of government." "If Mr. Obama does not stop Mr. Graham's assault on the courts and prosecutorial discretion, his ability to make national security will be compromised." A week earlier Holder and Gates had told Congress: "in order to protect the American people as effectively as possible ... we must be in a position to use every lawful instrument of national power – including both courts and military commissions."

Three retired military officers said trying the HVDs in MCs would be a mistake.[246] But Sen. McConnell and Rep. Smith sided with Sens. McCain and Lieberman. On CBS's *Face the Nation*, Graham reiterated his offer to support the administration in closing Guantánamo but only if it abandoned civilian trials. Sen. Bond objected: "I'm sure not going to horse-trade getting rid of one bad decision to let them make another bad decision." Sen. Feingold said "the best way to bring these terrorists to justice swiftly is through our civilian courts." The ACLU took a full-page ad in the *New York Times* showing an image of Obama morphing into Bush and declaring that Obama "must decide whether to keep his solemn promise to restore our Constitution and due process, or ignore his vow and continue the Bush–Cheney policies." Two former Bush administration officials supported civilian trials: John Bellinger III (legal adviser to both the DoS and the National Security Council) and Kenneth Wainstein (Assistant Attorney General for National Security). Tim Rutten wrote in his *Los Angeles Times* column: "if the president, who campaigned on a promise to restore the rule of law in the treatment of the jihadis, reverses course, it will be not only a lamentable triumph of politics over principle but an affront to common sense and some of our most valuable historical precedents." Darrel Vandeveld and Joshua Dratel (a former military prosecutor and a current civilian defense counsel in MCs) wrote in Salon that the MC was "untested, likely unconstitutional, and has yet to demonstrate a single credible result." The *Los Angeles Times* reiterated that "the 'where' of the trial was less important than the 'what' – a proceeding that would show the world that the United States was confident enough in its system of justice to afford the defendants the full protections of American law." The Constitution Project brought more than a dozen former judges, prosecutors, and diplomats to Congress to lobby for civilian trials. More than 200 members of September 11th Families for Peaceful Tomorrows did the same.

In mid-April Holder told the SJC that a trial in SDNY was "not off the table," and he was considering venues outside New York.[247] But Sen. Schumer said: "we know the administration is not going to hold the trial in New York. They should just say it already." Sen. Feinstein accused Republicans of politicizing national security in a "reprehensible" fashion, counseling Holder: "I've come to the conclusion that a lot of the attacks are just to diminish you, and I don't think you should buy into that at all." But Sen. Sessions told Holder that DoJ's handling of the issue had "shaken my confidence in your leadership." Speaking at the Constitution Society's award dinner a day later, Holder said the McCain–Lieberman bill barring civilian trials would "seriously harm our national security ... obscures some basic facts and allows campaign slogans to overtake reality."

At the end of April, OMC finally published its new manual.[248] David Frakt, who had been chief defense counsel in the previous two MCs, called it "substantially fairer than the 2006 version." "The standards for the admission of coerced statements and hearsay evidence ... now are much closer to the standards which apply in general courts-martial and federal court." But it contained some "very troubling language" about the standard of proof and still allowed prosecutions of acts that were not war crimes.

In July Eugene Sullivan (former chief judge of the US Court of Appeals for the Armed Forces) and Louis Freeh (former federal judge and FBI director) wrote a *Washington Post* op ed supporting a civilian trial for the HVDs, but suggesting it be held in Guantánamo.[249] "Our national honor as a country committed to the rule of law weighs heavily in favor of trying these accused terrorists in civilian federal courts." Sen. Feinstein wrote in a *Los Angeles Times* op ed that "the flurry of guilty pleas this year by high-profile terror suspects" had "dealt a serious blow" to those arguing that "the Obama administration is making America vulnerable by trying terrorists in federal criminal courts." "The decision of the best venue in which to prosecute a terror suspect should be the president's to make, and the call should be based on facts, not political rhetoric."

In October the *New York Times* contrasted the life sentence for Faisal Shahzad, who pleaded guilty in SDNY just five months after he tried to bomb Times Square, with the fact that the only defendant on trial in MCs "engineered to produce guilty verdicts, no matter how thin or tainted the evidence," was Omar Khadr, who had been held in Guantánamo for more than eight years.[250] The choice was between "justice in long-established federal courts that Americans can be proud of and the rest of the world can respect," or "illegal detentions and unending, legally dubious military tribunals. It is an easy one." Jack Goldsmith (who had headed the OLC under Bush) wrote in a *New York Times* op ed that all detainees should be held without trial rather than prosecuted in any forum. Ben Wittes (not a lawyer) wrote in a *Washington Post* op ed that KSM should be prosecuted in *both* a civilian court and military tribunal (ignoring double jeopardy problems).

On the anniversary of Holder's announcement of the civilian prosecutions, the *Washington Post* regretted that "Mr. Mohammed has yet to be brought to justice. The administration's paralysis is as confounding as it is damaging."[251] The government "has a moral and legal obligation, and strong policy reasons, to bring formal charges whenever possible." Congress's new ban on federal funds to bring detainees to the USA for trial was "an egregious encroachment on executive prerogatives – and one that the administration should have vigorously challenged." MCs "will likely be subject to legal challenges that could cause lengthy delays. But it's hard to imagine a delay longer than that caused by the administration's abdication."

When Holder said a decision was close, Schumer, King, and New York Governor Cuomo reiterated their opposition to a trial in New York and were echoed by politicians in Virginia and Pennsylvania (other possible venues).[252] Sen. McConnell called on the administration to "admit it was wrong and assure us just as confidently that terrorists will be tried from now on in the military commission system." Morris Davis wrote in a *New York Times* op ed that "there is no reason to assume that a military commission sentence will be more severe than one from a federal court."

The *Los Angeles Times*' wish list for 2011 included one that Obama "make good on his promises to … put accused terrorists on trial in civilian courts."[253] In his signing statement on H.R. 6523 (NDAA 2011), Obama vowed to seek repeal of the ban on spending money to transfer detainees to the USA for trial, but did not threaten to defy it. Sen. McConnell said the bill showed the "overwhelming bipartisan opposition in the Congress" to civilian trials. The *Washington Post* praised Obama for reiterating "the importance of preserving federal court prosecutions as an option." "Congress is to blame for the fear-mongering and political opportunism that gave rise to these unwise provisions. But the administration also bears responsibility for not fighting more aggressively."

On March 7, 2011 Obama finally issued executive orders reauthorizing military commissions.[254] HJC chair Smith was pleased the president had "finally seen the light on military commission trials," but called on the administration to "fully abandon the failed policy of trying terrorists in civilian courts." Sen. Grassley agreed. HASC chair McKeon criticized Obama for acting through "executive fiat" (just what Bush had done). Rep. Nadler condemned the "legally dubious military commissions" as "unworthy of this great nation." The *Washington Post* called the decision "both an admission of failure and a step in the right direction." The *Los Angeles Times* said that though MCs would now provide "more due process," the problem "is as much symbolic as it is substantive" because such trials "will be perceived as illegitimate throughout much of the world."

A month later – the day Obama launched his re-election campaign – Holder announced that the five HVDs would be tried by MCs. In November 2009 he said: "it became clear to me that the best venue for prosecution was in federal court. I stand by that decision today." "Unfortunately, since I made that decision, Members of Congress have intervened and imposed … unwise and unwarranted restrictions," which "undermine our counterterrorism efforts and could harm national security."

> I've read the files, know the facts, am familiar with the strategic issues in a way that members of Congress are not … Do I know better than them? Yes … and they should respect the role of the executive branch in making decisions of this type … We must face a simple truth: those restrictions [on bringing detainees to the USA] are unlikely to be repealed in the immediate future. And we cannot allow a trial to be delayed any longer for the victims of the 9/11 attacks or their families who have waited nearly a decade for justice.

(In November 2013 Holder reiterated that his plan to try the 9/11 suspects in civilian court had been "the right one" and "the defendants would be on death row as we speak."[255])

ACLU Director Anthony Romero predicted (correctly) that "delay is exactly what we'll get by trying the Sept. 11 suspects in the military commissions," whose "rules and procedures do not comport with the Constitution and international law and will only bring further legal challenges." The *New York Times* called this "a victory for Congressional pandering and an embarrassment for the Obama administration, which failed to stand up to it." The *Washington Post* said the original choice of a civilian trial had been "reasonable," but "the administration botched the matter." MC rules "have been improved … and now offer many of the legal protections embedded in civilian courts." Holder was "right to move forward, finally, with these trials." The *Los Angeles Times* deplored this "latest example of Obama, who was acidly critical of

George W. Bush's policies in the war on terror, embracing those policies or acquiescing in their continuation." "The fiasco of the Mohammed trial is an example of good intentions followed by inept execution." It warned that an MC trial "would make it easier for America's enemies to portray it as a show trial." Karen Greenberg (director of the New York University Center on Law and Security) wrote in a *Washington Post* op ed that "this trial could begin to restore the nation's confidence in its ability to administer justice to even the most vile criminals." The British writer William Shawcross wrote in a *New York Times* op ed that the Nuremberg trials (in which his father had been the chief British prosecutor) "offered far fewer protections to the Nazis in the dock than the military commissions ... military justice worked then and it can work again today."

A week later the *New York Times* warned: "it will never be possible to have military trials at Guantánamo that Americans can be fully proud of, or that the world will see as credible."[256] The decision was the "triumph of raw politics over the nation's security interests." Holder "ineptly failed to line up political support ... but that did not excuse the hyperventilating and unyielding opposition" of Bloomberg, Schumer, King, and other politicians. The Congressional funding ban was "a shocking example of politicians dictating a prosecutorial decision." "These most important of the 9/11 trials will take place in a system of questioned legitimacy, operating under untested rules, with no experience in concluding major terrorism trials." "To avoid an utter legal shambles and administer some justice," prosecutors should "not try to exploit the somewhat more lenient evidentiary rules in military commissions, or urge a fanciful redefinition of torture." OMC should provide "experienced military and civilian defense counsel" in "adequate numbers" and with "sufficient resources and leeway." The *Times* criticized the new MC rules, which required lawyers to announce the language they would speak with their clients. This was "absurd ... unless the government is improperly monitoring the conversations." The *Times* urged greater transparency and less security, criticizing "lack of timely access to trial filings and transcripts, and overclassification of evidence."

Signing the latest NDAA barring the use of funds to transfer detainees to the USA, President Obama criticized "the continuation of a dangerous and unprecedented challenge to critical executive branch authority to determine when and where to prosecute ... based on the facts and the circumstances of each case and our national security interests."[257]

In a *Los Angeles Times* op ed, Morris Davis warned of unlawful command influence, which a former chief judge of the Court of Appeals for the Armed Forces had called "the mortal enemy of military justice."[258] In November 2009 Obama had said no one would question his decision to prosecute HVDs in the civilian courts when KSM is "convicted and when the death penalty is applied to him." Holder had told the SJC: "failure is not an option. These are cases that have to be won. I don't expect that we will have a contrary result." Obama had just told a fundraiser that KSM "broke the law." Davis noted that "all participants in the military commissions are accountable to the commander-in-chief. Many, in addition to their status as uniformed military reserve officers, are career employees of the DoJ." Such statements "undermine confidence in justice by injecting the appearance of undue influence."

On May 31 the prosecution recommended capital charges against the five HVDs.[259] After the CA confirmed the charges against al-Nashiri in September 2011, defense lawyers moved to dismiss them or eliminate the death penalty. The European Parliament and human rights groups passed a resolution against the death penalty because of the CIA's abuse of al-Nashiri. Chief Prosecutor Martins promised to transmit the trial by video to viewing centers in the USA (for the media and relatives of 9/11 victims). The defense moved for an order requiring the government to declare whether it would continue to hold al-Nashiri if he were acquitted. Andrew Rosenthal commented in his *New York Times* column that one reason it had been a "horrible mistake" to use MCs is that they "do not seem to have the authority to actually free defendants."

In October the *Los Angeles Times* criticized the NDAA 2012 for continuing to ban the transfer of detainees to the USA for trial.[260] The measure was supported by SASC chair Levin and other Democrats on the committee. But Sens. Feinstein and Leahy (chairs of the Intelligence and Judiciary Committees) and 11 other Democratic members of those committees wrote Senate Majority Leader Reid opposing the provision. DoD General Counsel Jeh Johnson agreed that the choice of a forum should be left to "prosecutors and national security professionals." The *Philadelphia Inquirer* said Obama's "hands should not be tied to prevent bringing suspected terrorists to justice in the federal court system." But after the House eliminated the section banning the prosecution of al-Qaeda suspects in civilian courts and passed the bill 283–136, Obama dropped his veto threat. The *New York Times* warned that the "terrible new measures ... will make ... military trials a permanent part of American law" and "strip the F.B.I., federal prosecutors and federal courts of all or most of their power to arrest and prosecute terrorists and hand it off to the military, which has made clear that it doesn't want the job." "This is a complete political cave-in, one that reinforces the impression of a fumbling presidency." Although the law "allows the executive to grant a waiver for a particular prisoner to be brought to trial in a civilian court … the legislation's ban on spending any money for civilian trials for any accused terrorist would make that waiver largely meaningless." After Obama signed the bill, Holder called the "missed opportunity" to try the HVDs in New York his greatest disappointment. "We'd be finished with that trial by now, and it could be something we could point to and show that we can be fair even to those we despise."

Al-Nashiri was arraigned on November 9, the first time he had appeared in court since being seized nine years earlier.[261] He said his assigned lawyers were "doing a good job," and he understood he could change them. He chose to wear prison garb and promised to attend every hearing. Judge Pohl denied the defense motion to force the prosecution to say whether al-Nashiri would be released if he were acquitted; if not, the defense argued, there was less reason to deny him access to classified evidence. Pohl ordered the Guantánamo commander to stop his staff reading and translating al-Nashiri's communications with his lawyers. The defense asked the judge to rule on requests for funds for expert witnesses without consulting the prosecution, but Pohl said the CA had forbidden that. Prosecutors asked that the trial start in less than four months, even though discovery had not yet begun and the defense was waiting for 70,000 pages of documents, much of it classified. The defense asked for 10–24 months. Pohl gave it just two months to read all the documents and file any challenges. Martins said the charges included the "longstanding war crime" of perfidy and the "long-established offense" of murder. The official transcript was classified "top secret," even though the hearing had been observed by dozens of members of the press, the public, and victims' families.

The defense sought to subpoena Yemeni President Saleh, claiming that members of his government had been complicit in the bombings and he had "sought to limit the investigation of the Cole bombing" and "personally handled evidence."[262] DoS said he was immune. The defense sought to have al-Nashiri describe his CIA interrogation as part of a motion to have him unshackled while meeting with lawyers. The *Miami Herald* said Judge Pohl had gone "to absurd lengths" in agreeing with DoD to hear that motion in camera. "There's that pesky thing called the First Amendment that protects public access to the proceedings, particularly in a case that commands worldwide attention and raises significant issues. Beyond that, it's ridiculous to shield the public from testimony covering information already in the public domain." A dozen news organizations filed a motion seeking access to the hearing, the first time a nonparty had been heard. David A. Schulz, representing the media, wrote in a *New York Times* op ed that "the world will never accept the Guantánamo verdicts if significant testimony is closed for fear of embarrassment over detainee mistreatment." But Pohl mooted the issue by letting al-Nashiri meet his lawyers unshackled. HRW lawyer Reed Brody wrote a *Los Angeles Times* op ed about the deficiencies of the MCs. Pohl denied defense motions to dismiss the conspiracy and terrorism charges as *ex post facto* and for lack of jurisdiction, and to dismiss all the charges as a bill of attainder and a violation of equal protection, citing the CMCR decisions in *al-Bahlul*.[263]

As the HVD hearings began, JTF-GTMO commander RAdm. David Woods imposed a security review of legal mail to all defendants, rejecting assertions of lawyer–client privilege.[264] Marine Col. Jeffrey Colwell, chief military defense counsel, instructed his 40 lawyers not to sign agreements allowing such searches, which violated the rules of professional conduct, and to cease all written communication. He also told the lawyers not to comply with procedures for face-to-face meetings with their clients. He sent both orders to the pool of nearly a hundred civilian lawyers. The privilege review team was composed of DoD contractors who had been DoJ personnel, law enforcement, or intelligence. UCLA Law Professor Kal Raustiala wrote in a *Los Angeles Times* op ed that the "order is a mistake, one that threatens to jeopardize the progress made in reversing Guantánamo's tainted legacy as a legal black hole." ABA President Bill Robinson III urged Defense Secretary Panetta to rescind the policy. Judge Pohl summoned Woods to a hearing on less than 90 minutes' notice. When he was late, Pohl admonished prosecutors for "wasting a lot of time." If a Privilege Review Team (PRT) disputed a defense lawyer's certification that a document was privileged, Pohl declared that he, not Woods, would resolve the dispute.

On January 10, 2012 Chief Prosecutor Martins told the NYCB that MCs were "comparable to federal courts in their incorporation of all of the fundamental guarantees of a fair and just trial demanded by our values."[265] (He repeated that to the ABA in August: MCs "apply a well-defined body of law and rules from our respected courts-martial and federal courts and, like all judicial bodies, raise unresolved issues in a methodical way for reasoned and thoughtful resolution.") In February the defense moved to delay the trial until the summer so it could file memos arguing that capital charges should be dropped because PRTs violated lawyer–client privilege by reading their mail. But capital charges were filed on April 4. The *New York Times* warned that the defendants would be tried by "a constitutionally flawed military tribunal ... the worst way to administer justice to the 9/11 terrorists." MCs were "improved from the kangaroo courts that Mr. Bush created, but still profoundly flawed."

Prosecutors sought to start al-Nashiri's trial on March 3. Martins announced his retirement to signal he would forgo consideration by the Promotions Board. He declared: "justice is being done ... the current system is fair." Lisa Monaco, Assistant Attorney General for National Security, agreed MCs had the "same fundamental guarantees of fairness that are the hallmark of criminal trials." But Deputy Chief Defense Counsel Broyles objected that "this is the only court in the United States where you can plead guilty and still be given the death penalty." And Richard Kammen, representing al-Nashiri, said: "there is nothing about this system that the average American, if they were caught up in it, would see as being fair."

In May WD Wash Judge Bryan dismissed al-Nashiri's action against the CA (whose residence was in Washington State) seeking a declaration that the MC lacked jurisdiction because the acts for which the defendant was charged were not associated with hostilities.[266] Judge Bryan found that the MCA had stripped him of jurisdiction, CA MacDonald had sovereign immunity, and the District Court should abstain. The Ninth Circuit affirmed in December 2013.[267]

Pohl (who, as chief judge, had assigned himself both the HVD cases and al-Nashiri) ordered that the HVD arraignment be transmitted by video to eight sites, five for relatives of 9/11 victims.[268] He was by far the most experienced military judge in the Army. In the Abu Ghraib courts-martial he had declared the prison a crime scene (forbidding its demolition), refused to accept Lynndie England's guilty plea, and ordered many officers, up through CENTCOM commander Gen. Abizaid, to submit to defense questioning (see the companion volume *Law's Wars*). In May Benjamin Wittes wrote in the *Washington Post* that "there is reason to be optimistic that the long effort to bring the 9/11 conspirators to trial will finally succeed." Jack Goldsmith said Martins had given MCs "the appearance and the reality of more transparency." Martins insisted "we're going to have a fair trial." "The initial version of

commissions was flawed, but there has been a lot of work on reforms."
However, Cmdr. Ruiz (representing al-Hawsawi) said: "the odds continue to be silently and deliberately stacked against a fair process." The
defense had asked Pohl to return the capital charges to the CA because
of the obstacles defense lawyers had encountered. In his *New York Times*
column, Andrew Rosenthal criticized the ability of censors to cut off the
audio feed during hearings and the presumptive classification of any reference to the CIA. James Connell, representing al-Baluchi, challenged
the presumption that everything the defendants said was classified.[269]

The May 5 arraignment revealed the defendants' determination to
delegitimate the commissions. KSM refused to answer Pohl's questions
about whether he understood what was being said and whether he was
willing to be represented by his lawyers.[270] When David Nevin, his
civilian lawyer, said KSM was protesting the unfair process, Pohl said he
would assume KSM had no objections to representation. "He has that
choice" to be silent, "but he does not have a choice that would frustrate
this commission going forward." There were questions about whether
the headphones were working, whether defendants would wear them,
and whether the translation was adequate.

Defense lawyers tried to discuss the clothing defendants could wear
in court, but Pohl refused to address this. The Court Security Officer
periodically interrupted the sound. Bin 'Attash was in a restraint chair
because he had refused to leave his cell; Pohl offered to remove the
restraints if the defendant would pledge not to disrupt the proceedings,
but got no answer (because of the restraints). Pohl eventually removed
them after Capt. Schwartz, bin 'Attash's lawyer, made that promise.
When the defendants refused to wear headphones, Pohl directed consecutive translation over loudspeakers, causing confusion (as some
translators spoke over others) and delay (as everything was said twice).
Bin al-Shibh stood, knelt, and prayed (which Pohl tolerated). Pohl
advised each defendant of his right to counsel. When the accused
refused to answer his questions, Pohl appointed their detailed military counsel and civilian counsel. During their qualification process,
defense lawyers attempted (unsuccessfully) to raise the question of
access to their clients. Ruiz claimed he needed a translator to discuss
his own qualifications with al-Hawsawi and had not had one for the
last three years; Martins confirmed this but objected that Ruiz rejected
every translator the prosecution had offered. Bin al-Shibh interrupted,
complaining about conditions of confinement and shouting about
Qaddafi. When Pohl silenced him, bin al-Shibh said: "Maybe they are

going to kill us and say that we have committed suicide." But he quieted down when Pohl threatened to remove him.

Three defendants insisted the prosecution read aloud the 87-page charge sheet, which took two hours because it included the names of the 2,976 killed on 9/11. When all five defendants prayed for 20 minutes after a lunch break, Pohl warned: "I fully respect the accused's request for prayer. It's a right for them to have it. But a right can still be abused." Censors cut off the sound when a defense lawyer claimed his client had been tortured; but later comments about torture passed uncensored, and the government promised to include censored portions in the transcript. Cheryl Bormann, bin 'Attash's lawyer, wore a black abaya covering everything but her face and urged women on the prosecution team to dress more modestly. She asked the court to order guards not to forcibly extract defendants for the hearing, noting her client had "scars on his arms." Bin 'Attash removed his shirt to display them, but put it back on after Pohl admonished him.

Defense lawyers voir dired Pohl, who refused to answer questions he deemed inappropriate (such as his religious and political affiliations and why he had detailed himself to hear this case). Prosecutors asked for an August trial; the defense wanted at least a year's delay. After hours of motions the defendants refused to plead. At a news conference afterwards James G. Connell III (al-Baluchi's lawyer) said the defendants' refusal to acknowledge Pohl expressed "peaceful resistance to an unjust system." David Nevin (for KSM) denounced the "rigged game." ACLU Director Romero said "the commissions remain a cynical tool to obfuscate the fact that the U.S. sanctioned the use of torture at the highest level of government." It had filed a motion challenging the censorship. The *Wall Street Journal* accused military defense lawyers, "who know they can make a name for themselves," of helping the defendants "promote jihad and discredit American institutions, including the military system of justice." Bormann's request that women on the prosecution team dress modestly "was beyond any reasonable definition of what's necessary and proper for women working in a U.S. military courtroom." "The truth is that these will be the fairest, most transparent military tribunals in history." The *Los Angeles Times* said the commission might not be "a kangaroo court" but was still "an unacceptable alternative to a civilian trial." The *Miami Herald* denounced "the elaborate Guantánamo system attempts to square the circle – ostensibly offering a 'fair trial' to the accused who have been tortured, held in secret jails, and subjected to years of detention without charges." "For the process to have a shred of … credibility … the world must not only know what the terrorists did to America, but also what America did to them."

Pohl *sua sponte* ordered the prosecution to show cause why the five cases should not be severed, noting that issues of scheduling and evidence might hurt some defendants while helping others.[271] Al-Baluchi favored severance; bin al-Shibh called it premature; bin 'Attash lacked sufficient information to comment; and the other accused did not respond.

Lawyers for bin al-Shibh, al-Hawsawi, and al-Baluchi moved to dismiss because Bush, Obama, and others had made statements that could constitute "unlawful influence."[272] They sought testimony from both presidents, as well as Biden, Holder, and Graham. The *New York Daily News* accused their lawyers of having "horribly crossed the line from zealously advocating for their clients to acting as cheap, undignified propagandists." "This trial is not about the impartiality of the presiding judge."

KSM asked to wear a camouflage jacket and turban with traditional Pakistani clothing.[273] (At the May arraignment Pohl had refused a similar request by KSM and bin 'Attash, as well as one by al-Hawsawi to wear an orange jumpsuit.) Army Capt. Jason Wright, KSM's lawyer, said defendants in the Tokyo and Nuremberg tribunals had been allowed to choose their clothing. Prosecutors objected that "the detainee's attire should not transform this commission into a vehicle for propaganda." In July Pohl postponed the case during Ramadan, but denied a defense request to suspend hearings on Fridays.

In June al-Nashiri's lawyers filed a sealed motion asking Pohl to recuse himself, arguing both that he had an incentive to keep the case running (since he had been scheduled to retire in September 2010) and that he had no experience in capital cases.[274] Pohl denied the motion.

The media filed a motion opposing a prosecution proposal to close hearings on both defense funding and recusal and seeking access to information being withheld from the public. When Pohl closed the hearing on torture, al-Nashiri refused to attend. Pohl denied a defense motion to televise the trial. Al-Nashiri boycotted a hearing to protest the use of belly chains to move him from his cell. The prosecution wanted him brought to court (in chains) to explain his boycott!

Martins said: "the accused has to come to ensure the integrity of the trial." Objecting that the use of force could traumatize someone who had been tortured, the defense asked that medical experts evaluate their client. After 90 minutes of argument, Pohl ordered that al-Nashiri be produced. The next day al-Nashiri told the judge he would boycott future hearings if forced to wear chains, which hurt his "bad back." "If the guards do not treat me better, I have the right not to come. And let the world know that the judge sentenced me to death because I didn't show up to court due to chains." In August Pohl heard argument in the HVD trial about a 40-second audio delay to keep classified information from the audience, which was proposed by the prosecution and opposed by 14 media groups and the ACLU.[275]

When hearings resumed in October, Pohl asked if the accused understood that boycotting hearings could damage their defenses.[276] KSM said he did but added: "I don't think there is any justice in this court." Bin al-Shibh had no objection to the fact that his former lawyer, Cmdr. Lachelier, now represented al-Hawsawi. After lengthy debate over a prosecution request to bar the public from hearing testimony about interrogation, KSM said: "the president can take someone and throw him in the sea under the name of national security. He can legislate the killings under the name of national security." "Don't get affected by crocodile tears, because your blood is not made of gold and ours made of water. We are all human beings." Over prosecution objections, Pohl ruled that the accused had the right not to attend hearings. KSM, al-Baluchi, and al-Hawsawi boycotted the next day's hearing to protest a protective order barring lawyers from discussing harsh interrogation with their clients. In December Pohl issued a protective order prohibiting disclosure of information about how the accused were captured, where they were held, or their interrogation. In January he extended the ban to unclassified material. But he also modified the protective order so that defense counsel did not have to treat everything their clients said as "presumptively classified," only material that was actually classified or reasonably believed to be.

The next day military officials acknowledged that defense counsel offices were unsafe and promised they would be cleaned in time for the next hearing.[277] The military had acknowledged the problem a month earlier, but then declared the offices safe after cleaning them. Defense lawyers now showed photos of walls and air conditioning units coated with mildew and mold and floors littered with rat droppings, a dead crab, and lizards. At the end of the month Pohl rejected a defense motion to have the proceedings televised, which prosecutors had opposed.

In November al-Hawsawi moved to dismiss based on the DDC decision in *Hamdan* that the material support law could not apply retroactively.[278] In January 2013 CA MacDonald declined to withdraw conspiracy charges against the defendants, even though the DC Circuit had ruled in *al-Bahlul* that they were not law of war violations and the prosecution wanted to withdraw them.[279] MacDonald said: "Congress included conspiracy as a chargeable offense in the Military Commissions Acts of 2006 and 2009." After Martins said he would not resist defense motions to dismiss, Pohl ordered MacDonald to testify about preserving the charge. Pohl declined to rule on whether the Constitution applied, saying that al-Nashiri's lawyers were seeking an "advisory motion."[280] When the defense moved to dismiss the charges for the USS *Cole* attack on the ground that no armed conflict had existed at the time of the attack, Pohl refused, declaring that he owed deference to the judgment of the executive and legislative branches that "the United States government had simply been slow to recognize the existence of a state of hostilities then existing between the United States and al-Qaeda and its affiliates and franchises." Whether hostilities existed at the time was a question of fact, which the prosecution would have to prove to the jury. On February 4, 2013 Pohl granted the prosecution's request for an evaluation of al-Nashiri's competence to stand trial and two defense motions: to have Dr. Iacopino testify about the torture of al-Nashiri and to have Dr. Sandra Crosby examine him unshackled.[281]

During a January 2013 hearing, Pohl observed that "some external body" cut off the audio to the audience.[282] Furious, he said: "if some external body is turning the commission off under their own view of what things ought to be, with no reasonable explanation, we are going to have a little meeting about who turns that light on or off." The secret hearing lasted nearly three hours. The next day Pohl said the cut-off had been triggered when David Nevin discussed whether arguments would be open concerning a motion for the preservation of evidence at a detention facility (presumably a CIA black site). Pohl pronounced that "not a valid basis for the court to have been closed." A prosecutor told him that the "original classification authority" (presumably the CIA) could interrupt the audio. Pohl ordered there be no repetition. Defense lawyers said the incident created "paranoia" about whether their conversations had been eavesdropped. Martins denied the prosecution was doing so. But the Original Classification Authority could also hear what the microphones picked up. LtCdr. Reyes (representing al-Nashiri) filed an emergency motion to have a government witness "testify as to the extent of third party monitoring and censoring." Pohl accepted the defense lawyers' request to postpone further hearings until they interviewed audio technology officials about eavesdropping.

A week later Martins declared: "I can say unequivocally that no entity of the United States government is listening to, monitoring or recording communications between the five accused and their counsel at any location." Bormann interjected that the previous fall a guard had assured her that smoke detectors in the lawyer–client meeting rooms in Echo II were not microphones. "Well guess what, judge, it is a listening device" with "the ability to record." Navy Capt. Thomas J. Welsh, SJA, said he saw a law enforcement agent eavesdropping on a meeting between prosecution and defense lawyers, but had been assured by Col. John Bogdan, the JTF detention group commander, that "any listening to an attorney–client meeting is prohibited." James Connell, another defense lawyer, had learned that the raw feed from the courtroom transmitted conversations among defense counsel. The director of courtroom technology conceded that audio feeds could transmit ambient sound. Martins complained that defense lawyers were "shoveling" objections into the record, but agreed to remove the microphones in the courtroom. Saying "the sooner the better," Pohl proposed that microphones remain off unless turned on. The defense agreed, and Pohl so ordered, and then denied a defense motion to abate.

On February 4 bin 'Attash angrily stood up to protest that his cell had been searched while he was in court and personal papers confiscated, including privileged legal documents, as well as a photograph of Mecca and the 9/11 Report. A guard confirmed this. But Pohl cut off the outburst and threatened to expel bin 'Attash from court. Guards said most of the papers would be returned. In response to a motion by the HVD defense lawyers seeking 48-hour visits to the cells in which their clients were or had been detained, Pohl allowed groups of three to visit for 12 hours and take photos. But because of a dispute about classified evidence, only James Connell (representing al-Baluchi) made a visit.[283] In March the CMCR dismissed the petitions by media organizations and the ACLU challenging the closure of hearings because this had not yet occurred.

In April Kammen, representing al-Nashiri, complained that "defense emails have ended up being provided to the prosecution, material has disappeared off the defense server, and sometimes reappeared, in different formats, or with different names."[284] Ruiz, al-Hawsawi's military counsel, complained that the chief defense counsel's order to stop using servers and emails "essentially cripples our ability to operate." DoD acknowledged that 541,000 emails had been searched, but could not say how many were written by the defense. "This sort of human error is unfortunate but not out of the ordinary in complex litigation." A scheduled hearing was delayed for two months to let the defense investigate "information technology corruption and loss of relevant defense files." (In April 2014 the CMCR again rejected complaints by al Qosi, al-Hawsawi and bin al-Shibh about the computer breach. "It is an unfortunate reality that privileged documents inadvertently are produced to an adversary."[285])

In June Capt. Welsh, the SJA, confirmed to al-Nashiri's MC that the smoke detectors in cells at Camp Echo II did contain listening devices, but insisted they were not used to monitor lawyer–client interaction and had been removed in February when defense lawyers complained.[286] Col. Bogdan, the joint detention group commander, testified that he had been unaware of the listening devices until the defense raised the matter.

Pohl appointed a secret three-person military board to determine al-Nashiri's competence to stand trial.[287] In June 2013 it found he suffered from PTSD and depression but was competent. Days later both sides filed classified motions, and the judge held the first closed session since Obama's election. On June 11 a prosecutor declared the government had given defense lawyers all relevant evidence; but three days later a different prosecutor admitted the government had just discovered photos of al-Nashiri before he was waterboarded. Pohl granted a defense motion to compel Bogdan and Welsh to testify about eavesdropping.

The HVDs boycotted a pretrial hearing in June.[288] Pohl abruptly recessed it on June 19. After RAdm. Woods insisted (in response to Ruiz) that nobody told him the CIA had input into an order regulating the work of defense lawyers, Joanna Baltes, a DoJ lawyer, objected to naming the CIA. Ruiz said: "if she wants me to use the term 'agency who shall remain nameless' I can do that." After conferring with Baltes, Ruiz declared: "I will not be threatened by the prosecution." Pohl closed the court to the public. David Nevin protested.

In July the prosecution asked Pohl to set a September trial date, complaining that "the current practice of being in court for five days approximately every six weeks is inefficient."[289] In August Pohl held his first secret hearing without the accused but refused to withhold prosecution evidence from defense lawyers.[290] They moved to dismiss on several grounds: the CA performed both prosecutorial and judicial functions, the MCA of 2009 violated due process by subjecting only these defendants to MCs, and it violated the Define and Punish Clause. They also asked Pohl to suspend hearings until they received adequate resources. Prosecutors could not say when a new computer system would be ready to resolve concerns about lost emails, which had led the chief defense counsel to order his team not to exchange privileged documents by email. Work product had disappeared from defense computers, and lawyers were unable to file motions.

At a September hearing bin al-Shibh shouted: "I have a right to talk."[291] Pohl snapped back: "No you don't" and ordered him removed. When KSM protested military obstacles to his meetings with lawyers, Pohl silenced him as well. Al-Hawsawi chose not to attend. Defense lawyers renewed their complaints about computer security. Air Force Col. Karen Mayberry, chief military defense counsel, testified that DoD monitored defense computers. In the wake of a file transfer or "replication" the previous December, material had disappeared from defense computers. In January some lawyers were unable to access their hard drives at all. In February DoD executed a "dirty shutdown" of OMC computers (i.e., without appropriate backup), deleting additional files. Mayberry was told that defense work product could be searched and removed by military IT personnel. In April she responded by ordering defense counsel not to use the network for creating or storing privileged information. In June a comparison of the network drives with what they had contained before the December transfer identified hundreds of thousands of missing files, and even that was an underestimate. KSM's lawyers found documents altered by third parties and hidden files added to folders. Some defense staff learned that others were reading their internet searches. A separate migration of DoD email, which was not supposed to affect OMC, prevented some defense lawyers from emailing others. But Pohl denied the defense motion to delay proceedings while all this was resolved.

In October Bormann said that on September 25 guards removed, translated, and read privileged material from bin 'Attash's legal team. Ruiz said in February guards had searched al-Hawsawi's cell and seized a document that disclosed defense strategy and had been properly marked privileged.[292] Defense lawyers also moved to dismiss the charges because the court's protective order violated the accused's right under the CAT to describe their interrogations.

LtCdr. Kevin Bogucki complained that bin al-Shibh was being kept awake at night by sounds or vibrations, which prevented him from participating fully in the hearings. Pohl also heard motions to dismiss because of defense resource shortages before charges were referred and unlawful command influence.

In December Bogucki again complained that bin al–Shibh had been kept awake the previous night by noise and could not be "meaningfully" present.[293] Pohl said Bogucki had not made a motion. When Pohl asked if bin al-Shibh understood his rights, the defendant retorted: "I totally refuse to answer this question as long as the judge is taking position against me and against my allegations." When he launched into a monologue, Pohl instructed him to answer yes or no (fearing he would divulge classified information) and expelled him from the courtroom.

Bin al-Shibh shouted as he left: "I am not a war criminal; you are a war criminal." "It's a secret CIA prison. Nobody knows it. Nobody enters it. Nobody sees it." Over two more days he was expelled twice. At the prosecution's request, and over defense objections, Pohl ordered a mental health evaluation to investigate bin al-Shibh's claims of sleep deprivation. (He had made similar complaints in 2006; in 2009 a psychiatrist found he did not understand the legal proceedings.) Pohl also issued an order under seal that the government preserve evidence of the CIA's secret prisons. The defense argued its motion to dismiss the death penalty on the ground that it had been deprived of resources to uncover mitigation evidence (namely a translator to talk to al-Hawsawi). Bin al-Shibh refused to submit to the mental health investigation.[294] Bogucki said he would ask Pohl to include experts on the effects of torture in the evaluation and allow more time.

In January 2014 KSM issued a long, rambling "Statement to the Crusaders of the Military Commissions at Guantánamo," which he sought to transmit to Obama. The prison refused to deliver it because prisoners were limited to two pages of nonlegal correspondence a month.

DoD claimed that the letter was classified even though it had attached the letter to its own legal document. Pohl finally authorized its delivery three years later, just before the end of Obama's term.[295]

In August 2013 Pohl had scheduled al-Nashiri's trial for September 2014. But in February 2014 a conflict between the defendant and Kammen led Pohl to suspend a hearing.[296] A day later the two worked out their differences. Al-Nashiri had complained that he had no Arabic-speaking lawyer, two of his lawyers missed the hearing, and his lawyers attended secret hearings they could not describe to him. Days later Pohl held a second secret hearing on al-Nashiri's treatment in the secret CIA prison. Pohl set jury selection for October and the trial for December.

In February 2014 al-Nashiri's lawyers moved to dismiss charges of hijacking and hazarding the MV *Limburg* on the ground that it was not an international law of war crime cognizable by the MC, or alternatively that the ship was either a civilian or a belligerent-aligned oil tanker.[297] Other motions challenged jury selection and the MC appointment, and argued that the capital charges were *ex post facto*, or inappropriate for hazarding a vessel and perfidy, or a violation of the Eighth Amendment.

Also in February 2014 Bormann asked Pohl to order Martins to stop making "extrajudicial" observations.[298] In a *60 Minutes* interview the previous November the chief prosecutor had said defendants' statements following harsh interrogation by the CIA should be admissible. Bormann also asked Pohl to remove from the MC website the slogan "fairness*transparency*justice" and a chart comparing MCs to civilian courts. The defense argued its motion to dismiss for unlawful command influence.

Defense lawyers asked the government for a list of the countries in which al-Nashiri had been held and the names of those who guarded and interrogated him at the black sites.[299] Cmdr. Andreas Lockhart, the prosecutor, replied that the defense did not have the right to "double-check the government's work, and they certainly don't have the right to do their own independent investigation" of what happened to the defendant. "The name of the country or whatever particular location is not relevant for the purposes of what occurred." Cmdr. Mizer, al-Nashiri's military defense lawyer, replied that "you have to get back to the past to determine whether" his alleged confession "is just a dog barking on command." Defense lawyers could not discuss with him 14 percent of what they knew because it was classified. In a sealed order Pohl told prosecutors to give defense lawyers the names, dates, and places of detention and interrogation.

In April defense lawyers asked the DDC to enjoin al-Nashiri's MC because the *USS Cole* bombing predated the 9/11 attacks and the AUMF.[300] In August Judge Spath dismissed the charges for the 2002 attack on the French oil tanker MV *Limburg* because the prosecution had failed to produce any evidence.[301] In September prosecutors appealed to the CMCR about Spath's rejection of their theory of "wanton disregard" for the safety of Yemeni port workers; but the appeal was stayed because defense lawyers had challenged the CMCR's composition in the DC Circuit. In December DDC Judge Roberts refused to enjoin al-Nashiri's MC, abstaining from deciding until the end of the trial on the basis of comity and judicial economy.[302]

On April 22, 2014 the defense team again moved to disqualify Pohl, objecting to his hearing both al-Nashiri and the five HVDs, his failure (as a judge ten years earlier) to explore senior officers' responsibility for the Abu Ghraib abuses, and his appointment by the CA.[303] Pohl denied this motion.

Also in April 2014 Dr. Crosby, who had interviewed al-Nashiri for more than 30 hours, testified over prosecution objections that he suffered from chronic pain and anal-rectal complaints typical of "survivors of sexual assault."[304] He had scars on his wrists, legs, and ankles "consistent with the allegations and history that he gave me" and suffered from "irritability, anger, extreme emotional intensity to silence," which were "red flags" of trauma and torture. The military had insisted he be shackled during the examination and four guards be present, but Pohl backed Crosby's refusal. Three days later Pohl heard from a government psychiatrist, who had recently changed his diagnosis of al-Nashiri from PTSD to Narcissistic Personality Disorder and proposed to treat his anxiety disorder by exposing him to the experiences that triggered anxiety. Al-Nashiri (unsurprisingly) refused and therefore got no treatment. The defense asked that the proceedings be abated until al-Nashiri received appropriate treatment.

On April 14, 2014 defense lawyers told Pohl that FBI agents had questioned members of their team about the handling of evidence.[305] James Harrington said his court-appointed Court Security Officer (CSO) was asked about the January release to two media outlets of KSM's manifesto "An Invitation to Happiness." (The prosecution had earlier tried to learn how Channel 4 News in the UK and the Huffington Post had obtained it.) The CSO (a private contractor, who informed his employer) was asked to sign an agreement implying he might be asked to give the FBI more information.

Harrington said: "if we are the subject of some inquiry … by the FBI … then we have an interest in how that comes out and the question becomes whose interest do we protect first, ours or our client's." Pohl abruptly adjourned the hearing. Defense lawyers wanted to question three FBI agents and a prosecutor. Pohl ordered any defense team member contacted by the FBI to inform defense counsel, and he appointed AUSA Fernando Campoamor-Sanchez to investigate as a special trial counsel representing the government, but not the prosecutors.

In his secret report, Campoamor-Sanchez found that the FBI investigation did not concern the leak of the manifesto. Rather, the FBI had received information in November 2013 that a "nonattorney member of bin al-Shibh's defense team may have been involved in facilitating unauthorized communications with … unknown individuals located abroad," which "may have constituted a federal crime." The FBI opened a preliminary investigation but closed it on May 12. Pohl concluded that because no defense counsel was investigated, the MC did not need to inquire further. But a month later Nevin told Pohl that, starting in January 2013, the FBI had questioned at least four nonlawyer members of the defense team in two separate investigations. Until all the details were revealed, neither the lawyers nor their clients could know whether there was a conflict of interest. Pohl replied: "if there is no investigation, the conflict of interest claim must fail." Harrington said one of his investigators and one on the al-Hawsawi team had told the FBI in November 2013 that they suspected the CSO. "We have had basically a spy within our team for a number of months." Nevin said that in January 2013 the FBI had also investigated a linguist still working on KSM's defense team. Defense lawyers wanted to question the FBI officials who supervised the investigation. But Campoamor-Sanchez said the defense and Judge Pohl had all the relevant information, and any further inquiry could create error and a basis for appeal.

In June the CMCR delayed the al-Nashiri MC while it explored "options for re-nomination and re-confirmation of military judges as U.S.C.M.C.R. judges."[306] In July Pohl was replaced by Spath in the al-Nashiri MC because of a scheduling conflict.[307] Spath refused to recuse himself, even though he had prosecuted a case that Mizer (one of al-Nashiri's lawyers) was now appealing. Pohl had planned to rule on 59 outstanding motions even after stepping down, but Spath overruled him. Kammen sought to compel the government to reveal how it would execute al-Nashiri if he were sentenced to death and to order an MRI scan to investigate al-Nashiri's "organic brain damage" as mitigating evidence.[308] Poland asked the USA for diplomatic assurance that al-Nashiri would not be executed in light of the July 2014 European Court of Human Rights (ECHR) ruling that he suffered torture and cruel, inhuman, or degrading treatment while in the CIA's secret prison in Poland (see the companion volume *Law's Wars*).[309] Spath held that the government did not have to disclose its mode of execution and defense lawyers had not demonstrated the detention center's "deliberate indifference" to al-Nashiri's health care.[310] But less than two weeks later Spath ordered an MRI scan, which would delay the trial because a $1.65 million mobile MRI unit intended for Guantánamo had been sent to Georgia instead. In November Spath directed prosecutors to produce the Guantánamo commander for a hearing on why al-Nashiri could not be allowed a video or phone call with his parents, to whom he had not talked in 12 years.[311] (Two months later the ICRC enabled the HVDs to telephone their families for the first time in nearly a decade.[312]) In February 2015 Spath issued a secret amended protective order allowing al-Nashiri to speak about his treatment in custody.[313] Encouraged by this ruling, Connell asked Pohl to let al-Baluchi do so.[314]

The al-Nashiri prosecution team had been given the complete Senate Select Committee on Intelligence (SSCI) report to read and decide what the defense team could see.[315] Declaring that "in a fair system, they don't get to determine what we need," Kammen asked Spath to give the defense a copy of the report, or ensure it remained available (since SSCI was trying to recover and destroy all the copies). The prosecution resisted, and Spath denied the defense motion. But Spath abated the trial while two prosecution appeals were pending in the CMCR: one to restore the charges for the attack on the MV *Limburg* and the other to grant Yemeni dockworkers victim status.

In October 2015 the origins of one FBI investigation became clearer.[316] In August 2013 bin al-Shibh had asked his lawyers to send a message to his nephew in Yemen. A translator had a five-minute conversation with bin al-Shibh's brother, urging the nephew to study hard. Some defense team members, concerned about being prosecuted as Lynne Stewart had been (see Chapter 2), asked Harrington to report the call. He refused. After US officials learned of the incident in April 2014, the FBI contacted a defense team member to investigate whether the call contained coded messages to AQAP and told him not to discuss their visit. But several days later that member told Harrington, who moved to suspend the trial. Pohl ordered all government agencies to disclose any efforts to turn defense team members into confidential informants. In August 2015 DoJ reported that no one from the bin al-Shibh defense team would face criminal charges for the phone call. Pohl again appointed Campoamor-Sanchez to look into this, and he found that the investigation had ended and there could be no further conflict of interest.

In April 2014 Maj. Wright revealed that the Army had ordered him to attend a graduate course, removing him from the defense of KSM, with whom he had spent three years developing rapport.[317] Wright resigned to continue representing KSM as a civilian. "I chose the option which 100 percent of all defense lawyers would chose [*sic*]." After his resignation in August, Wright denounced the "show trial," which "can hardly be called a fair trial in any system in the world."

> Here you have government attorneys who tell a defendant, "I'm your attorney, I'm here to help you, and I'm going to be here 'til the end." And half-way through this process, the U.S. government – the same government that tortures you, the same government that's trying to kill you, the same government that provides the public defender – now gets to control when defense attorneys come and go.

In July Pohl severed bin al-Shibh from the other four HVDs to determine if he had the mental capacity to participate and whether he needed another lawyer because the FBI had questioned his defense team.[318] Prosecutors were opposed. Neither side had argued that bin al-Shibh was incompetent. Less than three weeks later Pohl reversed himself, but was still considering severance, which al-Hawsawi's lawyers also sought. In January 2015 Pohl rejected a prosecution motion to set a trial date because there were too many outstanding issues.[319] He also followed Judge Waits (in al-Hadi's prosecution) by ordering that female guards should not move detainees.[320]

In December 2014 Deputy Defense Secretary Robert Work ordered all MC judges to live in Guantánamo (rather than travel there for each hearing) and give those cases the highest priority.[321] He was reacting to a memo revealing that MCs had met for just 34 days in 2014, an average of five hours a day, at a cost of $78 million, which represented $2,294,117/day and $458,823/hour (excluding the cost of the 153 military personnel assigned to the MC). Defense lawyers promptly objected to what they denounced as unlawful command influence. Frakt moved that Spath step down from trying the capital murder charges against senior airman Charles A. Wilson III, who "deserves to have a judge that is able to give his undivided attention to the many complex and weighty issues in his case."[322] Pohl abated all MCs until DoD rescinded its order.

> Unless the intent is to make the military judge ignore his duty to exercise discretion under the law and instead move the case faster to shorten his stay at Guantánamo, the purported change will not, and cannot, have its intended effect. Moreover, any legitimate denial of delay requested by the defense immediately gives rise to an issue as to whether the military judge acted in the interests of justice or personal convenience.

Spath (who lived in Washington DC, and would have to resign as chief of the Air Force judiciary) ordered Marine MGen. Vaughn Ary, the CA, to testify about the order.[323] "Unlawful influence in any form is incredibly destructive to our process and we need to stop it and fix it, if it's here." Prosecutors sought to shield emails between Ary, Work, and DoD general counsel Stephen Preston, but Spath ordered the military to release 40 of 47 relevant documents. Six weeks later DoD rescinded the order, thereby averting Spath's directive that the three high-level DoD officials testify. But defense lawyers still moved to dismiss death penalty charges and exclude Ary, whose role included funding the defense and choosing the jury pool.

Declaring that Ary issued the order "knowing it could remove a sitting trial judge," Spath ordered DoD to replace Ary and the four lawyers working for him in the al-Nashiri case. "There is no doubt the action of the CA and his legal advisers at a minimum appeared to attempt to unlawfully influence the military judge in this proceeding." Spath halved the forthcoming hearing from two weeks to one to demonstrate that "this detailed trial judge feels no pressure to accelerate the pace of this litigation." The HVDs' lawyers also asked Pohl to disqualify Ary. (Waits was considering a similar request concerning al-Hadi.) Ary resigned in March 2015. The disclosed documents mentioned above revealed that DoD was considering seven more prosecutions: Mohd Farik bin Amin; Bashir bin Lap; Hambali (aka Riduan Isamuddin); Abdu Ali Sharqawi; Samad al Kazimi; Abdul Zahir; and Tariq Mahmoud el Sawah.[324] Morris Davis wrote about Ary's resignation in a *New York Times* op ed: "if a professional football team was on its seventh head coach and sixth quarterback in less than a dozen years, that team would almost certainly be a loser."[325]

In response to Sen. Ayotte's question at a SASC hearing in October, Defense Secretary Carter and JCS Chair Gen. Dunford denounced the "outrageous" ban on female guards.[326] A SOUTHCOM spokesperson said: "multiple soldiers" had filed "formal equal opportunity complaints." Marine Maj. Derek Poteet, one of KSM's lawyers, called it "extraordinarily inappropriate for these respected military and civilian leaders to inject themselves into matters that are currently under litigation in a military commission by a military judge, raising the specter of unlawful command influence." In May 2016 Pohl extended his ban for six months because of the "inappropriate," "disparaging" comments. "Senior military leaders should know better than to make these kinds of comments in a public forum during an ongoing trial."

HVD hearings resumed in February 2015 but stopped again when a new translator for bin al-Shibh was found to have worked on a CIA

black site where some of the defendants had been tortured.[327] Four of
the five HVDs recognized him. Harrington said "we vetted him," but
"he denied it." The defense moved to take his sworn testimony and
hold a pretrial hearing to conduct new background checks on the entire
team. In a sealed filing, Martins accused the defense of failing to do due
diligence in its vetting. Pohl ordered a third new translator.

Ruiz asked Pohl to intervene in al-Hawsawi's medical care, alleging
that the CIA had subjected him to what "some would call … sodomy,"
causing anal fissure, rectal prolapse and hemorrhoids, forcing him to sit
on a pillow.[328] Defense lawyers also asked Pohl to conform conditions of
confinement at secret Camp 7 to the Geneva Conventions. Prosecutors
replied that al-Hawsawi was "statutorily barred from asserting the
Geneva Conventions by the MCA of 09." Pohl ruled that the court
"does not have the authority to address issues concerning medical care."

In April 2015 Pohl canceled the third hearing in a row, citing a secret
DoJ filing about the FBI probe of defense lawyers, the unresolved issue of
severance, and pending release of the complete SSCI report.[329] In June
prosecutors reviewing that report found about 14,000 photos of black
sites where the HVDs had been held and tortured.[330] Defense attorneys
demanded to see them, calling it unacceptable to learn of the material
more than three years after arraignment.

Connell had moved in January 2013 to compel the production of
"documents and information" concerning where the "accused or a
potential witness have been confined," but Pohl never ruled on the
motion. Pohl canceled the August hearing because the conflict of
interest issue was unresolved.[331]

In October bin 'Attash asked to represent himself.[332] Martins was
opposed, as was Connell, who feared his own client, al-Baluchi,
would make the same request. Pohl and the two sides agreed on a 24-
page script for any accused who wanted to proceed pro se. Harrington
told Pohl that bin al-Shibh, who had been complaining of noises and
vibrations in his cell at night, said the problem had recurred and might
be caused by a covert DoD program discussed in court the previous
week (described below).[333] Nevin said KSM "has reported a similar
occurrence." On October 25 Pohl ruled that the FBI investigation
of the defense team raised no conflict of interest issue (even though
Campoanor-Sanchez disagreed). Within an hour bin 'Attash asked
to discuss firing his lawyers and representing himself. Pohl said the
request nonsensically "conflated three different legal principles" and
showed "why it's a bad idea to represent yourself." But two days later

bin 'Attash asked to discharge Bormann to a week after she had fired a long-serving mitigation expert who frequently consulted with him. Pohl sealed the transcript of this hearing, telling bin 'Attash: "ultimately it's your defense – and in this case it is your life – so ultimately you are the decision maker." But he denied the motion because bin 'Attash had not shown good cause. Pohl ordered the appointment of independent counsel for bin 'Attash, but then rescinded that order. When his two civilian lawyers declared an ethical responsibility to file motions over his opposition, bin 'Attash asked if he could prevent that. Pohl called it "a complicated legal issue" with no "simple yes or no answer." In February 2016, claiming "the attorneys have become the enemy," bin 'Attash sought to fire Schwartz; he had a new military lawyer, Maj. Matthew Seeger, but had met him only that week.[334] When Pohl refused to let bin 'Attash fire his lawyers or Bormann to quit the defense, the defendant announced he would boycott the proceedings and refuse all contact with military lawyers. Pohl directed bin 'Attash to stop writing him and ordered the chief defense counsel to assign bin 'Attash another lawyer to file pleadings.

Pohl also rejected a request to halt the proceedings because the Defense Secretary and JCS Chair had criticized his ban on female guards and reaffirmed the ban in December 2015.[335] In May 2016 Pohl denied a defense motion to make the ban permanent, but deferred rescission of his interim order for another six months. He denied a motion to dismiss on the ground of unlawful command influence, but acknowledged the "potential for statements ... to taint the panel," granting the defense expanded voir dire of jurors. SASC and HASC responded by adding a provision to the NDAA to nullify the ban and prohibit one in the future. Carter and Dunford declared that they had "had no intention to influence the military judges presiding over the military commissions ... we fully expect them to make their independent determinations on these and other matters."

The secret program discussed above was eavesdropping at Camp 7, which housed all MC defendants.[336] In his draft advisory to defendants seeking to represent themselves, Pohl warned: "you must assume anything you say in Camp 7 is not confidential and will be disclosed to the U.S. government." He planned to appoint Bormann and Schwartz as "standby counsel" for bin 'Attash. In December 2015 Pohl formally canceled his order severing bin al-Shibh and found him mentally fit to stand trial.[337] Ruiz then sought to sever al-Hawsawi and exclude the death penalty.[338] Pohl held a long hearing about the ban on female guards. In December lawyers for the five HVDs argued that statements by Bush, Obama, Holder, Carter, Dunford, and former SOUTHCOM commander Gen. Kelly (constituting unlawful command influence) and intelligence interference with lawyer–client privilege justified dismissal of the charges. Although prosecutors hoped to deliver all discoverable evidence by September 2016 (including 87 binders only the judge would see), two defense lawyers predicted pretrial litigation would take another five years.

In February 2016 DoD retroactively classified much of a 379-page public transcript of an October 2015 hearing concerning compliance with Pohl's order forbidding female guards from touching the HVDs.[339] This was resisted by 17 news organizations. Martins argued it was not Pohl who controlled redactions but the prison commander (who justified his actions in a secret declaration!). Pohl rejected the media's objections: "the fact that classified information was inadvertently released and publicly reported ... does not necessarily make that information fair game for unbridled further public disclosure."

In November 2014 al-Nashiri had petitioned the DC Circuit for writs of mandamus and prohibition on the ground that assignment of military judges to the CMCR violated the Constitution's Appointments and Commander-in-Chief Clauses. The Circuit Court had stayed proceedings in the CMCR; but on June 15, 2015 it denied the petition and dissolved the stay because al-Nashiri could raise those issues on appeal.[340] Seeking a rehearing in February 2016, Michel Paradis noted that the MC had neither held any hearings in a year nor set a date for the trial; even if trial began in 2018, the Circuit could not address those issues until 2024! But on August 30 the Circuit Court denied rehearing.[341] On June 9, 2016 the CMCR, now properly constituted, reversed Judge Spath's August 2014 dismissal of the charges against al-Nashiri for attacking the MV *Limburg*, holding that prosecutors could provide evidence of the attack during the trial.[342]

On December 19, 2013 Pohl had issued an order requested by the defense requiring the government to "preserve any existing evidence of any overseas detention facility used to imprison any of the defendants ... including maintaining any structure or fixture in its current state."[343] The defense learned in February 2016 that, six months after issuing the order, Pohl responded to a secret prosecution request by allowing the government to destroy that evidence and waited 18 months to order the government to provide the defense with a "redacted version," a "summary of a substitute." Defense lawyers asked

Pohl and the prosecution to recuse themselves because the action created the appearance that Pohl was "colluding with the government." The prosecution denounced this "despicable," "grandstanding," "perverse" "defense-manufactured nonsense" as a "willfully blind narrative," accusing KSM's lawyers of a "scorched-earth litigation strategy."

> [They] will apparently stop at nothing in their attempts to convince whoever may still be following their shrill antics that justice is simply not attainable at Guantánamo before a military commission. Their goal is not acquittal in this case; their goal, and their entire defense strategy, is that the case never, ever be tried.

Prosecutors blamed their failure to inform the defense for 18 months on "simple miscommunication" with Pohl, maintaining that it "caused no actual prejudice to the accused." Nevin countered that the prosecution's complicity in destruction of evidence was "despicable." Pohl declined to recuse himself.

In April 2016 chief defense counsel BGen. Baker prohibited his staff from living at Camp Justice after a joint military–civilian investigation found disturbing levels of mercury and formaldehyde in the air and arsenic in the soil.[344] An August 2015 study had rejected the notion of a cancer cluster because the types of cancer among the seven who contracted it were too disparate. (One was LtCdr. Kuebler, who died from cancer of the appendix.) Baker let his staff return to Camp Justice a month later.

On 20 July, 2016 bin 'Attash again sought to fire Bormann and Schwartz, expressing concern that Bormann controlled his other two lawyers, Maj. Matthew Seeger and Edwin Perry.[345] Baker argued that bin 'Attash could do this only by firing his entire team and representing himself. Despite Pohl's warning, bin 'Attash was determined to do so even though he could not be guaranteed a replacement and could not delay his trial for that reason. But Pohl ruled he could not fire the lawyers without showing good cause. When bin 'Attash shouted the next day "no lawyer at my table," Pohl had him removed. On July 25 bin 'Attash again complained about his lawyers, convincing Pohl to move them from the defense table to the back of the courtroom.

At a closed hearing a few days later Pohl said prosecutors had given him about half the evidence concerning secret prisons to which they believed the defense was entitled, and he had rejected "virtually all" the substitutions as inadequate.[346] The defense was now able to reveal that Pohl permitted the military to remove "fixtures" from the prison and, instead of letting the defense visit it, allowed prosecutors to substitute photos and diagrams.

On August 30, 2016 the DC Circuit denied another al-Nashiri mandamus petition challenging his MC on the ground that the criminal conduct charged did not occur during hostilities.[347] The Supreme Court denied certiorari the following year. Before the September 7 hearing, all four of al-Nashiri's military counsel left (Cmdr. Mizer was reassigned without his client's consent).[348] There was a new civilian prosecutor, Mark Miller (an AUSA in New Orleans). BGen. Baker reported "significant resourcing issues" because of the "lack of qualified military counsel" and complained that security clearance for two civilian counsel had been delayed for more than a year. But Spath denied a defense motion to abate until six months after counsel obtained that clearance: "we cannot abate these proceedings every time a new defense counsel is detailed." The next day Kammen (wearing a kangaroo lapel pin to show his contempt for the MC) renewed his criticisms, calling the CMCR "a Potemkin court [whose] only mission and only assignment is to help the prosecution when a judge has the temerity to say to the prosecution, 'you're wrong.'" A day after that Kammen complained that there was "no order" to the prosecution's 265,000 pages of discovery: "this system is hopelessly flawed." A few days later in a speech at Georgetown University's NATSECDEF Conference, Baker agreed the MCs were "a farce ... characterized by delay, government misconduct, and incompetence." "[E]ven the most routine client visit takes an entire week to accomplish." "Most recently, the government has been baiting one of the accused to fire his defense team and go pro se." Discovery practices were "unlike any undertaken by any prosecutor in any American court system."

> Here we are 15 years after 9/11 – or more generously, 4 years after the accused were arraigned – and the prosecution has not completed its discovery obligations. The redactions and deletions in what they have turned over will lead to what I predict is years of additional litigation ... for seven years – since charges were originally brought in the 9/11 case – the government has refused to provide the formal classification guidance required by Executive Order. The limited guidance that has been received has been inadequate, resulting in "spills" of classified information that cause significant delay, including the temporary seizure of computers ... More disturbingly, the classified evidence rules have been interpreted to allow the prosecution to secretly obtain permission from the military judge to secretly destroy critical exculpatory evidence

... My attempts to hire additional death penalty counsel, investigators, intel analyst [sic], and other critical resources have been continuously blocked by the Convening Authority.

When the HVD trial resumed in October 2016, bin al-Shibh claimed (for the first time) he could not understand Judge Pohl, saying (in English): "I need you to force your orders on the guard [to remediate the alleged vibrations and noises that interrupted his sleep] exactly the way you force the orders on me."[349] When Pohl replied "I'm not sitting here having you tell me what I need to do" and ordered the defendant to be quiet, bin al-Shibh retorted: "Either I'm going to leave or I'm going to talk or you are going to stop this abuse." Pohl expelled him. Ruiz explained that al-Hawsawi would miss future hearings to undergo a surgical procedure. Bin 'Attash reiterated that his lawyers, to whom he had not spoken in months, did not represent him.

A week later, Kammen compared the defense to "mushrooms kept in the dark" (quoting a Sixth Circuit reversal of a conviction after exposure of *ex parte* communications between prosecution and judge), calling the alleged "collaboration" "beyond unethical" and "a crime."[350] This provoked chief prosecutor Martins to lash out:

> We, as advocates here on this side of the courtroom, have been perhaps too sanguine that the trial judicial system will reign [sic] in such defense abuses, have perhaps erred too greatly on the side of equanimity and discipline, when a more appropriate posture may perhaps have been emphatic rebuttal of the nonsense that we hear from the other side of the courtroom so routinely. To rebut so-called learned counsel's antics in every instance or even more than occasionally could simply reward the defense with the delay and the disruption they do seek ... But here the innuendo and baseless accusations have crossed the line.

Kammen (wearing his kangaroo pin) retorted it was "an insult to kangaroos to call it a kangaroo court."

The December 5, 2016 hearing began with colloquy about whether al-Hawsawi, recovering from surgery for "third-degree prolapsed internal hemorrhoids," could attend court.[351] Ruiz sought to question the Special Medical Officer, who certified al-Hawsawi as medically fit.

RUIZ: Great system, Judge. Great system.
POHL: Mr. Ruiz, watch those kind of comments. You may not like this system but you won't disrespect this commission on the record like that. Do you understand me?
RUIZ: Judge, I think this whole commission is disrespectful.
POHL: I am not asking for your editorial opinion.

RUIZ: It is disrespectful to our flag and it's disrespectful to our system of justice.
POHL: Stop.
RUIZ: I think it is—
POHL: Stop. Sit down. You are done.
RUIZ: I am not done with my cross yet, Judge.
POHL: You are done for now. Sit down.
RUIZ [IRONICALLY]: I like the way this works.

When Swann, the prosecutor, objected to Ruiz connecting al-Hawsawi's surgery with his torture, observing that "a lot of people" have hemorrhoids, Ruiz replied angrily: "you weren't sodomized."

In April 2016, al-Hawsawi's lawyers disclosed that a computer error had let them see prosecution material (the "spill" Baker mentioned above).[352] Prosecutors sought an order to "scrub" all defense computers, shutting down each one for about six hours. In December the defense attacked Martins's decision to appoint a special trial counsel to investigate the computer error.[353] Pohl gave the defense eight weeks to argue it should be able to retain the information inadvertently disclosed. The next day was devoted to defense motions for discovery concerning the government's destruction of a black site, complete medical records for the five HVDs, recordings and transcripts of al-Qahtani's torture, and the unredacted SSCI report. Irritated by Martins's refusal to say whether DoD had a copy of the report, Pohl ordered the prosecution to respond.

After Trump's election defense lawyers again asked Pohl to preserve the SSCI report, arguing it contained "extremely important facts that can be offered in mitigation on behalf of Mr. Mohammed."[354] Martins resisted, dismissing it as just "opinions and analysis of the legislature." Pohl ordered the government to inform him in writing "whether the DoD is in possession of a copy," and ordered DoD to preserve the report and not return it to SSCI (whose chair had vowed to destroy it).[355]

In January 2017, when prosecutors said they wanted to begin the trial in March 2018, Jay Connell (for al-Baluchi) called this "hopelessly optimistic," and Jim Harring (for bin al-Shibh) said it was "not conceivable" and 2020 would be "more realistic."[356] Baker agreed 2018 was "unrealistic." The same day Pohl castigated the decision to cancel all 2017 reservations for temporary base housing for visiting MC staff, calling it "yet another example of how commission proceedings are slowed or halted by external forces making decisions without a full appreciation of the consequences those decisions have on the commissions. Such ad hoc decision-making goes to the very integrity of trial process."

He postponed several days of hearings on 33 motions because Bormann (bin 'Attash's only death penalty lawyer) had broken her arm and could not travel. In May 2017 Bormann and the other two defense lawyers asked to be relieved because Tim Semmerling, a former defense lawyer, had filed a (sealed) lawsuit in federal court, creating a conflict of interest.

In March 2017 the al-Nashiri prosecutors and defense lawyers clashed over allegations (eventually refuted) that the defense had wrongfully accessed prosecution computers and the prosecution had wrongfully obtained privileged defense communications, as well as allegations that the prosecution had failed to give the defense all discoverable evidence, including al-Nashiri's medical records.[357] Judge Spath granted a defense motion to compel testimony by John Rizzo, Jose Rodriguez, James Mitchell, and Bruce Jessen concerning CIA destruction of al-Nashiri's interrogation videotapes. Spath planned to start the trial in 2018, but acknowledged it would take months to seat the jury. Judge Pohl issued three public rebukes to the prosecution for "numerous" "misstatements," "misrepresentations, and mistakes," and ordered it to give the defense all the unredacted "torture memos." Connell sought all communications between the government and the filmmakers of *Zero Dark Thirty*, one of whose characters was modeled on his client, al-Baluchi. Lawyers for all the HVDs renewed a motion for disclosure of all government interceptions of privileged communications with their clients. Judge Pohl warned about "a potential train wreck of three cases coming to the same courtroom simultaneously" in 2018. Trying to solve that by holding trials from 7 a.m. to midnight "takes away from the seriousness of the case." Lawyers for Hadi sought the unredacted SSCI report and all its sources as well as the Panetta review. The parties debated whether al-Hadi's refusal to be transported to court by a female guard constituted voluntary waiver of the right to be present. Defense lawyers challenged the fact that the Convening Authority not only referred charges but also approved defense funding for experts, detailed panel members, and could modify their findings and sentence. Lawyers for al-Hawsawi and al-Baluchi made international and constitutional law arguments in support of motions asserting that the MC lacked jurisdiction. In April Judge Pohl dismissed charges of attacking civilian objects and destruction of property as barred by the five-year statute of limitations; but the CMCR reversed him two months later: "during hostilities, a statute of limitations applying a time limit to prosecute law of war violations is not practicable." After the Chief Military Defense

Counsel declared a "loss of confidence" in the integrity of "all poten-tial attorney–client meeting locations" following the disclosure that some had been recorded in violation of Judge Pohl's explicit order, SOUTHCOM commander Adm. Kurt Tidd ordered an AR 15–6 inves-tigation. In July Judges Pohl and Spath suspended their trials after the prison commander withdrew the boat that let them cross the bay separ-ately from 9/11 victims and families, counsel, and the press.

Attorney General Sessions blamed the repeated delays on the Obama administration's failure to "work[] through all the legal complications," which it "allow[ed] to linger and never get decided, so nothing ever happened."[358] The government charged the first new accused in years: Riduan Isamuddin (aka Hambali) for the 2002 Bali bombing 15 years earlier, declaring it would not seek the death penalty (perhaps because of the difficulties described above).

In August 2017 the DC Circuit granted a writ of mandamus vacating a CMCR decision concerning KSM because Scott Silliman, one of the judges, should have recused himself, having earlier called KSM one of "the major conspirators in the 9/11 attacks."[359]

CONCLUSION

Within months of the 9/11 attacks, President Bush and his adminis-tration made a calculated decision to try Guantánamo Bay detainees in MCs rather than civilian courts or courts-martial. Lawyers like Attorney General Ashcroft, Alberto Gonzales, and David Addington (legal advisers to the president and vice president) and William Haynes (DoD General Counsel) were determined to ensure convictions. MC prosecutor Morris Davis said Haynes told him: "we can't have acquittals …we have to have convictions." (As Chapter 3 shows, courts-martial were structured to acquit or impose only mild punishment, especially on senior officers.) Gonzales declared: "enemy war criminals are not entitled to the same procedural protections as people who violated our domestic laws." Administration officials predicted a mythical parade of horrors in civilian trials: Miranda warnings and defense lawyers on the battlefield, officers pulled out of combat to testify, difficulties in pre-serving the evidentiary chain of custody, delays, and fora that would give accused a political platform and terrorists a vulnerable target. At the same time, officials offered empty reassurances about MCs. Proceedings would be "full and fair" (a mantra repeated ad nauseam, like Bush's numbing protestations that "we do not torture"). Defendants would be charged only with "offenses against the international laws of war" (a promise broken as soon as it was made). Even after the Supreme Court rebuked the administration in *Hamdan*, Gonzales and senior DoD and DoJ lawyers (Dell'Orto and Bradbury) reiterated identical objections to civilian trials; and both the administration and Republican leaders in Congress sought to repudiate the US commitment to the Geneva Conventions. Bush cynically invited relatives of 9/11 victims to the White House to promise that the 14 HVDs he had dramatically extracted from the no longer secret CIA prisons – like rabbits from a magician's hat – would speedily be punished under the MCA he was urging Congress to pass. (He also hoped, vainly, to use national security fears to defeat Democrats in the forthcoming election, as he had done two years earlier.) The most vigorous and effective opposition to the administration's proposals came from military lawyers (the four JAGs) and senators with military experience: Warner (a former Navy Secretary), McCain (who had been tortured), and Graham (a career JAG lawyer). Although Gonzales (as White House counsel) had promised that detainees would have access to habeas corpus, after *Hamdan* (as Attorney General) he complained bitterly about the "hundreds of lawsuits from Guantánamo detainees that are clogging our court system," which the MCA was intended to eliminate. MCs would continue to admit hearsay and coerced confessions and deny defendants access to secret evidence. Two years later the administration filed death penalty charges against some HVDs to gin up support from the 9/11 families (whom it flew to Guantánamo for the arraignment), hoping to make it harder for Bush's successor to abort the prosecutions.

Obama appeared to restore some rule-of-law protections in trying detainees, as he did by ending torture and secret prisons and moving to close Guantánamo. He suspended the MCs and indicated that some HVDs would be tried in civilian courts. But though Holder initiated prosecutions in SDNY, he failed to secure support from local politicians (even Democrats). The administration's decision to reform the MCs and try al-Nashiri there made choices between these two fora seem arbitrary, even expedient. And the failed "underwear bomber" and Times Square attacks gave Republicans new opportunities to oppose civilian trials (even though both Abdulmutallab and Shahzad quickly pleaded guilty in civilian courts and received life sentences). If the administration hoped its capitulation on MCs would ensure Graham's support for closing Guantánamo, it was bitterly disappointed. Republicans cemented their congressional victory by legislating barriers against transferring Guantánamo detainees to the USA for civilian trial. When MCs resumed, their website repeated the empty promise of "Fairness* Transparency*Justice."

MCs themselves presented a very mixed picture. Some judges made principled decisions against the prosecution, if many of those setbacks were temporary. Both Allred and Brownback dismissed the charges against defendants whose CSRTs had not found them to be *unlawful* enemy combatants as the MCA required (but MCs quickly corrected that oversight). Allred granted Hamdan's motion to call the HVDs as witnesses (testifying by deposition) and shifted the burden to the prosecution to prove Hamdan's confession was voluntary because prosecutors had delayed in answering discovery requests. Although Henley excluded both of Jawad's "confessions," Parrish admitted the "confession" Khadr had made in Bagram when he had been even younger than Jawad. Judges sometimes let defense lawyers elicit evidence of torture (but SOPs had directed interrogators to destroy their notes). Allred denied a prosecutor's untimely objection to a jury instruction. Three judges barred Hartmann for improper behavior, leading to his removal as the CA's legal adviser. When the chief defense counsel removed Kuebler from Khadr's case, Parrish reinstated him, declaring that only the judge had that power. Juries seem to have taken their responsibilities seriously, deliberating eight hours over three days before acquitting Hamdan of conspiracy (while convicting him of material support) and sentencing him to just 5.5 years. At the sentencing hearing Allred excluded testimony by a prosecution witness injured in the 9/11 attack (with which Hamdan had no connection) and gave Hamdan credit for 61 months served, permitting his release in a few months, despite prosecution objections that he could be detained indefinitely as an EC. Judges were especially sensitive if their authority was challenged, as when DoD ordered them to live in Guantánamo, overruled judges' bans on female guards touching defendants, let guards read confidential lawyer–client communications, or denied judges a separate boat to travel to court. Spath halved the length of a hearing to defy the order that judges live in Guantánamo; and Pohl extended his ban on female guard escorts after the Defense Secretary and JCS Chair criticized it. And though all trials ended in guilty verdicts, some of those convictions did rest on evidence untainted by coercion (certainly Hamdan's, probably Khadr's, possibly Hicks's).

But MCs also compared unfavorably to their civilian counterparts in crucial ways. Pretrial proceedings often resembled trials in Alice in

Wonderland because MCs were *tabulae rasae*. Asked what law would govern, Chester lamely joked: "it's above my pay grade. The Supreme Court is going to tell us what to do." "I suppose we will look at military criminal law and federal criminal laws and procedures." Pressed to be more specific, he declined "to speculate as to what is or what is not controlling." Pohl even refused to say whether the Constitution applied in his courtroom! Parrish had to ask a defense lawyer about civilian protections for lawyer–client communications. Brownback denied saying that Hamdan had no right to a speedy trial and then, confronted with a tape of that statement, complained it had been made without his permission. Incompetent translations rendered testimony incomprehensible at best, seriously misleading at worst. Judges insisted on rigid protocols that made no sense in Guantánamo because defense lawyers were denied timely access to clients and prosecution evidence. Courts solicitously warned defendants seeking to proceed pro se that they would be seriously disadvantaged. But judges may have been more concerned about potential disruption and inefficiency: when al-Nashiri boycotted the hearings to protest guards' use of force, Pohl ordered the guards to use force to bring him to court to affirm his boycott. Judges capitulated to prosecution demands to withhold evidence from accused and excluded the public from hearings about that issue. They let DoD *retroactively* classify the transcript of a public hearing. They consulted prosecutors about defense requests to pay for expert witnesses. Kohlmann expelled Hicks's two civilian lawyers from the hearing in which their client pleaded guilty. Pohl ordered the government to preserve the secret prisons in which the HVDs had been tortured but then secretly heard and granted a prosecution request to permit their destruction. Perhaps because of this, Pohl then found inadequate the government's substitutions for the destroyed evidence and ordered DoD to preserve its copy of the unredacted SSCI report. Judges either rejected or postponed (until the inevitable DC Circuit review) the defense's fundamental threshold challenges to the proceedings (especially constitutional objections, such as those based on the Equal Protection and Define and Punish clauses). Pohl ruled that whether hostilities prevailed at the time of al-Nashiri's alleged crimes – a jurisdictional prerequisite – would be decided by the jury as an issue of *fact*. Juries were forced to perform the charade of sentencing al Qosi and Noor Uthman Mohammed when judges knew that secret plea bargains limited the sentences. Judges were repeatedly replaced during pretrial hearings, interrupting continuity and raising doubts about fairness. After Pohl refused multiple motions to disqualify him from hearing the HVD case, he was removed for a scheduling conflict. Changes of the CA, judges, prosecutors, defense lawyers, and governing law (the MCAs of 2006 and 2009) and the repeated withdrawal and refiling of charges protracted the proceedings and undermined their legitimacy.

Judges denied claims by both Hamdan and al-Bahlul that their charges were *ex post facto* and did not constitute war crimes, and the CMCR affirmed. It took the DC Circuit to reverse, declaring it "plain error" to charge material support or solicitation as war crimes; and the DDC ruled that material support could not be charged retroactively for acts committed before the MCA 2006. These two cases exposed judges' irreconcilable political differences. In *Hamdan*, DDC Judge Robertson was reversed by a divided DC Circuit, which was reversed in turn by a Supreme Court that split 5–3, producing six opinions extending over more than a hundred pages, followed by another Robertson opinion, an MC conviction that was upheld by an en banc CMCR in an 89-page opinion, and finally another reversal by a new DC Circuit panel. Even though al-Bahlul proudly proclaimed his actions, the CMCR took 150 pages to affirm the conviction, only to have that vacated by the DC Circuit, which in turn was displaced by the en banc Circuit in five opinions over 150 pages, leading to another panel decision requiring three opinions totaling 80 pages and finally another en banc reversal extending over 69 pages. The CMCR set aside Hicks's conviction, refusing to dismiss his appeal as untimely.

Defense lawyers engaged in zealous advocacy, vigorously challenging both prosecutors and judges (and even their own superior, the chief defense counsel). DoD retaliated against Swift for defending Hamdan, forcing him to retire after nearly a quarter century in the military by denying him a well-deserved promotion. Lawyers also confronted difficult and unusual ethical dilemmas when clients sought to appear pro se, refused to participate in the hearing, instructed lawyers not to participate, or exhibited signs of mental illness. These problems were compounded by the fact that clients had been abused by their captors for years, suffered from PTSD, were repeatedly shackled (when transferred to meetings with lawyers or to court), and had great difficulty trusting lawyers who differed from them linguistically and culturally, sometimes wore the uniform of their torturers, and visited Guantánamo briefly and infrequently.

313

Prosecutors were just as determined to win convictions and impose lengthy sentences. They sought to introduce highly prejudicial evidence about the bombings of US embassies in East Africa and the *USS Cole*, and especially the 9/11 attack itself, against defendants who bore no responsibility. They withheld exculpatory evidence and delayed or complied only partially when ordered to disclose it, "finding" as late as June 2015 some 14,000 photos of the black sites where HVDs had been tortured; but prosecutors rarely suffered any consequences because MCs lacked a *Brady* rule (imposing penalties for nondisclosure of exculpatory evidence). Borch apparently agreed with Haynes that MCs could not possibly acquit. Morris Davis was the typical hard-charging prosecutor, inflaming public opinion against the accused while condemning defense lawyers like Mori who tried to mobilize support for their clients. Indeed, Crawford sidelined Davis in negotiating a plea bargain for Hicks (a political deal struck between her former mentor Cheney and Australian Prime Minister Howard), perhaps fearing the prosecutor's resistance. It was stunning, therefore, when Davis switched sides, accusing Haynes and Hartmann of interfering with prosecutorial discretion for political reasons and then resigning. Other prosecutors also resigned in protest: Couch over the use of coerced testimony; Vandeveld because of the abuse of Jawad (whom he concluded was innocent); Carr and Preston following the failure to disclose exculpatory evidence; Wolf without giving reasons. DoD sought to prevent both Davis and Vandeveld from testifying for defendants. After criticizing Davis (his predecessor), Morris also resigned, complaining of political pressure. Even Crawford – Cheney's protégé – blocked the prosecution of Mohammed al-Qahtani because he had been tortured, and then she retired. (Both her predecessors, Altenburg and Hemingway, and her successor, Ary, also left following accusations of political interference.) All were career military lawyers who had been motivated by patriotism to volunteer for the MCs, but then jeopardized or jettisoned those careers for the sake of principle. Is there any other instance of such widespread prosecutorial revolt inspired by fidelity to the rule of law?

A variety of outsiders pressed MCs to respect the rule of law. Leading newspapers like the *New York Times, Washington Post,* and *Los Angeles Times* published numerous critical editorials and op eds (although the *Post* kept promoting a national security court, and conservative newspapers like the *Wall Street Journal* and *New York Daily News* reviled defense lawyers). ABA and NYCB leaders did the same. In three of America's closest allies – the UK, Canada, and Australia – influential voices in the media, the legal profession, and opposition parties (if not heads of state) called for the return of MC defendants. Federal judges exercised their power. Judge Robertson (a former Navy officer) enjoined Hamdan's MC (only to be reversed by a conservative DC Circuit panel and disabled by the MCA from intervening again). The Bush administration sought to soften judicial resistance by modifying MC rules in anticipation of federal court decisions. But some of the remaining features were particularly egregious, such as charging capital crimes against defendants unable to see all the evidence or seek review in an Art. III court. And Congressional attempts in the DTA and MCA to strip federal courts of habeas jurisdiction may have provoked the Supreme Court to defend its authority. Even Judge Kavanaugh – no fan of international law (especially customary international law) – had to concede that material support was not a war crime. Yet some judges unapologetically supported MCs. Conservatives called for deference to the executive. Roberts participated in *Hamdan* (and voted to reverse Robertson) while he was being considered for the Supreme Court. Invoking his son's service in the military (although he himself had never served), Scalia praised MCs before oral argument in *Hamdan* (and refused to recuse himself) and then – though he had fiercely assailed colleagues for citing *authentic* legislative history – rested his dissent on the *fictitious* legislative history fabricated by Kyl and Graham. But whereas political orientations (indicated by the appointing president's party) were strongly correlated with judges' decisions in civil damage actions by "war on terror" and terrorism victims (see Chapter 6), they were not significantly correlated with judges' reviews of military commissions (see Table 4.1).[360]

Table 4.1 Federal Judges' Rulings Reviewing Military Commissions, by Appointing President's Party

Appointing President	# Decisions for Accused	% Decisions for Accused	# Decisions for Prosecution	% Decisions for Prosecution	Total Decisions
Democrat	10	56	8	44	18
Republican	15	42	21	58	36
Total	25	46	29	54	54

Chi-Square = 0.93, p = .33

If the MC process was seriously flawed, its actions were even less satisfactory. First, although Rumsfeld insisted that Guantánamo housed "the worst of the worst," the first five people prosecuted hardly fit the description. Hamdan was an uneducated driver and mechanic and al Qosi a low-level cook, bodyguard, and driver. Khadr and Jawad were both juveniles at the time of their alleged acts. Hicks, who converted to Islam after a troubled youth, had a marginal and largely accidental connection to the "war on terror." Only al-Bahlul was a significant figure.

Second, many cases were resolved by plea bargains. True, so are most civilian criminal prosecutions. But MCs were designed to conduct show trials, which would show the world both the accused's iniquity and the quality of American justice. Yet the pressure to strike deals was even more intense in the MCs. *Defense* lawyers were told that was their job. Pleas were essential to conceal how horribly some defendants had been abused. Lenience was promised to persuade one detainee to testify against others (although these later trials often were endlessly postponed). Prosecutors cited successful deals to convince other defendants to plead guilty. Some did so because they (rightly) feared conviction, others out of (a justified) concern that even acquittal would not free them from Guantánamo.

Third, most of those convicted served short sentences: Hamdan just five months, Hicks less than a year (in Australia), al Qosi just two, Noor Uthman Mohammed less than three, and Khadr less than five (partly in Canada). Only al-Bahlul, who proudly proclaimed his guilt, was sentenced to life.

Fourth, many prosecutions were aborted, some permanently, others still in limbo. Unlike the completed prosecutions of the bit players described above, these inconclusive cases often involved defendants against whom there was evidence of involvement in significant terrorist activity. Al-Sharbi, Jabran al-Qahtani, and Kamin refused to participate, and their trials simply stopped, as did those of Zahir, Hadi, and al Kandari. Charges against Mohammed al-Qahtani, said to be the "20th hijacker," were repeatedly dropped because he had been tortured. Binyam Mohamed was linked to many other alleged high-profile terrorists: Richard Reid (the shoe bomber), José Padilla, abu Zubaydah, al-Hadi, al-Sharbi, Jabran al-Qahtani, and KSM. Again, however, the fact that he had been tortured made prosecution difficult, and Britain successfully pressed for his transfer and promptly released him. Of the 14 charged or slated for prosecution, only four were convicted (after guilty pleas) and served short sentences.

Finally, MCs encountered – and often foundered on – unique obstacles. I have already mentioned torture, which surfaced in and delayed or derailed the prosecutions of Mohammed al-Qahtani, Binyam Mohamed, Jawad, Khadr, and KSM, among others. Torture also raised doubts about the competence of bin al-Shibh, al-Baluchi, and al-Nashiri to stand trial (leading Pohl to sever bin al-Shibh from the HVD trial and then restore him). Al-Hawsawi's chronic rectal injuries from being sodomized forced repeated hearing postponements. But even torture – arguably the most fundamental rule-of-law violation – was dwarfed by two other kinds of problem. The first was attributable to the government, which often was its own worst enemy.

These were, after all, *military* commissions and therefore, unsurprisingly, quintessential embodiments of that indispensable military acronym SNAFU: situation normal, all fucked up. MCs were determined to secure convictions, were obsessed with secrecy, were entangled in labyrinthine bureaucracy, and were terminally incompetent. Especially in their early days, MCs did not accord defendants the equality of arms essential in death penalty cases. The shortage of military prosecutors, defense lawyers, and judges meant they were constantly being shifted from case to case, disrupting continuity and forcing proceedings to begin over again. Personnel had to be replaced when tours of duty ended or military lawyers retired or resigned. Khadr went through a dozen US lawyers (and was denied his choice of Canadians). All MC personnel wasted huge amounts of time (and money) flying to Guantánamo for brief, irregularly spaced hearings (particularly burdensome for civilian lawyers serving pro bono). Once there, they had to work in very difficult conditions; indeed, their offices sometimes were uninhabitable and their living quarters unhealthy. The military intranet was a shambles: defense documents disappeared or popped up in prosecution folders, forcing defense lawyers to stop using email or storing documents on servers; when the reverse happened, all defense computers had to be shut down and purged. Faulty file transfers and a "dirty" shutdown lost huge numbers of documents (at least temporarily). The military was able to monitor the defense's computers and internet searches. The pool of translators was small, and some were poorly trained or capable only of consecutive translation. Some HVDs had previously encountered one translator in a secret CIA prison where they had been tortured.

The military repeatedly violated lawyer–client privilege; rebuked by judges, it just switched to a different method.[361] The chief defense counsel felt compelled to ban all communication by snail mail, severely hobbling trial preparation. Guards searched defendants' cells in their absence, reading, copying, and seizing privileged documents. Microphones in cells could transmit defendants' conversations with lawyers; microphones in the courtroom regularly broadcast conversations among defense lawyers and clients. Judges openly acknowledged that the government systematically listened to all conversations among the five HVDs. FBI investigations of defense team members raised doubts about the integrity of the process, which were never entirely allayed. In August 2017 lawyers for the HVDs renewed motions "to permanently and verifiably disable any audio monitoring that may exist in attorney–client meeting spaces."[362] In October, prison guards seized computers and hard drives the government had given the HVDs, which contained privileged information.

The previous May, the government had notified MCs and defendants that lawyer–client communications had been compromised (presumably in the HVD case). A month later, Chief Military Defense Counsel BGen. Baker advised all defense counsel not to conduct lawyer–client meetings. Al-Nashiri's lawyers' request to disclose classified information about this to their client was denied, as were motions to compel production of relevant material and hold evidentiary hearings and to abate the proceedings. In October, Baker, acting on the advice of a "prominent legal ethicist" (Prof. Ellen Yaroshevsky), granted a request by al-Nashiri's three civilian lawyers to resign because they could not assure their client that communications with him were confidential.[363] That left him represented by only Lt. Alaric Piette (a 2012 Georgetown law graduate), who moved to abate pending the appointment of a new learned counsel (whose participation was required in a death penalty case). The judge, Col. Spath, promptly ordered the three to appear at the next hearing, claiming that the Trial Judiciary Rules of Court required that excusal "be approved by the military judge." Baker replied that the Manual for Military Commissions, under which the Rules had been promulgated, vested the official who appointed the lawyer (himself) with the power to excuse for good cause, which he had found. At the next hearing (which the three civilian lawyers declined to attend) Baker refused to testify under oath or rescind his decision. Spath threatened him with contempt, refusing to listen to his lawyer, whom he admonished for addressing Spath as "colonel" instead of "your honor." When Piette refused to proceed without learned counsel, Spath ruled that the current hearings did not involve the death penalty and threatened him, too, with contempt. (Contemporaneously, the chief military prosecutor declared he would no longer brief the press.) At the next hearing, Spath found Baker in contempt for engaging in "disorder," confining him to quarters for 21 days and imposing a $1,000 fine (although the CA suspended both until he could hear Baker's appeal). After Spath ordered the three civilian lawyers to appear by video from Virginia, threatening contempt, they again refused. Baker petitioned for habeas in DDC, and the three civilian lawyers filed preemptive habeas petitions in the jurisdictions to which they were admitted, in response to which a District Judge in Indianapolis enjoined enforcement of any order that Kammen appear in Virginia and prohibited marshals from seizing him. When prosecutors said that at the direction of Spath they would try to arrange for Prof. Yaroshevsky to testify remotely, her lawyer filed a preemptive habeas petition in SDNY to prevent US marshals from seizing her.

Government secrecy distorted the trials in numerous ways: defendants could not describe their torture to their own lawyers; any mention of torture or the CIA prompted the CSO to interrupt the audio feed, making it difficult for reporters and other observers to follow the proceedings. The CIA had its own off-switch, unknown even to the judge. The government repeatedly skirted or crossed the line of unlawful command influence – a fundamental threat to the MCs' fairness because of the military's rigid hierarchy and insistence that subordinates unquestioningly obey orders. Presidents Bush and Obama, their Attorneys General, and high civilian DoD officials proclaimed the depravity and guilt of the accused, especially the HVDs. DoD ordered judges to move to Guantánamo and countermanded judicial orders that female guards not touch defendants. The CAs' pivotal role blurred the separation of powers, which may have contributed to their replacement or resignation and those of their legal advisers.

If these flaws were theoretically remediable, the problems introduced by defendants were not. The government wanted trials to focus on their crimes. But the defendants sought to invert the proceedings, putting the government on trial for what they claimed were far worse crimes: centuries of mistreatment of Muslims, from the Crusades through the wars in Afghanistan and Iraq; a decade of rendition, detention, and torture in secret prisons and Guantánamo; and their own present conditions of confinement. (Defendants may have focused on the last because they had no other way to redress their most immediate grievances and no faith in the justice of the proceedings, much less any hope of acquittal or ultimate release, even if they won.) The government wanted MCs to showcase what it believed was incontrovertible proof of the defendants' guilt through a comprehensive presentation of damning evidence. But some HVDs boasted of their crimes – in the CSRTs, at arraignment, and repeatedly during subsequent hearings. The government wanted defendants represented by lawyers so trials would be orderly and appear fair. But many defendants (including Hamdan, Khadr, al-Bahlul, Jawad, al-Sharbi, Jabran al-Qahtani, Barhoumi, Binyam Mohamed, al Qosi, Kamin, al-Hadi, the five HVDs, and al-Nashiri) repeatedly fired their lawyers, insisting on representing themselves, or refused to participate at all. Acting pro se gave them a platform from which to declaim inflammatory rhetoric and use voir dire to insult judges. Firing lawyers was one of the few ways defendants could exercise agency and express anger. And they were unimpressed by judicial warnings that they would be disadvantaged by proceeding pro se because they had no faith in the fairness of MCs. Silencing them and forcing military defense lawyers to represent them created ethical dilemmas for the lawyers and undermined the appearance of fairness, already badly compromised by the fact that pro se defendants could not see all the evidence against them.

Judges wanted defendants to be present, especially if they were proceeding pro se; but defendants sought to discredit the entire process by staying in their cells. Defendants who did attend court refused to wear headphones, forcing the judge to switch from simultaneous to consecutive translation, straining the ability of translators, doubling the length of the proceedings, and creating a cacophony in which translators, witnesses, lawyers, and even the judge competed to be heard. Just as the civilian criminal justice system could not deter the suicidal 9/11 attackers, so MCs could not use the threat of conviction and execution to compel HVDs to respect its procedures.

Both administrations indulged in unrealistic boasts that they would prosecute some five dozen alleged terrorists. In 2001 Alberto Gonzales declared that MCs "can dispense justice swiftly" and "the American military justice system is the finest in the world." Obama's press secretary trumpeted: "KSM is going to meet justice, and he's going to meet his maker." But more than 15 years after Bush created the MCs, only about a quarter of the more than two dozen people originally charged had been convicted, and all but one of those were marginal figures who served sentences of just a few months or years. Nearly ten years after the HVDs were arraigned, their trials remain years away. The sister of a 9/11 victim, who had observed the proceedings in 2015, wrote in

2017: "A decade and a half of political posturing, wild spending, and the abandonment of our fundamental values in the rhetorical name of being 'tough on terrorism' have yielded nothing for any of us."[364] In a much-quoted dictum, Lord Chief Justice Hewart wrote that "not only must Justice be done; it must also be seen to be done."[365] But the MCs dispensed no justice, they were not seen, and they were never done.

CHAPTER FIVE

HABEAS CORPUS

Habeas corpus, whose origins date back to Magna Carta, is called the Great Writ because it is viewed as the ultimate bulwark against tyranny. Article I of the US Constitution limits suspension of the writ to "cases of rebellion or invasion" (neither of which has occurred in the "war on terror"). In his first inaugural address, Thomas Jefferson lauded the writ as one of the principles that form "the bright constellation which has gone before us." This chapter traces its vagaries throughout the 15 years after 9/11, posing the following questions.[1] How did judges divide in response to habeas petitions, with respect to both votes and the content and tone of judicial rhetoric? How did these cases compare with others in terms of opinion length, concurrences and dissents, appellate reversals, and en banc rehearings? What explains those differences, as well as exceptions to the overall pattern? How did Circuit Court judges treat District Judges (who decide issues of fact) and Supreme Court Justices (who determine doctrine)? How effective were habeas petitions in evaluating the government's grounds for detention and in releasing those unlawfully held?

EARLY PETITIONS

The Bush administration sent detainees to Guantánamo Bay because the OLC had opined that federal courts lacked jurisdiction to consider habeas petitions from them.[2] And indeed, the first petitions encountered insuperable barriers.[3] Just weeks after detainees were brought to the island prison, a group of Southern California journalists, lawyers, and clergy sought the writ in the CD Cal as next friend.[4] Judge Matz took just a month to dismiss the case, finding they lacked standing and, under *Johnson v. Eisentrager*,[5] no federal court would have jurisdiction over such a claim. Since the case had been filed "not one friend, relative, diplomatic or religious representative, fellow countryman or anyone with a direct tie to a particular detainee has authorized this petition. Common sense suggests that something is seriously awry in petitioners' claims to be the appropriate representatives of the detainees."[6]

The petitioners had not even alleged "that they *attempted* to communicate with the detainees." The Ninth Circuit affirmed.[7] Judge Wardlaw (joined by Berzon and Noonan) agreed that petitioners lacked next-friend and third-party standing. "[T]he Coalition has not demonstrated any relationship with the detainees," even though they had been visited by the ICRC and diplomats, and family members had filed petitions for others. But the judges vacated the decision that no federal court would have jurisdiction.

In the same District Court later that year, Belaid Gherebi filed a habeas petition as next friend for his brother Falen.[8] In May 2003 (before the 9th Circuit decision above), Judge Matz again found he lacked jurisdiction under *Eisentrager* because the USA did not exercise sovereignty in Guantánamo. But he reached "this conclusion reluctantly … because the prospect of the Guantánamo captives' [*sic*] being detained indefinitely without access to counsel, without formal notice of charges, and without trial is deeply troubling." The Executive Branch's 15-month delay in implementing "its stated intention to try these detainees" was "not consistent with some of the most basic values our legal system has long embodied. To compound the problem, recently reports have appeared in the press that several of the detainees are only juveniles." He issued "a prompt ruling to speed appellate review" in the hope that "a higher court will find a principled way" to provide a remedy.

The Ninth Circuit did just that.[9] Judge Reinhardt (joined by Shadur) began by maintaining that:

> even in times of national emergency – indeed, particularly in such times – it is the obligation of the Judicial Branch to ensure the preservation of our constitutional values and to prevent the Executive Branch from running roughshod over the rights of citizens and aliens alike. Here, we simply cannot accept the government's position that the Executive Branch possesses the unchecked authority to imprison indefinitely any persons, foreign citizens included, on territory under the sole jurisdiction and control of the United States, without permitting such prisoners

recourse of any kind to any judicial forum, or even access to counsel, regardless of the length or manner of their confinement.

The court read *Eisentrager* as requiring territorial jurisdiction, not sovereignty. "The United States has exercised 'complete jurisdiction and control' over the Base for more than one century." "We have also treated Guantánamo as if it were subject to American sovereignty." The court also found that personal jurisdiction over Defense Secretary Rumsfeld could be exercised by the District Court, which should decide the venue issue. Judge Graber dissented, arguing that the majority had misread *Eisentrager* and the Circuit Court should have delayed until the Supreme Court decided *Rasul* (see below). The Supreme Court granted certiorari, vacated the judgment, and remanded for consideration of venue in light of *Padilla* (see below).[10] The same Ninth Circuit panel then unanimously found that the District of Columbia was the proper venue.[11] DDC Judge Green held that the court had jurisdiction.[12]

THE SUPREME COURT DECIDES

Everything changed when the Supreme Court handed down its dramatic trio of rulings in *Hamdi*, *Padilla*, and *Rasul* on June 28, 2004. Yaser Esam Hamdi was seized in Afghanistan soon after 9/11 and sent to Guantánamo in January 2002 but transferred to the Naval Brig at Norfolk, Virginia in April when the military learned he had been born in Louisiana (to Saudi Arabian parents who moved back there soon thereafter). In May Frank Dunham, the Federal Public Defender, filed a habeas petition. At the end of the month ED Va Judge Doumar ruled that Hamdi, who had not yet met Durham, had a right to do so "because of fundamental justice provided by the Constitution." The day before the meeting the government obtained a stay from the Fourth Circuit.[13] Esam Fouad Hamdi (Yaser's father) then sought habeas. Judge Doumar found that Esam was an appropriate next friend, appointed Dunham to represent Yaser, and renewed his order. Again the government obtained a stay, and the Fourth Circuit (Wilkinson, with Wilkins and Traxler) remanded, finding that Dunham had no relationship to Hamdi.[14]

> [I]n the context of foreign relations and national security ... a court's deference to the political branches of our national government is considerable ... where as here the President does act with statutory authorization from Congress, there is all the more reason for deference.

Doumar had not considered the effect on "the government's ongoing gathering of intelligence." "[A]ny judicial inquiry into Hamdi's status as an alleged enemy combatant in Afghanistan must reflect a recognition that government has no more profound responsibility than the protection of Americans … allowing alleged combatants to call American commanders to account in federal courtrooms would stand the warmaking powers … on their heads."

On remand, Doumar expressed "concern over possible violations of Hamdi's rights as an American citizen" and asked rhetorically: "with whom is the war … that we're fighting?" and will it "never be over as long as there is any member [or] any person who might feel that they want to attack the United States of America"?[15] The government responded with an affidavit by Michael Mobbs. In a hearing on its sufficiency, Doumar expressed no doubt that Hamdi had a firearm or "went to Afghanistan to be with the Taliban." But he challenged "everything in the Mobbs' declaration," promising to "pick it apart … piece by piece." He even questioned whether Mobbs was a government employee and hinted that the government might have suppressed evidence. He concluded that the declaration "falls far short" of supporting detention. This was the first case "where an American citizen has been held incommunicado and subjected to an indefinite detention in the continental United States without charges, without any findings by a military tribunal, and without access to a lawyer." Because "the circumstances of Hamdi's surrender and detention are anything but clear," and there was "uncertainty regarding Hamdi's status," Doumar needed to "develop a factual background." He ordered the government to produce for his *ex parte* examination all of Hamdi's statements, interrogators' identities and notes, statements by Northern Alliance members, and the date of Hamdi's capture, and dates and locations of his detentions. "Under the facts that the Court has before it at this time," the government had not shown that "a military tribunal, appointed by the general courts-martial convening authority" had determined whether Hamdi was a Prisoner of War, as required by the Geneva Conventions and the Joint Service Regulations. Notwithstanding the deference owed the executive, "it is equally clear that the judiciary is entitled to a meaningful judicial review of those designations when they substantially infringe on the individual liberties, guaranteed by the US Constitution, of American citizens." "Meaningful judicial review" required a determination of whether Hamdi's classification as an enemy combatant satisfied Fifth Amendment due process. Mobbs's Declaration "falls far short of even ... minimal criteria." Although he was Special Adviser to the Undersecretary of Defense for Policy, the Declaration "does not indicate what authority a 'Special Advisor' has regarding classification decisions of enemy combatants" and said nothing about Hamdi's intelligence value. It gave no reason for holding him for 8–10 months, much of it in solitary, a "clearly ... unreasonable length of time," which showed that criminal charges "obviously" were not contemplated.

Indeed, years later a Freedom of Information Act (FOIA) request uncovered a Navy brig official's description of Hamdi in June 2003:

> I fear the rubber band is nearing its breaking point here and not totally confident I can keep his head in the game much longer ... in my opinion we're working with borrowed time. I would like to have some form of incentive program in place ... to keep him from whacking out on me.

Mobbs did not explain what he meant by alleging that Hamdi was "affiliated" with the Taliban, since he never alleged Hamdi belonged to or fought for them. Mobbs was "merely paraphrasing" Hamdi's alleged statements. "Due to the ease with which such statements may be taken out of context, the Court is understandably suspicious of the Respondent's assertions." Mobbs's Declaration "is little more than the government's 'say-so.' " By accepting it, the Court would "be abdicating any semblance of the most minimal level of judicial review ... acting as little more than a rubber-stamp."

> We must protect the freedoms of even those who hate us, and that we may find objectionable. If we fail in this task, we become victims of the precedents we create. We have prided ourselves on being a nation of laws applying equally to all and not a nation of men who have few or no standards. The warlords of Afghanistan may have been in the business of pillage and plunder.
>
> We cannot descend to their standards without debasing ourselves. We must preserve the rights afforded to us by our Constitution and laws for without it we return to the chaos of a rule of men and not laws.

When the government moved to certify this order for appeal, Doumar instead certified the question "whether the Mobbs Declaration, standing alone, is sufficient as a matter of law to allow a meaningful judicial review of Yaser Esam Hamdi's classification as an enemy combatant?" Taking this as an invitation to address "any issue fairly included," the same Fourth Circuit panel reversed.[16] The reasons for judicial deference were "not difficult to discern." The other branches were "organized to supervise the conduct of overseas conflict" and "most accountable to the people." "For the judicial branch to trespass upon the exercise of the warmaking powers would be an infringement of the right to self-determination and self-governance at a time when the care of the common defense is most critical." Whereas Padilla was "an American citizen captured on American soil," Hamdi was detained "during a combat operation undertaken in a foreign country" and "thus bears the closest imaginable connection to the President's constitutional responsibilities during the actual conduct of hostilities." The Non-Detention Act was directed at a repetition of Japanese internment and thus inapposite; if detention required an Act of Congress, the AUMF was sufficient. Because Congress had appropriated money to detain "persons … similar to prisoners of war," it was "difficult if not impossible to understand" how it had failed to authorize "their detention in the first instance." The Geneva Conventions were not self-executing and conferred no private right of action. Even if they applied, it was "anything but clear" that they required determination of Hamdi's status by an Art. III court.

The court set aside the order that the government produce Hamdi's statements, which "may contain the most sensitive and the most valuable information for our forces in the field." Doumar's order "went far beyond the acceptable scope of review" and created the risk "that judicial involvement would proceed increment by increment." "Litigation cannot be the driving force in effectuating and recording wartime detentions. The military has been charged by Congress and the executive with winning a war, not prevailing in a possible court case."

The court criticized Doumar for examining the Mobbs Declaration "line by line."

> To transfer the instinctive skepticism, so laudable in the defense of criminal charges, to the review of executive branch decisions premised on military determinations made in the field carries the inordinate risk of a constitutionally problematic intrusion into the most basic responsibilities of a coordinate branch.

No evidentiary hearing was "necessary or proper." Hamdi had *no* due process rights because "he has not been charged with any crime." But the court "emphasized" that it was not placing its "imprimatur upon a new day of executive detentions."

The Circuit voted 8–4 not to review en banc.[17] Dissenting, Judge Luttig said the case implicated "commanding constitutional interests" in balancing "the President's power to conduct war and the right of our

citizens to be free from governmental restraint except upon lawful justification." He wanted the Circuit to rule that "the appropriate standard
that is to govern the Judiciary's review of an individual's challenge to an
Executive designation of enemy combatant status" was "some factual
basis," which he "would likely" conclude had been satisfied here, since
"there is not even a hint of fabrication" in Mobbs's declaration. Stung
by Luttig's reference to the "analytical softness" of the panel opinion
he had written, Judge Traxler declared that "every resident within
Afghanistan … was in law an enemy, until determined by the Executive
to be a friend."

Judge Motz assailed the panel decision from the opposite perspective.
It had held "that a short hearsay declaration by … an unelected, otherwise unknown, government 'advisor,' – 'standing alone'" was "sufficient
as a matter of law to allow meaningful judicial review." This was "the
first time in our history that a federal court has approved the elimination
of protections afforded a citizen by the Constitution solely on the basis
of the Executive's designation of that citizen as an enemy combatant."

> We must not forget the lesson of *Korematsu* … In its deference to an
> Executive report that, like the Mobbs declaration, was filed by a member
> of the Executive associated with the military … the Court upheld
> the Executive's conviction of Korematsu for simply remaining in his
> home … The Executive's treatment of Hamdi threatens the freedoms
> we all cherish, but the panel's opinion sustaining the Executive's action
> constitutes an even greater and "more subtle blow to liberty."

Judge Wilkinson (who had been on the panel) criticized Judge Motz
for "not even quot[ing]" the constitutional provisions that "delegate the
conduct of war" to the executive and legislature. It was "incorrect" to
claim "there was no meaningful judicial review of Hamdi's detention."
To require more than the Mobbs Declaration "would be folly." "[T]he
paramount right is that of the citizens of our country to have their
democracy's most vital life-or-death decisions made by those whom the
Constitution charges with that task."

The Supreme Court granted certiorari on January 9, 2004, heard
argument on April 28 (the day the Abu Ghraib abuses were exposed),
and reversed two months later.[18] Justice O'Connor (writing for Chief
Justice Rehnquist and Justices Kennedy and Breyer) said the AUMF satisfied the Non-Detention Act's requirement of an Act of Congress. But
she "easily" rejected the government's claim that it was "'undisputed'
that Hamdi's seizure took place in a combat zone." To be an enemy

combatant "Hamdi would need to be 'part of or supporting forces hostile to the United States or coalition partners' and 'engaged in an armed conflict against the United States.'" That he resided in Afghanistan did not concede those essential findings or even that he had been "'captured in a zone of active combat' operations." "We have long since made clear that a state of war is not a blank check for the President when it comes to the rights of the Nation's citizens."

Hamdi was claiming "the most elemental of liberty interests – the interest in being free from physical detention by one's own government." "It is during our most challenging and uncertain moments that our Nation's commitment to due process is most severely tested; and it is in those times that we must preserve our commitment at home to the principles for which we fight abroad."

"'[T]he risk of an erroneous deprivation' of a detainee's liberty interest is unacceptably high under the Government's proposed rule," but the District Court's proposed procedures were "both unwarranted and too burdensome." Hamdi was entitled to "notice of the factual basis for his classification, and a fair opportunity to rebut the Government's factual assertions before a neutral decisionmaker," as well as access to counsel. But the government's evidence, which could include hearsay, was entitled to a rebuttable presumption.

Souter (joined by Ginsburg) concurred in the judgment but dissented in part: the AUMF did *not* satisfy the Non-Detention Act.

> In a government of separated powers, deciding finally on what is a reasonable degree of guaranteed liberty whether in peace or war ... is not well entrusted to the Executive Branch of Government, whose particular responsibility is to maintain security ... we are heirs to a tradition given voice 800 years ago by Magna Carta, which, on the barons' insistence, confined executive power by "the law of the land."

He agreed with Doumar that reliance on the president's "categorical pronouncement" that "Taliban detainees do not qualify as prisoners of war" was "at odds" with the military regulation "adopted to implement the Geneva Convention ... setting out a detailed procedure for a military tribunal to determine an individual's status." Therefore, he would release Hamdi.

Scalia dissented (joined by Stevens) because the plurality opinion did not go far enough. When Congress has not suspended the right to habeas corpus, "the Executive's assertion of military exigency has not been thought sufficient to permit detention without charge." "The very core of liberty secured by our Anglo-Saxon system of separated powers has been freedom from indefinite imprisonment at the will of the Executive." The Founders had expressed their "mistrust of military power permanently at the Executive's disposal." "Whatever the general merits of the view that war silences law or modulates its voice, that view has no place in the interpretation and application of a Constitution designed precisely to confront war and, in a manner that accords with democratic principles, to accommodate it."

Thomas also dissented because the plurality went too far: "due process requires nothing more than a good-faith executive determination." Anything more "will destroy the intelligence gathering function" by requiring the government "to divulge highly classified information."

On remand, Judge Doumar scheduled a hearing for the following week and ordered the government to give Hamdi's lawyers exculpatory evidence. Instead of complying, the government flew him to Saudi Arabia, which quickly released him.[19]

On his arrival in Chicago from Pakistan on May 8, 2002, José Padilla, an American citizen, was arrested on a material witness warrant issued by SDNY Judge Mukasey and flown to New York.[20] Padilla had over $10,000 in cash, together with cell phone numbers and email addresses of al-Qaeda operatives. Donna R. Newman, his court-appointed lawyer, moved to vacate the warrant. But on Sunday, June 9, two days before her motion was to be argued, the government notified Mukasey *ex parte* it was withdrawing the warrant because President Bush had designated Padilla an enemy combatant. DoD took custody and transferred him to the Navy brig in South Carolina. On June 11 Newman petitioned for habeas corpus, complaining that the Navy prohibited her from communicating with or visiting her client. The government opposed this with another Mobbs declaration.

The next day Attorney General Ashcroft announced on television from Moscow:[21] "We have disrupted an unfolding terrorist plot to attack the United States by exploding a radioactive 'dirty bomb.' We have acted with legal authority both under the laws of war and clear Supreme Court precedent." At a briefing the same day, Defense Secretary Rumsfeld asserted that Padilla "unquestionabl[y] was involved in terrorist activities." "[O]ur interest in his case is not law enforcement" but "to try and find out everything he knows." But Rumsfeld's deputy Paul Wolfowitz conceded that Padilla had been "in the very early stages of his planning. I don't think there was actually a plot beyond some fairly loose talk."

After requesting further briefs on Padilla's right to counsel, Mukasey decided on December 4. He criticized the government for "quot[ing] selectively" from the Fourth Circuit's *Hamdi* decision, which was "easily distinguishable" and "does not support the government's position here." The AUMF satisfied the Non-Detention Act's requirement of an Act of Congress. Although Mukasey was skeptical about most of Padilla's claims (and suggested that the standard of review was whether the government had "some evidence" for its contentions), the petitioner did have a statutory right to habeas, which "will be destroyed utterly if he is not allowed to consult with counsel." After reading both the sealed and redacted Mobbs declarations, Mukasey dismissed as "gossamer speculation" the government's "conjecture" that access to counsel would interfere with questioning – an objection that would deny *every* detainee such a right. Because Padilla had already met with counsel, "whatever speculative damage the government seeks to prevent may already have been done." Padilla's "able advocates" had "conducted themselves at all times in a fashion consistent with their status as … officers of the court."

The government responded to Mukasey's order that the parties discuss the terms of access to counsel by stalling in anticipation of another favorable Fourth Circuit decision in *Hamdi*, which occurred on January 8, 2003. The next day the government asked Mukasey to reconsider, offering an affidavit by Defense Intelligence Agency (DIA) Director Vice Adm. Lowell E. Jacoby, arguing that counsel would interfere with interrogation and was unnecessary given that only "some evidence" was required to hold Padilla. Newman objected that the government had missed the deadline for its motion and failed to seek leave to append an affidavit. The government denied this, but finally admitted it had no new facts to adduce. Mukasey denounced the government's "casuistry," which was "permeated with the pinched legalism one usually encounters from non-lawyers." But he overlooked the rule violations in the interest of national security.

Jacoby had declared that "any insertion of counsel" could "threaten[]" the perceived dependency and trust between the subject and interrogator." But Mukasey noted skeptically that the government had deliberately omitted "the particulars of Padilla's actual interrogation" and engaged in a "speculative" "forecast" about "a matter of human nature – Padilla's in particular – in which, most respectfully, there are no true experts." "[B]efore Padilla achieved his current status as a suspected terrorist, he was a criminal, and criminals are people with whom this court has at least as much experience as does Admiral Jacoby, and perhaps more."

Mukasey distinguished Hamdi, who "did not dispute that he was captured in a zone of active combat operations abroad," and directed the parties to discuss the conditions for access, which he would decide if they failed to agree.

> Lest any confusion remain, this is not a suggestion or a request that Padilla be permitted to consult with counsel, and it is certainly not an invitation to conduct a further "dialog" about whether he will be permitted to do so. It is a ruling – a determination – that he will be permitted to do so.

After the government refused to negotiate, Mukasey certified an interlocutory appeal.

On December 23 the Second Circuit affirmed in part and reversed in part.[22] Writing for herself and Judge Parker, Judge Pooler quickly found that the relationship between Newman and Padilla was a "significant one" despite its short duration and "the unique role Secretary Rumsfeld plays in this matter leads us to conclude he is a proper respondent." The President had no inherent constitutional authority "to detain American citizens on American soil outside a zone of combat." "The Constitution entrusts the ability to define and punish offenses against the law of nations to Congress, not the Executive." Although it "contemplates significant domestic abridgements of individual liberties" during "grave national emergencies," it "lodges these powers with Congress, not the President." "The Constitution's explicit grant of the powers authorized in the Offenses Clause, the Suspension Clause, and the Third Amendment, to Congress is a powerful indication that, absent express congressional authorization, the President's Commander-in-Chief powers do not support Padilla's confinement." The AUMF did not satisfy the Non-Detention Act's requirement that Congress "specifically authorize *detentions*."

Judge Westley (recently appointed by Bush) dissented. As commander-in-chief, the president had "inherent authority to thwart acts of belligerency." Because of the AUMF, his powers "were at their apogee." The majority created "a false distinction between the use of force and the ability to detain." If the Non-Detention Act precluded presidential detention without trial it was unconstitutional. But Westley agreed Padilla needed access to counsel to petition for habeas.

Two months later White House Counsel Alberto Gonzales told the ABA's mid-year meeting that citizens who betray their country do not deserve legal representation.[23] Such rights "must give way to the national security needs of this country to gather intelligence from captured enemy combatants."

> The stream of intelligence would quickly dry up if the enemy combatants were allowed contact with outsiders during the course of an ongoing briefing. The result would be the failure to uncover information that could prevent attacks. This is an intolerable cost, and we do not believe it is one required by the Constitution.

The Supreme Court granted certiorari. The evening after it heard argument, CBS broke the Abu Ghraib story. In May 2004 the DoJ claimed Padilla had confessed to the dirty bomb plot and other al-Qaeda activities. Deputy Attorney General Comey claimed: "We now know much of what Jose Padilla knows. And what we have learned confirms that the president of the United States made the right call."[24] The *Washington Post* complained that "the government has delivered a broadside smear against which no defense is possible."

The Supreme Court reversed on June 28 for improper venue.[25] Writing for Justices Scalia and Thomas, Chief Justice Rehnquist said the proper respondent was "the person who has custody," the Naval brig commander, requiring that the petition be filed in South Carolina. This rule "serves the important purpose of preventing forum shopping." Justices Kennedy and O'Connor concurred.

Justice Stevens vigorously dissented (joined by Souter, Ginsburg, and Breyer). The case raised "questions of profound importance to the nation." Padilla had been held "for two years – pursuant to a warrantless arrest." Newman had not been allowed to see him for 20 months and then only "as a matter of the Government's grace." The jurisdictional rule was "riddled with exceptions." "[I]f jurisdiction was proper when the petition was filed, it cannot be defeated by a later transfer of the prisoner to another district." "When the Government shrouded [its transfer] in secrecy, Newman had no option but to file immediately in the district where [Padilla's] presence was last officially confirmed." "[W]e should not permit the Government to obtain a tactical advantage as a consequence of an *ex parte* proceeding." It was "disingenuous at best to classify [Padilla's] petition with run-of-the-mill collateral attacks on federal criminal convictions." "This case is singular not only because it calls into question decisions made by the [Defense] Secretary himself, but also because those decisions have created a unique and unprecedented threat to the freedom of every American citizen." "Under the President's order, only the Secretary – not a judge, not a prosecutor, not a warden – has had a say in determining [Padilla's] location." "Having 'emphasized and jealously guarded' the Great Writ's 'ability to cut through barriers of form and procedural mazes' … surely we should acknowledge that the writ reaches the Secretary as the relevant custodian in this case." "When this case is analyzed under those traditional venue principles, it is evident that the Southern District of New York, not South Carolina, is the more appropriate place to litigate [Padilla's] petition." Although the Court did not need to reach the substantive issue, Stevens agreed with the Second Circuit that "the Non-Detention Act … prohibits – and the Authorization for the Use of Military Force … does not authorize – the protracted incommunicado detention of American citizens arrested in the United States." He concluded with a rhetorical flourish:

> At stake in this case is nothing less than the essence of a free society. Even more important than the method of selecting the people's rulers and their successors is the character of the constraints imposed on the Executive by the rule of law. Unconstrained Executive detention for the purpose of investigating and preventing subversive activity is the hallmark of the Star Chamber.
>
> Executive detention of subversive citizens, like detention of enemy soldiers to keep them off the battlefield, may sometimes be justified to prevent persons from launching or becoming missiles of destruction. It may not, however, be justified by the naked interest in using unlawful procedures to extract information. Incommunicado detention for months on end is such a procedure. Whether the information so procured is more or less reliable than that acquired by more extreme forms of torture is of no consequence. For if this Nation is to remain true to the ideals symbolized by its flag, it must not wield the tools of tyrants even to resist an assault by the forces of tyranny.

After Padilla refiled in South Carolina, Judge Floyd granted his petition on February 28, 2005, and ordered the government to release him within 45 days.[26] Padilla's case was much stronger than Hamdi's. Even Judge Wilkinson had agreed that "to compare this battlefield capture [of Hamdi] to the domestic arrest in *Padilla v. Rumsfeld* is to compare apples to oranges." Justice O'Connor's plurality opinion noted at least ten times that "the Court's holding that Mr. Hamdi's detention as an enemy combatant was constitutionally permissible was limited to the facts of that case." The government had offered no support for its claim that "a United States citizen is not 'in' the United States when he or she is 'in' a United States airport." Padilla's "alleged terrorist plans were thwarted at the time of his arrest." "There were no impediments whatsoever to the government bringing charges against him for … the array of heinous crimes that he has been effectively accused of committing." Floyd distinguished *Ex parte Quirin*,[27] where the petitioner had been charged with a crime, the war had had a definite ending, and the case preceded the Non-Detention Act. Floyd also quoted *Ex parte Milligan*:[28]

> No doctrine, involving more pernicious consequences, was ever invented by the wit of man than that any of [the Constitution's] provisions can be suspended during any of the great exigencies of government. Such a doctrine leads directly to anarchy or despotism, but the theory of necessity on which it is based is false; for the government, within the Constitution, has all the powers granted to it, which are necessary to preserve its existence.

The AUMF was not an Act of Congress for purposes of the Non-Detention Act. Invoking the Supreme Court's exhortation in *Ex parte Endo*[29] "to allow for the greatest possible accommodation between [fundamental] liberties and the exigencies of war" when "interpreting a wartime measure," Floyd declared:

> Certainly Respondent does not intend to argue here that, just because the President states that Petitioner's detention is "consistent with the laws of the United States, including the Authorization for Use of Military Force" that makes it so. Not only is such a statement in direct contravention to the well settled separation of powers doctrine, it is simply not the law.
> Moreover, such a statement is deeply troubling. If such a position were ever adopted by the courts, it would totally eviscerate the limits placed on Presidential authority to protect the citizenry's individual liberties.

The Fourth Circuit said in *Hamdi*: "where the exercise of Commander-in-Chief powers, no matter how well intentioned, is challenged on the ground that it collides with the powers assigned by the Constitution to Congress, a fundamental role exists for the courts." Justice Jackson had famously written in *Youngstown*:[30]

> the Constitution did not contemplate that the title Commander-in-Chief of the Army and Navy will constitute [the President] also Commander-in-Chief of the country, its industries and its inhabitants.

Floyd continued:

> The government's position would not only offend the rule of law and violate this country's constitutional tradition, but it would also be a betrayal of this Nation's commitment to the separation of powers that safeguards our democratic values and individual liberties. For the Court to find for Respondent would also be to engage in judicial activism. This Court sits to interpret the law as it is and not as the Court might wish it to be. Pursuant to its interpretation, the Court finds that the President has no power, neither express nor implied, neither constitutional nor statutory, to hold Petitioner as an enemy combatant …
>
> [S]imply stated this is a law enforcement matter, not a military matter … The difference between invocation of the criminal process and the power claimed by the President here … is one of accountability. The criminal justice system requires that defendants and witnesses be afforded access to counsel, imposes judicial supervision over government action, and places congressionally imposed limits on incarceration.

Alberto Gonzales (now Attorney General) accused the judge of disregarding the Supreme Court's holding in *Hamdi* that the government could detain an enemy combatant "for the duration of the hostilities" (conveniently ignoring Floyd's effort to distinguish *Hamdi* by quoting O'Connor's plurality opinion in that case).[31] This provoked surprisingly bipartisan criticism.

Fearing that "I will not live to see the end to the war on terror," Rep. Frank R. Wolf (R-Va) said: "we cannot continue to keep an American citizen." Rep. José E. Serrano (D-NY) urged the government to "bring [Padilla] to trial" if it had any evidence against him. A week later Gonzales threatened to do that if forced to release him (disregarding Comey's acknowledgment the previous year that "we obviously can't use any of the statements he's made in military custody, which will make that option challenging").

After the government's appeal was assigned to Judges Luttig, Michael, and Traxler, Justice O'Connor announced her retirement.[32] As suspense rose about her replacement, television cameras descended on Luttig, who was an obvious candidate (having worked in the Reagan White House, clerked for then Judge Scalia and Chief Justice Berger, helped prepare Souter and Thomas for their Supreme Court confirmation hearings, and argued for expanded presidential power in the DoJ of Bush's father, who had appointed Luttig to the bench in 1991). The appeal was argued two days later. A day after that Bush nominated John Roberts (Luttig's Reagan administration colleague). Chief Justice

Rehnquist died on September 3, 2005; three days later Bush nominated Roberts as Chief Justice, reopening O'Connor's seat.

Three days after that the Fourth Circuit overturned Floyd's decision, upholding Padilla's detention.[33] Luttig (writing for Michael and Traxler) found "no difference" between Hamdi and Padilla. Criminal prosecution "may well not achieve the very purpose for which detention is authorized in the first place – the prevention of return to the field of battle" – and often "would impede the Executive in its efforts to gather intelligence from the detainee." Judge Floyd had failed "to accord the President the deference that is his when he acts pursuant to a broad delegation of authority, such as the AUMF," which gave him "a power without which, Congress understood, the President could well be unable to protect American citizens from the very kind of savage attack that occurred four years ago almost to the day."

Gonzales exulted that the ruling reaffirmed "the president's critical authority to detain enemy combatants who take up arms on behalf of al-Qaeda" (although no court had found that Padilla – or any detainee – had done so).[34] Less than a month later Bush nominated Harriet Miers (Gonzales's successor as White House counsel) to succeed O'Connor. Luttig was disappointed a second time, but may have recognized the pressure on Bush to nominate a woman.

Miers withdrew on October 27 (perhaps acknowledging her lack of qualifications or fearing that the confirmation hearing would expose her complicity in the administration's civil liberties abuses). Four days later Bush nominated Samuel Alito (whose background and conservative pedigree resembled Luttig's), finally dashing Luttig's Supreme Court hopes.

On November 21, a week before the government had to respond to Padilla's petition for review, it surprised everyone by charging him in federal court.[35] (I discuss the prosecution in Chapter 2.) The government disingenuously called the decision – 42 months after his arrest – "a classic example of why the criminal justice system is one of those important tools" in the "war on terror." "[M]uch thought goes into how and why various tools are used in these complicated cases. The important thing is for someone not to come away thinking this whole process is arbitrary, which it is not." Factors included national security interests, the need to gather intelligence and the best and quickest way to obtain it, the concern about protecting intelligence sources and methods and ongoing information gathering, the ability to use information as evidence in a criminal proceeding, the circumstances of the manner in which the individual was detained, the applicable criminal charges, and classified evidence issues.

The government immediately moved to transfer Padilla from military to civilian custody and declared his Supreme Court appeal moot.[36] But one of Padilla's attorneys replied that the case "is anything but moot. The government still claims the power to seize American citizens in civilian settings in the United States and detain them in military prisons indefinitely and without charge ... it's a classic case of *capable of repetition yet evading review*" [emphasis in original]. "A senior attorney at the Solicitor General's Office informed me, on the very day the indictment was unsealed, that it was possible that Padilla would again be detained as an enemy combatant if he was found innocent of the criminal charges against him." The next day the government published Bush's order releasing Padilla from military custody, which "supersede[d]" his earlier order designating Padilla an enemy combatant but did not explicitly terminate that status. Padilla's South Carolina lawyer noted in a November 28 filing that because the new order "does not remove the designation of 'enemy combatant' ... the government continues to assert the authority to return Mr. Padilla to military custody." "Given the fast-moving developments and the current uncertainty that surrounds them, I respectfully request that these proceedings be stayed" until the Supreme Court heard the appeal. There was a pending request before Mag. Judge Carr in Charleston to create a framework to challenge the factual basis for Padilla's designation as an enemy combatant. The Fourth Circuit's September 9 decision had explicitly stated that "it is only on these facts that we consider whether the president has the authority to detain Padilla." Briefs were due on November 29. Believing that Padilla had already been removed from his jurisdiction, on November 28 Carr had held that the motion for a stay was moot.

The *New York Times* accused the administration of charging Padilla "just in time ... to prod Congress on extending the Patriot Act and to avoid having to argue the case before the Supreme Court."[37]

> If Mr. Padilla was seriously planning a "dirty bomb" attack, he can never be held accountable for it in court because the illegal conditions under which he has been held will make it impossible to do that. If he was only an inept fellow traveler in the terrorist community, he is excellent proof that the government is fallible and needs the normal checks of the judicial system ... The same is true of the hundreds of other men held at Guantánamo Bay and in the C.I.A.'s secret prisons.

Donna Newman found the government's timing "somewhat suspect" and condemned Gonzales for asserting "that Padilla's being held for three-and-a-half years in solitary confinement is irrelevant." Rep. Adam Schiff (D-Ca) said "the Justice Department cannot continue changing course each time action from the courts is imminent."

But though DoJ expected its motion to be pro forma, especially since Padilla supported it, the Fourth Circuit panel took the unusual step of requesting briefs on the question:

> whether, if the government's motion is granted, the mandate should be recalled and our opinion of September 9, 2005, vacated as a consequence of the transfer and in light of the different facts that were alleged by the president to warrant Padilla's military detention and held by this court to justify that detention, on the one hand, and the alleged facts on which Padilla has been indicted, on the other.[38]

Padilla's lawyers asked the court to retain jurisdiction, challenging the government's "extraordinary action of interfering with the Supreme Court's consideration of the case" while an appeal was pending.

A month later the Fourth Circuit *denied* the motion.[39] Luttig wrote that the case presented "an issue of such especial national importance as to warrant final consideration" by the Supreme Court, which the government's actions created "at least an appearance" it was "attempting to avoid." For three-and-a-half years the government had been "steadfastly maintaining that it was imperative in the interest of national security" that the military hold Padilla. While calling its transfer motion an "emergency application," the government "provided no explanation as to what comprised the asserted exigency." The "rule of law is best served by maintaining on appeal the status quo."

> The government's actions have left not only the impression that Padilla may have been held for these years ... by mistake ... [but also] that the government may even have come to the belief that the principle in reliance upon which it has detained Padilla for this time ... can, in the end, yield to expediency ... these impressions have been left ... at what may ultimately prove to be substantial cost to the government's credibility before the courts.

The *Washington Post* condemned the "appalling" treatment of Padilla.[40] The government had held him for three-and-a-half years "on President Bush's personal order" and "prevented him from speaking to his lawyers" for much of that time.

From the beginning, the government has made tactical concessions that were, to put it delicately, timed felicitously in relation to its litigation needs. Mr. Padilla, we were told, could not be allowed access to counsel without grave risk to the nation – but suddenly, as his case proceeded on its first trip to the Supreme Court, that risk seemed to melt away, and he was allowed to meet with his lawyer. National security required his continued military detention – until, with the case possibly heading to the high court again, it turns out that a trial would be okay after all.

Appealing to the Supreme Court, the government said the Fourth Circuit decision "defies both law and logic," was "based on a mischaracterization of events and an unwarranted attack on the exercise of executive discretion, and … would raise profound separation-of-powers concerns."[41] A trial on the original allegations would have compromised intelligence "sources and methods" (i.e., his years of mistreatment in custody). Padilla's lawyers sought review to "ensure the checks and balances." Calling it even "weirder" that the parties had "switched sides," the *Post* urged the Court to hear the case.

Instead, the Court summarily approved the transfer and declined to review the habeas petition.[42] Justice Kennedy took the unusual step of giving his reasons (in which Roberts and Stevens concurred). The Court should avoid "fundamental issues respecting the separation of powers." "In light of the previous changes in his custody status and the fact that nearly four years have passed since he first was detained, Padilla … has a continuing concern that his status might be altered again." If that happened, "courts of competent jurisdiction should act promptly to ensure that the office and purposes of the writ of habeas corpus are not compromised," and he could apply directly to the Supreme Court. Expressing her disappointment in Stevens's vote (which, with those of Souter and Kennedy, would have secured review), Ginsburg quoted his dissent in Padilla's earlier appeal, which said the case raised a question "of profound importance to the Nation." She added that "nothing the government has yet done purports to retract the assertion of executive power" and "nothing prevents the executive from returning to the road it earlier constructed and defended."

The *Washington Post* derided the decision as "face-saving permission for the government's backing down."[43] Although it was "unnerving[]" that "the administration retains the option of doing the same thing to someone else," it was reassuring that five Justices were on record "as casting grave doubt on the legality of the administration's authority to hold a person such as Mr. Padilla as an enemy combatant in the first place." The *New York Times* said the administration had avoided "an inevitable showdown" and accused the Court of having "ducked its duty." It denounced "Bush's sweeping claim to have the power to seize American citizens on American soil and toss them into indefinite detention outside the normal legal process." A repetition was "far from a hypothetical matter."

Five weeks after the Supreme Court denied review, Luttig abruptly resigned his lifetime appointment to become general counsel of Boeing.[44] The company was facing serious problems: a fine of up to $500 million for improperly acquiring documents from Lockheed Martin Corporation, allegations that it had illegally recruited a senior Air Force official who oversaw billions of dollars of Boeing contracts, and an investigation into an (aborted) $20 billion contract to lease air refueling planes. Ken Duberstein, a Boeing lead director and former chief of staff in the Reagan White House, had suggested Luttig because Boeing CEO Jim McNerney wanted to send a strong message about the company's ethics. Luttig insisted that "my decision has nothing whatever to do with the Supreme Court process." "No one can or should plan their life around the possibility of a Supreme Court appointment." Boeing offered a "singular opportunity" to remain in public service by working for an "American icon" (unconsciously corroborating Eisenhower's 1961 warning about the military–industrial complex). Furthermore, Luttig could not afford to send his two teenage children to college on a federal judge's $172,000 salary. He had rejected the transfer motion only because "I thought that it was appropriate that the Supreme Court would have the final review of the case." At his ceremonial departure, Luttig pointedly snubbed President Bush, standing next to him, to express "heartfelt thanks to your father, because of whom my professional dreams in life came true." (Although human motives are always opaque, it was striking that Luttig made an abrupt volte-face from peremptorily rejecting the habeas petitions of Hamdi and Padilla to suddenly showing concern for Padilla's legal rights after being passed over for a Supreme Court nomination a third time.)

On February 19, 2002, Shafiq Rasul and Asif Iqbal (British citizens), and David Hicks (an Australian) petitioned for habeas corpus. On May 1, Fawzi al Odah and 11 other Kuwaitis sought other relief, hoping to avoid dismissal as habeas petitioners. All were detained in Guantánamo. At the end of July, DDC Judge Kollar-Kotelly found under *Eisentrager* that she lacked jurisdiction to hear any petitions by aliens held in a place, like Guantánamo, outside the sovereign territory of the United States.[45] She sought to soften that denial with a double negative: her opinion "should not be read as stating that these aliens do not have some form of rights under international law."

The DC Circuit affirmed on March 11, 2003.[46] Judge Randolph (joined by Garland and Williams) agreed that under *Eisentrager* the petitioners had no constitutional rights. Randolph wrote separately that sovereign immunity barred any Alien Tort Statute (ATS) claim, and the Geneva Conventions were not self- executing. Letting courts "discover" customary international law would violate separation of powers; and to "allow judicial inquiry into military decisions" would "interfere with military functions in a manner the APA's [Administrative Procedure Act] exclusion was meant to forbid."

But on June 28, 2004 the Supreme Court reversed.[47] Justice Stevens quoted Justice Jackson's dissent in a case denying habeas corpus to aliens. "Executive imprisonment has been considered oppressive and lawless since John, at Runnymede, pledged that no free man should be imprisoned, dispossessed, outlawed, or exiled save by the judgment of his peers." *Eisentrager* was inapplicable because the petitioners "are not nationals of countries at war with the United States." "[F]or more than two years they have been imprisoned in territory over which the United States exercises ... plenary and exclusive jurisdiction," even if not "ultimate sovereignty." Concurring, Justice Kennedy emphasized that "Guantánamo Bay is in every practical respect a United States territory."

Justice Scalia dissented (joined by Rehnquist and Thomas), accusing the "carefree Court" of "an irresponsible overturning of settled law in a matter of extreme importance to our forces currently in the field" and "spring[ing] a trap on the Executive." "For this Court to create such a monstrous scheme in time of war, and in frustration of our military commanders' reliance upon clearly stated prior law, is judicial adventurism of the worst sort."

AL-MARRI

A fourth case, involving a lawful resident, elaborated these issues. Ali Saleh Kahlah al-Marri, a Qatari citizen, flew to the USA with his wife and children on September 10, 2001 to enroll for a master's in computer science at Bradley University in Peoria, Illinois, from which he had graduated ten years earlier.[48] The FBI questioned him twice in October and again for five hours in December. After refusing to consent to a search or take a polygraph test, he was arrested as a material witness on a warrant issued in SDNY. A search of his computer revealed information that could be used for credit card fraud, with which he was charged in January. A year later a superseding indictment added making false statements to the FBI and financial institutions and using someone else's ID to open an account in a federally insured bank. In May 2003, after the SDNY court dismissed the charges for lack of venue, he was arraigned under a new complaint in CD Ill and returned to Peoria. Although a pretrial conference and trial had been scheduled for July, Bush designated him an enemy combatant on June 23, the District Judge granted the government's motion to dismiss the indictment with prejudice, and al-Marri was transferred to the Naval brig in Charleston. Ashcroft explained that al-Marri "insisted on becoming a hard case" and "rejected government offers to improve his lot by cooperating with FBI investigators and providing information."[49] On August 1, CD Ill Judge Mihm granted the government's motion to dismiss al-Marri's petition for habeas for improper venue.[50] "[W]hether his removal from this district was or was not unseemly is not an issue for this Court to resolve."

The Seventh Circuit affirmed in March 2004.[51] Judge Easterbrook ridiculed the petition. Although al-Marri "likes" Illinois, "says, Peoria or bust," and "chafes at the prospect of litigating in South Carolina, the district court there and its appellate court are no less likely to respect his legal rights than are the courts in this circuit." The court also removed Bush as a respondent, since his naming "was not only unavailing but also improper."

When al-Marri renewed his habeas petition in South Carolina, Judge Floyd denied his motion for summary judgment in July 2005, rejecting "the premise that aliens to this country, at all times, have access to the same constitutional protections as its citizens" and finding that the AUMF gave the president the power to detain enemy combatants.[52] A year later Floyd denied the petition, now rejecting the very distinction from *Hamdi* that he had emphasized in *Padilla*.[53] *Hamdi* allowed admission of the hearsay statements in the declaration by Jeffrey N. Rapp (a career DIA officer), which satisfied the government's burden of providing al-Marri with the factual basis for his detention. It alleged that al-Marri had trained in bin Laden's camp for 15–19 months, had met Khalid Sheikh Mohammed and Mustafa Ahmed al-Hawsawi, and had been sent to the USA as a "sleeper agent" furnished with $10,000–15,000. He rarely attended classes at Bradley University. His computer contained research on weapons of mass destruction (WMDs), jihadi propaganda, and over 1,000 credit card numbers. In response, al-Marri "offered nothing more than a general denial," refusing "to come forward with evidence."

When al-Marri appealed to the Fourth Circuit, the government argued that the Military Commissions Act stripped federal courts of habeas jurisdiction.[54] Janet Reno (Clinton's Attorney General) joined seven other former DoJ officials in an amicus brief declaring that al-Marri's classification as an enemy combatant just before a hearing had "the appearance of manipulation of the judicial process." "The criminal justice system has proven that it can make the cases." DoJ replied that "the United States cannot afford to retreat to a pre-September 11 mindset that treats terrorism solely as a domestic law enforcement problem." In another amicus brief 30 constitutional law scholars warned:

> The government's interpretation would be vastly threatening to the liberty of more than 20 million non-citizens residing in the United States, exposing them to the risk of irremediable indefinite detention on the basis of unfounded rumors, mistaken identity, the desperation of other detainees subject to coercive interrogation, and the deliberate lies of actual terrorists.

A third amicus brief alleged that Rapp's declaration was based on statements extracted by torture from KSM and al-Hawsawi.

A May 2004 report by the Navy IG (disclosed in December 2006) found that al-Marri had been deprived of warm food, sleep, comfort items (mattress, pillow, toilet paper), and a Koran, and had been denied visits by the ICRC as part of his interrogation.[55] His "unique" solitary confinement for 16 months might violate US standards. Jonathan Hafetz, one of his lawyers, said this confirmed what he had alleged in a complaint challenging the conditions of confinement: "al-Marri felt he was losing his mind. He went months without hearing a human voice." In January 2007 he was still in solitary and had just gotten a letter (which his wife had sent ten months earlier) with words like "Allah" blacked out.

The Fourth Circuit reversed Judge Floyd in April.[56] Judge Motz began:

> For over two centuries of growth and struggle, peace and war, the Constitution has secured our freedom through the guarantee that in the United States, no one will be deprived of liberty without due process of

law. Yet more than four years ago military authorities seized an alien lawfully residing here.

She found that the MCA, "which simply amended a federal statute …
is not, and could not be, a valid exercise of Congress's powers under the
Suspension Clause." Although the government maintained that the
CSRT was an "adequate and effective" substitute for habeas, al-Marri
had never been and might never be offered one. But Judge Motz avoided
these "difficult constitutional questions" by concluding that the MCA
did not apply to al-Marri. President Bush may have "determined" that
al-Marri was an enemy combatant, but he did not determine that al-
Marri had been "properly detained" as the MCA also required. The
chairman of the House Judiciary Committee, who was floor manager for
the MCA, said it dealt with only the statutory grant of habeas, not the
constitutional right.

Turning to the merits, Motz quoted the Supreme Court: "Freedom
from imprisonment … lies at the heart of the liberty that [the Due
Process] Clause protects."[57] She cited *Hamdi* for the proposition that
the military cannot seize and indefinitely detain an individual – particularly when the sole process leading to his detention is a determination by the Executive that the detention is necessary – unless
the government demonstrates that he "qualif[ies]" for this extraordinary treatment because he fits within the "legal category" of enemy
combatant.

The government had offered evidence that Hamdi was "affiliated
with a Taliban military unit and received training," "took up arms with
the Taliban," "engaged in armed conflict against the United States," and
surrendered a Kalashnikov rifle when captured on the battlefield. The
government also offered evidence that Padilla "took up arms against
the United States forces in [Afghanistan] in the same way and to the
same extent as did Hamdi." Both cases relied on *Ex parte Quirin* to classify as an enemy combatant anyone affiliated during wartime with the
"military arm of the enemy government."[58] None of these cases rejected
the Supreme Court's earlier holding that Lambdin Milligan, a citizen
captured in the USA during the Civil War, could not be subjected
to military jurisdiction even though the government claimed he had
communicated with the enemy, conspired to seize munitions, and
joined in attempting to overthrow the government.[59] By contrast, the
government had only said that al-Marri "continues to pose a very real
threat of carrying out … acts of international terrorism." And it asked

345

the court to defer not to the military but a "multi-agency evaluation process" of Washington bureaucrats.

The Supreme Court had recently held in *Hamdan* that the conflict in Afghanistan was not international; therefore, there was no legal category of "enemy combatant." Even "assuming the Constitution permitted Congress to grant the President" the "awesome and unprecedented power" to "classify civilians as enemy combatants and so detain them in military custody," Congress "would have said so explicitly." Hence "the government has not offered … any authority that permits us to hold the AUMF empowers the president to detain al-Marri as an enemy combatant." Invoking Justice Jackson's opinion in *Youngstown* – "when the President takes measures incompatible with the expressed or implied will of Congress, his power is at its lowest ebb" – Judge Motz found that the Patriot Act's explicit prohibition of indefinite detention precluded the president's claim of inherent authority to detain al-Marri.

> [T]he Constitution does not allow the President to order the military to seize civilians residing within the United States and detain them indefinitely without criminal process … even if he calls them "enemy combatants" … [T]he Supreme Court has repeatedly catalogued our country's "deeply rooted and ancient opposition … to the extension of military control over civilians" … Unlike detention for the duration of a traditional armed conflict between nations, detention for the length of a "war on terror" has no bounds … To sanction … presidential authority to order the military to seize and indefinitely detain civilians, even if the President calls them "enemy combatants," would have disastrous consequences for the Constitution – and the country. For a court to uphold a claim of such extraordinary power … would effectively undermine all of the freedoms guaranteed by the Constitution.

Dissenting, Judge Hudson agreed that the MCA did not strip the court of jurisdiction. But the President had used his inherent authority and the AUMF properly to designate al-Marri an enemy combatant, who had received "all due process entitlements" he was owed.

The *New York Times* praised this "powerful" "ruling for justice," which "utterly rejected the president's claims" that the "war on terror" "gave him the power to decide who the combatants are and throw them into military prisons forever."[60] The court's "powerful arguments may be relevant to a large number" of Guantánamo detainees. A letter to the editor asked: "if the evidence is so strong, why does the Justice Department seek to avoid the scrutiny of a trial?" The *Washington Post* said al-Marri had been "treated in a way antithetical to American values." "This country does not simply 'disappear' people without hearings." The *Post* deplored the "ping-ponging of alleged terrorists such as Mr. Marri and Jose Padilla between civilian and military courts, depending on what suits the administration's legal interests."

Speaking at the Coast Guard Academy commencement in May, President Bush said the intelligence community believed al-Marri's potential targets included "water reservoirs, the New York Stock Exchange and United States military academies such as this one."[61]

After the Fourth Circuit agreed to rehear the case en banc, the *Washington Post* warned that "the full court, long a conservative bastion, appears likely to overturn the panel – and with some justification."[62] But it should not "back away from the panel's legitimate and unequivocal call for due process."

In spring 2008 al-Marri's lawyers moved for changes in his conditions of confinement.[63] He had been in virtual isolation for more than 2,700 days with just one phone call to his family; he was obsessed with noises, food, and "noxious fumes," and suspected his lawyers were part of a government conspiracy.

On July 15 the Fourth Circuit reversed in six opinions extending over more than a hundred pages.[64] Judges Williams, Wilkinson, Niemeyer, Traxler, and Duncan found that if the government's allegations were true, the AUMF had empowered the president to detain al-Marri as an enemy combatant. But Judges Motz, Michael, King, Gregory, and Traxler found that al-Marri had not been granted due process to challenge that designation. Judge Motz reprised her earlier opinion. The majority substituted "rhetoric and passion" for "faithful application of the Constitution." The Supreme Court had recently said in *Boumediene* that "security subsists ... in fidelity to freedom's first principles. Chief among these are freedom from arbitrary and unlawful restraint and the personal liberty that is secured by adherence to the separation of powers."

> [T]o justify al-Marri's indefinite military detention, the dissents resort to inventing novel definitions of enemy combatant, drawing on their own beliefs as to when detention is appropriate. That these judicially-created definitions differ so markedly from one another follows from the fact that each is simply the product of judicial conjecture ... by abandoning precedent and traditional law-of-war principles, Judge Williams renders the term "enemy combatant" utterly malleable ... by refusing to construe the AUMF through the lens of traditional law-of-war principles ... Judge

Wilkinson ignores a construction that avoids constitutional difficulties and instead chooses one that abounds in them.

Judge Traxler was troubled that al-Marri was required "to prove that he was not an enemy combatant by more persuasive evidence." If the government wanted to rely on hearsay evidence and be immune from discovery, it should demonstrate why it needed to do so. "I am aware of no case in which a person detained in this country has been stripped of the opportunity to contest the legality of his detention for refusing to participate in an unconstitutional process." Because *Hamdi*, *Padilla*, and this case showed that "the government frequently changes the manner in which it deals with alleged enemy combatants during the pendency of habeas proceedings ... al-Marri had every reason to fear that were he to give evidence on his behalf ... the government might then choose to transfer him back to civilian custody and use his own evidence against him." "[P]rotections we declare to be unavailable under the Constitution to al-Marri might likewise be unavailable to American citizens."

Judge Gregory wrote, "to express my intransigent belief that the Constitution requires a person detained in the United States under the ... AUMF receive a *determinate* level of due process" [original emphasis]. "[I]t is not only al-Marri's rights that are at stake, but rather the rights of every man, woman, and child who breathe the fragrant scent of liberty in this great land." "Just as we expressed our skepticism with the Government's attempt to transfer Padilla from the military to the civilian criminal system *three and a half years* after his initial detention, the Executive's decision to designate al-Marri an enemy combatant on the very eve of his civilian criminal trial raises a similar concern" [original emphasis].

Gregory concluded by quoting Thomas Jefferson's First Inaugural Address:

> The protection of habeas corpus was one of those principles which form the bright constellation which has gone before us and guided our steps through an age of revolution and reformation ... and should we wander from them in moments of error or of alarm, let us hasten to retrace our steps and to regain the road which alone leads to peace, liberty, and safety.

Judge Williams (joined by Duncan) wrote that because al-Marri was "*squarely* within the purposes of the AUMF" [original emphasis], it was "clear" he could be detained as an enemy combatant. Furthermore, "because al-Marri short-circuited the lower court's attempt to craft procedures meant to protect his due process rights, I would not reward his refusal to participate with a remand."

Judge Wilkinson wrote:

> The present case reminds that we live in an age where thousands of human beings can be slaughtered by a single action and where large swathes of urban landscape can be leveled in an instant ... Nuclear devices capable of inflicting enormous casualties can now fit inside a suitcase or a van ... For courts to resist this political attempt to meet these rising dangers risks making the judicial the most dangerous branch.

He criticized Judge Motz for overemphasizing "quaint and outmoded notions of enemy states and demarcated foreign battlefields," arguing for a law of war "so bound in obsolescence that it hinders a nation's ability to recognize new threats," embracing "a sense of rigidity and complacency ... that may lead to tragic results and lasting regrets." He accused his colleagues of "policymaking." Their interpretation of the AUMF was "incredible," a "paradox without parallel," which "grants the judiciary an expanding veto over future congressional efforts to protect this country." He warned that giving al-Marri more due process "will lead to more graymail, more fishing expeditions, and more thrashing litigiousness." "It is difficult to think of a more dangerous way to handle the highly sensitive information that is invariably used to apprehend terrorist sleeping agents such as al-Marri" than the plurality's proposed "most reliable available evidence" standard. "Taken to sufficient lengths, process can accomplish the dismemberment of meaningful democratic prerogatives and the frustration of vital substantive ends. Taken too far, process can essentially paralyze public officials in their attempt ... to provide even the most basic assurances of public safety." He concluded:

> The notion that the military detention of suspected al-Qaeda terrorists such as al-Marri somehow threatens to drag us even incrementally towards the degraded level of our adversaries is simply unfathomable ... Military detention, circumscribed carefully by the law of war's cardinal principle of discrimination, is no disproportionate response to those who aim to murder scores of thousands of civilians ... It is the *constitutional* function of the executive to act energetically in time of national peril ... The courts have been more actively involved in our current struggle than in any other war in our history [original emphasis].

Judge Niemeyer wrote that "because the district court in this case afforded al-Marri the habeas corpus process ... I would conclude that al-Marri has received all the process he was due."

The *New York Times* deplored the administration's "disturbing victory" in its "fierce battle for the power to lock people up indefinitely simply on the president's say-so."[65] "[T]he ruling supports President Bush's ludicrous argument that when Congress authorized the use of force against those responsible for the Sept. 11 attacks, it gave the president essentially unlimited powers." Al-Marri "was held on the basis of extremely thin hearsay evidence." "[T]he court's reasoning appears to apply equally to citizens." "People accused of bad deeds should be tried in court – not in sham proceedings."

Both sides appealed to the Supreme Court. In a *Los Angeles Times* op ed, al-Marri's lawyer, Jonathan Hafetz, invoked the 200-year-old principle "that people can't be imprisoned without being charged." Retired Gen. Antonio Taguba (who wrote the Abu Ghraib report) signed an amicus brief with other former military officers.[66] An amicus brief by former DoJ lawyers (including Janet Reno) and former federal judges (including Abner Mikva) called the en banc decision "a grave threat to the civil liberties of American citizens." In its own appeal, the government said it was "absurd" to claim that the president was exceeding the AUMF; "a contrary conclusion would severely undermine the military's ability to protect the nation against further al-Qaeda attack at home." The *New York Times* urged the Court "to make clear that a president cannot trample on individual rights by imprisoning people indefinitely simply by asserting that they are tied to terrorism." The *Washington Post* said the question the Court was being asked "at one point would have seemed ridiculous: Can the president detain indefinitely, without charge or trial, a person who was captured on US soil and is in the country legally?" The president's power to detain terrorism suspects under the AUMF required "a muscular legal process that gives detainees ample rights to challenge their detention." Placing the burden of disproof on al-Marri was "a perversion of justice."

The Court agreed to review on December 5, 2008, a month after Obama's election.[67] A lawyer for the Constitution Project expressed the hope he would "resoundingly reject the current administration's breathtaking claim." The ACLU legal director urged the Court to "ensure that people in this country cannot be seized from their homes and imprisoned indefinitely simply because the president says so." As a candidate, Obama had said: "I reject the Bush administration's claim that the president has plenary authority under the Constitution to detain US citizens without charges as unlawful enemy combatants." Three days after he was inaugurated, the Court granted the DoJ's request to delay filing its brief. A month later Attorney General Holder said the government planned to prosecute al-Marri criminally, reflecting "the changed approach this administration has taken." The Solicitor General asked the Supreme Court to dismiss the case, citing its decision in *Padilla* for the proposition that "no live controversy remains." A CD Ill grand jury charged al-Marri with material support. Hafetz welcomed the decision but said it should have been taken seven years earlier; he still planned to pursue Supreme Court review "to make sure that no American citizen or lawful resident will ever again be subjected to such treatment." The ACLU urged the administration to "unequivocally state that it will not repeat the abuse of executive authority that occurred in this case." HRF praised the decision as "yet another indication that President Obama is sticking to his pledge." AI called it "another crucial step in the right direction."

The *Washington Post* was pleased that "after nearly six years of detention," al-Marri "may finally get his day in court."[68] The *New York Times* called the decision "an important step toward bringing the government's terrorism-fighting efforts within the rule of law," but added that three years after the Court had "avoided" the issue in Padilla's case, "a Supreme Court showdown over the reprehensible enemy combatant policy is overdue."

A week after al-Marri was charged, the Court granted the government's motion to transfer him to civilian custody and vacated the Fourth Circuit judgment as moot (an action the government did not contest).[69] DSC Judge Carr denied bail, and CD Ill Judge Mihm tentatively scheduled trial for May 26. But al-Marri pleaded guilty at the end of April. Holder said the deal "reflects what we can achieve when we have faith in our criminal justice system and are unwavering in our commitment to the values upon which this nation was founded and the rule of law." David Kris, Assistant Attorney General for National Security, said the facts al-Marri admitted "demonstrate that he attended terrorist training camps, learned al-Qaeda tradecraft and was dispatched by the highest levels of al-Qaeda to carry out its terrorist objectives in America." Hafetz said: "it would be an outrage if he was given no credit for the period when he was stripped of his rights."

After a two-day sentencing hearing at the end of October, Judge Mihm sentenced al-Marri to more than eight years (the maximum was 15) and gave him credit for more than six in the Navy brig.[70] Al-Marri tearfully told the judge about years without any word from his wife and children, apologized for helping al-Qaeda, and said he no longer wished to harm the American people. Over the government's opposition, the judge took nine months off his sentence because of his harsh conditions of confinement. He was freed and returned to Qatar in January 2015.[71] Days later Qatar freed Matthew and Grace Huang, US citizens imprisoned for alleged mistreatment after their daughter died; DoS denied any connection.

BOUMEDIENE

The Supreme Court's decisions in *Rasul* and (to a lesser extent) *Hamdi* opened the door to habeas petitions by other Guantánamo detainees. And whereas even CCR lawyers had reservations when they first filed habeas petitions, the Supreme Court victories helped CCR recruit and coordinate hundreds of lawyers – from solo practitioners to those in the largest firms, as well as public defenders – to represent detainees pro bono.[72] Judge Kollar-Kotelly granted the lawyers the right to visit their clients without government monitoring.[73]

> They have been detained virtually incommunicado for nearly three years without being charged with any crime. To say that Petitioners' ability to investigate the circumstances surrounding their capture and detention is "seriously impaired" is an understatement.

Indeed, it was "nonexistent." The government had tried "to erode this bedrock prisnciple with a flimsy assemblage of cases." Its opposition was "thinly supported" and petitioners' claims "clearly" nonfrivolous. "Finally, this Court's ability to give Petitioners' claims the 'careful consideration and plenary processing' which is their due would be stymied were Petitioners to proceed unrepresented by counsel." In November Judge Green, assigned to supervise all the habeas petitions, promulgated elaborate rules for lawyer–client communication, explicitly approving Kollar-Kotelly's "well-reasoned opinion."

Declining to relinquish the petitions assigned to him, Judge Leon found they were based on "no viable legal theory."[74] He began by noting that the "al-Qaeda terrorist network orchestrated the most devastating terrorist attack in the history of the United States," in which the "United States economy was severely damaged." Congress "overwhelmingly passed a joint resolution authorizing the president to: '[U]se all necessary and appropriate force.'" The argument that "Congress did not *expressly* authorize the detention of enemy combatants not captured on or near the battlefields of Afghanistan is fanciful at best" [original emphasis]. "[P]etitioners are asking this Court to do something no federal court has done before: evaluate the legality of the Executive's capture and detention of nonresident aliens, outside of the United States, during a time of armed conflict." Hearing the petition would require the court to "inject itself into sensitive matters of foreign affairs, military policy, and other national security areas." Any "inadequacies in the law of 'traditional' warfare" required "a reevaluation of the laws by the *political branches*, not the judiciary" [original emphasis]. *Hamdi* affirmed the "clear and well-established principle of the law of war that detention may last for the duration of active hostilities." "Guantánamo is not a United States sovereignty." In *Rasul* the Supreme Court decided only jurisdiction, directing "lower courts to consider the very issue that it had not: the 'merits of petitioners [sic] claims.'" "[E]ven assuming, arguendo, that the petitioners do possess constitutional rights, which they do not, the Court notes that the CSRTs provide each petitioner with much of the same process afforded by Article 5 of the Geneva Conventions." The allegedly "deplorable" conditions of confinement created no right to habeas. Leon rejected claims based on treaties, which "as a general rule, are not privately enforceable."

Less than two weeks later Judge Green reached the opposite conclusion in 11 consolidated cases.[75] She, too, began with the "horrific and unprecedented attacks," but said the threat of terrorism "cannot negate the existence of the most basic fundamental rights for which the people of this country have fought and died for well over two hundred years." Many petitioners "may never have been close to an actual battlefield and may never have raised conventional arms against the United States or its allies." *Rasul* required "the recognition that the detainees at Guantánamo Bay possess enforceable constitutional rights" under the Fifth Amendment, which contains "one of the most fundamental rights recognized by the US Constitution." Although the Third and Fourth Geneva Conventions did not expressly grant private rights of action, Judge Green agreed with Judge Robertson that they were self-executing. Even though the president had declared that no Taliban fighter was a prisoner of war, "nothing in the Convention itself or in Army Regulation 190–8 authorizes the President of the United States to rule by fiat that an entire group of fighters covered by the Third Geneva Convention falls outside of the Article 4 definitions of 'prisoners of war.'" Detainees were not informed of the bases upon which they were detained, were not permitted access to counsel, were not given a formal opportunity to challenge their "enemy combatant" status, and were alleged to be held virtually incommunicado from the outside world.

Judge Green illustrated "the inherent lack of fairness of the CSRT's consideration of classified information not disclosed to the detainee" with this colloquy:

> TRIBUNAL PRESIDENT: We had to laugh, but it is okay.
>
> DETAINEE: Why? Because these are accusations that I can't even answer … You tell me I am from Al-Qaida, but I am not an Al-Qaida. I don't have any proof to give you except to ask you to catch bin Laden and ask him if I am a part of Al-Qaida. To tell me that I thought [to bomb the US Embassy in Sarajevo], I'll just tell you that I did not. I don't have proof regarding this. What should be done is you should give me evidence regarding these accusations because I am not able to give you any evidence. I can just tell you no, and that is it.

Green called the detainee's criticism "piercingly accurate."

Other hearings were just as fatally flawed. A "classified document formed the most important basis for the CSRT's ultimate determination" that Murat Kurnaz belonged to al-Qaeda, but it "was never provided to the detainee." His Personal Representative "is neither a lawyer nor an advocate and thus cannot be considered an effective surrogate to compensate for the detainee's inability to personally review and contest classified evidence against him." Furthermore, "the Personal Representative is obligated to disclose to the tribunal any relevant inculpatory information he obtains from the detainee." The only evidence against Kurnaz was that he "associated" with an Islamic missionary group, was an "associate" of and planned to travel to Pakistan with a man who planned (but did not execute) a suicide bombing, and accepted food, lodging, and schooling in Pakistan from a group known to support terrorist acts. Judge Green concluded that these facts "by themselves fall short of establishing that the detainee took any action or provided any direct support for terrorist actions."

Although Green's opinion was heavily redacted, a subsequent news account revealed the USA believed Kurnaz had been in contact with 9/11 leader Mohammed Atta, but had no evidence. Kurnaz's classified file contained a statement by the Command Intelligence Task Force that it "has no definite link/evidence of detainee having an association with Al-Qaeda or making any specific threat against the United

States."[76] His German lawyer said that when Kurnaz was arrested in Pakistan "during a routine check of a bus," he "had no weapons."[77]

Mamdouh Habib's file contained numerous "confessions," which he claimed had been made under torture in Egypt, where the USA had rendered him.[78] For similar reasons, Judge Green concluded that the CSRTs' reliance on the Command Intelligence Task Force "cannot be viewed to have satisfied the requirements of due process." An August 2, 2004 FBI report described the torture of Guantánamo detainees by forcing them to urinate or defecate on themselves because they were chained to the floor, denying them food or water, making them suffer intolerable heat or cold, and subjecting them to loud music. One "detainee was almost unconcious [sic] on the floor, with a pile of hair next to him. He had apparently been literally pulling his own hair out throughout the night." "What this Court needs to resolve at this juncture," Green wrote, is not the truth of these statements but "whether the petitioners have made sufficient allegations to allow their claims to survive the respondents' motion to dismiss. They had done so."

Judge Green also found that the definition of "enemy combatant" in the order creating the CSRTs was "significantly broader than the definition considered in *Hamdi*." Because it included "individuals who never committed a belligerent act or who never directly supported hostilities against the US or its allies," "the government claimed the authority to detain [a] little old lady in Switzerland who writes checks to what she thinks is a charity that helps orphans in Afghanistan but really is a front to finance al-Qaeda activities … a person who teaches English to the son of an al-Qaeda member … and a journalist who knows the location of Osama bin Laden but refuses to disclose it to protect her source."

Judge Green found that petitioners had stated valid Fifth Amendment claims, the CSRT procedures violated due process, and Taliban fighters had claims under the Third Geneva Convention unless specifically excluded from prisoner of war status by a competent Article 5 tribunal.

On September 8, 2005, the DC Circuit heard appeals from Judges Leon and Green in a case that would be referred to as *Boumediene*.[79] At the end of the year Congress passed the Detainee Treatment Act, stripping federal courts of habeas jurisdiction over Guantánamo detainees and substituting DC Circuit review of CSRT determinations and military commission decisions.[80] In January 2006 the government notified DDC it planned to move to dismiss all those cases.[81] Judge Walton promptly ordered his three petitioners (Almurbati, Battayav, and Gherebi) to show cause why their cases should not be dismissed.

In March the DC Circuit panel that had heard the Kuwaiti petitions the previous year heard reargument about whether the DTA was retroactive. In June the Supreme Court decided *Hamdan* (discussed in Chapter 4), finding that the DTA did not deprive courts of jurisdiction in habeas petitions pending at the time of its enactment. The Military Commissions Act, passed in October in response, declared that the DTA restriction applied to *all* habeas petitions. Sen. Feingold called it "a stain on our nation's history."

The *New York Times* denounced it as "our generation's version of the Alien and Sedition Acts."[82] In November the DC Circuit heard reargument in *Boumediene* about the MCA's retroactive effect. A group of retired federal judges submitted an amicus brief contending that the CSRT's willingness to hear evidence obtained by torture was a "fundamental flaw," which could not be remedied by limited Circuit Court review. Although the government had consented to the filing of this brief, an unsigned opinion by Sentelle and Randolph refused to accept it, citing an advisory opinion by the Judicial Conference of the United States that retired judges should not use their titles in litigation papers. Dissenting, Judge Rogers said this did not apply to amicus briefs. Judge Mikva (a retired DC Circuit judge who had signed the amicus brief) said "this was clearly aimed at me" for advocating that judges should not accept free trips to resorts for seminars sponsored by private groups. "They're so close to retirement age. They really should grow up."

After Judge Robertson dismissed Hamdan's habeas petition (citing the MCA) because he would soon be tried by a military commission, the *Los Angeles Times* urged the Supreme Court to "give habeas a chance."[83] Sen. Specter, who claimed he had voted for the MCA in the expectation that the Supreme Court would "clean it up," now joined Sen. Leahy to introduce the Habeas Corpus Restoration Act of 2006. The *Times* hoped Bush would not veto it. The *Washington Post* also supported the law.

> Stripping the courts of habeas jurisdiction over Guantánamo was a profoundly foolish step to stop judicial review of an administration whose behavior has repeatedly illustrated the crucial importance of such oversight. Virtually every step the administration has taken toward a fairer and more open system for the detention and prosecution of enemy combatants has come as the result of pressure, direct and indirect, of litigation.

A large group of law professors wrote the Congressional leaders of both parties in support of the Leahy bill.

At the end of January 2007 Attorney General Gonzales testified before the Senate Judiciary Committee.[84]

> GONZALES: [T]here is no express grant of habeas in the Constitution. There is a prohibition of taking it away.
>
> SEN. SPECTER (CHAIR): Now, wait a minute. The Constitution says you can't take it away except in case of rebellion or invasion. Doesn't that mean you have the right of habeas corpus?
>
> GONZALES: I meant by that comment the Constitution doesn't say every individual in the United States or every citizen is hereby granted or is assured the right of habeas corpus … It simply says that the right of habeas corpus shall not be suspended.

He later walked that back, calling habeas "very, very important. One of our most cherished rights."

In February 2007 Judge Randolph (joined by Sentelle) denied the *Boumediene* petitions, dismissing as "nonsense" the petitioners' "creative but not cogent" argument that Congress did not intend the MCA to apply to them.[85] The court found retroactive jurisdiction-stripping consistent with the Constitution's Suspension Clause, which preserved habeas corpus "as it existed in 1789," when it did not extend to petitioners outside the sovereign territory of the United States. Judge Rogers dissented, accusing the majority of "misreading the historical record and ignoring the Supreme Court's well-considered and binding dictum in *Rasul*." "The Suspension Clause limits the removal of habeas corpus … to times of rebellion or invasion unless Congress provides an adequate alternative remedy," which the CSRT was not.[86]

Sen. Graham praised the decision: "the determination of enemy combatant status belongs with our military. Civilian judges are not trained to determine who presents a threat to our nation."[87] But Sen. Leahy called the MCA "a dangerous and misguided law that undercuts our freedom and assaults our Constitution." The *Los Angeles Times* hoped the newly elected Democratic Congress would have "the fortitude to undo an injustice perpetrated by the Republican-controlled 109th." Calling the decision "another low moment for American justice," the *New York Times* warned that "American liberty" was "at the precipice." The MCA "raises insurmountable obstacles for prisoners to challenge their detentions." The *Washington Post* urged Congress to move quickly and not wait for the Supreme Court. "Congress has both a practical and a moral interest in ensuring that this basic human right is restored." In June the Senate Judiciary Committee voted 11–8 for Leahy's bill

(Specter joining the 10 Democrats).[88] Several weeks later Reps. Skelton and Conyers introduced a similar bill in the House.

On April 26, 2007 the Supreme Court denied certiorari.[89] Although voting to do so, Justices Stevens and Kennedy said that "if petitioners later seek to establish that the Government has unreasonably delayed proceedings under the Detainee Treatment Act," the Court "should act promptly." Justices Breyer, Souter, and Ginsburg voted to grant certiorari to "diminish the legal 'uncertainty' that now 'surrounds' the application to Guantánamo detainees of this 'fundamental constitutional principle.'" Sen. Leahy said the Court's refusal "underscores the need for Congress to act quickly," and Sen. Specter urged colleagues to support their bill. The New York Times agreed that the Court's inaction sent a "clear message" that "it is past time for Congress to undo the grievous damage done by President Bush's abuse of the Constitution."

Two months later five Justices voted to reverse that denial – a step the Court had not taken for about 40 years – but postponed consideration until the DC Circuit decided Bismullah and Parhat.[90] It may have been moved by a declaration by LtCol. Stephen Abraham, a 26-year military intelligence veteran who had served in the office administering the CSRTs, that their reviews were arbitrary and incomplete. On July 27 the DC Circuit withdrew its Boumediene decision.

Sen. Graham warned he was "not going to sit on the sidelines and watch this war be criminalized."[91] But the Washington Post exhorted Republicans not to block the Leahy–Specter bill. "Lawmakers should resist the temptation to punt the matter to the Supreme Court for a decision." The New York Times urged Congress to rectify the MCA's "grievous mistake." "The protection from arbitrary arrest, embedded in the Magna Carta and in the Constitution of the United States, is one of the most powerful weapons against tyranny in democracy's arsenal." It named leading conservatives who supported restoration of habeas. DoJ confirmed that as many as a fourth of its 56 civil appeals lawyers had opted not to represent the government in opposing habeas applications. The Washington Post again urged Congress to pass the Leahy–Specter bill quickly. Imprisonment without a hearing was "one of the sad and confounding legacies of the administration's war on terror." "[T]he federal courts are the only venues available that would allow detainees the immediate ability to emerge from what has essentially been a legal black hole." On the first day of the Supreme Court's 2007 term, the New York Times reiterated that it "should hold that the Constitution requires that the detainees be given their day in court."

But though the Senate passed Leahy's bill 56–43 (just six Republicans joined the Democrats), the vote was four short of the necessary 60.[92] Sen. Sessions asked if the USA wanted "to conduct warfare … in a way that allows those we capture to sue us?" Leahy replied that "casting aside the time-honored protection of habeas corpus makes us more vulnerable as a nation because it leads us away from our core American values and calls into question our historic role as defender of human rights around the world."

At the beginning of October, DDC Judge Kessler read the Supreme Court's grant of certiorari and the DC Circuit's withdrawal of its opinion as authority to consider a motion by Mohammed Rahman to enjoin his transfer to Tunisia.[93] She found that Tunisia had tried him in absentia under an *ex post facto* law and sentenced him to 20 years; given his severe health problems and the "serious threat of torture," she granted the injunction.

Many amici supported the *Boumediene* petitioners. Nearly 400 Euro MPs said the case "boils down to the simple, but crucial, question of whether the system of legal norms that purports to restrain the conduct of states vis-à-vis individuals within their power will survive the terrorist threat." The bar associations of 53 British Commonwealth countries said that if Guantánamo were under British rule, "it would be the English courts and not the executive which would be responsible for determining any issue relating to any 'enemy' status alleged against detained persons." The NYCB quoted Justice Kennedy's 1991 opinion that limiting access to lawyers constituted a danger to rights and a "severe impediment of the judicial function." Sen. Specter wrote that stripping the courts of habeas jurisdiction was "anathema to fundamental liberty interests" and the CSRT was so flawed it "demands robust habeas review."

The media weighed in again on the day of argument. The *Los Angeles Times* dismissed as "laughable" the government's claim that "the procedures at Guantánamo are a 'constitutionally adequate substitute' for habeas corpus."[94] The *Washington Post* castigated the government's "profoundly myopic and morally vacuous handling of detainees," whose detention for years "without any charge or process other than highly constricted hearings in which they have not been represented by lawyers or even fully informed of the evidence against them … offends the most fundamental tenets of justice and does incalculable harm to the nation's image and moral authority abroad."

The *New York Times* called habeas "an important bulwark against authoritarianism so vital that the Constitution expressly protects it." The "shabby regime set up by the MCA ... permits the use of secret evidence," bars detainees "from submitting some of the evidence they need," and does not let them "be represented by counsel." AI took a full-page advertisement in the *Times* urging Congress to return America to its core constitutional principles of justice and fairness by overturning the MCA, granting fair and timely trials, treating detainees humanely, and reinstating the time-honored right to be heard in court.

Four days later the *Los Angeles Times* wrote:

> The situation at Guantánamo is manifestly unjust. But would the predicament of those held there be any less unjust if they were being held in a prison in Egypt or Poland? We don't think so ... American courts should offer a similar avenue of appeal to foreigners in American custody, wherever the jail.

In June 2008 the Court reversed in 5 opinions spanning 75 pages.[95] Justice Kennedy (joined by Stevens, Souter, Ginsburg, and Breyer) held that because the petitioners had a constitutional right to habeas, for which the DTA's procedures were not "an adequate and effective substitute," the MCA was "an unconstitutional suspension of the writ." The majority began its constitutional inquiry by observing that the fact that "protection for the privilege of habeas corpus was one of the few safeguards of liberty specified in a Constitution that ... had no Bill of Rights" showed it "had a centrality" for the Framers. The Suspension Clause was designed to protect against "cyclical abuses." The historical evidence concerning the writ's geographic scope in 1789 was fragmentary and ambiguous. While conceding the government's claim that Cuba had *de jure* sovereignty over Guantánamo, the majority followed *Rasul* in finding that the USA exercised de facto sovereignty. It rejected the argument "that by surrendering formal sovereignty over any unincorporated territory to a third party ... it would be possible for the political branches to govern without legal constraint." Those branches did not have "the power to switch the Constitution on or off at will." "The test for determining the scope" of habeas "must not be subject to manipulation by those whose power it is designed to restrain." The majority distinguished *Eisentrager*: "there had been a rigorous adversarial process to test the legality of detention"; unlike Landsberg Prison, "in every practical sense Guantánamo is not abroad; it is within the constant jurisdiction of the United States." "The Government presents no credible arguments that the military mission at Guantánamo would be compromised if habeas corpus courts had jurisdiction to hear the detainees' claims."

Assessing the CSRT's adequacy as a substitute for habeas, the majority noted that "the detainee has limited means to find or present evidence to challenge the Government's case ... does not have the assistance of counsel and may not be aware of the most critical allegations." Because there were "no limits on the admission of hearsay evidence ... the detainee's opportunity to question witnesses is likely to be more theoretical than real." There was "considerable risk of error in the tribunal's findings of fact" because its process was "closed and accusatorial." Furthermore, Court of Appeals review was inadequate because it could not hear "evidence discovered after the CSRT proceedings concluded."

"In some of these cases six years have elapsed without the judicial oversight that habeas corpus ... demands." "The first DTA review applications were filed over two years ago, but no decisions on the merits have been issued ... the costs of delay can no longer be borne by those who are held in custody." "Security depends upon a sophisticated intelligence apparatus," but "security subsists, too, in fidelity to freedom's first principles. Chief among these are freedom from arbitrary and unlawful restraint and the personal liberty that is secured by adherence to the separation of powers." "The laws and Constitution are designed to survive, and remain in force, in extraordinary times. Liberty and security can be reconciled, and in our system they are reconciled within the framework of the law."

Justice Souter also concurred separately (joined by Ginsburg and Breyer). Although *Rasul* dealt with statutory habeas jurisdiction, "no one who reads the Court's opinion in *Rasul* could seriously doubt that the jurisdictional question must be answered the same way in purely constitutional cases." The dissents' suggestion "that the Court is somehow precipitating the judiciary into reviewing claims that the military ... could handle within some reasonable period of time" had a "hollow ring" given that some petitioners had been detained six years. "After six years of sustained executive detentions in Guantánamo, subject to habeas jurisdiction but without any actual habeas scrutiny, today's decision is no judicial victory, but an act of perseverance in trying to make habeas review and the obligation of the courts to provide it, mean something of value both to prisoners and to the Nation."

Chief Justice Roberts dissented (with Scalia, Thomas, and Alito). The DTA procedures were "the most generous set of procedural protections ever afforded aliens detained by this country as enemy combatants." "The majority merely replaces a review system designed by the people's representatives with a set of shapeless procedures to be defined by federal courts at some future date." "This whole approach is misguided." He implicitly rebuked Stevens and Kennedy for siding with the majority after initially voting against certiorari. The decision "is not really about the detainees at all but about control of federal policies regarding enemy combatants." "What alternative does the Court propose" to CSRTs? "Allow free access to classified information and ignore the risk the prisoner may eventually convey what he learns to parties hostile to this country, with deadly consequences for those who helped apprehend the detainee?" The "CSRT procedures provide ample opportunity for detainees to introduce exculpatory evidence – whether documentary in nature or from live witnesses." Roberts concluded by asking rhetorically "who has won?" and answering "Not the rule of law, unless by that is meant the rule of lawyers, who will now arguably have a greater role than military and intelligence officials in shaping policy for enemy combatants."

Justice Scalia dissented separately (joined by Roberts, Thomas, and Alito). Because "the writ of habeas corpus does not, and never has, run in favor of aliens abroad, the Suspension Clause ... has no application." "The game of bait-and-switch that today's opinion plays upon the Nation's Commander in Chief will make the war harder on us. It will almost certainly cause more Americans to be killed." The majority engaged in a "blatant *abandonment*" of "time-honored legal principle" [original emphasis]. The short-term consequences would be "devastating." At least thirty former detainees had "returned to the battlefield." The present decision will require "military officials to appear before civilian courts and defend their decisions." "[O]ne escalation of procedures that the Court is clear about is affording the detainees increased access to witnesses (perhaps troops serving in Afghanistan?) and to classified information." "'Manipulation' of the territorial reach of the writ by the Judiciary poses just as much a threat to the proper separation of powers as 'manipulation' by the Executive." "The Court's analysis produces a crazy result." "What drives today's decision is neither the meaning of the Suspension Clause, nor the principles of our precedents, but rather an inflated notion of judicial supremacy." "It is both irrational and arrogant to say that the answer" to the question "whether the constitution confers habeas jurisdiction on federal courts to decide petitioners' claims" "must be yes, because otherwise we would not be supreme." "[T]he Court's ultimate, unexpressed goal is to pre-serve the power to review the confinement of enemy prisoners held by the Executive anywhere in the world."

> Today the Court warps our Constitution in a way that goes beyond the narrow issue of the reach of the Suspension Clause, invoking judicially brainstormed separation-of-powers principles to establish a manipu-lable "functional" test for the extraterritorial reach of habeas corpus ... It blatantly misdescribes important precedents ... most tragically, it sets our military commanders the impossible task of proving to a civilian court ... that evidence supports the confinement of each and every enemy prisoner. The Nation will live to regret what the Court has done today.

Khalid Odah, whose son Fawzi was a petitioner, said: "after more than six long and painful years, justice for our family is finally within our reach."[96] CCR Director Michael Ratner optimistically predicted that "the government is going to have to release ... a high number of people." CCR lawyer Shayana Kadidal concurred: "the day before ... the day the government has to show up in court and justify holding these guys for six years ... is the day they are likely to get released." But Republicans continued to resist. President Bush said: "We'll abide by the Court's position. That doesn't mean I have to agree with it." He was considering legislation "so that we can safely say ... to the American people, 'we're doing everything we can to protect you.'" His press sec-retary said: "there's no question [the decision] has done damage to our ability to protect the country." Sen. Graham warned that the "tre-mendously dangerous and irresponsible ruling ... has conferred upon civilian judges the right to make military decisions." He hoped "there is some legislative enactments [sic] that we can pass that would protect our national security requirements."

Presidential candidates squared off.[97] Dismissing the petitioners as "unlawful combatants ... not American citizens," McCain declared that the Court had rendered "one of the worst decisions in the history of this country." Enemy combatants "never have been given the rights of citizens of this country." Courts would be "flooded" with lawsuits. "We are going to be bollixed up in a way that's terribly unfortunate. Our first obligation is the safety and security of this nation and the men and women who defend it. This decision will harm our ability to do that."

Obama praised the decision as "a rejection of the Bush administration's attempt to create a legal black hole at Guantánamo," which was "yet another failed policy supported by John McCain." "This is an important step toward reestablishing our credibility as a nation committed to the rule of law, and rejecting a false choice between fighting terrorism and respecting habeas corpus." (At a campaign rally the following September, Obama went further. Habeas corpus was "the foundation of Anglo-American law." "The reason you have that safeguard is because we don't always catch the right person ... You might think it's Barack the bomb thrower, but it's Barack the guy running for president." "Don't suggest that it's un-American to abide by what the Founding Fathers set up. It's worked pretty well for over two hundred years.")[98]

The *Washington Post* called it "a welcome victory for due process and the rule of law."[99] The CSRTs "make a mockery of detainees' ability to rebut government charges." Detainees "must be granted robust rights, including access to civilian lawyers and judges and the ability to challenge the evidence against them."

The *New York Times* praised the Court's "stirring defense of habeas corpus." "[T]here is an enormous gulf between the substance and tone of the majority opinion, with its rich appreciation of the liberties that the founders wrote into the Constitution, and the what-is-all-the- fuss-about dissent." But it was "sobering to think that habeas hangs by a single vote."

The *Times* also published laudatory letters. The CCR executive director called it "imperative that the lower courts move with full speed." Other writers said it would be "tragic if we throw away 200 years of constitutional wisdom" and urged "all those for whom the rule of law and our constitution mean everything" to "celebrate." In a *Times* op ed, Richard Epstein (a New York University law professor with libertarian and originalist views) praised the decision as "a rejection of the alarmist view that our fragile geopolitical position requires abandoning our commitment to preventing Star Chamber proceedings that result in arbitrary incarcerations." The *Los Angeles Times* said the Court "undid a compliant Congress's collusion" with the Bush administration in "denying due process of law to inmates at Guantánamo Bay Naval Base." Ben Wittes (a senior fellow at the Brookings Institution) wrote in a *Washington Post* op ed that "detainees should have real rights, starting with representation by competent counsel, cleared to see all evidence ... and a more meaningful opportunity to present evidence of their own." But the *Wall Street Journal* warned that "more Americans are likely to die as a result" of the decision and quoted Justice Jackson's observation that the Constitution is not a suicide pact, adding snidely: "about Anthony Kennedy's Constitution, we're not so sure." And two conservative commentators were hopeful that the decision would fuel Republican attacks on the Court.

A week after the decision Attorney General Mukasey reassured the American Enterprise Institute that *Boumediene* did not require the administration to "simply release [detainees] to return to the battle-field as indeed some have," while warning that "many" of the more than 200 "pose an extraordinary threat to Americans."[100] He was proposing legislation "to resolve the difficult questions left open by the Supreme Court." "First and foremost, Congress should make clear that our federal court [sic] may not order the government to bring enemy combatants into the United States." "We simply cannot afford to reveal to terrorists all that we know about them and how we acquired that information." "Soldiers fighting the war on terror … should not be required to leave the front lines to testify as witnesses in habeas proceedings." "[T]o suggest that the government must charge detainees with crimes or release them is to seriously misunderstand the principle of reasons [sic] why we detain enemy combatants in the first place. It has to do with self-protection, because these are dangerous people who pose threats to our citizens and to our soldiers."

The *New York Times* criticized this as another of "this administration's ceaseless efforts to undermine the Constitution and the rule of law," and derided Mukasey's claim that "all of these people … are aliens captured abroad in essentially battlefield conditions."[101]

> What the administration fears is that hearings for any prisoner will reveal how much abuse has been meted out by American interrogators and how thin and tainted the evidence is against most of the Guantánamo prisoners. It would be catastrophically irresponsible for Congress to rewrite the rules of justice according to Mr. Mukasey's cynical template.

But at the end of July four Republican Representatives introduced the Enemy Combatant Detention Review Act, cosponsored by Sens. Graham and Lieberman, which would do much of what Mukasey recommended. The *Washington Post* praised Congress for acting, but said the bill "comes too close to replicating some of the failed processes at Guantánamo." HASC held hearings on Boumediene.

POST-*BOUMEDIENE* CASES

The Supreme Court remanded to the DC Circuit, which remanded to the District Court.[102] Judge Hogan, who was managing all the cases, said on July 9, 2008: "The time has come to move these forward. Set aside every other case that's pending in the division and address this case first." The government filed a factual return containing a 53-page narrative and 650 pages of exhibits. The District Court held over 50 hours of hearings in response to petitioners' more than 80 discovery motions. Petitioners then filed their traverse: over 200 pages of narrative and 1,650 pages of exhibits.

On November 6 Judge Hogan issued a Case Management Order.[103] The government would provide the definition of enemy combatant and give petitioners "all reasonably available" evidence (including exculpatory), proffering classified evidence to counsel cleared to receive it unless the government sought an exception from the merits judge in camera. The judge should try to give the petitioner access to unclassified portions of the hearing "through available technological means." The government had to prove by a preponderance of evidence that detention was lawful. The merits judge could give government evidence a rebuttable presumption of accuracy and authenticity if the government proved such a presumption was "necessary to alleviate an undue burden presented by the particular habeas corpus proceeding." Hearsay would be admissible "if the movant establishes that the hearsay evidence is reliable and that the provision of nonhearsay evidence would unduly burden the movant or interfere with the government's efforts to protect national security."

Judge Leon promised to hear his 24 cases by Christmas, starting with *Boumediene*.[104] In November he listened to seven days of classified evidence and nearly four-and-a-half hours of argument, all in camera. Declaring that detainees did not have a constitutional right to confront or call witnesses, he had them testify by video. When the audio link failed, he ordered that tape recordings be sent overnight to Guantánamo. He adopted the DoD definition of "enemy combatant": anyone "who was part of or supporting Taliban or al-Qaeda forces, or associated forces." The government dropped its claims that the six *Boumediene* petitioners had plotted to blow up the US embassy in Sarajevo, as well as the claim (based on information from a convicted criminal whom the government itself called a liar) that one petitioner had obtained military training in Afghanistan and worked at a charity later designated as a terrorism sponsor. Although the government still alleged the petitioners planned to fight in Afghanistan, the only evidence was "a classified document from an unnamed source."

> [W]hile the information in the classified intelligence report ... was undoubtedly sufficient for the intelligence purposes for which it was prepared, it is *not* sufficient for the purposes for which a habeas court must now evaluate it. To allow enemy combatancy to rest on so *thin* a reed would be inconsistent with the Court's obligation under the Supreme Court's decision in *Hamdi* to protect petitioners from the risk of erroneous detention [original emphasis].

Finding that the government had "not provided the Court with enough information to adequately evaluate the credibility and reliability of this source's information," Judge Leon granted five petitions but denied Bensayah Belkacem's because the government had provided corroboration for the unnamed source's evidence that he was an al-Qaeda facilitator. At the end of July 2009 three petitioners had been transferred to Bosnia and one to France, but Saber Lahmar had no place to go. In August, his lawyers sought to block his transfer to Bosnia because he feared he would be deported to Algeria and tortured there.

In June 2010 the DC Circuit (Judge Ginsburg, joined by Henderson and Edwards) reversed the denial of Belkacem's petition.[105] Since the District Court's decision, the government had abandoned its claims that the alleged "senior al-Qaida facilitator" with whom Belkacem had contact actually *was* a senior al-Qaeda facilitator and that Belkacem had rendered support to al-Qaeda, as well as its legal argument that Belkacem could be detained under the president's commander-in-chief authority. In a decision redacted so thoroughly as to be incomprehensible, Ginsburg found that the corroboration on which Judge Leon had relied was insufficient and remanded for consideration of whether there was enough other evidence to prove that Belkacem was functionally part of al-Qaeda. Belkacem was released in December 2013.[106]

At the end of October 2008 Judge Sullivan said that the government's decision to withdraw allegations linking Binyam Mohamed to a dirty bomb just before the deadline for turning over exculpatory evidence "raises serious questions in this court's mind about whether those allegations were true."[107] "Someone is going to rue the day those allegations were made" if they turned out to be unfounded. When a DoJ lawyer claimed "we have simplified this case to its bare essence," Sullivan expressed skepticism: "that doesn't ring true; it rings hollow. The government has never been concerned with acting expeditiously here." Indeed, the DoJ lawyer said the government stood behind the dirty bomb plot. Sullivan also ordered the government to account for Mohamed's whereabouts from 2002 to 2004 (when he had been held in a secret CIA prison in Morocco). The day before the hearing a British court had ordered its government to turn over intelligence documents that lend "some support to [Mohamed's] claim that the confession was obtained after a period of two years incommunicado detention during which he was tortured."

At the end of December Judge Leon denied habeas to Hisham Sliti, finding that his "story about traveling to Afghanistan to kick a longstanding drug habit and find a wife is not credible," and to Moath al Alwi, finding he had close ties to the Taliban and al-Qaeda.[108]

In March 2005 CSRTs found that two Uighurs, Abu Bakker Qassim and A'del Abdu al-Hakim, "should no longer be classified as enemy combatants."[109] But the government did not tell the detainees and moved to stay the habeas petitions they filed that month without informing Judge Robertson of that finding. Although their lawyers twice asked about the CSRTs, the government did not reply. When counsel met their clients in Guantánamo in mid-July, they learned about the finding for the first time and filed an emergency motion to vacate the stay. On August 1, when the government asserted "the Executive's necessary power to wind up wartime detentions in an orderly fashion," Judge Robertson withheld a decision based on the parties' agreement that the men should be released "and the government's assurance that diplomatic efforts were being made to find a country that would accept the petitioners." At a December 12 hearing the government claimed "progress is being made," but would offer evidence only in camera; Judge Robertson refused, saying it "could have been offered only to coopt the court and seek further delay." Fearing the DTA would soon strip the courts of habeas jurisdiction (as discussed below), petitioners elicited Robertson's promise to decide within two weeks.

On December 22, Judge Robertson granted the petitions.[110] Although *Hamdi* upheld wartime detention to prevent prisoners from returning to the battlefield, "nothing in this record establishes that the government has or could reasonably have a concern that these petitioners would return to the battlefield if released." "The government's use of the Kafka-esque term 'no longer enemy combatants' deliberately begs the question of whether these petitioners ever were enemy combatants." But though he found their indefinite detention "unlawful," he lacked "the power to do what I believe justice requires." He had entertained, and the petitioners had accepted, "a simple order requiring the petitioners' release, without specifying how, or to where," but "the experiment cannot work." "An order requiring their release into the

United States – even into some kind of parole 'bubble,' some legal-fictional status in which they would be here but would not have been 'admitted' – would have national security and diplomatic implications beyond the competence of this court." He concluded despairingly "a federal court has no relief to offer."

The petitioners appealed directly to the Supreme Court, but it declined to act.[111] Instead, the DC Circuit scheduled an expedited hearing for May 2006. But just before that occurred, the administration transferred the petitioners to Albania, and in August the DC Circuit ruled this had mooted the case.[112]

In July 2007 the DC Circuit considered its procedures for reviewing CSRT determinations that eight other Uighurs were ECs.[113] Judge Ginsburg (joined by Henderson and Rogers) rejected the government's view that the court could consider only the CSRT record. "In order to review compliance" with the CSRT's own procedures, "the court must be able to view the Government information with the aid of counsel for both parties." That had to include all "reasonably available information in the possession of the US Government." Furthermore, "this court cannot discharge its responsibility … to determine whether a preponderance of the evidence supports the Tribunal's determination, unless a petitioner's counsel has access to as much as is practical of the classified information regarding his client" (although this did not include highly sensitive information). The court allowed a lawyer to visit a potential client twice before producing a written retainer or authorization by next friend. Three months later the panel denied rehearing.[114] In February 2008 the DC Circuit (5–5) denied rehearing en banc.[115] This deeply split decision unusually produced four opinions and an addendum with two more, extending over 17 pages. Judge Ginsburg (joined by Rogers, Tatel, Garland, and Griffith) wrote that:

> CSRT's status determination is the product of a necessarily closed and accusatorial process in which the detainee seeking review will have had little or no access to the evidence the Recorder presented to the Tribunal, little ability to gather his own evidence, no right to confront the witnesses against him, and no lawyer to help him prepare his case, and in which the decisionmaker is employed and chosen by the detainee's accuser … For this court to ignore that reality would be to proceed as though the Congress envisioned judicial review as a mere charade.

Judge Henderson (joined by Sentelle, Randolph, Brown, and Kavanaugh) voted for rehearing because the CIA, FBI, and NSA

Directors, DNI, and Deputy Secretary of Defense "detailed the grave national security concerns the *Bismullah* I holding presents." Judge Randolph (joined by Sentelle, Henderson, and Kavanaugh) warned that "vast reams of classified information" would go to detainees' lawyers, risking "serious security breaches for no good reason." "[T]he agencies charged with protecting the country against terrorist attacks ... warn that foreign intelligence services will cease cooperating with the United States if the panel opinion stands."

The government asked the DC Circuit to stay the panel decision and, warning of "drastic and immediate consequences," filed an emergency appeal, seeking to argue the case in the Supreme Court that term.[116] The petitioners resisted the stay, noting that seven detainees were in their seventh year of detention and Bismullah was in his fifth: "the human cost of further delay is simply too great." The *Washington Post* urged the Court to grant expedited review and rule against the government.

> Without the ability to examine the entire record, no court could pass judgment on whether the evidence presented to the tribunal was complete and in context; nor could it determine whether exculpatory evidence was omitted ... Justice cannot be served unless the tribunals themselves allow detainees such jurisprudential mainstays as the right to a lawyer and the right to review and rebut evidence against them.

On June 23 (11 days after deciding *Boumediene*), the Supreme Court granted certiorari in *Bismullah*, vacated the judgment, and remanded for consideration in light of *Boumediene*.[117] In January 2009 the original DC Circuit panel unanimously declined to review the CSRT decision at all, finding that Congress would not have passed the DTA knowing that the Supreme Court would hold that DC Circuit review of CSRT decisions could not serve as an exclusive alternative to habeas corpus.[118] (That left the Uighurs with habeas as their sole remedy.)

In June 2008 a different DC Circuit panel invalidated the CSRT, finding that Huzaifa Parhat (another Uighur) was an EC.[119] Judge Garland (joined by Sentelle and Griffith) wrote that it was "undisputed that he is not a member of al-Qaeda or the Taliban, and that he has never participated in any hostile action against the United States or its allies." The CSRT findings rested on classified documents "that provide no information regarding the sources ... and otherwise lack sufficient indicia of the statements' reliability." The CSRT relied "on the interview report of a single Uighur detainee," but did not consider "exculpatory evidence on the same point" by another detainee.

To prove that Parhat belonged to or supported forces associated with al-Qaida or the Taliban, which engaged in hostilities against the United States or its coalition partners, the CSRT relied on four government intelligence documents that repeatedly describe those activities and relationships as having "reportedly" occurred, as being "said to" or "reported to" have happened, and as things that "may" be true or are "suspected of" having taken place. But in virtually every instance, the documents do not say who "reported" or "said" or "suspected" those things.

Because neither the CSRT nor the court could "assess the reliability of the assertions," they "cannot sustain the determination that Parhat is an enemy combatant."

Parhat contends that the ultimate source of key assertions in the four intelligence documents is the government of the People's Republic of China, and he offers substantial support for that contention.

First, the government suggests that several of the assertions in the intelligence documents are reliable because they are made in at least three different documents. We are not persuaded.

Lewis Carroll notwithstanding, the fact that the government has "said it thrice" does not make an allegation true ... To the contrary ... many of those assertions are made in identical language, suggesting that later documents may merely be citing earlier ones ...

Second, the government insists that the statements made in the documents are reliable because the State and Defense Departments would not have put them in intelligence documents were that not the case. This comes perilously close to suggesting that whatever the government says must be treated as true.

Declining "to rubber-stamp the government's charges," the court remanded for another CSRT, but warned it would not countenance "endless 'do-overs'" and noted that habeas was still available. The court also denied (without prejudice) the government's motion to designate as "protected information" significant parts of the record because it relied "solely on spare, generic assertions."

On October 9, 2008, Judge Urbina took the extraordinary step of ordering the release into the USA of the 17 remaining Uighurs.[120] He began:

There comes a time when delayed action prompted by judicial deference to the executive branch's function yields inaction not consistent with the constitutional imperative. Such a time has come in the case of the 17 Uighurs in Guantánamo Bay, Cuba ... whom the

371

government has detained for 7 years without an opportunity for judicial redress until recently ... Because the Constitution prohibits indefinite detention without just cause, this court rules that the government's continued detention of the petitioners is unlawful. Furthermore, because separation-of-powers concerns do not trump the very principle upon which this nation was founded – the unalienable right to liberty – the court orders the government to release the petitioners into the United States.

The government had cleared ten Uighurs for release about two years before they petitioned for habeas in July 2005; it cleared another five in 2005, one in 2006, and the last in May 2007, saying it would treat them as "no longer enemy combatants." On July 23, 2008 Parhat filed a motion for release into the United States (which the others had joined). *Boumediene* "unequivocally extend[ed] to Guantánamo detainees the constitutional right to habeas corpus" and "re-emphasized the importance of the writ in preserving liberty." In response to the government's claim of authority to "wind up" the detentions, Judge Urbina held that the executive's constitutional authority to "wind up" detentions ceases once (1) detention becomes effectively indefinite; (2) there is a reasonable certainty that the petitioner will not return to the battlefield to fight against the United States; and (3) an alternative legal justification has not been provided for continued detention.

All three elements were met here.

> [T]he government has stymied its own efforts to resettle the petitioners by insisting (until recently) that they were enemy combatants ...
>
> [T]he court's authority to safeguard an individual's liberty from unbridled executive fiat reaches its zenith when the Executive brings an individual involuntarily within the court's jurisdiction, detains that individual and then subverts diplomatic efforts to secure alternative channels for release ... These efforts have failed for the last 4 years and have no foreseeable date by which they may succeed ... Because their detention has already crossed the constitutional threshold into infinitum and because our system of checks and balances is designed to preserve the fundamental right of liberty, the court grants the petitioners' motion for release into the United States.

Mukasey called the decision a disaster.[121] The government appealed. Solicitor General Garre said Urbina had overstepped his authority in giving his "unprecedented order."[122] The government was working hard to find countries to accept the detainees. The *Washington Post* urged President Bush to "do the right thing" and "use his executive powers to allow at least some of these detainees to settle in the United States," to demonstrate "that this country retains the capacity to do what is right and fair."

The DC Circuit reversed on February 18, 2009.[123] Judge Randolph (joined by Henderson) began with "the ancient principle that a nation-state has the inherent right to exclude or admit foreigners." A court could not "review the determination of the political branch ... to exclude a given alien" without express legal authority, which Judge Urbina had not cited. Urbina had invoked the maxim "ubi jus, ibi remedium"; Randolph replied: "not every violation of a right yields a remedy, even when the right is constitutional." "High-minded" sentiments that the petitioners "deserve to be released into this country after all they have endured" do not "represent a legal basis for upsetting settled law and overriding the prerogatives of the political branches." Judge Rogers concurred in the judgment on other grounds, but he rejected the court's reasoning as "not faithful to *Boumediene*" and "compromis[ing] the Great Writ as a check on arbitrary detention and the balance of powers." Randolph (with Henderson) rebutted her assertion at length and with biting sarcasm.

When the Obama administration reviewed the Uighur cases in March 2009, Rep. J. Randy Forbes (R), who represented the Northern Virginia district where they might be sent, said "I don't think people want people that could potentially be terrorists in the United States."[124] At the beginning of April the Uighurs' lawyers asked the Supreme Court to release them into the USA because a hundred countries (bowing to Chinese pressure) had refused to accept them. The *Washington Post* said: "the time has come for the United States to accept full responsibility for wrongly holding the Uighurs and to act boldly to rectify this miscarriage of justice." Obama should grant asylum to all those who "have not engaged in any acts of violence." On April 24 Obama called for seven of the remaining 17 to be released. In early June the *Post* said there was "still a small window of opportunity for President Obama to do right by the 17 men who have spent years behind bars even though they should never have been imprisoned." "Germany, which is home to a Munich-based Uighur community, recently declined to take nine of the detainees, in part because of the fear-mongering by US lawmakers and strong resistance from China." By opposing Supreme Court review of the DC Circuit's decision, the Obama administration threatened "to make the Uighurs modern victims of a real-life version of Jean-Paul Sartre's 'No Exit.'"

The Supreme Court granted certiorari on October 20. The *Washington Post* read this as a message to the government to "either provide real and meaningful freedom for the Uighurs now or risk that the Justices will do it – and possibly in a manner that could reach well beyond these cases." Despite the "difficult" legal questions, "the moral and ethical imperatives are clear and compelling." But Sen. McConnell warned that the Uighurs had received "weapons training" from a "terrorist organization." On March 1, 2010 the Court vacated the Circuit Court judgment, remanding for consideration of the fact that each detainee had received at least one offer of resettlement (although five had rejected two – from Palau and an unnamed country).[125] The *Washington Post* said the Court had "rightly dismissed the case" because the five "had undercut their legal and moral argument that they were continuing to be held against their will." On May 28 the Circuit Court reinstated its original opinion.[126] Since its last decision "Congress has prohibited the expenditure of any funds to bring any Guantánamo detainee to the United States" in seven bills, five still in effect. Judge Rogers concurred in the judgment, concluding: "Petitioners hold the keys to their release from Guantánamo for resettlement in an 'appropriate' country." The Supreme Court denied certiorari on April 18, 2011.[127] Justice Breyer (joined by Kennedy, Ginsburg, and Sotomayor) wrote separately that "these offers, the lack of any meaningful challenge as to their appropriateness, and the Government's uncontested commitment to continue to work to resettle petitioners transform petitioners' claim." The *Los Angeles Times* said the government had a "moral obligation" to resettle the Uighurs.[128] "The Court's unwillingness ... even to hear the case – compounds the injustice." (Two detainees were transferred to El Salvador in 2012 and the last three to Slovakia at the end of 2013, but none of these transfers was judicially mandated.)

Several cases involved US citizens held abroad. Ahmed Omar Abu Ali, arrested in Saudi Arabia in June 2003, claimed he was held there at the behest of the USA, which had interrogated him.[129] Contemporaneously, FBI agents had searched his Virginia home, and three other Americans were apprehended in Saudi Arabia, extradited to the USA, and charged with eight others with undergoing paramilitary training to engage in jihad.[130] Abu Ali's parents, who brought the petition, alleged he had been tortured.

DDC Judge Bates began his opinion by quoting a Supreme Court opinion describing habeas corpus as "the essential remedy to safeguard a citizen against imprisonment by State or Nation in violation of his

and held by the Muadh Ibn Jabal Brigade.[133] After two months he was freed by MNF-I, which delivered him to the Central Criminal Court of Iraq, where he was convicted of kidnapping and sentenced to death in a 15-minute hearing. Lamberth found that Munaf was in the actual custody of MNF-I, "who derive their ultimate authority from the United Nations and the MNF-I member nations acting jointly," and in the constructive custody of Iraq. "[N]o court in our country's history, other than *Omar*, has ever found habeas corpus jurisdiction over a multinational force comprised of the United States acting jointly with its allies overseas. And the law is legend that in time of actual hostilities or war, as in Iraq, courts should tread lightly and give the President, as Commander-in-Chief, the full power of his office."

Lamberth quoted an 1850 Supreme Court case holding that the president's decisions about how to deploy the armed forces "in the manner he may deem most effectual to harass and conquer and subdue the enemy" were "delicate, complex, and involve large elements of prophecy … They are decisions of a kind for which the Judiciary has neither aptitude, facilities nor responsibility and which has long been held to belong in the domain of political power not subject to judicial intrusion or inquiry." The DC Circuit affirmed.[134] Judge Sentelle (joined by Kavanaugh) found the decision compelled by *Hirota* as applied by *Finck*. Judge Randolph found that the District Court had jurisdiction, but habeas should be denied because Munaf had been convicted by an Iraqi court.

In June 2008 the Supreme Court reversed and remanded both cases (Souter, Ginsburg, and Breyer concurring in the result).[135] Chief Justice Roberts wrote that District Courts had jurisdiction to hear habeas petitions by "American citizens held overseas in the immediate 'physical custody' of American soldiers who answer only to an American chain of command." But the Court denied the injunctions, which "would interfere with Iraq's sovereign right to 'punish offenses against its laws committed within its borders.'" Petitioners' fears they would be tortured in Iraqi custody must "be addressed by the political branches." Judicial "second-guess[ing]" would "require federal courts to pass judgment on foreign justice systems and undermine the Government's ability to speak with one voice." The *Washington Post* praised the decision's "reasonable balance."[136] "The record shows that the two men have been afforded due process in Iraq, where they had legal representation and hearings before Iraqi judges." On remand, Judge Urbina denied Omar's petition.[137] The DC Circuit affirmed because "historically, a would-be transferee ... has possessed no right to judicial review of conditions the transferee might face in another country."[138]

In early January 2009 Judge Bates heard the habeas petitions of four men detained in the US Bagram prison in Afghanistan (known as the *Maqaleh* case). Criticizing the Bush administration for continuing to "espouse extreme theories about the detention of terrorism suspects" in "its waning days," the *Washington Post* urged the new Obama administration to give petitioners "a meaningful chance to challenge their detentions."[139] After three-and-a-half hours of argument, Bates expressed concern that the executive had created "a kind of law-free zone." Observing that the petitioners had been captured "nowhere near the battlefield in Afghanistan," he ordered the government to report in a week how many detainees it held in Bagram, how many had been captured outside Afghanistan, and how many were Afghan citizens. Because Obama's January 22 executive orders "indicating significant changes to the government's approach" to detention at Guantánamo "could impact the court's analysis" in these cases, Judge Bates gave the government four weeks to redefine "enemy combatant." But it declined to do so. The *Washington Post* called it "unacceptable" for the administration to argue "it can continue to hold people, some of whom were seized outside of Afghanistan, year after year, without charge or access to lawyers." They had even "fewer protections at their disposal than the Guantánamo inmates held under a flawed tribunal system." Of the 600 Bagram detainees, the 30 or so who had been detained outside Afghanistan were entitled to more procedural justice than was required for others under Art. 5 of the Geneva Convention.

At the beginning of April Bates denied the government's motion to dismiss three of the petitions in a 32-page opinion analyzing the application of *Boumediene* to Bagram. The process used to designate them as ECs was inadequate and "significantly less than the Guantánamo detainees ... received." They had no personal representative and could only submit a written statement without knowing the evidence against them. Although US jurisdiction in Bagram was "not quite as plenary as at Guantánamo," the "objective degree of control" exercised by the USA in the two sites was "not appreciably different." The "practical obstacles" of a habeas hearing were "in some ways greater ... because Bagram is located in an active theater of war"; but they "certainly are not insurmountable" and were "largely of the Executive's choosing." It would be "anomalous to allow respondents to preclude a detainee's habeas rights by choosing to put him in harm's way through detention in a theater of war." "[T]o the extent that respondents are alarmed by the prospect of pulling potential witnesses from the battlefield ... all four petitioners ... claim to have been captured outside Afghanistan, far removed from any battlefield – and were apprehended six or more years ago." But the Afghan citizenship of one (Wazir) created a "'practical obstacle[]' in the form of friction with the 'host' country," requiring dismissal of his petition.

Calling this "a serious blow to the Obama administration," the *Washington Post* urged it not to "prolong these men's detentions for many months without more appropriate review." It should grant the 30 captured outside Afghanistan immediate access to the federal court and consider moving the others to Guantánamo, "where their right to habeas corpus review would be unquestionable." Although the *Los Angeles Times* urged the government to "address the grievances" of the petitioners, it feared that in the future the military "might be tempted to surrender prisoners to foreign governments that would abuse them."

But the government appealed, arguing that in the future it would be "unable to move non-Afghan citizens captured across the border in Pakistan" to Afghanistan without judicial review, forcing it to reveal "the place of capture" and the "identity of US or foreign forces" that had participated. The *New York Times* was "disappoint[ed]" that the administration had acted "less nobly" in Bagram than in Guantánamo. It should focus on putting in place "a fair review process that complies with international and military law" rather than "wasting its energies in an appeal that simply recycles extravagant claims of executive power and perpetuates the detention policies of the Bush administration." After oral argument in January, the *Times* repeated that it had been "waiting – in vain – for the Obama administration to stop trying to block judicial scrutiny of some of the Bush administration's most outrageous policies." "[T]he prisoners at issue were not captured in the war zone." "The government's intimation that a few hearings would hurt the expanding war effort in Afghanistan is not credible."

In May 2010 the DC Circuit reversed. Judge Sentelle (joined by Tatel and Edwards) agreed with Judge Bates that the petitioners' status did not differ from that of the petitioners in *Boumediene*, and an Unlawful Enemy Combatant Review Board (UECRB) offered even less protection than the CSRT. But the USA did not exercise over Bagram the de facto sovereignty it enjoyed in Guantánamo. And the third *Boumediene* factor – "the practical obstacles inherent in resolving the prisoner's entitlement to the writ" – weighed "overwhelmingly" in favor of the government.

Sen. Graham hailed this "big win."

> Allowing a noncitizen enemy combatant detained in a combat zone access to American courts would have been a change of historic proportions. It also would have dealt a severe blow to our war effort. There is a reason we have never allowed enemy prisoners detained overseas in an active war zone to sue in federal court for their release. It simply makes no sense and would be the ultimate act of turning the war into a crime.

Praising Judge Bates's "narrowly focused" ruling, which "recognized that the logic of exempting POWs from judicial review cannot apply to a detainee who is imported to a war zone," the *New York Times* criticized the Circuit Court for having "overestimated the practical difficulty of affording court access and underestimated American control of Bagram." It was "especially distressing" that "the extravagant claim of executive power upheld by the court – to create a law-free zone at the Bagram lockup – was dreamed up by Mr. Bush and subsequently embraced by President Obama." The *Washington Post* warned of the "very real danger that the Bagram air base in Afghanistan could become the next Guantánamo." "Judicial checks – and clear and fair rules for detentions – are needed to prevent abuses of all kinds." Richard Epstein (a libertarian law professor at Chicago and NYU) denounced the "dangerous precedent."

On February 15, 2011 Judge Bates granted the Bagram detainees' motion to introduce new evidence about the commencement of civilian criminal trials for Afghan nationals at Bagram, the movement and retention of detainees in Afghanistan, and plans to continue holding non-Afghan detainees in Bagram. "[T]he proffered evidence is extensive (and arguably evolving) and, in some ways, its impact under the *Boumediene/Maqaleh* factors is subtle."[140] But on June 26, 2012, before Bates heard that case, Judge Gwin dismissed the habeas petition of Ziaur-Rahman, an Afghan held at Bagram, finding that it did not differ significantly from *Maqaleh*.[141] In September lawyers for the *Maqaleh* detainees offered new evidence, including a statement by President Karzai's chief of staff that the Afghan government did not want custody. But in October Judge Bates denied the habeas petition.[142] It was now more likely than it had been when the Circuit Court heard argument, that the USA would transfer custody of all detainees to Afghanistan, which was still a war zone. The same day Bates dismissed the amended petition of another Pakistani detainee, Hamidullah.[143] On November 15 Judge Lamberth denied the habeas petition of Amanatullah, a Pakistani held by the USA in Bagram.[144]

At the end of December 2013 the DC Circuit (Henderson, with Griffith and Williams) affirmed.[145] Because the Detainee Review Boards more closely resembled habeas review than the UECRBs they replaced, petitioners had a weaker case than the original *Maqaleh* petitioners. There was further evidence for the court's earlier conclusion that "American control over Bagram and its detention facilities lacks the permanence of US control over Guantánamo." "Not only have the political branches yet to announce an end to the war in Afghanistan, but the President has repeatedly declared that it is ongoing."

Majid Khan emigrated to the USA with his family from Pakistan in 1996, obtained asylum in 1998, graduated from high school in Baltimore in 1999, and returned to Pakistan to marry in 2002.[146] Pakistani security officials seized him in 2003 and handed him to the USA, which held him in secret prisons until Bush transferred him to Guantánamo in September 2006. CCR petitioned for habeas on his behalf just before passage of the MCA. In its response in November, the government argued that lawyers should not have access to Khan because he possessed top secret/sensitive compartmented information, including "locations of detention, conditions of detention, and alternative interrogation techniques." Gitanjali Gutierrez, his lawyer, said: "the government should not be able to torture someone and use that as a justification to keep that information from the American public." The same month Ramzi bin al-Shibh, another HVD just transferred to Guantánamo, also sought habeas.[147]

In January 2009 Judge Leon granted the habeas petition of Mohammed El-Gharani (who had filed on March 2, 2005).[148] The only evidence the government offered was statements by two Guantánamo detainees, whose credibility "has either been directly called into question by Government personnel or has been characterized by Government personnel as undetermined" and "is plagued with internal inconsistencies." Their stories "are not factually compatible." "Putting aside the obvious and unanswered questions as to how a Saudi minor from a very poor family could have even become a member of a London-based cell, the Government simply advances no corroborating evidence" for this allegation. "[A] mosaic of tiles bearing images this murky reveals nothing about the petitioner with sufficient clarity … that can be relied upon by this court."

The same month Judge Bates expressed impatience with the government's failure to comply with the Case Management Order requiring production of all the statements of petitioner Waleed Said Bn [sic] Said Zaid.[149] Bates could not take seriously the respondents' insistence that the process of merely *identifying* whether recordings, transcripts, or other versions of the petitioner's statements exist is "truly breathtaking in scope."

> It strains credulity to believe that the government, after several years of litigation, does not have electronic or other consolidated records pertaining to each Guantánamo detainee … Respondents have often replied to this Court's orders with eleventh-hour requests for enlargements of time or explanations why compliance is impossible or ill-advised. Respondents should not expect a sympathetic reception from the Court should they invoke that approach once again.

That month Judge Leon denied habeas to Ghaleb Nassar Al Bihani.[150] The government offered evidence that the Yemeni citizen living in Saudi Arabia had gone to Afghanistan in response to a fatwa endorsing jihad by the Taliban against the Northern Alliance, had received military training at an al-Qaeda camp, and had fought the Northern Alliance until his unit retreated in the face of US bombing, when he surrendered to the Northern Alliance. Judge Leon found that al Bihani's admission he had served as a cook was sufficient evidence. "[F]aithfully serving in an al-Qaeda affiliated fighting unit that is directly supporting the Taliban by helping to prepare the meals of its entire fighting force is more than sufficient 'support' to meet this Court's definition. After all, as Napoleon himself was fond of pointing out, 'an army marches on its stomach.'"

The DC Circuit affirmed in January 2010.[151] Noting that *Boumediene* had "provided scant guidance" concerning whom the president could detain and what procedure they were due, Judge Brown (joined by Kavanaugh) "aim[ed] to narrow the legal uncertainty that clouds military detention." The president's war powers were *not* "limited by the international laws of war," which were "not a fixed code" but "by nature contestable and fluid" and could be overridden by Congress (as in the AUMF). Therefore, "we have no occasion here to quibble over the intricate application of vague treaty provisions and amorphous customary principles." Al Bihani was detainable under the MCA's "purposefully and materially supported" language, which "clearly include[s] traditional food operations essential to a fighting force and the carrying of arms." In response to al Bihani's claim that he should be released because hostilities had ended, Judge Brown "defer[red] to the Executive's opinion on the matter." She rejected traditional habeas corpus.

> Requiring highly protective procedures at the tail end of the detention process for detainees like Al-Bihani would have systemic effects on the military's entire approach to war. From the moment a shot is fired, to battlefield capture, up to a detainee's day in court, military operations would be compromised as the government strove to satisfy evidentiary standards in anticipation of habeas litigation.

She found the government had proved support for al-Qaeda by a preponderance of the evidence.

In a separate concurrence, Judge Brown asked "whether a court-driven process is best suited to protecting both the rights of petitioners and the safety of our nation." Congress might "understandably be reluctant" to offer a legislative solution, "having been repeatedly rebuffed" by the Supreme Court. But it possessed "policy expertise, democratic legitimacy" and had taken an "oath to uphold and defend the Constitution." "[T]he old wineskins of international law, domestic criminal procedure, or other prior frameworks are ill-suited to the bitter wine of this new warfare." Judge Williams also concurred separately. The AUMF "clearly authorized the President to attack" the group in which al Bihani cooked and carried arms. But Williams dissociated himself from Brown's slighting of the international laws of war, which was "hard to square" with the Supreme Court's plurality opinion in *Hamdi*, or her "unnecessary" assertion that a preponderance of the evidence standard was constitutionally permissible.

In August 2010 the DC Circuit unanimously denied rehearing en banc, producing four opinions totaling more than 50 pages.[152] Judge Sentelle (with Ginsburg, Henderson, Rogers, Tatel, Garland, and Griffith) wrote that it was unnecessary "to determine the role of international law-of-war principles in interpreting the AUMF." Judge Brown, clearly stung, criticized her seven colleagues' "cryptic statement that exhibits no apparent function other than to mystify." The petition had asked the court to "take the radical step of incorporating all of international law as judicial enforceable constraints on the President's war powers." The "cumulative effect" of their opinion (and the two others discussed below) was "to muddy the clear holding of *Al-Bihani* that international law as a whole does not limit the AUMF's grant of war powers" and make "a rather common-place judicial proposition impenetrably obscure." The "government's eager concession that international law does in fact limit the AUMF ... warrants no deference from this court." She resisted the notion that her panel opinion had been dictum. She accused Judge Williams (see below) of "a hazy but ominous hermeneutics," whose "blithe[]" "nonchalance" was "only a mask for what is, at its core, a radical and sweeping claim, one at odds with our Constitution and caselaw," a "spring into judicial immodesty." Unlike international law, "our law is a closed and coherent system." "[S]ome of the tradeoffs traditionally struck by the laws of war no longer make sense." She feared that Judge Williams "would place ultimate control of the war in the one branch insulated from both the battlefield and the ballot box," inviting the "unpredictable and ad hoc rules judges would draw from the primordial stew of treaties, state practice, tribunal decisions, scholarly opinion, and foreign law that swirls beyond our borders." She was not reassured by "buzzwords, the pleasing sound of which nearly lulls the mind into missing the vision of judicial supremacy at the heart of Judge Williams' opinion."

Judge Kavanaugh wrote "at great length" to agree with Judge Brown, rejecting the "radical argument" that courts could "limit the scope of the President's war-making authority ... based on international-law norms that have never been enacted into domestic US law by American lawmakers."

> [I]t is hard to conceive of a task less appropriate for US judges – or less consistent with our constitutional structure – than judicial invocation, without a constitutional or congressional mandate, of uncertain and changing international-law norms to restrain the President and the US military in waging a congressionally authorized war abroad.

Judge Williams concurred separately to disagree with Judge Kavanaugh, arguing that international law norms could influence judicial interpretation of federal statutes, reflecting "the simple truth that the question of a word's meaning is an empirical one: what have persons in the relevant community actually meant when using the words that appear in a statute?" "[I]t seems improbable that in authorizing the use of all 'necessary and appropriate force' Congress could have contemplated employment of methods clearly and unequivocally condemned by international law."

In May 2009 Judge Kessler granted habeas to Alia Ali Bin Al Ahmed, who had "been detained since 2002, when he was a teenager."[153] "[J]ust before the Easter weekend" and five days before the hearing the government promised 2,000 pages of "newly available" material, but refused to reveal whether it was exculpatory. Calling it "clear" that the materials had been "packaged into a Factual Return and produced ... in another petitioner's case" a week earlier, Kessler granted Ahmed's motion to strike "on the grounds that there was no way that Petitioner could have carefully examined even the pared-down [200-page] Supplement at the last minute while preparing for this Merits Hearing." Although she followed Judge Hogan's Case Management Order in granting the government's evidence a rebuttable presumption of authenticity,[154] there was "absolutely no reason" to presume the facts were *accurate*. From the briefing and oral argument, indeed, it was clear their accuracy was "hotly contested" as second- and third-hand hearsay, or had been elicited by torture, or was not a verbatim account. Although the "mosaic approach" urged by the government "may well be" "a common and well-established mode of analysis in the intelligence community," it "certainly cannot govern the Court's ruling." In any case, "if the individual pieces of a mosaic are inherently flawed or do not fit together, then the mosaic will split apart." The government's "chief pieces of evidence" were four detainee statements. Judge Kessler agreed with Judge Leon that the detainee who also gave evidence in *El-Gharani* "cannot be credited." That detainee "has made accusations against a number of detainees," many of which "have been called into question by the Government." Statements by a second detainee were "riddled ... with equivocation and speculation" and "not entitled to significant weight." A third detainee exhibited mental health problems, made "inconsistent identifications" of Ahmed, and claimed his own statements were elicited by torture, which "the Government has presented no evidence to dispute." With respect to "the most serious charge," that Ahmed fought US forces, "the Court will not make the leap that the Government does, that simply because he was in Afghanistan, he was there to fight." She declined to rely on a "nine-word hearsay allegation" that "does not describe the [alleged military] training with any specificity." Furthermore, Ahmed's identification was based on "a fairly common nickname in Arab countries, somewhat equivalent to the use of 'Joe' or 'Buddy' in this country"; and his identification number in Bagram was also assigned to another detainee, who admitted military training. Basing its claim that Ahmed *traveled* with Taliban on the fact that he stayed at a guesthouse with some of them was "essentially a charge of guilt by association." "There is ample evidence in the record to indicate that guesthouses are common features of the region, serving as way stations for impoverished young men spending time away from home." "The fabric – or mosaic – simply will not hold; the connections are too weak and attenuated."

In March 2009, in response to an order by Judge Walton, the government stated it had dropped the term "enemy combatant" and changed its definition of whom it could detain from "individuals who were part of, or supporting, forces engaged in hostilities against the United States or its coalition partners and allies" to "persons who were part of, or substantially supported, Taliban or al-Qa[e]da forces or associated forces." Furthermore, it now based its detention authority solely on the AUMF (not the Commander-in-Chief's Article II powers).[155] Judge Walton approved both positions, interpreting "the government's 'substantial support' standard to mean individuals who were members of the 'armed forces' of an enemy organization at the time of their initial detention."

In May Judge Bates disagreed with Judge Walton, rejecting the government's definition of EC to include "substantial support."[156] "[E]ven given the deference accorded to the Executive in this realm ... it is ultimately the province of the courts to say 'what the law is'" (quoting *Marbury v. Madison*). "[A] detention authority that sweeps so broadly is simply beyond what the law of war will support." In September, Judge Hogan agreed with Judge Bates.[157]

Although the DoJ argued that its unclassified returns to more than a hundred habeas petitions should not be made public, Judge Hogan found that the government's "broad request usurps the Court's discretion" and ordered it to release them because the subject "remains a source of great public interest and debate."[158] The *Washington Post* called this decision "a wise compromise."

In June Judge Leon granted the habeas petition of Abdul Rahim Abdul Razak al-Janko.[159] The government claimed that al-Janko (a Syrian living in UAE) went to Afghanistan in 2000 to participate in jihad on behalf of the Taliban, spent five days at a guesthouse used by Taliban and al-Qaeda fighters helping to clean weapons, and attended the al Farouq training camp for 18 days. But though the government conceded he was then tortured by al-Qaeda into falsely admitting he was a US spy and was imprisoned for 18 months until the Taliban regime fell, Leon found that the government took "a position that defies common sense": that "a prior relationship between a detainee and al-Qaeda (or the Taliban) can[not] be sufficiently vitiated" by the "extreme treatment Janko was subjected to over a substantial period of time." "[T]o say the least, five days at a guesthouse in Kabul combined with eighteen days at a training camp does not add up to a longstanding bond of brotherhood." And his "extreme treatment" by the Taliban "evinces a total evisceration of whatever relationship might have existed!" The *Washington Post* applauded the decision, which was "all the more remarkable" because Leon had heard the first habeas petition and "concluded that there was no legal basis to allow such challenges." "[T]he revelations about Mr. Janko put the lie to the Bush administration's assertions – recently repeated by former Vice President Dick Cheney – that only the 'worst of the worst' were being held at Guantánamo."

Yasin Muhammed Basardah, a Yemeni, moved to Saudi Arabia, become addicted to and dealt in drugs, was arrested eight times for theft, and was repatriated to Yemen in 1995.[160] Recruited by a Pakistani-based charity, he went to Afghanistan for jihad, but told his CSRT: "I came in just for the money." He received military training at the al Farouq camp in spring 2001, became a cook and fighter, and hid with bin Laden in Tora Bora before fleeing to Pakistan, where he was arrested and handed to the USA. In Guantánamo he identified some sixty other detainees as having trained at al Farouq, stayed at Taliban or al-Qaeda guesthouses, protected bin Laden, or fought at Tora Bora. The military rewarded him with a single cell, McDonald's apple pies and coffee, chewing gum, a subscription to a truck magazine, a CD player, library books, a video game console, and other comfort items. He had requested asylum so he could join the American military. But by 2004 a military official assigned to represent another detainee at his CSRT wrote that Basardah "should not be relied upon" because he had put the detainee in an al-Qaeda camp three months before the man arrived in Afghanistan. Not a single man whom Basardah said was training at al Farouq on a specific date actually was in Afghanistan at the time. Judge Leon had granted habeas to el-Gharani partly because of doubt about Basardah's credibility. (After fingering the others, Basardah was reclassified as a lesser threat. The Guantánamo commander, Rear Adm. Thomas, recommended him for transfer in August 2008 "based on detainee's exceptional level of co-operation," and he was sent to Spain.[161])

In August 2009 Judge Kessler granted Mohammed al-Adahi's habeas petition.[162] She preferred Judge Walton's definition of ECs (in *Gherebi*) as "individuals who were members of the enemy organization's armed forces, as that term is intended under the laws of war" to Judge Bates's definition (in *Hamlily*) as "individuals who were 'part of ... Taliban or al-Qaida forces,' or associated forces," and not "merely 'substantial supporters' of those groups." Again she granted the government's evidence a presumption of authenticity but not accuracy, and repeated the reservations about the government's "mosaic theory" she had advanced in *Ali Ahmed*. "While it is true that Petitioner's familial ties to usama Bin Laden [*sic*] may suggest that he had access to the leadership of al-Qaida, such associations cannot prove that he was a member of al-Qaeda's 'armed forces.'" His attendance at the al Farouq training camp for 7–10 days before being expelled for violating its rules did not show he was a member of the enemy's "armed forces." His refusal "to comply with orders from individuals at al Farouq shows that he did not 'receive[] and execute[] orders' from the enemy's combat apparatus." The "Government has not established that Al-Adahi was a trainer at Al Farouq." "Petitioner's familiarity with other bodyguards does not, without more, compel the conclusion that he knew the men as a result of his service as a Bin Laden bodyguard." "[I]t appears that once his break with the group was initiated by al-Qaida, Al-Adahi accepted his expulsion and never attempted thereafter to become a member or supporter of al-Qaida, or to further its activities in any way." Kessler later learned that the government had not complied with her order to tape al-Adahi's participation in her hearing.

> Although he could not show prejudice, that is not the end of the analysis ... To ensure maximum public access to petitioner's testimony, and to comply with the intent of the court's original order, a transcript of petitioner's testimony shall be posted to the US District Court public information page ... [and] the government shall submit ... a detailed explanation of all steps it has taken to ensure that such errors shall not occur in the future.

In April Judge Leon denied the habeas petition of Hedi Hammamy, whose identity papers were found in the al-Qaeda cave complex after the battle of Tora Bora.[163] His claim that they had been stolen in Pakistan "rings hollow at best" and fails "to account for how his identity papers somehow mysteriously traveled the hundreds of miles ... to the highly secluded mountain hideaway of Tora Bora." Before he arrived in Afghanistan, Italian law enforcement had been about to charge him with supporting terrorism by furnishing false documents and currency.

In response to Ayman Saeed Batarfi's habeas petition, Judge Sullivan angrily ordered the government and its lawyers to show cause why they should not be held in contempt for failing to comply with his orders to disclose exculpatory information.[164] The government had persisted in relying on inexperienced DoD lawyers rather than experienced DoJ lawyers, with "the disturbing implication that the attorneys conducting the review in this and other habeas cases ... do not have the necessary experience with and knowledge of the government's *Brady* obligations." Noting that Batarfi had been "incarcerated for more than seven years without any adjudication," Judge Sullivan warned that "any delegation of a review for exculpatory evidence to attorneys who do not understand or are not familiar with *Brady* and its progeny under these circumstances is absolutely unacceptable and will not be tolerated further." "The Court will not tolerate any further delay by the government, particularly in the face of a clear violation of this Court's order to produce exculpatory evidence."

Two weeks later he found that the government had improperly withheld important psychiatric records concerning a government witness (possibly Basardah) who testified against Batarfi and a "significant" number of other detainees in CSRTs and military commissions.[165] He said angrily:

> [T]o hide relevant and exculpatory evidence from counsel and from the court under any circumstances, particularly here where there is no other means to discover this information and where the stakes are so very high ... is fundamentally unjust, outrageous and will not be tolerated ... How can this court have any confidence whatsoever in the United States government to comply with its obligations and to be truthful to the court? ... someone's going to pay a price ... the sanction is going to be high. I'll tell you quite frankly if I have to start incarcerating people to get my point across I'm going to start at the top.

He also criticized the government's last-minute decision to drop a military commission case against Batarfi.

> I'm not going to let this case drag on, or any of the other cases on my calendar, indefinitely while the government embarks on what it calls its diplomatic process, because I have seen in the past that that diplomatic process can indeed span months and years, and I have some serious concerns as to whether it's yet still another ploy ... to continue with his deprivation of his fair day in court.
>
> ... I mean this Guantánamo issue is a travesty ... a horror story ... and I'm not going to buy into an extended indefinite delay of this man's stay at Guantánamo.

He ordered the government to report to court on its progress every 14 days and to inform other District Judges of the psychological records relevant to their cases.

Although in 2008 a military commission judge excluded as coerced Mohammed Jawad's "confessions" (to having thrown a grenade that wounded two US soldiers), the statement of facts the government sub-mitted on June 1, 2009 in opposition to his habeas petition repeated those same "confessions."[166] The day before that filing, the Afghan gov-ernment protested his continued detention, alleging he had been just 12 when captured. A month later the USA said it would not oppose a motion to suppress evidence obtained through torture and coercion. When it sought more time at a July 16 hearing, Judge Huvelle denounced the "unbelievable case" as "an outrage"; it was "in a shambles" and "riddled with holes." She had suppressed every statement attributed to Jawad, which constituted "about 90 percent" of the government's return. When the DoJ lawyer explained she was "consulting internally," Huvelle retorted: "you can't prevail here without a witness who saw" the alleged attack, and "you can tell your superiors that."

> This is the most discovered case in the world. The idea that you should think that you have new and different [evidence] that you want to put in front of everybody is shocking to me, absolutely shocking … I'm not going to sit up here and wait for you to come up with new evidence at this late hour … I'm not going to have people running around trying to figure out a way to get this case out of the Court's jurisdiction for some other reason … We're having a merit proceeding very swift here. I'm not putting it off. This guy has been there seven years … He might have been taken there at the age of maybe 12 … I don't know what he is doing there.

When DoJ said it had just filed its non-opposition to the motion to suppress, Huvelle observed: "You should have figured this out months ago, years ago." When DoJ claimed to have identified "additional evi-dence," Huvelle said "you'll have to move faster … I'm not the least bit apologetic."

> If you are not relying on the gentleman's statements anymore, face it, this case is in trouble. I'm not going to wait to grant a habeas until you gear up a military commission. That's what I'm afraid of. Let him out. Send him back to Afghanistan … that's his home … your case has been gutted … You tell your superiors, I want a live witness … subject to real cross exam-ination like a real case instead of all of this intelligence and attributing it to people who are either cooperators, unknown, unidentified.

When DoJ protested that "this is a war time habeas proceeding ... not a normal situation where you call live witnesses," citing the "immense burdens ... involved in having to ... remove [them] off the battlefield and from Afghanistan," Huvelle replied: "there is nobody on the battlefield. The only people that you can dredge up here are Afghanistan people." Venting her anger at the government for "dragging this out for no good reason" after "your case fell apart," she gave it a week to decide whether to oppose Jawad's release.

> You'd better go consult real quick with the powers that be, because this is a case that's been screaming at everybody for years ... the idea that people would go to a military commission and say, "I'll only testify if you put a hood on me," is unbelievable. This is our government. Your case fell apart back then. So no, somebody ought to face the music.

DoJ cautioned that "we are not going to release anyone if it would endanger our national security."

At a July 22 hearing Judge Huvelle again demanded to know what the DoJ planned to use as evidence because 90 percent of its case was based on the excluded confessions. "There is no evidence otherwise." DoJ claimed the Obama administration had made "a dramatic break with the policies of the past" by deciding not to use the statements. Two days later the government said it would no longer treat Jawad as "detainable under the AUMF as informed by the laws of war," but added that this "does not resolve whether the current eyewitness testimony and other evidence or additional evidence that may be developed, would support a criminal prosecution." In a separate statement that day DoJ said the Guantánamo Review Task Force had "referred him for possible prosecution" and DoJ prosecutors had a statement by an eyewitness "that he saw Jawad throw a grenade that wounded two American service members." Its determination "whether evidence exists to support a criminal case in federal court" would be made "as soon as possible." Huvelle advised Attorney General Holder to give that decision "serious thought," because a prosecution would face "some serious issues," including the Speedy Trial Act, Jawad's arrest as a teenager, his torture, and whether he had been old enough at the time of the alleged acts to form the necessary intent. There "has been a consistent pattern" of government lawyers asking for more time, putting courts in "an untenable position." More than a year had elapsed since *Boumediene*. DoJ warned that if the court ordered Jawad released, it would take "several weeks" to resolve "logistical and other issues related to transfer arrangements." Jawad's lawyers replied that "the government of Afghanistan ... is prepared to receive Mr. Jawad immediately and unconditionally." Within hours of the government's July 24 statement, Judge Huvelle scheduled a hearing for July 30, at which she granted habeas, ordering the government to release Jawad by September 5 (because of the mandatory Congressional notification) and treat him "humanely." "After this horrible, long, tortured history, I hope the government will succeed in getting him back home. Enough has been imposed on this man to date."

The *New York Times* called the case "one of the most baffling" of the "many examples of the Bush administration's abusive and incompetent detainee policies." "[S]even years, one serious suicide attempt, and untold hours of physical and mental torture later, he remains [in Guantánamo], a wrecked young man held on an allegation ... without any credible evidence that he actually did [throw a grenade] or that he is a grave threat to American security." It denounced "the government's repeated attempts to delay the proceeding and the flimsiness of its case" and accused the Obama administration of "further[ing]" the "legal and human travesty perpetrated by the Bush team." "It should not have taken months and a formal motion to suppress the so-called evidence derived from torture to recognize that his military detention is illegitimate." It urged Holder to "heed Judge Huvelle's stern warning that bringing criminal charges now would raise serious issues." On August 24 Jawad was returned to Afghanistan, where he was greeted by President Karzai.

By late July 2009 judges had granted habeas to 26 petitioners (17 still detained) and denied it to five.[167]

At the end of July Judge Kollar-Kotelly granted habeas to Khalid Abdullah Mishal Al Mutairi, who had filed the oldest pending case more than seven years earlier.[168] She denied the government's evidence a presumption of authenticity or accuracy. "Based on the Government's own declarations, its raw intelligence has not been fully analyzed for its 'reliability, validity, and relevance.'" She warned of translation or transcription mistakes. For more than three years the government believed that Al Mutairi manned an anti-aircraft gun in Afghanistan because it made a mistake in his ID number. Judge Kollar-Kotelly followed Judge Bates in rejecting the government's claim that it could detain those who "substantially supported" enemy forces or "directly supported hostilities." Although she found Al Mutairi's own story not credible, she attributed this partly to the fact that he was "agitated" and "appears to have been goaded into making these statements by the linguist." The government had not proved he had trained with and become part of either al Wafa or al-Qaeda. The list of "captured al-Qaeda fighters" containing his name had been prepared by a prison guard to notify prisoners' families, not by al-Qaeda.

> [T]he Government has at best shown that some of Al Mutairi's conduct is consistent with persons who may have become a part of al Wafa or al-Qaida, but there is nothing in the record beyond speculation that Al Mutairi did, in fact, train or otherwise become a part of one or more of those organizations, where he would have done so, and with which organization.

In August Judge Urbina granted some of Abdul Raheem Ghulam Rabbani's discovery motions.[169] The government's reasons for withholding evidence provided "little confidence to the court that the government is fulfilling its disclosure obligations under the CMO." Judge Urbina ordered production of evidence that coercion, abuse, or torture had been used to obtain inculpatory statements.

> The mere fact that the petitioner allegedly recanted his prior inculpatory statements while at Bagram is insufficient to insulate subsequent statements from the taint of prior coerced statements, given the unbroken stream of interrogations to which the petitioner was subjected before and after Bagram as well as the highly coercive nature of the conduct alleged.

Although the government "vehemently" objected, Judge Urbina granted the motion to submit narrowly tailored interrogatories to KSM, for whom Rabbani allegedly had worked.

The same month Judge Robertson denied the petition of Adham Mohammed Ali Awad.[170] "[I]t seems ludicrous to believe" that Awad, who was marginally literate and had spent 7 of his 26 years in American custody, "poses a security threat now, but that is not for me to decide." After analyzing the evidence, which was so heavily redacted as to be incomprehensible, Robertson concluded:

> The case against Awad is gossamer thin. The evidence is of a kind fit only for these unique proceedings [redacted] and has very little weight. In the end, however, it appears more likely than not that Awad was, for some period of time, "part of" al-Qaida. At the very least Awad's confessed reasons for traveling to Afghanistan and the correlation of names on a list [redacted] clearly tied to al-Qaida make it more likely than not that he knew the al-Qaida fighters at the hospital and joined them in the barricade.

The DC Circuit affirmed.[171]

In August Judge Walton, departing slightly from Judge Hogan, ruled that in order to justify the admission of hearsay, the government had to demonstrate an "undue burden" and could not rely "upon its shortage of resources or its own mistakes."[172]

> [T]he more significant a fact the government seeks to establish through the use of hearsay is, the heavier its burden ... it is no excuse for the government's lawyers to assert that there are too many habeas corpus petitions ... the costs of this litigation, including the costs associated with providing sufficient manpower to properly litigate these cases, must be borne by the government, not fobbed off on the petitioners in the form of a blanket presumption of admissibility of otherwise inadmissible hearsay ... the result of this process might not be to the government's liking, but that is no reason to totally abandon well-established other-wise-applicable rules of evidence ... Ultimately, the government seems to suggest that because so much of its hearsay evidence is (in its view) internally consistent, the contents of *all* of its proffered hearsay evidence *must* be true, rather in the same way that a rumor must be true if enough people repeat it. But even the most widespread rumors are often inaccurate [original emphasis].

In August Judge Kollar-Kotelly denied the petition of Fawzi Khalid Abdullah Fahad Al Odah, who also had filed the oldest pending habeas case seven years earlier.[173] Again, she did not grant the government's evidence a presumption of accuracy or authenticity because, among other things, the government admitted erroneous dates in three separate reports. But the record supported "a reasonable inference that Al Odah may have ... been traveling to Afghanistan to engage in jihad."

> Al Odah's admissions against interest include his travel to Logar at the direction of a Taliban official, the surrender of his passport and other possessions to ... a member of the Taliban, his meeting with individuals who appeared to be armed fighters, his acceptance of an AK-47 rifle from one of the fighters, his travel into the Tora Bora mountains with armed men toward the armed conflict, where he remained through the Battle of Tora Bora and where he was ultimately captured carrying his AK-47 ... this evidence reflects that Al Odah made a conscious choice to ally himself with the Taliban instead of extricating himself form the country.

The DC Circuit affirmed.[174]

In September Chief Judge Lamberth said the "unprecedented" number of "difficult questions" made the judges' task "time consuming" because they were creating "precedents for future wars."[175] Classified material was involved in 200 cases: "if a court has one at a time, that's unusual." He had sent some to District Judges in Maryland and West Virginia. One of the judges' "great frustrations" was whether "they have the power to release" detainees into the United States.

That month Judge Kollar-Kotelly granted the habeas petition of Fouad Mahmoud Al Rabiah, another one of the earliest cases.[176] The 240-pound 50-year-old Kuwaiti father of four had been an aviation engineer for 20 years, had founded and managed health clubs, and "has a history of traveling to impoverished and/or war-torn countries for charitable purposes," including Bosnia, Kosovo, and Bangladesh. He went to Afghanistan for ten days on October 6, 2001 to deliver supplies to refugees, but was unable to return the way he had entered because Iran closed its border with Afghanistan. He wrote his family about this problem and his decision to travel to Peshawar, but was captured outside Jalalabad and handed to the USA. Judge Kollar-Kotelly found no evidence that the organizations for which he had volunteered had supported terrorism at the time. She did not credit the statement by another detainee (probably Basardah), who had given evidence against many other detainees. The government also relied on a witness whose "allegations are filled with inconsistencies and implausibilities." Another detainee "alleged that Al Rabiah attended a feast hosted by Usama bin Laden where Al Rabiah presented bin Laden with a suitcase filled with money, that Al Rabiah served in various fighting capacities in the Tora Bora mountains, and that Al Rabiah funneled money to mujahedeen in Bosnia in 1995. The Government has now withdrawn its reliance on almost all of [redacted] allegations."

The allegations "repeatedly change over time," several "are demonstrably false," and "there are multiple exhibits in the record demonstrating [redacted] unreliability as a witness." Judge Kollar-Kotelly disbelieved the allegation of another detainee who "was undergoing a cell relocation program at Guantánamo called the 'frequent flier program,' which prevented a detainee ... from resting," a sleep deprivation technique not authorized by the Army Field Manual. She credited an "early assessment made by an intelligence analyst that Al Rabiah should not have been detained." He only "confessed" to some of the allegations after being subjected to (redacted) interrogation techniques.

> Al Rabiah's confessions all follow the same pattern: Interrogators first explain to Al Rabiah the "evidence" they have in their possession ... Al Rabiah then requests time to pray (or to think more about the evidence)

before making a "full" confession. Finally, after a period of time, Al Rabiah provides a full confession to the evidence through elaborate and incredible explanations that the interrogators themselves do not believe.

The record is replete with examples of Al Rabiah's interrogators emphasizing a stark dichotomy – if he confessed to the allegations against him, his case would be turned back over to [redacted] so that he could return to Kuwait; if he did not confess, he would not return to Kuwait, and his life would become increasingly miserable.

Frustrated by the "numerous inconsistencies or implausibilities" in his confessions, interrogators threatened to render him to a country where he would be tortured and subjected him to sleep deprivation. "Al Rabiah's lead interrogator was disciplined for making similar threats during the same period toward a Guantánamo detainee who was also one of the alleged eyewitnesses against Al Rabiah."

Judge Kollar-Kotelly found the confessions "entirely incredible."

> [I]t defies logic that in October 2001, after completing a two-week leave form at Kuwait Airlines where he had worked for twenty years, Al Rabiah traveled to Tora Bora and began telling senior al-Qaeda leaders how they should organize their supplies in a six square mile mountain complex that he had never previously seen and that was occupied by people whom he had never previously met, while at the time acting as a supply logistician and mediator of supply disputes that arose among various fighting factions ... The fact that the Government has been forced by its theory of detention to search for the least detailed and least inculpatory version of Al Rabiah's confessions *in order for the evidence in this case to even make sense*, while simultaneously ignoring all of the details associated with the other versions of the same confessions, underscores the lack of reliability and credibility associated with the confessions themselves [original emphasis].

Although "the Government argued that Al Rabiah's confessions provided such specific details that they could not possibly have been imagined," the judge countered that "the specific details in these allegations served to undermine their credibility." They also were "often inconsistent." She attributed Al Rabiah's repetition of his "confessions" at his CSRT to the fact that "the interrogator who extracted Al Rabiah's confessions and punished his recantations, continued to make 'appearances' at Al Rabiah's interrogations ... after Al Rabiah's testimony in the CSRT proceedings." She concluded: "The Government's simple explanation for the evidence in this case is that Al Rabiah made confessions that the Court should accept as true. The simple response is that the Court does not accept confessions that even the Government's own interrogators did not believe." Al Rabiah was transferred to Kuwait on December 9.

On September 3 Judge Collyer denied habeas to Sufyian Barhoumi.[177] He had left his native Algeria after high school, eventually settling in London. In 1999, inspired by films showing Russian atrocities against Muslims in Chechnya, he trained at military camps in Afghanistan (including one associated with Abu Zubaydah) but never went to Chechnya. After the American attack he fled to Tora Bora and then Pakistan, where he was arrested with Abu Zubaydah and handed to the USA. Based on his testimony and the diaries of two other detainees, Judge Collyer concluded that he was "part of" Abu Zubaydah's militia, an "associated force that was engaged in hostilities against the United States." Circuit Court Judge Tatel (joined by Ginsburg and Kavanaugh) affirmed.

On November 19 Judge Kessler granted habeas to Farhi Saeed Bin Mohammed.[178] The government had met its burden of proof that Mohammed, who left his native Algeria after graduating from high school:

> traveled extensively in Europe both before and after September 11, 2001, by using false names, passports, and other official documents … that while in London Petitioner attended mosques which were well known to have radical, fundamentalist clerics advocating jihad. At one of the mosques he met a recruiter who then paid for and arranged his trip to Afghanistan along routes well-traveled by those wishing to fight with al-Qaeda and/or the Taliban against the United States and its allies … [and] that once Petitioner arrived in Afghanistan he stayed at a guesthouse with direct ties to al-Qaida and its training camps. But the Government's evidence fails to prove anything more.

The evidence that he had received military training rested on statements by Binyam Mohamed, whose allegations of torture the government did not contest. In concluding that this tainted later statements not made under torture, Kessler wrote that Binyam's "lengthy and brutal experience in detention weighs heavily with the Court."

> [For] two long years … he was physically and psychologically tortured. His genitals were mutilated. He was deprived of sleep and food. He was summarily transported from one foreign prison to another. Captors held him in stress positions for days at a time. He was forced to listen to piercingly loud music and screams of other prisoners while locked in a pitch-black cell.

She quoted scientific studies finding that torture's effects, including "confabulation," continued long after it ended. The allegation that Farhi Mohammed participated in battle "rests only on highly speculative evidence." "In short, at the point in his journey where the Government's evidence fails, Petitioner had not yet acquired a role within the 'military command structure' of al-Qaida and/or the Taliban, nor acquired any membership in these enemy forces."

Because Mohammed feared torture if he were sent to Algeria (where he had not lived for decades), Kessler enjoined his transfer there. When the government responded with three declarations, Kessler noted that two were months-old "boilerplate." In order to determine whether there was "real substance behind the conclusory phrases" in the declaration by DoS special envoy Daniel Fried, she ordered him to appear at a secret hearing. But the Circuit Court directed her to resolve the case without the testimony of Fried or any other government official, and summarily reversed her order protecting Mohammed against transfer to Algeria (both decisions were secret). Lawyers for Aziz Abdul Naji also sought an order against his repatriation to Algeria. But the Supreme Court denied an emergency stay (Ginsburg, Breyer, and Sotomayor dissenting, Kagan not participating). The *Washington Post* warned that "Algeria's shoddy human rights record has been well documented by NGOs." The *New York Times* said that any Algerian who sought to remain in Guantánamo "probably has a strong reason to fear the welcoming reception at home." Daniel Fried wrote the *Times* that the day its editorial appeared, Naji "was released after a few days in custody, as we had anticipated all along." "The administration had done its homework."

On December 15, Judge Urbina granted Saeed Mohammed Saleh Hatim's habeas petition.[179] The only evidence that he received military training at al Farouq was his statements during interrogation in Guantánamo and at his CSRT. But the government did not refute his claim that he had been repeatedly beaten and threatened with rape at Kandahar. These "unrefuted allegations of torture undermine the reliability of the statements made subsequent[ly]." Even if he attended al Farouq knowing it was an al-Qaeda camp, "there is scant evidence that while at al-Farouq the petitioner actually participated in al-Qaida's command structure" or – since he left early – at the time of his capture. Judge Urbina refused "to credit what is arguably the government's most serious allegation in this case" – that Hatim fought with al-Qaeda at Tora Bora – "based solely on one statement made years after the events in question" by Basardah, whose credibility had been rejected by Judges Leon and Kessler and "whose grasp on reality appears to have been tenuous at best." The DC Circuit reversed on February 15, 2011.[180] Judge Henderson (joined by Williams and Randolph) cited the Circuit's decision in *Al Bihani* that "those who purposefully and materially support" al-Qaida would be detained and its decisions in *Bensayah* and *Awad* that it was unnecessary to show that a detainee participated in the command structure. The District Court had also evaluated the evidence through an approach the Circuit had rejected in *Al-Adahi* and *Salahi*.

At the end of December Jack Goldsmith and Benjamin Wittes wrote in a *Washington Post* op ed that the president, not the courts, should determine detention policy.[181] Judges were "not experts in terrorism or national security and not politically accountable to the electorate."

On January 6, 2010 Judge Hogan denied the habeas petition of Musa'ab Al Madhwani.[182] Judge Hogan refused to credit evidence from al Madhwani's 23 Guantánamo interrogations because of the "harsh treatment" he suffered for 40 days in Pakistan and Afghanistan, including "being suspended in his cell by his left hand" in solitary confinement in a "pitch-black prison" and "blasted … with music twenty-four hours a day." His weight fell from 150 pounds to 104, and he exhibited a "severe dehydration that would normally require hospitalization in the United States." He "arrived at Guantánamo with a severe mental disorder." There was evidence that Guantánamo interrogators asked him to repeat the confessions he had made before arriving and made threats when he tried to retract them. "That the Government continued to drink from the same poisoned well does not thereby make the water clean."

But the harsh treatment did not taint his 2004 CSRT or 2005 ARB. Based on this "severely truncated body of evidence," Judge Hogan found that the government had not met its burden to prove that al Madhwani had gone from Yemen to Afghanistan for weapons training, but had proved he had actually received weapons training at the al Farouq camp for 25 days and thereafter voluntarily associated with al-Qaeda members in Afghanistan and Pakistan, including at an apartment where a firefight occurred. The DC Circuit (Henderson with Ginsburg and Tatel) affirmed.[183] Madhwani's testimony "reveals a wealth of incriminating detail."

On February 24 Judge Kessler denied habeas to Suleiman Awadh bin Agil al-Nahdi.[184] The government's authority to detain him under the AUMF did not turn on whether he posed a security threat.

The clandestine nature of Petitioner's travel to Afghanistan, as well as the unlikeliness, in one of the poorest areas of the world, of one stranger offering another a generous sum of money to travel abroad to receive military training, suggest ... that Al-Nahdi was being recruited by al-Qaida ... the fact that Petitioner willingly stayed in houses where he was advised not to go outside, where he was afraid to share his real name with other guests, where his passport was taken and held, and where he was shown jihadist videos strengthens the inference that Al-Nahdi knew he was associating with al-Qaida.

"[I]t is far more likely than not that ... by the time he was at Al Farouq" training camp "he fully understood ... he was associating with al-Qaida" and "more likely than not that Petitioner left Al Farouq and traveled to Tora Bora pursuant to a specific order from the camp's al-Qaida leadership." Once there, "he functioned as a guard within a command structure."

On March 10 Judge Kessler denied habeas to Fahmi Salem Al-Assani.[185] The government had shown he "was recruited by al-Qaida members in Yemen, that he subsequently traveled – at no cost to himself and through al-Qaida associated guesthouses – to Afghanistan, that he received military training at al-Qaida's Al Farouq camp, that while at the camp he became aware of its connection to al-Qaida and Usama Bin Laden," that he "received further training from Al Farouq leaders, that he traveled to Tora Bora under the command" of al-Qaeda leaders and "that he obeyed orders intended to organize his group into distinct units."

DDC Judges wanted Congress to clarify the detention rules.[186] Judge Walton said: "judges aren't in the business of making law – we interpret law. It should be Congress that decides a policy such as this that has a monumental impact on our society and makes a monumental impression on the world community." Chief Judge Lamberth said the judges were struggling "to adapt legal principles to a whole new sphere of ... existence that we've never witnessed in history as far as I know." "How confident can I be that if I make the wrong choice that he won't be the one that blows up the Washington Monument or the Capitol?" ECs could be held for the duration of hostilities, but how long would that last? "I don't know, and I don't think anybody on the face of the earth knows. So it makes it difficult for a legal judgment, and I think better suited for a legislative judgment." Judge Urbina said it was "an honor to have the responsibility of blazing the trail," but "also at times frustrating when not all the rules are clear and not all the specifics of how a matter should be dealt with are before us." Sen. Graham said the questions were "outside 'judges lane.' Congress should weigh in." He noted that at a December hearing Judge Hogan had called it "unfortunate" that "the legislative branch of the government, and the executive branch, have not moved more strongly to provide uniform, clear rules and laws for handling these cases."

Agreeing, the *Washington Post* urged Congress to create a national security court with "slightly more relaxed evidentiary standards" and published an op ed by Benjamin Wittes and Robert Chesney taking a similar position. David Cole retorted that it was "wildly optimistic to think that this Congress could agree on a detention standard," and in any case the questions were "not susceptible to bright-line rules but require careful case-by-case application of standards," which was "a job for judges, not Congress." And both HRF and HRW warned against a system of "preventive detention." But the Washington Legal Foundation took an ad in the *New York Times* to denounce "Lawyers for Terrorist Liberties."

> For the past nine years, domestic activists have advanced a litigation and demonization campaign aimed at wrapping homeland security in a legal and regulatory straight-jacket. These ideologues have sought full constitutional rights for foreign terror suspects … when the judiciary embraces … the radical legal theories propping up such civil liberties absolutism … as some unelected judges have, the ideas … become live threats to national security … Represented *pro bono* by high-priced lawyers, enemy combatants have flooded America's courts, and some have won get-out-of-jail free passes back to terrorist havens … Playing by the Queensbury rules advanced by activist ideologues will only transform our Constitution into a suicide pact. Can we afford to have the judiciary and bickering lawyers decide how to keep Americans safe from foreign terrorism? America cannot be secure when those protecting us are tied up in court or tied down by litigious activists.

And Sens. McCain and Lieberman introduced a bill on the interrogation, detention, and prosecution of enemy belligerents. But John J. Gibbons and Timothy K. Lewis (retired Third Circuit judges) replied in the *National Law Journal* that "determining whether a prisoner's detention is lawful has always been a judicial function, and a moment's reflection is enough to see that it could hardly be otherwise."

DDC Judges continued to decide habeas petitions. On March 24 Judge Lamberth denied the petition of Mukhtar Yahia Naji Al Warafi.[187] In August 2001 he responded to a fatwa by traveling from

Yemen to Pakistan to fight with the Taliban. After receiving military training in Afghanistan, he volunteered for further training at a medical clinic, where he cared for Taliban fighters. He was imprisoned by the Northern Alliance and shot during an uprising, before being handed to the USA. Based on this, Lamberth found it more probable than not that al Warafi was part of the Taliban and rejected the argument that he was not detainable as medical personnel under the First Geneva Convention, because that conferred no rights al Warafi could invoke. Like Judge Hogan in *Anam*, Lamberth was not convinced that al Warafi was a threat to national security and hoped that this decision did "not foreclose the government from continuing to review petitioner's file."

In February 2011 the DC Circuit affirmed in part and remanded.[188] Judges Ginsburg, Garland, and Williams agreed that al Warafi had been part of the Taliban but remanded for a determination of whether he had been "permanently and exclusively medical personnel" under the Geneva Conventions and Army Regulation 190–8. On September 1 Judge Lamberth found that al Warafi had not proven this.[189] "At the time of his surrender, petitioner carried no form of identification indicating his status as permanent medical personnel." In May 2013 the DC Circuit affirmed.[190]

On April 9 Judge Robertson granted the habeas petition of Mohamedou ould Slahi, who had been subjected to sleep deprivation and extreme heat and cold, threatened with death (by being thrown off a boat), and told that his mother would be seized and made the only female detainee in Guantánamo.[191] Although Slahi swore allegiance to al-Qaeda and bin Laden in 1991 in order to fight Russia, the government did not prove he continued to support the group. "The government had shown that Salahi was an al-Qaida sympathizer – perhaps a 'fellow traveler'; that he was in touch with al-Qaida members; and that from time to time, before his capture, he provided sporadic support to members of al-Qaida ... [but] its proof that Salahi gave material support to terrorists is so attenuated, or so tainted by coercion and mistreatment, or so classified, that it cannot support a successful criminal prosecution."

The government was concerned "he might renew his oath to al-Qaeda and become a terrorist" if released. "But a habeas court may not permit a man to be held indefinitely upon suspicion, or because of the government's prediction that he may do unlawful acts in the future." The government had failed to prove he was "part of" al-Qaeda "*at the time of his capture*" [original emphasis]. Sen. Kit Bond complained that "once again, the courts have put the rights of terrorist detainees above the safety of Americans. Unless Americans want unelected and unaccountable judges to make national security decisions, Congress must act now." On November 5 the DC Circuit reversed.[192] Although it did not presume that because Slahi swore allegiance to al-Qaeda in 1991 he was still a member when captured a decade later, it remanded for further inquiry in light of its decisions in *Awad* and *Bensayah*.

On April 10 Judge Kennedy granted habeas to Uthman Abdul Rahim Mohammed Uthman.[193] Two detainees who said he had been a bin Laden bodyguard were unreliable because there was "unrebutted evidence" that both had been tortured shortly before making the accusations. Although the government objected to that evidence as hearsay, Kennedy replied that "respondents themselves ask the Court to detain Uthman on the basis of hearsay." He also was unpersuaded that the detainees had correctly identified Uthman. One had called the alleged bin Laden bodyguard "Huthaifa Al-Anzi," which referred to an Arab tribe with which Uthman had no known connection.

> [T]he Court gives credence to evidence that Uthman (1) studied at a school at which other men were recruited to fight for Al-Qaeda; (2) received money for his trip to Afghanistan from an individual who supported jihad; (3) traveled to Afghanistan along a route also taken by Al-Qaeda recruits; (4) was seen at two Al-Qaeda guesthouses in Afghanistan; and (5) was with Al-Qaeda members in the vicinity of Tora Bora after the battle that occurred there.
>
> Even taken together, these facts do not convince the Court by a preponderance of the evidence that Uthman received and executed orders from Al-Qaeda.

On April 18 Judge Kennedy denied Yasein Khasem Mohammad Esmail's petition.[194] Although Kennedy credited some claims of mistreatment (forced nudity and subjection to cold), he disbelieved others (being threatened with a dog and thrown into a latrine). The lack of "evidence of the repeated beatings to which Esmail asserts he was subjected, call[s] into serious question the truthfulness of Esmail's most serious allegations of torture." "It is reasonable to infer based on the late addition of allegations [of being given electric shocks, hit with chains, and almost fully buried in the ground] that could reasonably be expected to appear in the First Declaration that Esmail has embellished his statements with false allegations in an effort to create an advantage for himself in this litigation."

Judge Kennedy found that Esmail

> (1) traveled to Afghanistan at the urging of an Al-Qaeda facilitator, (2) attended Al-Qaeda military training camps, (3) stayed at guesthouses which, if not exclusively patronized by Al-Qaeda members, were at least affiliated with that organization, (4) took a religious studies course at an Institute sponsored by Al-Qaeda, (5) remained in Afghanistan after the attacks of September 11, 2001, and (6) went to Tora Bora, the site of a major battle against the United States, where he acted as a fighter for Al-Qaeda.

The DC Circuit (Tatel, Brown, and Silberman) affirmed in April 2011.[195] Judge Silberman concurred separately to declare Esmail's "'story' phonier than a $4 bill." Whereas a "good judge" in the Court of Appeals "will vote to overturn a conviction if the prosecutor lacked sufficient evidence, even when the judge is virtually certain that the defendant committed the crime," "Guantánamo habeas petitions pose the infinitely greater downside risk to our country, and its people, of an order releasing a detainee who is likely to return to terrorism. One does not have to be a 'Posnerian' … to recognize this uncomfortable fact."

Therefore, the "preponderance of evidence standard" was "unnecessary – and moreover, unrealistic." "I doubt any of my colleagues will vote to grant a petition if he or she believes that it is somewhat likely that the petitioner is an al-Qaeda adherent or an active supporter." Silberman added:

> If it turns out that regardless of our decisions the executive branch does not release winning petitioners because no other country will accept them and they will not be released into the United States … then the whole process leads to virtual advisory opinions. It becomes a charade prompted by the Supreme Court's defiant – if only theoretical – assertion of judicial supremacy [in *Boumediene*] sustained by posturing on the part of the Justice Department, and providing litigation exercise for the detainee bar.

The *Washington Post* urged the Justices to "take note" of Silberman's "well-deserved jab over the Supreme Court's detainee ruling."[196] His "stinging critique" was justified because the Court's "lack of guidance has created confusion." But though the *Post* shared his "frustration" and "understandable irritation with other aspects of the judicial process," it disagreed with his "embrace of a lower standard."

On April 19 Judge Collyer declined to enjoin the government from repatriating Ahmed Belbacha to Algeria. After *Boumediene*, Belbacha won an injunction against his return,[197] but the government argued that the DC Circuit decision in *Kiyemba* held that District Judges could not make such orders.

On May 13 Judge Kennedy granted habeas to Ravil Mingazov.[198] He did not credit the evidence that Mingazov had joined the Islamic Movement of Uzbekistan (IMU) because Mingazov made "false or exaggerated" statements about his involvement out of fear of being sent back to Russia. Kennedy did not believe Mingazov fought with the Taliban against the Northern Alliance or attended any military training camp. He did not find Mingazov's travel itinerary after the defeat of the Taliban incriminating in the absence of evidence "that there was some other, easier route out of Afghanistan." His stay at a Jama'at al Tabligh Islamic Center was not incriminating without evidence that he had any connection to al-Qaeda. Evidence that he had stayed at Abu Zubaydah's house and Issa House did not show he was part of al-Qaeda.

> Mingazov's proximity to people engaged in military action, stays at guesthouses where members of Al-Qaeda may also have stayed … raise the suspicion that he was something more than an innocent traveler seeking a new home for his family. But respondents have not met their burden of proof as to their allegations that Mingazov became a member of IMU, fought with the Taliban, attended Al Farouq or any other military training camp, or became a member of Al-Qaeda.

On May 28 Judge Robertson denied habeas to Omar Mohammed Khalifh.[199] The "largely undisputed record" showed that he "associated extensively" with the Libyan Islamic Fighting Group in both Libya and Sudan, which "developed into involvement with al-Qaeda and bin Laden associates" in Sudan. He followed bin Laden to Afghanistan and received military training at al-Qaeda's Jihad Wahl training camp. He lost a leg from a mine while working as a Taliban minesweeper, after which he stayed at al-Qaeda guesthouses, which Robertson found a "quite powerful support to the inference that he was considered a member of al-Qaeda." Robertson was unconvinced Khalifh fought at Tora Bora and Taloqan. But "the government has shown more than probable cause to believe that Khalifh was part of al-Qaeda and associated forces through a steady string of activity right up until the time of his capture" in Pakistan in 2002. The DC Circuit dismissed the appeal in January 2011.[200]

On May 26 Judge Kennedy granted habeas to Mohammed Mohammed Hassan Odaini.[201] Odaini claimed his father, who worked for the Yemeni Security Service, sent him to Pakistan for religious studies at Jama'at al Tabligh in June 2001. Eight present or former Guantánamo detainees confirmed that in November 2002 he spent a single night at Issa House, where he was arrested with the other residents.

> [N]othing in respondents' presentation demonstrates by a preponderance of the evidence, or anything close to it, that Odaini's presence at Issa House supports his detention ... Remarkably, respondents find ways to argue that Odaini's statements to interrogators are so inconsistent and implausible as to call into serious question his truthfulness. They then make the leap that Odaini has been untruthful because he is covering up his involvement in Al-Qaeda ... Respondents argue that there is an inculpatory inference to be made from Odaini's connection to Jama'at Al Tabligh ... despite admitting repeatedly that Jama'at Al Tabligh is a large, respected movement with the legitimate purpose of teaching about the Islamic faith.

The record contained "several indications ... that respondents themselves have repeatedly concluded Odaini is not part of Al-Qaeda." Kennedy concluded:

> Respondents have kept a young man from Yemen in detention in Cuba from age eighteen to age twenty-six. They have prevented him from seeing his family and denied him the opportunity to complete his studies and embark on a career. The evidence before the Court shows that holding Odaini in custody at such great cost to him has done nothing to make the United States more secure. There is no evidence that Odaini has any connection to Al-Qaeda ... The Court therefore emphatically concludes that Odaini's motion must be granted.

For the *Washington Post*, the case rebutted the claim that the remaining detainees were "the worst of the worst."[202] It urged the administration to make an exception to its ban on transfers to Yemen to "correct this injustice." While the government was considering this, four men believed to be AQAP stormed Yemen's intelligence headquarters in Aden, killing at least 11 and freeing several detainees. Nevertheless, the administration agreed to repatriate Odaini on the ground that it had to comply with a court order.

On July 8 Sen. Christopher Bond (SSCI chair) thanked Gen. James L. Jones (National Security Adviser) for explaining that decision, but said the Committee wanted "to examine the Intelligence Community's intelligence threat assessments regarding Odaini and the other Guantánamo detainees," claiming that the CIA and DIA recommended against this transfer.

> It is only a matter of time before more detainees released by this
> administration are shown to have joined the ranks of recidivists
> released by the previous administration – a rate that now stands at over
> 20 percent ... I have lost patience with intelligence being withheld
> from the oversight committees, while potentially dangerous detainees
> continue to be released.

Nevertheless, Odaini was repatriated on July 13.

When Obaydullah petitioned for habeas in 2008, Judge Leon stayed
the petition because military commission charges had been sworn
against him; and Leon subsequently denied two motions to vacate the
stay even though the trial never began.[203] After Judge Ginsburg (joined
by Griffith and Williams) reversed the stay, Judge Leon denied the petition in October 2010.[204] There were "23 anti-tank mines of Italian and
Pakistani origin that were found in close proximity to the petitioner's
compound." "Obaydullah lied about his interest in them when first
confronted and then came up with a series of inconsistent and inherently ridiculous accounts as to their storage ... if petitioner really had
no ongoing interest in these mines, what on earth was he doing with a
notebook *on his person* that spelled out in detail how to assemble those
mines into remote control detonated IEDs" [original emphasis].

He told soldiers: "that the notebook contained notes and diagrams
regarding, of all things, a power generator." Judge Leon denied a petition
for reconsideration,[205] and the DC Circuit affirmed: Judges Henderson
and Garland because there was no reversible error, Judge Sentelle
because the appeal was not timely.[206] On January 30, 2013 Judge Leon
denied relief from the judgment on the basis of newly discovered evidence, and the DC Circuit affirmed.[207]

On July 8, 2010 Judge Friedman granted habeas to Hussain Salem
Mohammad Almerfedi.[208] The only evidence that he had stayed at
a guesthouse in Iran was a statement by another detainee, al-Jadani,
about "Hussain Al-Adeni," but "Hussain is a very common name, and
'Al-Adeni' could refer to any man from the city of Aden." Friedman also
found al-Jadani's four interrogations "inherently unreliable," and possibly based on multiple hearsay or rumor. "Information that came from
an unnamed group of detainees, for which the original source cannot
be pinpointed, amounts to no more than jailhouse gossip, if that." With
respect to other statements by al-Jadani, "the government essentially
urges the court to accept as true only the information ... that supports
petitioner's detention, while discounting information that conflicts
with its theory for detention." There was no evidence that Almerfedi:

who is uneducated, is a sophisticated traveler or document forger – skills that likely would be necessary for al-Qaeda facilitators. Furthermore, it is implausible that al-Qaeda would post petitioner to a guesthouse in Tehran, because it is undisputed that he does not speak Farsi ... There is no evidentiary basis on which to conclude that petitioner's association with [Jama'at al-Tabligh] or his stay in its Lahore Center, either standing alone or in conjunction with other evidence presented by the government, are adequate to justify petitioner's detention.

The DC Circuit reversed in June 2011.[209] Judge Silberman (with Kavanaugh) said Almerfedi admitted "he stayed for two and a half months at Jama'at Tablighi, an Islamic missionary organization that is a Terrorist Support Entity 'closely aligned' with al-Qaeda." "[I]f we add Almerfedi's travel route, which is quite at odds with his professed desire to travel to Europe (and brought him closer to the Afghan border where al-Qaeda was fighting), and also that he had at least $2,000 of unexplained cash on his person when captured ... the government's case that Almerfedi is an al-Qaeda facilitator is on firmer ground." Almerfedi's own "dubious account[s]" of his actions "amount to evidence in favor of the government." Silberman also found that "the district court clearly erred in finding unreliable al-Jadani's statements."

On July 13, 2010 the DC Circuit reversed Judge Kessler's grant of habeas to al-Adahi.[210] Judge Randolph (with Henderson and Kavanaugh) found that Judge Kessler had failed "to appreciate conditional probability analysis."

> Having tossed aside the government's evidence, one piece at a time, the court came to the manifestly incorrect – indeed startling – conclusion that "there is no reliable evidence in the record that Petitioner was a member of al-Qaeida and/or the Taliban" ...
>
> Al-Adahi tried to explain his personal audience with bin Laden on the basis that "meeting with Bin Laden was common for visitors to Kandahar" ... This is, as the government points out, utterly implausible ... the district court [ignored] the well-settled principle that false exculpatory statements are evidence – often strong evidence – of guilt ... The court characterized the rest of the evidence about Al-Adahi's meetings with bin Laden as "sensational and compelling" but not "actual, reliable evidence that would justify" detention ... The court's statements are incomprehensible.

Judge Kessler viewed evidence about these meetings as a distraction from "the essential focus – the nature of Al-Adahi's own conduct." The Circuit Court called these remarks "perplexing. If Al-Adahi's meetings with bin Laden were not his 'own conduct,' whose conduct were they?"

> Al-Adahi's voluntary decision to move to an al-Qaida guesthouse, a staging area for recruits heading for a military training camp, makes it more likely – indeed, very likely – that Al-Adahi was himself a recruit. There is no other sensible explanation for his actions …
>
> The district court ruled that Al-Adahi did not "receive and execute" orders because he violated the camp rule against smoking tobacco … That was error. Al-Adahi's violation of a rule or rules did not erase his compliance with other orders. One would not say that an Army trainee ceased to be part of the Army if he failed to shine his shoes or overslept one morning.
>
> We could go on, but what we have written thus far is enough to show that the district court clearly erred in its treatment of the evidence and in its view of the law.

The *Washington Post* applauded the reversal.[211] Judge Kessler's "deeply flawed" opinion "illustrates the perils of allowing trial judges to assess intelligence information through the lens of conventional rules of evidence." But the *Post* found it "just as worrisome" that the Circuit Court "flirted with – but stopped short of – allowing the government to meet an even lower standard of proof than the already relaxed standard now commonly required." Both decisions "prove once again the need for clearer rules," without which habeas petitions were "a kind of Guantánamo roulette, where the predilections of judges shape the rules and determine the outcomes. This serves no one well – not the detainees, not the government, and least of all the rule of law."

On July 20, 2010 Judge Walton denied the petition of Abd Al Rahman Abdu Abu al-Ghayth Sulayman.[212] Walton expressed concern "that much of the hearsay proffered by the government is unreliable" because it had failed to show the qualifications of the interpreters or provide a foundation for intelligence reports. But he believed two documents showing al-Ghayth had traveled from Yemen to Afghanistan with the help of a Taliban operative, stayed at guesthouses with other Taliban fighters, and gone to a "staging area" near battle lines, where he was given weapons. "It is nonsensical to think that the proprietor of a guesthouse who … was engaged in warfare with the Northern Alliance would allow a complete stranger to freeload for [seven months] during active hostilities." Although al-Ghayth claimed to have visited Afghanistan to find a job, a wife, and a home, he also admitted that he never really looked for them. "[T]he facts present overwhelming ... evidence that the petitioner was a 'part of' the Taliban armed forces."

On July 23, 2010 the DC Circuit asked detainees' lawyers in 31 cases to respond to a DoJ motion to vacate all District Court orders barring transfer until 30 days after detainees were notified, on the ground that authority to issue such orders had been nullified by *Kiyemba II* in April 2009. The detainees' lawyers asked the Circuit en banc to overrule *Kiyemba II* and not vacate any orders until this was resolved. The Supreme Court denied certiorari of *Kiyemba* in March 2010. On January 11, 2011, the DC Circuit denied en banc review.[213] Griffith (with Rogers and Tatel) dissented because the Suspension Clause as construed in *Boumediene* entitled detainees to notice of transfers (for the reasons advanced in his dissent in *Kiyemba II*).

On August 16, 2010 Judge Bates granted habeas to Adnan Farhan Abd Al Latif.[214] Because of persistent symptoms from a 1994 head injury, Latif claimed that he had accepted charitable assistance for further treatment in Pakistan and Afghanistan. Bates found that Latif's story, although "not without inconsistencies and unanswered questions," was "supported by corroborating evidence provided by medical professionals and is not incredible." The "inconsistencies to which respondents have pointed may be no more than misstatements or mistranslations." In October 2011 the DC Circuit vacated and remanded in three opinions extending over 43 pages.[215] Judge Brown wrote that: "intelligence documents of the sort at issue here are entitled to a presumption of regularity"; "the government official accurately identified the source and accurately summarized his statement"; and "neither internal flaws nor external record evidence rebuts that presumption in this case." Judge Brown criticized Judge Bates for the same error for which Judge Kavanaugh had recently criticized Judge Kessler in *al-Adahi*: failing to make findings about whether the petitioner was a credible witness. Latif's story might be "plausible," as Judge Bates had found, "and yet be very unlikely." If Latif again declined to testify on remand, that would be "another fact bearing on his credibility." Brown also criticized Bates for "explaining away some of the individual contradictions and coincidences in Latif's story one by one, as if each stood alone." Bates also erred in failing to consider that Latif followed a route "well traveled by al-Qaida and Taliban recruits." "[E]ven if a given inconsistency in a detainee's story does not go to the central question of his involvement with the Taliban or al-Qaida, it may be relevant nonetheless to the court's evaluation of his credibility, which in turn bears on the reliability of the Government's evidence." "The district court's failure to address certain relevant evidence leaves us with no confidence in its conclusions about the evidence it did consider." Judge Brown concluded that "*Boumediene*'s airy suppositions have caused great difficulty for the Executive and the courts" (citing the dissenters in that case). It "fundamentally altered the calculus of war, guaranteeing that the benefit of intelligence that might be gained – even from high-value detainees – is outweighed by the systemic cost of defending detention decisions." "*Boumediene*'s logic is compelling: take no prisoners."

Judge Henderson, concurring, would simply have reversed the grant of habeas because remanding "will be a waste of time and judicial resources." "If Latif were to repeat on the stand the same unpersuasive assertions he made in his declaration – assertions that are inconsistent with his earlier statements … the district court would have no choice but to disbelieve him." The dissent "misunderstands the clear error standard of review and its application in this case" and indulges in "high-pitched rhetoric."

Judge Tatel dissented:

> [R]ather than apply ordinary and highly deferential clear error review to the district court's findings of fact, as this circuit has done when district courts have found the government's primary evidence *reliable*, the court, now facing a finding that such evidence is *unreliable*, moves the goal posts … In imposing this new presumption [that "a government-produced document" is "accurate"] and then proceeding to *find* that it has not been rebutted, the court denies Latif the "meaningful opportunity" to contest the lawfulness of his detention guaranteed by *Boumediene* … Compounding this error, the court undertakes a wholesale revision of the district court's careful fact findings [original emphasis].

The presumption of regularity applies to "actions taken or documents produced within a process that is … transparent, accessible, and often familiar." But "the Report at issue here was produced in the fog of war by a clandestine method that we know almost nothing about." "[T]he presumption discards the unanimous, hard-earned wisdom of our district judges, who have applied their fact-finding expertise to a wide array of government hearsay evidence."

> Not content with moving the goal posts, the court calls the game in the government's favor … [by engaging] in an essentially de novo review of

the factual record, providing its own interpretations, its own narratives, even its own arguments ... I would conclude that the district court committed no clear error by finding that the Report was insufficiently reliable ... [or] by crediting Latif's account of what happened only insofar as it needed to, and that it adequately addressed other record evidence.

The *New York Times* said the DC Circuit's "wrongheaded rulings and analysis" had "gone off on the wrong track" and so thoroughly "eviscerated" *Boumediene* that no habeas petitions had been granted in the preceding 18 months. It urged the Supreme Court to "reject this willful disregard of its decision" by reviewing *Latif*, where "the appeals Court improperly replaced the trial court's factual findings with its own factual judgments" and "unfairly placed the burden on Mr. Latif to rebut the presumption that the government's main evidence was accurate." In its 15 habeas appeals, the DC Circuit had rendered "toothless" the standard for reviewing detentions. In the 2 years before July 2010, District Judges had granted 22 petitions and denied 15, but in the 16 months since then it had denied all 10 petitions.

On September 3, 2010 Judge Bates denied habeas to Shawali Khan.[216] During the anti-Soviet jihad Khan was a member of Hezb-I-Islam Gulbuddin (HIG), an associated force of the Taliban and al-Qaeda. Based on intelligence he found reliable, Judge Bates concluded that Khan had rejoined HIG after 9/11. The DC Circuit (Garland with Ginsburg and Sentelle) affirmed in September 2011.[217] In September 2014 Judge Bates again denied a motion for relief from judgment.[218] "[B]ecause Khan alleges that he is an innocent man who has been unlawfully detained at Guantánamo Bay for over a decade, and because the government's evidence in this case has never been overwhelming," the judge conducted "a somewhat more searching inquiry into the current state of the remaining evidence," but still found it more likely than not that Khan had been a "part of" HIG. That December Khan was transferred to Afghanistan, but renewed his petition, seeking relief from the "collateral consequences" of his detention. Judge Bates denied the petition because the DC Circuit had held that the remedy was unavailable to those no longer in custody.[219]

On January 11, 2011, Judge Leon denied habeas to Abdul Razak Ali (who now called himself Saeed Bakhouche).[220] On December 7, 2010 Leon had told Ali's counsel he had just received an *ex parte* filing classified top secret and had decided not to read it unless he needed to do so. But on December 23, the day after Leon told the parties he would announce his opinion on December 30, the DoJ *"for the first time"* told the court that its *ex parte* filing contained potentially exculpatory information about a government witness's credibility. Following an *ex parte* hearing with the government, Leon ruled that Ali's counsel had a need to know and a right to review the material. In order to withhold it, the government would have to prove that its use in a closed hearing would endanger national security. The government responded by withdrawing that witness, and Leon allowed Ali's counsel to re-present her closing argument. He found that Ali's capture in the same guesthouse as Abu Zubaydah in Faisalabad, Pakistan was sufficient to warrant detention and that Ali studied English at the guesthouse under Abu Zubaydah's training program. "Bakhouche's stubborn insistence that he had never been to Afghanistan, and did not know or interact in any way with Abu Zubaydah and his lieutenants in that relatively small guesthouse, was wholly incredible." The DC Circuit (Kavanaugh with Williams) affirmed on December 3, 2013.[221] Judge Edwards concurred:

> Our Nation's "war on terror" started twelve years ago, and it is likely to continue throughout Ali's natural life. Thus, Ali may well remain in prison for the rest of his life. It seems bizarre, to say the least, that someone like Ali, who has never been charged with or found guilty of a criminal act and who has never "planned, authorized, committed, or aided [any] terrorist attacks," is now marked for a life sentence ... The troubling question in these detainee cases is whether the law of the circuit has stretched the meaning of the AUMF and the NDAA so far beyond the terms of these statutory authorizations that habeas corpus proceedings like the one afforded Ali are functionally useless.

Praising Edwards's concurrence here and in *Hussain*, Linda Greenhouse wrote in the *New York Times* that "the Guantánamo saga isn't only about the 162 men still held there, or the hundreds who have come and gone. It's about the health of our own institutions, our own commitments. We look in the mirror of Guantánamo and see ourselves."[222]

On February 3, 2011 Judge Urbina denied the habeas petition of Mashour Abdullah Muqbel Alsabri.[223] He found that Alsabri "traveled to Afghanistan to fight with the Taliban or al-Qaida, stayed at Taliban or al-Qaida guesthouses, received military training at [an] al-Qaida facility, traveled to the battle lines and was captured during the same armed conflict." The DC Circuit (Garland with Kavanaugh and Ginsburg) affirmed in May 2012.[224]

In March 2011 the *New York Times* criticized the DC Circuit for having "dramatically restricted the *Boumediene* ruling" and urged the Supreme Court to correct this in Kiyemba's appeal, which concerned "judicial power and the duty to use it."[225] The *Times* noted that Judge Randolph, who wrote *Kiyemba* and *Boumediene* in the Court of Appeals, had said in a 2010 speech that the Justices were "wrong" in *Boumediene* and "all but expressed contempt for the holding." The *Times* commented that it was Randolph and the other Circuit Court judges who were "making the mess."

> In *Boumediene*, Justice Anthony Kennedy stressed that habeas is less about detainees' rights, important as they are, than about the vital judicial power to check undue use of executive power. The Appeals Court has all but nullified that view of judicial power and responsibility backed by Justice Kennedy and the court majority. The Supreme Court should remind the Appeals Court which one leads the federal judicial system and which has a solemn duty to follow it.

The same month the *Washington Post* praised Sen. Graham's Terrorist Detention Review Reform Act, which included important protections for detainees, including "a reaffirmation that testimony obtained by torture or coercion may not be used in court. Detainees may retain lawyers, and they are entitled to receive some exculpatory information in the government's possession."[226] It allowed a judge to presume that a prior association with al-Qaeda or the Taliban was ongoing but gave the detainee "the opportunity to rebut that presumption by showing that he took 'affirmative action to withdraw from the organization prior to … capture.'" "Unfortunately," the bill "tilts the scales too much in the government's favor," by authorizing detention based on "probable cause" to believe the individual had ties to al-Qaeda or associated forces, rather than proof of those ties by a preponderance of the evidence.

On April 4, the Supreme Court denied certiorari in *Odah* and *Awad* and in *Bihani*.[227] Linda Greenhouse wrote in a *New York Times* op ed on April 7 that it was "beginning to look" as though the Supreme Court was "finally finished with Guantánamo."[228] Despite the "nominal right to habeas corpus" after *Boumediene*, "no Guantánamo detainee has won a clean-cut victory on appeal" because of the Circuit Court's "forgiving" preponderance of the evidence standard and admission of hearsay. On April 11 the *Washington Post* urged the Court to "bring some clarity" by agreeing to hear *Kiyemba*.[229] But on April 18 it declined to do so.[230]

A week later McClatchy published data from WikiLeaks revealing that accusations by just eight detainees appeared in the files of at least 235 others.[231] Mohammed Basardah's evidence was used against at least 131 detainees even though a 2008 Guantánamo intelligence assessment said his "first-hand knowledge in reporting remains in question." Abdul Rahim Razak al-Janko accused 20 others; but his file said: "there are so many variations and deviations in his reporting, as a result of detainee trying to please his interrogators, that it is difficult to determine what is factual." Mohammad al-Qahtani, who accused 31, retracted the statements he had made after being waterboarded. Iban al-Shayk al-Libi, who named 38, also said he exaggerated. An analyst described Mohammed Hashim, who named 38, as "of an undetermined reliability and is considered only partially truthful." Abu Zubaydah, who named 12, had been waterboarded 83 times. Because Fawaz Naman Hamoud Abdullah Mahdi, who named six, had a "severe psychological disorder and deteriorating attention span … the reliability and accuracy of the information provided by [him] will forever remain questionable."

The *New York Times* called these documents "a chilling reminder of the legal and moral disaster that President George W. Bush created" at Guantánamo.[232]

> They describe the chaos, lawlessness and incompetence of his administration's system for deciding detainees' guilt or innocence and assessing whether they would be a threat if released …
>
> Evidence obtained from torture and the uncorroborated whispers of fellow prisoners fill the more than 700 classified documents. The administration should make its assessments of the remaining Guantánamo detainees public to the extent possible and free lawyers for detainees to fully communicate their clients' side of the story.

Instead, DoJ treated all the published WikiLeaks documents as classified and prohibited detainees' lawyers from downloading them.

On May 27 Judge Urbina denied habeas to Khirulla Said Wali Khairkhwa.[233]

> [T]he petitioner, like most other senior Taliban leaders, fought with the Afghan mujahideen in the 1980s, and, like other senior Taliban leaders with civilian titles, participated in the Taliban's military efforts to seize control of Afghanistan, serving as a commander of Taliban fighters during

the Taliban's assaults on Mazar-e-Sharif in 1997 and 1998. Even after his appointment as Governor of Herat in 1999, the petitioner remained integrally involved in the Taliban's military forces, operating within the Taliban's formal command structure and facilitating the movement of Taliban troops both before and after the commencement of Operation Enduring Freedom.

Throughout his tenure in the Taliban, the petitioner remained a prominent leader and a close ally of Mullah Omar ... Although the petitioner reached out to Hamid Karzai to discuss the possibility of surrender ... he never turned himself in and was captured at the home of a senior Taliban official.

The DC Circuit (Randolph with Rogers and Garland) affirmed in December 2012.[234]

On October 12, 2011 Judge Walton denied habeas to Abdul al-Qader Ahmed Hussain.[235] The government had proffered "damning" circumstantial evidence of Hussein's travel route, and "the petitioner's nonsensical version concerning his travel from Kabul to Lahore after the events of September 11, 2001, provides further justification for his detention." The DC Circuit (Griffith with Henderson) affirmed in June 2013.[236] Judge Edwards concurred. Noting that Hussain was a teenager when taken into custody and had spent 11 years in Guantánamo, Edwards said: "his petition for habeas relief should be granted, but his claim is doomed to fail because of the vagaries of the law." These cases had "presented extraordinary challenges for the judiciary." The Circuit had invoked "a 'preponderance of the evidence' standard while in fact requiring nothing more than substantial evidence to deny habeas petitions." The majority's invocation of the "walks like a duck" test was "invidious because, arguably, any young Muslim man traveling or temporarily residing in areas in which terrorists are known to operate would pass the 'duck test.'"

> Under the approach adopted by the majority, Hussain's petition is rejected because he could not offer a coherent story about his whereabouts during the times in question, not because the Government proved by a preponderance of the evidence that he was "part of" al-Qaeda, the Taliban, or associated forces ... Is it really surprising that a teenager, or someone recounting his teenage years, sounds unbelievable? What is a judge to make of this, especially here, where there is not one iota of evidence that Hussain "planned, authorized, committed, or aided the terrorist attacks that occurred on September 11, 2001, or harbored such ... persons"? ... I think we have strained to make sense of the applicable law, apply

the applicable standards of review, and adhere to the commands of the Supreme Court. The time has come for the President and Congress to give serious consideration to a different approach for the handling of the Guantánamo detainee cases.

On October 12, 2011 Judge Walton denied the habeas petition of Bostan Karim.[237] It was undisputed that he belonged to Jamaat al Tablighi; his attempt to conceal an inoperable cell phone from Pakistani authorities was additional "damning" circumstantial evidence.

Campaigning for the Republican presidential nomination, Newt Gingrich declared in January 2012 that "if the Court makes a fundamentally wrong decision, the president can ignore it."[238] The first one he would defy was the *Boumediene* decision "which ... is such an outrageous extension of the Court into the commander-in-chief's role. I will issue an instruction on the ... day I'm sworn in ... to the national security apparatus that it will not enforce *Boumediene* and it will regard it as null and void."

In the *New York Times* in May, Linda Greenhouse expressed hope that the Supreme Court would feel "a responsibility to get back into the game" because its silence had "basically permitted the Guantánamo issue to be outsourced" to the DC Circuit, whose "review of the government's evidence" had "been something very close to a rubber stamp."[239] "[T]o a startling degree, the conservative judges on the DC Circuit have been openly at war with the *Boumediene* decision." She could not "remember such open and sustained rudeness toward the Supreme Court by a group of lower court judges."

> [A] Court that had so much institutional pride just a few years ago ought to care enough now not to let itself be dissed by lower court judges who, in the system as I understand it, owe the Supreme Court obedience rather than on- and off-the-bench sniping. Let the Supreme Court take the reins back into its own hands and, as Chief Justice John Marshall famously promised, tell us what the law is.

Herman Schwartz (an American University law professor) noted that 9 of the 13 sitting DC Circuit Court judges had been appointed by Ronald Reagan and George W. Bush.[240] Three of the four Supreme Court decisions upholding detainees' rights reversed decisions by Randolph, who, in a 2010 speech to the Heritage Foundation, compared the Justices to Tom and Daisy Buchanan in *The Great Gatsby*: "they were careless people. They smashed up things ... and let other people clean up the mess they had made."

constitutional rights," adding that "this case requires the Court to give substance to those words." "[T]here is no principle more sacred to the jurisprudence of our country or more essential to the liberty of its citizens than the right to be free from arbitrary and indefinite detention at the whim of the executive." In challenging his jurisdiction, the government made the "sweeping" claim that it had the authority at its "discretion to deliver a United States citizen to a foreign country to avoid constitutional scrutiny" and "even to deliver American citizens to foreign governments to obtain information through the use of torture." Invoking *Rasul* and Scalia's dissent in *Hamdi*, Judge Bates declared that "a citizen cannot be so easily separated from his constitutional rights." "[T]he United States may not avoid the habeas jurisdiction of the federal courts by enlisting a foreign ally as an intermediary to detain the citizen." "[T]he executive's authority over foreign relations has never in our nation's history been deemed to override entirely the most fundamental rights of a United States citizen." Neither the act of state, separation of powers, or political question doctrine "extinguishes the fundamental right of a citizen to challenge his detention colorably alleged to be at the behest of the executive." Judge Bates ordered the parties to submit a proposal for an order governing jurisdictional discovery. But when Saudi Arabia extradited Abu Ali to the USA, where he was charged in the "paintball" cases, Bates dismissed the habeas petition as moot.[131]

In September 2006 DDC Judge Urbina granted a preliminary injunction against transfer to Iraqi custody of Shawqi Omar, a US citizen captured in his Baghdad home in 2004 and held at Camp Bucca.[132] The government appealed, claiming he was held by the MNF-I. In February 2007 the DC Circuit affirmed. Judge Tatel (joined by Edwards) wrote that "the fact that Omar has never been convicted of criminal activity … distinguishes this case from both *Hirota and Finck* [denying habeas], and rightly so, given that challenging extrajudicial detention is among the most fundamental purposes of habeas." Rejecting the government's claim that the case raised a political question, he said *Hamdi* "makes abundantly clear that Omar's challenge to his detention is justiciable." "[A] decision on the merits might well have implications for military and foreign policy, but that alone hardly makes the issue non-justiciable."

In October DDC Judge Lamberth rejected a similar request from Mohammad Munaf, a US citizen (married to a Romanian woman) who had traveled with Romanian journalists to Iraq, where he was captured

At the end of its 2011 Term the Supreme Court declined to review seven habeas cases: *Latif, al Alwi, al Bihani, Uthman, Almerfedi, al-Kandari,* and *al Madhwani.* The media were strongly critical. The *Los Angeles Times* wrote:[241]

> [F]or four years, the Supreme Court did its duty as a guardian of the Constitution by ruling that Congress couldn't prevent inmates at Guantánamo Bay from filing petitions for habeas corpus ... This week, the justices walked away from that responsibility ... the result is justice deferred for inmates and a continued embarrassment for the United States ... the justices have abdicated their authority and devalued their own achievement.

The *New York Times* agreed.[242] "[I]t is devastatingly clear that the Roberts Court has no interest in ensuring meaningful habeas review for foreign prisoners." The DC Circuit's rules were "unjustly one-sided in favor of the government." "In refusing to correct the appeals court's misguided rulings, the justices fail to support important principles proclaimed in *Boumediene* and diminish their own authority."

Three months after the Court declined to review his denial of habeas, Adnan Latif committed suicide.[243] David Remes, one of his lawyers, said: "every hope held out to him was dashed. He felt that his spirit was dying, that he couldn't continue to bear his conditions." Marc Falkoff, another of Latif's lawyers, said: "the real shock was that Obama chose to appeal the district court's order to release a prisoner whom his own task force had (privately) already designated for transfer home." The *New York Times* again criticized the Circuit Court's "manifestly incorrect decision."

In May 2013 Linda Greenhouse wrote in the *New York Times* that, in the first two years after *Boumediene,* District Judges granted 20 of the 34 habeas petitions they heard.[244] But after the DC Circuit decided *al-Adahi* in mid-2010 and the Supreme Court denied review in early 2011, District Judges granted only 1 of the 12 petitions and the DC Circuit reversed that one (*Latif*), creating a presumption that government evidence was reliable. In the only case the Supreme Court agreed to hear after *Boumediene* – concerning the Uighurs – the Obama administration changed the facts, leading the Court to dismiss the case.

In May 2013 the government withdrew its opposition to a habeas petition for Ibrahim Idris, an obese, diabetic, schizophrenic Sudanese. The District Court granted his petition in October, and he was transferred in December.[245]

A month after the Supreme Court's 2008 *Boumediene* decision, lawyers filed a habeas petition on behalf of abu Zubaydah.[246] Although the median time for resolving entire cases was slightly over two years for Judge Roberts, to whom the case was assigned, in May 2015 it had been pending for 6 years, 9 months and 12 days. The entire file was secret. Roberts never ruled on 16 motions, 13 filed by abu Zubaydah's lawyers, some alleging government misconduct. In January 2015 his lawyers finally asked Roberts to recuse himself for "nonfeasance." At the end of the Obama administration it still had not been decided.

At the end of July 2015 there were still ten active habeas petitions, including one claiming that Tariq ba Odah, who had been on hunger strike since February 2007, could starve to death.[247] Although DoS did not want the government to oppose his petition, DoD expressed concern that failure to do so would encourage others to engage in hunger strikes, and DoJ also wanted to resist. The Obama task force had recommended Odah's transfer in 2009, but he could not return to Yemen. In September the *New York Times* noted that the DoJ opposed every habeas petition. "If Mr. Obama ordered the Department to stop doing that, a federal judge could immediately release the detainees to a willing country, without requiring the Defense Secretary's signoff." Shayana Kadidal, a CCR lawyer representing detainees, wrote the same in a letter to the *New York Times* in November. Judge Friedman denied a petition by Saifullah Paracha attacking Congressional actions as bills of attainder, finding that he lacked standing and the MCA had stripped the court of jurisdiction; the DC Circuit affirmed.[248]

Just before the end of Obama's term, DDC Judge Collyer denied Sufyian Barhoumi's habeas petition and DDC Judge Kollar-Kotelly denied Abdul Latif Nasser's petition because, although the PRB had recommended transfer and Morocco had provided the necessary assurances, Defense Secretary Ashton had not certified the transfer.[249] In February 2017 DDC Judge Leon rejected Moath al Alwi's petition, deferring to the Executive Branch determination that the USA was still engaged in "active hostilities."[250] Leon was the fourth judge to do so.

CONCLUSION

When the Bush administration brought detainees from Afghanistan and Pakistan to Guantánamo, the prospect of using habeas corpus to challenge their detention seemed remote. The prisoners were noncitizens (with one accidental exception); and the administration had chosen Guantánamo on the OLC's advice that the base was beyond the protection of the Constitution and the reach of American courts. The first case was especially unpromising and was predictably dismissed for lack of standing because the petitioners had no relationship to the detainees – precisely what the Bush administration intended by forbidding all contact with prisoners and concealing their identities. But judges also dismissed petitions brought by legitimate "next friends" because the detainees were not citizens and the USA did not exercise *de jure* sovereignty over Guantánamo. (Judge Floyd also displayed greater sympathy for Padilla, a citizen, than for al-Marri, a legal resident.) *Eisentrager* was viewed as binding; and the AUMF was seen as an Act of Congress for the purposes of the Non-Detention Act.

Leading Bush administration officials strongly discouraged efforts to seek judicial review of detention. Attorney General Ashcroft, Deputy Attorney General Comey, and Defense Secretary Rumsfeld confidently and prematurely proclaimed Padilla's guilt. White House Counsel Gonzales (who later succeeded Ashcroft) declared that the right to counsel "must give way to the national security needs of this country to gather intelligence from captured enemy combatants."[251] Conservatives both inside the administration (Deputy Assistant Secretary of Defense Stimson) and outside (the Washington Legal Foundation) condemned lawyers who represented Guantánamo detainees pro bono. By contrast, leading national newspapers – including the *New York Times*, *Washington Post*, and *Los Angeles Times* – consistently advocated for the rule of law (although the *Post* also supported a specialized national security court and opposed judicial review of detention via habeas).

These diametrically opposed positions also divided judges. Using the appointing president's party as a proxy for the judge's political orientation, I found it was very significantly correlated with whether the judge responded favorably or unfavorably to a habeas petition, as shown in Table 5.1.

And because Republican appointees made 63 percent of the decisions and voted against petitioners 76 percent of the time, nearly two-thirds of the decisions favored the government.

The rhetoric deployed by these judges vividly exposed the ideological chasm. One group, whom I call liberal legalists, expressed sympathy for detainees held indefinitely without trial, anger at their mistreatment, and fidelity to basic constitutional principles, including civil liberties and judicial checks on executive power. They cited Magna Carta (Souter in *Hamdi*, Stevens in *Rasul*), condemned a process that

Table 5.1 Judges' Habeas Corpus Rulings, by Appointing President's Party

Party	# Favorable	% Favorable	# Unfavorable	% Unfavorable	Total number of petitions
Democrat	68	56	53	44	121
Republican	49	24	153	76	202
Total	117	36	206	64	323

Chi-Square = 31.304, p<.001

resembled the notorious Star Chamber (Stevens in *Padilla*), and quoted Justice Marshall's foundational assertion in *Marbury v. Madison* that "it is emphatically the province and the duty of the judicial department to say what the law is." Invoking the infamous internment of Japanese Americans during World War II, these judges argued that judicial capitulation to such abuses was uniquely destructive (Motz in *Hamdi*).

By contrast, a group of what Stephen Ellmann (in the South African context) termed "executive-minded" judges[252] called for deference to the president, military, and political branches in matters of national security, warfare, and foreign relations. As commander-in-chief, the president had "inherent authority to thwart acts of belligerency" (Wesley in *Padilla*). "In time of actual hostilities ... courts should tread lightly and give the President, as commander in chief, the full power of his office" (Lamberth in *Munaf*). These judges leveled accusations of "lawfare" against lawyers who advocated zealously on behalf of Guantánamo detainees. Silberman (in *Esmail*) dismissed habeas hearings as a mere "litigation exercise for the detainee bar." Habeas lawyers were guilty of "graymail," "fishing expeditions," and "thrashing litigiousness." Williamson (in *al-Marri*) warned apocalyptically that "process can accomplish the dismemberment of meaningful democratic prerogatives" and "paralyze public officials." Chief Justice Roberts denounced "the rule of lawyers, who will now arguably have a greater role than military and intelligence officials in shaping policy for enemy combatants" (*Boumediene*).

These judges expressed fear and loathing for international law (Randolph in *Rasul*), which was "uncertain and changing" (Kavanaugh in *al Bihani*). Brown (in *al Bihani*) was particularly vituperative: international law was "contestable and fluid," a "primordial stew" that "swirls beyond our borders." Treaties were "vague" and customary law "amorphous." Such alien contaminants could not be allowed to pollute the "closed and coherent system" of US domestic law (an unconscious appeal to the illusory ideal of nineteenth-century German pandectists). Two judges echoed Alberto Gonzales's cavalier dismissal of the "quaint" Geneva Conventions: "Some of the tradeoffs traditionally struck by the laws of war no longer make sense" (Brown in *al Bihani*); the law of war was "quaint and outmoded," "bound in obsolescence," displaying a "sense of rigidity and complacency" (Williamson in *al-Marri*).

These judges often began by commemorating the thousands killed in the 9/11 attacks (for which none of the petitioners bore any responsibility). And they indulged in an imaginary parade of horrors: military officers would have to interrupt their fighting to testify; judges would determine military tactics; vital intelligence would be lost or compromised; terrorists would attack the homeland with dirty bombs in suitcases (Williamson in *al-Marri*). Decisions about how to deploy the armed forces are "delicate, complex, and involve large elements of prophecy," for which the "judiciary has neither aptitude, facilities, nor responsibility" (Lamberth in *Munaf*). A habeas hearing would "compromise" military operations (Brown in *al Bihani*). Habeas would have "devastating" consequences, "make the war harder on us," and "almost certainly cause more Americans to be killed" (Scalia in *Boumediene*). Requiring anything more than "a good-faith executive determination" for detention "will destroy the intelligence gathering function" (Thomas in *Hamdi*). A habeas hearing would give detainees "free access to classified information," which they would communicate "with deadly consequences" (Roberts in *Boumediene*). Detainees' lawyers would obtain "vast reams of classified information," risking "serious security breaches for no good reason." "Foreign intelligence services will cease cooperating with the United States" (Randolph in *Bismullah*). The Supreme Court's *Boumediene* decision "guarantee[d] that the benefit of intelligence that might be gained – even from high-value detainees – is outweighed by the systemic cost of defending detention decisions" (Brown in *Latif*). Where Urbina invoked the Roman law maxim "ubi jus, ibi remedium" to grant habeas to the Uighurs, Randolph reversed, because "not every violation of a right yields a remedy, even when the right is constitutional."

Liberal legalists spoke the language of constitutionalism. Hamdi had a right to counsel "because of fundamental justice provided by the Constitution." The judiciary must conduct a "meaningful" review of enemy combatant designations "when they substantially infringe on the individual liberties, guaranteed by the U.S. Constitution, of American citizens." "We must preserve the rights afforded to us by our Constitution and laws for without it we return to the chaos of a rule of men and not laws" (all by Doumar in *Hamdi*). Hamdi's petition implicated "commanding constitutional interests," namely the "rights of our citizens to be free from government restraint except upon lawful justification" (Luttig). Judge Motz deplored "the first time in our history that a federal court has approved the elimination of protections afforded a citizen by the Constitution solely on the basis of the Executive's designation of that citizen as an enemy combatant" (*Hamdi*). Padilla's detention as an enemy combatant "created a unique and unprecedented threat to the freedom of every American citizen." "At stake in this case is nothing less than the essence of a free society." "[I]f this Nation is to remain true to the ideals symbolized by its flag, it must not wield the tools of tyrants even to resist an assault by the forces of tyranny" (Stevens).

Denying habeas would have "disastrous consequences for the Constitution – and the country" and "undermine all of the freedoms guaranteed by the Constitution" (Motz in *al-Marri*). At issue were "the rights of every man, woman and child who breathe the fragrant scent of liberty in this great land." Thomas Jefferson had hailed habeas as a "bright constellation," exhorting Americans: "should we wander ... in moments of error or of alarm, let us hasten to retrace our steps and to regain the road which alone leads to peace, liberty, and safety" (Gregory in *al-Marri*). Habeas was "the essential remedy to safeguard a citizen against imprisonment by state or nation in violation of his constitutional rights." There was "no principle more sacred to the jurisprudence of our country or more essential to the liberty of its citizens" (Bates in *Abu Ali*).

Liberal legalists declared that separation of powers required the judiciary to restrain the executive. Uncritically accepting the government's declarations would "be abdicating any semblance of the most minimal level of judicial review" and "acting as little more than a rubber-stamp" (Doumar in *Hamdi*). "The very core of liberty secured by our Anglo-Saxon system of separate powers has been freedom from indefinite imprisonment at the will of the Executive" (Scalia in *Hamdi*). To argue that "just because the President states that Petitioner's detention is 'consistent with the laws of the United States' ... that makes it so" "would totally eviscerate the limits placed on Presidential authority to protect the citizenry's individual liberties" (Floyd in *Padilla*). "Separation-of-powers concerns do not trump the very principle upon which this nation was founded – the unalienable right to liberty." Courts possessed the "authority to safeguard an individual's liberty from unbridled executive fiat" (Urbina in *Parhat*). "The executive's authority over foreign relations has never in our nation's history been deemed to override entirely the most fundamental rights of a United States citizen" (Bates in *Abu Ali*).

Liberal legalists urged judicial restraint, accusing government lawyers of inviting judicial activism. "This Court sits to interpret the law as it is and not as the Court might wish it to be" (Floyd in *Padilla*). Motz accused the en banc majority in *al-Marri* of engaging in "rhetoric and passion," "inventing" "judicially-created definitions," indulging in "judicial conjecture" and "abandoning precedent." When Randolph dismissed petitioners' arguments in *Boumediene* as "nonsense," Rogers retorted that the majority was "misreading the historical record and ignoring" the Supreme Court's decision in *Rasul*.

Liberal legalists were skeptical about the government's arguments. Its opposition to detainee access to lawyers was "thinly supported" with a "flimsy assemblage of cases" (Kollar-Kotelly in *Rasul*), based on "gossamer speculation" and "conjecture" (Mukasey in *Padilla*).

Refusing to "rubber-stamp" the government, Garland paraphrased Lewis Carroll's *The Hunting of the Snark*: "the fact that the government has 'said it thrice' does not make an allegation true" (*Parhat*). The government engaged in "casuistry ... permeated with the pinched legalism one usually encounters from non-lawyers" (Mukasey in *Padilla*). Judges had greater confidence in their own expertise than in the unsubstantiated conclusions of government officials. Mukasey noted that Padilla had been a criminal, "and criminals are people with whom this court has at least as much experience as does Admiral Jacoby, and perhaps more." Floyd expressed a similar sentiment: "simply stated, this is a law enforcement matter," with which he was very familiar, "not a military matter." Judges caustically criticized government tactics: Padilla's transfer to military custody was "shrouded in secrecy"; the government had sought a strategic advantage by its "ex parte proceeding" (Stevens in *Padilla*). Even Luttig, who generally favored the government, warned that its sudden indictment of Padilla created an "appearance" that it was trying to avoid Supreme Court review, implying that the principle on which it had relied to hold him for years as an enemy combatant could "yield to expediency."

Liberal legalists displayed sympathy for detainees, who had been held "virtually incommunicado for nearly three years without being charged with any crime" (Kollar-Kotelly in *Rasul*). "Their detention has already crossed the constitutional threshold into infinitum" (Urbina in *Parhat*). For eight years, from ages 18 to 26, the government had prevented Odaini "from seeing his family and denied him the opportunity to complete his studies and embark on a career." That "great cost to him has done nothing to make the United States more secure" (Kennedy). When constrained by precedent to deny habeas, liberal legalists did so "reluctantly," "deeply troubl[ed]" that this violated the "most basic values our legal system has long embodied," and expressed the hope that a higher court would correct the injustice (Matz in *Gherebi*). Even when denying habeas to Awad, Robertson dismissed the evidence as "gossamer thin," calling it "ludicrous" to believe he posed a threat. Although Robertson found the Uighurs' indefinite detention "unlawful," he sadly lacked "the power to do what I believe justice requires." Concurring in the denial of habeas to Razak Ali, Edwards regretted the "bizarre" and "troubling" consequence that he might be imprisoned for the rest of his life. The Circuit Court had "stretched the meaning of the AUMF and the NDAA so far beyond the terms of these statutory authorizations that habeas corpus proceedings like the one afforded Ali are functionally useless." Forced by "the vagaries of the law" to concur in another habeas denial, Edwards deplored that Hussain had been detained 11 years after being captured as a teenager. The court's "walks like a duck" test was "invidious" because "any young Muslim man traveling or temporarily residing in areas in which terrorists are known to operate would pass the 'duck test.'" (As an African American, Edwards may have been especially sensitive to such profiling.) Taking the unusual step of explaining why the Supreme Court was not reviewing the government's decision to transfer Padilla to civilian custody, Justice Kennedy (joined by Stevens and, surprisingly, Roberts) assured Padilla that all federal courts, including the Court's *original* jurisdiction, would be available if the government again declared him an enemy combatant. In its initial denial of certiorari in *Boumediene*, the Supreme Court promised to intervene if CSRTs were delayed (and two months later took the even more unusual step of reversing itself and agreeing to review).

Whereas executive-minded judges believed that national security demanded sacrifices of liberty, liberal legalists insisted that "particularly" "in times of national emergency" "it is the obligation of the Judicial Branch to ensure the preservation of our constitutional values and to prevent the Executive Branch from running roughshod over the rights of citizens and aliens alike." The executive does not possess "unchecked authority" (Reinhardt in *Gherebi*). "We have long since made clear that a state of war is not a blank check for the present when it comes to the rights of our Nation's citizens." "It is during our most challenging and uncertain moments that our Nation's commitment to due process is most severely tested; and it is in those times that we must preserve our commitment at home to the principles for which we fight abroad" (O'Connor in *Hamdi*). Terrorism "cannot negate the existence of the most basic fundamental rights for which the people of this country have fought and died for well over two hundred years" (Green in *In re Guantánamo Detainee Cases*). "Security subsists ... in fidelity to freedom's first principles" (Kennedy in *Boumediene*).

Executive-minded judges began (and ended) their legal analyses with security. "Government has no more profound responsibility than the protection of Americans." Courts owed "considerable" "deference" to the political branches "in the context of foreign relations and national security." The reasons were "not difficult to discern ... at a time when the care of the common defense is most critical" (Wilkinson in *Hamdi*). This is an "age where thousands of human beings can be slaughtered by a single action and where large swathes of urban landscape can be leveled in an instant." "For courts to resist this political attempt to meet these rising dangers risks making the judicial the most dangerous branch" (a reference to Alexander Bickel).[253] Indefinite detention was not a "disproportionate response to those who aim to murder scores of thousands of civilians" (Williamson in *al-Marri*). (Of course, there was no evidence that any of the petitioners ever harbored such an ambition.) Liberal legalists ignored the "uncomfortable fact" that detainees posed an "infinitely greater downside risk" than criminal accused (Silberman in *Esmail*). (In fact, the "recidivism statistics" discussed in the Guantánamo chapter of the companion volume *Law's Wars* show that ex-detainees were less likely to engage in terrorism than ordinary ex-prisoners were to commit crimes – unsurprising given that none of the ex-detainees had been convicted of any crime. Furthermore, all but about forty of the more than 700 detainees ultimately were released.) And 9/11 was "the most devastating terrorist attack in the history of the United States." The "economy was severely damaged." A habeas hearing would require the court to "inject itself into sensitive matters of foreign affairs, military policy, and other national security areas" (Leon in *Khalid*). Traxler criticized Doumar for granting habeas to Padilla, thereby failing "to accord the president the deference that is his when he acts pursuant to a broad delegation of authority, such as the AUMF." Such deference was necessary "to protect American citizens from the very kind of savage attack that occurred four years ago almost to the day" (Luttig in *Padilla*). "Call[ing] American commanders to account in federal courtrooms would stand the warmaking powers ... on their heads." Americans' "paramount right" was not liberty but "to have their democracy's most vital life-or-death decisions made by those whom the Constitution charges with that task" (Wilkinson in *Hamdi*). A habeas hearing would "interfere with military functions" (Randolph in *Rasul*). Some judges jumped to sweeping conclusions: "every resident within Afghanistan ... was in law an enemy, until determined by the Executive to be a friend" (Traxler in *Hamdi*). (The USA never declared war on Afghanistan.)

Executive-minded judges accused their liberal legalist colleagues of "carefree" "irresponsible" "judicial adventurism" (vintage Scalia in *Rasul*). The majority in *Boumediene* reached a "crazy result." Their "irrational and arrogant" opinion displayed an "inflated notion of judicial supremacy," which "warps our Constitution" and "blatantly misdescribes important precedents." "The Nation will live to regret what the Court has done today" (Scalia in *Boumediene*). Executive-minded judges also invoked the Constitution, which required "the executive to act energetically in time of national peril" (Williamson in *al-Marri*). Circuit Court judges, who were legally obligated to respect Supreme Court decisions, uncharacteristically took swings at *Boumediene*. Habeas hearings after *Boumediene* were a "charade prompted by the Supreme Court's defiant ... assertion of judicial supremacy" (Silberman in *Esmail*). "*Boumediene*'s airy suppositions have caused great difficulty for the Executive and the courts" (Brown in *Latif*). Speaking to the Heritage Foundation in 2010, Randolph borrowed from F. Scott Fitzgerald, calling the Supreme Court majority in *Boumediene* "careless people," who "smashed up things ... and let other people clean up the mess they had made."

These ideological differences generated an unusual number of reversals, dissents (many angry, some *ad hominem*), multiple lengthy opinions, en banc rehearings, and Supreme Court grants of certiorari (even an exceedingly rare reversal of a denial). Intrabench resentment may explain the DC Circuit's refusal to accept an amicus brief by retired judges *submitted with the government's consent* (because Mikva, one of the signers, had criticized his former colleagues for accepting

426

all-expense-paid vacations to address conservative gatherings at luxury resorts). In another DC Circuit case, Henderson accused Tatel of "high-pitched rhetoric" and "misunderstand[ing]" after Tatel claimed that the majority "moves the goal posts." The different outcomes of the two Ninth Circuit panels that heard habeas cases before *Rasul* (*Coalition* and *Gherebi*) underline the pivotal role of judicial personnel.

But political affiliation did not always predict outcome or rationale. Republicans exposed weaknesses in the government's cases, and Democrats acknowledged petitioners' connections to terrorist organizations. In finding for detainees, Doumar may have been influenced by his military background and Mukasey and Floyd by their criminal justice experience. Despite his initial hostility to petitioners, Leon sternly ordered the government to disclose exculpatory evidence to Abu Ali or withdraw its witnesses; and he granted five of the six petitions he heard after *Boumediene*. Sullivan rebuked the government's handling of Binyam Mohamed's petition. Luttig voted to deny the motion to transfer Padilla to civilian custody (which the government had expected to be pro forma and the detainee himself had endorsed), accusing the government of "expedient" unprincipled behavior. District Judges bemoaned the lack of standards to guide their hearing of petitions after *Boumediene*. Even when judges denied habeas (or were unable to free petitioners after granting it), the hearings offered a rare – often unique – opportunity to pierce the veil of secrecy the government had carefully constructed by hiding detainees in Guantánamo, holding CSRTs in camera, and demanding lawyers' silence as the price of representation. The administration's repeated rhetorical claims that these were the "worst of the worst" dissolved when the government's evidence was exposed as grossly inflated, unsubstantiated, contradictory, and lacking credibility. And before the SSCI finally succeeded in publishing its report on interrogation, habeas transcripts and opinions offered the *only* unbiased account of the abuses detainees had suffered.

After *Boumediene*, many DDC judges (including some Republicans) scrupulously scrutinized government returns to habeas petitions. Some judges were skeptical of the administration's "mosaic theory," refusing to discern a pattern of terrorist affiliation if some of the tiles were missing or flawed or the connecting "glue" was weak. They brought the perspective and standards of criminal justice to these hearings. Huvelle assailed Jawad's case as "an outrage" "riddled with holes." The government had been "dragging ... out for no good reason ... a case that's been screaming at everybody for years." District Judges criticized the government's failure to disclose all "reasonably available evidence," as required by Judge Hogan's Case Management Order. Declaring that this was "fundamentally unjust, outrageous and will not be tolerated," Sullivan threatened to incarcerate the responsible officials, starting at the top. "This Guantánamo issue is a travesty ... a horror story." Hogan ordered the government to release unclassified returns. To justify the admission of hearsay, Walton required the government to demonstrate an "undue burden," which could not be a shortage of resources or its own mistake. Echoing Garland's paraphrase of Lewis Carroll in *Parhat*, Walton rejected the government's argument "that a rumor must be true if enough people repeat it." Some judges declined to presume the accuracy of the government's evidence. Crediting detainees' allegations of torture, judges refused to rely on their "confessions" or their evidence against other detainees (a skepticism later validated by the disclosure that just *eight* Guantánamo detainees, many demonstrably unreliable, were the source of allegations against 235 others). Some judges rejected the Obama administration's new standard of "substantial support" for terrorism, invoking Justice Marshall in *Marbury*. Judges required evidence that petitioners had "received and executed orders" from terrorist organizations or otherwise were subordinated to their command structure. Robertson held that the government failed to prove that Slahi remained a member of al-Qaeda ten years after he joined. Some judges were reluctant to deny petitions based on the government's purely circumstantial evidence: a detainee's travel itinerary that paralleled those of terrorists, co-residence in guesthouses, acquaintanceship, even presence at battle sites.

But the DC Circuit, dominated by conservative Republican appointees (9 of the 13 judges participating in these cases), repeatedly overturned the DDC's grant of habeas petitions, effectively gutting the Supreme Court's *Boumediene* decision. As Tatel observed (dissenting in *Latif*), the Circuit Court conducted an unprecedented "de novo review of the factual record," producing a "wholesale revision of the district court's careful fact findings." Circuit Court judges were openly contemptuous of their lower court brethren. Reversing the grant of habeas to al-Adahi, Randolph sneered that Kessler did not "appreciate conditional probability analysis." He rejected her interpretation of the evidence, calling it "incomprehensible," "manifestly incorrect," "startling," "utterly implausible," and "perplexing." After Friedman granted habeas to Almerfedi, finding the evidence against him "inherently unreliable" "jailhouse gossip," Silberman reversed, choosing to believe the same evidence. Kennedy granted habeas to Odaini, finding that Jama'at al Tablighi, in whose guesthouse Odaini had stayed, was "a large, respected movement with the legitimate purpose of teaching about the Islamic faith." Again Silberman reversed, calling the organization "a Terrorist Support Entity 'closely aligned' with al-Qaeda." Kennedy accepted Odaini's explanation that he had $2,000 in cash when seized because he was trying to emigrate to Europe; Silberman found the cash was suspicious. Whereas District Judges repeatedly expressed skepticism about intelligence reports, Brown held they were "entitled to a presumption of regularity." Circuit Court judges overturned District Court findings on witness credibility, instructing lower courts to treat petitioners as less credible and government witnesses as more so. Circuit Court judges declared that false exculpatory evidence should not only be disbelieved but was also inculpatory. They instructed District Courts to draw inferences of culpability from petitioners' failure to testify. Circuit Court judges held it was unnecessary to find that detainees belonged to the command structure of terrorist organizations and that a "mosaic theory" of terrorist involvement could survive disproof of many of its component elements. The DC Circuit usurped the DDC's fact-finding functions, "call[ing] the game in the government's favor" (in Tatel's words) and thereby nullifying *Boumediene*'s holding that the Constitution entitled detainees to a "meaningful opportunity" to contest the lawfulness of their detention. And the Supreme Court silently acquiesced, refusing to grant certiorari in nearly a dozen subsequent cases.

The trajectory of post-9/11 habeas corpus was marked by two peaks of hope (the Supreme Court decisions in the summers of 2004 and 2008) surrounded by a pervasive slough of despond. The initial prospects for this remedy seemed very gloomy, given that petitioners were noncitizens secretly held in locations (Guantánamo and Bagram) chosen to avoid the jurisdiction of US courts. The government repeatedly responded to the threat of judicial oversight by using its executive power to dispatch petitioners who seemed likely to prevail: sending Hamdi from the USA to Saudi Arabia and Abu Ali from Saudi Arabia to the USA, moving Padilla and al-Marri back and forth between civilian and military custody. Even when District Judges ruled favorably on the substance in habeas cases, they were unable to release petitioners into the USA or compel or block their transfer abroad. The DC Circuit reversed most of the favorable rulings, and the Supreme Court abdicated its power to review. Even the Obama administration, which was publicly committed to closing Guantánamo, continued to oppose habeas petitions to the bitter end. Habeas petitions did periodically revive concern about indefinite detention without trial and expose the abuse detainees had suffered. But over the course of 15 long years, the Great Writ achieved very little.[254]

CHAPTER SIX

CIVIL DAMAGES ACTIONS

Civil damages actions perform three functions: compensating victims, judging and punishing past misconduct, and discouraging it in the future. Plaintiffs must prove fault, causation, and damages, a hurdle most of those injured by the US "war on terror" had little difficulty surmounting. Defendants' actions were clearly culpable, usually intentional. There rarely was doubt about causality (although there might be about command responsibility). And compensatory damages were substantial, potentially supplemented by punitive damages. Yet many of the most compelling claims foundered on defenses.[1] This chapter contrasts those failures with the atypical victories, grouping cases by substantive categories; but some of the most revealing language occurs when judges disagree within the confines of a single case. I also contrast compensation schemes for victims of the "war on terror" and of terrorism. I pose the following questions. What explains the success or failure of claims? Were there disproportionate numbers of split panels, reversals, and en banc hearings? What explains the differences in judges' votes, reasoning, and rhetoric (both content and tone)? What explains exceptions to the overall pattern? Do compensation schemes reflect similar differences?

UNSUCCESSFUL CASES

In the first of these cases, the owners of the Sudanese pharmaceutical plant destroyed by a US missile in 1998 in the mistaken belief it was producing chemical weapons for al-Qaeda sued for damages and declaratory relief. DDC Judge Roberts dismissed because the USA enjoyed sovereign immunity and the case involved a "nonjusticiable political question."[2] The DC Circuit (Griffith writing for Henderson) affirmed on the political question ground.[3] Ginsburg would have remanded the defamation claim to the District Court. The en banc Circuit affirmed on the same ground as the panel, although some judges did so because the plaintiffs "have not come close" to alleging "a cognizable cause of action."[4] The plaintiffs also lost in the Court of Federal Claims and the Court of Appeals for the Federal Circuit.[5]

Indefinite detention without trial and harsh interrogation generated many cases, almost all unsuccessful. In March 2005 five Iraqis detained at Abu Ghraib and four Afghans detained at Bagram sued Defense Secretary Rumsfeld and three military officers.[6] DDC Chief Judge Hogan dismissed this "lamentable case," declaring that a *Bivens* claim (for damages for violations of constitutional rights) "is clearly disfavored, as demonstrated by the fact that, in the 25 years or so since *Bivens* was decided, the Supreme Court has 'extended its holding only twice.'" Although the plaintiffs alleged "severe" abuses, the "inescapable conclusion" was that they were unprotected by the Fifth or Eighth Amendments; even if those rights were violated, they "were not clearly established at the time the alleged injurious conduct occurred." The Westfield Act would substitute the USA for these defendants, and the action would be dismissed under the Federal Tort Claims Act for failure to exhaust administrative remedies. *Rasul* was inapplicable because it dealt with habeas corpus. The recent Court of Appeals decision in *Boumediene* "removes any doubt about whether this Circuit views the Constitution as conferring any rights on nonresident aliens detained abroad."

Hogan adduced more basic reasons for dismissal:

> [A]uthorizing money damages remedies against military officials engaged in an active war would invite enemies to use our own federal courts to obstruct the Armed Forces' ability to act decisively and without hesitation in defense of our liberty and national interests …The discovery process alone risks aiding our enemies by affording them a mechanism to obtain what information they could about military affairs and disrupt command missions by wresting officials from the battlefield … Military discipline and morale surely would be eroded … Commanders likely would hesitate to act for fear of being held personally liable … It is established beyond peradventure that military affairs, foreign relations, and national security are constitutionally committed to the political branches of our government … [Any effort to determine] whether

certain acts constitute torture … would place the Court in the position of inquiring into the propriety of specific interrogation techniques and detention practices employed by the military while prosecuting wars.

The court should leave "to Congress the determination whether a damages remedy should be available."

When the Court of Appeals affirmed on similar grounds,[7] Judge Edwards wrote in dissent that plaintiffs should be able to proceed under the Alien Tort Statute.

> It is ironic that, under the majority's approach, *United States officials* who torture a foreign national in a foreign country are not subject to suit in an action brought under section 1350, whereas *foreign officials* who commit official torture in a foreign country may be sued under section 1350 … It is hard to fathom why Congress would pass a law that makes all government officials – except our own – subject to liability for torture committed overseas [original emphasis].

Shafiq Rasul and three other Guantánamo detainees sued for damages for detention and torture after their return to the UK. The DDC dismissed most of their claims on the same grounds as above, but allowed them to proceed under the Religious Freedom Restoration Act (RFRA) because a reasonable official would know that "flushing the Koran down the toilet and forcing Muslims to shave their beards" violated their rights.[8] The DC Circuit dismissed the RFRA claim because the plaintiffs were not protected "persons" under that statute for the same reason that they lacked constitutional rights.[9] But after the Supreme Court held in *Boumediene*[10] that detainees held outside the USA had some constitutional rights, it vacated the DC Circuit decision and remanded.[11] The *New York Times* hoped the Circuit now would uphold the claim.[12] "The Bush administration wanted Guantánamo to be a law-free zone in which military captors were free to mistreat prisoners with impunity. Part of the process of undoing that ugly legacy is making clear that detainees have the right to sue if they were tortured or otherwise abused."

But the Court of Appeals again dismissed the entire case in a brief *per curiam* opinion, resting its decision on qualified immunity, which was unaltered by *Boumediene*.[13] In a separate opinion, Judge Brown reiterated her belief that RFRA covered the plaintiffs. The *New York Times* found it "deeply distressing" to watch the DC Circuit "sink" to the standard of the Bush administration, which "came up with all kinds of ridiculously offensive rationalizations for torturing prisoners."[14] The Supreme Court should "have corrected that outlandish reading of the Constitution, legal precedent, and domestic and international statutes and treaties." By declining to review the latest decision, "the justices abdicated their legal and moral duty."

> The Court has granted the government immunity for subjecting people in its custody to terrible mistreatment. It has deprived victims of a remedy and Americans of government accountability, while further damaging the country's standing in the world. Contrary to the view of the lower appellate court, it was crystal clear that torture inflicted anywhere is illegal long before the Supreme Court's 2008 ruling … Moreover, the shield of qualified immunity was not raised in good faith. Officials decided to hold detainees offshore at Guantánamo precisely to try to avoid claims from victims for conduct the officials knew was illegal.

DDC Judge Leon, who had granted habeas to Abdul Rahim Abdul Razak al-Janko, later released from Guantánamo, dismissed his damages claim for alleged abuse because the MCA stripped federal courts of jurisdiction.[15] In any case, sovereign immunity was a bar. "War, by its very nature, victimizes many caught in its wake. Innocent civilians are invariably killed, and sometimes even mistakenly imprisoned. Our legal system was never designed to provide a remedy in our Courts for these inevitable tragedies, especially in a conflict like this where terrorists cunningly morph into their surroundings."

The DC Circuit affirmed because of the MCA's "unmistakable language."[16] Judge Henderson added:

> It may very well be that to deny the Appellant recovery for injuries incurred while in the United States's custody based solely on the unreviewed discretion of a tribunal the Supreme Court has labeled "closed and accusatorial" is rough justice … But that objection is to the statute's underlying policy and not to our interpretation thereof. The Constitution, subject to certain limitations, leaves exclusively to the Congress questions of fairness, justice, and the soundness of policy in the allocation of our jurisdiction … The Congress has communicated its directive in unmistakable language and we must obey.

DDC Chief Judge Lamberth followed *Rasul* in dismissing similar claims in 2013.[17] The DC Circuit affirmed.[18]

The families of Yasser al-Zahrani and Salah Ali Abdullah Ahmed al-Salami, who allegedly committed suicide in Guantánamo in June 2006, sued Rumsfeld and others in January 2009.[19] In a letter found after their deaths, they described being beaten by the "extreme reaction force," deprived of sleep for up to 30 days, forcibly shaved, denied medical care, and forced to witness the desecration of their Korans. DDC Judge Huvelle dismissed the case.[20] *Boumediene* had not altered the MCA's jurisdiction-stripping provision. Furthermore, the DC Circuit decision in *Rasul* foreclosed a *Bivens* remedy, defendants were entitled to qualified immunity, and the claim under the Alien Tort Claims Act was barred under the Federal Tort Claims Act (FTCA) because it arose in a foreign country.

The plaintiffs moved to reconsider after adding new testimony, including a witness who observed events on the night of the deaths (described in a *Harper's Magazine* article).[21] Judge Huvelle denied the motion.[22] He said the plaintiffs' claims "involve the treatment of detainees held at Guantánamo Bay, and, therefore, national security concerns." "[E]ven if every allegation of 'shocking conduct' in plaintiffs' proposed amended complaint and the *Harper's Magazine* article is true ... the highly disturbing nature of allegations in a complaint cannot be a sufficient basis in law" for action. The DC Circuit affirmed.[23]

Detainees had more mixed results when suing military contractors. Two groups of Iraqi detainees sued Titan Corp. (replaced by L-3 Communications Corp.) and CACI International, Inc. DDC Judge Robertson dismissed their claims under ATS and other federal statutes but not some common law claims.[24] He granted Titan summary judgment under the "combatant activities" exception to the FTCA because its linguists "were fully integrated into the military units to which they were assigned and ... performed their duties under the direct command and exclusive operational control of military personnel." But he denied CACI summary judgment because a jury could find that one of its employees "effectively managed" contract interrogators.

The DC Circuit dismissed all claims against both defendants under the FTCA's exception for discretionary activities, finding that the contractor was integrated into combat activities over which the military retained command authority.[25] Judge Silberman wrote: "[I]t is clear that all of the traditional rationales for *tort* law – deterrence of risk-taking behavior, compensation of victims, and punishment of tortfeasors – are singularly out of place in combat situations, where risk-taking is the rule" [original emphasis].

He created a new doctrine of "'battle-field preemption': the federal government occupies the field when it comes to warfare and its interest in combat is always 'precisely contrary' to the imposition of a non-federal tort duty." "The federal government's interest in preventing military policy from being subjected to fifty-one separate sovereigns ... is not only broad – it is *obvious*" [original emphasis]. "Arguments for preemption of state prerogatives are particularly compelling in times of war." "[T]he interests of any U.S. state ... are *de minimis* in this dispute– all alleged abuse occurred in Iraq against Iraqi citizens." "The breadth of displacement" of state law "must be inversely proportional to state interests, just as it is directly proportional to the strength of the federal interest." "[T]he application of international law to support a tort action on the battlefield must be equally barred." "Allowance of such suits will surely hamper military flexibility and cost-effectiveness, as contractors may prove reluctant to expose their employees to litigation-prone combat situations ... [and] will potentially interfere with the federal government's authority to punish and deter misconduct by its own contractors." The government had "forgone" the "numerous criminal and contractual enforcement options available." That it court-martialed military personnel at Abu Ghraib but took no action against contractors "indicates the government's perception of the contract employees' role."

Judge Garland dissented:

> Neither President Obama nor President Bush nor any other Executive Branch official has suggested that subjecting the contractors to tort liability for the conduct at issue here would interfere with the nation's foreign policy or the Executive's ability to wage war. To the contrary, the Department of Defense has repeatedly stated that employees of private contractors accompanying the Armed Forces in the field are *not* within the military's chain of command, and that such contractors *are* subject to civil liability [original emphasis].

The Supreme Court's decision in *Boyle*[26] interpreting the military exception to the FTCA "has never been applied to protect a contractor from liability resulting from the contractor's violation of federal law and policy." The majority "grants private contractors *more* protection than our soldiers and other government employees receive." It was "not clear" that states "have no interest in ensuring that their corporations refrain from abusing prisoners – even in a foreign country."

Four more Iraqi men sued CACI international, L-3 Services, and three individual contractors for alleged abuses in Abu Ghraib.[27] ED Va Judge Lee denied most of the motions to dismiss. The claims were justiciable and did not raise a political question because the defendants were private corporations. It was "plausible that the on site personnel engaged in conduct that higher-ups were wholly unaware of." Discovery was necessary to determine whether defendants enjoyed immunity and whether the interrogation complained of constituted "combatant activities" preempted by the FTCA. "[I]interrogation should not properly be understood to constitute actual physical force under *Skeels*[28] because the amount of physical contact available to an interrogator is largely limited by law and by contract, to the point where the amount of contact is unlikely equivalent to 'combat.'" Judge Lee rejected the defendant's claim that "the Court would have to conduct an extensive review of classified materials." "[M]atters are not beyond the reach of the judiciary simply because they touch upon war or foreign affairs." The SASC hearing[29] showed that "what happened at Abu Ghraib was wrong." "The public outcry against the abuse of detainees at Abu Ghraib was strong and compelling." While it is true that the events at Abu Ghraib pose an embarrassment to this country, it is the misconduct alleged and not the litigation surrounding that misconduct that creates the embarrassment ... the only potential for embarrassment would be if the Court declined to hear these claims on political question grounds.

"Immunity undermines a core belief of American jurisprudence that individuals must be held accountable for their wrongful acts." "The Court finds it doubtful that discovery will show that Defendants' actions were discretionary in light of Plaintiffs' allegations of legal and contractual violations." "[T]he Court is unpersuaded by Defendants' argument that subjecting a private, for-profit civilian corporation to a damages suit will interrupt or interfere with the prosecution of a war." "[P]ermitting this litigation against CACI to go forward actually advances federal interests ... because the threat of tort liability creates incentives for government contractors engaged in service contracts at all levels of government to comply with their contractual obligations to screen, train and manage employees." But Judge Lee dismissed the ATS claim "because such claims are fairly modern and therefore not sufficiently definite among the community of nations, as required under *Sosa*."

The Fourth Circuit reversed.[30] Judge Niemeyer wrote that:

> the potential liability under state law of military contractors for actions taken in connection with U.S. military operations overseas would ... affect the availability and costs of using contract workers ... present the possibility that military commanders could be hauled into civilian courts for the purpose of evaluating and differentiating between military and

> contractor decisions ... [and] undermine the flexibility that military necessity requires in determining the methods for gathering intelligence.

Judge King dissented because the court lacked jurisdiction to decide this interlocutory appeal. On the merits he would have rejected the discretionary function defense. "No federal interest implicates the torture and abuse of detainees. To the contrary, the repeated declarations of our executive, echoed by the Congress, expressly disavow such practices." "The plaintiffs allege that the contractor personnel acted contrary to military directives and law. The asserted basis of liability, then, is not one that would hamper the flexibility the military needs in determining how to gather intelligence, but rather one that would hold contractors to account for violating the bounds already set by the military."

The en banc Fourth Circuit reinstated the complaint.[31] Judge King wrote for ten other judges that the Court of Appeals had lacked jurisdiction. Judge Niemeyer dissented with two others, assailing the majority's reasoning as "regrettably threadbare" and "demonstrably flawed." Judge Wilkinson's dissent said the majority's "wrong" jurisdictional decision "inflicted significant damage on the separation of powers, allowing civil tort suits to invade theatres of armed conflict heretofore the province of those branches of government constitutionally charged with safeguarding the nation's most vital interests." The "abiding damage will long outlive the distressing [Abu Ghraib] photographs." This was a "novel ... violation of the most basic and customary precepts of both common and constitutional law." "[A]rrogating power to the Third Branch in a contest over military authority is the wrong call under our Constitution" and "contrary to decades of Supreme Court admonitions warning federal courts off interference with international relations." Although tort liability could "promote the public interest," it could "also lead to excessive risk-aversiveness." "Risks considered unacceptable in civilian life are sometimes necessary on a battlefield." The majority "raises thorny questions of whose law should apply" and "compromises the military's ability to utilize contractors in the future."

> The results of the rising tide of litigation will be both unpredictable and contradictory, as particular judges and juries debate and disagree over which methods of detention and interrogation are impermissible. And as detention of the enemy becomes a more litigious enterprise, the incentives to shortcut capture with more lethal and unmanned measures may rise ...

While there is a legitimate debate about how intelligence is best obtained, a tort suit is probably the very worst forum in which that issue can or should be resolved.

Only the government should be able to sue in contract for misconduct. Wilkinson deplored that an "era is ending ... through judicial ukase." "Perhaps this litigation is simply one of those small and tiny steps that weaken America only by increments and erode our constitutional structure only by degree. But I think that understates the matter."

On remand, Judge Lee dismissed the plaintiffs' ATS claims under the Supreme Court's recent *Kiobel* decision.[32] Choice of law rules mandated the application of Iraqi law to the other claims, but CPA Order 17 § 3(1) immunized contractors from Iraqi law and precluded liability for activity connected with military combat operations, including interrogation.

Anticipating another appeal to the Fourth Circuit, the *New York Times* condemned Judge Lee's "cramped reading" of *Kiobel*.[33] "Adding to the insult, the judge acceded to the contractor's outlandish request to hold the plaintiffs liable for its legal costs." The *Times* urged the Fourth Circuit to "give a few more victims a long-delayed chance for justice." The Court of Appeals reversed, holding that *Kiobel* did not bar the plaintiffs' ATS claim, but remanded on the political question defense.[34] Judge Keenan wrote that "plaintiffs' claims 'touch and concern' the territory of the United States with sufficient force," reflecting "extensive 'relevant conduct' in United States territory," including "the performance of a contract executed by a United States corporation with the United States government." The plaintiffs "allege acts of torture committed by United States citizens who were employed by an American corporation ... The alleged torture occurred at a military facility operated by United States government personnel." The alleged torturers "were hired by CACI in the United States." "CACI interrogators were required to obtain security clearances from the United States Department of Defense." "The plaintiffs also allege that CACI's managers located in the United States were aware of reports of misconduct abroad, attempted to 'cover up' the misconduct, and 'implicitly, if not expressly, encouraged' it."

As the trial finally began in February 2015 (nearly 7 years after the complaint was filed and 12 years after the alleged torts), the *New York Times* said the political question doctrine "should not be invoked to protect the civilian contractors in this case, who are not subject to the military justice system."[35] "The accountability gap becomes a larger concern as the military relies increasingly on contractors." But in June Judge Lee granted the motion to dismiss because the defendant was under the "plenary" and "direct" control of the military and "national defense interests were so 'closely intertwined' with the military decisions governing Defendant's conduct that a decision on the merits 'would require this court to question actual, sensitive judgments made by the military.' "[36] He dismissed the plaintiffs' ATS claims because "the Court lacks judicially manageable standards" for torture, "cruel, inhuman or degrading treatment," or war crimes. In October 2016 the Fourth Circuit again reversed, directing the District Court to determine whether the military actually exercised control over CACI (which would deprive the court of jurisdiction under the political question doctrine).[37] Judge Floyd concurred to insist that "while executive officers can declare the military reasonableness of conduct amounting to torture, it is beyond the power of even the President to declare such conduct lawful." "The determination of specific violations of law is constitutionally committed to the courts, even if that law touches military affairs." In September 2017 Judge Brinkema denied the motion to dismiss, ruling from the bench immediately after oral argument.

Of the Iraqis detained at Abu Ghraib and other US military bases, 72 sued L-3 Services and Adel Nakhla, who had been employed as a translator.[38] D Md Judge Messitte denied a motion to dismiss. "While a belligerent may lawfully inflict death and destruction upon the enemy, the law of war nevertheless places some limits on the wanton and malicious treatment of human lives ... One such universally recognized rule is that torture is prohibited." The case did not pose a political question because "plaintiffs do not challenge the constitutionally protected judgments of a political branch, only the decisions and actions of a private corporation and its employees," who "are alleged to have operated independently of the military and its policies." Only the government could assert a state secrets privilege. The court declined to follow the DC Circuit's decision in *Saleh*,[39] which "craft[ed] a new rule" of derivative sovereign immunity "that immunizes a contractor's rogue operations." Cruel, inhuman, and degrading treatment "is among the violations of the law of nations actionable under the ATS." "Instruments of international law, learned treatises, and the weight of judicial opinion suggest that war crimes claims under the ATS can be made against a private party and do not require state action" as long as the defendant acted "under color of law." "A person may have acted under color of law, yet still not have acted in an official capacity so as to gain the benefit of sovereign immunity."

The Fourth Circuit reversed for the reasons it gave in *al Shimari*.[40] Judge Niemeyer (who had dissented from the en banc majority there) found jurisdiction to hear this interlocutory appeal because of the "strong public policy interest, where wartime actions within a United States military prison are being challenged in a civilian court under state law" of "insulat[ing] the battlefield from the unjustified exertion of power by the courts of the 51 states and to free military operatives from the fear of possible litigation and the hesitancy that such fear engenders." He followed the DC Circuit's decision in *Saleh*: "the interest in battlefield preemption is the *complete eradication* of the 'imposition *per se*' of tort law …" [original emphasis]. Judge King (who had written for the en banc majority in *al Shimari*) dissented because the preemption defense was not equivalent to a claim of immunity and could not be the subject of a collateral appeal. Ultimately, Engility Holdings (successor to L-3) entered into a sealed settlement with 71 detainees for $5.28 million.[41]

If most of these opinions display scant sympathy for foreign victims, US citizens did not always fare better. When Iraqi police arrested Cyrus Kar in a taxi whose trunk contained washing machine timers (which could be used in IEDs but belonged to the driver), they delivered him to US forces, which held him for seven weeks, repeatedly abusing him.[42] He was released four days after the Detainee Status Board found him an "Innocent Civilian" and a day before the government had to answer his habeas petition. DDC Judge Robertson granted the motion to dismiss his damages action. Although "an army that is fully equipped with the latest technology can surely organize itself to convene a probable cause hearing in far less than 48 days," Kar's right to "a prompt probable cause hearing when detained in a war zone" was not sufficiently "clearly established" for a *Bivens* claim. Robertson also rejected a Fifth Amendment claim because "the government's inability or unwillingness to summon certain military personnel as witnesses and its refusal to turn over reports that might divulge interrogation techniques were acceptable given the interests at stake."

Donald Vance and Nathan Ertel worked for an Iraqi-owned contracting firm.[43] Believing that fellow employees were making payments to Iraqi sheikhs and engaging in illegal arms deals, Vance notified Iraqi-based US officials and (when rebuffed) told an FBI official in Chicago (for whom he claimed to work as an unpaid informant, contacting him up to twice a day). Both men alerted officials at the US

Embassy in Baghdad. When fellow employees confiscated the ID cards that let the men enter the Green Zone, they locked themselves in a room and called the Embassy for help. US military forces took them to the Embassy, which placed them in custody and then sent them to two military camps, where they suffered sleep and food deprivation, loud music, and threats, and were blindfolded and walked into walls. Ertel was released after one month, Vance after two. They sued Rumsfeld and others. ND Ill Judge Anderson denied a motion to dismiss:

> The allegations would substantiate plaintiffs' claim that Rumsfeld was aware of the direct impact that his newly approved treatment methods were having on detainees held in Iraq. In cases like this one in which much of the decision-making at issue took place behind closed doors, courts have shown a willingness to accept outside documentation of abuse as a factor supporting the plausibility of a plaintiff's allegations.

Anderson rejected Rumsfeld's claim of qualified immunity. "[F]ederal officials may not strip citizens of well-settled constitutional protections against mistreatment simply because they are located in a tumultuous foreign setting." The *Washington Post* objected: "[P]ersonal lawsuits against individual government officials should proceed only if there is plausible evidence that the named officials directly participated in the constitutional violation – a standard that Mr. Vance and Mr. Ertel's case does not meet with regard to Mr. Rumsfeld." They "should have availed themselves of processes within the military justice system to ferret out and punish miscreants."

The Seventh Circuit affirmed:[44]

> [A] reasonable official in Secretary Rumsfeld's position in 2006 would have realized that the right of a United States citizen to be free from torture at the hands of one's own government was a "clearly established" constitutional right and that the techniques alleged by plaintiffs add up to torture. If he were granted immunity the judicial branch – which is charged with enforcing constitutional rights – would be leaving our citizens defenseless to serious abuse or worse by another branch of their own government.

Praising the "courageous decision," the *New York Times* urged the Seventh Circuit not to reverse en banc. But it did. Judge Easterbrook refused to issue "a judicial order that would make the Secretary of Defense care less about the Secretary's view of the best military policy, and more about the Secretary's regard for his own finances."

José Padilla brought two lawsuits for his abuse in detention. He sued John Yoo for $1, based in part on Jack Goldsmith's assertion that Yoo's OLC memos were "legally flawed" and "tendentious in substance and tone."[45] The *Wall Street Journal* denounced this "political stunt intended to intimidate government officials." The *Washington Post* said the lawsuit had "dubious merit" unless Padilla could prove Yoo "was either incompetent or acting in knowing violation of the law." It deplored the "chilling effect on administration lawyers who may fear being held individually liable for giving candid advice." Yoo also expressed concern that "worrying about personal liability will distort the thinking of federal officials." "The prospect of having to waste large sums of money on lawyers will deter talented people from entering public service."

ND Cal Judge White denied the motion to dismiss.[46] "Although the Court does not rely on the state of current events to support its decision, it is aware that other branches of government and professional forums have not acted to provide an alternative remedy for the constitutional violations alleged in this case." He noted the "irony" that "Yoo drafted legal cover to shield review of the conduct of federal officials" but now "argues that the very drafting itself should be shielded from judicial review." The AUMF was not a special factor counseling hesitation in recognizing a *Bivens* action. The "possible constitutional trespass on a detained individual citizen's liberties where the detention was not a necessary removal from the battlefield" did not constitute "a core strategic warmaking power" urging judicial deference to executive discretion. "The treatment of an American citizen on American soil does not raise the same specter of issues relating to foreign relations" as did cases like *Arar* (discussed below). Padilla "has alleged sufficient facts to satisfy the requirement that Yoo set in motion a series of events that resulted in the deprivation of Padilla's constitutional rights."

The *Washington Post* said that though Yoo's "wrong" legal advice had been the "key" to giving the Bush administration "cover for many of its dubious 'war on terror' policies," the decision was "troubling." Denying Yoo immunity "would ignore the deep and sincere divisions among even neutral jurists." Moreover, Yoo "did not make the final policy decisions." The *Post* preferred an investigation by Congress or an independent commission.

Although constitutional law and legal ethics professors and even government lawyers filed amicus briefs on behalf of Padilla, the Ninth Circuit reversed, feeling compelled by the Supreme Court's dismissal of al-Kidd's action (discussed below).[47] When Yoo wrote his opinions, "the most germane precedent in existence," *Ex parte Quirin*, held that "a citizen detained as an unlawful combatant could be afforded *lesser* rights than ordinary prisoners" [original emphasis]. Although "the unconstitutionality of torturing a United States citizen was 'beyond debate' by 2001," Yoo was entitled to qualified immunity because it was not "clearly established" then "that the treatment to which Padilla says he was subjected amounted to torture." "[S]everal influential judicial decisions" at the time "declined to define certain severe interrogation techniques as torture."

The *New York Times* criticized this "misguided and dangerous ruling," which followed the Supreme Court's *Al-Kidd* decision that, to overcome qualified immunity, "existing precedent" must put any question about such a right "beyond debate."

> That is an unworkable standard and the Ninth Circuit decision shows why. The Bush administration manufactured "debates" – about torture and enemy combatants. Any future government can rely on this precedent to pull the same stunt as cover for some other outrage … The Ninth Circuit was wrong to swallow those deceits … [the] cruel, inhumane and shocking nature [of Padilla's treatment] badly violated his rights as a citizen … Even at the time, the issue was beyond debate, and Mr. Yoo should have known that.

The *Wall Street Journal* predictably denounced the "baseless … persecution of John Yoo by the white-shoe legal elite, which peddled the claims of a terrorist in order to harass the Bush administration lawyer for his national-security views."[48]

Padilla also sued Defense Secretaries Rumsfeld and Gates, Attorney General Ashcroft, and others, seeking the same remedy.[49] SC District Judge Gergel dismissed, finding no *Bivens* action.[50]

> The designation of Padilla as an enemy combatant and his detention incommunicado were made in light of the most profound and sensitive issues of national security, foreign affairs and military affairs. It is not for this Court, sitting comfortably in a federal courthouse nearly nine years after these events, to assess whether the policy was wise or the intelligence was accurate … one could easily imagine a massive discovery assault on the intelligence agencies of the United States Government … All of this would likely raise numerous complicated state secrets issues. A trial on the merits would be an international spectacle with Padilla, a convicted terrorist, summoning America's present and former leaders to a federal courthouse.

Furthermore, the defendants enjoyed qualified immunity. Given the conflicting decisions generated by Padilla's earlier habeas applications, it was "hard for the Court to imagine a credible argument that the alleged unlawfulness of Padilla's designation as an enemy combatant and detention were 'clearly established' at that time" or that his interrogation "was a violation of law."

The Fourth Circuit affirmed.[51] It approached the *Bivens* claim with "skepticism":

> The Constitution delegates authority over military affairs to Congress and to the President ... Where, as here, these two branches exercise their military responsibilities in concert ... the need to hesitate before using *Bivens* actions to stake out a role for the judicial branch seems clear ... Padilla's enemy combatant classification and military detention raise fundamental questions incident to the conduct of armed conflict. [A] judicially devised damages action would expose past executive deliberations affecting sensitive matters of national security to the prospect of searching judicial scrutiny ... [and] affect future discussions as well.

A *Bivens* action would "interrupt[] the established chains of military command" and "interfere[] with military and intelligence operations on a wide scale." Padilla had alternative remedies, as shown by the fact that he "challenged his military detention in habeas corpus proceedings before five different courts." That all the above "counsel[ed] hesitation" was "something of an understatement."

Federal courts were equally hostile to damage actions for extraordinary rendition. Maher Arar, a Canadian citizen, sued Ashcroft, FBI Director Mueller and others in EDNY for having been detained at JFK Airport in transit from Europe to Canada, denied access to counsel for two weeks, and then rendered to Syria, where he was tortured for a year. Judge Trager dismissed the lawsuit because it raised questions of national security and foreign relations.[52] The Torture Victims Protection Act applied only to US citizens suing someone acting under color of foreign law. Trager began his analysis of Arar's *Bivens* claim by quoting the Supreme Court's declaration of "the strong presumption in favor of judicial review of administrative action." The defendants' claim that the Immigration and Naturalization Act procedures were "fully capable of remedying the alleged torture and detention" "rings hollow." Arar's assertion that extraordinary rendition was unconstitutional "goes far beyond a mere challenge to the 'decision or action' to 'commence proceedings, adjudicate cases, or execute removal orders.'" Although defendants called Arar "an arriving alien seeking admission," Trager found "Arar was *not* seeking admission" [original emphasis]. Trager distinguished the leading *Eisentrager* case,[53] whose "detainees had 'never been or resided in the United States,' were 'captured outside of our territory and there held in military custody as[] prisoner[s] of war,' were 'tried by a Military Commission sitting outside the United States' and were 'at all times imprisoned outside the United States.'" "Arar, by contrast, was held virtually incommunicado – moreover, on U.S. soil – and denied access to counsel and process of any kind." *Rasul*[54] extended habeas "to a group of aliens with even less of a connection to the United States than Arar."

But even if Arar had adequately alleged a violation of Fifth Amendment substantive due process, his *Bivens* claim failed. Although Immigration and Naturalization Act (INA) procedures did not offer an alternative remedy, "this case raises crucial national security and foreign policy considerations, implicating 'the complicated multilateral negotiations concerning efforts to halt international terrorism,'" which "are most appropriately reserved to the Executive and Legislative branches of government. Moreover, the need for much secrecy can hardly be doubted." "One need not have much imagination to contemplate the negative effect on our relations with Canada if discovery were to ... [reveal] that certain high Canadian officials had, despite public denials, acquiesced in Arar's removal to Syria. Even a ruling sustaining state-secrets-based objections to a request for interrogatories, discovery demand or questioning of a witness could be compromising."

This case risked producing "what the Supreme Court has called in another context 'embarrassment of our government abroad' through 'multifarious pronouncements by various departments on our question.'" Judges "have neither the experience nor the background to adequately and competently define and adjudge the rights of an individual vis-à-vis the needs of officials acting to defend the sovereign interests of the United States." "Without explicit legislation, judges should be hesitant to fill an arena that, until now, has been left untouched – perhaps deliberately – by the Legislative and Executive branches."

While this was happening, Canada published an exhaustive three-volume report on Arar's rendition, paid him Can$10 million in compensation, and issued an official apology.[55]

The Second Circuit affirmed.[56] Judge Cabranes began by disparaging Judge Sack's dissent, which was "undermined by contradictory assertions and misstatements of the law" and failed to "grapple with the complicated legal questions arising from the extraterritorial application of the U.S. Constitution." "Such is the freedom enjoyed by the writer of a dissenting opinion. Those charged with rendering decisions that carry the force of law have no such freedom, however." "Whatever the emotive force of the dissent's characterization of the complaint, we cannot disfigure the judicial function to satisfy personal indignation." Arar's invitation "to devise a new *Bivens* damages action ... effectively invites us to disregard the clear instructions of the Supreme Court by extending *Bivens* ... to a new context requiring the courts to intrude deeply into the national security policies and foreign relations of the United States." His lawsuit would "probe deeply into the inner workings of the national security apparatus of at least three foreign countries ... the effective functioning of U.S. foreign policy would be affected, if not undermined." Arar had no right to counsel because he "lacked a physical presence in the United States." The alleged obstruction of his access to the courts failed to state a due process claim. The "relatively harsh conditions of detention" he alleged did not amount to "gross physical abuse" and were not "inflicted with punitive intent" or "unrelated to a legitimate government purpose." Finally, the INA review procedures were a "convincing reason" not to recognize a *Bivens* claim.

Judge Sack began his dissent by citing the Circuit's decision in *Iqbal v. Hasty* (discussed below):

> [M]ost ... rights ... do not vary with surrounding circumstances, such as the right not to be subjected to needlessly harsh conditions of confinement, the right to be free from the use of excessive force, and the right not to be subjected to ethnic or religious discrimination. The strength of our system of constitutional rights derives from the steadfast protection of those rights in both normal and unusual times.

"The majority reaches the wrong conclusion in large measure ... by treating Arar's claims as though he were an unadmitted alien seeking entry into the United States." The majority's assertion that he was not "physically present" in the USA was "a legal fiction peculiar to immigration law"; here it was "senseless." The majority's conception of "gross physical abuse" was "unduly narrow." But even that was violated when the defendants "physically caused him to be placed in the hands of someone ... for the purpose of having him tortured."

> The assessment of Arar's alleged complaint must take into account the entire arc of factual allegations that Arar makes – his interception and arrest; his questioning, principally by FBI agents, about his putative ties to terrorists; his detention and mistreatment at JFK Airport in Queens and the MDC [Metropolitan Detention Center] in Brooklyn; the deliberate misleading of both his lawyer and the Canadian Consulate; and his transport to Washington DC; and forced transfer to Syrian authorities for further detention and questioning under torture.

"[W]hether the defendants violated Arar's Fifth Amendment rights" does not "turn[] on whom they selected to do the torturing." Although "this Circuit has never explicitly decided whether a *Bivens* action can lie for alleged violations of substantive due process under the Fifth Amendment ... our cases imply that such a remedy is appropriate."

In another *Bivens* claim Judge Posner had written: "if ever there were a strong case for 'substantive due process,' it would be a case in which a person who had been arrested but not charged or convicted was brutalized while in custody." Sacks wrote that since "a federal inmate serving a prison sentence can employ *Bivens* ... [i]t would be odd if a federal detainee not charged with or convicted of any offense could not bring an analogous claim." INA procedures did not offer an alternative since Arar's "final order of removal was issued moments before his removal to Syria." It would have been "'clear to a reasonable officer' that attempting ... to obtain information from Arar under abusive conditions of confinement and interrogation, and then outsourcing his further questioning under torture to the same end, is 'unlawful.'" "[T]here is a long history of judicial review of Executive and Legislative decisions related to the conduct of foreign relations and national security." Those concerns "would be protected by the proper invocation of the state secrets privilege."

"During another time of national challenge," Justice Jackson had written:

> [M]y apprehensions about the security of our form of government are about equally aroused by those who refuse to recognize the dangers of Communism and those who will not see danger in anything else ... It is inconceivable to me that this measure of simple justice and fair dealing would menace the security of this country. No one can make me believe that we are that far gone.

The en banc Second Circuit affirmed the dismissal (7–4).[57] Chief Judge Jacobs found that special factors warranted hesitation in extending *Bivens* to the "new context" of extraordinary rendition. Congress alone had the "institutional competence" to create a civil remedy. "It is for the Executive in the first instance to decide how to implement extraordinary rendition." Arar "fail[ed] to specify any culpable action taken by any single defendant and does not allege the 'meeting of the minds' that a plausible conspiracy claim requires." "The only relevant threshold" for rejecting a *Bivens* action was "remarkably low": "that a factor 'counsels' hesitation." "[N]o account is taken of countervailing factors that might counsel alacrity or activism." This *Bivens* action "operates as a constitutional challenge to policies promulgated by the executive" and "would have a natural tendency to affect diplomacy, foreign policy, and the security of the nation." It "unavoidably influences government policy, probes government secrets, invades government interests, enmeshes government lawyers, and thereby elicits government funds for settlement." Hesitation was "counseled" by "the constitutional separation of powers" and "the limited institutional competence of the judiciary." The lawsuit would involve "a lot of classified material," whose "sensitivities" were "too obvious to call for enlarged discussion." The necessary concealment "would excite suspicion and speculation as to the true nature and depth of the supposed conspiracy." Thus "the preference for open rather than clandestine court proceedings is a special factor" counseling hesitation. "An investigation into the existence and content" of Syrian assurances that Arar would not be tortured "would potentially embarrass our government." The existence of classified documents exposed the government to graymail pressure to settle. Any government payment "tends to obviate any payment or contribution by individual defendants." It would be difficult to draw "the line between constitutional and unconstitutional conduct" in this "complex and rapidly changing legal framework." Judge Jacobs concluded by criticizing the dissenters' "emotional" and "overwrought" language.

Four judges dissented separately (each joining the others' opinions). Judge Sack accused the majority of "artificially dividing the complaint into a domestic claim that does not involve torture … and a foreign claim that does," in its "apparent determination to go to whatever lengths necessary to reach what it calls its 'dominant holding': that a *Bivens* remedy is unavailable." In doing so, "it unnecessarily makes dubious law." The Supreme Court's decision in *Iqbal* did not imply "that federal government miscreants may avoid *Bivens* liability altogether through the simple expedient of wearing hoods while inflicting injury." Furthermore, Arar had named some who personally violated his rights. With respect to the conspiracy allegation, "it is plain that the logistically complex concerted action allegedly taken to detain Arar and then transport him abroad implies an alleged agreement by government actors within the United States to act in concert." "[N]o one doubts that under Supreme Court precedent, interrogation by torture" "shocks the conscience." If the mere existence of special factors compelled the conclusion that a *Bivens* action was unavailable, "the bar to declining to allow a new *Bivens* claim ... would be chimerical." Those factors may counsel "hesitation," but "we have been 'hesitating' ... for nearly two years ... it cannot follow that having hesitated, we must therefore halt."

Bivens by its nature implicated "government interests," "enmeshes government lawyers, and elicits government funds for settlement ... authorizes courts to invalidate exercises in executive power ... attempt[s] to hold members of the executive accountable ... If these 'special factors' were persuasive grounds on which to deny *Bivens* actions ... they would not be permitted at all ... Civil rights actions influence policy ... [t]hat is their point." Sacks again quoted Justice Jackson in the original *Bivens* case: "The [government's] arguments for a more stringent test to govern the grant of damages in constitutional cases seem to be adequately answered by the point that the judiciary has a particular responsibility to assure the vindication of constitutional interests." The Circuit Court should direct the District Court to resolve the state secrets issue, as the government had invited during en banc argument, instead of "reaching out unnecessarily to decide a difficult issue related to separation of powers principles." Sacks suggested the majority was channeling Barry Goldwater: "Activism in the defense of 'liberty,' we gather, is no vice."[58]

Judge Parker began by quoting the categorical prohibition of the Convention Against Torture. The majority's "miscarriage of justice ... leaves Arar without a remedy in our court ... would immunize official misconduct ... distorts the system of checks and balances essential to the rule of law and ... trivializes the judiciary's role in these arenas." Executive and legislative powers in "the conduct of foreign policy and the maintenance of national security" were "not limitless" but rather "fixed by the same Constitution" in "both wartime and peacetime." There was "an enormous difference between being deferential and being supine in the face of governmental misconduct."

The judiciary's role was not "to serve as a help-mate to the executive branch" or "avoid difficult decisions for fear of complicating life for federal officials." "Always mindful of the fact that in times of national stress and turmoil the rule of law is everything, our role is to defend the Constitution ... by affording redress when government officials violated the law." Even the State Department had "repeatedly taken the position before the world community that this exact remedy [*Bivens*] is available to torture victims like Arar. If the Constitution ever implied a damages remedy, this is such a case – where executive officials allegedly blocked access to the remedies chosen by Congress." "When, as here, the executive branch takes measures incompatible with the express or implied will of Congress, its 'power is at its lowest ebb.'" "When presented with an appropriate case or controversy, courts are ... obliged ... to act, even in instances where government officials seek to shield their conduct behind invocations of 'national security' and 'foreign policy.'" A *Bivens* action "does not represent judicial interference in executive functions, as the majority would have it, but rather an effort to keep executive power within constitutional limits." Many previous "unilateral assertions of security and secrecy" had been "overblown," as in *Reynolds*[59] (which created the state secrets privilege) and the Pentagon Papers.[60] The Supreme Court had demonstrated its willingness to enter the area of foreign policy and national security even "against the express wishes of Congress." *Bivens* "does not create any new rights; it provides a mechanism for enforcing existing constitutional rights when no other avenue exists." "[T]he majority sets out to narrow *Bivens* to the point of vanishing." It "ignore[s] completely ... the gravity of the constitutional injuries alleged." Arar's pleading "provides as much factual support as a man ... could reasonably be expected to offer" after being "held in solitary confinement and then imprisoned for ten months in an underground cell." It was "hardly far-fetched" that Ashcroft and Mueller "oversaw Arar's detention and removal." His covert transfer to Syria "indicates involvement at the highest levels of government." The Department of Homeland Security's Office of the Inspector General "has itself confirmed the broad contours of Arar's mistreatment."[61]

Judge Pooler dismissed as dicta the majority's interpretations of *Bivens*, which "bear no relation" to its holdings. "Were the majority's dicta the rule, there would be no explanation for the Supreme Court's decision in *Bivens* in the first place." The majority's "simplistic framework would be contrary to the Supreme Court's *Bivens* decisions, which require that courts consider reasons both for and against recognizing the remedy."

> The majority's opinion was a result of its hyperbolic and speculative assessment of the national security implications of recognizing Arar's *Bivens* action, its underestimation of the institutional competence of the judiciary, and its implicit failure to accept as true Arar's allegations that defendants blocked his access to judicial processes so that they could render him to Syria to be tortured, conduct that shocks the conscience and disfigures fundamental constitutional principles.

Judge Calabresi predicted historians would view the decision with "dismay." "[I]n calmer times, wise people will ask themselves: how could such able and worthy judges have done that?" "In its utter subservience to the executive branch, its distortion of *Bivens* doctrine, its unrealistic pleading standards, its misunderstanding of the TVPA [Torture Victims Protection Act] and of [42 U.S.C.] § 1983, as well as its persistent choice of broad dicta where narrow analysis would have sufficed, the majority opinion goes seriously astray." Calabresi deplored the majority's "unwavering willfulness" in engaging in "extraordinary judicial activism." "Denying a *Bivens* remedy because state secrets might be revealed is a bit like denying a criminal trial for fear that a juror might be intimidated." The risks of graymail and government indemnification were "present in *every* tort suit against a government agent" [original emphasis]. "[A] civilized polity, when it errs, admits it and seeks to give redress." The majority insisted this "should be left entirely to congressional whim." But in the United States "courts are, almost universally, involved." This decision "hampers an admission of error ... decides constitutional questions that should be avoided" and is "on all counts, utterly wrong."

In Arar's appeal to the Supreme Court amicus briefs were filed by retired federal judges, the New York City Bar Association, the past and present UN Special Rapporteurs on Torture, Redress Trust (an organization of torture survivors), AI, Canadian human rights organizations and scholars, the Bar Human Rights Committee of England and Wales, and the European Center for Constitutional and Human Rights. But the Supreme Court denied certiorari.[62] Arar said:[63] "today's decision eliminates my last bit of hope in the judicial system of the United States. When it comes to 'national security' matters the judicial system has willingly abandoned its sacred role of ensuring that no one is above the law." The *New York Times* denounced the Court's "disgraceful" decision, a "bitterly disappointing abdication of its duty to hold officials accountable for illegal acts."[64]

In another extraordinary rendition claim, five men rendered to secret CIA prisons where they were tortured sued Jeppesen Dataplan, Inc., a Boeing subsidiary, which operated the planes.[65] After the government intervened and asserted state secrets, ND Cal Judge Ware dismissed under the *Totten* ban,[66] finding that allegations of covert US military or CIA operations in foreign countries against foreign nationals – "clearly a subject matter which is a state secret" – lay "at the core of Plaintiffs' case."[67] He did not analyze Director of the CIA (DCI) Hayden's classified declaration because of the Supreme Court's warning not to disclose "the very thing the privilege is designed to protect."

Anticipating the Ninth Circuit appeal, the *Los Angeles Times* hoped "the judges have the courage to stand up to the government. Better yet, we hope the Obama administration lawyers will ... reject the approach of the previous administration."[68] "If a man credibly claims to have been snatched from his home and family and tortured by or with the acquiescence of the government, he deserves a fair and impartial reckoning in court." "The history of the [state secrets] privilege suggests that the government may use it not so much to protect national security as to prevent its own illegal or embarrassing misadventures from coming to light."

The Ninth Circuit reversed, finding that "*Totten* has no bearing here, where third-party plaintiffs (not Jeppesen) seek compensation from Jeppesen (not the government) for tortious detention and torture (not unpaid espionage services)."[69] Judge Hawkins adopted this "narrow construction" of *Totten* because of "the Supreme Court's warning that 'occasion[s] for constitutional confrontation between the branches' should be avoided whenever possible." The government's theory that "the Judiciary should effectively cordon off all secret government actions from judicial scrutiny, immunizing the CIA and its partners from the demands and limits of the law" would "force[] an unnecessary zero-sum decision between the Judiciary's constitutional duty 'to say what the law is,' ... and the Executive's constitutional duty 'to preserve the national security.'"

> If the simple fact that information is classified were enough to bring evidence containing that information within the scope of the privilege, then the entire state secrets inquiry ... would fall exclusively to the Executive

Branch, in plain contravention to the Supreme Court's admonition that "[j]udicial control over the evidence in a case cannot be abdicated to the caprice of executive officers" without "lead[ing] to intolerable abuses."

When the Ninth Circuit granted en banc review, the *New York Times* urged it to "resist the Obama team's invitation to sacrifice democratic principles to avoid a politically embarrassing airing of policies and decisions that Mr. Obama himself has repeatedly condemned."[70] "Unless courts declare the conduct in question illegal, nothing will prevent another administration from arguing ... that kidnapping, secret detention, abuse and even torture were a perfectly acceptable response to national security concerns." The *Los Angeles Times* praised the three-judge panel for "rightly stating that to thwart a trial would 'perversely encourage the president to classify politically embarrassing information simply to place it beyond the reach of the judicial process.'"[71]

The en banc Ninth Circuit reversed by a single vote.[72] Judge Fisher chose not to resolve "the difficult questions of precisely which claims may be barred under *Totten*," preferring to fulfill the court's "obligation under *Reynolds* 'to review the [government's claim] with a very careful, indeed a skeptical eye, and not to accept at face value the government's claim or justification or privilege.'" After "thoroughly and carefully" reviewing all the declarations, the majority concluded there were "valid state secrets." "We are precluded from explaining precisely which matters the privilege covers lest we jeopardize the secrets we are bound to protect." Even if plaintiffs used only nonprivileged evidence, "any effort by Jeppesen to defend could unjustifiably risk disclosure of state secrets." Plaintiffs had other remedies: government reparations, Congressional investigation, private bills for compensation, and remedial legislation.

Judge Hawkins dissented because dismissal was justified under *Reynolds* "if and only if specific privileged evidence is itself indispensable." "[T]he doctrine is so dangerous as a means of hiding governmental misbehavior under the guise of national security, and so violative of common rights to due process, that courts should confine its application to the narrowest circumstances that still protect the government's essential secrets." When used to dismiss complaints "the result is a maximum interference with the due processes of the courts, on the most general claims of state secret privilege." Because "Jeppesen has yet to answer ... we have no idea what [its] defenses or assertions might be. Making assumptions about the contours of future litigation involves mere speculation." "The state secrets privilege, as an evidentiary privilege, is not relevant to the sufficiency of the *complaint*, but only to the sufficiency of evidence available to later *substantiate* the complaint" [original emphasis]. The "alternative remedies" offered by the majority were "insufficient." "Permitting the executive to police its own errors and determine the remedy to dispense would not only deprive the judiciary of its role, but also deprive Plaintiffs of a fair assessment of their claims by a neutral arbiter."

The *New York Times* regretted that the decision "diminishes any hope that this odious practice" of extraordinary rendition "will finally receive the legal label it deserves: a violation of international law." "The state secrets doctrine is so blinding and powerful that it should be invoked only when the most grave national security matters are at stake."[73] Tim Rutten wrote in his *Los Angeles Times* column that "the idea that injured parties can be denied legal redress because the executive branch wants the matter kept secret is an appalling novelty."[74] The *Los Angeles Times* declared that "of all the excesses of the post-9/11 war on terror, none was as outrageous as the practice of 'extraordinary rendition.'"[75] The Ninth Circuit had "compound[ed] the injustice" by ratifying the "extravagant claims" that a trial would disclose state secrets. "The decision to short-circuit the trial process is more than a misreading of the law; it's an egregious miscarriage of justice." "The Supreme Court should reopen the door that the 9th Circuit slammed shut." The *Washington Post* said the case "again points out the need for a new law" and urged support for the State Secrets Protection Act introduced by Sen. Leahy and Rep. Nadler.[76] By contrast with the USA, Sweden awarded SEK3 million ($433,000) and permanent residency to each of the two men whom the USA, with Swedish complicity, had rendered to Egypt, where they were tortured.[77] And Poland agreed to pay ECHR judgments of €130,000 to Abu Zubaydah and €100,000 to al-Nashiri for their detention and torture in a secret CIA prison.[78]

The third damages claim for rendition was brought by Khalid el-Masri, a German citizen seized by Macedonia on New Year's Eve 2003, interrogated for 23 days and then rendered by the CIA to its secret "Salt Pit" prison in Afghanistan, where he was held and harshly interrogated for four months before being dumped in Albania.[79] The CIA conceded it had detained him in error. He sued DCI Tenet and others, asserting a *Bivens* claim and two ATS claims.

ED Va. Judge Ellis dismissed the case, finding "no doubt that the state secrets privilege is validly asserted here," based on an *ex parte* reading of Tenet's declaration. "The entire aim of the suit is to prove the existence of state secrets." "El-Masri's private interests must give way to the national interest in preserving state secrets." If his allegations were true, he "deserves a remedy," but "the only sources of that remedy must be the Executive Branch or the Legislative Branch." The Fourth Circuit affirmed: "Contrary to El-Masri's assertion, the state secrets doctrine does not represent a surrender of judicial control over access to the courts." "That El-Masri is unfamiliar with the Classified Declaration's explanation for the privilege claim does not imply ... that the district court's ruling was simply an unthinking ratification of a conclusory demand by the executive branch." El-Masri's "personal interest in pursuing his civil claim is subordinated to the collective interest in national security." El-Masri commented: "above all, what I want from the lawsuit is a public acknowledgment from the U.S. government that I was innocent, a mistaken victim of its rendition program, and an apology for what I was forced to endure." The *New York Times* urged the Supreme Court to "scale back the use of this dangerous legal defense," which "could prevent judicial review of a wide array of unconstitutional actions by the executive branch." But the Court denied certiorari.

The last unsuccessful damages claims for "war on terror" tactics involved drone strikes. Former DCIs Panetta and Petraeus and former Joint Special Operations Command commanders McRaven and Votel were sued for killing three American citizens: Anwar al-Awlaki and his son Abdulrahman (brought by Nasser al-Awlaki, Anwar's father) and Samir Khan (brought by his mother Sarah).[80] DDC Judge Collyer dismissed the claims, and the plaintiffs abandoned their appeal.[81] Judge Collyer took judicial notice of the following: the Treasury Department had declared al-Awlaki a Specially Designated Global Terrorist; Umar Farouk Abdulmutallab (the "underwear bomber") said in his guilty plea that he had conspired with al-Awlaki, who also inspired Nidal Malik Hasan to attack Fort Hood. Attorney General Holder said al-Awlaki "was continuing to plot attacks when he was killed" and "it was not feasible to capture him." Judge Collyer rejected the government's invocation of the political question doctrine, whose "shifting contours and uncertain underpinnings" made it "susceptible to indiscriminate and overbroad application to claims properly before the federal courts." "The powers granted to the Executive and Congress to wage war and provide for national security does [sic] not give them *carte blanche* to deprive a U.S. citizen of his life without due process and without any judicial review." But because the deaths of Samir Khan and Abdulrahman al-Awlaki were allegedly caused by negligence, they did not raise *Bivens* claims. Judge Collyer found special factors arguing against a *Bivens* claim for the intentional killing of Anwar al-Awlaki. "In this delicate area of warmaking, national security, and foreign relations, the judiciary has an exceedingly limited role. This Court is not equipped to question, and does not make a finding concerning, Defendants' actions in dealing with AQAP generally or Anwar Al-Aulaqi in particular." "Permitting Plaintiffs to pursue a *Bivens* remedy under the circumstances of this case would impermissibly draw the Court into 'the heart of executive and military planning and deliberation.'"

Unsurprisingly, a lawsuit by Yemeni relatives of those killed by a drone strike was dismissed on the same ground.[82] DDC Judge Huvelle found that the case posed a nonjusticiable political question (while conceding that "plaintiffs may reasonably question whether this doctrine has been applied too deferentially to the executive branch"). The DC Circuit affirmed.

Brown, who wrote the opinion, also concurred separately, fearing that the doctrine of *El-Shifa* (which the court had followed) was "a wholly inadequate response to an executive decision ... implementing a standard operating procedure that will be replicated hundreds if not thousands of times." "Even the government acknowledges the 'inherent limitations' in its ability to calculate the precise effect of these strikes." It was "clear" that "the current generation of drone technology ... encourages the use of military force." True, "the Judiciary is simply not equipped to respond nimbly to a reality that is changing daily if not hourly."

> But this begs the question. If judges will not check this outsized power, then who will? ... every other branch of government seems to be passing the buck ... despite an impressive number of executive oversight bodies, there is pitifully little oversight within the Executive. Presidents are slow to appoint members to these boards, their operations are shrouded in secrecy, and it often seems the boards are more interested in protecting and excusing the actions of agencies than holding them accountable ... congressional oversight is a joke – and a bad one at that. Anyone who has watched the zeal with which politicians of one party go after the lawyers and advisers of the opposite party following a change of administration can understand why neither the military nor the intelligence agencies puts any trust in congressional oversight committees. They are too big. They complain bitterly that briefings are not sufficiently in-depth to aid them in making good decisions, but when they receive detailed information, they all too often leak like a sieve.

After quoting Sir Thomas More's adversary in Robert Bolt's *A Man for All Seasons*, declaring: "I'd cut down every law in England" to "get after the Devil," Brown concluded pessimistically: "The Court's opinion has not hacked down any laws, though we concede the spindly forest encompassing the political question doctrine provides poor shelter in this gale. But it is all a Judiciary bound by precedent and constitutional constraints may permissibly claim. It is up to others to take it from here."

Even US citizens or legal residents lost damage claims in conventional employment or civil liberties cases. Sibel Edmonds, an FBI contract linguist, was fired after complaining that translations were distorted by diplomatic considerations and accusing another linguist of blocking the translation of material involving acquaintances.[83] The DoJ IG sharply rebuked the FBI for failing to investigate Edmonds's allegations and firing her for making them. But DDC Judge Walton, "albeit with great consternation," granted Attorney General Ashcroft's motion to dismiss her wrongful dismissal and employment discrimination action on the ground of state secrets and potential disruption of domestic relations.[84] He based his decision on classified declarations he could not describe. The DC Circuit affirmed in an unpublished opinion, after hearing argument in a closed courtroom, and the Supreme Court declined to review.[85]

In late February 2002, Joseph C. Wilson IV, who had spent two decades in the diplomatic corps (much of it in Africa), was sent by the CIA to Niger at Vice President Cheney's suggestion to investigate a rumor that Saddam Hussein had bought enriched yellowcake uranium (which could be used to make a nuclear weapon).[86] Although Wilson reported that this was "highly doubtful," President Bush laid the groundwork for the Iraq war by declaring in his 2003 State of the Union message that "the British government has learned that Saddam Hussein recently sought significant quantities of uranium from Africa." On July 6 Wilson wrote in a *New York Times* op ed that he had "little choice but to conclude that some of the intelligence related to Iraq's nuclear weapons program was twisted to exaggerate the Iraq threat."[87] "[Q]uestioning the selective use of intelligence to justify the war in Iraq is neither idle sniping nor 'revisionist history.'" Five days later, DCI Tenet said Bush, Cheney, and other senior officials had not been briefed on Wilson's 2002 report because it "did not resolve whether Iraq was or was not seeking uranium from abroad." Cheney's aide, I. Lewis "Scooter" Libby, complained to NBC about Wilson's claim that the Vice President had initiated the Niger visit. Writing in the *Washington*

Post a week after Wilson's op ed, Robert Novak sought to discredit him by exposing his wife, Valerie Plame, as a covert CIA agent who had recommended Wilson for the mission. Libby was convicted of false statements, perjury, and obstruction of justice relating to his failure to cooperate with the investigation into the leak of Plame's identity. President Bush commuted his 30-month prison sentence (though not his $250,000 fine). Richard Armitage, deputy secretary of state, later admitted it was he who had told Novak about Plame.

Wilson and Plame sued Cheney, Libby, and Bush's adviser Karl Rove (later adding Armitage) for disclosing Plame's identity, abruptly ending her CIA career.[88] A year later DDC Judge Bates dismissed the case. The Westfall Act converted the action into one under the FTCA, and plaintiffs had not exhausted their administrative remedies. "[S]peaking with members of the press is within the scope of defendants' duties as high-level Executive Branch officials," even if their methods may have been "highly unsavory."[89] "Deference" to Congress "is no less proper when Congress denies rather than provides a remedy," as it did in the Privacy Act. For the court "to provide those remedies" under *Bivens* "would upset the careful balance created by the statutory scheme."

In November 2007 Scott McClellan, Bush's former press secretary, admitted his fall 2003 statement that Rove and Libby were "not involved" in the leak was "not true." Rove, Libby, Cheney, Bush, and Bush's chief of staff Andrew Card were all implicated in the lie. But the DC Circuit affirmed the dismissal.[90] Chief Judge Sentelle found that the Privacy Act offered an alternative remedy, even though the Wilsons could not obtain damages from any of these defendants because their omission had been "intentional." "We also cannot ignore that, if we were to create a *Bivens* remedy, the litigation of the allegations in the amended complaint would inevitably require judicial intrusion into matters of national security and sensitive intelligence information." Judge Rogers dissented. The Privacy Act offered the Wilsons no relief, and "the court's invocation of other special factors is based on unfounded and premature speculation about a risk of disclosure of secret or sensitive information," especially because the government had not yet invoked the state secrets doctrine. "Contrary to separation of powers ... the court effectively cedes to Congress the judiciary's defined role to decide issues arising under the Constitution."

Civil liberties claims fared no better. Three involved protests against Bush administration policies. Encountering Vice President Cheney at an outdoor mall in Colorado, Steven Howards said in a calm voice something like "I think your policies in Iraq are reprehensible."[91] Ten minutes later Secret Service agent Virgil D. Reichle Jr. handcuffed Howards and said he would be charged with assaulting Cheney. Local police filed misdemeanor harassment charges and jailed him for three hours, but the case was dismissed three weeks later when Cheney chose not to prosecute. The District Attorney said that though "the original indication was that [Howards] had pushed the Vice President," "later it looked to be that he had just spoken to him." When Howards sued Reichle, the Colorado District Judge denied a defense motion for summary judgment. The Tenth Circuit (2–1) let the case proceed.[92] Judge Seymour found that though Howards had lied about not touching Cheney, creating sufficient grounds for the arrest, it might have been retaliatory if the Secret Service agents had been "substantially motivated" by Howards's remarks. The *Los Angeles Times* warned that "a victory for Howards would needlessly encumber those charged with protecting the president – and the public." "The notion that a valid arrest becomes invalid because the arrested person was expressing himself is a radical concept and could have consequences far from the facts of this case." The Supreme Court reversed (8–0) because at the time "it was not clearly established that an arrest supported by probable cause could violate the First Amendment."[93]

Leslie Weise and Alex Young were ejected from a speech by President Bush in Denver in 2005 because they had bumper stickers criticizing the Iraq war. They sued Michael Casper and others in the president's advance team.[94] Although Colorado District Judge Daniel initially denied a motion to dismiss, he granted it after the plaintiffs conceded that the defendants had been closely supervised and could assert qualified immunity. The Tenth Circuit affirmed on the ground that "plaintiffs simply have not identified any First Amendment doctrine that prohibits the government from excluding them from an official speech on private property on the basis of their viewpoint."[95] Judge Holloway dissented. Weise "expressed an opinion on a matter of great public concern in a manner that has become very familiar in recent decades." Her expression did not "receive the protection to which it was entitled." She and her friends "were rudely, publicly, and forcefully ejected from a public meeting to which they had properly gained admission." "It is simply astounding that any member of the executive branch could have believed that our Constitution justified this egregious violation of Plaintiffs' rights." The District Court's reasoning was "severely misguided" and relied on "precedents that have no bearing on the questions." "The rights violated were clearly established because of the fundamental importance of the right of free speech on topics of public concern and because no reasonable officer could have believed that it was permissible under the Constitution to humiliate these Plaintiffs solely because one of them had legitimately exercised her right of free speech at another time and place."

Justice Ginsburg (writing for Justice Sotomayor) dissented from the denial of certiorari, complimenting Judge Holloway's "incisive dissent."[96] "I cannot see how reasonable public officials, or any staff or volunteers under their direction, could have viewed the bumper sticker as a permissible reason for depriving Weise and Young of access to the event." The Tenth Circuit claimed that "no specific authority instructs this court ... how to treat the ejection of a silent attendee from an official speech based on the attendee's protected expression outside the speech area." Justice Ginsburg retorted: "No 'specific authority' should have been needed; [f]or at least a [half]-century, this Court has made clear that" the government "may not deny a benefit to a person on a basis that infringes his constitutionally protected interests."

Michael Moss and six other demonstrators sued Secret Service agents Tim Wood and others for moving them away from President Bush during his October 2004 visit to Jacksonville, Oregon, while allowing supporters to remain closer.[97] Oregon District Judge Panner denied a motion to dismiss.[98] "It was clearly established in 2004 that viewpoint discrimination violates the First Amendment." The Ninth Circuit reversed because the plaintiffs had not adequately pleaded viewpoint discrimination, but gave them leave to amend.[99] On remand, the District Court found the pleadings adequate.[100] The Ninth Circuit affirmed.[101] "Public streets are 'the archetype of a traditional public forum.'" A "presidential advance manual" told White House staff to work with Secret Service agents to ensure that protest areas were "preferably not in view of the event site or motorcade route." Chief Judge Berzon said "there is simply *no* apparent explanation for why the Secret Service agents permitted only the pro-Bush demonstrators and not the anti-Bush protestors to remain along the president's after-dinner motorcade route" [original emphasis]. There was no qualified immunity. "It is 'beyond debate' that, particularly in a public forum, government officials may not disadvantage speakers based on their viewpoint." The panel unanimously denied a petition for rehearing and voted 2–1 against rehearing en banc. The Ninth Circuit declined to rehear it en banc.[102] Judge Berzon dismissed the dissenters' "speculative explanation" for moving the anti-Bush protesters as "non-responsive to the protestors' viewpoint discrimination claim."

> No "tape[] measure" is required ... to appreciate that demonstrators separated by more than a full square block, and two roadways, from the public official to whom and about whom they wish to direct a political message will be comparatively disadvantaged in expressing their views. Nor does one need a noise dosimeter to know that the President will be able to hear the cheers of the group left alongside his travel route but unable to hear the group restricted to an area about two square blocks away.

The dissent's explanation was "entirely hypothetical." "[A]t this stage of the case, the record is devoid of *any* explanation for the substantial difference in where the two groups of demonstrators were allowed to stand relative to the President's locations" [original emphasis].

This provoked a blistering dissent by Judge O'Scannlain (writing for seven others), who began by quoting the government's brief: "[t]he panel's decision in this case is a textbook case-study of judicial second-guessing of the on-the-spot judgment that Secret Service agents assigned to protect the President have made about security needs." O'Scannlain accused the panel of creating a "duty to act like concert ushers – ensuring with tape-measure accuracy that everyone who wants to demonstrate near the President has an equally good view of the show." "Having started with the wrong assumptions and asked the wrong question, it is no surprise that the panel arrives at the wrong answer." "It is hard to imagine how, in light of today's decision, Secret Service agents will navigate the treacherous path between the Scylla of our court's holdings in this case and the Charybdis of their duty to protect the President."

The Supreme Court unanimously reversed.[103] Justice Ginsburg assumed, without deciding, that *Bivens* extended to First Amendment violations. She quoted from O'Scannlain's dissent:

> No decision of which we are aware ... would alert Secret Service agents engaged in crowd control that they bear a First Amendment obligation "to ensure that groups with different viewpoints are at comparable locations at all times" ... Nor would the maintenance of equal access make sense in the situation the agents confronted.

Agents therefore had qualified immunity.

SUCCESSFUL CASES

Immediately after the 9/11 attack, the federal government used immigration charges to round up large numbers men believed to be Muslim or Arab, holding them indefinitely and mistreating them.[104] The DoJ OIG issued three reports documenting and criticizing the abuses. Ultimately, 13 BoP employees were disciplined, and the MDC warden retired. Ibrahim Turkmen and eight others sued Attorney General Ashcroft, FBI Director Mueller and FBI and BoP employees in EDNY in April 2002. Ehab Elmaghraby and Javaid Iqbal also sued in EDNY. Judge Gleeson assigned Magistrate Judges to manage discovery in both cases.[105] Magistrate Judge Pollak criticized the DoJ for delaying release of the BoP Office of Internal Affairs findings on BoP employees, giving it three weeks to comply. Magistrate Judge Gold ordered defendants to pay most of the cost of bringing the plaintiffs from Egypt for depositions, since "none of the plaintiffs are possessed of great material wealth" and "the primary benefit of this process is for the defendants." He expressed concern that the plaintiffs be allowed to communicate with their lawyers immediately on arriving at JFK Airport to "learn what is going on."

In January 2006 Judge Gleeson sustained the conditions of confinement claims.[106] He rejected the defense argument that "INA's comprehensive regulatory scheme constitutes a 'special factor'" counseling against a *Bivens* action.

> [U]nder the defendants' theory, the plaintiffs would not be entitled to compensation even if they were detained for twenty years before a Notice to Appear was filed, then for twenty years more after they were ordered removed, all with no telephone calls or access to a lawyer. That, of course, does not sound right … Nor am I persuaded that the events of September 11, 2001 provide any cause to relax enforcement of the rights guaranteed by our Constitution … the allegations of verbal and physical abuse alone permit the inference of an intent to punish … [S]trip searches and restraints seem excessive and arbitrary in light of the fact that plaintiffs were not accused of committing any violent crimes.

Gleeson rejected the claim of qualified immunity because it was "clearly established that conditions of confinement may not be imposed for the purpose of punishment." He authorized discovery about the involvement of Ashcroft and other high officials. He denied motions to dismiss several other claims: that the defendants deliberately interfered with the plaintiffs' religious practices; assignment of the plaintiffs to the Administrative Maximum Special Housing Unit (ADMAX SHU); denial of equal protection in conditions of confinement; communications blackout; and denial of access to counsel.

But Gleeson dismissed the detention claims based on allegations that the government used immigration charges to detain the plaintiffs longer than necessary to remove them in order to investigate terrorism. "After the September 11 attacks, our government used all available law enforcement tools to ferret out the persons responsible for those atrocities and to prevent additional acts of terrorism. We should expect nothing less." He was moved by the government's "legitimate foreign policy considerations and significant administrative burdens involved in enforcing immigration law," especially "immediately following a terrorist attack perpetrated on the United States by noncitizens, some of whom had violated the terms of their visas at the time of the attack." The plaintiffs did not have "a clearly established due process right to immediate or prompt removal." It made no difference that immigration law was a pretextual reason for detention. "[T]his approach may have been crude, but it was not so irrational or outrageous as to warrant judicial intrusion into an area in which courts have little experience and less expertise." "[R]egarding immigration matters … the Constitution assigns to the political branches all but the most minimal authority in making the delicate balancing judgments that attend all difficult constitutional questions."

When discovery resumed, Judge Gold supported CCR lawyer Rachel Meeropol, who was representing the plaintiffs, against DoJ lawyer Stephen Handler's objection that she had interrupted her client's examination by the government's psychiatrist. When Handler objected that the plaintiffs' document requests were untimely, Gold required the government to describe the duplicative effort compliance would require. "[M]aybe I'm giving [plaintiffs' lawyers] more benefit than [they] deserve. But I'm assuming that some of the difficulty [in] framing precise demands [for documents] stems from the fact that I have counsel here with clients who can't come into the United States."

He also ruled that the plaintiffs were entitled "to a representation that no member of the trial team is aware" that "somebody's listening to their conversations with their client." "I don't want them looking over their shoulder wondering whether you're getting phone calls from somebody at some National Security Agency saying, 'Guess what Reinert [Elmaghraby's lawyer] said to his client about you after you left the room the other day?'" When Handler represented that "the trial team does not have nor does it expect or intend to receive the contents of any such communications," Gold replied that any such intercepts "should not even implicitly inform the strategy of the trial lawyers." He also gave the plaintiffs more time to take depositions because they represented a class. He rejected the government demand that the plaintiffs pay the travel costs of witnesses from the District of Columbia to New York because the later locus was "much less expensive" for all and "it's certainly much easier for the government to bear the cost than for the individuals." When Handler objected to the duration of discovery, Gold noted that Handler had complained that "it's taking us months to review a huge volume of documents for privilege." Asked for a discovery deadline, Gold said "you're not going to tie me down." He granted most of Meeropol's discovery requests, overruling Handler's objections. After 11 MDC correctional officers were indicted (including four defendants in these cases), Gold refused the government's request to stay all discovery of them. One defendant was convicted. The government paid $300,000 to settle Elmaghraby's claim, without admitting liability. He reluctantly accepted it because he was ill in Egypt, unable to travel to the USA for discovery, in debt, and needed surgery for a thyroid problem aggravated in the MDC.

In the government's appeal of Iqbal's case, the Second Circuit allowed all but one of his claims to proceed.[107] Judge Newman saw "some merit in the argument in favor of a heightened pleading standard in this case" because "qualified immunity is a privilege that is essential to the ability of government officials to carry out their public roles effectively without fear of undue harassment by litigation." "But though some forms of governmental actions are permitted in emergency situations that would exceed constitutional limits in normal times ... most of the rights that the Plaintiff contends were violated do not vary with surrounding circumstances, such as the right not to be subjected to needlessly harsh conditions of confinement, the right to be free from the use of excessive force, and the right not to be subjected to ethnic or religious discrimination."

These rights also were clearly established. Iqbal adequately pleaded the involvement of all the defendants in his detention. "It is plausible to believe that senior officials of the Department of Justice would be aware of policies concerning the detention of those arrested by federal officers in the New York City Area in the aftermath of 9/11 and would know about, or condone, or otherwise have personal involvement in

465

the implementation of those policies." Iqbal had adequately pleaded his claims concerning conditions of confinement, excessive force, interference with the right to counsel, unreasonable searches, interference with religious practices, and racial and religious discrimination. But the procedural due process right concerning assignment to ADMAX SHU was not clearly established at the time.

When the government appealed, the *Washington Post* urged the Supreme Court to dismiss the case.[108] "Officials must be free to carry out their duties without fear of being hit with a lawsuit that could leave them liable for millions of dollars." The *New York Times* disagreed: "In this country, no one is supposed to be above the law." "When the government denies people their constitutional rights, high-ranking officials are often to blame. If courts are too willing to give them immunity, it will be difficult for the victims to learn how their rights were taken away or to stop such policies from continuing."

In April 2009 the Court dismissed the lawsuit for the insufficiency of its pleading.[109] Justice Kennedy wrote that:

> [T]he complaint does not show, or even intimate, that petitioners purposefully housed detainees in the ADMAX SHU due to their race, religion, or national origin. All it plausibly suggests is that the Nation's top law enforcement officers, in the aftermath of a devastating terrorist attack, sought to keep suspected terrorists in the most secure conditions available until the suspects could be cleared of terrorist activity.
>
> It should come as no surprise that a legitimate policy directing law enforcement to arrest and detain individuals because of their suspected link to the attacks would produce a disparate, incidental impact on Arab Muslims ... the arrests Mueller oversaw were likely lawful and justified by his nondiscriminatory intent to detain aliens who were illegally present in the United States and who had potential connections to those who committed terrorist acts ... discrimination is not a plausible conclusion.
>
> [W]e are impelled to give real content to the concept of qualified immunity for high-level officials who must be neither deterred nor detracted from the vigorous performance of their duties.

Justice Souter dissented (with Stevens, Ginsburg, and Breyer). Ashcroft and Mueller "made the critical concession that a supervisor's knowledge of a subordinate's unconstitutional conduct and deliberate indifference to that conduct are grounds for *Bivens* liability." The "Court's approach is most unfair to Iqbal," who "was entitled to rely on Ashcroft and Mueller's concession." "[W]hat is most remarkable about [the majority's] foray into supervisory liability is that its conclusion has no bearing on its resolution of the case." "[T]here is no principled basis for the majority's disregard of the allegations linking Ashcroft and Mueller to their subordinates' discrimination."

The *New York Times* criticized the Court's "disturbing campaign of closing the courthouse door to people who allege unfair treatment." "The Court's conservative majority is increasingly using legal technicalities to keep people from getting a fair hearing." "The mistreatment Mr. Iqbal alleges was not necessarily engineered from on high, but it might have been." By contrast, the *Washington Post* said "government officials are usually – and sensibly – shielded from being sued personally for actions they take in their official capacities." Officials could be held accountable "by public hearings, elections, prosecutions." "The Court has rightly set a high – but not insurmountable – bar" to private lawsuits.

Six months later the government paid $1.2 million to settle with five of the Turkmen plaintiffs.[110] Meeropol called it "a deterrent to the United States ever again rounding up innocent noncitizens based only on suspicion about their race and religion." But Yasser Abrahim, reluctantly accepting the deal after seven years of litigation, said "being held in that place for 249 days – $270,000 is not going to make up for that experience." Two other plaintiffs were still pursuing their claims, and on the day the settlement was agreed, CCR added five more. The Second Circuit affirmed Judge Gleeson's dismissal of the length of duration claims.[111] The defendants "had an objectively reasonable belief that the detentions were authorized." Furthermore, the plaintiffs cited no authority clearly establishing a due process right to immediate or prompt removal or an equal protection right to be free of selective enforcement of immigration laws based on national origin, race, or religion.

In his memoir, Ashcroft was unapologetic.[112] It was "worth it to detain and charge hundreds … in order to find one or more of the key men sent to America to facilitate a second wave of attacks on the United States." "If we can't bring them to trial, so be it." In fact, none of the 84 men detained in the MDC was ever charged with a terrorism offense, nor had a second wave been planned.

In January 2013 Judge Gleeson dismissed the claims against DoJ officials but upheld a claim against BoP officials, rejecting their qualified immunity defense for substantive due process violations but allowing it for claims deriving from the communications blackout.[113] In June 2015 the Second Circuit (Pooler and Wesley) upheld substantive due process, equal protection, Fourth Amendment, and conspiracy claims against DoJ and BoP officials and denied qualified immunity.[114] Judge Raggi dissented on the grounds ultimately endorsed by the Supreme Court (see below). When someone challenges "a national security policy pertaining to the detention of illegal aliens in the aftermath of terrorist attacks by aliens operating within this country, Congress, not the judiciary, is the appropriate branch to decide whether the detained aliens should be allowed to sue executive policymakers in their individual capacities for money damages."

In June 2017 the Supreme Court dismissed all the claims.[115] Justice Kennedy (writing for Justices Roberts, Alito, and Thomas) expressed a strong distaste for *Bivens* actions. "Claims against federal officials often create substantial costs, in the form of defense and indemnification." The "Legislature is in the better position to consider if 'the public interest would be better served' by imposing 'a new substantive liability.'" Congress' failure to do so was "telling." The plaintiffs had other remedies, such as injunctive relief and habeas corpus. Because the claims presented a "new context" for a *Bivens* action, the Court remanded to the Second Circuit to perform the requisite special factors analysis. Justice Breyer (writing for Justice Ginsburg) strongly endorsed *Bivens* actions. The context was not new, other remedies were not available, and special factors did not require rejection of the action.

> [T]here may well be a particular need for *Bivens* remedies when security-related Government actions are at issue. History tells us of far too many instances where the Executive or Legislative Branch took actions during time of war that, on later examination, turned out unnecessarily and unreasonably to have deprived American citizens of basic constitutional rights.

He quoted Lord Atkins: "amid the clash of arms, the laws are not silent." (Justices Sotomayor, Kagan, and Gorsuch did not participate.)

Federal courts rejected other *Bivens* claims for similar reasons. Doe, an unidentified US citizen, Army veteran, and military contractor, sued Rumsfeld and others, alleging he was detained for nine months by the military, three of them in solitary, and tortured.[116] DDC Judge Gwin denied a motion to dismiss Doe's *Bivens* claim because "Doe's American citizenship … cuts strongly in favor of affording him constitutional protections abroad and allowing judicial remedy for the constitutional violations he alleges." Gwin denied qualified immunity and found that Rumsfeld might be liable if he "crafted the policies for or authorized facially unconstitutional action." The DC Circuit reversed, finding that the involvement of the military and national security were special factors precluding a *Bivens* action.[117] "[A]llowing such an action would hinder our troops from acting decisively in our nation's interest."

Amir Meshal alleged that he was detained, interrogated, and tortured by US officials in three countries in the Horn of Africa.[118] DDC Judge Sullivan was "outraged" by Meshal's "appalling treatment." "To deny him a judicial remedy under *Bivens* raises serious concerns about the separation of powers, the role of the judiciary, and whether our courts have the power to protect our own citizens from constitutional violations by our government when those violations occur abroad." "Nevertheless, in the past two years three federal courts of appeals," including Sullivan's own, "have expressly rejected a Bivens remedy for citizens who allege they have been mistreated, and even tortured, by the United States of America in the name of intelligence gathering, national security, or military affairs." The DC Circuit affirmed the dismissal.[119] Judge Brown also found the allegations "quite troubling." But two special factors – "where the agents' actions took place during a terrorism investigation *and* those actions occurred overseas" [original emphasis] – precluded a *Bivens* claim. Although "the government had few concrete answers concerning what sensitive information might be revealed if the litigation continued" and "the actual repercussions are impossible to parse," "the unknown itself is reason for caution in areas involving national security and foreign policy." Judge Kavanaugh, concurring, was even more emphatic. He began: "The terrorists' stated goals are ... to destroy the State of Israel, to drive the United States from its posts in the Middle East, to replace more moderate Islamic leadership in nations such as Saudi Arabia, and to usher in radical Islamic control throughout the Middle East ... The war continues. No end is in sight." He concluded: "If we were to recognize a *Bivens* action in this case, U.S. officials undoubtedly would be more hesitant in investigating and interrogating suspected al-Qaeda members abroad."

Judge Pillard dissented: "Where FBI agents arbitrarily detain a United States citizen overseas and threaten him with disappearance and death during months of detention without charges, those agents' mere recitation of foreign policy and national security interests does not foreclose a constitutional damages remedy."

Abdullah al-Kidd (born Lavoni T. Kidd), a Muslim convert and former University of Idaho football star, was arrested on a material witness warrant in March 2003 while boarding a flight to Saudi Arabia, where he planned to pursue a doctorate in Islamic studies.[120]

The Magistrate Judge had issued the warrant on the basis of an FBI affidavit that "Kidd is scheduled to take a one-way, first class flight (costing approximately $5,000)." In fact, he had a round-trip coach ticket costing $1,700. He was stripped naked and kept in a small cell for hours. The government said he was essential to the prosecution of another University of Idaho student, Sami Omar al-Hussayen, who was later acquitted of computer-related terrorism charges.[121] Although Kidd was imprisoned for 16 days and then placed under restrictive court supervision for a year, he was never called to testify. (Nearly half of the 70 people held as material witnesses after 9/11 were never asked to testify.[122]) Al-Kidd sued Attorney General Gonzales and other DoJ officials in 2005. Judge Lodge denied a motion to dismiss based on sovereign immunity.[123] He found that Ashcroft had "spear-headed the post September 11, 2001 practice ... to use the material witness statute to detain individuals whom they sought to investigate" and "either knew or should have known the violations were occurring and did not act to correct the violations." "The allegations here relate to Mr. Ashcroft's actions which fall within the investigation realm of the type normally done by police" and therefore were not entitled to absolute prosecutorial immunity. The claim of qualified immunity raised factual questions.

The Ninth Circuit affirmed.[124] Judge Smith also rejected absolute immunity because the prosecutor was engaged in an investigatory function. Al-Kidd had alleged a constitutional violation by claiming "he was arrested without probable cause pursuant to a general policy, designed and implemented by Ashcroft, whose programmatic purpose was not to secure testimony, but to investigate those detained," and his "right not to be arrested as a material witness in order to be investigated or preemptively detained was clearly established in 2003." Smith distinguished the Supreme Court's recent *Iqbal* decision because Ashcroft stated that enhanced tactics, such as the use of the material witness statute, "form one part of the department's concentrated strategy to prevent terrorist attacks by taking suspected terrorists off the street," and that "[a]ggressive detention of lawbreakers and material witnesses is vital to preventing, disrupting or delaying new attacks."

However, the allegations of unconstitutional conditions of confinement failed the *Iqbal* test and were dismissed. Smith concluded by quoting William Blackstone that execution or confiscation of property was a "gross and notorious ... act of despotism ... But confinement of the person, by secretly hurrying him to gaol, where his sufferings are unknown or forgotten, is a less public, a less striking, and therefore a more dangerous engine of government." Smith commented:

> The Fourth Amendment was written and ratified, in part, to deny the government of our then-new nation such an engine of potential tyranny. And yet, if the facts alleged in al-Kidd's complaint are actually true, the government has recently exercised such a "dangerous engine of arbitrary government" against a significant number of its citizens, and given good reason for disfavored minorities ... to fear the application of such arbitrary power to them. We are confident that, in light of the experience of the American colonists with the abuses of the British Crown, the Framers of our Constitution would have disapproved of the arrest, detention, and harsh confinement of a United States citizen as a "material witness" under the circumstances, and for the immediate purpose alleged in al-Kidd's complaint. Sadly, however, even now, more than 217 years after the ratification of the Fourth amendment to the Constitution, some confidently assert that the government has the power to arrest and detain or restrict American citizens for months on end, in sometimes primitive conditions, not because there is evidence that they have committed a crime, but merely because the government wishes to investigate them for possible wrongdoing, or to prevent them from having contact with others in the outside world. We find this to be repugnant to the Constitution, and a painful reminder of some of the most ignominious chapters of our national history.

Judge Bea dissented. "Reading the minds of government officials is notoriously expensive, uncertain, and fraught with error. The very purpose of official immunity is to shield the purses of government officials from the high costs of civil damages lawsuits." "What Blackstone describes and condemns is simply not a description of this case." "Al-Kidd's confinement was neither indefinite nor in secret. He was detained on a warrant issued by a neutral magistrate. The duration of that confinement was subject to continuing judicial supervision. There is no allegation that al-Kidd was held incommunicado."

The *Washington Post* called the decision "wrong." Although the Justice Department had "misused" the material witness statute, "in 2003, no federal court had determined whether the Department had the right to use the law more freely in national security investigations." "[O]fficials should not have to fear personal lawsuits for performing their duties in good faith and in violation of no established legal precedent."

The Ninth Circuit denied review en banc.[125] Judge Smith reiterated that the case "involve[s] a warrantless search and seizure, as federal agents did not have a warrant to arrest al-Kidd for his commission of terrorism-related crimes." A reasonable official would know that the right violated was clearly established:

> [I]f anyone in the United States is presumptively on notice of cases involving federal law enforcement officers and the DOJ, it is the nation's top law enforcement officer ...
>
> However well-motivated Ashcroft's intentions may have been in creating, authorizing, supervising, and enforcing the misuse of the material witness statute in contravention of the Fourth Amendment, his motive does not presumptively immunize the policy, or himself, the nation's chief law enforcement officer, and others implementing and executing it, from complying with the rule of law.
>
> Fear of liability would not discourage aspirants to be Attorney General: the government was paying Ashcroft's attorney's fees and would indemnify any judgment.
>
> The truth is that there are legions of highly qualified attorneys who would gladly abandon almost any other position for the opportunity to serve as Attorney General of the United States. But it is critically important that whoever serves in that position be dedicated to the rule of law, and to upholding and defending the Constitution of the United States.

Justice Brandeis had warned in *Olmstead*:[126] "Experience should teach us to be most on our guard to protect liberty when the government's purposes are beneficent ... The greatest dangers to liberty lurk in insidious encroachment by men of zeal, well-meaning but without understanding."

Judge O'Scannlain wrote for seven other dissenters that the majority's conclusion "that the material witness statute itself is unconstitutional" was "preposterous." "The majority's decision to invalidate a statute passed by the First Congress and retained by every subsequent Congress should have *by itself* prompted us to rehear this case" [original emphasis]. (In fact, Smith had written: "the material witness statute ... *does not authorize arrests like the one in this case*" [original emphasis].) The decision "also distorts the bedrock Fourth Amendment principle that an official's subjective reasons for making an arrest are constitutionally irrelevant." "The majority's assertion that three sentences of dicta in a footnote to a subsequently reversed district court opinion clearly establish a right that the majority expended nearly three-thousand words describing is truly astonishing." O'Scannlain quoted the *Washington Post* editorial: "the majority has held that a former Attorney General might suffer personal liability solely for acting within the bounds of federal law. One shudders at the thought that this decision might deter the incumbent and future Attorneys General from exercising the full range of their lawful authority to protect the security of the United States." Judge Gould added his own dissent (writing for the same seven judges): "I fear that it will become more difficult to persuade a person of great talent and integrity to leave his or her current occupation in order to hold the nation's highest office."

After the Supreme Court granted certiorari, the *New York Times* said the case turned on the "sacrosanct principle" that "the government cannot arrest you without evidence that you committed a crime."[127] The justification for a material witness warrant had been "horribly twisted." The Obama administration's "forceful defense of this outrageous practice" was "disturbing." The *Los Angeles Times* said: "the Appeals Court makes a compelling argument for giving Kidd his day in court" and "the Supreme Court shouldn't stand in the way."[128] Kidd had settled lawsuits against jailors for conditions of confinement.[129] Five former Attorneys General filed an amicus for the government; 30 former federal prosecutors filed for al-Kidd. The *Washington Post* urged the Court to overturn the Ninth Circuit.[130] "[I]n 2003, there was no legal precedent on which Mr. Ashcroft could rely to determine whether the Department had the right to use the warrant more freely in national security matters." "As disconcerting as the Attorney General's actions were, he should not personally be on the hook for damages when such profound questions exist about the state of the law." The *Los Angeles Times* believed "the Court should allow Kidd's suit to proceed. But even if it doesn't, it should find a way to rule on the legality of the policy attributed to Ashcroft."[131] The *New York Times* accused the DoJ of using the material witness statute as "a ruse" to get around the refusal of Congress to give Bush authority to ignore the Non-Detention Act.[132] "The Supreme Court should say it has no power to do so."

A unanimous Supreme Court reversed.[133] Justice Scalia wrote for three others:

> [B]ecause al-Kidd concedes that individualized suspicion supported the issuance of the material-witness arrest warrant; and does not assert that his arrest would have been unconstitutional absent the alleged pretextual use of the warrant; we find no Fourth Amendment violation.
>
> Efficient and evenhanded application of the law demands that we look to whether the arrest is objectively justified rather than to the motive of the arresting officer.

Scalia also rejected a *Bivens* action. "At the time of all-Kidd's arrest, not a single judicial opinion had held that pretext could render an objectively reasonable arrest pursuant to a material-witness warrant unconstitutional." "The Court of Appeals seems to have cherry-picked the aspects of our opinions that gave colorable support to the proposition that the unconstitutionality of the action here was clearly established." "Qualified immunity gives government officials breathing room to make reasonable but mistaken judgments about open legal questions. When properly applied, it protects 'all but the plainly incompetent or those who knowingly violate the law' … Ashcroft deserves neither label." Justice Kennedy concurred (with Ginsburg, Breyer, and Sotomayor). "When faced with inconsistent legal rules in different jurisdictions, national officeholders should be given some deference for qualified immunity purposes." Concurring separately (with Breyer and Sotomayor), Justice Ginsburg questioned whether a material witness warrant was "'validly obtained' when the affidavit on which it is based fails to inform the issuing Magistrate Judge that 'the Government has no intention of using'" al-Kidd as a witness, he had cooperated with the FBI, and his parents, wife, and children were US citizens and residents. It also misrepresented that he had bought a first-class one-way ticket to Saudi Arabia when he had bought a tourist-class round-trip ticket. "[W]hat even arguably legitimate basis could there be for the harsh custodial conditions to which al-Kidd was subjected"? "[H]is ordeal is a grim reminder of the need to install safeguards against disrespect for human dignity, constraints that will control officialdom even in perilous times." Justice Sotomayor concurred separately (joined by Ginsburg and Breyer). "Whether the Fourth Amendment permits the pretextual use of a material witness warrant for preventive detention of an individual whom the Government has no intention of using at trial is, in my view, a closer question than the majority's opinion suggests."

The *New York Times* called it "a victory for … those who would shield Bush administration officials from accountability for their actions after Sept. 11, 2001." Although it was "the right decision," according to the *Washington Post*, "the government would be wrong to read it as a go-ahead to use material-witness law as a pretext for punitive detention." The *Los Angeles Times* regretted that "not for the first time, the Supreme Court has refused to hold high government officials responsible for outrageous abuses of human rights."

D Id Judge Lodge affirmed Magistrate Judge Williams's grant of summary judgment on most claims against one FBI agent and allowed al-Kidd to proceed to trial against another.[134] Judge Williams found that "the statements about the plane ticket, coupled with the omissions about al-Kidd's citizenship, family, and past cooperation, and the FBI's failure to contact him, were material to the probable cause determination regarding the impracticability of securing al-Kidd's presence at trial by subpoena." One defendant appealed, and the Ninth Circuit heard argument; but in January 2015 the parties settled.[135]

Suleiman Abdullah Salim (a Tanzanian allegedly subjected to harsh interrogation), Mohamed Ahmed Ben Soud (a Libyan interogatee) and the estate of Gul Rahman (an Afghan who died under interrogation) won a preliminary victory against James Mitchell and John "Bruce" Jessen (the psychologists who designed and conducted the earliest EITs) when ED Wash Judge Quackenbush rejected the political question doctrine and derivative sovereign immunity and found that the MCA had not stripped him of jurisdiction.[136] In a pretrial motion, the defendants perversely compared themselves to German scientists and bankers acquitted of war crimes because the poison gas and money they provided to the Nazis were only "raw materials" for the Holocaust.[137] But after Judge Quackenbush denied motions for summary judgment and to dismiss, the parties reached a secret settlement, in which the defendants continued to deny responsibility.[138]

One case offers the greatest contrast with the unsuccessful lawsuits. On March 11, 2004 terrorists bombed commuter trains in Madrid, killing 191 and wounding 1,600.[139] Spanish National Police lifted fingerprints from a bag of detonators. On March 13, the FBI could not find a match; but after receiving higher-resolution photos, its computer produced 20 candidates. The fourth-ranked prints belonged to Brandon Mayfield, an American lawyer who had converted to Islam and married an Egyptian immigrant. He was an Army veteran and had not left the USA since 1994. The identification was confirmed by a Supervisory Fingerprint Specialist, an "independent fingerprint examiner," and a senior FBI manager; but Mayfield alleged that all three knew he was Muslim. The FBI began surveillance, obtained a FISC order to bug his home and office, tapped his phones, and conducted several "sneak and peak" searches of both. On April 13 Spanish National Police (SNP) told the FBI that the prints did not belong to Mayfield, repeating this on April 21 when the FBI traveled to Spain. Nevertheless, an FBI investigator submitted an affidavit to federal court declaring a "100% positive identification" of Mayfield and saying nothing about SNP's disagreement. The affidavit noted that Mayfield attended a mosque and advertised his legal services in *Jerusalem Enterprises*, which it called the "Muslim Yellow Pages." The federal judge ordered that the fingerprints be submitted to an expert, chosen by Mayfield, who confirmed the identification. This led to further searches of Mayfield's home and office, and his arrest and imprisonment on a material witness warrant on May 6. On May 19 SNP told the FBI it had matched the fingerprint to an Algerian. The next day the FBI released Mayfield, who sued for civil rights violations. The District Court denied motions to dismiss. But though the government appealed, it settled in November 2006, paying Brandon $1.9 million and his wife and three children $25,000 each, destroying the materials obtained through FISA, returning all other materials seized, and declaring:

> The United States of America apologizes to Mr. Brandon Mayfield and his family for the suffering caused by the FBI's misidentification of Mr. Mayfield's fingerprint and the resulting investigation ... The United States acknowledges that the investigation and arrest were deeply upsetting ... and ... regrets that it mistakenly linked Mr. Mayfield to this terrorist attack.

The government insisted, however, that "This Stipulation for Compromise Settlement and Release is not, and should not be construed as, an admission of liability or fault on the part of the United States." The DoJ OIG published a highly critical report of the FBI's conduct.[140]

Other victims of the US "war on terror" won equally unambiguous victories. Abdallah Higazy, an Egyptian student legally in the USA, was arrested soon after 9/11 when an aviation radio was allegedly found in his room at the Millennium Hilton Hotel near the World Trade Center.[141] On the ninth day of a ten-day detention on a material witness warrant, Higazy confessed to owning the radio. Michael Templeton, the FBI agent conducting a polygraph examination, had called Higazy a "baby" for complaining of intense pain in his arm and inability to breathe, declaring that "a nine-year-old could tolerate his pain." Banging on the table and screaming that Higazy was a liar, Templeton threatened that if he did not cooperate, the FBI would make his brother in Egypt "live in scrutiny" and "make sure that Egyptian security gives [his] family Hell." Templeton admitted knowing that the laws governing

Egyptian security forces "are different than ours, that they are probably allowed to do things in that country where they don't advise people of their rights, they don't – yea, probably about torture, sure." About three weeks later an airline pilot returned to the Millennium Hotel to retrieve his radio, which had been found in *his* room, a floor below Higazy's. Two days later Higazy was released after 34 days in prison. He sued the hotel, its employees, and Templeton for his detention and treatment. Finding that Templeton's conduct "cannot be classified as conscience-shocking or constitutionally oppressive," SDNY Judge Buchwald granted summary judgment to all the defendants except for Higazy's false arrest claim.[142] The Second Circuit reversed and remanded, holding that the agent was not immune from a civil rights claim.[143] "On January 11, 2002, it was clearly established that the FBI could not coerce a confession and later use that confession in a criminal case." The FBI did not contest the allegation that Higazy's "confession" had been coerced. Two years later the government settled Higazy's claim for approximately $250,000.

The government also paid $2.5 million to settle the claims of the widow and children of Robert Stevens, the first victim of the 2001 anthrax attacks.[144] The litigation exposed slack rules and sloppy record-keeping at the US Army Medical Research Institute of Infectious Diseases at Fort Detrick (where the anthrax was believed to have originated). But the agreement required that much of the evidence remain secret; and the government did not admit liability.

Although local governments vigorously resisted claims for violating the civil liberties of anti-war protesters, they ultimately settled most of them. Of the nearly 2,000 arrested during demonstrations against the 2004 Republican National Convention in summer 2004, 600 sued New York City for false arrest and imprisonment and the conditions of their confinement.[145] Charges had been dropped against 90 percent – some 400 because videotapes contradicted police evidence; 157 pleaded guilty (usually so they could return home); and just 22 were convicted at trial. The city resisted the ACLU's motion to release arrest records, arguing that this could disclose police intelligence (which could be useful to terrorists) or reveal environmental conditions on Pier 57 (a former bus depot used as a holding pen), hurting its commercial development. The city argued that medical reports on police officers who complained about illness after working at Pier 57 were "unreliable" and "likely to contain misinformation." It claimed that material disclosed to the plaintiffs' counsel, including 27 police videotapes of mass arrests, was privileged and "highly personal and private." It sought to withhold its "R.N.C. Executive Summary" of June 24, 2004 because "it discusses the potential for terrorist activity" and disclosure "would chill the candor of executives of the N.Y.P.D." The city also sought to withhold depositions of three police chiefs about possible disruptions and three reports on environmental conditions at Pier 57. But it eventually settled 112 cases for $2.1 million. And after Judge Sullivan had found that more than 200 people had been illegally arrested on Fulton Street and urged settlement, the city paid about $18 million (an average of $6,400/plaintiff) to resolve the remaining 430 individual cases and a class action for about 1,200. New York Civil Liberties Union (NYCLU) Director Donna Lieberman called it the "largest protest settlement" in American history. The *New York Times* said the city had spent more than $35 million for "an expensive legal course in basic civil liberties," which taught it that "mass arrests without probable cause to arrest each individual are illegal."

Plaintiffs also won conventional tort actions against private parties. Shawn Esfahani, a naturalized citizen who had fled Iran in 1980 after Khomeini's revolution and who then owned Eastern Shore Toyota in Daphne, Alabama, won a defamation lawsuit against Bob Tyler Toyota in Pensacola, Florida, whose employees had told prospective car buyers that Esfahani was an Iraqi "terrorist" funneling money to other terrorists.[146] The jury deliberated just three hours before awarding $2.5 million compensatory damages and $5 million punitive damages. Esfahani said: "The feeling I received in the courtroom for the truth to come out was worth a lot more than any money anybody can give me." Abas Idris, a Muslim security guard, quit his job with Andrews International in February 2010 after the company failed to take seriously his complaints that fellow workers and supervisors called him a terrorist and al-Qaeda member.[147] He won $65,000 in lost wages and emotional distress and $400,000 punitive damages.

CLAIMS BY TERRORISM VICTIMS

Whereas courts tended to be obstructionist, skeptical, and begrudging toward claims by suspects or dissenters in the US "war on terror," they were sympathetic, credulous, and encouraging with respect to terrorism victims.[148] Plaintiffs initially encountered procedural obstacles. SDNY Judge Casey and the Second Circuit rejected the claims of 9/11 victims against the Saudi High Commission and Saudi princes because of lack of personal jurisdiction and sovereign immunity, offering the small consolation that "our government has other means at its disposal – sanctions, trade embargos, diplomacy, military action – to achieve its foreign policy goals and to deter (or punish) foreign sovereigns."[149] But after a different Second Circuit panel let a claim against Afghanistan proceed (discussed below) and circulated its opinion to the rest of the Circuit, effectively overruling the earlier opinion in a "mini-en-banc" procedure, the Court of Appeals directed District Judge Daniels to reopen the dismissed claims.[150] Bob Kerrey, a 9/11 Commission member, said the staff "felt strongly that they had demonstrated a close Saudi connection to the two hijackers," but the report had omitted this for political reasons.

Other courts did all they could to favor plaintiffs, often explicitly expressing sympathy. Overturning a Magistrate Judge's recommendation to grant a motion to dismiss and rejecting sovereign immunity, DDC Judge Lamberth held Iran responsible for the 1996 attack on Khobar Towers in Saudi Arabia, entering a $253 million default judgment for relatives of the 19 people killed.[151] He condemned Iran's "intentional, extreme, and outrageous" conduct, adding: "This court takes note of plaintiffs' courage and steadfastness in pursuing this litigation and their efforts to take action to deter more tragic suffering of innocent Americans at the hands of terrorists. Their efforts are to be commended."

A man sued bin Laden and the Transitional Islamic State of Afghanistan under the Anti-Terrorism Act for his wife's death, invoking the noncommercial tort exception to the Foreign Sovereign Immunities Act (FSIA).[152] Affirming the denial of a motion to dismiss, the Second Circuit wrote: "Afghanistan's proposed narrow reading of the noncommercial tort exception would not so much be a reading of the statute as it would be a decision that the terrorism exception amounts to a partial repeal by implication of the noncommercial tort exception."[153]

David Boim was shot dead in Israel's Occupied Territories by Hamas a year before it was designated a terrorist organization.[154] His parents sued Mohammed Khalil Salah, the Holy Land Foundation for Relief and Development, the American Muslim Society and the Islamic Association for Palestine, alleging they had paid Hamas for speaking engagements and distributed its propaganda. Denying a motion to dismiss, ND Ill Judge Lindberg found that plaintiffs had adequately pleaded a cause of action for aiding and abetting international terrorism under the Anti-Terrorism Act (ATA).[155] The Seventh Circuit affirmed, rejecting the defendants' First Amendment claims.[156] "[I]f we failed to impose liability on aiders and abettors who knowingly and intentionally funded acts of terrorism, we would be thwarting Congress' clearly expressed intent to cut off the flow of money to terrorists at every point along the causal chain of violence." After a Magistrate Judge ruled the Boims did not have to show the defendants aided or were aware of the attack, but only that they "were involved in an agreement to accomplish an unlawful act," Judge Lindberg entered summary judgment on liability,[157] and the jury awarded $52 million in damages, which the statute trebled.

The Seventh Circuit reversed and remanded for a new trial on liability because the Magistrate Judge made three errors: giving collateral estoppel effect to another Circuit's finding that Holy Land Foundation funded Hamas; relieving the plaintiffs of the burden of proving that the American Muslim Society and Salah caused Boim's death; and *sua sponte* granting summary judgment against the Quranic Literacy Institute.[158] "We must resist the temptation to gloss over error, admit spurious evidence and assume facts not adequately proved simply to side with the face of innocence and against the fact of terrorism."

When the Seventh Circuit granted an en banc rehearing, DoJ supported the plaintiffs. Writing for seven others, Judge Posner upheld most of the District Court's decision, adopting expansive notions of causation and mens rea.[159] Section 2333 "makes good sense as a counterterrorism measure. Damages are a less effective remedy against terrorists and their organizations than against their financial angels." "We know that Hamas kills Israeli Jews, and Boim was an Israeli citizen, Jewish, living in Israel, and therefore a natural target for Hamas." "A knowing donor to Hamas – that is, a donor who knew the aims and activities of the organization – would know that Hamas was gunning for Israelis ... that Americans are frequent visitors to and sojourners in Israel, that many U.S. citizens live in Israel ... and that donations to Hamas, by augmenting Hamas's resources, would enable Hamas to kill or wound, or try to kill, or conspire to kill more people in Israel." "[I]f you give money to an organization that you know to be engaged in terrorism, the fact that you earmark it for the organization's nonterrorist activities does not get you off the liability hook." "Hamas's social welfare activities reinforce its terrorist activities both directly by providing economic assistance to the families of killed, wounded, and captured Hamas fighters and making it more costly for them to defect ... and indirectly by enhancing Hamas's popularity among the Palestinian population and providing funds for indoctrinating schoolchildren." "Anyone who knowingly contributes to the nonviolent wing of an organization that he knows to engage in terrorism is knowingly contributing to the organization's terrorist activities." It did not matter that the alleged terrorist acts occurred long after the donation. "Terrorism campaigns often last for many decades. Think of ... Palestine, where Arab terrorism has been more or less continuous since 1920. Seed money for terrorism can sprout acts of violence long after the investment." "[A]s Hamas engaged in violence as a declared goal of the organization, anyone who provides material support to it, knowing the organization's character, is punishable ... whether or not he approves of violence." The majority dismissed with respect to Salah and remanded with respect to the Holy Land Foundation.

Judge Rovner (writing for Judge Williams) objected that the majority "have opted to 'relax[]' – I would say eliminate – the basic tort requirement that causation be proven," believing that "otherwise there would be a wrong and an injury but no remedy because the court would be unable to determine which wrongdoer inflicted the injury." Plaintiffs were not "unable" to show causation; "rather ... they did not even make an attempt." "[T]he majority simply deems [causation] a given." It reached other "remarkable" conclusions, eliminating "any need for proof that the aid was given with the intent to further Hamas's terrorist agenda." Such "judicial activism at its most plain ... poses a genuine threat to First Amendment freedoms." "[O]ne who gives money to any Hamas entity, even if it is a small donation to help buy an x-ray machine for a Hamas hospital, is liable from now until the end of time for any terrorist act that Hamas might thereafter commit against an American citizen outside of the United States." "Rather than sustain the panel's unexceptional demand that the expert [witness]'s sources be proven reliable ... the majority gives its blessing to circumventing the rules of evidence altogether." "The murder of David Boim was an unspeakably brutal and senseless act ... Terrorism is a scourge, but it is our responsibility to ask whether it presents so unique a threat as to justify the abandonment of such time-honored tort requirements as causation. Our own response to a threat can sometimes pose as much of a threat to our civil liberties and the rule of law as the threat itself."

Judge Wood also dissented in part. "[I]n our zeal to bring justice to bereaved parents" in this "heart-breaking" case, "we must not lose sight of the need to prove liability on the facts that are presented to the court. Assumptions and generalizations are no substitute for proof." "The majority is saying that even if an independent day care center receives $1 from organization H known to be affiliated with Hamas, not only the day care center but also anyone who gave to H is liable for all acts of terrorism by Hamas operatives from that time forward against any and all Americans who are outside the United States. That is a proposition of frightening, and I believe unwise, breadth."

The family of Aharon Ellis, an American killed by Palestinian gunmen in Israel in 2002, sued the Palestine Liberation Organization (PLO).[160] SDNY Judge Marrero held that neither it nor the Palestinian Authority was a "state" within the meaning of FSIA and there were no nonjusticiable political questions. "Defendants' claim of statehood for Palestine reduces to an intense enduring aspiration that, however devoutly wished, apparently still seems more boosted by impassioned protestations and pretensions than affirmed by the juridically recognized ensigns of a sovereign nation." Marrero noted "the incongruity and conflict with statutory intent" of the defendants' argument that the case involved nonjusticiable political questions.

> Plaintiffs' claims allege unprovoked savagery that encompasses even murder. Defendants' view essentially would ask the Court to hold that, even if the facts were to verify the accusations here, a wanton massacre of innocents would still be "nonjusticiable." This proposition cuts against the grain of what compels the business of the courts. It would rub every syllable of justice out of the concept of justiciability and do equal violence to the ATA. In American jurisprudence, the instances in which atrocities committed against United States nationals are deemed beyond the justiciable reach of the law and in which our courts are thus utterly unable to perform their ordained functions, are rare indeed … The jurisdictional force of the ATA aims precisely to further narrow the scant exceptions, so as to extend the law to the vindication of rights and reparation of international injuries that otherwise would not be rectifiable in our courts.

After entering a default judgment on liability, Judge Marrero adopted the Magistrate Judge's recommendations for treble damages totaling $192,740,660.13.

When PLO Chairman Mahmoud Abbas sought guidance from Secretary of State Condoleezza Rice, she "encourage[d]" him, "as I would any government, to respond to U.S. legal proceedings in good faith and a timely manner." Judge Marrero agreed to set aside the judgment and reopen the case because the Palestine Authority (PA)'s new leadership had retained new counsel and decided to defend. "Given the transcendental [*sic*] scope" of the political issues at stake, "a judgment concerning such questions, involving liability assessed in hundreds of millions of dollars, ordinarily should not be decided by default." But he required the PLO to post bond for the entire judgment. When its lawyers offered $15 million, claiming their clients were "teetering on the verge of bankruptcy," the plaintiffs' lawyer retorted that "hundreds of millions of dollars" had been concealed by Yasser Arafat (who died in 2004). The court ordered the defendants to post $20 million immediately and another $5 million a month up to a total of $120 million. The defendants had reached confidential settlements after two previous default judgments for more than $100 million.

A SDNY jury awarded damages of $218.5 million (tripled to $655.5 million) against the same defendants to the estates of four people killed and to three dozen injured in six terrorist attacks in 2002–04.[161] The Second Circuit reversed for lack of personal jurisdiction.[162] (DDC judges had dismissed three similar claims on the same ground.[163]) "The overwhelming evidence shows that the defendants are 'at home' in Palestine, where they govern." "The terror machine gun attacks and suicide bombings that triggered this suit and victimized these plaintiffs were unquestionably horrific. But the federal courts cannot exercise jurisdiction in a civil case beyond the limits prescribed by the due process clause of the Constitution."

The estate and family of Yaron and Efrat Ungar sued the PA under the ATA for murdering them in 1996. The D RI Court denied in part the motion to dismiss, rejecting a claim of nonjusticiability, and entered a default judgment for $116,409,123.[164] The First Circuit affirmed.[165] Judge Selya found that, given the passage of the ATA, "the district court's decision denying immunity did not impede the constitutional prerogatives of the political branches over foreign policy." "[T]he defendants' assertion that the district court made a political statement in calibrating the size of the award ... is wholly unsupported." But the Court of Appeals overturned the District Court's categorical refusal to allow defendants to seek to reopen the case.[166] Defendants "blame political extremism within the PLO and the PA for their earlier decision to default" and "insist they have had a good-faith change of heart." Before the District Court reconsidered the motion to reopen, the Magistrate Judge ruled that the plaintiffs could seek to execute on Israeli tax transfers to the PA.[167]

Layne Morris and Tabitha Speer sued Ahmed Said Khadr, alleging that his son Omar (a Guantánamo detainee) had thrown a hand grenade in Afghanistan, blinding Morris and killing Speer's husband, Chris.[168] (I discuss Omar Khadr's military commission in Chapter 4.) D Utah Judge Cassell found subject matter jurisdiction under the ATA, even though that excluded an "act of war," defined as "armed conflict between military forces of any origin."

> [E]ven if al-Qaeda established "military" camps, it does not automatically follow that graduates of those camps are operating as a "military force" when they use skills learned there. A person might receive what can legitimately be called "military" training but employ it in a terroristic fashion to achieve terroristic ends ... Al-Qaeda is not a "nation"; the people who fight in its behalf thus cannot be "armed forces" or the "military." It is, instead, a "group" that systematically uses violent and destructive acts in its attempts to coerce the United States into acceding to its demands ... The court refuses to be al-Qaeda's advocate and force plaintiffs to prove that, in fact, al-Qaeda's members are not "military forces of any origin" ... the burden should fall on Mr. Khadr to prove that.

The court also found it had personal jurisdiction over Khadr.

> In terrorism cases, courts have employed the "effects doctrine" to establish the requisite minimum contacts for personal jurisdiction. Under this doctrine, "jurisdiction may attach if the defendant's conduct is aimed at or has an effect in the forum." Terrorism cases provide textbook examples of "unabashedly malignant actions" aimed at the United States whose effects are "directed at [and] felt" here ... Two families in this country no doubt continue to feel these horrific effects every day. And plaintiffs have made a prima facie showing that Mr. Khadr actively participated in and helped plan al Qaeda's terrorist agenda – so much so, in fact, that he convinced his son to risk his life and attack American soldiers.

In a default judgment (with service of process by publication), the court awarded Speer $31.5 million and Morris $2.7 million, both to be trebled. Judge Cassell apologized for the fact that the ATA did not allow him to award the other $2.5 million claimed by Morris's family. "To avoid any confusion, the court in no way means to minimize the harms suffered by Mr. Morris's family," whom he encouraged to sue. Expecting that Omar might win a Can$20 million lawsuit against the Canadian government for wrongful imprisonment, the plaintiffs sued him for $44.7 million in a Utah state court, winning a default judgment for treble damages of $134.2 million.[169] (Canada later settled with Omar for Can$10.5 million, which these plaintiffs sought to attach.)

Technology companies, including Google, Twitter, and Facebook, were sued by victims and survivors for disseminating communications by terrorists involved in attacks in Orlando (Florida), Paris, and Jordan.[170] A judge dismissed the Jordanian case on the ground that Twitter was protected by the Communications Decency Act 1996. EDNY Judge Garaufis dismissed two suits against Facebook.

The Arab Bank was sued by 297 plaintiffs in EDNY under the ATA for deaths and injuries in 24 Hamas attacks in 2001–04. They claimed it had allowed Osama Hamdan, a Hamas spokesman, to have an account.[171] Magistrate Judge Pohorelsky held that "foreign bank secrecy concerns must yield to United States interests in combating terrorism, as expressed in the Anti-Terrorism Act." Judge Gershon criticized Arab Bank's "grudging production" of documents. "The years of delay caused by defendant's refusals weigh against a finding of good faith … Defendant's conduct places it at a location approaching willfulness on the 'continuum of fault.'"

As a result, Gershon let the jury infer that the bank provided financial services to designated terrorist organizations and individuals and processed payments to terrorists for the Saudi Committee, and she restricted the bank's ability to rebut. The Second Circuit declined to review. When the Arab Bank appealed to the Supreme Court, it sought advice from the administration, which split: DoS supported the bank; tax and Treasury officials supported the plaintiffs; and DoJ refused to intervene against US victims of terrorist attacks. The Supreme Court declined to hear the appeal. After two days of deliberation, a jury held the Arab Bank liable. The bank denounced the District Court's "improper sanction," which produced a "show trial." A separate trial would determine damages, which could reach $1 billion when trebled.

In lawsuits filed by East African embassy bombing victims, DDC Judge Bates awarded $955 million against Iran (which defaulted) and Sudan (which stopped participating after losing its jurisdictional challenge).[172] He said: "damages awards cannot fully compensate people whose lives have been torn apart; instead, they offer only a helping hand. But that is the very least that these plaintiffs are owed." He awarded $622 million to other victims suing the same defendants, adding: "The court commends the dedicated, creative, and courageous resolve of all the plaintiffs – and their conscientious attorneys – in the cases brought against the terrorists … They have helped to ensure that terrorism, and its support by defendants, will not ultimately succeed in achieving its long-term goals."

In other lawsuits Judge Bates awarded $8.4 billion to victims of the 1982 and 1984 Beirut embassy bombings, and Judge Lamberth awarded $453 million to victims of the 1983 bombing of the US Marine barracks in Beirut, writing: "Iran must be punished to the fullest extent legally possible for the bombing in Beirut. This horrific act harmed countless individuals and their families, a number of who [sic] receive awards in this lawsuit." DDC judges awarded more than $20 billion against Iran between 2008 and 2014.

Because almost all these judgments occurred by default, plaintiffs faced significant obstacles in executing them; but judges were very sympathetic to their efforts. Eighteen groups of creditors (encompassing more than a thousand individuals) sought to execute billions of dollars of judgments against the Islamic Republic of Iran.[173] SDNY Judge Forrest denied motions by UBAE, Clearstream Banking, and Bank Markazi to prevent Citibank from using $2 billion of their assets to satisfy the judgments, rejecting arguments that this raised questions of foreign relations or political questions. "'Enough is enough' is the reductionist version of plaintiffs' response to Clearstream's motion to vacate. This Court agrees." Forrest granted summary judgment to the plaintiffs for $1.75 billion in assets.

> [I]n opposition to this motion, defendants have filed the proverbial kitchen sink with arguments. As the Court has reviewed the thousands of pages of briefing on and in support of these motions, building in a crescendo to the instant motion, it cannot help but be reminded of the grand finale in a Fourth of July fireworks show – all arguments thrown in and set off at once ... the basic question and the dispositive legal principles do not require descent into those waters – or into that sink, to mix metaphors.

The Second Circuit affirmed.[174]

In February 2012 President Obama issued EO 13,599 blocking Bank Markazi assets. In August Congress passed the Iran Threat Reduction and Syria Human Rights Act (ITRSHRA), declaring the assets subject to execution. Judge Forrest awarded the office building at 650 Fifth Avenue, worth more than $500 million, to plaintiffs who had sued Iran, finding that the companies owning it "are" the government of Iran under federal law.[175] In April 2016 the Supreme Court (6–2) affirmed, holding that the ITRSHRA did not violate separation of powers.[176] The law "is an exercise of congressional authority regarding foreign affairs, a domain in which the controlling role of the political branches is both necessary and proper." On remand, a SDNY jury quickly decided that the Alavi Foundation's share of the building (now worth $1 billion), as well as its other US properties, could be seized to satisfy the judgment.[177] The Supreme Court has agreed to review a Seventh Circuit decision holding that nine U.S. plaintiffs could not execute a $71.5 million District Court judgment for a 1997 suicide bombing by attaching thousands of Persepolis tablets (which the Iranian government had loaned to the University of Chicago) because Iran had not been using the tablets for commercial purposes.[178]

Courts also were very sympathetic to 9/11 victims' claims against *domestic* defendants. More than 9,000 rescue and cleanup workers at the World Trade Center sued 90 government agencies and private companies for illnesses and injuries.[179] SDNY Judge Hellerstein approved a $500 million settlement of the first 93 claims, capping legal fees at 15 percent.[180] The World Trade Center Captive Insurance Company, given $1.1 billion by the Federal Emergency Management Agency, disbursed $712.5 million (later supplemented by $47 million from the Port Authority) in individual payments ranging from $3,500 to more than $1.8 million. Finding earlier settlements insufficient, Hellerstein took "judicial control," declaring: "I will not preside over a settlement based on fear and ignorance." "The niceties of federal practice have to go second to the compelling needs of people to get a recovery that is almost, almost, almost within their grasp." He disallowed some expenses claimed by plaintiffs' lawyers so as to leave more money for the plaintiffs. The family of Mark Bavis, a UA175 passenger, insisted on a public trial, refusing United's offer to admit liability and try only damages.[181] But though relatives of other victims were supportive, the Bavis family ultimately settled. Michael Bavis, Mark's twin brother, said the public filing "tells an important story as to why this happened." Cantor Fitzgerald, which lost 658 of its nearly 1,000 New York employees, settled its $1.1 billion claim for $135 million (exclusively for business and property losses).[182]

COMPENSATION FUNDS

Congress also created the September 11th Victim Compensation Fund, which paid more than $7 billion to 97 percent of the attack's victims, an average of $1.8 million each. It also distributed 559 grants totaling $528 million to individuals and businesses affected by the attack.

A House committee then voted to appropriate another $5.1 billion for the first decade of a fund to compensate up to 60,000 people (other than first responders) living or working near ground zero and to reopen the September 11th Victim Compensation Fund, raising the cap to $8.4 billion.[183] The *New York Times* wrote: "the badly needed legislation ... is a chance to make good on [the] vow" to "never forget the victims of Sept. 11." The *Times* assailed Republican obstructionism as "feckless and cruel," a "shameful bout of election-year politicking," and "an insult, especially to the tens of thousands of ordinary citizens who pitched in selflessly for weeks in the cleanup." After the House passed the James Zadroga 9/11 Health and Compensation Act, the *Times* asked angrily: "Is it too much to ask Senate Republicans to show bipartisanship and responsibility?" When they balked, the *Times* denounced their "callous move." Supported by Rudy Giuliani, the Republican former NYC mayor, a reduced version passed ($1.8 billion for medical monitoring and treatment and $2.5 billion to reopen the 9/11 Fund for five years). Sen. Coburn (R-Ok) said "every American recognizes the heroism of the 9/11 first responders." Sen. McConnell (Republican minority leader) said "there was never any doubt about supporting the first responders."

As mandated by the Zadroga law, Dr. John Howard, Director of the National Institute of Occupational Safety and Health, concluded from a meta-analysis of 18 published studies that there was little evidence that exposure to contaminants at the World Trade Center caused cancer. Nevertheless, the new fund's advisory committee concluded there was justification for covering 14 broad categories of cancer. Because etiology was indeterminate, *any* cancer sufferer who had been exposed could claim. Dr. Howard declared: "Requiring evidence of positive associations from studies of 9/11-exposed populations exclusively does not serve the best interests of the patients." Dr. Alfred I. Neugut, an oncologist and professor of epidemiology at Columbia's Mailman School of Public Health, said the "difficult decision" was "primarily motivated by concern for a sympathetic population. The scientific evidence is currently weak." The *New York Times* praised this "reasonable and humane step." Even though some experts found the causal evidence "weak ... we have a moral obligation to ensure that those harmed by exposure at ground zero get the medical and financial help they need." (Of course, the *Times* had just admitted it could not be known whether cancer sufferers had been "harmed by exposure at ground zero.") Six months after the decision a NYC Health Department study of 55,700 people – the largest to date – found no increase in the cancer rate among those exposed at ground zero compared with the general population and no greater incidence among those with more intense exposure. Still, the NYC Health Commissioner agreed with Dr. Howard. "You don't want to wait 20 to 30 years to get a definitive answer." Although the fund required volunteers to produce orders, instructions, or confirmation of tasks performed at Ground Zero, or medical records created when they were in the exposure zone, the fund administrator acknowledged it was hard for applicants to recreate records and would assume they were honest. (In fact, there were only a few documented incidents of fraud.)

Little more than a week after the April 15, 2013 Boston Marathon bombing, the Boston mayor and Massachusetts governor had raised more than $10 million for One Fund Boston to compensate victims, whose friends and relatives had created dozens of smaller funds.[184] By the end of June, One Fund Boston had $60.9 million and had compensated 232 people, paying nearly $2.2 million each to two double amputees and the families of the four killed, nearly $1.2 million each to 14 people who lost one limb, nearly $1 million each to ten people who spent at least 32 nights in hospital, $125,000 each to 18 people hospitalized for two nights, and $8,000 each to 143 people treated but not admitted to hospital.[185] As with World Trade Center victims, all disbursements were tax-free, insurance payments were disregarded, and beneficiaries still could sue and accept payments from other funds. The Fund subsequently received another $20 million.[186]

It is illuminating to compare these judgments and compensation fund disbursements with payments under the Foreign Claims Act for civilian casualties in the "war on terror."[187] Unlike compensation fund payments, collateral sources were deducted; unlike tort awards, there were no punitive damages. A claim was not payable if it related to combat or was "not in the best interest of the United States." Between fall 2001 and spring 2007 the USA distributed about $32 million in Afghanistan and Iraq. In 2005–06 it denied 404 of 490 death claims, paying an average of just $4,200 for the 86 it granted; it seemed more sympathetic to property damage claims. DoD also paid nominal "solatia" for combat-related injuries: approximately $30 million in 2003–04, just $2.7 million in Afghanistan in 2011–13. After the Haditha massacre (one of the worst atrocities), the USA paid just $38,000 for all 24 men, women and children killed; it paid nothing in Mahmudiya, where soldiers raped a young girl and burned her body and killed her family.[188] (I discuss both incidents in Chapter 3.) In 2005–06 it gave solatia to only 70 of 233 claims excluded by Foreign Claims Commissions as combat-related. Army guidelines in Helmand in 2010 anticipated giving $1,500–2,500 for the death of a child or adult. When a drone killed 15–23 Afghan civilians and injured many others, the USA paid $2,900 to each one injured and $4,800 for each death.[189] (The USA paid nothing for hundreds of drone deaths in Pakistan, presumably because it never acknowledged these covert CIA operations.)

These paltry amounts were justified by noting that the average Afghan annual income was well under $1,000. But political pressures could greatly inflate payments. The USA paid $916,000 following the massacre by Sgt. Robert Bales in Kandahar, Afghanistan: $50,000 for each of 17 deaths and $11,000 for each of the six wounded.[190] (I also discuss this in Chapter 4.) After CIA contractor Raymond Davis shot to death two men in Pakistan who allegedly had tried to rob him, the USA paid *diyya*[191] of $1.2 million to the family of each in order to extricate Davis from the country.[192] (I discuss this in the companion volume *Law's Wars*.) And in an earlier incident, the USA made a "voluntary humanitarian payment" of $4.5 million to the families of the three killed and 27 injured by its mistaken bombing of the Chinese embassy in Belgrade in 1999, and $28 million to China for property damage.[193]

CONCLUSION

The "war on terror" profoundly distorted American tort law. Even the crude win/loss figures reveal this. Victims of the "war" (US citizens as well as aliens) lost almost every case challenging the federal executive: detention of immigrants after 9/11; Guantánamo Bay detainees (even after courts granted them habeas corpus); Abu Ghraib (even though Bush and Rumsfeld expressed regret and courts-martial convicted some soldiers); secret prisons (even though Obama closed them and less culpable nations like Poland and Lithuania paid detainees); torture and harsh interrogation (even though these were later prohibited and shown to be ineffective); rendition (even victims of unambiguous mistakes, like Arar and el-Masri, and even though much less culpable nations like Canada and Sweden paid compensation); targeted killing (even of US citizens killed in error); and denials of civil liberties and loss of employment. Victims prevailed only against foot soldiers (like those who took the rap for Abu Ghraib), cities (which could not invoke the doctrines protecting the federal executive, discussed below), and private individuals and companies. The only

Table 6.1 Judges' Rulings on "War on Terror" Victims' Civil Damages Claims, by Appointing President's Party

Appointing President	# Pro- Plaintiff	%	# Anti- Plaintiff	%	Total Rulings
Democrat	63	58	46	42	109
Republican	23	16	118	84	141
Total	86	34	164	66	250

Chi-square = 46.89, p<.001

exceptions were two gross miscarriages of justice (Mayfield and Higazy), which were attributed to careless errors by low-level federal officials (in addition, Mayfield was a US citizen).

The distortion is highlighted by contrasting two categories of judges: those favoring the government (whom I call deferential) and those favoring victims (whom I call rights-oriented). Once again, using the party of the nominating president as a proxy for the judge's political orientation, I found a highly significant statistical correlation between judges' political orientations and their votes on "war-on-terror" victims' claims (see Table 6.1).[194]

The breadth of their disagreements – about everything from fundamental premises to procedural conventions (e.g., the aversion to interlocutory appeals) – reveals how profoundly the law was politicized. Deferential judges deployed apocalyptic language: an "era is ending" through "judicial ukase"; this will "weaken America" (Wilkinson). Judges extended the decades-long conservative campaign against tort law (funded by manufacturers and doctors[195]) to protect the federal executive from the recently concocted threat of "lawfare": the "rising tide of litigation" concerning warfare (Wilkinson). Judges argued that only Congress could create damages claims (denying the basic premise of *Bivens*). That "a factor 'counsels' hesitation" became the "remarkably low" threshold for rejecting a *Bivens* action, which judges justified because such a claim "unavoidably influences government policy, probes government secrets, invades government interests, enmeshes government lawyers, and thereby elicits government funds for settlement" (Jacobs). Allowing these cases to proceed would "invite enemies to use our own federal courts to obstruct the Armed Forces' ability to act decisively and without hesitation in defense of our liberty and national interests" and erode "military discipline and morale" (Hogan). Judges rejected *Bivens* claims because the rights asserted were not "clearly established" at the time of their alleged violation: denial of a prompt probable cause hearing following detention in a war zone; Padilla's years of solitary confinement; freedom from retaliatory arrest for exercising First Amendment rights; demonstrators' access to the president without viewpoint discrimination; freedom from detention on the pretext of immigration enforcement in order to investigate terrorism. (This approach allowed the government to argue that a right was not "clearly established" if a single federal judge refused to recognize it.) Judges rejected a *Bivens* action by finding "alternative remedies," such as INA review (although Arar was seeking to *leave* the USA, not stay), remedial legislation, military justice, Congressional investigations, independent commissions, or *ex gratia* payments (even though none of these afforded redress). Sometimes the arguments were mutually contradictory: the Privacy Act offered a remedy even though it was unavailable in this case (Sentelle); failure of the Privacy Act to offer a remedy was a reason for rejecting a *Bivens* action (Bates).

Judicial hostility to these actions revealed other biases. "Our legal system was never designed to provide a remedy" for the "inevitable tragedies" of war, especially when those seeking redress were "terrorists" who "cunningly morph into their surroundings" (Leon). (These tragedies were hardly "inevitable.") The "traditional rationales for tort law ... are singularly out of place in combat situations, where risk-taking is the rule." Lawsuits would "surely hamper military flexibility and cost-effectiveness" (Silberman). Tort liability could "lead to excessive risk-aversiveness" (Wilkinson). Contractor liability would "affect the availability and costs of using contract workers" and "undermine the flexibility that military necessity requires in determining the methods for gathering intelligence" (Niemeyer). (Conservatives who otherwise insisted that government regulation demonstrate its cost-effectiveness refused to require that an executive waging a "war on terror" consider the costs of its actions, including accident costs.) Deferential judges minimized the harms inflicted: mass detention after 9/11 had only an "incidental impact on Arab Muslims," justified by their "potential connections to those who committed terrorist acts." ("Potential connections"! None was found.) "Discrimination is not a plausible conclusion" (Kennedy). (But *only* Arab and Muslim immigrants were detained, and none was convicted of terrorism.)

Deferential judges insisted that separation of powers demanded that the executive have unrestrained power to deploy the military. "[M]ilitary affairs, foreign relations, and national security are constitutionally committed to the political branches of our government" (Hogan). Civil actions would "invade theatres of armed conflict heretofore the province of those branches of government constitutionally charged with safeguarding the nation's most vital interests" (Wilkinson). A tort suit was "the very worst forum" to decide "how intelligence is best obtained." Judges "have neither the experience nor the background to adequately and competently define and adjudge the rights of an individual vis-à-vis the needs of officials acting to defend the sovereign interests of the United States." (Adjudicating "the rights of an individual" is precisely what courts are mandated to do.) Courts cannot consider "the propriety of specific interrogation techniques and detention practices employed by the military while prosecuting wars" (Hogan). (But some techniques and practices are prohibited by statutes, treaties, and the Constitution.) Where the executive and legislature "exercise their military responsibilities in concert ... the need to hesitate before using *Bivens* actions to stake out a role for the judicial branch seems clear" (Wilkinson). "[T]he complicated multilateral negotiations concerning efforts to halt international terrorism" (by mistakenly rendering Arar to torture in Syria) are "most appropriately reserved to the Executive and Legislative branches" (Trager). The discretion essential to the executive was extended to contractors "fully integrated" into the military. Although these conservative judges routinely invoked "states' rights" to constrain the federal government, now they embraced the "strong public policy interest" in "insulat[ing] the battlefield from the unjustified exertion of power by the courts of the 51 states." The federal government had an "*obvious*" interest in preempting state law, whereas state interests were "*de minimis*" (Silberman). Although the MCA might dispense "rough justice," that was the prerogative of Congress.

Deferential judges enthusiastically embraced sovereign immunity, without which officials would be improperly swayed by fear of litigation and liability (even though the government defended and indemnified them). Judges worried that "a person of great talent and integrity" might decline to serve as Attorney General (Kennedy). (There was no evidence for that proposition; and not all would call Ashcroft or Gonzales "a person of great talent and integrity.") Judges claimed indemnification undermined tort law's deterrent effect (while arguing inconsistently that risk aversion was inappropriate in a war context) (Jacobs).

As cheerleader, the *Washington Post* claimed that officials could be held accountable by "public hearings, elections, prosecutions" – knowing full well these were empty promises.

Deferential judges expressed fear of "embarrassment of our government abroad" from "multifarious pronouncements by various departments" (Trager). (It was the government's actions that had embarrassed it.) Trial of Arar's claims could "undermine" the "effective functioning of U.S. foreign policy" by "prob[ing] deeply into the inner workings of the national security apparatus of at least three foreign countries" (Cabranes). (Canada courageously exposed and condemned the errors of its own national security apparatus. Did Syria merit such solicitude?) The USA might be embarrassed by an investigation into Syria's assurances that it would not torture Arar (Jacobs). "A trial on the merits would be an international spectacle with Padilla, a convicted terrorist, summoning America's present and former leaders to a federal courthouse" (Gergel).

Deferential judges used the state secrets doctrine prophylactically to abort civil actions at their earliest stages because even identifying secret documents, witnesses or facts "could be compromising." "[W]e are precluded from explaining precisely which matters the privilege covers lest we jeopardize the secrets we are bound to protect" (Fisher; see also Walton). It was better to bar the courthouse door at the outset rather than risk having to close it during trial (even the initial hearing on the state secrets issue sometimes was closed). The "sensitivity" of classified material was "too obvious to call for enlarged discussion" (Jacobs). (But it was generally acknowledged – including by the Obama administration – that far too much information is needlessly classified.) Mere "private" or "personal" interests must yield to "national" and "collective" interests (Ellis and Fourth Circuit) (a striking inversion of the usual conservative hierarchy of values).

By contrast, rights-oriented judges emphasized the responsibilities of the judiciary rather than the prerogatives of the executive or legislature, rejected "senseless" fictions (that Arar had never been "present" in the USA) and pretextual arguments, rebuked government delay and stonewalling, invoked *conservative* arguments against judicial activism and the universal preference for avoiding constitutional questions and conflicts between co-equal branches (by confining the state secrets doctrine to questions of the admissibility of evidence, which were peculiarly within the competence of judges), and expressed concern and regret when they could not protect victims. It was perverse to apply the ATS to torture by foreign officials but not that by Americans (Edwards) or confer greater immunity on contractors than on the military (Garland), especially since actions against contractors did not raise political questions (Lee). States had significant interests in ensuring that domiciled corporations obeyed the law (Garland).

Conservative judges sought to apply RFRA (Brown). The alternative remedies precluding a *Bivens* action were chimerical: the INA was useless to Arar when he received his deportation order just moments before being sent to Syria; the DoJ OIG's scathing reports (on immigrant detention and the mistreatment of Mayfield) offered no redress. That a *Bivens* action could influence policy was an argument in its favor, not against it. Judges found it plausible that high officials (like Ashcroft and Rumsfeld) directed their subordinates' actions, especially when national security seemed threatened. Judges found the alleged abuse of material witness warrants "a painful reminder of some of the most ignominious chapters of our national history."

Rights-oriented judges insisted on their responsibility under the Supreme Court's foundational decision in *Marbury* v. *Madison* "to say what the law is." There was "an enormous difference between being deferential and being supine in the face of governmental conduct" (Parker). "[T]he judiciary has a particular responsibility to assure the vindication of constitutional interests" (Sack quoting Jackson). Judges resisted assertions of a "state of exception." "[M]atters are not beyond the reach of the judiciary simply because they touch upon war or foreign affairs." Even the law of war "places some limits on the wanton and malicious treatment of human lives" (Messitte). Gleeson was not "persuaded that the events of September 11, 2001 provide any cause to relax enforcement of the rights guaranteed by our Constitution." Rights "do not vary with surrounding circumstances" (Newman; Sack). Al-Kidd's "ordeal is a grim reminder of the need to install safeguards against disrespect for human dignity, constraints that will control officialdom even in perilous times" (Ginsburg). "The strength of our system of constitutional rights derives from the steadfast protection of those rights in both normal and unusual times." The limits on executive and legislative power were "fixed by the same Constitution" in "both wartime and peacetime" (Parker). Indeed, "in times of national stress and turmoil" the rule of law is "everything." Rights-oriented judges invoked illustrious predecessors: "my apprehensions about the security of our form of government are about equally aroused by those who refuse to recognize the dangers of Communism and those who will not see danger in anything else" (Sack, quoting Jackson); "the greatest dangers to liberty lurk in insidious encroachment by men of zeal, well-meaning but without understanding" (Smith, quoting Brandeis).

These judges were unmoved by fear of embarrassing the government: "it is the misconduct alleged and not the litigation surrounding that misconduct that creates the embarrassment" (Lee). They were skeptical of immunity, which "undermines a core belief of American jurisprudence that individuals must be held accountable for their wrongful acts." Rather than "interrupt[ing] or interfer[ing] with the prosecution of a war," a suit against contractors actually "advances federal interests ... because the threat of tort liability creates incentives for government contractors ... to comply with their contractual obligations" (Lee). There should be no immunity because "no federal interest implicates the torture and abuse of detainees."

The deep divisions between these two categories of judges produced unusual numbers of reversals, split panels, and en banc rehearings, in the course of which judges harshly criticized their colleagues. The majority's reasoning was "regrettably threadbare" and "demonstrably flawed" (Niemeyer). The dissent made "contradictory assertions and misstatements of the law" and failed to "grapple with complicated legal questions." It abused "the freedom enjoyed by the writer of a dissenting opinion" in pursuit of "emotive force" and "disfigure[d] the judicial function to satisfy personal indignation" (Cabranes). Dissenters indulged in "emotional" and "overwrought" language (Jacobs). The majority "unnecessarily makes dubious law," creating "artificial" distinctions in its "apparent determination to go to whatever lengths necessary" to reject a *Bivens* action (Sack). The majority opinion was a "miscarriage of justice" (Parker). The majority's "simplistic framework" engaged in "hyperbolic and speculative assessment of the national security implications" and "disfigure[d] fundamental constitutional principles" (Pooler). The majority displayed "utter subservience to the executive branch ... distortion of *Bivens* doctrine ... unrealistic pleading standards ... misunderstanding of the TVPA and of § 1983" and "persistent choice of broad dicta where narrow analysis would have sufficed." Its "unwavering willfulness" represented "extraordinary judicial activism." It "goes seriously astray" and was "on all counts, utterly wrong" (Calabresi). The lower court was "severely misguided" and relied on precedents that "have no bearing on the questions" (Holloway). "Having started with the wrong assumptions and asked the wrong

Table 6.2 Judges' Rulings on Civil Damages Claims by "War on Terror" Victims and Terrorism Victims

	# Pro-Plaintiff	%	# Anti-Plaintiff	%	Total Rulings
"War on Terror" Victims	86	34	164	66	250
Terrorism Victims	35	65	19	35	54
Total	121	43	183	57	304

Chi-square = 17.15, p<.001

question, it is no surprise that the panel arrives at the wrong answer." "One shudders" at the panel's "preposterous" and "truly astonishing" decision, which "distorts the bedrock Fourth Amendment principle that an official's subjective reasons for making an arrest are constitutionally irrelevant" (O'Scannlain). "[T]here is no principled basis for the majority's disregard of the allegations linking Ashcroft and Mueller to their subordinates' discrimination" (Souter). The majority's "remarkable" conclusions were "judicial activism at its most plain," "a genuine threat to First Amendment freedoms." The opinion "gives its blessing to circumventing the rules of evidence altogether" and "eliminate[s] … the basic tort requirement that causation be proven" (Rovner).

When I compared the votes of *all* judges on claims by (mostly foreign) "war-on-terror" victims against the USA with votes on claims by US terrorism victims against mostly foreign defendants, I found a highly significant difference between antipathy toward the former claims and sympathy for the latter – two-thirds of the decisions in both categories – further demonstrating the politicization of these cases (see Table 6.2).[196]

But once again judges' political affiliations were reflected in their votes: judges appointed by Republican presidents were far more sympathetic to terrorism victims than those appointed by Democratic presidents, although the difference was no longer statistically significant (presumably because sympathy for US victims and antipathy for sponsors of terrorism transcended political orientation) (see Table 6.3). Appointees of both parties were consistent across the two categories: Republican appointees favored the government over "war-on-terror" victims 84% of the time and terrorism victims over state

Table 6.3 Judges' Rulings on Terrorism Victims' Civil Damages Claims, by Appointing President's Party

Appointing President	# Pro-Plaintiff	%	# Anti-Plaintiff	%	Total
Democrat	14	50	14	50	28
Republican	21	81	5	19	26
Total	35	65	19	35	54

Chi-square = 5.60, p = 0.18

sponsors of terrorism 81% of the time; Democrat appointees voted for "war-on-terror" victims 58% of the time and terrorism victims 50% of the time.[197]

Courts initially rebuffed such claims, deferring to executive concerns to preserve good relations with Saudi Arabia (a crucial ally) or rebuild Iraq after the American invasion (and make it an ally against Iran). But when the executive favored such claims (against Hamas, the PLO, and Iran), the judiciary warmly embraced them, easily overcoming obstacles courts had found insurmountable when "war-on-terror" victims were claiming. Some judges displayed uncharacteristic – arguably unseemly – partisanship. Judge Lamberth "commended" the plaintiffs' "courage and steadfastness." Judge Bates expressed sympathy for "people whose lives have been torn apart." Damages were "the very least that these plaintiffs are owed." He, too, "commend[ed] the dedicated, creative, and courageous resolve of all the plaintiffs – and their conscientious attorneys," who "have helped to ensure that terrorism, and its support by defendants, will not ultimately succeed." (This contrasted sharply with vilification of lawyers who waged "lawfare" against the USA and judicial tirades against "litigiousness." And it credited unexecuted tort judgments with an unproved, and probably fictitious, impact on terrorism.) Iran's "horrific act harmed countless individuals and their families" and "must be punished to the fullest extent legally possible." Judge Cassell declared that terrorism was "unabashedly malignant action," whose victims suffer its "horrific effects every day." Judge Posner took unusually broad judicial notice: "We know that Hamas kills Israeli Jews, and Boim was an Israeli citizen, Jewish, living in Israel, and therefore a natural target for Hamas." In Palestine, "Arab terrorism has been more or less continuous since 1920" (as had British colonialism and then Zionism, which

Posner did not see fit to mention). Judge Marrero condemned "unprovoked savagery that encompasses even murder" and "wanton massacre of innocents." He rejected the political question defense, which would "rub every syllable of justice out of the concept of justiciability." Courts must "perform their ordained functions" (precisely those that conservative judges shirked when dismissing claims by "war-on-terror" victims). (Perhaps encouraged by these displays of partisanship, a hundred members of the US military wounded in Iraq and survivors of those killed have sued five US and European corporations for allegedly facilitating the sale of weapons involved in those attacks.[198])

Even dissenters expressed sympathy for terrorism victims. Judge Rovner declared that "the murder of David Boim was an unspeakably brutal and senseless act" and "terrorism is a scourge." Judge Wood called it a "heart-breaking" case. But these dissenters (like the rights-oriented judges discussed above) felt compelled to respect the law. The Seventh Circuit panel said:

> We must resist the temptation to gloss over error, admit spurious evidence and assume facts not adequately proved simply to side with the face of innocence and against the facts of terrorism … [and reject] abandonment of such time-honored tort requirements as causation. Our own response to a threat can sometimes pose as much of a threat to our civil liberties and the rule of law as the threat itself.

And when the en banc Seventh Circuit ruled for the Boims, Judge Wood reiterated that "we must not lose sight of the need to prove liability on the facts that are presented to the court." The majority's expansive concept of causation exhibited a "frightening, and I believe unwise, breadth."

Having interpreted the substantive law to let plaintiffs prevail on the merits, judges construed procedural law to help them execute their judgments (often obtained by default). Judges expressed impatience with recalcitrant defendants. Declaring that "enough is enough," Judge Forrest accused defendants of filling "the proverbial kitchen sink with arguments," which she simply disregarded. Judge Gershon penalized the Arab Bank's "grudging production" and "willfulness" by limiting its rebuttal of the inference that it provided financial services to designated terrorist organizations. Refusing "to be al-Qaeda's advocate," Judge Cassell required Ahmad Khadr to prove it was a "military force" whose actions fell outside the ATA. Cassell found personal jurisdiction by reading the "effects doctrine" to apply whenever the defendant's conduct "is aimed at or has any effect in the forum." He even apologized for his inability to compensate the Morris family (who were not plaintiffs) and urged them to sue.

Courts also displayed strong sympathies for 9/11 victims suing domestic defendants for negligence. Citing plaintiffs' "compelling needs," Judge Hellerstein took the unusual step of rejecting as insufficient a settlement *they* had accepted and slashed their lawyers' contingent fees and expenses. Federal, state, and local governments and private individuals created generous compensation funds for 9/11 victims, first responders, and World Trade Center neighbors, and then for Boston Marathon bombing victims. In the "best interests of patients" these schemes relaxed the requirement to prove exposure to toxic substances and disregarded scientific studies finding no evidence of causation (as Judge Posner had done for the Boims). Payments were on the order of a *thousand* times larger than those to victims of the US "war on terror" in Afghanistan and Iraq (partly because the latter took account of the extreme poverty in Afghanistan and Iraq, whereas "compensation" for American victims of terrorism jettisoned the tort maxim that damages seek to restore victims to the *status quo ante*).

The rule of law is most essential – and most in jeopardy – at those moments when the nation, or some group within it, feels existentially threatened. One such period began with the Red Scare following World War I and extended through the Korean War (with a brief interruption during World War II, when the Soviet Union was an indispensable ally against Germany). The rule of law repeatedly failed to protect civil liberties during those tumultuous decades; yet we know with hindsight that domestic communism never was a threat. The "war on terror" has corrupted civil law remedies in the same way, denying its victims redress while engaging in contortions to compensate victims of terrorism. Lady Justice is depicted wearing a blindfold so she cannot be tempted to display favoritism in balancing her scales; confronted with the "war on terror," deferential judges did not just peek – they ripped off the blindfold altogether. Although a handful of rights-minded judges courageously resisted these political pressures, it may take decades for the legal system to acknowledge and correct the distortions – too late to help those whom (like rape victims) it victimized a second time.

CHAPTER SEVEN

CIVIL LIBERTIES

Although both this volume and *Law's Wars* address the tensions between liberty and security, the present chapter focuses on threats to core civil liberties, approaching them from two perspectives.[1] First, I discuss fundamental rights: expression and assembly, travel, immigration, and privacy. Then I present six narratives of Islamophobia: siting mosques (especially one near the World Trade Center), burning the Koran, insulting Mohammed, moral panics over sharia and radical Islam, and the 2016 presidential campaign. These controversies raise several questions. How were civil liberties violations exposed? Who supported the victims? How did violators respond to being challenged? Which violations were remedied, which were not, and what explains the differences? How did government officials and civil society deal with Islamophobia while continuing to respect free speech rights?

FREEDOM OF EXPRESSION

Responses to the abridgment of free speech illuminate the uneven impact of 9/11 on fundamental constitutional rights. When the DoJ closed immigration hearings for Arabs and Muslims detained soon after the attack, the *Detroit Free Press* successfully won an injunction reopening them from ED Mich Judge Edmunds and the Sixth Circuit.[2] Jittery police abused people photographing public places. When Jim McKinniss took photos of an ExxonMobil refinery, a Los Angeles Police Department (LAPD) officer patted him down, photographed and fingerprinted him, and asked if he was a terrorist. A federal judge called this "disturbing." "Vigilance is not an excuse for not being aware of where the constitutional line is."[3] Robert Taylor was arrested for taking photographs in a NYC subway station, addressing the arresting officers in an "unreasonable voice," and "impeding traffic." The city dropped the first charge, admitting that photography was allowed. A year earlier it had paid more than $30,000 to settle the lawsuit of a photographer who had been handcuffed and detained. Visual activists and artists gathered 26,000 signatures to successfully oppose severe new restrictions on filming on city streets.[4] After the Federal Protective Service confiscated the camera of a news photographer taking pictures of a demonstration in front of the federal courthouse in lower Manhattan, it settled his lawsuit by agreeing to inform employees that the public could "photograph the exterior of federal courthouses from public accessible spaces."[5] In May 2005 Rakesh Sharma, an Indian documentary filmmaker, spent 30 minutes filming Indian taxi drivers in New York from the Park Avenue median looking toward the Met Life building.[6] Police questioned him for two hours, insisting he needed a city permit. Sharma complained that the officer shoved and cursed him: "there were many other tourists shooting scenes in the city. They were not being bothered by anyone." The ACLU, which represented him, said permits (which required millions of dollars of insurance) were not mandatory for someone filming alone with a handheld video camera.

Some judges upheld the free speech rights of anti-war demonstrators. Eighteen members of the Granny Peace Brigade were arrested and charged with disorderly conduct for protesting the Iraq war outside the Times Square military recruiting station in October 2005. The prosecutor called it a "simple and straightforward" case of "obstructing pedestrian traffic," while the defense lawyer claimed his "respectful, orderly, justified and patriotic" clients sought "to alert an apathetic public." Three women – 86, 87, and 91 years old – said they wanted to enlist. The state judge found them not guilty: "there was no blockage of pedestrian traffic and anyone who wanted to enter the recruiting center could do so."[7] A Maryland federal judge dismissed charges against 13 peace activists protesting outside the NSA, finding that its security officer lacked authority to charge them: the law prohibited entering, not remaining on, the property, and the NSA never told the protesters to leave.[8] Invoking the First Amendment, D Az Judge Wake enjoined a prosecution for selling T-shirts proclaiming "Bush Lied – They Died," brought under a state law prohibiting the selling of products using the names of military casualties without the families' permission.[9]

As we saw in Chapter 6 on civil damages actions, most of those demonstrating during the 2004 Republican National Convention in New York had their charges dismissed or were acquitted. June Brashares, who carried a sign declaring "Bush Lies People Die," was accused of assaulting a convention volunteer with the heel of her shoe, inflicting a gash requiring ten stitches. The prosecutor called her a cunning woman, who had snuck into a private affair to provoke a nationally televised disruption. But the jury acquitted, finding that her footwear had no heels. Of the 1,670 prosecuted by the Manhattan District Attorney, 91 percent were dismissed or acquitted.[10] Anti-war groups also won the right to demonstrate in Central Park.[11] Although the city had excluded them on the pretext of protecting the Great Lawn's turf, the challengers uncovered a Parks Department email stating: "It is very important that we do not permit any big or political events for the period between August 23 and September 6, 2004." The Parks Commissioner had emailed Mayor Bloomberg in June: "Following your call I spoke to [Police Commissioner] Ray[mond Kelly] about 10 minutes ago. Coincidentally, our lawyer and [Assistant] Chief [John B.] McManus [who oversaw police strategy for the Republican National Committee (RNC)] and the [City] Law Department are meeting at this very minute to agree on the language and strategy of the letter rejecting the Arab-American rally on the Great Lawn." After a federal judge denied a motion to dismiss the lawsuit, the Parks Department rescinded the rule it had used to deny the permit, paid $25,000 to each group that had sued, and reimbursed their $500,000 in legal costs.

Courts struck down content discrimination, no matter how offensive the message. Reacting to the Council on American–Islamic Relations (CAIR)'s "MyJihad" campaign, publicizing the peaceful meanings of jihad, Pamela Geller's American Freedom Defense Initiative (AFDI) sought to buy an advertisement in NYC subway stations entitled "Support Israel. Defeat Jihad," exhorting readers to "support the civilized man" in "any war between the civilized man and the savage."[12] After the Metropolitan Transportation Authority (MTA) rejected it for "demeaning language," SDNY Judge Engelmayer ordered the ad be displayed. MTA responded by unanimously adopting a new rule prohibiting any ad it "reasonably foresees would incite or provoke violence or other immediate breach of the peace" and requiring all viewpoint ads to state that MTA did not endorse them. Jewish and Christian groups bought ads endorsing love over hate. Many AFDI ads were defaced, but it planned more (to be placed out of the reach of vandals) with photos of the World Trade Center and an alleged quotation from the Koran about casting "terror into the hearts of the unbelievers." The *Washington Post* urged the DC Metro to stop deferring action on a similar ad in the name of "public safety."

AFDI revived the controversy in 2014 by proposing five ads, one showing a man in a *keffiyeh* (traditional Middle Eastern headscarf) declaring: "Killing Jews Is Worship that Draws Us Close to Allah" (a statement it attributed to Hamas MTV) and captioned: "That's his jihad. What's yours?" When SDNY Judge Koeltl struck down MTA's rejection of the ad under its revised standard, it quickly prohibited *all* ads about "disputed economic, political, moral, religious or social issues." The MTA chairman explained: "we can't get so deluded and diverted from what our main function is, which is to provide transportation." Under the new policy, MTA banned satirical ads it had approved for a 2013 *Muslim* docu-comedy, *The Muslims Are Coming!* The Philadelphia area Southeastern Pennsylvania Transportation Authority (SEPTA) enacted a similar ban after AFDI won a federal court order requiring SEPTA to display a series of ads declaring "Jew Hatred: It's in the Quran," one with a photo of Hitler and a Palestinian Arab nationalist who had supported him (sporting a similar mustache). Washington DC adopted the same blanket ban after AFDI sought to buy an ad displaying the winning entry in its "Jihad Watch Muhammad Art Exhibit and Cartoon Contest" in Garland, Texas. Under the caption "Support Free Speech," it showed a grimacing Mohammed brandishing a sword and proclaiming "You can't draw me," while the cartoonist responded: "that's why I draw you." The *New York Times* said: "there is no question that images ridiculing religion, however offensive they may be to believers, qualify as protected free speech," but the contest "was not really about free speech. It was an exercise in bigotry and hatred." The *Times* found it "hard to see" how "freedom of expression" is "advanced by inflicting deliberate anguish on millions of devout Muslims who have nothing to do with terrorism." AFDI sued again when the MTA banned an ad – claiming Muslims believed that "killing Jews is worship that draws us close to Allah" – on the ground that the likeliest interpretation "by most people would be that it urges Muslims to kill or attack Jews as a religious obligation." (Is that really the likeliest interpretation?) In October 2015 SDNY Judge McMahon ordered the MTA to accept film ads for *The Muslims Are Coming!* – a comedy by two Muslims – because MTA had not shown the ads were political, and the authority had not displayed viewpoint neutrality.[13] The *New York Times* said the MTA should "roll back the April ban on ads with political messages."

Xavier Alvarez was convicted under the federal Stolen Valor Act for falsely claiming (at a meeting of a water district board, of which he was a member) that he had been a Marine for 25 years and had been awarded a Congressional Medal of Honor.[14] The US District Judge held that the First Amendment did not protect known falsehoods. But the Ninth Circuit reversed and denied en banc review. The *New York Times* and other news organizations filed an amicus brief for Alvarez. The Supreme Court agreed the law was unconstitutional, but Breyer and Kagan (concurring) suggested they would support "a more finely tailored statute," which required "a showing that the false statement caused specific harm." (A bill to prohibit making such misrepresentations with intent to obtain "anything of value" was already before Congress.) The *Washington Post* agreed with the Court that "it is precisely in tolerating 'inconvenient' speech that the First Amendment is tested and must be upheld." The House quickly passed the new law 410–3, and the Senate unanimously agreed. In a later case, the Ninth Circuit dismissed the conviction of an ex-Marine for wearing medals he had not earned.

But other free speech claims failed. We saw in Chapter 6 on civil actions that courts denied damages to Leslie Weise and Alex Young for being expelled from a Bush speech and to Steven Howards for being convicted for touching Cheney at a Colorado event. A couple arrested for wearing T-shirts declaring "Regime Change Starts at Home" and "Love America, Hate Bush" at a Bush speech at the West Virginia state capitol sued, and obtained a 2002 "Presidential Advance Manual" directing screeners to look for "folded cloth signs" and ensure that those near the stage be "*extremely* supportive of the administration" [original emphasis].[15] A roving "rally squad" should use large signs displaying "favorable messages" as shields between the demonstrators and the main press platform and lead supportive chants of "USA! USA! USA!" to drown out protesters. "As a last resort, security should remove the demonstrators from the event site." The *Washington Post* observed that "censoring nonviolent speech at a publicly funded event would seem to run afoul of … the U.S. Constitution." The Supreme Court unanimously upheld the conviction of a demonstrator for trespassing on Vandenberg Air Force Base.[16]

The First Amendment offers no protection against private restraints. At a United States Bridge Federation awards dinner in Shanghai, the victorious women's team displayed a sign declaring: "We did not vote for Bush.[17] The Federation required the offenders to sign an apology it drafted and sentenced them to a year's suspension, another year's probation, and 200 hours of community service "that furthers the interests of organized bridge." The Federation president said: "this isn't a free speech issue. There isn't any question that private organizations can control the speech of people who represent them." But the *New York Times* called "this sort of censorship … un-American, unsporting and counterproductive." Sen. Joseph Lieberman successfully pressured YouTube to remove hundreds of videos allegedly produced by Islamist terrorist organizations or their supporters.[18] Rep. Anthony Weiner did the same for al-Awlaki videos.[19] During the 2008 Republican National Convention, CBS Outdoor canceled a contract for a Minneapolis billboard display of photos showing soldiers between tours in Iraq and Afghanistan gazing vacantly, claiming they "looked to us like they were representing deceased soldiers."[20] CVS and Walgreens banned a *Rolling Stone* issue on the ground that its cover photo glamorized Dzhokhar Tsarnaev.[21] CVS said that: "as a company with deep roots in New England and a strong presence in Boston we believe this is the right decision out of respect for the victims of the attack and their loved ones." The *New York Times* attributed this "hysteria" to an August heat wave.

Even public employers could restrain employee speech. We saw in Chapter 5 that Bassem Youssef and Sibel Edmonds lost their damages claims. After questioning Abdel-Moniem Ali el-Ganayni (an Egyptian-born naturalized US citizen and nuclear physicist) about his religious beliefs, money he sent overseas, and criticism of the Iraq war and alleged FBI mistreatment of Muslims, the US Department of Energy (DoE) revoked the security clearance he had held for 17 years (rendering him unemployable).[22] WD Pa Judge McVerry dismissed his lawsuit when DoE claimed to have reliable information it could not make available that he was a security risk. The Third Circuit affirmed because courts could not review the merits of security clearance revocations. The National Geospatial Intelligence Agency revoked Mahmoud M. Hegab's security clearance because his wife, Bushra Nusairat, worked for Islamic Relief USA, even though that charity partnered with the US Agency for International Development (USAID) and DoS to provide food and public health and education programs.[23] Both el-Ganayni and Hegab were US citizens. Morris Davis lost a lawsuit challenging his dismissal by the Library of Congress for writing a *Washington Post* op ed criticizing the MCs (of which he had been chief prosecutor).[24] A CIA software contractor lost her security clearance and job after blogging on the intelligence community's classified internet about the CIA cafeteria's bad food, stagflation, and the Middle East war.

State and local government employees fared no better. Umar Abdul-Jalil, director of the NY Department of Corrections Ministerial Services Unit, was suspended for failing to state he had been speaking as a private citizen when declaring that the "greatest terrorists in the world occupy the White House," Jews controlled the media, and Muslims were tortured in Manhattan jails.[25] Rep. Peter King asserted that "a person with those views should not be allowed to serve in any government agency." The NYC Department of Education suspended Debbie Almontaser as principal of the Khalil Gibran International Academy.[26] Although the Equal Employment Opportunities Commission (EEOC) vindicated her denial of any connection to T-shirts with the slogan "Intifada NYC," she resigned under pressure.

But some employees prevailed. The federal Air Marshall Service issued a policy declaring that employees could not "criticize or ridicule" the agency "by speech, writing, or other expression" or release information about it without authorization. Frank Terreri (president of the employee association), suspended for criticizing a colleague who (with management authorization) had disclosed that marshals boarded planes before other passengers, was reinstated after suing in federal court.[27] Disneyland successfully prohibited a Muslim woman from wearing a hijab as a hostess because it clashed with the restaurant's early 1900s-America theme. But the Supreme Court gave short shrift to a retailer who justified a similar ban on the ground that a hijab was "not Abercrombie look."[28] Announcing the decision from the bench, Justice Scalia called the case "really easy." "The company's claim of ignorance about Ms. Elauf's reason for wearing her head scarf is hard to believe." The *New York Times* praised the decision as "a common-sense reading of the Civil Rights Act, and a good reminder for employers that the best policy is one of inclusiveness and accommodation." Abercrombie said it had since altered its policy to let workers "be more individualistic" because of the company's "longstanding commitment to diversity and inclusion."

The media devoted the most attention to one of its own. During a discussion of "political correctness" with Bill O'Reilly on *Fox News*, Juan Williams said:[29]

I'm not a bigot. You know the kind of books I've written about the civil rights movement in this country. But when I get on a plane, I got to tell you, if I see people who are in Muslim garb and I think, you know, they are identifying themselves first and foremost as Muslims, I get worried. I get nervous.

When O'Reilly expressed sympathy, saying "Muslims attacked us on 9/11," Williams replied that it was as wrong to generalize about Muslims as it would be to malign Christians because of Timothy McVeigh. After Muslim advocacy groups and liberal commentators expressed anger, National Public Radio (NPR) fired Williams, saying it had repeatedly warned him about making speculative statements or voicing opinions in other venues that would be unacceptable on NPR and "undermined [his] credibility as an analyst." After Obama's inauguration, Williams had said on *The O'Reilly Factor* that Michelle's "instinct is to start with this 'blame America,' you know, 'I'm the victim.'" NPR's chief executive, Vivian Schiller, said at the Atlanta Press Club that Williams should have discussed his feelings about Muslims with "his psychiatrists or his publicist." Although she quickly retracted that remark – "I spoke hastily and I apologize to Juan and others for my thoughtless remarks" – she justified the firing because "if someone keeps not following your guidance, you have to make a break." "This is not a First Amendment issue."

Williams, who had appeared on NPR for almost a decade, called his dismissal "an outrageous violation of journalist standards and ethics by management that has no use for a diversity of opinion, ideas or diversity of staff (I was the only black male on the air)." Such "one-party rule ... leads to enforced ideology" and "journalists being sent to the gulag for raising the wrong questions and displaying independence of thought." "I am open to being misinterpreted only if you snipt [sic] one line out of what I said." But he was unrepentant: "there's a reality. You cannot ignore what happened on 9/11, and you cannot ignore the connection to Islamic radicalism." Fox promptly gave him a multiyear contract worth nearly $2 million. Conservatives expressed outrage. Sarah Palin tweeted that Williams "got a taste of left's hypocrisy." Mike Huckabee planned to boycott NPR, which "has discredited itself as a forum for free speech." Newt Gingrich said Congress should consider "cutting off their money." House Speaker John Boehner agreed it was "reasonable to ask why Congress is spending taxpayers' money to support a left-wing radio network."

The *Washington Post* defended Williams, who had been a staff writer. "[N]o one has a perfect record." His words "could be offensive to some, if construed as an endorsement of negative stereotyping. But the full broadcast makes clear that Mr. Williams intended the opposite." NPR had proved Williams's point that "political correctness can lead to some kind of paralysis where you don't address reality." The conservative commentator Reuel Marc Gerecht wrote in a *Washington Post* op ed that the comments "were hardly a firing offense." "Williams was right to suggest that there is a troubling nexus between the modern Islamic identity and the embrace of terrorism as a holy act." The *Los Angeles Times* said: "NPR overreacted." Although "hurtful" and "ignorant," Williams's statements "were not a fiery fomenting of hatred." "If our first reaction to every statement that makes us uncomfortable is unmitigated horror and a swift kick out the door, we run the risk of closing off all honest debate about difficult subjects." In a *New York Times* op ed the liberal journalist Robert Wright wondered if Fox News would have given Williams "a $2-million pat on the back" had he made a homophobic comment. Islamophobia "alienates Muslims, raising the risk of homegrown terrorism." The *New York Times* warned that cutting off funding because of "NPR's ham handed" response to Williams's "foolish and hurtful remarks" would be "the worst possible outcome."

Little more than two months after the firing, Vivian Schiller resigned after being denied her annual bonus, as did the senior vice president for news. The NPR board chairman said: "we learned that we should slow down the process." An independent review found Williams's firing consistent with his contract but urged NPR to examine its code of ethics.

Expressions of blatant bias provoked prompt, strong, generally effective rebuttals. When Keith Ellison was elected as the first Muslim member of Congress in November 2006, conservative talk radio host Dennis Prager said he should relinquish his seat if he insisted on taking the oath of office on the Koran, "an act of hubris that perfectly exemplifies multicultural activism – my culture trumps America's culture."[30] "America is interested in only one book, the Bible." When members of the Holocaust Museum board rebuked Prager (who also was a member), he denied having expressed any "bigotry" and accused them of succumbing to Muslim pressure. "I completely respect Congressman-elect Ellison's right to take an oath on the Koran, and regret any language that suggested otherwise." But Prager then dug himself deeper: "My entire effort in the Keith Ellison matter has been to draw attention to the need to acknowledge the Bible as the basis of America's moral values."

Rep. Virgil H. Goode Jr. (R-Va) aggravated the situation by warning that Ellison's election posed a serious threat to traditional values. Goode wanted to restrict immigration "so that we don't have a majority of Muslims elected to the United States House of Representatives." Condemning such "colossally stupid" "bigotry," the *Washington Post* wondered whether Congress "can afford a lawmaker of Mr. Goode's caliber." He retorted: "I do not apologize, and I do not retract my letter." The *New York Times* said Ellison "behaved with extreme grace," while Prager and Goode helped demonstrate "how very fast things can get both nutty and unpleasant once the founding fathers' wise decision to avoid institutionalizing any religious faith gets breached."

Overall, free speech did not fare badly in the wake of 9/11. Unsurprisingly, there were some ill-advised attempts to regulate it by overzealous officials and legislatures. But individual abuses did not become policy. Courts unhesitatingly struck down content discrimination. The media consistently defended the right to express unpopular views while also displaying the courage to condemn hateful speech. Transportation authorities, by contrast, showed a lack of political spine by eliminating *all* controversial ads – a capitulation sadly reminiscent of the South's massive resistance to racial integration, when Prince Edward County, Virginia closed its public schools and Mississippi drained public swimming pools. But if the core of free speech remained largely intact, its periphery was always endangered. Courts were overprotective of presidential security at the expense of dissenting speakers. Public entities could limit employee speech, and private actors were unconstrained by the First Amendment (if they could not discriminate). NPR's firing of Juan Williams exposed the difficulty of striking the right balance between the media's need to determine editorial policy by limiting employees' political speech, the imperative of applying that policy evenhandedly, and employees' own rights of expression.

TRAVEL[31]

Passengers

Given the circumstances of the 9/11 attack, it is unsurprising that Muslims were particularly vulnerable when flying. A US Airways passenger about to travel from Minneapolis to Phoenix passed a note to the flight attendant that "6 suspicious Arabic men," who had been saying "Allah" before the flight and "cursing U.S. involvement with Saddam," had then "spaced out in their seats."[32] The six, who had been attending a North American Imams Federation conference, were led off the plane in handcuffs, questioned separately for five hours, and then released. US Airways refunded their money, barring them from later flights. After investigating, it insisted staff actions had been justified. The six sued US Airways and the complaining passenger. Minneapolis imams met with the Airports Commission, which was considering a "meditation room" for all faiths.

Tarik Farag and Amro Elmasry were detained after flying from San Diego to JFK Airport, allegedly because they switched seats, often checked their watches, and spoke in Arabic.[33] EDNY Judge Block held they could not be arrested simply because of their race.

AirTran removed six adults and three children flying from Washington DC to Orlando after two teenage girls told the flight attendant that two of the women had said that sitting near the engine might be dangerous.[34] The two men in their group (an anesthesiologist and a lawyer) with beards and the four women with headscarves were going to a religious retreat. The pilot refused to fly them, and the flight left two hours late without them. Because AirTran would not rebook them, they had to pay another carrier. AirTran said it had followed federal rules: "people got on and made comments they should [not] have … it just so happened these people were of Muslim faith and appearance." The Transportation Security Administration (TSA) said the pilot acted appropriately: "someone heard something that was inappropriate, and then the airline decided to act on it. We certainly support [the pilot's] call to do that." CAIR complained to the Department of Transportation. After the media reported the incident, AirTran offered the group a refund and free return trip and apologized to *all* the passengers on the flight.

Two US residents of Yemeni descent traveling to Yemen from Birmingham, Alabama, were detained in Amsterdam at the request of the USA after a search of their unaccompanied luggage and that of a third Yemeni who was to have joined their flight in Chicago found $7,000 in cash, a box cutter, three large knives, pill bottles, and cell phones and watches taped together.[35] They were released without charges.

In August 2006 JetBlue and TSA barred an Iraqi-born US resident from a Washington DC to Oakland flight until he covered a T-shirt declaring "We Will Not Be Silent" in English and Arabic. A TSA employee told him that wearing a shirt with Arabic script was like going to the bank in a shirt that said "I am a robber." JetBlue seated him in the rear of the plane.[36] The airline and the TSA employees settled his lawsuit for $240,000 but did not apologize. In August 2009 a student was handcuffed at Philadelphia International Airport and questioned for four hours because he was learning Arabic from flash cards, which TSA called "anomalous" behavior and "erratic" conduct.[37] A supervisor asked his views on 9/11 and what language bin Laden spoke. The FBI interrogated him about whom he had met during a semester abroad. A January 2010 US Airways flight from La Guardia to Louisville was diverted to Philadelphia when a 17-year-old Orthodox Jewish boy traveling with his 13-year-old sister donned tefillin (leather boxes containing scriptural passages) and started davening (praying).[38] Asked what he was doing, the boy explained to a flight attendant he was praying. She told the pilot "there was an item wrapped around his head" by straps, which "did appear to be cables or wires to her." After the plane landed in Philadelphia, police boarded with guns drawn and handcuffed the boy. In Spring 2016 a UC Berkeley senior was removed from a flight when he was overheard talking on his cell phone in Arabic. Days later a University of Pennsylvania economics professor was taken off a flight when a seatmate mistook his differential equations for Arabic and reported him to a flight attendant. In August two Muslim American women were removed from a plane when they talked to other passengers about being denied food and water while takeoff was delayed for five hours and then photographed a flight attendant who threatened them (and was not wearing a name badge). Returning to the USA after a world tour, two YouTube stars were removed from a flight in Heathrow after one of them was heard speaking Arabic.

Even when not flying, immigrants were particularly vulnerable at or near borders. A report by the NYCLU and the NYU Law School Immigration Rights Clinic found that Customs and Border Patrol agents were boarding domestic trains and buses in upstate New York far from the Canadian border, inspecting passenger IDs, and arresting illegal immigrants.[39] These were not terrorists seeking to infiltrate the USA: three-quarters had been in the country at least a year and 12 percent more than ten years; only about one percent were entering for the first time. The Department of Homeland Security (DHS) Customs and Border Patrol (CBP) tripled the number of agents in Vermont, added boats and helicopters, deployed new technology, and proposed to build a fence in Derby Line (pop. 776) on the US–Canadian border. An agent warned that if a "kid throws a Frisbee over here, he can come and get it. But if he got the Frisbee and kept walking down to the Arby's to get a soda, we're going to stop you." At the other end of the US–Canadian border, CBP agents were screening and arresting passengers on domestic ferries in Washington's San Juan Islands.

The ACLU sued on behalf of several travelers alleging discrimination, including Dr. Sam Hamade, a Lebanese-born Canadian citizen seeking US citizenship, who had been detained at least six times driving across the border to his job as senior resident at Upstate Medical University in Syracuse, NY.[40] Abdulameer Habeeb had been in the USA for ten months as a legal refugee from Iraq when he stepped off an Amtrak train near the Canadian border in Havre, Montana in April 2003 to stretch his legs.[41] A CBP agent asked if had registered under the "special registration" system (which did not apply to refugees) and then arrested him. He was strip-searched, held three nights in county jail, walked through the Havre airport in handcuffs, flown to Seattle, and held four more days. After the charges were dismissed by the US District Court in Montana, the US Attorney in Seattle apologized for the "good faith mistake," insisting it was not "racial profiling" but just "a legal matter according to what his status was."

Even citizens faced greater scrutiny at the border. The Electronic Frontier Foundation and the Asian Law Caucus sued to compel the government to disclose its policies on border searches of cell phones and computers, and challenged whether it could ask travelers about their political views, religious practices and other First Amendment activities.[42] DHS declared it could seize, search and retain electronic devices at border crossings and share their contents with other agencies and private entities for translation and data decryption. David House (an advocate for Chelsea Manning) had his laptop, camera, thumb drive, and cell phone seized and held for seven months after returning to the USA in November 2010. In response to an ACLU complaint, the government agreed to destroy all copies of the data it had downloaded and eliminate him from the search list for future trips. Laura Poitras, the American filmmaker who publicized Edward Snowden's disclosures of illegal NSA surveillance, was repeatedly stopped when returning to the USA.[43]

Sen. Russell Feingold (D-Wisc) drafted the Travelers Privacy Protection Act to limit this power. Rep. Loretta Sanchez (D-Ca) had introduced legislation requiring CBP agents to protect confidentiality, limit how long devices could be retained, and inform owners if data were copied or shared. The *Washington Post* wanted a requirement of "reasonable suspicion." The *Los Angeles Times* urged Congress "to curb this exponential invasion of privacy" and supported a bill by Rep. Zoe Lofgren (D-Ca) to outlaw computer searches. The Obama administration reaffirmed the search policy but proposed to limit most CBP searches to 5 days and ICE searches to 30 days, and provide periodic audits. The Association of Corporate Travel Executives remained critical. But DHS said that of the more than 221 million travelers the previous year, it had searched only a thousand laptops, just 46 in depth.

The *Los Angeles Times* applauded an ACLU challenge, which claimed that 6,671 laptops had been searched in a 20-month period. Plaintiffs included criminal defense lawyers and the National Press Photographers Association. The lead plaintiff, Pascal Abidor, a dual US–French citizen doing a Ph.D. in Islamic studies at NYU, was pulled off the train from Montreal, frisked, handcuffed, jailed for several hours, and questioned about his religious and political views when his computer (which was held for 11 days) was found to contain research material in Arabic and news photos of Hezbollah and Hamas rallies. Because the judiciary was "inhospitable" toward such suits (two Circuits had upheld searches), the *Los Angeles Times* endorsed the Feingold and Lofgren bills. So did the *New York Times*, which urged "a balance that grants sufficient leeway to protect the nation's borders without allowing the intimate details of people's lives and work to be searched, seized and copied on a whim." The *Los Angeles Times* was right about the courts: EDNY Judge Korman held the plaintiffs lacked standing because, given the "10 in a million chance" of a search, "there is not a substantial risk that their electronic devices will be subject to search or seizure without reasonable suspicion." "The precautions plaintiffs may choose to take to 'mitigate' the alleged harm associated with the remote possibility of a border search are simply among the many inconveniences associated with international travel." Even if plaintiffs had standing, the government did not need reasonable suspicion to search. After the Ninth Circuit upheld a border search of a laptop found to contain child pornography, the *New York Times* called on the Supreme Court to protect the "privacies of life."[44] But the en banc Ninth Circuit then held that an extended search required reasonable suspicion (though it also found that standard met in this case). Subsequently, the DDC excluded evidence obtained during such a search.

Travelers also surrendered privacy in their quotidian lives, far from any border. The NYCLU challenged searches of bags in the subways, instituted in response to the July 7, 2005 London bombings.[45] A lawyer for NYC claimed the searches "keep terrorist planning and operations off balance," "effectively harden[ing] New York City targets and driv[ing] terrorist planning elsewhere." The Deputy Police Commissioner for Intelligence said "unpredictability is the enemy of the terrorist." The Deputy Police Commissioner for Terrorism maintained that the program "dramatically improves the security posture of this huge sprawling subway system." Riders were "free" to decline a search and just try another station. Plaintiffs replied that searches were too infrequent to be effective; their testers encountered just 34 in 3,288 visits to subway stations over four weeks; and a survey found that only 32 percent of riders felt they increased security. SDNY Judge Berman denied the plaintiffs' request for information about when and where searches had been conducted, accepting the argument that unpredictability was crucial, and found for the city. "Because the threat of terrorism is great and the consequences of unpreparedness may be catastrophic, it would seem foolish not to rely upon those qualified persons in the best position to know." Sealed evidence proffered by the city showed there had been daily searches from July 22 to November 6. The program "adds uncertainty and unpredictability" to terrorist planning, increasing the chances an attack would fail. The flow of passengers had not been "significantly impeded or interrupted." Noting that the city had not found any evidence of terrorism, NYCLU appealed, but the Second Circuit affirmed. Boston (which had been the first city to search subways, during the 2004 Democratic National Convention but stopped after a legal challenge) followed New York's example and planned to add behavior recognition teams.

Watchlists[46]

If the above incidents sometimes produced a remedy (albeit late and inadequate), challenges to terrorism watchlists generally failed.[47] TSA's Terrorist Identities Datamart Environment (TIDE) list grew tenfold, from 100,000 names in 2003 to over a million in 2009, when 1,600 new names were being proposed daily. DoJ IG audits in 2005, 2007, 2008, and 2009 criticized the inclusion of inappropriate names (38 percent of one sample) and deficiencies in the process for correcting or eliminating them. At a time when the "selectee" list contained fewer than 16,000 names and the no-fly list fewer than 2,500, a DoJ IG report found that TIDE still wrongly included 24,000 names while omitting some actual suspects. The DHS IG criticized TSA for detaining people with a common last name like Khan. A Government Accountability Office (GAO) audit found that nearly half the names triggering a response were a mistake. The list included young children, members of Congress, war heroes, and nuns. Sen. Edward Kennedy had been stopped at Reagan Airport. Sen. Ted Stevens said his wife Catherine was repeatedly asked whether she was Cat Stevens (the British pop singer who had changed his name to Yusuf Islam in 1978). Nelson Mandela was on the list until Congress passed a bill removing him in 2008. Kiernan O'Dwyer, a veteran American Airlines pilot, was stopped 80 times between 2003 and 2007, perhaps confused with Ciaran O'Dwyer, who was born on the same day but who was serving a five-year prison sentence. TSA rejected as possibly forged a CBP letter stating "you are not, nor have you ever been, on record as a criminal suspect"; and, unlike foreign flight crews, he could not submit his fingerprints. One major airline had 9,000 false hits a day; even federal air marshals had been stopped from checking in. The 30,000-name no-fly list included 14 of the 19 dead 9/11 hijackers. When challenged, TSA said others might use their names. Rental and mortgage companies and car dealers made similar mistakes in denying service when using the online Treasury Department's Office of Foreign Asset Control 250-page list of 3,300 organizations and individuals.

Remedial efforts were frustrating and often unsuccessful. In 2007–09, 81,793 travelers asked to be removed; 25,000 cases were still pending; the selectee list had grown to 20,000 and the no-fly list to 8,000 (including about 400 US citizens). The *New York Times* wrote: "a half-billion-dollar emergency program to repair the nation's main and deeply flawed terrorist watchlist is 'on the brink of collapse,' according to a Congressional investigation." After Michael Kirby contacted members of Congress, supplying notarized copies of his driver's license, birth certificate, and Social Security number, the DHS Traveler Redress Inquiry Program (TRIP) confirmed he was not the person on the travel watchlist, but said: "you're still subject to additional screening and clearance when you come to the airport." Airline clerks noted there were six other Michael Kirbys on the list. In 2009 DHS created Secure Flight, requiring travelers to provide their full name, birth date, and gender in order to reduce mistaken identifications. After Abdulmutallab's failed attempt to detonate a bomb as his plane landed in Detroit, pressure increased to expand the no-fly list. The *New York Times* said the case made "chillingly clear" that the "complicated, expensive and hugely onerous" security system had "serious flaws." Errors kept appearing. Although the TSA "mythbuster" website insisted that "no 8-year-old is on a T.S.A. watchlist," Michael Winston Hicks, aged eight, had been on the selectee list since he was a baby. He was patted down at age two and frisked more aggressively at eight. Another boy was stopped twice, at ages six and seven.

The *Washington Post* denounced the no-fly list as "essentially a black hole." In 2011 the *New York Times* said: "the government's bloated terrorist watchlist remains a flawed security tool in need of greater transparency and accountability." By 2012 the no-fly list had 21,000 names; a year later TIDE had 875,000 (up from 540,000 in 2008). *The Intercept* reported that TIDE had more than a million names in June 2013, about 680,000 of them on watchlists: 47,000 (including 800 Americans) on the no-fly list and 16,000 (including 1,200 Americans) on the "selectee" list. According to the National Counterterrorism Center's 166-page "March 2013 Watchlisting Guidance," a single White House official could place "entire categories" of people on the no-fly and selectee lists. By June 2014 the no-fly list had 64,000 names and TIDE had 1.1 million (including 25,000 US citizens and legal permanent residents).

Judicial challenges encountered numerous obstacles. When the ACLU sued in July 2010 on behalf of ten American citizens and legal residents, some stranded abroad, D Ore Judge Brown dismissed, finding she lacked authority over TSA policies. But after the Ninth Circuit reversed, she held that the plaintiffs had a "constitutionally protected liberty interest" in international air travel, rejecting government claims that sharing classified evidence with targets would undermine national security. The *Washington Post* urged the government to accept her decision "as an opportunity for reform." The White House promised to change the rules for challenging a no-fly listing, but the plaintiffs' lawyers rejected the process as insufficient. Four Muslim men sued when offered removal from the list only if they became informants. In October 2015 the Sixth Circuit reversed a District Court's grant of a motion to dismiss Saeb Mokdad's challenge to the no-fly list.[48]

By contrast, the People's Mujaheddin Organization of Iran (Mujaheddin-e-Khalq (MEK)), classified as terrorist by the Clinton administration in 1997, waged a successful campaign to be removed from the list (supported by many prominent conservatives).[49] Although DoS (under Secretary Clinton) claimed MEK remained committed to violence (and trained women suicide bombers) and much of its information on Iran's nuclear program was false, the Department delisted MEK two weeks before a deadline imposed by the DC Circuit.

The tortuous path toward redress can be illustrated by a single narrative.[50] It is based on ND Cal Judge Alsup's decision, which government redactions often rendered incomprehensible, as shown by the following excerpt: "Given the Kafakesque [redacted] treatment imposed on Dr. Ibrahim, the government is further ordered expressly to tell Dr. Ibrahim [redacted] (always subject, of course, to future developments and evidence that might [redacted])."

Rahinah Ibrahim, a Malaysian citizen, earned architecture degrees from the University of Washington in 1987 and the Southern California Institute of Architecture in 1990. In 2000 she returned to the USA under an F-1 visa to pursue a Ph.D. in construction engineering and management at Stanford. In November 2004 FBI Special Agent Kevin Kelley used the National Crime Information Center (NCIC) Violent Gang and Terrorist Organizations File to nominate her for the TSA no-fly list. (When Kelley learned in September 2013 that she had been added, he admitted he had checked the wrong box, having intended to nominate her for a different (redacted) database.) When Ibrahim arrived at San Francisco Airport on January 2, 2005 (in a wheelchair because she was recovering from surgery) to fly home with her 14-year-old daughter, she was arrested, handcuffed, and held in a cell for two hours before being told that her name had been removed from the no-fly list. She flew to Malaysia the next day but with a Secondary Security Screening Selection boarding pass.

That day one visa office official emailed another:

> I have a stack of pending [visa] revocations that are based on VGTO entries. These revocations contain virtually no derogatory information. After a *long* and frustrating game of phone tag … we're going to revoke them … there is no practical way to determine what the basis of the investigation is for these applicants … [so] we will accept that the opening of an investigation itself is a prima facie indicator of potential ineligibility.

Because Ibrahim's visa was in this stack, it was revoked on January 31. In an email exchange on February 8, a DoS official told the US Embassy in Kuala Lumpur:

> The short version is that [Ibrahim's] visa was revoked because there is law enforcement interest in her as a potential terrorist. This is sufficient to prudentially revoke a visa but doesn't constitute a finding of ineligibility. The idea is to revoke first and resolve the issues later in the context of a new visa application … My guess based on past experience is that she's probably issuable.

When Ibrahim tried to return to Stanford in March, she learned for the first time at the airport that her visa had been revoked. She immediately sought review by filing a Passenger Identity Verification Form (PIVF) and then (after government communications whose content was redacted) sued for damages and injunctive relief in January 2006. (As discussed in Chapter 6 on civil actions, the defendants settled her damages claim for $225,000.) TSA responded to her PIVF in March 2006 in an opaque bureaucratese that obscured her status: "where it has been determined that a correction to records is warranted, these records have been modified to address any delay or denial of boarding that you may have experienced." In December 2009 she was denied a visa to attend hearings in this lawsuit on the ground that she was a "terrorist." In 2011 she became Dean of the Faculty of Design and Architecture of Universiti Putra Malaysia. She again sought a visa in September 2013 to attend further court proceedings; but though she received no answer before the trial, the government admitted there that it had been denied. Her daughter, an American citizen by birth, also was not allowed to fly to attend the trial. (The court wrote that "the snafu was the result of government error ... as will be outlined at the end of the findings of fact." But those findings were redacted.)

After two District Court decisions, two appeals, and "rounds of contentious discovery motions," the District Court barred classified documents on state secrets grounds but rejected other government objections. Although the government promised it would "not affirmatively seek to prevail in this action based upon information that has been withheld on grounds of privilege," it sought to do just that. In response to the government's summary judgment motion, Judge Alsup expressed exasperation that "the vast majority of the hearing time ... was concerned over whether or not the trial should be public and whether certain information listed on plaintiff's demonstratives was subject to various privileges." After he denied the government's summary judgment motion, it sought reconsideration "because the core of the case had been excluded as state secrets." "At least ten times, the Court reluctantly asked the press and the public to leave the courtroom" in response to government assertions of a "sensitive security information" privilege and a "law enforcement privilege."

Alsup began his conclusions of law:

> At long last, the government has conceded that plaintiff poses no threat to air safety or national security and should never have been placed on the no-fly list. She got there by human error ... leading to the humiliation, cuffing, and incarceration of an innocent and incapacitated air traveler ... a bureaucratic analogy to a surgeon amputating the wrong

digit ... plaintiff has endured a litany of troubles in getting back into the United States ... [and] reasonably suspects that those troubles are traceable to the original wrong ... After so much gnashing of teeth and so much on-the-list-off-the-list machinations ... due process requires ... that the government remediate its wrong by cleaning and/or correcting all of its lists and records ... and by certifying that such ... has been accurately done as to every single government watchlist and database [by April 15, 2014].

Judge Alsup recognized Ibrahim's constitutional rights to travel and to be free from incarceration, and "the stigma and humiliation of a public denial of boarding and incarceration." He found that TRIP "is inadequate, at least on this record." He declined her request for a pre-determination hearing on the ground that it "would aid terrorists in their plans to bomb and kill Americans." "[U]ntil concrete, reviewable adverse action occurs against a nominee, the Executive Branch must be free to maintain its watchlists in secret." But "[t]he government's legitimate interest in keeping secret the composition of the no-fly list should yield, on the facts of this case, to a particularized remedy isolated by this order only to someone even the government concludes poses no threat to the United States. Everyone else in this case knows it. As a matter of remedy, she should be told that [redacted]." Although the state secrets privilege prevented courts from reviewing visa denials, Alsup ordered the government to inform Ibrahim of the reasons for her denials in 2009 and 2013 and tell her she was eligible to apply for a waiver.

Invoking the public's "well-recognized right to access its courts," Judge Alsup rebuked the government. "In stubborn resistance to letting the public and press see the details of this case, the government has made numerous motions to dismiss on various grounds, including an overbroad complete dismissal request based on state secrets. When it could not win an outright dismissal, it tried to close the trial from public view." The statutory privilege it invoked "recognizes that information more than three years old should ordinarily be deemed too stale to protect." "[V]irtually all of the [sensitive security information] about the [Terrorist Screening Database] is publicly known." He therefore ordered release of his entire opinion, but gave the government three months to seek redactions – producing the butchered version quoted above. The *New York Times* criticized the government for subjecting Ibrahim and her pro bono lawyers to "eight years of confounding litigation and coordinated intransigence" and then resisting Alsup's release of his opinion. The "terror watchlists remain pointlessly overbroad" and "operate under a veil of secrecy so thick that it is virtually impossible to pierce it when mistakes are made."

Scanners

The failure to detect Abdulmutallab's "underwear" bomb on Christmas Day 2009 led the Obama administration to consider mandating full-body scans.[51] TSA planned to install 150 scanners in early 2010 and buy another 300. Former DHS secretary Michael Chertoff claimed that "if they'd been deployed, this would pick up this kind of device." (It was later revealed that his Chertoff Group represented Rapiscan, which manufactured the machines.) Conservatives, who usually championed national security, now raised privacy concerns. Rep. Jason Chaffetz (R-Ut) sponsored a bill (which passed the House 310–118) to limit the devices to secondary screening. "I don't think anybody needs to see my 8-year-old naked in order to secure" an airplane. A coalition of 24 privacy organizations wrote DHS Secretary Napolitano: "Your agency will be capturing the naked photographs of millions of American air travelers suspected of no wrongdoing." An ACLU lawyer objected that "these scanners show starkly detailed images of the human body, which amount to an assault on the dignity of passengers and can be personally humiliating." FlyersRights, claiming 25,000 members, complained that "the price of liberty is too high." Its members, especially women, were "frantic" about their bodies being seen.

But the scans had supporters. The founder of the Association for Airline Passengers Rights said, dismissively, it was no "different than if you go to the beach and put on a bikini." The head of the Federal Law Enforcement Officers Association retorted to critics that "a bomb detonating on a plane is the biggest invasion of privacy a person can experience." The president of the Los Angeles Airport Peace Officers Association insisted that "all available technology and tools must be used to fix an obvious gap in security that puts airline travelers and crew members at risk." And the *Washington Post* said passengers on flights to the USA should be scanned "whenever possible." "Concerns about privacy must be balanced with law enforcement's ability to meet the terrorist threat with tools that work." It subsequently wrote that "there's nothing to fear from the use of full-body scanners at airports." The Netherlands (from where Abdulmutallab had flown to Detroit) agreed to use them on all US-bound passengers. Some critics warned the scans could cause cancer, although scientists denied there was any evidence for this. When the Sikh Coalition, United Sikhs, and the Sikh American Legal Defense and Education Fund expressed concern to DHS and TSA officials about racial profiling, they were told turbans would be treated as a "per se anomaly," giving agents discretion to conduct additional screening.

The Electronic Privacy Information Center (EPIC) feared TSA might save the images, despite promising not to do so. Documents that EPIC obtained by suing TSA for violating passengers' Fourth Amendment rights confirmed that scanners would have that capability. Chaffetz said this was "in direct contradiction to multiple assurances." "We don't need to look at naked 8-year-olds and grandmothers to secure airplanes." But he favored scans for all 550,000 on the watchlist. The ACLU was concerned about colostomy bags, mastectomy scars, and adult diapers. The International Air Transport Association (IATA), US Travel Association, and Allied Pilots Association criticized TSA for the intrusive and time-consuming scrutiny at airport checkpoints. IATA said "it is not acceptable to treat passengers as terrorists until they prove themselves innocent." The Allied Pilots Association urged members to refuse to submit for privacy and health reasons.

A few people committed or advocated civil disobedience. In November, John Tyner, a software engineer, refused to be scanned at San Diego Airport and videotaped himself being patted down, warning: "if you touch my junk, I'll have you arrested." The YouTube video quickly went viral. We Won't Fly promoted a mass protest on Thanksgiving Eve (the busiest flying day in the year), urging followers to refuse full-body scans in order to generate long lines for the more time-consuming pat-down (thereby intensifying outrage). Brian Sodergren launched a website for National Opt-out Day for the same day. A Las Vegas company sold rubber patches to cover body parts; a Colorado company hawked underwear that blocked X-rays. The ACLU declared that scanners "produce strikingly graphic images of passengers' bodies, essentially taking a naked picture." At a Senate Homeland Security Committee hearing, Chairman Joseph Lieberman (I-Ct) asked TSA Director John Pistole why scanners were "justified" but also defended them. Sen. George Lemieux (R-Fla) assailed the pat-downs: "I wouldn't want my wife to be touched in a way that these folks are being touched." There had been numerous passenger complaints in the three weeks since TSA began using more aggressive pat-downs. The US Travel Association and the ACLU had gotten more than 2,000 reports, many from people whose surgeries had created "anomalies." A woman wearing an insulin pump was angry at being patted down every time. An elementary school teacher said of a TSA agent: "I didn't really expect her to touch my vagina through my pants." An Alaska State Representative – patted down because she wore an artificial breast following a mastectomy – was traumatized for weeks because she had been sexually molested as a child. The second time this happened she chose a two-day ferry ride home. The Alaska legislature passed a resolution declaring "no one should have to sacrifice their dignity in order to travel." Two pilots sued DHS and TSA. New York City Council members asked the city to ban scanners at its airports. Rep. Ron Paul (R-Tex) introduced the American Traveler Dignity Act to ban body scans. "It establishes that airport security screeners are not immune from any U.S. law regarding physical contact with another person, making images of another person, or causing physical harm through the use of radiation-emitting machinery on another person."

Most of the media joined the chorus. The (conservative) *Washington Times* blamed "TSA's demeaning new 'enhanced pat-down' procedures" on "the Obama administration's willful blindness to the threat from Islamic radicals." "The agency wants every American to enter a literal position of surrender while being undressed by an x-rated x-ray machine." The *New York Times* saw "no excuse for the bumbling, arrogant way the TSA has handled questions and complaints." "There are far too many reports of T.S.A. agents groping passengers, using male agents to search female passengers, mocking passengers and disdaining complaints." Although scanners probably were not unconstitutional, "the lawsuits are a healthy process that will require the government to prove that the scanners are reliable and more effective than other devices." The *Times* published letters calling for profiling. George Will agreed in his *Washington Post* column: "if grandma is coming to our house" for Thanksgiving, "she may be wanded while barefoot at the airport" because the Fourteenth Amendment "requires the amiable nonsense of pretending that no one has the foggiest idea of what an actual potential terrorist might look like." In her *Post* column, Kathleen Parker denounced the "Kafkaesque farce that most closely resembles a college fraternity psychology experiment devised around a keg," and asked if "touching a 13-year-old boy or girl, possibly the most sensitive creature on the planet, is supposed to be just hunky-dory?" Charles Krauthammer complained in his *Post* column that "nowhere do more people meekly acquiesce to more useless inconvenience and needless indignity for less purpose." "The only reason we continue to do this is that people are too cowed to even question the absurd taboo against profiling – when the profile of the airline attacker is narrow, concrete, uniquely definable and universally known." But the *Los Angeles Times* called "fears about the scanners ... overblown." "Having seen the less-than-titillating images produced by the scanners, we doubt that they'll show up on internet porn sites anytime soon – or that even if they did, the subjects in them would be remotely recognizable." "If you can't handle such a minor inconvenience, perhaps you should stay on the ground."

Profiling quickly attracted other cheerleaders. The (conservative) Heritage Foundation wanted to limit body scans and pat-downs to those who raised suspicion. A former Federal Aviation Administration director of aviation security urged more profiling. Several commentators expressed enthusiasm for what the *Washington Times* called Israel's "sophisticated intelligence analysis which allows them to predict which travelers constitute a possible threat and which do not." This was no different from "the types of techniques that police on the beat use every day." A sympathetic former DHS Assistant Secretary for Policy said Israel focused on "the travelers' country of origin, their profession, visas ... places they have visited, people they know and the color of their skin." But others urged caution. A Haitian American leaving Israel was asked "what kind of a name is Dreyfuss?" (his interlocutor apparently had never heard of the famous victim of French anti-Semitism) and was "directed to a very long line" of "Arabs or Africans," all of whom had their luggage inspected. "A booklet from the Peres Center for Peace ... seemed to raise alarm." When he identified himself as a journalist, "my books were put back, my suitcase was snapped shut, and I was on my way home." An Israeli security expert confirmed that Israel concentrated on Arabs and some foreign nationals. Donna Shalala, Clinton's Secretary of Health and Human Services, was questioned for two-and-a-half hours because of her last name.

Nevertheless, a poll found that 70 percent of Americans favored profiling: most by nationality, half by appearance, and 32–40 percent by race, religion, and sex. Rush Limbaugh denounced "Obama-led government agents ... acting like perverts." Sarah Palin tweeted: "TSA: Why politically incorrect 2 'profile' anyone re: natl security issues? We profile individuals/suspects in other situations! Profile away." Calling pat-downs a "humiliating and degrading, totally unconstitutional intrusion," Mike Huckabee said Obama should subject his wife, daughters, and mother-in-law to them. The *New York Times* accused Republicans of being "happy to trade away a long and proud history of civil liberties over a few moments of inconvenience in the airport." But Roger Cohen wrote in his *Times* column that "the unfettered growth of the DHS and the T.S.A. represent a greater long-term threat to the prosperity, character, and wellbeing of the United States than a few madmen in the valleys of Waziristan or the voids of Yemen." TSA should "focus on the very small proportion of travelers who might present a threat." Although the *Washington Post* said "limiting the use of enhanced security techniques to those who fit a certain profile (Muslim men or those with Arabic names, for example) would be as foolish as it would be wrong," it favored "behavioral" profiling.

TSA responded by exempting pilots (but not flight attendants) from scans and pat-downs but invoked Abdulmutallab's attack as grounds for making no other changes. It noted that only 1 percent of travelers had opted for pat-downs. Polls found that two-thirds of Americans supported full-body scans and 70 percent of frequent travelers were willing to sacrifice privacy for security. In the first two weeks of intensified screening only about 700 of the 28 million passengers complained. The We Won't Fly website received 600,000 hits in the two weeks before Thanksgiving. At Phoenix Airport, students planned to offer travelers devices to register the radiation from scanners and give TSA agents gloves to do pat-downs. A passengers' rights group was going to be televised monitoring screening in San Francisco Airport. Campaign for Liberty, connected to Ron Paul, planned to distribute fliers at Reagan Airport. But the protest was a bust, with only 39 people opting out of scans in Atlanta, one in Charlotte, 113 in Los Angeles, and 300 in Boston.

In February 2011 TSA piloted new software producing a gray, cookie-cutter outline of the human form with little red boxes identifying anomalies. Pistole claimed: "it addresses the privacy issues that have been raised." FlyersRights agreed it was "a great step forward." Pistole also favored "more risk-based and intelligence-driven" screening. The US Travel Association proposed a program in which "trusted travelers" who provided fingerprints and other identifying information in advance would not have to remove clothing. But highly publicized incidents continued to plague TSA. Parents posted a video on YouTube showing an agent brushing the back of her hand along their 6-year-old daughter's back and inspecting around her waistline. Her mother said on television: "we struggle to teach our kids to protect themselves, to say 'no, it's not okay to touch me in this way in this area.' Yet, here we are saying it's okay." Calling it "another example of mistreatment of an innocent American at the hands of TSA," Rep. Chaffetz demanded an explanation. Days later he introduced a bill requiring parental permission before a pat-down. TSA responded that terrorists could use children to carry explosives. Reacting to this incident in her *New York Times* column, Maureen Dowd described the pat-down of "a distinguished federal official" after a scan found an ileostomy bag. Ignoring the TSA notification the passenger had proffered "so as to discreetly inform the T.S.A. agent of my medical condition," the agent "did a hand search of my groin, breasts, under the waistband of my slacks and around my ostomy bag."

After a former Miss USA claimed to have been groped at Dallas-Fort Worth Airport, 70 state legislators introduced a bill making it a felony to touch private areas, even through clothing, without probable cause to believe the person was carrying something illegal. TSA responded that of the 252 million subjected to body scans, less than 3 percent were patted down, and fewer than a thousand of those seven million complained. But though the Texas House passed the bill, it initially failed in the state Senate after the federal government threatened to halt all flights to Texas; and after it passed the Senate, it failed to get the four-fifths vote the House needed to reconsider it. In July the DC Circuit rejected EPIC's constitutional challenge. In January 2014 a passenger with a metal knee and hip implants challenged the pat-downs, but the First Circuit found no violation of the Fourth Amendment and no claim under the Rehabilitation Act.

After *USA Today* reported that "newly released" DHS documents revealed 25,000 security breaches at US airports since November 2001, DHS accused Rep. Chaffetz of illegally disclosing "sensitive security information." Rep. Darrell Issa (Homeland Security Committee chair) condemned this "meritless" retaliation for Congressional efforts to address "TSA deficiencies." Chaffetz (National Security, Homeland Defense, and Foreign Operations subcommittee chair) launched inquiries into passenger complaints against TSA agents and TSA security-related personnel actions against its employees. At separate hearings in November, senators expressed concerns about radiation, insensitive treatment of passengers with medical conditions, and children on the terrorist watchlist. The TSA reauthorization bill would require improved screening of those with metal implants, prosthetics, or physical disabilities. Sen. Schumer (D-NY) and New York State Sen.

Michael Gianaris called for a passenger advocate program after a woman claimed to have been strip-searched at JFK Airport (which was located in Gianaris's district). The 85-year-old woman asked to be patted down, fearing the body scanner would affect her defibrillator.

Instead, the search made her miss her flight and wait two-and-a-half hours. TSA denied she had been stripped, insisting that "all passengers are treated with dignity and respect," but it planned to establish a hotline for those with disabilities or medical conditions. After a scanner set off an alarm in January 2012, Sen. Rand Paul refused a pat-down and missed his flight (but was allowed to board a later one without the pat-down). He condemned TSA as an "out of control" "police state," which "gropes and grabs our children, our seniors, and our loved ones and neighbors with disabilities." His "Plan to Restore America" would eliminate TSA. Just before the Republican National Convention in September 2012, Paul mimed the backscatter-machine stance in a speech, asking the audience: "Is this the pose of a free man?"

Although Pistole praised TSA's Screening Passengers by Observation Techniques (SPOT) program, which claimed to identify potential terrorists by their "micro-expressions," journalists revealed that Behavioral Detection Officers (BDOs) in New Jersey and Hawaii targeted Mexicans in order to demonstrate productivity. Rep. Bennie G. Thompson (D-Miss) had raised questions as House Homeland Security Committee chair in August 2010 and again in November 2011 as ranking minority member. A GAO report found that 39 percent of arrests from SPOT referrals were for immigration violations. Pistole replied that BDOs could not distinguish unlawful immigrants from terrorists because both feared discovery. Nine months later 32 BDOs at Boston's Logan Airport (the testing ground for an expanded use of behavioral detection) filed written complaints about profiling (after taking their concerns to the ACLU). In order to meet managers' demands for criminal referrals, BDOs targeted blacks, Hispanics, other minorities, and those from the Middle East, believing they were more likely to be carrying drugs or have outstanding arrest warrants or immigration problems. DHS Secretary Napolitano responded by requiring BDOs and their managers to attend a four-hour class on why racial profiling was unacceptable and ineffective.

In June 2013 the DHS IG found that TSA had never assessed SPOT's effectiveness or instituted a comprehensive training program for BDOs. Rep. Thompson planned to offer an amendment to the DHS appropriation bill to terminate SPOT, which had cost

$1 billion. The *New York Times* commented that "erratic and sub-jective screening wastes time and money – and worse, can be a pre-text for illegal profiling." Pistole replied that SPOT was "a proven and unobtrusive way for officers to look out for possible threats and illegal activity. Looking and listening for behavioral cues like facial expressions, body language or other mannerisms that may indicate a security risk are simply common sense and a far cry from profiling, which is imprecise and ineffective."

Five months later, however, GAO repeated that "until TSA can pro-vide scientifically validated evidence demonstrating that behavioral indicators can be used to identify passengers who may pose a threat to aviation security, the agency risks funding activities that have not been determined to be effective." Less than one percent of the more than 30,000 passengers annually identified as suspicious were arrested, and *none* of those charges related to terrorism. A meta-analysis of 200 studies found that identification of liars based on behavior was no better than chance, and even worse in the absence of verbal cues. Pistole responded: "I can personally attest to the effectiveness of behavior detection principles." "T.S.A. is not looking for a stereotypical liar, but rather for a high-risk passenger exhibiting behavior patterns historically observed in people intending to carry out terrorist attacks and other egregious crimes."

In January 2013 TSA canceled its contract with Rapiscan (which had failed to meet a Congressional deadline for adopting software to protect privacy), substituting machines that concealed all iden-tifying details. TSA planned to identify "trusted travelers" eligible for lighter screening based on information collected by airlines and travel agents, including birth date, passport number, travel itinerary, and discount. Pistole said they would start with elite frequent flyers "because we knew from intelligence that they were less likely to be a possible terrorist." The German Federal Commissioner for Data Protection and Freedom of Information questioned whether the program met the requirement that it be effective, proportional, and nondiscriminatory. A Libyan-born American citizen complained that on each of his eight trips between June and October 2013 "they pat me down. Then they pull out every single article of clothing in my bag" and swab his luggage for explosives.

After the Christmas Day bomb attempt, the USA also required more intense scrutiny of citizens from 14 nations, even if they had not lived there for years. Nigeria (Abdulmutallab's birthplace) objected that "it is unfair to discriminate against over 150 million people because of the behavior of one person." Algeria protested: "discrimination against the citizens of Algeria, who do not pose any particular risk to the people of the United States." The *Los Angeles Times* agreed that "the vast majority of people from these countries are not violent, religious extremists." "[I]n treating entire nations as potential suspects, we will drive away like-minded business partners and political allies." Pakistani politicians on a DoS tour of the USA canceled their domestic flights after refusing to submit to a full-body scan because it "makes you naked, and in making you naked, they make the whole country naked." Three months after introducing more intense scrutiny the USA dropped it in favor of individual intelligence. But foreign dignitaries continued to criticize their treatment. DoD apologized after nine Pakistani military officers traveling to CENTCOM in Tampa were removed from an airplane when one made what a flight attendant considered an "inappropriate remark." India's Foreign Minister protested when its Ambassador to the USA was pulled out of line and patted down at a Mississippi airport, the second time this had happened in three months. TSA suggested it was because she was wearing "bulky" clothes, i.e., a sari. In November 2011 the USA apologized after the former Indian president was frisked at JFK Airport.

The variety of travel restrictions after 9/11, though initially confusing, reveals *whose* rights are protected and *in which* circumstances. Muslims arbitrarily and rudely ejected from airplanes obtained little redress, while other mistreated passengers received greater sympathy. Although the Circuits split, some federal judges upheld privacy rights against border searches of electronic devices, perhaps because the targets were ordinary Americans (like the judges themselves). The overbreadth of terrorist watchlists – eventually containing more than a million names – and their many, often ludicrous, errors persisted, despite widespread and repeated criticism, both within the federal government and by the media. Yet MEK was able to mobilize enough political clout among conservatives to pressure Secretary of State Clinton to remove it. One district judge boldly exposed and denounced the errors, secrecy, and cover-ups in the mistreatment of Rahinah Ibrahim, only to have his own opinion mangled and obscured by government censors.

The different responses to watchlists and airport scanners are illuminating. Watchlists affect relatively few people, most of them foreign, Muslim, or both. Scanners affect *all* of the more than 800 million annual air travelers, most of them non-Muslim citizens. Critics – many just seizing another pretext to attack Obama – pushed two hot button issues – sex (nudity) and health (cancer) – to foment widespread moral panic. (In fact, scanners were the brainchild of Pistole, who had been *Bush's* Assistant Director of the FBI, and were championed by Chertoff, *Bush's* first DHS Secretary, who personally profited from them after leaving office.) Rightly unpersuaded, courts found no constitutional violation; and a technological fix allayed anxieties about voyeurism. (Scanners exposed travelers to much less radiation than they experienced during flight.) But conservatives persisted in exploiting American individualism, widespread anger at the worsening experience of air travel, and suspicion of government (especially Washington), calling for profiling (which would transform scans into watchlists, limiting their impact to Muslims). Pistole encouraged this by maintaining uncritical enthusiasm for SPOT, even though he was never able to adduce evidence for this hugely expensive program's effectiveness. Frequent business travelers were offered special treatment (an obvious class bias). Prominent individuals secured apologies for mistreatment. And nations successfully resisted discrimination against their citizens (especially the most prominent). This mixed bag of resistance to the arbitrary, costly, and dubiously effective impediments to travel since 9/11 reflects the vagaries of politics rather than legal norms. (A DHS IG investigation found that screeners failed to detect weapons and other prohibited items 95 percent of the time in a covert test.[52])

IMMIGRATION

Immigrants were vulnerable to civil liberties violations because they possessed the fewest constitutional rights and the 9/11 attackers were foreign.[53] In November 2002 the National Security Entry Exit and Registration System required all men over 16 who were citizens of 25 listed countries to be photographed, fingerprinted, and interviewed under oath.[54] Of the 83,000 who responded, nearly 20 percent were put into deportation proceedings, and 1,200 were charged with immigration offenses. Only 11 of the more than 65,000 who registered the first year were found to have ties to terrorists. The Portland, Oregon, city attorney (whose father had been Eisenhower's Attorney General and Nixon's Secretary of State) refused Attorney General Ashcroft's request to help interview 5,000 men, citing an Oregon law that prohibited questioning anyone who was not a crime suspect. When the program was terminated in April 2011, at least one man was still fighting deportation. As we saw in Chapter 6 on civil actions, detainees lost all damages claims except those concerning conditions of confinement.

Long after 9/11, immigrants continued to be subject to expulsion. A 16-year-old girl who had emigrated from Bangladesh at the age of five was deported when the FBI discovered her visits to an internet chat room containing sermons by a London imam encouraging suicide bombing.[55] Federal authorities also used the threat of deportation to persuade immigrants to become informants.[56] Yassine Ouassif, a 24-year-old Moroccan permanent resident who had immigrated legally in January 2001, was blocked from returning to the USA in September 2005, and then had his Green Card suspended when he managed to do so. He was then threatened with detention if he did not inform, and was told it would take two years to fight deportation and that he would lose.

Challenges to other immigration rulings faced huge hurdles. Grants of visas are notoriously arbitrary. Tariq Ramadan, a Swiss academic (and grandson of the founder of the Muslim Brotherhood) was invited to speak by the American Academy of Religion, the American Association of University Professors and PEN American Center, and was offered a chair by Notre Dame University, but he was barred under the USA Patriot Act (he accepted a chair at Oxford).[57] When he reapplied for a visa after receiving more than forty invitations to speak in the USA, he was declared a "public safety and national security risk" because in 2000 he had donated $1,300 to a French-based committee for charity and aid to Palestinians, which allegedly supported Hamas (before it was declared a terrorist organization). The Second Circuit ordered the government to let him show he had not known his donation would go to Hamas.

The ACLU, PEN American Center and other organizations sued on behalf of Adam Habib, a South African academic who had a Ph.D. from City University of New York (CUNY) and who had been a frequent visitor to the USA until his visa was revoked in 2006. The New York Times urged Secretary of State Clinton to "end ideological exclusions and to review dubious visa denials." When she granted visas to both Ramadan and Habib, the Times renewed its call "to end ideological exclusion."

Goverdhan Mehta – President of the Paris-based International Council for Science (an advocate for free access to scientific research), director of the Indian Institute of Science, and science adviser to the Indian Prime Minister – was denied a visa to speak at an international conference in the USA (which he had visited dozens of times) after traveling 200 miles to a US consulate and waiting three hours for an interview, in which he was accused of deception about the nature of his research and told to fill out a detailed questionnaire and return.[58] Although the USA apologized and offered a visa, he canceled his trip.

Surprisingly, those jailed while fighting deportation were more successful. Ahilan Nadarajah was arrested for an immigration violation in October 2001.[59] Although Immigration Court judges twice granted him asylum, DHS detained him as a terrorist while it appealed. In March 2006 the Ninth Circuit found his five-year detention "plainly unreasonable." "The government does not possess the authority under the general detention statutes to hold Nadarajah ... indefinitely." After prosecutors unsealed an indictment against the Holy Land Foundation (HLF), they arrested Abdel-Jabbar Hamdan on immigration charges (for overstaying a 1979 student visa). An Immigration Court judge ordered him deported but blocked DHS from sending him to Jordan, where he might be tortured. DHS kept him in prison because of a donation to HLF, which allegedly supported Hamas. A magistrate judge found that this violated a Supreme Court decision limiting such detention to six months. The Board of Immigration Appeals affirmed the deportation, finding he should have known HLF was funding "Hamas-controlled charitable organizations and support to the orphans and families of Hamas martyrs and prisoners." But CD Cal Judge Hatter ordered the government to free Hamdan, threatening DHS Secretary Chertoff with contempt if he failed to do so. ED Va Judge Friedman ordered the release of Majed T. Hajbeh, a Palestinian imprisoned for four years because the government could not deport him to Jordan (where he had been convicted in absentia) or find another country to take him.[60] The most dramatic victory followed a 20-year fight against deportation by two alleged members of the Popular Front for the Liberation of Palestine, when a federal judge condemned the government's "gross failure" to comply with his order to provide potentially exculpatory information, creating "an embarrassment to the rule of law."[61] The government heeded exhortations by the *Washington Post*, *Los Angeles Times*, and *New York Times* not to appeal.

Some asylum seekers received unexpected support from an unusual alliance of liberals (HRW, HRF) and conservatives (including Concerned Women for America and the National Association of Evangelicals). A Hudson Institute fellow and former Reagan administration lawyer condemned as "indefensible" asylum denials based on a broad definition of "material support" to terrorist groups.[62] Gary Bauer, President of American Values, said enforcement had "lapsed into ludicrousy [sic]." The Bush administration responded by proposing to allow waivers for combatants fleeing authoritarian governments in Myanmar, Tibet, Vietnam, Laos, and Cuba. But journalists and human rights organizations continued to document delays in processing applications for visas, green cards, citizenship, and asylum, especially for Muslims.[63]

Sens. Joseph Lieberman (D-Ct) and Scott Brown (R-Mass) and Reps. Jason Altmire (D-Pa) and Charlie Dent (R-Pa) introduced the Terrorist Expatriation Act to strip citizenship from those the Secretary of State found (without a judicial hearing) had joined terrorist organizations or provided material support to them.[64] The sponsors claimed this would prevent such people from reentering the USA and make them eligible for MC prosecution. Lieberman said his target was Adam Gadahn (a notorious al-Qaeda spokesman), but the *New York Times* noted that Gadahn had already been indicted for treason. Secretary of State Clinton said the administration would take "a hard look" at the bill. "United States citizenship is a privilege. It is not a right. People who are serving foreign powers – or in this case, foreign terrorists – are clearly in violation ... of that oath which they swore when they became citizens." (The vast majority acquire citizenship by birth, not oath.) In an unusual role reversal, House Speaker Nancy Pelosi (D-Ca) supported the "spirit" of the measure, but House Minority Leader John Boehner warned that "until they are convicted of some crime, I don't see how you would attempt to take their citizenship away ... under the United States Constitution." Georgetown law professor David Cole wrote in a *Washington Post* op ed that the bill was "a meaningless form of symbolism that plays on patriotic fervor and xenophobic anxiety but would have no legal effect." The *Los Angeles Times* called the proposal "unnecessary and open to abuse." University of California, Irvine School of Law dean Erwin Chemerinsky wrote in a *Los Angeles Times* op ed that its provisions were "dangerous and ineffective, violations of basic civil liberties, and they are almost surely unconstitutional." The *Washington Post* said the bill "wouldn't be very useful" and "seriously threatens civil liberties." Having attracted only one other sponsor during the six weeks after it was introduced, the bill died a quiet death at the end of the Congressional session.

Not surprisingly, immigrants enjoyed few legal protections when the federal government responded to the 9/11 attacks with wholesale interrogation, detention, and deportation of Muslim and Arab men.

Yet each instance of successful resistance to the government's abuse of its largely unrestrained power is illuminating. Although courts could not review visa decisions (as even Judge Alsup conceded in Rahinah Ibrahim's case), Ramadan and Habib won visas when persistent pressure by educational and cultural institutions coincided with a change in the White House. Noncitizens who lost their deportation cases convinced courts to free them from indefinite detention when the government could not find a recipient country where they would be safe from torture. Conservatives usually eager to pander to American xenophobia had a soft spot for asylum seekers at risk because they had helped the USA or challenged regimes the conservatives disliked. And a foolish bill's gratuitous proposal to strip citizenship attracted few sponsors. Only politics explains why immigrants, otherwise bereft of legal protections, sometimes prevailed.

POLICE BEHAVIOR

In the wake of 9/11, a variety of government agencies surveilled and arrested protesters engaging in constitutionally protected activity. Three years after the DoJ IG criticized FBI behavior, the ACLU reported that the Bureau continued to violate civil liberties.[65] But the controversy was especially heated in New York, whose police department was bound by the 1985 consent decree resolving the 1971 *Handschu* litigation brought by 16 political organizations.[66] The decree prohibited police investigations without "specific information" of involvement in or preparation for criminal activity and required police to get permission from the *Handschu* Authority (two police officers and a civilian appointed by the mayor) to investigate a mix of constitutionally protected and criminal activity. In 2003 the Corporation Counsel persuaded SDNY Judge Haight (who had approved the original decree) to abolish the *Handschu* Authority, eliminate the requirement that police have specific evidence a crime was being committed, and authorize police to "attend any event open to the public, on the same terms and conditions of the public generally" in order "to investigate and thwart terrorists," but retain only evidence related to potential criminal activity. Four days after Haight's ruling, NYPD arrested 350 protesters against the Iraq war, asked many about their political views and activities, and charged almost all with disorderly conduct. Commissioner Raymond W. Kelly explained: "we live in a more dangerous, constantly changing world." But Eileen Clancy, founder of I-Witness Video, gave the *New York Times* tapes showing at least ten undercover agents carrying protest signs, holding flowers, and riding bicycles at Iraq war protests, mass bicycle rallies, and a street vigil for a bicyclist killed while riding. Judge Haight found that in February and March 2003 (before he changed the guidelines) NYPD had videotaped anti-war rallies and questioned those arrested about their politics. The *Times* called it "a sad day" when NYPD was "caught using underhanded tactics to spy on and even distort political protests and mass rallies." During the 2004 Convention police had made "a deliberate effort to incite violence that would in turn justify a tough police response." "Mayor Michael Bloomberg's record on free speech is already pretty poor. Unless he wants to make a disregard for New Yorkers' rights part of his legacy, he should make sure that the police understand what civil liberties mean in a democracy."

Five internal NYPD documents obtained in a lawsuit by animal rights demonstrators arrested during the February 2002 World Economic Forum disclosed that commanders used "proactive arrests," covert surveillance, and psychological tactics to control protesters. A police captain praised subordinates for seizing demonstrators who were "obviously potential rioters." A draft report by the Disorder Control unit proposed resuming covert tactics repudiated by the city 30 years earlier, including: "utilize undercover officers to distribute misinformation within the crowds." Another report endorsed the "staging of massive amounts" of armored vehicles, prisoner wagons and jail buses to "cause [demonstrators] to be alarmed." Those arrested were held up to 40 hours without seeing a judge (twice as long as those arrested for murder, rape, or robbery the same day); all the charges were dropped or dismissed.

Nearly 400 people were arrested in Union Square on August 31, 2004, jailed for up to 48 hours, and charged with disorderly conduct and parading without a permit. NYPD Inspector James Essig swore in a criminal complaint the next day that police had warned the group "they were blocking vehicular traffic, had to disperse and would be arrested if they did not." But in subsequent litigation Essig first could not "recall specifically what I said," then claimed he had "attempted to" order them to disperse, and finally admitted not doing so.

NYPD's own remedial processes were toothless. The Civilian Complaint Review Board received 63 complaints about police activity during the Convention, but found no misconduct in 32, dropped 18, was unable to identify the officer in 7, and substantiated just 3. It charged Deputy Chiefs Stephen Paragallo and Terence Monahan with abuse of authority for ordering the arrest of large numbers of demonstrators without giving them an opportunity to disperse. But it recommended only an "instruction" for Paragallo, which Commissioner Kelly declined to issue, declaring that policing during the Convention "was one of the Police Department's finest hours" and "protected the city against a potential terrorist attack while accommodating massive, peaceful protest." Police were not obligated to give a warning before making arrests.

The city paid over $400,000 to settle 13 of 635 claims by the 1,800 arrested during the Convention. It had sought to seal legal briefs in the cases, but SDNY Magistrate Judge James C. Francis IV, citing "the patent inadequacy" of the city's "formulaic incantation of harm," ordered it to disclose records of arrests, videotapes, and testimony. In February 2007 Judge Haight ordered the police to destroy videotapes of people exercising constitutionally protected rights at a Harlem march and a homeless demonstration at Gracie Mansion. Calling the police conduct "egregious," Haight admitted his 2003 order was not "a model of clarity." The modified *Handschu* decree had allowed investigation and videotaping only if there were indications that unlawful activity might occur and only after securing permission from the Deputy Commissioner of the Intelligence Division. Neither condition had been satisfied. Emphasizing the "quantum difference between a police officer and a little old lady (or other tourist or private citizen) videotaping or photographing a public event," Haight warned that future violations could lead to contempt citations. The *New York Times* praised him for curbing the police, who "have more and more overstepped by routinely and indiscriminately videotaping demonstrations of every kind, even peaceful ones."

NYPD continued to resist discovery on the ground that the media would "fixate upon and sensationalize" documents that "contain information filtered and distilled for analysis by intelligence officers accustomed to reading intelligence information" but could be "misinterpreted." Retorting that the documents revealed that the Intelligence Division had sent undercover detectives around the world to collect information on political activists, most of whom had shown no intent to break the law, the *New York Times* declared that "the police may have overreached and misused surveillance authority" and seem "to have spent a lot of effort infiltrating and compiling dossiers on groups that clearly posed no danger."

Mr. Bloomberg has made it no secret that he does not like protests ... The city has lost its best forum – Central Park's Great Lawn – for the large demonstrations that once defined New York as a center of free speech. New Yorkers expect the Police Department to keep them safe, but not at the cost of their constitutional rights. So, pardon us while we fixate [on the documents].

City lawyers accused the NYCLU of leaking the documents to the *Times*, an "egregious violation" of the court order against disclosure (but they later admitted not knowing the source). Reversing himself, Judge Francis ordered the police to give the NYCLU and the *Times* 600 pages of summary reports on police preparation for the Convention, which revealed that detectives visited at least 15 cities in the USA, Canada, and Europe, posing as activists or sympathizers and participating in meetings by church groups and anti-war and environmental organizations. An unrepentant Commissioner Kelly reiterated that the NYPD "did an outstanding job of protecting this city during the Convention. People wanted to come here to shut down the city."

After NYPD presented evidence that the 2005 demonstrations had involved unlawful activity, Judge Haight reversed his threat to hold it in contempt for violating his 2003 modification of the *Handschu* decree, declaring he could punish only constitutional violations. "It would be unduly burdensome for this court to police every alleged violation of the N.Y.P.D. guidelines no matter how slight." But "if the N.Y.P.D. should break its promise to the court" to follow the 2003 modification, "I am not required to sit idly by with my hands tied." Judge Francis then ordered release of nearly 2,000 pages of raw intelligence and other documents (while concealing the identities of undercover officers and confidential informants, as well as police investigative methods).

Judge Francis refused to consider a sealed affidavit by David Cohen, Deputy Commissioner for Intelligence, because "secret argument is antithetical to our adversary system of justice." When the city subpoenaed all I-Witness Video tapes (including some 150 shot by volunteers and others, which it had archived), Eileen Clancy called this "a gross abuse of subpoena power," agreeing to turn over only arrest footage. When Judge Francis again ordered NYPD to release documents it appealed. The *New York Times* "wonder[ed] what the New York City Police Department is trying to hide" and urged it "to lift the secrecy surrounding its actions." The Second Circuit reversed, holding that plaintiffs had not shown a "compelling need" for the documents.

In August 2008 the city agreed to pay over $2 million to 52 people arrested at protests during the opening days of the Iraq war. The only two tried were acquitted. The city spent another $1 million on its defense, assigning five lawyers to the case for four years and creating a special appellate team; 55 police officers and supervisors were deposed, many losing two days of work. In November, NYPD revealed that in April 2007, two weeks before Judge Haight heard the NYCLU complaint about unlawful videotaping, the Department had revised its rules to videotape only "when it appears that unlawful conduct is about to occur, is occurring, or has occurred during the demonstration." Criticizing the Department for not notifying it or the court of the change, the NYCLU sought costs for the 17 months of unnecessary litigation and an order that the city inform it of future changes.

In October 2010 SDNY Judge Sullivan upheld the disorderly conduct arrests during the Republican National Convention of two men holding anti-abortion signs on a 7th Avenue sidewalk facing Madison Square Garden. Asserting their right to be within "sight and sound" of conventioneers, the two had refused 17 orders to leave. But two years later Judge Sullivan found that arrests of more than 200 on Fulton Street during the Convention lacked probable cause. "An individual's participation in a lawbreaking group may, in appropriate circumstances, be strong circumstantial evidence of an individual's own illegal conduct. But, no matter the circumstances, an arresting officer must believe that every individual arrested personally violated the law ... The Fourth Amendment does not recognize guilt by association." However, he upheld the Department's "no-summons" policy because "intelligence sources" revealed that "demonstrators aimed to 'shut down the city of New York and the R.N.C.' through 'continuous unlawful behavior'" and "would be undeterred by the issuances of summonses."

In 2011 AP investigative reporters Adam Goldman and Matt Apuzzo published an exposé of NYPD undercover work (for which they received a Pulitzer Prize and the Harvard Kennedy School's Goldsmith Prize). David Cohen, the 35-year CIA veteran who became Deputy Commissioner for Intelligence in 2002, and his deputy Larry Sanchez (with 15 years of overseas CIA experience) were instrumental in having the CIA train an NYPD detective and second to the Department a former CIA station chief in Pakistan and Jordan. The undercover program began in response to the 2003 suicide bombings in Casablanca and the 2005 Madrid train bombing linked to Moroccan terrorists (even though there was no evidence that Moroccans posed a threat in

New York). Cohen sent police to Pakistani neighborhoods to stop cars on pretext so they could search for outstanding warrants or suspicious behavior and turn suspects into informants. When NYPD applied to relax the *Handschu* restrictions, Cohen wrote Judge Haight that "in the case of terrorism, to wait for an indication of crime before investigating is to wait far too long." After Haight agreed, noting that the old rules "addressed different perils in a different time," NYPD created the Demographic Unit, dividing the city into zones and assigning undercover police to monitor ethnic neighborhoods. (The Department initially denied the Unit's existence and then said it had been closed.) Because Cohen wanted the squad to "rake the coals, looking for hot spots," police who monitored bookstores, bars, cafes, and nightclubs became known as "rakers." NYPD regularly shredded documents discussing their activities. It also sent informants known as "mosque crawlers" to take notes on sermons. (Because the FBI could not do that, its officials in New York ordered agents not to accept information from mosque crawlers.) NYPD also conducted surveillance in New Jersey.

David Petraeus, the new DCI, said in response to these revelations that the Agency's IG had begun an investigation. DNI James Clapper admitted it was "not a good optic to have C.I.A. involved in any city-level police department." Rep. Rush Holt (D-NJ) called it "profiling, plain and simple." "[I]n America, you don't put people under suspicion without good reason." Several New York State senators wanted an investigation. Lawyers monitoring the *Handschu* decree asked Judge Haight to examine the disclosures. At a hearing packed with Muslim organizers and civil liberties lawyers, NYC Council Member Brad Lander said: "it looks like we are targeting Muslim neighborhoods and communities." Commissioner Kelly replied that the Department followed leads involving "the possibility of unlawful activity" "wherever these leads may take us." The Demographics Unit (now called the Zone Assessment Unit) mapped "a lot of different communities." A CIA employee "works with us" as an adviser and provides "information, usually coming from perhaps overseas," but "doesn't have access to our investigative files." NYPD claimed to have foiled 14 terrorist plots since 9/11. (When an investigative reporter called the boast exaggerated, Kelly retorted: "after a plot is thwarted, always somebody would say … it couldn't happen … Of course, if something happened, then it's our fault.") Sen. Dianne Feinstein (D-Ca) said the CIA has "no business or authority in domestic spying, or in advising the NYPD how to conduct local surveillance."

Three dozen members of Congress urged federal investigations. But conservative newspapers backed the NYPD. The *New York Post* said there was "a very good reason why anti-terror investigations often lead to the Muslim American community. It's because that's where the threat often resides." The *New York Daily News* called the investigative reporting "overheated, overhyped."

The exposé increased mistrust of the police in the Muslim community. Some Muslims opened meetings on campuses and in mosques by saying "hello to whoever might be spying." At a "know your rights" session at Brooklyn College, a CUNY law professor called most police investigations "a fishing expedition … the safest thing you can do for yourself, your family and for your community, is not to answer." The Muslim community sought an independent commission to investigate police and CIA operations. Fourteen Muslim leaders boycotted the mayor's annual interfaith breakfast and sought a meeting with Bloomberg to discuss the surveillance; another three dozen supported their protest. But overall attendance was up, including about 60 Muslims – one wearing an "I AM NOT A TERRORIST!" t-shirt. In his weekly radio broadcast, Bloomberg insisted the police did not "target any neighborhood." He added disingenuously: "It's like saying you are going after people that are my height with brown hair. If a perpetrator is described that way in the neighborhood, you look at everybody in the neighborhood that's got brown hair, my height, you stop them." (Would he have felt the same if NYPD profiled Jews?)

Although the CIA IG found no wrongdoing in the partnership with NYPD, it also found that the Agency had failed to obtain its general counsel's prior approval (as required by a presidential order) and violated its own rules by sending a senior clandestine operative to New York in July 2011 (the CIA promptly withdrew him). Noting that the NYPD fell outside the jurisdiction of the city's Department of Investigations, two Brennan Center lawyers called for an independent NYPD inspector general. After a new AP story revealed that NYPD had urged officers to "expand and focus intelligence" at Shiite mosques, 30 Muslim and legal advocacy groups and New York Attorney General Eric Schneiderman called for an investigation.

Other journalists uncovered evidence of additional surveillance. NYPD officers investigated students at universities throughout the Northeast, talking to professors, sending undercover agents on student trips, and trawling websites. Richard Levin, president of Yale (one of the targets) declared, "in the strongest possible terms, that police surveillance based on religion, nationality, or peacefully expressed political opinion is antithetical to the values of Yale, the academic community, and the United States." New York's City College, another target, criticized "any investigation of any student organization based on the political or religious content of its ideas." NYPD replied that "some of the most dangerous western al-Qaeda linked/inspired terrorists since 9/11 were radicalized and/or recruited at universities in Muslim Student Associations." Bloomberg dismissed the critics: "I don't know why keeping the country safe is antithetical to the values of Yale." Three prominent civil liberties lawyers wrote the *New York Times* that "law enforcement agencies should be prohibited from compiling a permanent database of individuals who are not engaged in suspected or actual criminal activity, especially protected First Amendment activity." The *Times* agreed: "today Muslims are the target ... Tomorrow it will be another vulnerable group whose lawful behavior is blended into criminal activity."

Revelations that NYPD also surveilled mosques and businesses in Newark provoked Mayor Cory Booker to condemn such actions as "deeply offensive"; his Police Director assured residents that "this type of activity is not what the Newark Police Department would ever do." New Jersey Governor Chris Christie called the reports "disturbing," wondering whether "this NYPD action was born out of arrogance, or out of paranoia, or out of both." NYPD "think their jurisdiction is the world. Their jurisdiction is NYC." But though Christie asked his Attorney General (AG) to investigate, it turned out that the AG and his predecessor had known about the surveillance at the time, and Christie's own predecessor had signed two executive orders authorizing the operation. The FBI Special Agent in Charge of the Newark office was critical: "when people pull back cooperation, it creates additional risk, it creates blind spots." But FBI Director Mueller told the House Appropriations Committee that "Kelly and the NYPD have done a remarkable job in protecting New York." When it emerged that White House grant money had paid for the surveillance, the administration promptly denied any control over how it was spent. Commissioner Kelly accused critics of using the media "to spread misinformation," declaring: "it would be folly for us to focus only on the five boroughs of New York City." "[T]he tactics and strategies that we've used on the streets of this city have indeed saved lives." Bloomberg said his city's safety was not "a political football to play with." Former mayor Ed Koch said the *New York Times* editorial "endangers the lives of eight million residents." The *Times* replied that these responses "overlook the real-life consequences of the surveillance."

After Gov. Christie withdrew his criticism of the NYPD because his Attorney General said it had broken no law, Muslim leaders considered appealing to the DoJ. Some, represented by Muslim Advocates, sued New York City. A New Jersey State Assemblyman (who was also a Jersey City detective) introduced a bill to require out-of-state police to notify the state Attorney General, head of the State Police and chief law enforcement officer in any locality surveilled. The revelations had repercussions across the country. Muslim and Sikh leaders in Los Angeles pressured LAPD to limit the federal Suspicious Activities Reporting program to criminal behavior. San Francisco required a public hearing by the Police Commission before the San Francisco Police Department (SFPD) renewed its cooperation with the FBI.

Goldman and Apuzzo published new files showing that NYPD collected information on businesses owned by second- and third-generation Muslim Americans but not the Jewish majority among Syrian immigrants or the Coptic minority among Egyptians. Although Bloomberg had said in response to the initial reports that "we don't stop to think about religion," he still claimed "we're doing the right thing." Attorney General Holder expressed concern about the surveillance, which was being reviewed. A poll found that 58 percent of voters approved of the police behavior, including pluralities of blacks, Hispanics, and Democrats. But the *New York Times* called the operation "a possible violation" of the *Handschu* decree, and two dozen NYC Council Members proposed the creation of an Inspector General for the NYPD.

In a deposition in one of the cases alleging violation of the *Handschu* guidelines, NYPD Assistant Chief Thomas Galati of the Counterterrorism and Intelligence Bureau defended the Demographics Unit by maintaining the Department "has not commenced an investigation" based on information "related to Demographics." "I never made a lead from rhetoric that came from a Demographics report." (Why, then, did the NYPD waste resources on such activity?) But his account offered further evidence that the Unit profiled Muslims engaged in constitutionally protected activity. Describing "rakers" who overheard two Pakistani men complaining in Urdu that airport security policies singled out Muslims, Galati commented: "I'm seeing Urdu. I'm seeing them identify the individuals involved in that are Pakistani. I'm using that information for me to determine that this would be a kind of place that a terrorist would be comfortable in. Most Urdu speakers from that region would be of concern, so that's why it's important to me."

Similarly, eavesdropping in a Lebanese café might let analysts learn that customers were from south Lebanon. "That may be an indicator of possibility that that is a sympathizer to Hezbollah because southern Lebanon is dominated by Hezbollah." Based on this information, lawyers monitoring the *Handschu* decree told Judge Haight in February 2013 that "the N.Y.P.D. has deceived this court and counsel, as well as the public, concerning the character and scope of its activities in violation of the guidelines." The *New York Times* said the lawyers

> had made a strong case that the city has simply ignored those guidelines in its anti-terrorism fight and is targeting Muslim groups because of their religious affiliation, not because they present any risk … If the assertions by the *Handschu* lawyers are borne out in court, the judge should consider appointing an independent monitor to review Department investigations.

In March 2013 Creating Law Enforcement Accountability and Responsibility (CLEAR) (a CUNY Law School project) and two organizations representing Muslim and Asian Americans published a report on NYPD surveillance of Muslims. Three months later CLEAR and NYCLU sued the city and NYPD to stop the surveillance, asking the judge to appoint a police monitor. After reports that NYPD installed a video camera to record those attending a Brooklyn mosque and tried to engage congregants there and elsewhere in inflammatory conversations, the *New York Times* hoped courts would decide whether the Muslim surveillance program was constitutional. "What already seems clear is that these surveillance policies create suspicion and mistrust, which does not help the police department or anyone else."

In June 2013 EPIC obtained a declassified summary of the CIA IG's December 2011 report finding that four Agency analysts had been assigned to police departments. Larry Sanchez believed there were "no limitations" on his activities because he was on unpaid leave from the Agency; another agent read "unfiltered" police reports. NYPD replied it was "proud of our relationship with C.I.A." In August the *Washington Post* revealed that in seeking to persuade Judge Haight to relax the *Handschu* decree, David Cohen had told him mosques could be used "to shield the work of terrorists from law enforcement scrutiny by taking advantage of restrictions on the investigation of First Amendment activity." NYPD had proposed Terrorism Enterprise Investigations

(TEIs), allowing police to monitor speech whenever the "facts or circumstances reasonably indicate" that two or more were plotting terrorism or other violent crimes. In the first eight months of the new *Handschu* rules, NYPD opened at least fifteen TEIs, at least ten targeting mosques. When the FBI refused NYPD's request to bug a mosque, police used informants to secretly record sermons and conversations. Declaring that this "indefensible" surveillance program "has turned out to be even more aggressive than earlier reports had shown," the *New York Times* applauded the City Council for overriding Bloomberg's veto and establishing a police inspector general. The ACLU and 125 organizations nationwide asked DoJ to investigate NYPD surveillance.

Immediately after his 2013 election as mayor, Bill de Blasio announced that his new Police Commissioner, William Bratton, would review intelligence gathering. David Cohen and Richard Daddario (head of the counterterrorism unit) promptly resigned. During de Blasio's first week in office, the city settled most of the demonstrators' outstanding lawsuits for $18 million. The city's total cost for all the cases (including legal expenses) exceeded $35 million, making it the "largest protest settlement" in American history, which the *New York Times* called "an expensive legal course in basic civil liberties." In a meeting with de Blasio, Attorney General Holder extended the FBI's ban on profiling to national security investigations and the protected categories from race to religion, national origin, gender, and sexual orientation. In April 2014, after Muslim and Arab groups met with Bratton, NYPD abolished the Demographics Unit. "In the future, we will gather that information, if necessary, through direct contact between the police precincts and the representatives of the communities they serve." The *New York Times* praised this "important step" in abolishing an "indefensible program" and urged the city to reinstate the *Handschu* Authority. But NYPD continued to operate its Citywide Debriefing Team, which interrogated Muslims arrested for non-terrorism offenses (such as arguing with a parking enforcement officer, prostitution, driving or operating a vending cart without a license), asking about religious practices and seeking to turn those charged into informants. Although the new Deputy Commissioner of Intelligence claimed these were "noncoercive sessions where people had the ability to opt out at any time," the *New York Times* accused the Department of "still running a program that singles out Muslims in a problematic way."

In June 2015 SDNY Magistrate Judge James Orenstein approved a settlement of the NYCLU lawsuit.[67] NYPD would not investigate solely based on religion, race or ethnicity, would use undercover officers only when other options were impractical, and would consider the effect of its actions on religious groups. A civilian lawyer, appointed by the mayor for a five-year term and approved by a federal judge, would review intelligence files and report misconduct to the Commissioner, the mayor, or a judge. In August 2016 the NYPD Office of the Inspector General (NYPD OIG) issued a report criticizing the Department for not complying with the *Handschu* guidelines: missing deadlines to seek extensions of investigations into political activity, and failing to explain the role of undercover officers and confidential informants. In October Judge Haight rejected the settlement, citing the NYPD OIG finding of "near-systemic failure." NYPD had become "accustomed to disregarding" court orders. "The proposed role and powers of the civilian representative do not furnish sufficient protection from potential violations of the constitutional rights of those law-abiding Muslims and believers in Islam who live, move and have their being in this city." Declaring that "the NYPD has had a long history of trampling on the constitutional rights of law-abiding citizens," the *New York Times* said Haight was "right not to accept the settlement." (A month later, after meeting Trump, Rep. Peter T. King (R-NY) urged a national surveillance program modeled on what he called the "forward-leaning" and "very effective" NYPD program.) In March 2017 NYPD agreed to Haight's more stringent conditions, empowering the civilian monitor to raise questions about ongoing investigations and report violations to the court, which would have to approve elimination of the monitor. The city also paid $1.67 million to those surveilled. But three months later the NYCLU sued the NYPD for giving a Glomar response – it could neither confirm nor deny – to two requests for information about surveillance; and the Department opposed a City Council bill requiring it to report the equipment it used to surveil and how it stored the data it obtained.

In February 2014 D NJ Judge Martini dismissed a 2012 lawsuit challenging NYPD surveillance of mosques because the eight Muslim plaintiffs "have not alleged facts from which it can be plausibly inferred that they were targeted solely because of their religion.[68] The more likely explanation for the surveillance was to locate budding terrorist conspiracies." "The motive for the program was not solely to discriminate against Muslims, but to find Muslim terrorists hiding among the ordinary law-abiding Muslims." Any injuries the plaintiffs suffered "flow from The Associated Press's unauthorized disclosure" of the surveillance. In October 2015 the Third Circuit reversed. Judge Ambro wrote:

> We have been down similar roads before. Jewish-Americans during the Red Scare, African-Americans during the civil rights movement and Japanese-Americans during World War II are examples that readily spring to mind. We are left to wonder why we cannot see with foresight what we see so clearly with hindsight, that loyalty is a matter of the heart and mind, not race, creed or color.

Police in other jurisdictions were more responsive to criticism. LAPD was accused of conducting an extensive program to map its estimated half million Muslims (the largest concentration after New York).[69] A week earlier Deputy Chief Michael P. Downing, head of the Anti-Terrorism Bureau, had told the Senate Homeland Security and Governmental Affairs Committee that the program's goal was to identify communities "susceptible to violent, ideologically-based extremism and then use a full-spectrum approach guided by an intelligence-led strategy." In order to weave "enclaves" in "closed vulnerable communities" into "the fabric of the larger society," police had to "get to know people's names. We need to walk into homes, neighborhoods, mosques and businesses." Downing now insisted "this has nothing to do with intelligence." Salam al-Marayati, executive director of the Muslim Public Affairs Council (MPAC), commended Downing for being "very forthright in his engagement with the Muslim community" and offered to provide input while "making sure that people's civil liberties are protected." But Shakeel Syed, executive director of the Islamic Shura Council of Southern California, complained he had not been told of the program even though he was a member of Chief Bratton's Forum of Religious Advisers. Syed completely rejected it, as did Muslim Advocates. Hussam Ayloush, head of the Los Angeles chapter of CAIR, said mapping "turns the LAPD officers into religious political analysts." "Who is going to decide who are the moderates? Are Muslims who criticize the war in Iraq moderate?" The Southern California ACLU expressed "grave concern." Executive Director Ramona Ripston called it "nothing short of racial profiling." University of Southern California's Center for Risk and Economic Analysis of Terrorism Events was reconsidering its participation in the program.

Chief Bratton denied the police would engage in "targeting or profiling." "It is an effort to understand communities." Mayor Villaraigosa assured the Muslim community of Downing's "good intentions." While acknowledging that "today's LAPD is a far cry" from the abuses of the Red Squad, Zoot Suit riots, and spying on political opponents, the *Los Angeles Times* remained "uncomfortable with the idea of the Police Department compiling maps of those it sees as susceptible to violence. That starts from the premise that race or nationality or religion defines susceptibility – a prescription for profiling if ever we've heard one."

When Downing, at al-Marayati's urging, withdrew the plan before meeting with Muslim leaders, the MPAC director praised this "great step for democracy." "Extending mapping of a criminal nature to a mainstream community ... was offensive to Muslim Americans." Muslims had been supported by the Roman Catholic Archdiocese, Episcopal Diocese, progressive Jewish and Christian organizations, and Japanese Americans. Arif Alikhan, Deputy Mayor for Homeland Security and Public Safety, had told Bratton and Downing that the proposal was "causing fear and apprehension in the Muslim community and was counterproductive." The *Los Angeles Times* found the decision "heartening": LAPD might "be learning to listen, not just bark orders."

Four years later the Los Angeles Sheriff's Department (which patrolled the county) took a different approach. Sgt. Mike Abdeen (a Palestinian American) responded to calls from Muslim parents to counsel their children. Declaring that "we're not going to win the war against terrorism without Muslims," Sheriff Leroy D. Baca created a Muslim American Homeland Security Advisory Group. Downing now explained that "the purpose of our outreach engagement is not to be able to knock on the door and say, tell me where the next terrorist is. It's about building resilient communities and neighborhoods." He and six LADP officers attended Friday prayers at the Islamic Center of Southern California, talking to worshippers afterwards.

At the request of Maryland's Democratic Governor Martin O'Malley, Stephen Sachs, a former Maryland Attorney General, produced a "blistering" 93-page report revealing that for 14 months Maryland State Police had infiltrated meetings, rallies, and email lists, and had added 53 people to state and federal terrorism databases for protesting against the Iraq war and capital punishment.[70] This surveillance was "an instructive example of the abuses that can result when the mere invocation of 'terrorism' is understood to override constitutional protections." Sachs recommended prohibiting covert surveillance of an advocacy group unless the Superintendent made a written finding of a reasonable, articulable suspicion that it had engaged in or planned a violation of the law and a less intrusive method of investigation was unlikely to produce equivalent results. Thomas Hutchins, the former Superintendent, had claimed the program targeted "fringe people ... who wish to disrupt the government." Condemning this "knuckle-headed" instance of homeland security "mania," the *New York Times* said this "chilling free-speech distinction" was "not found in the Constitution." State Police were apologizing to those surveilled. The *Washington Post* said: "Maryland should do everything in its power to ensure such an alarming violation of civil liberties doesn't happen again." "[I]nvestigators were closer to finding a good snickerdoodle recipe than they were to uncovering a scintilla of intelligence about wrongdoing." The *Post* supported a bill prohibiting all police (state and local) from "collecting, disseminating, or maintaining certain information" gathered through covert spying unless the intelligence was lawfully obtained and directly related to criminal activity.

After the second attack on the World Trade Center in less than a decade, New York understandably feared it remained in the crosshairs of Islamic terrorists. NYPD responded to this sense of vulnerability by enlarging its powers in two ways. First, it persuaded Judge Haight to relax the *Handschu* guidelines and refrain from using his contempt power to enforce the modified decree. As journalists and independent observers revealed, police then recorded, infiltrated, and disrupted demonstrations (against the war and for other causes), arrested peaceful protesters, and mistreated detainees. Prosecutors managed to convict very few (at least some of whom had engaged in constitutionally protected conduct). But the rest faced repeated obstacles in seeking legal redress (a problem other observers have repeatedly documented).[71] The Civilian Complaint Review Board and NYPD top brass refused to discipline higher officials. Courts (a partial shield against unfounded criminal prosecutions) denied access to police records in civil damages actions. And the city settled cases only slowly and grudgingly – until de Blasio replaced Bloomberg.

Second, NYPD surveilled Muslim communities (even in New Jersey) and infiltrated informants into mosques it could not enter undercover. This, too, was exposed by dedicated investigative reporters, whose stories provoked outrage in the media and among civil libertarians, legislators, and especially Muslims. But courts remained unsympathetic, and the city and police were unyielding. Bloomberg could not distinguish between searching for a specific perpetrator identified by height and hair color and profiling an entire

THE "GROUND ZERO" MOSQUE AND OTHERS

religious or ethnic community. Once again, it took the de Blasio administration to end the abuses. (The experiences in Los Angeles and Maryland also demonstrated the essential role of state and local leadership.) In the end it was politics, not law, which offered protection from discriminatory policing.

THE "GROUND ZERO" MOSQUE AND OTHERS[72]

In December 2009 Feisal Abdul Rauf, a Sufi imam who had been leading Friday afternoon prayers in a lower Manhattan storefront, announced a plan to build a mosque near "where a piece of the wreckage fell" to send "the opposite statement to what happened on 9/11." (Critics later noted that Rauf had said on television on September 30, 2001: "I wouldn't say the United States deserved what happened, but the United States' policies were an accessory to the crime that happened.") Sharif el-Gamal, a developer whose company bought the building, hoped "to provide a place of peace." Bloomberg's spokesman said: "the building owners have a right to do what they want." His Office of Immigrant Affairs was more supportive: "New York Muslims have as much of a commitment to rebuilding New York as anybody." The advisory team for the National September 11 Memorial and Museum (which included Rauf's wife, Daisy Khan) felt that "the idea of a cultural center that strengthens ties between Muslims and people of all faiths and backgrounds is positive."

Seven months later, however, Rep. Rick Lazio (R-Long Island), seeking the Republican gubernatorial nomination, asked Attorney General Holder to investigate the project's finances. Carl Paladino, a Buffalo developer campaigning for the same nomination, promised to expropriate the property to keep it out of Muslim hands. Bernard Kerik, the former NYPD Commissioner, now in prison for fraud, also declared his opposition. Sarah Palin urged "peace-seeking Muslims" to "refudiate [sic]" the "unnecessary provocation." Sen. John McCain seconded his former running mate. Newt Gingrich called the proposal "clearly an aggressive act that is offensive." "There should be no mosque near Ground Zero in New York so long as there are no churches or synagogues in Saudi Arabia." A Republican political action committee produced a television commercial against it. A man whose son died in the 9/11 attack complained: "it's going to hurt." Polls suggested that a majority of Americans opposed the mosque. The Anti-Defamation League (ADL) sympathized with opponents: "survivors of the Holocaust are entitled to feelings that are irrational. Their anguish entitles them to positions that others would categorize as irrational or bigoted." The president of the National Jewish Council for Learning and Understanding retorted: "the ADL should be ashamed of itself." Bloomberg reiterated his support: "What is great about America, and particularly New York, is we welcome everybody, and if we are so afraid of something like this, what does that say about us?" The *Los Angeles Times* called Bloomberg's remarks "the best 'refudiation' of Palin, Gingrich and others."

With the Statue of Liberty as a backdrop, Bloomberg declared: "we would betray our values if we were to treat Muslims differently than anyone else ... to cave to popular sentiment would be to hand a victory to the terrorists ... our first responders defended not only our city but also our country and our Constitution ... We honor their lives by defending ... the freedoms the terrorists attacked."

The local Community Board 1 overwhelmingly supported the project; the Landmarks Commission unanimously denied protection to the building the mosque would replace. But a firefighter who survived 9/11 sued to block the project; and a man whose son died there called it "a slap in the face." The *New York Times* condemned Republicans for "shamelessly playing the politics of fear." It would be a "disservice" to the memories of those who died on 9/11 "to give into the very fear that the terrorists wanted to create and, thus, to abandon the principles of freedom and tolerance." The project was "as important a test of the separation of church and state as any we may see in our lifetime." But the *Times* published letters on both sides. A couple who lost a son, daughter-in-law, and granddaughter condemned the "victory mosque," asking if it was being paid for by "the same people who financed 9/11?" The brother of a dead firefighter called it "disrespectful ... astoundingly insensitive," lacking "common decency." But a woman whose husband died in the Lockerbie bombing had learned that "unabated anger is not the road that leads to healing." A man warned that the ADL's logic would render "most acts of hatred ... excusable." And a Muslim hoped the project would "embolden moderate Muslims in America" and "send a clear message to Muslim extremists that they have not been able to sow anti-Muslim prejudice in America." In his *New York Times* column, Thomas Friedman urged the USA to tell the world "we are a country that will even tolerate a mosque near the site of 9/11." The *Washington Post* concurred: to use 9/11 "to smear the entire religion of Islam" would "be to give in to the extremists who want to finish what those hijackers started." In his *Los Angeles Times* column, Doyle McManus predicted that "if this mosque is blocked by popular prejudice or political dema-goguery, that's when bin Laden will claim a second victory."

Although the White House press secretary initially said the presi-dent did not want to "get involved in local decision-making," Obama declared at a White House dinner celebrating Iftar (the daily end of the Ramadan fast): "as a citizen, and as president, I believe that Muslims have the same right to practice their religion as anyone else in this country." Noted First Amendment lawyer Floyd Abrams wrote the *New York Times*: "as a legal matter, there is nothing to debate." A Community Board member said opposition to this project was based "not on sensitivities but on bigotry, pure and simple." But one opponent denounced the mosque's proximity to "sacred ground," and another condemned "an act of colossal insensitivity." A Protestant min-ister said deferring to such feelings would be the " 'religious' thing to do." Gingrich accused Obama of "pandering to radical Islam." House Minority Leader Boehner called Obama's "decision to endorse" the mosque "deeply troubling." "The fact that someone has the right to do something doesn't necessarily make it the right thing to do." Rep. Peter T. King (R-NY) said Obama was "wrong" to "cave in to polit-ical correctness." The Muslim community was "abusing" its right "by needlessly offending so many people who have suffered so much." A former RNC Chairman said Obama "has a very disdainful view of the American people." The president appeared to backtrack: "I was commenting very specifically on the right people have that dates back to our founding," not "on the wisdom of making the decision to put a mosque there." Senate Majority Leader Reid underlined that distinc-tion: "the First Amendment right protects freedom of religion," but "the mosque should be built someplace else." But Rep. Jerrold Nadler (D-NY), who represented the constituency, hoped "people will realize that everybody's liberty is at stake here."

In his *New York Times* column, Ross Douthat said the America "that understands itself as a distinctive culture ... speaks English, not Spanish," and "looks back to a particular religious heritage" was "right to press for something more from Muslim Americans." "Too often, American Muslims institutions have turned out to be entangled with ideas and groups that most Americans rightly consider beyond the pale." But the *Times* wished Obama "hadn't diluted the message" and was "disturbed" by Reid. And the *Washington Post* regretted that "rather than provide clarity and leadership," Obama "muddled his stance." In his *New York Times* column, Nicholas Kristof mocked the claim of sacred land, having found two strip clubs (the New York Dolls Gentlemen's Club and the Pussycat Lounge) just blocks from the World Trade Center. "Today's crusaders against the Islamic Community Center are promoting" a "paranoid intolerance," which "many American Republicans share with al-Qaeda" and which believes "the west and the Islamic world are caught inevitably in a 'clash of civilizations.'"

New York Gov. Paterson proposed to look for state-owned land for the mosque further away from Ground Zero. And while defending religious freedom, Archbishop Timothy M. Dolan called for "attention" to those who "wonder about the wisdom" of locating the mosque "near such a wounded site." But the project leaders refused to move. When Reps. King and Ileana Ros-Lehtinen (R-Fla) denounced DoS for sending Rauf to speak in the Middle East, the Department responded that Rauf "brings a moderate perspective to foreign audiences on what it's like to be a practicing Muslim in the United States," and it posted Bloomberg's speech on its website in English, Arabic, and Farsi.

Some Democratic candidates distanced themselves from the president. Rep. Charlie Menacon (D-La), hoping to unseat a Republican Senator, claimed to "support freedom of religion," but said putting a mosque near Ground Zero "isn't appropriate." Jeff Greene, seeking the Florida Democratic senatorial nomination, said "common sense and respect" were a "sensible reason to build the mosque someplace else." Florida's Democratic gubernatorial nominee agreed. Republicans also differed. Libertarian Grover Norquist criticized Gingrich for pursuing "a distraction from a winning game plan" in the November election. Gingrich retorted that his "principled" position was based on "the outrage of triumphalist radical Islamists choosing a deliberately provocative site." Norquist's Muslim wife joined other prominent Muslim Republicans: "we cannot support victory" in November "at the expense of the U.S. Constitution or the Arab and Muslim community in America." A demonstration against the mosque was organized by conservatives, including Gingrich, John Bolton (Bush's UN Ambassador), and Pamela Geller (who once claimed Obama was Malcolm X's illegitimate son).

Accusing Republicans of "pandering" to prejudice, the *Washington Post* said most Muslims found al-Qaeda repugnant. The "hurt feelings" of 9/11 survivors "reflect misunderstandings or prejudice," to which the response should be "education, not appeasement." Republicans "have been almost universally eager to exploit the issue for political purposes."

CAIR deplored this "nadir of Islamophobic rhetoric," which Daisy Khan likened to "metastasized anti-Semitism." Breaking an unwritten rule of New York politics against exploiting 9/11 images in campaign ads, Lazio used videos of the burning World Trade Center, asked where the mosque was getting its money from, and called Rauf "a terrorist sympathizer" – provoking immediate condemnation from police and firefighter unions (whose members had died in the attack). The *New York Times* attributed Lazio's behavior to his failure to attract public support or raise funds, but said that "can never excuse, his increasingly hysterical attacks." And it praised Attorney General Andrew Cuomo, the Democratic gubernatorial candidate, for asking: "what are we about if not religious freedom?" But Sheldon Silver, the Democratic New York Assembly Speaker whose district included Ground Zero, urged the project sponsors to "take into very serious consideration the kind of turmoil that's been created and look to compromise." The ACLU deputy legal director and NYCLU executive director wrote the *Times* that "preventing Muslims ... from freely practicing their faith is unconstitutional and conflicts with our core American values." The mother of two Iraq war veterans warned that "the uproar over the proposed Islamic center is at odds with what the United States is trying to do in Iraq and Afghanistan right now and actually puts our troops in danger." In his *Los Angeles Times* column, Tim Rutten denounced "rhetorical bigotry more disgraceful and dangerous than anything admitted to our national conversation for decades." In his *New York Times* column, Paul Krugman asked "where are the statements, from the former president [Bush] or those in his inner circle, preaching tolerance and denouncing anti-Islam hysteria?"

El-Gamal declared that he was in charge, not Rauf, even though he had not incorporated the non-profit that would run the center or chosen an architect. He promised not to accept money linked to "un-American" values for the anticipated $100 million project. Rauf denounced opposition by a "tiny, vociferous minority" seeking political advantage during "the election season." The New York Islamic Leadership Council (including 55 mosques and groups) demonstrated at City Hall. But two polls found that large majorities of New Yorkers (71 and 66 percent) thought the mosque should move. Nationwide opposition was even greater: 83 percent of Republicans, 65 percent of Independents, and 53 percent of Democrats. The *New York Times* called "the hate-filled signs carried recently by protesters" "chilling" and denounced "opportunistic politicians" like Lazio, and Palladino, who "foment this noxious anger." It stood with "the 27 percent who say the mosque should be built in lower Manhattan because moving it would compromise American values." But proclaiming that Islam preaches "hate, violence and death," internet evangelist Bill Keller planned a "9/11 Christian Center" at Ground Zero as a counterweight to the "victory mosque." Rauf wrote in the *New York Times*: "My life's work has been focused on building bridges between religious groups and never has that been as important as it is now." The center would have "separate prayer spaces for Muslims, Christians, Jews, and men and women of other faiths" and "a multifaith memorial dedicated to victims of the Sept. 11 attacks." The Union for Reform Judaism and the (Conservative) Rabbinical Assembly supported the project; the American Jewish Committee did so as long as the organizers agreed to "fully reveal their sources of funding and to unconditionally condemn terrorism inspired by Islamist ideology." But an Orthodox Upper East Side rabbi called the mosque insensitive and "provocative."

On the eve of the ninth anniversary of 9/11, Obama said that the "inalienable" right to practice one's religion freely meant "that if you could build a church on a site ... you should be able to build a mosque on the site." "We are not at war against Islam. We are at war against terrorist organizations that have distorted Islam or falsely used the banner of Islam to engage in their destructive acts." "Millions of Muslim Americans" were "going to school with our kids" and were "our neighbors ... our friends ... our coworkers." Muslim American soldiers were "putting their lives on the line for us." The *Washington Post* and the *New York Times* praised the speech. The *Times* called the "physical rebirth" of lower Manhattan "cause for celebration," a "far more fitting way to defy the hate-filled extremists who attacked the United States" than "the intolerance and fear that have mushroomed across the nation." Five ministers of the Collegiate Church of New York took a full-page *New York Times* ad supporting the community center. On September 11, 2010 demonstrations for and against the mosque each mustered about two thousand people. But Tariq Ramadan (the Swiss Muslim academic barred from the USA) wrote in the *Washington Post* that the Ground Zero mosque was "not a wise decision." "This is the moment to go beyond rights and reach for the common good." Rauf said he was "exploring all options" to "resolve this problem." El-Gamal was willing to create space for other religions but only if that did not curtail Muslim worship. He had changed the name from Cordoba House to Park51 (its address) after critics invoked the thirteenth-century Muslim conquest of Christian Cordoba (overlooking the fact that two centuries later Christian Spain expelled its Jews after defeating the Muslims). The Islamic Leadership Council of Metropolitan New York, CAIR, Islamic Circle of North America, and Muslim American Society declared their support. El-Gamal planned Islamic (i.e., interest-free) financing for the $140 million project. Rauf and his wife received threats, which NYPD treated as hate crimes. He planned a nationwide tour to explain the project. A few weeks later, however, el-Gamal unilaterally announced he would be the sole spokesman and fund-raiser, although Rauf and Khan would remain on the board. Services at Park51 would be conducted by Abdallah Adhami, who had been imam of another lower Manhattan mosque for years. (Adhami resigned three weeks later after it was revealed that he blamed homosexuality on childhood abuse.) When Rauf reiterated his willingness to move the mosque, el-Gamal balked, declaring that Rauf "has no authority or control over this project." Rauf capitulated, saying he would "concentrate on broader issues, interfaith dialogue, which has always been my work." El-Gamal rejected Donald Trump's offer to buy the property for 25 percent more than he paid if he would move at least five blocks from Ground Zero. "Are we supposed to move so we can create a Muslim-free zone, Muslim-free blocks?" "I have been trying for eight years now to help my community. It's just not in my DNA to give up." A New York Supreme Court judge held that the firefighter lacked standing to challenge the Landmarks Preservation Commission decision.

The Islamic Center finally opened in September 2011 with little fanfare and no protesters. El-Gamal expressed regret that he had not "engaged the 9/11 family members because our intention was never to hurt or antagonize anyone." A month later, however, Con Edison, which owned part of the property, threatened to evict the Center for failing to pay an alleged $1.7 million in back rent. In February 2013 Robert Deak, who had donated $167,000 to the Center, sued Rauf and Khan for diverting the money to their personal use; they counterclaimed against Deak for inflating the value of a condominium he sold the Center for $1.5 million; the suits were settled by Deak paying $1.35 million. In April 2014 el-Gamal scaled back his plan from a 15-story interfaith community center to a three-story museum "dedicated to exploring the faith of Islam and its arts and culture," with a prayer sanctuary. And in May 2017 el-Gamal said he would build a 43-story tower of luxury condominiums containing a much smaller Islamic museum and public plaza.

Mosques in other locales encountered mixed reactions.[73] European countries (unconstrained by the First Amendment) were much more restrictive. A Swiss referendum banned the construction of minarets.[74] A French court canceled the building permit for the Grand Mosque of Marseille, allegedly out of concern about parking.[75] In the first 11 years after 9/11 DoJ opened more than 28 investigations of campaigns to prevent mosque construction. During the five months of 2010 when the Ground Zero mosque controversy was most intense, the ACLU identified 30 projects facing opposition.[76] The Sheboygan, Wisconsin city council unanimously supported a proposal (though only after residents reviled its sponsor at a public hearing).[77] Members of the Utica (New York) United Methodist Church welcomed a proposal to save their building by converting it to a mosque. The mayor asked: "where would we be today if no one welcomed the Italians, like my father, the Irish, the Polish who became the backbone of this community." Opposition to a planned mosque and community center in Willowbrook (a Chicago suburb) was based on parking, traffic, and water runoff.[78] A three-decade-old mosque in rural Waterport, New York suffered vandalism, arson, and gun shots. At a June 2010 meeting to discuss converting a Catholic convent on Staten Island into a mosque, a woman challenged Ayman Hammous, president of the local branch of the Muslim American Society: "wouldn't you agree that every terrorist, past and present has come out of a mosque?" The 400-member audience drowned out his denial. Another woman falsely declared the Society was on the terrorist watchlist. Robert Spencer (author of the Jihad Watch blog) accused the Society of ties to Hamas, Hezbollah, and the Muslim Brotherhood. Others asked if Hammous believed sharia was superior to democracy and how he felt about Israel. Shortly before the contentious three-hour meeting ended, a Marine Lance Corporal who had mediated between warring tribes in Afghanistan asked if the mosque would "work to form a cohesive bond with the people of this community." Hammous agreed, but the crowd booed. A week later the parish pastor sought to rescind the deal.

In Temecula, California, 150 families sought to build a 25,000-square-foot Islamic community center on land they owned. Members of the local Tea Party picketed Friday prayers with dogs (viewed as unclean by Muslims). One warned that Muslims would outnumber Christians in 20 years and impose sharia. The senior pastor of the local Baptist church condemned Islam's "fundamental teachings" and the "documented stories of the terror that radical Islam promotes." But at an August 2010 meeting supporters (including the Mormon secretary of the local Interfaith Council) outnumbered opponents four to one. And after an eight-hour hearing in which the city attorney advised that the decision had to be based on mundane concerns, not Islam, the City Council unanimously approved the project.

In Murfreesboro (a Nashville suburb), hundreds of protesters, accompanied by unsuccessful Republican candidates for governor and Congress, denounced a proposed mosque. An "ex-Muslim" claimed a mosque was "a place where war is started ... where ammunition was stored." But the past and present local chairmen of the Republican and Democratic Parties concurred that Rutherford County had followed the law in approving the plan. Nearly a thousand people participated in opposing demonstrations. Weeks later a suspicious fire burned much of the construction site; shots were fired a day later; and mosques in the vicinity increased security. The US Attorney defended the mosque against a challenge to the building permit, which claimed that Islam was not a religion but a political cause. A state court rejected the challenge but then reversed itself, finding that the Planning Commission had not adequately noticed the meeting at which it approved the plan. A month later the US Attorney filed charges against a man for threatening the mosque. DoJ and the mosque also sued in federal court, obtaining a temporary restraining order (TRO) to let construction proceed. Just before the end of Ramadan in August 2012 the mosque obtained the necessary permits and opened for worship.

After Republican presidential candidates inflamed anti-Muslim hatred (discussed below), a sheriff's deputy terminated a meeting to discuss expanding the Islamic Center of Fredericksburg, Virginia when protesters denounced the "evil cult" and declared "every one of you are terrorists."[79] Following the December 2015 San Bernardino shooting, the mosque abandoned its effort. In neighboring Culpepper County, the Board of Supervisors rejected a sewage permit application (only the second denial in 20 years), blocking a Muslim congregation from building a mosque. After 39 public hearings over nearly four years, the Planning Board of Bernards Township, New Jersey denied a permit to the Islamic Society of Basking Ridge to build a mosque. Admitting during a lawsuit that it did not consider the mosque to be a church because it met on Friday evenings, the township ultimately capitulated, agreeing to pay the Islamic Society $3 million. Bensalem, a Philadelphia suburb, had granted variances to an Indian Orthodox Church, two Hindu temples, and some faith-based private schools, but denied it to the Bensalem Majid Mosque. The Dudley, Massachusetts zoning board of appeals denied a permit for a Muslim cemetery. Newton County (35 miles from Atlanta) was about to approve a mosque until militia from a neighboring county threatened to demonstrate with guns drawn. Sterling Heights (17 miles from Detroit) settled a DoJ lawsuit and reversed its prior rejection of a permit for the American Islamic Community Center. But Bayonne, New Jersey blocked an attempt to build its first mosque; and Culpepper County, Virginia denied a pump-and-haul sewage permit for a mosque after granting all 26 previous requests, including nine for churches.

The experience of Muslims seeking to establish mosques in the United States after 9/11 revealed both the strengths and weaknesses of efforts to protect religious freedom. Initial unconcern about the "Ground Zero" mosque (a typical New York "fuggedaboudit" response) was quickly supplanted by suspicion as conservative Republicans cynically sought to exploit ignorance and fear for partisan political advantage. Claiming (with some evidence) to speak on behalf of most Americans (who tend to be indifferent or hostile to civil liberties for unpopular minorities – precisely why we need a Bill of Rights), they recruited relatives of 9/11 victims, who asserted a unique moral entitlement to decide the future of "hallowed ground." But the attack on the mosque generated broad resistance. Major newspapers unanimously supported the mosque. The Community Board approved the proposal, and the Landmarks Commission and courts refused to block it. Perhaps because a distressingly large proportion of Americans believed the conservatives' myth that Obama was Muslim, the president equivocated before endorsing the mosque. But Bloomberg consistently gave it strong backing. When conservatives advanced the debating point that some Muslim countries did not tolerate churches or synagogues, Bloomberg replied that the country – and especially New York City – should show that Americans were better. (This recalled the powerful argument against torture advanced by Sen. McCain, who this time sadly echoed the incoherent demagoguery of his former running mate Sarah Palin.) When critics invoked majoritarian sentiment, defenders could respond with the need to display special sensitivity toward "discrete and insular minorities" like Muslim Americans.[80]

If the *right* of Muslims to build the mosque was beyond question – and successfully defended – its *appropriateness* raised different questions. Even proponents disagreed about its purpose. Rauf, more concerned with its ecumenical potential, seemed willing to find a different site. El-Gamal, as the developer, was wedded to the site but eager to jettison Rauf and the adverse publicity he attracted. Both experienced financial difficulties. In the end, el-Gamal drastically reduced the project's physical size, narrowed its scope from a community center to a mosque, and focused on maximizing his profit. After the mosque opened with little fanfare, public interest evaporated.

Conservatives found other issues; and the news cycle had long since ended. Even localities that did not share New York's long history as a magnet for immigrants eventually accepted mosques (as they had the residents who sought to worship there). The fact that Americans are more likely to attend church than citizens of other advanced industrial countries paradoxically strengthened the claims of Muslims to practice their religion.

BURNING THE KORAN[81]

If the civil liberties regarding mosques were relatively straightforward, expressions of Islamophobia posed more complex challenges. In 2008 the fundamentalist Westboro Baptist Church, which gained notoriety with its profoundly offensive homophobic demonstrations at military funerals, burned a Koran – and nobody noticed. A year later "Reverend" Terry Jones (who styled himself "Dr." based on an honorary degree from an unaccredited bible school) posted a sign declaring "Islam is of the devil" outside his grandiosely named Dove World Outreach Center, a 50-member unaffiliated Christian church in rural Florida. The *Gainesville Sun* responded by investigating his profit-making eBay sales of furniture stored on church property. (The church had chronic financial problems, and its land was for sale.) That fall the church produced Islamophobic t-shirts, which children wore to school and adults displayed on provocative visits to the University of Florida campus.

In July 2010 Jones announced he would burn the Koran on the 9/11 anniversary, quickly garnering 150 media interviews, including an appearance on CNN, where he pronounced: "What we're doing has no middle of the road. You have to believe it is totally, totally good or absolutely of the devil." The worldwide publicity led to protests in Afghanistan. CNN, Fox News, the *New York Times* and the Associated

Press decided not to publish photos of the Koran-burning. Gen. David Petraeus warned it would endanger US forces in Afghanistan (which he commanded). The US Embassy in Kabul said: "Americans from all religious and ethnic backgrounds reject the offensive initiative by this small group in Florida." Speaking as commander-in-chief, Obama warned "that this stunt that [Jones] is pulling could greatly endanger our young men and women in uniform." DoS denounced the "un-American" action. A group of former high-level national security officials condemned it, calling the Koran "a sacred text for millions of Americans and others around the world." Local clergy sought to dissuade Jones. An emergency interfaith summit of religious leaders in Washington denounced "the derision, misinformation and outright bigotry." After they met with Attorney General Holder, DoJ reiterated its "strong commitment to prosecuting hate crimes." Rev. Richard Cizik, president of the New Evangelical Partnership for the Common Good, said the act would "bring dishonor to those who love Jesus Christ." Geoff Tunnicliffe, head of the World Evangelical Alliance (one of the largest such organizations), told Jones that Christian leaders and missionaries around the world were opposed. The Alliance's US chapter (the National Association of Evangelicals) asked Muslims not to judge "all Christians by the behavior of one extremist." Prominent conservatives like Sarah Palin and Glenn Beck denounced the burning. The Pope opposed it. The American Bible Society and other religious groups took a full-page ad in the *New York Times* declaring: "Burning the Qur'an Does Not Illuminate the Bible." The *Los Angeles Times* wrote that burning the Koran "supports the terrorists' narrative that America is waging war on Islam." Local clergy planned an interfaith prayer service. The Gainesville mayor and city commissioners telephoned Jones. Hundreds were expected to demonstrate outside the church against the burning. Although he had gotten more than a hundred death threats and was carrying a pistol, Jones was determined to send "a warning to radical Islam" that "if you attack us, we will attack you." "Instead of possibly blaming us for what could happen, we put the blame where it belongs – on the people who would do it."

After meeting him, Imam Muhammad Musri, president of the Islamic Society of Central Florida, hoped Jones would change his mind. Defense Secretary Gates telephoned Jones during the meeting to warn of the danger to members of the armed forces. On television, Obama urged Jones to "understand[] that what he's proposing to do is completely contrary to our values as Americans." He denied the administration had "elevated this story." "In the age of the Internet," it could "cause us profound damage around the world, so we've got to take it seriously." Two days before the anniversary Jones appeared with Musri to announce he had canceled his plan, claiming Rauf had agreed to meet them in New York and relocate his proposed mosque away from Ground Zero. "We are absolutely strong on that. It is not the time to do it." Rauf denied agreeing to the move, saying "we are not going to toy with our religion ... nor are we going to barter"; and el-Gamal flatly declared: "we're not moving." Insisting they still planned to meet in New York on 9/11, Jones said he had "suspended" the burning, swayed not by the risk to Americans but rather the promise to move the mosque – "a sign from God." But then complaining that Musri "clearly lied to us," Jones said he would "rethink our decision" because the reaction it provoked revealed "that there is a violent element of Islam, much more violent than we had anticipated."

When Jones flew to LaGuardia Airport on September 10 and checked into a hotel in Queens, NYPD warned his life was in danger. In a conference call with Tunnicliffe and others he promised never to burn the Koran and discussed an appropriate apology, saying on NBC's *Today* show that the plan was "totally canceled." Instead of trying to meet Rauf, he flew home. More than a thousand people demonstrated in Gainesville on September 10 and another 200 at his church the next day. More than 10,000 people protested in Afghanistan, causing widespread property damage, two deaths, and many injuries. In three subsequent demonstrations by thousands, some flaunting Taliban flags, at least three more were killed and many injured. In Kashmir, at least fourteen civilians and two security officers died and at least sixty were injured. At a subsequent demonstration by thousands, 4 were killed and 30 wounded. Addressing a thousand Iranian protesters calling for Jones's death, Ayatollah Khamenei blamed the plan on "Zionist think tanks." The *New York Times* deplored the "intolerance and fear that have mushroomed across the nation ... fed by the kind of bigotry exhibited by the would-be book burner in Florida." Jones and his supporters were "trying to tear down more than two centuries of religious tolerance." Michael Gerson warned in the *Washington Post* that "the idea that an unbalanced pastor with an internet connection and a poster can cause our nation's highest military and civilian leaders to respond is an invitation to global crackpotocracy." But Richard Cohen wrote in the *Post* that Jones had sought to make a "political statement" and warned that "this was not the first time the threat of violence in the Islamic world has had a chastening effect here."

In January 2011 Jones's renewed threat to "put the Koran on trial" provoked no reaction. On March 20 he held an "International Judge the Qu'ran Day," conducting a mock trial based on the testimony of two Muslim converts to Christianity. Jones presided as judge over a prosecutor (another Muslim convert to Christianity) and defense attorney (an imam, who quit the proceedings prematurely). After the jury of parishioners found the Koran guilty of five "crimes against humanity," an online poll sentenced it to burning. (Because Gainesville had changed its fire code after Jones's earlier threat, this occurred indoors.) Jones said he executed the sentence not with "any pleasure" but "because we feel a deep obligation to stay with the court system of America." "It was as fair a trial as we could have."

These theatrics attracted little media attention, and the video on the church's website (subtitled in Arabic) received relatively few hits. US embassies in Afghanistan and Pakistan called the burning "disrespectful, intolerant, divisive and unrepresentative of American values." Pakistan President Asif Ali Zardari condemned the act. Afghan President Hamid Karzai urged the USA to prosecute Jones and was echoed by the acting head of the Ulema Council of Afghanistan. Three mullahs organized a protest of 20,000 people at a United Nations compound in Mazar-i-Sharif, leading to the deaths of seven UN workers and five Afghans. The most prominent mullah said Afghanistan should sever relations with the USA unless it arrested Jones. Obama observed that "the desecration of any holy text, including the Koran, is an act of extreme intolerance and bigotry"; but "to attack and kill innocent people in response is outrageous, and an affront to human decency and dignity." After two more days of rioting in Kandahar, there was a total of 24 dead and more than 100 wounded; and an assault on a US military installation in Kabul led to at least three more deaths. Afghan police in Mazar-i-Sharif and Paktia Province turned their guns on US soldiers and Afghan police, killing three and wounding others. Gen. Petraeus and NATO's civilian representative reiterated their "condemnation of any disrespect to the Holy Qur'an and the Muslim faith" and, "in particular, the action of an individual in the United States who recently burned the holy Qur'an." Karzai repeated that "those people who are responsible for burning the holy Koran should be arrested soon." Sen. Graham (who, as a lawyer, should have known better) appeared to agree: "free speech is a great idea, but we're in a war. During World War II, we had limits on what you could do if it inspired the enemy." He wanted to do "anything we can to push back here in America against acts like this that put our troops at risk."

Jones, though "devastated," denied responsibility for the deaths, which showed that "Islam is not a religion of peace. It is time that we call these people to accountability [sic]." "It was intended to stir the pot; if you don't shake the boat, everyone will stay in their complacency [sic]." He played a tape of the September 8, 2010 conversation in which Musri said Rauf "is willing to relocate … the mosque from Ground Zero … to an alternative location that is not controversial at all, away from Ground Zero." (Musri called it a fake.) Jones's parishioners were carrying guns, and three police cars were stationed at his church, which had received nearly $20,000 in donations since August. One conservative (Michael Graham) wrote in an op ed that Jones "hasn't done anything wrong. Nothing." But another (Jonah Goldberg) called that "nuts."

When Jones planned a demonstration several weeks later outside the Islamic Center of America in Dearborn, Michigan (one of the largest Arab American communities), a prosecutor asked a state judge to determine whether Jones posed a threat to the peace. After a jury found he did (in a one-day trial in which Jones represented himself), he was briefly arrested but freed after paying $1 for a peace bond. He railed against "extremist Muslim influences" for over three hours on the City Hall steps, but often was drowned out by opponents. A year later he burned several more Korans and an image of Mohammed at his church, but got little media coverage.

The events surrounding Jones's burning of the Koran presented almost a mirror image of those concerning the lower Manhattan mosque. Rauf and el-Gamal sought to minimize publicity; Jones craved the limelight (posing a dilemma for opponents, who risked conferring the notoriety he desired). They preached respect for all religions (and were repaid with wild accusations of Muslim "triumphalism"); he proclaimed the primacy of Christianity and the evil of Islam. They regretted the distress expressed by some 9/11 families; he deliberately offended all Muslims. The mosque's opponents repeatedly (if unsuccessfully) resorted to law to block the project; all of Jones's American critics accepted his right to burn the Koran – a classic example of Holmes's "freedom for the thought that we hate."[82] (Strident demands for Jones's punishment from governments in Afghanistan and Pakistan highlighted America's commitment to this bedrock principle.) Whereas the mosque project elicited a gaggle of conservative opponents, Jones attracted almost no supporters. Indeed, the broad spectrum of his critics – including conservatives Sarah Palin (who had opposed the mosque) and Glenn Beck – affirmed America's vibrant civil society and validated Brandeis's argument that the best remedy for "falsehood and fallacies" is "more speech, not enforced silence."[83] (Islamophobes may have been embarrassed by Jones's class background and buffoonish behavior.) Jones's critics invoked not only the American tradition of religious tolerance dating back to the Founders, but also prudential fears about the harms he would cause. For while the Supreme Court has rightly rebuffed as a "heckler's veto" any effort to justify governmental restraints on speech by reference to the harms adversaries might inflict,[84] critics accurately predicted that burning the Koran would provoke violence. Cocooned within his profound ignorance and smugly convinced of his moral inerrancy, Jones ignored their warnings, with the tragic result that dozens died and hundreds were injured. But the fickleness of the public's attention and the media's drive for newer news pushed Jones out of a spotlight he never should have enjoyed.

"INNOCENCE OF MUSLIMS"[85]

On September 11, 2012 terrorists attacked the US consulate in Benghazi, killing Ambassador Stevens and three other Americans. The next day Secretary of State Clinton said some attributed the attack "to inflammatory material posted on the Internet" (described below). She reiterated "America's commitment to religious tolerance," but maintained "there is no justification" for the attack. President Obama also rejected "all efforts to denigrate the religious beliefs of others," but emphasized "there is absolutely no justification to this type of senseless violence." A day later Clinton repeated that "the United States rejects both the content and the message of that video" (posted on the Internet) and "deplores any intentional effort to denigrate the religious beliefs of others." In a meeting with the Moroccan Foreign Minister, Clinton condemned both the "disgusting and reprehensible" video and the Benghazi attack. Later that day DoS spokeswoman Victoria Nuland acknowledged "there are plenty of people around the region citing this disgusting video as something that has been motivating." On September 15 Obama again said the video had inspired "angry mob[s]" in the Middle East and reaffirmed that the USA "has a profound respect for people of all faiths ... and we reject the denigration of any religion – including Islam." On September 18 Obama said the government had "denounced" the "offensive" video, which "extremists and terrorists used as an excuse to attack a variety of our embassies, including the consulate in Libya." The same day White House spokesman Jay Carney said: "it was the video that caused the unrest in Cairo, and the video and the unrest in Cairo … precipitated some of the unrest in Benghazi and elsewhere." On September 20 Obama said: "the natural protests that arose because of the outrage over the video were used as an excuse by extremists to see if they can also directly harm U.S. interests." But as time passed, both the admin-istration and its critics abandoned any attempt to link the Benghazi attack to the video.

The producer of the video was initially identified as Sam Bacile, a 52-year-old Israeli American real estate developer in California, who claimed to have raised $5 million from a hundred Jewish donors to make the film. (It later emerged that he was an Egyptian Copt, who had raised $80,000 from that community, including his second ex-wife.) A 14-minute trailer uploaded to YouTube in July (which drew 1.6 million views) began with Egyptian security forces letting Muslims burn Egyptian Coptic homes before cutting to scenes portraying Muhammad as a buffoon, womanizer, homosexual, child molester, and a greedy, bloodthirsty thug. Terry Jones said it showed "the destructive ideology of Islam." He commemorated 9/11 by screening the film and a depiction of a lynched devil dressed in a white turban for "International Judge Muhammed Day." Morris Sadek posted the film with Arabic subtitles on the website of his National American Coptic Assembly.

After Egyptian television aired trailer excerpts (dubbed into Arabic) on September 8 and 10 (before any attacks), the US Embassy in Cairo condemned "the continuing efforts by misguided individuals to hurt the religious feelings of Muslims." "Respect for religious beliefs is a corner-stone of American democracy. We firmly reject the actions by those who abuse the universal right of free speech to hurt the religious beliefs of others." Mitt Romney (cynically pursuing political advantage in the impending election) denounced the Embassy statement as "akin to apology … a severe miscalculation." When criticized, he reiterated that "apology for America's values is never the right course," maintaining the administration should have defended the filmmaker's right to free speech. It was "disgraceful that the Obama administration's first response was not to condemn attacks on our diplomatic missions but to sympathize with those who waged the attacks." Republicans closed ranks. Romney was supported by Sen. Jim DeMint and Rep. Howard McKeon. Sen. Jon Kyl said the Embassy statement was "like a judge telling the woman that got raped, 'you asked for it because of the way you dressed.'" Sen. James Inhofe condemned Obama's "failed foreign policy of appeasement and apology."

Thousands protested outside the Cairo Embassy, some attacking it, while Egyptian security waited five hours to remove them. Demanding an apology, the Muslim Brotherhood urged the USA to prosecute the "madmen" who made the video, but then said it did "not hold the American government or its citizens responsible for the acts of the few that abuse the laws protecting freedom of expression." Turkish President Erdogan condemned "insults against the supreme values of Islam," but rejected "any act of violence, any act of terror, especially to hurt innocent people." Defending his "political movie," "Bacile" said he had not expected the violent response and had gone into hiding. CAIR urged Muslims not to give the "extremist producers" of this "trashy film" the "cheap publicity they so desperately seek." Nevertheless, protests persisted in Egypt, Yemen, Iran, Morocco, Sudan, Tunisia, Bangladesh, Qatar, Kuwait, Iraq, the West Bank, and Gaza. Egyptian President Morsi said the Benghazi attack was "unacceptable," but "the prophet Muhammad and Islamic sanctities are red lines for all of us." The president of the Islamic Society of North America said he and other American Muslim leaders had been assuring colleagues in Egypt, Libya, Tunisia, and Mauritania that the filmmakers "do not represent the American people."

The *New York Times* castigated both Romney for his "extraordinary lack of presidential character" and the filmmakers for "damage to the interests of the United States and its core principle of respecting all faiths." Denying there had been any apology, the *Washington Post* said Obama had "struck the right note." "Religious tolerance, as much as freedom of speech, is a core American value. The movie … is a despicable piece of bigotry; it was striking that Mr. Romney had nothing to say about such hatred directed at a major religious faith." Thomas Friedman wrote in his *New York Times* column that though he did not "like to see anyone's faith insulted," even the "stupid and ugly" video did not justify violence. Before demanding an apology, Muslims should "look at the chauvinistic bile that is pumped out by some of their own media." Others quickly took sides. Charles Lane wrote in his *Washington Post* column that the Obama administration's criticism of the video "seemed to reward violence." Sarah Chayes wrote in a *Los Angeles Times* op ed that "even under the most restrictive current standard" of Holmes's clear-and-present-danger test, the video was "not, arguably, free speech protected under the U.S. Constitution." Anthony Lewis apparently concurred: "if the result is violence, and that violence was intended, then it meets the [imminence] standard." (Neither was a lawyer; but as a prominent journalist and author on legal topics, including a book entitled *Freedom for the Thought That We Hate*, Lewis should have known better.) Salman Rushdie (whose novel *The Satanic Verses* had provoked a fatwa) disagreed: it was "very important that we hold our ground." "Terrible ideas, reprehensible ideas, do not disappear if you ban them." "It's not for the American government to regret what American citizens do."

Steve Klein, one of the video's producers and an anti-Islamic activist who had met "Bacile" at Media for Christ, hoped viewers "will come to understand just how violent Muhammad was." The filmmakers wanted to seduce Muslims into watching what they expected to be a celebration of Islam and then expose "the truth, the facts, the evidence and the proof" that it was evil. But the reception showed that "if you merely say anything that's derogatory about Islam, then they immediately go to violence." JCS Chair Gen. Dempsey asked Jones to withdraw his support for the film. Although it had been promoted by leaders of the Coptic diaspora in the USA, Bishop Serapoin of the Coptic Orthodox Diocese of Los Angeles condemned it: "Our Christian teaching is we have to respect people of other faiths."

Afghanistan banned YouTube. Because of the "very difficult situation in Libya and Egypt," Google temporarily suspended its service there but did not remove the video, which was "clearly within our guidelines." Coincidentally, *Charlie Hebdo* published caricatures of Mohammed, some showing him naked (leading to the 2015 attack on its editors). Editor Stephane Charbonnier maintained the images "would shock only those who wanted to be shocked." French Foreign Minister Laurent Fabius had urged the magazine to delay publication. Although the "principle of freedom of expression ... should not be undermined," he questioned whether it was "sensible or intelligent to pour oil on the fire." France closed embassies, schools, cultural centers, and consulates in 20 countries. Egypt's ruling Freedom and Justice Party asked France to take action against the magazine (which was legally possible in the absence of a First Amendment). Pakistani hackers claimed to have blocked the *Charlie Hebdo* website. Egypt charged seven Coptic Christians and Terry Jones (all of whom were outside the country). The German

Interior Minister promised to use "all available legal means" to stop the *Bürgerbewegung pro Deutschland* (the far-right Citizens Movement for Germany) from screening the full 74-minute video. A Toronto Hindu group planned to show it to expose Islam's negative portrayal of Hindus.

Although the USA bought ads on a half-dozen Pakistani television stations disavowing the video, and Pakistan declared a holiday to encourage peaceful protests, 23 people were killed and more than 200 injured when 15,000 demonstrated in Karachi. Pakistan's Foreign Affairs Minister summoned the Embassy's chargé d'affaires to demand the USA remove the video. Pakistan's federal railway minister offered a $100,000 reward from his personal funds for anyone who killed the filmmaker, inviting the Taliban and al-Qaeda to do so. Although incitement to murder was a crime (and rioters against the video had destroyed a cinema owned by his brother), he was "ready to be hanged in the name of the prophet Muhammad." Pakistan promptly repudiated his action; but the Taliban took him off its "hit list." A businessman offered to put up another $400,000. A group of 5,000 demonstrated in Sri Lanka; more than a hundred were injured in protests in Bangladesh. Al-Qaeda leader Ayman al-Zawahiri urged Muslims to fight in response to the insult. Pakistan blocked YouTube, renewing the ban three months later; Egypt suspended it for a month. Pakistani President Ashraf asked the UN to outlaw blasphemy. But Obama told the UN General Assembly that the USA valued its First Amendment "because in a diverse society, efforts to restrict speech can become a tool to silence critics, or oppress minorities." "[G]iven the power of faith in our lives ... the strongest weapon against hateful speech is not repression, it is ... the voices that rally against bigotry and blasphemy." The *New York Times* and the *Washington Post* praised the speech. But in the same venue Egyptian President Morsi condemned the video's "unacceptable" "obscenities," which were "part of an organized campaign against Islamic sanctities."

"Bacile" was revealed to be Nakoula Basseley Nakoula, 55, who operated a gas station and had been convicted of check-kiting (a type of fraud) in June 2010, for which he had been imprisoned for 21 months and made to pay restitution of $794,700. A federal magistrate judge ordered him held without bond pending a probation revocation hearing on charges that he had lied to law enforcement officers. He pleaded to four charges related to maintaining two identities and was sentenced to a year (the government had sought two). His lawyer was defiant: "President Obama may have gotten Osama bin Laden, but he didn't kill the [Muslim] ideology." Nakoula grandstanded from prison: "I thought, before I wrote this script, that I should burn myself in a public square to let the American people and the people of the world know this message that I believe in." Cindy Lee Garcia, who appeared in the video and had since received death threats, sued him for fraud and slander, claiming she had been unaware of the film's anti-Muslim content. (Nakoula had called the principal character "George" when shooting the film, later dubbing in Mohammed.) In response, a Ninth Circuit panel ordered YouTube to take down the trailer, but the en banc court reversed on the ground that Garcia lacked a copyright interest and could not establish irreparable harm.

Like Jones, Nakoula was an outsider who embodied a lethal combination of ignorance and arrogance. He claimed to want to liberate Muslims from the blinders of Islam by opening their eyes to its evils, subtitling the trailer in Arabic and uploading it to YouTube. But his real goal seems to have been to ignite what Samuel Huntington[86] predicted would be an inevitable "clash of civilizations," perversely mirroring what Osama bin Laden may have hoped to achieve by the 9/11 attacks. Nakoula's success likely exceeded his naive expectations when Muslims around the world vented their fury at the USA by violently demonstrating for their faith with tragic losses of life and limb, vividly illustrating the claim by some Islamists that "we love death more than you love life." (This foreshadowed the attack on *Charlie Hebdo* two years later for having published caricatures of Mohammed contemporaneously with Nakoula's video.) Both Nakoula and Jones endangered members of the US military and Foreign Service. As with the Koran-burning, no American lawyer contested Nakoula's legal right to make and disseminate the video. Indeed, the Ninth Circuit rebuffed Garcia's copyright claim (although Nakoula's pretextual imprisonment for violating probation may have been an effort to silence him). Despite calls from leaders of Muslim countries, the First Amendment precluded the regulation of hate speech in the United States[87] (unlike the situation in many European countries). But the government's responses were still controversial. Conservatives attacked the Obama administration for not defending Nakoula's free speech rights as vigorously as it had championed Muslims' right to establish mosques; and they assailed the administration's apologies for the offense to Muslims as an invitation to violence. Neither critique was persuasive. Government dissemination of its views is entirely consistent with free speech ideals; and calls for religious tolerance in no way condone or encourage violence.

SHARIA[88]

Islamophobes also sought to foment fear of sharia (Islamic law). Sarah Palin warned that if sharia "were to be adopted, allowed to govern in our country, it will be the downfall of America." In July 2010 Andrew McCarthy wrote in the *National Review*: "some Islamists employ mass-murder attacks while others prefer a gradual march through our institutions ... the goal of both, though, is the same. It's about sharia." The same month Newt Gingrich told the American Enterprise Institute that "sharia is a mortal threat to the survival of freedom in the United States and in the world as we know it," the "heart of the enemy movement from which the terrorists spring forth." "The victory of Sharia would clearly mean the end of the government Lincoln was describing." Two months later he got a standing ovation by telling the Values Voter Summit: "We should have a federal law that says sharia law cannot be recognized in any court in the United States."

The movement's ringleader was David Yerushalmi, a Hasidic lawyer who pronounced in 2006 that "most of the fundamental differences between races are genetic." As general counsel of the conservative Center for Security Policy he wrote a 172-page book, *Shariah: The Threat to America*, and drafted a model statute: American Laws for American Courts. After Tennessee and Louisiana passed an early version (which did not mention sharia), other states took up the banner. Oklahoma State Rep. Rex Duncan introduced a ballot measure that would amend the state constitution to mandate that state courts "rely on federal and state law" and forbid them from "considering or using" international law or sharia. (A similar bill had been introduced in South Carolina; and Arizona was considering one to bar state judges from relying on "any body of religious sectarian law or foreign law.") Citing a New Jersey family court judge who invoked sharia in denying a restraining order to a wife who had been raped by her husband (a decision quickly reversed on appeal), Duncan called his proposal a "preemptive strike." "Oklahoma does not have that problem yet." (Muslims formed less than one percent of the state's population.) "But why wait until it's in the courts?" Sharia tribunals in Britain were "a cancer." (No UK court administered sharia.) "This is a war for the survival of America." After being termed out, he won a close race for County District Attorney, boosted by sponsoring the measure. State Rep. Mike Reynolds, a cosponsor, hailed "an awakening of people concerned about Christian values in our nation." State Rep. Cory Williams (who was one of ten Democrats opposed and facing re-election) complained that his challenger's mailers depicted him next to a shadowy figure in Arab headdress, suggesting that Williams was part of "an international movement, supported by militant Muslims and liberals," to establish sharia throughout the world. He won by 280 votes, but other Democrats lost. Act! For America (founded by Brigitte Gabriel, a Lebanese Maronite) spent $60,000 on radio ads and 600,000 robocalls featuring Jim Woolsey, an Oklahoma native and former CIA director.

Oklahoma voters embraced the law 7–3, but CAIR promptly challenged it, and WD Ok Judge Miles-LaGrange issued a temporary restraining order because the law "may be viewed as specifically singling out shariah law, conveying a message of disapproval of plaintiff's faith." Duncan denounced the decision, which "thwarts the will of the people." But the Tenth Circuit affirmed. Mosques in Oklahoma City and Tulsa were deluged with hate mail, including a video of a man destroying a mosque. The *Los Angeles Times* denounced the measure as "a symptom of a grave sickness in the heartland ... inspired by paranoia, xeno-phobia and ignorance that should offend ... anyone who believes in the principles enshrined by the U.S. Constitution." The *New York Times* applauded the TRO, which "save[d] Oklahoma from its pernicious folly and ... prevent[ed] other states from following the same path"; but it regretted that "the issue helped drive the high Republican turnout at the polls in Oklahoma that, combined with the national Republican wave, helped give the party veto-proof control of the legislature and a Republican governor for the first time."

Republicans seeking the 2012 presidential nomination continued to exploit populist fears (displaying a mix of incoherence and ignor-ance). Rick Santorum told a political dinner in New Hampshire that "Sharia law is incompatible with American jurisprudence and our Constitution." It "is not just a religious code. It is also a government code." Donald Trump said on Bill O'Reilly's television program that the Koran "teaches some very negative vibe ... when you look at people blowing up all over the streets that are in some countries over in the middle east ... there's tremendous hatred out there." Several months later Herman Cain chimed in: "Sharia law is what they are to infuse in to our ... what I'm saying is American laws in American courts." People "are objecting to the fact that Islam is both religion and of a set of laws, sharia law. That's the difference between any one of our other trad-itional religions where it's just about religious purposes." (*Kashruth?*) In a debate among Republican candidates Mitt Romney said: "we're not going to have Shariah law applied in U.S. Courts." Declaring that sharia "must be resisted across the United States," Michelle Bachmann endorsed anti-sharia legislation.

The campaign provoked criticism. The chairman of the Muslim Writers Guild of America explained that "Islam requires that people must voluntarily abide by Shariah in order for it to be applied." The executive director of ACLU of Tennessee drew encouragement from the fact that during the recent state legislative session several hundred Muslims had traveled to the state capitol, urging legislators to oppose a bill that would have undermined constitutional protections for Muslims. Joined by civil liberties and civil rights groups and clergy of many faiths, they succeeded in stripping the original bill of its most egregious provisions.

A Nashville hotel canceled reservations for "The Constitution or Sharia: A Freedom Conference." When his nomination of Sohail Mohammed as the first Muslim on the New Jersey Superior Court provoked opposition, Gov. Christie said on YouTube: "this shariah law business is crap. It's just crazy, and I'm tired of dealing with crazies." The New York Times hoped "those words will shame his friends on the Republican right and finally quiet all the candidates who are cynically trawling for votes claiming, absurdly, that Muslim religious law is threatening to take over the American legal system." Eliyahu Stern, Assistant Professor of Religious Studies and History at Yale, wrote in a New York Times op ed that "anti-shariah legislation fosters a hostile environment that will stymie the growth of America's tolerant strands of Islam."

But in May 2012 the Kansas House of Representatives unanimously passed a bill declaring that state courts, administrative agencies, and tribunals could not base rulings on any foreign law or legal system that would not grant parties rights guaranteed by state and federal constitutions; the Senate approved 33–3, and Gov. Sam Brownback signed it. In a pending divorce, the husband had asked that property be divided according to a prenuptial agreement the couple had made in Lebanon and spousal maintenance be limited to three months under sharia. Sen. Susan Wagle (R-Wichita) said: "in this great country of ours and in the state of Kansas, women have equal rights. They stone women to death in countries that have Shariah law." Sen. Tim Owens, the Republican judiciary committee chair, voted against the bill, which would "put Kansas in a light that says we are intolerant of any other faith." In 2014 Alabama voters passed a similar law 72 percent to 28 percent, joining Arizona, North Carolina, and South Dakota.

The campaign against sharia was a classic example of moral panic, a concept formulated by Joseph Gusfield to understand the American temperance movement and by Stanley Cohen to explain English fears of Mods and Rockers,[89] and subsequently applied to such diverse phenomena as comic books, fluoridated drinking water, television, marijuana and other drugs, homosexuality, and transgender people. The anti-sharia campaign revived painful memories of the treatment of the German language and culture during World War I, the internment of Japanese Americans during World War II, and rabid anti-communism after both wars. But perhaps it more closely resembled the recrudescence of anti-Semitism in countries like Poland, where the Jewish population had been virtually exterminated. None of the states enacting such laws – Louisiana, Tennessee, Oklahoma, Kansas, Alabama, Arizona, North Carolina, and South Dakota – had significant Muslim populations (by contrast with urban agglomerations in states like New York, California, Michigan, Illinois, and Minnesota, which seemed tolerant of, or at least indifferent to, Islam). Rather, unscrupulous politicians who had never previously displayed any enthusiasm for feminism suddenly vied to defend Muslim women from patriarchal oppression under sharia.

Opinion polls, plebiscites, legislative action, and elections all revealed the dangers of unbridled majoritarianism. Fortunately, the overreaction shamed some Republicans, aroused the mainstream media, and provoked rebuffs from the courts.

HOUSE HOMELAND SECURITY COMMITTEE HEARINGS ON MUSLIM "RADICALIZATION"[90]

Immediately after being sworn in as Homeland Security Committee chair following the Republican capture of the House in November 2010, Rep. Peter T. King (NY) announced hearings on Muslim "radicalization," declaring that though Democrats had "denounced" him for raising the idea when he was in the minority, law enforcement officials were "constantly telling me how little cooperation they get from Muslim leaders." "We have to break through this politically-correct nonsense which keeps us from debating and discussing what I think is one of the most vital issues in this country, that we are under siege by Muslim terrorists." The American–Arab Anti-Discrimination Committee legal director accused King of "bigoted intentions." The Muslim Public Affairs Council executive director said King was treating Muslims "as a suspect community." Opposing the plans to build the Ground Zero mosque, King had said: "this is such a raw wound, and they are just pouring salt into it." The *New York Times* called King's "sweeping slur on Muslim citizens ... unacceptable," agreeing with Rep. Keith Ellison (D-Mn, the sole Muslim in Congress) that King's words were "very scary." King had said there were "too many mosques in this country," 85 percent of them run by radical extremists. In the preface to his 2004 novel *Vale of Tears*, he had written that it "describes how vulnerable we can become ... if we fail to recognize that our terrorist foes comprise a worldwide network with operatives active within our borders."

A coalition of 55 religious and civil rights groups condemned the hearings: "engaging in fear mongering and divisive rhetoric ... only weakens the fabric of our nation and distracts us from actual threats." Nearly a hundred members of Congress asked King to cancel the hearings or broaden their scope. Rep. Bennie G. Thompson (D-Miss), the committee's ranking minority member, asked King to include right-wing threats. Conservatives criticized Thompson for calling only Muslim witnesses. Rep. Ellison planned to testify that "if you put every single Muslim in the U.S. in jail, it wouldn't have stopped Jared Loughner" in Colorado, or the Virginia Tech killings, or the Oklahoma City bombing, or the murder at the Holocaust Museum in Washington. King rebuffed that as "political correctness at its worst." "If we included these other violent events in the hearings, we'd be sending the false signal that we think there's a security threat equivalency between al-Qaeda and the neo-Nazi movement, or ... gun groups. There is none." (Non-Muslim extremists had killed nearly twice as many Americans since 9/11 as had Muslim extremists; in a 2015 survey of 382 law enforcement agencies, 74 percent said anti-government extremism was one of the top three terrorist threats, while just 39 percent identified al-Qaeda and like-minded groups.[91]) At a forum organized by Muslim Advocates, Los Angeles County Sheriff Baca said that as a member of the Major City Police Chiefs Association and the National Sheriffs Association, he had heard no complaints about Muslim non-cooperation.

DHS Secretary Napolitano said "the [national security] threat today may be at its most heightened state since the attacks nearly 10 years ago." Calling this "shift" a "game changer," King warned of a "nightmare scenario": a launch "from the suburbs" of a "dirty bomb, which would put that metropolitan area off-limits, besides the massive loss of human life." On CNN's *State of the Nation*, he said relatives of men who had been radicalized would testify about "how this originated in mosques." Ellison replied on the same program that investigating "a religious minority" was "the wrong course of action." The *Los Angeles Times* said King "has not identified" a "growing threat ... and certainly not at a level that would justify singling out one religion to be targeted for special scrutiny." The hearings "run the risk of exacerbating" the "real and widespread" "anti-Islamic feeling in this country." Critics recalled that King himself had strongly supported a terrorist group – the IRA – and compared Gerry Adams, the leader of Sinn Féin, to George Washington, denouncing the British government as "a murder machine."

Denis McDonough, Deputy National Security Adviser, assured the All Dulles Area Muslim Society that the administration "will not stigmatize or demonize entire communities because of the actions of a few." In his *New York Times* column, Bob Herbert warned that the hearings "can only serve to further demonize a group of Americans already being pummeled by bigotry and vicious stereotyping." The *New York Times* deplored King's "slanders and misstatements," agreeing that the hearings "seem designed to stoke fear against American Muslims." In his *Washington Post* column, Eugene Robinson said the hearings' premise "offends our nation's founding ideals." "This is religious persecution – and it's un-American and wrong!" In his *Washington Post* column, Richard Cohen said: "the government has no business examining any peaceful religious group because a handful of adherents have broken the law." Rabbis created the group Stand Together: Rabbis Speak Out against Islamophobia. The *Washington Post* called King's false claim that 80 percent of US mosques were controlled by radical leaders "deeply troubling and disparaging to the vast majority of Muslims who are peaceful, law-abiding and productive members of this country." But there was a "need for a candid conversation about the real phenomenon of homegrown terrorism."

Defiantly assuring supporters he would not "back down to the hysteria created by my opponents," King opened the hearings by acknowledging that "the overwhelming majority of Muslim Americans are outstanding Americans," but insisting "there are realities we cannot ignore." "To back down would be a craven surrender to political correctness." Ellison replied that "we need to conduct a thorough, fair analysis and to do no harm. The approach of today's hearing, I fear, does not meet these standards." King was assigning "collective blame to a whole group" and "stereotyping and scapegoating." Thompson warned the hearings could increase "fear and mistrust" among Muslim Americans. Denouncing CAIR as "discredited," an "unindicted co-conspirator or joint venturer" in the HLF prosecution (see Chapter 2), King congratulated the FBI for cutting off high-level contact with the Council. But his only evidence was a 1970s poster by the Puerto Rican independence movement warning "Don't talk to the FBI," once spotted in a CAIR office but quickly removed. And FBI Director Mueller had recently said officials regularly worked with CAIR chapters on investigations. Nevertheless, other Republicans joined King's attack: Rep. Chip Cravaack (MN) said CAIR was founded by two men the FBI had identified as "Hamas members." Rep. Frank R. Wolf (Va) accused CAIR of "an attempt to stifle debate and obstruct cooperation with law enforcement."

The *New York Times* said King "demeaned the crucial issue of home-land security – and himself – building a Congressional hearing around his foolish, provocative and hurtful claims of widespread radicalization of Muslim Americans," for which he offered "not a scintilla of substan-tiation." He did not call a single police witness or any large, established Muslim American organization, preferring to feature "two aggrieved witnesses offering anecdotal tales about radicalized relatives, as if that proved his case." "The only good news is that Congressman King's main success was how he punctured his own bloviations." The *Times* contrasted King's "xenophobic allegation" with a hearing conducted by Sen. Richard Durbin (D-Ill), which revealed that Muslims, though forming just 1 percent of the population, were victims in 14 per-cent of religious discrimination cases. King's hearings inspired NY State Sen. Gregory R. Ball (R-Putnam County) to hold his own (and ask King to testify). Eight Democratic State Senators objected: "by including Islamic law as a topic of the hearing, you conflate the religious observances and practices of a faith into security matters."

King's second set of hearings focused on Islamic radicalization in prisons. But noting that non-Muslim white, Latino, Asian, and African American gang members also left prison more violent than when they entered, Rep. Laura Richardson (D-Ca) called the hearings "racist and discriminatory." King retorted that "we are not going to spread our-selves out, investigate everything, which means investigate nothing." His third and fourth hearings focused on al-Shabaab in the USA and the US military, which provided "the most sought-after targets of vio-lent extremists." But Paul Stockton, Assistant Secretary of Defense for Homeland Defense and America's Security Affairs, who was called by

King, testified that "al-Qaeda would love to convince Muslims around the world that the United States is at war with Islam" and "I'm not going to aid and abet that effort to advance their propaganda goals."

Many observers drew the obvious parallels between King's hearings and those of Sen. Joseph McCarthy nearly sixty years earlier. Like McCarthy, King was an outsider seeking to expose weakness within the administration by manipulating diffuse feelings of insecurity stemming from a wide variety of causes: 9/11 and the few dramatic terrorist attacks or attempts that followed; the wars the USA initiated in Afghanistan and Iraq and seemed unable to win; economic anxieties (some clearly justified after the housing bubble burst); and xenophobic fear of immigrants. King had already sought political visibility by opposing the Ground Zero mosque.

But he failed to achieve anything like McCarthy's impact for several reasons. History had thoroughly discredited the Wisconsin senator: domestic communism never posed a significant threat. Terrorism experts repeatedly documented that white extremists posed a much greater danger than Muslims. The targets of the two demagogues were different: despite its enemies' slanders, Islam is a religion, not a political movement like communism (which *did* want to overthrow American capitalism, even though it never had any chance of doing so). King's target was too large, respectable, and diverse: an estimated seven million American Muslims, compared with the few thousand members of the Communist Party in the 1950s. McCarthy was a far more effective and ruthless politician, bullying witnesses into invoking the Fifth Amendment, seen at the time as an admission of guilt. Few dared challenge him. By contrast, Congressional Democrats stood up to King, the mainstream media condemned the hearings, and leading law enforcement officials refused to support him. For all of King's hype, the hearings turned out to be a non-event.

THE 2016 PRESIDENTIAL CAMPAIGN

After eight years of the Obama presidency, the Republican campaign to succeed him quickly deteriorated into a vicious competition in Islamophobia. In June 2015 Ben Carson declared: "we should not be bringing anyone in[to]" the country from the Middle East until we "have in place a very excellent screening mechanism."[92] (He cited the Boston Marathon bombers; but they had come from Dagestan, not the Middle East: Dzhokhar Tsarnaev aged 9 in 2002 and his brother Tamerlan aged

18 in 2004.) A Donald Trump campaign stop in New Hampshire a few days later produced the following exchange.[93]

> AUDIENCE MEMBER: We have a problem in this country. It's called Muslim. We know our current president is one.
> TRUMP: Right.
> AUDIENCE MEMBER: You know he's not even an American.

Refusing to correct his interlocutor then or later, Trump said "the bigger issue is that Obama is waging a war against Christians in this country." Ted Cruz and Rick Santorum declined to comment. Carson declared he "absolutely would not agree ... that we [should] put a Muslim in charge of this nation." The *Washington Post* said Carson's words "betrayed appalling ignorance of the U.S. Constitution and a fundamental misunderstanding of what this country is about." The *New York Times* agreed: "this latest sordid mess ... touches on bedrock American values, constitutional principles and American history." John Kasich and Bobby Jindal refused to address such a "hypothetical question." Carson then compounded his error by reiterating that "we do not put people at the leadership of our country whose faith might interfere with carrying out the duties of the Constitution" (reviving memories of the anti-Catholic slurs against Kennedy in 1960, Al Smith in 1928, and James Blaine in 1884). Asked about the effect of those comments on his campaign, Carson bragged that "within 24 hours we raised $1 million."

Mike Huckabee opposed admitting any Syrian refugees because "we could be inviting some of the most violent and vicious people on earth ... it's insane." "They don't speak our language."[94] (Few refugees are native-English speakers.) Falsely claiming (after the November 2016 attacks in Paris) that Obama wanted to admit 250,000 Syrians, Trump said: "you'd have to be insane." Cruz called it "absolute lunacy." Paul, Kasich, and Christie concurred. More than thirty governors vowed to refuse Syrian refugees. Trump called for deporting those already in the USA. The government had to "strongly consider" closing mosques that nurtured "absolute hatred." He claimed to have "predicted terrorism" in his 2000 book "because I can feel it, like I feel a good location, o.k.?" Syrian refugees were a "Trojan Horse." Jeb Bush urged admitting only those who "can prove you're a Christian." Cruz agreed. The *Times* called the suggestion "idiotic." The *Post* deplored the candidates' "downright ugly" rhetoric. President Obama responded that a "religious test" was "offensive and contrary to American values." Rep. Michael McCaul (R-Tex) introduced a bill to restrict the admission of Syrian refugees. The *Times* condemned such "election-year pandering to the xenophobia that rears up when threats from abroad arise." Although Obama threatened to veto the bill, which "would provide no meaningful additional security," it passed the House by a veto-proof margin (50 Democrats joining 239 Republicans). The administration raised fines for airlines that failed to verify the identities of passengers flying to the USA and required foreign countries to ask if they had traveled to conflict zones. Sens. Jeff Flake (R-Az) and Dianne Feinstein (D-Ca) introduced a bill eliminating visa waivers for anyone who had traveled to Syria or Iraq in the previous five years, which the *Times* called "a far more constructive way to flag dangerous people." It passed the House overwhelmingly (407–19).

Trump said he would "absolutely" require Muslims in the USA to register and would deport Syrian refugees already in the country.[95] "It's all about management." "I want surveillance of certain mosques, o.k.? We've had it before and we'll have it again." "Security is going to rule … We're going to have to do certain things that were frankly unthinkable a year ago" (an implicit invocation of Cheney declaration days after 9/11: "we also have to work … the dark side"). On 9/11 Trump claimed to have "watched in Jersey City, New Jersey, where thousands and thousands of people were cheering as [the World Trade Center] was coming down." (When the New Jersey State Police and Gov. Christie denied this ever occurred, Trump insisted "it did happen, I saw it." Carson also said: "I saw the film of it," but later admitted confusing New Jersey with the Middle East.) Trump said: "you have to take out [terrorists'] families." Carson equated a refugee seeking entry to "a rabid dog running around your neighborhood." Rand Paul introduced an amendment prohibiting the use of federal funds to assist refugees or asylum seekers.

Other Republican candidates offered a more nuanced Islamophobia. Bush said "talk about closing mosques … registering people – that's just wrong." But he added: "there is a special important need to make sure that Christians from Syria are being protected." Although Cruz was "not a big fan of government registries," "it is the height of lunacy for a government official to welcome in tens of thousands of refugees when we know that among them will be ISIS [Islamic State of Iraq and Syria] terrorists." Although Christie conceded that "the indiscriminate closing of mosques or the establishment of a national registry based on religion will do nothing to keep us safer," he opposed admitting even "orphans under 5." Only Democrats balked. Martin O'Malley asked "how is that at all American?" Bernie Sanders cautioned: "we will not destroy ISIS by undermining the Constitution and our religious freedoms." Hillary Clinton said: "We cannot allow terrorists to intimidate us into abandoning our values and humanitarian obligations. Turning away orphans, applying a religious test, discriminating against Muslims, slamming the door on every single Syrian refugee – that's just not who we are."

The *New York Times* denounced "repugnant religious litmus tests," warning of "the danger of self-inflicted injury … the risk that society will lose its way."[96] "History teaches that failing to hold a demagogue to account is a dangerous act." Its columnists concurred. Andrew Rosenthal noted the "inescapable … similarities to the registration of Jews in Nazi Germany." Frank Bruni denounced resort to "the repressive, regressive methods of our enemies." Nicholas Kristof quoted a tweet he had received: "The Statue of Liberty Must Be Crying with Shame." Readers might remember "this family: a carpenter named Joseph, his wife, Mary, and their baby son, Jesus." Washington State Gov. Inslee wrote in an op ed that "the American character is being tested." The *Washington Post* said: "the only way to beat a bully is to stand up to him." Its columnists agreed. David Ignatius said Trump "has displayed a level of irresponsibility that borders on recklessness." Ruth Marcus warned that "this coarsening of dialogue helps create a climate that nurtures the current explosion of anti-Muslim bias … among leading Republican presidential candidates."

After the San Bernardino massacre on December 2, 2015, Cruz declared: "we are at a time of war."[97] "We will carpet bomb [ISIS] into oblivion. I don't know if sand can glow in the dark, but we're going to find out." (The tactic wasn't so successful in Southeast Asia.) Christie agreed: "we are in the midst of the next world war." Bush attacked Obama and Clinton for not denouncing "the brutal savagery of Islamic terrorism." "[W]e need to declare war on them." "There are no radical Christians that are organizing to destroy western civilization." Trump assailed Obama for refusing to name "radical Islamic terrorism." The *Times* noted that since 9/11, 45 people in the USA had been killed by terrorists, 48 by white supremacists and right-wing extremists, and more than 200,000 by ordinary criminals.

Trump demanded a ban on immigration by *all* Muslims, whose "hatred" was "beyond comprehension." Bush called him "unhinged." Rubio declared the proposal "offensive and outlandish," but also insisted "there is no middle ground" in this "clash of civilizations." Leading

Republicans, including Paul Ryan, Mitch McConnell, and Dick Cheney, rejected Trump's call. Clinton condemned it as "reprehensible, prejudiced and divisive." But Cruz "commend[ed] Donald Trump for standing up and focusing America's attention on the need to secure our borders." He introduced bills to let states exclude refugees and to bar all refugees from Syria, Iraq, Somalia, or any country with territory "substantially controlled by IS [Islamic State] or any foreign terrorist organization." Paul wanted to ban refugees from 30 countries with "large jihadist movements." Newt Gingrich thought Trump's idea "may be too strong," but "something jarring is very helpful in leading to a national debate in [sic] how big this problem is." Trump responded to the criticism by invoking FDR, "a president highly respected by all," who "did the same thing" when interning Japanese Americans. Trump claimed Paris police refused to enter "radicalized" neighborhoods and London police "are afraid for their own lives" (citing no evidence because the claims were patently false). Democratic candidates continued to champion tolerance. Sanders said "we must never forget what happened under the racist ideology of the Nazis, which led to the deaths of millions and millions of people, including [family] members of mine." Invoking the example of Danes who defied Nazi attempts to identify and exterminate Jews by donning yellow stars, O'Malley said: "if Donald Trump wants to start a registry in our country of people by faith, he can start with me." In his first visit to a mosque (the Islamic Society of Baltimore), Obama recited phrases from the Koran, declared that Muslims were part of "one American family," and warned Americans against remaining "bystanders to bigotry."

Trump's provocation produced the desired result.[98] In his *New York Times* column, Frank Bruni seconded Sen. Graham's suggestion to "tell Donald Trump to go to hell." The *Times* warned that Trump was not unique; his Republican rivals "have been peddling their own nativist policies for months or years." "The fascism behind the agenda of the right wing on immigrants and foreigners has long been as plain as day." In the *Washington Post*, Ruth Marcus said Trump had crossed "an incrossable [sic] line," Kathleen Parker called him "IS's secret weapon," Charles Lane accused him of "sloppy thinking," Dana Milbank termed him "America's Modern Mussolini," Colbert King heard "echoes [of] the red scare era," E.J. Dionne Jr. warned of the proposed ban's "slippery slope," David Ignatius said Trump's "anti-Muslim rhetoric will live in infamy" (echoing FDR's famous phrase about Pearl Harbor), Eugene Robinson decried "a new era of pitchfork populism," and even conservative

Charles Krauthammer could not "get over" the ban's "sheer absurdity." The *Post* assailed Trump's "lunatic and offensive" pronouncements.

On the 150th anniversary of the Thirteenth Amendment, Obama denounced "bigotry in all its forms," calling for equality "no matter what ugliness might bubble up." A public poll found that two-thirds believed the ban "goes against the founding principles of this country." Partnership for New York City took a full-page ad in the *Times*, noting that 3,160,471 New Yorkers "came to our city from another country … we welcome their contributions to the strength and vitality of our great city. Just as we have since 1768." #WeAreBetterThanThis (a broad coalition) also took a full-page ad decrying "the surge of divisive rhetoric that sows the seeds of more violence to come." The *Times* urged companies "that have emblazoned the Trump name on their properties and products" to "think hard about whether they want to be associated with the outrageous things coming out of Donald Trump's mouth." The *Post* criticized a Republican Party "that breeds presidential contenders who would monitor schools and mosques, shut down parts of the Internet and exclude certain immigrants for no reason beyond the faith they profess." It called for "a sharp and clear response from everyone who cares about fairness and decency, democracy and tolerance." On Martin Luther King Day the *Post* said: "when we start judging people based on categories they belong to, we diminish ourselves."

Trump's first television ad at the beginning of 2016 called for a ban on Muslim immigrants, displaying images of terrorism and masked men in front of Arabic script.[99] At the Republican presidential debate a week later, Christie said: "we should take no Syrian refugees of any kind." Rubio agreed: "if we do not know who you are, and we do not know why you are coming … you are not getting into the United States of America." Cruz wanted to suspend "all refugees from nations that ISIS or al Qaeda control [sic] significant territory." A month later Trump told an apocryphal story about General Pershing executing alleged Muslim terrorists in the Philippines with bullets dipped in pigs' blood, and claimed: "for 25 years, there wasn't a problem." "We better start using our heads, or we're not going to have a country, folks." The *Post* called Republican leaders' silence on Trump "inexcusable – and irrational." At the next debate a week later Trump reiterated that "there is tremendous hate" among "large portions" of the world's Muslims. The *Post* contended that such "hateful spewing … should be unacceptable." But after the bombings in Brussels on March 22, 2016, Cruz said: "we need to empower law enforcement to patrol and secure Muslim neighborhoods before they become radicalized." Trump claimed absurdly that Brussels used to be "a beautiful place with zero crime, and now it's a disaster city." The *Times* warned against "the impulse after a barbaric attack … to rein in civil liberties and freedoms." The *Post* reminded Cruz that NYPD had terminated its "covert" and "deeply controversial" surveillance of Muslim communities. But Trump reiterated that "we have to look very seriously at the Mosques. Lots of things happening in the Mosques, that's been proven." This wave of vituperation seems to have been effective: in little more than three months the proportion of Americans opposing a Muslim ban fell by half, from two-thirds to little more than a third.

After the June 12 Orlando terrorist attack, Trump again called for a ban on immigrants from any part of the world with "a proven history of terrorism" against the USA or its allies.[100] (Britain? Canada?) American "Muslims have to work with us. They know what's going on. They know that [the Orlando shooter] was bad. They knew the people in San Bernardino were bad. But you know what? They didn't turn them in." Obama condemned "language that singles out immigrants and suggests entire religious communities are complicit in violence." "Are we going to start treating all Muslim Americans differently?" The *Washington Post* warned that "to generalize about … 'the Muslims' is to set the nation down a dangerous road it has trod, to its eventual regret in the past." Newt Gingrich advocated doing just that: "we originally created the House Un-American Activities Committee to go after Nazis … We're going to presently have to go take similar steps here." "Western civilization is in a war. We should frankly test every person here who is of a Muslim background, and if they believe in sharia, they should be deported." "Anybody who goes on a website favoring ISIS or al Qaeda or other terrorist groups, that should be a felony." A bill to bar all refugees secured the support of 86 House Republicans. The *New York Times* condemned this "meanspirited and illogical proposal," noting that only five of the 800,000 refugees admitted to the USA since 9/11 had been arrested for terrorism, and none was charged with an attack in the USA.

Trump repeated that "we have to be very strong in terms of looking at the mosques" because "this is a problem that if we don't solve it, it's going to eat our country alive." He also called for profiling because "we have to start using common sense." The *Post* asked "what, exactly, does a 'possible [terrorist]' look like? Brown? Male? Bearded? Wearing a thawb [Arab robe]?" When Trump rephrased his ban to cover "terror countries," the *Post* called that "gibberish." The *Times* said the response to terrorism "cannot be to abandon the respect for human rights, equality, reason and tolerance that is the aspiration of all democratic cultures." Michael Morrell (former deputy and acting DCI) wrote in a *Times* op ed that Trump's Muslim ban "clearly contradicts the foundational values of our nation." In another rhetorical evasion, Trump called for "extreme vetting" to exclude those who do not "share our values and respect our people," or who "believe that sharia law should supplant American law." The *Times* said this would "undermine the very American values of tolerance and equal treatment that he said he wanted to encourage." After Trump aired his first ad for the general election, the *Times* warned that "the message of hatred and paranoia that is inciting millions of voters will outlast the messenger." Trump spoke "frontier gibberish." After the September bomb explosions in New York City and New Jersey, Trump again called for police profiling of Muslims. The *Post* found Trump's "knock the hell out of 'em" "bombast" "equally disturbing." In the second presidential debate, Trump said his "Muslim ban is something that in some form has morphed into a [sic] extreme vetting from certain areas of the world." He did not want "hundreds of thousands of people coming in from Syria … We know nothing about their values and we know nothing about their love for our country."[101]

After Trump's election, the *Times* exhorted him to "immediately and unequivocally repudiate the outpouring of racist, sexist, xenophobic, anti-Semitic and homophobic insults, threats and attacks being associated with your name."[102] When Trump named Stephen Bannon as his chief strategist, the *Times* repeated that the president "has a duty to unequivocally denounce [the alt-right's] toxic propaganda." Instead, Trump tweeted on November 29 that citizens who burn the American flag should face "loss of citizenship or year in jail." "I want to protect Article I, Article II, Article XII – go down the list." (The Constitution has only ten Articles.) The *Times* observed that when Trump swore to defend the Constitution during his inauguration, "we the people will have good reason to doubt he knows what he's talking about." The *Post* said: "in one tweet, Trump trashes two constitutional amendments." Michael Flynn, Trump's pick as National Security Adviser (forced to resign after 24 days), denounced Islam as a "political ideology" that hides "behind what we call freedom of religion," compared it to metastasized cancer, and declared "fear of Muslims is RATIONAL." Trump's Attorney General Jefferson Sessions (named after the President of the Confederacy, not the United States) agreed that a "toxic ideology" was at the root of Islam. He thought religion should play a role in vetting immigrants since "many people do have religious views that are inimical to the public safety of the United States." After a terrorist attack at Ohio State University in November, 2016, Trump reiterated his threat to "suspend immigration from regions where it cannot be safely processed." (The perpetrator, Abdul Razak Ali Artan, had entered as a Somali refugee aged 16 in 2014 and had displayed no signs of radicalization.) Publishing all of Trump's executive orders and proposals, the *Times* warned they "would damage America's credibility as a guardian of human rights, anger allies and undermine civil liberties at home."

A week after being inaugurated (and just after noting it was Holocaust Remembrance Day), Trump issued an executive order barring all refugees and citizens from seven Muslim countries and granting Christians and other minority religions priority over Muslims.[103] He said: "we only want to admit those into our country who will support our country, and love deeply our people," maintaining (falsely) that under Obama "if you were a Muslim you could come in, but if you were a Christian, it was almost impossible." "Christians in the Middle East have been executed in large numbers. We cannot allow this horror to continue!" Trump claimed his order was "working out very nicely." But it was opposed by religious and political leaders, business executives, academics, and the leaders of the UK, France, Germany, Italy, and Pakistan.

Republican Sens. McCain, Graham, and Corker and the conservative Koch network were critical. George W. Bush's daughter tweeted: "this is not the America I know." The *New York Times* denounced the "cruelty" of this "un-American" "bigoted, cowardly, self-defeating policy." The UN special rapporteurs on migrants, racism, human rights, counterterrorism, torture, and freedom of religion said the ban "breaches Washington's human rights obligations." And US District Judges in EDNY and ED Va immediately issued injunctions. The *Post* called it "an affront to values upon which this nation was founded." Rudy Giuliani explained on *Fox News*: "When [Trump] first announced it, he said, 'Muslim Ban.' He called me up. He said, 'put a commission together. Show me the right way to do it legally' … we focused on, instead of religion, danger … which is a factual basis … perfectly legal."

When Acting Attorney General Sally Yates refused to defend the order because she was not convinced it was lawful, Trump immediately fired her. Stephen Miller (a senior Trump adviser, who was not a lawyer) said: "it's sad that our politics have become so politicized that you have people refusing to enforce our laws." More than a thousand DoS employees (the largest number ever) signed a dissent cable opposing the ban.

On February 3, 2017 WD Wash Judge Robart (a George W. Bush appointee) issued a TRO against the ban because the court "must intervene to fulfill its constitutional role in our tripartite government." Trump denounced the "terrible," "ridiculous" decision by the "so-called judge," which "takes law-enforcement away from our country," and the White House called the decision "outrageous." Washington Gov. Inslee said this attack was "beneath the dignity" of the presidency and could "lead America to calamity." Even conservatives expressed dismay. University of Chicago law professor Eric Posner denounced the "indefensible" assault on Robart's integrity. Berkeley law professor John Yoo expressed "grave concerns about Mr. Trump's use of presidential power." Harvard law professor Charles Fried called it: "inappropriate … indecent … unpresidential." Sen. Sasse (R-Neb) said: "we don't have so-called judges." Senate Majority Leader McConnell thought it "best to avoid criticizing judges individually." MSNBC host Joe Scarborough pronounced it "simply unacceptable" for Trump to "question the legitimacy of a federal judge." But Trump was unrepentant: "just cannot believe a judge would put our country in such peril. If something happens blame him and court system." "The judge opens up our country to potential terrorists." "Because the ban was lifted by a judge, many very bad and dangerous people may be pouring into our country. A terrible decision." "What is our country coming to when a judge can halt a Homeland Security travel ban." And Vice President Pence declared that "the president of the United States has every right to criticize the other two branches of government." Trump repeated that "courts seem be so political" but then threatened (inconsistently) to "see you in court." The *New York Times* disagreed with Pence: "coming from the president, it is a threat to the rule of law." Hoping to elicit support for his Supreme Court nomination, Judge Neil Gorsuch cautiously told senators that "any criticism of a judge's integrity and independence" was "disheartening and demoralizing."

When a Ninth Circuit panel upheld Robart's injunction, Trump attacked the "political," "disgraceful" ruling. Although DoJ sought to delay a hearing on a permanent injunction, Judge Robart accepted Trump's challenge to "see you in court" and issued it. Stephen Miller called "the rulings from these courts … flawed, erroneous and false," telephoning the EDNY US Attorney at home to instruct him how to defend the travel ban (thereby violating a DoJ memo issued by Holder). ED Va Judge Brinkema also issued an injunction, finding that "the 'Muslim ban' was a centerpiece of the president's campaign for months, and the press release calling for it was still available on his website." "Maximum power does not mean absolute power." The *New York Times* asked: "where could the demonizing and dehumanizing of the foreign born lead but to a whiter America?" It called for "protesting and public actions" by "churches, universities, schools, philanthropies, health systems, corporations, farmers and artists."

Trump's revised executive order, excluding Iraq from the countries whose citizens were banned, as well as Green Card and visa holders, prompted three lawsuits.[104] D Hi Judge Derrick Watson (an Obama appointee) blocked the new EO, which a "reasonable, objective observer" would view as having been "issued with a purpose to disfavor a particular religion, in spite of its stated, religiously neutral purpose." He cited "significant and unrebutted evidence of religious animus driving the promulgation of the executive order." Trump's "plainly worded statements" as a candidate "betray the executive order's stated secular purpose." He had said in March 2016: "we're having problems with the Muslims, and we're having problems with Muslims coming into the country." There was "nothing 'veiled'" about the December 2015 campaign press release, which said "Donald J. Trump is calling for a total and complete shutdown of Muslims entering the United States." When asked about this in June 2016, Trump had replied: "so you call it territories. Okay?" Asked a week later if he had changed his line, Trump retorted: "I actually don't think it's a rollback. In fact, you could say it's an expansion … People were so upset when I used the word Muslim. Oh, you can't use the word Muslim … And I'm okay with that, because I'm talking territory instead of Muslim."

Stephen Miller had said in February 2017 that the revised order was intended to have "the same basic policy outcome" as the first. D Md Judge Theodore Chuang (another Obama appointee) issued a preliminary injunction, also finding that the order's likely purpose was "effectuation of the proposed Muslim ban" Trump had promised. "Simply because a decision maker made the statements during a campaign does not wipe them" from judicial memory. Trump denounced Watson's "unprecedented judicial overreach," declaring that his "terrible decision" was motivated by "political reasons." He also criticized the Ninth Circuit panel's decision, which "makes us look weak, which by the way we no longer are, believe me." "I have to be nice, otherwise, I'll be criticized for speaking poorly about our courts. Among the most dishonest people in the world, I will be criticized." Days later he defiantly told a fundraising dinner: "somebody said I should not criticize judges. O.K. I'll criticize judges." (The Ninth Circuit voted 5–5 not to rehear the appeal en banc, provoking an angry dissent from Judge Bybee, an author of Bush's notorious "torture memos." But Bybee also said: "the personal attacks on the distinguished District Judge and our colleagues were out of all bounds of civic and persuasive discourse.") Trump added that since the new order was just "a watered-down version of the first one … we ought to go back to the first one, and go all the way, which is what I wanted to do in the first place." Attorney General Sessions said he was "amazed that a judge sitting on an island in the Pacific can issue an order that stops the President of the United States from what appears to be clearly his statutory and constitutional power." Declaring that the Ninth Circuit "has a terrible record of being overturned," Trump tweeted: "See you in the Supreme Court!" (79 percent of Ninth Circuit cases appealed to the Supreme Court were overturned, compared with 70 percent from all circuits, making this rate the third highest in the country.) Reince Priebus, Trump's Chief of Staff, said: "the Ninth Circuit went bananas." Trump said he "absolutely" was considering breaking up the Ninth Circuit, whose decisions were "like, semi-automatic."

The Fourth Circuit (10–3) also declined to reverse D Md Judge Chuang's injunction.[105] Chief Judge Gregory wrote:

> [T]hen-candidate Trump's campaign statements reveal that on numerous occasions, he expressed anti-Muslim sentiment, as well as his intent, if elected to ban Muslims from the United States … the government has repeatedly asked this court to ignore evidence, circumscribe our own review, and blindly defer to executive action, all in the name of the Constitution's separation of powers. We decline to do so, not only because it is the particular province of the judicial branch to say what the law is, but also because we would do a disservice to our constitutional structure were we to let its mere invocation silence the call for meaningful judicial review … to the extent that our review chills campaign promises to condemn and exclude entire religious groups, we think that a welcome restraint.

After the London Bridge attack in June 2017, Trump repudiated the statement by his Press Secretary Sean Spicer that "it's not a travel ban," tweeting that "the lawyers and the courts can call it whatever they want, but I am calling it what we need and what it is a TRAVEL BAN." He preferred "the original Travel Ban, not the watered down, politically correct version." "The Justice Department should ask for an expedited" Supreme Court hearing because "the courts are slow and political!" (He had recently exulted over appointing the conservative Neil Gorsuch to the Court.)

The 2016 Presidential campaign and its aftermath offer frightening evidence of how quickly fundamental attitudes toward immigrants and religious minorities can be inverted. By demagoguery and bullying, Donald Trump induced his Republican rivals to join in trying to sound the most Islamophobic (a competition to which some were already predisposed). Republican candidates shared his contempt for both truth and law. Trump lied that he had predicted 9/11 and seen thousands in New Jersey cheering the attack, that Obama wanted to admit 250,000 Syrians, that police were afraid to enter Muslim neighborhoods in Paris and London, that Muslims had transformed a previously crime-free Brussels into a "disaster city," that Gen. Pershing had used bullets coated with pigs' blood to execute Filipinos, and that American Muslims concealed from police their advance knowledge of the San Bernardino and Orlando attacks. Trump advocated patently illegal actions: deporting refugees (without any process), banning Muslim immigrants, registering and profiling Muslims in the USA, surveilling and closing mosques, and jailing flag burners or rescinding their citizenship. His rivals were no better. Carson could not distinguish between New Jersey, the Middle East, and Dagestan, and declared that a Muslim could not be president. Bush embraced preferences for Christians over Muslims. Cruz called for police surveillance of Muslim neighborhoods and wanted to "carpet bomb [ISIS] into oblivion" (recalling Rick Santorum's earlier threat to "bomb them back to the seventh century" and Gen. Curtis LeMay's to bomb Vietnam "back into the Stone Age").

Republicans blithely defied Santayana's warning that those who cannot remember the past are doomed to repeat it: Gingrich calling for a revival of the House Committee on Un-American Activities, Trump claiming to channel FDR by citing the Japanese American internment as a *good* precedent and issuing his Muslim ban on Holocaust Remembrance Day. Although causality is always uncertain, there was extensive evidence that anti-Muslim hate crimes increased.[106] Fortunately, these attacks elicited expressions of solidarity with

Muslims,[107] advocacy of tolerance by businesses[108] and celebrities,[109] and criminal prosecutions.[110]

The hatred also provoked vociferous criticism. The *New York Times* and *Washington Post* published numerous editorials, and their columnists were even more scathing.[111] All the Democratic presidential candidates assailed Trump's views. But none of these could devise a strategy to counter what both leading newspapers denounced as "gibberish." Just as Herman Kahn broke a taboo a half century ago by "thinking about the unthinkable" idea of thermonuclear war,[112] and Dick Cheney declared we would "have to work, through … the dark side,"[113] so Trump promised to do the "frankly unthinkable": crossing an "incrossable" line and saying what had been unsayable. The opposition's inefficacy was suggested when the proportion of Americans opposing a "Muslim ban" dropped by half in just three months and then, catastrophically, was confirmed by Trump's election six months later.

Trump quickly disabused any hope that taking office might make him more presidential. Just a week after the inauguration he issued the first EO on immigration (with little apparent input from the usual battery of government lawyers). On the advice of Rudy Giuliani, he targeted "terror countries" rather than Muslims. When his acting Attorney General refused to follow the law, he fired her (reviving memories of Nixon's Saturday Night Massacre) and followed that up by firing FBI Director Comey (for investigating Trump's Russian connections). After a thousand DoS employees signed a dissent cable, Trump proposed drastic cuts in the Department's budget (initially 37 percent, then 28 percent). Most disturbingly, when federal judges blocked the EO, he assailed them personally (just as he had as a candidate), apparently convinced that the best defense is an offense. But whereas his vicious attacks on political opponents (Obama, Clinton) and the media were red meat for his base (and expanded it), the judiciary was another matter. Judges do not suffer defiance gladly. They base their authority on the fundamental constitutional principle of separation of powers (garnering sympathy and support from even conservative legal scholars, brethren on the bench, and some Republican leaders). And Trump's demagoguery – so effective in winning the election – exposed his EOs to judicial scrutiny. Five District Judges, a unanimous 9th Circuit panel, a split en banc 9th Circuit, and 10 of the 13 members of the 4th Circuit struck down the EOs. Although this is not the end of the story, it does reveal the capacity of some institutions to resist presidential tyranny.

CONCLUSION

It is unsurprising, if distressing, that civil liberties were repeatedly violated after the USA suffered the 9/11 attack and feared a repetition. My concern here is evaluating responses to those violations by comparing more and less effective remedies. Some unambiguous abridgements were easily repulsed, such as content discrimination in expression and limitations on free exercise of religion. Most people saw little danger in either free speech or mosques (although this varied geographically); and some recognized the difficulty of protecting Christian and Jewish institutions from state intervention while urging restrictions on Islam by invoking the transparent fiction that it was not a religion. Mayor Bloomberg championed the "Ground Zero" mosque while defending NYPD profiling of Muslims. DoJ advocated for Muslim communities seeking to construct mosques. Even an authoritarian organization like the military displayed increasing tolerance toward Sikh religious practices (turbans and beards).[114] But transportation authorities cravenly sought to avoid controversy by suppressing *all* political speech. Alleged concern for the safety of the president and vice president became a pretext for shielding them (and their supporters) from dissenting voices. And employees were forced to surrender some free speech in the workplace. Most Muslims whose travel rights were infringed had few remedies against either airlines or the federal government, even though they were precisely the "discrete and insular minorities" the Supreme Court said the Fourteenth Amendment was intended to protect. But prominent individuals received apologies, powerful countries successfully protested discrimination against their citizens; and pressure from conservatives could remove an organization like MEK from the terrorist watchlist. By contrast, courts and administrators showed greater solicitude for the generality of travelers whose privacy rights were threatened by border searches of their electronic devices and airport screening of their bodies. Indeed, the non-Muslim majority repeatedly sought to replace the mild inconveniences they experienced with profiling of minority Muslims. Once again, the party of the appointing president was very significantly correlated with judges' support for civil liberties (see Table 7.1).[115]

Immigrants enjoyed few rights; even a courageous judge like Alsup could offer only limited remedies and helplessly watch his opinion be butchered. Yet asylum seekers were more likely to succeed if they feared persecution by regimes conservatives opposed. Investigative reporters

Table 7.1 Judges' Rulings in Civil Liberties Cases, by Appointing President's Party

Appointing President	Judge Upholds Civil Liberties (#)	Judge Upholds Civil Liberties (%)	Judge Rejects Civil Liberties (#)	Judge Rejects Civil Liberties (%)	Total
Democrat	71	77	21	23	92
Republican	37	47	42	53	79
Total	108	63	63	37	171

Chi-Square = 16.81, p<.001

and volunteer observers played an essential role in exposing NYPD violations of the rights of demonstrators and surveillance of Muslim communities, provoking widespread condemnation of those abuses. But the Department's internal remedies were predictably toothless, and the city stonewalled the civil actions. It took the replacement of Bloomberg by de Blasio and intervention by federal courts to end abuses and compensate victims.

The stories of Islamophobia are perversely encouraging when contrasted with their precursors. Whereas high government officials fomented popular hatred of German Americans in World War I, Japanese Americans in World War II, and radicals after both wars, most government officials condemned Islamophobia in the wake of 9/11. (Could they have learned from history?) Less than a week after the attack, President Bush visited the Islamic Center of Washington DC, quoted from the Koran, and declared solidarity with American Muslims.[116] If Obama equivocated about the Ground Zero mosque, he firmly repudiated Koran-burning and insults to Mohammed; Bloomberg was even more outspoken. Mainstream media were united in condemning Islamophobia; if they briefly shone a spotlight on publicity-seeking Islamophobes, the inexorable news cycle quickly diverted public attention to other stories. Courts and agencies steadfastly protected freedoms of religion and speech, while civil society – notably ecumenical groups of religious leaders – advocated religious tolerance.[117] Police, prosecutors, and courts arrested, convicted, and sentenced perpetrators of hate crimes.[118] Neither opportunistic state and federal politicians nor lone actors like Jones and Nakoula succeeded in igniting a moral panic. It was difficult to defend free speech rights to burn the Koran and insult Islam without acknowledging that freedom of religion included the right of Muslims to build mosques and follow sharia. Yet Trump's campaign and election demonstrated how quickly an unscrupulous demagogue could inflame smoldering Islamophobia, inciting anger and suspicion toward Muslims and immigrants, mosques, and sharia. The Trump administration energetically disseminated "alternative facts" and brazenly displayed its contempt for law, the Constitution, and the judiciary. Whereas both Bush and Obama repeatedly insisted Islam was not the enemy, Trump and his Republican rivals embraced the "clash of civilizations," declaring the USA to be at war with radical Islam. There is evidence that anti-Muslim hate crimes increased after Trump's election.[119]

The attacks on domestic civil liberties after 9/11 were deplorable. When the government claimed national security was at risk – as in the round-up of Muslim and Arab immigrants, presidential safety, or the overinclusive terrorist watchlist – the legal system failed to correct these wrongs. But in most other instances civil liberties eventually were restored, even if this depended significantly on factors outside the legal system: the media, civil society, and the configuration of *political* forces (as the 2016 election confirmed).

CHAPTER EIGHT

REVERSIBLE ERROR?

War is hell, inflicting grievous harms on both victims and perpetrators. But though law suffers its own wounds, war may offer it a form of purgatory, from which redemption is possible. Law can correct some of war's harms as well as its own errors. The present volume examined six settings in which law was challenged: criminal prosecutions, habeas corpus, military commissions, civil damages actions, courts-martial, and civil liberties. This conclusion evaluates the ways in which each of these legal institutions and processes did or did not respect fundamental rule-of-law ideals and then compares them with each other and with the five contested sites analyzed in the companion volume *Law's Wars*: Abu Ghraib, Guantánamo Bay, interrogation, electronic surveillance, and civilian casualties. It ends by locating the fate of law in the US "war on terror" within the historical context of other efforts to confront and redress grievous wrongs.

THE LEGAL ARMORY

Criminal Prosecutions

Within the courthouse walls, prosecutions of terrorism-related offenses resembled those for ordinary crimes, exhibiting the strengths and weaknesses of the American criminal justice system. Prosecutors filed appropriate charges and fulfilled their discovery obligations (if some politicized trials by inflammatory invocations of 9/11, Osama bin Laden and al-Qaeda, even when these were unrelated to the alleged offenses). Defense lawyers engaged in zealous advocacy without suffering conservatives' slurs (unlike the pro bono lawyers filing habeas petitions for Guantánamo detainees). Cases proceeded expeditiously, and most were resolved by guilty pleas (as usual). Judges carefully voir dired prospective jurors, and displayed laudable restraint toward the rare obstructive accused (e.g., Moussaoui) and exemplary fairness in handling defense objections to tainted evidence (even when central to the prosecution case, as in Ghailani). Jurors deliberated at length, a few individuals bravely holding out against the rest of the panel (if others later claimed, unsuccessfully, to have capitulated to undue pressure).

This core of due process could be preserved, however, only because it was surrounded by less visible but troubling distortions. The most significant was the material support statute, rarely deployed before 9/11 but subsequently charged against virtually all alleged terrorists, markedly facilitating conviction. Because of the potentially catastrophic harm to victims, as well as the political fallout, the government was determined to anticipate terrorism rather than rely on imprisonment after the fact to incapacitate and deter (as it does for other crimes). Indeed, some terrorists showed themselves impervious to deterrence by seeking martyrdom. The government therefore prioritized intelligence gathering over collecting admissible evidence, with the result that the exclusionary rule could not perform its prophylactic function of discouraging government misconduct (such as the lengthy solitary confinement Padilla and al-Marri suffered in the Navy brig). The government also relied heavily on undercover agents and confidential witnesses (sometimes forgiving the latter's crimes). Both necessarily engaged in deceit, sowing distrust and anger in Muslim communities. Although some prosecutions rested heavily on the accused's own words (e.g., Mehanna), they skirted First Amendment concerns by alleging only actions. Entrapment could never be proved because the accused always had done *something* to advance the alleged crime. But the decision to charge inchoate offenses and intervene early engendered doubts about whether the more clueless accused – who lacked expertise, weapons, and commitment – would have done anything without encouragement by the UA or cooperating witness. Some accused seemed to be life's losers, and were profoundly ignorant of Islam as either a religion or a political movement. Some were consumed by a generalized anger, rendering them susceptible to suggestions about possible targets. Others sought to escape dreary, impoverished lives by gaining a sense of meaning, 15 minutes of fame, or unimaginable material rewards. While focused on many who might never have consummated a terrorist attack, the criminal justice system failed to identify the few real domestic threats since 9/11, like Abdulmutallab, Shahzad, and Tsarnaev (and others who died before they could be prosecuted).

What followed conviction also raised questions. These accused were sentenced to decades in prison – perhaps appropriate for what they allegedly intended but harsh given that almost none caused actual harm. As a result, hundreds of men will spend much of their lives in jail, at enormous cost to themselves and their families, as well as the taxpayers who foot the bill for incarceration. Prison may intensify their commitment to terrorism or even instill it for the first time (as D Minn Judge Davis acknowledged in seeking alternative dispositions for young Somali American men attracted to al-Shabab).[1] These costs of potential false positives must be weighed against the speculative costs of the possible false negatives: what these men might have done if not incarcerated. The "war on terror" (like its inspiration, the hideously expensive nearly half-century long "war on drugs") has spawned a huge investigative and correctional apparatus, which must keep producing convictions in order to demonstrate the persistence and magnitude of the danger, thereby justifying its constantly expanding budget and playing the fear card against political opponents.

Habeas Corpus

The Bush administration detained nearly 800 men in Guantánamo Bay believing it had hidden them from judicial scrutiny. (Lawyers could not even learn their names – a prerequisite for offering representation in habeas petitions.) John Yoo had produced authoritative OLC memos offering such assurance, at the bidding of Gonzales and Addington (legal advisers to Bush and Cheney). After all, detainees were noncitizens, some had been seized on battlefields, and they were held outside sovereign US territory while hostilities persisted. Lower court judges (even those later favorably disposed toward petitioners) readily agreed that the Supreme Court's *Eisentrager* decision barred judicial review. All this changed when the Court's landmark decision in *Rasul* (likely influenced by the shocking exposé of Abu Ghraib just weeks earlier) opened the courthouse doors. Both in that case (and the Court's later *Boumediene* decision) and in the DC District and Circuit Courts, judges quickly divided into two camps, inhabiting different normative and even empirical universes. These differences produced an unusual number of divided panels (both concurrences and dissents), appellate reversals, en banc rehearings, and grants of certiorari. Opinions were suffused with elevated rhetoric, hyperbole, even personal attacks on judicial brethren. Both sides viewed the issues as momentous, apocalyptic. Liberal legalists saw fundamental freedoms at stake: "We must not wield the tools of tyrants even to resist an assault by the forces of tyranny" (Stevens dissenting in *Padilla*); "a state of war is not a blank check for the present when it comes to the rights of our Nation's citizens" (O'Connor in *Hamdi*). These judges repeatedly invoked the Constitution and its ancient precursor, Magna Carta. They were skeptical about the government's claims and sympathetic toward detainees facing indefinite imprisonment without any meaningful hearing (and expressed regret when legally unable to grant relief). Executive-minded judges, by contrast, believed the nation's very existence was in danger; without it there would be *no* liberties. Americans' "paramount right" was the commander-in-chief's unlimited power (Wilkinson in *Hamdi*). Some executive-minded judges joined conservatives outside the courts in criticizing pro bono lawyers for even filing habeas petitions (a position so anathema to the adversary system that it forced one of the rare resignations by a Bush administration official). These judges foretold a parade of horrors. Terrorists "aim to murder scores of thousands of civilians," who "can be slaughtered by a single action"; "large swathes of urban landscape can be leveled in an instant" (Williamson in *al-Marri*). Judges made dubious factual assertions without evidence. The "economy was severely damaged" by 9/11 (Leon in *Khalid*). Merely allowing habeas review would have "devastating" consequences, which would "make the war harder on us" and "almost certainly cause more Americans to be killed" (Scalia in *Boumediene*). Liberal legalists resented the executive's efforts to curtail judicial power; executive-minded judges deferred to the commander-in-chief, denigrating their brethren's expertise in military matters. Just as in criminal prosecutions, liberal legalists could point to actual harm to America's constitutional fabric, whereas executive-minded judges could only speculate about possible harms on the battlefield or at home. The exceptions to this ideological divide are equally revealing: Mukasey and Doumar citing their criminal justice experience to reject military "experts"; Floyd invoking his own military service; Mukasey, Luttig, Doumar, Floyd, and even Scalia moved by the fact that Padilla was a US citizen held on US soil; Leon and Sullivan resenting executive limits on judicial power.

At the end of the day, however, none of this mattered to the detainees. Congress passed Bush's MCA, stripping the courts of habeas jurisdiction, and the conservatives appointed to the DC Circuit by Republican presidents reversed the petitions granted by District Judges. Justice Jackson's ringing dissent in *Korematsu*[2] is all too apt:

> Much is said of the danger to liberty from the Army program for deporting and detaining these citizens of Japanese extraction. But a judicial construction of the due process clause that will sustain this order is a far more subtle blow to liberty than the promulgation of the order itself. A military order, however unconstitutional, is not apt to last longer than the military emergency … But once a judicial opinion rationalizes such an order to show that it conforms to the Constitution, or rather rationalizes the Constitution to show that the Constitution sanctions such an order, the Court for all time has validated the principle of racial discrimination in criminal procedure and of transplanting American citizens. The principle then lies about like a loaded weapon, ready for the hand of any authority that can bring forward a plausible claim of an urgent need.

Military Commissions
Just as Bush sought to insulate detainees from the gaze of Art. III judges by immuring them in Guantánamo and secret prisons, so he created military commissions to minimize the accused's procedural rights and maximize the likelihood of conviction, hoping to derive political advantage from the threatened prosecutions. Lacking political will, skill, or both, Obama failed to prosecute the HVDs in SDNY (or to close Guantánamo). Each new terrorist attempt revived pressure (fortunately resisted) to try the suspects in military commissions rather than civilian courts.

But aside from keeping the HVDs out of the criminal justice system, MCs have proven ineffective at best – the proverbial sledgehammer to crack a nut – and a fiasco at worst. The first five completed commissions targeted small fry: two car drivers (Hamdan and al Qosi), two juveniles (Khadr and Jawad), and a naive young Australian adventure-seeker (Hicks). Plea bargains in those and other cases prevented the commissions from either demonstrating that Guantánamo detainees were "the worst of the worst" or showcasing the virtues of American justice. Most of the sentences negotiated were short (especially after defendants were credited with time served, enhanced by having been subjected to EITs and harsh conditions of confinement). Torture made it impossible to prosecute some detainees and raised doubts about the mental competence of others, while the need to keep that torture under wraps excluded prosecution evidence. The commissions' ineluctable politicization surfaced with embarrassing frequency, forcing DoD to remove three Convening Authorities (Altenberg, Hemingway, and Ary) and one of their legal advisers (Hartmann). Another Convening Authority, Crawford (a Cheney protégé), resigned after blocking al-Qahtani's prosecution because he had been tortured. Apparently repulsed by the unfairness of the process, prosecutors also quit (Couch, Vandeveld, Carr, Preston, Wolf, and Morris), and one even switched sides (Davis). Most MC judges were less experienced than their civilian counterparts and were constantly replaced as they redeployed, completed tours of duty, or retired (sometimes in disgust at the process). Because commissions did not follow the *Brady* rule, prosecutors suffered no consequences for obstructing or delaying discovery. Defense lawyers were highly skilled and dedicated, but they lacked adequate resources (and certainly equality of arms with the prosecution). They had difficulty gaining the trust of clients who had been harshly abused by other Americans (some wearing the same uniform as the military lawyers); and they confronted the troubling ethical issue of how to represent an accused who boycotted the process. Interpreters were slow, sometimes incompetent. Lawyer–client confidentiality was constantly compromised by microphones capable of transmitting conversations, government scrutiny of written communications, and IT glitches. Commission judges refused to address defense challenges to their jurisdiction, committing what even the conservative DC Circuit called "plain error" in hearing charges that were either not war crimes or retroactive (material support). All participants (except the detainees!) had to fly to Guantánamo for the periodic pretrial hearings, which often resembled the stop-go traffic on California freeways (while courts-martial flew by in the HOV [high occupancy vehicle] lane).

None of this was necessary. The government had ample evidence against the HVDs, who in any case proudly proclaimed their responsibility. Judge Brinkema demonstrated the capacity of federal courts to try a defiant, disruptive defendant (Moussaoui); a federal jury convicted Ghailani even after Judge Kaplan excluded a key prosecution witness. All that had been achieved – 16 years after Bush created the military commissions, 10 after he sent the HVDs to Guantánamo for trial, and 6 after Holder abandoned civilian prosecutions – was the chaos that inevitably ensues when a criminal process is created from scratch and entrusted to a novice institution subject to unacceptable political influences.

Courts-Martial

The US military is proud of the UCMJ and the courts-martial that administer it. Highly visible trials demonstrate both the system's procedural fairness and its willingness to impose harsh sentences: 35 years for Chelsea Manning, death for Nidal Hasan (whose targets were national security and US military). When the victims were foreigners in war zones, however, military justice differed from its civilian counterpart in many ways. The fog of war often seemed to obscure the courts' vision. Military investigators lacked the expertise of the FBI and police departments; they often arrived at the scene long after the alleged crime; and even when evidence was collected, it went missing with alarming frequency. Soldiers displayed a loyalty to their comrades at least as intense as that of the Mafia and with the same consequence: *omertà*. Anger at incessant attacks by an invisible enemy killing and maiming their buddies led soldiers to dehumanize the entire civilian population they were ostensibly protecting. The very nature of warfare required soldiers to be trained for and ordered to engage in actions that would be heinous crimes off the battlefield. Enemy casualties were one of the few markers of success; soldiers displayed their "kills" like film cowboys notching their .45's. In most trials the contested issue was not what had happened (as in the classic "whodunit" mystery) but whether it was justified (as in white-collar crime). The lines drawn by the law of war between permitted and prohibited behavior are unavoidably ambiguous. In courts-martial, moreover, they are applied by what can truly be called a jury of the defendant's peers: fellow soldiers, of at least equal rank, usually with combat experience. And in the name of essential military discipline, courts-martial are subordinate to commanders, who determine the charge and can modify the penalty.

The outcomes of courts-martial for alleged crimes in Afghanistan and Iraq were predictable: acquittals were more frequent and punishments more lenient than they would be in civilian courts. (The analogy to police shootings of black men is unavoidable.) The likelihood of punishment was inversely related to the accused's rank. Again, the exceptions are revealing. Civilian courts severely punished military contractors and ex-soldiers. Courts-martial convicted and sentenced those whose actions lacked any colorable military justification (thereby demonstrating that the problem was just a few bad apples): Abu Ghraib's sexualized abuse, thrill-seeking murders by the 5th Stryker Combat Brigade, rape in Mahmudiyah, and Bales's massacre of women and children. Courts-martial were less forgiving of actions off the battlefield: corruption, drug abuse, and some sexual offenses. And the military showed itself capable of investigating and correcting systemic abuses affecting Americans: at Walter Reed Army Hospital, Arlington National Cemetery, and the Dover Air Force Base mortuary.

Civil Damages Actions

Civil actions by "war-on-terror" victims faced an array of obstacles that defeated nearly every plaintiff: the Supreme Court's grudging creation of a "disfavored" *Bivens* remedy; constitutional rights allegedly "not clearly established" at the time of the harmful actions; the requirement to exhaust administrative remedies and the existence of other illusory remedies (criminal prosecution, Congressional action, elections); qualified immunity; state secrets (blocking lawsuits, not just excluding evidence); and the MCA's jurisdiction-stripping provisions. As they had in response to habeas petitions, federal judges split into two camps – which I called rights-oriented and deferential – whose disagreements again produced an unusual number of split panels (both concurrences and dissents), appellate reversals, en banc rehearings, inflammatory rhetoric, and attacks on fellow judges. Rights-oriented judges quoted Justice Marshall's foundational assertion in *Marbury* v. *Madison* that courts have a duty "to say what the law is."[3] They rejected claims of a "state of exception," viewed rights as even more imperative when national security was threatened, and were skeptical of sovereign immunity. They invoked *conservative* arguments: against judicial activism and for avoiding constitutional questions and inter-branch conflicts. Deferential judges, by contrast, dismissed the plaintiffs' injuries as the "inevitable" tragedies of war, where "risk-taking is the rule," and blamed "terrorists" who "cunningly morph into their surroundings." These judges endowed the executive with powers unlimited by statute, treaty, or the Constitution. Conservative judges who routinely required regulatory agencies to conduct a cost–benefit analysis before taking any action rejected such a constraint on the military (whose power to harm was infinitely greater); they casually dismissed the states' rights they usually championed and uncharacteristically declared that "personal" interests must yield to those of the "collective." Originalists created novel doctrines like "battlefield preemption." Judges who routinely accused lawyers of "lawfare" for suing the government on behalf of "war-on-terror" victims lavished praise on lawyers who sued on behalf of terrorism victims. Judges who adamantly insisted on the US government's immunity readily dismissed the immunity of other governments, which allegedly sponsored terrorism. These judges relaxed or disregarded tort law's essential requirement of causation and bent over backward to help terror victims execute default judgments. As they did in denying habeas petitions, these judges advanced wholly speculative arguments without offering any evidence: that claims against the government would obstruct its "war on terror," claims against terrorists could end terrorism, and qualified lawyers would decline to serve as Attorney General if threatened with liability.

Here, too, the rare successful claims exposed how the "war on terror" distorted tort law. The USA paid $2 million to Brandon Mayfield, an American lawyer it erroneously detained for two weeks, but nothing to Maher Arar, the Canadian it rendered to Syria, where he was tortured for a year (for which his own government apologized and paid him Can$10 million). A few plaintiffs won judgments against low-level federal employees, local governments, and private businesses. And both courts and compensation funds were far more solicitous of and generous to US victims of terrorism than to foreign victims of the US "war on terror."

Civil Liberties

The response to civil liberties violations reflected strengths and weaknesses of the law pre-dating 9/11 (for instance, the Constitution does not protect freedom of speech or religion from private restraint). Perhaps because protests did not significantly affect the "war on terror," courts generally vindicated First Amendment rights (although often years after their violation and not when presidential "security" seemed threatened). New York City's experience decades earlier with anti-war and civil rights protests had induced the federal court to create rules and institutional structures to oversee NYPD misconduct (the *Handschu* consent decree). Here, too, judges resented defiance of their authority. Civil liberties violations were more likely to go unremedied when an individual victim was thought to be a Muslim or noncitizen and more likely to be redressed when victims were members of the general public: compare individuals removed from flights or placed on watch lists (actions that were almost impossible to challenge) with mass opposition to airport screening (and proposals to substitute profiling of Muslims); or the exemption from border searches of laptops and smart phones (carried by almost everyone, especially business travelers). As elsewhere, government officials exaggerated the possible cost of false negatives (including damage to their own political futures) while minimizing the cost of false positives to "others" from registries, round-ups, detentions, mistreatment and deportation of immigrants, grossly overinclusive watch lists, denials of habeas to Guantánamo detainees, and material support prosecutions. Political influence could secure special treatment: declassification of MEK as a terrorist organization, travel by foreign government officials in the USA, visas for notables. New Jersey resented NYPD incursions into its territory just as foreign governments had resented NSA's violations of their sovereignty or drone attacks. And the media played a crucial role in exposing police misconduct (as it did with respect to secret prisons and surveillance).

Responses to Islamophobia were one of the few encouraging findings of this book. Whereas the Civil War and Reconstruction spawned Jim Crow, the KKK, and lynching of African Americans, and the two World Wars and Cold War prompted harsh mistreatment of German and Japanese Americans and suspected communists and other radicals, multiple efforts since 9/11 have failed to incite a widespread moral panic against Islam (although it is too soon to evaluate the ultimate effect of Trump's vile lies and actions as candidate and president). Nine days after the attack, Bush called Islam "good and peaceful," declaring that "the enemy of America is not our many Muslim friends. It is not our many Arab friends." "No one should be singled out for unfair treatment or unkind words because of their ethnic background or religious faith."[4] Cynical politicians and demagogues trying to stir up hatred by opposing the construction of mosques almost always failed, most notably at Ground Zero in New York (a city of immigrants, where Mayor Bloomberg took an uncharacteristically principled stance), although NIMBY sentiments temporarily prevailed elsewhere. Terry Jones's Koran-burning stunt and Basseley Nakoula's childishly offensive film garnered the attention they craved; but both were condemned by a broad spectrum of civil and religious leaders. Campaigns against the illusory threat of sharia were blocked by courts upholding the First Amendment and never gained significant momentum.

Islamophobia and al-Qaeda represented two sides of the same coin, both fervently believing in, indeed seeking, a "clash of civilizations." Each tried to provoke the "enemy" into revealing its true nature. Osama bin Laden hoped the 9/11 attack would incite the USA to respond, mobilizing the entire Muslim *ummah* (community) to take revenge for centuries of mistreatment. (Bush's September 16, 2001 reference to his "war on terror" as a "crusade"[5] and his 2003 decision to attack Iraq, seeking to vindicate his father's honor, tragically fulfilled bin

Laden's expectation, engendering a war without end, if one that divided rather than united Muslims.) Jones and Basseley Nakoula succeeded in incensing Muslims around the world; but since they could only vent their anger locally, the deaths, injuries, and damage they wreaked on fellow Muslims did not motivate Americans to declare war on Islam. (However, attacks in Europe – Paris, Brussels, London, Stockholm – and the USA – San Bernardino, Orlando, New York, New Jersey, Ohio State University, and a Minneapolis mall – continued to fuel Islamophobic, anti-immigrant, and populist sentiments.)

Comparing the Six Legal Domains

Similarities and differences in how legal institutions and processes responded to the "war on terror" illuminate the resilience and vulnerability of the rule of law. Politics pervasively distorted law. Federal judges at all three levels approached habeas corpus petitions, civil damages actions by "war-on-terror" victims, and civil liberties claims from fundamentally different standpoints, which correlated very significantly ($p < .001$) with whether they had been appointed by a Democratic or Republican president. Those irreconcilable differences produced an unusual number of concurrences and dissents, appellate reversals, and en banc rehearings. Judges held radically different views of the world, attacking each other and arguing in apocalyptic terms that either essential liberties or the nation's very survival were at stake. (A few judges behaved atypically out of resentment at what they saw as government disrespect: unwarranted claims of criminal justice expertise, unnecessary invocation of state secrets, defiance of court judgments or consent decrees. And military service seems to have shaped the actions of judges as well as prosecutors and legislators.) Judges who had railed against "lawfare" by habeas petitioners and "war-on-terror" victims seeking damages from the government (all of them noncitizens and most of them Muslim) lauded Americans for suing state sponsors of terrorism (even when those lawsuits challenged conventional legal boundaries). "War-on-terror" victims lost two-thirds of their claims; terrorism victims won two-thirds of theirs. Party differences were not statistically significant in decisions on claims by terrorism victims ($p = .18$), presumably because Democratic appointees also sympathized with victims and detested state sponsors of terrorism. Republican appointees decided for terrorism victims 81% of the time and against "war-on-terror" victims 84% of the time; Democratic appointees were almost evenly divided in both categories (50:50 and 58:42).

By contrast with habeas petitions and civil damages claims, criminal prosecutions and courts-martial proceeded more routinely. There was no significant difference between decisions by Republican and Democratic appointees in criminal prosecutions; indeed, Democratic appointees were more favorable to prosecutors than were Republican (70% versus 59%). Because more Democratic appointees made such decisions (43 versus 27), two-thirds of all decisions favored the prosecution. Similarly, there was no significant difference between Republican and Democratic appointees in federal court reviews of military commissions (although here 56% of Democrats favored the accused while 58% of Republicans favored the prosecution). One reason may have been that criminal prosecutions, military commissions, and courts-martial seek to assert rather than contest the authority of the executive (including the military). To put it another way: habeas petitions and civil damages actions by "war-on-terror" victims wield law as a sword to free a prisoner from detention or extract money from the government, whereas law functions as a shield against government action in criminal prosecutions, courts-martial, and military commissions. Criminal accused could mobilize a broad range of well-established procedural protections, including a presumption of innocence; even military commissions granted defendants some conventional rights; by contrast, detainees filing habeas petitions for release from Guantánamo confronted a presumption that the government's evidence against them was accurate. Civil liberties cases were litigated in the context of a long struggle to establish constitutional rights, e.g., the *Handschu* consent decree with the NYPD; most plaintiffs were invoking law as a shield; and none was accused or suspected of terrorism. Democratic appointees were more favorable to civil liberties claims (77%) than Republican appointees (47%), a difference that again was statistically significant ($p<.001$). And because more Democrats than Republicans rendered those decisions (92 versus 79), nearly two-thirds of the decisions were favorable.

Lawyers representing the HVDs have used law as a shield to challenge every facet of the military commissions' novel institutional structure, substantive law, and procedure, with the predictable result that trials remain a distant prospect more than ten years after Bush dispatched the accused to Guantánamo for that purpose. Politicians repeatedly played the fear card, demanding military commission trials for all those who committed or attempted terrorist acts in the USA; and prosecutors sought to inflame civilian juries by irrelevant references to al-Qaeda, bin Laden, and 9/11. The government failed to achieve either of its goals – demonstrating the enemy's depravity and the virtue of its own justice system – because civilian prosecutions and the early military commissions dealt almost exclusively with small-fry who pleaded guilty in exchange for shorter sentences. (The government disclosed its political motivation by flying 9/11 families to Guantánamo and even accelerating commission hearings before elderly relatives died.) If the HVDs ever are tried, they are likely to keep challenging the forum's legitimacy while boasting about the crimes with which they are charged. Similarly, courts-martial held in the USA years after soldiers had committed atrocities in Afghanistan and Iraq failed to ensure that justice was "seen to be done" by foreign victims of the "war on terror"; even bringing a slew of witnesses to Bales's trial did not satisfy the Afghan community he had massacred, which wanted to try and execute him itself.

Ambiguity had diametrically opposed effects on civilian and military criminal trials. Civilian prosecutions of Muslim Americans for material support, often based on interactions with informants, led to harsh punishments for inchoate crimes that might never have culminated in harm. By contrast, courts-martial invoked the fog of war to exculpate or mitigate the punishment of American soldiers who had killed or wounded Afghan or Iraqi civilians. To put it differently, civilian prosecutions of Muslims favored false positives; courts-martial of US soldiers favored false negatives. Background variables like grief for a buddy, harsh living conditions, or substance abuse – which would never diminish responsibility in civilian prosecutions – excused or mitigated crimes in courts-martial. The defense of entrapment *never* prevailed in civilian courts; courts-martial sometimes found that defendants had not been properly Mirandized or there had been unlawful command influence. (Military commissions were chronically tainted by political interference, forcing the replacement of Convening Authorities and a legal adviser; but none of this led to acquittal.) Neither courts-martial nor military commissions enjoyed the insulation from political influence that is the hallmark of civilian courts. Nor did military tribunals ensure equality of arms: the underfunded defense in military commissions operated under numerous disabilities; CIC and NCIS investigating criminal allegations against soldiers lacked both expertise and the ability to collect evidence in foreign countries. Juries in civilian prosecutions convicted almost every accused (even if it took three trials); juries in courts-martial – true peers of the accused in terms of rank and combat experience – often acquitted. (Military commission juries – if they are ever empaneled – will be the *enemies* of the HVDs – typical victor's justice.) Judges often granted motions to dismiss at the outset of civil damages actions brought by "war-on-terror" victims; by contrast, military commissions refused to address threshold challenges to their jurisdiction (forcing defendants to undergo a trial whose judgment might be overturned on appeal to a civilian court, as some already have been). Courts almost never awarded damages to "war-on-terror" victims (a rare exception was Brandon Mayfield, an American lawyer imprisoned in the USA because of the government's unambiguous mistake); but courts displayed great solicitude in awarding compensation to terrorism victims and helping them execute default judgments. Similarly, compensation schemes were extremely generous toward terrorism victims (even jettisoning tort law's indispensable causation requirement) while callously stinting "war-on-terror" victims.

Justice was unequal in other ways. Law systematically imposed responsibility for misconduct on those at the lowest levels while protecting their superiors: in courts-martial (at Abu Ghraib and for later killings in Afghanistan and Iraq) and in civil damages actions (because of sovereign immunity). Most of the hundreds of Muslims quickly and easily convicted of material support by civilian courts were life's losers: poor, immigrant, ill-educated, some neither understanding Islam nor observing its strictures, and most acting alone or in tiny groups. Sixteen years after they were created, military commissions remained years away from even beginning the trials of HVDs, whose appeals may drag on for decades. On one hand, the legal system consistently devalued the costs of false positives inflicted by the "war on terror" on "others" (noncitizen, foreign, Muslim) through watch lists, travel restrictions, mistreatment of immigrants, surveillance of Muslim communities, detention in Guantánamo, prosecutions of inchoate crimes, restrictions of civil liberties, harsh interrogation, rendition, and civilian casualties of warfare. On the other, the legal system exaggerated the inescapably speculative costs of possible false negatives on Americans (domestic terror attacks, military casualties). Executive-minded deferential judges readily accepted government assertions that were not, and often could not be, substantiated: Guantánamo detainees would engage in terrorism if released, criminal prosecutions prevented attacks, liability for damages would interfere with prosecution of the "war on terror," and peaceful demonstrators threatened security. The few habeas corpus petitioners who prevailed (at least temporarily) were US citizens

(Padilla and Hamdi). Courts-martial were more likely to convict and severely punish those who committed crimes against American soldiers or challenged military authority than those who committed far more heinous crimes against Afghans and Iraqis. The rule of law survived within a protected core – the civilian courtroom – only because government had significantly compromised it elsewhere: through legislation authorizing material support prosecutions or stripping courts of jurisdiction over habeas petitions or civil damages claims, executive action creating military commissions and transferring prosecutions there from civilian courts, and doctrines of state secrets or immunity aborting civil damages actions.

Comparing the Fate of the Rule of Law across the Two Volumes

The companion volume *Law's Wars* examines the defense of the rule of law in other settings: Abu Ghraib, Guantánamo Bay, interrogation, surveillance, and foreign battlefields. Comparing that experience with the six legal domains offers additional insights.

If sunlight is the best disinfectant, as Justice Brandeis opined, the executive does a poor job of exposing misconduct to what Brandeis called the remedy of publicity.[6] Secrecy lets government silence skeptics and critics by declaring: if you knew what we know, you would acknowledge the necessity of our actions. BGen. Taguba's report on Abu Ghraib was supposed to remain secret, and the military investigations its disclosure prompted often were heavily redacted. FISC hearings and judgments were secret (and the process not adversarial). The executive briefed the two intelligence committees (often just its leaders) in closed meetings after pledging them to secrecy, thereby coopting them. The 6,000-page SSCI report on rendition, detention, and interrogation is still secret. Guantánamo, extraordinary renditions, and secret prisons were designed to hide inmates and conceal the torture they suffered. And the Bush White House directed the OLC (whose members were appointed by Ashcroft) to craft secret memos authorizing its own abuses; some memos written under both Bush and Obama remain secret.

By contrast, almost all civilian court hearings are public; civilian courts compel prosecutors to disclose exculpatory evidence to the defense; and perhaps most importantly, all courts, unlike either the executive or the legislature, *must* give reasons for their decisions (though FISC's remained secret until recently). Courts-martial and military commissions are more opaque than civilian courts; but even they disclose most of the evidence to (the usually sparse) observers and give reasons for their judgments. (The absence of a *Brady* rule, however, means that prosecutorial failure to disclose exculpatory evidence to the defense is not punished.) This greater transparency lets the public see the judicial process and debate its judgments. (But judges bow, if sometimes reluctantly, to government demands to hear evidence in camera, even *ex parte*, and redact their judgments in the name of state secrecy, sometimes rendering them incomprehensible.) Imagine what might have happened had the Bush and Obama administrations' OLC memos – drafted without the benefit of an adversary process and exempt from further review – been made public when they were written, rather than only after the Abu Ghraib scandal exploded.

The Bush administration sought to carve out spaces free from law, or at least less constrained by it: Guantánamo Bay, extraordinary renditions, secret prisons, CIA "ghost prisoners" concealed from the ICRC, US military (and sometimes contractors) immune from Afghan or Iraqi justice, CSRTs and ARBs instead of courts hearing habeas petitions, retroactive immunity for those conducting interrogation and surveillance, the non-adversarial FISC (stacked with Republicans by the Republican Chief Justice) rather than Art. III courts hearing FISA warrant applications, prosecutions of alleged terrorists in military commissions and military personnel in courts-martial instead of in civilian courts, doctrines of sovereign immunity and state secrets limiting federal courts' civil jurisdiction, and the jurisdiction-stripping provisions of the DTA and MCA. But courts pushed back: affirming the right of Guantánamo detainees to petition for habeas, finding that military commissions were fatally flawed and lacked jurisdiction over some charges, letting some civil actions proceed despite the government's invocation of state secrets, and making FISC hearings more adversarial and requiring its judges to publish some judgments. Although judges appointed by Republican presidents tended to favor the executive (in habeas petitions, civil damages actions by "war-on-terror" victims, and civil liberties claims), even they sometimes displayed political independence. And military service seemed to influence the behavior of legislators, judges, the general counsels of the four DoD branches, the JAGs, and MC judges, prosecutors, and defense counsel.

Just as legal institutions discounted the undeniable cost of false positives the USA imposed on "others" in its "war on terror" while exaggerating the speculative cost of false negatives (i.e., attacks on Americans that would have occurred but for the US "war on terror"), so similar distortions are found in the companion volume *Law's Wars*.

Prisoners tortured at Abu Ghraib disclosed no "actionable intelligence." Many Guantánamo Bay detainees had no intelligence value, and the vast majority did not engage in terrorism when released. Most electronic surveillance uncovered nothing of value – as acknowledged by NSA's own metaphorical justification that it was searching for a needle in a haystack (inevitably finding hay, not needles). The SSCI report concluded that EITs rarely if ever elicited useful intelligence that could not have been obtained in other ways. And none of the civilian casualties in Afghanistan or Iraq would have occurred without the "war on terror," which in 16 years has failed to defeat the Taliban, al-Qaeda, or ISIS.

Although the media played an indispensable role in defending the rule of law, its efficacy varied with the circumstances. Media disclosures of the Taguba report and Abu Ghraib photos were pivotal in forcing public debate about those abuses. By contrast, FOIA actions failed to extract thousands of other such photos (allegedly displaying even worse abuses). Media reporting – of surveillance or interrogation, for instance – could force a legislative or executive response and lay the foundation for a civil action. Media and NGO observers helped ensure that criminal courts and military commissions respected procedural safeguards. Media exposés could shame the military into initiating courts-martial for abuses it had covered up. Publicity exposed Islamophobic moral panic to criticism: opposition to the Ground Zero and other mosques, Koran-burning, *The Innocence of Muslims* film, and campaigns against sharia and Muslim immigrants. Journalists' investigations of NYPD surveillance of Muslim communities generated lawsuits and increased political pressure to end the practice.

Juxtaposing the myriad rule-of-law violations analyzed in these two volumes permits some provisional observations about the relative efficacy of different forms of remedial action. The Democratic-controlled SSCI was more effective than the courts in discovering and disclosing the details of rendition, detention, and interrogation; but Congress would not have acted without the earlier investigations by journalists and NGOs. On his second day in office Obama closed the secret prisons and ended EITs; Congress confirmed the latter order but frustrated his efforts to empty Guantánamo. Media (and Snowden) were more effective than the courts in disclosing surveillance. But Bush, Obama, and both parties in Congress crafted legislation that let NSA continue most of its activities, while offering Americans slightly more protection. It was not courts granting habeas petitions but rather the executive (pressured by the media and Congress) that almost emptied Guantánamo. Exposés by the media and NGOs and domestic anger in Afghanistan, Pakistan, Iraq, and Yemen increased pressure on the US military to limit civilian casualties; legal remedies were virtually power-less. Obama's rules and procedures limited targeted killing (following public outrage at citizen victims); civil actions were toothless. Although courts-martial tried the soldiers who committed the Abu Ghraib abuses, courts did not otherwise address or resolve the issues discussed in *Law's Wars*: improving conditions of confinement at Guantánamo or freeing detainees, ending EITs or electronic surveillance, or reducing civilian casualties from air strikes or night raids (actions that never prompted courts-martial). The irrelevance of courts may be partly attributable to the fact that the only one of those practices directly affecting Americans – surveillance – was necessarily invisible. (By contrast, the public was far angrier about airport scanners, which were less corrosive of privacy but more tangible.) Direct action had unpre-dictable and often transitory consequences: hunger strikes sometimes improved conditions of confinement in Guantánamo; local protests in Afghanistan and Pakistan temporarily curtailed US airstrikes; buffoons like Terry Jones and Basseley Nakoula briefly grabbed public attention while tragically provoking bloodshed in the Muslim world.

But the most important conclusion of these books is the central paradox that the fate of the rule of law – whose *raison d'être* is to pro-tect against politically motivated state abuses – itself depends on politics. *Law's Wars* documents that political party control of the White House and Congress was the single most powerful determinant of the responses to Abu Ghraib, Guantánamo Bay, interrogation, surveil-lance, secret prisons, extraordinary rendition, and civilian battlefield casualties. The difference between judges appointed by Republican and Democratic presidents was greatest in decisions challenging electronic surveillance: the former favored government 83% of the time, the latter favored plaintiffs 68% of the time (p<.00002).

The present volume confirms that party influence on the nomination and confirmation of federal judges is the single most powerful influence on the role of courts. Republicans blocked many of Obama's judicial nominations, including Merrick Garland for the Supreme Court, and then quickly confirmed Trump's nomination of Neil Gorsuch (after jettisoning the long-standing Senate precedent requiring 60 votes to end a filibuster). Trump launched personal attacks on federal judges with whom he disagreed and threatened to break up the Ninth Circuit.

The lesson is clear: champions of the rule of law must focus on the electoral process.

LA LONGUE DURÉE

The 16 years of the Bush and Obama administrations offer a troubling picture of the performance of American institutions in defending the rule of law during the "war on terror." Trump and Congressional Republicans have shown alarming signs of contempt for the rule of law. Rather than end these books on that pessimistic note, however, I propose taking a longer historical perspective (if not nearly as lengthy as that of the French *Annales* school, from which I borrowed this section heading). There is considerable evidence that it takes a generation or more for governments and civil society institutions to confront and correct grievous wrongs.[7] This is unsurprising, given the difficulty most people experience in offering family or friends a convincing apology for significant misconduct (as exemplified by deathbed confessions). Multiply that by the vastly higher stakes and number of actors involved, often with divergent interests, and it is amazing that collectivities *ever* manage to acknowledge serious wrongdoing.

Jennifer Lind has compared the responses of Germany and Japan to their wartime conduct.[8] Both quickly began paying compensation: Germany in the Luxembourg Agreement (1952); Japan to its Southeast Asian conquests starting in 1955 and Korea in 1965.[9] But though it often is said that "actions speak louder than words," it took both countries much longer to say those words. Konrad Adenauer, Germany's first postwar Chancellor, foreshadowed Bush on Abu Ghraib by blaming the Holocaust on a few bad apples: "the German people abhorred the crimes committed against the Jews and did not participate in them."[10] Anticipating Obama on EITs, Adenauer called for a "*tabula rasa*," urging Germans to "put the past behind us" because "many have subjectively atoned for a guilt that was not heavy." But in 1970 President Gustav Heinemann and Chancellor Willy Brandt acknowledged Germany's responsibility for the war; and Brandt fell on his knees when words failed him in the Warsaw ghetto.[11] In 1977 Helmut Schmidt became the first Chancellor to visit a concentration camp (Auschwitz); and the following year he apologized for Kristallnacht. Perhaps because honor plays such a prominent cultural role in Japan, it took the government until 1972 to apologize to China for invading Manchuria in 1931 and massacring civilians in Nanjing in 1937.[12] And Japanese apologies have been repeatedly undermined by: official visits to the Yasukuni shrine (honoring convicted war criminals); distortions, elisions, and obfuscations in histories and schoolbooks; and equivocation about the forced prostitution of Koreans (so-called "comfort women").[13] Both countries continued to deal with their guilt decades later. In 1995 Prime Minister Murayama apologized to Asian countries for "colonial rule and aggression."[14] In 2015 Japan apologized to the "comfort women" and created a compensation fund.[15] The following year Prime Minister Abe became the second Japanese leader to visit Pearl Harbor.[16] And a year after that President Steinmeier made the first official visit to Rome's Ardeatine Caves, where German soldiers murdered 335 civilians in 1944 in revenge for a partisan attack on Nazi soldiers.[17] More than 60 years after the end of World War II, Germany is still investigating Einsatzgruppen members.[18]

I have unsystematically collected other instances of institutions confronting serious wrongdoing. Because my primary concern is *when* they do so, I have included a wide variety of actions – acknowledgment, apology, compensation, criminal punishment, and regime change – without inquiring how those responses might be interrelated or how they were received. These examples can only be suggestive about timing: there is no way to define the entire population of serious wrongs in order to compare the totality of institutional responses (including inaction). Nor do I deny that some wrongs are remedied much earlier (e.g., crimes against humanity by Burundi President Pierre Nkurunziza)[19] and others may never be redressed. Nevertheless, the number and variety of occasions when institutions have addressed a previous generation's wrongs offer hope that the USA may one day reckon with its egregious violations of the rule of law during its "war on terror."

Victors seek to try war crimes as soon as possible.[20] After VE Day (May 8, 1945) and VJ Day (September 2, 1945), the Allies lost little time in trying the Axis leaders: in Manilla (October 29–December 7, 1945), Nuremberg (November 20, 1945–October 1, 1946), and Tokyo (April 29, 1946–November 12, 1948).[21] International tribunals take longer. The ICC began the trial of former Ivory Coast President Gbagbo six years after his alleged crimes against humanity.[22] The ICC convicted former Democratic Republic of the Congo Vice President Bemba 14 years after the war crimes occurred.[23] The ICTR completed its work 20 years after the genocide.[24] The ICC sentenced Radovan Karadzic, President of Republika Srpska, more than 20 years after the Bosnian genocide.[25] Culpable countries either fail to try war criminals or procrastinate. Rwanda's courts did not begin trials until 22 years after the Tutsi genocide.[26] The German Bundestag passed a general amnesty law in 1949 and expanded it in 1954; German courts sentenced only 21 men during that period. But trials resumed in 1963, and Germany ultimately abolished the statute of limitations and is still trying war criminals more than 70 years after the end of the war.[27] The Extraordinary Chambers in the Courts of Cambodia have convicted only a handful of men for the genocide committed 40 years earlier.[28] In 2014–16 Bangladesh finally tried and executed Islamists for war crimes perpetrated during the 1971 independence war.[29] South Africa famously subordinated prosecution to reconciliation through its Truth Commission.[30] And Latin American nations like Brazil[31] and Colombia[32] experienced decades of struggle over the choice between amnesty and punishment.

Religious and educational institutions take a generation or more to confront sexual and other abuses of their vulnerable young charges by men in authority – priests and teachers – and their own cover-ups (see Table 8.1). Ms. magazine devoted a special issue to sexual harassment in November 1977, and Catherine MacKinnon published a book on the subject two years later; but it took four decades before accusations against Harvey Weinstein opened the floodgates (discussed below).[33]

Governments seem to take similar amounts of time to acknowledge mistreatment of gay people. Britain, Germany, and Australia waited 50 years to pardon those convicted of homosexuality.[34] In October 2017, after former Prime Minister Heath had died, British police acknowledged having sufficient evidence to interview him under caution concerning allegations of child sexual abuse a half century earlier.[35] It took 70 years for DoD to grant retroactive honorable discharges to gay veterans and DoS to apologize for discriminating against gay employees.[36] Addressing racism is just as dilatory. Alabama acknowledged the victims of lynching some 65–160 years after those atrocities took place.[37] Only in 2005 did a federal court convict a perpetrator of the notorious 1964 murders of three civil rights workers in Philadelphia, Mississippi.[38] Georgetown University admitted its involvement in slavery nearly two centuries after the fact.[39] Prime ministers apologized to Native Canadian children 125 years after the first were forcibly incarcerated in residential schools, and also apologized for the country's racist immigration policy a century after its adoption.[40]

Governments also take decades, sometimes centuries, to deal with the wrongs they commit against their own people, including those they

Table 8.1 Length of Time between Commission of Wrong and
Response: Religious and Educational Institutions

Subject	Wrong	Response	Years elapsed
Religious Institutions			
Deaths of illegitimate children in Irish Mother-and-Baby Home[41]	1950s	2017	*c.*60
Pope Francis creates tribunal to judge bishops for covering up sexual abuse[42]	?	2015	+/−50
Sexual abuse of children by Catholic priests in Australia[43]	1980	2017	*c.*40
Australia charges Cardinal Pell with sexual abuse[44]	1966	2017	50
Roman Catholic Dioceses of NY and Brooklyn compensate sexual abuse victims[45]	1930s and 1960s–	2016	50–80
Church of Jesus Christ of Latter-Day Saints admits founder Joseph Smith married 55 women, some just 14 or already married[46]	1820–40s	2014	*c.*200
Sexual abuse victim sues former Catholic bishop of Phoenix[47]	1970s	2016	40
Church of England documents cover-up of sexual abuse[48]	1970s–90s	2017	20–40
Investigator documents physical and sexual abuse of more than 500 boys in Regensburg (Germany) Catholic Church choir[49]	1945–92	2017	25–72
23 women accuse Roman Catholic priest in Queens[50]	1972–94	2017	23–45
Educational Institutions			
British Christian evangelical leader brutally caned nude schoolboys for masturbation[51]	1970s	2017	*c.*40
Sexual abuse at American Boychoir School[52]	1960s–80s	2002	20–40
St. George's School compensates sexual abuse victims[53]	1974–2004	2016	10–40
Horace Mann apologizes for sexual abuse[54]	1960s–90s	2013	20–50
Penn State football coach Jerry Sandusky convicted of abusing underprivileged youth[55]	1977–	2011	35

(*continued*)

Table 8.1 (*continued*)

Subject	Wrong	Response	Years elapsed
Phillips Exeter Academy acknowledges sexual abuse[56]	1970s–80s	2017	35–45
Fessenden School addresses sexual abuse[57]	1960s–70s	2016	40–50
South African tennis coach sentenced for sexual abuse[58]	1980s–90s	2016	20–30
Choate admits 12 former teachers sexually molested students[59]	1960s–	2017	50
Phillips Andover Academy acknowledges sexual abuse[60]	1960s	2017	50
Kent Denver Day School, Colorado, finds sexual abuse[61]	1983	2017	34
Loomis Chaffee School admits headmaster sexually abused students[62]	1960s	2017	50
Williston Northampton School admits headmaster sexually abused students[63]	1970s	2017	40
KIPP NYC Charter School Network investigates sexual abuse[64]	2000s	2017	10+

colonized (see Table 8.2). I have grouped countries by continent for ease of presentation and to show that the pattern is global.

Similar postwar behavior characterizes even non-aggressor governments. It took a century for Germany to acknowledge complicity in Turkey's Armenian genocide[65] and 20 years for a court to find the Dutch government partly responsible for failing to stop Serbs from killing Muslims in Srebrenica.[66] Private companies are equally slow: Mitsubishi acknowledged the forced labor of Chinese prisoners and began paying compensation 75 years after World War II.[67] Because of its enormity, the Holocaust raised difficult questions of complicity. It took 70 years for France to compensate those its national railroad deported to German death camps and for Monaco to ask Jews for forgiveness for its collaboration.[68] It took 75 years for Ukraine to commemorate the Babi Yar massacre of Jews and for Romania to promise restitution for its complicity in the Holocaust.[69] There are continuing efforts to recover Jewish art stolen by Nazis.[70]

Table 8.2 Length of Time between Commission of Wrong and Response: Governments

Subject	Wrong	Response	Years elapsed
Asia			
Taiwan museum memorializes Kuomintang (KMT) suppression of nationalist opposition[71]	1947	1997	50
KMT massacre of 28,000 Taiwanese[72]	1947	2017	70
Taiwan apologizes to aboriginal peoples[73]	Over centuries	2016	70 years after KMT takeover
Indonesia investigates military massacres of communists[74]	1965–66	2016	50
Reconciliation after Sri Lankan civil war[75]	1983–2009	2015	30
Australian Prime Minister Rudd apologizes to indigenous peoples[76]	Over centuries	2008	Centuries
Korea acknowledges forced prostitution for US soldiers[77]	1960–70s	2017	50
Europe			
Britain charges ex-soldiers with killing IRA commander[78]	1972	2016	44
Britain apologizes for and compensates abuse of Mau Mau[79]	1950s	2013	60
Britain charges six, including police, with Hillsborough Stadium Disaster[80]	1989	2017	28
Serbia arrests Serbs for Bosnian war massacre[81]	1993, 1995	2014–15	20
EU plans war crimes tribunal for massacre of Kosovars by ethnic Albanians[82]	1999	2014	15

(continued)

Table 8.2 (continued)

Subject	Wrong	Response	Years elapsed
Argentine judge asserts universal jurisdiction over Spanish officials for torture under Franco[83]	1939–75	2014	70
Germany to redress genocide in Namibia[84]	1904–08	2017	110
Germany acknowledges atrocities in Tanganyika[85]	1890–1919	2017	100+
Dutch government compensates families of Indonesians executed in war of independence[86]	1940s	2015	70
Latin America			
Peru punishes ex-soldiers for killing civilians[87]	1985	2016	30
Peru tries former military dictator for abductions[88]	1978	2016	38
Peru Truth Commission documents 70,000 deaths in dirty-war against Shining Path[89]	1980–2000	2014	30+
Argentina convicts military officers for dirty war crimes[90]	1970s	2016	40
Argentine president vows to determine guilt for Jewish center bombing[91]	1994	2016	22
El Salvador Supreme Court annuls 1993 amnesty for civil war massacre[92]	1981	2016	35
USA extradites Salvadoran ex-colonel; El Salvador arrests ex-military officers[93]	1980s	2015–16	30
USA awards civil damages for Pinochet-era killing of Allende supporter[94]	1973	2016	44

618

Chile convicts 2 for Pinochet-era assassination of US citizens[95]	1973	2016	44
Chile charges seven former Pinochet military officers in killing of US protester[96]	1986	2015	30
Chile investigates Pablo Neruda's death[97]	1973	2017	44
Brazil acknowledges torture by military dictatorship[98]	1964–85	2014	30–50
Guatemala arrests ex-military for civil war massacre[99]	1981–86	2016	30–35
Guatemala convicts ex-police officer for massacre[100]	1980	2015	35
Guatemala to retry Gen. Efraín Ríos Montt for Mayan genocide[101]	1982–83	2015	40+
Surinam denies indemnity to ex-President Bouterse for killing opponents[102]	1982	2015	33
Former Communist Countries			
Albania investigates communist-era disappearances[103]	1944-	2017	30–70
Romania sentences prison warden for communist-era abuses[104]	1956–63	2016	50–60
Poland honors partisans killed by communists[105]	1946	2016	70
Russian civil society memorializes Stalin's victims[106]	1936–38	2015	80
Africa			
Chad convicts ex-President Habré of war crimes[107]	1980s	2016	30–35
South Africa prosecutes security police for apartheid-era crimes[108]	1983	2016	33
Tunisia's Truth and Dignity Commission hears testimony about torture[109]	1950s-	2016	60
Burkina Faso issues warrant for ex-President Compaoré for assassinating his predecessor, Capt. Sankara[110]	1987	2015	28

(continued)

Table 8.2 (*continued*)

Subject	Wrong	Response	Years elapsed
Spain will try 11 former Moroccan officials for genocide in the former Western Sahara[111]	1976–91	2015	40
Kenyan President Uhuru Kenyatta apologizes for killings of Somalis and post-election violence[112]	1984 2007–08	2015	30 8
North America			
USA remedies Japanese American internment[113]	1941–45	1976, 1988	30–40
US apologizes for abductions and detentions of Japanese Latin Americans during World War II[114]	1940s	1999	55
Canada apologizes for sexual harassment by the Royal Canadian Mounted Police[115]	1974–	2016	c.40
Canada apologizes for placing Native Canadian children in residential schools, pays Can$1.6 billion and creates Truth and Reconciliation Commission.[116]	1876–1996	2008	10–130
Canada to pay Can$750 million to 30,000 Native Canadian children forcibly adopted by non-Native parents[117]	1960s–80s	2017	30–50
USA decontaminates Agent Orange in Vietnam[118]	1961–72	2016	44–55
Memphis compensates black sanitation strikers[119]	1968	2017	50
US Army court-martials retired major general for child rape[120]	1980s	2017	c.30
Georgia arrests five people for heinous killing of black man[121]	1983	2017	34

620

Governments can wait decades to redress other forms of misconduct. It took 40 years for Chicago to compensate police abuse victims and nearly a century for Montana to posthumously pardon a World War I protester.[122] The US government took decades to apologize for: the notorious Tuskegee Study of Untreated Syphilis in the Negro Male (65 years from its inception),[123] deliberately infecting Guatemalans with syphilis (also 60 years),[124] and exposing US soldiers to radiation (50 years).[125] Britain took 40 years to investigate the National Health Service's use of contaminated blood to treat patients (many hemophiliac), infecting thousands with HIV and hepatitis C and killing 2,400.[126] It took Florida nearly 70 years to apologize for falsely convicting four African American men of raping a white woman and lynching two of them.[127]

Some world leaders have shown particular dedication to addressing old wrongs. In 1999 President Clinton apologized for CIA support of Guatemalan government abuses during its civil war (40 years) and a year later for the US role in the 1953 coup against Iranian Prime Minister Mosaddegh (50 years).[128] President Obama acknowledged in Laos the suffering US bombs caused during the Vietnam War (50 years), in Havana US efforts to "exert control over Cuba" (50 years), in Hiroshima the grievous harm inflicted by two atomic bombs (70 years), and in Buenos Aires tacit US approval of the 1976 military coup and failure to "speak out" against human rights abuses during the dirty war (40 years).[129] Pope Francis apologized for the Church's role in the 1994 Rwandan genocide (23 years),[130] condemned Turkey's 1915–17 Armenian genocide (100 years),[131] apologized in Bolivia for the Church's "grave sins" during colonialism (centuries),[132] met sexual abuse victims in Philadelphia and condemned as "sacrilegious" the actions of priests and cover-ups by bishops (50 years),[133] and said the Church should apologize to gay peoples (centuries).[134] In 2017 French President Macron commemorated the 75th anniversary of the round-up of 13,000 Jews at the Véldrome d'Hiver and their deportation to Auschwitz-Birkenau by acknowledging the Vichy government's responsibility and admitting "not a single German" was directly involved.[135]

This (admittedly unsystematic) compilation of institutional engagements with past wrongs suggests a variety of research questions about the dynamics of the process. Like the "justice cascade" of human rights described by Kathryn Sikkink, the examples concerning sexual abuse in the Catholic Church and US private schools show how each acknowledgment encourages and facilitates others by reinforcing the norm violated, affirming complainants, and making cover-ups riskier.[136] Accusations of sexual misconduct against Miramax executive Harvey Weinstein moved hundreds of women (and some men) to accuse him and others in the entertainment industry, and then inspired similar actions in a wide range of environments: federal and state governments, Silicon Valley, restaurants, hotels, sports, the arts, fashion, journalism, and academia, as well as the British Parliament, France, and academia in India.[137] The exposé of Ireland's Magdalen Laundries for "fallen women" led to investigations of unmarried mothers forced to surrender their children for adoption and multiple abuses in "mother-and-baby homes" for unmarried mothers, including pharmaceutical company vaccine trials on the children and dissections and mass burials of dead children.[138] Admitting one wrong makes it easier for the perpetrator to acknowledge others (perhaps because the consequences no longer seem so fearsome) and increases pressure to do so. Religious and educational institutions may be particularly susceptible to such influence because they are publicly committed to higher values and compete for moral superiority. (Nations and commercial enterprises can be drawn into similar competitions.) By contrast, partial or qualified acknowledgments may undermine the plausibility of later admissions.

Vulnerability inhibits victims from complaining but endows those who do with greater moral authority. Institutions find it easier to acknowledge the misconduct of individuals, especially subordinates, than collective guilt. That is one reason why those at the bottom of the hierarchy tend to bear the brunt of any punishment; another is the difficulty of proving command responsibility (since superiors take precautions to ensure deniability). Physical distance may also facilitate acknowledgment: a metropole finds it easier to admit wrongs committed in a colony (especially one it has liberated). Rather than revealing weakness, acknowledgment of a wrong may alter the balance of power by securing the support of victims (which can include former colonies) and increasing legitimacy while delegitimating opponents (as more culpable or less repentant). The most extreme manifestation of this strategy is regime change: punishing perpetrators of past wrongs can entrench the transformation. Redress imposed externally – for instance, by international criminal tribunals or other nations' courts asserting universal jurisdiction – may be faster but appear less legitimate.

The lapse of time (whose duration can vary widely) may be necessary for several reasons. A generation (or more) may have to transpire before perpetrators and supporters lose power (or die); sometimes their descendants (more often the second generation) seek absolution by acknowledging their ancestors' wrongdoing. The alleged threats (usually to national security), invoked to justify the wrongs, diminish with time, as they did in the aftermath of the two World Wars, the Cold War, the "Troubles" in Northern Ireland, and the transition to democracy in South Africa. (The 2017 guilty plea by a Northern Ireland Protestant paramilitary leader to more than 200 terrorist crimes dating back to 1991 may be the first step in exposing police complicity in those crimes.[139]) Some threats are acknowledged to have been minimal or nonexistent. Regime change may be an essential prerequisite: the Tunisian Truth and Dignity Commission began hearings in November 2016, nearly six years after the overthrow of President Ben Ali.[140] Norms change slowly, such as those concerning the sexual exploitation of women or children, homosexuality, racism, colonialism, human experimentation, torture, police practices, and warfare. It took a century and a half for Southern states to begin removing or modifying Confederate flags and monuments, but the movement then snowballed.[141] Australia and New Zealand are replacing racially offensive place names adopted during colonialism.[142] A century and a half later, Canada is considering whether to remove its first Prime Minister Sir John A. Macdonald, whose racist beliefs led to forced schooling of more than 100,000 indigenous children, from currency, place names, and memorials.[143] Overturning a criminal conviction may be one of the less costly remedies (though not for the crime's victims). The stronger the emerging normative consensus, the greater the pressure to correct violations, which may be one reason why a defeated Germany repudiated the Holocaust immediately and unequivocally, whereas Japan (having suffered horrendous destruction from two atomic bombs) persisted in justifying its colonial conquests and the Pearl Harbor attack as legitimate responses to American imperialism.

Failures to address or correct past wrongs are equally illuminating. Some events may be too recent. Nepal's Truth and Reconciliation Commission has yet to resolve 58,000 abuse complaints dating from the 1996–2006 Maoist rebellion.[144] Some perpetrators are too powerful. Although a British court found Vladimir Putin complicit in the 2006 assassination of former KGB operative Alexander Litvinenko in London, nothing is likely to happen to the Russian president.[145] In 2017 Putin unveiled a "Wall of Sorrow" he commissioned to "remember the tragedy of repressions," but opposed any "settling of scores." Critics objected that the government "is trying to pretend that political repression is a thing long since past."[146] Some victims are too weak and disorganized, especially compared to their adversaries. Families of the 85 people killed in the 1994 bombing of a Jewish community center in Buenos Aires are still waiting for the Argentine government to investigate Iran's involvement.[147] Illegitimate children forced to work as virtual slaves on Swiss farms (*Verdingkinder*) over the last hundred years have obtained neither recognition nor redress.[148] Disappearances of Aboriginal girls and women on a remote Canadian highway have remained unsolved for more than fifty years.[149] One thousand Sephardic immigrant families are seeking information from the Israeli government about babies who allegedly died soon after birth in the 1950s (but may have been secretly adopted by Ashkenazim).[150]

A crime's magnitude can discourage governments from addressing it. Efforts at denazification after World War II and lustration after the fall of communism foundered on the pervasiveness of complicity. Poland's Constitutional Court upheld a 2015 law limiting recovery of property stolen by Nazis and Communists.[151] The Netherlands resists returning paintings Nazis stole from Jews.[152] The USA has never confronted the consequences of slavery, or even the more than 4,000 lynchings after Emancipation.[153] Britain rejected reparations for slavery in Jamaica.[154] The USA has never apologized for firebombing Dresden and Tokyo, dropping atomic bombs on Hiroshima and Nagasaki, bombing Vietnam and Cambodia, or supporting brutal dictators throughout the world. It has never acknowledged the victims of more than 200 above-ground nuclear tests in 1946–62 or damage from four hydrogen bombs that accidently fell in Spain in 1966.[155] Turkey continues to deny committing genocide in Armenia (although a Turkish historian in the USA keeps accumulating evidence to document it).[156] Neither Greece nor Turkey has acknowledged expelling the other's nationals from its territory in the early twentieth century. Spain has never confronted the horrors of its civil war or the crimes of Franco's dictatorship (although 42 years after his death, its parliament voted to remove his remains from the Valley of the Fallen).[157] Israel has never acknowledged the Nakba. China has outlawed apologies for the Cultural Revolution's abuses and closed a museum commemorating its victims.[158] Russia vetoed a UN resolution condemning the 1995 Srebrenica massacre.[159] Indonesia still refuses, 50 years later, to confront its killing of 500,000 to 1 million people during the anticommunist purges of 1965–66, and countries like the USA have failed to acknowledge complicity.[160]

Remediation efforts can have perverse consequences. Campaigns to correct injustices can provoke backlash, as when Civil War apologists, white racists, and most recently President Trump defended Confederate memorials.[161] Governments sometimes undermine earlier acknowledgments. Although Japan apologized for and agreed to compensate Korean "comfort women" in a "final and irreversible" 2015 resolution, it recalled its ambassador two years later to protest a comfort woman statue erected outside its Busan consulate. As a candidate, Moon Jae-in (elected South Korean president in May 2017) repudiated the 2015 agreement because Japan did not accept "legal" responsibility or create a *government* compensation fund.[162] In 2015 Prime Minister Abe sent a ritual gift to the Yasukuni Shrine containing the tombs of war criminals.[163] The Philippines reburied disgraced president Ferdinand Marcos in its national cemetery in 2016.[164] Argentina's Supreme Court shortened the sentence of a man convicted of crimes during the 1976–83 military dictatorship, prompting hundreds of thousands to demonstrate and a nearly unanimous Congress to legislate against any other reductions.[165] And critics of human rights activism have argued that focusing attention on particular wrongs to individuals or collectivities may distract from systemic problems, such as racism, inequality, or environmental damage.

One reason I chose to study the fate of the rule of law in the US "war on terror" was my experience in researching the role of law in the struggle against apartheid in South Africa. As I explain in the preface to *Law's Wars*, the USA seemed to offer a much more favorable environment for the rule of law: a written constitution; a 200-year tradition of judicial review by independent judges appointed by presidents of both parties, which regularly exchanged control of the executive and legislature; a large diverse, respected legal profession committed to the rule of law; a vibrant, well-resourced civil society; and a free media. Whereas most white South Africans (erroneously) believed nonracial democracy posed an existential threat, neither al-Qaeda, the Taliban, or ISIS has ever endangered the existence of the USA, notwithstanding the false alarms of self-styled Cassandras. Yet the US record since 9/11 displays a deeply troubling mix of victories and defeats for the rule of law. As the above historical reflections suggest, however, that judgment may be premature. The South African National Party began constructing apartheid immediately after winning the 1948 election. It took nearly half a century, until 1994, for a democratic election to transfer power to the black majority. Whereas the black South Africans oppressed by apartheid were 85 percent of the population, and all were citizens (despite the fiction of independent "homelands"), "war-on-terror" victims are relatively few, dispersed across distant war-torn nations with no power over the USA, and almost all noncitizens. They confront the world's most powerful nation. But I cling to the belief their time will come and hope those who fought tenaciously for the rule of law since 9/11 – both victims and their champions – draw comfort from the successful struggles of South Africans and other oppressed peoples, and inspiration from Martin Luther King Jr.'s promise that "the arc of the moral universe is long, but it bends towards justice."

APPENDIX: TABLES

Chapter 2

Table A1 Criminal Prosecutions

First Named Accused	Court	Judge	For prosecution or accused (P/A)	Appointing President's party
Hayat (Lodi)	ED Cal	Burrell	P	R
	9th Cir.	Berzon	P	D
		Schroeder	P	D
		Tashima	A	D
Batiste (Liberty City 7)	ND Fla	Lenard	P	D
	11th Cir..	Tjoflat	P	R
		Martin	P	D
		Dawson	P	D
Cromitie (Newburgh 4)	SDNY	McMahon	A	D
	2nd Cir.	Newman	P	D
		Raggi	P	R
		Jacobs	A	R
Mehanna	D Mass	O'Toole	P	D
	1st Cir.	Selya	P	R
		Howard	P	R
		Thompson	P	D
Ghailani	SDNY	Kaplan	A	D
	2nd Cir.	Cabranes	P	D
		Laval	P	D
		Parker	P	R

(*continued*)

Table A1 (*continued*)

First Named Accused	Court	Judge	For prosecution or accused (P/A)	Appointing President's party
Abu Ali	ED Va	Lee	P	D
	4th Cir.	Wilkinson	P	R
		Traxler	P	D
		Motz	A	D
	ED Va	Lee	P	D
Al-'Owhali	2nd Cir.	Cabranes	P	D
		Feinberg	P	D
		Newman	P	D
Ahmed	SDNY	Castel	A	R
Al-Moayad	EDNY	Johnson	P	R
	2nd Cir.	Wesley	A	R
		McLaughlin	A	R
		Parker	A	R
Koubriti	ED Mich	Rosen	A	R
Stewart	EDNY	Koeltl	A	D
	2nd Cir.	Walker	P	R
		Sack	P	D
		Calabresi	P	D
	EDNY	Koeltl	P	D
Siddiqui	SDNY	Berman	P	D
	2nd Cir.	Wesley	P	R
		Carney	P	D
		Mauskopf	P	R
Bujol	SD Tex	Hittner	P	R
Medanjunin	EDNY	Gleeson	P	D
Moussaoui	ED Va	Brinkema	A	D
Muhtorov	D Colo	Kane	A	D
Abdulmutallab	ED Mich	Edmunds	A	D
Abu Ghaith	SDNY	Kaplan	A	D
Ressam	WD Wash	Coughenour	A	R

Table A1 (*continued*)

First Named Accused	Court	Judge	For prosecution or accused (P/A)	Appointing President's party
	9th Cir.	Alarcon	P	D
		Rymer	P	R
		Berzon	P	D
	WD Wash	Coughenour	A	D
	9th Cir.	Alarcon	P	D
		Clifton	P	R
		Fernandez	A	R
	9th Cir. en banc	Clifton	P	R
		Graber	P	D
		McKeown	P	D
		Bybee	P	R
		Reinhardt	P	D
		Wardlaw	P	D
		Kozinski	P	R
		Schroeder	A	D
		Paez	A	D
		Berzon	A	D
		Murguia	A	D
	WD Wash	Coughenour	A	D
Awadallah	SDNY	Scheindlin	A	D

Chapter 4

Table A2 Federal Court Reviews of Military Commissions

Defendant	Court	Judge	Appointing President's Party	For defendant (Y/N)
Hamdan	DDC	Robertson	D	Y
	DC Cir.	Randolph	R	N
		Roberts	R	N
		Williams	R	N
	USSC	Stevens	R	Y
		Breyer	D	Y
		Kennedy	R	Y
		Souter	R	Y
		Ginsburg	D	Y
		Scalia	R	N
		Thomas	R	N
		Alito	R	N
	DDC	Robertson	D	N
	DC Cir.	Kavanaugh	R	Y
		Sentelle	R	Y
		Ginsburg	R	Y
Hicks	DDC	Kollar- Kotelly	D	N
	DC Cir.	Kavanaugh	R	N
		Griffith	R	N
		Randolph	R	N
Al-Bahlul	DC Cir.	Henderson	R	Y
		Rogers	R	Y
		Tatel	D	Y
	DC Cir. en banc	Henderson	R	Y
		Garland	D	Y
		Tatel	D	Y
		Griffith	R	Y
		Rogers	R	Y

Table A2 (*continued*)

Defendant	Court	Judge	Appointing President's Party	For defendant (Y/N)
		Brown	R	N
		Kavanaugh	R	Y
	DC Cir.	Rogers	R	Y
		Tatel	D	Y
		Henderson	R	N
	DC Cir. en banc	Henderson	R	N
		Brown	R	N
		Griffith	R	N
		Kavanaugh	R	N
		Millett	D	N
		Wilkins	D	N
		Rogers	R	Y
		Tatel	D	Y
		Pillard	D	Y
Jawad	DDC	Huvelle	R	Y
Al-Nashiri	WD Wash	Bryan	R	N
	9th Cir.	McKeown	D	N
		Alarcon	D	N
		Ikuta	R	N
	DDC	Roberts	D	N
	DC Cir.	Henderson	R	N
		Rogers	R	N
		Pillard	D	N
	DC Cir.	Griffith	R	N
		Sentelle	R	N
		Tatel	D	Y

Chapter 6

Table A3 Civil Damages Actions by "War-on-Terror" Victims

Case	Court	Judge	Appointing President's Party	For Plaintiff (Y/N)
Iraq Detainees	DDC	Hogan	R	N
	DC Cir.	Sentelle	R	N
		Henderson	R	N
		Edwards	D	Y
Rasul	DDC	Urbina	D	Y
	DC Cir.	Henderson	R	N
		Brown	R	Y
		Randolph	R	N
al-Janko	DDC	Leon	R	N
	DC Cir.	Henderson	R	N
		Rogers	D	N
		Tatel	D	N
Celikgogus	DDC	Lamberth	R	N
	DC Cir.	Silberman	R	N
		Kavanaugh	R	N
		Garland	D	Y
Shimari	ED Va	Lee	D	Y
	4th Cir.	Niemeyer	R	N
		Shedd	R	N
		King	D	Y
	4th Cir. en banc	King	D	Y
		Traxler	D	Y
		Motz	D	Y
		Gregory	D	Y
		Duncan	R	Y
		Agee	R	Y
		Davis	D	Y

Table A3 (*continued*)

Case	Court	Judge	Appointing President's Party	For Plaintiff (Y/N)
		Keenan	D	Y
		Diaz	D	Y
		Floyd	D	Y
		Wilkinson	R	N
		Niemeyer	R	N
		Shedd	R	N
	ED Va	Lee	D	N
	4th Cir.	Keenan	D	Y
		Floyd	D	Y
		Cogburn	D	Y
	ED Va	Lee	D	N
Qureshi	D Md	Messitte	D	Y
	4th Cir.	Niemeyer	R	N
		Shedd	R	N
		King	D	Y
Kar	DDC	Robertson	D	N
Vance	ND Ill	Anderson	R	Y
	7th Cir.	Manion	R	Y
		Evans	D	Y
		Hamilton	D	Y
	7th Cir. en banc	Easterbrook	R	N
		Posner	R	N
		Flaum	R	N
		Manion	R	N
		Kanne	R	N
		Rover	R	Y
		Wood	D	Y
		Williams	D	Y
		Sykes	R	N

(*continued*)

Table A3 (*continued*)

Case	Court	Judge	Appointing President's Party	For Plaintiff (Y/N)
		Tinder	R	N
		Hamilton	D	Y
Padilla	ND Cal	White	R	Y
	9th Cir.	R Fisher	D	N
		R Smith	R	N
		Pallmeyer	D	N
Padilla	DSC	Geigel	D	N
	4th Cir.	Wilkinson	R	N
		Motz	D	N
		Duncan	R	N
Arar	EDNY	Trager	D	N
	2nd Cir.	Cabranes	D	N
		McLaughlin	R	N
		Sack	D	Y
	2nd Cir. en banc	Jacobs	R	N
		McLaughlin	R	N
		Cabranes	D	N
		Raggi	R	N
		Wesley	R	N
		Hall	R	N
		Livingston	R	N
		Sack	D	Y
		Calabresi	D	Y
		Pooler	D	Y
		Parker	R	Y
Mohamed	ND Cal	Ware	R	N
	9th Cir.	Hawkins	D	Y
		Schroeder	D	Y
		Canby	D	Y

Table A3 (*continued*)

Case	Court	Judge	Appointing President's Party	For Plaintiff (Y/N)
	9th Cir. en banc	Fisher	D	N
		Bea	R	N
		Hawkins	D	Y
		Schroeder	D	Y
		Canby	D	Y
		Thomas	D	Y
		Paez	D	Y
		Kozinski	R	N
		Tallman	D	N
		Rawlinson	D	N
		Callahan	R	N
el-Masri	ED Va	Ellis	R	N
	4th Cir.	King	D	N
		Shedd	R	N
		Duncan	R	N
al-Awlaki	DDC	Collyer	R	N
Edmonds	DDC	Walton	R	N
	DC Cir.	Ginsburg	R	N
		Sentelle	R	N
		Henderson	R	N
Wilson	DDC	Bates	R	N
	DC Cir.	Sentelle	R	N
		Henderson	R	N
		Rogers	D	N
Howards	10th Cir.	Seymour	D	Y
		Lucero	D	Y
		Kelly	R	N
	USSC	Roberts	R	N
		Scalia	R	N

(*continued*)

Table A3 (*continued*)

Case	Court	Judge	Appointing President's Party	For Plaintiff (Y/N)
		Thomas	R	N
		Kennedy	R	N
		Alito	R	N
		Ginsburg	D	N
		Sotomayor	D	N
		Breyer	D	N
Weise	D Colo	Daniel	D	N
	10th Cir.	Kelly	R	N
		Tacha	R	N
		Holloway	D	Y
Moss	D Ore	Panner	D	Y
	9th Cir.	Tashima	D	N
		M Smith	R	N
		Wu	R	N
	D Ore	Panner	D	Y
	9th Cir.	Berzon	D	Y
		Ebel	R	Y
		R Smith	R	Y
	9th Cir. en banc	O'Scannlain	R	N
		Kozinski	R	N
		Gould	D	N
		Tallman	D	N
		Bybee	R	N
		Callahan	R	N
		Bea	R	N
		Ikuta	R	N
		Berzon	D	Y
		Ebel	R	Y
		R Smith	R	Y

Table A3 (*continued*)

Case	Court	Judge	Appointing President's Party	For Plaintiff (Y/N)
	USSC	Ginsburg	D	N
		Sotomayor	D	N
		Breyer	D	N
		Roberts	R	N
		Scalia	R	N
		Thomas	R	N
		Alito	R	N
`		Kennedy	R	N
		Kagan	D	N
Turkmen	EDNY	Gleeson	D	Y
Iqbal	2nd Cir.	Newman	D	Y
		Cabranes	D	Y
		Sack	D	Y
	USSC	Kennedy	R	N
		Scalia	R	N
		Stevens	R	Y
		Souter	R	Y
		Thomas	R	N
		Breyer	D	Y
		Roberts	R	N
		Alito	R	N
Kidd	D Id	Lodge	R	Y
	9th Cir.	M Smith	R	Y
		Thompson	R	Y
		Bea	R	N
	9th Cir. en banc	O'Scannlain	R	N
		Kozinski	R	N
		Kleinfeld	R	N
		Gould	D	N

(*continued*)

Table A3 (*continued*)

Case	Court	Judge	Appointing President's Party	For Plaintiff (Y/N)
		Tallman	R	N
		Callahan	R	N
		Bea	R	N
		Ikuta	R	N
		Thompson	R	Y
		M Smith	R	Y
	USSC	Scalia	R	N
		Kennedy	R	N
		Thomas	R	N
		Ginsburg	D	N
		Breyer	D	N
		Roberts	R	N
		Alito	R	N
		Sotomayor	D	N
		Kagan	D	N
	D Id	Lodge	R	Y
Higazy	SDNY	Buchwald	R	N
	2nd Cir.	Pooler	D	Y
		Koeltl	D	Y
		Jacobs	R	Y

Table A4 Civil Damages Actions by Terrorism Victims

Case	Court	Judge	Appointing President's Party	For Plaintiff (Y/N)
9/11 Victims	SDNY	Case	D	N
	2nd Cir.	Jacobs	R	N
		Cabranes	D	N
		Vitaliano	R	N
	SDNY	Daniels	D	N
	2nd Cir.	Cabranes	D	N
		Raggi	R	N
		Rakoff	D	N
?	DDC	Lamberth	R	Y
Doe	DDC	Roberts	D	Y
	2nd Cir.	Kearse	D	Y
		Calabresi	D	Y
		Wesley	R	Y
Boim	ND Ill	Lindberg	R	Y
	7th Cir.	Rovner	R	Y
		Wood	D	Y
		Evans	D	Y
	ND Ill	Lindberg	R	Y
	7th Cir. en banc	Posner	R	Y
		Easterbrook	R	Y
		Flaum	R	Y
		Kanne	R	Y
		Rovner	R	N
		Wood	D	N
		Evans	D	N
		Williams	D	Y
		Sykes	R	Y
		Tinder	R	Y
Ellis	SDNY	Marrero	D	Y

(*continued*)

Table A4 (*continued*)

Case	Court	Judge	Appointing President's Party	For Plaintiff (Y/N)
Ungar	D RI	Lagueux	R	Y
	1st. Cir	Selya	R	Y
		Campbell	R	Y
		Lipez	D	Y
Speer	D Utah	Caseell	R	Y
Linde	SDNY	Gershon	D	Y
?	DDC	Bates	R	Y
?	DDC	Lamberth	R	Y
?	DDC	Bates	R	Y
Peterson	SDNY	Forrest	D	Y
	2nd Cir.	Winter	R	Y
		Walker	R	Y
		Cabranes	D	Y

Chapter 7

Table A5 Civil Liberties Cases

Case	Court	Judge	Upholds Civil Liberties (Y/N)	Appointing President's Party
Detroit Free Press	ED Mich	Edmunds	Y	R
	6th Cir.	Keith	Y	D
		Daughtry	Y	D
		Carr (DJ)	Y	D
Frazier	D Az	Wake	Y	R
National Council of Arab Americans	SDNY	Pauley	Y	D
American Freedom Law Center	DDC	Collyer	Y	R
AFDI	SDNY	Engelmayer	Y	D
AFDI	SDNY	Koeltl	Y	D
Muslims Are Coming	SDNY	McMahon	Y	D
Alvarez	CD Cal	Klausner	N	R
	9th Cir.	Smith	Y	R
		Nelson	Y	D
		Bybee	N	R
	USSC	Kennedy	Y	R
		Roberts	Y	R
		Ginsburg	Y	D
		Sotomayor	Y	D
		Breyer	Y	D
		Kagan	Y	D
		Alito	N	R
		Scalia	N	R

(continued)

Table A5 (*continued*)

Case	Court	Judge	Upholds Civil Liberties (Y/N)	Appointing President's Party
		Thomas	N	R
Apel	CD Cal	Walter	N	R
	9th Cir.	Silverman	Y	D
		Rawlinson	Y	D
		Tunheim (DJ)	Y	D
	USSC	Roberts	N	R
		Kennedy	N	R
		Breyer	N	D
		Scalia	N	R
		Ginsburg	N	D
		Kagan	N	D
		Sotomayor	N	D
		Alito	N	R
		Thomas	N	R
Swisher	D Id	Winmill	N	D
	9th Cir.	Ikuta	N	R
		Alarcon	N	D
		Tashima	N	D
	9th Cir. en banc	Ikuta	Y	Rr
		Thomas	Y	D
		Reinhardt	Y	D
		Kozinski	Y	R
		Mckeown	Y	R
		Berzon	Y	D
		Clifton	Y	R
		Nguyen	Y	D
		Bybee	N	R
		Smith	N	R
		Watford	N	D

Table A5 (*continued*)

Case	Court	Judge	Upholds Civil Liberties (Y/N)	Appointing President's Party
el-Ganayni	WD Pa	Mcverry	N	R
	3rd Cir.	Smith	N	R
		Fisher	N	R
		Stapleton	N	R
EEOC	ND Ok	Frizzell	Y	R
	10th Cir.	Holmes	N	R
		Kelly	N	R
		Ebel	Y	R
	USSC	Scalia	Y	R
		Roberts	Y	R
		Kennedy	Y	R
		Ginsburg	Y	D
		Breyer	Y	D
		Sotomayor	Y	D
		Kagan	Y	D
		Alito	Y	R
		Thomas	N	R
Farag & Elmasry	EDNY	Block	Y	D
Abidor	EDNY	Korman	N	R
Cotterman	D Az	Collins	Y	D
	9th Cir.	Tallman	N	D
		Rawlinson	N	D
		Fletcher	Y	D
	9th Cir. en banc	McKeown	N	R
		Kozinski	N	R
		Thomas	N	D
		Wardlaw	N	D
		Fisher	N	D
		Gould	N	D

(*continued*)

Table A5 (*continued*)

Case	Court	Judge	Upholds Civil Liberties (Y/N)	Appointing President's Party
		Merguia	N	D
		Christen	N	D
		Callahan	N	R
		Clifton	N	R
		Smith	Y	R
? (subway search)	SDNY	Berman	N	D
Aalah ali Ahmed	D Ore	Anna Brown	Y	D
Mokdad	ED Mich	Victoria Roberts	N	D
	6th Cir.	Gibbons	Y	R
		Gilman	Y	D
		Batchelder	Y	R
	ED Mich	Roberts	Y	D
Ibrahim	ND Cal	Alsup	N	D
	9th Cir.	Kozinski	Y	R
		Otero (DJ)	Y	R
		N Randy Smith	N	R
	ND Cal	Alsup	Y	D
Ruskai	1st Cir.	Kayatta	N	D
Ramadan	SDNY	Crotty	N	R
	2nd Cir.	Newman	Y	D
		Feinberg	Y	D
		Raggi	Y	R
Habib	D Mass	O'Toole	Y	D
Nadarajah	SD Cal	Burns	N	R
	9th Cir.	Thomas	Y	D
		Tallman	Y	D
		Fitzgerald	Y	D
Abdel-Jabbar Hamdan	CD Cal	Hatter	Y	D

Table A5 (*continued*)

Case	Court	Judge	Upholds Civil Liberties (Y/N)	Appointing President's Party
Majed Hajbeh	ED Va	Friedman	Y	D
Handschu	SDNY	Haight	N	R
		Haight	Y	R
		Mag Judge Francis	Y	R
		Mag Judge Orenstein	Y	R
		Haight	Y	R
?	SDNY	Sullivan	N	R
?	SDNY	Sullivan	Y	R
Hassan	D NJ	Martini	N	R
	3rd Cir.	Ambro	Y	D
		Fuentes	Y	D
		Roth	Y	R
DoJ (Murfreesboro)	MD Tn	Campbell	Y	D
Garcia	CD Cal	Fitzgerald	Y	D
	9th Cir.	Kozinski	N	R
		Gould	N	D
		N Randy Smith	Y	R
	9th Cir. en banc	McKeown	Y	R
		Thomas	Y	D
		Berzon	Y	D
		Rawlinson	Y	D
		Clifton	Y	R
		Callahan	Y	R
		Smith	Y	R
		Murguia	Y	D
		Christen	Y	D

(*continued*)

Table A5 (*continued*)

Case	Court	Judge	Upholds Civil Liberties (Y/N)	Appointing President's Party
		Watford	Y	D
		Kozinski	N	R
CAIR	WD Ok	Miles-Lagrange	Y	D
	10th Cir.	Matheson	Y	D
		O'Brien	Y	R
		McKay	Y	D
Muslim ban	WD Wash	Robart	Y	D
	D Mass	Gorton	Y	R
	ED Va	Brinkema	Y	D
	D Hi	Watson	Y	D
	9th Cir.	Canby	Y	D
		Clifton	Y	R
		Friedland	Y	D
	9th Cir. en banc	Canby	Y	D
		Clifton	Y	R
		Friedland	Y	D
		Berzon	Y	D
		Reinhardt	Y	D
		Kozinski	N	R
		Callahan	N	R
		Bea	N	R
		Ikuta	N	R
		Bybee	N	R
	D Md	Chuang	Y	D
	4th Cir.	Gregory	Y	D
		Motz	Y	D
		King	Y	D
		Diaz	Y	D

Table A5 (*continued*)

Case	Court	Judge	Upholds Civil Liberties (Y/N)	Appointing President's Party
		Floyd	Y	D
		Harris	Y	D
		Traxler	Y	D
		Keenan	Y	D
		Wynn	Y	D
		Thacker	Y	D
		Niemeyer	N	R
		Shedd	N	R
		Agee	N	R

NOTES

In order to avoid distracting readers with the numerous citations, they are grouped together in notes that contain all the sources for one or more related paragraphs.

ACRONYMS

1st Lt.	First Lieutenant (Army)
2nd Lt.	Second Lieutenant (Marines)
ABA	American Bar Association
ABC	American Broadcasting Company
ACLU	American Civil Liberties Union
AFJ	Alliance for Justice
AFP	Agence France-Presse
AI	Amnesty International
AP	Associated Press
AWOL	Absent Without Official Leave
BBC	British Broadcasting Corporation
BG	*Boston Globe*
BH	*Boston Herald*
BS	*Baltimore Sun*
CA	Military Commissions Convening Authority (also called Appointing Authority)
Capt.	Captain
CBC	Canadian Broadcasting Corporation
CCR	Center for Constitutional Rights
CD Cal	US District Court for the Central District of California
CHRGJ	NYU Center for Human Rights and Global Justice
CLEAR	Creating Law Enforcement Accountability and Responsibility
CMCR	Court of Military Commission Review

CNN	Cable News Network
Col.	Colonel
Cpl.	Corporal
CQ	*Congressional Quarterly*
CRS	Congressional Research Service
CSM	Christian Science Monitor
CST	*Chicago Sun-Times*
CT	*Chicago Tribune*
D Az	US District Court for the District of Arizona
D Id	US District Court for the District of Idaho
DDC	US District Court for the District of Columbia
DoD	US Department of Defense
DoJ	US Department of Justice
DoJ IG	US Department of Justice Inspector General
DoJ OIG	US Department of Justice Office of the Inspector General
ED Mich	US District Court for the Eastern District of Michigan
ED Va	US District Court for the Eastern District of Virginia
EDNY	US District Court for the Eastern District of New York
FAA	Federal Aviation Administration
FISA	Foreign Intelligence Surveillance Act
FP	*Foreign Policy*
G	*Guardian* (UK)
HASC	House Armed Services Committee
HBO	Home Box Office
HRF	Human Rights First
HRW	Human Rights Watch
HuffPost	Huffington Post
Humvee	High Mobility Multipurpose Wheeled Vehicle (HMMWV)
ISIL	Islamic State of Iraq and the Levant
ISIS	Islamic State of Iraq and Syria
JFK	John F Kennedy Airport
LAPD	Los Angeles Police Department
LAT	*Los Angeles Times*
LAX	Los Angeles Airport
LCpl.	Lance Corporal
Lt.	Lieutenant

LtCol.	Lieutenant Colonel
KSM	Khalid Sheikh Mohammed
Maj.	Major
MC	military commission
MDC	Metropolitan Detention Center (federal prison in Brooklyn)
MGen.	Major General
MH	*Miami Herald*
MPR	Minnesota Public Radio
MSgt.	Master Sergeant
MST	*Minneapolis Star-Tribune*
MTA	Metropolitan Transportation Authority
NBC	National Broadcasting Company
NCIS	Naval Criminal Investigative Service
NCT	*North County Times* (California)
ND Cal	US District Court for the Northern District of California
NLJ	*National Law Journal*
NPR	National Public Radio
NSA	National Security Agency
NYC	New York City
NYLJ	*New York Law Journal*
NYPD	New York Police Department
NYRB	*New York Review of Books*
NYT	*New York Times*
O	*The Oregonian*
OARDEC	Office for the Administrative Review for the Detention of Enemy Combatants
PFC	Private First Class
PLO	Palestine Liberation Organization
POW	Prisoner of War
Pvt.	Private
PTSD	post-traumatic stress disorder
RNC	Republican National Committee
ROE	Rules of Engagement
SB	*Sacramento Bee*
SDNY	US District Court for the Southern District of New York
SEALs	Sea, Air and Land Teams (Navy)
SFC	Sergeant First Class

SFPD	San Francisco Police Department
Sgt.	Sergeant
SJC	Senate Judiciary Committee
SPC	Specialist
SSgt.	Staff Sergeant
TRAC	Transaction Records Access Clearinghouse (Syracuse University)
TSA	Transportation Security Administration
UCMJ	Uniform Code of Military Justice
UPI	United Press International
WD Wash	U.S. District Court for the Western District of Washington
WP	*Washington Post*
WSJ	*Wall Street Journal*
WTC	World Trade Center

CHAPTER 1   JUDGING THE JUDGES

1   On the essential role of courts, especially in wartime, see Fiss (2015).
2   Cover (1975: 6).
3   Wacks (1984a, 1984b); Dugard (1984, 1987); Robertson (1989).
4   Baum (1977).
5   Abel (1995: 528).
6   E.g., Gage (2009). On "executive-minded" South African judges during apartheid, see Ellmann (1992).
7   Lewis (2007: 102–03).
8   *Schenck* v. *U.S.*, 249 U.S. 47 (1919); Walker (1990: 26).
9   *Shaefer* v. *U.S.*, 251 U.S. 466, 501 (1919).
10   For other civil liberties violations, see Muller (2007); Reeves (2015).
11   *Hirabayashi* v. *U.S.*, 320 U.S. 81 (1943); Walker (1990: 145–47); Stone (2004: 27–99).
12   *Korematsu* v. *U.S.*, 323 U.S. 214 (1944); Lewis (2007: 113); Stone (2004: 204–05).
13   *Dennis* v. *U.S.*, 341 U.S. 494 (1951); Powe (2009: 166); Martelle (2011); Weiner (2012: 155).
14   Walker (1990: 192, 242); Powe (2009: 164–65).
15   *U.S.* v. *U.S. District Court*, 407 U.S. 297 (1972); Stone (2004: 496).
16   Stone (2004: 84, 126).
17   Murphy (1979: 186–212); Stone (2004: 161, 224–25).
18   Walker (1990: 43–44); Stone (2004: 225); Weiner (2012: 37–40).
19   Stone (2004: 164, 169).

20 *Abrams* v. *U.S.*, 250 U.S. 616 (1919); Stone (2004: 192ff.); Lewis (2007: 28–34).
21 Chafee (1919). On Holmes's volte-face, see Acheson (1965); Ragan (1971); Finan (2007: 32).
22 *Abrams* v. *U.S.*, 250 U.S. 616 (1919).
23 *Gitlow* v. *New York*, 268 U.S. 652 (1925); Lewis (2007: 108).
24 *Whitney* v. *California*, 274 U.S. 357 (1927); Lewis (2007: 35–36).
25 *U.S.* v. *Schwimmer*, 279 U.S. 644 (1929); Lewis (2007: 27).
26 *Stromberg* v. *California*, 283 U.S. 359 (1931); Walker (1990: 90–92); Lewis (2007: 27).
27 *Minersville School District* v. *Gobitis*, 310 U.S. 586 (1940); *West Virginia State Board of Education* v. *Barnette*, 319 U.S. 624 (1943); Walker (1990: 109); Lewis (2007: 114).
28 *Schneiderman* v. *U.S.*, 320 U.S. 118 (1943); Walker (1990: 160).
29 Walker (1990: 242); Powe (2009: 164–65, 194).
30 *Peters* v. *Hobby*, 349 U.S. 331 (1955).
31 *Cole* v. *Young*, 351 U.S. 536 (1956).
32 *Pennsylvania* v. *Nelson*, 350 U.S. 497 (1956).
33 *Slochower* v. *Board of Regents*, 350 U.S. 551 (1956).
34 Powe (2009: 167–68).
35 Stone (2004: 483–85).
36 Scott (2013: 95–133).
37 Stone (2004: 477).
38 Balbus (1974); Trubek (1977).
39 Stone (2004: 450, 470–71).
40 *U.S.* v. *Seeger*, 380 U.S. 163 (1965).
41 Walker (1990: 279–80); Stone (2004: 450).
42 *Tinker* v. *Des Moines Independent Community School District*, 393 U.S. 503 (1969); Walker (1990: 280–81).
43 *Street* v. *New York*, 394 U.S. 576 (1969).
44 *Cohen* v. *California*, 403 U.S. 15 (1971); Lewis (2007: 132).
45 *Brandenburg* v. *Ohio*, 395 U.S. 444 (1969), overruling *Whitney* v. *California*, 274 U.S. 357 (1927).
46 Tolley (1990–91: Table 1).
47 Lewis (2007: 4).
48 Stone (2004: 84).
49 Weiner (2012: 45–54).
50 Barkan (1985).
51 Hite & Unger (2013); Robben (2004).
52 Simmons (2009: 285–95); Hilbink (2007).
53 Davis (2014: 2–26, 192–93).
54 Ibid. 30–41, 177–82, 185–203.
55 Ibid. 30–37, 51, 177–82.
56 Simmons (2009: 297–303).
57 *Sharif* v. *C.O. Homefront Command*, 50(4) P.D. 485–91 (1996).
58 Barak (2001).
59 Woffinden (1987).

60 For normative and historical accounts of the tension between liberty and security, see Wilson (2005); Gross & Ni Aoláin (2006); Dyzenhaus (2006); Lane & Oreskes (2007); Gould & Lazares (2007); Posner & Vermeule (2007); Wittes (2008); Fisher (2008); Bobbitt (2008); Honig (2009); Springer (2010); Glennon (2010); Unger (2012); Ryan (2015). For comparative analyses, see Hussain (2003); Gross (2006); Horne (2006) (Algeria); Brysk & Hafir (2008); Donohue (2008); Mokhtari (2009); Lazar (2009); Roach (2011); Anderson (2011) (Kenya); Masferrer & Walker (2013).

61 Fisher (2008: 137–46); Agamben (2005: 20); Neff (2010: chap. 2).

62 Murphy (1979: 53–54, 73–103, 107, 186–226); Walker (1990: 12–15); Stone (2004: 156, 181, 188 ff.); Finan (2007: 7–8, 13, 26); Fisher (2008: 110); Brinkley (2008: 30–33); Weiner (2012: 5, 14–16, 24–36); Walker (2012: chap. 2).

63 Walker (1990: 43–44); Stone (2004: 230–31); Fisher (2008: 116); Weiner (2012: 21–23); Walker (2012: chap. 3).

64 Murphy (1979: 49, 153–78, 230–34).

65 Walker (1990: 134–36, 154); Rankin & Dallmayr (1964: 47); Walker (2012: chap. 4).

66 Yoo (2008: 56–58).

67 Walker (1990:154–59): Weiner (2012: 109).

68 *Ex parte Quirin*, 317 U.S. 1 (1942); Danelski (1996); Weiner (2012: 112).

69 Fisher (2008: 144–52); Stone (2004: 283ff.).

70 Walker (1990: 137–47); Stone (2004: 292, 296–302); Fisher (2008: 140–42).

71 Walker (1990: 282–86); Stone (2004: 440–45); Walker (2012: chap. 8); Keys (2014: 57–62); Moyn (2014).

72 Allison (2007: 5–20, 35–45, 70–88); Solf (1972); Kalven & Zeisel (1966).

73 Allison (2007: 93–103).

CHAPTER 2   CRIMINAL PROSECUTIONS

1 Quoted in Barrio, "By Any Means Necessary," *American Lawyer* (11.14.08).

2 Prepared Remarks for the US Mayors Conference, Speeches of Attorney General John David Ashcroft, www.justice.gov.ag/speeches-8 (last accessed March 1, 2018).

3 Hunt (2010); Said (2015); Bergen (2016).

4 Abrams (2005).

5 Lichtblau, Johnston & Nixon, "F.B.I. Struggling to Handle Wave of Finance Cases," NYT (8.19.08); HRW and Columbia Law School (2014: 62); Chesney (2007b).

6 Eggen, "Terrorism Prosecutions Drop," WP (9.4.06); Lichtblau, "Study Finds Sharp Drop in the Number of Terrorism Cases Prosecuted," NYT (9.4.06); "Nation in Brief," WP (11.6.06); DoJ OIG, The Department of

Justice's Internal Controls Over Terrorism Reporting, Audit Report 07-20 (Feb. 2007); "Audit Finds Flaws in Terror Statistics," NYT (2.21.07); Meyer, "Data on Terrorism Littered with Flaws," LAT (2.21.07). See also TRAC, Who Is A Terrorist? Government Failure to Define Terrorism Undermines Enforcement, Puts Civil Liberties at Risk (2009), which gives different figures for declinations: 2002 – 31%; 2005 – 61%; 2008 – 73%.

7   TRAC, Terrorism Enforcement: International, Domestic and Financial (2007); TRAC, "National Internal Security/Terrorism Prosecutions for January 2008 (2008); TRAC, National Internal Security/Terrorism Prosecutions for November 2008 (2008).

8   Quoted in Barrio, "By Any Means Necessary," *American Lawyer* (11.14.08).

9   See also the Lackawanna 6: Temple-Raston (2007); Wypiejewski, "Living in an Age of Fire," *Mother Jones* (March/April 2003). See Precht (2003) for a defense lawyer's argument that the criminal justice system failed in the prosecution of Mohammad Salameh for the 1993 World Trade Center bombing.

10   Goodman, "U.S. Says 2 Georgia Men Planned a Terror Attack," NYT (4.22.06); deStefano, "U.S.-born Man to Be Charged in Terrorism Case," LAT (4.22.06); Rashbaum, "New Accusations against Georgia Man Keep Him in Custody," NYT (4.29.06); "Canada Arrests 17 in Alleged Terror Plot," LAT (6.4.06); "More Charges in Georgia Terrorism Case," NYT (7.20.06); Eggen, "Georgia Pair Charged in Plot to Strike Capitol, World Bank," WP (7.20.06); "Georgia: Not Guilty Plea in Terror Case," NYT (7.28.06); Sheridan, "Terrorism Probe Points to Reach of Web Networks," WP (1.24.08); Johnson, "American Convicted on Terror Charges in Atlanta," WP (6.10.09); Brown, "Georgia Man Is Convicted in Conspiracy," NYT (6.11.09); Bluestein, "Georgia Terror Suspect: Jihad Chatter Was 'Empty Talk,'" WP (8.4.09); "Georgia: Defending Himself," NYT (8.4.09); "American Is Convicted of Aiding Terrorists," NYT (8.13.09); Rotella, "U.S. Man Guilty in Terror Case," LAT (8.13.09); DoJ Press Release (8.12.09); DoJ Press Release (12.14.09); "Georgia: Terror Video Sentencing," NYT (12.15.09); Hussain, "New Film Delves into FBI Arrests of Youths for Terrorism Crimes They Might Commit," *The Intercept* (3.6.16).

11   "Canada Arrests 17 in Alleged Terror Plot," LAT (6.4.06); "2 in Toronto-NYC Train Terror Plot Found Guilty," WP (3.21.15).

12   For another successful pretextual conviction, for tax fraud, see *U.S. v. Mubayyid*, 567 F.Supp.2d 223 (D.Mass 2008), aff'd in part, 658 F.3d 34 (1st Cir. 2011).

13   Walsh & Stanton, "Two in Lodi accused of al-Qaeda links," SB (6.8.05); Murphy & Johnston, "California Father and Son Face Charges in Terrorism Case," NYT (6.9.05); Tempest, Krikorian & Romney, "Ties to Terror Camps Probed," LAT (6.9.05); Marshall, "Bail Denied to Californian in Terror Case," NYT (6.11.05); "National Briefing," NYT (6.22.05); "6 Men Got Terrorist Training, Pair Say," LAT (7.9.05); La Ganga & Tempest, "2 Lodi Men to Be Deported; U.S. Will Drop Charges," LAT (7.16.05); Magagnini, "Lodi imam denied bond," SB (8.10.05); Romney

& Simmons, "Pakistani Cleric Agrees to Leave U.S.," LAT (8.16.05); Marshall, "Deportation Set for Imam in F.B.I. Case," NYT (8.16.05); Walsh, "Suspect Allegedly Pledged Holy War," SB (8.24.05); "Man Indicted on Terrorism Charges," WP (9.23.05); "National Briefings," NYT (9.23.05); Walsh, "Bail OK'd in Lodi Terror Case," SB (9.27.05); Walsh, "Judge Approves Bail in Lodi Case," SB (10.27.05); Walsh, "Bail Is Denied in Lodi Case," SB (1.5.06); Walsh, "A Late Surprise for Lodi Defense," SB (2.10.06); Archibold, "Diverging Views of Californian at Terror Trial," NYT (2.17.06); Tempest, "Man Trained to Be Terrorist, Prosecutor Says," LAT (2.17.06); Walsh, "Suspect Got FBI Prompts," SB (2.22.06); "Lodi Man Said Hospitals and Markets Were Possible Targets," LAT (2.22.06); Tempest, "FBI Informer Begins His Testimony in Terror Trial," LAT (2.23.06); Walsh, "Hayat Self-Assured in New Tapes," SB (2.24.06); "Informant Recalls Talk of Jihad by Lodi Man," LAT (2.24.06); Walsh, "Defense Attacks FBI's Man in Lodi," SB (3.3.06); Bailey, "Attorney Says Lodi Terror Suspect Told Tall Tales to FBI Mole," LAT (3.3.06); Tempest, "Lodi Man Describes Terrorist Training," LAT (3.8.06); Walsh, "Jury Hears of Terror Plot," SB (3.9.06); Bailey, "Informant Says He Saw al Qaeda's No. 2," LAT (3.14.06); Romney, Bailey & Meyer, "Sighting of Terrorist in Lodi Questioned," LAT (3.15.06); "Lodi Men Had Jihad Book, Judge Told," LAT (3.16.06); Tempest, "Onetime Clerk Is at Center of Lodi Trial," LAT (3.21.06); Tempest, "Informant's Tactics Are Questioned," LAT (3.22.06); Geis, "California Town Is Latest Site of U.S. Terrorism Prosecution," WP (3.23.06); Tempest, "Terror Case Unproved, Former Juror Says," LAT (3.23.06); Walsh, "Doubt Cast on al-Zawahri Sighting," SB (3.30.06); Tempest, "Al Qaeda in Lodi 'Unlikely,'" LAT (3.30.06); Magagnini, "Judge Rejects Defense Witness at Hayat Trials," SB (4.1.06); Tempest, "Tape Recording Surfaces in Lodi Terrorism Trial," LAT (4.5.06); Archibold, "Prosecution Sees Setback at Terror Trial in California," NYT (4.10.06); Tempest, "Lodi Terror Trial Enters Final Round," LAT (4.11.06); Bailey, "Defense Rests in Lodi Terror Trial," LAT (4.12.06); Tempest, "Lodi Terror Case Goes to the Jury," LAT (4.13.06); Tempest, "Jury in Lodi Case Asks to See Video," LAT (4.14.06); Korber, "Hayat Judge Revises Words to Jury," SB (4.21.06); Korber, "Request from Hayat Jury Buoys Defense," SB (4.22.06); Tempest, "Terrorism Trial Hits a Roadblock," LAT (4.25.06); Archibold & Kearns, "In California Terror Case, A Mistrial for a Father, but a Son Is Guilty," NYT (4.26.06); Walsh & Korber, "U.S. Claims Victory in Lodi Terror Case," SB (4.26.06); Tempest & Bailey, "Conviction for Son, Mistrial for Father in Lodi Case," LAT (4.26.06); Korber, "U.S. Hails its Hayat Strategy," SB (4.27.06); Broder, "Federal Victory in Terror Case May Prove Brief, Experts Say," NYT (4.27.06); Tempest & Bailey, "Lodi Terrorism Conviction Was a Rout, Jury Says," LAT (4.27.06); Romney, "Lodi Muslims Stung by Verdict; Some Fear a Youth Backlash," LAT (4.27.06); Walsh, "Hayat Juror Says Vote Was Coerced," SB (4.28.06); Tempest, "Lodi Case Juror Alleges Bullying," LAT (4.29.06); Marshall, "Juror Says She Was Pressured to Convict Defendant in California Terror Trial," NYT (4.29.06); Magagnini & Carreon, "Hayat

Lawyer: Toss Verdict," SB (3.29.06); Tempest, "In Lodi Terror Case, Intent Was the Clincher," LAT (5.1.06); Walsh, "A New Hayat Jury Issue," SB (5.4.06); Tempest, "U.S. to Retry Father in Lodi Case," LAT (5.6.06); Archibold, "Prosecution Sees Setback at Terror Trial in California," NYT (5.10.06); Walsh, "Hayat Agrees to Plea Deal," SB (6.1.06); "Lodi Man Is Released in Plea Bargain," LAT (6.1.06); MacFarquhar, "Echoes of Terror Case Haunt California Pakistanis," NYT (4.27.07); "Walsh, "New Hayat Trial Denied," SB (5.18.07); "California: Appeal Fails in Terror Case," NYT (5.19.07); Marshall, "24-Year Term for Californian in Terrorism Training Case," NYT (9.11.07); Arax, "The Agent Who Might Have Saved Hamid Hayat," LAT 17 (5.28.06); Waldman, "Islam on Trial?" *The Atlantic* (9.12.06); Arax (2009); VanSickle, "Part 1: Small-town 'Terrorists'; Part 2: Deceit and Terror," *The Intercept* (11.19.16).

14 Waldman, "Prophetic Justice," *The Atlantic* (October 2006).
15 *U.S. v. Hayat*, 2007 WL 1454280 (E.D. Ca. 2007).
16 *U.S. v. Hayat*, 710 F.3d 875 (9th Cir. 2013).
17 O'Neil, "Seven Are Charged with Plot to Blow Up Sears Tower," NYT (6.23.06); Schmitt, "7 Arrested in Miami in Alleged Terrorist Plot," LAT (6.23.06); Whorisky & Eggen, "7 Held in Miami in Terror Plot Targeting Sears Tower," WP (6.23.06); Shane & Zarate, "F.B.I. Killed Plot in Talking Stage a Top Aide Says," NYT (6.24.06); Williams & Schmitt, "FBI Says 7 Terror Suspects Were Mostly Talk," LAT (6.24.06); Whoriskey & Eggen, "Terror Suspects Had No Explosives and Few Contacts," WP (6.24.06); Drew & Lichtblau, "Two Views of Terror Suspects: Die-Hards or Dupes," NYT (7.1.06); Blum, "6 Held in Terror Case Denied Bail," LAT (7.6.06); Pincus, "FBI Role in Terror Probe Questioned," WP (9.2.06); Shane & Bergman, "Adding Up the Ounces of Prevention," NYT (9.10.06); Williams, "Are They Terrorists or 'Naïve Losers'?" LAT (10.3.07); Whoriskey, "Trial Begins for 7 Accused of Plotting to Destroy Sears Tower," WP (10.3.07); Goodnough, "Trial Starts for Men in Plot to Destroy Sears Tower," NYT (10.3.07); Weaver, "Liberty City 7 'Wanted to Wage Jihad,' Jury Told," MH (10.3.07); Sedensky, "Informant: Suspect Wanted al-Qaida Help," MH (10.4.07); Weaver, "Liberty City Seven Leader Is on Video Discussing Targets," MH (10.6.07); Weaver, "Liberty City Seven Defense Faces Setbacks," MH (10.23.07); Weaver, "Liberty City 7 'Were on Path to Jihad,'" MH (10.31.07); Weaver, "Liberty City 7: I Was Pretending, Terror Suspect Says," MH (11.8.07); Menendez, "Liberty City 7 Trial Runs Like a B-Movie," MH (11.18.07); Weaver, "Closing Arguments Coming for Liberty City 7," MH (11.22.07); Anderson, "Testimony Ends in Miami Terrorism Case," MH 11.27.07); Anderson, "Prosecutor: Fla. Group Was Terror Cell," MH (11.29.07); Williams, "Liberty City 7: A Case of Conspiracy or Entrapment?" LAT (11.30.07); Semple, "Closing Arguments Begin in Trial of Men Charged in Plot to Destroy Sears Tower," NYT (11.30.07); Semple, "Defense Ends its Arguments in Terrorism Trial in Miami," NYT (12.1.07); Weaver, "Liberty City 7 Case Goes to Jury," MH (12.4.07); Blum, "Jury in Terrorism Trial Is Deadlocked," LAT (12.7.07); Weaver, "Liberty City 7 Jurors Apparently Deadlocked," MH (12.7.07);

Anderson, "Sears Tower Terror Jury Told to Work On," MH (12.10.07); Whoriskey, "Terrorism Case Ends in Mistrial; 1 Acquitted," WP (12.14.07); Semple, "U.S. Falters in Terror Case against 7 in Miami," NYT (12.14.07); "Florida: Retrial Begins in Sears Tower Case," LAT (2.2.08); "Ex-Terror Suspect Is Charged Anew," NYT (2.27.08); Weaver, "Federal Court: Liberty City Terror Trial Nears End," MH (3.27.08); Weaver, "2nd Jury Weighs Liberty City Terror Case," MH (3.31.08); Anderson, "Jury in Terrorism Case Asks If Oath to al-Qaeda a Crime," MH (4.1.08); "Florida; Stalemate for Terror Jury," NYT (4.12.08); "Jury Fails to Reach Verdict in Terror-Conspiracy Case," MH (4.12.08); "Florida: Jury Told to Keep At It in Bomb Case," LAT (4.16.08); "Liberty City Terror Jury: We Can't Agree," MH (4.15.08); Weaver, "Mistrial Declared in Liberty City Terror Trial," MH (4.16.08); Cave, "Mistrial for 6 in Sears Tower Terror Case," NYT (4.17.08); Blum, "Another Mistrial in Florida Terrorism Case," LAT (4.17.08); Gage, "2nd Mistrial in 'Liberty City 7' Case," WP (4.17.08); Gentile, "Six Suspects Will Be Tried a Third Time in Sears Plot," NYT (4.24.08); Blum, "Florida Terrorism Case to Be Retried," LAT (4.24.08); Weaver, "Liberty City 6 Face Third Terrorism Trial," MH (4.24.08); "A Trial Too Far," WP (5.2.08); "Ex-Terror Suspect May Be Deported," WP (12.6.08); Cave, "After 2 Mistrials, Prosecutors Try Again to Prove Jihad Plot," NYT (1.27.09); Anderson, "Sept. 11 a Factor in Fla. Terror Retrial," MH (1.27.09); Weaver, "Racial Concerns Halt Jury Selection in Liberty City Six Terror Retrial," MH (2.12.19); Gentile, "U.S. Begins Third Effort to Convict 6 in Terror Case," NYT (2.19.09); Madkour, "3rd Trial Starts for 6 Men Accused of Terror Plot," MH (2.18.09); Weaver, "Judge Dismisses Sick Juror, Suspends Deliberations in Terror Trial," MH (4.30.09); Weaver, "Jury Deliberations Begin in Third Liberty City Terror Trial," MH (5.2.09); Weaver, "Jury Deliberations in Terror-Conspiracy Retrial Delayed Again," MH (5.2.09); Weaver, "Judge Removes Juror in Liberty City Six Terror Trial," MH (5.5.09); Blum, "5 Convicted in Terrorism Trial," LAT (5.13.09); Cave & Gentile, "Five Convicted in Plot to Blow Up Sears Tower As Part of Islamic Jihad," NYT (5.13.09); Weaver, "Five Members of Liberty City Six Guilty in Terror Plot," MH (5.13.09); "Florida: Sentences for Lesser Players in Terrorism Plot," NYT (11.19.09); "Florida: Sentencing in Tower Plot," NYT (11.20.09).

18 *U.S.* v. *Augustin*, 661 F.3d 1105 (11th Cir. 2011), cert. den. 132 S.Ct. 2118, 2444, 2447 (2012).

19 Meyer, "Four Accused in N.Y. Bomb Plot," LAT (5.21.09); Susman, "Disbelief over a 'Chilling Plot,'" LAT (5.22.09); Wilson, "Case against 4 Ex-Convicts: Steps and Missteps, On Tape," NYT (5.22.09); Baker, "Suspects in Terror Bombing Plot; Drug Arrests and Prison Conversions," NYT (5.22.09); Rashbaum & Fahim, "Informer's Role in Bombing Plot," NYT (5.23.09); Wakin, "Imams Reject Talk That Islam Radicalizes Inmates," NYT (5.24.09); Rayman, "The Alarming Record of the F.B.I.'s Informant in the Bronx Bomb Plot," *Village Voice* (7.8.09); Moynihan, "Bronx Terror Case May Depend on Testimony of Informant," NYT (9.18.09); Sulzberger, "Defense Cites Entrapment in Terror Case," NYT

(3.18.10); Glaberson, "Trial for 4 Accused of Trying to Bomb Synagogues in the Bronx Is Delayed," NYT (6.15.10); NYT (6.26.10); Fahim, "Agent Wanted Backup Charge in Synagogue Bomb Case, Defense Says," NYT (8.27.10); Fahim, "Informer Says Defendant Wanted to be a Martyr," NYT (8.27.10); Fahim, "On Tapes, Terror Suspect Brags and Reveals His Hate," NYT (8.31.10); Fahim, "Recordings Reveal Informer's Role in Synagogue Bomb Plot," NYT (9.9.10); Fahim, "Trial in Synagogue Plot Is Delayed over Questions about Defendant's Mental Health," NYT (9.15.10); Fahim, "Lawyer Tries to Discredit Informer in Synagogue Bomb-Plot Case," NYT (9.16.10); Fahim, "Informer in Bomb Plot Describes His Two Lives," NYT (9.17.10); Fahim, "Defense Presses Informer in Synagogue Bomb Case," NYT (9.21.10); Fahim, "Informer in Synagogue Plot Accused of Bullying Suspect," NYT (9.22.10); Fahim, "Judge Shouts at Witness in Synagogue Bomb Case," NYT (9.24.10); Fahim, "Terror Witness Returns, Facing Gentler Questioning," NYT (9.28.10); Fahim, "Witness's Last Turn in Synagogue Bomb Case," NYT (9.30.10); Fahim, "Behind the Scenes at a Bomb-Plot Trial," NYT (10.4.10); Fahim, "Focus as Bomb-Plot Trial Nears End: Were 4 Men Predisposed to Commit a Crime?" NYT (10.5.10); Fahim, "Defense Seeks Mistrial for 4 in Plot, Citing Error," NYT (10.12.10); Fahim, "4 Convicted of Attempting to Blow Up 2 Synagogues," NYT (10.19.10); Susman, "Four Convicted in New York Synagogue Bomb Plot," LAT (10.19.10); Rayman, "Were the Newburgh 4 Really Out to Blow Up Synagogues?" *Village Voice* (3.2.11); Moynihan, "Entrapment Is Reasserted in Appeal in Synagogue Bombing Case," NYT (3.25.11); Weiser, "Three Men Draw 25-year Sentences in Plot to Bomb Two Bronx Synagogues," NYT (6.30.11); Katz, "U.S. Tricked Man Convicted of Plot to Bomb Synagogues: Lawyer," Reuters (2.2.12); Lyons, "FBI Informant in Upstate Stings, Including Albany, Surfaces in Pittsburg Case," Times Union (3.17.12); Weiser, "Judges Question Tactics in Bronx Bomb Case," NYT (11.6.12); Laguardia (2013). HBO made an award-winning documentary, *The Newburgh Sting* (2004).

20 Wilson, "2 Albany Men Are Convicted in Missile Sting," NYT (10.11.06); *United States* v. *Aref*, 2007 WL 603508 (N.D.N.Y. 2007), aff'd, 285 Fed. App'x 784 (2nd Cir. 2008).
21 *United States* v. *Cromitie*, 2011 WL 1842219 (S.D.N.Y. 2011).
22 *United States* v. *Cromitie*, 727 F.3d 194 (2nd Cir. 2013).
23 Meyer, "Boston-Area Man Charged in Alleged Terrorist Plot," LAT (10.22.09); Hsu, "Massachusetts Man Arrested on Terror Charges," WP (10.22.09); Zaremba, "Feds to Cite 'Library' in Terror Trial," BH (10.20.11); Valencia, "Sudbury Terrorism Suspect's Trial to Begin," BG (10.23.11); Valencia, "Jury Picking Begins in Terrorism Plot Case," BG (10.25.11); Valencia, "Jurors at Mehanna Trial Will Be Shown Video That Includes bin Laden Speech," BG (10.27.11); Valencia & Finucane, "Prosecutors Say Mehanna Supported Terrorists," BG (10.28.11); Sweet, "Feds: Tarek Mehanna Was al-Qaeda Mouthpiece," BH (10.28.11); Valencia & Finucane, "Investigators Conduct Secret Search of Mehanna's Home in Sudbury in 2006," BG (10.29.11); Valencia, "Terror Suspect's

Friend Recounts Talks," BG (11.4.11); Valencia, "Defense Depicts Mehanna as a Scholar," BG (11.5.11); Valencia & Finucane, "Witness Says Mehanna Sought Terror Training," BG (11.15.11); Valencia, "Mehanna Friend Said to Seek Camps for Training," BG (11.16.11); Valencia, "FBI Agent Recounts Visit to Terror Suspect," BG (11.17.11); Valencia, "Witness Testifies about Terror Suspect's Influence," BG (11.18.11); Valencia, "Mehanna Counseled Nonviolence, in '06," BG (11.22.11); Valencia, "Mehanna's Father Grew Worried, Witness Says," BG (11.23.11); Valencia, "Ex-Friend Says Goal of Mehanna's Trip Was Terror Training," BG (11.29.11); Valencia, "Mehanna Did Not Regret Trip to Yemen, U.S. Alleges," BG (12.1.11); Valencia, "Prosecution Analyst Outlines al Qaeda Strategy," BG (12.3.11); Valencia, "Mehanna Lawyers Challenge Analyst," BG (12.6.11); Valencia, "Analyst Again under Fire at Tarek Mehanna Trial," BG (12.7.11); Valencia, "Defense Depicts Less-Radical Mehanna," BG (12.8.11); Valencia, "Yemen Trip Called a Search for Schooling," BG (12.9.11); Valencia, "Mehanna Defense Sums Up Case," BG (12.10.11); Valencia, "Mehanna Defense Focuses on Language in Terror Case," BG (12.14.11); Valencia, "Accused al Qaeda Supporter's Defense Rests," BG (12.15.11); Valencia, "Mehanna Defense Hits Prosecutors," BG (12.16.11); Valencia, "Closing Arguments Given in Terror Suspect's Trial," BG (12.17.11); Valencia, "Tarek Mehanna Guilty of Terror Charges," BG (12.20.11); Sweet, "Sudbury Man Guilty in Terror Plot," BH (12.21.11); Goodenough, "U.S. Citizen Is Convicted in Plot to Support al Qaeda," NYT (12.21.11); "From Words to Deeds," BH (12.21.11); Schworm, "Mehanna Conviction Stirs Outcry on Rights," BG (12.22.11); "Mass. Terror Convict Asks Judge to Consider His Background as Teacher, Pharmacist," WP (4.10.12); Valencia & Element, "Federal Prosecutors Ask for 25-Year Sentence for Sudbury al Qaeda Supporter Tarek Mehanna," BG (4.11.12); Tarek Mehanna Sentencing Statement (4.12.12); DoJ Press Releases (4.13.12); Valencia & Finucane, "Tarek Mehanna, Homegrown Terrorist from Boston Area Who Promoted al Qaeda on the Internet, Sentenced to 17½ Years," BG (4.13.12); March, "A Dangerous Mind?" NYT (4.22.12).

24 *United States v. Mehanna*, 735 F.3d 32 (1st Cir. 2013), cert. denied, 135 S.Ct. 49 (2014).

25 Melia, "Pentagon Official Rejects Death Penalty Bid for Africa Embassy Bombing Suspect Held at Gitmo," LAT (10.3.08); Glaberson, "President to Transfer First Detainee to U.S.," NYT (5.22.09); Finn, "The First Guantánamo Detainee Arrives in U.S.," WP (6.9.09); Finn, "Guantánamo Bay Detainee Brought to U.S. for Trial," WP (6.10.09); Weiser, "In U.S. Court, Guantánamo Detainee Pleads Not Guilty to Embassy Bombing Charges," NYT (6.10.09); Weiser & Shane, "U.S. Says It Will Preserve Secret C.I.A. Jails for Terrorism Cases," NYT (7.3.09); Weiser, "Bomb Suspect Can't Keep His Military Lawyers," NYT (11.19.09); Weiser, "Terrorism Trial May Point Way for 9/11 Cases," NYT (11.23.09); Weiser, "Terrorism Suspect Seeks Dismissal over Delay in Trial," NYT (12.2.09); Weiser, "Mental State of Suspect May Be Issue in Terror Case," NYT

(12.18.09); Weiser, "Judge Is Asked to Reject Terror Defendant's Claim That He Didn't Receive a Speedy Trial," NYT (12.19.09); Weiser, "U.S. Told to Review Files on Terror Case Detention," NYT (2.10.10); Wesier, "No Dismissal in Terror Case on Claim of Torture in Jail," NYT 5.11.10); Weiser, "Judge Refuses to Dismiss Terror Suspect's Case," NYT (7.14.10); "Let the Legal System Work," LAT (7.17.10); Weiser, "Dispute over Witness in Embassy Bombing Case," NYT (9.3.10); Weiser, "Witness in 1998 Bombings Is Identified at a Hearing," NYT (9.20.10); Weiser, "Gauging Jurors' Fears before a Trial Starts," NYT (9.25.10); Weiser, "Report Shows Detainee's Insight into Legal Process," NYT (9.27.10); Weiser, "Missing from First Civilian-Court Trial of a Guantánamo Detainee: His Statements," NYT (10.5.10); Weiser, "Judge Bars Major Witness from Terrorism Trial," NYT (10.7.10); Finn, "Ruling in '98 East Africa Embassy Bombings Case Is Setback for U.S.," WP (10.6.10); "Prosecutors in Guantánamo Bay Suspect's Terror Trial Won't Appeal Witness Ban," WP (10.10.10); Serrano, "Prosecutors Will Not Appeal Ruling in Embassy Bombing Case," LAT (10.10.10); Weiser, "No Appeal in Exclusion of Witness in Terror Trial," NYT (10.11.10); Weiser, "Trial of Man Once Held at Guantánamo Opens," NYT (10.13.10); Susman, "Africa Embassy Bombing Suspect's Civilian Trial Begins in New York," LAT (10.12.10); Weiser & Moynihan, "Some Clues about Jurors in Trial of Former Detainee," NYT (10.14.10); Weiser, "Judge Says Key Figure in Embassies Bombing Case Isn't Credible," NYT (10.15.10); Weiser, "Candid Talks by Detainee Were Caught on U.S. Tapes," NYT (10.27.10); Weiser, "Solemn End to Trial for '98 Attacks," NYT (11.4.10); Weiser, "Prosecution Closes in Trial of Detainee," NYT (11.9.10); Weiser, "Ex-Detainee's Defense Calls Him a Dupe in its Closing," NYT (11.10.10); Weiser, "No Verdict in Terror Trial of Ex-Detainee," NYT (11.12.10); Weiser, "Juror Asks to Leave Embassy Bombing Trial," NYT (11.16.10); Finn, "Ahmed Ghailani, Gitmo Detainee, Acquitted of All but 1 Charge in N.Y.," WP (11.18.10); Weiser, "Detainee Acquitted on Most Counts in '98 Bombing," NYT (11.18.10); Williams & Baum, "U.S. Civilian Court Acquits Ex-Guantánamo Detainee of all Major Terrorism Charges," LAT (11.18.10); Weiser, "Trial Omitted Statements by Ghailani," NYT (11.18.10); "The Ghailani Verdict," NYT (11.19.10); Davis, "A Terrorist Gets What He Deserves," NYT (11.19.10); Finn & Kornblut, "Analysis: Verdict Dims Outlook for Civilian Trials of Terrorism Detainees," WP (11.19.10); Kornblut & Finn, "White House Undeterred after Ghailani Terror Case Verdict," WP (11.18.10); "Acquittal in Terror Case Shows Justice System's Strengths," WP (11.19.10); Serrano, "U.S. to Go Ahead with Terrorism Trials," LAT (11.19.10); "Justice Was Served in Ghailani Case," LAT (11.19.10); Thiessen, "Try Ahmed Ghailani at Gitmo," WP (11.22.10); Haberman, "Don't Agree with Verdict? It's Injustice," NYT (11.23.10); Weiser, "Ex-Detainee Wants Judge to Dismiss Conviction on Single Count in Bombings," NYT (12.18.10); Weiser, "Ghailani Prosecutors Challenge Defense Request for Dismissal," NYT (1.13.11); Weiser, "Life Sentence Is Requested in Bomb Case," NYT

(1.7.11); Weiser, "Embassy Bombing Suspect Was Told of Plot, Filing Says," NYT (1.15.11); Weiser, "Ghailani's Lawyers Detail Terror Defense Strategy," NYT (1.18.11); Weiser, "Ex-Detainee Gets Life Sentence in Embassy Blasts," NYT (1.26.11); Finn, "Gitmo Detainee Ghailani Gets Life Sentence in Embassy Plot," WP (1.26.11); Weiser, "Former Detainee's Appeal Cites Long Wait for a Trial," NYT (5.9.13). For a moving account of the pre-9/11 trial of other conspirators, see Hirsch (2006).

26 *United States v. Ghailani*, 743 F.Supp.2d 242 (S.D.N.Y. 2009).
27 *United States v. Ghailani*, 687 F.Supp.2d 365 (S.D.N.Y. 2010); *United States v. Ghailani*, 751 F.Supp.2d 498 (S.D.N.Y. 2010).
28 *United States v. Ghailani*, 751 F.Supp.2d 502 (S.D.N.Y. 2010).
29 *United States v. Ghailani*, 751 F.Supp.2d 508 (S.D.N.Y. 2010).
30 *United States v. Ghailani*, 751 F.Supp.2d 515 (S.D.N.Y. 2010).
31 *United States v. Ghailiani*, 2010 WL 4006381 (S.D.N.Y. 2010).
32 *United States v. Ghailani*, 733 F.3d 29 (2d Cir. 2013)
33 See Lawson, "The Fear Factory," *Rolling Stone* (1.25.08) (use of informant against Derrick Shareef); Al Jazeera, Informants (2014); Laguardia (2013); Aaronson, "The Informants," *Mother Jones* (8/11); CHRGJ (2011); "Who Is 'Mel'? US Terror Case May Unmask NY Police Mole," CBS New York (4.11.17).
34 On the difficulty of proving entrapment generally, see Valdes (2005). On the particular difficulties in terrorism prosecutions, see Norris (2015, 2016); Norris & Grol-Prokopczyk (2016).
35 Feuer & Rashbaum, "2 Charged with Plotting to Bomb Train Station," NYT (8.29.04); Rashbaum, "Subway Bomb Plot Suspect Tells of Confusion at Arrest," NYT (1.25.06); Elliott, "A Terror Case that Resonates Close to Home," NYT (3.6.06); Rashbaum, "Subway Terror Case to Offer Insight into the Use of Moles," NYT (4.24.06); Rashbaum, "Police Informer in Terror Trial Takes Stand," NYT (4.25.06); Rashbaum, "In Tapes of Subway Plot Suspect, a Disjointed Torrent of Hatred," NYT (4.26.06); Rashbaum, "Terror Jury Hears Talk of Bombing Subway Stop," NYT (4.27.06); Rashbaum, "Informer in Bomb Plot Trial Tells of His Visits to Mosques," NYT (5.2.06); Rashbaum, "Detective Was 'Walking Camera' among City Muslims, He Testifies," NYT (5.19.06); Rashbaum, "Jury Convicts Pakistani Immigrant in a Plot to Blow Up a Subway Station," NYT (5.25.06); Elliott, "Undercover Work Deepens Police–Muslim Tensions," NYT (5.27.06); Rashbaum, "Terror Trial Opens Window on Shadowing of Muslims," NYT (5.28.06); Rashbaum, "Man Sentenced to 30 Years for Plot to Blow up Manhattan Subway Station," NYT (1.9.07).
36 Wilson, "2 Albany Men Are Convicted in Missile Sting," NYT (10.11.06).
37 Feuer, "Recordings Open Window on World of a Would-Be Terrorist from the Bronx," NYT (5.8.07); Soufan (2011: 518–24).
38 Watanabe & Glover, "Man Says He Was FBI Informant," LAT (2.26.09).
39 DoJ Press Release (9.24.09); McKinley, "Friends' Portrait of Texas Suspect at Odds with F.B.I.'s," NYT (9.28.09); "Texas: Not-Guilty Plea in Bombing Case," NYT (10.27.09); DoJ Press Release (5.26.10).

40 Sweeney, "Guilty Plea Expected in Terrorism Case," CT (7.12.12); "Chicagoan Accused of Plotting to Be Suicide Bomber for al-Qaeda, al-Shabab to Plead Guilty," WP (7.12.12); Meiser, "Chicago Man Pleads Guilty to Terrorism Charge," CT (7.31.12).

41 "Illinois: Man Charged in Explosives Plot," NYT (9.21.10); "Chicago Fake-Bomb Suspect to Change Plea to Guilty in Deal with Federal Prosecutors," WP (12.21.11); DoJ Press Release (4.23.12); "Would-Be Wrigley Field Backpack Bomber to Be Sentenced in Chicago," WP (5.30.13).

42 Goldstein & Rashbaum, "City Bomb Plot Suspect Is Called Fan of Qaeda Cleric," NYT (11.21.11); "'Al-Qaeda Sympathizer' Accused of NYC Bomb Plots," WP (11.21.11); Susman, "New York Police Arrest 'Lone Wolf' Bomb Plot Suspect," LAT (11.21.11); Rashbaum & Goldstein, "Informer's Role in Terror Case Is Said to Have Deterred F.B.I.," NYT (11.22.11); "Bomb Plot Suspect's Mom Apologizes to New Yorkers," WP (11.22.11); Baum & Susman, "New York Bomb Plot Suspect Didn't Seem Radical to Neighbors," LAT (11.22.11).

43 Rashbaum, & Moynihan, "Most Serious Charges Are Rejected in Terror Case," NYT (6.16.11).

44 Johnson, "Lawyer: Man to Plead Guilty in Seattle Terror Plot," BG (12.7.11); DoJ Press Release (12.8.11); Myers, "Man Pleads Guilty in Plot to Attack Seattle Military Site," Reuters (12.7.12); "Washington: Sentencing in Terror Plot," NYT (3.26.13); Pearce, "California Man Gets 17-Year Prison Term in Seattle Terrorist Plot," LAT (4.18.13).

45 Seipel, "San Jose Neighbors Stunned by Alleged Terrorist Living in Their Midst," *San Jose Mercury News* (2.9.13); FBI Press Release (2.8.13); Salonga, "San Jose Man Gets 15 Years in Prison for Oakland Bank Bombing Plot," *San Jose Mercury News* (2.27.14).

46 Osnos, "The Imam's Curse," *The New Yorker* (9.21.15).

47 Thompson, "Trafficking in Terror," *The New Yorker* (12.14.15).

48 See Fordham Law School Center on National Security, Case by Case: ISIS Prosecutions in the United States, March 1, 2014–June 30, 2016 (7.6.16).

49 Savage, "American Woman Indicted on Terror Charges in Plot to Kill Swedish Cartoonist," NYT (3.10.10); Johnson, "Jihad Jane, an American Woman, Faces Terrorism Charges," WP (3.10.10); Urbina, "Militant Views Were Expressed Online but Unknown to Neighbors," NYT (3.11.10); Drogin & Portnoy, "Jihad Jane? To Most She Was Just Colleen," LAT (3.11.10); Johnson & Robbins, "Relatives Believe Woman Arrested in Ireland Became Radical Muslim," NYT (3.14.10); Johnson, "Colorado Woman Linked to Swedish Murder Plot, 'Jihad Jane,'" WP (3.14.10); Riccardi, "Ireland Frees American Woman in Terrorist Plot," LAT (3.14.10); "Mom Says Daughter Held in Ireland Terror Plot," LAT (3.13.10); Quinn & Burns, "Irish Hearing Provides Details on a Suspected Plot to Kill a Swedish Cartoonist," NYT (3.16.10); Urbina, "Woman Pleads Not Guilty in Terror Case," NYT (3.19.10); Burn, "Irish Port Town Puzzled to Find Itself Part of a Multinational Terrorism Inquiry," NYT (33.20.10); "Second American Woman Charged in 'Jihad-Jane' Case," WP (4.3.10); "Pennsylvania: Silent Plea in Terrorism Case," NYT (4.8.10); "2nd

Woman Charged in Plot to Kill Artist Pleads Not Guilty," WP (4.8.10); "Pennsylvania: Plea Change for 'Jihad Jane,'" NYT (1.29.11); Dale, "'Jihad Jane' Terror Suspect Pleads Guilty in Pennsylvania," WP (2.2.11); "Pennsylvania: Guilty Plea in Terror Case," NYT (3.9.11); Hall, "'Jihad Jane' Codefendant Pleads Guilty to Terrorism Charge," LAT (3.10.11); Bennett, "Teenager Charged in 'Jihad Jane' Case," LAT (8.27.11); Bishop, "Howard County Teen Indicted on Terrorism Charges," BS (10.21.11); Hermann, "Ellicott City Teen Pleads Not Guilty to Terrorism Charges," BS (10.25.11); "Md. Teen Plans Guilty Plea in Terror Case in Pa.," AP (3.5.12); Dalby, "Ireland: Suspect in Terrorism Case Faces Extradition to U.S.," NYT (3.1.13); Shiffman, "Jihad Jane: Despite Cooperation, U.S. Seeks 'Decades' in Prison," Reuters (1.1.14); Hurdle, "10 Years for Plot to Murder Cartoonist," NYT (1.7.14); "Colorado Mother Sentenced to 8 Years in Terror Case," WP (1.9.14); "Pennsylvania: Young Immigrant Gets 5 Years in 'Jihad Jane' Conspiracy," NYT (4.18.14).

50 Ruiz, Goldman & Apuzzo, "Terror Suspect Brought to U.S. for Trial, Braking from Trump Rhetoric," NYT (7.22.17).

51 "Two New Jersey Men Arrested in Terrorism Charges," LAT (6.6.10); Rashbaum, "2 Men Seized at J.F.K. Accused of Plotting Jihad," NYT (6.7.10); Pérez-Peña & Barron, "2 Held in Terrorism Case Appear in Federal Court," NYT (6.8.10); Serrano, "New Jersey Men Arraigned on Terrorism Charges," LAT (6.8.10); Fahim, Pérez-Peña & Zraick, "From Troublemaking Teenagers to International Terror Suspects," NYT (6.12.10); Zraick, "Terror Suspects in New Jersey Plead Guilty," NYT (3.4.11); "Two New Jersey Men with al Qaeda Links Sentenced to Prison," Reuters (4.15.13); Jones, "Judge Rejects Plea from Men Who Joined al Qaeda Affiliate," Reuters (5.22.13).

52 "2 Charged in Plot to Attack NYC Synagogues Are Due in Court Wed.," WP (6.15.11); Rashbaum, & Moynihan, "Most Serious Charges Are Rejected in Terror Case," NYT (6.16.11); "Defense Lawyers: NYC Temple Plot Case Misuses State Terror Law, Should Be Tossed Out," WP (11.10.11); Moynihan, "Lawyers for Man Accused in Terrorism Plot Make Case for Dismissal," NYT (3.14.12); "Judge: NYC Temple Terror Plot Case Can Go Forward," Fox News (6.25.12); Goldstein & Hughes, "F.B.I. Criticizes Officer's Role in a Terror Case," NYT (9.19.12); Italiano, "Temple 'Terror Plotter' Eyes Deal," *New York Post* (9.19.12); Moynihan, "Queens Man Pleads Guilty in Plot to Blow Up Manhattan Synagogue," NYT (12.5.12); "10-Year Term in Synagogue-Bomb Plot," NYT (3.15.13); Buettner, "Man Sentenced in Plan to Bomb Manhattan Synagogue," NYT (4.27.13).

53 Savage & Shane, "U.S. Accuses Iranians of Plotting to Kill Saudi Envoy," NYT (10.12.11); Ignatius, "What Iran's Alleged Terror Plot Tells U.S.," WP (10.12.11); Dilanian, Richter & Bennett, "U.S. Sees Alleged Assassination Plot as Radical Shift for Iran," LAT (10.12.11); "Iran's Terror Plot," WSJ (10.12.11); "The Charges against Iran," NYT (10.13.11); "Alleged Assassination Plot Serves as a Warning about Tehran," WP (10.13.11); Cooper, "Obama Says Facts Support Accusation

of Iranian Plot," NYT (10.14.11); Gladstone, "Iran Says Saudi Plot Defendant Belongs to Exile Group," NYT (10.19.11); Shane, "U.S. Denies Iran Claims that Saudi Plot Defendant Belongs to Exile Group," NYT (10.20.11); Weiser, "Not-Guilty Plea in Plot to Kill Saudi Ambassador to the U.S.," NYT (10.25.11); "UN 'Deplores' Alleged Plot to Kill the Saudi Ambassador to U.S. and Points Finger at Iran," WP (11.19.11); Weiser, "Questions over Whether Terror Suspects' Aid in Inquiries Was Voluntary," NYT (11.24.11); Weiser, "Judge Sets Trial Date in Alleged Plot to Kill Saudi Official," NYT (2.8.12); Weiser, "Mental Illness Cited in Challenge to Terror Case," NYT (7.17.12); "Trial Date Moved for Man in Saudi Ambassador Plot," WSJ (8.17.12); Weiser, "Man Accused of Plot on Envoy Wasn't Mentally Ill, U.S. Argues," NYT (10.4.12); Weiser, "Psychiatrist Details Talks with Suspect in Bomb Plot," NYT (10.5.12); DoJ Press Release (10.17.12); DoD Press Release (5.30.13).

54 Goodnough, "Man Is Held in a Plan to Bomb Washington," NYT (9.29.11); Finn, "Man Accused of Plotting to Hit Pentagon and Capitol with Drone Aircraft," WP (9.29.11); Serrano, "Man Held in Alleged Terrorist Plot on Washington," LAT (9.29.11); "FBI: Mass. Man Had 'Mission' against Pentagon," CBS News (11.4.11); "Massachusetts Main Charged with Plotting to Fly Explosives into Pentagon Ordered Held on Bail," WP (11.29.11); DoJ Press Release (7.11.12); DoJ Press Release (11.1.12); Bidgood, "Massachusetts Man Gets 17 Years in Terrorist Plot," NYT (11.1.12); Letter from Acting U.S. Attorney to Federal Public Defender (6.26.12).

55 "4 California Men Charged in Terror Plot, F.B.I. Says," NYT (11.20.12); Lopez, "4 Held in Alleged Terror Plot," LAT (11.20.12); Feldman, "California Men Plead Not Guilty in Plot to Join al Qaeda," CT (12.6.12); Hansen, "Terrorism Trial Underway for Men Accused of Trying to Join al Qaeda," LAT (8.18.14); "Jury Finds 2 Men Guilty in Federal Terror Trial," ABC News (9.25.14).

56 Miller & Hayasaki, "Arrests Made in Alleged JFK Plot," LAT (6.3.07); Faiola & Mufson, "N.Y. Airport Target of Plot, Officials Say," WP (6.3.07); Meyer, "A Potential Threat Seen in America's Backyard," LAT (6.3.07); Garvey, "Alleged Plot's Damage Would Have Been Limited," LAT (6.3.07); Buckley & Rashbaum, "4 Men Accused of Plot to Blow Up Kennedy Airport Terminals and Fuel Lines," NYT (6.3.07); Powell & Rashbaum, "Court Papers Portray Plot as More Talk Than Action," NYT (6.4.07); Miller, "A Down-and-Out Terrorism Suspect," LAT (6.4.07); Barry & Wilensky-Lanford, "Many Guyanese in New York Are Puzzled by Terror Arrests," NYT (6.5.07); Faiola & Shulman, "In 'Little Guyana,' Disbelief over Terrorism Arrests," WP (6.4.07); "Suspects in Alleged JFK Plot to Be Extradited," LAT (8.7.07); Rashbaum, "Extradition Ordered for Three Suspects in Airport Bomb Plot," NYT (8.7.07); Meyer, "3 Extradited in Alleged Airport Plot," LAT (6.26.08); Sulzberger, "Trial Is Set to Start in a Plot to Bomb Kennedy Airport," NYT (6.30.10); Sulzberger, "Tapes of Defendant Plotting to Blow Up Kennedy Airport Are Played for Jury," NYT (7.16.10); Moynihan, "Suspect Denies Role

in Kennedy Airport Plot, Saying He Sought to Build a Mosque," NYT (7.21.10); Sulzberger, "2 Men Convicted of Airport Plot," NYT (8.3.10); Long, "2 Men, Including Guyana Ex-Official, Convicted in Plot to Blow Up JFK Airport Fuel Tanks," LAT (8.2.10); Moynihan, "Life Sentence for Plotting to Set Off Blasts at J.F.K.," NYT (12.16.10); Moynihan, "15-Year Sentence for Conspirator in Airport Plot," NYT (1.14.11); Moynihan, "Life Sentence for Leader of Terror Plot at Kennedy," NYT (2.18.11); Secret, "Trinidadian Gets Life Sentence in J.F.K. Bomb Plot," NYT (1.14.12); Maddux, "Jihadist 'Plotted' from Jail," *New York Post* (8.15.12); "Appeals Court Upholds Trinidadian's Conviction in N.Y. Airport Bomb Plot," NYT (7.13.13).

57 DoJ Press Release (11.2.11); Shane, "4 Georgia Men Arrested in Terror Plot," NYT (11.2.11); Warrick, "Alleged Ricin Plot in Georgia Was a Long Shot," WP (11.3.11); Severson & Brown, "Georgia Men Held in Plot to Attack Government," NYT (11.3.11); "Georgia Terror Suspects Allegedly Inspired by Online Novel," LAT (11.3.11); Sverdlik, "Elderly Georgia Men Plead Not Guilty in Toxin Plot Case," Reuters (11.10.11); Junod, "Counter-Terrorism Is Getting Complicated," *Esquire* (1.30.12); "2 Suspects in Georgia Terror Plot Plead Guilty of Conspiring to Obtain Explosives, Silencer," WP (4.11.12); "Georgia: 2 Waffle House Plotters Are Sentenced," NYT (8.23.12); Blinder, "Defendant Admits Sending Letter with Ricin to Obama," NYT (1.18.14); Blinder, "Two in Ricin Terrorism Plot Are Each Sentenced to 10 Years in Prison," NYT (11.15.14).

58 Brune & Palmer, "Plot to Attack N.Y. Tunnels Disrupted, Authorities Say," LAT (7.7.06); Hsu & Wright, "Plot to Attack N.Y. Foiled," WP (7.8.06); Baker & Rashbaum, "3 Held Overseas in Plan to Bomb New York Target," NYT (7.8.06); Meyer & Barry, "Plot on N.Y. Tunnels Alleged," LAT (7.8.06); Lipton, "Recent Arrests in Terror Plots Yield Debate on Preemptive Action by Government," NYT (7.9.06); Meyer, "Alleged Plot Possibly Went Beyond N.Y. Tunnels," LAT (7.10.06).

59 Russakoff & Eggen, "Six Charged in Plot to Attack Fort Dix," WP (5.9.07); Kocieniewski, "6 Men Arrested in a Terror Plot against Ft. Dix," NYT (5.9.07); Meyer & Hayasaki, "6 Charged in Plot to Strike Army Base," LAT (5.9.07); Faiola & Russakoff, "The Terrorists Next Door?" WP (5.10.07); Fahim & Elliott, "In Large Immigrant Family, Religion Guided Three in Fort Dix Plot: Working People with Mostly Workaday Lives," NYT (5.10.07); Kocieniewski, "In Large Immigrant Family, Religion Guided Three in Fort Dix Plot: Informer's Role Draws Praise and Questions," NYT (5.10.07); Hayasaki & Meyer, "Neighbors Saw Changes in Suspects," LAT (5.10.07); Wilensky-Lanford & Rohde, "Relatives Noticed Changes in Accused Plotters," NYT (5.11.07); Meyer, "As Terrorism Plots Evolve, FBI Relies on Agent John Q. Public," LAT (5.12.07); Fahim, "U.S. Judge Promises Speedy Trial, and Leg Shackles, in Fort Dix Terror Case," NYT (6.15.07); "6 Plead Not Guilty in Ft. Dix Case," LAT (6.15.07); Fahim, "Clerk Accused of Fixing Tickets for Suspect in Ft. Dix Terror Plot," NYT (6.16.07); Mulvihill, "Trial to Begin for Men Accused of Planning to Kill

Soldiers on New Jersey Military Base," LAT (9.29.08); Meyer, "'Ft. Dix Six' Informants in Hot Seat Too," LAT (10.19.08); Mulvihill, "Opening Arguments Begin Monday in Trial of Men Accused of Plotting to Kill Fort Dix Soldiers," LAT (10.29.08); Mulvihill, "Key Informant with a Shady History to Take the Stand in Fort Dix Terror Plot Trial," LAT (10.27.08); Mulvihill, "Defense Lawyers Question Informant in Terror Case," WP (11.6.08); Von Zielbauer, "Five Are Convicted of Conspiring to Attack Fort Dix," NYT (12.23.08); Barnes, "Five Convicted of Plotting to Kill Ft. Dix Soldiers," LAT (12.23.08); "3 Brothers Sentenced to Life for Holy War Plot at Ft. Dix," NYT (4.29.09); "Judge Sentences Two More in Ft. Dix Conspiracy," LAT (4.30.09); "Defendant in Fort Dix Terror Plot Expected to Plead Guilty," NYT (10.27.07); "Life Sentences Upheld for Brothers Convicted in Terror Plot," AP (6.1.16).

60 "25-Year-Old Man Arrested in Florida Bomb Plot," NYT (1.9.12); Levesque & Thalji, "Alleged Terror Plot Targeted in Tampa," *Tampa Bay Times* (1.10.12); "Sami Osmakac, Accused of Terrorism, Fit to Stand Trial," ABC News (2.21.13); Wright, "Pinellas Terror Suspect Plans Entrapment Defense," Fox (4.24.13); "Trial Delay for Sami Osmakac, Accused of Plotting Terrorist Attacks on Tampa," WTSP.com (10.8.13); Phillips, "Jury Finds Sami Osmakac Guilty of Terrorism," *Tampa Bay Times* (6.11.14); "Sami Osmakac Gets 40 Years in Prison for Plotting Terrorist Attacks in Tampa," *Tampa Bay Times* (11.5.14).

61 DoJ Press Release (11.26.10); "Somali-Born Teenager Held in Oregon Bomb Sting," NYT (11.27.10); Miner, Robbins & Eckholm, "F.B.I. Says Oregon Suspect Planned 'Grand' Attack," NYT (11.28.10); "Somali-Born Teen Held in Oregon Car-Bomb Plot," LAT (11.27.10); Markon, "FBI Foils Elaborate Bomb Plot in Oregon," WP (11.28.10); Drogin & Choi, "Teen Held in Alleged Portland Bomb Plot," LAT (11.28.10); Schmidt & Savage, "In U.S. Sting Operations, Questions of Entrapment," NYT (11.30.10); Yardley, "Entrapment Is Argued in Defense of Suspect," NYT (11.30.10); Drogin & Choi, "Oregon Terrorism Suspect Pleads Not Guilty," LAT (11.30.10); "'Stinging' Would-Be Terrorists," LAT (12.17.10); Ross, "Mohamed Mohamud Trial: Was He Tricked into Terrorism?" Daily Beast (4.23.12); Denson, "Mohamed Mohamud Lawyers Denied Access to Surveillance Warrants in Terrorism Case," O (5.8.12); Denson, "Mohamed Mohamud Bomb Plot Case: FBI Agent Recounts Airport Interview with Terrorism Suspect about No-Fly List," O (9.24.12); Denson, "Judge Rules Portland Bomb-Plot Suspect Mohamud Can't Have FBI Informant's Identification," O (9.26.12); Duara, "Prosecutors Ask to Use Word 'Terrorist' at Trial," *San Francisco Chronicle* (11.7.12); Johnson, "In 2010 Portland Bomb Plot, a Question of Manipulation or Violent Extremism," NYT (1.11.13); Duara, "Undercover Agent Details Terrorism-Sting Specifics," ABC News (1.14.13); Johnson, "Harsher View of Bombing Suspect Is Revealed on Tapes," NYT (1.16.13); Denson, "Portland Terrorism Trial: Mohamed Mohamud Made 'Goodbye Video,'" O (1.16.13); Duara & Dubois, "Oregon Terrorism Suspect Portrayed as Inexperienced,"

AP (1.16.13); Denson, "Portland Terrorism Trial: FBI Agents Trace Trail That Led Them to Mohamed Mohamud," O (1.24.13); Denson, "Portland Terrorism Trial: 'This Is Bad … Mohamed's Been Arrested,' Parents Recall," O (1.29.13); Denson, "Portland Terrorism Trial: 'This Case Is a Tragedy,' Mohamed Mohamud's Lawyer Says," O (1.30.13); Johnson, "Federal Jury Weighs Case in Bomb Plot in Portland," NYT (1.30.13); Johnson, "Oregon Man Convicted in Holiday Bombing Plot," NYT (1.31.13); Denson, "Mohamed Mohamud Found Guilty in Portland Terrorism Trial," O (1.31.13); Denson, "Mohamed Mohamud Apologizes, but His Fate in Portland Bomb Plot Rests in Judge's Hands," O (8.23.13); Savage, "Warrantless Surveillance Continues to Cause Fallout," NYT (11.21.13); Johnson, "Judge Suspends Sentencing of Would-Be Bomber after NSA Revelations," NPR (11.26.13); Nakashima, "Man Convicted in Terror Case Seeks Evidence from Warrantless Spying," WP (1.14.14); Savage, "Justice Dept. Defends Its Conduct on Evidence," NYT (2.15.14); "Oregon: 30-Year Sentence in Bomb Plot," NYT (10.2.14); *U.S. v. Mohamud*, 843 F.3d 420 (9th Cir. 2016).

62 Fahim & Rashbaum, "Former City Resident Is Accused of Trying to Join Terrorists," NYT (10.27.10); Serrano, "American Arrested in Terrorism Case Was Denied Entry to Pakistan," LAT (10.28.10); Secret, "Staten Island Man Is Convicted of Lying about Plans to Join Terrorists," NYT (3.26.13); "NYC Man Sentenced to 13 Years for Lying about His Plans to Join al-Qaeda," WP (9.20.13).

63 Finn, Hsu & Gibson, "Feds Arrest N. Va. Man in D.C. Metro Bomb Plot," WP (10.28.10); Tavernise, "Details Emerge on Man Charged in Plot on Subway," NYT (10.29.10); Hsu, "Suspect in D.C. Metro Bomb Plot Sought to Fight U.S. Troops Overseas, Records Say," WP (10.29.10); "Virginia: 23-Year Sentence for Subway Bomb Plot," NYT (4.12.11).

64 Fenton & Bishop, "Arrest Made in Plot to Blow up Baltimore-Area Military Recruiting Center," LAT (12.8.10); Savage & Gately, "Man Arrested in Bomb Plot in Maryland," NYT (12.9.10); Calvert, "Baltimore Man Charged in Bomb Case Appeared to Drift into Islamic Extremism," LAT (12.10.10); "Lawyer Argues Entrapment in Bomb Plot," NYT (12.14.10); "Md. Man Caught in FBI Sting Pleads Guilty to Plot to Bomb Military Recruiting Center," WP (1.26.12).

65 Finn, "FBI: Saudi Student Bought Materials for Bomb, Considered Bush Home as Target," WP (2.24.11); Serrano, "FBI Charges Saudi in Alleged Terrorism Plot," LAT (2.24.11); Savage & Shane, "U.S. Arrests Saudi Student in Bomb Plot," NYT (2.25.11); McKinley & Wheaton, "Saudi Student to Be Arraigned in Bomb Plot," NYT (2.26.11); Finn, "FBI: Saudi Student Bought Materials for Bomb, Considered Bush Home as Target," WP (2.26.11); Williams, "In Texas Courtroom, Saudi Denies Plotting Bomb Attacks," NYT (3.28.11); Clark, "Lubbock Terror Suspect Requests Psychiatric Exam," KCBD (11.9.11); "Attorney for Saudi Man Charges in Alleged Terror Plot Files Notice to Pursue Insanity Defense," AP (11.10.11); "Judge Rules Saudi Man Accused in Terror Bomb Plot

Mentally Competent," WP (2.21.12); Carver, "Terror Suspect Aldawsari's Trial Moved to Amarillo, Set for June," *Lubbock Avalanche-Journal* (4.18.12); Nett, "Language of 'Attempted Use' Provides Vague Area for Aldawsari Jury," *Lubbock Avalanche-Journal* (6.19.12); "Texas: No Defense Is Given in Bomb-Making Trial," NYT (6.26.12); Nett, "Aldawsari Trial to Jury," *Lubbock Avalanche-Journal* (6.26.12); "Saudi Is Convicted in Bomb Attempt," NYT (6.27.12); DoJ Press Release (6.26.12); Clark, "Lubbock's Nationally Known Terror Suspect Objects to Conviction," KCBD (7.26.12); "Saudi Student Jailed for Plot to Attack Bush's Home," BBC News (11.4.12); Graczyk, "Conviction Upheld in Saudi Student Texas Bomb Plot," *Washington Times* (1.24.14).

66 Reeves, "Uzbek Man Pleads Guilty in Plot to Kill Obama," WP (2.11.12); Mackay, "Alabama Uzbek Who Plotted to Kill Obama Was Victim of Social Media, His Lawyer Says," NYT (7.14.12).

67 Savage, "F.B.I. Arrests Man in a Suspected Terrorist Plot near the U.S. Capitol," NYT (2.18.12); Horowitz, Wan & Wilber, "Federal Agents Arrest Amine el Khalifi," WP (2.18.12); Serrano, "Would-Be Attacker Arrested near U.S. Capitol, Officials Say," LAT (2.18.12); Frazier, "How the FBI Invents Terrorists like the U.S. Capitol 'Suicide Bomber,'" Daily Beast (2.19.12); Wilber, "Inside an FBI Anti-Terrorist Sting Operation," WP (11.25.12); "Man Accused in Plot to Blow Up Capitol Set to Enter Guilty Plea," WP (6.22.12); "Court Papers: FBI Promised 'Martyrdom Payments' to Target of Sting in Capitol Bomb Plot," WP (9.11.12); "Moroccan Sentenced in Plot to Bomb Capitol," NYT (9.15.12).

68 DoJ Press Release (10.17.12); Horwitz, "Man Arrested in Purported Plot to Bomb New York Federal Reserve," WP (10.17.12); "Exchange Student Indicted in Attempted Bombing of Federal Reserve Bank," CNN (11.16.12); Smythe, "N.Y. Federal Bomb-Plot Sting Suspect Pleads Not Guilty," Bloomberg (11.27.12); Secret, "Bangladeshi Admits Trying to Blow up Federal Bank," NYT (2.8.13); Secret, "30-Year Prison Sentence in Plot to Bomb U.S. Bank," NYT (8.9.13).

69 HRF (2008).

70 "Ex-bin Laden Spokesman Sulaiman abu Ghaith: U.S. Tortured Me on Plane," Politico (7.25.13); Beekman, "Osama bin-Laden's Son-in-Law Sulaiman abu Ghaith Treated Like Royalty on Flight to New York, Says U.S. Marshall," New York Daily News (9.18.13); Wachtel, "Lawyer Says bin Laden's Son-in-Law Was Disoriented during Interrogation," Fox News (10.8.13).

71 Herbert, "Tyranny of Fear," NYT (8.17.06); Hays, "False Accusation Creates a 9/11 Footnote," AP (9.9.06).

72 "US Wants Man Named in Plot to Kill Bush Held in Jail," NYT (2.23.05); Hendren, "Man Indicted in Plot to Kill the President," LAT (2.23.05); "Prosecutors Deny Plot Suspect's Torture Claims," LAT (2.24.05); "The Case of Ahmed Omar Abu Ali," NYT (2.24.05); "Security a Bar for Bush Plot Suspect," LAT (8.30.05); Lichtblau, "U.S. Details Charges against Student Linked to Plot against Bush," NYT (9.20.05); "National Briefing," NYT (10.20.05); *United States* v. *Abu Ali*, 395 F.Supp.2d 338 (E.D. Va. 2005);

National Briefing," NYT (10.25.05); Markon, "Judge Allows Statement by al Qaeda Suspect," WP (10.25.05); *U.S. v. Ali*, 350 F.Supp.2d 28 (E.D.Va. 2004); Lichtblau, "Trial Starts for Student in Plot to Kill President," NYT (11.1.05); Barakat, "Terror Suspect: 'Everyone Makes Mistakes,'" WP (11.2.05); "National Briefs," NYT (11.17.05); Markon, "Va. Man Convicted in Plot to Kill Bush," WP (11.23.05); Stout, "Student from Virginia Is Convicted of Plotting with al Qaeda to Assassinate Bush," NYT (11.23.05).

73 *In re Terrorist Bombings of U.S. Embassies in East Africa*, 552 F.3d 177 (2nd Cir. 2008), 553 F.3d 93 (2nd Cir. 2008), 553 F.3d 150 (2nd Cir. 2008), cert. den. 556 U.S. 1283 (2009); Weiser, "Interpreter for F.B.I. Thinks Interrogators Beat Terrorism Suspect," NYT (4.16.09).

74 Weiser, "Questions over Whether Terror Suspects' Aid in Inquiries Was Voluntary," NYT (11.24.11); Weiser, "Mental Illness Cited in Challenge to Terror Case," NYT (7.17.12); Weiser, "Man Accused of Plot on Envoy Wasn't Mentally Ill, U.S. Argues," NYT (10.4.12); Weiser, "Psychiatrist Details Talks with Suspect in Bomb Plot," NYT (10.5.12); DoJ Press Release (10.17.12).

75 Savage & Schmitt, "U.S. to Prosecute a Somali Suspect in Civilian Court," NYT (7.6.11); DeYoung, "U.S. Indicts Somali on Terrorism Charges," WP (7.5.11); Finn, "Somali's Case a Template for U.S. As It Seeks to Prosecute Terrorism Suspects in Federal Court," WP (3.30.13).

76 Weiser, "Hearing on Terror Suspect Explores Miranda Warning," NYT (12.13.11); Weiser, "Judge in Terrorism Case Orders Hunt for E-mails," NYT (1.13.12).

77 Klasfeld, "Suspected Bomb Plotter Challenges CIA Detention," Courthouse News Service (10.8.14); Weiser, "Suspected Qaeda Operative Tries to Quash Rights Waiver," NYT (10.16.14).

78 Worth, "Yemeni Cleric Is Sentenced to 75 Years in Terrorism Case," NYT (7.29.05); "Yemeni Sheikh Gets 75 Years for Backing Terror," WP (7.29.05); Weiser, "Appeals Court Overturns Two Terror Convictions, Citing Errors by Judge," NYT (10.3.08); Hsu, "Convicted Yemeni Cleric to Be Deported," WP (8.8.09); *U.S. v. al-Moayad*, 545 F.3d 139 (2nd Cir. 2008).

79 Lichtblau, "U.S. Had Doubts about Lesser Case against Terror Suspects," NYT (5.13.05); Eggen, "Prosecutor, Agent Indicted in Detroit," WP (3.30.06); Lichtblau, "Ex-Prosecutor in Terror Inquiry Is Indicted," NYT (3.30.06); Slevin, "Detroit 'Sleeper Cell' Prosecutor Faces Probe," WP (11.20.05); Shenon, "Ex-Prosecutor 'Crossed Over the Line,' Jury Told," NYT (10.31.07); Shenon, "Ex-Prosecutor Acquitted of Misconduct in 9/11 Case," NYT (11.1.07). *U.S. v. Koubriti*, 336 F.Supp.2d 676 (E.D. Mich. 2004).

80 **Mohamed Osman Mohamud**: Savage, "Warrantless Surveillance Continues to Cause Fallout," NYT (11.21.13); Johnson, "Judge Suspends Sentencing of Would-Be Bomber after NSA Revelations," NPR (11.26.13); Nakashima, "Man Convicted in Terror Case Seeks Evidence from Warrantless Spying," WP (1.14.14); Savage, "Justice Dept. Defends Its Conduct on Evidence," NYT (2.15.14).

Adel Daoud: Janssen, "Attorney for Teen Terror Suspect Wants to See Secret Evidence," CST (11.29.13); Meisner, "Judge Rejects Looking into If

Surveillance Program Led to Terrorism Charge," CT (1.20.14); Tarn, "U.S. Appeals Ruling to Let Lawyers See Secret Files," AP (3.31.14); Meisner, "Lawyers for Terrorism Suspect Say Government Embellishes Claims of National Security," CT (5.5.14); Schlickerman, "Attorneys for Terror Suspect Kicked Out of 'Secret' Court Hearing," CST (6.4.14); Schmadeke, "Terrorism Suspect's Lawyer Clashes with Appeals Judge in Do-Over," CT (6.9.14); Nakashima, "Appeals Court Overturns Lower Court Order Permitting Disclosure of Secret FISA Material," WP (6.16.14).

Raees Alam Qazi and Sheheryar Alam Qazi: Kravets, "Feds Won't Say if NSA Surveilled New York Terror Suspects," Wired's Threat Level (5.13.13).

Basaaly Moalin: Brumfield, "Four Somalis in U.S. Found Guilty of Supporting Terrorists Back Home," CNN (2.23.13); Vitka, "The Dragnet's Day in Court," *Slate* (9.30.13); Sharma, "San Diego Somalis Want New Trial after NSA Revelations," KPBS (12.13.13).

Reaz Qadir Khan: Barrett, "DoJ Notifies Terror Suspect Evidence Gathered through NSA Program," WSJ (4.3.14).

Jamshid Muhtorov: Barnes & Nakashima, "U.S. Tells Terror Suspect It Will Use Surveillance Evidence, Setting Up Possible Legal Challenge," WP (10.25.13); Gurman, "Terror Suspect Wants Details of Case against Him," AP (10.20.14); Farivar, "In 2016, Terror Suspects and 9-Eleven Thieves May Bring Surveillance to Supreme Court," Ars Technica (1.1.16).

Mohamed Mohamud: Hansen, "Xmas Bomber Case Appeal Challenges NSA Surveillance," AP (7.6.16); Savage, "Terrorism Conviction of a Wiretapped American Is Upheld on Appeal," NYT (12.6.16).

Mohamed Younis al-Jayab; Yahya Farooq Mohammad: Savage, "Warrantless Surveillance in Terror Case Raises Constitutional Challenge," NYT (4.26.16).

81 DeYoung, "Obama Aide Defends Trial for Suspect in Xmas Day Attempt to Bomb Plane," WP (1.4.10); "The Ramzi Yousef Standard," WSJ (1.6.10); Savage, "Nigerian Man Is Indicted in Attempted Plane Attack," NYT (1.7.10).

82 Baker, "Arrest Renews Debate about Rights of Suspects in Terrorism Cases," NYT (5.5.10); "Arrests Made for Alleged Immigration Violations as Times Square Bombing Attempt Is Investigated," LAT (5.13.10); Yost, "Attorney General: Criminal Justice System Proving its Strength," (5.13.10); Rashbaum & Shane, "F.B.I. Raids Tied to Case in Times Square," NYT (5.14.10).

83 Savage & Schmitt, "U.S. to Prosecute a Somali Suspect in Civilian Court," NYT (7.6.11); DeYoung, "U.S. Indicts Somali on Terrorism Charges," WP (7.5.11); Cassata, "Mitch McConnell Criticizes Handling of Ahmed Abdulkadir Warsame," HuffPost (7.6.11); "Obama Administration Shows How to Treat a Terrorist Suspect," LAT (7.9.11); "Terrorism and the Law," NYT (7.17.11).

84 Letter from U.S. Attorney Preet Bharara to Defense Counsel Priya Chaudhry and Lee Ginsberg (12.20.11); Goldman & Weiser, "How Civilian Prosecution Gave the U.S. a Key Informant," NYT (1.27.16).

85 "Iraqi Pleads Guilty to Trying to Assist al-Qaida," NPR (12.16.11); DoJ Press Release (1.29.13).
86 Mazzetti & Rashbaum, "Bin Laden Relative with Qaeda Past to Have New York Trial," NYT (3.8.13); Santora & Rashbaum, "Bin Laden's Son-in-Law Is Arraigned in New York Court," NYT (3.8.13); Miller & Finn, "Osama bin Laden's Son-in-Law Captured, Turned Over to U.S.," WP (3.8.13); Santora & Rashbaum, "Bin Laden Relative Pleads Not Guilty in Terrorism Case," NYT (3.9.13).
87 Munoz, "Captured al Qaeda Leader 'To Be Treated Like Anyone Else' Says Top Democrat," The Hill (10.7.13); Munoz, "GOP Senators: Put al Qaeda Chief in Gitmo," The Hill (10.8.13); Lazar, "GOP Senators Want al-Libi Transferred to Guantánamo," ABC News (10.8.13); AI, "USA: Abduction in Libya Violates Human Rights, Undermines Rule of Law" (10.7.13).
88 Baker, Schmitt & Schmidt, "U.S. Captures Top Suspect in Benghazi Siege, Pentagon Says," NYT (6.17.14); Steinhauer & Savage, "U.S. Defends Prosecuting Benghazi Suspect in Civilian Rather Than Military Court," NYT (6.17.14); O'Keefe, Lowery & Sullivan, "Republicans Call for Captured Benghazi Suspect to Be Held at Guantánamo," WP (6.17.14); Savage, "U.S. Asserts Self-Defense in Benghazi Suspect Case," NYT (6.18.14); Schmidt, Apuzzo, Schmitt & Savage, "Trial Secondary as U.S. Questions a Libyan Suspect," NYT (6.20.14); Davis, "No to Guantánamo for Ahmed abu Khattala," NYT (6.19.14); "The Capture of a Benghazi Suspect Has Lessons for the Obama Administration," WP (6.18.14); Balluck, "McCaul Blasts Trial of Benghazi Suspect," The Hill (6.29.14); Milbank, "Benghazi Suspect abu Khattala's Hearing Shows Merits of Civilian Courts," WP (7.3.14); Hsu, "Accused Benghazi Ringleader Abu Khattala Challenges U.S. Evidence in New Court Files," WP (5.2.17); Gerstein, "Benghazi Suspect's Defense Claims Coercion," Politico (5.4.17); Tillman, "Benghazi Suspect Argues Prosecutors Shouldn't Get to Use Any Statements He Made at Sea," BuzzFeed (6.7.17).
89 "House Intelligence Committee Chairman Says There's Enough Evidence to Convict Bombing Suspect," WP (4.21.13); Savage, "G.O.P. Lawmakers Push to Have Boston Suspect Questioned as Enemy Combatant," NYT (4.22.13); "How to Handle a Terrorism Case," NYT (4.22.13); Horwitz, Markon & Johnson, "CIA, FBI, Military Interrogators Ready to Question Boston Bombing Suspect," WP (4.22.13); O'Keefe, "What Will Congress Do about the Boston Bombings," WP (4.22.13); Rosenthal, "What's the Difference Between McVeigh and Tsarnaev?" NYT (4.22.13); Lane, "An Update for Miranda Rights," WP (4.23.13); "Charging the Boston Marathon Suspect," WP (4.23.13); "Enemy Combatants in Boston," WSJ (4.21.13); MacDaffy, "Boston, Bombs, and Lindsey Graham," Daily Kos (4.23.13); Yager, "Top Intelligence Panel Lawmaker Blasts Justice Department over Miranda Rights," The Hill (4.26.13); "President on Terror Suspect, the Rule of Law Applies," St. Louis Post-Dispatch (4.24.13); Keefe, "The Worst of the Worst," The New Yorker (9.14.15); "Massachusetts: No Retrial for Marathon Bomber,"

NYT (1.16.16) (O'Toole Decision); Thadani, "Boston Bomber's Lawyers Seek to Overturn Conviction, Death Sentence," *USA Today* (2.1.16) (appeal to 1st Circuit).

90 Ruiz, Goldman & Apuzzo, "Terror Suspect Brought to U.S. for Trial, Breaking from Trump Rhetoric," NYT (7.22.17); "A Terrorism Trial in the Federal Courts," NYT (7.25.17); Wala, Letter to the Editor, NYT (7.31.17).

91 Lichtblau, "Scholar Is Given Life Sentence in 'Virginia Jihad' Case," NYT (7.14.05).

92 Lichtblau, "From Advocacy to Terrorism, a Line Blurs," NYT (6.5.05); Dahlburg, "Ex-Professor, 3 Others Face Terrorism Trial," LAT (6.6.05); "U.S. to Deport Palestinian It Failed to Convict," NYT (4.15.06); Hsu, "Former Fla. Professor to Be Deported," WP (4.18.06); Stacy, "Sentencing Expected Today in Terror Case of Former Fla. Professor," WP (5.1.06); Steinhauer, "19 Months More in Prison for Prof. in Terror Case," NYT (5.2.06); "A Plea Deal in Florida," WP (5.2.06).

93 Weiser, "Muslim Cleric 'Was Committed to War' Prosecutor Says in Terrorism Trial," NYT (4.18.14); Weiser, "Hostage Testifies about Post-Rescue Meeting with Imam Charged in Kidnapping," NYT (5.8.14); McVeigh, "Abu Hamza Denies Yemen Kidnapping Role as New York Terror Trial Continues," G (5.12.14); Weiser, "Cleric Convicted of All Terrorism Charges," NYT (5.20.14); Erlanger, "From Cameron, a Sense of Justice Delayed but Achieved," NYT (5.20.14); Weiser, "Life Sentence for British Cleric Who Helped Plan 1998 Kidnappings in Yemen," NYT (1.10.15).

94 Weiser, "Lawyers in Terrorism Case Seek Access to 9/11 Suspect," NYT (2.5.14); Weiser, "Bin Laden Aide Began Qaeda Propaganda Day after 9/11, U.S. Says," NYT (3.6.14); Weiser, "Interrogation of Bin Laden Relative Is Recounted," NYT (3.14.14); Weiser, "Interactions of bin Laden and Son-in-Law Detailed in an F.B.I. Document," NYT (3.12.14); Weiser, "At Trial, Son-in-Law Recalls a Cave Meeting with bin Laden on 9/11," NYT (3.20.14); "Ex-al-Qaeda Spokesman Recalls 9/11 with bin Laden," WP (3.20.14); Weiser, "Jurors Convict Abu Ghaith, bin Laden Son-in-Law, in Terror Case," NYT (3.27.14); Weiser, "Abu Ghaith, a Bin Laden Adviser, Is Sentenced to Life in Prison," NYT (9.24.14); Stempel, "Bin Laden's Son-in-Law; U.S. Conviction Upheld; U.S. Says 'Justice Done,'" Reuters (9.28.17).

95 Preston, "Lawyer in Terror Case Apologizes for Violating Special Prison Rules," NYT (9.29.06); Preston, "Lawyer, Facing 30 Years, Gets 28 Months, to Dismay of U.S.," NYT (10.17.06); Barr, "Terrorist's Lawyer Gets Two-Year Term," LAT (10.17.06); Weiser & Eligon, "Conviction of Sheik's Lawyer for Assisting Terrorism Is Upheld," NYT (11.18.09); Moynihan, "Radical Lawyer Convicted of Aiding Terrorist Is Jailed," NYT (11.20.09); Eligon, "Sentence Is Sharply Increased for Lawyer Convicted of Aiding Terror," NYT (7.16.10); Susman, "Judge Extends Sentence of Attorney Who Defended Terrorist," LAT (7.16.10); Weiser, "10-Year Sentence for Lawyer in Terrorism Case Is Upheld," NYT

NOTES TO PAGES 84–87

(6.29.12); Weiser, "Judge Orders Release of Dying Lawyer Convicted of Aiding Terrorism," NYT (1.1.14). *U.S. v. Stewart*, 590 F.3d 93 (2nd Cir. 2009), 686 F.3d 156 (2nd Cir. 2012), cert. den. 134 S.Ct. 54 (2013).

96 Leonnig, "Pakistani Tortured, Her Attorney Says," WP (9.5.08); Weiser, "Court to Hear New Reports on Pakistani Scientist's Fitness for Trial," NYT (7.6.09); Weiser, "Pakistani Scientist Interrupts Competency Hearing with Repeated Outbursts," NYT (7.7.09); "Pakistani Neuroscientist Fit to Stand Trial: U.S. Judge," Reuters (7.29.09); Weiser, "Pakistani Ruled Fit to Stand U.S. Trial in October," NYT (7.30.09); "Pakistani Neuroscientist Says Boycotting U.S. Trial," Reuters (1.15.10); Hughes, "Pakistani Scientist Found Guilty of Firing at Americans," NYT (2.4.10); Weiser, "Pakistani Sentenced to 86 Years for Attack," NYT (9.24.10); Ingram, "Pakistani Woman Embraced by Islamic State Seeks to Drop U.S. Legal Appeal," Reuters (9.18.14); *United States v. Siddiqui*, 699 F.3d 690 (2nd Cir. 2012), cert. den., 133 S.Ct. 2371 (2013). See generally Scroggins (2012).

97 "Texas: Man Accused of Aiding al Qaeda," NYT (6.4.10); Schiller, "Accused Texas Terrorist Speaks Out for First Time," *Houston Chronicle* (11.6.11); "Texan Tells Court He Didn't Aim to Help al Qaeda," BG (11.8.11); Schiller, "Texan Tells Court He Did Not Want to Help al-Qaida," *Houston Chronicle* (11.8.11); Schiller, "Accused Terrorist Secretly Recorded Talking Jihad," *Houston Chronicle* (11.10.11); FBI Press Release (11.14.11); DoJ Press Release (5.24.12).

98 "Muslim Soldier at Ky. Post Objecting to War Charged with Possession of Child Pornography," WP (6.15.11); Goodman, "Soldier Held Amid Claim of Terror Plot at Fort Hood," NYT (7.29.11); Finn & Ukman, "Awol Soldier Accused of Plotting Fort Hood Attack," WP (7.29.11); Cloud, "Soldier Suspected of Planning Ft. Hood Attack," LAT (7.29.11); Fernandez & Dao, "Soldier Arrested in Suspected Bomb Plot Had Series of Disputes with Army," NYT (7.30.11); Powers & Serrano, "Ft. Hood Suspect Cries Name of Defendant in 2009 Rampage," LAT (7.30.11); "Testimony Expected to Wrap Up in Trial of Soldier Accused of Planning to Bomb Fort Hood Troops," WP (5.24.12); DoJ Press Release (5.25.12); "Soldier Guilty in Plot to Bomb a Restaurant near Ft. Hood," NYT (5.25.12); "Texas: Soldier Who Plotted Attack Gets Life Sentence," NYT (8.11.12).

99 Meyer, "New York Homes Raided in Terrorism Case," LAT (9.15.09); Hsu & Johnson, "N.Y. Homes Raided in Terror Probe," WP (9.15.09); Hernandez & Zraick, "Terrorism Task Force Raids Queens Apartments," NYT (9.15.09); Zraick & Johnston, "Man Whose Visit Touched Off Raids in Queens Denies Any Terrorist Link," NYT (9.16.09); Baker, "Reasons Unclear for Terrorist Fears," NYT (9.18.09); Rashbaum, "Terror Suspect Is Charged with Preparing Explosives," NYT (9.25.09); Johnston & Shane, "Terror Case: 'Scary' Ingredients," NYT (9.25.09); Johnson & Hsu, "Terrorism Suspect Planned Peroxide Bombs, Officials Say," WP (9.25.09); Rashbaum & Robbins, "Terror Suspect Is Held without Bail and Transferred to New York for Trial," NYT (9.26.09); Correll, "Suspected

Terrorist May Have Planned 9/11 Anniversary Attack," LAT (9.26.09); Rashbaum, "Suspect Pleads Not Guilty in Bomb-Conspiracy Case," NYT (9.30.09); Rashbaum, "Queens Man Is Charged with Murder Conspiracy and Receiving Qaeda Training," NYT (1.10.10); Sulzberger & Rashbaum, "Guilty Plea Made in Plot to Bomb New York Subway," NYT (2.23.10); Susman & Serrano, "Guilty Plea in New York Terrorism Case," LAT (2.23.10); Johnson & Hsu, "Najibullah Zazi Pleads Guilty in New York Subway Bomb Plot," WP (2.23.10); Rashbaum & Zraick, "Government Says al Qaeda Leaders Ordered New York Suicide Bombings," NYT (4.24.10); Markon, "al-Qaeda Leaders Said to Have Ordered Attack on NY Subway System," WP (4.24.10); Secret, "Homegrown Bomb Plot Is Rarity for Open Court," NYT (4.16.12); Teng, "Sister and Mother Testify at Trial of Alleged Subway Bomb Plotter," CNN (4.26.12); Marzulli, "Would-Be Subway Bomber Cries in Court as Family Describes FBI Swat Raid on Apartment," New York Daily News (4.26.12); Secret, "Terror Defendant Convicted in New York Subway Plot," NYT (5.2.12); Secret, "Man Convicted of a Terrorist Plot to Bomb Subways Is Sent to Prison for Life," NYT (11.17.12); DoJ Press Release (11.16.12).

100 DoJ Press Release (7.27.09); Johnson & Hsu, "Seven Face Terrorism Charges in North Carolina," WP (7.28.09); Meyer, "7 Held in North Carolina on Terrorism Charges," LAT (7.29.09); Robertson, "Arrests in Terror Case Bewilder Associates," NYT (7.29.09); Robertson, "Wife Disputes Jihad Charge against Husband and Sons," NYT (7.30.09); Robertson, "North Carolina Man Admits to Aiding a Jihadist Plot," NYT (2.10.11); Robertson, "North Carolina: Second Guilty Plea in Terror Case," NYT (6.8.11); Zucchino, "Jury Considers North Carolina Terrorism Case," LAT (10.12.11); Zucchino, "Three U.S. Muslims Convicted in Terrorism Case," LAT (10.14.11); Dalesio, "Brothers Sentenced for Roles in North Carolina Terror Plot," AP (12.21.11); "US Judge: 15 to 45 Years for 3 Men Convicted in Terror Ring That Plotted Jihadi Attacks," WP (1.13.12); "FBI: Man Convicted in Homegrown Terror Plot in North Carolina Wanted Witnesses against Him Beheaded," WP (1.25.12); "North Carolina Woman Held without Bond on Charge of Hiring Hit Man to Kill Witnesses in Terror Case," WP (2.3.12); Biesecker," Convicted North Carolina Terror Plotters Get Long Prison Terms," ABC News (8.25.12); Biesecker, "Man Sentenced in North Carolina Plot to Behead Terror Witness," AP (5.10.13).

101 Schwirtz & Santora, "Man Is Accused of Jihadist Plot to Bomb a Bar in Chicago," NYT (9.16.12); Meisner, "Terror Suspect Also Charged with Soliciting Murder," CT (8.30.13); "Suspected Terrorist Adel Daoud's Trial May Be Delayed," CST (12.10.15) (fitness to stand trial hearing); "Judge Blasts Repeated Delays in Jailed Man's Terrorism Trial," AP (2.24.16).

102 DoJ Press Release (7.6.16) (Yahya Farooq Mohammad).

103 Markon, "Lawyers Restored for Moussaoui," WP (11.15.03); Markon, "Court Reins in Terror Suspect," WP (12.30.03); Markon, "Terrorism Trial's Strategies Revealed," WP (11.14.05); "Moussaoui Disrupts Start

of Jury Selection," NYT (2.6.06); "Outbursts Get Moussaoui Repeatedly Ejected from Court," LAT (2.7.06); Lewis, "Moussaoui Ejected Four Times for Disrupting Jury Selection," NYT (2.7.06); "Judge Removes Moussaoui from Courtroom," NYT (2.7.06); Serrano, "Moussaoui Barred from Rest of Jury Phase after Outburst," LAT (2.15.06); Lewis, "Judge Ejects 9/11 Suspect after Outburst," NYT (2.15.06); Markon, "Judge Bars Moussaoui from Courtroom," WP (2.15.06); Serrano, "Jury Selection for 9/11 Plotter," LAT (2.16.06); Lewis, "Defendant in 9/11 Case Heeds Judge," NYT (2.16.06); Lewis, "Moussaoui Now Ties Himself to 9/11 Plot," NYT (3.28.06); Serrano, "Moussaoui Says He Was to Fly 5th Plane," LAT (3.28.06); Markon and Dwyer, "Moussaoui Says He Was to Fly 5th Plane," WP (3.28.06); Lewis, "Jurors Permit Death Penalty for Moussaoui," NYT (4.4.06); Markon & Dwyer, "Moussaoui Found Eligible for Death," WP (4.4.06); Serrano, "Terrorist a Step Closer to Death," LAT (4.4.06); Serrano, "Defiant Moussaoui Testifies," LAT (4.14.06); Markon & Dwyer, "Moussaoui Tells Court 9/11 Toll Was Too Low," WP (4.14.06); Lewis, "Moussaoui, Testifying Again, Voices Glee over Witnesses' Accounts of Sept. 11 Grief," NYT (4.14.06); Markon & Dwyer, "Sister, Experts Testify on Moussaoui's Troubled Childhood," WP (4.18.06); Lewis, "Moussaoui's Childhood Is Presented as Mitigating Factor," NYT (4.18.06); Serrano, "Moussaoui's Sisters Defend 'Sweetheart,'" LAT (4.18.06); Serrano, "Jurors Give Moussaoui Life Term," LAT (5.4.06); Lewis, "Moussaoui Given Life Term by Jury over Link to 9/11," NYT (5.4.06); Markon & Dwyer, "Jurors Reject Death Penalty for Moussaoui," WP (05.4.06); *U.S. v. Moussaoui*, Crim. No. 01-455-a (ED Va. 5.3.06); "At Sentencing, Moussaoui Is Defiant," NYT (5.4.06); Serrano, "With Judgment, Moussaoui Is Silenced at Last," LAT (5.5.06); Lewis, "A Last Moment in the Spotlight for Moussaoui," NYT (5.5.06).

104 Rotella, "Jet Passengers Overpower Would-Be Bomber," LAT (12.26.09); Meyer, "Authorities Probe Possible al Qaeda Ties to Foiled Plane Attack," LAT (12.27.09); O'Connor & Baker, "Passenger Tried to Ignite Device on Jet, U.S. Says," NYT (12.26.09); "Michigan: Man Accused in Bomb Plot Is Allowed to Be His Own Lawyer," NYT (9.14.10); Chapman, "Judge Overrules Terror Suspect's Request for Evidence," NYT (10.15.10); Davey, "Trial to Start in Attempt to Use Bomb Aboard Jet," NYT (10.4.11); Davey, "Jury Sought for Nigerian Held in Bid to Bomb Jet," NYT (10.5.11); Serrano, "Defendant in Underwear Bomb Case Has Outburst in Court," LAT (10.5.11); Finn, "Underwear Bomber Trial Set to Begin with Abdulmutallab Representing Himself," WP (10.9.11); Davey, "Would-Be Plane Bomber Pleads Guilty, Ending Trial," NYT (10.13.11); White, "Guilty Plea in Underwear Bomb Plot," WP (10.13.11); Muskal, "'Underwear Bomber' Pleads Guilty in Airline Plot," LAT (10.13.11); Bunkley, "Would-Be Plane Bomber Is Sentenced to Life in Prison," NYT (2.17.12); Bennet, "Would-Be Bomber of Jetliner Gets Life Sentence," LAT (2.17.12); Snell, "'Unchanged,' Abdulmutallab Gets 4 Life Terms," *Detroit News* (2.17.12).

105 Rodriguez & King, "Times Square Bomb Attempt: Terror Group's Claim of Responsibility Met with Skepticism," LAT (5.3.10); Hsu, Markon & Wilgoren, "Faisal Shahzad, U.S. Citizen from Pakistan, Arrested in Times Square Bomb Attempt," WP (5.4.10); Rashbaum, "U.S. Deployed Hundreds of Agents Based on Bombing Suspect's Leads," NYT (5.21.10); Weiser, "A Guilty Plea in Plot to Bomb Times Square," NYT (6.22.10); Susman, "N.Y. Bomb Defendant Pleads Guilty," LAT (6.21.10); Markon, "Shahzad Pleads Guilty in Failed Times Square Bombing, Warns of Future Attacks," WP (6.22.10); Weiser, "Call to Taliban after Bomb Attempt in Times Square," NYT (9.29.10); "Life Sentence Sought in Failed Times Square Bombing," LAT (9.30.10); Wilson, "Shahzad Gets Life Term for Times Square Bombing Attempt," NYT (10.6.10); Markon, "Would-Be Times Square Bomber Gets Life in Prison," WP (10.5.10); Baum, "Failed Times Square Bomber Faisal Shahzad Gets Life in Prison," LAT (10.6.10).

106 "Guilty Plea in New York 'Mini-al Qaeda' Cell Case," WSJ (6.18.12).

107 "U.S. Sentences Pakistani over Taliban Smuggling Plot," AFP (1.6.12).

108 Browning, "Minnesota Man Accused of Terrorism Goes on Trial Monday," MST (9.30.12); Forliti, "Families, Agents Testify in Minnesota al-Shabab Case," *San Francisco Chronicle* (10.3.12); Browning & Shah, "Recruit Describes Jihad Activities at Somalis Site," MST (10.4.12); "Witness: Minnesota Man Gave $500 to Help American Recruit of al-Shabab Terror Group in Somalia," WP (10.4.12); "Witness: Minnesota Man Accused of Aiding al-Shabab Recruiting Not Part of Planning Sessions," Fox News (10.10.12); Browning, "FBI at Somali Terror Trial: 'He Was Flip-Flopping,'" MST (10.16.12); Browning & Shah, "Minneapolis Man Found Guilty of Aiding Somalia Terrorist Group," MST (10.19.12); "Minnesota: Man Convicted of Aiding Terror in Somalia," NYT (10.18.12); Temple Raston, "Minnesota Case Re-Opens Wounds among Somalis," NPR (10.19.12); Williams, "Kamal Said Hassan, Mahamud Said Omar Sentenced in al-Shabab Terrorism Trial," Minnesota Public Radio News (5.14.13); Forliti, "Sentences Continue in Minnesota Somali Terror Case," HuffPost (5.14.13); Chanen, "Woman Pleads Guilty to Perjury in Case Involving Raising Money for Fighters in Somalia," MST (8.30.13); Furst, "Somali Convicted in Terrorist Case Can Withdraw His Appeal, Judge Decides," MST (9.4.13); "Day 8: Friend-Turned-Informant Testifies in Minnesota Terror Trial," KSTP Eyewitness News (5.19.16).

109 *U.S. v. Lindh*, 198 F.Supp.2d 739 (E.D.Va. 2002); *U.S. v. Lindh*, 227 F.Supp.2d 565 (E.D. Va. 2002); Romero & Temple-Raston (2008: chap. 1).

110 DoJ Press Release (10.27.09); Coen & St. Clair, "Two Chicago Men Charged in Terrorist Plot," LAT (10.28.09); Johnson, "2 Charged by U.S. with Plotting Attacks," WP (10.28.09); Johnston, "2 in Chicago Held in Plot to Attack in Denmark," NYT (10.28.09); DoJ Press Release (12.7.09); Thompson & Johnston, "U.S. Man Accused of Helping Plot 2008 Mumbai Attack," NYT (12.7.09); Johnson & Hsu, "U.S.

Citizen Charged with Conspiring to Aid Terrorists in 2008 Mumbai Attack," WP (12.7.09); DoJ Press Release (3.18.10); Thompson, "A Witness Overshadows a Terrorism Defendant," NYT (6.8.11); Sweeney, "Prosecutors Seek Lighter Sentence for Man Convicted in Mumbai Massacre," CT (1.23.13); Rotella, "Businessman Gets 35-Year Prison Sentence for His Role in Mumbai Terrorist Attacks in 2008," WP (1.25.13); "India Says 35 Years Isn't Enough for American Convicted in U.S. for Role in Mumbai Terror Attack," WP (1.25.13).

111 "Pennsylvania: Plea Change for 'Jihad Jane,'" NYT (1.29.11); Dale, "'Jihad Jane' Terror Suspect Pleads Guilty in Pennsylvania," WP (2.2.11); "Pennsylvania: Guilty Plea in Terror Case," NYT (3.9.11); Hall, "'Jihad Jane' Codefendant Pleads Guilty to Terrorism Charge," LAT (3.10.11); "Md. Teen Plans Guilty Plea in Terror Case in Pa.," AP (3.5.12); Shiffman, "Jihad Jane: Despite Cooperation, U.S. Seeks 'Decades' in Prison," Reuters (1.1.14); Hurdle, "10 Years for Plot to Murder Cartoonist," NYT (1.7.14); "Colorado Mother Sentenced to 8 Years in Terror Case," WP (1.9.14); "Pennsylvania: Young Immigrant Gets 5 Years in 'Jihad Jane' Conspiracy," NYT (4.18.14).

112 Shane, "2 Americans in Cases Tied to Terrorism," NYT (7.22.10); Hsu & Chandler, "Graduate of Va.'s Oakton High Charged with Trying to Join Terrorist Group," WP (7.22.10); Hsu, "Zachary Adam Chesser of N.Va. Pleads Guilty to Supporting Somali Terrorists," WP (10.21.10); Gerstein, "Second South Park Threat Suspect to Plead Guilty," Politico (2.9.12); "Founder of Radical Muslim Site Sentenced to 11½ Years for Threats to 'South Park' Creators," WP (6.22.12).

113 Rashbaum & Mekhennet, "Long Islander Helped Qaeda, Then Informed," NYT (7.23.09); Meyer, "U.S. Man Fought for al Qaeda Abroad," LAT (7.23.09); Rotella & Meyer, "A Young American's Journey into al Qaeda," LAT (7.24.09); Cowan, Lequeriere, Mekhennet, Powell & Rashbaum, "From Captured U.S. Recruit, How al Qaeda Vets and Trains Foreign Applicants," NYT (7.24.09); Meyer & Rotella, "He Forged His Own Path into al Qaeda," LAT (7.26.09); Secret, "Homegrown Bomb Plot Is Rarity for Open Court," NYT (4.16.12); Cruickshank, "Lawyers Call for Release of US Terrorist Who Helped 'Dismantle' al Qaeda," CNN (5.6.17); Cooper & Levenson, "American al Qaeda Recruit to Be Released from Prison," CNN (5.11.17).

114 Bidgood, "Boston Suspect's Friend Changes Plea to Guilty," NYT (8.20.14); Lavoie, "Marathon Bomb Suspects' Pal to Plead Guilty to Lying to FBI," AP (1.12.15).

115 Markon & Dwyer, "Moussaoui's Lies Led to 9/11, Jury Told," WP (3.7.06); Lewis, "Prosecutor Urges Death for Concealing Sept. 11 Plot," NYT (3.7.06); Serrano, "Jury Is Told Papers Link Plotter to 9/11," LAT (3.7.06); Markon & Dwyer, "Moussaoui Unfazed as 9/11 Attacks Detailed," WP (3.8.06); Serrano, "Al Qaeda Expert Offers Few Details at Moussaoui Trial," LAT (3.8.06); Lewis, "Prosecutors at Sept. 11 Trial Lay Out Activities of Hijackers," NYT (3.8.06); Dwyer & Markon, "Flight Instructor Recalls Unease with Moussaoui," WP (3.10.06); Serrano,

"Moussaoui Called a Bad Pilot, but Determined to Fly," LAT (3.10.06); Lewis, "Agent Says He Thought Moussaoui Knew about Plot," NYT (3.10.06); Markon, "Terror Case 'Delicate,' Judge Warns Prosecutors," WP (3.11.06); Lewis, "Judge Raises Possibility of Mistrial in Moussaoui Sentencing," NYT (3.13.06); "Witness Coaching Sidetracks Moussaoui Trial," LAT (3.13.06); Serrano, "Judge in Moussaoui Trial Faces a Delicate Task," LAT (3.19.06); Serrano, "Witness Lists FAA Measures Available for a pre-9/11 Tip," LAT (3.23.06); Lewis, "Case for Moussaoui Execution Seems Bolstered by 2 Witnesses," NYT (3.23.06); Lewis, "Prosecution of Moussaoui Finishes Up," NYT (3.24.06); Serrano, "FBI Agent Says 9/11 Plot Was within Grasp," LAT (3.24.06); Markon & Dwyer, "Moussaoui Shouts His Intention to Take the Stand," WP (3.24.06); Lewis, "Moussaoui Now Ties Himself to 9/11 Plot," NYT (3.28.06); Serrano, "Moussaoui Says He Was to Fly 5th Plane," LAT (3.28.06); Markon & Dwyer, "Moussaoui Says He Was to Fly 5th Plane," WP (3.28.06); Lewis, "Defense Tries to Undo Damage Moussaoui Did," NYT (3.29.06); Meyer, "A New Name in 9/11 Plot Surfaces," LAT (3.29.06); Serrano, "FBI Agent Says Moussaoui Was Looking to Make a Deal," LAT (3.29.06); Markon & Dwyer, "Moussaoui Offered to Implicate Himself," WP (3.29.06); Markon & Dwyer, "In Closing, Moussaoui Trial Rests on His Lies," WP (3.30.06); Serrano, "Moussaoui Case Goes to Jury," LAT (3.30.06); Lewis, "Moussaoui Sentencing Case Goes to the Jury," NYT (3.30.06); Lewis, "Jury Begins Deliberating Moussaoui's Fate," NYT (4.25.06); Markon & Dwyer, "Moussaoui's Fate Is in the Jury's Hands," WP (4.25.06); Serrano, "Jurors Give Moussaoui Life Term," LAT (5.4.06); Lewis, "Moussaoui Given Life Term by Jury over Link to 9/11," NYT (5.4.06); Markon & Dwyer, "Jurors Reject Death Penalty for Moussaoui," WP (5.4.06); U.S. v. Moussaoui, Crim. No. 01-455-a (ED Va. 5.3.06).

116 Duara, "Prosecutors Ask to Use Word 'Terrorist' at Trial," San Francisco Chronicle (11.7.12); Wax (2008).
117 Zraick, "Terror Suspects in New Jersey Plead Guilty," NYT (3.4.11).
118 Weiser, "Bin Laden's Son-in-Law Seeks a New Lawyer, but There's a Snag," NYT (5.21.13); Wachtel, "Lawyer Says bin Laden's Son-in-Law Was Disoriented during Interrogation," Fox News (10.8.13); Weiser, "In Terrorism Case, New Path to Testimony from 9/11 Suspect," NYT (2.14.14); Weiser, "Bin Laden Relative's Trial May Fuel Debate over Trying Terrorism Cases in Civilian Courts," NYT (3.3.14); Hurtado, "Bin Laden Son-in-Law Jury Won't Hear of Mistaken Identity," Bloomberg (3.2.14); Weiser, "Bin laden Aide Began Qaeda Propaganda Day after 9/11, U.S. Says," NYT (3.6.14); Weiser, "Trial Judge Will Not Allow 9/11 Architect's Testimony," NYT (3.19.14); Weiser, "Lawyers Sum Up Cases at Bin Laden Relative's Trial," NYT (3.25.14); Weiser, "Jurors Convict Abu Ghaith, bin Laden Son-in-Law, in Terror Case," NYT (3.27.14).
119 Mitchell, "After Five Years without Trial, Uzbek Terror Suspect Jamshid Muhtorov Is Ordered Released from Colorado Custody," Denver Post

(6.23.17); Mitchell, "Federal Appeals Court Halts Release of Colorado Terror Suspect," *Denver Post* (6.29.17).

120 Markon, "Moussaoui Prosecutors Defy Judge," WP (7.15.03); Markon, "Moussaoui Granted Access to Witnesses," WP (8.30.03); Markon, "U.S. Refuses to Produce Al Qaeda Officials as Witnesses," WP (9.11.03); Markon, "Terrorism Trial's Strategies Revealed," WP (11.14.05); Lewis, "Jury in Virginia Will Decide Life or Death for Moussaoui," NYT (2.6.06); Serrano, "Moussaoui Trial Strategy Outlined," LAT (2.6.06); Dwyer, "9/11 Families to Watch Moussaoui Face Fate," WP (2.6.06); Markon, "The Man Who Wasn't There on 9/11," WP (3.4.06); Serrano, "Moussaoui Barred from Rest of Jury Phase after Outburst," LAT (2.15.06); Lewis, "Judge Ejects 9/11 Suspect after Outburst," NYT (2.15.06); Markon, "Judge Bars Moussaoui from Courtroom," WP (2.15.06); Serrano, "Jury Selection for 9/11 Plotter," LAT (2.16.06); Lewis, "Defendant in 9/11 Case Heeds Judge," NYT (2.16.06); "Moussaoui Jury Pool Nears Completion," NYT (2.23.06); "Jury for Moussaoui Penalty Trial Is Seated," NYT (3.6.06); Dwyer & Markon, "Flight Instructor Recalls Unease with Moussaoui," WP (3.10.06); Serrano, "Moussaoui Called a Bad Pilot, but Determined to Fly," LAT (3.10.06); Lewis, "Agent Says He Thought Moussaoui Knew about Plot," NYT (3.10.06); Markon, "Terror Case 'Delicate,' Judge Warns Prosecutors," WP (3.11.06); Lewis, "Judge Raises Possibility of Mistrial in Moussaoui Sentencing," NYT (3.13.06); "Witness Coaching Sidetracks Moussaoui Trial," LAT (3.13.06); Markon & Dwyer, "Judge Halts Terror Trial," WP (3.24.06); Savage & Schmitt, "Moussaoui Case Is Latest Misstep in Prosecutions," LAT (3.14.06); Serrano, "Judge Weighs Next Steps in Moussaoui Trial," LAT (3.14.06); Lewis, "Judge Calls Halt to Penalty Phase of Terror Trial," NYT (3.14.06); Markon & Dwyer, "Federal Witnesses Banned in 9/11 Trial," WP (3.15.06); Lewis, "Judge Penalizes Moussaoui Prosecutors by Barring Major Witnesses," NYT (3.15.06); Labaton & Wald, "Lawyer Thrust into Spotlight after Misstep in Terror Case," NYT (3.15.06); Serrano, "Judge Curbs Terror Trial," LAT (3.15.06); Markon, Morello & Branigin, "Lawyer in 9/11 Case Placed on Leave," WP (3.16.06); Serrano & Neuman, "U.S. Tries to Salvage Unraveling 9/11 Trial," LAT (3.16.06); Liptak, "Crossing a Fine Line on Witness Coaching," NYT (3.16.06); Lewis & Wald, "Moussaoui Prosecutors Seek Security Officials' Testimony," NYT (3.16.06); Serrano, "9/11 Prosecutors Granted a Reprieve," LAT (3.18.06); Lewis, "Judge Gives Prosecutors New Chance in Terror Case," NYT (3.18.06); Lewis, "Defense Tries to Undo Damage Moussaoui Did," NYT (3.29.06); Meyer, "A New Name in 9/11 Plot Surfaces," LAT (3.29.06); Serrano, "FBI Agent Says Moussaoui Was Looking to Make a Deal," LAT (3.29.06); Markon & Dwyer, "Moussaoui Offered to Implicate Himself," WP (3.29.06); Lewis, "One Verdict Decided, 9/11 Jury Faces Second," NYT (4.5.06); Serrano, "Jurors Will Relive 9/11 in Life-or-Death Case," LAT (4.6.06); "9/11 Recording Can Be Played, Judge Says," NYT (4.6.06); Markon & Dwyer, "Moussaoui Gets Some Unusual Help," WP (4.20.06); Lewis, "Jury Hears

9/11 Relatives against Killing Moussaoui," NYT (4.20.06); Serrano, "Families of 9/11 Victims Testify for Moussaoui," LAT (4.20.06); Serrano, "Jurors Give Moussaoui Life Term," LAT (5.4.06); Lewis, "Moussaoui Given Life Term by Jury over Link to 9/11," NYT (5.4.06); Markon & Dwyer, "Jurors Reject Death Penalty for Moussaoui," WP (5.4.06); U.S. v. Moussaoui, Crim. No. 01-455-a (ED Va. 5.3.06); "At Sentencing, Moussaoui Is Defiant," NYT (5.4.06); Serrano, "With Judgment, Moussaoui Is Silenced at Last," LAT (5.5.06); Lewis, "A Last Moment in the Spotlight for Moussaoui," NYT (5.5.06). U.S. v. Moussaoui, 591 F.3d 263 (4th Cir. 2010).

121 "Michigan: Man Accused in Bomb Plot Is Allowed to Be His Own Lawyer," NYT (9.14.10); Chapman, "Judge Overrules Terror Suspect's Request for Evidence," NYT (10.15.10); "Underwear Bomber Seeks Lesser Sentence Than Life," Reuters (2.13.12).

122 Weiser, "Bin Laden's Son-in-Law Seeks a New Lawyer, but There's a Snag," NYT (5.21.13); "N.Y. Judge Sees No Evidence of Spying in Terror Case," USA Today (7.8.13); "Judge Says Statements by Bin Laden's Son-in-Law Can Be Used in Terrorism Case," NYT (11.27.13); Weiser, "Lawyers in Terrorism Case Seek Access to 9/11 Suspect," NYT (2.5.14); Weiser, "In Terrorism Case, New Path to Testimony from 9/11 Suspect," NYT (2.14.14); Weiser, "Bin Laden's Relative's Lawyers Claims Mistaken Identity as Trial Nears," NYT (2.28.14); Weiser, "Bin Laden Relative's Trial May Fuel Debate over Trying Terrorism Cases in Civilian Courts," NYT (3.3.14); Hurtado, "Bin Laden Son-in-Law Jury Won't Hear of Mistaken Identity," Bloomberg (3.2.14); Weiser, "Juror Loses Job for Serving in Terror Trial," NYT (3.8.14); Weiser, "Shoe-Bomb Plot Revisited at Trial of Bin Laden Relative," NYT (3.11.14); Weiser, "At Trial of Bin Laden Relative, Witness Describes Meeting 9/11 Mastermind," NYT (3.11.14); Weiser, "Prosecutors Argue against Allowing 9/11 Mastermind's Testimony," NYT (3.18.14); Weiser, "Trial Judge Will Not Allow 9/11 Architect's Testimony," NYT (3.19.14); Moynihan, "Prominent Lawyer Will Plead Guilty to Impeding the I.R.S.," NYT (4.14.14); Stempel, "Bin Laden Son-in-Law; US Conviction Upheld; U.S. Says 'Justice Done,'" Reuters (9.28.17).

123 Kershaw, "Terrorist in '99 U.C. Case Is Sentenced to 22 Years," NYT (7.28.05); "Appellate Panel to Hear Arguments in LAX Millennium Bomb Plot Sentencing," LAT (11.13.06); Weinstein, "Court Voids Sentence in LAX Plot," LAT (1.17.07); Steinhauser, "Appeals Court Vacates Term of Algerian in Bomb Plot," NYT (1.17.07); "Washington: Judge Won't Increase Plotter's Sentence," NYT (12.4.08); Murphy, "Would-Be LAX Bomber Is Resentenced to 22 Years," LAT (12.4.08); Schwartz, "Appeals Court Throws Out Sentence in Bombing Plot, Calling It Too Light," NYT (2.3.10); Lovett, "Appeals Court Overturns Millennium Bomb-Plot Sentence," NYT (3.13.12); Johnson, "New Sentence Is Imposed in Bomb Plot from 1999," NYT (10.25.12); U.S. v. Ressam, 474 F.3d 597 (9th Cir. 2007), rev'd, 128 S.Ct. 1858

(2008), 538 F.3d 1166 (9th Cir. 2010), 629 F.3d 793 (9th Cir. 2010), 679 F.3d 1069 (9th Cir. 2012).

124 *United States* v. *Abu Ali*, 2006 WL 1102835 (E.D.Va 2006), rev'd, 528 F.3rd 210 (4th Cir. 2008), cert. den., 555 U.S. 1170 (2009); 410 Fed. Appx. 673 (4th Cir. 2011).

125 Mulvihill, "Trial to Begin for Men Accused of Planning to Kill Soldiers on New Jersey Military Base," LAT (9.29.08).

126 Seelye, "Accord Calls for Jury Pool of 2,000 in Boston Bombing Trial," NYT (9.13.14).

127 Lichtblau, "From Advocacy to Terrorism, a Line Blurs," NYT (6.5.05); Dahlburg, "Ex-Professor, 3 Others Face Terrorism Trial," LAT (6.6.05); Hsu & Eggen, "Fla. Professor Is Acquitted in Case Seen as Patriot Act Test," WP (12.7.05); Lichtblau, "Not Guilty Verdicts in Florida Terror Trial Are Setback for U.S.," NYT (12.7.05); Licthblau, "Professor in Terror Case May Face Deportation," NYT (12.8.05); Whoriskey, "Ex-Professor Won Court Case but Not His Freedom," WP (12.14.05).

128 Shennon, "2 Egyptians Indicted on Explosives Charge," NYT (9.2.07); Whoriskey, "YouTube Bomb Video Brings Scrutiny," WP (10.1.07); "Explosives Suspect Denied Separate Trial," WP (11.30.07); "South: Florida: F.B.I. Backs Students on Explosives," NYT (2.1.08); "FBI Says 'Bombs' Were Fireworks," LAT (2.1.08); "Florida: Plea Deal in Bomb Video Case," NYT (6.19.08); "Florida: Verdict in Explosives Case," NYT (4.4.09); "Florida: After Acquittal, An Arrest," NYT (4.7.09); "Florida: Jurors Denounce Arrest," NYT (4.16.09).

129 Von Zielbauer, "Five Are Convicted of Conspiring to Attack Fort Dix," NYT (12.23.08); Barnes, "Five Convicted of Plotting to Kill Ft. Dix Soldiers," LAT (12.23.08).

130 Preston, "Lawyer Convicted in Terror Case Lied on Stand, A Juror Says," NYT (10.21.06).

131 Finn, "Ahmed Ghailani, Gitmo Detainee, Acquitted of All but 1 Charge in N.Y.," WP (11.18.10); Weiser, "Detainee Acquitted on Most Counts in '98 Bombing," NYT (11.18.10); Williams & Baum, "U.S. Civilian Court Acquits Ex-Guantánamo Detainee of all Major Terrorism Charges," LAT (11.18.10).

132 "Terrorism Jury Balks," NYT (10.4.07); Krikorian, "Holy Land Verdict Is Sealed," LAT (10.19.07); Krikorian, "Mistrial in Holy Land Terrorism Financing Case," LAT (10.23.07); Whoriskey, "Mistrial Declared in Islamic Charity Case," WP (10.23.07); Eaton, "U.S. Prosecution of Muslim Group Ends in Mistrial," NYT (10.23.07); Liptak & Eaton, "Financing Mistrial Adds to U.S. Missteps in Terror Prosecutions," NYT (10.24.07).

133 Preston, "With 9/11 Trial Set to Begin, Prosecution Appeal Delays It," NYT (6.1.05); Preston, "Prosecutors Seek Removal of the Judge in a Terror Case," NYT (12.13.05); "Mistrial in San Diego Student's 9/11 Perjury Case," LAT (5.5.06); Brick & Garland, "Mistrial for Student Accused of Lying to 9/11 Inquiry," NYT (5.5.06); Brick & Garland,

"After Mistrial, Another Prologue Begins in Epic Perjury Case Related to 9/11," NYT (5.6.06).

134 Chesney (2005; 2007a).

135 Nakashima, "U.S. Charges Iran-Linked Hackers with Targeting Banks, New York Dam," WP (3.24.16).

136 Rubin, "LAX Gunman Who Targeted TSA Officers Is Sentenced to Life in Prison," LAT (11.7.16).

137 Botelho & Ellis, "San Bernardino Shooting Investigated as 'Act of Terrorism,'" CNN (12.5.15); Finnegan, "Last Days," *The New Yorker* (2.22.16).

138 Caplan & Hayden, "At Least 50 Dead in Orlando Gay Club Shooting," ABC News (6.12.16).

139 Santora, Rashbaum, Baker & Goldman, "Ahmad Khan Rahami Is Arrested in Manhattan and New Jersey Bombings," NYT (9.19.16).

140 Smith & Pérez-Peña, "Friends Say Minnesota Attacker Was 'Normal American Kid,'" NYT (9.20.16).

141 "Alaskan Veteran Is Indicted in Fort Lauderdale Airport Rampage," NYT (1.27.17).

142 Kilcannon & Goldstein, "Sayfullo Saipov, the Suspect in the New York Terror Attack, and His Past," NYT (10.31.17).

143 NYU Law School (2011: 19); Zabel & Benjamin (2008: 32); HRW and Columbia Law School Human Rights Institute (2014: 62). The Supreme Court upheld the statute: Holder v. Humanitarian Law Project, 130 S.Ct. 2705 (2010), a case that did not involve the "war on terror."

144 Goodnough & Shane, "Padilla Is Guilty on All Charges in Terror Trial," NYT (8.17.07).

145 NYU Law School (2011: 4, 26); HRW and Columbia Law School Human Rights Institute (2014: 21, 41, 45, 47, 54); Aaronson, "The Informants," *Mother Jones* (8.11); Al Jazeera, "Informants" (2014); Lichtblau, "F.B.I. Steps Up Use of Stings in ISIS Cases," NYT (6.7.16). "U.S. Hands Down Longest-Ever Sentence for ISIL Support," Al Jazeera (3.18.16) (Mufid Elfgeeh; recorded conversations with two paid informants); Ibrahim & Yen, "Alleged ISIS Conspirator Said to Have Bragged about Ability to Take Down Minnesota State Police Planes," Minnesota Public Radio (12.22.15) (Abdirizak Warsame); Mueller, "Rochester Man Charged with Planning Attack on Behalf of ISIS," NYT (1.1.16) (Emanuel I. Lutchman); O'Brien, "Milwaukee Man Charged with Weapons Possession, Allegedly Planned Mass Shooting," Reuters (1.26.16) (Samy Mohamed Hamzeh); Mazzetti, "Virginia Man Is Accused of Trying to Join ISIS," NYT (1.17.16) (Joseph Hassan Farrokh and Mahmoud Amin Mohamed Elhassan); DoJ Press Release (2.23.16) (John T. Boker); "Washington: Gun Charges for Man Said to Back ISIS," NYT (2.9.16) (Daniel Seth Franey); Stein, "American Snitch: Inside the Life of a Counterterrorism Informant," *Newsweek* (2.21.16) (Saeed Torres, who informed on Tarik Shah, Khalif Ali Al-Akili); Goldstein, "F.B.I. Agent Testifies about Conversation with Suspect in ISIS Case," NYT (3.3.16) (Tairod Pugh); DoJ Press Release (3.9.16) (Cheng Le);

Shane, "An Amateur vs. ISIS: A Car Salesman Investigates and Ends Up in Prison," NYT (4.24.16) (Toby Lopez); Weaver, "Man Accused of Plot to Blow Up Synagogue," MH (5.3.16) (James G. Medina); Lissarrague, "Day 8: Friend-Turned-Informant Testifies in Minnesota Terror Trial," ABC (5.19.16) (Abdirahman Bashir informed on Abrirahman Daud and Mohamed Farah); Kheel, "Ex-National Guardsman Arrested, Accused of Offering to Help ISIS Attack U.S.," *The Hill* (7.5.16) (Mohamed Bailor Jalloh); DoJ Press Release (7.8.16) (Haris Qamar); Kearney, "U.S. Counterterrorism Agents Arrest Michigan Man with Grenades," Reuters (8.2.16) (Sebastian Gregerson aka Abrurrahman bin Mikaayl); DoJ Press Release (8.3.16) (Nicholas Young); DoJ Press Release (8.4.16) (Jamal Hendricks); Zavadski, "FBI Agent Apparently Egged on 'Draw Muhammad' Shooter," Daily Beast (8.4.16) (Elton Simpson); Rector, "Maryland Man Accused of Plotting Attack on U.S. Service Member for ISIS," BS (10.4.16) (Nelash Mohamed Das); Hussain, "18-Year-Old Arrested in Terrorism Charges Is Mentally 'Like a Child,'" The Intercept (8.3.16) (Mahin Khan); Stack, "Brooklyn Man Arrested, Accused of Supporting IS," NYT (11.22.16) (Mohamed Rafik Naji); Weiner, "20-year-old Says He Planned ISIS Terror Attacks in Virginia, North Carolina," WP (11.29.16) (Justin Sullivan); Daugherty, "Suffolk Man Charged with Trying to Support Islamic State Wanted Shootout with FBI, Feds Say," *Virginian Pilot* (1.4.17) (Lionel Nelson Williams aka Harun Ash-Shababi).

146 Hoffman et al. (2015).
147 But see Austen, "Canada Judge Rules that Police Entrapped Couple in Bomb Plot," NYT (7.30.16).
148 Weiser, "Departing Judge Offers Blunt Defense of Ruling in Stop-and-Frisk Case," NYT (5.2.16).
149 "Suspected Terrorist Adel Daoud's Trial May Be Delayed," CST (12.10.15) (hearing on fitness to stand trial); Hurdle & Pérez Peña, "Gunman Said He Shot Philadelphia Officer for ISIS, Police Say," NYT (1.9.16) (Edward Archer: mental illness, criminal convictions); Chambers, "Alleged ISIS Supporter Indicted on Non-Terror Charges," *Detroit News* (2.17.16) (Khalil abu-Rayyan: mental illness); Mueller, "Rochester Man Charged with Planning Attack on Behalf of ISIS," NYT (1.1.16) (Emanuel I. Lutchman: mental illness); "N.Y. Man Admits Planning Islamic State-Inspired New Year's Eve Attack," Reuters (8.11.16) (Lutchman); Hussain, "18-Year-Old Arrested in Terrorism Charges Is Mentally 'Like a Child,'" *The Intercept* (8.3.16) (Mahin Khan).
150 Yourish, Buchanan and Williams, "ISIS in America," NYT (2.5.16) (analysis of 82 convictions).
151 Aaronson, "The Released," *The Intercept* (4.20.17).
152 Turner & Schulhofer (2005) (secrecy can be reconciled with due process); Zabel & Benjamin (2008: 2); Abel (2011) (José Padilla trial).
153 Laguardia (2013: 201); U.S. Department of Justice, Office of the Inspector General: Audit Division, The Department of Justice's Internal Controls over Terrorism Reporting (2007); Chesney (2007c: 858–72);

NYU Law School Center on Law and Security, Terrorist Trial Report Card: September 11, 2001–September 11, 2009 (January 2010), September 11, 2001–September 11, 2010 (2010), September 11, 2001–September 11, 2011 (2011); TRAC/FBI, New Findings (12.5.06).

154 Laguardia (2013: 190, 212); NYU Law School (2011: 2, 7–8, 12); Chesney (2007c: 872–88); Zabel & Benjamin (2008: 26); "ISIS in America," NYT (2.5.16); Goldman, Yang & Muyskens, "The Islamic State's Suspected Inroads into America," WP (5.12.16).

155 Barakat, "U.S. Charges Defense Contractor with Afghan Killing," WP (11.20.08); Maraca, "Army Contractor Pleads Guilty in Detainee Shooting," WP (2.4.09); White, "No Jail Time in Retribution Killing Overseas," WP (5.9.09).

156 Zucchino, "Afghans Growing War of U.S. Security Contractors," LAT A1 (8.13.09); Department of Justice Press Release (1.7.10); Risen, "Two Former Blackwater Guards Are Charged with Murder in an Afghan Shooting," NYT A10 (1.8.10); Markon, "Two Defense Contractors Indicted in Shooting of Afghans," WP A3 (1.8.10); Zucchino, "Iraqis Settle Lawsuits over Blackwater Shootings," LAT (1.8.10); Dujardin, "Murder Trial of Military Contractors in Afghanistan Ends in Mistrial," LAT (9.27.10); Risen, "Efforts to Prosecute Blackwater Are Collapsing," NYT (10.21.10); "Virginia: Manslaughter Verdicts in Death of Afghan Civilian," NYT (3.12.11); Vergaris, "Blackwater Contractors Convicted in Virginia Trial," WP (3.12.11); Sizemore, "2nd Ex-Blackwater Contractor Gets 30 Months for Manslaughter," *Virginian Pilot* (6.28.11).

157 Bergengruen, "Lindsey Graham Wants NY Bomber Treated as Enemy Combatant," McClatchy DC (9.20.16); Ruiz, Goldman & Apuzzo, "Terror Suspect Brought to U.S. for Trial, Breaking from Trump Rhetoric," NYT (7.22.17).

158 Montemayor & Koumpilova, "Terror Suspects Will Test Deradicalization Program," MST (3.2.16); McKelvey, "Terrorism Trial Highlights U.S. Deradicalization Effort," BBC News (6.2.16); Montemayor, "Minnesota Judge, Attorneys Looking at Other ISIL-Related Cases ahead of Local Sentencings," MST (8.12.16); Montemayor, "'I'm Not a Terrorist,' Minnesota ISIL Case Defendant Tells Judge in a Letter," MST (11.4.16); DoJ Press Release (11.14.16) (Abdullahi Yusuf). But he sentenced some to long terms: Yen, "Third Isis Sentence of the Day: 10 Years," MPR News (11.15.16).

159 See the Table A1 in the Appendix.

160 Barrett, "Trial to Begin Monday for Suspect in Manhattan, New Jersey 2016 Bomb Spree," WP (10.2.17); DoJ Press Release (10.16.17); Wilson, "New Jersey Man Is Found Guilty on All Counts in Chelsea Bomb Attack," NYT (10.17.17).

161 Savage & Goldman, "At Trial, a Focus on the Facts, Not the Politics, of Benghazi," NYT (10.1.17); Savage, "At Benghazi Trial, Attack Survivors Recount a Night of Horror," NYT (10.3.17); Wilson, "Key Evidence in

Chelsea Bombing Trial: Articles on Building Bombs," NYT (10.3.17); Sirota, "Benghazi Trial Enters Second Week," HRF (10.19.17).

162 DoJ Press Release (10.30.17).

163 Qiu, "Trump Calls Terrorism Trial Process 'A Joke,' Despite Hundreds of Convictions," NYT (11.2.17); Savage, "Nettlesome Legal Question in a Suggestion to 'Send Him to Gitmo,'" NYT (11.2.17); Berman & Zapotosky, "Investigators Probe New York Attack Suspect's Communications While Trump Calls for Death Penalty," WP (11.2.17); Watkins, "Donald Trump Laments He's 'Not Supposed' to Influence DoJ, FBI," CNN (11.3.17); Rucker & Zapotosky, "Trump Breaches Boundaries by Saying DOJ Should Be 'Going After' Democrats," WP (10.4.17); Savage & Goldman, "Following Trump's Lead, Republicans Grown Quiet on Guantánamo," NYT (11.5.17); "No, "Guantánamo Is Not a 'Very Fine Place' to Hold Terrorism Suspects," WP (11.5.17).

CHAPTER 3 COURTS-MARTIAL

1 For historical accounts of military justice, see Allison (2007); Nelson (2008). For accounts of crimes, see Wood (2006); Roberts (2013); Gezari (2013).

2 On the role of contractors, see Singer (2003); Chesterman & Lehnhardt (2007).

3 McGirk, "Collateral Damage or Civilian Massacre in Haditha?" *Time* (3.19.06); Ghosh, "After Haditha, the Silence," *Time* (3.23.06); McGirk, "One Morning in Haditha," *Time* (3.27.06); Ghosh, "Too Little, Too Late on Haditha?" *Time* (4.11.06); Shanker, "Inquiry Implies Civilian Deaths in Iraq Topped Initial Report," NYT (5.19.06); Perry, "House to Look into Probe of Pendleton Marines," LAT (5.20.06); Shanker, Schmitt & Oppel, "Military Expected to Report Marines Killed Iraqi Civilians," NYT (5.26.06); Ricks, "Top Marine Visits Iraq as Probe of Deaths Widens," WP (5.26.06); Cooper, "The Haditha Scandal's Other Casualty," *Time* (5.26.06); Perry & Barnes, "Photos Indicate Civilians Slain Execution-Style," LAT (5.27.06); Knickmeyer, "In Haditha, Memories of a Massacre," WP (5.27.06); Perry, "Marines Held in the Slaying of Iraqi Man," LAT (5.28.06); Duffy, "The Shame of Kilo Company," *Time* (5.28.06); Ghosh, "On Scene: Picking Up the Pieces in Haditha," *Time* (5.29.06); Donnelly, "Did Marines Kill 'In Cold Blood'?" *Time* (5.29.06); Oppel & Mahmoud, "Witness Accounts Tie Marines to Killings of 24 Iraqi Civilians," NYT (5.29.06); Spiegel, "Lawmakers Suspect Cover-Up by Senior Officers," LAT (5.29.06); Marshall, "On a Marine Base, Disbelief over Charges," NYT (5.30.06); "Thorough Inquiry on Marines Promised," LAT (5.30.06); Schmitt & Cloud, "Files Contradict Account of Raid in Iraq," NYT (5.31.06); "What Happened at the Iraqi My Lai?" LAT (5.31.06); Richter, "Iraq Envoy Wants Slaying Inquiry," LAT A18

(5.31.06); Oppel, "More Than 40 Are Killed in Iraqi Insurgent Attacks," NYT (5.31.10); Stack & Salman, "A Town Awoke to Slaughter," LAT (6.1.06); Stolberg, "In First Comments on Case, Bush Promises Justice in Military Investigation of Civilian Deaths," NYT (6.1.06); White & Ricks, "Investigators of Haditha Shootings Look to Exhume Bodies," WP (6.2.06); Perry, "Murder Charges Likely for Marines in Iraq Deaths," LAT (6.2.06); Oppel, "Premier Accuses U.S. of Attacking Civilians in Iraq," NYT (6.2.06); Stack & Roug, "More Ethics Training Ordered for GIs in Iraq," LAT (6.2.06); Cloud & Schmitt, "Initial Response to Marine Raid Draws Scrutiny," NYT (6.3.06); "A Hard Look at Haditha," NYT (6.4.06); Ricks, "In Haditha Killings, Details Came Slowly," WP (6.4.06); Cloud & Schmitt, "Senators Press Pentagon on Haditha Hearings," NYT (6.7.06); White, "Marine Says Rules Were Followed," WP (6.11.06); Perry, "Lawyers Defend Marines in Raid," LAT (6.12.06); Tyson, "General Leading Haditha Probe Known for Integrity," WP (6.16.06); Broder, "Contradictions Cloud Inquiry into 24 Iraqi Deaths," NYT (6.17.06); Barnes & Perry, "Marines Missed 'Red Flags,' Study Finds," LAT (6.21.06); Schmitt & Cloud, "General Faults Marine Response," NYT (7.8.06); Ricks, "Haditha Probe Finds Leadership Negligent," WP (7.9.06); Walker, "Marine Corps Stays Silent on Contents of Haditha Report," NCT (7.14.06); Cloud, "Inquiry Suggests Marines Excised Files on Killings," NYT (8.18.06); Ricks, "Officer Called Haditha Routine," WP (8.19.06); Bennett, "Sergeant in Haditha Case Was Recommended for Medal," NCT (8.30.06); White, "Family Stands by a Marine under Investigation," WP (11.22.06); Von Zielbauer, "At Least 5 Marines Are Expected to Be Charged in Haditha Deaths," NYT (12.6.06); Von Zielbauer, "Captain to Face Charges in Marines' Killings of Iraqis, Lawyer Says," NYT (12.20.06); Von Zielbauer & Marshall, "Marines Charge 4 with Murder of Iraq Civilians," NYT (12.22.06); White & Geis, "4 Marines Charged in Haditha Killings," WP (12.22.06); White, "Death in Haditha," WP (1.6.07); Von Zielbauer, "U.S. Inquiry Backs Charges of Killing by Marines in Iraq," NYT (1.7.07); "Witness Accounts of Attack on Civilians Revealed," LAT (1.7.07); Bennett, "Haditha Lawyers Protest Leak, Claims News Reports Could Taint Jury Pool," NCT (1.15.07); Walker, "Hearing Set for High-Ranking Marine Charged in Haditha Case," NCT (3.6.07); Walker, "Attorneys for Accused Haditha Officer Fire Another Salvo," NCT (4.3.07); White, "Charges Against Marine in Iraq Killings Dropped," WP (4.18.07); Perry, "Marine Prosecutors Provide Immunity in Exchange for Testimony on Iraqi Killings," LAT (4.20.07); White, "Marine Officer Receives Immunity in Haditha Killings Case," WP (4.20.07); Von Zielbauer, "Marine Officer to Testify on Iraq Killings in Exchange for Immunity," NYT (4.21.07); White, "Report on Haditha Condemns Marines," WP (4.21.07); Von Zielbauer, "Military Cites 'Negligence' in Aftermath of Iraq Killings," NYT (4.22.07); Watkins, "Civilian-Death Report Faults Command," WP (4.24.07); Walker, "Marine's Attorneys Ask for Investigation in Haditha Case," NCT (4.25.07); Walker, "Haditha Case Set to Unfold Starting May 8," NCT

(4.27.07); Walker, "Officer Testifies Marines Did Nothing Wrong at Haditha," NCT (5.8.07); Walker, "Marine 1st Sergeant Says He Pressed for Haditha Probe," NCT (5.9.07); Von Zielbauer, "Officer Says Civilian Toll in Haditha Was a Shock," NYT (5.9.07); "Officer Defends Action that Killed 24 Iraqis," LAT (5.9.07); "Marine Tells of Civilians Shot to Death," LAT (5.10.07); Walker, "General Testifies Haditha Killings Appeared as Conflict Deaths," NCT (5.11.07); Geis, "Haditha Deaths Raised No Red Flags," WP (5.11.07); Von Zielbauer, "Marine Says His Staff Misled Him on Killings," NYT (5.11.07); Walker, "Legal Affairs Officer: Haditha Decision Not Criminal," NCT (5.14.07); Walker, "Accused Haditha Officer Tells Court He Did Nothing Wrong," NCT (5.15.07); Walker, "Haditha Hearing Shows Leadership Mind-Set," NCT (5.16.07); Von Zielbauer, "Lawyers on Haditha Panel Peer into Fog of War," NYT (5.17.07); Walker, "Request for Generals at Next Haditha Hearing Denied," NCT (5.22.07); Watkins, "Marine Describes Haditha Death Scene," WP (5.30.07); Walker, "Iraqis Told Haditha Deaths Were Unfortunate," NCT (5.31.07); Von Zielbauer, "2 Marines Deny Suspecting Haditha War Crimes," NYT (5.31.07); Perry, "Marine Recalls Scene of Haditha Killings," LAT (5.31.07); Walker, "Experts Say Haditha Killings Demanded Immediate Probe," NCT (6.1.07); Walker, "General Says Chessani Should Have Told Him More," NCT (6.1.07); Von Zielbauer, "Lawyers in Haditha Case Say Gunshots, not Grenades, Killed Many Victims," NYT (6.1.07); Perry, "Haditha Killings Detailed at Hearing," LAT (6.1.07); Walker, "General Questions Whether Commander Fully Detailed Haditha Killings," NCT (6.2.07); Geis, "Iraqis Sought Probe of Killings," WP (6.2.07); Von Zielbauer, "General Says Bosses Knew of '05 Killings in Iraqi Town," NYT (6.2.07); Perry, "General Blames Report in Haditha Case," LAT (6.2.07); Perry, "Marine Defends His Commander," LAT (6.3.07); Von Zielbauer, "At Trial, Colonel's Role in Haditha is Questioned," NYT (6.3.07); Walker, "Legal Officer Says No One Questioned Haditha Deaths," NCT (6.5.07); Perry, "No 'Bad Guys' Amid the 19 Bodies," LAT (6.5.07); Perry, "Marines Balked at Haditha Inquiry," LAT (6.6.07); Perry, "Haditha Deaths Were Seen as Combat-Related," LAT (6.7.07); Von Zielbauer, "Web Sites Rally Support for G.I.'s in Legal Trouble," NYT (7.22.07); Perry, "Marine Says He Erased Photos of Slain Iraqis," LAT (6.8.07); Von Zielbauer, "At Haditha Hearing, Dueling Views of a Battalion Commander," NYT (6.8.07); "Haditha Investigator Calls for a Dismissal," NYT (6.10.07); Perry, "Marine Denies Wrongdoing in Haditha Case," LAT A4 (6.10.07); Walker, "Accused Haditha Shooter Gets Day in Court," NCT (6.12.07); Perry, "Officer's Role at Haditha Argued," LAT (6.12.07); Walker, "Haditha Deaths Came on Day of Chaotic Battle," NCT (6.13.07); Von Zielbauer, "U.S. Inquiry Hurt by Iraq Violence, Investigators Say," NYT (6.13.07); Walker, "Accused Marine Says He Acted Properly in Haditha Shootings," NCT (6.14.07); Walker, "Hearing Officer Challenges Haditha Prosecution," NCT (6.15.07); Von Zielbauer, "Forensic Experts Testify That 4 Iraqis Killed by Marines Were Shot from a Few Feet Away," NYT (6.15.07);

Perry, "Men in Haditha Pointed Guns, Marine Says," LAT (6.15.07); Von
Zielbauer, "A Marine Tutorial on Media 'Spin,'" NYT (6.25.07); Perry,
"Details Emerge of a Deadly Day in Haditha," LAT (7.2.07); Walker,
"Haditha Hearing Officer Has More Work Ahead," NCT (7.11.07);
White, "Investigator Urges Clearing of Marine in Killings at Haditha,"
WP (7.12.07); Von Zielbauer, "Web Sites Rally Support for G.I.'s in Legal
Trouble," NYT (7.22.07); Watkins, "Marine Said Deadly Force in Haditha
Seemed Appropriate," WP (7.17.07); Figueroa, "Agent Says Pendleton
Marine Knew He Shot Child," NCT (7.19.07); Figueroa, "Marine: 'I
Didn't Know There Was Women and Children,'" NCT (7.24.07); Perry,
"Defining the Time to Kill," LAT (7.31.07); White, "Charges Dropped
Against 2 Marines in Haditha Killings," WP (8.10.07); Perry, "Marine's
War Crimes Hearing to Begin," LAT (8.30.07); White, "Haditha
Investigator Urges Dropping of Marine's Case," WP (8.24.07); Von
Zielbauer, "Inquiry Urges End to Charges Against Marines," NYT
(8.24.07); Von Zielbauer, "Marines' Trials in Iraq Killings Are Withering,"
NYT (8.30.07); Perry, "Marine's War Crimes Hearing to Begin," LAT
(8.30.07); Vick, "Witness Describes Iraq Killing," WP (9.1.07); Von
Zielbauer, "At Marine's Hearing, Testament to Violence," NYT (9.1.07);
Perry, "3 Officers Censured in Iraqi Deaths," LAT (9.6.07); White, "3
Marine Officers Censured in Haditha Case," AP (6.9.07); Von Zielbauer,
"General and 2 Colonels Censured for Poor Investigation into Haditha
Killings," NYT (9.6.07); Perry, "Marine Denies Role in 12 Iraqi Deaths,"
LAT (9.7.07); Von Zielbauer, "Marine's Defense Team Ends Haditha
Hearing Abruptly," NYT (9.7.07); White, "Marine Corps Exonerates
Captain in Iraq Killings," WP (9.19.07); Von Zielbauer, "Investigator Said
to Find Case Against Marine Weak," NYT (10.5.07); White, "Reduced
Charges Urged in Iraq Case," WP (10.5.07); Perry, "Marines Face Trials in
Haditha Deaths," LAT (10.20.07); Carter, "2 Marines to Face Courts-
Martial in Haditha Killings," WP (10.20.07); Perry, "Marine General Bids
Farewell," LAT (11.3.07); Perry, "Marine to Stand Trial in Haditha
Killings," LAT (1.1.08); Von Zielbauer, "2 More Marine Trials in Killings
of 17 Iraqis," NYT (1.1.08); "Marine Faces Reduced Charges in Iraq
Killings," WP (1.1.08); White, "No Murder Charges Filed in Haditha
Case," WP (1.4.08); Figueroa, "Attorney: Gen. Mattis to Testify Monday
in Haditha Case," NCT (5.30.08); Figueroa, "Mattis Testifies No One
Influenced Haditha Decision," NCT (6.2.08); Figueroa, "Undue Influence
Decision in Hands of Judge," NCT (6.3.08); Figueroa, "Jury Selection
Begins in First Haditha Court-Martial," NCT (5.28.08); Figueroa,
"Attorney: Accused Marine 'Fall Guy' in Haditha Case," NCT (5.29.08);
Figueroa, "Colonel Testifies Officer Said There Were No Haditha Photos,"
NCT (5.30.08); Figueroa, "Judge Drops Obstruction Charge in Haditha
Case Mid-Trial," NCT (6.3.08); Figueroa, "Haditha Marine Acquitted,"
NCT (6.4.08); Fiske, "U.S. Military Judge Dismisses Obstruction Charge
in Haditha Killings Case," Jurist (6.4.08); Carter, "Marine after Not Guilty
Verdict: 'It Was Surreal,'" WP (6.5.08); Walker, "Marine Corps Striking
Out in Haditha Prosecutions," NCT (6.5.08); Walker, "Charges against

Haditha Commander Dismissed," NCT (6.17.08); Perry, "Charges Dropped against Marine Officer," LAT (6.18.08); Walker, "Marine Corps Appealing Dismissal Ruling for Chessani," NCT (6.18.08); Carter, "Prosecutors Appeal Dismissal of Haditha Charges," WP (6.19.08); "Prosecutors Appeal Dismissal of Haditha Charges," NYT (7.29.08); Perry, "Dismissal of Iraq Charges Upheld," LAT (3.18.09); "Camp Pendleton: Reinstatement of War Crimes Charges Urged," LAT (4.18.09); "Marine Escapes Charges in 24 Killings in Iraq," LAT (8.29.09); Perry, "Marine to Face Court-Martial in Killings of 24 Iraqi Civilians," LAT (3.27.10); Perry, "Court-Martial to Begin for Camp Pendleton Marine in Iraqi Killings," LAT (1.6.12); Perry, "Jury Chosen for Court-Martial of Marine in 24 Iraqi Deaths," LAT (1.7.12); "Prosecutor: Marine Made Fatal Assumptions, Lost Control of Himself in Major Iraq War Crime," WP (1.9.12); Perry, "Court-Martial Begins in Marine Killing of 24 Iraqis," LAT (1.9.12); Perry, "Ex-Marine Testifies at Squad Leader's Court-Martial in Iraqi Deaths," LAT (1.11.12); Perry, "Marine Testifies Squad Leader Asked Him to Lie about Iraqi Killings," LAT (1.12.12); Perry, "ROE a Key Issue in Marine's Court-Martial," LAT (1.19.12); "Marine in Haditha Killings Trial Has to Decide: Fight or Take a Deal," LAT (1.20.12); Perry, "Marine's Court-Martial Resumes with No Plea Deal," LAT (1.21.12); Perry, Williams & Gold, "Marine's Trial Ends without a Conviction in 2005 Iraq Killings," LAT (1.24.12); "In Iraqi Town of Haditha, Disbelief at Light Sentence for Marine Who Led Raid that Killed 24," WP (1.24.12); Schmidt, "Anger in Iraq after Plea Bargain over 2005 Massacre," NYT (1.25.12); Perry, "Marine Gets No Jail Time in Killing of 24 Iraqi Civilians," LAT (1.25.12); Salman & McDonnell, "In Iraq, Haditha Case Is Reminder of Justice Denied," LAT (1.25.12); "Iraq Will Take Legal Action to Ensure Justice for Civilians Killed in US Raid, Official Says," WP (1.26.12); Savage & Bumiller, "An Iraqi Massacre, A Light Sentence and a Question of Military Justice," NYT (1.28.12); "California: Marine Convicted in Killings Is Discharged," NYT (2.22.12). See Langewiesche (2006); Rath (2008).

4 "U.S. Opens Inquiry into Civilian's Death in a Marine Raid," NYT (5.25.06); Perry, "Murder Charges Likely for Marines in Iraq Deaths," LAT (6.2.06); Walker & Sterrett, "Lawyer for Navy Corpsman Calls for Investigation, Sets Up Defense Fund," NCT (6.6.06); Sterrett & Walker, "Carlsbad Attorney Critical of Leaks in Marine Probe," NCT (6.7.06); Sterrett & Walker, "Attorney: Suspects Threatened with Death Penalty," NCT (6.7.06); Perry, "Lawyer Decries Sailor's Brig Stay," LAT (6.7.06); Perry, "Parents Fear Marine's Case Tainted by Haditha Killings," LAT (6.11.06); Sterrett, "Marine Corps Unshackles Troops under Investigation," NCT (6.17.06); Perry & Barnes, "Haditha Report to Fault Oversight, Official Says," LAT (6.17.06); "Marines, Sailor to Be Charged with Murder," NYT (6.21.06); Sterrett & Walker, "Prosecution Document Details Alleged Slaying," NCT (6.22.06); "8 U.S. Troops Charged in Iraqi's Death," LAT (6.22.06); White & Geis, "8 Troops Charged in Death of Iraqi," WP (6.22.06); Perry, "Base Rally Backs 8 Accused Troops," LAT (6.25.06); Walker, "Attorneys: Accused Troops Won't Testify against Each

Other," NCT (7.25.06); Perry, "Six Marines Charged with Criminal Abuse in Iraq," LAT (8.4.06); Marshall, "6 Marines Are Charged in Assault," NYT (8.5.06); Figueroa, "Accused Hamdania Marine Wants to Head Straight to Trial," NCT (8.16.06); "Charges Filed against Marine Lieutenant in Hamdania Case," NCT (8.16.06); Figueroa, "Demand for Immediate Trial Signals Change in 'Pendleton 8' Case," NCT (8.20.06); Figueroa & Walker, "Pretrial Hearing Waiver Denied Hamdania Defendants," NCT (8.23.06); Walker & Figueroa, "Death Penalty Pulled Off the Table for Encinitas Marine," NCT (8.30.06); Walker & Figueroa, "Marines Signal End of Pretrial Hearings in Two Hamdania Cases," NCT (8.31.06); Geis, "Hearings Begin for Marines Accused of Killing Iraqi," WP (8.31.06); Perry, "Two Marines Admit Killing Iraqi Man," LAT (8.31.06); Walker, "Next Hamdania Hearing Set for Tuesday," NCT (9.6.06); Marshall, "Death Penalty Not Sought for Marine in Killing of Iraqi," NYT (9.13.06); Walker, "Tactics Suggest Hamdania Attorneys Expect Courts-Martial," NCT (9.14.06); Figueroa, "Attorney Says Court-Martial Recommended for Encinitas Marine," NCT (9.15.06); Walker, "Courts-Martial Ordered for Three Hamdania Defendants," NCT (9.25.06); Perry, "3 Marines to Be Tried in Death of Iraqi Man," LAT (9.26.06); "3 Marines to Face Courts-Martial," NYT A12 (9.26.06); Walker, "Video Clips of Corpsman Accused in Hamdania Killing Released," NCT (10.3.06); Figueroa & Walker, "Plea Deal Said in the Works for Hamdania Defendant; Navy Corpsman May Be First to Strike Deal with Prosecutors," NCT (10.4.06); Perry, "Sailor Charged in Iraqi's Slaying to Testify Against 7 Codefendants," LAT (10.6.06); Perry, "Sailor Sentenced to One Year in Iraqi's Slaying," LAT (10.7.06); Walker, "Sergeant Said to Be Ready to Rebut Bacos Testimony," NCT (10.10.06); Figueroa & Walker, "Sergeant Accused in Iraqi Man's Killing Appears in Court," NCT (10.17.06); "Lawyer Says Marine Will Plead Guilty in Iraqi Murder Case," NYT (10.21.06); Walker & Figueroa, "Encinitas Marine Pleads Guilty in Hamdania Killing," NCT (10.26.06); "Marine Admits Role in Killing of Iraqi," LAT (10.27.06); Marshall, "Marine on Trial Tells of Killing Unarmed Iraqi," NYT (10.27.06); "3rd Defendant in Slaying of Iraqi Man Reportedly Will Plead Guilty," LAT (10.31.06); Walker, "Jackson Pleads Guilty to Conspiracy to Obstruct Justice, Aggravated Assault in Hamdania Slaying Case," NCT (11.6.06); Walker, "Jodka Sentenced to 18 Months for His Role in Hamdania Killing," NCT (11.15.06); Perry, "Marine Gets 18 Months in Slaying of Iraqi," LAT (11.16.06); Marshall, "Third Guilty Plea in Killing of Iraqi by a Marine Patrol," NYT (11.7.06); "Marine Faces Trial in Killing," LAT (11.15.06); Von Zielbauer, "Soldier to Plead Guilty in Iraq Rape and Killings," NYT (11.15.06); Walker, "Marine Says He Asked NCIS for Attorney but Wasn't Given One," NCT (11.21.06); "California: Marine Is Sentenced," NYT (11.22.06); Walker, "Hearing Set for Marine Officer Charged in Hamdania Assault," NCT (1.5.07); Walker, "Iraqis to Be Brought to U.S. to Testify in Hamdania Assault Case," NCT (1.11.07); Walker, "Attorney Says Agents Made Up Assault Case Evidence," NCT (1.12.07); Bennett, "Tough Going for Defense Funds in

Haditha Case," NCT (1.17.07); Walker, "Marine Wants Jury Trial in Awad Killing," NCT (1.17.07); Walker, "Marine Pleads Guilty to Murder in Killing of Retired Iraqi Police Officer," NCT (1.19.07); "Marine Corporal Pleads Guilty in Killing of Unarmed Iraqi," NYT (1.19.07); Walker, "NCIS Agent Says His Notes Conflict with Witness Statement," NCT (1.26.07); Walker, "Witness for Accused Marine Lieutenant Threatened with Perjury Charge," NCT (1.27.07); Walker, "Attorney: Accused Marine Lieutenant Is Really a 'Hero,'" NCT (1.28.07); "Marine Witness Warned of Possible Perjury Charges," LAT (1.28.07); "Walker, "Marine Withdraws Guilty Pleas, Now Says He Was Obeying Orders," NCT (2.9.07); "Marine Withdraws a Plea," NYT A28 (2.10.07); Walker, "Pennington Pleads Guilty to Two Counts in Awad Killing," NCT (2.13.07); "California: Plea Deal in Iraqi's Death," NYT A16 (2.14.07); Walker, "Marine Used Hand of Slain Iraqi to Slap Victim's Face," NCT (2.16.07); Perry, "Marine Gets 8 Years for Iraqi's Death," LAT A10 (2.18.07); Walker, "Accused Marine Will Be Evaluated by Board," NCT (3.1.07); "California: Marine Is Arraigned a Second Time," NYT A13 (3.2.07); Walker, "Hamdania Commander Warned about Excessive Force," NCT (3.3.07); Walker, "Statements Made by Accused Marine Ruled Admissible," NCT (3.6.07); Watkins, "Sailor, First to Plead Guilty in Iraqi Killing, Is First Set Free," NCT (3.14.07); Walker, "Hutchins' Statement Ruled Admissible at Trial," NCT (3.14.07); Walker, "Hamdania Lieutenant Ordered to Court-Martial," NCT (3.19.07); Walker, "Assault Charges Dropped against Lieutenant in Hamdania Case," NCT (5.1.07); Figueroa, "Judge: Jurors Not to Be Told Marine Faces Life in Prison in Hamdania Case," NCT (5.11.07); Figueroa, "Jurors Will Not Hear of Short Sentences in Hamdania Case," NCT (5.31.07); Walker, "Lieutenant in Hamdania Case Reprimanded, Restricted to Base," NCT (6.1.07); Figueroa, "Accused Marine Wants Jury to Hear Classified Info in Murder Trial," NCT (6.13.07); Figueroa, "Attorney Points to Combat Stress in Defense of Accused Marine," NCT (6.14.07); Figueroa, "Judge: Jury Will Not Hear Marine's CNN Interview," NCT (6.14.07); Walker, "First Trial Begins in Hamdania Killing," NCT (7.9.07); Walker, "Troops Detail Hamdania Killing," NCT (7.11.07); Walker, "Marine Acquitted of Murder, Convicted of Conspiracy, Kidnapping," NCT (7.19.07); Walker, "Convicted Marine Asks Jury for Leniency," NCT (7.19.07); Von Zielbauer, "Web Sites Rally Support for G.I.'s in Legal Trouble," NYT (7.22.07); Walker, "Trials Under Way for Last Two Marines," NCT (7.23.07); Walker, "Hamdania Squad Leader Described as Murder Plot 'Mastermind,'" NCT (7.24.07); Figueroa, "Marine Testifies He Was 'Frustrated' by Release of Iraqi Suspects," NCT (7.26.07); Perry, "Defining the Time to Kill," LAT (7.31.07); Figueroa, "Magincalda Pleads for Mercy," NCT (8.2.07); Perry, "Marine Not Guilty of Most Serious Charge," LAT (8.2.07); Von Zielbauer, "Marine Corps Squad Leader Is Guilty of Unpremeditated Murder in Killing of an Iraqi Man," NYT (8.3.07); Perry, "Another Marine Guilty in Slaying of Iraqi," LAT (8.3.07); Perry, "Man Sentenced to 15 Years in Iraq Killing," LAT (8.4.07); Perry, "2 Marines in Hamandiya Slaying Freed from Brig," LAT

(8.8.07); Perry, "Marine in Case of Slain Iraqi Is Freed," LAT (8.11.07); "Marine Sent to Camp Pendleton after Murder Conviction Overturned in Iraqi War Crimes Case," LAT (5.7.10); Perry, "Marine Convicted of Killing Iraqi Civilian Back on Duty at Camp Pendleton," LAT (7.5.10); "Marine's Murder Conviction Is Overturned," NYT (6.27.13); "Marine Guilty of Murder in Retrial for 2006 Killing of Iraqi Civilian," NBC News (6.17.15); "California: Jury Calls for Marine's Discharge in Killing," NYT (6.19.15); Filkins, "The Warrior Monk," *The New Yorker* (5.29.17).

5 Finer, "Troops Facing Murder Probe," WP (7.1.06); Wong, "G.I.'s Investigated in Slayings of 4 and Rape in Iraq," NYT (7.1.06); White, "Ex-Soldier Charged in Killing of Iraqi Family," WP (7.4.06); Spiegel, "Former GI Charged in Murder, Rape," LAT (7.4.06); Cloud & Semple, "Ex-G.I. Held in 4 Slayings and Rape in Iraq," NYT (7.4.06); Barnes, "U.S. Sees Possible Links between Incidents in Iraq," LAT (7.5.06); Wong, "Inquiry into Iraq Killings Focuses on Supervision of Soldiers," NYT (7.5.06); Cloud, "Ex-G.I. in Rape-Killing Case Left Army under Mental Illness Rule," NYT (7.6.06); Salman & Kennedy, "In Cold Blood: Iraqi Tells of Massacre at Farmhouse," LAT (7.6.06); "Former GI Pleads Not Guilty in Iraq Case," LAT (7.7.06); White, "Ex-Soldier Pleads Not Guilty to Raping Woman and Killing Family in Iraq," WP (7.7.06); Wong, "2 American Officials Apologize for Crime," NYT (7.7.06); Colvin, "Criminal Case Throws Spotlight on US–Iraqi Ties," Reuters (7.7.06); Daragahi, "At Least 12 Iraqis Killed in Mosque Attacks," LAT (7.8.06); King, "Not Just Another Abuse Scandal," WP (7.8.06); Finer & Partlow, "Four More GIs Charged with Rape, Murder," WP (7.10.06); Daraghi, "5 More Soldiers Facing Charges," LAT (7.10.06); "Accused Soldiers Identified," LAT (7.11.06); Marshall, "Soldier's Lawyer Requests Order of Silence," NYT (7.13.06); Dwyer & Worth, "Accused G.I. Was Troubled Long Before Iraq," NYT (7.14.06); White, "Soldiers Plan to Argue Rape Tied to Distress," WP (7.21.06); Von Zielbauer, "Lawyers for Accused G.I. Say Confession Was Forced," NYT (7.22.06); Worth & Marshall, "G.I. Crime Photos May Be Evidence," NYT (8.5.06); Semple & O'Neil, "Iraq Incident Was Fueled by Whiskey, G.I. Says," NYT (8.7.06); Partlow, "U.S. Soldier Reportedly Describes Rape Scene," WP (8.7.06); Roug, "Scene of Slain Iraqi Family Described," LAT (8.7.06); Roug, "Testimony Tells of Rape, Killings in Iraq," LAT (8.8.06); Von Zielbauer, "Soldier Who Testified on Killings Says He Feared for His Life," NYT (8.8.06); Roug, "Witnesses Tell of Troop Stress Before Attack," LAT (8.9.06); Von Zielbauer, "Investigator Recommends Courts-Martial for 4 Soldiers," NYT (9.4.06); "Troops to Face Courts-Martial on Charges," NYT (10.18.06); Roberts, "Military Will Try 11 in Iraq Slayings," WP (10.19.06); "Kentucky: Ex-Soldier Indicted in Killings in Iraq," NYT (11.3.06); Barrouquere, "Ex-Soldier Accused in Deaths of Iraqis," LAT (11.8.06); "G.I. to Plead Guilty in Iraq Plot," LAT (11.15.06); "Soldier Admits to Iraq Rape, Killings," LAT (11.16.06); White, "Soldier Pleads Guilty in Iraq Rape Trial," WP (11.15.06); Von Zielbauer, "Soldier Pleads Guilty in Iraq Rape and Killings," NYT (11.15.06); "Soldier Pleads Guilty to Murder," LAT

(2.21.07); "Soldier Weeps Describing Role in Rape and Killing in Iraq," NYT (2.22.07); "Soldier Gets 100 Years in Prison in Rape, 4 Slayings," LAT (2.23.07); "Soldier Admits Lesser Crimes in Iraq Killings," NYT (7.31.07); "Soldier Receives 100 Years in Rape of Iraqi Girl, Killings," LAT (8.5.07); Von Zielbauer, "Rape of Iraqi Girl and Killing of Family Gets G.I. 100 Years," NYT (8.5.07); Barrouquere, "Former Soldier to Face Civilian Trial for Alleged Crimes in Iraq," WP (8.27.08); Robertson & Kakan, "Ex-G.I. Guilty of Rape and Killings in Iraq," NYT (5.9.09); Dao, "Civilian Jury Considers Death Penalty for Ex-G.I.," NYT (5.21.09); Dao, "Ex-Soldier Gets Life for Killings in Iraq," NYT (5.22.09); Santora & al-Salhy, "Iraq Tribes Are Upset by Sentence Given to G.I.," NYT (5.23.09); "Kentucky: Ex-Soldier Sentenced," NYT (9.5.09); "Kentucky: Conviction Is Challenged," NYT (12.1.09); Zucchino, "Soldier Convicted in Rape, Murder of Iraqi Girl Is Found Hanged," LAT (2.18.14); U.S. v. Green, 654 F.3d 637 (6th Cir. 2011); Frederick (2010).

6 Barnes & Spiegel, "Military Investigates U.S. Killings of Iraqis at Checkpoint," LAT (6.16.06); Perry & Barnes, "Haditha Report to Fault Oversight, Official Says," LAT (6.17.06); Shanker & Oppel, "Criminal Inquiry Begins in Killings of 3 Iraqis by U.S. Soldiers," NYT (6.18.06); Shanker & Tavernise, "Murder Charges for 3 G.I.'s in Iraq," NYT (6.20.06); Barnes, "3 U.S. Soldiers Charged with Murder," LAT (6.20.06); Caldwell, "Accused Soldiers Say They Were Ordered to Kill," Houston Chronicle (7.21.06); Worth, "Lawyers for 4 Accused Soldiers Say They Acted on Orders," NYT (7.23.06); Worth, "Sergeant Tells of Plot to Kill Iraqi Detainees," NYT (7.28.06); Von Zielbauer, "G.I.'s Say Officers Ordered Killing of Young Iraqi Men," NYT (8.3.06); Caragahi & Barnes, "Officers Allegedly Pushed 'Kill Counts,'" LAT (8.3.06); Fleishman, "At Hearing, Witness Says Troops Fired at Fleeing Iraqis," LAT (8.4.06); Von Zielbauer, "Prosecutor Calls Accused G.I.'s War Criminals," NYT (8.5.06); Von Zielbauer, "4 G.I.'s Tell of How Iraqi Raid Went Wrong," NYT (8.7.06); Tyson, "Army Official Recommends Court-Martial for Soldiers," WP (9.3.06); Alonso-Zaldivar, "4 Soldiers Eligible for Execution if Convicted," LAT (9.3.06); Von Zielbauer, "Army Officer Calls for Death in Slaying Case," NYT (9.3.06); "Two from 101st Airborne Arraigned in Iraqi Deaths," LAT (10.27.06); Von Zielbauer, "Soldier Reaches Plea Deal in the Killing of 3 Iraqis," NYT (1.4.07); Von Zielbauer, "Army Says Improper Orders by Colonel Led to 4 Deaths," NYT (1.21.07); Von Zielbauer, "G.I. Gets 18-Year Prison Term for Killing 2 Captive Iraqis," NYT (1.26.07); Zucchino, "Soldier Pleads Guilty in Detainees' Deaths," LAT (1.26.07); Zucchino, "Hometown Fights for Man Charged in Iraq Slayings," LAT (2.25.07); Zucchino, "Army Squad Is at Odds in Trial," LAT (3.14.07); Zucchino, "Superior Says He Asked Why Iraqis Had not Been Killed," LAT (3.15.07); Zucchino, "Sergeant Denies Ordering 3 Iraqis Killed," LAT (3.16.07); Zucchino, "Jury Spares Sergeant," LAT (3.17.06); "Jury Endorses 10-Year Term for Iraq Soldier," LAT (3.20.07); "SSG Girouard makes an East Tenn. Homecoming," WVLT (10.10.09); United States v. Girouard, 2010 WL 3529415 (A. Ct. Crim. App. Apr. 23,

2010); Scott, "Former Soldier Ray Girouard Starts Life Over with Cleared Name," WBIR (4.12.12); *United States* v. *Girouard*, U.S. Ct. of Appeals for the Armed Forces (4.14.12); Philipps, "Shared Mission to Pardon U.S. Soldiers Who Killed Civilians," NYT (5.20.16). See generally Mestrovic (2009).

7 "Army: Afghan Civilians Killed by Grenades, Shot," LAT (6.16.10); Whitlock, "Members of U.S. Platoon in Afghanistan Accused of Killing Civilians for Sport," WP (9.18.10); Whitlock, "Army Monitored Stryker Brigade, Hit Hard in Afghanistan, for Signs of Stress," WP (9.18.10); Yardley & Schmitt, "5 U.S. Soldiers Accused of Killing Afghan Civilians," NYT (9.20.10); "Why Did Warnings about Murders by Soldiers in Afghanistan Go Unheeded?" WP (9.22.10); Yardley, "Army Limits Use of Images of Casualties in G.I.'s Case," NYT (9.25.10); Whitlock, "Army Soldier Says Staff Sgt Plotted Afghans' Killings," WP (9.27.10); Riccardi, "U.S. Army Sergeant Described as Ringleader in Slaying of Afghan Civilians," LAT (9.28.10); Yardley, "Drug Use Cited in Killings of 3 Civilians," NYT (9.28.10); Savage, "Case of Soldiers Accused in Afghan Civilian Killings May Be Worst of Two Wars," NYT (10.4.10); Yardley, "Young Soldier Both Revered and Reviled," NYT (10.5.10); Shah & Rubin, "Relatives Tell of Civilians Killed by U.S. Soldiers," NYT (10.5.10); "Washington: Court-Martial Recommended in Afghan Killings," NYT (10.18.10); "Soldier to Face Court-Martial in Afghan Civilian Deaths," LAT (10.16.10); Whitlock, "Brigade Linked to Afghan Civilian Deaths Had Aggressive, Divergent War Strategy," WP (10.14.10); Bumiller & Yardley, "G.I.'s Accused in Deaths Were Isolated from Officers," NYT (10.16.10); Whitlock, "Stryker Unit Sought to Defend Killing at Heart of Afghan Murder Probe," WP (10.26.10); Yardley, "Sergeant Accused of Killing Afghan Civilians Faces Hearing," NYT (11.10.10); Whitlock, "Army Alleges that Sergeant Led 'Kill Team' Targeting Afghan Civilians," WP (11.10.10); Murphy, "War Crimes Hearing Begins for Soldier in Afghan Deaths," LAT (11.10.10); Zimmerman, "War Is Hell," LAT (11.3.10); "Deal for Soldier in Afghan Case," NYT (12.2.10); "Washington: Court Martial for Soldier," NYT (12.4.10); "Soldier Faces Court-Martial in Killings," NYT (1.7.11); Whitlock, "Soldier in Army War-Crimes Case Signs Plea Deal in Killings of Afghan Civilians," WP (1.26.11); "U.S. Soldier Accused of Killing 3 Afghans for Sport Will Face Military Trial," LAT (2.1.11); Yardley, "Soldier May Testify against Comrades in Afghan Killings, Lawyer Says," NYT (2.12.11); Whitlock, "Der Spiegel Publishes Photos of U.S. Soldiers Posing with Dead Afghan Civilian," WP (3.20.11); Rubin, "Photos Imperil U.S. Relations with Afghanistan," NYT (3.22.11); Yardley, "Soldier Is Expected to Plead Guilty in Afghan Killings Case," NYT (3.23.11); Yardley, "Soldier Gets 24 Years for Killing 3 Afghan Civilians," NYT (3.24.11); Murphy, "U.S. Soldier Pleads Guilty to Murder of Three Afghans," LAT (3.24.11); "U.S. Army Calls Photos of Soldiers Posing with Afghan Corpses 'Disturbing,'" WP (3.28.11); King, "Karzai Denounces Alleged 'Trophy' Killings in Afghanistan," LAT (3.31.11); Murphy, "Soldier Pleads Guilty

to Manslaughter in Afghan's Killing," LAT (8.6.11); "Army Private Gets 7 Years for Murder of Unarmed Afghan Teen," LAT (9.24.11); Bernton, "Lewis-McChord Soldier Gets 7-Year Sentence for Murder of Afghan," *Seattle Times* (9.24.11); Ashton, "'Kill Team' Suspect Holms Sentenced to Seven Years in Jail for Afghan Murder," *Tacoma News Tribune* (9.24.11); Ukman, "Staff Sgt. Calvin Gibbs, Alleged Leader of Stryker 'Kill Team,' Set to Face Court-Martial," WP (10.28.11); "Sergeant Charged in Thrill Killings of 3 Afghan Civilians Admits Cutting Fingers from Bodies," WP (10.31.11); Murphy, "Court Martial Begins for Sergeant Accused of Killing Civilians," LAT (10.31.11); Yardley, "Trial Opens in Court-Martial of Soldier Tied to Afghan Killings," NYT (11.1.11); Yardley, "Soldier Is Convicted of Killing Afghan Civilians for Sport," NYT (11.11.11); Johnson, "U.S. Soldier Found Guilty in Afghan Thrill Killings," Seattle Post-Intelligencer (11.11.11); "Washington: Army Drops Charges against Soldier in Civilian Deaths," NYT (2.4.12). See also Mogelson, "A Beast in the Heart of Every Fighting Man," NYT (4.27.11); Boal (2011); Krauss, "The Kill Team" (2013) (documentary film).

8   Partlow & Pincus, "Iraq Bans Security Contractor," WP (9.18.07); Parker, "U.S. Rushes to Smooth Iraq's Anger over Blackwater," LAT (9.18.07); Tavernise, "U.S. Contractor Banned by Iraq over Shootings," NYT (9.18.07); Tavernise & Glanz, "Iraqi Report Says Guards for Blackwater Fired First," NYT (9.19.07); Tavernise & Glanz, "Guards' Shots Not Provoked, Iraq Concludes," NYT (9.21.07); Fainaru & Raghavan, "Blackwater Faced Bedlam, Embassy Finds," WP (9.28.07); Glanz & Tavernise, "Blackwater Role in Shooting Said to Include Chaos," NYT (9.28.07); Risen, "State Department Starts Third Review of Private Security in Iraq," NYT (9.28.07); Raghavan & DeYoung, "5 Witnesses Insist Iraqis Didn't Fire on Guards," WP (9.29.07); Glanz & Rubin, "From Errand to Fatal Shot to Hail of Fire to 17 Deaths," NYT (10.3.07); Raghavan, Partlow & DeYoung, "Blackwater Faulted in Military Reports from Shooting Scene," WP (10.5.07); Susman & Salman, "Iraqi Guard's Widow Reports No Compensation," LAT (10.8.07); Raghavan, "Iraqi Probe Faults Blackwater Guards," WP (10.8.07); Glanz & Rubin, "Blackwater Shootings 'Deliberate Murder,' Iraq Says," NYT (10.8.07); Zavis, "Blasts, Other Violence Kill 37 Iraqis," LAT (10.9.07); Susman & Berthelsen, "Private Security Guards Kill 2 in Iraq," LAT (10.10.07); Oppel & Gordon, "U.S. Military and Iraqis Say They Are Shut Out of Inquiry," NYT (10.11.07); Glanz, Oppel & Kamber, "New Evidence that Guards Took No Fire," NYT (10.13.07); Raghavan & White, "Blackwater Guards Fired at Fleeing Cars, Soldiers Say," WP (10.12.07); "U.S. Deal Slows Blackwater Inquiry," LAT (10.30.07); DeYoung, "Immunity Jeopardizes Iraq Probe," WP (10.30.07); Johnston, "State Department Made Immunity Offer to Firm's Guards," NYT (10.30.07); Berthelsen & Salman, "Iraqi Witnesses Discuss Blackwater Shooting," LAT (10.31.07); "Justice in Iraq," LAT (10.31.07); DeYoung, "Senior Democrats Want Blackwater Case Details," WP (10.31.07); Johnston & Broder, "F.B.I. Says Guards Killed 14 Iraqis without Cause," NYT (11.14.07); DeYoung, "Contractors'

Actions Labeled Unjustified," WP (11.15.07); "Prosecuting Blackwater," NYT (11.16.07); Fainaru & Leonnig, "Grand Jury to Probe Shootings by Guards," WP (11.20.07); Johnston & Broder, "U.S. Prosecutors Subpoena Blackwater Employees," NYT (11.20.07); Apuzzo, "Blackwater Grand Jury Hears Two Witnesses," WP (11.29.07); "Blackwater Probe Reportedly Focuses on 3," WP (12.8.07); Risen & Johnston, "Justice Department Briefed Congress on Legal Obstacles in Blackwater Case," NYT (1.16.08); Thompson, "From Texas to Iraq, and Center of Blackwater Case," NYT (1.19.08); "Pentagon Letter Complicates Blackwater Case," WP (2.3.08); Apuzzo & Jordan, "Blackwater Inquiry Turns to Baghdad," WP (2.21.08); Wilber & DeYoung, "Justice Department Moves toward Charges against Contractors in Iraq Shooting," WP (8.17.08); Wilber, "Blackwater Guards Indicted in Deadly Baghdad Shooting," WP (12.6.08); Thompson & Risen, "5 Guards Face U.S. Charges in Iraqi Deaths," NYT (12.6.08); Wilber & Tate, "Contractors' Attorneys Lash Out at Justice Department," WP (12.7.08); Thompson & Zoepf, "Lawyers Say U.S. Reckless in Charges for 5 Guards," NYT (12.7.08); "Blackwater Drama Unfolds on 2 Cross-Country Stages," LAT (12.8.08); Zoepf & Kakan, "U.S. Prosecutor Goes to Iraq to Work on Blackwater Case," NYT (12.8.08); Wilber, "Contractors Charged in '07 Iraq Deaths," WP (12.9.08); Thompson & Risen, "Plea by Blackwater Guard Helps U.S. Indict 5 Others," NYT (12.9.08); "Contractors on Trial," WP (12.9.08); Zoepf & Ali, "Iraqi Victims and Families Talk with U.S. Prosecutors," NYT (12.14.08); "A Blackwater Hole," LAT (12.15.08); Risen, "Guards Plead Not Guilty in '07 Killing in Baghdad," NYT (1.7.09); Wilber, "Judge Refuses to Dismiss Charges against Blackwater Guards," WP (2.18.09); Risen, "Prosecutors in Iraq Case See Pattern by Guards," NYT (9.14.09); Wilber, "Judge Closes off Pretrial Blackwater Hearing," WP (10.15.09); "Sealing the Courtroom," WP (10.17.09); "Open Up Blackwater's Closed Hearing," LAT (10.22.09); "U.S. to Drop Manslaughter Charges against Blackwater Guard," LAT (11.21.09); Apuzzo, "Blackwater Shooting Charges All Dismissed by Judge," WP (12.31.09); C. Savage, "Charges Voided for Contractors in Iraq Killings," NYT (1.1.10); D. Savage, "Judge Throws Out Blackwater Guards' Charges in Iraqi Deaths," LAT (1.1.10); Wilber, "Charges Dismissed against Blackwater Guards in Iraq Deaths," WP (1.1.10); Williams, "Iraqis Angered at Dropping of Blackwater Charges," NYT (1.2.10); Hastings, "Day of Mixed Emotions in Baghdad: Elation for U.S., but Anger for Iraqis," WP (1.2.10); Leland, "Iraq Says Deal Is Near on the Last of 5 Hostages," NYT (1.4.10); "Judge Made the Right Call in Blackwater Case," WP (1.6.10); "Privatized War, and Its Price," NYT (1.11.10); "It's a Police Matter," LAT (1.9.10); Palazolo, "Prosecutors Can Seek a New Indictment in Blackwater Case," www.mainjustice (1.19.10) (last accessed 2.1.10, also available on Facebook or Twitter); Shadid, "Biden Says U.S. Will Appeal Blackwater Case Dismissal," NYT (1.24.10); Sly, "Biden Says U.S. Will Appeal Blackwater Ruling," LAT (1.24.10); Londoño, "Justice Department to Appeal Dismissal of Blackwater Indictment, Biden Says," WP (1.24.10); Vicini, "U.S. Court

Reinstates Blackwater Iraq Shooting Case," Reuters (4.22.11); Risen, "Ex-Blackwater Guards Face Renewed Charges," NYT (4.23.11); Wilber & Hsu, "Judge Ordered to Revisit Blackwater Guard Shooting Case," WP (4.23.11); Serrano, "Charges Revived against Guards in Blackwater Case," LAT (4.23.11); Schmidt, "Reopening of Blackwater Case Confuses Iraqi Victims," NYT (4.26.11); "Ruling Revives Blackwater Shooting Case," LAT (5.2.11); "New Charges in 2007 Blackwater Shootings in Iraq, Aljazeera America (10.17.13); Tillman, "Prosecution of Blackwater Guards Survives Early Challenge," *Legal Times* (3.16.14); Tillman, "Ex-Blackwater Guard Wins Challenge of Manslaughter Indictment," *Legal Times* (4.7.14); Tillman, "Feds Charge Ex-Blackwater Guard with Murder," *Legal Times* (5.9.14); Apuzzo, "Trying to Salvage Remains of Blackwater Case," NYT (5.12.14); Apuzzo, "In a U.S. Court, Iraqis Accuse Blackwater of Killings in 2007," NYT (6.26.14); Apuzzo, "Witnesses Testify against Ex-Blackwater Colleagues in Case of 2007 Iraq Killings," NYT (7.16.14); Yost, "Defense: Gov't Suppressed Evidence in Blackwater," AP (7.28.14); Apuzzo, "Blackwater Jurors Urged to Give Iraqis Justice," NYT (8.28.14); "Blackwater Guards Found Guilty in Iraq Shootings," AP (10.22.14); Hsu, St. Martin & Alexander, "Four Blackwater Guards Found Guilty in 2007 Iraq Shootings of 31 Unarmed Civilians," WP (10.23.14); Apuzzo, "Blackwater Guards Found Guilty in 2007 Iraq Killings," NYT (10.23.14); "A Verdict on Blackwater," NYT (10.23.14); Semple, "In Iraq, Relief after News of Blackwater Convictions," NYT (10.24.14); Lamothe, "Erik Prince on Blackwater Verdicts: "A Lot of Politics Surrounding This," WP (10.24.14); Apuzzo, "Ex-Blackwater Guards Sentenced to Long Prison Terms in 2007 Killings of Iraqi Civilians," NYT (4.13.15); Apuzzo, "Court Rejects a Murder Conviction and Voids 3 Sentences in Blackwater Case," NYT (8.4.17); *U.S. v. Slatten* (4th Cir. 8.3.17); Scahill (2008: 3–37).

9 *United States* v. *Slough*, 677 F.Supp.2d 112 (D.D.C. 2009).
10 *United States* v. *Slough*, 679 F.Supp.2d 55 (D.D.C. 2010).
11 *United States* v. *Slough*, 641 F.3d 544 (D.C. Cir. 2011), cert. den. 132 S.Ct. 2710 (2012).
12 *United States* v. *Slough*, 36 F.Supp.3d 37 (D.D.C. 2014).
13 *United States* v. *Slatten*, 22 F.Supp.3d 9 (D.D.C. 2014).
14 *U.S.* v. *Slatten*, 2017 WL 3318837 (D.C. Cir. 2017) (Henderson, Rogers, Brown).
15 "U.S. Officials Say Army Soldier Suspected of Shooting More Than a Dozen Afghans," WP (3.11.12); Londoño & Hamdard, "U.S. Soldier Detained after Opening Fire on Afghans; 15 killed," WP (3.11.12); Shah & Bowley, "U.S. Sergeant Is Said to Kill 16 Civilians in Afghanistan," NYT (3.12.12); Londoño, Hamdard & Branigin, "Taliban Vows Revenge for Killings by U.S. Soldier," WP (3.12.12); Shah & Bowley, "An Afghan Comes Home to a Massacre," NYT (3.13.12); Shah & Rosenberg, "Militants Attack Afghan Delegation at Site of Killing Spree," NYT (3.13.12); "Horror in Kandahar," NYT (3.13.12); "Afghanistan on Edge," LAT (3.13.12); Whitlock & Leonnig, "Military Searches Soldier's Records for Clues in Killings of Afghan Civilians," WP (3.13.12); Landler, "Obama

Promises Thorough Inquiry into Afghan Attack," NYT (3.14.12); "Afghan Official Says Surveillance Video Shows U.S. Soldier Surrendering after Civilians Killed," WP (3.14.12); Cushman & Bowley, "Suspect in Afghan Deaths Flown to Kuwait as Evidence Arises That He Acted Alone," NYT (3.15.12); "Panetta Assures Afghans of Justice Despite Shooting Suspect's Transfer," LAT (3.15.12); Snider, "Karzai Urges American Pullback after Massacre," CNN (3.15.12); Sanchez, "Afghan Fury as US Soldier Accused of Massacre is Flown to Kuwait," *Telegraph* (3.15.12); Schmitt & Yardley, "Accused G.I. 'Snapped' under Strain, Official Says," NYT (3.16.12); "U.S. Suspect in Afghan Killings Flown out of Kuwait," AP (3.16.12); Dao, "U.S. Identifies Army Sergeant in Killing of 16 in Afghanistan," NYT (3.17.12); Davenport, Leonnig & Flaherty, "Soldier Accused in Afghan Shooting Spree Identified as Staff Sgt. Robert Bales," WP (3.17.12); Dao, "At Home, Asking How 'Our Bobby' Became War Crime Suspect," NYT (3.19.12); Schwartz, "The Military Path to Justice Could Be Lengthy," NYT (3.20.12); Cooper & Protess, "Suspect Was Once Accused of Financial Fraud," NYT (3.20.12); Yardley, "U.S. Sergeant Faces 17 Counts of Murder in Afghan Killings," NYT (3.22.12); "Afghan Shootings Carried Out in 2 Operations, Inquiry Finds," NYT (3.24.12); Londoño & Hamdard, "U.S. Pays 'Blood Money' to Victims of Afghan Massacre," WP (3.24.12); Nordland, "Unborn Afghan Child Said to Be 17th Victim of Shootings," NYT (3.26.12); Dao & Shah, "Details Offered on How Suspect Could Have Left Afghan Base," NYT (3.29.12); Leonnig, "Staff Sgt. Robert Bales Describes PTSD-like Symptoms, Lawyer Says," WP (3.29.12); Dao & Yardley, "U.S. Soldier's Lawyer Says Access Denied to Evidence," NYT (3.31.12); "Washington: Soldier Won't Comply with Sanity Review after Massacre," NYT (4.14.12); Dao, "Charges Amended for Soldier Accused in Civilian Deaths," NYT (6.2.12); Londoño, "U.S. Soldier Charged in Kandahar Massacre to Make First Court Appearance," WP (11.5.12); Johnson, "Pretrial Hearing Starts for Soldier Accused of Murdering 16 Afghan Civilians," NYT (11.6.12); Londoño, "U.S. Soldier Charged in Kandahar Massacre Showed No Remorse, Fellow Soldier Says," WP (11.6.12); Murphy, "Afghan Killing Spree Hearing: 'It's Really Bad,' Bales Allegedly Said," LAT (11.6.12); "At Hearing, Focus Turns to Soldier's Mind-Set," NYT (11.7.12); "Testimony: Sergeant's Actions after Afghanistan Massacre Suggest He Knew What He Was Doing," WP (11.7.12); Londoño, "In U.S. Soldier's War Crimes Hearing, Afghans to Take Center Stage," WP (11.7.12); Murphy, "Bales Said, 'You Guys Are Going to Thank Me,' Soldiers Testify," LAT (11.7.12); "Agent: Weeks before U.S. Forces Could Visit Crime Scene in Afghan Massacre after Severe Reaction," WP (11.8.12); Johnson, "Two Views of Officer Emerge in Afghan Case," NYT (11.8.12); "Victims, Relatives to Testify from Afghanistan in Hearing of US Soldier Charged in Massacre," WP (11.9.12); Johnson, "At Soldier's Hearing, Grisly Descriptions of Chaos and Horror," NYT (11.10.12); Johnson, "Young Afghans Recount Horror Stories at Bales Hearing," AP (11.12.12); Johnson, "Army Seeks Death Penalty in Afghan Massacre," NYT (11.14.12); Johnson, "Army

Seeking Death Penalty in Massacre of 16 Afghans," NYT (12.20.12);
"U.S. Soldier Charged in Afghan Massacre Had PTSD: Lawyer," Reuters
(1.18.13); "Afghan Woman Recounts How U.S. Soldier Killed Her
Husband in Rampage," WP (5.16.13); Dao, "Soldier Is Expected to Plead
Guilty in Afghan Massacre," NYT (5.30.13); Johnson, "Soldier Accused
of Killing Afghan Civilians to Testify," NYT (6.5.13); Johnson, "Guilty
Plea by Sergeant in Killing of Civilians," NYT (6.6.13); Durrani, "Afghan
Fury as U.S. 'Massacre' Soldier Escapes Death," AFP (6.6.13); Healy,
"Villagers Tell of Slaughter by a Soldier in Kandahar," NYT (8.21.13);
Healy, "Defense Tries to Soften Image of Soldier Who Killed 16 Afghans,"
NYT (8.22.13); Healy, "Apology, but No Explanation, for Massacre of
Afghans," NYT (8.23.13); Healy, "Soldier Sentenced to Life without
Parole for Killing 16 Afghans," NYT (8.24.13); "Villagers Unsatisfied by
Life Sentence for Robert Bales," WP (8.24.13).

16 Klay (2014: 129–67).

17 Lamothe, "Marine Who Urinated on Dead Taliban Has Conviction
Thrown Out Due to General's Meddling," WP (11.9.17).

18 LeDuff, "New York Marine Convicted of Assaulting Iraqi Prisoners,"
NYT (9.3.04); McKelvy, "Brass Tacks," The Nation (12.26.05) (Sgt. Gary
Pittman and Maj. Clarke Paulus, who beat to death a suspect in the cap-
ture of PFC Jessica Lynch).

19 See, e.g., Felstiner et al. (1981); Abel (1985).

20 Abel (1988: chaps. 9, 16); Abel (1989: chap. 7).

21 Philipps, "Shared Mission to Pardon U.S. Soldiers Who Killed Civilians,"
NYT (5.20.16).

22 Savage & Bumiller, "An Iraqi Massacre, a Light Sentence and a Question
of Military Justice," NYT (1.28.12); see also Savage, "Case of Soldiers
Accused in Afghan Civilian Killings May Be Worst of Two Wars," NYT
(10.4.10).

23 See also Horton, "Devin Kelley's Air Force Punishment Exposes Flaws
with Military Justice, Observers Say," WP (11.13.17).

24 See Ohman (2005: App. 2).

25 "Army Clears 2 Reservists Discharged on Abuse Allegations," LAT
(8.20.05); "World Briefing," NYT (11.18.05); "U.S. Soldier Convicted
in Abuse," LAT (1.29.06); "G.I. Is Guilty of Abusing Afghan Prisoners,"
NYT (1.29.06); "U.S. Soldier Sentenced for Prisoner Abuse," NYT
(1.30.06) (Sgt. Kevin D. Myricks; SPC James R. Hayes); "No Jail for
Soldier Charged in Assault," LAT (8.15.07) (SFC Timothy L. Drake).

26 Walker, "Marine Sniper Facing Manslaughter Charges," NYT (6.5.08);
Perry, "Court Martial Not Advised for Marine in Iraq Deaths," LAT
(7.15.08) (Sgt. John Winnick II); Kulish, Drew & Rosenberg, "Navy
SEALs, a Beating Death and Claims of a Cover-Up," NYT (12.17.15)
(Seal Team 2 in Kalach Village, Oruzgan Province, Afghanistan); "What
Went Wrong with Navy SEALs," NYT (12.18.15); Whitlock, "Senator
Pressures Navy to Take Action against Admiral in Charge of SEALs,"
WP (12.19.15); Drew, "Investigation of SEAL Conduct in Afghanistan
Is Reopened," NYT (1.15.16); Lamothe, "Army Reopens Investigation

into Detainee's Death after Special Force Soldier's Fox News Interview,"
WP (12.9.16) (Maj. Mathew I. Golsteyn first admitted killing the detainee
during a polygraph test for the CIA).

27 Taylor, "Tactical Psyops Stopped in Afghanistan, for Now," ArmyTimes.
com (10.28.05); "Officers Face Reprimands in Burning of Taliban Fighters'
Bodies," NYT (11.27.05) (MGen. Jason Kamiya); Bumiller, "Two Marines
Face Charges," NYT (9.24.12); "Washington: Marine Sentenced in
Taliban Urination Case," NYT (12.21.12); "U.S. Marine Pleads Guilty
to Urinating on Corpse of Taliban Fighter in Afghanistan," G (1.16.13);
"North Carolina; Marine Admits He Desecrated Corpses," NYT (1.17.13);
"North Carolina: Case against Marines Widens," NYT (2.9.13); Hauser,
"Marine Who Urinated on Taliban Corpses Says He Has No Regrets,"
NYT (7.18.13) (SSgt. Edward W. Deptola; SSgt. Joseph W. Chamblin).

28 Jaffe, "Investigators Recommend Punishment for Koran Burning," WP
(6.20.12); Bumiller, "Two Marines Face Charges," NYT (9.24.12).

29 "Captain Is Convicted of Assaults," LAT (3.17.05); "In Brief: Colorado
Officer in Iraqi Assaults Gets Prison, Keeps Rank," LAT (3.18.05) (Capt.
Shawn L. Martin); "Officials: Officers Staged Mock Executions," Fox
News (5.17.05) (2nd Lt. Yancy).

30 "Soldier Defends His Killing of Iraqi As 'the Honorable Thing,'" LAT
(3.31.05); "Military Panel Convicts Soldier," LAT (4.1.05); "Convicted
GI Will Not Serve Time," LAT (4.2.05); "Army Officer Convicted in
Iraqi's Death Is Freed," NYT (4.2.05) (Capt. Rogelio Maynulet); Perry &
Miller, "Marines Getting a New Message," LAT (7.9.06); Worth, "U.S.
Military Braces for Flurry of Criminal Cases in Iraq," NYT (7.9.06) (SSgt.
Cardenas J. Alban; SSgt. Johnny Horne).

31 Filkins, "The Fall of the Warrior King," NYT Magazine (10.23.05) (LtCol.
Nathan Sassaman).

32 "National Briefing," NYT (11.18.05); Milburn, "Soldier Says He Lied
When Implicating Leader in Killing," AP (11.18.05); "National Briefing,"
NYT (12.6.05) (Pvt. Michael Williams; SPC Brent May; Lt. Erick
J. Anderson); Von Zielbauer, "Green Berets Face Hearing on Killing of
Suspect in Afghan Village," NYT (9.18.07); Von Zielbauer, "Green Beret
Hearing Focuses on How Charges Came About," NYT (9.19.07); Von
Zielbauer, "Hearing in Killing of Afghan Puts Army War Effort on Trial,"
NYT (9.20.07) (MSgt. Troy Anderson; Capt. Dave Staffel); "Reservist Is
Found Guilty," NYT (12.14.07); "World Briefing: Middle East: Iraq: Marine
Discharged over Killing," NYT (12.15.07) (LCpl. Delano Holmes);
DeSantis, "Hearing Begins for Marine Accused of Killing 2 Iraqis," NYT
(4.27.05); DeSantis, "National Briefing South: North Carolina: Accused
Marine Is Praised," NYT (4.29.05); DeSantis, "Prosecution Presses Murder
Case Against Marine," NYT (5.1.05); DeSantis, "Call to Drop Murder
Case against Marine," NYT (5.14.05); Moore, "Rebuilding in the Gulf,"
WorldNetDaily (4.14.05); DeSantis, "Marine Cleared in Deaths of 2
Insurgents in Iraq," NYT (5.27.05); Zucchino, "Marine Cleared in Killing
of 2 Iraqi Detainees," LAT (5.27.05); "North Carolina Officer to Resign,"
NYT (6.3.05); Williams (2012–13) (Ilario Pantano).

33 "Soldier Faces Trial in Iraqi Man's Death," NYT (2.25.05); "Witness: Slain Iraqi Had Been Cooperating," LAT (5.26.05); "Soldier Charged in Iraqi Killing Is Acquitted," NYT (5.27.05) (SSgt. Shane Werst); Davey, "An Iraqi Police Officer's Death, a Soldier's Varying Accounts," NYT (5.23.05); Salvato, "Soldier Says Killing of Iraqi Was Self-Defense," NYT (5.24.05); Salvato, "On Day of Court-Martial, Soldier Pleads Guilty in Death of Iraqi Officer," NYT (7.26.05) (Cpl. Dustin M. Berg); Partlow, "Guardsmen Charged in Iraqi's Death," WP (6.26.06); "Pa. Guardsman Cleared in Iraqi's Death," WP (7.23.06); White, "Killing by Guardsman in Iraq Called Appropriate," WP (7.22.06) (SPC Nathan B. Lynn; Sgt. Milton Ortiz Jr.); Kakesako, "Schofield Soldier Wants Murder Trial Dismissed," *Honolulu Star Bulletin* (10.19.07); "G.I. Cleared of Murder in Killing," NYT (2.21.08); "Military Jury Acquits Soldier in Killing of Iraqi," *Honolulu Advertiser* (4.25.08); Kakesako, "Clemency Frees Shore," *Honolulu Star Bulletin* (5.21.08) (SPC Christopher Shore; SFC Trey Corrales).

34 Gall, "U.S. Military Investigating Death of Afghan in Custody," NYT (3.4.03); Gall, "New Charges Raise Questions on Abuse at Afghan Prisons," NYT (9.17.04); Jehl, "Army Details Scale of Abuse of Prisoners in an Afghan Jail," NYT (3.12.05); Golden, "In U.S. Report, Brutal Details of 2 Afghan Inmates' Deaths," NYT (5.20.05); Golden, "Army Faltered in Investigating Detainee Abuse," NYT (5.22.05); "Karzai Demands Custody of All Afghan Prisoners," NYT (5.22.05); Watson & Kazem, "Afghan Leader to Seek Control over Detainees," LAT (5.22.05); "Patterns of Abuse," NYT (5.23.05); Sanger, "Bush Deflects Afghan's Request for Return of Prisoners," NYT (5.24.05); Hart, "Afghan Detainee's Leg Was 'Pulpified,' Witness Says," LAT (3.23.05); Hart, "Soldier Facing Trial in Death of Prisoner Wins Round," LAT (4.4.05); "Jail Term for Soldier in Abuse Case," NYT (5.23.05); "World Briefings," NYT (8.5.05); Golden, "Abuse Cases Open Command Issues at Army Prison," NYT (8.8.05); "U.S. Soldier Found Guilty in Beating," LAT (8.18.05); "Soldier Guilty of Assault Is Demoted but Avoids Jail," LAT (8.19.05); "National Briefing," NYT (8.24.05); Roberts, "Soldier Gets 75 Days in Prison, Discharge, for Prisoner Assault," *El Paso Times* (8.31.05); "Afghans Decry Sentences for GIs," LAT (8.25.05); "World Briefing," NYT (11.5.05); Caldwell, "Pentagon: Top al-Qaeda Operative Escaped," NYT (11.2.05); Schmitt & Golden, "Details Emerge on a Brazen Escape in Afghanistan," NYT (12.4.05); "Reservist Acquitted of Abuse," WP (2.24.06); Golden, "Charges Dropped in Afghanistan against U.S. Officer in Beating Deaths of Afghan Inmates," NYT (1.8.06); "Charges Dropped in Afghanistan Abuse Probe," LAT (1.8.06); Golden, "Years after 2 Afghans Died, Abuse Case Falters," NYT (2.13.06); Golden, "In Final Trial, G.I. Is Acquitted of Abusing Jailed Afghans," NYT (6.2.06).

35 "A Region Inflamed," NYT (11.28.03); Fisher, "The Struggle for Iraq: Human Rights," NYT (5.10.04); Schmitt, "The Reach of War: Abuse," NYT (7.3.04); "Army Charges 4 Soldiers with Murder in the Death of an Iraqi General During Interrogation," NYT (10.5.04); HRF, Torture on Trial (January 13, 17–20, 24, 2006); Riccardi, "Trial Illuminates Dark Tactics of Interrogation," LAT (1.20.06); Riccardi, "Dead Iraqi's Role

Described in Army Murder Case," LAT (1.21.06); Riccardi, "Interrogator Convicted in Iraqi's Death," LAT (1.22.06); Schmitt, "Army Interrogator Is Convicted of Negligent Homicide," NYT (1.23.06); "Army Officer Gets Reprimand for Iraqi Death," NYT (1.24.06); Emery, "No Jail for Carson GI," *Denver Post* (1.24.06); Riccardi, "Mild Penalties in Military Abuse Cases," LAT (1.25.06); White, "Sentence in Death of Iraqi Angers Son," WP (1.25.06); LaPlante, "Iraq's 'Blacksmith Hotel,'" *Salt Lake Tribune* (1.25.06); "Abusive G.I.'s Not Pursued, Survey Finds," NYT (2.23.06); Johnston, "U.S. Inquiry Falters on Civilians Accused of Abusing Detainees," NYT (12.16.06); "Pattern Cited in Killings of Civilians by U.S.," NYT (9.4.07).

36 "Hearing to Begin in Abuse Case," LAT (3.20.05); Perry, "Navy SEAL Goes on Trial in Death of Iraqi Prisoner at Abu Ghraib," LAT (5.24.05); Cloud, "Seal Officer Hears Charges in Court-Martial in Iraqi's Death," NYT (5.25.05); Perry, "CIA Operative Testifies He Saw SEAL Beating Prisoner," LAT (5.25.05); Perry, "SEALs Instructed to Treat Prisoners Well," LAT (5.26.05); Cloud, "Seal Officer's Trial Gives Glimpse of C.I.A.'s Role in Abuse," NYT (5.26.05); Perry, "Navy Lieutenant Denies Assaulting Iraqi Prisoner," LAT (5.27.05); Perry, "SEAL Officer Not Guilty of Assaulting Iraqi," LAT (5.28.05).

37 This is all too common in warfare. Zimmerman, "War Is Hell," LAT (11.3.10).

38 Von Zielbauer, "Marines Dispute Accounts of Excessive Force in Afghans' Deaths," NYT (9.5.07); Von Zielbauer, "Marine Inquiry into Afghan Killings to Look at 2 Officers, Lawyer Says," NYT (10.21.07); Von Zielbauer, "Afghan Civilians Were Killed Needlessly, Ex-Marine Testifies," NYT (1.9.08); Zucchino, "Marine Testifies He Saw No Enemy Fire," LAT (1.9.08); Von Zielbauer, "4 Say Marines Took Fire in Attack on Afghans," NYT (1.10.08); Zucchino, "Marine Shooter Seeks Immunity in Afghan Case," LAT (1.11.08); Zucchino, "Frustration in Marines Shooting Inquiry," LAT (1.18.08); Zucchino, "2 Afghans Testify in Marine Inquiry," LAT (1.22.08); Zucchino, "Army Colonel Again Criticizes Marine Unit," LAT (1.24.08); Zucchino, "Marine Humvee Was Shot At, Army Expert Testifies," LAT (1.26.08); Zucchino, "No Answers in Marine Inquiry," LAT (1.29.08); Zucchino, "Marine Court Hears Dueling Depictions of Accused," LAT (1.30.08); Zucchino, "Did Marines Kill Wildly, or Not?" LAT (2.5.08); Thompson, "No Charges for 2 Marines Accused in Afghan Deaths," AP (5.23.08).

39 Perry, "Marines Face Scrutiny in Iraqi Deaths," LAT (7.5.07); "U.S. Inquiry into Falluja Deaths," NYT (7.7.07); "National Briefing: West: California: Marine Charged in Deaths," NYT (12.9.07); "Marine Charged in Iraq Shooting," LAT (5.15.08); Walker, "Military: Hearing Set on Fallujah Detainee Killings," NYT (7.9.08); Perry, "Marine Tells of Killing Iraqi Prisoners," LAT (7.11.08); Figueroa, "Military: 'Debate' Preceded Fallujah Killings," NYT (7.10.08); Perry, "Killing Still Haunts Marine," LAT (4.2.09); Figueroa, "Military: Prosecutor Says Fallujah Killing about 'Right and Wrong,'" NYT (7.11.08); Walker, "Trial Recommended in Fallujah Killing," NYT (7.18.08); Perry, "2 Marines Found in Contempt of

Court," LAT (8.23.08); Perry, "Riverside Jury Gets Crash Course in Marine Culture," LAT (8.26.08); Perry, "Ex-Marine's Testimony Links Squad Leader to Iraqi Prisoner Killings," LAT (8.27.08); "Federal Jury Acquits Ex-Marine in Iraqi's Death," AP (8.28.08); Bjelland, "Former Marine Found Not Guilty in Iraq Deaths," *Riverside Press-Enterprise* (8.28.08); Perry, "Contempt Charges Dropped Against 2 Marines in Fallouja Case," LAT (9.24.08); Carter, "Attorneys in Marine Detainee Death Trials Say Delay Is Ploy to Force Comrade's Testimony," LAT (10.3.08); Perry, "2nd Marine is Acquitted in Fatal Shootings of Prisoners in Fallouja," LAT (4.10.09); North, "Murder Charges Dismissed against Marine," KABC-TV (9.29.09) (Ryan Weemer; Jermaine A. Nelson; Jose Luis Nazario Jr.).

40 **1st Lt. Michael C. Behenna**: 15 years. "2 U.S. Soldiers Face Murder Charges," LAT (8.3.08); "Hearing Begins for U.S. Soldier Charged with Killing Iraqi Detainee," LAT (9.13.08); Gera, "Iraq: Hearing Opens for U.S. Soldier Charged with Fatally Shooting an Iraqi Detainee," LAT (9.21.08); "Kentucky: Officer Sentenced in Iraqi Shooting," LAT (3.1.09); Mozingo, "A Deadly Interrogation in Iraq," LAT (9.13.09); Mozingo, "An Unlikely Witness Provides One Last Hope for Soldier in Murder Case," LAT (9.14.09); *U.S. v. Behenna*, 71 M.J. 228, 2012 WL 2684980 (U.S. Court of Appeals for the Armed Forces 2012).

Sgt. Michael P. Leah, Jr.: life, reduced to 20 years; SFC Joseph P. Mayo: 35 years; **SFC John E. Hatley**: life, reduced to 40 years. Von Zielbauer, "U.S. Soldiers Executed Iraqis, Statements Say," NYT (8.27.08); "3 U.S. Soldiers Charged with Murder in Iraq Deaths," LAT (9.17.08); Finn, "3 Soldiers Charged in Iraqi Deaths," WP (9.18.08); "3 G.I.'s Charged in 4 Iraqi Deaths," NYT (9.18.08); "G.I. Sentenced to 7 Months," NYT (9.19.08); "U.S. Soldier Pleads Guilty in Killings in Iraq," LAT (10.3.08); Frey, "U.S. Army Sergeant to Face Court-Martial for Murder in Slayings of Iraqi Prisoners," WP (11.12.08); "U.S. Soldier Will Face Court-Martial in Deaths," LAT (1.8.09); "Iraq: Court-Martial for U.S. Sergeant," NYT (1.14.09); Frey, "Army Medic Is Sentenced for Murder of Iraqi Detainees," WP (2.21.09); "U.S. Soldier Apologizes for Role in 4 Iraqis' Deaths," LAT (3.31.09); Whitlock, "Army Sergeant Pleads Guilty to Murder in Iraqi Prisoner Deaths," WP (3.31.09); "Iraq: U.S. Soldier Pleads Not Guilty in Killings," NYT (4.15.09); "GI Guilty of Murdering Iraqis," LAT (4.16.09); Hood, "Town Rallies Behind Convicted Soldier," LAT (6.20.09); "Soldiers' Sentences Reduced," NYT (8.14.09).

Pvt. David W. Lawrence: life, reduced to 10 years. Perry, "Army Private Accused of Murder in Afghan Prisoner's Death," LAT (11.30.10); Vaughan, "Fort Carson Soldier Pleads Guilty to Killing Taliban Commander," *Denver Post* (5.25.11). 1st Lt. Clint Laurance: 20 years. Londoño, "Army Officer Convicted in Shooting Deaths of 2 Afghans," WP (8.2.13).

Sgt. Evan Vela got 10 years for premeditated murder and covering it up; **SPC Jorge Sandoval** and **SSgt. Michael Hensley** were acquitted of the serious charges. Parker, "2 U.S. Soldiers Charged with Murder, Planting Weapons," LAT (7.1.07); Farrell, "3d American Soldier Charged in Murder of an Iraqi Civilian," NYT (7.3.07); White & Partlow, "U.S. Aims to Lure Insurgents with 'Bait,'" WP (9.24.07); Von Zielbauer, "Snipers Killed Iraqis Who Took 'Bait,' Soldiers Testify," NYT (9.25.07); Kratovac, "Soldier Pleads Not Guilty in Killing of Iraqis," WP (9.27.07); Parker, "Soldier Describes Killing Unarmed Iraqi," LAT (9.28.07); Von Zielbauer, "Testimony in Court-Martial Describes a Sniper Squad Pressed to Raise Body Count," NYT (9.28.07); Parker, "Soldier Describes Killing Unarmed Iraqi," LAT (9.28.07); Von Zielbauer, "Testimony in Court-Martial Describes a Sniper Squad Pressed to Raise Body Count," NYT (9.28.07); Von Zielbauer, "Army Sniper Acquitted of Murder in 2 Deaths," NYT (9.29.07); "Iraq Seeks Long-Term U.S. Security Pact," NYT (9.30.07); Parker, "Sniper Team Tells of Pressure from Above," LAT (10.5.07); Von Zielbauer, "Court-Martial to Open in Killings of 3 Iraqis," NYT (11.6.07); Parker, "U.S. Army Sniper on Trial in Baghdad," LAT (11.7.07); Parker, "Witness Recalls Less at Iraq Sniper Trial," LAT (11.8.07); Parker, "Panel Acquits GI of Murder, "LAT (11.8.07); Von Zielbauer, "Military Jury Acquits Army Sniper of Premeditated Murder in Killings of 3 Iraqis," NYT (11.9.07); Parker, "U.S. Sniper Sentenced to Time Served," LAT (11.10.07); Parker, "Sniper Accused of Murder Disputes Statement," LAT (12.8.07); Moore, "At Court-Martial, G.I. Sniper Tells of Ordering the Killing of an Unarmed Iraqi," NYT (2.9.08); Parker, "Sniper Unit Chief Tells of Ordering Slaying," LAT (2.9.08); Parker, "Army Sniper on Trial Tells of Killing Iraqi," LAT (2.10.08); Parker, "Army Sniper Gets 10 Years for Killing of Iraqi Civilian," LAT (2.11.08); Moore, "G.I. Gets 10-Year Sentence in Killing of Unarmed Iraqi," NYT (2.11.08).

41 Philipps, "Army Fraud Crackdown Uses Broad Net to Catch Small Fish, Some Unfairly," NYT (5.28.17).

42 Shanker, "Concern Grows over Top Military Officers' Ethics," NYT (11.13.12); Baldor, "General Demoted for Lavish Travel and Spending," AP (11.14.12).

43 Whitlock, "'Fat Leonard' Probe Expands to Ensnare More than 60 Admirals," WP (11.5.17).

44 "California: 64 Sailors to Be Discharged for Drug Use," NYT (10.21.11); "California: More Navy Ousters for Drugs," NYT (11.22.11).

45 **Sgt. Hasan K. Akbar**: death for killing two officers and wounding 14 soldiers; but a jury acquitted. **SSgt. Alberto B. Martinez:** two fragging deaths. "U.S. Soldier to be Tried in 2 Officers' Deaths," LAT (10.3.06); "North Carolina: Soldier Is Arraigned in Killings," NYT (11.4.06); Von Zielbauer, "After Feud and 2 Deaths in Iraq, Soldiers and Families Are Torn," NYT (6.16.08); Thompson, "Fort Bragg Trial to Start in Case of Army Soldier Accused of 'Fragging' 2 Superior Officers," LAT (10.22.08); Von Zielbauer, "G.I. Offered to Plead Guilty, Then Went Free in Iraq Deaths," NYT (2.21.09); Zucchino, "Widows Pursue Justice in Soldiers' Slaying," LAT (4.8.10).

   Pvt. Nicholas D. Mikel: 25 years for shooting at fellow soldiers. "Soldier Gets 25 Years for Shooting at Others," LAT (4.21.06).

   Sgt. William Kreutzer: life for premeditated murder of a soldier and wounding 18 others. "North Carolina; Soldier Gets Life Term," NYT (3.25.09).

Sgt. Joseph Bozicevich: life for two premeditated murders of soldiers. "Soldiers Say Accused Sgt. Exclaimed, 'Just Kill Me,'" LAT (4.14.09); "Army Sergeant Gets Life Sentence for Killing Fellow Soldiers," Reuters (8.10.11); "Ga. Soldier Sentenced to Life without Parole in 2008 Slayings of 2 US Soldiers in Iraq," WP (8.10.11).

Sgt. John M. Russell: life for premeditated murder of five military personnel. Londoño, "Five U.S. Soldiers' Deaths Came at Hands of Comrade, Military Says," WP (5.11.09); Londoño, "U.S. Military Identifies Sergeant Charged in Baghdad Shooting," WP (5.12.09); Sly, "Suspect in Iraq Had Drawn Concern," LAT (5.13.09); Dao & Alvarez, "Soldier in Iraq Shooting Had Been Ordered to Receive Psychological Counseling," NYT (5.13.09); "Attorneys for Soldier Charged with 2009 Iraq Shootings Begin Defense at Military Hearing," WP (8.10.11); Myers, "U.S. Soldier to Hear Charges for 2009 Iraq Shootings," Reuters (11.19.12); Johnson, "U.S. Soldier Charged in 2009 Iraq Shootings to Appear in Court," Reuters (3.12.13); "John Russell: Sergeant Who Killed Fellow U.S. Troops in Iraq Gets Life Sentence," Reuters (5.16.13); "Washington: Plea Deal Reported in Killings in Iraq," NYT (4.20.13); "Soldier Found Guilty of Premeditated Murder," NYT (5.14.13).

MSgt. Timothy B. Hennis: death after *three* trials for killing a woman and two children. "North Carolina: Tried 3 Times, Soldier Faces Death," NYT (4.16.10).

SPC Neftaly Platero: life for killing two soldiers and injuring a third. Fadel, "U.S. Soldier Accused of Fatally Shooting Fellow Troops after Argument in Iraq," WP (9.28.10); "Neftaly Platero Sentenced: Life in Prison for Georgia Soldier Who Murdered Two Army Roommates," AP (6.13.12).

46 SSgt. Michael G. Rhoades: dishonorably discharged for cruelty and impeding an investigation. Eckholm, "With Problems in Recruiting, the Military Reins in Abuses at Boot Camp," NYT (7.26.05).

SSgts. David J. Roughan and Fernando Galvan: acquitted for a drowning death; similar treatment in training deaths and injuries at other bases. Perry, "2 Marines Ordered to Face Court-Martial in Drowning," LAT (5.5.06); "Marine Not Guilty in Death," LAT (10.6.06); "Charges Dismissed in Death of a Marine," LAT (10.13.06); Blumenthal, "Army Moves to Curb Abuses in Program for Injured Recruits," NYT (5.12.06).

Sgt. Jerrod Glass: six months for assaults and abuse of recruits. Perry, "San Diego Drill Instructor Faces a Court Martial on 91 Counts of Assault," LAT (8.24.07); Perry, "Drill Instructor Ignored Training Rules, Prosecutor Says," LAT (11.7.07); Perry, "Marine Tells of Abusive Treatment," LAT (11.9.07); Perry, "Dog Handler Testifies at Court-Martial of Ex-Drill Instructor," LAT (11.10.07); Perry, "Jury Gets Marine Assault Case," LAT (11.14.07); Perry, "Marine Drill Instructor Convicted of Abuse," LAT (11.15.07); Perry, "Ex-Drill Instructor Gets Six Months," LAT (11.16.07).

47 Semple, "Army Charges 8 in Wake of Death of a Fellow G.I.," NYT (12.22.11); Semple, "After Charging 8, Army Is Scrutinized on Hazing," NYT (12.23.11); Londoño & Davenport, "8 U.S. Soldiers Charged in

Death of Comrade in Afghanistan," WP (12.21.11); "A Soldier's Death," NYT (12.23.11); Chen, "Private Chen's Family Learns More about Hazing by Fellow G.I.'s," NYT (1.6.12); Semple, "Most Serious Charge in a Private's Death May Be Dropped," NYT (1.24.12); "U.S. Military Investigators Recommend 4 Troops Be Court-Martialed over Suicide in Afghanistan," WP (3.6.12); Semple, "Any Trial in Soldier's Death Would Be at Fort Bragg," NYT (4.12.12); Semple, "Army Prosecutor Details Racial Abuse That Preceded Soldier's Suicide," NYT (7.25.12); Semple, "Soldier Talked of Suicide over Hazing, Friend Says," NYT (7.27.12); Semple, "At Court-Martial, Testimony That Soldier Who Committed Suicide Was to Be Transferred," NYT (7.29.12); Semple, "Sergeant Acquitted of Driving a Suicide," NYT (7.31.12); Semple, "Jury Recommends 30-day Sentence for Sergeant in Army Hazing Case," NYT (8.1.12); Chu, "Military Hazing Has Got to Stop," NYT (8.4.12); Semple, "Army Officer Reaches Deal in Suicide of a Private," NYT (12.18.12).

48 Lamothe, "15 Marine Drill Instructors Face Allegations of Hazing and Assault at Paris Island," WP (6.30.16); Hauser, "20 Marines Face Discipline after Muslim Recruit's Death Is Ruled a Suicide," NYT (9.9.16); Lamothe, "Marine Drill Instructor Accused of Running a Clothes Dryer with a Muslim Recruit Inside," WP (9.14.16); School, "Parris Island Hazing Scandal: Three Marines Face Court-Martial," *Marine Times* (12.13.16); Lamothe, "Marine Drill Instructors Accused of Using a 'Dungeon' on Recruits and Drinking on the Job," WP (1.6.17); Lamothe, "Marines Move Forward with Prosecution of Drill Instructor Accused of Putting Recruit in Dryer," WP (4.8.17); Lamothe, "Marine Recruit Needed Skin Grafts to Treat Chemical Burns Suffered at Boot Camp, Documents Reveal," WP (5.4.17); Reitman, "The Making – and Breaking – of Marines," NYT (7.9.17); Laverty, "Trial Opens for Marine Drill Instructor Accused of Abusing Muslim Recruits during Whiskey-Fueled Assaults," WP (11.1.17); Laverty, "What Happens in the Squad Bay Stays in the Squad Bay," WP (11.7.17); Laverty, "Marine Drill Instructor Sentenced to 10 Years in Prison for Targeting Muslim Recruits," WP (11.10.17).

49 "Florida: 50 Years for Rapes by Air Force Officer," LAT (3.1.07); Millette, "Captain Gets 50 Years in Sodomy Case," US Air Force Office of Special Investigations (3.19.07).

50 "Navy Chaplain Gets 2 Years for Sex Abuse," LAT (12.7.07).

51 Hauser, "Green Beret Who Hit Afghan Child Rapist Should Be Reinstated, Lawmakers Say," NYT (3.4.16); Schuppe & Kube, "Army Reverses Expulsion of Charles Martland, Green Beret Who Hit Afghan Rapist," NBC News (4.29.16); Hauser, "Green Beret Who Beat Up Afghan Officer for Raping Boy Can Stay in Army," NYT (4.30.16).

52 White, "4-Star General Relieved of Duty," WP (8.10.05); Schmitt, "4-Star General Is Dismissed over Conduct," NYT (8.10.05); Huffington, "At Rummy's Bizarro Pentagon, Torture Is Rewarded While Sex Is a Firing Offense," HuffPost (8.10.05); "An Army Affair," WP A22 (8.11.05); "Make War, Not Love," *St. Petersburg Times* (8.12.05). The military was

investigating another alleged adultery. Shanker, "South Carolina: General Faces Adultery Investigation," NYT (5.22.13).

53 Lamothe, "'Inappropriate Sexual Acts' Prompt Air Force to Retroactively Demote Retired General Two Ranks," WP (2.2.17).

54 "U.S. Is Detaining a Senior Officer," NYT (4.26.07); Partlow & Raghavan, "U.S. Officer in Iraq Accused of Aiding Enemy," WP (4.27.07); Cave, "American Col. Accused of 'Aiding Enemy' at Prison in Iraq," NYT (4.27.07); Cave, "Officer Testifies Against U.S. Military Jailer in Iraq," NYT (5.1.07); Susman, "Case against U.S. Officer in Iraq Profiled," LAT (5.1.07); Susman, "GI Who Oversaw Iraq Jail Faces Court Martial," LAT (6.15.07); "Va. Officer to Go on Trial on Charges of Aiding Foe," WP (10.14.07); Kratovac, "Iraq: Soldier's Trial for Aiding Enemy," LAT (10.15.07); "Court-Martial Opens for GI Accused of Aiding Iraqi Enemy," LAT (10.16.07); "Colonel Cleared of Aiding Enemy," NYT (10.20.07). See also Shanker, "Concern Grows over Top Military Officers' Ethics," NYT (11.13.12) (James H. Johnson III demoted, fined, and discharged for bigamy with an Iraqi woman and business dealings with her family).

55 Jaffe, "Navy's Quick Condemnation of Raunchy Videos Wins Praise from Gay Rights Groups," WP (1.3.11); Bumiller, "Navy Captain Is Investigated over Videos," NYT (1.4.11); Jaffe, "Navy Fires Capt. Owen Honors over Raunchy Video," WP (1.5.11); Cloud & Bennett, "Navy Removes Captain over Anti-gay Videos," LAT (1.5.11); Bumiller, "Navy Officers Face Censure over Videos on Carrier," NYT (3.4.11); "Virginia: Navy Officer Censured for Raunchy Videos," NYT (3.19.11); "Captain Censured over Lewd Videos Submits Comments in Support for Retaining Him in Navy," WP (8.9.11); "Virginia: Raunchy Videos Won't Mean the End of a Captain's Navy Career," NYT (8.25.11).

56 Sang-Hung, "American Soldier Sentenced for Raping a South Korean Woman," NYT (11.1.11) (10 years); Fackler, "Japanese Court Convicts 2 U.S. Sailors in Okinawa Rape," NYT (3.1.13) (Christopher Browning got 10 years, Sklyer Dozier Walker 9 years); "Marine Sentenced to 40 Years for Rape," AP (12.4.06) (LCpl. Daniel Smith; overturned on appeal).

57 Draper, "In the Company of Men," NYT (11.30.14); Lamothe, "Marine Corps Takes New Step to Separate Troops Caught Sexually Harassing Others," WP (5.10.17); Weiser, "Court Halts Former Cadet's Lawsuit against Her Superiors at West Point," NYT (8.31.17).

58 "No Retrial for Freed Marine," LAT (5.9.09).

59 Nakamura, "U.S. Military Sanctions 10 in Colombia Prostitution Scandal," WP (7.19.12); "Report Says Military Members Brought Prostitutes to Colombia Hotel; Let Dogs Soil Rooms," WP (8.3.12).

60 Williams, "General Charged with Sexual Misconduct," NYT (9.28.12); Whitlock, "Disgraced Army General, Jeffrey A. Sinclair, Receives Fine, No Jail Time," WP (3.20.14).

61 "The Military's Approach to Sexual Assault Has to Change," WP (5.10.13).

62 "31 Women Identified as Victims in Air Force Sex Inquiry," NYT (6.29.12); "Texas: Court-Martial Is Under Way for Instructor Accused of Rape," NYT (7.17.12); Dao, "Instructor for Air Force Is Convicted in Sex Assaults," NYT (7.21.12); "Air Force Instructor Sentenced to 20 Years in Sexual Assault," NYT (7.22.12); "Mississippi: Air Force Instructor Sentenced," NYT (4.25.13); "Texas: Five Former Commanders Punished in Air Force Sex Scandal," NYT (5.2.13).

63 Whitlock, "Air Force General's Reversal of Pilot's Sexual-Assault Conviction Angers Lawmakers," WP (3.9.13); Risen, "Hagel Open to Review of Sexual Assault Case," NYT (3.12.13); "Sexual Assaults and Military Justice," NYT (3.13.13); Savage, "Amid Criticism, Pentagon Is Seeking Overhaul of the Court-Martial System," NYT (4.9.13); Steinhauer, "Military Courts Are Called Outdated on Sex Crimes," NYT (5.9.13); Whitlock, "Military Leaders Open to Power Shift in Sexual-Assault Investigations," WP (5.17.13); Steinhauer, "Women in the Senate Confront the Military on Sex Assaults," NYT (6.3.13); Whitlock, "U.S. Military Chiefs Balk at Taking Sex-Assault Cases Out of Commanders' Hands," WP (6.4.13); Steinhauer, "Joint Chiefs' Answers on Sex Crimes Dismay Senators," NYT (6.5.13); Steinhauer, "A Sexual-Assault Measure to Be Cut from Military Bill," NYT (6.12.13); "An Escalating Fight over Military Justice," NYT (7.30.13).

64 Whitlock & Gibbons-Neff, "More High-Ranking Officers Being Charged with Sex Crimes against Subordinates," WP (3.20.16).

65 Gibbons-Neff, "How the Marine Corps' Widening Nude Photo Scandal Has Spread Throughout the Military," WP (3.11.17); "The Marines' Nude Photo Scandal Is a Sorely Needed Wake-Up Call," WP (3.11.17); Gibbons-Neff, "Lawmakers Skewer Top Marine Officer over Nude-Photo Scandal," WP (3.15.17); Gibbons-Neff, "First Marines Punished for Online Conduct Following Nude-Photo Scandal," WP (4.8.17); Lamothe, "Army Suspends Drill Sergeants at Fort Benning amid Allegations of Sexual Assault against Trainees," WP (8.23.17).

66 Sonez, "Dover Mismanagement Requires Congressional Action, Some Lawmakers Say," WP (11.10.11); Whitlock & Ukman, "Panetta Orders Review of Discipline in Dover Mortuary Probe," WP (11.11.11); "Our Fallen Veterans Deserve Better," WP (11.11.11).

67 "Virginia: Ship Commander Fired (NYT (3.3.11); "California: Captain Loses Command of Destroyer," NYT (4.29.11).

68 Hastings, "The Runaway General," *Rolling Stone* (6.25.10); Shanker, "Pentagon Inquiry into Article Clears McChrystal and Aides," NYT (4.19.11); Cloud, "Pentagon Report Contradicts Article that Led to Gen. Stanley McChrystal's Ouster," LAT (4.19.11).

69 "U.S. Fires Senior Officer for Remarks on Afghans," NYT (11.5.11).

70 "Balking Sailor Is Sentenced," NYT (5.13.05) (three months hard labor and demotion); Mohammed, "Enlistee Flees Return to Iraq," LAT (9.22.06); Khalil, "L.A. Man Faces Trial for Desertion," LAT (3.6.07); "L.A. Man in Desertion Case Freed," LAT (4.19.07) (SPC Agustin Aguayo: eight months' time served and discharge); "Sgt. Who Left His Base in Protest

of Iraq Is Sentenced," LAT (10.13.06); Goodstein, "A Soldier Hoped to Do Good but Was Changed by War," NYT (10.13.06) (Sgt. Ricky Clousing: three months and discharge); "Colorado: Missing Marine," NYT (10.6.06); Roberts, "Marine Lance Hering Accepts Plea for Disappearing Act," *Denver Westword* (10.6.09) (LCpl. Lance Hering: probation); "Specialist Pleads Guilty to Awol," NYT (2.6.07); "Soldier Gets 2 Months for Desertion," AP (2.5.07) (SPC Melanie McPherson: three months and discharge); "Soldier Gets 7 Months for Going Awol," LAT (2.23.07) (SPC Mark Wilkerson: seven months and discharge); "Louisiana: Antiwar Vet Gets General Discharge," LAT (6.14.07) (Marine Cpl. Adam Kokesh: discharge); Priest & Hall, "A Soldier's Officer," WP (12.2.07); "The Case of Lt. Whiteside," WP (12.6.07); Priest & Hall, "Leniency Suggested for Officer Who Shot Herself," WP (12.11.07); "Events Surrounding the Case of 1st Lt. Elizabeth Whiteside," WP (1.30.08) (1st Lt. Elizabeth Whiteside: honorable discharge after two suicide attempts); Frosch, "Soldier Who Deserted to Canada Draws 15-month Term," NYT (8.23.08) (PFC Robin Long: 15 months and discharge); McKinley, "Soldier Who Didn't Obey Orders Is Jailed," NYT (8.6.09) (SPC Victor Agosto: one month and discharge); "Maryland: Obama-Doubting Army Doctor Sentenced," NYT (12.17.10) (LtCol. Terrence Lakin: six months and discharge); "Nebraska: Air Force Discharges 'Birther,'" NYT (8.18.11) (SSgt. Daryn Moran: discharge).

71 Kifner & Egan, "Officer Faces Court-Martial for Refusing to Deploy to Iraq," NYT (7.23.06); Watanabe, "Loyal to Country or Conscience?" LAT (10.16.06); Watanabe, "Dissenting Officer Faces Court-Martial," LAT (11.12.06); Watanabe, "Dissent Case Will Test Limits of Officers' Speech," LAT (1.7.07); "Military Injustice," LAT (1.8.07); Watanabe, "Officer Facing Court-Martial Denounces War," LAT (1.18.07); Yardley, "Trial Starts for Officer Who Refused to Go to Iraq," NYT (2.6.07); Tizon, "Instead of Iraq, a Battle All His Own," LAT (2.5.07); "Mistrial Called in Lieutenant's Court-Martial," WP (2.8.07); Verhovek, "Mistrial Declared for War Objector," LAT (2.8.07); "Iraq Objector Faces Another Court-Martial," LAT (2.24.07); "Washington: Second Court-Martial in Iraq Protest," NYT (3.1.07); "War Objector's 2nd Court-Martial Blocked," LAT (11.8.07); "Army Officer Who Refused Iraq Duty Is Allowed to Resign," NYT (9.27.09); Murphy, "Army to Discharge Officer Who Refused to Go to Iraq," LAT (9.29.09).

72 Hsu & Johnson, "Authorities Scrutinize Links between Fort Hood Suspect, Imam Said to Back al-Qaeda," WP (11.9.09); Johnston & Shane, "U.S. Knew of Suspect's Tie to Radical Cleric," NYT (11.10.09); Rucker, Johnson & Nakashima, "Hasan E-mails to Cleric Didn't Result in Inquiry," WP (11.10.09); "Hasan's Attorney Says His Goal Is a Fair Trial," LAT (11.12.09); Rucker & Nakashima, "Hasan Charged with 13 Counts of Murder," WP (11.13.09); Schwartz, "Experts Outline Hurdles in Trying to Defend Hasan," NYT (11.16.09); Jaffe & Pershing, "Army Panel to Examine Hasan's Career," WP (11.17.09); "Understanding Fort Hood," WP (11.21.09); Bumiller & Shane, "Pentagon Faults Supervision

in Fort Hood Case," NYT (1.16.10); "Subpoenas Sought for Information on Shootings," NYT (4.16.10); Hsu, "Two Senators Subpoena Obama Administration for Information on Fort Hood Shootings," WP (4.20.10); "Impasse on Rampage Files," NYT (4.28.10); "Texas: Death Penalty to Be Sought in Fort Hood Case," NYT (4.29.10); Serrano, "Battles Brew over Fort Hood Shooting Suspect's Past," LAT (5.22.10); Serrano, "Hearing Set to Begin into Ft. Hood Shootings," LAT (10.11.10); Krauss, "Defendant in Court for Hearing at Ft. Hood," NYT (10.13.10); Zucchino, "Hearing Delayed in Ft. Hood Shooting Case," LAT (10.13.10); Krauss, "Witnesses Recount Horror at Ft. Hood," NYT (10.14.10); Zucchino, "Survivors of Ft. Hood Shootings Testify," LAT (10.14.10); Gerhart, "Mental Health Specialists Were Hit Hard at Fort Hood, Victims Testify," WP (10.15.10); Zucchino, "More Wounded Soldiers Recount Horrors of Ft. Hood Rampage," LAT (10.15.10); McKinley, "At Hearing on Fort Hood Attack, Few Clues," NYT (10.16.10); Gerhart, "Though Hours of Wrenching Testimony, Ft. Hood Psychiatrist Nidal Malik Hasan Shows No Emotion," WP (10.16.10); "Soldiers Identify Hasan as Ft. Hood Shooter," LAT (10.16.10); Zucchino, "Police Officers Describe Fort Hood Gunfight," LAT (10.21.10); Zucchino, "Suspect in Ft. Hood Rampage Sought High-Tech Gun, Salesman Says," LAT (10.22.10); Zucchino, "Lawyers for Ft. Hood Suspect Decline to Put On a Defense," LAT (11.16.10); "Texas: Defense Offers No Evidence in Fort Hood Case," NYT (11.16.10); "Texas: Trial Sought in Fort Hood Case," NYT (11.18.10); Steinhauer, "Authorities Faulted in Fort Hood Attack," NYT (2.4.11); Wan & Sonmez, "Senate Probe Faults Army, FBI for Missing Warning Signs before Fort Hood Attack," WP (2.3.11); Serrano, "Senators Criticize FBI and Pentagon in Ft. Hood Shooting Case," LAT (2.3.11); McKinley, "Texas: Capital Trial Is Suggested in Rampage at Fort Hood," NYT (3.5.11); Fernandez, "Major Is Arraigned in Fort Hood Killings," NYT (7.21.11); "Army Judge Who Was at Fort Hood on Day of Shooting Rampage Won't Step Aside in Suspect's Case," WP (12.1.11); "Texas: Third Delay Possible in Fort Hood Rampage," NYT (6.19.12); "Texas: Judge Denies another Delay in Fort Hood Trial," NYT (6.30.12); "Fort Hood Suspect May Be 'Forcibly Shaved' before Trial," CNN (7.25.12); Brown, "Terrorism Expert May Testify at Fort Hood Trial," ABC News (8.9.12); Hennessy-Fiske, "Judge Fines Ft. Hood Suspect for Beard, Denies Trial Delay," LAT (8.14.12); Fernandez, "Fort Hood Shooting Trial Delayed Pending Ruling on Beard," NYT (8.16.12); Fernandez, "Impasse over Suspect's Beard Spurs Debate in Fort Hood Shooting Case," NYT (8.23.12); Fernandez, "Texas: Appeals Court Declines to Rule on Forced Shaving of Defendant," NYT (8.28.12); Fernandez, "Fort Hood Shooting Suspect's Beard Must Be Shaved, Military Judge Rules," NYT (9.7.12); Rizzo, "U.S. Asks Court to Deny Fort Hood Shooter's Appeal," CNN (11.20.12); Fernandez, "Court Ousts Trial Judge in Rampage at Ft. Hood," NYT (12.3.12); Fernandez, "Texas: New Judge in Fort Hood Shooting Case," NYT (12.5.12); "Texas: Fort Hood Defendant Is Allowed to Keep Beard," NYT (12.19.12); Chumley, "Judge Denies Fort Hood Shooting Suspect's Attempt to Plead

Guilty," *Washington Times* (3.12.13); Fernandez, "Shooting Suspect Seeks to Represent Himself in Trial at Fort Hood," NYT (5.30.13); Fernandez, "Judge Says Ft. Hood Shooting Suspect May Act as His Own Lawyer in Court," NYT (6.4.13); Fernandez, "Fort Hood Suspect Says Rampage Was to Defend Afghan Taliban Leaders," NYT (6.5.13); Fernandez, "Fort Hood Suspect Given More Time to Prepare Defense, Most Likely Delaying Trial," NYT (6.6.13); Fernandez, "Lawyers Torn over Suspect in Rampage at Fort Hood," NYT (6.12.13); Fernandez, "Judge Rejects Fort Hood Shooting Suspect's Defense Strategy," NYT (6.15.13); "Six Possible Jurors Dismissed in Fort Hood Shooting Case," NYT (7.10.13); "Texas: Fort Hood Suspect Questions Possible Jurors," NYT (7.11.13); "Fort Hood Shooting Suspect Nidal Hasan Barred from Seeing Evidence Obtained by FISA Spying for His Self-Defense," CBS News (7.12.13); Fernandez, "Victims to Again Face Gunman in Fort Hood Trial," NYT (8.5.13); "Prosecutor in Fort Hood Trial Tells Jury Hasan Planned to 'Kill as Many Soldiers as He Could,'" WP (8.6.13); Fernandez, "Defendant in Fort Hood Shooting Case Admits Being Gunman," NYT (8.7.13); Kember, "Trial of Nidal Hasan, Accused Fort Hood Gunman, Begins after Delays," WP (8.7.13); Fernandez, "Lawyer Says Fort Hood Defendant's Goal Is Death," NYT (8.8.13); "Standby Lawyers Demand Removal from Fort Hood Trial, Say They're Being Forced to Violate Rules," WP (8.8.13); Fernandez, "Judge Denies Ex-Defense Team's Bid to Limit Role in Fort Hood Suspect's Trial," NYT (8.9.13); Manning, "The Fort Hood Attack Was Terrorism. The Army Should Call It That," WP (8.8.13); Fernandez, "Witnesses Relive Horror of Fort Hood Attack," NYT (8.10.13); Fernandez, "Fort Hood Gunman Told Panel That Death Would Make Him a Martyr," NYT (8.12.13); Fernandez, "Sergeant Who Confronted Fort Hood Gunman Faces Him in Court," NYT (8.17.13); Fernandez, "Fort Hood Gunman E-mailed Supervisors over Concerns," NYT (8.20.13); "Soldier Accused in 2009 Fort Hood Shootings Rests Case without Calling Witnesses," WP (8.21.13); Fernandez, "Calling No Witnesses, Defendant in Fort Hood Shooting Rests His Case," NYT (8.22.13); Fernandez, "Jury Begins Work on Fort Hood Shooting," NYT (8.23.13); "With Death Sentence on Line, Widows of Fort Hood Slain Describe Lost Moments with Fallen," WP (8.27.13); Fernandez, "Judge Denies Defense Lawyers' Request in Fort Hood Case," NYT (8.28.13); Lapidis, "Should Hasan Get the Death Penalty?" NYT (8.29.13); Fernandez, "Death Penalty for Rampage at Fort Hood," NYT (8.29.13); Kember, "Nidal Hasan Sentenced to Death for Fort Hood Shooting Rampage," WP (8.29.13).

73 Bumiller, "Army Leak Suspect Is Turned In, by Ex-Hacker," NYT (6.8.10); "Soldier Detained in Connection with Giving Iraq Military Video to WikiLeaks," LAT (6.7.10); Nakashima, "Online Contact Says He Turned In Analyst Who Wanted to Leak Information," LAT (6.8.10); Nakashima, "Messages from Alleged Leaker Bradley Manning Portray Him as Despondent Soldier," WP (6.10.10); Myers, "Charges for Soldier Accused of Leak," NYT (7.6.10); Greenwald, "The Inhumane Conditions of Bradley Manning's Detention," Salon.com (12.15.10); Shane, "Accused

Soldier in Brig as WikiLeaks Link Is Sought," NYT (1.14.11); Nakashima, "Lawyer for Bradley Manning, Army Figure in WikiLeaks Case, Alleges Prison Mistreatment," WP (1.21.11); Shane, "Lawyer Protests Status of Soldier in Leaks Case," NYT (1.22.11); Nakashima, "Bradley Manning, WikiLeaks' Alleged Source, Faces 22 New Charges," WP (3.3.11); Savage, "Soldier Faces 22 New WikiLeaks Charges," NYT (3.3.11); Savage, "Soldier in Leaks Case Was Jailed Naked, Lawyer Says," NYT (3.4.11); Savage, "Soldier in Leaks Case Will Be Made to Sleep Naked Nightly," NYT (3.5.11); Nakashima, "In Brig, WikiLeaks Suspect Bradley Manning Ordered to Sleep without Clothing," WP (3.6.11); Shane, "Obama Defends Detention Conditions for Soldier Accused in WikiLeaks Case," NYT (3.12.11); Oliphant, "Is Treatment of WikiLeaks Suspect Bradley Manning Fueling State Department–Pentagon Dispute?" LAT (3.12.11); Hillary Rodham Clinton Press Statement (3.13.11); Crowley Statement (3.13.11); Landler & Shear, "Official Exits State Dept. after Jabs at Pentagon," NYT (3.14.11); Richter, "State Department Spokesman P.J. Crowley Resigns," LAT (3.14.11); Sheridan, "State Department Spokesman Quits after Criticizing WikiLeaks Suspect's Treatment," WP (3.14.11); "The Abuse of Private Manning," NYT (3.15.11); "Punishing Pfc. Manning," LAT (3.15.11); "Pfc. Bradley Manning Doesn't Deserve Humiliating Treatment," WP (3.16.11); Adam, "Britain to Reassert Worries about WikiLeaks Suspect Bradley Manning's Treatment," WP (4.6.11); "Kansas: Leaks Suspect to Join Other Inmates," NYT (4.29.11); Pilkington, "Manning Held under Better Conditions ahead of Trial," G (5.5.11); Nakashima & Tate, "Army Pfc. Manning to Face Pretrial Hearing in WikiLeaks Case," WP (12.16.11); Shane, "Private in WikiLeaks Spying Case Goes to Court," NYT (12.17.11); Nakashima, "Bradley Manning's Attorney in WikiLeaks Case Seeks Presiding Officer's Recusal," WP (12.17.11); Nakashima & Tate, "Soldier's Gender Identity Issues Raised in WikiLeaks Case," WP (12.18.11); "Pretrial Hearing Continues as Prosecution Seeks to Connect Manning's Disclosures to WikiLeaks," WP (12.18.11); Bennett, "Testimony in Manning's WikiLeaks Case Shows Breadth of Evidence," LAT (12.18.11); Savage, "Private Accused of Leaks Offers Partial Guilty Plea," NYT (11.9.12); Savage, "Judge Says Harsh Detention Is Not Cause to Drop Charges in WikiLeaks Case," NYT (1.9.13); Tate & Nakashima, "Judge Refuses to Dismiss Charges against WikiLeaks Suspect Bradley Manning," WP (1.9.13); Savage, "Soldier Admits Providing Files to WikiLeaks," NYT (3.1.13); Tate & Londoño, "Bradley Manning Pleads Guilty to 10 Lesser Charges, Explains Motive," WP (3.1.13); Shane, "Soldier to Face More Serious Charges in Leak," NYT (3.2.13); Savage, "Manning Is Acquitted of Aiding the Enemy," NYT (7.31.13); Dishneau, "Manning's Possible Sentence Cut to 90 Years," *Stars and Stripes* (8.6.13); Savage, "Manning, Facing Prison for Leaks, Apologizes at Court-Martial Trial," NYT (8.14.13); Huetteman, "At Sentencing Hearing, Lawyers for Manning Urge Leniency," NYT (8.20.13); Tate, "Judge Sentences Bradley Manning to 35 Years," WP (8.21.13); Savage & Huetteman, "Manning Sentenced to 35 Years for a Pivotal Leak of U.S. Files," NYT (8.22.13); Shaer, "The Long, Lonely Road of Chelsea Manning," NYT (6.12.17); Nicks (2012); Madar (2013).

74 Savage, "Chelsea Manning Tried Committing Suicide a Second Time in October," NYT (11.4.16); Savage, "Chelsea Manning Asks Obama to Cut Sentence to Time Served," NYT (11.14.16); Nakashima, "Chelsea Manning Petitions Obama for Clemency on her 35-Year Prison Sentence," WP (11.15.16); McFadden, Monahan, Arikin & Connor, "Army Leaker Chelsea Manning on Obama's 'Short List' for Commutation," NBC News (1.11.17); Savage, "Chelsea Manning to Be Released Early as Obama Commutes Sentence," NYT (1.17.17); Ryan, Horwitz & Tate, "In Manning Clemency Call, Obama Sought to Reduce Sentence Viewed as 'Nuts,'" WP (1.19.17); Pilkington, "Chelsea Manning Leaks Had no Strategic Impact on US War Efforts, Pentagon Finds," G (6.20.17).

75 Oppel, "Bowe Bergdahl to Face Court-Martial on Desertion Charges," NYT (12.15.15); "A Bad Call on the Bergdahl Court-Martial," NYT (12.16.15); "The Soldier Donald Trump Called a Traitor," NYT (11.27.16); Oppel, "Bergdahl, Callled 'Dirty Rotten Traitor' by Trump, Seeks End to Charges," NYT (1.20.17); Kheel, "Military Judge: Trump Comments about Bergdahl 'Disturbing,'" The Hill (2.13.17); Oppel, "Judge Says Trump's Statements Did Not Prejudice Case against Bergdahl," NYT (2.25.17); Kheel, "Appeals Court Upholds Decision Not to Toss Bergdahl Case over Trump Comments," The Hill (3.14.17); Oppel, "Bowe Bergdahl, Called a 'Traitor' by President Trump, Pleads Guilty," NYT (10.17.17); Kheel, "Bergdahl Lawyers Renew Efforts to Have Case Tossed over Trump Comments," The Hill (10.18.17); Drew, "Military Judge in Bergdahl Case Worries about Trump Impact," MH (10.23.17); Oppel, "Bergdahl's Odd Journey from Victim to Criminal," NYT (10.24.17); Oppel, "Sgt. Bergdahl's Sentence May Be Lighter Because of Trump's Comments," NYT (10.31.17); Horton, "Bowe Bergdahl Should Spend 14 Years in Prison and Lose His Medical Benefits, Army Says," WP (11.2.17); Horton, "Bowe Bergdahl, the Fomer Hostage Who Pleaded Guilty to Desertion, Avoids Prison," WP (11.4.17).

76 Sherrill (1970). Clemenceau is supposed to have said: "Ainsi la justice militaire n'est pas la justice, la musique militaire n'est pas la musique."

CHAPTER 4   MILITARY COMMISSIONS

1 Carney, "McCain Doubles Down on Waterboarding Criticism," The Hill (2.9.16).

2 66 Fed. Reg. 57831 (11.16.01); Bravin (2013: 38–39). For critiques and comparisons of military commissions with other criminal procedures, see Glazier (2003; 2006; 2008); Kannaday et al. (2012); Ni Aoláin & Gross (2013); Center for American Progress, Sizing Up the Bush Military Commissions: Comparison of Models of Due Process (n.d.). For the most detailed account of an earlier Military Commission (MC), documenting

many problems similar to those discussed in this chapter, see Ryan (2012). For other histories, see Fisher (2005); Richards (2007); Smith (2012); Scheiber & Scheiber (2016) (Hawai'i in World War II).

3 Elsea (2014).

4 Toner & Lewis, "White House Push on Security Steps Bypasses Congress," NYT (11.15.01).

5 "Department of Justice Oversight," SJC Hearing (11.28.01); Mahler (2009: 61).

6 Gonzales, "Martial Justice, Full and Fair," NYT (11.30.01).

7 147 Cong. Rec. S3277 (12.14.01); "John Ashcroft Misses the Point," NYT (12.7.01); ABA Task Force on Terrorism and the Law, Report (1.4.02); Safire, "Seizing Dictatorial Power," NYT (11.15.01); Safire, "Kangaroo Courts," NYT (11.26.01).

8 Because the government chose to detain and try accused in Guantánamo because of its inaccessibility, coverage of trials was limited. For summaries of some hearings, see HRF Military Commission Trial Observation, "A New Week at Guantánamo" (11.8.04); "Enter the Federal Court" (11.8.04); "Background" (1.9.06); "Preview" (1.10.06); "Chatty Prosecutors and the Old Camp X-Ray" (1.11.06); "Boycott – United States v. Al Bahlul" (1.12.06); "The Guantánamo Spin Zone" (1.13.06); "Military Commissions in Context as Guantánamo Enters Its Fifth Year" (2.28.06); "Flaws in the Process and Dracula?" (3.1.06); "Yes, Commissions Can Allow In Evidence Obtained under Torture" (3.1.06); "Not Full and Fair" (3.2.06); "Today's Score from Guantánamo – Constitution – 1, No Constitution – 3" (7.18.08); "Fig Newtons and Fundamental Rights" (7.19.08); "Is That What You're Wearing to Trial?" (7.22.08); "Why Are You Doing This?" (7.23.08); "Military Commission Trial Shows Its True Colors" (7.24.08); "When Did the Conflict with al Qaeda Start?" (7.30.08); " 'Black Clouds' of Coercion over Guantánamo" (7.31.08); "The Madan War Crimes Trial: An Illusion of Justice" (8.7.08); "Not All Crimes Are War Crimes" (8.15.08); "Representing the Unwilling" (8.18.08).

9 Hathaway (2007); Mahler (2009: 90–92); for accounts by Hamdan's lawyers, see Katyal (2006); Swift (2007).

10 Mahler (2009: 118).

11 Mahler (2009: chap. 9); Bravin (2013: chaps. 8, 10).

12 *Hamdan v. Rumsfeld*, 344 F.Supp.2d 152 (DDC 2004); Mahler, "The Bush Administration vs. Salim Hamdan," NYT (1.8.06).

13 Denbeaux & Denbeaux (2006).

14 Golden, "U.S. Is Examining a Plan to Bolster the Rights of Detainees," NYT (3.27.05); DoD Press Release 897-05, "Secretary Rumsfeld Approves Changes to Improve Military Commission Procedures" (7.31.05); Lewis, "U.S. Alters Rules for War Crime Trials," NYT (9.1.05).

15 Johnston & Lewis, "Lawyer Says Military Tried to Coerce Detainee's Plea," NYT (6.16.05); Mahler (2009: 190).

16 *Hamdan v. Rumsfeld*, 415 F.3d 33 (D.C. Cir. 2005); Lewis, "Ruling Lets U.S. Restart Trials at Guantánamo," NYT (7.16.05); Serrano, "Guantánamo Military Tribunals Are Upheld," LAT (7.16.05).

17 VandeHei, "Judge Heard Terrorism Case As He Interviewed for Seat," WP (8.17.05).
18 Gillers, Luban & Lubet, "Improper Advances: Talking Dream Jobs with the Judge Out of Court," Slate.com (8.17.05); Gillers, Luban & Lubet, "Roberts' Bad Decision," LAT (9.13.05); Kirkpatrick, "Nominee's Role in Tribunal Case Draws Democrats' Interest," NYT (8.25.05).
19 *Hamdan* v. *Rumsfeld*, 126 S.Ct 622 (2005); Bazelon, "Hear Me, Hear Me: The Case of the Year at the Supreme Court May Duck," *Slate* (10.27.05).
20 "Sins of Commission," WP (3.27.06).
21 "No Legal Rights for Enemy Combatants, Scalia Says," WP (3.27.06); "Supreme Court: Detainees' Rights – Scalia Speaks His Mind," *Newsweek* (4.3.06).
22 Land, "Scalia's Recusal Sought in Key Detainee Case," WP (3.28.06).
23 "Over-the-Top Justice," NYT (4.2.06).
24 Eggen & White, "U.S. Seeks to Avoid Detainee Ruling," WP (1.13.06); "Administration Asks Justices to Dismiss Appeal," NYT (1.13.06); Denniston, "Analysis: Hamdan and a Few Minutes in the Senate," Scotusblog (3.23.06); Dean, "Senators Kyl and Graham's Hamdan v. Rumsfeld Scam," Findlaw.com (7.5.06); Bazelon, "Hamdan Hoax, Part 3," *Slate* (7.26.06); Kropf, "Graham's Faux Debate," Charleston Post & Courier (7.12.06).
25 "The President and the Courts," NYT (3.20.06).
26 Bravin, "White House Will Reverse Policy, Ban Evidence Elicited by Torture," WSJ (3.22.06); Rosenberg, "U.S. Bars Any Evidence Resulting from Torture," MH (3.23.06); Shanker, "Barring Evidence from Torture Is Considered," NYT (3.23.06); DoD, Military Commission Instruction No. 10 (3.24.06).
27 "The Law vs. the Government," LAT (3.29.06).
28 *Hamdan* v. *Rumsfeld*, 548 U.S. 557 (2006).
29 Hess, "Bush May Seek Law of War Changes in UCMJ," UPI (6.29.06); Greenhouse, "The Ruling on Tribunals: The Overview," NYT (6.30.06); Yost, "War on Terror Ruling Worries GOP Lawmakers," AP (7.2.06); Liptak, "The Court Enters the War, Loudly," NYT (7.2.06); "Fox News Sunday with Chris Wallace" (7.2.06); Yoo, "The High Court's Hamdan Power Grab," LAT (7.7.06).
30 Reynolds, "Congress Tackles the Guantánamo Challenge," LAT (7.1.06); Zernicke, "A Top Senate Republican Is Uncertain on Legislation for Military Tribunals for Terror Suspects," NYT (7.1.06); Abramowitz & Weisman, GOP Seeks Advantage in Ruling on Trials," WP (7.1.06); "Lawmakers Seek Action after Ruling on Detainees," NYT (7.3.06); "Schmitt, "Congress Faces Dilemma on Terror Trials," LAT (7.3.06).
31 "A Victory for Law," WP (6.30.06); "Let There Be Law," WP (7.2.06); "Congress's Turn," WP (7.9.06).
32 "Bush vs. the Constitution," LAT (6.30.06).

33 "The Fragile Kennedy Court," NYT (7.7.06); "Signs of Life in Congress," NYT (7.9.06).
34 Rosenberg, "Lawyer Is Denied Promotion," MH (10.8.06).
35 "The Cost of Doing Your Duty," NYT (10.11.06).
36 Flaherty, "U.S. Will Give Detainees Geneva Rights," AP (7.11.06).
37 "Gitmo, Meet Geneva," LAT (7.13.06).
38 Herbert, "The Law Gets a Toehold," NYT (7.13.06).
39 Zernike & Stolberg, "Detainee Rights Create a Divide on Capitol Hill," NYT (7.10.06); Flaherty, "U.S. Will Give Detainees Geneva Rights," AP (7.11.06); Milbank, "It's Bush's Way or the Highway on Guantánamo Bay," WP (7.12.06); Babington & Abramowitz, "U.S. Shifts Policy on Geneva Conventions," WP (7.12.06); Shane, "Terror and Power: Bush Takes a Step Back," NYT (7.12.06); Chairman Hunter Opening Statement, HASC (7.12.06).
40 "New Rules for Gitmo," LAT (7.11.06).
41 "The Rule of Law: Recognizing the Power of the Courts, Finally," NYT (7.12.06).
42 Weisman, "Battle Looms in Congress over Military Tribunals," WP (7.13.06); Spiegel, "Bush Lawyers Decry Plan for War Crimes Court," LAT (7.13.06); Flaherty, "Military Lawyers Clash with White House," AP (9.7.06).
43 "Bush Won't Seek Military Tribunals, McCain Says," NYT (7.13.06); Zajac, "Gonzales Takes Issue with Justices' Detainees Ruling," CT (7.14.06); Smith & Weisman, "Policy Rewrite Reveals Rift in Administration," WP (7.14.06).
44 "A Process for Prisoners," WP (7.13.06).
45 Zernike, "Military Lawyers Urge Protections for Detainees," NYT (7.14.06); "Wisdom on Detainees," WP (7.14.06); Weisman, "Senators Gain Momentum to Change Military Tribunal System," WP (7.15.06).
46 "The Real Agenda," NYT (7.16.06).
47 Herbert, "The Definition of Tyranny," NYT (7.17.06).
48 Herbert, "Leading to Low Ground," NYT (7.20.06).
49 Spiegel & Schmitt, "New Plan Is Proposed for Detainees," LAT (8.3.06); Zernike, "White House Asks Congress to Define War Crimes," NYT (8.3.06).
50 Weisman & Abramowitz, "White House Shifts Tack on Tribunals," WP (7.20.06).
51 Cloud & Stolberg, "White House Bill Proposes System to Try Detainees," NYT (7.26.06); Smith & White, "Proposal Calls for Tribunal-Style Trials," WP (7.27.06); Cloud & Stolberg, "Rules Debated for Trials of Detainees," NYT (7.27.06).
52 Savage, "Military Lawyers See Limits on Trial Input," BG (8.27.06).
53 "A Flawed Proposal," WP (7.29.06).
54 Spiegel & Schmitt, "New Plan Is Proposed for Detainees," LAT (8.3.06); Zernike, "White House Asks Congress to Define War Crimes," NYT (8.3.06).

55 "Listening to the Lawyers," NYT (8.5.06).
56 "Justice after Guantánamo," LAT (8.4.06).
57 Goldsmith & Posner, "A Better Way on Detainees," WP (8.4.06).
58 Stolberg, "President Moves 14 Held in Secret to Guantánamo: Seeks Tribunals," NYT (9.7.06); Sanger, "A Challenge to Congress," NYT (9.7.06); Zernike & Lewis, "Proposal for New Tribunals for Terror Suspects Would Hew to the First Series," NYT (9.7.06).
59 "Ending the Lawlessness," WP (9.7.06).
60 "Barely Legal War-Making," LAT (9.7.06).
61 Zernike, "Lawyers and G.O.P. Chiefs Resist Proposal on Tribunal," NYT (9.8.06); Zernike, "Crucial Senator Says a Few Problems Remain in Bill on Terror Tribunals," NYT (9.9.06); Zernike, "Looking for Agreement on Tribunals for Detainees," NYT (9.9.06).
62 "A Solution for Trials," WP (9.9.06).
63 Smith, "White House Gains Concessions in Senate Measure on Tribunals," WP (9.12.06); Rosen, "Graham Thinks Terror Bill Fatally Flawed," The State (Columbia, South Carolina) (9.12.06); Jonnelly & Perine, "Senate GOP Still Split over Rules for Trying Terror Detainees," CQ Today (9.12.06); Zernike, "Deal Reported Near on Rights of Suspects in Terror Cases," NYT (9.13.06); Allen, "Senate Republicans Defy Bush over Terrorism Trials," WP (9.13.06).
64 Ike Skelton, Press Release (9.13.06); Allen, "Senate Republicans Defy Bush over Terrorism Trials," WP (9.13.06).
65 "A Crucial Choice," WP (9.14.06).
66 Judges Gibbons, Hufstedler, Jones, Lewis, Norris, Pratt, Sarokin, Sessions, and Wald to Congress (9.13.06).
67 Simon, Barnes & Hook, "Senate Panel Rebuffs Bush on Detainees," LAT (9.15.06); Hulse, "An Unexpected Collision," NYT (9.15.06); Hulse, Zernike & Stolberg, "How 3 G.O.P. Veterans Stalled Bush Detainee Bill," NYT (9.17.06).
68 "Stampeding Congress," NYT (9.15.06).
69 Herbert, "The Kafka Strategy," NYT (9.18.06).
70 "No Rubber Stamp for Bush," LAT (9.17.06).
71 Graham interview in Newsweek (9.18.06).
72 Donnelly & Kady, "Senate GOP Dissidents Reject New White House Detainee Language," CQ Today (9.19.06); Babington & Weisman, "Dissidents' Detainee Bill May Face Filibuster," WP (9.20.06); Zernike, "White House Drops a Condition on Interrogation Bill," NYT (9.20.06); "5 Ex-Joint Chiefs Oppose Bush Detainee Effort: Sen. McCain," Dow Jones (9.20.06); Babington, "House Panel Supports Tribunal Plan, 20 to 19," WP (9.21.06); Lewis & Zernike, "Measures Seek to Restrict Detainees' Access to Courts," NYT (9.21.06); Milbank, "Bush's Bill Suffers a Torturous Day in Committee," WP (9.21.06); Zernike, "Top Republicans Reach an Accord on Detainee Bill," NYT (9.22.06).
73 "A Bad Bargain," NYT (9.22.06); Simon & Barnes, "Defense Lawyers Assail Legislation on Detainees," LAT (9.23.06); Smith, "On Rough Treatment, a Rough Accord," WP (9.23.06).

74   "Rush to Error," WP (9.27.06).
75   Babington, "House Approves Bill on Detainees," WP (9.28.06); Hulse & Zernike, "House Passes Detainee Bill as It Clears Senate Hurdle," NYT (9.28.06).
76   "Rushing Off a Cliff," NYT (9.28.06).
77   Benjamin & Shapiro, "Tortured Justice," Salon (9.28.06); Babington & Weisman, "Senate Approves Detainee Bill Backed by Bush," WP (9.29.06); Zernike, "Senate Approves Broad New Rules to Try Detainees," NYT (9.29.06); Fletcher, "Bush Attacks 'Party of Cut and Run,'" WP (9.29.06); McManus, "Detainee Bill Boosts GOP," LAT (9.30.06).
78   "Profiles in Cowardice," WP (10.1.06).
79   Dodd, "What My Father Saw at Nuremberg," LAT (10.1.06).
80   "President Bush Signs Military Commissions Act of 2006," White House News Release (10.17.06); Fletcher, "Bush Signs Terrorism Measure," WP (10.18.06); Schmitt & Barnes, "Bush Signs Tough Rules on Detainees," LAT (10.18.06).
81   "Head of Military Commissions Quits," WSJ (11.15.06); DoD Press Release 151-07 (2.7.07).
82   *Hamdan v. Rumsfeld*, 464 F.Supp.2d 9 (DDC 2006).
83   Rosenberg, "Driver for Bin Laden to Face Charges," MH (5.11.07).
84   Williams & Barnes, "Tribunals Are Dealt Another Legal Setback," LAT (6.5.07); Glaberson, "Court Advances Military Trials for Detainees," NYT (9.25.07).
85   "Challenge to Military Trial Panels Turned Down," LAT (10.2.07).
86   Williams, "Bid [sic] Laden's Driver to Argue He's POW," LAT (12.6.07); Glaberson, "Defense Challenges Enemy Combatant Status of Detainee," NYT (12.6.07); Williams, "Hamdan Is Called More Than Driver," LAT (12.7.07); Glaberson, "Detainee's Loyalty to bin Laden Is at Issue in Hearing," NYT (12.7.07); "Judge: Gitmo Trial for bin Laden Driver," NYT (12.20.07).
87   Davis, "The Guantánamo I Know," NYT (6.26.07).
88   Glaberson, "War-Crimes Prosecutor Quits in Pentagon Clash," NYT (10.6.07); White, "Ex-Prosecutor Alleges Pentagon Plays Politics," WP (10.20.07); Glaberson, "Ex-Prosecutor Says He Was Pushed toward Closed Trials at Guantánamo," NYT (10.20.07).
89   Bravin, "Pentagon Forbids Marine to Testify," WSJ (11.8.07); Bravin, "Guantánamo Testimony Is Blocked," WSJ (12.9.07); see Goodman, "Torture at Guantánamo: Lt. Col. Stuart Couch on His Refusal to Prosecute Abused Prisoner," *Democracy Now!* (2.22.13).
90   Davis, "AWOL Military Justice," LAT (12.10.07).
91   Hartmann, "There Will Be No Secret Trials," LAT (12.19.07).
92   Rosenberg, "Brief: Guantánamo Detainee 'Traumatized,'" MH (2.3.08); Glaberson, "Detainees' Mental Health Is Latest Legal Battle," NYT (4.26.08); White, "From Chief Prosecutor to Critic at Guantánamo," WP (4.29.08); "Ex-Prosecutor Calls War Tribunals Tainted," LAT (4.29.08); White, "Guantánamo Detainee Rejects Court Procedure," WP (4.30.08); Glaberson, "An Apologetic Boycott in Good-Natured Banter," NYT

(4.30.08); White, "Justice System for Detainees Is Moving at a Crawl," WP (5.6.08).

93 Glaberson, "Judge Drops General from Trial of Detainee," NYT (5.10.08); Glaberson, "Judge's Guantánamo Ruling Bodes Ill for System," NYT (5.11.08); Glaberson, "Detainee's Trial Delayed until Justices Rule," NYT (5.17.08).

94 Glaberson, "Detainee's Trial Delayed until Justices Rule," NYT (5.17.08); Glaberson, "Two Subplots in Guantánamo's Long Legal Story," NYT (7.4.08); Wilber, "Former Driver for Bin Laden Seeks Delay in Military Trial," WP (7.4.08).

95 Markon, "Lawyers Want Detainees to Testify in Terror Trial," WP (7.15.08); Glaberson, "Detainee's Lawyers Make Claim on Sleep Deprivation," NYT (7.15.08); Meyer, "Judge Allows Guantánamo Inmates to Testify," LAT (7.15.08); Markon & White, "Detainee Describes Treatment," WP (7.16.08); Glaberson, "Detainee Challenges Guantánamo By Describing Life There," NYT (7.16.08).

96 *Hamdan v. Gates*, 565 F.Supp.2d 130 (DDC 2008); Shane & Glaberson, "Rulings Clear Military Trial of a Detainee," NYT (7.18.08); "Guantánamo Bay: Defense Can Talk to Detainees," LAT (7.19.08).

97 Markon, "Detainee's Trial in Military System Begins Today," WP (7.21.08); Glaberson & Lichtblau, "Guantánamo Detainee's Trial Opens, Ending a Seven Year Tangle," NYT (7.22.08); Williams, "Evidence on Terror Suspect Barred," LAT (7.22.08); Rosenberg, "Trial Arguments Describe World of al Qaeda," MH (7.22.08); Rosenberg, "Conspiracy Idea Floated at War-Crimes Trial," MH (7.23.08); Williams, "Bin Laden's Driver Knew 9/11 Target, Lawyer Says," LAT (7.23.08); Glaberson, "Two Sides at Guantánamo Trial Paint Starkly Different Pictures of the Defendant," NYT (7.23.08); Markon, "Hamdan Had 2 Missiles When Arrested," WP (7.23.08); Williams, "Defendant Walks Out of His Guantánamo War Crimes Trial," LAT (7.24.08); Melia, "FBI Agents Testify at Guantánamo War Crimes Trial," MH (7.24.08); Williams, "Hamdan Case Is Built on His Own Words," LAT (7.25.08); Rosenberg, "U.S. Released Bin Laden's Chief Bodyguard," MH (7.25.08); Rosenberg, "Driver: U.S. Let Bin Laden Escape," MH (7.26.08); Williams, "Hamdan Helped bin Laden Succeed, Agent Says," LAT (7.26.08); Glaberson, "Prosecution States Its Case in First Guantánamo Trial," NYT (7.26.08); Markon, "Goal of Hamdan Trial: Credibility," WP (7.27.08); Williams, "The Agency Name That Dare Not Be Spoken," LAT (7.27.08); Rosenberg, "Experts Open Second Week of Driver's Trial," MH (7.28.08); Melia, "U.S. Produced Al-Qaida Movie Played at Gitmo Trial," MH (7.28.08); Rosenberg, "Movie on Al Qaeda Unveiled at Tribunal," MH (7.29.08); Glaberson, "A U.S. Trial By Its Looks, but Only So," NYT (7.29.08); Williams, "Guantánamo Jurors Shown Graphic Film on al Qaeda," LAT (7.29.08); Rosenberg, "Witness Fails to ID Bin Laden's Driver," MH (7.30.08); Williams, "Prosecution Doesn't Rest in Hamdan Case," LAT (7.30.08); Rosenberg, "Jihad Expert: Driver

Doesn't Fit Elite Profile," MH (7.30.08); Melia, "Guantánamo: Judge Allows DisputedInterrogation," MH (7.30.08); Rosenberg, "Alleged 9/11 Mastermind Won't Testify," MH (7.30.08); Glaberson, "Lawyers for Detainee Assert Coercion," NYT (7.31.08); Williams, "Hamdan's Lawyers Want Agent's Testimony Blocked," LAT (7.31.08); MuhammadAlly, " 'Black Clouds' of Coercion over Guantánamo," HRF Law and Security Blog (7.31.08); Williams, "Two Army Officers Testify for Hamdan, in Secret," LAT (8.1.08); Glaberson, "Prosecution Rests, Then Terror Trial Enters Secret Session to Hear Defense Testimony," NYT (8.1.08); Rosenberg, "Witness Says Bin Laden Driver Made Loyalty Pledge," MH (8.1.08); Rosenberg, "Defense Rests at Bin Laden Driver's Trial," MH (8.1.08); Rosenberg, "Defense Rests at Trial of Osama bin Laden's Driver," MH (8.1.08); "Verbatim: Accused al Qaeda Kingpin on Driver," MH (9.1.08); Markon, "Hamdan Seen as 'Not Fit' for Terror," WP (8.2.08); Williams, "Hamdan 'Not Fit' for Attacks," LAT (8.2.08); Glaberson, "Terror Trial Nears End as Defense Rests Case," NYT (8.2.08); Rosenberg, "9/11 Architect: Bin Laden Driver No Terrorist," MH (8.2.08); Williams, "Jury Is Out for Hamdan and the Tribunal Process," LAT (8.4.08); Glaberson, "Lawyer Suggests Detainee Aided U.S. in Afghanistan," NYT (8.5.08); Williams, "Hamdan Case Goes to the Jury," LAT (8.5.08); Sutton, "Mistrial Avoided in Guantánamo Court Case," Reuters (8.5.08); Glaberson, "Terrorism Trial Judge Admits Possible Error on Jury Instructions," NYT (8.6.08); Williams, "Defending Hamdan: The Capture and Defense of Bin Laden's Driver," The Complex Terrain Laboratory (9.22.08).

98 Markon, "Hamdan Guilty of Terror Support," WP (8.7.08); Williams, "Mixed Verdict at Terror Tribunal," LAT (8.7.08); Williams, "Yemeni Gets 5½ Years in Prison," LAT (8.8.08); Glaberson, "Panel Convicts bin Laden Driver in Split Verdict," NYT (8.8.08); Glaberson, "Panel Sentences bin Laden Driver to a Short Term," NYT (8.8.08); Markon & White, "Bin Laden Driver Gets 5½ Years; U.S. Sought 30," WP (8.8.08); White, "Detainee May Not Go Free after Sentence," WP (8.10.08); McChesney, "Juror Questions U.S. Pursuit of Salim Hamdan," "All Things Considered," NPR (8.10.08).

99 "Trial by Tribunal," WP (8.10.08); "A Mixed Verdict," LAT (8.7.08); "The United States v. The Driver," NYT (8.10.08); Keefe, Cartoon, *Denver Post* (8.7.08); "Justice at Gitmo," LAT (8.12.08).

100 Melia, "Guantánamo Prosecutors Want Redo of Convict's Sentence," AP (9.26.08); Finn, "Detainee's Time Served Is Challenged," WP (10.18.08); Finn, "Judge Rejects Government Call to Reconsider Hamdan Sentence," WP (10.31.08); Williams, "Freed Guantánamo Prisoner Arrives Home in Yemen," LAT (11.26.08); "Hamdan Released in Yemen," LAT (1.10.09).

101 Rosenberg, "Full Panel to Decide bin Laden Driver's Appeal," MH (9.3.10); Savage, "In Setback for Military Tribunals, Bin Laden Driver's Conviction Is Reversed," NYT (10.16.12).

102 *U.S. v. Hamdan*, 801 F.Supp.2d 1247 (CMCR 2011).

103 *Hamdan* v. *U.S.*, 696 F.3d 1238 (D.C. Cir. 2012); Savage, "In Setback for Military Tribunals, Bin Laden Driver's Conviction Is Reversed," NYT (10.16.12).

104 Hicks (2010: 281); see Sales (2007).

105 Hicks (2010: chaps. 23–30).

106 Ibid. 329 n.8.

107 Bonner, "Australia Uneasy about U.S. Detainee Case," NYT (4.10.05).

108 Lewis, "Detainee Trials to Resume Soon, Rumsfeld Says," NYT (7.19.05); Lewis, "Two Prosecutors Faulted Trials for Detainees," NYT (8.1.05); Bravin, "Two Prosecutors at Guantánamo Quit in Protest," WSJ (8.1.05); "Military Denies Rigging Guantánamo Tribunals," WP (8.2.05); Tuttle, "Gitmo Trials Rigged," *The Nation* (2.20.08); Ephron, "Gitmo Grievances," *Newsweek* (5.18.08).

109 Hicks (2010: 146–47); Sales, "Leaked Emails Claim Guantánamo Trials Rigged," ABC News (8.1.05); Umansky, "The Six Gitmo Prosecutors Who Protested," ProPublica (10.1.08); Bravin (2013: 136–38).

110 Bonner, "Australian Group Campaigns to Free Guantánamo Prisoner," NYT (8.28.05); Hicks (2010: 146–47).

111 "Pentagon Planning to Resume Commissions," NYT (9.21.05).

112 *Hicks* v. *Bush*, 397 F.Supp.2d 6 (D.D.C. 2005); Lewis, "Judge Halts Guantánamo Trial," NYT (11.16.05).

113 Hicks (2010: 347, 359); "British Court Expected to Grant Citizenship to Detainee," NYT (12.13.05); "Court Backs Citizenship Bid By Terror Suspect," LAT (4.14.06).

114 Hicks (2010: 363–64).

115 Ibid. 366–68.

116 "Military Drafts New Detainee Charges," LAT (2.3.07); "Australian Is Charged in Terror Case," NYT (3.2.07); White, "Australian Detainee Is Charged under '06 Law," WP (3.2.07); Bonner, "Growing Calls in Australia for Terror Suspect's Return," NYT (3.3.07); Nason, "Mori Charges Could Be Laid after Trial," *The Australian* (3.3.07); Allard, "Hicks Trial at Risk If Mori Taken Off Case," *The Age* (3.5.07); Bonner, "Terror Cases Prosecutor Assails Defense Lawyer," NYT (3.5.07); "Guantánamo Intimidation," WP (3.6.07); "Arraignment Set for Australian Suspect," LAT (3.8.07); Statement of Col. Morris D. Davis to HASC Hearing (7.30.08); Hicks (2010: 379).

117 *Hicks* v. *Bush*, 2007 WL 902303 (D.D.C. 2007).

118 Williams, "Guantánamo Bay Tribunals to Begin Again," LAT (3.26.07); Glaberson, "Detainee's Lawyers Seek Removal of Chief Prosecutor," NYT (3.26.07); Glaberson, "Plea of Guilty from a Detainee in Guantánamo," NYT (3.27.07); Wizner, ACLU Blog (3.27.07); White, "Australian's Guilty Plea Is First at Guantánamo," WP (3.27.07); Williams, "Australian Pleads Guilty at Guantánamo," LAT (3.27.07).

119 Glaberson, "Australian to Serve Nine Months in Terrorism Case," NYT (3.31.07); Williams, "Terror Detainee to Get Nine Months," LAT (3.31.07); Williams, "Hicks' Plea Deal Strikes Some Experts as a

Sham," LAT (4.1.07); Richter, "A Trial That Was Uncomfortably Close to Stalinist Theatre," *The Age* (4.1.07); White, "Australian's Plea Deal Was Negotiated without Prosecutors," WP (4.1.07); Bonner, "Critics Say Australian Leader Was Alert to Politics in Detainee Deal," NYT (4.1.07); Glaberson, "Some Bumps at Start of War Tribunals at Guantánamo," NYT (4.1.07); Faiz, "Suspicion of Cheney Intervention Surrounds Guantánamo Plea Bargain," ThinkProgress (4.2.07); "U.S. Detainee May Be Able to Speak to News Media," NYT (4.5.07); Nason, "Secret Trials for Terrorists, Says U.S. Judge," *The Australian* (6.29.07); Elliott, "Hicks Case Rushed to Suit Howard – US," *Herald Sun* (Australia) (2.25.08).

120 "Spectacle at Guantánamo," WP (4.4.07).

121 Wizner, "Tribunals of the Absurd," LAT (4.5.07).

122 "Terror Detainee Back in Australia," NYT (5.20.07); Bonner, "Australia Terrorism Detainee Leaves Prison," NYT (12.29.07); "Ex-Guantánamo Inmate Is Released," LAT (12.29.07).

123 Hicks (2010); Leopold, "An Interview with Former Detainee David Hicks," Truthout (2.16.11); "Australia Notifies Ex-Guantánamo Detainee It May Seize Any Profits from His Autobiography," WP (7.21.11); Rosenberg, "Australia Abandons Bid to Seize Freed Guantánamo Detainee's Book Profits," MH (7.24.12).

124 "Convicted Guantánamo Prisoner Files Appeal," NYT (11.6.13).

125 Rosenberg, "War Court's First Convict Wants His Get-out-of-Guantánamo Guilty Plea Canceled," MH (8.20.14).

126 *Hicks v. United States*, CMCR 13-004 (2015).

127 Lewis, "Pentagon Charges 5 More in Guantánamo Bay Camp," NYT (11.8.05); Cover, "Military Commission Trial Observation," HRF (1.11–13.06); Williams, "Teen Detainee Boycotts His War Crimes Trial," LAT (4.6.06); Golden, "Boycott Threat Roils Guantánamo Hearing," NYT (4.6.06); Patel, "Military Commission Trial Observation," HRF (4.3.06); Rosenberg, "Canadian Teen Protests 'Solitary Confinement' at Guantánamo," MH (4.5.06). For Canadian accounts of Khadr, see Williamson (2012) (sympathetic); Shephard (2015) (sympathetic); Levant (2012) (hostile).

128 Bravin, "At Guantánamo, Even 'Easy' Cases Have Lingered," WSJ (12.18.06).

129 "Military Drafts New Detainee Charges," LAT (2.3.07); Williams, "Second Terror Suspect Charged," LAT (4.25.07).

130 White & Murray, "Guantánamo Ruling Renews the Debate over Detainees," WP (6.6.07).

131 Rosenberg, "War Court Tosses Case against Young Captive," MH (6.4.07); White, "Charges against Guantánamo Detainee Set for Trial Dropped over Limit in Law," WP (6.5.07); Williams & Barnes, "Tribunals Are Dealt Another Legal Setback," LAT (6.5.07); Liptak, "Tribunal System, Newly Righted, Stumbles Again," NYT (6.5.07); Glaberson, "Military Judges Dismiss Charges for 2 Detainees," NYT (6.5.07); White & Murray, "Guantánamo Ruling Renews the Debate over Detainees," WP (6.6.07); "Stuck in Guantánamo," WP (6.7.07); Savage & Williams,

"Tribunals Seen As Only Way to Try Terrorists," LAT (6.7.07); "U.S. Review of Decision on Detainees," NYT (6.9.07); Farley, "Guantánamo Inmate Stirs Debate in Canada," LAT (6.24.07).

132 Glaberson, "Military Says It Can Repair Guantánamo Trial Defects," NYT (8.25.07); *U.S. v. Khadr*, 717 F.Supp. 2d 1215 (CMCR 2007); Glaberson, "Court Advances Military Trials for Detainees," NYT (9.25.07); White, "Court Reverses Ruling on Detainees," WP (9.25.07).

133 "Canadian Detainees Terror Case to Proceed," LAT (11.7.07); Williams, "Canadian's Terrorism Trial Is Expected to Be Rocky," LAT (11.8.07); Williams, "Terror Case Could Turn on Eyewitnesses," LAT (11.9.07); Glaberson, "Decks Are Stacked in War Crimes Cases, Lawyers Say," NYT (11.9.07); Glaberson, "Witness Names to Be Withheld from Detainee," NYT (12.1.07).

134 Alberts, "Defence Seeks Dismissal on Grounds Khadr Was Child Soldier," Canwest News (1.17.08).

135 Glaberson, "Guantánamo Judge Is Urged to Get On with Proceedings," NYT (4.12.08); Williams, "Detainee Lawyer Says Death Was Possibly by Friendly Fire," LAT (4.12.08); Austen, "Lawyer Urges Canada to Try a Citizen Held by U.S. Forces," NYT (4.30.08).

136 Williams, "Charges Dropped for '20th Hijacker,'" LAT (5.14.08); Glaberson, "Army Judge Is Replaced for Trial of Detainee," NYT (5.31.08); Williams, "Judge Critical of War Crimes Case Is Ousted," LAT (5.31.08).

137 Melia, "Defense Lawyer: US Urged Interrogators at Gitmo to Destroy Notes in Case They Had to Testify," WP (6.9.08).

138 Freeze & Akkad, "Canada's Secret Documents on Khadr's Treatment Revealed," *Globe and Mail* (7.9.08); Austen, "Citing New Report, Lawyers for Canadian Detainee Denounce Abuse," NYT (7.11.08); Noronha, "Video of Interrogation of Gitmo Prisoner Released," WP (7.15.08); Yum, "Transcript: Video Showing Omar Khadr Released by Lawyers," *National Post Canada* (7.15.08); Austen, "Blurry Peek at Questioning of a Guantánamo Inmate," NYT (7.16.08).

139 Akkad, "Khadr Lawyers Demand Independent Psychologist Assessment," *Globe and Mail* (8.13.08).

140 Rosenberg, "Guantánamo General Banned from Khadr Case," MH (9.4.08); Rosenberg, "Judge Delays Omar Khadr War Crimes Trial," MH (9.11.08); Akkad, "Khadr's Lawyers Argue for Trial Delay," *Globe and Mail* (10.22.08).

141 *Khadr v. Bush*, 587 F.Supp.2d 225 (D.D.C. 2008).

142 Finn, "Evidence in Terror Case Said to Be in Chaos," WP (1.14.09).

143 Canwest News Services (4.8.09); Edwards, "Khadr Looks to Retain Civilian Lawyer," Canwest News Service (7.15.09); Danzig, "Khadr Case Goes Nowhere at Gitmo (Again)," HuffPost (10.7.09); Melia, "Rather Than Shutting Down, Guantánamo Gears Up for More Detainee Trials in 2010," Canadian Press (12.25.09); Finn, "Former Boy Soldier, Youngest Guantánamo Detainee, Heads toward Military Tribunal," WP (2.10.10); "The U.S. vs. Omar Khadr," CBC (2.21.10).

144 Finn, "Military Tribunal Opens Hearings on Guantánamo Detainee Omar Khadr," WP (4.29.10); Finn, "Video Shows Detainee Building Bombs in Afghanistan," WP (4.30.10); Finn, "U.S. Seeking a Plea Agreement in Case of Guantánamo Detainee," WP (5.1.10); Ackerman, "Most Dramatic Testimony of Post-9/11 Era Expected at Gitmo," *Washington Independent* (5.3.10).

145 "Tainted Justice," NYT (5.24.10).

146 *Khadr v. Obama*, 724 F.Supp.2d 61 (D.D.C. 2010).

147 Much of this comes from transcriptions by Lisa Hajjar, who observed the hearing. See also Vladeck, "Frustration Boycotts, and the Arkansas Ethics Rules," Balkanization (7.12.10); "Defense Disputes Claim of Confession by Detainee," NYT (8.13.10).

148 Verkaik, "Guantánamo Critic Removed from Jury," *Independent* (8.13.10); Rosenberg, "Army Defender Collapses in Khadr Courtroom," MH (8.12.10); Rosenberg, "Judge: Nobody Tortured Terror Suspect Omar Khadr," MH (8.20.10).

149 Peters, "Pentagon Eases Some Rules on Guantánamo Coverage," NYT (9.11.10); "The Administration's Press Censorship," NYT (9.18.10).

150 Savage, "Judge Delays Resumption of Guantánamo Trial," NYT (10.15.10); Sutton, "U.S. Canadian Lawyers Working on Deal for Youngest Detainee," WP (10.15.10); DoD Press Release (10.25.10); Savage, "Deal Averts Trial in Dispute Guantánamo Case," NYT (10.26.10); Finn, "Youngest Guantánamo Detainee Pleads Guilty," WP (10.26.10); Savage, "Symbolic Term for Ex-Qaeda Soldier," NYT (11.1.10).

151 "Warped Justice," NYT (11.9.10).

152 Shephard, "Omar Khadr's Lawyers Question Pentagon's Star Witness," *The Star* (4.18.11).

153 Murphy, "Feds Coy on Khadr's Repatriation," *Toronto Sun* (11.2.11); Savage, "Delays Keep Former Qaeda Child Soldier at Guantánamo, Despite Plea Deal," NYT (3.24.12); Davis, "Federal Government Blames U.S. for Stalled Omar Khadr Repatriation," *Ottawa Citizen* (3.27.12); Shephard, "Omar Khadr: U.S. Defence Secretary Signals Guantánamo Prisoner Will Soon Be Transferred to Canada," *Toronto Star* (3.28.12); Austen, "Canada: Request to Leave Guantánamo," NYT (4.19.12); Shephard, "Omar Khadr Transfer Request from Gitmo Now in Ottawa's Hands," *Toronto Star* (4.19.12); Shephard, "Omar Khadr's Lawyers, Senator Romeo Dallaire Head to Ottawa to Demand Gitmo Prisoner's Release," *Toronto Star* (6.20.12); Gillies, "Lawyers for Guantánamo Prisoner Say Canada Stonewalling on Khadr," MH (6.22.12); Shephard, "Omar Khadr: Delayed Transfer from Guantánamo Bay to Canada Goes to Court," *Toronto Star* (7.13.12); "The New Villain at Guantánamo Is Canada," Bloomberg (7.15.12); Smith, "Omar Khadr Wants Quick Decision on Return from Guantánamo Bay to Canada," *Vancouver Sun* (7.15.12); Stone, "Omar Khadr Videos, Reports Needed before Guantánamo Detainee Can Be Returned to Canada: Vic Toews," *Toronto Star* (7.20.12); Shephard, "Omar Khadr: U.S. Officials

Dismiss Suggestions Canada Was 'Duped' into Taking Guantánamo Prisoner," *Toronto Star* (7.27.12); Dallaire & Whitman, "Ten Years On, Khadr Saga Remains a National Shame," *Ottawa Citizen* (7.26.12); diLeonardo, "U.N. Official Calls for Transfer of Khadr to Canada," Jurist (7.27.12); Perkel, "U.S. Set to Hand Over Omar Khadr Videotapes to Canadian Government," *National Post* (8.13.12); Shephard, "Canada Blames U.S. for Omar Khadr Transfer Delays," *Toronto Star* (9.13.12); DoD, "Detain Transfer Announced" (9.29.12); "Lawyer for Former Guantánamo Detainee Repatriated to Canada Desperate to Be a Normal Canadian," WP (9.30.12); Koring, "Validity of Khadr's Guilty Plea in Doubt," *Globe & Mail* (2.28.13); "Former Guantánamo Prisoner, Now in Canada, to Appeal U.S. Terror Convictions," WP (4.28.13); "Lawyer Says Ex-Gitmo Detainee Transferred from Ontario Prison after Threat on his Life," WP (5.29.13); "Ex-Guantánamo Detainee Omar Khadr to Appear in Court in Canada to Challenge Adult Detention," WP (9.24.13); Rosenberg, "Canadian Appeals his Guantánamo 'Child Soldier' Conviction," MH (11.18.13).

154 Noronha, "Canadian Judge Orders Release of Ex-Guantánamo Detainee," WP (4.24.15); Gilies, "Canada Seeks Stay of Bail against Former Gitmo Inmate," WP (5.4.15); "Canada Tries to Stop Release of Ex-Gitmo Inmate Omar Khadr," WP (5.5.15); Austen, "Omar Khadr, Former Guantánamo Detainee, Is Released on Bail in Canada," NYT (5.8.15); Blanchfield, "Supreme Court Rejects Federal Government's Argument that Omar Khadr Is an Adult Offender," National Press (5.14.15).

155 Motions to disqualify Judge Pollard (denied 10.17.14, 11.13.15), clerk (denied 12.11.14), Judge Sillman (denied 10.20.14), all judges (denied 10.17.14). Two judges were replaced: Jamison by Weber (7.30.14) and Ward (retiring) by Cook (12.17.14); *In re Khadr*, 823 F.3d 92 (D.C. Cir. 2016).

156 Shephard, "Khadr to Get Apology, Compensation over $10m as Lawsuit Settled," *The Star* (7.3.17); Gillies, "Injured U.S. Soldier, Widow Go after Money Canada Will Give to Omar Khadr," *The Star* (7.4.17); Austen, "Canada Apologizes and Pays Millions to Citizen Held at Guantánamo Bay," NYT (7.8.17); Paperny, "Canada Judge Rejects U.S. Widow's Bid to Freeze Ex-Guantánamo Detainee's Assets," Reuters (7.13.17).

157 Bravin (2013: chap. 8).

158 Cloud, "Terror Suspect Upsets Plan to Resume Trials in Cuba," NYT (1.12.06); Cover, HRF (1.11.06).

159 Sutton, "Prosecutor Likens Guantánamo Defendants to Vampires," Reuters (2.28.06).

160 Williams, "Defender Says Detainees Should Be Able to Represent Themselves," LAT (4.8.06); Patel, HRF (4.7.06).

161 Barrett, "Representing the Unwilling," HRF Law and Security Blog (8.15.08).

162 Sutton, "Al Qaeda Media Chief Stands Mute at Guantánamo," WP (10.27.08); McFadden, "Guantánamo Prisoner and Lawyer Boycott

Trial," AP (10.27.08); Rosenberg, "Terror Trial to Showcase Gadgetry, Spy-Plane Imagery," MH (10.28.08); McFadden, "U.S.: Yemeni Suspect Made Videos Glorifying al-Qaeda," MH (10.28.08); Rosenberg, "Guantánamo War Court Shows Martyrdom Video," MH (10.29.08); Rosenberg, "Bin Laden Propagandist Smiles as Jury Sees His Film," MH (10.30.08); McFadden, "3 from New York Terror Case to Testify at Gitmo Trial," MH (10.30.08); Rosenberg, "Jury Deliberates at Gitmo Propaganda Trial," MH (10.31.08); Rosenberg, "Swift Verdict at Gitmo Terror Trial – Sealed until Monday," MH (10.31.08); DoD Press Release (11.3.08); Finn, "Guantánamo Jury Sentences bin Laden Aide to Life Term," WP (11.4.08); Glaberson, "Detainee Convicted on Terrorism Charges," NYT (11.4.08); see Temple-Raston (2007) (Lackawanna 6).
163 *U.S. v. Al Bahlul*, 820 F.Supp.2d. 1411 (CMCR 2011).
164 *Al Bahlul v. U.S.*, 2013 WL 297726 (DC Cir 2013); Sutton, "Court Overturns another Guantánamo Conviction," Reuters (1.25.13).
165 Sutton, "United States Scales Back Plans for Guantánamo Prosecutions," Reuters (6.12.13); Rosenberg, "Prosecutor: Court Ruling Cuts Vision for Guantánamo War Crimes Trials," MH (6.16.13).
166 *Bahlul v. United States*, 767 F.3d 1 (D.C. Cir. 2014).
167 *Bahlul v. United States*, 792 F.3d 1 (D.C. Cir. 2015); Savage, "Guantánamo Detainee's Conviction Is Thrown Out on Appeal," NYT (6.12.15).
168 "A Rebuke to Military Tribunals," NYT (6.18.15).
169 *Bahlul v. United States*, 840 F.3d 757 (D.C. Cir. 2016); Savage, "Guantánamo Detainee's Conspiracy Conviction Upheld, but Legal Issue Lingers," NYT (10.20.16).
170 Rosenberg, "Conviction of Guantánamo's Lone Lifer Won't Be Reviewed by Supreme Court," MH (10.10.17).
171 Williams, "Charges Filed against Guantánamo Inmate," LAT (10.12.07); Glaberson, "Detainee at Guantánamo Is Charged in 2002 Attack," NYT (10.12.07); Rosenberg, "War Crimes Tribunals," MH (6.2.08); White, "Detainee's Attorney Seeks Dismissal over Abuse," WP (6.8.08); Rosenberg, "Afghan Detainee Claims Abuse at Guantánamo," MH (6.19.08); Barrett, "The GTMO Incentive Program," HRF Law and Security Blog (8.18.08).
172 Rosenberg, "Judge Bans General from Guantánamo Trial Role," MH (8.14.08).
173 Rosenberg, "Army Prosecutor Quits Gitmo War Court Case," MH (9.24.08); Meyer, "Guantánamo Prosecutor Quits Amid Controversy," LAT (9.25.08); Finn, "Guantánamo Prosecutor Quits, Says Evidence Was Withheld," WP (9.25.08); Glaberson, "Guantánamo Prosecutor Is Quitting in Dispute over a Case," NYT (9.25.08); Melia, "Guantánamo Prosecutor Quits over Detainee Case," MH (9.25.08); "Guantánamo Ex-Prosecutor Demands Immunity to Testify," LAT (9.26.08); Melia, "Former War Crimes Court Prosecutor Blasts Tribunals," MH (9.27.08); Lewis, "Official American Sadism," 55(14) NYRB 45 (9.25.08); Meyer, "Guantánamo Prosecutor Who Quit Had Grave Misgivings

about Fairness," LAT (10.12.08); Sullivan, "Confessions of a Former Guantánamo Prosecutor," Salon (10.23.08).

174 Melia, "Former Prosecutor Says Ruling Wrecks U.S. Case," MH (10.29.08); McFadden, "Gitmo Judge Tosses Out Detainee's 2nd Confession," AP (11.20.08); Denniston, "Jawad Torture Case Put on Hold, SCOTUS blog (2.4.09); www.mc.mil.

175 Finn, "Evidence in Terror Cases Said to Be in Chaos," WP (1.14.09); Eviatar, "Military Lawyer Claims U.S. Paid Gitmo Prosecution Witnesses," Washington Independent (8.4.09); Eviatar, "Lead Military Lawyer Confirms Afghan Witnesses Said They Were Paid by U.S.," Washington Independent (8.4.09).

176 Eviatar, "Documents Suggest Detainee Abuses by Defense Department," Washington Independent (9.25.09).

177 Bravin, "The Conscience of the Colonel," WSJ (3.31.07); Bravin, "'Imagine the Worst Possible Scenario': Why a Guantánamo Prosecutor Withdrew from the Case," The Atlantic (February 2013); Bravin (2013: chaps. 4, 7).

178 Lewis, "Pentagon Charges 5 More in Guantánamo Bay Camp," NYT (11.8.05); Patel, "Military Commissions Preview," HRF (4.24.06, 4.27.06); Williams, "Detainee Defiantly Admits Charges," LAT (4.28.06).

179 Sharbi v. Bush, 430 F.Supp.2d 1 (D.D.C. 2006); "Judge Delays Hearing in Terrorism Case," LAT (5.13.06).

180 Williams, "Judge Critical of War Crimes Case Is Ousted," LAT (5.31.08); "U.S. Drops Charges against 5 Gitmo Detainees," AP (10.21.08); Williams, "U.S. Drops Charges against 5 Terrorism Suspects," LAT (10.22.08); Finn, "Charges Against 5 Detainees Dropped Temporarily," WP (10.22.08); Glaberson, "U.S. Drops War Crimes Charges for 5 Guantánamo Detainees," NYT (10.22.08).

181 Lewis, "Pentagon Charges 5 More in Guantánamo Bay Camp," NYT (11.8.05); Patel, "Military Commissions," HRF (4.25.06); Williams, "A Dilemma for Defenders," LAT (4.30.06).

182 "U.S. Drops Charges against '20th Hijacker' Facing Guantánamo Trial," AP (5.13.08); Williams, "Charges Dropped for '20th Hijacker,'" LAT (5.14.08); Glaberson, "Case against 9/11 Detainee Is Dismissed," NYT (5.14.08); White & Tate, "Charges against 9/11 Suspect Dropped," WP (5.14.08).

183 "Torture's Blowback," WP (5.16.08).

184 Glaberson, "Detainee Will Face New War-Crimes Charges," NYT (11.18.08); Woodward, "U.S. Tortured Detainee, Overseer Says," LAT (1.14.09); Woodward, "Detainee Tortured, Says U.S. Official," WP (1.14.09).

185 Williams, "Defense: Drop Terror Charges," LAT (1.17.09).

186 Patel, HRF (4.26.06); Williams, "A Dilemma for Defenders," LAT (4.30.06); Williams, "U.S. Drops Charges against 5 Terrorism Suspects," LAT (10.22.08).

187 Golden, "Guantánamo Terror Suspect Mocks Tribunal," NYT (4.7.06); Williams "Terror Suspect's Lawyer Risks Contempt Citation," LAT (4.7.06); Patel, HRF (4.7.06); Williams, "Guantánamo Detainee to Be Charged," LAT (6.4.08); Finn, "Key Allegations against Terror Suspect Withdrawn," WP (10.15.08); Bonner, "Detainee to Return to Britain, as Efforts to Prove Torture Claims Continue," NYT (2.23.09); Sullivan, "Former Guantánamo Detainee Returns to London," WP (2.23.09); "Freed Detainee Arrives Back in UK," BBC (2.23.09); Bonner, "Plea Bargain Was Weighed for Guantánamo Detainee," NYT (3.24.09).

188 "U.S. Charges 10th Guantánamo Detainee," LAT (1.21.06); Pantesco, "Guantánamo Military Judge Unsure of What Laws Govern Detainee Trial," Jurist (4.4.06); Bravin, "U.S. Resumes Military Trials at Guantánamo," WSJ (4.4.06); Williams, "Guantánamo Judge Delays Suspect's Tribunal 3 Months," LAT (4.5.06).

189 "Charged Detainee Is Hijacker's Brother-in-Law," WP (12.22.07); Rosenberg, "Document: Judge Sets May 27 Guantánamo Hearing," MH (5.6.09); Rosenberg, "Judge Won't Delay May 27 War Court Session," MH (5.10.09); Rosenberg, "Army Judge Postpones Guantánamo Hearing," MH (5.19.09); Rosenberg, "Pentagon Charges Saudi at Guantánamo with Aiding Terror in al-Qaeda Case," MH (8.30.12); Bravin (2013: 264–71); "Charges against Ahmed Mohammed Ahmed Haza al Darbi Referred to Military Commission (2.5.14); Lawfare (2.20.14); Goldman, "Brother-in-Law of 9/11 Hijacker Expected to Plead Guilty at Guantánamo Bay," WP (2.20.14); Savage, "Guantánamo Detainee Pleads Guilty in 2002 Attack on Tanker off Yemen," NYT (2.21.14).

190 Rosenberg, "Al-Qaida Terrorist Turned Informant Apologizes at Guantánamo, Gets 13-Year Sentence," MH (10.13.17).

191 Finn, "Guantánamo Detainee with Baltimore Ties Is Charged with War Crimes," WP (2.15.12); Savage, "'High Value' Detainee Is Said to Reach Tentative Deal," NYT (2.23.12); Rosenberg, "Guantánamo Plea Deal Unveils New Trial Strategy," MH (2.28.12); "Former Maryland Resident Once Labeled a 'Ghost Prisoner' Pleads Guilty at Guantánamo Tribunal," WP (2.29.12); Finn, "Plea Deal in Terror Suspect's Military Trial Sparks Debate," WP (3.1.12); Shane, "Testimony on al Qaeda Is Required in Plea Deal," NYT (3.1.12); Rosenthal, "Majid Khan's Plea Deal," NYT (2.29.12); "A Terrorist's Fair Deal," WP (3.5.12).

192 Rosenberg, "Guantánamo Prisoner Postpones Terror Plea Sentencing for 3 Years," MH (11.3.15).

193 Lawfare (9.15.16).

194 Williams, "3rd Guantánamo Detainee to Boycott Trial," LAT (4.11.08); Glaberson, "U.S. Detainee Says He'll Boycott His Trial," NYT (4.11.08); Finn, "Resumed Military Panels Face New Challenges," WP (12.4.09); Savage, "Guantánamo Detainee Pleads Guilty in Terrorism Case," NYT (7.8.10); Robles, "Bin Laden Driver to War-Court Convict," MH (7.8.10); "Bin Laden Chef Sentenced to 14 Years in Jail," BBC (8.11.10); *United States v. Al Qosi*, 28 F.Supp.3d 1198 (CMCR 2014); *In re Al Qosi*,

602 Fed.Appx. 542 (DC Cir 2015); Rosenberg, "Freed Guantánamo Convict Back in the Fight," MH (4.21.17); Simpson, "Appeal of Guantánamo Conviction Hits Snag over Legal Representation," Reuters (7.12.17).

195 "Detainee Dragged to Gitmo Court," AP (5.21.08); Rosenberg, "Afghan Detainee Dragged into War Court with Scrapes," MH (5.21.08); Rosenberg, "War Crimes Tribunals," MH (6.2.08); Rosenberg, "Guantánamo War Court Gavels Back into One-Day Session," MH (11.18.09); Danzig, "If You Believe Guantánamo Makes Us Safer You Should Have Been There," HuffPost (11.19.09).

196 Williams, "U.S. Drops Charges against 5 Terrorism Suspects," LAT (10.22.08); Finn, "Charges against 5 Detainees Dropped Temporarily," WP (10.22.08); Rosenberg, "Guantánamo War Court Resumes Hearings amid Uncertainty," MH (4.7.10); Savage, "Detainee Who Pleaded Guilty Describes Terror Training," NYT (2.18.11); Sutton, "Sudanese Prisoner Finishes Guantánamo Sentence, Will Head Home," Reuters (12.3.13); Savage, "Sudanese Detainee to Be Sent Home from Guantánamo," NYT (12.5.13); "U.S. Dismisses Guantánamo Conviction after Prisoner Sent Home," NYT (1.10.15); Rosenberg, "Pentagon Throws Out Foot Soldier's Guantánamo War Court Conviction," MH (1.10.15).

197 Savage, "Guantánamo Bay Prosecutors Accuse Detainee of Conspiracy," NYT (2.15.14); Savage, "Guantánamo Detainee Arraigned in Case That Could Help Decide Fate of Tribunals," NYT (6.18.14); Rosenberg, "Judge Orders Prison to Stop Using Female Guards to Move Prisoner to Lawyer Meeting," MH (11.11.14); Rosenberg, "Guantánamo Prosecutors: Prison Needs Female Guards Touching, Moving Ex-CIA Captives," MH (11.17.14); Lawfare (1.18.15); Lawfare (1.27.15); Rosenberg, "Female Guards File Discrimination Complaints against Guantánamo Judges," MH (1.27.15); Rosenberg, "Defense Lawyer Asks Guantánamo Judge to Expand the Female Guard No-Touch Rule," MH (1.29.15); Rosenberg, "Navy Judge Named in Discrimination Complaint Lifts Guantánamo Female Guard No-Touch Order," MH (3.1.15); Rosenberg, "Alleged al-Qaeda Commander Fires Legal Team, Paralyzing Guantánamo Trial," MH (9.22.15); Chief Prosecutor Mark Martins, Remarks at Guantánamo Bay (5.16.16); Rosenberg, "Alleged al-Qaeda Commander Returns to Guantánamo War Court, Seeks Delay," MH (7.12.16); Rosenberg, "Alleged al-Qaida Commander Gets New, Marine Judge at Guantánamo War Court," MH (10.27.16); Lawfare (11.18.16); Rosenberg, "Troops Force Alleged al-Qaida Commander into Guantánamo War Court," MH (1.9.17); Rosenberg, "Accused al-Qaida Commander Asks, If Found Innocent of War Crimes, Can I Leave Guantánamo?" MH (4.25.17).

198 Rosenberg, "U.S. Deliberately Withheld Medical Care at Guantánamo, Federal Lawsuit Claims," MH (7.26.17).

199 Rosenberg, "Pentagon Drops Kuwaiti's War Crimes Charges," MH (6.29.12).

200 See Shawcross (2012).

201 Glaberson, "6 at Guantánamo Are Said to Face Trial," NYT (2.9.08); Glabersosn, "U.S. Said to Seek Execution for 6 in Sept. 11 Case," NYT (2.11.08); "Out of Order," LAT (2.12.08); "The 9/11 Trials," WP (2.13.08); "Unnecessary Harm," NYT (2.13.08).

202 Davis, "Unforgivable Behavior, Inadmissible Evidence," NYT (2.17.08); Tuttle, "Gitmo Trials Rigged," *The Nation* (2.20.08); Fox, "Ex-Prosecutor to Serve as Defense Witness in Terror Case," WP (2.22.08).

203 "Ex-Prosecutor Calls War Tribunals Tainted," LAT (4.29.08); Glaberson, "Ex-Prosecutor Tells of Push by Pentagon on Detainees," NYT (4.29.08); White, "Colonel Says Speaking Out Cost a Medal," WP (5.29.08).

204 Zagorin, "Why the Gitmo Cases Are in Disarray," *Time* (5.14.08); Bravin (2013: 322).

205 Williams, "Guantánamo Lawyers Want Case Tossed," LAT (5.17.08).

206 Ephron, "'Fair, Open, Just, Honest': A Chat with the Adviser to the Gitmo Military Commissions," *Newsweek* (6.2.08).

207 Zagorin, "US Justice on Trial at Gitmo," *Time* (6.4.08); MuhammedAlly, "Undermining American Justice," HRF blog (6.6.08); White, "9/11 Architect Tells Court He Hopes for Martyrdom," WP (6.6.08); White, "A Mythic Figure, in Person," WP (6.6.08); Glaberson, "Arraigned, 9/11 Defendants Talk of Martyrdom," NYT (6.6.08); Williams, "Five 9/11 Suspects Defiant in Court," LAT (6.6.08); 200 *HRF Law and Security Digest* (6.6.08).

208 "The Guantánamo Court," WP (6.7.08); White, "Detainees May Be Denied Evidence for Defense," WP (6.15.08).

209 Glaberson, "Guantánamo Detainee Faces War Crimes Charges in Attack on Destroyer," NYT (7.1.08); White, "Charges Are Filed in Cole Bombing," WP (7.2.08); Finn, "Military to Try USS Cole Suspect," WP (12.20.08); Finn, "Military Judge Denies Obama Request to Suspend Guantánamo Hearings," WP (1.29.09); Glaberson, "Judge Refuses to Delay a Case at Guantánamo," NYT (1.30.09); Williams, "Guantánamo Judge Says He's Forging Ahead," LAT (1.30.09); Finn, "Guantánamo Judge Denies Obama's Request for Delay," WP (1.30.09); "Washington: Charges to Be Dropped in Cole Case," NYT (2.6.09).

210 Meyer, "Judge Urges 9/11 Suspects to Accept Legal Help," LAT (7.10.08); Rosenberg, "Detainee Refuses to Leave Cell for Hearing," MH (7.10.08); Meyer, "9/11 Plotters Tell Judge of Legal Woes," LAT (7.11.08); Glaberson, "Detainees, As Lawyers, Test System of Tribunals," NYT (7.11.08).

211 Coughenour, "The Right Place to Try Terrorism Cases," WP (7.27.08).

212 "Workable Terrorism Trials," WP (7.27.08).

213 Meyer, "Guantánamo Judge Enlists Help of Sept. 11 Suspects," LAT (9.23.08); Finn, "Judge Lets 9/11 Defendants Urge Detainee to Appear," WP (9.23.08); Meyer, "Sept. 11 Plotter Turns Tables on Military Judge," LAT (9.24.08); Melia, "9/11 Mastermind Takes Lead Role in Gitmo Courtroom," MH (9.23.08); Rosenberg, "Alleged 9/11 Architect: Terror Trial an 'Inquisition,'" MH (9.24.08).

214 Finn, "Defense Lawyers Get Access to Secret Guantánamo Camp," WP (10.28.08).
215 Barkow, "Translation Problems Hinder Military Commission Proceedings," *HRF Law and Security Digest* (9.24.08); Finn, "Lawyers Criticize Quality of Guantánamo Interpreters," WP (10.14.08).
216 Finn, "Guantánamo War-Crime Trials Advisor Is Reassigned," LAT (9.20.08); Meyer, "Guantánamo Tribunals Overseer under Investigation," LAT (10.25.08); "Air Force Probes General for Actions at Guantánamo," WP (10.26.08); Rosenberg, "'War Court Czar' Wants to Retire," MH (11.1.08).
217 Rosenberg, "9/11 Kin to Watch Terror Trial at Guantánamo, by Lottery," MH (10.27.08).
218 Finn, "Top Judge at Guantánamo Announces Retirement," WP (11.18.08); Rosenberg, "Army Col. Named Chief Judge at Guantánamo," MH (12.15.08).
219 Glaberson, "Alleged 9/11 Plotters Offer to Confess at Guantánamo," NYT (12.8.08); "Top 9/11 Suspects to Plead Guilty," BBC News (12.8.08); "Guantánamo Detainees Ask to Give 9/11 Confessions," G (12.8.08); Glaberson, "5 Charged in 9/11 Attacks Seek to Plead Guilty," NYT (12.9.08); Williams, "Chaos at Guantánamo Tribunal," LAT (12.9.08); Finn, "Five 9/11 Suspects Offer to Confess," WP (12.9.08); Warrick, "Offer of Plea Serves Mohammed and Bush," WP (12.9.08); "Trial by Absurdity," WP (12.10.08); Glaberson, "Relatives of 9/11 Victims Add a Passionate Layer to Guantánamo Debate," NYT (12.10.08); Williams, "A Family Feud over the Fate of Guantánamo," LAT (12.11.08).
220 Zagorin, "Trying to Tie Obama's Hands on Gitmo," *Time* (12.8.08).
221 Finn, "Judge's Order Could Keep Public from Hearing Details of 9/11 Trials," WP (1.7.09); Finn, "Officials Expecting Halt to 9/11 Proceedings," WP (1.20.09).
222 "Obama Moves to Delay Tribunals at Guantánamo," LAT (1.21.09); Finn, "Obama Seeks Halt to Legal Proceedings at Guantánamo," WP (1.21.09); Rosenberg, "Obama Seeks Freeze in Guantánamo War Court Trial," MH (1.21.09); "First Steps at Guantánamo," NYT (1.22.09); "Justice and Security," WP (1.22.09).
223 Zeleny & Bumiller, "Suspects Will Face Justice, Obama Tells Families of Terrorism Victims," NYT (2.7.09); Finn & Eggen, "Obama Talks to Sept. 11, USS Cole Families about Guantánamo Prison," WP (2.7.09); Haberman, "Justice, Not Revenge, Is Her Motive," NYT (2.10.09).
224 Glaberson, "Detainees Say They Planned Sept. 11, and Voice Pride in It," NYT (3.10.09); Finn, "Military Judge's Release of Pleading by 9/11 Defendants Draws Criticism," WP (3.11.09).
225 Glaberson, "U.S. May Revive Guantánamo Military Courts," NYT (5.2.09); Finn, "Obama Set to Revive Military Commissions," WP (5.9.09); Barnes, "Obama to Renew Tribunals," LAT (5.15.09); Glaberson, "Vowing More Rights for Accused, Obama Retains Tribunal System," NYT (5.16.09); Williams & Barnes, "Obama Hasn't Fixed Image of Tribunals," LAT (5.16.09); Shear & Finn, "Obama to Revamp

Military Tribunals," WP (5.16.09); "Photographs and Kangaroo Courts," NYT (5.17.09); "Sticking with Tribunals," WP (5.17.09); "Obama's Military Tribunals," WSJ (5.16.09).

226 Glaberson, "Obama Considers Allowing Pleas by 9/11 Suspects," NYT (6.6.09); Barnes, "Fewer Detainees to Be Tried in U.S.," LAT (6.18.09); Ackerman, "Obama Military Commissions Vision Takes Shape," *Washington Independent* (7.7.09); Johnston, "In Senate, Debate on Detainee Legal Rights," NYT (7.8.09); 250 *HRF Law and Security Digest* (7.10.09).

227 "Undoing the Damage," NYT (7.12.09); "Detainees on Trial," WP (10.15.09).

228 Barrett, "Dozens of Gitmo Cases Referred to U.S. Prosecutors," AP (8.3.09); Finn, Markon & Wilber, "Va., N.Y. Districts Vie for 9/11 Case," WP (8.4.09); "Senators Call on President to Prosecute 9-11 Mastermind by Military Commission," Sen. Graham Press Release (8.6.09); "Justice Delayed," NYT (9.13.09).

229 Shane, "Sept. 11 Defendant Seeks a Trial and a Platform," NYT (11.21.09).

230 Finn, "Detainee Files Emergency Writ to Halt Hearings," WP (9.11.09); *In re Al-Shibh*, 2010 WL 2898997 (D.C. Cir. 2010).

231 Stout, "House Allows Guantánamo to Transfer Some to U.S.," NYT (10.16.09); "Holder, Gates, Oppose Restrictions on Gitmo Trials," AP (11.3.09); "Washington: Senate Votes on Terrorism Trials," NYT (11.6.09).

232 DoD News Release 889-09 (11.13.09); Montopoli, "Republicans Outraged over Terrorism Trial," CBS News Political Hotsheet (11.13.09); Meyer & Savage, "Strong Reaction to Announcement of 9/11 Trial in New York Court," LAT (11.14.09); Savage, "Accused 9/11 Mastermind to Face Civilian Trial in N.Y.," NYT (11.14.09); Kleinfield & Healy, "Trial Venue Leaves 9/11 Families Angry or Satisfied," NYT (11.14.09); Finn & Johnson, "Alleged Sept. 11 Planner Will Be Tried in New York," WP (11.14.09); Johnson, "For Holder, Much Wrestling over Decision," WP (11.14.09); Frumin, "Giuliani on 9/11 Trials," TPM Livewire (11.15.09); Yoo, "The KSM Trial Will Be an Intelligence Bonanza for al Qaeda," WSJ (11.16.09).

233 Savage, "Trial without Major Witness Will Test Tribunal System," NYT (12.1.09); Finn, "Administration Halts Prosecution of Alleged USS Cole Bomber," WP (8.26.10); Serrano, "Saudi Charged in First Guantánamo Tribunal under Obama," LAT (4.21.11); Finn, "Capital Charges Brought against Guantánamo Detainee Abd al-Rahim al-Nashiri in USS Cole Attack," WP (4.20.11); Rosenberg, "Defenders: USS Cole Bombing Case Too Tainted for Death Penalty Trial," MH (7.16.11); "Death Penalty Possible for Guantánamo Detainee," NYT (9.29.11); Finn, "Death Penalty Case Set for USS Cole Defendant," WP (9.29.11); Rosenberg, "Pentagon Oks Capital Trial for USS Cole Bombing," MH (9.29.11); Rosenthal, "Catch-22 Alive and Well in Guantánamo Bay," NYT (11.3.11).

234 Memorandum for the CA (7.15.11).
235 Hakim, "Paterson Calls Obama Wrong on 9/11 Trial," NYT (11.17.09).
236 "Poll: Most Oppose Terror Trials in Open Court," CBS News (11.17.09).
237 "Plan for Mohammed's Trial Upholds U.S. Values," LAT (11.14.09); "A Return to American Justice," NYT (11.14.09); "Terrorism on Trial," WP (11.14.09).
238 "Eric Holder Defends Decision to Try 9/11 Terrorists in Federal Court," LAT (11.18.09); Meyer, "Obama and Holder Defend Plans to Try Sept. 11 Suspects," LAT (11.19.09); Savage, "Holder Defends Decision to Use U.S. Court for 9/11 Trial," NYT (11.19.09); Johnson, "Holder Answers to 9/11 Relatives about Trials in U.S.," WP (11.19.09).
239 Baker, "Security for Terrorism Trials Estimated at $200 Million a Year," NYT (1.7.10); "Julie Menin," NYT (1.17.10); "NY Congressman Introduces Bill to Keep 9/11 Trials Out of Civilian Courts," LAT (1.28.10); Barbaro & Baker, "Bloomberg Balks at 9/11 Trial, Dealing Blow to White House," NYT (1.28.10).
240 Shane, "Site for Terror Trial Isn't Its Only Obstacle," NYT (1.31.10); "White House Says Cities Have a Say in Holding Terror Trials," WP (2.1.10); "Government Retreating on Civilian Trial for Accused Terrorist," WP (2.1.10); "The War on Terror's Legal Battle," LAT (2.3.10).
241 Reilly, "Obama: 'Pretty Rank Politics' Delaying 'Gitmo' Closure," MainJustice (2.2.10); Ramonas, "Senators Offer Bill to Block Trial of 9/11 Conspirators," MainJustice (2.2.10); Reilly, "Mukasey Says It's 'Amateur Night' at the Department of Justice," MainJustice (2.2.10).
242 Soufan, "Tribunal and Error," NYT (2.12.10).
243 Kornblut & Johnson, "Obama Will Help Select Location of KSM Terrorism Trial," WP (2.12.10); Barrett & Feller, "Administration May Abandon Civilian 9/11 Trial," AP (2.12.10); Kantor & Savage, "Getting the Message," NYT (2.15.10).
244 "Letter to the Editor," NYT (2.21.10).
245 Savage, "Senator Proposes Deal on Handling of Detainees," NYT (3.4.10); Kornblut & Finn, "Obama Advisers Set to Recommend Military Tribunals for Alleged 9/11 Plotters," WP (3.5.10); Barnes & Parsons, "White House Reconsiders Holding Terror Trials in Civilian Court," LAT (3.5.10); "Trial and Error," NYT (3.5.10).
246 Savage, "White House Delays on Location of 9/11 Trial," NYT (3.6.10); "Senator Offers Guantánamo Bay Deal if 9/11 Trials Move to Military Tribunals," WP (3.8.10); Apuzzo & Barrett, "Obama Still Wants U.S. Trial for Some Gitmo Suspects," AP (3.8.10); Rutten, "No Reason for Obama to Backtrack," LAT (3.10.10); Vandeveld & Dratel, "Military Commissions: A Bad Idea," Salon (3.10.10); "The Guantánamo Diversion," LAT (3.13.10); Johnson, "Critics: Military Trial of Suspects Could Open Cases to Legal Uncertainty," WP (3.14.10).
247 Savage, "Holder Won't Rule Out 9/11 Trial in New York," NYT (4.15.10); Hsu, "Attorney General Eric Holder Stands His Ground at

Senate Hearing," WP (4.15.10); Hsu, "Holder Prefers Keeping Option of Civilian Courts for Terrorism Suspects," WP (4.16.10).

248 Frakt, "New Manual for Military Commissions Disregards the Commander-in-Chief, Congressional Intent and the Laws of War," HuffPost (4.29.10).

249 Sullivan & Freeh, "Try Sept. 11 Suspects in the U.S. District Court for Guantánamo," WP (7.16.10); Feinstein, "For Terrorism Trials, Civilian Courts Are Up To the Job," LAT (7.20.10).

250 "Civil Justice, Military Injustice," NYT (10.6.10); Goldsmith, "Don't Try Terrorists, Lock Them Up," NYT (10.9.10); Wittes, "The Right Way to Try KSM," WP (10.29.10).

251 "9/11 Mastermind Must Be Tried," WP (11.5.10).

252 Finn & Kornblut, "Opposition to U.S. Trial Likely to Keep Mastermind of 9/11 Attacks in Detention," WP (11.13.10); Davis, "A Terrorist Gets What He Deserves," NYT (11.19.10).

253 "Our List of Wishes for 2011," LAT (1.1.11); Finn & Kornblut, "Obama Decries Curbs on Trying Detainees in U.S.," WP (1.7.11); "President Obama Should Fight Barriers to Guantánamo Civilian Trials," WP (1.7.11).

254 Shane & Landler, "Obama Clears Way for Guantánamo Trials," NYT (3.8.11); Stern, "Obama's Decision on Guantánamo Detainees Roundly Criticized on Right, Left," CQ Today (3.7.11); Serrano, "Obama to Resume Military Trials for Guantánamo Detainees," LAT (3.8.11); "Mr. Obama's Gitmo Order Is a Half Step in the Right Direction," WP (3.9.111); "Mired in Guantánamo," LAT (3.9.11); "Statement of the Attorney General on the Prosecution of the 9/11 Conspirators," DoJ (4.4.11); Finn, "KSM To Be Tried by Military Commission," WP (4.4.11); Savage, "In a Reversal, Military Trials for 9/11 Cases," NYT (4.5.11); Serrano, "Obama Administration Won't Pursue Civilian Trials for 9/11 Suspects," LAT (4.5.11); "Cowardice Blocks the 9/11 Trial," NYT (4.5.11); "Right Call on Sept. 11 Defendants, Military Trials," WP (4.5.11); "Obama Administration's Anti-Terror Architecture: Too Much Like Bush," LAT (4.10.11); Greenberg, "Even at Guantánamo, a 9/11 Trial Can Serve Justice," WP (4.9.11); Shawcross, "Lessons from Nuremberg," NYT (4.10.11).

255 Horwitz, "Holder Says His Plan to Try 9/11 Suspects in Civilian Court in New York Was 'Right One,'" WP (11.4.13).

256 "Guantánamo, On Trial," NYT (4.17.11).

257 Statement by the President on H.R. 1473 (4.15.11).

258 Davis, "Manning and Mohammed Cases: Tilting the Scales of Justice," LAT (4.28.11).

259 "9/11 Defendants Charged at Guantánamo with Terrorism and Murder," NYT (6.1.11).

260 "Civilian Courts the Right Place for Terrorism Trials," LAT (10.23.11); Ukman, "Detention Legislation Divides Democrats," WP (10.25.11); "Don't Retreat from Freedoms," Philadelphia Inquirer (12.6.11); Savage, "Obama Drops Veto Threat over Military Authorization Bill after

in Fight of His Career," WP (5.4.12); Savage, "U.S. to Restart Tribunal, Aiming to Show It's Fair," NYT (5.5.12); Rosenthal, "Justice Delayed, Torture Classified," NYT (5.5.12).

269 "Guantánamo Detainee Contests Court's Secrecy Rule," AFP (4.20.12).

270 Lawfare (5.5.12); Military Commission Transcript (5.5.12); Savage, "At a Hearing 9/11 Detainees Show Defiance," NYT (5.6.12); Finn, "9/11 Detainees Work to Disrupt Opening of Arraignment at Guantánamo Bay," WP (5.6.12); Savage, "9/11 Defendants' Hearing Was Rigged, Lawyers Say," NYT (5.7.12); Finn, "9/11 Detainee's Attorney Promises Long, Hard Fight after Hearing at Guantánamo," WP (5.7.12); Romero, "Guantánamo's 9/11 Show Trials," G (5.8.12); "The KSM Trial Spectacle," WSJ (5.8.12); Seibel, "Use of White Noise to Block Sound at Guantánamo Hearing Was an Error, Pentagon Says," MH (5.9.12); "Justice and the Guantánamo Trial," MH (5.9.12); Margolin, "Husband of 9/11 Victim Goes to Gitmo to Spare Plotters from Death Sentence," *New York Post* (5.14.12); "Justice and the 9/11 Defendants," LAT (5.17.12); "Judge in 9/11 Case at Guantánamo Weighs Splitting Up Defendants and Holding Multiple Trials," WP (5.18.12).

271 Rosenberg, "9/11 Defenders Send Mixed Message on Whether to Split Up Guantánamo Trial," MH (6.1.12).

272 "Bush, Obama Asked to Testify in Motion to Dismiss Sept. 11 Case at Guantánamo," WP (5.24.12); "Guantánamo Lawyers Make Mockery of Court," *New York Daily News* (5.25.12).

273 "Sept. 11 'Mastermind' Wants to Wear Military-Style Clothing at Guantánamo Trial," NYT (6.13.12); "Muslim Holy Period Delays Sept. 11 Case at Gitmo," NYT (7.16.12).

274 Rosenberg, "USS Cole Case Defense Wants Guantánamo Judge to Recuse Himself," MH (6.16.12); Rosenberg, "Media Oppose Guantánamo Hearing Closure," MH (7.13.12); "Judge Won't Step Down in Case of Cole Attack," NYT (7.17.12); Rosenberg, "Accused Planner of Attack on USS Cole Shuns Guantánamo Court Session," MH (7.19.12); "Judge Refuses to Televise Gitmo Trial," IOL News (9.14.12); Rosenberg, "USS Cole Defenders Seek Three-Month Delay," MH (9.26.12); "Judge Pauses Guantánamo Hearing over Defendant's Courtroom Presence," WP (10.24.12); Savage, "Terrorism Suspect Threatens to Boycott His Trial," NYT (10.25.12).

275 Rosenberg, "Media, ACLU to Argue against Censorship at Guantánamo," MH (8.2.12); "Judge in Sept. 11 Trial at Guantánamo Asked for Rules That Would Shield Torture Testimony," WP (10.14.12).

276 Lawfare (10.15–17.12); Savage, "Defendants in Sept. 11 Case Cooperate as Proceedings Resume at Guantánamo," NYT (10.16.12); London & Tate, "Alleged Sept. 11 Mastermind, Four Others in Court for Pretrial Hearing," WP (10.16.12); Tate & London, "KSM Accuses U.S. of Justifying Murder, Torture in Name of Security," WP (10.17.12); Serrano, "Three 9/11 Suspects Opt Out of Pretrial Hearing," LAT (10.17.12); Rosenberg, "Accused 9/11 Architect Wears Hunting Vest to Guantánamo

Court," MH (10.17.12); Finn, "Testimony on CIA's Treatment of 9/11 Suspects Will Be Kept Secret, Judge Rules," WP (12.13.12); Serrano, "Judge Restricts More Material in 9/11 Trial," LAT (1.4.13).

277 Lawfare (10.19.12); "Gov't Told to Fix Mold, Rat Problems at Guantánamo Offices to Avoid Delay in Terror Trial," WP (10.5.12); "Military to Clean Guantánamo Legal Offices Said to Be Contaminated with Rat Droppings, Mold," WP (10.18.12); "Lawyers for Sept. 11 Defendants at Guantánamo Ask U.S. Defense Secretary to Televise Trial," WP (11.1.12); Rosenberg, "Defense Attorneys Ask Panetta to Televise 9/11 Trial from Guantánamo," MH (11.1.12); "Judge: No Television Broadcast of Guantánamo," MH (1.3.13).

278 "9/11 Plotter Wants Case Thrown Out," AFP (11.6.12).

279 Savage, "Military Prosecutor to Keep Conspiracy Charge," NYT (1.19.13).

280 Savage, "Military Judge Rejects Defense Requests at Terror Hearing," NYT (1.8.13).

281 Lawfare (2.4.13).

282 Rosenberg, "Guantánamo Judge Says 'External Body' Was Wrong to Censor War Court," MH (1.29.13); Finn, "Guantánamo Judge Declines to Explain Mysterious Censoring," WP (1.29.13); Savage, "Guantánamo Lawyers Seeking 48-Hour Visits," NYT (1.29.13); Savage, "Judge Overrules Censors in Guantánamo 9/11 Hearing," NYT (1.30.13); Rosenberg, "Guantánamo Defense Attorneys Worry about Eavesdropping," MH (1030.13); Munoz, "Gitmo Censor Controversy Spawns Fears of Additional Surveillance," The Hill (1.31.13); Savage, "Judge Stops Censorship in Sept. 11 Case," NYT (1.31.13); Lawfare (2.11–14.13); Savage, "9/11 Case Is Delayed as Defense Voices Fears on Eavesdropping," NYT (2.12.13); Finn, "At Guantánamo, Microphones Hidden in Attorney–Client Meeting Rooms," WP (2.13.13); "Defendant in Sept. 11 Case Makes Angry Outburst over Searches at Guantánamo," WP (2.14.13); Savage, "Legal Clashes at Hearing for Defendants in 9/11 Case," NYT (2.15.13); McGeal, "Guantánamo Trials Plunged into Deeper Discord As Confidence in Court Wanes," G (2.17.13); Rosenberg, "Judge: No Sleepover but Lawyers Can Spend 12 Hours in Guantánamo's Secret Prison," MH (2.21.13); Pitter, "Listening In," FP (2.21.13).

283 Fox, "Window Opens on Secret Camp within Guantánamo," AP (4.13.14).

284 Currier, "Gitmo Defense Lawyers Say Somebody Has Been Accessing Their Emails," ProPublica (4.11.13); Finn, "Pentagon Acknowledges E-Mail Mix-Up among Guantánamo Bay Lawyers," WP (4.12.13); "Judge OKs Delay in Sept. 11 Case at Guantánamo over Pentagon Data Breach," WP (4.18.13).

285 U.S. v. Al Qosi, 28 F.Supp.3d 1198 (CMCR 2014).

286 Lawfare (6.13.13).

287 Rosenberg, "Torture Expert Testifies at Guantánamo in USS Cole Case," MH (2.5.13); Rosenberg, "Guantánamo Captive Accused in USS Cole Bombing Suffers from PTSD, Depression," MH (6.3.13); Rosenberg,

"New Layer of Secrecy at Guantánamo Court," MH (6.10.13); Rosenberg, "Guantánamo Judge Orders First Closed Session of Obama War Court," MH (6.13.13); Rosenberg, "Guantánamo Prosecutor Uncovers Secret CIA Photos of Accused Bomber," MH (6.26.13); Rosenberg, "Judge Sets USS Cole Trial Date for Next Year at Guantánamo," MH (8.26.13).

288 "Defendants Sit Out Guantánamo Pretrial Hearing in 9/11 Case," WP (6.18.13); Rosenberg, "Accused 9/11 Plotters Back in Guantánamo War Court," MH (6.18.13); Rosenberg, "Red Cross to Guantánamo Judge: Don't Give 9/11 Defense Lawyers Our Confidential Records," MH (6.18.13); Rosenberg, "Guantánamo Prosecutors Say Arguments on Waterboarding Should Be in Secret Session," MH (6.19.13); Rosenberg, "Judge Orders Abrupt Recess at 9/11 Hearings at Guantánamo," MH (6.20.13).

289 Fox, "Judge Asked to Move Along 9/11 Case at Guantánamo," ABC News (7.2.13).

290 Rosenberg, "Guantánamo Judge Holds First Secret Hearing of 9/11 Trial," MH (8.20.13); Lawfare (8.22.13); "Defense Seeks to Dismiss Some of the Charges in 9/11 Case at Guantánamo," WP (8.24.13); Rosenberg, "Pentagon Tech Troubles Could Stall 9/11 Hearings," MH (8.23.13); Lawfare (8.23.13); Rosenberg, "Guantánamo Judge Makes Secret Ruling on Secret Motion in Secret Hearing," MH (9.11.13).

291 Rosenberg, "Protesting 9/11 Defendants, Sick Defense Attorney Shut Down Guantánamo Hearing," MH (9.16.13); Kember, "At Guantánamo, Defense Attorneys Complain of 'Monitoring' of Their Internet Activities," WP (9.18.13); Lawfare (9.18–19.13); Eviatar, "Time to Retire the Military Commissions," Just Security (9.23.13); "Military Judge Refuses to Delay 9/11 Cases at Guantánamo Bay," WP (10.2.13).

292 Lawfare (10.22–24.13); Rosenberg, "At Guantánamo, 9/11 Hearing Probes Cell Searches, Seizures," MH (10.24.13).

293 Lawfare (12.17–18.13); Savage, "Suspect in 9/11 Case Is Ejected from a Guantánamo Court after Outbursts," NYT (12.18.13); Rosenberg, "Guantánamo Guards Remove 9/11 Defendant from Court – Twice – After Noisy Protests," MH (12.17.13); "Guantánamo Prisoner Again Ejected from Hearing," WP (12.18.13); "Mental Exam Set for 9/11 Suspect at Guantánamo," NYT (12.20.13); Rosenberg, "Guantánamo Judge Orders U.S. to Preserve Evidence of CIA 'Black Sites,'" MH (12.20.13); "Psychologist Found Accused Sept. 11 Plotter to Be Mentally Incompetent in 2009," WP (12.26.13).

294 "9/11 Accused Said to Refuse Guantánamo Mental Exam," MH (1.23.14); Rosenberg, "Alleged 9/11 Conspirator Stymies Mental-Health Board," MH (1.31.14).

295 Letter from KSM to Obama (1.8.15); Rosenberg, "Man Who Bragged about Planning 9/11 Is Allowed to Send a Letter to Obama," MH (1.11.17); Rosenberg, "Special Delivery: Alleged 9/11 Plotter's Letter Reaches White House," MH (1.16.17); Rosenberg, "About the KSM Letter You Read: The Pentagon Now Says It's Classified," MH (2.10.17).

296 Rosenberg, "USS Cole Bombing Hearing Halted at Guantánamo; Defendant May Fire Lawyer," MH (2.18.14); Rosenberg, "Alleged USS Cole Bomber Apologizes for Delay, Calls Guantánamo Court 'Strange,'" MH (2.19.14); Rosenberg, "Lawyers, Judge Hold Secret Hearing on CIA Black Sites," MH (2.23.14); Rosenberg, "Guantánamo Judge Pushes USS Cole Trial to Dec. 4," MH (3.4.14).

297 Lawfare (2.19–21.14).

298 "Motion Is Filed to Silence Prosecutor in Sept. 11 Case," NYT (2.7.14); Lawfare (2.19.14).

299 Rosenberg, "Guantánamo Defense Attorneys Want CIA Names to Prepare USS Cole Case," MH (4.9.14); Rosenberg, "Guantánamo Judge to CIA: Disclose 'Black Site' Details to USS Cole Defense Lawyers," MH (4.17.14).

300 Gerstein, "Alleged USS Cole Bomber Seeks to Halt Guantánamo Trial," Politico (4.24.14).

301 Rosenberg, "New Guantánamo Judge Throws Out Limburg Charges in USS Cole Case," MH (8.11.14).

302 Al-Nashiri v. Obama, 76 F.Supp.3d 218 (D.D.C. 2014).

303 Lawfare (4.2.14).

304 Lawfare (4.25–29.14); Rosenberg, "Expert Testifies Accused USS Cole Bomber Was Tortured," MH (4.24.14); Rosenberg, "Guantánamo Holds Rare War-Court Session to Hear from Captive's Psychiatrist," MH (4.27.14).

305 Lawfare (4.14–17.14); "FBI Said to Question Member of 9/11 Case Defense," WP (4.15.14); "Lawyers in 9/21 Case at Gitmo Seek to Question FBI," WP (4.17.14); Savage, "Official Denies F.B.I. Was Investigating Manifesto Leak," NYT (4.22.14); Savage, "F.B.I. Closes Investigation into Guantánamo Defense Aide," NYT (5.22.14); Savage, "Guantánamo Detainees' Lawyers Seek Further Delays," NYT (6.16.14); Lawfare (6.16.14); Dishneau, "Khalid Sheikh Mohammed Lawyer Wants Details of FBI Investigations," Stars and Stripes (8.14.14).

306 Rosenberg, "Prosecution Gets New Delay in USS Cole Proceedings," MH (6.29.15).

307 Rosenberg, "Guantánamo Judge Steps Down from USS Cole Case, Names Air Force Successor," MH (7.10.14); Rosenberg, "New Guantánamo Judge Takes Charge of USS Cole Case, Won't Step Down," MH (8.4.14).

308 Rosenberg, "Defense Lawyers Want to Know How a Guantánamo Convict Would Be Executed," MH (8.5.14); Rosenberg, "Guantánamo Argument: Does USS Cole Defendant Have Brain Damage," MH (8.7.14).

309 Rosenberg, "Poland Asks U.S. to Spare Alleged USS Cole Bomber from Execution," MH (4.1.15).

310 Rosenberg, "Judge: Accused USS Cole Attack Plotter Gets Adequate Health Care at Guantánamo," MH (3.30.15); Rosenberg, "Guantánamo Judge Orders MRI of USS Cole Defendant's Brain, Abates Trial," MH (4.10.15).

311 Rosenberg, "Judge to Probe Guantánamo's No-Skype Policy for Ex-CIA Prisoners," MH (11.16.14).

312 Tate & Ryan, "High-Value Guantánamo Detainees Call Home for the First Time in Nearly a Decade," WP (1.24.15).

313 Lederman, "Al-Nashiri Can Now Speak about His Treatment," Just Security (2.23.15).

314 Ackerman, "9/11 Trial Dealt Blow As Defendant Asks for Alleged CIA Torture Records," G (6.30.14).

315 Rosenberg, "USS Cole Defense Lawyers Want Entire Senate 'Torture Report,'" MH (3.4.15); Rosenberg, "War Court Judge Denies USS Cole Defense Lawyers Full 'Torture Report,'" MH (4.30.15).

316 Lawfare (10.28.15); Rohde, "How a 5-Minute Phone Call Put 9/11 Trial on Hold for More Than a Year," Reuters (10.2.15); Fox, "Judge May End Impasse That Halted 9/11 Case at Guantánamo," AP (10.18.15).

317 "Army Drives 9/11 Mastermind's Lawyer to Sacrifice His Military Career," HuffPost (4.21.14); "Guantánamo Defense Lawyer Resigns, Says U.S. Case Is 'Stacked,'" NPR (8.31.14).

318 Goldman, "Military Judge Severs Accused 9/11 Plotter from Guantánamo Proceeding," WP (7.25.14); Ramstack, "Guantánamo Judge Rules 9/11 Suspect Should Be Tried with Others," Reuters (8.13.14).

319 Rosenberg, "Judge Rebuffs Prosecution Bid to Set 9/11 Trial Date," MH (1.2.15).

320 "Guantánamo Order Bars Women from Moving Accused in 9/11 Case," AP (1.17.15).

321 Lerman, "Guantánamo Judges Told to Stay Put and Get Trials Moving," Bloomberg (1.8.15); Rosenberg, "Defense Lawyers Cry Foul over Rule Change Requiring War Court Judges to Move to Guantánamo," MH (1.13.15); Rosenberg, "Side Issues Slow Progress toward 9/11 Trial at Guantánamo," MH (2.8.15); Lederman, "Judge Pohl's Rebuke of DoD's Unorthodox Effort to Accelerate the 9/11 Trial," Just Security (2.26.15); Rosenberg, "Pentagon Scraps Judges' Guantánamo Move Order, 9/11 Cases Unfrozen," MH (2.27.15); Rosenberg, "Sept. 11 Defense Lawyers Ask Army Judge to Disqualify Guantánamo War Court Overseer," MH (3.13.15).

322 Rosenberg, "Airman Asks Judge to Quit Murder Trial over Pentagon's 'Guantánamo-First' Rule," MH (1.16.15).

323 Rosenberg, "Guantánamo Judge Orders Senior Pentagon Official to Testify on Meddling Motion," MH (2.24.15); Ramstack, "High Cost, Slow Pace of Guantánamo Proceedings Become Issue at Hearing," Reuters (2.23.15); Rosenberg, "Pentagon Scraps Judges' Guantánamo Move Order; 9/11 Cases Unfrozen," MH (2.27.15); Rosenberg, "War Court Judge Orders Pentagon to Replace USS Cole Trial Overseer," MH (3.3.15); Ryan, "Senior Official Resigns after Flap over Relocating Judges to Guantánamo," WP (3.19.15).

324 Rosenberg, "Pentagon Envisions up to 7 More Guantánamo Trials," MH (3.27.15).

325 Davis, "Guantánamo's Charade of Justice," NYT (3.28.15).

326 Rosenberg, "Senior Defense Dept. Officials Decry Guantánamo Judge's Female Guard Ban," MH (10.27.15); "Judge Says He Will Lift Restrictions on Female Guantánamo Guards," NYT (5.1.16); Rosenberg, "Guantánamo Judge Invites Pentagon Brass to Clear up Their Role in Female Guard Controversy," MH (5.10.16).

327 Lawfare (2.9.15); Rosenberg, "Pentagon: 9/11 Defense Team Linguist Was CIA Asset," MH (2.10.15); Rosenberg, "9/11 Lawyers Trade Barbs over CIA 'Black Site' Translator Turned Guantánamo Defense Linguist," MH (2.12.15).

328 Rosenberg, "9/11 Defendant Still Suffering from CIA 'Black Site' Injuries, Lawyer Says at Guantánamo," MH (2.12.15); Rosenberg, "9/11 Judge: War Court Can't Order Guantánamo Healthcare," MH (3.21.15).

329 Rosenberg, "Judge Cancels This Month's 9/11 Hearing at Guantánamo," MH (4.6.15).

330 Goldman, "CIA Photos of 'Black Sites' Could Complicate Gitmo Trials," WP (6.28.15).

331 "U.S. Military Cancels Hearing for September 11 Suspects," Reuters (8.16.15).

332 Rosenberg, "Accused 9/11 Plotter Asks about Self-Representation at Guantánamo War Court, Snags Hearing," MH (10.19.15); Johnson, "Lawyers Debate Self-Representation for Guantánamo 9/11 Suspects," Reuters (10.20.15); Rosenberg, "Alleged 9/11 Plotter Asks Army Judge to Fire His Death-Penalty Attorney," MH (10.28.15); Rosenberg, "Guantánamo Judge Overrules Sept. 11 Defendant's Bid to Fire His Lawyer," MH (10.30.15); Rosenberg, "Sept. 11 Hearing Wraps Up with Spotlight on Female Guards," MH (10.30.15).

333 Lawfare (11.3.15); Rosenberg, "Defense Lawyer to Guantánamo Judge: Secret Program May Be Depriving 9/11 Defendant of Sleep," MH (10.25.15); Rosenberg, "Sept. 11 Gitmo Trial Judge Decides Conflict Issue, Hits New Snag," MH (10.26.15).

334 Rosenberg, "Accused 9/11 Terrorist Tries to Fire Legal Team at Guantánamo," MH (2.17.16); Rosenberg, "Guantánamo Judge Rejects Attempts to Upend Sept. 11 Defense Team," MH (2.17.16).

335 Fox, "Judge Keeps Ban on Women Guards Touching High-Security Prisoners at Guantánamo, For Now," Star Tribune (12.11.15); Chief Prosecutor Mark Martins, Remarks at Guantánamo Bay (5.16.16); Savage, "Congress Moves to Nullify Judge's Order on Guantánamo Guards," NYT (5.20.16); Rosenberg, "Pentagon Brass Try to Clear Up Their Role in Female Guard Controversy," MH (5.27.16).

336 Rosenberg, "Secret Program at Secret Guantánamo Prison Hears Everything," MH (11.13.15).

337 Lawfare (12.11–14.15); Rosenberg, "Guantánamo Judge Formally Restores Five-Man 9/11 Trial," MH (12.4.15); Chief Prosecutor Mark Martins, Remarks at Guantánamo Bay (2.13.16).

338 Rosenberg, "Defense Lawyers: U.S. Leaders' Prejudice Stains Sept. 11 Death-Penalty Trial," MH (12.11.15); Rosenberg, "No Unlawful

Influence on Pentagon Official in 9/11 Case, Guantánamo Judge Rules," MH (4.11.16).

339 Rosenberg, "Guantánamo Prosecutor Defends Retroactive Censorship of Public Hearing in 9/11 Case," MH (2.4.16); Rosenberg, "Attorneys Joust over Right of Public to Vanished Open-Court Guantánamo Testimony," MH (2.22.16); Rosenberg, "Guantánamo Judge Approves Retroactive Censorship of Open-Court Hearings," MH (10.12.16).

340 *In re al-Nashiri*, 791 F.3d 71 (D.C. Cir. 2015).

341 Doyle, "Lawyer for Suspect in USS Cole Bombing Foresees Appeal in 2024," MH (2.17.16); *In re al-Nashiri*, 835 F.3d 110 (D.C. Cir. 2016).

342 *U.S. v. Al-Nashiri*, CMCR 14-001 (6.9.16).

343 Savage, "Judge Allowed Destruction of Evidence in 9/11 Case, Defense Says," NYT (5.12.16); Ackerman, "Judge 'Manipulated' 9/11 Attacks Case, Court Document Alleges," G (5.31.16); Ackerman, "Guantánamo Bay Lawyers Deny Colluding with Judge in Key 9/11 Case," G (6.8.16).

344 Rosenberg, "Citing Health Concerns, Marine General Bans War Court Defense Staff from Living at Guantánamo's Camp Justice," MH (4.12.16); Rosenberg, "Navy Health Teams Still Analyzing Guantánamo's Camp Justice," MH (11.15.16); Rosenberg, "Marine General Returns Defense Lawyers to Trailer Park at Guantánamo's Camp Justice," MH (5.20.16).

345 Rosenberg, "New Question Burdens 9/11 Trial: Can Death-Penalty Case Proceed without Capital Defender?" MH (7.20.16); Rosenberg, "Judge Ejects Unruly 9/11 Defendant from Court," MH (7.21.16); Lawfare (7.22.16, 7.23.16, 7.28.16).

346 Rosenberg, "Guantánamo Judge: 9/11 Prosecutor's Proposed Trial Evidence Is So Far Inadequate," MH (7.25.16); Rosenberg, "9/11 Defense Lawyers: Judge Let U.S. Secretly Destroy CIA Black Site Evidence," MH (7.25.16).

347 *In re Al-Nashiri*, 2016 LEXIS 15974 (D.C. Cir. 2016).

348 Rosenberg, "After 18-Month Hiatus USS Cole Trial Participants Return to Guantánamo," MH (9.7.16); Rosenberg, "USS Cole Case Lawyers Debate Extraterritorial Reach of Guantánamo's War Court," MH (9.9.16); Lawfare (9.9.16, 9.10.16, 9.13.16, 9.15.16).

349 Lawfare (10.14.16).

350 Lawfare (10.21.16), citing *U.S. v. Barnwell*, 477 F.3d 844 (6th Cir. 2007).

351 Lawfare (12.8.16); Rosenberg, "Guantánamo Doctor: 'Sodomized' 9/11 Captive Was Treated for Hemorrhoids," MH (12.5.16).

352 Gerstein, "Classified Information 'Spill' Reported at Guantánamo Military Commission," Politico (5.10.16).

353 Lawfare (12.8.16, 12.9.16).

354 Rosenberg, "Quick, 9/11 Lawyers Argue, Preserve Senate 'Torture Report' before Trump Takes Office," MH (12.7.16); Rosenberg, "Guantánamo Lawyer: We Need to Hear from the Torturers," MH (12.15.16); Rosenberg, "9/11 Trial Judge Orders Pentagon to Preserve Its Copy of the CIA 'Torture Report,'" MH (1.10.17).

355 Rosenberg, "9/11 Trial Judge Orders Pentagon to Preserve Its Copy of the CIA 'Torture Report,'" MH (1.10.17).

356 Rosenberg, "Guantánamo Hearings to Go Forward Minus One Death-Penalty Defender," MH (1.22.17); Rosenberg, "Guantánamo Prosecutor Wants to Start 9/11 Trial in March 2018," MH (1.25.17); "Lawyer's Accident Trips Up 9/11 Case at Guantánamo," ABC News (1.25.17); Rosenberg, "Guantánamo's 9/11 Hearing Could Hit Snag on First Day," MH (5.14.17); Rosenberg, "Guantánamo's 9/11 Case Judge: Civil Suit No Problem for This Week's Hearing," MH (5.15.17).

357 Lawfare (March 8, 12, 13, 16, 17, 20, 21, 23, 24, 27; April 3, 27, 29; May 23, 2017); Rosenberg, "Shadowy Dispute over Evidence Casts Doubt on 2018 Start of 9/11 Trial," MH (3.5.17); Rosenberg, "Guantánamo Judge Orders CIA Testimony on Destroyed 'Black Site' Videotapes," MH (3.7.17); "Army Judge Drops 2 Non-Capital Charges in Guantánamo's 9/11 Case," MH (4.7.17); Rosenberg, "Guantánamo War Court Isn't Legitimate, Sept. 11 Defense Lawyers Argue," MH (5.18.17); Rosenberg, "Did Someone Illegally Record Legal Meetings: Southcom Investigates," MH (6.19.17); Rosenberg, "Pentagon Appeals Panel Overrules Guantánamo Judge, Reinstates Two 9/11 Trial Charges," MH (6.29.17); Rosenberg, "Guantánamo Judges Freeze Sept. 11 USS Cole Terror Cases in Speedboat Showdown," MH (7.7.17).

358 Savage, "Sessions Says Guantánamo Is a 'Very Fine Place' for New Suspects," NYT (3.10.17); Ard, "U.S. Charges Guantánamo Detainee with 2002 Bali Bombing," McClatchy (6.24.17); Rosenberg, "Pentagon Won't Seek Death Penalty in Guantánamo's Bali Bombing Case," MH (6.28.17).

359 In re Khalid Shaikh Mohammad, No. 17–1156 (DC Cir. 8.9.17).

360 See the Table A2 in the Appendix.

361 Denbeaux et al. (2013).

362 Lawfare (9.1.17).

363 Rosenberg, "Defense Lawyers Quit. Not So Fast, Says War Court Judge, Who Orders Them to Guantánamo," MH (10.23.17); Rosenberg, "Civilian Lawyers Defy Judge's Order to Travel to Guantánamo for War Court Showdown," MH (10.29.17); Rosenberg, "USS Cole Prosecutors Want No-Show Civilian Attorneys Found in Contempt of War Court," MH (10.30.17); Rosenberg, "Guantánamo Judge Orders Contempt Hearing to Try to End Defense Revolt at War Court," MH (11.1.17); Rosenberg, "Pentagon's War Crimes Prosecutor Begins a Media Blackout at Guantánamo," MH (12.1.17); Lawfare (11.2.17); Crawford, "Guantánamo Defense Lawyer Punished for Disobeying Judge," CNN (11.2.17); Rosenberg, "Gitmo Judge Sends Marine General Lawyer to 21 Days Confinement for Disobeying Orders," MH (11.1.17); Lamothe, "In a Highly Unusual Move, an American General Is Sentenced to Confinement at Guantánamo Bay," WP (11.2.17); Lawfare (11.2.17); Rosenberg, "Resigned USS Cole Case Lawyers to Defy War Court Judge's Order – Again," MH (11.2.17); Coyle, "Guantánamo Chief Defense Counsel, Confined for Contempt, Gets Temporary Freedom," NLJ (11.3.17); Rosenberg, "Federal Judge Blocks Military Judge from

Having U.S. Marshals Seize Defense Attorney," MH (11.4.17); Lawfare (11.14.17).

364 Rodriguez, "Guantánamo Is Delaying Justice for 9/11 Families," NYT (11.14.17).

365 *R* v. *Sussex Justices, ex p McCarthy*, [1924] KB 256.

CHAPTER 5 HABEAS CORPUS

1 See Ball (2007). For a history of habeas in the USA, see Wert (2010).
2 Philbin and Yoo to Hayes, "Possible Habeas Jurisdiction over Aliens Held in Guantánamo Bay, Cuba" (12.28.01).
3 See generally Hafetz (2011; 2016).
4 *Coalition of Clergy* v. *Bush*, 189 F.Supp.2d. 1036 (C.D. Calif. 2002).
5 339 US 763 (1950).
6 *Coalition of Clergy* v. *Bush*, 189 F.Supp.2d. 1036 (C.D. Calif. 2002).
7 *Coalition of Clergy, Lawyers, and Professors* v. *Bush*, 310 F.3d 1153 (9th Cir. 2002), cert. denied, 538 US 2031 (2003).
8 *Gherebi* v. *Bush*, 262 F.Supp.2d 1064 (C.D. Calif. 2003).
9 *Gherebi* v. *Bush*, 352 F.3d 1278 (9th Cir. 2003).
10 *Bush* v. *Gherebi*, 542 US 952 (2004).
11 *Gherebi* v. *Bush*, 374 F.3d 727 (9th Cir. 2004).
12 *Gherebi* v. *Bush*, 338 F.Supp.2d 91 (2004).
13 *Hamdi* v. *Rumsfeld*, 294 F.3d 598 (4th Cir. 2002) (Hamdi I).
14 *Hamdi* v. *Rumsfeld*, 296 F.3d 378 (4th Cir. 2002) (Hamdi II).
15 *Hamdi* v. *Rumsfeld*, 243 F.Supp.2d 527 (E.D.Va. 2002).
16 *Hamdi* v. *Rumsfeld*, 316 F.3d 450 (4th Cir. 2002) (Hamdi III).
17 *Hamdi* v. *Rumsfeld*, 337 F.3d 335 (4th Cir. 2003) (Hamdi IV).
18 *Hamdi* v. *Rumsfeld*, 542 US 507 (2004).
19 Brinkley & Lichtblau, "Held 3 Years by US, Saudi Goes Home," *International Herald Tribune* (10.13.04); Markon, "Hamdi Returned to Saudi Arabia," WP (10.12.04).
20 *Padilla* v. *Bush*, 233 F.Supp.2d 564 (S.D.N.Y. 2002).
21 Ari Fleischer, Press Briefing (6.12.02) www.white-house.gov/news/releases/200206.12-5-html (last accessed June 12, 2004); Fainaru, "Lawyer Challenges Al-Muhajir's Detention," WP (6.12.02).
22 *Padilla* v. *Rumsfeld*, 352 F.2d 695 (2nd Cir. 2003).
23 Gonzales, Remarks to the ABA Standing Committee on Law and National Security (2.24.04), www.abanet.org/natsecurity/judge_gonzales.pdf.
24 Remarks of Deputy Attorney General Comey Regarding Jose Padilla (6.1.04) www.justice.gov/archive/dag/speeches/2004/dag6104.htm; "No Defense Possible," WP (6.4.04).
25 *Rumsfeld* v. *Padilla*, 542 US 426 (2004).
26 *Padilla* v. *Hanft*, 2005 US Dist. LEXIS 2921 (February 28, 2005); 2005 WL 465691 (D.S.C.); Lewis, "Judge Says Terror Suspect Can't Be Held

As an Enemy Combatant," NYT (3.1.05); Serrano, "Judge Rules Terror Suspect Must Be Charged or Freed," LAT (3.1.05).

27 317 US 1 (1942).
28 71 US 2 (1866).
29 323 US 283 (1944).
30 *Youngstown Sheet & Tube Co.* v. *Sawyer*, 343 US 579 (1952).
31 "Gonzales Defends Detention," LAT (3.2.05); Schmitt, "US May Still Charge 'Enemy Combatant,' Gonzales Says," LAT (3.8.05).
32 Jackman, "US a Battlefield, Solicitor General Tells Judges," AP (7.20.05); "Padilla Should Be Charged, His Lawyer Tells Appellate Panel," LAT (7.20.05).
33 *Padilla* v. *Hanft*, 423 F.3d 326 (4th Cir. 2005).
34 Markon, "US Can Confine Citizens Without Charges, Court Rules," WP (9.10.05).
35 "US Indicts Padilla after 3 Years in Pentagon Custody," NYT (11.22.05); Lichtblau, "In Legal Shift, US Charges Detainee in Terrorism Case," NYT (11.23.05); Eggen, "Padilla Is Indicted on Terrorism Charges," WP (11.23.05); Jehl & Lichtblau, "Shift on Suspect Is Linked to Role of Qaeda Figures," NYT (11.24.05); Lewis, "Indictment Portrays Padilla as Minor Figure in a Plot," NYT (11.24.05); Liptak, "In Terror Cases Administration Sets Its Own Rules," NYT (11.27.05).
36 Denniston, "Padilla's Status: The Same, or Changing?" Scotusblog (12.2.05).
37 "Um. About That Dirty Bomb?" NYT (11.23.05).
38 Lewis, "Terror Trial Hits Obstacle, Unexpectedly," NYT (12.2.05); Greenhouse, "Justices Are Urged to Dismiss Padilla Case," NYT (12.18.05).
39 *Padilla* v. *Hanft*, 432 F.3d 582, 585 (4th Cir. 2005); Leis, "Court Refuses US Bid to Shift Terror Suspect," NYT (12.22.05); Markon, "Court Bars Transfer of Padilla to Face New Terrorism Charges," WP (12.22.05).
40 "Mr. Padilla in Captivity," WP (12.23.05).
41 Lichtblau, "Supreme Court Is Asked to Rule on Terror Trial," NYT (12.29.05); Markon, "US Defends Conduct in Padilla Case," WP (12.29.05); "Padilla Wants High Court Ruling," LAT (12.31.05); "The 4th Circuit v. Mr. Bush," WP (1.2.06).
42 *Padilla* v. *Hanft*, 547 US 1062 (2006); Greenhouse, "Justices to Let US Transfer Padilla to Civilian Custody," NYT (1.5.06); Savage, "High Court OKs Moving Padilla to Jail," LAT (1.5.06); Lane, "Justices Won't Review Padilla Case," WP (4.4.05); Greenhouse, "Justices Decline Terror Case of a US Citizen," NYT (4.4.06); "Supreme Court Rejects Challenge to Bush War Powers," LAT (4.3.06); Savage, "High Court Declines to Take Up 'Dirty Bomber' Case," LAT (4.4.06).
43 "Permission to Back Down," WP (4.4.06); "The High Court Punts," NYT (4.4.06).
44 Lewis, "Judge Leaves Appeals Court for Boeing," NYT (5.11.06); "Federal Appellate Judge to Be Boeing's Top Lawyer," LAT (5.11.06); Bravin & Lunsford, "New Task: Appease McCain," WSJ (5.11.06).

45 *Rasul v. Bush*, 215 F.Supp.2d 55 (D.D.C. 2002).
46 *Al Odah v. United States*, 321 F.3d 1134 (2003).
47 *Rasul v. Bush*, 542 US 466 (2004).
48 *U.S. v. Al-Marri*, 230 F.Supp.2d 535 (S.D.N.Y. 2002); Bazelon, "Meet the New Padilla," *Slate* (4.10.06).
49 Ashcroft (2006: 168–69).
50 *Al-Marri v. Bush*, 274 F.Supp.2d 1003 (C.D. Ill. 2003).
51 *Al-Marri v. Rumsfeld*, 360 F.3d 707 (7th Cir. 2004), cert. denied, 543 US 809 (2004).
52 *Al-Marri v. Hanft*, 378 F.Supp.2d 673 (D.S.C. 2005).
53 *Al-Marri ex rel. Berman v. Wright*, 443 F.Supp.2d 774 (D.S.C. 2006); Eggen, "US Suffers Setback in Case of Alleged Enemy Combatant," WP (4.21.06).
54 "Virginia: US: Terror Law Covers Immigrants," LAT (11.14.06); Eggen, "Reno Joins Criticism of Anti-Terror Strategy," WP (11.22.06).
55 Leonnig, "04 Pentagon Report Cited Detention Concerns," WP (12.14.06); Liptak, "In a War with Vague Boundaries: A Terror Detainee Longs for Court," NYT (1.5.07).
56 *Al-Marri v. Wright*, 487 F.3d 160 (4th Cir. 2007); Leonnig, "Judges Rule against US on Detained 'Combatant,'" WP (6.12.07); Meyer, "Indefinite Detention Struck Down," LAT (6.12.07); Liptak, "Judges Say US Can't Hold Man as 'Combatant,'" NYT (6.12.07).
57 *Zadvydas v. Davis*, 533 US 678 (2001).
58 *Ex parte Quirin*, 317 US 1 (1942).
59 *Ex parte Milligan*, 71 US (4 Wall.) 2 (1866).
60 "A Ruling for Justice," NYT (6.12.07); Letter to the Editor, NYT (6.13.07); "Dealing with Mr. Marri," WP (6.13.07).
61 Schmidt, "Trail of an 'Enemy Combatant': From Desert to US Heartland," WP (7.20.07).
62 "Justice for an 'Enemy Combatant,'" WP (8.25.07).
63 "Court Considers Enemy Combatant Case," LAT (11.1.07); Liptak, "Court Takes Second Look at Enemy Combatant Case," NYT (11.1.07); White, "Lawyers Fear for Marri's Sanity," WP (5.4.08).
64 *Al-Marri v. Pucciarelli*, 534 F.3rd 213 (4th Cir. 2008); Liptak, "Court Ruling Favors Bush in Powers on Detainees," NYT (7.16.08).
65 "Detaining Mr. Marri," NYT (7.20.08).
66 Kinnard, "Federal Prosecutors Defend Administration's Right to Hold Accused Enemy Combatant," LAT (10.31.08); Markon, "High Court May Consider Legality of Detention," WP (11.9.08); Hafetz, "2,000 Days in Detention," LAT (11.25.08); "Indefinite Detention," NYT A30 (11.25.08); "The President's Prisoner," WP (12.12.08).
67 Liptak, "Justices to Rule on Detainee Held in US Torture Case," NYT (12.6.08); Savage, "Supreme Court to Hear 'Enemy Combatant' Case," LAT (12.6.08); Barnes, "Justices to Decide Legality of Indefinite Detention," WP (12.6.08); Liptak, "Early Test of Obama Views on Power over Detainees," NYT (1.3.09); DoJ Press Release (2.27.09); ACLU Press Release (2.27.09); Johnston & Lewis, "In Reversal, US Plans to Try Qaeda

Suspect in Civilian Court," NYT (2.27.09); Meyer & Savage, "Charges Expected in 'Combatant' Case," LAT (2.27.09); Johnson & Tate, "Prosecutors Prepare Charges against Final 'Enemy Combatant' in US," WP (2.26.09); Johnson & Tate, "'Combatant' Case to Move from Tribunal to US Court," WP (2.27.09); HRF, Press Release (2.27.09); Johnson, "Terrorism Suspect Headed to US Court," WP (2.28.09); Schwartz, "A Terrorism Case Test Obama May Not Want," NYT (2.28.09).

68 "Mr. Marri's Day in Court," WP A14 (3.6.09); "A Necessary Supreme Court Showdown," NYT (3.6.09).

69 *Al-Marri v. Spagone*, 555 US 1220 (2009); Barnes & Johnson, "Court Puts Off Decision on Indefinite Detention," WP (3.7.09); Johnson & Finn, "Suspected al-Qaeda Agent Gets Hearing," WP (3.18.09); Johnson, "Continued Detention of Marri Is Ordered," WP (3.19.09); Hood, "Suspected al Qaeda Operative Pleads Not Guilty," LAT (3.24.09); DoJ Press Release (4.30.09); Hood & Meyer, "Ali Saleh Kahlah Marri Admits Helping 9/11 Architects," LAT (5.1.09); Johnson, "Marri Admits Conspiring with al-Qaeda Operatives," WP (5.1.09); Schwartz, "Plea Agreement Reached with Agent for al Qaeda," NYT (5.1.09); Eviatar, "The Significance of Ali al-Marri's Guilty Plea," *Washington Times* (5.2.09); Finn & Johnson, "Detainee Compromises Likely," WP (5.4.09).

70 Schwartz, "Admitted Qaeda Agent Receives Prison Sentence," NYT (10.30.09); Johnson, "Judge Credits Time Served in Sentencing al-Qaeda Aide," WP (10.30.09).

71 "Qatari Held in US Since 2001 Returns Home," AFP (1.17.15); Kirchick, "Exclusive: Freed Al Qaeda Agent Was Part of Proposed Swap for Jailed Americans," Daily Beast (1.26.15).

72 Denbeaux & Hafetz (2009); Fletcher et al. (2011); Sullivan, "The Minutes of the Guantánamo Bar Association," *New York Magazine* (6.26.06).

73 Lewis, "US Allows Lawyers to Meet Detainees," NYT (7.3.04); Marquis, "Pentagon Will Permit Captives at Cuba Base to Appeal Status," NYT (7.8.04); Hendren & Mazzetti, "Pentagon Reportedly Aimed to Hold Detainees in Secret," LAT (7.9.04); Gearan, "Prisoner Gets First Chance to Tell Story," AP (7.31.04); *Al Odah v. US*, 346 F.Supp.2d 1 (D.D.C. 2004); *In re Guantánamo Detainee Cases*, 344 F.Supp.2d 174 (D.D.C. 2004).

74 *Khalid v. Bush*, 355 F.Supp.2d 311 (D.D.C. 2005).

75 *In re Guantánamo Detainee Cases*, 355 F.Supp.2d 443 (D.D.C. 2005).

76 OARDEC, "Summary of Evidence for Combatant Status Review Tribunal: KARNAZ [sic] Murat," DoD (9.22.04).

77 Leonnig, "Panel Ignored Evidence on Detainee," WP (3.27.05); Kurnaz (2008).

78 See Habib (2009).

79 Lewis, "Appeals Court Weighs Prisoners' Right to Fight Detention," NYT (11.7.06); Liptak, "Appeals Court Rejects Brief Submitted by Ex-Judges," NYT A15 12.30.06); Fleming (2016).

80 §1005.

81 Lewis, "US to Seek Dismissal of Guantánamo Suits," NYT A13 (1.4.06); White, "Impact of Detainee Act Debated in Court," WP (3.23.06).

82 Statement of US Senator Russ Feingold on the President Signing the Military Commissions Act (10.17.06); "Rushing Off a Cliff," NYT (9.28.06).
83 Lewis, "Judge Sets Back Guantánamo Detainees," NYT A32 (12.14.06); "Give Habeas a Chance," LAT (12.18.06); "Fix Needed," WP (12.21.06).
84 Savage, "Habeas Corpus and an Era of Limits," LAT (1.30.07).
85 *Boumediene v. Bush*, 476 F.3d 981 (D.C. Cir. 2007).
86 *Al Odah v. U.S.*, 127 S. Ct. 3067 (2007).
87 Labaton, "Court Endorses Curbs on Appeal by US Detainees," NYT (2.21.07); Savage, "Court Denies Guantánamo Legal Rights," LAT (2.21.07); White, "Guantánamo Detainees Lose Appeal," WP (2.21.07); "Restore the Writ," LAT (2.21.07); "American Liberty at the Precipice," NYT (2.22.07); "A Congressional Duty," WP (2.23.07); Letters to the Editor, "When Our Freedom Is at Stake," NYT (2.26.07).
88 Savage, "Senate Urges Trials at Guantánamo," LAT (6.8.07); AFJ Press Release (6.22.07).
89 *Boumediene v. Bush*, 550 US 1301 (2007); Goldstein, "Justice Won't Hear Detainee Rights Cases – for Now," WP (4.3.07); Greenhouse, "Supreme Court Turns Down Detainees' Habeas Corpus Case," NYT (4.3.07); Savage, "Justices Refuse Detainees," LAT (4.3.07); "Guantánamo Follies," NYT (4.6.07).
90 *Boumediene v. Bush*, 551 US 1160 (2007); "Supreme Court Will Hear Cases on Detainees," NYT (6.29.07); Savage & Williams, "High Court to Reconsider Guantánamo," LAT (6.30.07); Glaberson, "In Shift, Justices Agree to Review Detainees' Case," NYT (6.30.07); Brown, "Justices to Weigh Detainee Rights," WP (6.30.07); Hafetz (2011: 157).
91 NPR, Morning Edition (7.16.07); "Justice at Guantánamo," WP (7.18.07); Schwartz, "Justice Department Lawyers Refuse Detainee Cases," US News (8.30.07); Greenhouse, "Guantánamo Legal Battle Is Resuming," NYT (9.2.07); "Restoring American Justice," NYT (9.17.07); "Justice for Detainees," WP (9.18.07); "The Roberts Court Returns," NYT (9.30.07).
92 Weisman, "GOP Blocks Bid on Rights of Detainees," WP (9.20.07); Hulse, "Senate Republicans Block Detainee Right of Appeal," NYT (9.20.07).
93 *Alhami v. Bush*, DDC CA 05-359 (10.2.07).
94 Greenhouse, "For Justices, Another Day on Detainees," NYT (12.3.07); "Gitmo Inmates Deserve Protection," LAT (12.5.07); "Their Day in Court," WP (12.5.07); "A Key Moment for Justice," NYT (12.5.07); "The Supreme Court's Habeas Hearing," LAT (12.9.07).
95 *Boumediene v. Bush*, 553 US 723 (2008).
96 White and Wilber, "Detainees Now Have Access to Federal Court," WP (6.13.08); Barnes, "Justices Say Detainees Can Seek Release," WP (6.13.08); Greenhouse, "Detainees in Cuba Win Major Ruling in Supreme Court," NYT (6.13.08); Glaberson, "Guantánamo Detention Camp Remains, but Not Its Legal Rationale," NYT (6.13.08); Savage,

"Constitution Applies to Detainees, Justices Say," LAT (6.13.08); Spiegel & Meyer, "Basis for Offshore Prison Is Undercut," LAT (6.13.08); Abramowitz, "Administration Strategy for Detention Now in Disarray," WP (6.13.08); Abramowitz, "Critics Study Possible Limits to Habeas Corpus Ruling," WP (6.14.08).

97 Zernike, "McCain and Obama Split on Justices' Ruling," NYT (6.13.08); Greenhouse, "Over Guantánamo, Justices Come under Election Year Spotlight," NYT (6.14.08); Helprin & Shear, "McCain Denounces Detainee Ruling," WP (6.14.08).

98 Isaac (2016: 27).

99 "The Justices' Refrain," WP (6.13.08); "Justice 5, Brutality 4," NYT (6.13.08); "Due Process at Gitmo," LAT (6.13.08); Letters to the Editor, NYT (6.14.08); Epstein, "How to Complicate Habeas Corpus," NYT (6.21.08).

100 DoJ, Transcript of Remarks by Attorney General Michael B. Mukasey at the American Enterprise Institute for Public Policy Research (7.21.08).

101 "Mr. Mukasey's Justice," NYT (7.27.08); "Detainees' Day in Court," WP (9.17.08).

102 *Boumediene v. Bush*, 282 Fed. Appx 844 (D.C. Cir. 2008); "Judge Orders Detainee Hearings," LAT (7.9.08).

103 *In re Guantánamo Bay Detainee Litigation*," 2008 WL 4858241 (D.D.C. 2008); *In re Guantánamo Bay Litigation*, DDC (12.16.09), Misc. No. 08-0442 (TFH).

104 *Boumediene v. Bush*, 579 F.Supp.2d 191 (D.D.C. 2008); Denniston, Scotusblog (8.21.08); Judge Leon's Oral Ruling (10.27.08); Wilber, "Cases Against Detainees Have Thinned," WP (11.2.08); Wilber, "Judge Is Told 6 Algerians Should Remain Detained," WP (11.7.08); Glaberson, "Judge Opens First Habeas Corpus Hearing on Guantánamo Detainees," NYT (11.7.08); Savage, "Judge Orders Release of 5 Guantánamo Prisoners," LAT (11.21.08); Statement by 10 Prominent Conservatives Urging Government to Comply with Judge Ricardo Urbino's Order to Release Uighurs, 224 *HRF Law and Security Digest* (11.21.08); Glaberson, "Judge Declares Five Detainees Held Illegally," NYT (11.21.08); Wilber, "Detention Challenges Are Far Off for Many," WP (7.31.09).

105 *Bensayah v. Obama*, 610 F.3d 718 (D.C. Cir. 2010); Savage, "Appeals Court Sides with Guantánamo Detainee," NYT (7.4.10).

106 DoD, "Detainee Transfer Announced" (12.5.13).

107 "National Briefing: Washington, D.C.," LAT (10.31.08); Finn & Wilber, "Motives of Justice Lawyers Questioned in Detainee's Case," WP (10.31.08); Glaberson, "Questioning 'Dirty Bomb' Plot, Judge Orders US to Yield Papers on Detainee," NYT (10.31.08).

108 *Sliti v. Bush*, 592 F.Supp.2d 46 (D.D.C. 2008); *Al Alwi v. Bush*, 593 F.Supp.2d 24 (D.D.C. 2008), aff'd, 653 F.3d 11 (D.C. Cir. 2011); Glaberson, "Judge Agrees with Bush in Ruling on 2 Detainees' Status," NYT (12.31.08).

109   White, "Unable to End 'Unlawful' Detention, Judge Says," WP (12.23.05).
110   *Qassim v. Bush*, 407 F.Supp.2d 198 (D.D.C. 2005).
111   Leonnig, "Chinese Detainees' Lawyers Will Take Case to High Court," WP (1.17.06); White, "Supreme Court Won't Hear Chinese Detainees' Case," WP (4.14.06); Yost, "Chinese Detainees Released to Albania," WP (5.6.06); *Qassim v. Bush*, 466 F.3d 1073 (D.C. Cir. 2006).
112   See Willett (2016).
113   *Bismullah v. Gates*, 501 F.3d 178 (D.C. Cir. 2007) (*Bismullah* I).
114   *Bismullah v. Gates*, 503 F.3d 137 (D.C. Cir. 2007).
115   *Bismullah v. Gates*, 514 F.3d 1291 (D.C. Cir. 2008); "Guantánamo Ruling Is a Setback for Bush," LAT (2.2.08); Glaberson, "Guantánamo Decision Rebuffs Government," NYT A9 (2.2.08).
116   Greenhouse, "A Second Case on Detainees Complicates Supreme Court Deliberations," NYT (2.6.08); Greenhouse, "Bush Appeals to Justices on Detainees Case," NYT (2.15.08); Greenhouse, "Detainees at Guantánamo Fight Further Appeal Delay," NYT (2.22.08); "Justice at Guantánamo: Once Again the Bush Administration Is Trying to Curtail It," WP (2.19.08).
117   *Gates v. Bismullah*, 554 U.S. 913 (2008).
118   *Bismullah v. Gates*, 551 F.3d 1068 (D.C. Cir. 2009).
119   *Parhat v. Gates*, 532 F.3d 834 (D.C. Cir. 2008); Glaberson, "Evidence Faulted in Detainee Case," NYT (7.1.08); Wilber & White, "Judges Cite Need for Reliable Evidence to Hold Detainees," WP (7.1.08).
120   *In re Guantánamo Bay Detainee Litigation*, 581 F.Supp.2d 33 (D.D.C. 2008).
121   "Mr. Mukasey's Modest Proposal," WSJ (7.22.08).
122   Wilber, "Appeals Court Hears Uighur Detainees' Case," WP (11.25.08); "Guantánamo Justice," WP (11.27.08); Willett, "Judging Detainees on the Facts," BG (11.30.08).
123   *Kiyemba v. Obama*, 555 F.3d 1022 (D.C. Cir. 2009).
124   Glaberson & Williams," Chinese Inmates at Guantánamo Pose a Dilemma," NYT (4.1.09); Williams, "Detainees' Release into US Is Urged," LAT (4.7.09); "Justice for the Uighurs," WP (4.18.09); Barnes, "US May Accept Muslim Detainees," LAT (4.24.09); Goldstein, "Swedish Court Secures Ex-Guantánamo Uighur's Asylum Quest," CSM (4.30.09); "Freedom for the Uighurs," WP (6.6.09); Savage, "Supreme Court to Decide Who Can Free Guantánamo Prisoners," LAT (10.21.09); Liptak, "Justice to Decide on US Release of Detainees," NYT (10.21.09); Barnes, "Supreme Court to Hear Uighurs' Case," WP (10.21.09); "The Clock Is Ticking," WP (10.21.09); McConnell, "A Lesson from the Uighurs," NLJ (11.9.09); "Uighurs' Gambit," WP (3.3.10).
125   *Kiyemba v. Obama*, 558 US 969 (2009), 559. US 131 (2010).
126   *Kiyemba v. Obama*, 605 F.3d 1046 (D.C. Cir. 2010).
127   *Kiyemba v. Obama*, 131 S. Ct. 1631 (2011).
128   "US Should Resettle Uighurs Held at Guantánamo," LAT (4.22.11).
129   *Abu Ali v. Ashcroft*, 350 F.Supp.2d 28 (D.D.C. 2004).

130 See the "paintball" cases in Bohn & Frieden, "'Virginia jihad' members found guilty," CNN.com (3.5.04).
131 *Abu Ali v. Gonzales*, 387 F.Supp.2d 16 (D.D.C. 2005).
132 *Omar v. Harvey*, 416 F.Supp.2d 19 (D.D.C. 2006); "US Appeals Ruling on American Held in Iraq," NYT (9.12.06); "Court Blocks Moving American's Case to Iraq Court," NYT (2.10.07); *Omar v. Harvey*, 479 F.3d 1 (D.C. Cir. 2007).
133 *Mohammed v. Harvey*, 456 F.Supp.2d 115 (D.D.C. 2006).
134 *Munaf v. Geren*, 482 F.3d 582 (D.C. Cir. 2007); White, "US Citizen Sentenced to Death in Iraq Loses Appeal," WP A3 (4.7.07).
135 Savage, "Americans Held in Iraq Reach Supreme Court," LAT (12.8.07); *Munaf v. Geren*, 553 US 674 (2008); Johnson, "Ability to Challenge Transfer to Foreign Custody Is Limited," WP A3 (6.13.08).
136 "Appeal from Abroad," WP A14 (6.22.08).
137 *Omar v. Geren*, 689 F.Supp.2d 1 (D.D.C. 2009).
138 *Omar v. McHugh*, 646 F.3d 13 (D.C. Cir. 2011).
139 "Overreaching at Bagram," WP (1.7.09); Denniston, summary of argument, Scotusblog (1.8.09); Denniston, "US: No Habeas Rights at Bagram," Scotusblog (2.20.09); Pickler & Apuzzo, "Obama Backs Bush: No Rights for Bagram Prisoners," WP (2.20.09); "A Reckoning at Bagram," WP (3.7.09); *Maqaleh v. Gates*, 620 F.Supp.2d 51 (D.D.C. 2009); *Wazir v. Gates*, 629 F.Supp.2d 3 (D.D.C. 2009); Wilber & DeYoung, "3 Detained in Afghanistan Can Take Challenges to US Court," WP (4.3.09); Savage, "Afghan Detainees Win Ruling," LAT (4.3.09); Savage, "Judge Rules Some Prisoners at Bagram Have Right to Habeas Corpus," NYT (4.3.09); "The Constitution's Reach," WP (4.7.09); "Due Process for All," LAT (4.9.09); 239 *HRF Law and Security Digest* (4.10.09); "Obama to Appeal Detainee Ruling," NYT (4.11.09); Smith, "Obama Follows Bush Policy on Detainee Access to Courts," WP (4.11.09); "The Next Guantánamo," NYT (4.13.09); Schwartz, "Court Backs War Powers over Rights of Detainees," NYT (1.6.10); Savage, "Court Upholds US Right to Hold Guantánamo Prisoners," LAT (1.6.10); Wilber, "Appeals Court Upholds Ruling to Detain Terror Suspect," WP (1.6.10); Denniston, "Parsing Boumediene," Scotusblog (1.7.10); "A Bagram Reckoning," NYT (1.18.10); Savage, "An Appeals Panel Denies Detainees US Court Access," NYT (5.22.10); Savage & Parsons, "Court: No Habeas Rights for Prisoners in Afghanistan," LAT (5.21.10); *Maqaleh v. Gates*, 605 F.3d 84 (D.C. Cir. 2010); "Backward at Bagram," NYT (6.1.10); "The New Gitmo?" WP (6.7.10); Epstein, "A Constitutional Parody on Habeas Corpus," Forbes (6.1.10).
140 *Al Maqaleh v. Gates*, 2011 WL 666883 (D.D.C. 2011).
141 *Wahid v. Gates*, 876 F.Supp.2d 15 (D.D.C. 2012).
142 Savage, "US Hearings Again Sought for 3 Detainees," NYT (9.25.12); *Al Maqaleh v. Gates*, 899 F.Supp.2d 10 (D.D.C. 2012); Savage, "Judge Denies Hearing Request from 3 Afghanistan Detainees," NYT (10.19.12).

143 *Hamidullah* v. *Obama*, 899 F.Supp.2d 3 (D.D.C. 2012).

144 *Amanatullah* v. *Obama*, 904 F.Supp.2d 45 (D.D.C. 2012).

145 *Maqaleh* v. *Hagel*, 738 F.3d 312 (D.C. Cir. 2013).

146 CCR, Press Release: "CCR Files Habeas Petition on Behalf of Majid Khan" (10.3.06).

147 Leonnig & Tate, "Sept. 11 Plotter Asks Court for Lawyer, Trial," WP A3 (10.26.06).

148 *El Gharani* v. *Bush*, 593 F.Supp.2d 144 (D.D.C. 2009); Wilber, "Citing Weak Evidence, Judge Orders Guantánamo Detainee Freed," WP A11 (1.15.09).

149 *Zaid* v. *Bush*, 596 F.Supp.2d 11 (D.D.C. 2009).

150 *Al Bihani* v. *Obama*, 594 F.Supp.2d 35 (D.D.C. 2009); "Yemeni to Stay in US Custody," LAT (1.29.09); Wilber, "US Can Continue Yemeni's Detention," WP (1.29.09); Pickler, "Judge OKs Holding Taliban Cook Now at Guantánamo," MH (1.28.09).

151 *Al-Bihani* v. *Obama*, 590 F.3d 866 (D.C. Cir. 2010).

152 *Al-Bihani* v. *Obama*, 619 F.3d 1 (D.C. Cir. 2010), cert. denied, 131 S. Ct. 1814 (2011); Savage, "Appeals Court Backs Away from War Powers Ruling," NYT (9.1.10).

153 *Ahmed* v. *Obama*, 613 F.Supp.2d 51 (D.D.C. 2009); Wilber, "Release of Yemeni Held at Guantánamo Ordered," WP (5.13.09).

154 *Ahmed* v. *Bush*, 585 F.Supp.2d 127 (D.D.C. 2008).

155 DoJ Press Release (3.13.09); *Gherebi* v. *Obama*, 609 F.Supp.2d 43 (D.D.C. 2009).

156 *Hamlily* v. *Obama*, 616 F.Supp.2d 63 (D.D.C. 2009).

157 *Anam* v. *Obama*, 653 F.Supp.2d 62 (D.D.C. 2009).

158 *In re Guantánamo Bay Detainee Litigation*, DDC Misc. No. 08-0442 (6.1.09); Wilber, "US Challenged on Sealing of Detainee Files," WP (3.16.06); Pickler, "Judge: Gitmo Legal Documents Must Be Public," HuffPost (6.1.09); "Secrecy vs. Sunshine," WP (7.2.09).

159 *Al Ginco* v. *Obama*, 626 F.Supp.2d 123 (D.D.C. 2009); "Another Detainee Debacle," WP (6.28.09).

160 Wilber, "Detainee-Informer Presents Quandary for Government," WP (2.3.09).

161 Leigh, "Star Informer Freed after Implicating 123 Prisoners," G (4.25.11).

162 *Al-Adahi* v. *Obama*, 2009 WL 2584685 (D.D.C. 2009); Wilber, "Defense Dept. Faulted for Not Taping Detainee," WP (12.11.09).

163 *Hammamy* v. *Obama*, 604 F.Supp.2d 240 (D.D.C. 2009).

164 *Batarfi* v. *Bush*, 602 F.Supp.2d 118 (D.D.C. 2009).

165 Taylor, "Judge: US Hid Witness' Mental Illness in Guantánamo Cases," McClatchy Newspapers (4.7.09).

166 Eviatar, "US Relies on Tortured Evidence in Habeas Case," *Washington Independent* (6.23.09); ACLU Press Release (7.15.09); *Jawad* v. *Obama*, Transcript of Hearing before Judge Huvelle (7.16.09); Glaberson, "US Judge Challenges Evidence on a Detainee," NYT (7.23.09); AI, USA, "Moving the Goalposts, Prolonging the Detention" (7.27.09); Rosenberg, "Karzai Government Offers to Fetch Young Afghan from Guantánamo,"

MH (7.28.09); Glaberson, "Obama Faces Court Test over Detainee," NYT (7.29.09); Denniston, "Afghan Ordered Freed, Trial Unsure," Scotusblog (7.30.09); *Bacha* v. *Obama*, 2009 WL 2365846 (D.D.C. 2009); Glaberson, "Judge Orders a Detainee to Be Freed in August," NYT (7.31.09); Taylor, "Young Afghan Detainee to Head Home after Years at Guantánamo," *Pittsburgh Post-Gazette* (7.31.09); "Justice Too Long Delayed," NYT (8.5.09).

167 Lee, "Their Own Private Guantánamo," NYT (7.23.09); Lee, "An Examination of 31 Gitmo Detainee Lawsuits," ProPublica (7.22.09).

168 *Mutairi* v. *United States*, 644 F.Supp.2d 78 (D.D.C. 2009).

169 *Rabbani* v. *Obama*, 656 F.Supp.2d 45 (D.D.C. 2009); Cushman, "Detainee to Question 9/11 Suspect," NYT (8.23.09); Wilber, "Judge Allows Access to Guantánamo Detainees," WP (8.23.09).

170 *Awad* v. *Obama*, 646 F.Supp.2d 20 (D.D.C. 2009).

171 *Awad* v. *Obama*, 608 F.3d 1 (D.C. Cir. 2010).

172 *Bostan* v. *Obama*, 662 F.Supp.2d 1 (D.D.C. 2009).

173 *Al Odah* v. *United States*, 648 F.Supp. 2d 1 (D.D.C. 2009).

174 *Al Odah* v. *United States*, 611 F.3d 8 (D.C. Cir. 2010).

175 Rosenberg, "Judges Siding with Detainees in Guantánamo Habeas Cases," MH (9.7.09).

176 *Al Rabiah* v. *United States*, 658 F.Supp.2d 11 (D.D.C. 2009); Rosenberg, "Judge: Free Kuwait Engineer at Guantánamo," MH (9.17.09); "Kuwaiti Ordered Released from Guantánamo Bay," NYT (9.26.09).

177 *Barhoumi* v. *Obama*, No. 05-1506 (D.D.C. Sept. 3, 2009); *Barhoumi* v. *Obama*, 609 F.3d 416 (D.C. Cir. 2010).

178 *Mohammed* v. *Obama*, 689 F.Supp.2d 38 (D.D.C. 2009), 704 F.Supp.2d 1 (D.D.C. 2009); Rosenberg, "Judge Orders Algerian Freed from Guantánamo," MH (11.20.09); Denniston, "Testing the Government's Word," Scotusblog (6.10.10); Finn, "Six Detainees Would Rather Stay at Guantánamo Bay Than Be Returned to Algeria," WP (7.10.10); "Precautions Are Needed If Algerian Detainees Are Sent Home," WP (7.16.10); "Justices Decide US May Send Two Detainees Back to Algeria," NYT (7.18.10); Finn, "Guantánamo Detainee Naji Sent Back to Algeria against His Will," WP (7.20.10); Letter to the Editor, NYT (7.30.10).

179 *Hatim* v. *Obama*, 677 F.Supp.2d 1 (D.D.C. 2009); Wilber, "2008 Habeas Ruling May Pose Snag As US Weighs Indefinite Detentions," WP (2.13.10).

180 *Hatim* v. *Gates*, 632 F.3d 720 (D.C. Cir. 2011).

181 Goldsmith & Wittes, "No Place to Write Detention Policy," WP (12.22.09).

182 *Anam* v. *Obama*, 696 F.Supp.2 1 (D.D.C. 2010); Wilber, "US Can Continue to Detain Yemeni," WP (12.15.09).

183 *Al-Madhwani* v. *Obama*, 642 F.3d 1071 (D.C. Cir. 2011); cert denied, 132 S.Ct. 2739 (2012).

184 *Al-Adahi* v. *Obama*, 692 F.Supp.2d 85 (DDC 2010).

185 *Al-Adahi* v. *Obama*, 698 F.Supp.2d 48 (DDC 2010).

186 Lee, "Judges Urge Congress to Act on Indefinite Terrorism Detainees," ProPublica (1.22.10); "The Case for Clear Standards on Holding the Worst of the Detainees," WP (2.6.10); Wittes & Chesney, "The Courts' Shifting Rules on Guantánamo Detainees," WP (2.5.10); Letter to the Editor, WP (2.9.10); "Lawyers for Terrorist Liberties," NYT (2.22.10); Gibbons & Lewis, "Always a Judicial Function," NLJ (3.22.10).
187 *Al Warafi v. Obama*, 704 F.Supp.2d 32 (D.D.C. 2010).
188 *Al Warafi v. Obama*, 409 Fed.Appx. 360 (D.C. Cir. 2011).
189 *Al Warafi v. Obama*, 821 F.Supp.2d 47 (D.D.C. 2011).
190 *Al Warafi v. Obama*, 716 F.3d 627 (D.C. Cir. 2013). The court denied rehearing en banc on August 26, and the Supreme Court denied certiorari: *Al Warafi v. Obama*, 134 S.Ct. 2134 (2014).
191 *Salahi v. Obama*, 710 F.Supp.2d 1 (D.D.C. 2010); Rosenberg, "Detainee Abused at Guantánamo Ordered Freed," MH (3.22.10); Rosenberg, "Judge OK's Holding Yemeni Who Says He Was Clinic Worker in Afghanistan," MH (3.25.10); Finn, "Federal Judge Orders Release of Guantánamo Bay Detainee," WP (4.10.10); Slahi (2015).
192 *Salahi v. Obama*, 625 F.3d 745 (D.C. Cir. 2010).
193 *Abdah v. Obama*, 708 F.Supp.2d 9 (D.D.C. 2010).
194 *Abdah v. Obama*, 709 F.Supp.2d 25 (D.D.C. 2010).
195 *Esmail v. Obama*, 639 F.3d 1075 (D.C. Cir. 2011).
196 "A Well-Deserved Jab over the Supreme Court's Detainee Ruling," WP (4.11.11).
197 *Belbacha v. Bush*, 520 F.3d 452 (D.D.C. 2008).
198 *Al Harbi v. Obama*, 2010 WL 2398883 (D.D.C. 2010).
199 *Khalifh v. Obama*, 2010 WL 2382925 (D.D.C. 2010).
200 *Khalifh v. Obama*, 2011 WL 321713 (D.C. Cir. 2011).
201 *Abdah v. Obama*, 717 F.Supp.2d. 21 (D.D.C. 2010).
202 "Meet One Gitmo Inmate Who Can't Be Described As 'the Worst of the Worst,'" WP (6.16.10); Finn, "US Considers Partially Lifting Ban on Transfer of Detainees to Yemen," WP (6.19.10); "11 Killed as Militants Storm Yemen Jail," NYT (6.20.10); Finn, "US to Repatriate Guantánamo Detainee to Yemen after Judge Orders Him Released," WP (6.26.10); DoJ Press Release (7.13.10).
203 *Obaydullah v. Obama*, 609 F.3d 444 (D.C. Cir. 2010).
204 *Obaydullah v. Obama*, 744 F.Supp.2d 344 (D.D.C. 2010).
205 *Obaydullah v. Obama*, 2011 WL 1100492 (D.D.C. 2011).
206 *Obaydullah v. Obama*, 688 F.3d 784 (D.C. Cir. 2012), cert. denied, 133 S.Ct. 2855 (2013).
207 *Obaydullah v. Obama*, 920 F.Supp.2d 14 (D.D.C. 2013), aff'd, 554 Fed. Appx. 12 (D.C. Cir 2014).
208 *Almerfedi v. Obama*, 725 F.Supp.2d 18 (D.D.C. 2010); Savage, "Rulings Raise Doubt on Policy on Transfer of Yemenis," NYT A9 (7.9.10).
209 *Almerfedi v. Obama*, 654 F.3d 1 (D.C. Cir. 2011), cert. denied, 132 S.Ct. 2739 (2012).

Revisions," NYT (12.15.11); "Politics over Principle," NYT (12.16.11); Savage, "A Partisan Lightning Rod Is Undeterred," NYT (12.18.11).

261 Savage, "Accused al-Qaeda Leader Is Arraigned in U.S.S. Cole Bombing," NYT (11.10.11); Rosenberg, "Guantánamo Trial for Cole Bombing Suspect Delayed for a Year," MH (11.10.11); Temple-Raston, "At Guantánamo Hearing, Alleged Cole Mastermind Is 'All Swagger,'" NPR (11.10.11); Gerver, "Coverage of al-Nashiri's Arraignment," Lawfare (11.11.11); van Schaack, "Guantánamo Hearing Shows Stark Deficiencies of Military Justice," San Jose Mercury News (11.21.11); Gerstein, "DoD: Transcript of Public Guantánamo Hearing 'Top Secret,'" Politico (1.16.12); Pitter, "Guantánamo's System of Injustice,'" Salon (1.19.12).

262 Rosenberg, "State Dept: Guantánamo Lawyers Can't Question Yemeni Leader," MH (2.9.12); Rosenberg, "Secrecy Likely to Surround Guantánamo Testimony of Alleged USS Cole Bomber," MH (3.27.12); "Absurd Lengths," MH (4.10.12); Rosenberg, "First Amendment Lawyer in Guantánamo to Challenge Closures," MH (4.11.12); Savage, "Ruling Averts Testimony by Detainee for Now," NYT (4.12.12); Brody, "No Real Justice in Guantánamo," LAT (4.19.12); Schulz, "Guantánamo Trials Should Be Open," NYT (4.19.12).

263 U.S. v. Al-Nashiri, Rulings (5.7.12, 5.29.12, 6.19.12).

264 Fox, "Guantánamo Leader Signs Order Opposed by Lawyers," AP (12.30.11); Finn, "Guantánamo Bay Lawyers to Halt Written Communication," WP (1.12.12); Transcript of Military Commission (1.17–18.12); Raustiala, "Another Guantánamo Taint," LAT (1.18.12); Rosenberg, "Guantánamo Commander: Contractors Read Inmate Lawyers' Mail," MH (1.18.12);"Defense Lawyer Challenges Guantánamo Prison Mail Rule As Illegal 'Intelligence Monitoring,'" WP (2.9.12); Herridge, "Two 9/11 Suspects on Gitmo Hunger Strike, Sources Say," Fox News (3.13.12).

265 BGen. Mark Martins, Address to the New York City Bar (1.10.11); Temple-Raston, "Sept. 11 Case a Litmus Test for Military Commissions," NPR (1.5.12); Pitter, "Guantánamo's System of Injustice," Salon (1.19.12); Temple-Raston, "Top Prosecutor at Guantánamo Military Commissions to Retire," NPR (2.2.12); Rosenberg, "Defenders Seek 9/11 Trial Delay, Blame Guantánamo Legal Mail Dispute," MH (2.2.12); Temple-Raston, "A Prosecutor Makes the Case for Military Trials," NPR (4.3.12); "The Road We Need Not Have Traveled," NYT (4.8.12); Reilly, "Guantánamo Lawyers: Obama Gets Away with Legal Moves Bush Wouldn't Have," TPM Muckraker (4.17.12); Remarks of Brigadier General Mark Martins to ABA Judicial Division (8.4.12).

266 Al-Nashiri v. MacDonald, 2012 WL 1642306 (WD Wash. 2012).

267 Al-Nashiri v. MacDonald, 741 F.3d 1002 (9th Cir. 2013).

268 "U.S. to Screen Guantánamo Arraignment at 8 Sites," WSJ (4.27.12); Rosenberg, "9/11 Judge Has Handled Tough Cases Before," MH (4.29.12); Wittes, "Will Military Commissions Survive KSM?" WP (5.4.12); Finn, "Brig. Gen. Mark Martins, Lead Prosecutor in 9/11 Case,

210 *Al-Adahi v. Obama*, 613 F.3d 1102 (D.C. Cir. 2010), cert. denied, 562 US 1194 (2011); Savage, "Reversal Upholds Detention of Yemeni at Guantánamo," NYT (7.14.10); see Denbeaux et al. (2012).

211 "Gitmo Gambling," WP (7.24.10).

212 *Sulayman v. Obama*, 729 F.Supp.2d 26 (D.D.C. 2010).

213 *Abdah v. Obama*, 630 F.3d 1047 (D.C. Cir. 2011).

214 *Abdah v. Obama*, 2010 WL 3270761 (D.D.C. 2010).

215 *Latif v. Obama*, 666 F.3d 746 (D.C. Cir. 2011), reissued, 677 F.3d 1175 (D.C. Cir. 2011), cert. denied, 132 S.Ct. 2741 (2012); "Reneging on Justice at Guantánamo," NYT (11.20.11); Liptak, "The 'Fill in the Blanks' Court Game of Indefinite Detention," NYT (12.13.11).

216 *Khan v. Obama*, 741 F.Supp.2d 1 (D.D.C. 2010).

217 *Khan v. Obama*, 655 F.3d 20 (D.C. Cir. 2011).

218 *Khan v. Obama*, 2014 WL 4843907 (D.D.C. 2014).

219 *Khan v. Obama*, CA 08-1101 (D.D.C. 2016), following *Gul v. Obama*, 652 F3d 12 (DC Cir 2011); Savage, "Federal Judge Dismisses Lawsuit of Former Guantánamo Detainee," NYT (10.25.16).

220 *Ali v. Obama*, 741 F.Supp.2d 19 (D.D.C. 2011).

221 *Ali v. Obama*, 736 F.3d. 542 (D.C. Cir. 2013).

222 Greenhouse, "The Mirror of Guantánamo," NYT (12.12.13).

223 *Alsabri v. Obama*, 764 F.Supp.2d 60 (D.D.C. 2011).

224 *Alsabri v. Obama*, 684 F.3d 1298 (D.D.C. Cir. 2012).

225 "A Right without a Remedy," NYT (3.1.11).

226 "Another Attempt to Craft Rules for Detainee Cases," WP (3.24.11).

227 Barnes, "Supreme Court Declines to Clarify Rights of Guantánamo Bay Detainees," WP (4.11.11).

228 Greenhouse, "Gitmo Fatigue at the Supreme Court," NYT (4.7.11).

229 "A Well-Deserved Jab over the Supreme Court's Detainee Ruling," WP (4.11.11).

230 *Kiyemba v. Obama*, 131 S.Ct. 1631 (2011).

231 Rosenberg & Lasseter, "WikiLeaks: Secret Guantánamo Files Show US Disarray," McClatchy (4.24.11); Lasseter & Rosenberg, "Wikileaks: Jihadist(?) at Gitmo Gave Evidence against 255 Others," McClatchy (4.25.11).

232 "The Guantánamo Papers," NYT (4.26.11); Savage, "Lawyers for Guantánamo Detainees Allowed to See Leaked Files," NYT (6.11.11).

233 *Khairkhwa v. Obama*, 793 F.Supp.2d 1 (D.D.C. 2011).

234 *Khairkhwa v. Obama*, 703 F.3d 547 (D.C. Cir. 2012).

235 *Hussein v. Obama*, 821 F.Supp.2d 67 (D.D.C. 2011).

236 *Hussain v. Obama*, 718 F.3d 964 (D.C. Cir. 2013). It denied en banc rehearing on August 21, and the Supreme Court denied certiorari, 34 S.Ct. 1621 (2014).

237 *Bostan v. Obama*, 821 F.Supp.2d 80 (D.D.C. 2011).

238 McGreal, "Newt Gingrich: I Would Ignore Supreme Court As President," G (1.19.12).

239 Greenhouse, "Goodbye to Gitmo," NYT (5.16.12).

240 Schwartz, "Imprisonment without End at Guantánamo," Politico (9.21.12).

241 "Bad Judgment on Guantánamo," LAT (6.12.12).

242 "The Court Retreats on Habeas," NYT (6.13.12).

243 Savage, "Guantánamo Detainee, A Former Hunger Striker, Dies," NYT (9.11.12); Rosenberg, "Dead Guantánamo Detainee Won, Then Lost Court-Ordered Release," MH (9.11.12); Savage, "Military Identifies Guantánamo Detainee Who Died," NYT (9.12.12); Tate, "Guantánamo Detainee Found Dead Had Recently Gone on Hunger Strike," WP (9.12.12); Azmy, "The Face of Indefinite Detention," NYT (9.15.12); "Death at Guantánamo Bay," NYT (9.16.12); Falkoff, "A Death at Gitmo," LAT (9.20.12).

244 Greenhouse, "Gitmo's Other Prisoner," NYT (5.30.13).

245 Clark, "US Transfers Two More Guantánamo Detainees," MSNBC (12.19.13).

246 Bonner, "'Incommunicado' Forever: Gitmo Detainee's Case Stalled for 2,477 Days And Counting," ProPublica (5.12.15).

247 "While Guantánamo Logjam Endures, Some Prisoners Could Be Freed," NYT (7.30.15); Savage, "Guantánamo Hunger Striker's Petition Divides Officials," NYT (8.8.15); "How to Close Guantánamo," NYT (9.20.15); Kadidal, Letter to the Editor, NYT (11.5.15).

248 *Paracha v. Obama*, 194 F.Supp.3d 7 (D.D.C. 2016), aff'd, No. 16–5248 (D.C. Cir. 2017).

249 "Guantánamo Captive Who Wants to Open a Pizza Parlor in Algiers Loses Pre-Trump Bid for Release," MH (1.18.17); *Nasser v. Obama*, 2017 WL 237568 (D.D.C. 2017).

250 Tillman, "This Guantánamo Detainee Argued He Should Go Free Because the War Is Over – a Judge Disagreed," BuzzFeed (2.23.17); *Al-Alwi v. Trump*, 2017 WL 728177 (D.D.C. 2017).

251 Gonzales, Remarks to the ABA Standing Committee on Law and National Security (2.24.04) www.abanet.org/natsecurity/judge_gonzales .pdf.

252 Ellmann (1992).

253 Bickel (1962).

254 See Rakoff, "The Magna Carta Betrayed?" NYRB (2.11.16).

CHAPTER 6 CIVIL DAMAGES ACTIONS

1 For critiques of the reluctance of courts to allow such actions, see Davis (2008); Rudenstine (2016).

2 *El-Shifa Pharmaceutical Industries Co. v. U.S.*, 402 F.Supp.2d 267 (D.D.C. 2005).

3 *El-Shifa Pharmaceutical Industries Co. v. U.S.*, 559 F.3d 578 (D.C. Cir. 2009).

4 *El-Shifa Pharmaceutical Industries Co. v. U.S.*, 607 F.3d 836 (D.C. Cir. 2010).

5 *El-Shifa Pharmaceutical Industries Co. v. U.S.*, 55 Fed. Cl. 751 (Court of Fed. Claims 2003), aff'd, 378 F.3d 1346 (Ct. App. Fed. Cir. 2004).

6 *In re Iraq and Afghanistan Detainees Litigation*, 479 F.Supp.2d 85 (D.D.C. 2007); Gerstenzang, "Rumsfeld Sued Over Abuse of Prisoners," LAT (3.2.05); Herbert, "Is No One Accountable?" NYT (3.28.05); Human Rights First, "Suit Against Rumsfeld to Be Heard in Federal Court in the District of Columbia," Media Alert (6.22.05); Tapper & Griffin, "Former Iraqi Detainees Allege Torture by U.S. Troops," ABC News (11.14.05); "Prisoners Allege Use of Lions," NYT (11.16.05); Leonnig, "Ex-Detainees Seek to Sue U.S. Officials," WP (12.8.06); Von Zielbauer, "Former Detainees Argue for Right to Sue Rumsfeld over Torture," NYT (12.9.06); Smith, "U.S. Denies Liability in Torture Case," WP (12.9.06). For an analysis of 41 Bivens claims by "war-on-terror" victims, see Pfander (2017), who found a success rate of just 22 percent.

7 *Ali v. Rumsfeld*, 649 F.3d 762 (D.C. Cir. 2011).

8 *Rasul v. Myers*, 414 F.Supp.2d 26 (D.D.C. 2006).

9 *Rasul v. Myers*, 512 F.3d 644 (D.C. Cir. 2008).

10 *Boumediene v. Bush*, 128 S.Ct. 2229 (2008).

11 *Rasul v. Myers*, 555 U.S. 1083 (2008); Savage, "Supreme Court Revives Lawsuit by Former Detainees," LAT (12.16.08); Liptak, "Justices Restore Suit Brought by Ex-Detainee Citing Torture," NYT (12.16.08).

12 "The Right to a Day in Court," NYT (12.24.08).

13 *Rasul v. Myers*, 563 F.3d 527 (D.C. Cir. 2009).

14 "Yes, It Was Torture and Illegal," NYT (1.4.10).

15 *Al Janko v. Gates*, 831 F.Supp.2d 272 (D.D.C. 2011); Hsu, "Freed Guantánamo Detainee Sues U.S. Military over Alleged Torture," WP (10.6.10); Rosenberg, "Torture Victim Sues Obama Administration over 'Kafkaesque Nightmare,'" MH (10.9.10).

16 *Al Janko v. Gates*, 741 F.3d 136 (D.C. Cir. 2014), cert. denied 135 S. Ct 1530 (2016).

17 *Celikgogus v. Rumsfeld*, 920 F.Supp.2d. 53 (D.D.C. 2013).

18 *Allaithi v. Rumsfeld*, 753 F.3d 1327 (D.C. Cir. 2014).

19 "Families Demand Justice for Abuse and Deaths of Wrongfully Detained Sons at Guantánamo," CCR Press Release (1.29.09). For a compelling argument that they did not commit suicide, see Hickman (2015).

20 *Al-Zahrani v. Rumsfeld*, 684 F.Supp.2d 103 (D.D.C. 2010).

21 Horton, "The Guantánamo 'Suicides': A Camp Delta Sergeant Blows the Whistle," *Harper's Magazine* (1.18.10).

22 "US Judge Dismisses Hearing into Guantánamo 'Suicides,'" AFP (9.30.10).

23 *Al-Zahrani v. Rodriguez*, 669 F.3d 315 (D.C. Cir. 2012); "Guantánamo Suicide Suit Disallowed," NYT (2.22.12).

24 *Ibrahim v. Titan Corp.*, 391 F.Supp.2nd 10 (D.D.C. 2005); *Saleh v. Titan Corp.*, 436 F.Supp.2d 55 (D.D.C. 2006).

25 *Saleh v. Titan Corp.*, 580 F.3d 1 (D.C. Cir. 2009), cert. denied, 131 S.Ct. 3055 (2011).

26 *U.S. v. Boyle*, 469 U.S. 241 (1985).

27 *Al Shimari v. CACI Premier Technology, Inc*, 657 F.Supp.2d 700 (E.D. Va. 2009); "Former Iraqi Detainees Sue U.S. Military Contractors," NYT

(6.30.08); Dishneau, "Renton Man Sued in Iraq Torture Claim," AP (7.1.08).

28 *Skeels* v. *U.S.*, 72 F. Supp. 372 (W.D. La. 1947).
29 Discussed in *Law's Wars*, my companion volume.
30 *Shimari* v. *CACI International, Inc.*, 658 F.3d 413 (4th Cir. 2011).
31 *Shimari* v. *CACI International, Inc.*, 679 F.3d 205 (4th Cir. 2012) (en banc).
32 *Al Shimari* v. *CACI International, Inc.*, 951 F.Supp.2d 857 (E.D. Va. 2013); *Kiobel* v. *Royal Dutch Petroleum Co.*, 569 U.S. 108 (2013); Censer, "Judge Weighs Motions That Could Result in Dismissal of Abu Ghraib Claims against CACI," WP (5.20.13). On extraterritorial jurisdiction, see Raustiala (2009); Putnam (2016).
33 "Abu Ghraib, 10 Years Later," NYT (4.23.14).
34 *Al Shimari* v. *CACI Premier Technology, Inc.*, 758 F.3d 516 (4th Cir. 2014).
35 "Will Anyone Pay for Abu Ghraib?" NYT (2.5.15).
36 *Al Shimari* v. *CACI Premier Technology, Inc.*, 119 F.Supp.3d 434 (E.D. Va. 2015).
37 *Al Shimari* v. *CACI Premier Technology, Inc.*, 840 F.3d 147 (4th Cir. 2016).
38 *Al Qureshi* v. *Nakhla*, 728 F.Supp.2d 702 (D. Md. 2010).
39 *Saleh* v. *Titan Corp.*, 436 F.Supp.2d 55 (D.D.C. 2006), aff'd, 580 F.3d 1 (D.C. Cir. 2009), cert. denied, 131 S.Ct. 3055 (2011).
40 *Al Qureshi* v. *Nakhla*, 657 F.3d 201 (4th Cir. 2011).
41 Cushman, "Contractor Settles Case in Iraq Prison Abuse," NYT (1.9.13).
42 "L.A. Man Detained in Iraq Sued U.S.," WP (7.9.06); Weinstein, "Filmmaker Sues U.S. over Iraq Detention," LAT (7.8.06); *Kar* v. *Rumsfeld*, 580 F.Supp.2d 80 (D.D.C. 2008).
43 *Vance* v. *Rumsfeld*, Amended Complaint, N.D. Ill. 06 C 6964 (2.12.07); Robinson, "Donald Rumsfeld Torture Lawsuit Clears Hurdle, Allowed to Proceed," HuffPost (3.5.10); "U.S. Citizens Who Say They Were Tortured Get Their Day in Court," WP (8.31.10); Phinney, "American Tortured in Iraq Sues Rumsfeld," Truthout (4.7.07); *Vance* v. *Rumsfeld*, 694 F.Supp.2d 957 (N.D. Ill. 2010).
44 *Vance* v. *Rumsfeld*, 653 F.3d 591 (7th Cir. 2011); "Court Won't Dismiss Rumsfeld from Suit," UPI (8.8.11); "Holding Rumsfeld Accountable," NYT (8.14.11); "Remedies for Misconduct in War Zones," NYT (2.7.12); *Vance.* v. *Rumsfeld*, 701 F.3d 193 (7th Cir. 2012) (en banc), cert. denied, 133 S.Ct. 2796 (2013); "Supreme Court Ends Torture Suit against Donald Rumsfeld," Politico (6.10.13).
45 Goldsmith (2007); Liptak, "Padilla Sues U.S. Lawyer over Detention," NYT (1.5.08); "Yale and the Terrorist," WSJ (1.10.08); Yoo, "Terrorist Tort Travesty," WSJ (1.19.08).
46 Gerstein, "Judge: Will Obama Defend Yoo?" AP (3.7.09); Schwartz, "Judge Weighs Dismissing Case Involving Torture Memorandums," NYT (3.7.09); *Padilla* v. *Yoo*, 633 F.Supp.2d 1005 (N.D. Calif. 2009); Schwartz, "Judge Allows Civil Lawsuit over Claims of Torture," NYT (6.14.09); "Padilla v. Yoo," WP (6.20.09).

47 *Padilla* v. *Yoo*, 678 F.3d 748 (9th Cir. 2012); "California: Court Throws Out Suit against Bush Lawyer," NYT (5.3.12).

48 "John Yoo's Vindication," WSJ (5.4.12).

49 Richey, "In Padilla Interrogation, No Checks or Balances," CSM (9.4.07); Richey, "Padilla Sues US Officials over Confinement," CSM (9.24.07).

50 *Lebron* v. *Rumsfeld*, 764 F.Supp.2d 787 (D.S.C. 2011); Richey, "Rumsfeld Seeks to Throw Out Padilla Case," CSM (2.13.11).

51 "Padilla Lawyers Appeal to Reinstate Torture Suit," AP (10.27.11); *Lebron* v. *Rumsfeld*, 670 F.3d 540 (4th Circuit 2012), cert. denied, 132 S.Ct. 2751 (2012).

52 *Arar* v. *Ashcroft*, 414 F.Supp.2d 250 (E.D.N.Y. 2006).

53 *Eisentrager* v. *Johnson*, 339 U.S. 763 (1950).

54 *Rasul* v. *Bush*, 542 U.S. 466 (2004).

55 Arar Commission, Report of the Events Relating to Maher Arar (2006); Office of the Prime Minister, Press Release: Prime Minister Releases Letter of Apology to Maher Arar and His Family and Announces Completion of Mediation Process (1.26.08) http://pm.gc.ca/eng/media.asp?id=1509 (last accessed February 1, 2008).

56 *Arar* v. *Ashcroft*, 532 F.3d 157 (2nd Cir. 2008); Feuer, "Court Dismisses Rendition Suit," NYT (7.1.08).

57 Weiser, "Appeals Court Hears Case of Canadian Citizen Sent by U.S. to Syria, and Confined," NYT (12.10.08); *Arar* v. *Ashcroft*, 585 F.3d 559 (2nd Cir. 2009) (en banc); Weiser, "Appeals Court Rejects Suit by Canadian Man over Detention and Torture Claim," NYT (11.3.09).

58 Goldwater said during his presidential campaign on July 16, 1964: "I would remind you that extremism in the defense of liberty is no vice! And let me remind you also that moderation in the pursuit of justice is no virtue!"

59 *United States* v. *Reynolds*, 345 U.S. 1 (1953).

60 *New York Times Co.* v. *United States*, 403 U.S. 713 (1971).

61 Department of Homeland Security, Office of Inspector General, The Removal of a Canadian Citizen to Syria (OIG-09-18) (March 2008).

62 *Arar* v. *Ashcroft*, 560 U.S. 978 (2010).

63 CCR Press Release (6.14.10).

64 "No Price to Pay for Torture," NYT (6.16.10).

65 ACLU News Release (5.30.07); Rose, "'Torture Flight' Airline Sued by MI5 Informer," *Observer* (8.5.07).

66 *Totten* v. *U.S.*, 92 U.S. 105 (1875).

67 *Mohamed* v. *Jeppesen Dataplan, Inc.*, 539 F.Supp.2d 1128 (N.D. Calif. 2008).

68 Schwartz, "Claims of Torture Abroad Face Test Monday in Court," NYT (2.6.09); "Torture on Trial?" LAT (2.7.09).

69 *Mohamed* v. *Jeppesen Dataplan, Inc.*, 579 F.3d 943 (9th Cir. 2009).

70 *Mohamed* v. *Jeppesen Dataplan, Inc.*, 586 F.3d 1108 (9th Cir. 2009); Williams, "Suit by 5 Ex-Captives of CIA Can Proceed, Appeals Panel Rules," LAT (4.28.09); Johnson, "Appeals Court Rejects 'State Secrets' Claim, Revives Detainee Suit," WP (4.29.09); Savage, "Court Lets Ex-Detainees Proceed with Civil Torture Case," NYT (4.29.09); "Impunity or Accountability," NYT (12.15.09).

71 "We're Making a List," LAT (12.25.09).
72 *Mohamed v. Jeppesen Dataplan, Inc.*, 614 F.3d 1070 (9th Cir. 2010), cert. denied, 131 S.Ct. 2442 (2011); Savage, "Court Dismisses a Case Asserting Torture by C.I.A.," NYT (9.9.10); Finn, "U.S. Appeals Court Dismisses Suit Against Firm in 'Extraordinary Rendition' Case," WP (9.8.10).
73 "Torture Is a Crime, Not a Secret," NYT (9.9.10).
74 Rutten, "A Post-9/11 Betrayal Endures," LAT (9.11.10).
75 "Hiding Torture, Legally," LAT (9.10.10).
76 "Security Secrets and Justice," WP (9.13.10).
77 "Swedish Official: Residency Granted to Ex-Terror Suspect Deported from Sweden to Egypt by CIA," WP (7.4.12).
78 "Poland to Pay $262,000 to Inmates Held at Secret CIA Prison," WP (2.18.15).
79 *El-Masri v. Tenet*, 437 F.Supp.2d 530 (E.D. Va.2006), aff'd sub nom. *El-Masri v. United States*, 479 F.3d 296 (4th Cir. 2007), cert. denied, 128 S.Ct. 373 (2007); "Virginia: Torture Suit Tossed for Security's Sake," LAT (3.3.07); Liptak, "U.S. Appeals Court Upholds Dismissal of Abuse Suit against C.I.A., Saying Secrets Are at Risk," NYT (3.3.07); el-Masri, "I Am Not a State Secret," LAT (3.3.07); "Too Many Secrets," NYT (3.10.07); see Satterthwaite (2009).
80 Savage, "Relatives Sue Officials over U.S. Citizens Killed by Drone Strikes," NYT (7.19.12).
81 *Al-Aulaqi v. Panetta*, 35 F.Supp.3d 56 (D.D.C. 2014); Savage, "Relatives of Victims of Drone Strikes Drop Appeal," NYT (6.3.14).
82 *Jaber v. U.S.*, 155 F.Supp.3d 70 (D.D.C. 2016), aff'd, 2017 WL 2818645 (D.C. Cir. 2017).
83 DoJ IG, A Review of the FBI's Actions in Connection with Allegations Raised by Contract Linguist Sibel Edmonds (January 2005); Files, "Appeals Court Backs Dismissal of Suit on F.B.I.," NYT (5.7.05); Greenhouse, "Justices Reject F.B.I. Translator's Appeal on Termination," NYT (11.29.05).
84 *Edmonds v. United States Department of Justice*, 323 F.Supp.2d 65 (D.D.C. 2004).
85 *Edmonds v. Department of Justice*, 161 Fed.Appx. 6 (D.C. Cir. 2005).
86 Wilson (2005); Wilson (2007).
87 Wilson, "What I Didn't Find in Africa," NYT (7.6.03).
88 Weiss & Lane, "Vice President Sued by Plame and Husband," WP (7.14.06); Schmitt, "Cheney, Rove and Libby Are Sued in Agent's Unmasking," LAT (7.14.06); Lewis, "Ex-C.I.A. Officer Sues Cheney and Others over Leak," NYT (7.14.06); Schmitt, "Plame Condemns 'Shameful Conduct,'" LAT (7.15.06); Deane, "Couple Reiterate Claims They Were Punished," WP (7.15.06); Leonnig, "Plame's Suit against Top Officials Dismissed," WP (7.20.07); "Former Press Secretary Blames Bush, Cheney for Misstatement about Leak," LAT (11.21.07); McClellan (2008).
89 *Wilson v. Libby*, 498 F.Supp.2d 74 (D.D.C. 2007).
90 *Wilson v. Libby*, 535 F.3d 697 (D.C. Cir. 2008).

91 Johnson, "Man Sues Secret Service Agent over Arrest after Approaching Cheney and Denouncing War," NYT (10.4.06); Liptak, "Supreme Court to Consider the Arrest of a Cheney Critic," NYT (12.6.11); Barnes, "Supreme Court to Decide Whether Man Arrested for Confronting Cheney Can Sue," WP (12.6.11); "Steven Howards and the Limits of Free Speech," LAT (12.8.11).

92 *Howards v. McLaughlin*, 634 F.3d 1131 (10th Cir. 2011).

93 *Reichle v. Howards*, 132 S.Ct. 2088 (2012).

94 "Colorado: Suit Filed over Ejection from Speech," NYT (3.17.07); *Weise v. Casper*, 2008 WL 4838682 (D. Colo. 2008).

95 *Weise v. Casper*, 593 F.3d 1163 (10th Cir. 2010).

96 *Weise v. Casper*, 131 S.Ct. 7 (2010).

97 Barnes, "Supreme Court to Review Whether Agents Violated Rights of Bush Protesters," WP (11.27.13).

98 *Moss v. Wood*, 2007 WL 2915608 (D. Ore. 2007).

99 *Moss v. Wood*, 572 F.3d 962 (9th Cir. 2009).

100 *Moss v. United States Secret Serv.*, 750 F.Supp.2d 1197 (D. Ore. 2010).

101 *Moss v. Wood*, 675 F.3d 1213 (9th Cir. 2012).

102 *Moss v. United States Secret Service*, 711 F.3d 941 (9th Cir. 2013).

103 *Wood v. Moss*, 134 S.Ct. 2056 (2014).

104 DoJ IG, The September 11 Detainees: A Review of the Treatment of Aliens Held on Immigration Charges in Connection with the Investigation of the September 11 Attacks (June 2003); DoJ IG, Supplemental Report on September 11 Detainees' Allegations of Abuse at the Metropolitan Detention Center in Brooklyn, New York (December 2003); DoJ IG, Analysis of the Second Response by the Department of Justice to Recommendations in the Office of the Inspector General's June 2003 Report on the Treatment of September 11 Detainees (January 2004); DoJ IG, Analysis of the Response by the Federal Bureau of Prisons to Recommendations in the OIG's December 2003 Report on the Abuse of 9.11 Detainees at MDC in Brooklyn (March 2004); Schmitt & Serrano, "Inaction in New York Prison Abuse Stirs Anger," LAT (5.21.05); Bernstein, "Top Officials Told to Testify in Muslims' Suit," NYT (9.29.05); Bernstein, "U.S. Is Settling Detainee's Suit in 9/11 Sweep," NYT (2.28.06); Bernstein, "Magistrate Rules that Government Must Reveal Monitoring," NYT (5.31.06); Bernstein, "Judge Rules that U.S. Has Broad Powers to Detain Noncitizens Indefinitely," NYT (6.15.06); Cole, "Manzanar Redux," LAT (6.16.06); Perrotta, "U.S. Told to Show if Lawyers' Talks with Suspects Tracked," NYLJ (10.4.06); Bernstein, "Judges Zero In on Treatment of a Detainee," NYT (10.5.06); Serrano, "9/11 Prisoner Abuse Suit Could Be Landmark," LAT (11.20.06); DoJ OIG (2003); Bali (2003; 2006); CHRGJ & Asian American Legal Defense and Education Fund (2011).

105 Accounts of discovery are based on motions and hearings.

106 *Turkmen v. Ashcroft*, 2006 WL 1662663 (E.D.N.Y. 2006).

107 *Iqbal* v. *Hasty*, 490 F.3d 143 (2d Cir. 2007); Bernstein, "Relatives of Interned Japanese-Americans Side with Muslims," NYT (4.3.07); Neumeister, "Ashcroft Can Remain in Detainee's Suit," WP (6.14.07).

108 Greenhouse, "Court to Hear Challenge from Muslims Held after 9.11," NYT (6.17.08); Barnes, "Court to Rule in Suit against Ashcroft, Others," WP (6.17.08); "Court Will Decide Reach of Lawsuit," LAT (6.17.08); "Finding Fault," WP (12.8.08); "Accountability and the Court," NYT (12.10.08).

109 *Ashcroft* v. *Iqbal* 556 U.S. 662 (2009); Savage, "Former Detainee's Lawsuit Is Tossed," LAT (5.19.09); Liptak, "Justices Void Ex-Detainee's Suit against 2 Officials," NYT (5.19.09); Barnes, "Court Says Detainee's Lawsuit Can't Proceed," WP (5.19.09); "Abuse and Accountability," WP (5.19.09); "Throwing Out Mr. Iqbal's Case," NYT (5.20.09).

110 Bernstein, "U.S. to Pay $1.2 Million to 5 Detainees over Abuse Lawsuit," NYT (11.3.09).

111 *Turkmen* v. *Ashcroft*, 589 F.3d 542 (2nd Cir. 2009).

112 Ashcroft (2006).

113 *Turkmen* v. *Ashcroft*, 915 F.Supp.2d 314 (E.D.N.Y 2013).

114 *Turkmen* v. *Hasty*, 789 F.3d 218 (2nd Cir. 2015).

115 *Ziglar* v. *Abbasi*, 2017 WL 2621317 (2017).

116 *Doe* v. *Rumsfeld*, 800 F.Supp.2d 94 (D.D.C. 2011).

117 *Doe* v. *Rumsfeld*, 683 F.3d 390 (D.C. Cir. 2012).

118 *Meshal* v. *Higgenbotham*, 47 F.Supp.3d 115 (D.D.C. 2014).

119 *Meshal* v. *Higgenbotham*, 804 F.3d 417 (D.C. Cir. 2016).

120 Eggen, "Ashcroft Is Denied Immunity in Case," WP (9.29.06).

121 Barrett (2006).

122 HRW & ACLU, Witness to Abuse: Human Rights Abuses Under the Material Witness Law Since September 11 (June 2005).

123 *Al-Kidd* v. *Gonzales*, 2006 WL 5429570 (D. Id. 2006).

124 *Al-Kidd* v. *Ashcroft*, 580 F.3d 949 (9th Cir. 2009); Schwartz, "Federal Court Rules against Ashcroft," NYT (9.5.09); Johnson, "Court Allows Lawsuit against Ashcroft," WP (9.5.09); "Suing Mr. Ashcroft," WP (9.12.09).

125 *Al-Kidd* v. *Ashcroft*, 598 F.3d 1129 (9th Cir. 2010); "Idaho: Suit against Ashcroft Proceeds," NYT (3.19.10).

126 *Olmstead* v. *U.S.* 277 U.S. 438 (1928).

127 *Ashcroft* v. *Al-Kidd*, 131 S.Ct. 415 (2010); Liptak, "Justices to Hear Appeal by Ashcroft over Detention Suit," NYT (10.19.10): Barnes, "Supreme Court to Decide whether Ashcroft Can Be Sued by Detained Citizen," WP (10.19.10); "An Indefensible Defense," NYT (10.24.10).

128 "The Ashcroft Appeal," LAT (10.25.10).

129 Liptak, "Supreme Court to Hear Material Witness Case," NYT (2.21.11).

130 "High Court Should Overturn Kidd v. Ashcroft," WP (3.1.11).

131 "Don't Shield Ashcroft," LAT (3.5.11).

132 "Indefensible Detention," NYT (3.11.11).

133 *Ashcroft* v. *Al-Kidd*, 131 S.Ct. 2074 (2011); Savage, "Supreme Court Rejects Suit against John Ashcroft," LAT (6.1.11); Liptak, "Justices Block Suit over Use of Material Witness Law against Detainee," NYT (6.1.11); "Qualified Immunity, Unqualified Doubt," NYT (6.1.11); "The Right Call on John Ashcroft," WP (5.31.11); "Supreme Court, The Ashcroft Immunity," LAT (6.10.11).

134 *Al-Kidd* v. *Gonzales*, 2012 WL 4470852 (D. Id. 2012); Bronner, "Citizen Held after 9/11 Wins Right to Be Tried," NYT (9.29.12).

135 ACLU, "Abdullah al-Kidd v. United States, et al.," ACLU Blog of Rights (1.15.15).

136 *Salim* v. *Mitchell*, 183 F.Supp.3d 1121 (E.D. Wash. 2016), CV-15-0286-JLQ (1.27.17); Fink & Risen, "Lawsuit Aims to Hold 2 Contractors Accountable for C.I.A. Torture," NYT (11.28.16); Fink, "Judge Allows Lawsuit against Psychologists in C.I.A. Torture Case," NYT (1.28.17); Siems, "These CIA Torture Victims May Finally Have a Chance at Justice," *The Nation* (6.26.17); Fink, "2 Psychologists in C.I.A. Interrogations Can Face Trial, Judge Rules," NYT (7.28.17).

137 Ackerman, "CIA's Mad Torture Scientists: We're Like Those Who Made Gas for the Nazis," Daily Beast (7.25.17).

138 Fink, "2 Psychologists in C.I.A. Interrogations Can Face Trial, Judge Rules," NYT (7.28.17); Siems, "Creators of the CIA's Enhanced Interrogation Program to Face Trial," G (8.8.17); ACLU, "CIA Torture Psychologists Settle Lawsuit" (8.17.17); Fink, "Settlement Reached in C.I.A. Torture Case," NYT (8.18.17).

139 *Mayfield* v. *U.S.*, D. Ore Civil No. 05-1427-AA (9.26.07). For a thorough account, see Wax (2008).

140 DoJ OIG (2006).

141 Feuer, "Lawsuit Is Reinstated for Man Wrongly Suspected in 9/11," NYT (10.20.07); Eggen, "Second Court Ruling Redacts Information about Interrogation," WP (10.25.07); Weiser, "9/11 Wrongful-Accusation Suit Settled," NYT (9.25.09).

142 *Higazy* v. *Millennium Hotel & Resorts*, 346 F.Supp.2d 430 (S.D.N.Y. 2004).

143 *Higazy* v. *Templeton*, 505 F.3d 161 (2^d Cir. 2007).

144 Shane, "U.S. Settles Suit over Anthrax Attacks," NYT (11.30.11); Markon, "Federal Government Settles Suit in Fatal Anthrax Attacks," WP (11.30.11).

145 Dwyer, "City Fights Efforts to Release 2004 Convention Arrest Records," NYT (12.13.06); Moynihan, "New York Is Said to Settle Suits over Arrests at 2004 G.O.P. Convention," NYT (12.23.13); Dwyer, "Mass Arrests during '04 Convention Leave Big Bill and Lingering Mystery," NYT (1.8.14); Weiser, "New York City to Pay $18 Million over Convention Arrests," NYT (1.16.14); "The Convention and the Damage Done," NYT (1.17.14).

146 Dugan, "Owner of Car Dealership Labeled 'Taliban Toyota' Wins Millions," Reuters (11.1.11).

147 "San Francisco Jury Awards $465,000 to Muslim Security Guard Who Says He Was Called a Terrorist," WP (1.25.12).

148 For a successful $10 billion claim by Kenyan victims of the US Embassy bombings against the Sudanese government, see *Sheikh* v. *Republic of Sudan*, 172 F.Supp.3d 124 (DDC 2016).

149 *In re: Terrorist Attacks on September 11, 2001*, 349 F.Supp.2d 765 (S.D.N.Y. 2005); 392 F.Supp.2d 539 (SDNY 2005), aff'd, 538 F.3d 71 (2ᵈ Cir. 2008), cert. denied sub nom. *Federal Insurance Co.* v. *Kingdom of Saudi Arabia*, 557 U.S. 935 (2009). Plaintiffs encountered similar obstacles when Judge Daniels took over the case after Judge Casey's death. *In re: Terrorist Attacks on September 11, 2001*, 464 F.Supp.2d 335 (S.D.N.Y. 2006), rev'd, 714 F.3d 118 (2ᵈ Cir. 2013), cert. denied sub nom. *O'Neill* v. *Al Rajhi Bank*, 134 S.Ct. 2870 (2014).

150 *In re: Terrorist Attacks on September 11, 2001*, 464 F.Supp.2d 335 (S.D.N.Y. 2006), rev'd, 714 F.3d 118 (2ᵈ Cir. 2013), cert. denied sub nom. *O'Neill* v. *Al Rajhi Bank*, 134 S.Ct. 2870 (2014); Goldhaber, "The Global Lawyer: Forget 'Arab Bank.' 'In re 9/11' Is Back," *American Lawyer* (10.15.14).

151 Lewis, "Judge Links Iran to '96 Attack in Saudi Arabia," NYT (12.23.06); Leonnig, "Iran Held Liable in Khobar Attack," WP (12.23.06).

152 *Doe* v. *bin Laden*, 580 F.Supp.2ᵈ 93 (D.D.C. 2008).

153 *Doe* v. *bin Laden*, 663 F.3d 64 (2nd Cir. 2011).

154 "$156 Million Jury Award Overturned in Terrorist Case," LAT (12.29.07); Fears, "Ruling against Muslim Group Is Overturned," WP (12.29.07).

155 18 U.S.C. § 2333; *Boim* v. *Quranic Literacy Institute*, 127 F.Supp.2d 1002 (N.D. Ill. 2001).

156 *Boim* v. *Quranic Literacy Institute*, 291 F.3d 1000 (7th Cir. 2002).

157 *Boim* v. *Quranic Literacy Institute*, 340 F.Supp.2d 884 (N.D. Ill. 2004).

158 *Boim* v. *Holy Land Foundation for Relief and Development*, 511 F.3d 707 (7th Cir. 2007).

159 *Boim* v. *Holy Land Foundation for Relief and Development*, 549 F.3d 685 (7th Cir. 2008) (en banc), cert. denied, *Boim* v. *Salah*, 558 U.S. 981 (2009).

160 Weiser, "Palestinians Get 2nd Try in Terror Suit, but at a Price," NYT (9.8.08); *Knox* v. *Palestine Liberation Organization*, 306 F.Supp.2d 424 (S.D.N.Y. 2004); *Knox* v. *Palestine Liberation Organization*, 230 F.R.D. 383 (S.D.N.Y. 2005); *Knox* v. *Palestine Liberation Organization*, 442 F.Supp.2d 62 (S.D.N.Y. 2006); *Knox* v. *Palestine Liberation Organization*, 248 F.R.D. 420 (S.D.N.Y. 2008); *Knox* v. *Palestine Liberation Organization*, 2009 WL 1591404 (S.D.N.Y. 2009), 628 F.Supp.2d 507 (S.D.N.Y. 2009).

161 Weiser, "Palestinian Groups Are Found Liable at Manhattan Terror Trial," NYT (2.24.15); Booth & Deane, "U.S. Jury Blames Palestinian Groups for Attacks," WP (2.24.15); Booth & Eglash, "Palestinians Vow to Appeal U.S. Ruling Blaming PLO for Terrorists Attacks," WP (2.25.15); the unreported case was *Sokolow* v. *Palestine Liberation Organization*.

162 *Sokolow* v. *Palestine Liberation Organization*, Second Circuit Nos. 15-3135-cv(L) and 15-3135-cv (XAP) (4.12.16).

163 *Estate of Klieman* v. *Palestinian Authority*, 82 F.Supp.3d 237 (D.D.C. 2015); *Livnat* v. *Palestinian Authority*, 82 F.Supp.3d 19 (D.D.C. 2015); *Safra* v. *Palestinian Authority*, 82 F.Supp.3d 37 (D.D.C. 2015).

164 *Estates of Ungar* v. *Palestinian Authority*, 153 F.Supp.2d 76 (D.R.I. 2001); 228 F.Supp.2d 40 (D.R.I. 2002); aff'd, *Unger* v. *Palestinian Authority*, 2003 WL 21254790 (1st Cir. 2003); *Estates of Ungar* v. *Palestinian Authority*, 304 F.Supp.2d 232 (D.R.I. 2004); *Estates of Ungar* v. *Palestinian Authority*, 315 F.Supp.2d 164 (D.R.I. 2004); 325 F.Supp.2d 15 (D.R.I. 2004).

165 *Ungar* v. *Palestine Liberation Organization*, 402 F.3d 274 (1st Cir. 2005), cert. denied sub nom. *Palestine Liberation Organization* v. *Ungar ex rel. Strachman*, 546 U.S. 1034 (2005).

166 *Ungar* v. *Palestine Liberation Organization*, 599 F.3d 79 (1st Cir. 2010), reversing *Estates of Unger* v. *Palestinian Authority*, 613 F.Supp.2d 219 (D.R.I. 2009).

167 *Estates of Ungar* v. *Palestinian Authority*, 715 F.Supp.2d 253 (D.R.I. 2010).

168 *Morris* v. *Khadr*, 415 F.Supp.2d 1323 (D.Ut. 2006).

169 Price, "Blinded Soldier, Widow Sue Former Gitmo Prisoner," MH (5.26.14); Clifford, "The Cost for Arab Bank Is a Complex Calculation," NYT (9.24.14); Walsh, "Widow May Have Legal Case Against Terrorist," Western Journalism (7.5.17).

170 Fung, "Tech Companies 'Profit from ISIS,' Allege Families of Orlando Shooting Victims in Federal Lawsuit," WP (12.20.16); Jureck, "EDNY Dismisses Suits against Facebook on Hamas Attacks," Lawfare (5.18.17).

171 *Linde* v. *Arab Bank, PLC*, 384 F.Supp.2d 257 (E.D.N.Y. 2005); *Linde* v. *Arab Bank*, 463 F.Supp.2d 310 (E.D.N.Y. 2006); *Almog* v. *Arab Bank, PLC*, 471 F.Supp.2d 257 (E.D.N.Y. 2007); *Linde* v. *Arab Bank*, 269 F.R.D. 186 (E.D.N.Y. 2010); *Linde* v. *Arab Bank, PLC*, 706 F.3d 92 (2nd Cir. 2013); *Arab Bank, PLC* v. *Linde*, 134 S.Ct. 2869 (2014). Clifford & Silver-Greenberg, "Terrorism Trial of Mideast Bank Worries the Financial World," NYT (8.13.14); Clifford, "Hamas Transactions Got through in Error, Bank Says," NYT (8.14.14); Clifford, "Victim of Suicide Bombing Testifies at Bank's Terror Trial," NYT (8.20.14); Larson & Smythe, "Arab Bank Chairman Tells Jury Terrorism Hurts Business," Bloomberg (9.8.14); Clifford, "Witness for Arab Bank Says Disputed Payments Were Humanitarian," NYT (9.12.14); Clifford, "In Closing Arguments, Arab Bank's Role in Flagging Terrorists Is Debated," NYT (9.19.14); Clifford, "Arab Bank Liable for Supporting Terrorist Efforts, Jury Finds," NYT (9.23.14).

172 Tillman, "Judge Awards Embassy Bombing Victims $955 Million," *Legal Times* (3.31.14); Tillman, "Embassy Bombing Victims Awarded $8 Billion," NLJ (7.25.14); "D.C. Judge Awards $622 Million to Victims of 1998 Embassy Bombings," *Legal Times* (10.15.14); *Opati* v. *Republic of Sudan*, 60 F.Supp.3d 68 (D.D.C. 2014).

173 *Peterson* v. *Islamic Republic of Iran*, 2013 WL 1155576 (S.D.N.Y. 2014).

174 *Peterson* v. *Islamic Republic of Iran*, 758 F.3d 185 (2nd Cir. 2014); Triedman, "Terrorism Victims to Share $2 Billion," NLJ (7.14.14).

175 Beekman, "Iran Loses Manhattan Skyscraper to Terror Victims," *New York Daily News* (3.31.14).

176 *Bank Markazi v. Peterson*, 136 S.Ct. 1310 (2016).

177 Wang, "Manhattan Skyscraper Linked to Iran Can Be Seized by U.S., Jury Finds," NYT (6.29.17).

178 Williams, "Supreme Court Takes up Dispute over Iran Antiquities in Terror Case," NBC News (6.27.17).

179 Navarro, "Effort to Settle Sept. 11 Lawsuits," NYT (2.5.10).

180 Weiser, "Judge's Approval Is Sought in 2 Lawsuits from 9/11," NYT (3.5.10); Navarro, "Deal Is Reached on Health Costs of 9/11 Workers," NYT (3.12.10); Navarro, "Judge Rejects Deal on Health Claims of Workers at Ground Zero," NYT (3.20.10); Navarro, "Empathetic Judge in 9/11 Suits Seen by Some as Interfering," NYT (5.3.10); Sulzberger & Navarro, "Accord on Bigger Settlement for Ill Ground Zero Workers," NYT (6.11.10); Navarro, "Already under Fire, Lawyers for 9/11 Workers Are Ordered to Justify Some Fees," NYT (8.27.10); Navarro, "9/11 Workers Would Get $47 Million More in a New Pact," NYT (10.15.10); "The Long Recovery from 9/11," NYT (10.25.10); Navarro, "$27.5 Million for 9/11 Workers," NYT (11.7.10); Navarro, "Over 95 Percent of 9/11 Workers Approve Settlement," NYT (11.20.10).

181 Weiser, "Among 9/11 Families, the Final Holdout on a Settlement Wants Its Day in Court," NYT (9.11.10); Weiser, "A 9/11 Judge Sets a Timer for a Month," NYT (4.28.11); Weiser, "Family and United Airlines Settle Last 9/11 Wrongful-Death Suit," NYT (9.20.11).

182 Weiser, "Cantor Fitzgerald to Settle 9/11 Lawsuit against American Airlines," NYT (12.14.13); Weiser, "Cantor Fitzgerald Settles 9/11 Suit against American Airlines for $135 million," NYT (12.18.13).

183 "The Ongoing Toll from 9/11," NYT (3.23.10); "The Continuing Pain of 9/11," NYT (6.2.10); Hernandez, "Plan to Aid 9/11 Victims Is Rejected in House," NYT (7.30.10); "Feckless and Cruel," NYT (7.31.10); "The Continuing Human Damage," NYT (9.11.10); Hernandez, "House Passes Bill to Help with 9/11 Health Care," NYT (9.29.10); "The Long Recovery from 9/11," NYT (10.25.10); Chen, "Mayor Will Push Senators to Pass 9/11 Health Bill," NYT (11.13.10); Hernandez, "Republicans Block U.S. Health Aid for 9/11 Workers," NYT (12.10.10); "The Senate Stands for Injustice," NYT (12.10.10); Hernandez, "Congress Passes 9/11 Health Bill after Cost Is Cut," NYT (12.23.10); Hartocollis, "Scant Evidence to Link 9/11 to Cancer, U.S. Report Says," NYT (7.27.11); Moynihan, "Police Union Seeks Data for Cancer Links to 9/11," NYT (2.13.12); Hartocollis, "Logistics Hang over a Ruling on 9/11 Cancer," NYT (5.29.12); Hartocollis, "Sept. 11 Health Fund Given Clearance to Cover Cancer," NYT (6.8.12); "Ground Zero Cancers," NYT (6.14.12); Hartocollis, "No Clear Link between Cancer and 9/11 Debris, Study Finds," NYT (12.19.12); "Ground Zero Fund Opens to Applicants," NYT (10.3.11); Hartocollis, "Volunteers at Ground Zero Now Face a Demand for Proof," NYT (1.1.13); Hartocollis, "9/11 Health Fund Pays Out its First 15 Awards," NYT (1.29.13).

184 Goodnough, "For Wounded, Daunting Cost; For Aid Fund, Tough Decisions," NYT (4.23.13).
185 Bernstein, "Boston Marathon Bombing Victims Will Split $60.9 Million" WP (6.29.13).
186 Bernstein, "Boston Marathon Bombing Victims to Get $20 Million More," WP (6.28.14).
187 Witt (2008). Records are fragmentary and unreliable, but other sources agree that these numbers are roughly accurate. Currier, "Our Condolences: How the U.S. Paid for Death and Damage in Afghanistan," The Intercept (2.27.15).
188 Tracy, "Sometimes in War, You Can Put a Price on Life," NYT (5.16.07).
189 "Behind U.S. Condolence Payments for Afghan Civilians," LAT (4.13.11).
190 Londoño & Hamdard, "U.S. Pays 'Blood Money' to Victims of Afghan Massacre," WP (3.24.12).
191 In Muslim law, a payment by an aggressor to a victim to avoid retaliation.
192 Gall & Mazzetti, "Hushed Deal Frees C.I.A. Contractor in Pakistan," NYT (3.16.11).
193 Dumbaugh, "Chinese Embassy Bombing in Belgrade: Compensation Issues," Congressional Research Service (2000).
194 See the table in the Appendix.
195 Haltom & McCann (2004).
196 See Table A3 in the Appendix.
197 See Table A4 in the Appendix.
198 Harris, "Lawsuit Claims Three American-Based Companies Financed Terrorism in Iraq," NYT (10.18.17).

CHAPTER 7   CIVIL LIBERTIES

1 For analyses of the threats in the first years after 9/11, see Lawyers Committee for Human Rights (2002, 2003a, 2003b); for documentation of effect on Islamic charity, see ACLU (2009); for perspectives by Muslims, see Bayoumi (2015); Kundnani (2014); Nguyen (2005); for perspectives by Sikhs, see Sidhu et al. (2009); see also Giridharadas (2015).
2 Detroit Free Press v. Ashcroft, 195 F.Supp.2d 937 (E.D. Mich. 2002), aff'd, 303 F.3d 681 (6th Cir. 2002).
3 Krasnowski, "Judge Says Incident Shows Torrance Police Officers Need Training," Daily Breeze (1.24.06).
4 Dwyer, "No Photo Ban in Subways, Yet an Arrest," NYT (2.18.09).
5 Dunlap, "Right Upheld to Photograph U.S. Buildings," NYT (10.19.10).
6 Getlin, "Movie Project Develops into a Legal Battle," LAT (1.16.06).
7 "18 Antiwar 'Grannies' on Trial in New York," LAT (4.21.06); Haberman, "What Did You Do in the War, Grandma?" NYT (4.21.06); Hartocollis,

"With 'Grannies' in Dock, a Sitting Judge Is Bound to Squirm," NYT (4.27.06); "18 Antiwar 'Grannies' Are Found Not Guilty," LAT (4.28.06); Hartocollis, "Setting Grandmotherhood Aside, Judge Lets 18 Go in Peace," NYT (4.28.06).

8   "Maryland: Charges Dropped in Protests," NYT (1.27.07).

9   "Arizona: 'Bush Lied' T-shirt Is Cleared," LAT (8.21.08).

10 Jacobs, "Banner-Bearing Protester at Convention is Acquitted," NYT (6.24.05).

11 Cardwell, "In Court Papers, a Political Note on '04 Protests," NYT (7.31.06); Feuer, "Antiwar Groups Claim Victory in Settlement over Central Park's Great Lawn," NYT (1.9.08).

12 Flegenheimer, "Ad Calling Jihad 'Savage' Is Set to Appear in Subway," NYT (9.19.12); "Metro Should End Its Delay of Running 'Defeat Jihad' Ad," WP (9.24.12); Flegenheimer, "M.T.A. Amends Rules after Pro-Israel Ads Draw Controversy," NYT (9.28.12); Masoodi, "Pro-Muslim Subway Ads to Hang Near Anti-Jihad Ads," NYT (10.5.12); "Judge Orders Metro to Display Provocative Ads," NYT (10.6.12); Flegenheimer, "Controversial Pro-Israel Ad Campaign to Expand to Buses," NYT (10.6.12); Flegenheimer, "Controversial Group Plans More Ads in Subway Stations," NYT (12.14.12); Southall, "Group to Sue after M.T.A. Rejects Ad that Refers to Muslims Killing Jews," NYT (9.20.14); "Pennsylvania: Ads with Adolf Hitler Appear on Buses," NYT (4.3.15); Fitzsimmons, "Judge Orders M.T.A. to Run a Bus Ad it Rejected," NYT (4.22.15); Fitzsimmons, "M.T.A. Board Votes to Ban Political Ads on Subways and Buses," NYT (4.30.15); "Free Speech vs. Hate Speech," NYT (5.7.15); Siddons, "Washington Bans Political Ads from Public Transit," NYT (5.29.15); McCaughey, "Don't Censor My Commute," NYT (6.1.15); Czajkowski, "Countering Hostility with Jokes," NYT (7.9.15).

13 Stempel, "New York's MTA Must Run 'Muslim' Movie Posters in Subways – Judge," Reuters (10.7.15); "The M.T.A. Board Should Loosen Up on Advocacy Ads," NYT (10.27.15).

14 Liptak, "Justices Take Case on Lying about Honors from Military," NYT (10.18.11); Barnes, "Supreme Court to Review Free Speech Issue on Lying about Military Honors," WP (10.18.11); "Honor and Free Speech," NYT (2.23.12); Dao, "Lying about Earning War Medals Is Protected Speech, Justices Rule," NYT (6.29.12); "The Supreme Court Defends the Right to Lie," WP (6.30.12); "House Tries Again, Passing New Stolen Valor Act," NYT (9.14.12); Maze, "Senate Passes Revised Stolen Valor Act," Air Force Times (12.3.12); Hauser, "Ex-Marine Can Wear Medals He Didn't Earn," NYT (1.14.16); U.S. v. Alvarez, 2008 WL 8683050 (CD Cal 2008), rev'd, 617 F.3d 1198 (9th Cir. 2010), aff'd, 587 U.S. 709 (2012); U.S. v. Swisher, 790 F.Supp.2d 1215 (D Id 2011), aff'd, 771 F.3d 514 (9th Cir. 2014), rev'd, 811 F.3d 299 (9th Cir. en banc 2016).

15 Baker, "White House Manual Details How to Deal with Protesters," WP (8.22.07); "Don't Read This, Mr. President!" WP (9.10.07).

16 U.S. v. Apel, 676 F.3rd 1202 (9th Cir. 2012), rev'd, 134 S. Ct 1144 (2014).

17 Strom, "Display of Anti-Bush Sign Has Competitive Bridge World in an Uproar," NYT (11.14.17); "Don't Shut Up and Play," NYT (11.15.07).

18 "Joe Lieberman, "Would-Be Censor," NYT (5.25.08); Bennett, "YouTube Is Letting Users Decide on Terrorism-Related Videos," LAT (12.13.10); Howard, "Lieberman Urges Google to Implement Terrorist-Flagging Feature," Slate.com (11.22.11).

19 Burns & Helft, "YouTube Withdraws Cleric's Videos," NYT (11.4.10).

20 Saulny, "Battles over Billboard Space Precede G.O.P. Gathering," NYT (8.30.08).

21 Cohen, "CVS and Walgreens Ban an Issue of Rolling Stone," NYT (7.18.13); McGregor, "CVS Won't Sell Rolling Stone Issue Featuring Boston Bombing Suspect," WP (7.18.13); "Judging Rolling Stone By Its Cover," NYT (7.19.13).

22 Hamill, "Scientist, Claiming Bias, Sues U.S. over Revoked Clearance," NYT (6.27.08); "Pennsylvania: Scientist's Firing," NYT (11.7.08); "Egyptian-Born Scientist Leaves U.S. after Losing Suit," NYT (11.29.08); El-Ganayni v. U.S. Dept. of Energy, 2008 WL 4890171 (W.D. Pa. 2008), 2008 WL 5101756 (W.D. Pa. 2008), aff'd, 591 F.3d 176 (3rd Cir. 2010).

23 O'Keefe, "Worker Suing Intelligence Agency Claims Anti-Muslim Bias," WP (11.1.11).

24 Serwer, "Lawsuit on Behalf of Gitmo Critic Can Proceed," American Prospect (3.31.11); "Appeals Court Hears Case of Ex-Gitmo Prosecutor Fired from Library of Congress over Writings," WP (11.11.11);

25 Gold, "Chaplain of New York Jails Suspended over Speech," LAT (3.11.06); "The Mayor and the Imam," NYT (3.18.06); Getlin, "N.Y. Chaplain's Suspension Ignites Debate," LAT (3.20.06).

26 Elliott, "Federal Panel Finds Bias in Ouster of Principal of Arab-American School," NYT (3.13.10); Medina, "Principal of City's Only Arabic-Language Public School Resigns Her Post Suddenly," NYT (3.17.10); Medina, "Ex-Principal of Arabic School Won't Sue City," NYT (5.26.10).

27 Lipton, "Some U.S. Security Agents Chafe under Speech Limits," NYT (4.26.05).

28 "Hold the Hijab," LAT (8.24.10); Greenhouse, "Offended Muslims Speak Up," NYT (9.24.10); Liptak, "Muslim Woman Denied Job over Head Scarf Wins in Supreme Court," NYT (6.2.15); Equal Employment Opportunity Commission v. Abercrombie & Fitch Stores, 798 F.Supp.2d 1272 (N.D.Ok. 2011), rev'd, 731 F.3d 1106 (10th Cir. 2012), rev'd, 135 S.Ct. 2028 (2015); "Head Scarves Before the Supreme Court," NYT (6.2.15).

29 Wilgoren, "NPR Fires Juan Williams over Anti-Muslim Remarks," WP (10.21.10); Padilla, "NPR Commentator Loses Job over Muslim Remark," LAT (10.21.10); Farhi, "Juan Williams at Odds with NPR over Dismissal," WP (10.22.10); Gerecht, "Juan Williams, The Truthful Dissident," WP (10.22.10); "NPR's Hasty Decision to Fire Pundit Juan Williams," WP (10.22.10); Gold, "In Wake of NPR Controversy, Fox News Gives Juan Williams an Expanded Role," LAT (10.22.10); Gold, "Prominent Muslims Fear NPR Analyst's Firing May Fan Hostility," LAT (10.22.10); "NPR's Overreaction," LAT (10.22.10); Stelter, "Two Takes

on NPR and Fox on Juan Williams," NYT (10.22.10); Stelter & Jensen, "Criticism of Firing by NPR Heightens as Broadcaster Defends the Decision," NYT (10.23.10); Wright, "Islamophobia and Homophobia," NYT (10.27.10); "The Noise about Public Radio," NYT (10.30.10); Jensen, "NPR Executive Who Fired Juan Williams Resigns," NYT (1.7.11).

30 Zeller, "No Koran in Congress, Fewer Muslims to America?" NYT (12.20.06); Swarns, "Holocaust Museum Rebukes Member for Koran Comment," NYT (12.22.06); "Washington: Bush Is Urged to Act on Criticism of Muslim," NYT (12.23.06); "A Bigot in Congress," WP (12.22.06); Shear & Craig, "Good Has Often Inspired Political Ire," WP (12.23.06); "Fear and Bigotry in Congress," NYT (12.23.06).

31 See Kahn (2013); Schneier (2012).

32 Sander, "6 Imams Removed from Flight for Behavior Deemed Suspicious," NYT (11.22.06); Lydersen, "Diversity of Opinion on Imams' Dispute with Airline," WP (12.8.06); "Muslim Clerics Sue Airline and Passengers," NYT (4.1.07).

33 Robbins, "Judge Rules that Suspects Cannot Be Detained Because of Ethnicity," NYT (11.25.08).

34 Gardner, "9 Muslim Passengers Removed from Jet," WP (1.2.09); Gardner & Hsu, "Airline Apologizes for Booting 9 Muslims," WP (1.3.09); Dizikes, "Muslim Families Are Taken Off Flight," LAT (1.3.09); Robbins, "9 Muslims Are Pulled from Plane and Denied Re-Entry; Airline Belatedly Apologizes," NYT (1.3.09).

35 Shane & Schmitt, "Officials Detain Two Airline Passengers, Fearing a Test of a Terrorist Plot," NYT (8.31.10); Finn, "Pair Held after Odd Items Turn Up in Luggage," WP (8.31.10); Shane, "Detained Yemenis Are Thought to Be Unconnected to Terrorism, Official Says," NYT (9.1.10); "The Netherlands: 2 Yemenis Freed," NYT (9.2.10).

36 Hsu & Freeman, "JetBlue, TSA Workers Settle in T-Shirt Case," WP (1.6.09); Schwartz, "Iraqi Gets $240,000 Settlement in T-Shirt Incident at U.S. Airport," NYT (1.8.09).

37 "Pennsylvania: Student of Arabic Sues over Detention," NYT (2.9.10); Hsu, "College Student Sues U.S. for Detainment at Pennsylvania Airport," WP (2.11.10).

38 Barron, "A Flight Is Diverted by a Prayer Seen as Ominous," NYT (1.22.10); Stack, "College Student Is Removed from Flight after Speaking Arabic on Plane," NYT (4.17.16); Rampell, "Ivy League Economist Ethnically Profiled, Interrogated for Doing Math on American Airlines Flight," WP (5.8.16); Hauser, "2 Muslim American Women Ordered Off American Airlines Flight," NYT (8.6.16); Bromwich, "YouTube Stars Say They Were Removed from Delta Flight for Speaking Arabic," NYT (12.22.16).

39 Semple, "Report Faults Border Patrol on Bus and Train Searches," NYT (11.9.11); Glascock, "Security Checks on Domestic Washington Ferries Roil Islanders," LAT (6.30.08); Richburg, "Homeland Security Comes to Vermont," WP (8.24.08).

40 MacFarquhar, "Terror Fears Hamper U.S. Muslims' Travel," NYT (6.1.06).

41 MacFarquhar, "Detention Was Wrong, and U.S. Apologizes," NYT (8.24.07).

42 "Looking into Laptops," LAT (11.11.06); Nakashima, "Clarity Sought on Electronic Searches," WP (2.7.08); Nakashima, "Travelers' Laptops May Be Detained at Border," WP (8.1.08); "Search and Replace," WP (8.13.08); "Laptop Searches Go Too Far," LAT (9.29.08); Nakashima, "Bush's Search Policy for Travelers Kept," WP (8.28.09); "Congress Must Act to End Electronic Fishing Expeditions at the Border," LAT (9.13.10); "Searching Your Laptop," NYT (11.16.10); Shipler, "Can You Frisk a Hard Drive?" NYT (2.20.11); "Shielding the Privacies of Life," NYT (4.23.11); Stellin, "Border Agents' Power to Search Devices Is Facing Increasing Challenges in Court," NYT (12.5.12); Stellin, "The Border Is a Back Door for U.S. Device Searches," NYT (9.10.13); Stellin, "District Judge Upholds Government's Right to Search Electronics at Border," NYT (1.1.14); Nakashima, "Judge Upholds Search of Passengers' Laptops," WP (1.1.14); Tillman, "Laptops Are Not Searchable like Handbags, Judge Tells Feds," NLJ (5.11.15).

43 Greenwald, "U.S. Filmmaker Repeatedly Detained at Border," Salon (4.8.12); "'CitizenFour' Filmmaker Says U.S. Harassed Her," NYT (7.14.15).

44 U.S. v. Cotterman, 2009 WL 465028 (D Az. 2009), rev'd, 637 F.3d 1068 (9th Cir. 2011), rev'd en banc, 709 F.3d 952 (9th Cir. 2013), cert. den., 134 S.Ct. 899 (2014).

45 Chan, "Bag Searches on Subway to Go On Trial," NYT (11.1.05); Chan, "Testimony Completed in Suit over Searches in Subways," NYT (11.2.05); Chan, "Terrorism Expert Advised City on Searches," NYT (11.7.05); Preston, "Police Searches in the Subways Are Upheld," NYT (12.3.05); Feuer, "U.S. Appeals Court Upholds Bag Searches on Subways," NYT (8.12.06); Zezima, "Police to Start Inspecting Bags on Boston Subway," NYT (10.5.06).

46 See de Goede & Sullivan (2015).

47 DoJ OIG (2005, 2007, 2008, 2009); Pincus & Eggen, "325,000 Names on Terrorism List," WP (2.15.06); "Names on U.S. Terror List Quadruple," LAT (2.15.06); Lipton, "Flexible Rules Are Urged in Detention of Travelers," NYT (7.25.06); DeYoung, "Terror Database Has Quadrupled in Four Years," WP (3.25.07); Nakashima, "Ordinary Customers Flagged as Terrorists," WP (3.27.07); Nakashima, "Terror Suspect List Yields Few Arrests," WP (8.25.07); Nakashima, "Terrorism Watchlist Is Faulted for Errors," WP (9.7.07); Shenon, "Inspection Notes Errors in Terror List," NYT (9.7.07); "Illinois: Ruling on Watchlists," NYT (4.24.08); "'We'll Have to Check, Sir,'" NYT (5.15.08); "That Troubled Terrorism List," NYT (8.24.08); Sharkey, "Sorry, Pal. You're Innocent, But You're Still on our Lists," NYT (8.26.08); Sharkey, "Mom and Dad Are Cleared, but Junior's Another Story," NYT (9.9.08); Hsu, "Government to Take Over Airline Passenger Vetting," WP (10.23.08); "FBI Terrorist Watchlist Errors Cited," LAT (5.7.09); Lichtblau, "Terror List Wrongly Includes 24,000,

While Some Actual Suspects Escaped It," NYT (5.7.09); Pincus, "1,600 Are Suggested Daily for FBI's List," WP (11.1.09); "The System Failed," NYT (12.30.09); Tankersley, "U.S. No-Fly List Criticized after Attempted Plane Bombing," LAT (12.31.09); Alvarez, "Meet Mikey, 9: U.S. Has Him on Watchlist," NYT (1.14.10); McIntyre, "Ensnared by Error on Growing U.S. Watchlist, with No Way Out," NYT (3.7.10); "A.C.L.U. Sues over No-Fly List," NYT (7.1.10); "U.S. Citizens Need a Better Way to Challenge Flight Ban," WP (7.14.10); "Antiterror Measures at Home," NYT (10.2.11); "U.S. No-Fly List Doubles in Past Year to 21,000 Known or Suspected Terrorists," WP (2.1.12); "Oregon: Lawsuit Challenging No-Fly List Is Allowed to Proceed," NYT (7.27.12); Hosenball, "Number of Names on U.S. Counterterrorism Database Jumps," Reuters (5.2.13); Carson, "Muslims Challenging U.S. 'No Fly' List Win Partial Court Victory," Reuters (8.30.12); "Nelson Mandela Was on the U.S. Terrorist Watchlist until 2008," HuffPost (12.6.13); Kravets, "Scholar Wins Court Battle to Purge Name from U.S. No-Fly List," *Wired* (1.14.14); "A Rebuff to Overbroad Watchlists," NYT (1.22.14); Millman, "Judge Questions Secrecy Shrouding 'No Fly' List," WSJ (3.17.14); "Terror Watchlists Run Amok," NYT (4.19.14); Goldman, "Lawsuit Says FBI Uses No-Fly List in Bid to Recruit Muslim Informants," WP (4.22.14); "Judge Tells Government that Secret List Barring Suspect Passengers Doesn't Fly," WP (6.28.14); Barakat, "U.S. Terrorist Database Growing at Rapid Rate," AP (7.18.14); Scahill & Devereaux, "Blacklisted: The Secret Government Rulebook for Labeling You a Terrorist," The Intercept (7.24.14); Savage, "Over Government Objections, Rules on No–Fly List Are Made Public," NYT (7.24.14); Goldman, "Document Details Procedure for Placing Terrorist Suspects on Government Watchlist," WP (7.24.14); Savage, "Secret Papers Describe Size of Terror Lists Kept by U.S.," NYT (8.6.14); "The 'Terrorist Screening Database': Are They All Terrorists?" LAT (8.12.14); "White House Promises to Change Rules for Removal from No-Fly List," NYT (8.20.14); Goldman, "U.S. to Inform Americans Whether They Are on 'No-Fly' List, and Possibly Why," WP (4.15.15); Markon, "Terror Watchlists Have Grown Dramatically since 9/11," WP (6.18.16).

48 *Mokdad v. Lynch, 2013 WL8840322* (E.D. Mich. 2013), rev'd, 804 F.3d 807 (6th Cir. 2015), on remand, 2016 WL 4205909 (ED Mich 2016).

49 Kessler, "Court Tells State Department to Reconsider Terrorist Label for Iran Opposition Group," WP (7.17.10); Warrick, "U.S. to Remove Iranian Group from Terror List, Officials Say," WP (9.21.12); Gerstein, "Eric Holder, James Clapper State Secrets Privilege Claims Disclosed in No-Fly List Lawsuit," Politico (4.24.13).

50 *Ibrahim v. Department of Homeland Security*, 2006 WL 2374645 (N.D.Cal. 2006), rev'd in part, 538 F.3d 1250 (9th Cir. 2008), 2009 WL 4021757 (N.D. Cal. 2009), rev'd, 669 F.3d 983 (9th Cir. 2012), 62 F.Supp.3d 909 (ND Cal. 2014).

51 Kornblut, "Obama Addresses Airline Security in Low-Key Fashion," WP (12.28.09); Lipton, "With Safety Gaps Revealed, A Surge in Security,"

NYT (12.29.09); "In the Wake of Flight 253, the TSA Must Get More Anti-Terrorist Tools," WP (12.29.09); Schwartz, "Debate over Full-Body Scans v. Invasion of Privacy Flares Anew," NYT (12.30.09); Healy & Simons, "Full-Body Scans to Be Used for Amsterdam–U.S. Flights," NYT (12.31.09); Kindy, "Ex-Homeland Security Chief Head Said to Abuse Public Trust by Touting Scanners," WP (1.1.10); Lipton, "Strict Airport Screening to Remain for Citizens of 14 Nations," NYT (1.4.10); Rucker, "TSA Tries to Assuage Privacy Concerns about Full-Body Scans," WP (1.4.10); Dixon, "The Chink in Airports' Armor," LAT (1.5.10); Kim, "L.A. Airport Police Union Urges Full-Body Scans at Checkpoints," LAT (1.5.10); Lipton, "New Air Security Checks from 14 Nations to U.S. Draw Criticism," NYT (1.5.10); "Airline Security and the Real World," LAT (1.6.10); "There's Nothing to Fear from the Use of Full-Body Scanners at Airports," WP (1.7.10); Wald, "Cancer Risks Debated for Type of X-Ray Scan," NYT (1.9.10); Wald, "Documents Send Mixed Signal on Airport Scanners," NYT (1.13.10); Savage, "The Fight against Full-Body Scanners at Airports," LAT (1.13.10); Perlez, "Angered by U.S. Security Measures, Pakistani Lawmakers Return Home as Heroes," NYT (3.10.10); Zeleny, "Security Checks on Flights to U.S. to Be Revamped," NYT (4.2.10); Kornblut & Hsu, "U.S. Changing the Way Air Travelers Are Screened," WP (4.2.10); Cloud, "Personal Traits Will Be Used to Screen U.S.-Bound Air Passengers," LAT (4.2.10); "Pakistanis Removed from Flight," NYT (8.31.10); Maguire, "American Sikhs Decry Screenings," NYT (11.7.10); "Obama's Hand in Your Crotch," *Washington Times* (11.15.10); "Shut Up and Be Scanned," LAT (11.17.10); ACLU email (11.17.10); Parker, "Facing Scrutiny, Officials Defend Airport Pat Downs," NYT (11.17.10); Bennett & Steffen, "TSA Chief Defends Body Scanners, Pat-Downs," LAT (11.18.10); Stellin, "Flier Patience Wears Thin at Checkpoints," NYT (11.19.10); Stellin, "Pat-Downs at Airports Prompt Complaints," NYT (11.19.10); Krauthammer, "Don't Touch My Junk," WP (11.19.10); "TSA's Security Charade," *Washington Times* (11.20.10); "The Uproar over Pat-Downs," NYT (11.20.10); Letters to the Editor, NYT (11.20.10); Will, "The T.S. of A. Takes Control," WP (11.21.10); Parker, "Enduring the Bare Necessities in Airport Screening," WP (11.21.10); Bennett, "TSA Exempts U.S. Airline Pilots from Pat-Downs and Body Scans," LAT (11.21.10); Nixon, "T.S.A. Grants Airline Pilots an Exception to Screenings," NYT (11.21.10); Shane, "Administration to Seek Balance in Airport Screenings," NYT (11.22.10); Tarm, "Security Protest Could Disrupt Thanksgiving Travel," WP (11.22.10); Halsey, "Scientists Say They Have Solution to TSA Scanner Objections," WP (11.22.10); Abrams, "TSA Chief Says No Change in Screening Policy," WP (11.22.10); Puzzanghera, "'Invasive' Airport Pat-Downs Not Going Away for the Holidays," LAT (11.22.10); Barry, "At a Checkpoint, Terror Fears and Testy Travelers," NYT (11.23.10); Cooper, "Administration to Seek Balance in Airport Screening," NYT (11.23.10); Cohen & Halsey, "Poll: Nearly Two-Thirds of Americans Support Full-Body Scanners at Airports," WP (11.23.10); Memoli & Saillant, "TSA Aims to Ease

Passengers' Worries," LAT (11.23.10); Riccardi, "He's Selling TSA-Proof Underwear," LAT (11.23.10); Kravitz, "Protesters' Body Scanner Opt-Out Day Could Bring Nationwide Delays at Airports," WP (11.24.10); Marcus, "Don't Touch My Junk? Grow Up, America," WP (11.24.10); Memoli, "Officials Brace for Possible 'Opt Out' Protests at Airports," LAT (11.24.10); Robertson, "Passengers Unmoved by Protests against Scan," NYT (11.25.10); Parker, "T.S.A. Chief Visits Airport to Buck Up Employees and Defend Tactics," NYT (11.25.10); Dreyfuss, "On Airport Security, Do We Really Want to Be like Israel?" WP (11.25.10); "The TSA Was Right to Add Pat-Downs to Its Security Arsenal," WP (11.25.10); Cohen, "The Real Threat to America," NYT (11.26.10); Zacharia, "Israeli Air Security Experts Insist Their Methods Better Than U.S.," WP (11.27.10); "India: Airport Pat-Down Draws Protest," NYT (12.10.10); Halsey, "TSA Debuts Less-Revealing Software for Airport Scanners," WP (2.2.11); Murphy, "Alaska Legislator's 'No' to TSA Pat-Downs Wins Praise at Home," LAT (2.25.11); Halsey, "Panel Urges TSA to Implement 'Trust Travelers' Program," WP (3.16.11); O'Keefe, "TSA, Congress to Review Screening Procedures after Pat-Down of 6-Year-Old Girl," WP (4.14.11); O'Keefe, "Bill Requires TSA Seek Parental OK Before Patting-Down a Child," WP (4.19.11); Dowd, "Stripped of Dignity," NYT (4.20.11); Brown, "Texas Bill Would Make Invasive Pat-Downs a Felony," WP (5.1.11); Williams, "Texan Defends Proposed Ban on 'Intrusive' Airport Searches," NYT (6.16.11); Caesar, "Texas Bill to Restrict Airport Pat-Downs Dies," LAT (6.30.11); Savage, "Court Rejects Challenge to Airport Body Scanners," LAT (7.16.11); Rein, "Lawmakers Dispute TSA's Definition of 'Sensitive' Information," WP (7.16.11); Halsey, "TSA Introduces Software That Uses Less-Revealing Body Scanner Images," WP (7.21.11); "US Embassy Apologizes after Former Indian President Frisked at Airport," WP (11.14.11); Stellin, "Screening Still a Pain at Airports, Fliers Say," NYT (11.22.11); Davidson, "Lawmaker Challenges TSA on Claims of Ethnic Profiling," WP (11.29.11); "Tennessee: Airport Security Stops Senator," NYT (1.24.12); O'Keefe, "Sen. Rand Paul Declines TSA Pat-Down Is Escorted from Security Checkpoint," WP (1.24.12); Schmidt & Lichtblau, "Racial Profiling Rife at Airport, U.S. Officers Say," NYT (8.12.12); Schmidt, "Mandatory Class for Airport Officers Accused of Profiling," NYT (8.18.12); Lapidos, "Is This the Pose of a Free Man?" NYT (9.15.12); Nixon, "Unpopular Full-Body Scanners to Be Removed from Airports," NYT (1.19.13); Stellin, "Airport Screening Concerns Civil Liberties Groups," NYT (3.12.13); Schmidt, "Report Says T.S.A. Screening Is Not Objective," NYT (6.5.13); "That Extra Hurdle at the Airport," NYT (6.17.13); Letter to the Editor, NYT (6.21.13); Stellin, "Security Check Now Starts Long Before You Fly," NYT (10.21.13); Davidson, "Report Casts Doubt on Major TSA Program Designed to Spot Potential Airline Terrorists," WP (11.15.13); Qualters, "Disabled Passenger Takes Airport Pat-Downs to First Circuit," NLJ (1.2.14); *Ruskai v. Pistole*, 775 F.3d 61 (1st Cir. 2014); Wegman, "Once You're on the No-Fly List, It's Hard to Get Off," NYT (2.8.14); Tierney, "At Airports, a

Some," LAT (1.12.07); Fears, "U.S. Anti-Terrorism Laws Hold up Asylum Seekers," WP (8.13.07).

63 Freedman, "Delays in Muslims' Cases Spur Interfaith Call to Action," NYT (9.5.09); HRF (2009); Bernstein, "Immigration Detention System Lapses Detailed," NYT (11.3.09); Cody, "Travelers with Muslim Names Find Themselves Fighting for U.S. Visas," WP (4.1.10); Arango, "Visa Delays Put Iraqis Who Aided U.S. in Fear," NYT (7.13.11); Bennett, "Iraqi Refugees in U.S. Rechecked for Terrorism Links," LAT (7.19.11); Healy, "Afghans Who Risked Lives for U.S. Are Left in Dark on Visas," NYT (8.5.11); "As Threatened Afghans Await U.S. Refuge, Former Ambassador Warns Visa Program Hurts U.S. Mission," WP (8.9.11); Tariq, "U.S. Pullout Leaves Iraqi Interpreters out on a Limb," LAT (11.7.11); Sieff, "Alleged Terrorism Ties Foil Some Afghan Interpreters' U.S. Visa Hopes," WP (2.2.13).

64 Savage "Bill Targets Citizenship of Terrorists' Allies," NYT (5.7.10); Cole, "Bill to Expatriate Those Who Support Terrorists More Symbol Than Substance," WP (5.8.10); "A Lieberman Loser," LAT (5.10.10); Chemerinsky, "Even Terrorism Suspects Have Rights," LAT (5.11.10); "Sens. Lieberman and Brown Offer the Wrong Solution on Dealing with Citizen Terrorists," WP (5.17.10); Viser, "Brown Renews Call for Terrorist Expatriation Act," BG (6.22.10); Kasperowicz, "Lawmakers Seek to Strip Citizenship from People Supporting Terrorism against U.S.," *The Hill* (10.13.11).

65 DoJ OIG (2010); ACLU (2013).

66 *Handschu v. Special Services Division*, Memorandum Opinion and Order (SDNY 2.27.08); Dwyer, "New York Police Covertly Join In at Protest Rallies," NYT (12.22.05); "Surveillance, New York Style," NYT (12.23.05); Dwyer, "Surveillance Prompts a Suit: Police v. Police," NYT (2.3.06); Dwyer, "Charges, But No Penalty, for a Chief's Role in a Convention Arrest," NYT (3.8.06); Dwyer, "Police Memos Say Arrest Tactics Calmed Protest," NYT (3.17.06); Hartocollis, "Police Lied about Arrests, Group Says," NYT (3.23.06); Baker, "2 Top Officers Are Criticized for '04 Arrests," NYT (5.10.06); Baker, "Some Suits Are Settled in '04 Arrests amid Protests," NYT (7.21.06); "Convention Arrests to Be Made Public," NYT (1.23.07); Dwyer, "Judge Tells Police to Stop Routinely Taping Public Events without Cause," NYT (2.16.07); "Smile, You're on N.Y.P.D. Camera," NYT (2.17.07); Dwyer, "City Police Spied Broadly before G.O.P. Convention," NYT (3.25.07); Dwyer, "City Asks Court Not to Unseal Police Spy Files on Convention," NYT (3.26.07); "The Police and the Spy Unit," NYT (3.27.07); Feuer, "Secrecy Order on Police Files Still Stands," NYT (3.27.07); Moynihan, "Judge Orders Police Department Files on Preconvention Surveillance Opened," NYT (5.17.07); Feuer, "In Shift, Judge Eases Limits on Surveillance by the Police," NYT (6.14.07); McFadden, "Judge Orders Release of '04 Republican Convention Surveillance Reports," NYT (8.7.07); Neumeister, "Judge: NYC Can't Use Secret Arguments," AP (1.22.08); Moynihan, "City Seeks to See Tapes of Protests from

2004," NYT (6.20.08); "The Convention Papers," NYT (8.19.08);
Dwyer, "52 Arrests, $2 Million Payout, and Many Questions," NYT
(8.20.08); Weiser, "Plaintiffs Are Surprised by New Rules on Taping,"
NYT (11.11.08); Dwyer, "In the Courts, a Merry-Go-Round on Police
Surveillance of Gatherings," NYT (11.12.08); Johnston & Rashbaum,
"New York Police Fight with U.S. on Surveillance," NYT (11.20.08);
Baker, "New York Can Keep Police Surveillance Data Secret, U.S. Judges
Rule," NYT (6.10.10); Hartocollis, "Judge Backs 2 Protesters' Arrest
during G.O.P. Meeting in 2004," NYT (10.2.10); *Marcavage v. City of
New York*, 2010 WL 3910355 (S.D.N.Y. 2010), aff'd, 689 F.3d 98 (2nd
Cir. 2012), cert. den., 133 S.Ct. 1492 (2013); Eligon, "A Never-Ending
Lawsuit Turns 40," NYT (5.6.11); Goldman & Apuzzo, "With CIA
Help, NYPD Moves Covertly in Muslim Areas," AP (8.24.11); Mazzetti,
"C.I.A. Examining Legality of Work with Police Dept.," NYT (9.14.11);
"NYPD Had Surveillance on U.S. Citizens Based on Ethnicity, Not Any
Possible Crimes," WP (9.22.11); Rashbaum, "Judge Is Asked to Allow
Review of Police Dept. Monitoring of Muslim Communities," NYT
(10.4.11); Goldstein, "City Council Grills Kelly on Police Surveillance
of Muslims," NYT (10.7.11); "What's the CIA Doing at NYPD?
Depends Whom You Ask," CBS News (10.17.11); Powell, "Police Eyes
Hovering over Muslims," NYT (10.18.11); "Angry over NYPD Spying,
Muslim Activists Urge against Calling Police, Adding to Mistrust,"
WP (11.14.11); "Hectoring the Heroes," *New York Post* (12.26.11);
Taylor, "14 Muslim Leaders Plan Boycott of Breakfast with Mayor,"
NYT (12.29.11); "NYC Mayor Bloomberg Doesn't Address Boycott of
Interfaith Event by Muslims Upset over Spying," WP (12.30.11); Taylor,
"At Mayor's Interfaith Breakfast, Some Respectful Dissents," NYT
(12.31.11); "Top CIA Lawyer Never Approved NYPD Collaboration
That Built Widespread Muslim Spying Program," WP (1.20.12); "CIA
to Pull Officer from NYPD after Internal Probe," WSJ (1.26.12); Patel
& Gotein, "It's Time to Police the N.Y.P.D.," NYT (1.30.12); Sacribey,
"Muslims Petition again for NYPD Probe," WP (2.3.12); "NYPD
Investigation of Muslims: Civil Rights Groups Ask for Probe," LAT
(2.3.12); "NYPD Monitored Muslim Students across Northeast," LAT
(2.20.12); Baker & Taylor, "Bloomberg Defends Police's Monitoring of
Muslim Students on Web," NYT (2.22.12); "Ex-Director of Newark, N.J.,
Police Says No Local Officers Were Used in NYPD Spying on Muslims,"
WP (2.22.12); "NYPD Built Secret Files on New Jersey, Long Island
Mosques," WSJ (2.22.12); "Newark Mayor Calls for Probe of NYPD
Spying on Muslims," WP (2.23.12); "White House Grant Money Paid
for NYPD Blanket Surveillance of Muslims, Mosques," WP (2.27.12);
Goldstein, "Kelly Defends Surveillance of Muslims," NYT (2.28.12);
Powell, "Police Monitoring and the Climate of Fear," NYT (2.28.12);
Letter to the Editor, NYT (2.28.12); "Surveillance, Security and Civil
Liberties," NYT (3.4.12); Baker, "Police Leader's Evolving Efforts to
Defend Surveillance," NYT (3.7.12); Baxter, "Secret NYPD Surveillance
in N.J. Was Not So Secret, Former Officials Say," Star Register (3.7.12);

Baker, "F.B.I. Official Faults Police Tactics on Muslims," NYT (3.8.12);
"The N.Y.P.D. and Muslims," NYT (3.9.12); Goldman & Apuzzo, "New
Files Show More Muslim NYPD Targets," BG (3.10.12); Goldstein,
"Most of City's Voters Back Police's Surveillance of Muslims, Poll
Finds," NYT (3.13.12); "Police Powers in New York," NYT (3.18.12);
"Christie Accepts Monitoring of Muslims," NYT (5.25.12); Finnigan,
"LAPD Modifies Surveillance Program of Muslims," LAT (5.21.12);
Burack, "Law Restricts SFPD–FBI Collaboration," *San Francisco
Examiner* (5.9.12); Sullivan, "NJ Muslims File Federal Suit to Stop
NYPD Spying," AP (6.6.12); Silber, "Who Will Defend the Defenders?"
Commentary (June 2012); Elliott, "Fact-Check: How the NYPD
Overstated Its Counterterrorism Record," ProPublica (7.10.12); Raz,
"Counterterrorism and the NYPD," NPR (7.15.12); Friedersdorf, "The
Problem with the NYPD's Interstate Spy Squad," *The Atlantic* (7.26.12);
"The Convert," *This American Life* (8.10.12); "NYPD Official: Muslim
Spying by Secret Demographics Unit Generated No Leads, Terrorism
Cases," WP (8.21.12); Weiser, "Judge Rules That Mass Arrests at a
2004 Protest Were Illegal," NYT (10.1.12); "N.J. Bill Would Require
Surveillance Notification," WSJ (10.15.12); Greenberg, "New York: The
Police and the Protesters," NYRB 58 (10.11.12); Goldstein, "Lawyers Say
Surveillance of Muslims Flouts Accord," NYT (2.4.13); "Spying on Law-
Abiding Muslims," NYT (2.10.13); CLEAR et al. (2013); "Civil Rights
Groups Sue NYC Mayor and Top Cop over Post-9/11 Muslim Surveillance
Programs," WP (6.18.13); "More Overreach by the N.Y.P.D.," NYT
(6.24.13); Savage, "C.I.A. Report Finds Concerns with Ties to New York
Police," NYT (6.27.13); "The C.I.A. and the N.Y.P.D.," NYT (7.6.13);
"Documents: NYPD Labels Mosques Terrorism Enterprises to Record
Sermons and Spy on Imams," WP (8.28.13); "Spying on Muslims," NYT
(9.9.13); "NYC Defends Muslim Surveillance in Court," WP (9.12.13);
"NY Judge Asked to Bar NYPD Monitoring of Muslims," WSJ (10.2.13);
Horwitz, "ACLU Asks Justice to Probe Surveillance of Muslims by NYC
PD," WP (10.24.13); Goodman, "Intelligence and Counterterrorism
Commissioners Leave NYPD," NYT (12.19.13); Moynihan, "New York
Is Said to Settle Suits over Arrests at 2004 G.O.P. Convention," NYT
(12.23.13); Dwyer, "Mass Arrests during '04 Convention Leave Big
Bill and Lingering Mystery," NYT (1.8.14); Weiser, "New York City to
Pay $18 Million over Convention Arrests," NYT (1.16.13); Apuzzo &
Goldman, "The NYPD Division of Un-American Activities," *New York
Magazine* (8.25.13); Apuzzo, "U.S. to Expand Rules Limiting Use of
Profiling by Federal Agents," NYT (1.16.14); "The Convention and the
Damage Done," NYT (1.17.14); "Judge Finds Surveillance of Mosques
Was Allowed," NYT (2.21.14); Apuzzo & Goldstein, "New York Drops
Unit that Spied on Muslims," NYT (4.16.14); "Spying at the N.Y.P.D.,"
NYT (4.17.14); Goldstein, "New York Police Recruit Muslims to Be
Informers," NYT (5.10.14); "Muslims and the N.Y.P.D.," NYT (5.26.14);
Moynihan, "New York City Fights an Appeal by Muslims Who Say They
Were Watched," NYT (10.8.14); Apuzzo & Goldman (2013).

67 "New York Reaches Outline of Settlement over Muslim Surveillance," Reuters (6.22.15); Apuzzo & Baker, "New York to Appoint Civilian to Monitor Police's Counterterrorism Activity," NYT (1.8.16); Baker & Rojas, "New York Police Broke Surveillance Rules after 9/11, Inquiry Finds," NYT (8.24.16); Apuzzo & Goldman, "Judge Rejects Settlement over Surveillance of Muslims by NYPD," NYT (10.31.16); "A Judge Keeps His Eye on Police Spies," NYT (11.2.16); Apuzzo, Haberman & Kaplan, "Congressman Proposes National Surveillance Program after Trump Meeting," NYT (12.16.16); Mathias, "Rep. Peter King Urges Donald Trump to Create a Federal Muslim Surveillance Program," HuffPost (12.15.16); Apuzzo & Goldman, "After Spying on Muslims, N.Y.P.D. Agrees to Even More Oversight," NYT (3.6.17); "A Way to Control Police Spying," NYT (3.15.17); Keshner, "Former Federal Judge to Serve as Civilian Watchdog on NYPD Muslim Surveillance," *New York Daily News* (3.21.17); Keshner, "Judge Greenlights Settlement in NYPD Muslim Surveillance Suit," *New York Daily News* (3.21.17); Feuer, "Activists Sue Police Dept. over 'Can't Confirm or Deny' Tactic," NYT (6.15.17); Prendergast, "NYPD Anti-Terror Chief: Surveillance Bill Would Help Terrorists," *New York Post* (6.18.17).

68 *Hassan v. City of New York*, 2014 WL 654604 (D.N.J. 2014), rev'd, 804 F.3d 277 (3rd Cir. 2015); Weiser, "Lawsuit over New York Police Surveillance of Muslims Is Revived," NYT (10.13.15).

69 Winton, Renaud & Pringle, "LAPD to Build Data on Muslim Areas," LAT (11.9.07); MacFarquhar, "Protest Greets Police Plan to Map Muslim Angelenos," NYT (11.9.07); Winton, Watanabe & Krikorian, "LAPD Defends Muslim Mapping Effort," LAT (11.10.07); "Mapping L.A. Muslims," LAT (11.13.07); Winton & Watanabe, "LAPD's Muslim Mapping Plan Killed," LAT (11.15.07); Krikorian & Watanabe, "Experts See Value in Data on Muslims," LAT (11.16.07); "Right Move on Muslim Mapping," LAT (11.16.07); MacFarquhar, "Los Angeles Police Scrap Mapping Plan, Elating Muslims," NYT (11.16.07); Goodstein, "Police in Los Angeles Step Up Efforts to Gain Muslims' Trust," NYT (3.10.11).

70 "Citizen Terrorists Deleted," NYT (10.10.08); "Spying Gone Awry," WP (10.10.08); Drogin, "Spying on Pacifists, Environmentalists and Nuns," LAT (12.7.08); Sachs (2008).

71 Chevigny (1969); Skolnick (1966).

72 Blumenthal & Mowjood, "Muslim Prayers and Renewal near Ground Zero," NYT (12.8.09); Hernandez, "Vote Endorses Muslim Center near Ground Zero," NYT (5.26.10); Haberman, "In Islamic Center Fight, Lessons in Prepositions and Fear-Mongering," NYT (7.27.10); "Let Religious Freedom Ring," LAT (7.30.10); Barbaro, "Debate Heating Up on Plans for Mosque near Ground Zero," NYT (7.31.10); Barbaro & Hernandez, "Mosque Plan Clears Hurdle in New York," NYT (8.4.10); "A Monument to Tolerance," NYT (8.4.10); Letters to the Editor, NYT (8.4.10); Friedman, "Broadway and the Mosque," NYT (8.4.10); "A Vote for Religious Freedom," WP (8.4.10); McManus, "A Mosque

near Ground Zero: It's the Wise Choice," LAT (8.8.10); Barnard, "For Muslim Center Sponsors, Early Missteps Fueled a Storm," NYT (8.11.10); Lee, "U.S. State Department Sending Imam of Proposed New York Mosque to Middle East," WP (8.12.10); "Obama Remarks during Iftar Dinner at the White House," WP (8.13.10); Stolberg, "Obama Backs Islam Center near 9/11 Site," NYT (8.14.10); Letters to the Editor, NYT (8.14.10); Nicholas & Love, "Obama Supports Plan for Mosque near Ground Zero," LAT (8.14.10); Nicolas & Santa Cruz, "Obama Again Defends Right to Put Mosque near Ground Zero," LAT (8.15.10); Stolberg, "Obama Says Mosque Remarks Were about Rights," NYT (8.15.10); Nicholas, "Mosque Takes Obama Off-Message on Gulf Coast," LAT (8.15.10); Hertzberg, "Zero Grounds," *The New Yorker* (8.16.10); Douthat, "Islam in Two Americas," NYT (8.16.10); Hulse, "G.O.P. Seizes on Islamic Center near Ground Zero as Election Issue," NYT (8.17.10); "The Constitution and the Mosque," NYT (8.17.10); "President Obama Needs to Show Strong Leadership on the Mosque Debate," WP (8.17.10); Cillizza, "Democrats Divided over Proposed NYC Mosque," WP (8.17.10); Hook & Hamburger, "New York Mosque Debate Splits GOP," LAT (8.17.10); Boorstein, "In Flap over Mosque near Ground Zero, Conservative Writers Gaining Influence," WP (8.18.10); "Where Are the Republicans Who Will Reject Pandering and Prejudice?" WP (8.19.10); Hernandez, "Archbishop Offers to Mediate Islamic Center Controversy," NYT (8.19.10); Thompson & Sonmez, "To N.Y. Muslims, Islamic Center near Ground Zero Would Be More Than a Mosque," WP (8.19.10); Barnard, "Parsing the Record of Feisal Abdul Rauf," NYT (8.21.10); Kristof, "Taking bin Laden's Side," NYT (8.22.10); Barbaro, "In Governor's Race, Lazio Finds an Issue in the Furor over Islamic Center," NYT (8.23.10); Grynbaum, "Two Sides Face Off in Protests over Muslim Center," NYT (8.23.10); Letters to the Editor, NYT (8.24.10); "Mr. Lazio's Bid for Attention," NYT (8.24.10); Barbaro, "As Bloomberg Affirms Muslim Center Support, Assembly Speaker Differs," NYT (8.25.10); Letters to the Editor, NYT (8.25.10); Rutten, "More Than a Mosque," LAT (8.25.10); Barnard & Haughney, "Islamic Center also Challenges a Young Builder," NYT (8.27.10); Krugman, "It's Witch-Hunt Season," NYT (8.30.10); Shaheen, "There Is No Struggle between Islam and America, Imam Says," *The National* (Abu Dhabi) (8.30.10); "New Yorkers Strongly Oppose Mosque near Ground Zero, Poll Shows," LAT (8.31.10); "Who Else Will Speak Up?" NYT (8.31.10); Baum, "New York Muslim Leaders Defend Islam," LAT (9.1.10); Barbaro & Connelly, "New York Poll Finds Wariness on Muslim Site," NYT (9.3.10); Santos, "In a Room near Ground Zero, a Preacher Rails against Islam," NYT (9.6.10); Cohen & Dropp, "Most Americans Object to Planned Islamic Center near Ground Zero, Poll Finds," WP (9.9.10); Vitello, "For Holy Days, Weighing Words on Islamic Center," NYT (9.9.10); Zucchino & Susman, "Florida Pastor Says He May Burn Korans After All," LAT (9.10.10); "A Call to Reconciliation," NYT (9.10.10); "On the Eve of 9/11, President Obama Shares a Message on

Unity," WP (9.11.10); Susman & Drogin, "Tension Marks This Year's 9/11 Remembrance," LAT (9.11.10); "Sept. 11, 2010: The Right Way to Remember," NYT (9.11.10); Barnard & Fernandez, "On Anniversary of Sept. 11, Rifts amid Mourning," NYT (9.12.10); Ramadan, "Even Now, Muslims Must Have Faith in America," WP (9.12.10); Baum, Susman & Drogin, "Angry Tones Mix with Somber at Sept. 11 Memorials," LAT (9.12.10); DeYoung, "N.Y. Imam: 'Every Option' Being Considered on Islamic Community Center," WP (9.13.10); Barnard, "One Project, One Faith, and Two Men Who Differ," NYT (9.17.10); Barnard, "After Day of Intense Talks, Muslim Leaders United behind Community Center," NYT (9.21.10); Barnard, "Muslim Center's Developer to Use Islamic Loan Plan," NYT (9.30.10); "Imam's Wife Tells of Death Threats," NYT (10.4.10); Barnard & Feuer, "Outraged and Outrageous," NYT (10.8.10); Vitello, "Imam Behind Project Plans U.S. Speaking Tour," NYT (12.24.10); Semple, "Opponent Seeks to Block Construction of Downtown Mosque," NYT (1.11.11); Vitello, "Amid Rift, Imam's Role in Islam Center Is Sharply Cut," NYT (1.15.11); Vitello, "Imam Stirs Confusion Regarding Islamic Center," NYT (2.1.11); Moynihan, "Fight on Islamic Center Flares Anew As Ex-Firefighter Takes His Case to Court," NYT (3.16.11); Baum, "The Man behind the Manhattan Mosque," LAT (4.6.11); Moynihan, "Judge Rules Ex-Firefighter Cannot Sue over Mosque," NYT (7.11.11); "Once-Controversial Islamic Center Opens in New York," LAT (9.22.11); Flegenheimer, "Rent Dispute Endangers Mosque Plan," NYT (10.17.11); Otterman, "Donor, Citing Fraud, Sues Imam Tied to Mosque near Ground Zero," NYT (2.6.13); Kaminer, "Ex-Leader of Planned Mosque near Ground Zero Settles Suit with Donor," NYT (6.8.13); Nussbaum (2012: chap. 6); Otterman, "Developer Scales Back Plans for Muslim Center near Ground Zero," NYT (4.30.14); Kaysen, "Condo Tower to Rise Where Muslim Community Center Was Proposed," NYT (5.13.17).

73 Vitello, "Heated Opposition to a Proposed Mosque," NYT (6.11.10); Dwyer, "A Marine, a Mosque, a Question," NYT (6.20.10); "Reason Prevails over Planned Mosque in Temecula," LAT (8.4.10); Goodstein, "Around Country, Mosque Projects Meet Opposition," NYT (8.8.10); Applebome, "In This Town, Open Arms for a Mosque," NYT (8.19.10); Gowen, "Far from Ground Zero, Other Plans for Mosques Run into Vehement Opposition," WP (8.23.10); Brown, "Arson Case at Mosque in Tennessee Spreads Fear," NYT (8.31.10); Schwartz, "Zoning Law Aside, Mosque Projects Face Battles," NYT (9.4.10); Otterman, "A Mosque Invisible to Many Is a Target," NYT (9.4.10); "Tennessee: U.S. Attorney Defends Constitutionality of Mosque," NYT (10.19.10); Serrano, "Justice Dept. Says Opposing Tenn. Mosque Could Be a Crime," LAT (10.19.10); "Tennessee: Court Battle over Murfreesboro Mosque," NYT (11.12.10); "Tennessee: Bid to Stop Mosque Fails," NYT (11.18.10); "California: Mosque Is Approved," NYT (1.27.11); "Temecula's Mosque Moment," LAT (1.28.11); "No Room for Tolerance," NYT (9.19.11); "Tennessee: Judge Rescinds Approval of New Mosque," NYT (5.30.12);

Severson, "Texas Man Is Accused of Threatening Tennessee Mosque," NYT (6.22.12); Severson, "Judge Allows Muslims to Use Tennessee Mosque," NYT (7.18.12); "Tennessee: More Delays for Permitting of Mosque," NYT (7.20.12); Brown & Hauser, "After Struggle, Tennessee Mosque Opens," NYT (8.11.12); "Ramadan in Murfreesboro," NYT (8.20.12).

74 Cumming-Bruce & Erlanger, "Swiss Ban Building of Minarets on Mosques," NYT (11.29.09).

75 De la Baume, "France: Court Cancels Permit for Grand Mosque of Marseille," NYT (10.28.11).

76 ACLU, Nationwide Anti-Mosque Activity (n.d.), https://action.aclu.org.maps/map-nationwid-anti-mosque-activity (last accessed February 15, 2018).

77 Ghosh, "Islamophobia: Does America Have a Muslim Problem?" Time (8.30.10).

78 Ruzich, "DuPage Zoning Panel Opposes Plan for Mosque Near Willowbrook," CT (1.14.11); "Naperville Not Putting Out Welcome Mat for Islamic Religious Center," CT (10.7.11).

79 "A Harvest of Anti-Muslim Hatred," WP (11.25.15); Dwyer, "Muslims Sue over Denial of Bid to Build Mosque in New Jersey Suburb," NYT (3.11.16); Shepherd, "A Muslim Community in Virginia Feels the Heat of Extremists' Sins," NYT (6.22.16); Shepherd, "Township Saw a Zoning Issue. The Justice Department Saw Religious Discrimination," NYT (8.7.16); Bidgood, "Muslims Seek New Burial Ground, and a Small Town Balks," NYT (8.29.16); Wootson, "Georgia Officials Were Set to Approve a New Mosque – Until an Armed Militia Threatened to Protest," WP (9.14.16); "Northern Virginia, County Bigwigs Cry 'Sewage' to Block a Mosque," WP (12.16.16); Foderaro, "The Mosque Next Door: City Law vs. Houses of Faith," NYT (12.21.16); Victor, "Muslim Group Wins Right to Build Mosque in Michigan City," NYT (2.22.17); Otterman, "Mosque Is Blocked in New Jersey, but Dispute Is Far from Over," NYT (3.11.17); Dwyer, "A New Jersey Township Wielded its Zoning Rules as a Barrier to Islam," NYT (5.24.17); Rojas, "Settlements with New Jersey Suburb Clear the Way for a Proposed Mosque," NYT (5.31.17).

80 United States v. Carolene Products, 304 U.S. 144, 152 n.4 (1938).

81 Nakamura, "Petraeus Condemns Florida Church's Plan to Burn Korans," WP (9.7.10); Cave, "In Florida, Many Lay Plans to Counter a Pastor's Message," NYT (9.8.10); Goodstein, "Concern Is Voiced over Religious Intolerance," NYT (9.8.10); Bahrampour & Boorstein, "U.S. Officials, Religious Leaders Condemn Plan to Burn Koran on 9/11," WP (9.8.10); Zucchino, "Reaction to Proposed Koran Burning Doesn't Faze Florida Church," LAT (9.8.10); Stein, "Koran Burning Spurs Ex-CIA Official to Lead Protest," WP (9.8.10); "Another Voice Raised against Bonfire," NYT (9.9.10); Boorstein, "Evangelical Leaders Try to Reach Out to the Pastor Who Plans to Burn the Koran," WP (9.9.10); Nakamura, "Burning the Koran: Muslim World Reaction," WP (9.9.10); Nakamura & Azraq, "Afghans Protest Florida Church's Plan to Burn Korans," WP (9.9.10); "Florida Cancels Plan to Burn Korans on Sept. 11," LAT (9.9.10);

Muskal, "Obama Urges Florida Pastor to Drop Plan to Burn Koran on 9/11 Anniversary," LAT (9.9.10); Hudak, "Florida Imam Hopeful Church Will Call Off Koran-Burning Event," *Orlando Sentinel* (9.9.10); "Don't Fan the Flames," LAT (9.9.10); Stelter, "A Fringe Pastor, a Fiery Stunt and the Media Spotlight's Glare," NYT (9.10.10); "Burning the Qur'an does not illuminate the Bible," NYT (9.10.10); Cave & Barnard, "Florida Minister Wavers on Plans to Burn Koran," NYT (9.10.10); Thompson & Bahrampour, "Obama Denounces Planned Koran Burning, Renews Call for Religious Tolerance," WP (9.10.10); Zucchino & Susman, "Florida Pastor Says He May Burn Korans After All," LAT (9.10.10); "Muslim World: Concerns Linger after Florida Pastor Says He Might Burn Korans After All," LAT (9.10.10); Farenthold & Gowen, "9/11 Commemorations Begin as America Examines its Relationship with Islam," WP (9.11.10); "Florida Pastor Says His Church Will Never Burn the Koran," LAT (9.11.10); Cave, "Gainesville, Aghast, Disavows Pastor's Talk of Burning Koran," NYT (9.11.10); "Sept. 11, 2010: The Right Way to Remember," NYT (9.11.10); Baktash, "Clashes Follow Afghan Protest over U.S. Pastor's Plan to Burn Koran," LAT (9.11.10); Rubin, "2 Afghans Killed in Protest over Koran," NYT (9.13.10); Boorstein, "Gainesville Turned Upside Down by Koran-Burning Threat, even after Cancellation," WP (9.12.10); Yardley & Kumar, "In Kashmir, Reports of Koran Desecration in the U.S. Bring Violent Reactions," NYT (9.14.10); Worth, "Ayatollah Speaks of Plot to Abuse Koran," NYT (9.14.10); Gerson, "The Internet: Enabling Pastor Terry Jones and Crazies Everywhere," WP (9.14.10); Cohen, "Pastor Terry Jones, as Right as John Brown," WP (9.14.10); Londoño & Hamdard, "Kabul Protest over Canceled Koran Burning in U.S. Turns Violent," WP (9.15.10); King, "Dozens Injured in Kabul Protest over Koran-Burning Threat," LAT (9.15.10); "India: Police Kill 4 Protesters," NYT (9.16.10); Nordland, "2 Afghans Are Killed in Protests over Koran," NYT (9.17.10); "Jim Wallis on the Story behind Pastor Terry Jones's Change of Heart," WP (9.19.10); "Afghan Officials: 7 Killed at UN Office When Quran Burning Protest Turns Violent," WP (4.1.11); Najfizada & Nordland, "Afghans Avenge Florida Koran Burning, Killing 12," NYT (4.2.11); Alvarez & Van Natta, "Pastor Who Burned Koran Demands Retribution," NYT (4.2.11); Partlow & Londoño, "At Least Seven Foreigners Killed in an Attack on U.N. Compound in Northern Afghanistan," WP (4.2.11); King, "Koran Burning Sparks More Violence in Afghanistan," LAT (4.2.11); Fausset, "Pastor of Church that Burned Koran Calls Afghan Mob Killings 'Very Tragic,'" LAT (4.2.11); Shah, "Afghan Protest over Quran Burning Leaves 9 Dead," MH (4.2.11); Boorstein, "Koran Burning by Florida Pastor Initially Went Unnoticed," WP (4.2.11); Alvarez, "Koran-Burning Pastor Unrepentant in Face of Furor," NYT (4.3.11); Shah & Nordland, "Protests over Koran Burning Reach Kandahar," NYT (4.3.11); Partlow, "Protests over Koran Burning Spread in Afghanistan, with 9 Dead in Kandahar," WP (4.3.11); Sieff, "Florida Pastor Terry Jones's Koran Burning Has Far-Reaching Effect," WP (4.3.11); King, "9 More Killed in Afghan Protests over Koran-Burning," LAT (4.3.11); Partlow & Hamdard,

"Afghan Protests over Koran Burning in Florida Are Calmer on 3rd Day," WP (4.3.11); Shah & Nordland, "Violence Continues in Afghanistan over Koran Burning in Florida," NYT (4.4.11); King, "Taliban Exploits Afghan Riots over Koran Burning," LAT (4.4.11); Nordland, "Afghan Officer Turns against U.S. Soldiers, Killing 2," NYT (4.5.10); Rutten, "Florida Pastor Terry Jones and the Far Reach of Free Speech," LAT (4.6.11); Gall, "Taliban Seen Stirring Mob to Violence," NYT (4.10.11); Goldberg, "Free Speech and Burning Korans," LAT (4.12.11); Alvarez, "Pastor Who Burned Koran Says He Was Duped into Holding Back," NYT (4.17.11); "Pastor Is Jailed in Michigan over Planned March at Mosque," NYT (4.23.11); Chapman, "Michigan: Koran-Burning Pastor Draws a Boisterous Crowd," NYT (4.30.11); Erdbrink, "Iran Denounces Florida Pastor over Koran Burning," NYT (5.1.12).

82 *United States* v. *Schwimmer*, 279 U.S. 644 (1929) (dissent).
83 *Whitney* v. *California*, 274 U.S. 357 (1927).
84 *Gregory* v. *Chicago*, 394 U.Ss. 111 (1969) (Black, concurring); *Hill* v. *Colorado*, 530 U.S. 703 (2000).
85 "Benghazi Timeline," FactCheck.org (posted 10.26.12; updated 5.2.14); Kirkpatrick, Cowell & Myers, "U.S. Envoy to Libya Is Killed in Attack," NYT (9.12.12); DeYoung & Birnbaum, "U.S. Ambassador to Libya, 3 other Americans Killed in Benghazi," WP (9.12.12); Malika-Henderson & Boorstein, "Anti-Muslim Film Director in Hiding, Following Libya, Egypt Violence," WP (9.12.12); Kirkpatrick & Myers, "Libya Attack Brings Challenges for U.S.," NYT (9.13.12); Arrabyee & Cowell, "Turmoil Spreads to U.S. Embassy in Yemen," NYT (9.13.12); Goodstein, "American Muslim Leaders Condemn Attacks," NYT (9.13.12); Baker & Parker, "A Challenger's Criticism Is Furiously Returned," NYT (9.13.12); Nagourney, "Origins of Provocative Video Are Shrouded," NYT (9.13.12); "Murder in Benghazi," NYT (9.13.12); Malika-Henderson, "Anti-Muslim Film Director in Hiding, Following Libya, Egypt Violence," WP (9.13.12); Farhi, "Doubts Grown about Source of Anti-Muslim Film behind Attacks," WP (9.13.12); Kessler, "An Embassy Statement a Tweet, a Major Misunderstanding," WP (9.13.12); "Mr. Romney's Rhetoric on Embassy Attacks Is a Discredit to His Campaign," WP (9.13.12); Arghandiwal, "Afghanistan Bans YouTube to Block Anti-Muslim Film," Reuters (9.13.12); Kirkpatrick & Cowell, "Anti-American Protests over Film Enter 4th Day," NYT (9.14.12); Miller, "As Violence Spreads in Arab World, Google Blocks Access to Inflammatory Video," NYT (9.14.12); Rubin, "Afghanistan Tries to Block Video and Head Off Rioting," NYT (9.14.12); Nagourney & Kovaleski, "Man of Many Names Is Tied to a Video," NYT (9.14.12); Boorstein, Constable & Markon, "Origins of Controversial Anti-Muslim Video Remain a Mystery," WP (9.14.12); Lovett, "Man Linked to Film in Protests Is Questioned," NYT (9.16.12); Clark, "French Magazine Publishes Cartoons Mocking Mohammed," NYT (9.19.12); "Egypt: 8 Charged over Anti-Islam Film," NYT (9.19.12); Friedman, "Look in Your Mirror," NYT (9.19.12); Khazan, "German, Canadian Groups Plan Public Screenings of 'Innocence of Muslims,'" WP (9.19.12); Lane, "There's No

Place for Censorship-by-Riot," WP (9.20.12); Chayes, "Does 'Innocence of Muslims' Meet the Free-Speech Test?" LAT (9.18.12); Hussain & Leiby, "In Pakistan, 20 Killed on Day of Protest against Incendiary Video," WP (9.21.12); Welsh, "Pakistani Minister Offers Bounty over Anti-Islam Video," NYT (9.23.12); Keller, "The Satanic Video," NYT (9.24.12); "Pakistan Disowns Minister's Bounty on Filmmaker, Protests against Anti-Islam Film Roll On," WP (9.24.12); Cooper, "Obama Tells U.N. New Democracies Need Free Speech," NYT (9.26.12); "President Obama at the U.N.," NYT (9.26.12); "Mr. Obama's Refreshing Defense of Free Speech," WP (9.26.12); "Pakistan Taliban's 'Amnesty' for Bounty Minister, Not in Hit List Now," AFP (9.26.12); Gearan, "Egypt's President Morse Tells U.N.: Insults to Muhammad 'Unacceptable,'" WP (9.26.12); Barnes, "Man Tied to Anti-Islam Video Held on Probation Charge," NYT (8.28.12); "Al-Qaeda Leader al-Zawahri Urges Muslims to Fight U.S. over Prophet Film," WP (10.13.12); Barnes, "Man behind Anti-Islam Video Gets Prison Term," NYT (11.8.12); Kovaleski & Barnes, "From Man Who Insulted Muhammad, No Regret," NYT (11.26.12); "Calif. Judge Denies Another Bid by Actress to Take Down Anti-Muslim Film from YouTube," WP (11.30.12); Ahmed, "YouTube Ban, Spurred by Anti-Islamic Video, Is Met with Shrugs," NYT (12.6.12); Masood, "Pakistan Lifts YouTube Ban, for 3 Minutes," NYT (12.30.12); "Egypt Court Orders Block on YouTube Access," NYT (2.10.13); *Garcia v. Nakoula*, 2012 WL 12878355 (CD Cal 2012), rev'd sub nom. *Garcia v. Google*, 743 F.3d 1258 (9th Cir. 2014), superseded by 766 F.3d 929 (9th Cir. 2014), rev'd 786 F.3d 733 (9th Cir. en banc 2015); "Appeals Court Orders YouTube to Remove Anti-Muslim Film," WP (2.26.14).

86 Huntington (1996).

87 *R.A.V. v. City of St. Paul*, 505 U.S. 377 (1992).

88 Boorstein, "For Critic of Islam, 'Sharia' Becomes Shorthand for Extremism," WP (8.25.10); Robinson, "Sharia as the New Red Menace," WP (9.21.10); Sulzberger, "Voters Face Decisions on a Mix of Issues," NYT (10.6.10); Riccardi, "Measure Would Outlaw Islamic Law in Oklahoma–Where It Doesn't Exist," LAT (10.29.10); Smith, "Judge Blocks Oklahoma's Ban on Islamic Law," CNN (11.8.10); "Overwrought in Oklahoma," LAT (11.12.10); McKinley, "Oklahoma Surprise: Islam as an Election Issue," NYT (11.15.10); "Intolerance and the Law in Oklahoma," NYT (11.29.10); McKinley, "Judge Blocks Oklahoma's Ban on Using Shariah Law in Court," NYT (11.30.10); Elliott, "It's Official: Sharia Will Be an Issue in 2012," Salon.com (3.14.11); Brody, "Donald Trump Says Something in Koran Teaches a 'Very Negative Vibe,'" CNN.com (4.12.11); Robinson, "Stand Up to Herman Cain's Bigotry," WP (7.19.11); Alliott, "The Man behind the Anti-Shariah Movement," NYT (7.31.11); Letters to the Editor, NYT (8.6.11); "Some Very Good Sense," NYT (8.19.11); Stern, "Don't Fear Islamic Law in America," NYT (9.3.11); "Nashville Hotel Backs Out of Anti-Sharia Conference," LAT (10.25.11); Gerson, "The Problem with Gingrich's Simplistic Attack on Sharia," WP (12.13.11); Shane, "In Islamic Law, Gingrich Sees a Mortal

Threat," NYT (12.22.11); Eckholm, "Oklahoma: Court Upholds Blocking of Amendment against Shariah Law," NYT (1.11.12); "Legislature Approves Bill to Bar Use of Islamic Law, Other Foreign Codes, in Kansas Courts," WP (5.13.12); "Kansas: Law Bans the Use of Foreign Legal Codes," NYT (5.26.12); Howerton, "Voters in This State Overwhelmingly Pass Amendment to Ban Sharia Law, Other 'Foreign Laws' – Here Are the Details," The Blaze (11.5.14); *Awad v. Ziriax*, 754 F.Supp.2d 1298 (W.D.Ok. 2010), aff'd, 670 F.3d 1111 (10th Cir. 2012).
89 Gusfield (1963); Cohen (1972).
90 Hernandez, "Muslim 'Radicalization' Is Focus of Planned Inquiry," NYT (12.17.10); Freedlander, "Peter King on Muslim Hearings," New York Observer (12.20.10); "Homeland Blather," NYT (1.2.11); Wan, "Long Island Muslims Fear Their Congressman's Hearings Could Inflame Islamophobia," WP (1.23.11); Serrano, "Coalition Urges Halt to House Hearings on Muslim Radicalization," LAT (2.3.11); Goodstein, "Muslims to Be Hearings' Main Focus," NYT (2.8.11); Schmitt, "Lawmakers Hear of Threat by Domestic Terrorists," NYT (2.10.11); Finn, "Terrorist Threat May Be at Most 'Heightened State' since 9/11, Napolitano Says," WP (2.9.11); Serrano, "U.S. Terrorism Threat at 'Heightened' State," LAT (2.9.11); "Targeting Muslims," LAT (2.10.11); Finn, "As Rep. Peter King's Muslim Hearings Approach, His Past Views Draw Ire," WP (3.5.11); Stolberg, "White House Seeks to Allay Muslims' Fears on Terror Hearings," NYT (3.7.11); Letter to Rep. King from 55 organizations (3.7.11); Nicholas, "White House Seeks to Reassure Muslims," LAT (3.7.11); Herbert, "Flailing after Muslims," NYT (3.8.11); "Peter King's Obsession," NYT (3.8.11); Robinson, "Stoking Irrational Fears about Islam," WP (3.8.11); Cohen, "Rep. Peter King's Hearings on Islamic Radicalization: Fuel for the Bigots," WP (3.8.11); Shane, "For Lawmaker Examining Terror, A Pro-I.R.A. Past," NYT (3.9.11); Bennett & Baum, "Rep. Peter King's Hearing on American Muslims a 'Very Personal Quest,'" LAT (3.9.11); Stolberg, "Domestic Terrorism Hearing Stirs Passion," NYT (3.10.11); Boorstein & Farenthold, "Peter King Tempers Rhetoric on Muslims as Congressional Hearing Gets Underway," WP (3.10.11); Fahrenthold & Boorstein, "Rep. Peter King's Muslim Hearings: A Key Moment in an Angry Conversation," WP (3.10.11); "Homegrown Islamic Radicalization: Worth Studying," WP (3.10.11); Oliphant, "Rep. Peter King Opens Muslim 'Radicalization' Hearing, Saying It 'Must Go Forward,'" LAT (3.10.11); Stolberg & Goodstein, "Domestic Terrorism Hearing Opens with Contrasting Views on Dangers," NYT (3.11.11); Stanley, "Terror Hearing Puts Lawmakers in Harsh Light," NYT (3.11.11); Farenthold & Boorstein, "Rep. Peter King's Muslim Hearing: Plenty of Drama, Less Substance," WP (3.11.11); Robinson, "Peter King's Modern-Day Witch Hunt," WP (3.11.11); Shane, "Congressional Hearing Puts Muslim Civil Rights Group in the Hot Seat Again," NYT (3.12.11); "Mr. King's Sound and Fury," NYT (3.12.11); Milbank, "Rep. King's Red Scare," WP (3.13.11); "The Truth about Muslims," NYT (4.2.11); Vitello, "Critics Call Terrorism Hearing

in Manhattan Anti-Muslim," NYT (4.7.11); Serrano, "Parties Clash over Hearing on Muslim Radicalization," LAT (6.16.11); Yager, "Rep. King's Fourth Muslim-American Radicalization Hearing to Focus on Military," *The Hill* (12.6.11); Herrige, "Military a Growing Terrorist Target, Lawmakers Warn," Fox News (12.6.11); Yager, "Military Communities 'Most Sought-After' Target for Terrorists in US, Says GOP," *The Hill* (12.7.11); "GOP Rep. King Defends Hearings on Muslim Radicalization, Terrorism Ties," Fox News.com (6.20.12); Lisee " 'Radicalization Hearings on Muslim [*sic*] Return to Capitol," WP (6.21.12); "U.S. Congress Debates Threat from Islamists," AFP (6.21.12).

91 Kurzman & Schanzer, "The Growing Right-Wing Terror Threat," NYT (6.16.15); Shane, "Homegrown Extremists Tied to Deadlier Toll than Jihadists in U.S. since 9/11," NYT (6.25.15).

92 Richardson, "Carson Links Boston Marathon Bombers, Refugee Crisis," *The Hill* (9.13.15).

93 Rogers, "Donald Trump Does Not Correct a Man Who Called Obama a Muslim," NYT (9.19.15); Rappeport, "Jeb Bush Says President Obama is 'an American' and 'a Christian,' " NYT (9.19.15); "Prejudice on Display in the Republican Campaign for President," WP (9.22.15); Rappeport & Flegenheimer, "Ben Carson Can't Change Subject after Contentious Remark," NYT (9.23.15); "The Republican Attack on Muslims," NYT (9.23.15); Scott, "Ben Carson: Money Pouring in after Muslim Comments," CNN (9.23.15).

94 Kaczynski, "Huckabee: Don't Admit Syrian Refugees because They Might Be 'Violent and Vicious People,' " BuzzFeed (9.24.15); Baily, "Donald Trump Says He Would Consider Closing Down some Mosques in the U.S.," WP (10.21.15); Martin, "In Presidential Campaign, It's Now Terrorism, Not Taxes," NYT (11.16.15); Hulse, "Parties Split on Response but United Behind France," NYT (11.17.15); Healy & Bosman, "G.O.P. Governors Vow to Close Doors to Syrian Refugees," NYT (11.17.15); Haberman, "Donald Trump Questions Whether Syrian Refugees Are 'Trojan Horse,' " NYT (11.17.15); Rappeport, "Donald Trump Repeats Call to Inspect Mosques for Signs of Terrorism," NYT (11.17.15); "After the Paris Attacks, Vilifying Refugees," NYT (11.17.15); "After Paris, America Cannot Abandon Refugees in Need," WP (11.17.15); Lichtblau, "White House Affirms Syrian Refugee Plan despite Paris Attacks," NYT (11.18.15); Parker, "Jeb Bush Urges Caution on Accepting Syrian Refugees," NYT (11.18.15); Herszenhorn & Shear, "Republicans Call for Halt to Syrian Refugee Program," NYT (11.18.15); Robbins, "Mallow Welcomes a Syrian Family to Connecticut as Christie Shuns Refugees," NYT (11.19.15); "Refugees from the War Aren't the Enemy," NYT (11.19.15); Werner, "Obama Threatens to Veto House GOP Bill on Syrian Refugees," AP (11.18.15); deBonis, "Senators Eye New Restrictions on Visa Waivers after Paris Attacks," WP (11.18.15); Steinhauer & Shear, "House Approves Tougher Refugee Screening, Defying Veto Threat," NYT (11.20.15); Harris & Schmidt, "U.S. Tightens Visa-Waiver Program in Bid to Deter Militants," NYT (12.1.15); "A Safeguard against Threats

from Abroad," NYT (12.3.15); Marcos, "House Votes Overwhelmingly to Restrict Visa Waivers for Travelers," *The Hill* (12.9.15).

95 Gabriel, "Donald Trump Says He'd 'Absolutely' Require Muslims to Register," NYT (11.20.15); Rappeport, "Muslim Group Assails Remarks by Donald Trump and Ben Carson," NYT (11.20.15); "Rand Paul Refugee Amendment," Scrbd (11.19.15); Walker, "Donald Trump Has Big Plans for 'Radical Islamic' Terrorists and 'That Communist' Bernie Sanders," Yahoo! Politics (11.19.15); Haberman & Pérez-Peña, "Donald Trump Sets Off a Furor with Call to Register Muslims in the U.S.," NYT (11.21.15); Rappeport, "Terrorism and Refugees Dominate Week in Presidential Race," NYT (11.21.15); Haberman, "Donald Trump Calls for Surveillance of 'Certain Mosques' and a Syrian Refugee Database," NYT (11.22.15); Corasanti, "Donald Trump Insists He Saw Celebrations in New Jersey on Sept. 11," NYT (11.23.15); Rappeport, "Ben Carson Clarifies Remarks on Muslims Celebrating on 9/11," NYT (11.24.15); Dwyer, "A Definitive Debunking of Donald Trump's 9/11 Claims," NYT (11.25.15); Gass, "Trump: We Have to Take Out ISIL Members' Families," Politico (12.13.15).

96 "The Price of Fear," NYT (11.21.15); Rosenthal, "Donald Trump's Horrifying Plan for American Muslims," NYT (11.21.15); Bruni, "How ISIS Defeats Us," NYT (11.22.15); Kristof, "The Statue of Liberty Must Be Crying with Shame," NYT (11.22.15); Inslee, "Why My State Won't Close Its Door to Syrian Refugees," NYT (11.21.15); "Mr. Trump's Applause Lies," NYT (11.24.15); "Republicans Need to Stand Up To Trump's Bullying," WP (11.24.15); "Repugnant Religious Litmus Tests," NYT (11.25.15); Ignatius, "Donald Trump Undermines Our Fight against the Islamic State," WP (11.25.15); Marcus, "The Danger of Ignoring Religious Bigotry," WP (11.25.15).

97 "Tough Talk and a Cowardly Vote," NYT (12.4.15); Barbaro & Gabriel, "After San Bernardino Attack, Republican Candidates Talk 'War,'" NYT (12.6.15); Baker & Schmitt, "California Attack Has U.S. Rethinking Strategy on Homegrown Terror," NYT (12.6.15); Healy & Barbaro, "Donald Trump Calls for Barring Muslims from Entering U.S.," NYT (12.8.15); "Bizarre Responses to a Plea for Reason," NYT (12.8.15); Haberman, "Donald Trump Deflects Withering Fire on Muslim Plan," NYT (12.9.15); Fernandez & Preston, "Anxiety Grows in Texas with Syrians Due to Arrive Soon," NYT (12.9.15); Sullivan & Johnson, "Trump's Proposal to Keep Out Muslims Crosses a Line for Many in Both Parties," WP (12.9.15); Tharoor, "The Republican Obsession with 'Radical Islam' Is a Smokescreen for Something Else," WP (12.10.15); Corasanti, "Bernie Sanders Warns of Demagogues and Division in Mosque Visit," NYT (12.17.15); Democratic Presidential Debate (1.17.16); Harris, "Obama in Mosque Visit, Denounces Anti-Muslim Bias," NYT (2.3.16).

98 Bruni, "What to Tell Donald Trump," NYT (12.9.15); Marcus, "Donald Trump Has Crossed an Incrossable [sic] Line of Bigotry," WP (12.9.15); Parker, "Donald Trump: The Islamic State's Secret Weapon?" WP (12.9.15); Milbank, "Donald Trump, America's Modern Mussolini,"

WP (12.9.15); "It's Time for Republicans to Renounce Donald Trump's Candidacy," WP (12.9.15); Davis, "Obama Calls for End to Bigotry, in Implicit Rebuke of Donald Trump," NYT (12.10.15); Dionne, "The Slippery Slope to Trump's Proposed Ban on Muslims," WP (12.10.15); "The Trump Effect and How It Spreads," NYT (12.10.15); Lane, "Trump's Muslim Ban Falls into a Tradition of American Sloppy Thinking," WP (12.10.15); Krauthammer, "Why Take the Trump Stunt Seriously?" WP (12.11.15); Ignatius, "Trump's Anti-Muslim Rhetoric Will Live in Infamy in American History," WP (12.11.15); Robinson, "Donald Trump Ushers in a New Era of Pitchfork Populism," WP (12.11.15); King, "Donald Trump's Anti-Muslim Rhetoric Echoes the Red Scare Era," WP (12.12.15); "Facts & Figures: Most Oppose Barring Muslims from America," NYT (12.12.15); Partnership for New York City, Advertisement, NYT (12.10.15); #WeAreBetterThanThis, Advertisement, NYT (12.10.15); "The Tarnished Trump Brand," NYT (12.13.15); "For Republicans, Bigotry Is the New Normal," WP (12.17.15); "Despite What Donald Trump Says, Americans Are Better Than This," WP (12.24.15); "What Would Martin Luther King Do?" WP (1.18.16).

99 Rappeport, "Donald Trump's First Television Ad Focuses on Immigration," NYT (1.4.16); RNC Debate (1.14.16); Johnson, "Trump Tells Story about Killing Terrorists with Bullets Dipped in Pigs' Blood, Though There's No Proof of It," WP (2.20.16); "Republican Leaders' Silence on Trump Is Inexcusable – and Irrational," WP (2.23.16); "The GOP's Uncivil Debate Was Full of Ignorant Stereotyping," WP (3.12.16); McCaskill & Collins, "Cruz Calls for Patrols of Muslim Neighborhoods," Politico (3.22.16); "After Brussels, Trump, Cruz Slam Obama, Call for Halts to Immigration Programs," Fox News (3.22.16); "Standing with Brussels against Terrorism and Fear," NYT (3.23.16); "Mr. Cruz's Irresponsible Rhetoric on Muslims in America," WP (3.26.16); Anderson Cooper Interview with Donald Trump (3.29.16); Easley, "Half of Voters Back Muslim Travel Ban, Patrols of Muslim Neighborhoods," Morning Consult (3.29.16).

100 Martin & Burns, "Blaming Muslims after Attack, Donald Trump Tosses Pluralism Aside," NYT (6.13.16); "Donald Trump's Assault on Our Values," WP (6.14.16); "Mr. Obama's Powerful Words about Terrorism," NYT (6.15.16); "Gingrich: Let's Create a New Version of House Un-American Activities Committee," TalkingPointsMemo. com (6.14.16); Hudson, "House Republicans Seek Blanket Ban on All Refugees," FP (6.15.16); Diamond, "Trump Doubles Down on Calls for Mosque Surveillance," CNN (6.15.16); Mahler, "Donald Trump Calls for Profiling to Stop Terrorists," NYT (6.19.16); "Who 'Looks Like' a Terrorist in America?" WP (6.21.16); "Slamming Shut America's Door," NYT (6.22.16); "Mr. Trump's Gibberish on Muslims," WP (6.30.16); Rappeport, "Newt Gingrich Echoes Donald Trump with Remarks on Muslims and Terrorism," NYT (7.15.16); "Our Best Defense against Terrorism," NYT (7.16.16); Morell, "Spooks for Hillary," NYT (8.5.16);

Zezima, "Donald Trump Calls for 'Extreme Vetting' of People Looking to Come to the United States," WP (8.15.16); "Mr. Trump's Foreign Policy Confusions," NYT (8.16.16); "How Can America Recover from Donald Trump?" NYT (8.21.16); Burns & Confessore, "After Bombings, Hillary Clinton and Donald Trump Clash over Terrorism," NYT (9.20.16); "After the Weekend's Attacks, Clinton Acted like a Leader. Trump Did Not," WP (9.20.16).

101 Presidential Debate (10.9.16).

102 "Denounce the Hate, Mr. Trump," NYT (11.10.16); "Michael Flynn: An Alarming Pick for National Security Adviser," NYT (11.19.16); "Trump Has Made Some Dangerous Appointments," WP (11.19.16); Warrick & Hauslohner, "Trump's Security Picks Deepen Muslim Worries about an Anti-Islamic White House," WP (11.20.16); "Donald Trump Rages, at the Wrong Target," NYT (11.22.16); Savage, "Trump Calls for Revoking Flag Burner's Citizenship. Court Rulings Forbid It," NYT (11.30.16); Liptak, "Trump vs. The Constitution," NYT (11.30.16); "Mr. Trump, Meet the Constitution," NYT (11.30.16); "In One Tweet, Trump Trashes Two Constitutional Amendments," WP (11.30.16); "The Ohio State Attack Teaches Us to Be Cautious – but Not to Shut our Doors," WP (12.4.16); Zapotosky, Horwitz & Nakashima, "Sessions Emphasizes the Primacy of the Law over His Political Views," WP (1.10.17); "'I Think Islam Hates Us,'" NYT (1.26.17).

103 Shear & Cooper, "Trump Bars Refugees and Citizens of 7 Muslim Countries," NYT (1.28.17); Shear, Kulish, Fung & Jan, "Tech Firms Recall Employees to U.S., Denounce Trump's Ban on Refugees from Muslim Countries," WP (1.29.17); Feuer, "Judge Blocks Trump Order on Refugees Amid Chaos and Outcry Worldwide," NYT (1.29.17); "Donald Trump's Muslim Ban Is Cowardly and Dangerous," NYT (1.29.17); "Pandering to Fear," WP (1.29.17); Wang, "Trump Asked for a 'Muslim Ban,' Giuliani Says – and Ordered a Commission to Do It 'Legally,'" WP (1.30.17); "Pakistan Interior Minister Decries Trump's Ban," NYT (1.30.17); Smale, "European Leaders Reject Trump's Refugee Ban as Violating Principles," NYT (1.30.17); Baker, "Travelers Stranded and Protests Swell over Trump Order," NYT (1.30.17); Fung & Wong, "'Apple Would Not Exist without Immigrants': Companies at Trump's Technology Summit React to His Travel Ban," WP (1.30.17); Apuzzo, Lichtblau & Shear, "Acting Attorney General Orders Justice Dept. Not to Defend Refugee Ban," NYT (1.30.17); Shear, Landler Apuzzo & Lichtblau, "Trump Fires Acting Attorney General Who Defied Him," NYT (1.31.17); Gettleman, "State Dept. Dissent Cable on Trump's Ban Draws 1,000 Signatures," NYT (2.1.17); Seik, "'Not the America I Know': George W. Bush's Daughter Wants You to Remember His Speech on Islam," WP (2.2.17); Kulish, Dickerson & Savage, "Court Temporarily Blocks Trump's Travel Ban, and Airlines Are Told to Allow Passengers," NYT (2.4.17); Zapotosky, Aratani & Jouvenal, "Federal Judge Temporarily Blocks Trump's Entry Order Nationwide," WP (2.4.17); Landler, "Trump Attacks Judge Who Blocked Visa Ban,"

NYT (2.4.17); Landler, "Appeals Court Rejects Request to Immediately Restore Travel Ban," NYT (2.5.17); Posner, "Gorsuch Must Condemn Trump's Attack on a Judge," NYT (2.5.17); Yoo, "Executive Power Run Amuck," NYT (2.6.17); Scarborough, "Trump's Reckless Shot at a Federal Judge," WP (2.6.17); Baker, "Trump Clashes Early with Courts, Portending Years of Legal Battles," NYT (2.6.17); "President Trump's Real Fear: The Courts," NYT (2.7.17); Zapotosky & Barnes, "Trump Suggests Only Politics Could Lead Court to Rule against his Immigration Order," WP (2.8.17); Davis, "Neil Gorsuch's Criticism Wasn't Aimed at Trump, Aides Say in Reversal," NYT (2.10.17); Baker, "Trump Vows Quick Action to Stop Terrorism after Setback in Court," NYT (2.11.17); "The 9th Circuit Makes the Right Call on Trump's Travel Ban," WP (2.11.17); Geidner & Tillman, "Courts Still Proceeding with Lawsuits – and a New Injunction – against Trump's Travel Ban," BuzzFeed (2.13.17); Hensch, "White House Adviser Stephen Miller: 'Nothing Wrong' with Trump's Travel Order," The Hill (2.21.17); Siegel, "Stephen Miller Called Brooklyn U.S. Attorney at Home and Told Him How to Defend Travel Ban in Court," New York Daily News (2.18.17); "Breaking the Anti-Immigrant Fever," NYT (2.19.17).

104 Burns, "Hawaii Sues to Block Trump Travel Ban," NYT (3.9.17); Burns, "Trump's New Travel Ban May Be Hard to Beat. But States Are Trying," NYT (3.10.17); Burns, "2 Federal Judges Rule against Trump's Latest Travel Ban," NYT (3.16.17); Shear, "Who Undercut President Trump's Travel Ban? Candidate Trump," NYT (3.16.17); Fabian, "Trump Blasts Court Ruling Blocking Revised Travel Order," The Hill (3.15.17); Shelbourne, "Appeals Court Won't Rehear Case on Trump's Original Travel Ban," The Hill (3.15.17); Davis, "Trump Urges Unity on Health Overhaul," NYT (3.16.17); Lawfare (3.16.17); Liptak, "Campaign Pledges Haunt Trump in Court," NYT (3.17.17); Fabian, "Trump Blasts Court Ruling Blocking Revised Travel Order," The Hill (3.15.17); Thrush, "'I'll Criticize Judges,' Trump Says, Hours after a Scolding for Doing Just That," NYT (3.22.17); Beavers, "Hawaii Attorney General Slams Sessions for Remark about Federal Judge," The Hill (4.20.17); Baker, "Defiant Trump Vows to Take Immigration Case to Supreme Court," NYT (4.25.17); Westwood, "Trump 'Absolutely' Looking at Breaking up 9th Circuit," Washington Examiner (4.26.17); Washington v. Trump, 2017 WL 462040 (W.D.Wa. 2017), aff'd, 847 F.3d 1151 (9th Cir. 2017), denying reconsideration en banc, 858 F.3d 1168 (9th Cir. 2017).

105 Liptak, "Appeals Court Will Not Reinstate Trump's Revised Travel Ban," NYT (5.26.17); Baker, "Trump Doubles Down on Original 'Travel Ban,'" NYT (6.5.17); Liptak & Baker, "Trump Promotes Original 'Travel Ban,' Eroding His Legal Case," NYT (6.6.17); International Refugee Assistance Project v. Trump, 2017 WL 1018235 (D.Md. 2017), aff'd, 857 F.3d 554 (4th Cir. en banc 2017).

106 Dickerson & Saul, "Campuses Confront Hostile Acts against Minorities after Donald Trump's Election," NYT (11.10.16); Guerra,

"University of Michigan Student Wearing a Hijab Was Threatened with Being Set on Fire, Police Say," WP (11.14.16); Lichtblau, "Attacks on Muslim Americans Fuel Increase in Hate Crime, F.B.I. Says," NYT (11.15.16); Larimer, "A Hiker Wore a Bandanna for Sun Protection. Then She Found an Anti-Muslim Note on Her Car," WP (11.19.16); Nir & Southall, "Rally in Brooklyn Park Condemns Swastikas and 'Go Trump' Graffiti," NYT (11.21.16); Guerra, " 'Trump Is President … They'll Deport You Soon': Man Filmed Unloading on Muslims Uber Driver," WP (11.21.16); "Threats of an Anti-Muslim Holocaust," NYT (11.29.16); Guerra, " 'It's a Sickness': Letters Calling for Genocide of Muslims Sent to Mosques Across the Country," WP (11.30.16); Nir, "Finding Hate Crimes on the Rise, Leaders Condemn Vicious Acts," NYT (12.6.16); North, "The Scope of Hate in 2016," NYT (12.29.16); Mele, "Man Kicked J.F.K. Airport Worker Wearing Hijab, Prosecutor Says," NYT (1.27.17); "Majar, "India Condemns Deadly Shooting in Kansas as a Possible Hate Crime," NYT (2.24.17); Hedgpeth & Moyer, "Violent Threats Made in Letters to Two Muslims Facilities in Maryland," WP (3.1.17); Stack & Victor, "Hate Group Numbers in U.S. Rose for 2nd Year in a Row, Report Says," NYT (2.15.17); Wang, "A Man Assumed a Store's Indian Owners Were Muslim. So He Tried to Burn it Down, Police Say," WP (3.1.17); Barry, "Officials in U.S. and India Condemn Shooting of Sikh Man in Washington State," NYT (3.5.17); North, "What It Feels Like When a Mosque Is Threatened," NYT (3.10.17); Wootson, " 'Go Back to Your Country, Terrorist': Man Accused of Attacking Restaurant Employee with a Pipe," WP (3.13.17); Burch, "Spread of Hate Crimes Has Lawmakers Seeking Harsher Penalties," NYT (4.30.17); Haag, "Two Killed in Portland after Trying to Stop Anti-Muslim Rant, Police Say," NYT (5.27.17).

107 Goodstein, "Both Feeling Threatened, American Muslims and Jews Join Hands," NYT (12.6.16).

108 Maheshwari, "In Year of Anti-Muslim Vitriol, Brands Promote Inclusion," NYT (1.2.17).

109 Guerra, "Katy Perry's Chilling PSA Against Creating a Database of Muslims in the Country," WP (1.17.17); Soros, "When Hate Surges," NYT (3.17.17).

110 Rojas, "Man Gets 20-Year Sentence for Hate Crimes at a Queens Mosque," NYT (12.15.16); Stevens, "Kansas Man Indicted on Hate Crime Charges in Shooting of Indian Immigrants," NYT (6.10.17).

111 "Hateful Acts Are on the Rise, and It's Trump's Responsibility to Take a Stand," WP (11.17.16); "1942 All Over Again?" NYT (11.18.16); "Michael Flynn: An Alarming Pick for National Security Adviser," NYT (11.19.16); "Trump Has Made Some Dangerous Appointments," WP (11.19.16); "An Un-American Registry," WP (11.21.16); "Donald Trump Rages, at the Wrong Target," NYT (11.22.16); "Who Belongs in Trump's America?" NYT (2.28.17).

112 Kahn (1962).

113 Interview on NBC (9.16.01).
114 Phillips, "Sikh Soldier Allowed to Keep Beard in Rare Army Exemption," NYT (12.14.15); Phillips, "Sikh Soldier Sues Defense Dept., Citing Religious Discrimination," NYT (3.1.16); but see Rogers, "Citadel Denies Student's Request to Wear a Hijab," NYT (5.11.16).
115 See Table A5 in the Appendix.
116 "'Islam is Peace' Says President," White House Press Release (9.17.01).
117 Goodstein, "Both Feeling Threatened, American Muslims and Jews Join Hands," NYT (12.6.16).
118 Klasfield, "Creepy Social Media Trail in NYC Hate Crime Case," Courthouse News (8.28.15); Stack, "Hate Crime Inquiry Opened into Vandalism of Sikh Temple in California," NYT (12.10.15); Rojas, "Arson Is Suspected at a California Mosque," NYT (12.12.15); Rojas, "'Person of Interest' Detained in Mosque Fire in California," NYT (12.13.15); Stack, "California Police and F.B.I. Open Hate Crimes Inquiry into Vandalism of Mosques," NYT (12.14.15); "Two Teenagers Charged in Hate Crime Attack against Muslim Man in the Bronx," NYT (1.23.16); "Man Who Shot at Connecticut Mosque Is to Plead Guilty to Hate Crime," NYT (2.9.16); "Oregon Man Gets Probation for Fire at Mosque," NYT (3.3.16); Chokshi, "'Take It Off! This Is America!': Man Who Yanked Hijab Pleads Guilty to Religious Obstruction," WP (5.14.16); "Decorated Officer Charged with Threatening Muslims in North Carolina," NYT (6.11.16); "New York Man Due in Court, Charged with Slaying Muslim Imam, Assistant," NYT (8.16.16); Janny, "FBI Joins Investigation into June Shooting of Somali-American Men," *Minneapolis Star-Tribune* (8.16.16); Hauser, "Oklahoma Man Is Charged with Killing Lebanese-American Neighbor," NYT (8.24.16); Johnson, "Man Gets 15 Years for Somali Café Attack in North Dakota," Reuters (9.6.16); Mele, "Arrest Made in Arson at Mosque That Orlando Nightclub Gunman Attended," NYT (9.14.16); Mele, "2 Face Hate Crime Charges in Attack on Sikh Man in California," NYT (10.15.16); Smith, "3 Held in Bomb Plot against Somalis in Kansas," NYT (10.15.16); Rojas, "Man Gets 20-Year Sentence for Hate Crimes at a Queens Mosque," NYT (12.15.16); Mele, "Man Kicked J.F.K. Airport Worker Wearing Hijab, Prosecutor Says," NYT (1.27.17); but see Najarro, "No Jail Term for Threats against a Muslim Man," NYT (7.8.15).
119 Khan, "Attacks on American Muslims Are Un-American. Under Trump, They're On The Rise," WP (7.22.17).

CHAPTER 8   REVERSIBLE ERROR?

1 CRS reported that about 50 "homegrown violent jihadists" would be released in the decade following January 2017. Reichmann, "Should Springing of US Terrorism Convicts Alarm Americans?" AP (8.6.17).

2   323 U.S. 214, 245-46 (1944).
3   5 U.S. 137, 177 (1803).
4   Transcript of President Bush's Address to a Joint Session of Congress (9.20.01), www.cnn.com/2001/US/09/20/gen.bush.transcript (last accessed February 15, 2018).
5   Waldman & Pope, "'Crusade' Reference Reinforces Fears War on Terrorism Is Against Muslims," WSJ (9.21.01).
6   Brandeis & Abrams (1967).
7   See Wilson & Brown (2009); Engle et al. (2016a).
8   Lind (2008). For a comparison of Lebanon, Cyprus, South Africa, and Chile, see Kovras (2017).
9   Lind (2008: 34).
10 Herf (1997: 209, 271) and Frei (2002: 6), quoted in Lind (2008: 110).
11 Lind (2008: 127–28).
12 Ibid. 160–62.
13 Ibid. 84–85.
14 Fifield, "Abe Urged to Uphold Japan's Apology for Wartime Aggression," WP (4.20.15).
15 "South Korea, Japan Reach Landmark Deal on WWII Sex Slaves," NYT (12.28.15); Kim & Park, "South Korea, Japan Agree to Irreversibly End 'Comfort Women' Row," Reuters (12.28.15); Soble & Choe, "South Korean and Japanese Leaders Feel Backlash from 'Comfort Women' Deal," NYT (12.29.15); Fifield, "Cracks Appear in Japan–South Korea Deal on Wartime Sex Slaves," WP (12.31.15); Choe, "South Korea Illegally Held Prostitutes Who Catered to G.I.s Decades Ago, Court Says," NYT (1.20.17).
16 Soble & Sanger, "Shinzo Abe to Become First Japanese Leader to Visit Pearl Harbor," NYT (12.5.16); "Shinzo Abe at Pearl Harbor: 'Rest in Peace, Precious Souls of the Fallen,'" NYT (12.27.16).
17 "German President Visits Site of Rome's WWII-era Massacre," WP (5.3.17).
18 "Germany Investigating 2 Former SS Death Squad Members," WP (9.28.17).
19 Bruce, "U.N. Group Accuses Burundi Leaders of Crimes Against Humanity," NYT (9.5.17).
20 See Pugliese & Hufford (2006). But they often fail. Stover et al. (2016). On the turn to criminal law – the "anti-impunity" movement" – and its opponents, see Engle (2015, 2016); Engle et al. (2016a, 2016b).
21 Ryan (2012).
22 Rothschild, "Trial of Ivory Coast's Laurent Gbagbo Will Test International Criminal Court," NYT (1.27.16).
23 Simons, "Congolese Politician, Jean-Pierre Bemba, Sentenced to 18 Years for War Crimes," NYT (6.21.16).
24 Cowell, "20 Years After, Rwanda Pauses to Recall Carnage," NYT (4.7.14); "Apology over Rwanda Genocide," NYT (4.17.14).

Misplaced Faith in Body Language," NYT (3.24.14); Letter to the Editor, NYT (4.12.14); Hicks, "How Useful Is TSA 'Behavior Detection' at Airports?" WP (1.24.15).

52 Smith, "Head of T.S.A. Out after Tests Reveal Flaws," NYT (6.2.15).

53 Sarat (1997).

54 Elliott, "Caught in a Net Thrown for Terrorists," NYT (5.24.05); Asthana, "Domestic Detainee from 9/11 Released," WP (7.21.06); Yardley, "In the Defense of Basic Rights, an Official Led a City's Defiance," NYT (9.8.06); Mendoza, "One Man Still Locked Up from 9/11 Sweeps," WP (10.14.06); Dolnick, "A Post-9/11 Registration Effort Ends, but Not its Effects," NYT (5.31.11).

55 Bernstein, "Questions, Bitterness and Exile for Queens Girl in Terror Case," NYT (6.17.05).

56 Romney, "Pressured to Name Names," LAT (8.7.06).

57 Preston, "Lawsuit Filed in Support of Muslim Scholar Barred from U.S.," NYT (1.26.06); "A.C.L.U. Intervenes for Muslim Scholar," NYT (3.16.06); Preston, "Hearing for Muslim Barred by U.S.," NYT (4.14.06); Asthana, "Advocates Say U.S. Bars Many Academics," WP (8.4.06); "Muslim Scholar Barred by U.S. Denies Support for Terrorism," NYT (9.26.06); MacFarquhar, "Free Speech Groups Sue over Visa Denial," NYT (9.26.07); Liptak, "Say What You Like, Just Don't Say It Here," NYT (10.22.07); Eligon, "Patriot Act Faulted in Denial of Visa for Muslim Scholar," NYT (10.26.07); "Barring of Muslim Flawed," LAT (7.18.09); "Visas and Speech," NYT (9.17.09); Lyall, "In Shift, U.S. Lift Visa Curbs on Professor," NYT (1.21.10); "Visas and Censorship," NYT (4.14.10); American Academy of Religion v. Chertoff, 2007 WL 4527504 (SDNY 2007), rev'd, 573 F.3d 115 (2009); American Sociological Association v. Chertoff, 588 F.Supp.2d 166 (D.Mass. 2008).

58 Vedandtam, "Scientist's Visa Denial Sparks Outrage in India," WP (2.23.06); Sengupta, "3 Indian Scientists Protest Delay in Getting U.S. Visas," NYT (2.24.06); Vedantam, "U.S. Approves Visa for Indian Scientist," WP (2.24.06).

59 "Judge Urges Release of Chief Fundraiser for Islamic Charity," LAT (3.23.06); Reza, "Detainee's Release May Be Coming," LAT (3.26.06); Reza, "Muslim Should Be Deported, Board Rules," LAT (4.12.06); Reza, "Freedom Ordered for O.C. Man Who Was Terror Suspect," LAT (7.28.06); Reza, "Judge Reiterates: Free Jailed Man," LAT (7.29.06); Nadarajah v. Gonzales, 443 F.3d 1069 (9th Cir. 2006).

60 "Judge Orders Detainee's Release," NYT (5.31.07).

61 Weinstein, "20-Year Bid to Deport 2 Is Dismissed," LAT (1.31.07); "A Shameful Prosecution," NYT (2.14.07); "Drop This Case," WP (2.22.07); "And Then There Were Two," LAT (2.27.07); MacFarquhar, "U.S. Stymied 21 Years, Drops Bid to Deport 2 Palestinians," NYT (11.1.07).

62 Swarns, "Terror Laws Cut Resettlement of Refugees," NYT (9.28.06); Fears, "Conservatives Decry Terror Laws' Impact on Refugees," WP (1.8.07); Swarns, "Administration Offers Plan to Ease Rules on Asylum," NYT (1.12.07); Gaquette, "Door to U.S. Asylum Cracked Open for

25 "Karadzic Convicted of Genocide, Gets 40-Year Sentence," NYT (3.24.16); Simons, "Radovan Karadzic, a Bosnian Serb, Is Convicted of Genocide," NYT (3.24.16).

26 "Rwanda Takes Genocide Suspect into Custody from Congo: Officials," NYT (3.20.16); see Miller (2016).

27 Lind (2008: 108, 110, 128); "Court OK's Trial of Auschwitz Guard for Early 2015," WP (12.16.14); Moyer, "Why We Could Be Hunting Nazis until the 2040s," WP (9.16.14); Smale, "Former SS Member, on Trial in Germany, Says He Was 'Morally Complicit' at Auschwitz," NYT (4.21.15); Smale, "Oskar Gröning, Ex-SS Soldier at Auschwitz, Gets Four-Year Sentence," NYT (7.15.15); Smale, "A Front-Row Seat to Germany's Long Reckoning with Its Past," NYT (6.17.16); Eddy, "Former Auschwitz Guard Apologizes at Trial in Germany," NYT (4.29.16); Eddy, "Trial of Reinhold Hanning, Ex-Auschwitz Guard, Opens in Germany," NYT (2.11.16).

28 Bernstein, "The Insoluble Question," NYRB 64 (4.3.14); Fuller & Wallace, "2 Senior Khmer Rouge Leaders Are Convicted in Cambodia, Decades after Rule," NYT (8.7.14); "Cambodian War Tribunal Charges Another Ex-Member of Khmer Rouge," NYT (3.27.15); Mydans, "11 Years, $300 Million and 3 Convictions. Was the Khmer Rouge Tribunal Worth It?" NYT (4.10.17); Ciorcari & Heindel (1998); Giry, "Married Off by the Khmer Rouge, and 'Nobody Could Help Me,'" NYT (9.10.16); Hinton (2016).

29 "Bangladesh: War Tribunal Issues a Death Sentence," NYT (11.25.14); "A Top Islamist Is Executed by Bangladesh," NYT (4.11.15); Alam, "Bangladesh Tribunal Sentences 3 to Death for 1971 War Crimes," WP (7.18.16); Barry & Manik, "Bangladesh Braces for Violence after Opposition Leader, Motiur Rahman Nizami, Is Executed," NYT (5.10.16); "Islamist Party Figure Executed in Bangladesh for '71 Atrocities," NYT (9.3.16).

30 Davis (2016).

31 Veçoso (2016).

32 Garcia & Engle (2016).

33 "Sexual Harassment and How to Stop It," Ms. (November 1977); MacKinnon (1979, 2017); see Bennett, "The 'Click' Moment; How the Weinstein Scandal Unleased a Tsunami," NYT (11.6.17).

34 "Alan Turing Law Grants Posthumous Pardons to Gay Men in Britain," NYT (1.31.17); Jacobs, "He Was Convicted for Being Gay. 42 Years Later, He Wants an Apology," NYT (10.27.16); Chan, "Thousands of Men to Be Pardoned for Gay Sex, Once a Crime in Britain," NYT (10.20.16); Chan, "Germany Says It Will Rescind Convictions for Homosexuality," NYT (5.11.16); "Australian State Apologizes to Men Convicted for Gay Sex," WP (5.11.17); Shimer, "Germany Wipes Slate Clean for 50,000 Men Convicted Under Anti-Gay Law," NYT (6.23.17).

35 "UK Police: We'd Quiz Ex-Prime Minister Heath on Sex Claims Were He Alive," WP (10.5.17).

36 Hauser, "Gay Veteran, 91, Gets Honorable Discharge after 69 Years," NYT (1.10.17); Gearan, "John F. Kerry Apologizes for State

Department's Past Discrimination against Gay Employees," WP (1.9.17).

37 Robertson, "Memorial in Alabama Will Honor Victims of Lynching," NYT (8.15.16).

38 Robertson, "Mississippi Ends Inquiry into 1964 Killing of 3 Civil Rights Workers," NYT (6.20.16); Roberts, "Marcus D. Gordon, Judge in 'Mississippi Burning' Case, Dies at 84," NYT (5.27.16).

39 Swarns, "Georgetown University Plans Steps to Atone for Slave Past," NYT (9.1.16); Swarns, "Intent on a Reckoning with Georgetown's Slavery-Stained Past," NYT (7.10.16); "Georgetown University Is Trying to Make Right the Sale of Human Beings," NYT (6.26.16).

40 "Prime Minister Stephen Harper's Statement of Apology," CBC News (6.11.08); Tharoor, "Canada's Trudeau Makes Formal Apology for Racist Komagata Maru Incident," WP (5.18.16).

41 Barbash, "Decades-Old Mass Gave of Children of Unwed Mothers Confirmed in Ireland," WP (3.4.17).

42 Povoledo & Goodstein, "Pope Creates Tribunal for Bishop Negligence in Child Sexual Abuse Cases," NYT (6.10.15).

43 "Australia and the Church's Sex Abuse Scandal," NYT (2.13.17); Cole, "Australian Police Investigate Abuse Accusations against Cardinal Pell," NYT 7.28.16).

44 Williams, "Australian Cardinal and Aide to Pope Is Charged with Sexual Assault," NYT (6.28.17); Cave, "How Cardinal Pell Rose to Power, Trailed by a Cloud of Scandal," NYT (6.30.17).

45 Otterman & Schmidt, "New York Archdiocese Offers Compensation Program for Sexual Abuse Victims," NYT (10.6.16); Otterman, "7 Victims Name Priests Who Sexually Abused Them as Children," NYT (5.18.17); Otterman, "Brooklyn Diocese Seeks to Compensate Sex Abuse Victims," NYT (6.22.17); Otterman, "Former Priest Says Revered Colleague Was a Predator," NYT (10.30.17).

46 Egan, "Sex and the Saints," NYT (11.30.14).

47 Stevens, "Lawsuit Accuses Former Phoenix Bishop of Sexually Abusing Boy," NYT (8.4.17).

48 Bilefsky, "Church of England 'Colluded' with Bishop to Hide Sex Abuse, Report Says," NYT (6.22.17).

49 Stanley-Becker, "Hundreds of Boys Abused at Storied Catholic Choir in Germany, New Report Says," WP (7.18.17); Eddy, "'Culture of Silence' Abetted Abuse of at Least 547 German Choir Boys, Inquiry Finds," NYT (7.19.17).

50 Otterman, "23 Women Accuse Former Queens Priest of Abusing Them as Children," NYT (10.12.17).

51 Yeginsu, "Dozens Say Christian Leader Made British Boys 'Bleed for Jesus,'" NYT (3.4.17).

52 Schemo, "Years of Sex Abuse Described at Choir School in New Jersey," NYT (4.16.02).

53 Seelye, "Ex-Students at St. George's School Reach Pact on Sex Abuse Accusations," NYT (8.3.16).

54 Flanagan, "The Dark Hallways of Horace Mann," *The Atlantic* (January–February 2016); Leonhardt, "The Conspiracy of Inaction on Sexual Abuse and Harassment," NYT (11.6.17).

55 Viera, "Former Coach at Penn State Is Charged with Abuse," NYT (11.5.11).

56 Cronin, "5 Former Phillips Exeter Staffers Accused of Sexual Misconduct," WMUR (3.2.17); Seelye, "Former Exeter Official Charged with Sexual Assault from 1970s," NYT (5.13.16); Pérez-Peña, "Phillips Exeter Deans Failed to Report Sex Assault Case," NYT (11.14.17).

57 Smithy & Lavoie, "An Email Obtained by The Associated Press Shows that an Elite Rhode Island Boarding School Where Dozens of Alumni Say They Were Abused Is Negotiating Possible Settlements with Lawyers for More than 30 People," US News (5.9.16).

58 Imray, "South Africa: Bob Hewitt Appeal Rejected, Must Go to Jail," WP (6.9.16).

59 Harris, "Sexual Abuse at Choate Went On for Decades, School Acknowledges," NYT (4.14.17); Feuer, "Choate's Stance on Sexual Abuse Was 'I'd Rather Let It Go At That,'" NYT (4.15.17); Harris, "Choate Scrutinized on Reporting of Abuse Claims," NYT (4.26.17); Harris, "2 Choate Life Trustees Resign Amid Sexual Abuse Investigation," NYT (4.28.17).

60 Harris, "Second Phillips Andover Sex Abuse Report Includes Teacher Named by Choate," NYT (7.31.17).

61 Harris, "Third School Report Finds Sexual Misconduct by Choate Teacher," NYT (8.1.17).

62 Bidgood, "'Credible' Claims Found Against an Ex-Headmaster," NYT (8.9.17).

63 Ibid.

64 Harris, "KIPP NYC Charter School Network Is Investigating Claims of Past Sex Abuse," NYT (9.28.17).

65 "German Parliament to Label Killings of Armenians Genocide," WP (4.20.15); Fraser, "Erdogan: Turkey's Ancestors Never Committed Genocide," WP (4.23.15); Smale & Eddy, "German Vote on Armenian Genocide Riles Tempers, and Turkey," NYT (6.1.16); Smale & Eddy, "German Parliament Recognizes Armenian Genocide, Angering Turkey," NYT (6.2.16).

66 Bilefsky, "Court Finds Netherlands Responsible for Srebrenica Deaths," NYT (7.16.14); "Court: Dutch Not Liable for Most Srebrenica Deaths," WP (7.16.14); Chan, "Netherlands Partly Liable for 1995 Massacre of Bosnian Muslim Men, Court Rules," NYT (6.27.17).

67 Ramzy, "Mitsubishi Materials Apologizes to Chinese World War II Laborers," NYT (6.1.16).

68 Bilefsky, "France to Pay Holocaust Survivors over Deportations," NYT (12.5.14); "Monaco Seeks Forgiveness for Deporting Jews during WWII," NYT (8.27.15).

69 Roth, "Ukraine Marks 75th Anniversary of Killing of Jews at Babi Yar," NYT (9.29.16); Gillet, "Romania Takes Steps Toward Restitution to Holocaust Survivors," NYT (5.10.16).

70 Cohen, "The Story Behind 'Woman in Gold': Nazi Art Thieves and One Painting's Return," NYT (3.30.15); Hickley, "Case of Looted Klee Is Settled," NYT (7.27.17).

71 Forsythe, "Taiwan Turns Light on 1947 Slaughter by Chiang Kai-shek's Troops," NYT (7.14.15).

72 Wang, "For Decades, No One Spoke of Taiwan's Hidden Massacre. A New Generation Is Breaking the Silence," WP (2.28.17); Horton, "Taiwan Commemorates a Violent Nationalist Episode, 70 Years Later," NYT (2.26.17).

73 Ramzy, "Taiwan's President Apologizes to Aborigines for Centuries of Injustice," NYT (8.1.16).

74 Kutner, "A City Turns to Face Indonesia's Murderous Past," NYT (7.12.15); Hutton, "Indonesia Moves to Investigate Anti-Communist Atrocities," NYT (4.26.16); Cochrane, "Indonesia Rules Out Criminal Inquiry of Anti-Communist Purges," NYT (4.18.16).

75 "Sri Lanka Plans Fresh Inquiry into Human Rights Abuses during Civil War," G (1.29.15); Bastians & Harris, "Sri Lanka to Free Tamils and Return Their Land," NYT (1.30.15); Harris, "Sri Lanka Premier Starts with Fixing Civil War Ills," NYT (2.22.15); Gowen, "Can Reconciliation Heal Sri Lankan War Wounds?" WP (6.13.15); Cumming-Bruce, "Sri Lanka Lays Out Plan for Reconciliation," NYT (9.14.15).

76 "Apology to Aborigines," BBC News (2.12.08).

77 Choe, "South Korea Illegally Held Prostitutes Who Catered to G.I.s Decades Ago, Court Says," NYT (1.20.17).

78 O'Shea, "2 Ex-Soldiers Face Charges in '72 Killing of I.R.A. Commander," NYT (10.16.16).

79 Elkins, "Britain Has Said Sorry to Mau Mau. The Rest of the Empire is Still Waiting," G (6.7.13); "Mau Mau Torture Victims to Receive Compensation – Hague," BBC News (6.6.13); Cowell, "Britain to Compensate Kenya Victims of Colonial-Era Torture," NYT (6.6.13).

80 Bilefsky, "Hillsborough Stadium Disaster: Verdict Faults Police for Fans 'Unlawfully Killed,'" NYT (4.26.16); Bilefsky, "Six Are Charged in 1989 Hillsborough Stadium Disaster in England," NYT (6.28.17).

81 Lyman, "15 Serbs Are Arrested in Connection with 1993 Massacre," NYT (12.5.14); Cowell, "Serbia Arrests Eight Suspected in 1995 Srebrenica Massacre," NYT (3.18.15); "Serbia Prosecutors Charge 8 in Srebrenica Massacre," NYT (9.10.15).

82 "Kosovo: EU Plans War Crimes Tribunal," NYT (4.5.14).

83 Yardley, "Facing His Torturer as Spain Confronts Its Past," NYT (4.6.14); Gilbert, "Argentine Judge Orders Arrest of Spanish Ex-Officials," NYT (11.2.14).

84 "Germany Moves Toward Calling Namibian Massacre Genocide," NYT (7.10.15); Onishi, "A Colonial-Era Wound Opens in Namibia," NYT

(1.21.17); Onishi, "Germany Grapples with its African Genocide," NYT (12.29.16).
85 Domasa, "Tanzania to Seek German Reparations for Colonial Acts," WP (2.8.17).
86 "Dutch Govt Must Compensate Indonesia War Widows, Children," WP (3.11.15).
87 "Peru Sentences Ex-Soldiers to Prison for Killing Villagers in 1985," NYT (9.1.16).
88 "Peru: Former Dictator Is to Be Tried in 1978 Abductions of His Opponents," NYT (9.10.15).
89 "Peru Families Receive Bodies of Dirty War Victims," WP (10.28.14).
90 "Another Sentence for Argentina Ex-Dictator," WP (10.8.14); "15 Jailed for Life in Argentina 'Dirty War' Trial," WP (10.24.14); Gilbert, "Ex-Military Officers Convicted of Human Rights Crimes during Argentina Dictatorship," NYT (8.25.16); Gilbert, "Argentine Court Confirms a Deadly Legacy of Dictatorships," NYT (5.28.16).
91 Gilbert, "Twisting Inquiry into Buenos Aires Bombing Takes New Turn," NYT (1.31.16); Politi, "Argentine Court Reopens Investigation of Ex-President in '94 Bomb Case," NYT (12.29.16).
92 "Seeking Justice in El Salvador," NYT (7.22.16); Malkin & Palumbo, "Salvadoran Court Overturns Wartime Amnesty, Paving Way for Prosecutions," NYT (7.14.16).
93 Haberman, "Laying Out a Case for Departing Human Rights Abusers," NYT (11.10.14); Preston, "U.S. Delays Deportation of Salvadoran Ex-Official Accused in '80s Killings," NYT (3.31.15); Preston, "U.S. Deports Salvadoran General Accused in '80s Killings," NYT (4.8.15); Malkin, "U.S. Judge Approves Extradition of Former Salvadoran Colonel," NYT (2.5.16); Malkin, "El Salvador Arrests Ex-Military Officers in 1989 Jesuit Killings," NYT (2.6.16); Preston, "Florida: Ex-Leader of Salvadoran Military Deported," NYT (1.8.16); Katz, "U.S. Wants Former Salvadoran Ally to Face Justice in 1989 Massacre," NYT (9.13.15).
94 Bonnefoy, "Florida Jury Finds Former Chilean Officer Liable in '73 Killing," NYT (6.27.16); Ryan, "CIA Found 'Convincing Evidence' Chilean Dictator Was Behind 1976 D.C. Attack," WP (9.23.16).
95 Bonnefoy, "2 Sentenced in Murders in Chile Coup," NYT (1.28.15).
96 Bonnefoy, "Chilean Court Rules U.S. Had Role in Murders," NYT (7.1.14); "Chile: 7 in Pinochet's Military Charged in Death of Protester," NYT (7.24.15); Bonnefoy, "Officers Arrested in 1986 Burning Death of U.S. Student in Chile," NYT (7.21.15).
97 Dorfman, "Neruda, Pinochet and Rumors of Murder," NYT (10.30.17).
98 Romero, "Brazil Releases Report on Past Rights Abuses," NYT (12.10.14).
99 Malkin, "Guatemala Arrests Former Military Officers in Connection with Massacres," NYT (1.6.16).
100 "Victims of 1982 Guatemala Massacre Laid to Rest," WP (7.31.14); Malkin, "Guatemala: Former Police Official Is Convicted in 1980 Embassy Siege," NYT (1.19.15).

101 Malkin, "Genocide Retrial Is Set for Guatemalan Former Dictator," NYT (8.25.15).
102 "Suriname: Judges Say President's Trial over Killings in 1982 Should Continue," NYT (12.2.15).
103 Brunwasser, "As Albania Reckons with its Communist Past, Critics Say It's Too Late," NYT 2.26.17).
104 Gillet, "Brutal Romanian Prison Warden, 90, Loses Appeal of 20-Year Sentence," NYT (2.10.16).
105 "State Burial in Poland for WWII Heroes Slain by Communists," US News (8.28.16).
106 Tavernise, "Russian Project Honors Stalin's Victims and Stirs Talk on Brutal Past," NYT (9.20.15).
107 Simons, "Ex-Leader of Chad Goes on Trial for Crimes against Humanity," NYT (7.20.15); Petesch, "Chad Ex-Dictator Habré to Stand Trial Sought for Decades," WP (7.18.15); Searcey, "Hissène Habré, Ex-President of Chad, Is Convicted of War Crimes," NYT (5.30.16); Barry & Searcey, "Hissène Habré, Ex-Ruler of Chad, Loses War Crimes Appeal," NYT (4.27.17).
108 Cowell, "Truth, Reconciliation and Now, a Prosecution in South Africa," NYT (2.19.16); Chutel, "Tutu Asks Why It Took Years to Prosecute Apartheid Murder," WP (2.11.16); Swenson, "An Anti-Apartheid Activist Died in Police Custody in 1971. New Testimony Points to Murder," WP (8.1.17).
109 Gall, "Silenced for Decades, 'Victims of Despotism' Air Torture Claims in Tunisia," NYT (11.18.16); Kottoor, "'They Crushed Me': Tunisians Reveal Abuses They Endured before the Arab Spring," WP (12.16.16).
110 "Burkina Faso Issues Arrest Warrant for Ex-President Blaise Compaoré," NYT (12.21.15).
111 Gall, "Spanish Judge Accuses Moroccan Former Officials of Genocide in Western Sahara," NYT (4.10.15).
112 "Kenya: Official Apology for Past Wrongs," NYT (4.22.15).
113 Civil Liberties Act of 1988; Stone (2004: 305).
114 *Mochizuki* v. U.S., 43 Fed. Cl. 97 (1999).
115 Austen, "Women in Royal Canadian Mounted Police Get an Apology for Years of Harassment," NYT (10.6.16).
116 Austen, "Canada Agrees to Pay Millions in Lawsuit over Forced Adoptions," NYT (10.7.17).
117 Ibid.
118 Malloy, "U.S. Helping Defuse Vietnam's Dioxin Hot Spots Blamed on Agent Orange," WP (4.8.16).
119 Blinder, "Decades Later, Memphis to Compensate Black Sanitation Strikers of 1968," NYT (7.26.17).
120 Whitlock, "In Rare Spectacle, Army Court-Martials a Retired General," WP (8.26.17).
121 Stevens & Fortin, "Five Arrested in Georgia in 'Heinous' 1983 Killing," NYT (10.16.17).

122 Smith & Davey, "Chicago to Pay $5 Million to Victims of Police Abuse," NYT (5.6.15); Lewis (2007: 101–102); Work (2005).
123 "Remarks by the President in Apology for Study Done in Tuskegee," White House Office of Press Secretary (5.16.97).
124 McNeil, "U.S. Apologizes for Syphilis Tests in Guatemala," NYT (10.1.10).
125 Advisory Committee on Human Radiation Experiments (1996); Haberman, "Veterans of Atomic Test Blasts: No Warning, and Late Amends," NYT (5.29.16).
126 "UK's May Orders Probe into Contaminated Blood Scandal," WP (7.11.17).
127 Fortin, "Florida Apologizes for 'Gross Injustices' to Four Black Men, Decades Later," NYT (4.27.17).
128 Fisher, "Obama, Acknowledging U.S. Misdeeds Abroad, Quietly Reframes American Power," NYT (9.7.16).
129 Ibid.
130 Winfield, "Pope Begs Forgiveness for Church Role in Rwanda Genocide," WP (3.20.17).
131 Povoledo, "Pope Francis Condemns 'Genocide' of Armenians before Visit to Memorial," NYT (6.24.16).
132 Yardley & Neuman, "In Bolivia, Pope Francis Apologizes for Church's 'Grave Sins,'" NYT (7.9.15).
133 Yardley, "Pope Acknowledges Cover-Ups by Bishops," NYT (9.28.15).
134 "Pope Francis Says Church Should Apologize to Gays," NYT (6.26.16).
135 Goldman, "Macron Denounces Anti-Zionism as 'Reinvented Form of Anti-Semitism,'" NYT (7.17.17).
136 Sikkink (2011); Karlin, "Emma Willard Report Reveals History of Sexual Misconduct," Albany Times Union (4.19.17); Harris, "Brearley, Manhattan Girls' School, Pursuing Allegations of Past Abuse," NYT (11.13.17); Harris, "Suit Alleges Past Sexual Abuse at Connecticut Boarding School," NYT (5.18.17) (Kent School); Bidgood, "St. Paul's School Acknowledges Decades of Sexual Misconduct," NYT (5.23.17); Bidgood, "New Hampshire Will Investigate St. Paul's School over Sex Abuse," NYT (7.14.17); Harris, "Brearley Tells of Staff Sexual Misconduct," NYT 10.28.17); see Felstiner et al. (1981).
137 Kantor & Twomey, "Harvey Weinstein Paid Off Sexual Harassment Accusers for Decades," NYT (10.5.17); Codrea-Rado, "#MeToo Floods Social Media with Stories of Harassment and Assault," NYT (10.16.17); Nagourney & Medina, "In Sacramento, Fury over Pervasive Harassment," NYT (10.18.17); Bilefsky & Peltier, "France Considers Fines for Catcalls as Women Speak Out on Harassment," NYT (10.18.17); Chokshi, "Growing List of Women with Stories of Abuse," NYT (10.19.17); Mather, "Maroney Claims a Team Doctor Molested Her," NYT (10.19.17); Fortin, "Two Face Accusations of Sexual Misconduct," NYT (10.23.17); Schuesser, "Editor Admits to 'Offenses' against Women and Loses Deal," NYT (10.25.17); Feuer, "Women Accuse Knight Landesman, Art World Mainstay, of Sexual Harassment," NYT (10.26.17); Koblin & Grynbaum,

"Top Political Journalist Faces Multiple Charges of Harassment," NYT (10.27.17); Fortin, "More Women Accuse James Toback of Sexual Harassment," NYT (10.29.17); Friedman & Paton, "A Scapegoat for the Fashion Industry?" NYT (10.29.17); Gall & Peltier, "2 Frenchwomen Accuse Prominent Islamic Scholar of Sexual Assault," NYT (10.30.17); Bidgood, Jordan & Nagourney, "Sexual Misconduct in California's Capitol Is Difficult to Escape," NYT (10.30.17); McAuley, "Weinstein Scandal Sparks an Uproar in France," WP (10.30.17); Castle, "Wave of Sex Harassment Claims Surfacing in Britain's Parliament," NYT (10.31.17); Gabler, Twohey & Kantor, "New Accusers Expand Claims against Weinstein into the 1970s," NYT (10.31.17); Paulson, "Spacey Apologizes after Accusation of Misconduct," NYT (10.31.17); Ember, "Complaints Lead Publisher to Take Leave of Absence," NYT (10.31.17); McMillan, "The Cost of Raunchy Kitchen Talk," NYT (10.31.17); Seelye & Saul, "Dartmouth College Professors Investigated over Sexual Misconduct Allegations," NYT (11.1.17); Sadurni, "Columbia Professor Accused of Sexual Harassment Steps Down," NYT (11.1.17); Doshi, "After #MeToo, a Facebook List Names South Asian Academics. Some Say It's a Step Too Far," WP (11.1.17); Farhi, "Top Newsroom Official at NPR Resigns amid Harassment Allegations," WP (11.1.17); Castle, "Michael Fallon, U.K. Defense Secretary, Quits over Inappropriate Conduct," NYT (11.2.17); Abrams, "Top Producer Faces Harassment Allegations," NYT (11.2.17); "Kevin Spacey to Seek Help as Accusations Fly," NYT (11.3.17); "French Women Ask Macron for Attack Plan against Sexual Abuse," WP (11.5.17); Gall, "Tariq Ramadan Is On Leave from Oxford after Rape Allegations," NYT (11.8.17); Pogrebin, "Art Fair Director Ousted over Claims of Harassment," NYT (11.9.17); Ryzik, Buckley & Kantor, "Detailing Lewd Acts, 5 Women Accuse a Comic of Misconduct," NYT (11.10.17); Fausset, Martin & Robertson, "G.O.P. Reels as Sex Allegations Arise against Senate Candidate," NYT (11.10.17); Holson, "A Dubious List Grows," NYT (11.12.17); Robertson & Bidgood, "Silence Lifts in Statehouses as Harassment Scandals Bring Swift Penalties," NYT (11.13.17); Nicholson & Moore, "Capitol Hill Has a Sexual Harassment Problem," WP (11.14.17); Martin & Stolberg, "Fifth Woman Accuses Senate Candidate Roy Moore of Sexual Misconduct," NYT (11.14.17); Miller, Benner & Kantor, "Harassment Claims Topple a Tech Financier," NYT (11.14.17); Alcindor & Rogers, "Congress Struggles to Confront Harassment as Stories Pile Up," NYT (11.14.17).

138 Barry, "The Lost Children of Tuam," NYT (10.29.17); Phelan, Letter to the Editor, NYT (11.6.17).

139 O'Laughlin, "Guilty Plea by Ulster Loyalist May Shed Light on Police Collusion," NYT (6.23.17).

140 Gall, "Tunisia's Truth-Telling Renews a Revolution's Promise, Painfully," NYT (4.22.17).

141 Mele, "New Orleans Begins Removing Confederate Monuments, under Police Guard," NYT (4.24.17); Decuir, "Good Riddance to Confederate Monuments," NYT (4.28.17); "Monuments of

White Supremacy," NYT (5.9.17); Tisserand, "A Racism Harder Than Stone," NYT (5.9.17); Mele, "Jefferson Davis Statue in New Orleans Is Removed," NYT (5.11.17); Blinder, "Tributes to the Confederacy: History, or a Racial Reminder in New Orleans?" NYT (5.14.17); Robertson, "New Orleans Removes Beauregard Statue, and Subdued Crowds Look On," NYT (5.17.17); Bosman, "Few in St. Louis Knew Confederate Memorial Existed. Now, Many Want It Gone," NYT (5.26.17); "On Monument Avenue, Richmond Will Start Recognizing Its Real History," WP (6.24.17); "Change J.E.B. Stuart High School's Name," WP (7.26.17); Stack & Caron, "State Leaders Call for Confederate Monuments to Be Removed," NYT (8.14.17); Horton, "Protesters in North Carolina Topple Confederate Statue following Charlottesville Violence," WP (8.14.17); Stack & Caron, "After Violent Weekend, Calls Beyond Virginia to Remove Civil War Statues," NYT (8.15.17); Goldman, "Baltimore Removes Confederate Statues in Overnight Operation," NYT (8.16.17); Bloch, McCarthy, Stack & Andrews, "The Confederate Symbols Being Removed," NYT (8.17.17); Tchekmedyian, Khan, and Rocha, "Hollywood Forever Cemetery Removes Confederate Monument after Calls from Activists and Threats of Vandalism," LAT (8.16.17); Nir & Otterman, "Cuomo Says Confederate Names on New York Streets Should Go," NYT (8.17.17); "After Racist Rage, Statutes Fall Quietly," NYT (8.17.17); "It's Time for a Full and Fair Reckoning with Confederate Statues," WP (8.18.17); Stevens, "M.T.A. to Modify Subway Station Design Resembling Confederate Flag," NYT (8.18.17); Astor & Fandos, "Descendants Say Confederate Statues Can Go," NYT (8.20.17); Bromwich, "University of Texas at Austin Removes Confederate Statutes in Overnight Operation," NYT (8.21.17); Gabriel, "Far From Dixie, Outcry Grows Over a Wider Array of Monuments," NYT (8.25.17); Newman, "Planned Review of Statues Leaves de Blasio to Parse Role of History and Culture," NYT (8.31.17); Newman & Wang, "Calhoun Who? Yale Drops Name of Slavery Advocate for Computer Pioneer," NYT (9.3.17); Haag, "Dallas Can Remove Robert E. Lee Statue, Judge Rules," NYT (9.7.17); King, "The Removal of Confederate Windows at National Cathedral Was No Cause for Celebration," WP (9.9.17); Bosman, "Battle over Confederate Monuments Moves to the Cemeteries," NYT (9.21.17).

142 Kwai, "Australian State Removes Racially Offensive Place Names," NYT (8.29.17).
143 Austen, "Canada, Too, Faces a Reckoning with History and Racism," NYT (8.29.17); Freeman, "As America Debates Confederate Monuments, Canada Faces Its Own Historical Controversy," WP (8.29.17).
144 Schultz, "A Decade after Nepal's Maoist Rebellion, Little Justice for Victims," NYT (1.29.17).
145 Witte & Birnbaum, "Putin Implicated in Fatal Poisoning of Former KGB Officer at London Hotel," WP (1.21.16).

146 MacFarquhar, "Critics Scoff as Kremlin Erects Monument to the Repressed," NYT (10.31.17).

147 Gilbert, "Twisting Inquiry into Buenos Aires Bombing Takes New Turn," NYT (1.31.16); Politi, "Argentine Court Reopens Investigation of Ex-President in '94 Bomb Case," NYT (12.29.16).

148 Wild, "Slavery's Shadow on Switzerland," NYT (11.10.14).

149 Levin, "Dozens of Women Vanish on Canada's Highway of Tears, and Most Cases Are Unsolved," NYT (5.24.16).

150 Kershner, "Israeli Mystery of Lost Babies Gets New Chapter: 200,000 Secret Records," NYT (12.28.16).

151 Berendt, "Polish Court Limits World War II-Era Restitution Claims in Warsaw," NYT (7.27.16); Segal, "Holocaust Survivors in Poland Find Restitution Claims 'Like a Carousel,'" NYT (5.11.17).

152 Segal, "Obstacles on the Path to Return Looted Art," NYT (5.13.17).

153 Bittker (1972); "The Horror of Lynchings Lives On," NYT (12.3.16).

154 Bilefsky, "David Cameron Grapples with Issue of Slavery Reparations in Jamaica," NYT (9.30.15).

155 Haberman, "Veterans of Atomic Test Blasts: No Warning, and Late Amends," NYT (5.29.16); Phillips, "Decades Later, Sickness among Airmen after a Hydrogen Bomb Accident," NYT (6.19.16).

156 Arango, "'Sherlock Holmes of Armenian Genocide' Uncovers Lost Evidence," NYT (4.22.17).

157 "Spain Parliament Calls for Franco's Remains to Be Moved," WP (5.11.17).

158 Johnson, "China's Brave Underground Journal: Part I," NYRB 70 (12.18.14); Tatlow, "Fate Catches Up to a Cultural Revolution Museum in China," NYT (10.2.16).

159 DeYoung, "Russian Veto of U.N. Resolution on Srebrenica Infuriates U.S., Allies," WP (7.8.15).

160 Cochrane, "Indonesia Takes a Step Back from Reckoning with a Past Atrocity," NYT (9.30.17); Bevins, "In Indonesia, the 'Fake News' that Fueled a Cold War Massacre Is Still Potent Five Decades Later," WP (9.30.17); Beech, "U.S. Stood by as Indonesia Killed a Half-Million People, Papers Show," NYT (10.18.17).

161 Fausset, "Tempers Flare Over Removal of Confederate Statues in New Orleans," NYT (5.7.17); Selk, "'The Battle of New Orleans': David Duke Expects Confederate Statue Defenders to Mass on Sunday," WP (5.6.17); "New Orleans Needs Help Moving Confederate Statues – and Stopping Extremists in the Way," WP (5.10.17); Bromwich, "White Nationalists Wield Torches at Confederate Statue Rally," NYT (5.15.17); "A Protest in Virginia with Echoes of the Klan," NYT (5.17.17); Spencer & Stevens, "23 Arrested and Tear Gas Deployed after a K.K.K. Rally in Virginia," NYT 7.9.17); Saul, "Edging Out of a Confederate Shadow, Gingerly," NYT (8.10.17); Spencer & Stolberg, "Virginia Town Is on Edge Over Confederate Statue," NYT (8.12.17); Stolberg & Rosenthal, "White Nationalist Protest Leads to Deadly Violence," NYT (8.13.17); Sullivan, "Trump Says It Is 'Foolish' to Remove Civil War Statues," NYT

(8.17.17); Fandos, Fausset & Blinder, "Charlottesville Violence Spurs New Resistance to Confederate Symbols," NYT (8.17.17); Robertson, Blinder & Fausset, "In Monument Debate, Calls for an Overdue Reckoning on Race and Southern Identity," NYT (8.19.17); Tavernise, "New Monuments to the Confederacy Are Rising, on Private Property," NYT (8.31.17).

162 Panda, "The 'Final and Irreversible' 2015 Japan–South Korea Comfort Women Deal Unravels," The Diplomat (1.9.17); Choe, "Leaders of South Korea and China Talk, and U.S. Missile Defense Is On The Table," NYT (5.12.17).

163 Fackler, "Shinzo Abe, Japanese Premier, Sends Gift to Contentious Yasukuni Shrine," NYT (4.21.15).

164 Paddock, "Hero's Burial for Ferdinand Marcos Draws Protests from Dictator's Victims," NYT (11.18.16); Gomez, "Philippine Gov't Historian Resigns over Dictator's Burial," WP (11.29.16).

165 Politi, "Argentines Fight Court's Leniency for Human Rights Crimes," NYT (5.13.17).

REFERENCES

CHAPTERS 1 AND 8

Abel, Richard L. 1995. *Politics by Other Means: Law in the Struggle Against Apartheid, 1980–1994*. New York: Routledge.

Acheson, Dean. 1965. *Morning and Noon*. New York: Houghton Mifflin.

Advisory Committee on Human Radiation Experiments. 1996. *Final Report*. New York: Oxford University Press.

Agamben, Giorgio. 2005. *State of Exception* (trans. Kevin Attell). Chicago: University of Chicago Press.

Allison, William Thomas. 2007. *Military Justice in Vietnam: The Rule of Law in an American War*. Lawrence: University Press of Kansas.

Anderson, David. 2011. *Histories of the Hanged: The Dirty War in Kenya and the End of Empire*. New York: W. W. Norton.

Balbus, Isaac. 1974. *The Dialectics of Legal Repression: Black Rebels before the American Criminal Courts*. New York: Russell Sage Foundation.

Barak, Aharon. 2001. "Democracy, Terror and the Courts." Speech at Haifa University (December 16).

Barkan, Steven E. 1985. *Protesters on Trial: Criminal Justice in the Southern Civil Rights and Vietnam Antiwar Movements*. New Brunswick, NJ: Rutgers University Press.

Baum, Lawrence. 1977. "Judicial Specialization, Litigant Influence, and Substantive Policy: The Court of Customs and Patents Appeals," 11 *Law & Society Review* 823.

Bittker, Boris. 1972. *The Case for Black Reparations*. New York: Random House.

Bobbitt, Philip. 2008. *Terror and Consent: The War for the Twenty-First Century*. New York: Alfred A. Knopf.

Brandeis, Louis D. and Richard M. Abrams. 1967 (first published 1913). *Other People's Money and How the Bankers Use It*. New York: Harper & Row.

Brinkley, Alan. 2008. "World War I and the Crisis of Democracy," in Daniel Farber (ed.), *Security and Liberty: Conflicts between Civil Liberties and National Security in American History*. New York: Russell Sage Foundation.

Brysk, Alison and Gershon Hafir (eds.). 2008. *National Insecurity and Human Rights: Democracies Debate Counterterrorism*. Berkeley: University of California Press.

Chafee, Zechariah. 1919. "Freedom of Speech in War Times," 32 *Harvard Law Review* 932.

Ciorciari, John D. and Anne Heindel. 1998. *Hybrid Justice: The Extraordinary Chambers in the Courts of Cambodia.* Ann Arbor: University of Michigan Press.

Cover, Robert M. 1975. *Justice Accused: Antislavery and the Judicial Process.* New Haven: Yale University Press.

Danelski, David J. 1996. "The Saboteurs' Case," 21 *Journal of Supreme Court History* 61.

Davis, D. M. 2016. "The South African Truth Commission and the AZAPO Case: A Reflection Almost Two Decades Later," in Karen Engle, Zinaida Miller and D. M. Davis (eds.). *Anti-Impunity and the Human Rights Agenda.* New York: Cambridge University Press.

Davis, Jeffrey. 2014. *Seeking Human Rights Justice in Latin America: Truth, Extra-Territorial Courts, and the Process of Justice.* New York: Cambridge University Press.

Donohue, Laura K. 2008. *The Cost of Counterterrorism: Power, Politics, and Liberty.* New York: Cambridge University Press.

Dugard, John. 1984. "Should Judges Resign? – A Reply to Professor Wacks," 101 *South African Law Journal* 286.

1987. "Omar: Support for Wacks's Ideas on the Judicial Process," 3 *South African Journal on Human Rights* 295.

Dyzenhaus, David. 2006. *The Constitution of Law: Legality in a Time of Emergency.* New York: Cambridge University Press.

Ellmann, Stephen. 1992. *In a Time of Trouble: Law and Liberty in South Africa's State of Emergency.* New York: Oxford University Press.

Engle, Karen. 2015. "Anti-Impunity and the Turn to Criminal Law in Human Rights," 100 *Cornell Law Review* 1069.

2016. "A Genealogy of the Criminal Turn in Human Rights," in Karen Engle, Zinaida Miller and D. M. Davis (eds.). *Anti-Impunity and the Human Rights Agenda.* New York: Cambridge University Press.

Engle, Karen, Zinaida Miller and D. M. Davis (eds.). 2016a. *Anti-Impunity and the Human Rights Agenda.* New York: Cambridge University Press.

2016b. "Introduction," in Karen Engle, Zinaida Miller and D. M. Davis (eds.). *Anti-Impunity and the Human Rights Agenda.* New York: Cambridge University Press.

Felstiner, William L. F., Richard L. Abel and Austin Sarat. 1981. "The Emergence and Transformation of Disputes: Naming, Blaming, Claiming ...," 14 *Law & Society Review* 631.

Finan, Christopher M. 2007. *From the Palmer Raids to the Patriot Act: A History of the Fight for Free Speech in America.* Boston, MA: Beacon Press.

Fisher, Louis. 2008. *The Constitution and 9/11: Recurring Threats to America's Freedoms.* Lawrence: University Press of Kansas.

Fiss, Owen. 2015. *A War Like No Other: The Constitution in a Time of Terror* (Trever Sutton ed.). New York: New Press.

Frei, Norbert. 2002. *Adenauer's Germany and the Nazi Past* (trans. Joel Golb). New York: Columbia University Press.

Gage, Beverly. 2009. *The Day Wall Street Exploded: A Story of America in its First Age of Terror*. New York: Oxford University Press.

Garcia, Helena Alviar and Karen Engle. 2016. "The Distributive Politics of Inequality and Anti-Indemnity: Lessons from Four Decades of Colombia Peace Negotiations," in Karen Engle, Zinaida Miller and D. M. Davis (eds.). *Anti-Impunity and the Human Rights Agenda*. New York: Cambridge University Press.

Glennon, Michael J. 2010. *The Fog of Law: Pragmatism, Security and International Law*. Stanford: Stanford University Press.

Gould, Benjamin and Liora Lazares (eds.). 2007. *Security and Human Rights*. Oxford: Hart.

Gross, Emanuel. 2006. *The Struggle of Democracy against Terrorism: Lessons from the United States, the United Kingdom, and Israel*. Charlottesville: University of Virginia Press.

Gross, Owen and Fionnuala Ni Aoláin (eds.). 2006. *Law in Times of Crisis: Emergency Powers in Theory and Practice*. New York: Cambridge University Press.

Herf, Jeffrey. 1997. *Divided Memory: The Nazi Past in the Two Germanys*. Cambridge, MA: Harvard University Press.

Hilbink, Lisa. 2007. *Judges beyond Politics in Democracy and Dictatorship: Lessons from Chile*. New York: Cambridge University Press.

Hinton, Alexander Isban. 2016. *Man or Monster? The Trial of a Khmer Rouge Torturer*. Durham, NC: University of North Carolina Press.

Hite, Katherine and Mark Unger. 2013. *Sustaining Human Rights in the 21st Century: Strategies from Latin America*. Baltimore: Johns Hopkins University Press.

Honig, Bonnie. 2009. *Emergency Politics: Paradox, Law, Democracy*. Princeton: Princeton University Press.

Horne, Alastair. 2006. *A Savage War of Peace: Algeria 1954–1962* (first published 1977). New York: New York Review Books Classics.

Hussain, Nasser. 2003. *The Jurisprudence of Emergency: Colonialism and the Rule of Law*. Ann Arbor: University of Michigan Press.

Kalven, Harry Jr. and Hans Zeisel. 1966. *The American Jury*. Boston, MA: Little Brown & Co.

Keys, Barbara. 2014. *Reclaiming American Virtue: The Human Rights Revolution of the 1970s*. Cambridge, MA: Harvard University Press.

Kovras, Iosif. 2017. *Grassroots Activism and the Evolution of Transitional Justice: The Families of the Disappeared*. New York: Cambridge University Press.

Lane, Eric and Michael Oreskes. 2007. *The Genius of America: How the Constitution Saved Our Country – and Why It Can Happen Again.* New York: Bloomsbury.

Lazar, Nomi Claire. 2009. *States of Emergency in Liberal Democracies.* New York: Cambridge University Press.

Lewis, Anthony. 2007. *Freedom for the Thought That We Hate: A Biography of the First Amendment.* New York: Basic Books.

Lind, Jennifer. 2008. *Sorry States: Apologies in International Politics.* Ithaca, NY: Cornell University Press.

MacKinnon, Catherine. 1979. *Sexual Harassment of Working Women.* New Haven: Yale University Press.

2017. *Butterfly Politics.* Cambridge, MA. Harvard University Press.

Masferrer, Aniceto and Clive Walker (eds.). 2013. *Counter-Terrorism, Human Rights and the Rule of Law: Crossing Legal Boundaries in Defence of the State.* London: Edward Elgar.

Martelle, Scott. 2011. *The Fear Within: Spies, Commies, and American Democracy on Trial.* New Brunswick, NJ: Rutgers University Press.

Miller, Zinaida. 2016. "Anti-Impunity Politics in Post-Genocide Rwanda," in Karen Engle, Zinaida Miller and D. M. Davis (eds.). *Anti-Impunity and the Human Rights Agenda.* New York: Cambridge University Press.

Mokhtari, Shadi. 2009. *After Abu Ghraib: Exploring Human Rights in America and the Middle East.* New York: Cambridge University Press.

Moyn, Samuel. 2014. "From Antiwar Politics to Antitorture Politics," in Austin Sarat, Lawrence Douglas and Martha Merrill Umphrey (eds.), *Law and War.* Stanford: Stanford University Press.

Muller, Eric L. 2007. *American Inquisition: The Hunt for Japanese American Disloyalty in World War II.* Chapel Hill: University of North Carolina Press.

Murphy, Paul L. 1979. *World War I and the Origin of Civil Liberties in the United States.* New York: W. W. Norton.

Neff, Stephen C. 2010. *Justice in Blue and Gray: A Legal History of the Civil War.* Cambridge, MA: Harvard University Press.

Posner, Eric and Adrian Vermeule. 2007. *Terror in the Balance: Security, Liberty, and the Courts.* New York: Oxford University Press.

Powe, Lucas A. 2009. *The Supreme Court and the American Elite, 1789–2008.* Cambridge, MA: Harvard University Press.

Pugliese, Elizabeth M. and Larry G. Hufford (eds.). 2006. *War Crimes and Trials: A Historical Encyclopedia from 1850 to the Present.* Santa Barbara: ABC-Clio.

Ragan, Fred D. 1971. "Justice Oliver Wendell Holmes, Jr., Zechariah Chafee, Jr., and the Clear and Present Danger Test for Free Speech: The First Year, 1919," 58 *Journal of American History* 39.

Rankin, Robert S. and Winfried R. Dallmayr. 1964. *Freedom and Emergency Powers in the Cold War.* New York: Appleton-Century-Crofts.

Reeves, Richard. 2015. *Infamy: The Shocking Story of the Japanese American Internment in World War II*. New York: Henry Holt.

Roach, Kent. 2011. *The 9/11 Effect: Comparative Counter-Terrorism*. New York: Cambridge University Press.

Robben, Antonius. 2004. *Political Violence and Trauma in Argentina*. Philadelphia: University of Pennsylvania Press.

Robertson, Michael. 1989. "The Participation of Judges in the Present Legal System: Should Judges Resign?" in Hugh Corder (ed.), *Democracy and the Judiciary*. Cape Town: Juta.

Ryan, Allan A. 2012. *Yamashita's Ghost: War Crimes, MacArthur's Justice, and Command Accountability*. Lawrence: University Press of Kansas.

2015. *The 9/11 Terror Cases: Constitutional Challenges in the War against al Qaeda*. Lawrence: University Press of Kansas.

Scott, Katherine A. 2013. *Reining in the State: Civil Society and Congress in the Vietnam and Watergate Eras*. Lawrence: University Press of Kansas.

Sikkink, Kathryn. 2011. *The Justice Cascade: How Human Rights Prosecutions Are Changing World Politics*. New York: W. W. Norton & Co.

Simmons, Beth A. 2009. *Mobilizing for Human Rights: International Law in Domestic Politics*. New York: Cambridge University Press.

Solf, Waldemar, 1972. "A Response to Telford Taylor's Nuremberg and Vietnam: An American Tragedy," 5 *Akron Law Review* 66.

Springer, Paul J. 2010. *America's Captives: Treatment of POWs from the Revolutionary War to the War on Terror*. Lawrence: University Press of Kansas.

Stone, Geoffrey R. 2004. *Perilous Times: Free Speech in Wartime from the Sedition Act of 1798 to the War on Terrorism*. New York: W. W. Norton.

Stover, Eric, Victor Peskin and Alexa Koenig. 2016. *Hiding in Plain Sight: The Pursuit of War Criminals from Nuremberg to the War on Terror*. Oakland: University of California Press.

Tolley, Howard B. Jr. 1990–91. "Interest Group Litigation to Enforce Human Rights," 105 *Political Science Quarterly* 617.

Trubek, David M. 1977. "Complexity and Contradiction in the Legal Order: Balbus and the Challenge of Critical Thought about Law," 11 *Law & Society Review* 529.

Unger, David. 2012. *The Emergency State: America's Pursuit of Absolute Security at All Costs*. New York: Penguin.

Veçoso, Fabia Fernandes Carvalho. 2016. "Whose Exceptionalism? Debating the Inter-American View on Amnesty and the Brazilian Case," in Karen Engle, Zinaida Miller and D. M. Davis (eds.). *Anti-Impunity and the Human Rights Agenda*. New York: Cambridge University Press.

Wacks, Raymond. 1984a. "Judges and Injustice," 101 *South African Law Journal* 266.

1984b. "Judging Judges: A Brief Rejoinder to Professor Dugard," 101 *South African Law Journal* 295.

Walker, Samuel. 1990. *In Defense of American Liberties: A History of the ACLU.* New York: Oxford University Press.

2012. *Presidents and Civil Liberties from Wilson to Obama.* New York: Cambridge University Press.

Weiner, Tim. 2012. *Enemies: A History of the FBI.* New York: Random House.

Wilson, Richard Ashby (ed.). 2005. *Human Rights in the "War on Terror."* New York: Cambridge University Press.

Wilson, Richard Ashby and Richard D. Brown (eds.). 2009. *Humanitarianism and Suffering: The Mobilization of Empathy.* New York: Cambridge University Press.

Wittes, Benjamin. 2008. *Law and the Long War: The Future of Justice in the Age of Terror.* New York: Penguin Books.

Woffinden, Bob. 1987. *Miscarriages of Justice.* London: Hodder & Stoughton.

Work, Clemens P. 2005. *Darkest Before Dawn: Sedition and Free Speech in the American West.* Albuquerque: University of New Mexico Press.

Yoo, John. 2008. "FDR, Civil Liberties, and the War on Terrorism," in Daniel Farber (ed.), *Security and Liberty: Conflicts between Civil Liberties and National Security in American History.* New York: Russell Sage Foundation.

CHAPTERS 2–7

Aaronson, Trevor. 2013. *The Terror Factory: Inside the FBI's Manufactured War on Terrorism.* New York: IG Publishing.

Abel, Richard L. 1985. "£'s of Cure, Ounces of Prevention," 73 *California Law Review* 1003.

1988. *The Legal Profession in England and Wales.* Oxford: Basil Blackwell.

1989. *American Lawyers.* New York: Oxford University Press.

2011. "Law under Stress: The Struggle Against Apartheid in South Africa, 1980–94 and the Defense of Legality in the United States after 9/11," 26 *South African Journal on Human Rights* 217.

Abrams, Norman. 2005. "The Material Support Terrorism Offenses: Perspectives Derived from the (Early) Model Penal Code," 1 *Journal of National Security Law & Policy* 5.

ACLU (American Civil Liberties Union). 2009. *Blocking Faith, Freezing Charity: Chilling Muslim Charitable Giving in the "War on Terrorism Financing."* New York: ACLU.

2013. *Unleashed and Unaccountable: The FBI's Unchecked Abuse of Authority.* New York: ACLU.

Allison, William Thomas. 2007. *Military Justice in Vietnam: The Rule of Law in an American War.* Lawrence: University Press of Kansas.

Apuzzo, Matt and Adam Goldman. 2013. *Enemies Within: Inside the NYPD's Secret Spying Unit and Bin Laden's Final Plot against America.* New York: Simon & Schuster.

Arax, Mark. 2009. *West of the West: Dreamers, Believers, Builders, and Killers in the Golden State*. New York: Public Affairs.

Ashcroft, John. 2006. *Never Again: Securing America and Restoring Justice*. New York: Center Street.

Bali, Asli. 2003. "Changes in Immigration Law and Practice after September 11: A Practitioner's Perspective," 2 *Cardozo Public Law, Policy and Ethics Journal* 161.

    2006. "Scapegoating the Vulnerable: Preventive Detention of Immigrants in America's 'War on Terror,'" 30 *Studies in Law, Politics and Society* 25.

Ball, Howard. 2007. *Bush, Detainees, and the Constitution: The Battle over Presidential Power in the War on Terror*. Lawrence: University Press of Kansas.

Barrett, Paul M. 2006. *American Islam: The Struggle for the Soul of a Religion*. New York: Farrar, Straus and Giroux.

Bayoumi, Moustafa. 2015. *The Muslim American Life: Dispatches from the War on Terror*. New York: New York University Press.

Bergen, Peter. 2016. *United States of Jihad: Investigating America's Homegrown Terrorists*. New York: Crown Publishers.

Bickel, Alexander. 1962. *The Least Dangerous Branch: The Supreme Court at the Bar of Politics*. New York: Bobbs-Merrill.

Boal, Mark. 2011. "The Kill Team. How U.S. Soldiers in Afghanistan Murdered Innocent Civilians," *Rolling Stone* (March 27).

Bravin, Jess. 2013. *The Terror Courts: Rough Justice at Guantánamo Bay*. New Haven: Yale University Press.

Chesney, Robert M. 2005. "The Sleeper Scenario: Terrorism-Support Laws and the Demands of Prevention," 42 *Harvard Journal on Legislation* 1.

    2007a. "Anticipatory Prosecution in Terrorism-Related Cases," in John L. Worrall and M. Elaine Nugent-Borakove (eds.), *The Changing Role of the American Prosecutor*. Albany: SUNY Press.

    2007b. "State Secrets and the Limits of National Security Litigation" (Wake Forest University Legal Studies Paper No. 946676), available at SSRN: https://ssrn.com/abstract=946676.

    2007c. "Federal Prosecution of Terrorism-Related Offenses: Conviction and Sentencing Data in Light of the 'Soft-Sentence' and 'Data-Reliability' Critiques," 11 *Lewis & Clark Law Review* 851.

Chesterman, Simon and Chia Lehnardt (eds.). 2007. *From Mercenaries to Market: The Rise and Regulation of Private Military Companies*. New York: Oxford University Press.

Chevigny, Paul. 1969. *Police Power: Police Abuses in New York City*. New York: Pantheon Books.

CHRGJ (Center for Human Rights and Global Justice). 2011. *Targeted and Entrapped: Manufacturing the "Homegrown Threat" in the United States*. New York: New York University Law School.

CHRGJ (Center for Human Rights and Global Justice) and Asian American Legal Defense and Education Fund. 2011. *Under the Radar: Muslims Deported, Detained, and Denied on Unsubstantiated Terrorism Allegations.* New York: New York University Law School.

CLEAR (Creating Law Enforcement Accountability & Responsibility), Muslim American Civil Liberties Coalition and Asian American Legal Defense and Education Fund. 2013. *Mapping Muslims: NYPD Spying and its Impact on American Muslims.* New York: CLEAR.

Cohen, Stanley. 1972. *Folk Devils and Moral Panics: The Creation of the Mods and Rockers.* London: MacGibbon and Kee.

Davis, Jeffrey. 2008. *Justice Across Borders: The Struggle for Human Rights in U.S. Courts.* New York: Cambridge University Press.

De Goede, Marieke and Gavin Sullivan. 2015. "The Politics of Security Lists," 2015 *Society and Space* 1.

Denbeaux, Mark and Joshua Denbeaux. 2006. *No-Hearing Hearings: An Analysis of the Government's Combatant Status Review Tribunals at Guantánamo.* Newark, NJ: Seton Hall Law School.

Denbeaux, Mark P. and Jonathan Hafetz (eds.). 2009. *The Guantánamo Lawyers: Inside a Prison Outside the Law.* New York: New York University Press.

Denbeaux, Mark, Jonathan Hafetz, Sara Ben-David, Nicholas Stratton and Lauren Winchester. 2012. *No Hearing Habeas: D.C. Circuit Restricts Meaningful Review.* Newark, NJ: Seton Hall Law School Center for Policy & Research.

Denbeaux, Mark P., Adam Kirchner, Josh Wirtshafter and Joseph Hickman. 2013. *Spying on Attorneys at GTMO.* Newark, NJ: Seton Hall Law School Center for Policy & Research.

DoJ OIG (Department of Justice, Office of the Inspector General). 2003. *The September 11 Detainees: A Review of the Treatment of Aliens Held on Immigration Charges in Connection with the Investigation of the September 11 Attacks.* Washington, D.C.: DoJ OIG.

2005. *Review of the Terrorist Screening Center* (Audit Report 05-27) (June). Washington, D.C.: DoJ OIG.

2006. *A Review of the FBI's Handling of the Brandon Mayfield Case.* Washington, D.C.: DoJ OIG.

2007. *Follow-up Audit of the Terrorist Screening Center* (Audit Report 07-41) (September). Washington, D.C.: DoJ OIG.

2008. *Audit of the U.S. Department of Justice Terrorist Watchlist Nomination Process* (Audit Report 08-16) (March). Washington, D.C.: DoJ OIG.

2009. *The Federal Bureau of Investigation's Terrorist Watchlist Nomination Practices* (Audit Report 09-25) (May). Washington, D.C.: DoJ OIG.

2010. *A Review of the FBI's Investigations of Certain Domestic Advocacy Groups* (September). Washington, D.C.: DoJ OIG.

Ellmann, Stephen J. 1992. *In a Time of Trouble: Law & Liberty in South Africa's State of Emergency*. Oxford: Clarendon Press.

Elsea, Jennifer K. 2014. *Comparison of Rights in Military Commissions and Trials in Federal Criminal Court* (Congressional Research Service 7-5700). Washington, D.C.: CRS.

Felstiner, William L. F., Richard L. Abel and Austin Sarat. 1981. "The Emergence and Transformation of Disputes: Naming, Blaming, Claiming …," 14 *Law & Society Review* 631.

Fisher, Louis. 2005. *Military Tribunals and Presidential Power: American Revolution to the War on Terrorism*. Lawrence: University Press of Kansas.

Fleming, Mark. 2016. "The *Boumediene* Case after the Supreme Court," in Jonathan Hafetz (ed.), *Obama's Guantánamo: Stories from an Enduring Prison*. New York: New York University Press.

Fletcher, Laurel E., Alexis Kelly and Zulaikha Aziz. 2011. "Defending the Rule of Law: Reconceptualizing Guantánamo Habeas Attorney," 44 *Connecticut Law Review* 617.

Frederick, Jim. 2010. *Black Hearts: One Platoon's Descent into Madness in Iraq's Triangle of Death*. New York: Broadway Paperbacks.

Gezari, Vanessa M. 2013. *The Tender Soldier: A True Story of War and Sacrifice*. New York: Simon & Schuster.

Giridharadas, Arnand. 2015. *The True American: Murder and Mercy in Texas*. New York: W. W. Norton & Co.

Glazier, David W. 2003. "Kangaroo Court or Competent Tribunal: Judging the 21st Century Military Commission," 89 *Virginia Law Review* 2005.

  2006. "Full and Fair by What Measure?: Identifying the International Law Regulating Military Commission Procedure," 24 *Boston University International Law Journal* 55.

  2008. "A Self-Inflicted Wound: A Half-Dozen Years of Turmoil over the Guantánamo Military Commissions," 12 *Lewis & Clark Law Review* 131.

Goldsmith, Jack. 2007. *The Terror Presidency: Law and Judgment inside the Bush Administration*. New York: Norton.

Gusfield, Joseph. 1963. *Symbolic Crusade: Status Politics and the American Temperance Movement*. Urbana: University of Illinois Press.

Habib, Mamdouh. 2009. *My Story: The Tale of a Terrorist Who Wasn't*. Brunswick, Australia: Scribe Publications.

Hafetz, Jonathan. 2011. *Habeas Corpus after 9/11: Confronting America's New Global Detention System*. New York: New York University Press.

  (ed.). 2016. *Obama's Guantánamo: Stories from an Enduring Prison*. New York: New York University Press.

Hathaway, Oona. 2007. "Hamdan v. Rumsfeld: Domestic Enforcement of International Law," in John E. Noyes, Laura A. Dickinson and Mark W. Janis (eds.), *International Law Stories*. St. Paul: Foundation Press.

Langewiesche, William. 2006. "Rules of Engagement," *Vanity Fair* (November).

Lawyers Committee for Human Rights (LCHR). 2002. *A Year of Loss: Reexamining Civil Liberties since September 11*. New York: LCHR.

2003a. *Imbalance of Powers: How Changes to U.S. Law and Policy since 9/11 Erode Human Rights and Civil Liberties*. September 2002–March 2003. New York: LCHR.

2003b. *Assessing the New Normal: Liberty and Security for the Post-September 11 United States*. New York: LCHR.

Levant, Ezra. 2012. *The Enemy Within: Terror, Lies and the Whitewashing of Omar Khadr*. Toronto: McClelland & Stewart.

Madar, Chase. 2013. *The Passion of Bradley Manning: The Story behind the WikiLeaks Whistleblower*. New York: Verso.

Mahler, Jonathan. 2009. *The Challenge*. New York: Picador.

McClellan, Scott. 2008. *What Happened: Inside the Bush White House and Washington's Culture of Deception*. New York: PublicAffairs.

Mestrovic, Stjepan G. 2009. *The "Good Soldier" on Trial: A Sociological Study of Misconduct by the US Military Pertaining to Operation Iron Triangle*. New York: Algora Publishing.

Nelson, Deborah. 2008. *The War behind Me: Vietnam Veterans Confront the Truth about U.S. War Crimes*. New York: Basic Books.

Nguyen, Tram. 2005. *We Are All Suspects Now: Untold Stories from Immigrant Communities after 9/11*. Boston, MA: Beacon Press.

Ni Aoláin, Fionnuala and Oren Gross (eds.). 2013 *Guantánamo and Beyond: Exceptional Courts and Military Commissions in Comparative Perspective*. New York: Cambridge University Press.

Nicks, Denver. 2012. *Private: Bradley Manning, WikiLeaks, and the Biggest Exposure of Official Secrets in American History*. Chicago: Chicago Review Press.

Norris, Jesse J. 2015. "Why the FBI and Courts Are Wrong about Entrapment and Terrorism," 84 *Mississippi Law Journal* 1257.

2016. "Entrapment and Terrorism on the Left: An Analysis of Post-9/11 Cases," 19 *New Criminal Law Review* 236.

Norris, Jesse J. and Hanna Grol-Prokopczyk,. 2016. "Estimating the Prevalence of Entrapment in Post-9/11 Terrorism Cases," 104 *Journal of Criminal Law & Criminology* 609.

Nussbaum, Martha C. 2012. *The New Religious Intolerance: Overcoming the Politics of Fear in an Anxious Age*. Cambridge, MA: Belknap Press.

NYU (New York University) Law School, Center on Law and Security. 2011. *Terrorist Trial Report Card: September 11, 2001–September 11, 2011*. New York: NYU Law School, Center on Law and Security.

Ohman, Mynda G. 2005. "Integrating Title 18 War Crimes into Title 10: A Proposal to Amend the Uniform Code of Military Justice," 57 *Air Force Law Review* 1.

Pfander, James E. 2017. *Constitutional Torts and the War on Terror*. New York: Oxford University Press.

Precht, Robert E. 2003. *Defending Mohammad: Justice on Trial*. Ithaca, NY: Cornell University Press.

Putnam, Tonya L. 2016. *Courts without Borders: Law, Politics, and U.S. Extraterritoriality*. New York: Cambridge University Press.

Rath, Ann. 2008. "Rules of Engagement," *PBS's Frontline* (February 19).

Raustiala. Kal. 2009. *Does the Constitution Follow the Flag? The Evolution of Territoriality in American Law*. New York: Oxford University Press.

Richards, Peter Judson. 2007. *Extraordinary Justice: Military Tribunals in Historical and International Context*. New York: New York University Press.

Roberts, Mary Louise. 2013. *What Soldiers Do: Sex and the American GI in World War II France*. Chicago: University of Chicago Press.

Romero, Anthony D. and Dina Temple-Raston. 2008. *In Defense of Our America*. New York: William Morrow.

Rudenstine, David. 2016. *The Age of Deference: The Supreme Court, National Security, and the Constitutional Order*. New York: Oxford University Press.

Ryan, Allan A. 2012. *Yamashita's Ghost: War Crimes, MacArthur's Justice, and Command Accountability*. Lawrence: University of Kansas Press.

Sachs, Stephen H. 2008. Review of Maryland State Police Covert Surveillance of Anti-Death Penalty and Anti-War Groups from March 2005 to May 2006.

Said, Wadie E. 2015. *Crimes of Terror: The Legal and Political Implications of Federal Terrorism Prosecutions*. New York: Oxford University Press.

Sales, Leigh. 2007. *Detainee 002: The Case of David Hicks*. Melbourne: Melbourne University Press.

Sarat, Austin. 1977. "Studying American Legal Culture: An Assessment of Survey Evidence," *11 Law & Society Review* 427.

Satterthwaite, Margaret L. 2009. "The Story of El-Masri v. Tenet: Human Rights and Humanitarian Law in the 'War on Terror,'" in Deena R. Hurwitz and Margaret L. Satterthwaite (eds.), *Human Rights Advocacy Stories*. New York: Foundation Press.

Scahill, Jeremy. 2008. *Blackwater: The Rise of the World's Most Powerful Mercenary Army*. New York: Nation Books.

Scheiber, Harry and Jane L. Scheiber. 2016. *Bayonets in Paradise: Martial Law in Hawai'i*. Honolulu: University of Hawai'i Press.

Schneier, Bruce. 2012. *Liars and Outliers: Enabling the Trust that Society Needs to Thrive*. Indianapolis: Wiley.

Scroggins, Deborah. 2012. *Wanted Women: Faith, Lies, and the War on Terror: The Lives of Ayaan Hirsi Ali and Aafia Siddiqui*. New York: HarperCollins.

Shawcross, William. 2012. *Justice and the Enemy: Nuremberg, 9/11, and the Trial of Khalid Sheikh Mohammed*. New York: PublicAffairs.

Shephard, Michelle. 2015. *Guantánamo's Child: The Untold Story of Omar Khadr*. Hoboken, NJ: John Wiley & Sons.

Sherrill, Robert. 1970. *Military Justice Is to Justice as Military Music Is to Music*. New York: Harper & Row.

Sidhu, Dawinder S., Neha Singh Gohil and Amy Chua. 2009. *Civil Rights in Wartime: The Post- 9/11 Sikh Experience*. Farnham: Ashgate.

Singer, P. W. 2003. *Corporate Warriors: The Rise of the Privatized Military Industry*. Ithaca, NY: Cornell University Press.

Skolnick, Jerome. 1966. *Justice without Trial: Law Enforcement in Democratic Society*. New York: John Wiley & Sons

Slahi, Mohamedou Ould. 2015. *Guantánamo Diary*. New York: Little Brown.

Smith, Charles Anthony. 2012. *The Rise and Fall of War Crimes Trials: From Charles I to Bush II*. New York: Cambridge University Press.

Soufan, Ali H. 2011. *The Black Banners: The Inside Story of 9/11 and the War Against al-Qaeda*. New York: W. W. Norton & Co.

Swift, Charles. 2007. "The American Way of Justice," *Esquire* (March).

Temple-Raston, Dina. 2007. *The Jihad Next Door: The Lackawanna Six and Rough Justice in the Age of Terror*. New York: Public Affairs.

Turner, Serrin and Stephen J. Schulhofer. 2005. *The Secrecy Problem in Terrorism Trials*. New York: New York University Law School, Brennan Center for Justice.

Valdes, Stephen G. 2005. "Frequency and Success: An Empirical Study of Criminal Law Defenses, Federal Constitutional Evidentiary Claims, and Plea Negotiations," 153 *University of Pennsylvania Law Review* 1709.

Wax, Steven T. 2008. *Kafka Comes to America: Fighting for Justice in the War on Terror*. New York: Other Press.

Wert, Justin L. 2010. *Habeas Corpus in America: The Politics of Individual Rights*. Lawrence: University Press of Kansas.

Willett, Sabin. 2016. "Twelve Years After," in Jonathan Hafetz (ed.), *Obama's Guantánamo: Stories from an Enduring Prison*. New York: New York University Press.

Williams, Alan F. 2012–13. "Overcoming the Unfortunate Legacy of Haditha, the Stryker Brigade 'Kill Team,' and Pantano: Establishing More Effective War Crimes Accountability by the United States." 101 *Kentucky Law Journal* 337.

Williamson, Janice. 2012. *Omar Khadr, Oh Canada*. Montreal: McGill-Queen's University Press.

Wilson, Joseph C., IV. 2004. *The Politics of Truth: Inside the Lies that Led to War and Betrayed My Wife's CIA Identity: A Diplomat's Memoir*. New York: Carroll & Graf.

Wilson, Valerie Plame. 2007. *Fair Game: How a Top CIA Agent Was Betrayed by Her Own Government*. New York: Simon & Schuster.

Witt, John Fabian. 2008. "Form and Substance in the Law of Counterinsurgency Damages," 41 *Loyola Los Angeles Law Review* 1455.

Wood, Trish. 2006. *What Was Asked of Us: An Oral History of the Iraq War by the Soldiers Who Fought It*. New York: Back Bay Books.

Zabel, Richard B. and James J. Benjamin Jr. 2008. *In Pursuit of Justice: Prosecuting Terrorism Cases in Federal Courts*. New York: Human Rights First.

INDEX

Kamins, Barry M., 204
Kammen, Richard, 285
Kane, John L., 92
Kaplan, Lewis A., 62
Karim, Bostan, 416
Kar, Cyrus, 441
Karadzic, Radovan, 613
Kariokoo, Dar es Salaam, 62
Karzai, Hamid, 157, 562
Kasich, John, 578
Kavanaugh, Brett, 216, 240, 369, 376, 381, 383, 396, 407, 412, 469
Keenan, Barbara M., 439
Keith, Damon, 8
Kelly, Raymond, 46, 273, 534
Kennedy, Anthony, 192, 328, 333, 340, 342, 358, 360, 374, 466, 468, 474
Kennedy, Henry H., 402, 404
Kenny, Steven, 217
Kessler, Gladys, 359, 384, 386, 396, 398, 399
Khadr, Ahmad Said, 483
Khadr, Omar Ahmed, 222
Khairkhwa, Khirulla Said Wali, 414
Khalid, Mohammad Hassan, 72, 91
Khalifh, Omar Mohammed, 404
Khalilzad, Zalmay, 142
Khan, Daisy, 549
Khan, Hafiz, 71
Khan, Majid Shoukat, 253, 380
Khan, Muhammad Adil, 27
Khan, Naseem, 26
Khan, Samir, 456
Khan, Shawali, 411
Khoury, Andre, 55
Kimber, James S., 105
King, Angus, 81
King, Colbert, 581
King, Peter, 193, 273, 507, 551, 573
King, Peter J., 46, 68, 80, 81
King, Robert B., 347, 438, 441
Klay, Phil, 170
Kline, John, 106
Kodirov, Ulugbek, 76
Koeltl, John G., 84, 504
Kohl, Kenneth, 161
Kohlmann, Evan F., 59, 213
Kohlmann, Ralph, 250
Kohlmann, Ralph H., 220, 261
Kollar-Kotelly, Colleen, 218, 341, 352, 391, 393, 394
Korematsu, 598
Korman, Edward R., 514
Koubriti, Karim, 78
Krauthammer, Charles, 582
Kris, David, 270
Kristof, Nicholas, 551, 580
Krugman, Paul, 553

KSM (Khalid Sheikh Mohammed), 213, 259
Kunk, Thomas, 141
Kurnaz, Murat, 354
Kyl, Jon, 189, 193, 566

L-3 Services, 440
Lachelier, Susan, 254
Lackawanna Six, 239
Lackland Air Force Base, 179
LaGrange, Miles, 571
Lahmar, Saber, 367
Lamberth, Royce C., 162, 375, 380, 393, 399, 400, 434, 479, 486
Landis, Kenesaw M., 2
Lane, Charles, 82, 581
LaRose, Colleen, 72, 91
Latif, Adnan, 417
Latif, Abu Khalid Abdul, 71
Laval, Pierre, 70
Lazio, Rick, 549, 553
Leahy, Patrick, 195, 273, 275, 356
Ledford, Andrew K., 177
Lee, Gerald B., 77, 436, 439, 440
LeMay, Curtis, 589
Lemorin, Lyglenson, 37
Lenard, Joan A., 39
Leon, Richard J., 352, 366, 368, 380, 381, 385, 387, 406, 411, 418, 434
Lever, Henry D., 132
Levin, Carl, 81, 110, 189, 200, 270
Levin, Richard, 540
Lewin, Nicholas, 66
Lewis, Anthony, 567
Lewis, Derek I., 132
Lewis, James, 13
Lewis, Timothy K., 400
Libby, I. Lewis "Scooter," 458
Liberty City, Florida, 35
Liberty, Evan S., 161
Lichte, Arthur, 179
Lieberman, Joseph, 79, 273, 365, 533
Limbaugh, Rush, 524
Lincoln, Abraham, 13
Lind, Jennifer, 612
Lindberg, George W., 479
Lindh, John Walker, 90
Lippman, Walter, 18
Livingston, Robert, 12
Llaneza, Matthew, 71
Lockhart, Andreas, 295
Lodge, Henry Cabot, 13
Lodge, Edward, 470, 475
Lodi, 26
Lofgren, Zoe, 514
Lopezromo, Saul H., 132
Luttig, J. Michael, 327, 336, 339, 341

CAMBRIDGE STUDIES IN LAW AND SOCIETY

Constituting Religion: Islam, Liberal Rights, and the Malaysian State
Tamir Moustafa

The Invention of the Passport: Surveillance, Citizenship and the State, Second Edition
John C. Torpey

Law's Trials: The Performance of Legal Institutions in the US "War on Terror"
Richard L. Abel

Law's Wars: The Fate of the Rule of Law in the US "War on Terror"
Richard L. Abel

Transforming Gender Citizenship: The Irresistible Rise of Gender Quotas in Europe
Eléonore Lépinard and Ruth Rubio-Marín

Muslim Women's Quest for Justice: Gender, Law and Activism in India
Mengia Hong Tschalaer

Haltom, William and Michael McCann. 2004. *Distorting the Law: Politics, Media, and the Litigation Crises.* Chicago: University of Chicago Press.

Hickman, Joseph. 2015. *Murder at Camp Delta: A Staff Sergeant's Pursuit of the Truth About Guantánamo Bay.* New York: Simon & Schuster.

Hicks, David. 2010. *Guantánamo: My Journey.* North Sydney: William Heinemann.

Hirsch, Susan F. 2006. *In the Moment of Greatest Calamity: Terrorism, Grief and a Victim's Quest for Justice.* Princeton: Princeton University Press.

Hoffman, Bruce, Edwin Meese III and Timothy J. Roemer. 2015. *The FBI: Protecting the Homeland in the 21st Century.* Washington, D.C.: FBI.

HRF (Human Rights First). 2008. *Torture Justice: Using Coerced Evidence to Prosecute Terrorism Suspects.* New York: HRF.

2009. *Denial and Delay: The Impact of the Immigration Law's "Terrorism Bars" on Asylum Seekers and Refugees in the United States.* New York: HRF.

HRW (Human Rights Watch) and Columbia Law School (CLS) Human Rights Institute. 2014. *Illusion of Justice: Human Rights Abuses in U.S. Terrorism Prosecutions.* New York: HRW and CLS.

Hunt, Jennifer C. 2010. *Seven Shots: An NYPD Raid on a Terrorist Cell and its Aftermath.* Chicago: University of Chicago Press.

Huntington, Samuel P. 1996. *The Clash of Civilizations and the Remaking of the World Order.* New York: Simon & Schuster.

Isaac, Gary A. 2016. "The Wrong Person: How Barack Obama Abandoned Habeas Corpus," in Jonathan Hafetz (ed.), *Obama's Guantánamo: Stories from an Enduring Prison.* New York: New York University Press.

Kahn, Herman. 1962. *Thinking about the Unthinkable.* New York: Horizon Press.

Kahn, Jeffrey. 2013. *Mrs. Shipley's Ghost: The Right to Travel and Terrorist Watchlists.* Ann Arbor: University of Michigan Press.

Kannaday, Christopher, Peter Masciola and Michel Paradis. 2012. "The 'Push-Pull' of the Law of War – The Rule of Law and Military Commissions," in Ana Maria Salinas de Frias, Katja Samuel and Nigel White (eds.), *Counter-Terrorism: International Law and Practice.* New York: Oxford University Press.

Katyal, Neal Kumar. 2006. "Comment: Hamdan v. Rumsfeld: The Legal Academy Goes to Practice," 120 *Harvard Law Review* 65.

Klay, Phil. 2014. *Redeployment.* New York: Penguin.

Kundnani, Arun. 2014. *The Muslims Are Coming: Islamophobia, Extremism, and the Domestic War on Terror.* New York: Verso.

Kurnaz, Murat. 2008. *Five Years of My Life: An Innocent Man in Guantánamo.* New York: Palgrave Macmillan.

Laguardia, Francesca. 2013. "Terrorists, Informants, and Buffoons: The Case for Downward Departure as a Response to Entrapment," 17 *Lewis & Clark Law Review* 171.